MIDDLE CLASSES IN
DEPENDENT COUNTRIES

CLASS, STATE, & DEVELOPMENT

Series Editor:
DALE L. JOHNSON
Department of Sociology, Rutgers University

Class, State, & Development intends to provide class analysis perspectives on questions of the state and of development. Volumes will emphasize critical Marxist approaches to the class structure and class relations of advanced capitalist societies, the social basis of contemporary states—both democratic and authoritarian—and the social and economic development of Latin America, Asia, Africa, and the Middle East. This series is published in cooperation with the Department of Sociology, Rutgers University.

EDITORIAL BOARD
(at Rutgers University)

Volumes in this series:

Volume 3   **CLASS, STATE, & DEVELOPMENT**

MIDDLE CLASSES IN DEPENDENT COUNTRIES

EDITED BY
DALE L. JOHNSON

SAGE PUBLICATIONS
Beverly Hills   London   New Delhi

For information address:

SAGE Publications, Inc.
275 South Beverly Drive
Beverly Hills, California 90212

SAGE Publications India Pvt. Ltd.
C-236 Defence Colony
New Delhi 110 024, India

SAGE Publications Ltd
28 Banner Street
London EC1Y 8QE, England

Printed in the United States of America

Library of Congress Cataloging in Publication Data

Main entry under title:

Middle classes in dependent countries.

   (Class, state, and development ; v. 3)
   Includes bibliographical references.
   1. Middle classes—Political activity—Addresses, essays, lectures. 2. Middle classes—Developing countries—Political activity—Addresses, essays, lectures. I. Johnson, Dale L. II. Series: Class, state & development ; v. 3.
HT684.I58   1984   305.5′5   84-12713
ISBN 0-8039-2375-9

FIRST PRINTING

Contents

Part Three   Classes in the Socialist Transition

Preface

This volume is not an anthology of diverse perspectives on a particular problem area. It is a book with a certain unity that has emerged from a major research thrust within the Graduate Department of Sociology at Rutgers University. Each contribution represents original work undertaken by Rutgers faculty or graduate students who are concerned to develop a more historical and dialectical social science than is current in the field. We have selected intermediate classes and the historical process of development as the theme of the volume and class analysis as the method. Of major concern is the recent proliferation of military dictatorship in the peripheral areas we have researched. Case studies included here amply document the salient roles of intermediate classes in forming the idea of the nation and in constructing territorial states. In the contemporary period intermediate classes provide principal social bases for different forms of the state, including military dictatorship.

Middle Classes in Dependent Countries is a sequel to Volume 1 of the book series "Class, State, & Development," edited at Rutgers and published by Sage. The first volume, *Class & Social Development: A New Theory of the Middle Classes,* explores theoretical issues in an attempt to construct a historical and dialectical theory of social class. The book places a great deal of emphasis on intermediate classes, as these formations have been insufficiently addressed in the literature on social class. Substantively, the first volume examines the historical formation and current class situation of intermediate classes in the advanced industrial countries, especially the United States. The present book shifts the emphasis to the qualitatively distinct positioning of intermediate class formations in Latin America and the Caribbean, Asia, and the Middle East.

The empirical/historical conditions forming intermediate groups in the social structure and conditioning their roles in the development process and in politics are quite distinct between advanced capitalist and dependent and underdeveloped countries and markedly divergent within the Third World regions as well. The common thread holding studies of intermediate classes together in such diverse context is our major theoretical premise: The process of capitalist development in the world system polarizes social structures—concentrated and centralized capital at the one pole, classes of people dispossessed of other means of subsistence and incorporated, directly or indirectly, to waged labor at the other pole. This bi-polarization is a highly uneven, relational process; as it unfolds, pre-existing "middle classes," such as independent producers, farmers, and small businessmen, are dispossessed of productive property; "new middle classes" of professional, technical, and administrative labor are formed to intervene in or mediate the capital/labor relation.

Several of the chapters represent ideas, here revised and extended, first appearing within Ph.D. dissertations; and (with firm prodding by the editor, Johnson) most chapters have gone through several revisions over a period that extended into years. Though a very large share of responsibility for errors and misinterpretations are those of the editor, the book is an intellectual product of the collective activity of the authors.

Chesapeake Center   Dale Johnson

Adolf's Ghost

The ghost of Adolf Hitler animates
the calculated antics
of General Pinocchio Pinochet.
"Extirpating Chile's cancer"
the Generals,
bankrolled by their friends
in corporate board rooms abroad,
removed the Nation's heart
and replaced it with
a Made-in-USA machine.

In Chile,
Latin America and Asia,
Pentagon programmed
militarism
imprisons the valiant,
tortures reason,
degrades the noble,
strains to devour
what remains of civilization.

Militarism infuses mentalities
of the Powerful
everywhere where
stirrings of the Many
frighten the Few.
Yesterday in Chile,
Today in Salvador,
This social disease
infects the consciousness
of the petty-privileged.
Ex-Señor Presidente Eduardo Frei,
President-by-Junta-blessing Napoleón Duarte

and their middle class followers
made doublethink
of the words
"Christian" and "Democrat."

The germ of this social disease?
The substance of work and life
that the Few appropriate
from the Many.
Exploitation
denies justice,
impels rebellion,
buys social privilege,
incites reaction.

Militarism is embedded
in a panoply of institutional forms
that facilitates thievery,
oppresses and suppresses
the victims.

With printed lies,
subtle distortions,
and electronic messages
of the culture of domination
the social disease
feeds on
subverted consciousness
and obliterated humanity.

Militarism
is the death agony
of a system
that has lived out its time.

—*Dale L. Johnson*

Part One: Historical Studies of

Class Formation

Dale L. Johnson: Class and Social Development: Toward a Comparative and Historical Social Science

An Argentine sociologist, José Nun, once wrote an article that achieved considerable acclaim entitled "The Middle Class Military Coup in Latin America" (Nun, 1968). His object of analysis was mainly the 1964 Brazilian and 1966 Argentine military interventions. Others have since portrayed these interventions as other than "middle class" in nature, but in Peru from 1968–1974 military officers energetically imposed a series of profound reforms that bore the distinct stamp of a middle class "populist" project (Bamat, Chapter 9, this volume). In the Chilean counterrevolution of 1973 hundreds of thousands of shopkeepers, truck owners, bureaucrats, and professionals massed on the streets in militant opposition to the socialist measures of the Popular Unity government. In Jamaica during the late 1970s Michael Manley and the People's National Party vainly attempted to bring about a democratic socialism that was the political vision of a "bureaucratic-entrepreneurial" sector (Keith and Keith, Chapter 3, this volume) of the island's fledgling "brown middle class" (Karch, Chapter 4). In the Third World nationalism is an ideology of middle class origin, not an expression of a "national bourgeoisie," nor of the aspirations of ordinary people (Ahmad, Chapter 2). The communist state of Afganistan is a government of feuding professionals and functionaries, not a peoples' state. In Soviet-type societies bureaucratic functionaries have transformed themselves into a new kind of ruling class (Stoleroff, Chapter 10).

The formation of intermediate classes is a historical process with great regional and national variations. We trace the evolution of intermediate classes (1) in relation to the uneven development of the capitalist mode of production in different regions and (2) in relation to the construction of states that act as agents of class formation. We view social classes as groupings of subjects meshed within networks of antagonistic social relations more than as defined empirical entities to be described and counted. Intermediate classes cannot be looked at in isolation from other classes. Examined therefore are (3) the places of intermediate groupings in the social division of labor, the functions they perform in their work activities, and the nature of their relations with dominant classes, on the one side, and subordinated classes, on the other side. Finally, (4) we examine the salient roles of intermediate classes in the development process and in politics within distinct national contexts.

(1) *Uneven Development.* Intermediate class formations have first to be seen as products of the historical process of development of the capitalist mode of production (MOP), for pre-capitalist modes do not form intermediate elements to any appreciable degree.[1] Since the capitalist MOP has come into being and matured in a highly uneven manner on a world scale, this makes a comparative framework on the place of intermediate formations indispensable. For example, two of the cases examined in this volume, Argentina and Bangladesh, could hardly offer greater disparities and contrasts. Argentina is fully enmeshed in a process, shortly to be explored, of "dependent development." Bangladesh remains trapped in a stage of "classic underdevelopment."

Argentina, a nation free of direct colonialism for 150 years, a country of immigrants many of whom brought business and industrial skills and capital, has rich agricultural resources and a primarily industrial economy, well developed civil and cultural institutions, and a middle class of professionals, scientists and technicians, and administrators that rivals the mature industrial nations of Western Europe. The Argentine intermediate groups are locked into highly conflictive relations with an economically predominant class of bankers, industrialists, and big ranchers and with a sizeable and militant working class.

Bangladesh became a nation only in 1971. The rich history of the region of Bengal is recounted by Shahidullah in Chapter 5. Today, Bangladesh has no industry or capitalist or working class to speak of and a vast peasantry that, as a consequence of agrarian reforms, displacement of Hindu landlords with independence, and war, does not have to defer to big landlords (a class once created in Bengal by British colonial policy). In its historical formation, the Bengali middle class is a true intermediate class; the British educated and employed a class of indigenous functionaries to administer the colonial state that stood between English commercial interests, whose interests were primarily in jute, and the jute producers and the colonized population generally. With the exit of the British in 1947, a new nation, Pakistan, became divided between West and East (Bengal). The government administrators and capitalists of the West rapidly developed an agrarian "intenral colony" in the East. The aspirations of Bengali intermediate strata and businessmen were blocked at every turn, leading finally to war and secession. After 1971, sectors of the intermediate class came together to become a governing class, with sectors drawing upon the resources of the state to enrich themselves, others using the machinery of government to contain the peasantry, and others losing out to military heavyhandedness. Bangladesh remains in a condition of extreme dependency on foreign assistance, loans, and investments and the export of primary products; the governing class, itself under the firm direction of its military contingent, now mediates between international centers of power and the vast pauperized population.

(2) *States and Class Formation.* Throughout the Third World the activities of states have been primary sources of the formation of intermediate class categories. Where capitalism has transformed traditional economies most extensively on the periphery (parts of Latin America), the state has developed an institutional gigantism and range of activities that often surpasses the mature states of the advanced industrial countries. In less developed societies the state tends to grow to the limits of resources that can be taxed or otherwise appropriated by government. Middle class personnel occupy the multiplying niches of the state apparatuses. The "overdevelopment" of the state (in comparison to the growth of states with development in the West) is in part due to late development; dependent states trying to manage underdeveloped economies in chronic crisis took imported Keynesian principles even further than in the West. In part, this overdevelopment compensates for the presence of weak classes of local capitalists, or even their virtual nonexistence: States assume entrepreneurial functions, giving birth to technocratic, managerial, and technical groupings that do not owe their existence to private property. The bloating of the public bureaucracy is also due to systems of clientelism, often associated as well with graft and corruption (at the point of being almost unbelievable in countries like Nigeria and Mexico), most of which are modern patronage systems, not carryovers of traditional ways; political parties often become instruments for the advancement of the careers of middle class personnel, as well as of the political and social aspirations of the class.

Ahmad's chapter documents the centrality of the state in the formation of social classes, especially intermediate classes. In his study of several Middle and Near Eastern societies, he goes even further in defining the intermediate class/state nexus. The state through its "overdevelopment" not only forms expansive intermediate classes, these same classes have been the most important forces in forming the state.

Modern states in this part of the Third World were constructed, either under colonial rule or in defensive reaction to imperialism, prior to the emergence of a capitalist class as a dominant class. A capitalist type state was a pre-condition for the establishment of the dominance of the capitalist mode of production over pre-capitalist modes. The power of nationalist movements defined the very idea of a nation in areas where the concept of nation was submerged well into the twentieth century by legacies of ancient empires, by colonialism, and by the territorial co-existence of diverse ethnic, religious, and language groups. Nations became defined with the drawing of the territorial frontiers of states, often resulting in the dominance of one ethnic-religious group over several others. Intermediate groups became the main inventors and carriers of nationalism. Ahmad suggests that the class content of nationalism is determined

> in the very process of its emergence, by the power bloc which appropriates it and gives expression to it in the course of the struggle for hegemony. That may lead to revolution, as in Vietnam, or to a bureaucratic dictatorship of the radical nationalist type, as in Algeria, or to clericil fascism, as in Iran. The class content of nationalism is determined, in other words, by the alliance of classes that utilizes nationalist ideology in the construction of its own power and thus comes to speak, symbolically and with concrete political effect, for what is called the nation.

These alliances, in most instances, have been spearheaded by sectors of the intermediate classes. The mobilizing power of nationalism and the strategic positioning of intermediate strata in the state apparatuses, in the trade unions and other institutions of civil society, and in the economy enable intermediate strata to gain powers, seize initiatives, and struggle for political dominance over other classes, including old classes of landowners and new groupings of capitalists.

(3) *The Place of Intermediate Formations.* Perhaps the main reason for the relative overdevelopment of peripheral states is chronic economic crisis, social distress, and political instability that, contrary to the expectations of developmentalists, tends to increase with development. The spread and growth of the capitalist mode of production under conditions of dependency greatly accelerates the level of class conflict and social struggles of all types at regional, national, and localized levels. The behemoth of state power attempts to manage, channel, contain, and repress conflict and struggle. Middle class state functionaries therefore become front line contestants in the broad field of social struggle.

The "place" of intermediate groupings, in general, is to perform mediating functions in antagonistic social relations. At the highest levels, as managers and staff technocrats of private capital and state enterprises, they are delegated day-to-day control functions. At lower levels of private and public bureaucracies they perform the technical aspects of coordination, supervision, and the development of the forces of production. Other categories are responsible for accounting and sales; still others, such as teachers, producers of culture, and social and health workers, work to reproduce the labor force and existing social relations. Capitalist development proliferates these "places" and "functions".

In the book *Class and Social Development* (1982) I warned against adopting a purely "functional" view of intermediate classes. An intermediate class is not composed simply of agents charged to keep the lid on and reproduce what is. The authors in this volume each reject even a "radical functionalist" analysis of intermediate classes. These classes are subordinated to superior powers as well as superordinate to the dominated classes; intermediate class personnel are not merely agents, they are also active subjects of the historical process of development.

(4) *Political Roles of Intermediate Classes*. In recent decades, intermediate classes have become highly visible actors in international dramas of reform, nationalist assertions, revolution, counterrevolution, and dictatorship. Achieving an understanding of the social bases of contemporary forms of peripheral states is the main end of the present volume. To accomplish this, considerable attention is given to the historical formation and present character of locally dominant classes. For it is only in the relations between dominant/intermediate/subordinate classes that sense can be made of the state. This is particularly important in Latin America, where local bourgeoisies, while weak and divided in comparison to the bourgeoisies of the center countries, are nevertheless the dominant social forces. In most of Asia and in Africa and the Middle East local bourgeoisies are only incipiently formed and the intermediate classes, while less expansive than in Latin America, achieve an inordinate importance as a social base of state power.

Situated between the low level of development of the polar classes of capitalism in Africa and much of Asia and the Middle East and the stronger presence of capitalist and working classes in Latin America are several new nations of the Commonwealth: Caribbean, Jamaica, Trinidad, and Barbados. These island states are creations of British colonialism, and they still bear the stamp of the slave-plantation societies that marked the first several centuries of their existence. Classes of white men still own and control the bulk of the islands' productive resources; brown men administer institutions' and black men and women toil in the fields, hotels, and new factories. During slavery, the dominant class was the plantocracy, and behind the planters were the British merchants. When the interests of the British merchants were displaced in the formation of England's colonial policy by industrial interests, slavery was abolished, free trade supplanted protected markets, and sugar production slipped into crisis. A corporate plantation economy, headed by an agro-commercial oligarchy, nevertheless emerged in the Caribbean colonies. This oligarchy, especially since the 1950s, gradually has extended its domain to industry, tourism, and other modern business activity. In this long evolution a certain place was grudgingly acceded to lesser social elements especially to those of mixed ancestry. The historical evolution of West Indian dominant and intermediate classes are studied in some depth in the chapters by Karch and by Keith and Keith.

Karch notes: "In effect, the intermediate classes as the governing group of the islands still perform the same function that they did under the plantation system. They remain a buffer grouping between the predominantly white bourgeoisie and the mainly black masses." Keith and Keith provide a detailed study of the social formation and political history of the Jamaican brown middle class. They suggest that the democratic socialism espoused by the Peoples National Party, until it was ousted by elections in 1980, was a comprehensive program sponsored by a particular sector of the Jamaican intermediate class, the "bureaucratic-entrepreurial fraction." This program resonated throughout the middle ranks and mobilized a considerable popular support.

The major thrust of the book is an understanding of the changing features of state power, especially the strong trend on a world scale towards authoritarianism. This prime concern with the social origins of dictatorship and democracy has become a major theme of literature in the field of international development. There are few works, however, that explore this concern from our perspective of historical and comparative social science. There are a growing number of very good historical accounts of particular countries; there are some books that examine new state forms in a particular region, especially Latin America (Saul, 1979, is very good on Africa); the few cross-regional studies tend to be anthologies containing diverse studies employing different methods and perspectives. It is next to impossible for a single author to grasp the complexities of these issues in the very different settings of Africa, Asia, Latin America, the Caribbean, and the Middle East. We hope that our readers will examine this edited volume as a book (not an anthology) employing a common theory and method to similar problems in diverse geographical areas.

The "social origins of dictatorship and democracy" is of course the title of the classic study by Barrington Moore, Jr. Moore's method is comparative social history and the scholarship of this work is noteworthy in modern social science. Another excellent contribution is Theda Skocpol (1979).

Social Origins of Dictatorship and Democracy is concerned with the historical paths to the development of modern political forms. Moore's case studies include England and the United States (liberal democratic forms), Germany and Japan (fascist), and China and Russia (communist). These paths are mainly determined by the outcome of relations between the principle classes of pre-capitalist and capitalist societies: landlords, peasants, commercial and industrial bourgeoisies, and workers. This too is our approach.

His scholarship is particularly strong in studies of lords and peasants and the importance of the commercialization of agriculture in shaping the political as well as economic direction of development. At the same time, in seeking to bring lords and peasants from the margins to the mainstream of history, he seems to give an undue weight to the historical importance of these classes. In the Third World cases studied here, we have not found precapitalist classes among the major actors of recent periods. This is because, in most cases, classes in ascendence, not those in decline, are the makers of history. Thus, our main emphasis is upon the relations between bourgeoisie, intermediate, and working classes. In particular cases, the relations between local bourgeoisies and landowners is important in the way that Moore indicated in his studies of the social origins of fascism: an alliance between local bourgeoisies and landowners is a reactionary one tending toward authoritarian solutions to political struggle. Similarly, the struggles of peasants, those on the land and the millions forced into marginal existence in the cities, for land, bread, work, and sheer existence, is a critical factor in the larger panorama of crisis and struggle. But nowhere today are either landlords or peasants responsible for underdevelopment and dictatorship.

The great weakness of Moore's work is the absence of imperialism in his framework of class analysis. His study of the English bourgeoisie is as if its activities were confined to bringing democracy to the British Isles. In his lengthy analysis of India there is only occasional mention of the impact of British colonialism on Indian social structure and development. This, of course, is rectified in the case studies of this book.

While Moore's conception of political forms of societies is perfectly adequate, his notion of the state is a narrowly institutional one. The royalty or the bureaucracy are viewed as actors in the same sense as the classes. Below are presented some initial comments on the state, followed by a lengthier theoretical discussion in Chapter 6 and various case studies.

A Preliminary Note
on the State

There are as many conceptions of the nature of the state as there are broad political positions on the ideological spectrum. The long dominant liberal-democratic conception eulogizes the state that stands above society. With disinterested if sometimes muted wisdom and twarted justice, yet passion for the social good, the state arbitrates social conflict and arranges for social harmony and the progress of the nation. Principled conservatives view the state as a parasitic institution trampling the liberties of individuals and suppressing the wondorous workings of private enterprise. Fascists esteem the state as an embodiment of natural law, the fountain of civilization, and the spiritual essence of mankind. Marxists variously view the state as the executive committee of the ruling class or the "condensation" of prevailing production relations.

Prominent twentieth century political theorists—Weber, Parsons, Dahl, Poulantzas and many others—have given scholastic formulation to the rich classic tradition of Western political theory and provided a firmer intellectual basis for the various ideological notions.

Undoubtably none of these ideological views of the state are entirely remiss in capturing an element of truth about this institution so fundamental to the contemporary world. Marx was right, in the most fundamental sense. Capitalist states are instruments of the capitalist class in that they persistently promote the interests of the powerful and pursue policies of capitalist development. How else could it be in societies where economic power is so concentrated? So too are the liberal political theorists correct. In Western democracies legislatures function more or less effectively to represent sectional interests. Even in the face of concentrated class power, the interests of working people are ignored only at the peril of regime stability. The state functions (in Talcott Parsons' functionalism) in a goal-oriented policy which in the real world comes down to favoring capital and its expansion but always within the limits established by another prime function, to ameliorate the injustices and social conflicts of capitalist development, thus guarding its legitimacy. The legitimacy that states have achieved in advanced industrial societies even lends a certain truth, especially in times of social breakdown and economic crisis when legitimacy becomes more precarious, to fascistic and militaristic ideas of the corporate embodiment of the common will. Capitalist states are also, rather obviously, parasitic institutions, luxuriously consuming monies appropriated from the citizenry and harboring entrenched and immobile bureaucracies.

The authors in this volume hold that only the tradition of Marxist class analysis holds the promise of formulating a theory of the capitalist state that transcends the limits of ideological postures. Chapter 6 surveys different currents within this tradition: instrumentalist, structuralist, Hegelian, and derivationist thinking about the nature of the state. The main assumption, drawing upon these currents, of our approach can be summed in the following proposition: The state is an institutional expression of class relations. This is a complex proposition; its meaning will emerge in the course of the book.

Marxist thinking about the state draws heavily upon Western European theory and historical experience. We think that this enthnocentrism both limits the adequacy of theoretical and political concerns central to Western Marxism and, when applied to non-Western situations, distorts prevailing realities.

The Marxist formulation of "dictatorship as the exceptional form of the capitalist state" is one such distorted tenet. There are only a handful of democratic countries and upwards of 100 states in the world today assume the form of dictatorship. And some of these are the most ferocious tyrannies known in world history. They can be accounted for only as "expressions" of underlying class relations, national and international.

During the decade 1964–1974, the more economically advanced, socially developed and politically progressive nations of Latin America and Asia succumbed one by one to the heeled boot of reaction: Brazil, Indonesia, Argentina, the Philippines, Uruguay, Chile. These new militarized states bore little resemblance to the traditionalistic dictatorships of the Banana Republics and other peripheral, subordinate countries. In their phase of ascendance, they bore the stamp of classic European fascisms—militaristic regimes riding the crest of the mobilized power of a broad alliance of reactionary elements from all the socially privileged classes. After the seizure of power, however, these regimes departed from the classically fascist forms of mobilization and ideological pronouncements, rapidly deactivating their social bases and institutionalizing the brutal police states of the *juntas*.

The decade was also the era of unrestrained United States offensive against revolutionary nationalism in Indo-China and against the perceived threats of democratic and reform nationalisms in the Great Power's backyard. The strategically located U.S. client regimes of Iran, South Korea, and Taiwan were armed to the teeth and opened-up to the newest forms of foreign political controls and penetration by transnational capital. Traditional oligarchic states on the American continent were buttressed. Millions of dollars of economic and military aid poured into unstable nations—Pakistan, Bolivia, Guatemala—that were vacilating between civilian and conservative military regimes. The aging fascisms of Spain and Portugal persisted well into the 1970s in spite of changing circumstances in Europe.

The power of the United States to intervene or manage events in different corners of the globe is today to some degree constrained, although the Reagan administration is trying, with some success, to remove these constraints. Arms and aid from abroad and threats of intervention cannot indefinitely shore up decrepit regimes. Dictatorship, while remaining a reality for suffering hundreds of millions, is on the defensive. The dictatorship of the Shah of Iran has spectacularly collapsed, though the political results are not what one would hope. The Somoza dynasty has been crushed by the force of popular uprising. It will not be easy for the United States to reverse Nicaragua's revolution. The insurrection against the murderous El Salvador regime relentlessly grinds on. Greece, Spain, Portugal, and the Dominican Republic have managed democratic transitions without changes in fundamental structures. The pressures for democratization are very strong in Brazil. In the Philippines the rule of Marcos and the army precariously persist. Taiwan has been abandoned by the Americans in favor of their new ally against the Soviets. The Pinochet dictatorship has made Chile a pariah among nations and the Argentine dictatorship has disintegrated. Military governments in Pakistan and Uruguay lack legitimacy even among their former civilian supporters. Dictatorships can endure for considerable periods without great political support by repression and political bargaining. But there is nothing permanent about any particular form of the state; military dictatorships are not omnipotent.

Examined in this book are the main features of the distinct forms of the capitalist state and the conditions of their historical emergence, consolidation, and disintegration. In this introductory essay I try to bring together several of the themes developed in the book and to draw out elements of underlying method.

A historical approach requires periodization and implies a concept of "stages of development." In general the development of the capitalist mode of production on the periphery, even leaving aside a century and more of colonialism in much of the Third World, has passed through three distinct stages: classic underdevelopment, a stage produced by imperialism from about 1870 to the Great Depression; national development, a stage only achieved in a number of nations of Latin America and is very limited elsewhere (such as India in the post-colonial period); dependent development, a recent stage of development on the periphery corresponding to the complete internationalization of capital. New patterns of international accumulation are affecting most Third World countries and are moving a number of nations out of classic underdevelopment. This rapid change is very impressive in South Korea and the Philippines, and has firmly transcended the stage of national development in the major nations of Latin America.

I should note that the concept of stages of development is formulated here as a heuristic ordering device (most applicable to Latin American cases) more than as an analytic construct. Full theoretical exploration of the problem of periodization of the capitalist mode of production in its highly uneven development on the periphery would require more space, and effort, than is available.

Stages of Development

Third World countries are often assumed to be or to remain underdeveloped because of the slow movement of the economic, social, and political forces of development and "modernization." The mainstream social science literature is replete with studies of "traditionalism," "backward-ness," "obstacles to development" and the like. Critical and Marxist social science, elaborated with considerable scope and sophistication since the 1960s, largely has been concerned to demonstrate that capitalist develop-ment and modernization are the sources of underdevelopment, not its solution. There are few who have not concluded that imperialism and dependence inhibit, frustrate, block, and deform any real development on the periphery.[2] And these inhibitions and deformations are no less so in countries like Brazil, Mexico, Taiwan, and South Korea where there has been a considerable "development with dependence" (e.g. rapid growth of GNP) or "associated dependent development" (concepts developed by Car-doso, 1979).

However, insofar as the theoretical perspectives of imperialism and dependence imply the absence of, or slow rates of, economic and social change, there is, at the very least, a problem of misplaced emphasis. For in the twentieth century, and with ever increasing force and rapidity in recent decades, the capitalist mode of production and the dependent forms that it assumes in the periphery have experienced profound transformation.

Appreciation of the depth and rapidity of change has been submerged by the stagnationist theses of the dependency literature. The idea of the de-velopment of underdevelopment that emerged out of early dependency work has largely, as the critics allege, failed to gain an adequate perspective on the different stages of capitalist development either within the imperial center or on the dependent periphery.

Over the last century, the mode of production in center countries has experienced a transition to and the consolidation, crisis, and reconsolidation on a world scale of one historical stage, the stage of monopoly capitalism and imperialism. During this same century, the nations of the Southern Cone of South America, for example, have passed through three qualitatively distinct historical stages in the development of dependent forms of the capitalist mode of production: the stages of the development of classic underdevelopment, of national development, and dependent development.

While all of Latin America had entered before the beginnings of the twentieth century the stage of classic underdevelopment, only a few na-tions—Argentina, Brazil, Uruguay, Chile, Mexico—entered into a new stage of development, national development, beginning about 1930 (with a transitional phase going back to World War I) and ending in the early 1950s. Although most of the remaining Latin American countries have recently begun a process of incipient industrialization, these nations never experi-enced a stage of national development and passed directly from classic underdevelopment into the most recent stage of dependent development.

Nations such as South Korea, Taiwan, the Philippines, Indonesia, Pakistan, Iran, Egypt, and Nigeria have passed directly from colonial or neo-colonial domination to the stage of dependent development.

"Stages of development" do not refer to a simple periodization of history, but to analytically distinct historical epochs in which the mode of production, social structural formations, and patterns of class relations have characteristics qualitatively different from earlier periods. In the European experience, the stages are conventionally termed feudalism, the transition to capitalism (sometimes termed mercantilism), competitive (or laissez faire) capitalism, and monopoly capitalism and imperialism.[3] It is also possible to empirically derive successive "phases" of development within broad historical stages. It was the dynamics of European and later North American development through these distinct stages that gave—in interrelation with specific histories within Asia, Africa, and Latin America—fundamental direction, though a very different direction, to the transformation of peripheral societies from earlier to later stages of development.

At the analytic level, there are only a limited variety of modes of production: primarily feudalism, capitalism, and socialism. At the historical level, however, a particular mode of production can assume a wide range of concrete forms. British capitalist development, for example, took different forms than the German, especially in respect to class formations and the nature of state activity; and the American and Japanese were quite distinct from each other and the European. Nonetheless, the historical outcomes of this development permit observers today to think of a particular broad form of contemporary capitalism: the advanced industrial capitalism of Europe, North America, and Japan.

Capitalist development in Asia, Africa, and Latin America came about in direct relation with European (and later North American) colonialism and imperialism. As a consequence, the development of the capitalist mode of production in the "peripheral" regions was established and came about in different ways—summed up by the concept of dependency—than in the European and North American "center." While it is theoretically improper to speak of a "dependent mode of production," it is clearly necessary to analyze very concretely the regional and national variations in the development of the capitalist mode of production on the periphery. Generalizing what is common to the regional and national variations of this process, we can postulate the existence of a great number of countries who share a common condition—they are "dependent" and "underdeveloped."

There is no conceptual scheme of stages of development that can be uniformly applied to the different Third World regions, since the form of penetration by Western colonialism has varied and indigenous economic and social structures have articulated in different ways with Western encroachment (Ahmad's chapter here examines the differences between colonized and non-colonized countries of the Near East region). In general, the transition to a new stage of development on the periphery is highly structured by modalities in the internationalization of capital during the period. Here scant attention is given to this, which has been addressed well by others, in favor of an emphasis on "internal" developments, from the perspective of the dialectics of assymetrical dependency relations.

Internal to the dependent nations of peripheral regions, economic development, under the changing forms of relations of dependence, results in transformation in the social structure; these transformations are the main determinants of how the "internal" articulates with international structuring forces. (Elsewhere I have conceptualized the "external-internal" nexus as a dialectic of "general and proximate determinants" [Chilcote and Johnson, 1983: chap. 7]). The class practices and ideological conflicts of the different contending social forces shift; new "power blocs" emerge. And these struggles and shifts in turn result in changes in the social basis, structure, function, and form of the state. State managers attempt to implant a new hegemony with changed formulae of political rule and strategies of economic development. Development strategies are adjusted to current trends and exigencies in the international relations of dependency and to internal economic changes and social-political contingencies. The transition to a new stage of development always involves great disjunctures; frequently the transition is a period of multifaceted economic and political crises. When economic and political crises coincide with sharp upturns in class struggle, the concept of "organic crisis" is used. The economic, social, political, and ideological changes actively sought by the strongest social forces in these situations I will refer to as the "hegemonic project."

Latin American cases provide a brief illustration of the political concomitants of the transition from one stage of development to another. In the 1930s and 1940s in parts of Latin America "reformist-nationalist" and "populist" projects were actively pursued by newly forged "power blocs" that excluded the old oligarchies formed in the prior development stage. In the 1960s and 1970s, the most important projects, the "national security states" of the Southern Cone, have a very different content and social base than those of the stage of national development. These projects and their roots are explored in separate chapters in some depth in case studies of Peru, Jamaica, Chile, and the Southern Cone countries. Below is a sketch of the historical framework.

Classic Underdevelopment

Leaving aside the colonial and post-independence (1830–1870) periods, all of Latin America passed into the stage of the development of classic underdevelopment, roughly from 1870 to 1930.

The main structural features of classic underdevelopment are well known: (1) Integration into the international economy of the period created externally dependent economies producing primary products from agriculture and mining for export; industrial development was greatly inhibited. (2) National oligarchies composed of export-import merchants and large landowners battled among themselves but exercised a firm domination over the other classes—the peasantry and workers producing the exported wealth and the weak classes of artisans, small businessmen, and professionals and salaried employees. (3) As instruments of class rule of dependent, traditional oligarchies, governments pursued development strategies based on "England's greatest export"—free trade and laissez faire doctrines. These doctrines were congruent with the place of the Latin American region as an exporter of primary products and importer of manufactures in the stage of monopoly capitalism and imperialism then being consolidated on a world scale under the sway of British industrialists, merchants, and Navy. These economic and social structures and the policies and activities of local states and dominant classes frustrated the possibility of independent national development. At the same time, the productive forces in primary-export sectors of commercial agriculture and mining achieved a considerable growth in the first decades of the twentieth century and the class relations within these sectors became increasingly sharp. There were also developmental spin-offs of the development of underdevelopment in transportation and other social overhead facilities, as well as a considerable flourishing of commerce in the main urban centers and ports. The limited successes of this development, which were most substantial in Argentina and Uruguay in the first decades of this century, gradually formed new social interests hampered in their further formation and social aspirations by the structural limits of underdevelopment and by the domination of traditional oligarchies. These new social forces included petty bourgeoisies tied to slowly developing local markets, sizeable strata of salaried professionals and administrators, small groupings of largely immigrant industrialists, and an incipient working class.

National Development

International crises—two world wars and depression—disrupted the export-import economy and the economic base of the dominant class and made possible a process of incipient industrialization in some countries, especially of the Southern Cone. The rupture of the pre-existing bonds of international dependence brought about a severe internal crisis to the old order, out of which a stage of national development came about.

While the dependency literature does not have a coherent stage theory of development, this "development from the inside" as opposed to the "development from the outside" of the previous stage (stages as conceptualized by dependency-oriented development economists), is consistent with Frank's thesis (Cockcroft, Frank, and Johnson, 1972: chaps. 1 and 2) that national development based upon local production and the nationalist and reformist assertions of social-political forces comes about when the reigns of dependency are loosened.

Industrial developments greatly strengthened the new social interests already in formation. Oligarchic states corresponding to classic underdevelopment at first tried to meet the crisis with new policies, but all eventually collapsed in the face of an offensive by broad multi-class coalitions pursuing reform and nationalist projects. These coalitions confronted economically and politically weakened oligarchies. Populist states emerged early in Brazil and later in Argentina, Mexico experienced violent upheaval, and democratic states pursuing social reform and state guided economic development gained office in Chile and Uruguay. In South America, multiclass coalitions of progressive social forces achieved tenuous footholds in state institutions, participating with the traditional ruling elements (whose hegemony was under serious challenge by the transitional crisis, but who maintained a conservative political presence) in formulating new strategies of national development and modernizing the state. The considerable economic development achieved resulted in strengthened national capitalism in which the state actively pursued many capital accumulation and entrepreneurial functions.

Transition to Dependent Development

Yet national development was not to proceed unhindered by either international forces or internal factors. At the international level, the multinational or transnational corporation spread investments of a new type throughout the world, precipitating great changes in recipient countries, especially in those nations with the strongest industrial systems. Accelerated penetration of transnational capital coincided with an important internal development in those nations that emerged from depression and war with strengthened national capitalisms: the growing presence of a modernizing capitalist class. By the 1940s and 1950s, traditional oligarchies had assumed a less aristocratic and more bourgeois face and began to modernize themselves, under the tutelage of the state, by reconstituting a firmer economic base in finance and industry. Structurally, the bourgeoisies, though politically still placed on the defensive by populist and reform coalitions, took on a similar complexion to the dominant classes of the metropolitan countries: interest groups composed of big capitalists engaged in ownership or control of diverse corporate activity, that is, the structure of finance capital.

The dual ascendence of transnational capital and local finance capital combined to pummel Third World nations, with special force in South America, into a new stage of "dependent development."

In the post-World War II period imperialism in the form of American capital and United States hegemony as a superpower became integrally reinserted in Latin America. The effects of this resurgence of internaional capitalism, directed from a single power center, rapidly gave a new character to the Latin American economies and to their place in the emerging world of transnational capital. By the early 1950s, Brazil, Mexico, Argentina, Chile, and Uruguay had entered a phase of transition. By the 1960s Latin American countries, such as Venezuela, Peru, and Colombia, which had not experienced a stage of national development passed directly from classic underdevelopment into dependent development. In the Southern Cone countries the national development proceeding from import substitution industrialization and the associated processes of internal development of the two world wars and intervening depression had run up against severe barriers (Brazil) or largely come to a halt (Argentina, Uruguay, and Chile). From the mid-1950s to the 1970s, the explosive growth of transnational corporate investments in industry, commerce, finance, and services and the growing weakness or collapse of the multi-class coalitions undergirding developmentalist states fully established the conditions for a qualitatively new stage of development. The modern forms of monopoly capital of the metropole were reproduced in the most advanced sectors of the dependent periphery. Groups of local finance capitalists greatly strengthened their position and established closer and closer ties to the operations of transnational corporations. Class relations assumed a new and explosive quality. An industrial working class matured. The middle strata split, some moving to the revolutionary left, the great majority to the reactionary right. The new stage of dependent development superseded the prior stage of national development. The political consequences became extremely grave.

The Social Roots of Politics
in the Transition

The emergence phase of contemporary military dictatorship in South America came about in the transition to dependent development. These new faces of fascism (the term is used rhetorically here) are among the most important international phenomena since the fascism and world war of the 1930s and 1940s.

The periods preceding the establishment of rightist military dictatorships have been characterized by deep transitional crises, particularly in the economic sphere, by mounting class conflict, by progressive delegitimation of the system among substantial sectors of the popular classes and among elements of the middle class, and by weak and ineffective reform or populist governments. These governments attempted to pursue a strategy of national development and a politics of reconciliation among classes and interest groups, that in the crisis situation proved unworkable. Dramatic changes in the form and activities of states followed from these circumstances.

The key to understanding the proximate determinants of changing forms of the state—in this case from reform and populist to militarized authoritarian states—resides in an analysis of changing class relations both within the dominant class and between this class and its allies and other social forces. During the 1950s and 1960s throughout the Southern Cone, a fraction of the local bourgeoisie, groupings of finance capitalists directly tied to transnational capital, was reconstituted as the leading sector of the class. However, this fraction did not enjoy hegemony. A growing economic strength, yes; but not economic predominance, much less a broader hegemony. The interests involved were subordinated to transnational capital on the one hand and to a state bureaucracy that reflected the political presence of the multi-class coalition occupying state offices on the other hand. The constraints on capital accumulation were numerous and the economic situation difficult. Moreover, the bourgeoisie as a whole was fractionalized. Uneven development had preserved the most reactionary fractions of the dominant class, the agrarian bourgeoisie tied to the export economy and the *latifundistas* producing for local markets. The often family-based groups of finance capitalists competed fiercely among themselves in developing a multi-sectoral economic base. Patronage from the state favored some business interests as versus others, depending on political relationships to the bureaucracy and corruption. A genuine national bourgeoisie of industrial capital had not developed, but there were numerous medium-sized capitals in national industry and commerce, divided into ethnic communities: Lebanese, Jews, Italians, Spaniards, Germans, and so on. The development of capitalism had subordinated the simple commodity mode of production, but a numerous petty bourgeoisie articulated into the capitalist mode of production still existed.

The stage of national development in the 1930s and 1940s had considerably expanded the middle segments of society. The new *capas medias* of salaried professionals, technicians, and administrators of the private and public bureaucracies began, as their social position and social privileges became elevated, to turn their backs to a politics of nationalism and progress and to exhibit the life styles and values marketed by cultural imperialism—

consumerism, status striving, competitiveness, careerism, and political conservatism. During the stage of dependent development the new middle strata became mainly dependent for their livelihoods, life styles, and social privileges upon the transnational corporations or upon the favors of local capital or the state. The subsidiaries of transnational corporations provided technical and administrative jobs, especially to those educated abroad. Local business and government agencies began to pay salaries high enough to enable increasing numbers to buy homes in the suburbs, drive to work in a car, and hire a maid. Their jobs were to supervise and add technical competence to a modernized labor process that extracted and appropriated the income and wealth produced by workers and to administrate the governmental agencies that facilitated private capital accumulation and contained the assertions of the subordinate classes.

The political problem for the leading fraction of the local bourgeoisie, the finance capitalists and their international partners was the construction of a new power bloc in which they could translate their economic interests into the exercise of hegemony. In the emergence phase of the national security state in Brazil, Uruguay, Argentina, and Chile this was accomplished, with direct participation and backing from United States corporations and government agencies, by forging an alliance of the various fractions of the bourgeoisie, substantial segments of the middle strata and petty bourgeoisie, and the military. An almost classically fascist mobilization of these forces created political situations that made military intervention possible and successful: Brazil in 1964 and 1968; Argentina in 1955, 1966, and 1976; Chile and Uruguay in 1973.

The Possibilities and Limits of National Capitalist Development

It is well to take a modest excursion here into some of the specifics of national development experience, for a genuine "stage of national development" remains today the dream of developmentalists and modernizers throughout the world. The Shah of Iran died in 1980 in total bewilderment that his "White Revolution" and the modernization generously supported by the Americans was not understood as national development by the Iranian people. Juan Peron passed from the scene in 1974 not understanding that populist formulae of the 1940s could not fit the circumstances of Argentina in the 1970s.

Moreover, most of the attempts to construct socialism—tied in parts of the world to anti-colonial struggles and everywhere to nationalist ideology—have been frustrated or greatly deformed. (Clive Thomas's book on economic pitfalls is excellent, 1974). The Algerian revolution threw out the

French, but fizzled as a socialist revolution. Nasserism succumbed with Nasser and Peruvian populism with General Velasco. Democratic socialism never achieved democracy, much less socialism, in Jamaica and Guyana. Chilean socialism was aborted in blood and tiny Grenada mopped up by U.S. marines. Where recent social revolutions have been successful, their continued existence is threatened (with the probable exceptions of Vietnam and Cuba, and possibly Zimbabwe). Some of the regimes have fallen far short of realizing their revolutionary aspirations. The "communism" of the feuding intermediate strata in Afganistan requires the presence of large numbers of Soviet troops. Ethiopian socialism is a highly authoritarian military regime that massacres its opponents and wages massive war against Eritrian nationalists and socialists. Other emerging socialisms internally strong face the formidable power of the United States, which has drawn the line in Central America and energetically tries to reverse the Nicaraguan Sandinista revolution.

We have included several studies in this volume that scrutinize the possibilities and limits of national development, both "national capitalist" and "socialist." Keith and Keith analyze the historical and social roots of the failure of democratic socialism of the People's National Party of Jamaica. Ahmad touches on the origins of the Afghan regime and of the 1979 Iranian revolution that turned toward "clerical fascism." Two studies deal explicitly and in depth with class relations in societies in transition. These are sharply contrasting cases, Peru and the USSR, yet instructive in getting at the broader issues of frustrated revolution and the formation of new dominant classes with sufficient power to freeze genuine revolutionary possibilities (USSR) or reverse the possibilities of even achieving development of a strong national capitalism (Peru).

Frustrated National Capitalism:
Peru

The Peruvian experience under the government of General Velasco (1968–1974) in trying to construct a "non-capitalist and non-communist" path to national development is a highly instructive one. It went a good deal further, but collapsed even more quickly than Latin America's prior cases of "populism," such as the Vargas regime in Brazil or Peron's Argentina.[4] It reveals both the real possibility of forging new "power blocs" within nations arrested within the confines of underdevelopment and the even more pressing limitations, national and international in origin, that are placed these days on the success of such projects.

Where national capitalist development has been successfully pursued, specific sets of circumstances have prevailed. (1) The forces of colonialism or imperialism have been constrained, either through successful anti-colonial struggle or international crisis that inhibits the exercise of imperial intrusion. (2) The power of pre-existing dominant classes has been undermined by the weakening of imperial support and/or by internal crisis of the prevailing order of underdevelopment. (3) A multi-class coalition of opposition forces coalesces into an effective power bloc and is able to gain a foothold in state power. Intermediate classes figure prominently in this coalition. (4) The state assumes a highly interventionist character. A series of reforms are enacted or imposed that undermine the old order and facilitate the emergence of new patterns of economic and social development. The level of state investment in productive facilities greatly increases and government agencies manage the overall development process.

In Peru in 1968 a group of nationalist and reformist military officers, led by General Velasco, overthrew a conservative civilian government, initiating a rapid process of deep structural reform and instituting a highly statist model of development. This military intervention occurred in a moment when the impact of the international forces of dependent development had not yet been extensive in Peru. The period was also one of stagnation of the coastal plantation export economy that had been the chief feature of Peruvian underdevelopment and the main source of power of the Peruvian oligarchy for many decades.

The reform project imposed by the military had the unmistakeable markings of a "middle class military coup." In gestation through three decades of nationalist, reformist, and anti-oligarchic agitation by middle class forces, the project sought a strong state, agrarian reform to break-up coastal plantations and traditionalist sierra haciendas, industrialization to promote an internal market, and increased popular participation in the political process. Middle class technocrats and ideologues were visible in key advisory roles, and military leaders themselves had middle class origins. The economic fortunes of the middle class were promoted through income redistribution, rising salaries, provision of consumer durables, and government housing subsidies.

Yet certain anomalies in characterizing the regime as "middle class" arose over its years (1968–1975) in power. A growing gap appeared between the rhetoric and reality of a government that declared itself anti-capitalist and anti-imperialist while primarily favoring big capital and becoming ever more indebted to international financial interests. As Bamat documents (see also Bamat, 1983), there was a consistent rise in enterprise profits as a share of national income and a considerable consolidation of monopoly capital. Taxes on corporate profits declined steadily between 1968 and 1974, while the tax burden remained on the middle class. As time went on it became apparent that the regime, while unequivocally hostile to the old oligarchy, promoted the interests of an urban-industrial bourgeoisie. Prior to 1968 this class had modestly formed on the basis of a limited industrialization, but its economic weight had not been appreciable *vis-à-vis* the oligarchy and its social-political presence much less visible than that of the clamoring middle segments. Perhaps then we are dealing with the assertions of a "national bourgeoisie" hiding behind the barracks?

The class character of political regimes is an issue that bears directly on the question of the possibilities and limits of national development elsewhere in the world. The relative clarity of the issues in the Peruvian case make an examination valuable.

The most notable effort of the Peruvian populist project was its direct attack on the core of the dominant class. The economic base of the oligarchy of agro-exporters/bankers together with that of traditional agricultural interests was eliminated by the agrarian and banking reforms. But in no way was the Velasco regime an "instrument" of a modernizing, national industrial bourgeoisie. To be sure, an "urban-industrial" bourgeoisie, with interests in objective conflict with the old agro-export faction, was in formation prior to the 1968 coup. This fraction of the local bourgeoisie was also generally favored by the policies of the Velasco government. Industrial development proceeded, even with the uncertainties of what was interpreted by industrialists as an unfavorable investment climate. Industrial profits increased and taxes on profits decreased; the state gave incentives to private capital for industrial investments, took over strategic but unprofitable industries, and vastly expanded its own infra-structural and productive investments. Moreover, local industrial capital became heavily entertwined with transnational capital throughout the 1960s and 1970s.

Yet Bamat is able to document amply (see also Bamat, 1983) that the urban-industrial bourgeoisie had no part whatsoever in the 1968 coup. Moreover, the pre-existing mechanisms of articulation between the entire bourgeoisie and the state were completely ruptured by the exclusion by military bureaucrats of trade associations, political parties and other instruments of class and interest organization from access to the means of policy formation. In fact, the industrialists, together with all other business interests placed themselves in opposition to the military government. Bamat analyzes the form of this opposition: They informally cultivated allies among certain military officers; in the early 1970's the National Industrial Society even engaged in tactics of direct confrontation; and throughout the trying period businessmen pursued actions that Bamat terms "tactical containment." In addition, nationalist and statist policies made international capital, the United States government, and international lenders generally hostile to the Velasco regime, severely restricting international credits and holding back investments.

Bamat's major point is plainly that an "instrumentalist" interpretation of the Peruvian regime will not do. His is a "structuralist" explanation. The Peruvian reform was an "expression" of the relative power of social forces in struggle. The course of this struggle was such that the "logic" of relations of capitalist production and reproduction could not be broken. "The overall effect of their years of authoritarian military rule has been the reproduction, expansion, and 'modernization' of capitalism in Peru. . . . The populist reform project of the military never broke with the logic of capitalist accumulation and never overcame its fear of the independent organization of the popular masses" (Bamat, 1983: 141). Given the firmly entrenched character of capitalist social relations in Peru, the reform and development policies of the regime only consolidated the position of the already emerging urban-industrial bourgeoisie, while the reform rhetoric incited a militant working class in formation.

Peru's reform experience made the urban-industrial bourgeoisie into the predominant faction of the Peruvian bourgeoisie. They achieved this predominance, on the one hand, through the mediation of a populist political project that was not under their own direct control and, on the other hand, through a strategy of sustained struggle against the regime until it was toppled by a conservative military coup in 1975 which dismantled the prior reforms. Moreover, rather than conciliating class conflict, the overriding ambition of the middle strata and technocratic military reformers, the experience added a considerable "class-for-itself" dimension to the structural polarization of classes in Peru.

Gilbert has filled in many of the gaps left by Bamat. The Velasco regime elaborated a set of reform policies and a development model that was consistent with the class dynamic of Peru in the late 1960s:

> In brief, the model favored already privileged urban classes over urban and rural masses by promoting a pattern or industrialization which was import intensive and oriented toward middle class consumers. Concurrently, it sought to reduce and rationalize the role of foreign capital in the economy. The class orientation of this model actually intensified external economic dependence, while policy toward foreign capital evoked hostility from centers of international capitalist power. The net result was severe vulnerability to balance of payment problems which, in turn, forced political capitalation (1980:15–16).

An alliance of military populists and technocrats and "old" and "new" intermediate classes could not successfully perform a grand balancing act between the increasingly combative, polarizing classes, the bourgeoisie and the working class and peasantry, to push through a technocratic state capitalism (that the reformers termed "neither capitalist nor communist").

The reform project was an ideological creation of this alliance and it proceeded rapidly until, as Bamat implies, it ran up against the "structural logic" of the system.

Aníbal Quijano has portrayed the salient place of *capas medias* in Peruvian class relations and their role in the coalition of forces during the Velasco regime:

> One of the most important and illustrative political phenomena of Peruvian history since the 1930's has been the especially relevant role of the *capas medias*, first as head of a coalition of democratic and nationalist forces facing the oligarchy-imperialist coalition, and later as an intermediate political force between the bourgeoisie and workers and between the sectors of the bourgeoisie. . . . And all this has been based, until recently, even in the "Jacobin" style of the Velasco attempt at solutions to the problems of Peruvian capitalism, as an answer to the sharpening of class confrontation (1978:59).

Gall quotes a Peruvian militant as saying: "What we are seeing is a so-called revolution of the middle class on the make, an alliance between military and civilian technicians of the middle class, mainly interested in jobs for themselves" (Gall, 1971:289).

An analysis of the key political role of the *capas medias* is elaborated in greater depth by Germaná (1983).

Since the 1975 conservative military intervention, the Peruvian *capas medias* have become decidedly subordinated. And the main reason is the rapid process of class polarization. The bourgeoisie, as both Bamat and Quijano (1983) demonstrate, has been reconsolidated on a new base and greatly strengthened. In spite of the elimination by the reforms of the old oligarchy of plantation owners and bankers, the newly consolidated urban/industrial bourgeoisie is far from a true "national bourgeoisie." Meanwhile, the working class has matured and achieved a considerable organizational and political capacity (Quijano, 1983). Its numbers augmented by industrialization and proletarianization in pre-capitalist sectors and among the marginal sectors of the petty bourgeoisie, its ranks penetrated by revolutionary ideology, and its class situation slammed by the economic crisis and state repression in the post-1974 period, the urban working class (and to a lesser extent rural workers) is a highly combative social force, set squarely against its now modernized, sophisticated, and assertive antagonist, the local bourgeoisie and its prop and ally, international capital. In this polarization the role of the middle strata as intermediate forces, much less as principle social forces defining the course of struggle, is considerably reduced. While the populist and nationalist reforms of the 1968–1974 period demonstrated the great importance of the political role of sectors, this period of the middle strata's most radical expression was also "recognition and requiem for a history of half a century" (Quijano, 1978:60). The loss of the intermediating role of the *capas medias* (just as in the populist and reform projects of the Southern Cone during the stage of national development) "is the paradoxical price of their own work" (Quijano, 1978:60).

Middle classes do not chart independent paths to national development, even with the backing of military force and in favorable circumstances. The demise of Peruvian populism was locally rooted in the ascendence of the local bourgeoisie, one without any pretensions of a "national bourgeoisie," and of the working class, with a decline in the mediating and larger political role of the intermediate strata. These tendencies of internal class polarization are greatly reinforced by the "general determinants" of the international forces of dependent development.

Undoubtably this situation is not unique to Peru. Studies employing the perspectives indicated above of such once promising cases as Algeria and Egypt will probably indicate similar factors in their demise as models of national development. Short of genuine social revolution, the prospects for national development do not appear hopeful.

At the moment, social revolution appears as a real possibility in Central America and other countries will follow in due time. A main question facing these revolutions is how to achieve economic development without sacrificing social justice and political democracy. An analysis of class relations in existing socialism follows that will reflect on this question.

A Note on Class Relations in the Socialist Transition

In the West, Marxism is a theory of the development of capitalist society and a critical approach to the inner workings of the prevailing order. It aspires to be both a science of history and a vehicle of liberation; and Marxism has in fact guided successful revolutionary transformations and will undoubtedly continue to do so as struggles in areas such as Central America are resolved in the direction of revolutionary change. In the East, a sterile, mechanical Marxism that serves as an ideology of domination prevails. Serious analyses of class relations in the Soviet Union, Eastern Europe, China and other existing socialist orders mainly emanate from the West and remain few and relatively undeveloped. Among Eastern European analysts, I would agree with Marcrakovski: "Soviet-type society is neither socialist nor capitalist, nor is it a mixture of the two systems. It is a class society *sui generis,* a different kind of class society existing alongside capitalism" (1978:15).

This view seems increasingly accurate for China as well, though it is of doubtful validity for the younger revolutionary societies of Cuba and Vietnam, and is certainly not applicable to Angola or Nicaragua. If some existing socialisms have convuluted into *sui generis* class societies, this means that a class theory adequate to the task of analyzing these societies is necessary. Even more importantly, it means that Marxism as critical theory and liberating ideology must be applied, not only to existing socialisms, but also to the strategy of making a revolution that minimizes the chances, once capitalism is vanquished, of yet another form of class society emerging.

Of course the critical thrust of theory cannot make revolutions or assure their purity. Revolutions are made by mobilized peoples in specific historical conditions that inevitably limit the liberating potential. But genuine development is the liberation of people from conditions of poverty, exploitation, and oppression. A genuine revolution aims at the abolition of classes, for it is class society that produces and deepens poverty, exploitation, and oppression (on this concept of development see Johnson, 1973).

The Bolshevik Revolution opened the way for economic development, but the Revolution did not abolish classes. In the Soviet Union the crimes of Stalin and the continuation today of the dominance of a heavy handed, conservative class of bureaucratic functionaries has given socialism a bad name. But this should not be allowed to obscure the historical gains the Soviet Revolution still symbolizes—and the hope and potential that socialism holds for the many millions of exploited and brutally oppressed peoples throughout the world.

In the concluding chapter of this volume, Alan Stoleroff attacks the notion that the Soviet Union is a "socialist" society, or one in transition to socialism. He argues that a political revolution carried out by a revolutionary party that represents the interests of the proletariat and that succeeds in abolishing the sway of private property over the means of production does not, in itself, present the necessary and sufficient conditions for abolishing capitalism and its classes. Stoleroff contends that "Soviet-type social formations" are species of capitalist societies in which only the juridicial form of property has been altered. Other features of the capitalist mode of production are operative: the social division of labor is based on a radical separation of the direct producers from the means of production and their subordination to a class of non-productive controllers of the accumulation and labor processes; commodity production predominates; labor power is a commodity; and the capitalist categories of wages, prices, and profits are working principles of the economy. Soviet-type systems are "state capitalism;" they are class societies in the fullest sense. The polar classes are the state bourgeoisie (composed of two factions, managers of the state and enterprise level directors) and the proletariat. Set between these classes is an intermediate class of state functionaries and socially privileged categories of administrative and technical employees. The class structure is nearly identical to that of advanced capitalism, save that the economic base of the dominant class is control of social property rather than private property.

While I do not agree with much of Stoleroff's analysis, this is a provocative work that extends the debate on the character of Eastern socialism carried on by Sweezy, Bettleheim, Mandel, and others (see especially Sweezy, 1978, and Bettleheim, 1976, 1978). This debate takes on an extraordinary significance with the events of Poland since 1980. Clearly, the Polish state and working class are locked into a struggle of unprecedented proportions. The military dictatorship is a, hopefully vain, attempt to maintain an ossified system. Poland represents perhaps hopeful indications of future upheavals that hold the promise of displacing the conservative East European regimes and moving toward a more democratic, if not revolutionary, socialism.

There is no question that Soviet-type systems are class societies. In Poland, the clash of Solidarity and the Polish state has all the features of a momentous class struggle that pits an entrenched dominant class based on concentrated state property, the Party, and the state apparatus against a class conscious, militant and unprecedentedly mobilized working class. But the argument that Poland or the USSR are capitalist societies in which only the juridicial form of property has been altered, giving rise to a state bourgeoisie that supercedes the bourgeoisie of private property, is quite another matter.

The Soviet Union represents a new type of class society qualitatively distinct from previous class societies. The 1917 Soviet Revolution precipitated a revolutionary process in which the dominant class of Czarist Russia was destroyed, in which pre-capitalist forms of production were thoroughly uprooted, and in which the fledgling institutions of Russia's backward capitalism were demolished. Social property completely displaced private property; centralized planning eliminated commodity markets; the basis of accumulation was radically altered.

At the same time, political developments of the Stalin era represented a counter-revolutionary process; not one that harkened back to capitalism, but one that smothered the potential of a genuine transition to a vastly higher level of social development; one in which a new class, formed in the specific conditions of post-revolutionary society and based in the Party and the state apparatus, waged a relentless struggle against the peasantry, the working class, and any and all communists not party to the Stalinist project. The "excesses" and barbarisms of the Stalin period were not aberrations of a bureaucratic caste that had "deformed" the workers' state. They were systematic outcomes of a class war declared by an emergent class against the Soviet people. The class that emerged victoriously did not depend upon the resurrection of capitalist political economy (as Stoleroff contends), it was formed, in fierce struggle, in the context of subverting revolutionary transformations, social property and planning, into the basis of consolidation of a new class power.

Leon Trotsky observed in 1939: "Either the Stalin regime is an abhorrent relapse in the process of transforming bourgeois society into a socialist society, or the Stalin regime is the first stage of a new exploiting society. If the second prognosis proves correct, then, of course, the bureaucracy will become a new exploiting class" (cited in Sweezy, 1978:8). Trotsky was firmly convinced that the Stalin regime was "an abhorrent relapse" that would be demolished in the post-war period by the force of Soviet workers (aided by post-war European revolutions). That this did not eventuate indicates that in fact the "bureaucracy" had succeeded in dismantling the Soviets, turning the trade unions into instruments of social control, capturing the Communist Party as its instrument of power, and making the state its own. In short, a "new exploiting class" was formed in the class struggles that emerged within the revolutionary transformations and adverse conditions created by the 1917 Revolution.

Notes

1. In countries like the United States, Canada, and Australia, it might be said that a "petty commodity" mode of production grew up with the capitalist mode, until, after the mid-nineteenth century, it became increasingly subordinated to the capitalist mode of production and eventually eliminated during the stage of monopoly capitalism. The independent producers of the simple commodity mode could be said to form a class intermediate between capitalists (and other elements such as plantation owners) and workers, but their place in the social order is quite distinct from intermediate classes under advanced capitalism.

2. Bill Warren (1980) argues that imperialism promotes development. Some tendencies in European Marxism implicitly share his view; but see the devastating critique of Warren and this thinking generally by Ahmad (Chilcote and Johnson, eds., 1983: Chapter 1).

3. Ernest Mandel suggests that the capitalist mode of production has passed through "epochs," the epoch of competitive capitalism (roughly from 1780–1880) and the epoch of imperialism (1880–1940). Since World War II, Western capitalist societies have entered a third epoch to which is given the cumbersome title "late capitalism." In each epoch Mandel finds vast technological changes, long waves of industrial expansion and contraction, and cyclical crises of overaccumulation (Mandel, 1968).

4. Space limits discussion of the populist reform experiences of Argentina, Brazil, Chile, Mexico, and Uruguay. The literature available is ample and quite good. An excellent general work is Ianni (1975).

References

Bamat, Thomas
1983 "Peru's Velasco Regime and class domination after 1968." Latin American Perspectives 37/38 (Spring/Summer): 128–150.

Bettleheim, Charles
1976 Class Struggles in the U.S.S.R. Volume 1. New York: Monthly Review Press.
1978 Class Struggle in the U.S.S.R. Volume 2. New York: Monthly Review Press.

Cardoso, Fernando Henrique
1979 Dependence and Development in Latin America. Berkeley: University of California Press.

Chilcote, Ronald H. and Dale L. Johnson (eds.)
1983 Theories of Development: Mode of Production or Dependency? Beverly Hills, CA: Sage.

Cockcroft, James D., André Gunder Frank, and Dale L. Johnson
1972 Dependence and Underdevelopment: Latin America's Political Economy. Garden City, NY: Doubleday.

Gall, Norman
1971 "The Master is Dead." Dissent 18: 281–320

Germaná, César
1983 "The middle strata and the problem of class alliances." Latin American Perspectives 37/38 (Spring/Summer): 171–184.

Gilbert, Dennis
1980 "The end of the Peruvian revolution: a class analysis." Studies in Comparative International Development 15 (Spring): 15–37

Ianni, Octavio
1975 La Formación del Estado populista en América Latina. México: Ediciones Era.

Johnson, Dale L.
1973 The Sociology of Change and Reaction in Latin America. Indianapolis: Bobbs-Merrill.

Johnson, Dale L. (ed.)
1982 Class and Social Development. A New Theory of the Middle Classes. Beverly Hills, CA: Sage.

Marcrakovski, Narc
1978 Towards an East European Marxism. New York: St. Martin's Press.

Moore, Barrington, Jr.
1966 Social Origins of Democracy and Dictatorship. Lord and Peasant in the Making of the Modern World. Boston: Beacon.

Nun, José
1968 "The middle class military coup in Latin America." Pp. 145–185 in James Petras and Maurice Zeitlin (eds.) Latin America: Reform or Revolution? New York: Fawcett.

Quijano, Aníbal
1978 "La luchade classes en el Perú actual." Cuadernos Políticos 15 (January–March): 44–61
1983 "Imperialism, social classes, and the state in Peru, 1890–1930." Pp. 107–138 in Ronald H. Chilcote and Dale L. Johnson (eds.) Theories of Development: Mode of Production or Dependency? Beverly Hills, CA: Sage.

Saul, John
1979 The State and Revolution in Eastern Africa. New York: Monthly Review Press.

Thomas, Clive
1974   Dependence and Transformation: The Economics of the Transition. New York: Monthly Review Press.
Skocpol, Theda
1979   States and Social Revolution. New York: Cambridge University Press.
Sweezy, Paul
1978   "Is there a ruling class in the U.S.S.R.?" Monthly Review (October): 1–17.
Warren, Bill
1980   Imperialism: Pioneer of Capitalism. London: New Left Books.

Aijaz Ahmad: Class, Nation, and State: Intermediate Classes in Peripheral Societies

The present text is designed to explore some initial propositions regarding the intermediate and auxiliary classes in Asian and Middle Eastern formations, as these have been historically constituted through the epochal experiences of colonization and peripheral capitalist development. The enhanced power of these classes in our societies is rooted in the historical genesis of the peripheral state, and in the specific composition of classes that is a corollary of that genesis. It would have been more appropriate, then, to argue the case in the shape of particular historical narratives than to pose the question only in its generality, on the theoretico-abstract level. The construction of such detailed narratives is, unfortunately, not possible in so brief a text. The present study is therefore divided into four sections. In the first section, we state the general argument with little reference to particular histories. In the three subsequent sections—on the composition of the "governing caste," on the military elite, and on nations and nationalisms— we try to document our theoretical propositions with as many specific facts as space would allow.

It should be clarified at the very outset what is meant by the intermediate and auxiliary classes. We of course assume that a given mode of production in a class society is comprised, principally, of two polar classes. Capitalism, for example, is comprised, principally, of a capitalist class and the proletariat. This principal aspect does not, however, exhaust the totality of that mode of production, and surely not of the society based upon that mode. The reproduction of any mode occurs within a complex social organization which includes a number of forms of property, countless ways of appropriating labor, and myriad tasks of circulation, administration, education, and so on. Intermediate and auxiliary classes are reproduced in that wider space and would include, initially, all classes which are not the polar classes of a particular dominant mode of production.

We also assume that classes are not necessarily homogeneous entities, and that it is a particular characteristic of capital, as well as of landed property, that it is highly fractionalized. For instance, the essential labor relation is usually the same in a manufacturing plant that employs, let us say, fifty relatively unskilled workers, and a more advanced industrial enterprise based upon higher levels of technology and perhaps thousands of workers; owners in both cases are members of the capitalist class; but their locations in society are quite different, and some of their interests overlap while others do not. They are united in defense of capitalism, but they diverge in all sorts of other ways. This becomes altogether clear when we analyze landed property. In West Asia, for example, the essential labor relation, and hence the defining characteristic of the mode of production, is normally the same on a farm of, say, thirty acres and on a huge estate of thousands of hectares; the independant proprietor and the semi-feudal lord are, in that initial sense, members of the same landowning class. But little else unites them. The lord is opposed to re-distribution of land and imposition of agricultural tax; the independent proprietor wants re-distribution, because he is not affected by it, and supports a kind of agricultural tax that provides exemptions and even subsidies to small farms. For purposes of our present analysis, therefore, we make a fundamental distinction between scales of property. Small landowners, rich and middle peasants, the merchants of rural and semi-rural townships, small-scale manufacturers, retailers, and so on, are included here among the intermediate and auxiliary classes. The professional petty bourgeoisie has arisen mainly from these classes and shares many of the same interests and attitudes. Many of the radical reform movements, whether of the populist or of the revolutionary kind, have drawn the bulk of their cadres from these classes, as well as from among the professional petty bourgeoisie, precisely because their interests are sufficiently different from those of the dominant sectors of capital and landed property to allow, even sometimes to require, the politics of opposition.

General Premises

Our basic argument is that far from being mere "agents" of the ruling classes or a mere "vascillating mass," as they are often portrayed in Marxist literature, the intermediate and auxiliary classes of the periphery occupy a strategic field in the economy and politics of their countries, thus obtaining powers and initiatives which make it possible for them to struggle for political dominance over other classes, including the bourgeoisie. Thus, these classes play a key role in the construction of political reaction as well as in the process of radicalization and even revolution. What political role they play in a given conjuncture, and whether they would align themselves with the class above or the class below, is highly influenced by the historical constitution of the conjuncture itself. Since the balance of force is usually in favor of the bourgeoisie and the landed elite, and since imperialism usually inserts itself into the dominated periphery in collaboration with those upper classes, the intermediate classes are normally predisposed to work within that alignment. In the exceptionally unstable situation prevailing in the periphery, however, that is not always the case, and the intermediate classes are quite capable of reorganizing their own political practices accordingly. Their only loyalty is to the pursuit of their own hegemony, and in the course of that pursuit they may align themselves, depending upon the prevailing configuration of power, with the bourgeoisie or the proletariat, the big landowners or the peasantry, or with a melange of class fractions, which is usually the case.

The drive for hegemony on the part of the intermediate classes stems, principally, from the overwhelming role of the state in all aspects of the peripheral societies, including the economic, and from the powerful presence of the intermediate classes in apparatuses of the state. It is through the agency of the state that the personnel drawn from these classes strives to dominate the whole of civil society as such. On the ideological level, this is expressed in a certain fetishization of the state, and the creation of a whole range of disparate and mutually contradictory ideologies—e.g., Western-style developmentalism, the "socialism" of the radical-nationalists with its emphasis on "nationalizations," the ethno-religious fascism of the Khomeini variety—which are nonetheless united in viewing the state as the principal agency of social transformation. Thus, an analysis of the peripheral intermediate classes shall hinge largely upon (1) the historical genesis and the contemporary form of the peripheral state; (2) the manner in which this state arose, historically, prior to the emergence of a fully-fledged bourgeois class and still continues to guide and even dominate that class; (3) the "overdevelopment" of the state in relation to the largely disenfranchised civil society; and (4), the presence of the personnel of the intermediate classes in the actual exercise of the power of that state.

Conversely, this drive for hegemony is facilitated by the comparative weakness of the polar classes, namely the owners of large-scale private property on the one hand, the peasantry and the working classes on the other. This "weakness" can take any number of forms. In the capitalist sector, for example, the bourgeoisie may suffer from a structural subordination of the private sector to the public sector, so that it relies upon the state for undertaking the fundamental tasks of capitalist production. In the oil-producing countries, particularly, the bourgeoisie is dependent upon the state because oil and gas revenues are deposited directly into the state treasury. Elsewhere, as in Egypt or Syria, the private sector is subordinated to the public sector thanks to the "nationalizations" undertaken by the radical strata of the petty bourgeoisie who have wielded state power in those countries (e.g., under Nasser in Egypt, under the Ba´ath in Syria and Iraq, under the FLN in Algeria, under Qaddafi in Libya). Thus, the precise combination of factors might be different in different countries, but the bourgeoisie tends to be, in most cases, unable to take charge of the state in an unambiguous fashion.

The proletariat, on the other hand, tends to be numerically small, culturally very underprivileged, and generally lacking in the experience as well as the means to create effective autonomous organizations. The creation of proletarian parties and trade unions is everywhere mediated, therefore, by the crucial presence of the radical petty bourgeoisie in such organizations. In the agricultural sector, meanwhile, the historic experience of agrarian reforms is that they restrict large-scale landed property to lesser or greater extent, thus augmenting the power of the rich and middle peasants and enhancing the resources of an intermediate class of semi-rural commercial bourgeoisie which often overlaps with medium-sized landholdings. And, in strengthening capitalist relations in the countryside, agrarian reforms tend also to strengthen the role of the state—in organizing rural credit, providing the technology of the so-called Green Revolution, and constructing a whole range of new structures, from irrigation works to cooperatives and marketing organizations. The landless peasantry rarely benefits from these reforms. Rather, the bulk of it remains tied to landlords in such elaborate and acute ties of dependence, and it is so fragmented and widely dispersed, that it is usually unable to organize itself for sustained resistance, while the organizational role in militant mobilization of the peasantry is taken up largely by cadres drawn from the rich and middle peasantries (Alavi, 1965).

These peculiar features of state and civil society in the peripheral formations of Asia and the Middle East—e.g., the "overdevelopment" of the state in relation to the classes of civil society, the relative weakness of the polar classes, the enhanced powers, by contrast, of the intermediate classes— stem not from some sort of historical exceptionalism that might render them unintelligible to the Marxist method. Rather, the past and present experiences of a historical nature which distinguish them from metropolitan capitalism require modifications in perspective and analytic procedure. The crux of the matter is that the social formations we are discussing here are, by and large, transitional in character, where capitalism is dominant but not universal and where a variety of non-capitalist forms exist not only alongside capitalism, occupying their own effective space, but also intertwined with the capitalist mode itself, with profound effects on the social relations of capitalist production per se. The balance of class powers, and hence the modalities of class struggle in such peripheral formations, have characteristics that correspond to this transitional character of the systems of production. Likewise, the genealogy of the capitalist state in the periphery ought also to be studied not so much on the theoretico-abstract level of the capitalist mode of production as such, but in relation, fundamentally, to the specific modalities of the transition as it has unfolded in the actual histories of these formations.

A passage from Antonio Gramsci sheds rather interesting light on what we mean by the modalities of peripheral transition:

> In the typical peripheral countries . . . a broad spectrum of intermediate classes stretches between the proletariat and capitalism: classes which seek to carry on policies of their own, with ideologies which influence broad strata of the proletariat, but which particularly affect the peasant masses [Gramsci, 1978: 409].

Here, Gramsci is of course speaking of the Southern Question in Italy in the first three decades of this century, and when he speaks of the peripheral countries he has in mind essentially the Slavic countries and some other regions of Southern and Eastern Europe. But the passage contains several ideas which can be useful for a contemporary analysis. First, that the class structure of a peripheral society is different from that of mature capitalism, and that society is not so very much polarized between "the proletariat and capitalism"; indeed, there is a wide social space between the polar classes. Second, that this space is occupied not by the petty bourgeoisie alone, which is doubtless a strategic class of the capitalist mode of production, but by "a broad spectrum of intermediate classes," in the plural. Third, that these classes are not mere agents of other classes but, rather, they pursue "policies of their own." Fourth, that these classes generate ideologies that are designed not only to cement their own self-organization but also to establish their hegemony over much of the proletariat, and especially over the peasantry.

We shall develop this framework below, and add two crucial ideas that are absent from the above passage. The first is that the difference between the metropolitan and the peripheral formations exists not only on the level of civil society wherein the composition and balance of class forces provides a wide social space for the hegemonic projects of the intermediate classes, but also on the level of the state formation whereby these intermediate classes seek to establish their dominance over civil society by monopolizing the apparatuses of the state itself. The second idea, which is linked to the first, is that the intermediate classes have "policies" and "ideologies" which seek dominance not only over the proletariat and the peasantry but over the fundamental propertied classes as well.

In other words, classes exist as historical actors in so far as they struggle against other classes, and struggle is often for dominance. The intermediate classes are not passive bearers who merely serve the interests of other classes. Rather, like the polar classes, they too form multi-class alliances. In accordance with the actual balance of class powers obtaining in particular conjunctures, these intermediate classes may well accept, provisionally or for entire historical epochs, the leadership of a more powerful class. However, these political strategies and practical restrictions do not imply that an intermediate class foregoes that which is constitutive of the existence of a class as such, namely the struggle for dominance over other classes. Now, Gramsci's formulation that the intermediate classes possess "ideologies" that "influence" the working classes would appear to be rather weak, lest we remember that in the Gramscian problematic, ideology refers not to a "false consciousness" or to purely subjective conditions but to those cognitive processes that shape the real actions of human beings in the real world; "influence," then, is a radically practical undertaking whereby one class establishes its leadership over another. Understood this way, Gramsci's formulation helps us understand the real life-process of a whole range of ideologies, from the communist to the nationalist to the ethno-religious. Strata arising from inside the intermediate classes have historically sought to insert themselves into the politics of the working classes on the basis of these ideological interpellations, while the social conditions of peripheral development make it all the more likely that the working class organizations would be dominated by these strata.

In context, we shall argue that exceptional powers tend to be concentrated in the hands of the intermediate and auxiliary classes precisely because the peripheral state arose, as a rule, prior to the formation of the bourgeoisie as a politically dominant class, and as a pre-condition for the insertion of capitalism into non-capitalist societies, so that effective political power was exercised, in this process of transition, not necessarily by those who owned large-scale capital but primarily by those who actually organized this new type of state. This is true of Pakistan and Bangladesh, which were colonized, and of Iran which was never colonized but where the colonial powers played a key role in the construction of the capitalist state, as well as of Turkey and Afghanistan where the colonial impact remained indirect, limited and ambiguous, and where the new type of state arose at least partially in opposition to colonial encroachment. In each case, we witness the emergence of powerful strata, organized for the most part in apparatuses of the state, which arose from inside civil society, often from agrarian property and/or the bureaucracy of the antecedent non-capitalist state, but which detach themselves increasingly from that society and exercise special kinds of power over it, including the power of organizing relationships among the various propertied classes and mediating the relationship between these classes and the metropolitan bourgeoisie. The disproportionate power of what Marx and Engels used to call "the governing caste" thus comes from the fact, above all, that the state is the principal agency through which the dominance of the capitalist mode is established, so that the peripheral state is everywhere a highly interventionist state, itself acting as the largest capitalist firm, as well as directing and re-organizing every sector of the economy. Moreover, it is through the peripheral state that imperialism establishes its own dominance over the imperialized formation. This collaborative relationship between the metropolitan bourgeoisie and the indigenous "governing caste" greatly augments the power of the latter over the indigenous populace in general.

The Peripheral State and the "Governing Caste"

The dissolution of the precapitalist state and the construction, instead, of a state of the capitalist type occurred under very different circumstances in different countries of Asia and the Middle East. In Pakistan, it is indeed a post-colonial state, in the sense that the sovereign state which arose at the moment of de-colonization, in 1947, was based firmly on apparatuses, systems of governance, and even the personnel which had been assembled already by the British colonialists, while the dissolution of the precapitalist state(s) had taken place much earlier, in the nineteenth century, with the triumph of colonialism. But it is difficult and even misleading to generalize from that experience.

In Iran, for example, the peripheral state came into being only in the first half of the present century, and this process was extended in time from the abortive Constitutionalist Revolution of 1905–11 to the full length of the Reza Shah regime during the inter-War period (Halliday, 1979; Keddie, 1981; Abrahamian, 1982). British tutelage was substantial, but the context was one of semi-colonialism, and with the passage of time Reza Shah attempted to increase his room of maneuver by playing off the British against the Germans. And, in yet another contrast, the first major attempts to create a state of the capitalist type in Egypt date back not to the British Occupation of 1882, but to the very early years of the nineteenth century when the patriotic prince, Muhammed Ali, had sought to organize such a state, military-bureaucratic in form as a nationalist response to the Napoleonic invasion and the continuing threat of renewed European assaults. For him, the creation of a military-bureaucratic regime, the modernization of the Armed Forces, and the accentuation of commodity production and even industrialization under state supervision, were means of obtaining the centralized apparatus and the augmented economic surplus which he thought were essential for the defense of Egypt (Dodwell, 1931; Issaw, 1966: Part VI). Preponderant power of the state over civil society has been a characteristic of Egypt since times immemorial, and since the period of Muhammed Ali, at least, the state-associated strata have played the key role not only in systems of governance but also in systems of production and property (Abdel-Malek, 1968).

In more recent decades, this type of regime has arisen also from a rather different set of dynamics, viz., the military-bureacratic consolidation of the national liberation movements (e.g., in Kemalist Turkey, in Algeria under the FLN, in Bangladesh since 1971) as well as the radical-nationalism of the "progressive" coup (e.g., the politics of Nasserism in Egypt, under the Báath in Syria and Iraq, in Afghanistan since 1978). These distinct regimes have adopted different policies toward imperialism. Their ideologies have been surely diverse, ranging from the bourgeois etatism of Turkey to the full-blown "communism" of Afghanistan. And, each regime has modified the balance of class forces in the respective countries in very different ways. The common feature in all these cases, however, is the emergence and consolidation of a governing caste, comprised mostly of personnel that arose initially from among the intermediate classes, and which then consolidated its own dominance over the state so as to utilize the apparatuses of the state for dominating the classes of civil society. Colonialism played no role in creating any of the regimes we have cited here, and several of these arose in fact in opposition to colonial and/or imperialist domination. In each case, an indigenous military formation played the crucial role, while leadership for each formation was provided by persons who arose initially from the intermediate classes and became professional soldiers on their way to political power.

Again, in an entirely different sort of dynamic prevailing in the present-day oil-producing countries of the Gulf region, the pre-eminent role of the state-associated strata is owed simply to the fact that oil and gas revenues are deposited directly into the state treasury. Perhaps for the first time in history, we have a type of state that is fabulously wealthy but that obtains most of its revenues not from domestic taxation or expropriation of domestic labor but from exploitation largely of foreign labor migrating to oil centers and from production and sale of industrial raw materials on the international market. In a single stroke, the state has become completely dominant in the economic sphere, while the capitalist class is comprised mainly of commercial and rentier bourgeoisies that are entirely dependent upon the largesse of the state. Vast new bureaucracies have mushroomed everywhere, with high salaries, sumptuous privileges, and unprecedented powers. Rapid investments are made to generate new technical and managerial personnel from among the intermediate classes, and it is these personnel who then consolidate the state not only as an awesome military machine or as the chief administrator but also as simply the largest capitalist firm, for infrastructural construction, industrial investment, import/export networks, real estate development, the creation of credit, and so on. This preponderant role of the state in the economic sphere exists regardless of ideological commitments to statism or to maximization of private enterprise. In the case of pre-revolutionary Iran, for example, the state accounted for over 60 percent of all industrial investment in 1975, and during the period 1973–78, the state invested over $46 billion in industry, while the private sector invested just over $23 billion, or roughly half of what the state had invested. Significantly, over two-thirds of this private investment was itself owed to credit provided by the state. One is again reminded of Marx's characterization of the state, in his discussion of primitive accumulation, as an agency that creates the bourgeoisie, "hothouse-fashion."

The overwhelming economic power of the governing caste, and the dependence of the bourgeoisie upon this caste is of course altogether clear in the case of those countries—e.g., Nasserist Egypt, FLN's Algeria, Qaddafi's Libya—where official ideology describes itself as socialist. And, we have already cited the case of monarchical Iran as typical of those oil-producing countries that are entirely committed to private enterprise but where the state plays the pivotal role in all areas of economic production. However, the predominant economic role of the state is not a matter of oil revenues or radical/nationalist programs. The role is premised, rather, on the objective requirements of peripheral capitalist development, regardless of the character of ideologies or the volume of revenues. In Afghanistan prior to 1978, when there was no pretence of socialism, more than half the industry was in the state sector; 51 percent of all those who had nine or more years of schooling were said to be working in the Education Ministry; and the Army alone, not to speak of the civil bureaucracy, was four times as numerous as the entire working class, including the workers in the state-owned gas fields (Halliday, 1978; Dastarac and Levant, 1980). In Pakistan, the principal industrial units during the "take-off" of the 1950s were created by the state, through the Industrial Development Corporation, and were then sold to private firms, usually on credit; Ghulam Faruq, the Chairman of that Corporation, later emerged as one of the major industrialists in the country (Amjad, 1974). Then, in an effort to resolve the crisis that ensued from the separation of Bangladesh in 1971, the Government of Pakistan took over all the indigenous commercial banks, leaving only foreign banks in private hands; the state thus became also the chief banker in the country, even in the commercial sphere. Likewise, in the 1970s, investment by the state in the public industrial sector was four times larger than the aggregate private industrial investment (Ahmad, 1978).

We shall return to the question of the pre-eminent role of the state presently. It is worth emphasizing, meanwhile, that the distinguishing characteristics of the peripheral state, culminating in all events in the dominant role of the governing caste, arise not from the specific experience of colonialism as such, but from the historical peculiarities of capitalist development in our region, and from the assimilation of our societies to the objective requirements of the expanding world market. What defines the experience of the region as a whole is the externally inserted presence of the metropolitan bourgeoisie, the growing generalization of capitalist relations and commodity production at home, and the emergence of the peripheral-capitalist state as the articulating principle for the internal and external dynamics. Whether it arose as a consequence of colonialism, as in Pakistan, or in opposition to colonialism, as in Turkey, the peripheral state was designed to overcome, even to conceal, a certain absence, namely the absence of an indigenous bourgeois class capable of mastering the state. In some ways, this type of state is a specifically peripheral, particularly shoddy attempt to replicate the Bismarckian "revolution from above": it accelerates commodity production, transforms the landowners into a bourgeoisie of the ground-rent, constructs the supremacy of generalized commerce, and lays the foundations for industrial production. This occurs under the leadership not of a bourgeois class but of a 'governing caste' and, in a context of dependency, results in distorted forms of capitalist development.

The "Governing Caste" and the Military Elite

The case of the Armed Forces is even more complex. Conventional Marxist wisdom has it that the military becomes a dominant apparatus in the typical contemporary state of the periphery—i.e., in the so-called post-colonial state—as a result of the predominance of the colonial army in the past (Alavi, 1972). In some cases, that is true, but applied to the region as a whole, the proposition is factually incorrect and analytically barren. The argument was first made in relation to Pakistan as a typical case, and it is entirely true that the basic structure of those Armed Forces indeed came into being during the colonial period, the small number of the military officers who were inherited from the colonial Army have wielded power through thirty years of post-colonial history, and Great Britain, the ex-colonial power, continued to guide the expansion of the post-colonial army in the initial phase, from 1947 to 1951. But even in the case of Pakistan, where the argument is more applicable than in most other places, the military apparatus that was inherited from colonialism was in fact itself quite rudimentary, and the real proliferation of the apparatus is largely a post-colonial affair. Thus, local officers had begun to get admitted into the British Indian Army during World War I, but when Pakistan came into being, in 1947, it inherited neither an Air Force nor a Navy, and the Army it did inherit had no officer above the rank of colonel. By contrast, the first thirty years after de-colonization witnessed such immense expansion of the Armed Forces that, by the time of the coup in 1977, these Forces were comprised of roughly half a million. By 1982, the Army alone had over fifty Generals, Pakistani troops and ground personnel were stationed in eighteen countries, and the Air Force was beginning to take delivery of F-16s, the most sophisticated fighter-aircraft in the world. This relatively recent expansion of the military apparatus thus reflects the post-colonial structure and its articulation with United States efforts to build-up military forces around the world, much more than the colonial one.

In Iran, foreign patronage and imperialist domination were no doubt intimately connected with the development of the Armed Forces, but the dynamic is not reducible to a paradigm of colonialism, in the sense that Iran was never really colonized, and the whole process has to be understood in the perspective of an evolving capitalist state under a monarchy that was externally dependent on European powers but that organized the Armed Forces in its own largely autonomous space. Thus, when Reza Shah marched on Tehran in February 1921, with the agreement of the British, he had a humdrum force of well below 20,000. By 1925, he had created a unified Army of 40,000. In 1930, his forces stood at 80,000, and then rose to 125,000 by 1941. Throughout this period, while Reza Shah struggled to become more independent of the British by aligning himself increasingly with the Germans, the military budget constituted roughly one-third of all state expenditures. Under his son, the more recent Shah, the military budget rose from $67 million in 1953 to $844 million in 1970, and then up to to $9,400 million in 1977. By 1976, the Armed Forces, standing at 300,000, accounted for over 5% of all non-agricultural employment, while perhaps an equal number depended on the military for employment in infrastructural construction and related services (Halliday, 1979: 64–103). Thus, the Irani Armed Forces surely had historic, vital links with global imperialism but it would be simplistic to view them as a colonial construct.

Elsewhere, matters are even more ambiguous. The creation of a modern Army was first undertaken in Egypt in the early part of the nineteenth century, as a reaction against Napoleon's invasion. Over the next half century, first under Muhammed Ali and then under Khediv Ismael, the number of European technicians and military officers kept growing, augmenting the structure of dependence, but colonialism, in the proper sense, came later, with the British Occupation of 1882. The colonial authorities then played a key role in re-organizing the Armed Forces. Even so, Egypt remained technically a part of the Ottoman Empire until 1919 and then became nominally independent in 1936. Colonial presence, especially in its military form, was overwhelming, but—from the uprising of Urabi Pasha on the eve of the occupation to the National Party of Mustafa Kamel, and from the mass uprisings of 1919 to the organization of bourgeois opposition under men like Sa´ad Zaghlul—Egypt retained a space of autonomy for itself, and colonialism proved to be one moment among others in the prolonged evolution of the bourgeois state and its apparatuses in Egypt. Besides, the modern predominance of the military apparatus is owed to an altogether different conjunction of facts: the Free Officers' coup in 1952, in opposition to the Palace and its British patrons, which brought Nasser to power and led to the nationalization of the Canal; the Tripartite Invasion (by Britain, France, and Israel) in 1956; the Israeli invasion of 1967; and, the concommitant rise of a huge military apparatus whereby the Soviet Union, for example, trained over a million Egyptian soldiers (Abdel-Malek, 1968; Hussein, 1974). These factors were combined with a system of governance in which the military became the principal instrument of rule for both Nasser and Sadat—and now Hosni Mubarak, who is himself an ex-General of the Air Force. One should keep in mind also that more than a century before Nasser sent his Army to fight off the Saudis in the Yemen, Muhammed Ali, the legendary Egyptian ruler, had also dispatched his troops to the Hejaz (in modern-day Saudi Arabia) to suppress Wahabbi power. Neither enterprise was even remotely connected with the European colonization of Egypt.

Some other cases can be summarized more quickly. The governing caste that was built around a nucleus of military officers and that came to dominate the post-colonial state in Algeria arose not out of the structures of French colonialism but in opposition to it, from inside the Army of National Liberation. Similarly, the military-bureaucratic elite is no doubt the decisive force in Bangladesh today, but this elite arose not from the British colonial state but in the process of the secessionist movement of 1971 and in the course of the subsequent bureaucratic consolidation of power in the ravaged nation. The upper crust of this elite is comprised of men who were junior officers in the Pakistan Army during the 1960s, while the junior officers of today are recruits from the movement of 1971 and thereafter.

Finally, the case of Saudi Arabia represents yet another variant in this highly variegated regional configuration. The army of Abdel-Aziz al-Saud, which affected the territorial consolidation of the country in the early 1920s and thus constituted the historical basis for the modern Armed Forces of Saudi Arabia, had nothing at all to do, one way or another, with colonialism. Rather, at the height of its drive for power in 1924, that army fought its main battles against the Sherrif of Mecca, the then darling of the British. Reconciliation with and subordination to imperialism came after the consolidation of domestic power (Philby, 1968).

In brief, then, the military surely is, as a norm, the predominant apparatus of state in the majority of our countries, but in great many cases this contemporary position has little or nothing to do with a genealogical origin in the colonial armies of the past. The phenomenon is related, more often, to the way these states came into being in the first place, the articulations of power that developed in the absence of a leading bourgeois class, and, in many cases, the mode of their assimilation into the global impieralist system. Factors are too many to be analyzed in depth here, but a few can be mentioned in passing.

First, in the absence of a hegemonic bourgeoisie, and in conditions where the politics of the masses are essentially insurrectionary, the peripheral state is based on transparent coercion and repression. The repressive apparatus thus has an inherent tendency in this situation to subsume the political apparatus as well. In the process, the Armed Forces tend to appropriate the bulk of the national revenues. Second, in a host of countries, from Turkey to Afghanistan to Saudi Arabia, the military structure was already the leading structure of the state prior to the assimilation of that state into the imperialist system. In these cases, the modern army arose from inside the old army, transforming itself and greatly expanding its regular and permanent personnel in the process, but this self-transformation was designed precisely to preserve and even to increase its leading role. Third, with the single exception of Iran, all the anti-monarchical revolutions of the post-war period were carried out not by forces arising from below but by groups of "progressive" officers who then substituted monarchical regimes with military regimes. In terms of class powers, there was often a very considerable shift, from large-scale property, especially landed property, toward sectors of the intermediate classes; but in institutional terms, these anti-monarchical revolutions have almost always led to the supremacy of the military officers. Fourth, even within the liberation movements, from Turkey to Algeria, the military organization tended to overshadow the political organization, with the political apparatus often coming into being as an effect of the military organization, so that the task of organizing the new state after independence was taken up by the military organization as the leading force.

Finally, the territorial consolidation of the bourgeois state is in most cases a recent and unstable phenomenon, so that the Armed Forces take up a prominent role in these countries as guarantors of beleaguered frontiers, a task that may not be within their capacity but which is nonetheless the basis for their claim upon national revenues. Thus, Pakistan came into being only in 1947, and its boundaries were cut in half in 1971. Even today, there are secessionist movements in three of its four principal linguistic regions, with the Baloch nationality having fought a full-scale war in the 1970s. Territorial boundaries of the state are thus far from having become permanent. In the case of Afghanistan, territorial consolidation occurred only in the last quarter of the nineteenth century and was completed as late as 1919, with the conclusion of the Third Anglo-Afghan War; successive Afghan governments have thereafter claimed the northwestern province of Pakistan, thus indicating that the Afghan state is yet to achieve the frontiers it would consider legitimate. Similarly, Persia has of course existed since times immemorial, but Iran as we know it today is a phenomenon of the twentieth century, when the monarchical regime of Reza Shah (1926–1941) moved, in the words of Ervand Abrahamian, "to consolidate his power by building and strengthening his support on three pillars—the new Army, the government bureaucracy, and the court patronage. For the first time since the Safavids, the state was able to control society through extensive instruments of administration, regulation, and domination" (Abrahamian, 1982: 135–136). The "control" nevertheless failed to take root. Even today, the Kurdish nationality is waging a full-scale war of resistance and survival against the centralized Irani state. A similar dynamic is at work in the Arab world. As indicated earlier, the creation of the Saudi state is an affair of the 1920s. A number of other states, such as Syria, Lebanon and Jordan, emerged as sovereign entities only after World War II. The modern division between the states of North and South Yemen has some historical basis in the colonial past but is a result, specifically, of the conflicts of the 1960s. And the unity of the United Arab Emirates (UAE) is only about a decade old. Conversely, parts of Syria have been annexed by Israel, Lebanon is currently in the process of being blown to pieces, and the fate of Jordan is unclear. The best that can be said of the two Yemens is that although they are caught in an intricate set of regional conflicts and imperialist interventions, they have so far avoided a full-scale, mutually destructive war. Needless to add, many of these frontiers were drawn by colonial armies, but many others were either drawn by indigenous forces or represented, at best, uneasy compromises between the colonial powers and the indigenous ruling coalitions.

All this has had at least four major consequences. One, almost every state has territorial claims against one or more of its neighbors. Second, most frontiers are altogether arbitrary, signifying a conquest, and the territorial consolidation of particular countries has meant the division and dispersion of numerous ethno-linguistic nationalities—Kurds, Balochs, Azerbaijani Turks, Pashtuns, Tajiks, Turkomans, to name only a few—across internationally recognized frontiers. Conversely, movements for re-consolidation of these nationalities promise to upset the territorial consolidation of existing states. Third, most of these are in reality multi-national societies but tend to simulate the appearance and modes of governance of nation-states. In practice, power tends to be concentrated in the hands of a particular ethnic or religious group (the Alawis in Syria, the Maronites in Lebanon) or nationality (Punjabis in Pakistan, Persians in Iran, Pashtuns in Afghanistan), while the dominant group presents itself as the repository of "national unity," circumventing a distribution of power that might more truly correspond to the multi-national character of our societies. Fourth, state power is premised everywhere on coercive minority regimes, with no ties of representation with the majority of the population. This whole structure requires the predominance of the military apparatus, which then inserts itself into each of the four elements summarized above, viz., in the politics of territorial claims upon neighbors, in preventing the consolidation of nationalities that are dispersed across frontiers, in establishing the supremacy of particular ethno-linguistic groups and nationalities over others, and in underwriting the power of the coercive minority regimes.

The imperialist dimension is grafted on top of these aggregated violences. It is the historic fact of our age that the major means of military violence are produced by the metropolitan bourgeoisies but utilized, more often than not, and almost as a fact of daily existence, by the rulers of the periphery. None of these armies would be what they are without the means of mass destruction they recieve from the metropolitan exporters of weaponry. It is in this sense that imperialism is the constitutive element and the stabilizing factor in the whole global structure of military violence, the problem is not the colonialism of the past but the imperialism of the present, and the repressive apparatus becomes the supreme apparatus of state and the state itself becomes not hegemonic, in the Gramscian sense, but simply absolutist and predatory.

Nation, Nationalism, and the Intermediate Class

We have proposed in the preceding sections that in the concrete conditions prevailing in our region, the peripheral state of the modern type arises prior to the emergence of the bourgeoisie as the politically dominant class, which makes it possible for those segments of the intermediate and auxiliary classes that occupy the apparatuses of the state to exercise extraordinary powers over all classes of civil society. We have pointed also to the relative general weakness of the polar classes as such, so that while some fractions of the intermediate classes seek to utilize the apparatuses of state to establish their dominance over the whole of civil society, other fractions may occupy significant positions in workers' organizations, leftwing political parties, and mass movements of the populist and radical kind. In the latter context, the classic case is of course that of the segment of the Afghan petty bourgeoisie that led the revolution of April 1978. And, there is an enormously broad experience of communist parties and liberation movements throughout the region, and indeed in other parts of the world, that can be analyzed to substantiate this point. Here, however, we wish to comment briefly on a much misunderstood phenomenon, namely that of nationalism, which tends everywhere to be the classic terrain for the politics of the intermediate classes, while the ideology of nationalism itself takes myriad forms, as we shall see.

The best known variety of the nationalist ideology is of course the one that arises in opposition to colonial occupation or imperialist exploitation. In a case like that of Algeria, for example, where a settler colony population dominated the whole of the indigenous society, nationalism was of course directed outward, and since the intensity of colonization had prevented the emergence of an Algerian bourgeoisie, the nationalist movement was dominated wholly by the developing Third Estate. Then, the mass organizations and the internal guerrilla army were thoroughly battered in the course of the revolutionary war, and it was from among the administrative elite of the exile government and the officers' corps of the external army that the governing caste of post-independence Algeria really arose (Hambrachi, 1966; Amin, 1970; Blair, 1970; Cleg, 1971). It is significant, moreover, that the Europeanized segment of the urban petty bourgeoisie, led by men like Ferhat Abbas, had historically accepted the purported ideology of "assimilation," whereby this privileged segment was promised full citizenship rights within the French nation. This segment went into opposition during the 1940s, demanding that the policy of selective assimilation be implemented, and its leaders joined the liberation movement in the 1950s only after those hopes were at length frustrated (Wolfe, 1969). In any case, anti-colonial nationalism is only one form of the nationalist ideology, albeit the best known.

There are other cases, however, where the nationalist opposition is directed not against the externally inserted colonial power but against indigenous forces, and especially against the centralized state. Thus, the Pakistan Movement which arose among the Muslims of British India and succeeded in carving out a new country for itself, represented a nationalism that was directed not against the colonial authority of the British but against the Hindu majority inside the subcontinent. Similarly, the movement of Bengali nationalism which later created its own state in Bangladesh, in 1971, again represented a nationalist force that was directed against the independent post-colonial state of Pakistan itself, precisely because the military-bureaucratic regime was based among the non-Bengali minorities, obstructing the consolidation of the bourgeois class in East Bengal and greatly restricting the presence and power of the Bengali petty bourgeoisie in organs of the state (Alavi, 1971). And, in virtually every country of our region there are nationalisms of various minorities, such as the Baloch in

Pakistan and Iran, or the Kurds in Turkey, Iran and Iraq. Any one of these nationalisms may be progressive or reactionary, and their objectives may vary, from secession to regional autonomy to domination over the constituted state. In virtually all cases, however, we find that the political organization is largely dominated by persons drawn from among the intermediate classes, and it is they, more than any other class or social stratum, who tend to gain from the success of such a movement. There are of course material reasons for all that. Such movements arise precisely among nationalities and regions where a consolidated bourgeois class does not exist, where the propertied classes find themselves barred from participation in the centralized state, and where the petty bourgeoisie finds itself systematically excluded from the higher circles of the civilian and military bureaucracies. Membership in the organs of the state becomes the critical question because it is in these organs that power is concentrated. Thus, in the Indian sub-continent, for example, the Muslim fraction of the bourgeoisie had wanted to become free of the dominance of the Hindu fraction but was structurally so weak and regionally so isolated that it was unable to organize a secessionist movement under its own leadership. That organizational role was performed by the Muslim fraction of the Third Estate in colonial India, and it is primarily from that fraction that a new governing caste of bureaucrats and military officers arose after Pakistan came into being as a separate, sovereign state. Likewise, there is today no consolidated bourgeois class among the Kurds in Turkey or Iran or Iraq; nor is there one among the Baloch in Pakistan. Logically, then, it is the so-called "educated middle class" which plays the key role in organizing dissidence among these nationalities, usually in a relationship of collaborative competition with the landowning classes.

Then, there are what we might call the assimilative or corporatist nationalisms—Pan-Arabism, Pan-Islamism, and so on—that characteristically arise either among the traditional sectors of the intermediate classes and among strata whose location in the capitalist economy is highly precarious (e.g. Pan-Islamism, in its myriad forms) or among segments of the modern Third Estate (e.g. Pan-Arabism). Frequently, there may even be an overlap, in pursuit of collaborative action and mutual advantage. In the Arab countries, for example, there is a broad ideological discourse among the urban petty bourgeoisie these days which holds, rather unconvincingly, that there is no difference between Pan-Islamism, which is manifestly an idea of religious particularity, and Pan-Arabism, which has historically symbolized commonality of action between the Muslim and Christian sections of the Arab population. Of course, the supra-national character of the respective ideologies is itself highly mystificatory. Militant Pan-Arabism is now forty years old. Its spokesman have wielded enormous power in Egypt under

Nasser, in Libya under Qaddafi, in Syria and Iraq under the respective factions of the Báath. Every Arab ruler has paid homage to the idea, in one form or another. The material fact nonetheless is that each Arab country is incorporated into the global imperialist system as a particular nation-state, and the ruling class of each country has a highly differentiated character. It is unlikely that the utopian notions of pan-Arabism would ever dissolve these material specificities. Similarly, Pan-Islamicists are now in possession of state power in Iran, and they command significant political movements in a number of other countries. Yet, they are themselves so profoundly fractionalized, and the nation-state within which each of the movements exists is so very much a reality, that their dream of a supra-national Islamic imperium is altogether unlikely ever to materialize. One might even suggest that the assertion of a supra-national ideology is more often than not a way of masking the essentially national character of the ambition. The Pan-Arabist ideology of the Iraqi Báath, for example, is in reality little more than a mask for the ambition of the Iraqi state to dominate the whole of the Gulf region. Similarly, the Islamic Societies in Egypt today are doubtless Pan-Islamicist in their ideology, but the real function of that ideology is not to work toward the creation of a global Islamic polity but to harness the forces of opposition and disaffection against the Egyptian state. In any event, and regardless of ideological mystifications, when we look at the biographical and sociological profile of the leading cadres either in the Pan-Islamicist movements (e.g. the Muslim Brotherhood and the Islamic Societies in Egypt and elsewhere, the Shii opposition in Iraq, the NSP and NAP in Turkey, the Jamáat-e-Islami in Pakistan) or the leaders of the Pan-Arabist movements (the Nasserists, the Báathists, the founders of the Arab National Movement), we are struck by the predominance and even virtual monopoly of personnel drawn from among the intermediate classes.

Finally, there is what we have designated as 'radical nationalism', e.g. the FLN in Algeria, Nasserism in Egypt and beyond, the Arab Báath in its original formation in Syria and elsewhere, and in some respects the Bhutto regime in Pakistan. This radical nationalism normally has three characteristics. One, it obtains legitimacy from its origins in anti-colonialism and its claim to be anti-imperialist. Thus, the FLN arose as a liberation movement against French colonialism. The Báath arose initially in Syria under French occupation and has thereafter utilized anti-Zionism as a legitimizing principle. Nasserism was born not in a colonial setting but surely in response to the defeat of the Egyptian Army in the war of 1948 against Israel, and it became a hegemonic ideology after the nationalization of the Suez Canal and especially after successful resistance against the Tripartite Agression of 1956. The Bhutto regime, less radical than some others, was born nonetheless on a platform of anti-imperialism and sought to at least re-negotiate its contract with the imperialist powers. The second characteristic of radical nationalism is that it tends also to converge with what we have called assimilative nationalism. All the expressions we have cited here with regard to the Arab world—Nasserism, the Báath, the FLN—were Pan-Arabist, while the radicalism of the Bhutto regime in Pakistan was coordinated increasingly with Pan-Islamism. Conversely, the Pan-Islamicists of the Khomeini movement in Iran have made full use of the anti-imperialist platform of the radical-nationalists in their own populist mobilizations. Third, in the domain of ideological mystifications that conceal the actual class practices, it is characteristic of radical nationalism that it presents itself, sooner or later, either as a socialism (if its thrust is essentially secular) or as a third way (Islam; neither communism nor capitalism). In practice, of course, these slogans of socialism and the third way tend to support highly authoritarian regimes based upon the predominance of the public sector over the private, a wave of nationalizations, some agrarian reforms, and concentration of political power in the hands of a single party that increasingly becomes a political bureaucracy and converges with administrative and military bureaucracies, with the whole pyramid leading to a charismatic personal dictatorship at the top.

Now, the ideology of nationalism does not have an a priori class content that is integral to it prior to its emergence in particular historical circumstances. The class content is determined, rather, in the very process of its emergence, by the power bloc that appropriates it and gives expression to it in the course of the struggle for hegemony. That may lead to revolution, as in Vietnam, or to a bureaucratic dictatorship of the radical-nationalist type, as in Algeria, or to clerical fascism, as in Iran. The class content of nationalism is determined, in other words, by the alliance of classes that utilizes nationalist ideology in the construction of its own power and thus comes to speak, symbolically and with concrete political effect, for what is called the nation. In all events, the category of "the nation" is attractive to the intermediate classes because of the highly productive ambiguity of the term. On the one hand, there are oppressions that are fundamentally national in character; colonialism is the obvious example of it, but there is also the rampant subordination and exploitation of the oppressed nationalities within the boundaries of the existing sovereign states, which then constitutes the objective basis for the emergence of separatist nationalisms. There are national projects to be undertaken; the reconstitution and consolidation of the Palestinian nation, for example, is a crucial nationalist undertaking. And, regardless of the perversity of models imported from the capitalist metropoles, the development of the productive forces in the periphery is a real task which can be addressed, in the present historical phase at any rate, only at the level of the nation-state. Similarly, Pan-Arabism does incorporate, for all its utopianism, realities which are at once primordial and contemporary. In other words, there are concrete material reasons why the ideology of nationalism has such immense mobilizing power. On the other hand, the category of the nation is attractive for the intermediate classes also because of its predilection to suppress the class question and to pose the question of liberation on the level of "the people" or even on the level of the (classless) state. It is precisely because of its supra-class appearance and its immense mobilizing power that the ideology of nationalism becomes the classic terrain for the construction of hegemony, on the part of any class which seeks to lead the other classes of civil society.

It should be understood also that the nation is not a metaphysical, supra-historical category that might exist outside, above, or prior to class practices and/or configurations of power. Rather, the nation, and national-ism as its ideological accompaniment, comes into being only under particu-lar historical circumstances, as a realization of a hegemonic project, created by a leading class or an alliance of class forces able to muster the requisite power for their act of creation and realization. For example, the Turkish nation, as we know it today, is a product of the Kemalist Revolution and of the state that was created in the process. Before that, there was only the Ottoman Empire, and the nationalisms which preceded the Kemalist variant in Turkey were of three kinds. There was, first, an "Ottoman" nationalism, corresponding to the territoriality of the Empire, which sought to bestow equal rights of citizenship on all subjects of the Sultan—Muslim or non-Muslim, Slavic or Arab or Turk—provided that the unity of Empire was maintained. Then, second, there was a powerful Pan-Islamic nationalism, which reflected the claim of the Sultan that he was caliph of all Muslims everywhere; it was a nationalism not so much of an imperial territory as of a religious faith which thought of itself as an empire. Third, there was also a Pan-Turkic nationalism, focused primarily upon the Central Asian territor-ies conquered by the Russian Czars but peopled, nevertheless, by speakers of the Turkish language. The idea that there was a secular Turkish nation which corresponded neither to the Ottoman Sultanate, nor to the Islamic faith, nor to the totality of the Turkic people—and the idea, moreover, that this Turkish nation corresponded quite precisely to a brand new national territory, created in the aftermath of World War I, and consisting of not much more than Anatolia and the adjoining provinces—this idea was a new one, given ideological content and material shape by the Kemalist Revolu-tion itself, in the process of dealing with the rest of the world (Ahmed, 1969; Inalric; 1973; Lewis, 1961; Merdin, 1962; Mortimer, 1982, 126–58). Nor is this process of re-defining a nation peculiar to Turkey.

The Afghan nation is likewise a product of the territorial consolidation of a particular country over a long period of time, between about 1840 and 1919, through a series of wars undertaken by a state that created the nation in the process of its own consolidation. That is to say, Afghanistan is a nation-state only in so far as there is a leading force, or a hegemonic bloc, upholding the identity of nation and state. In its internal composition, of course, the Afghan nation is in reality a multinational society comprised of many ethno-linguistic entities, such as the Pashtuns, Tajiks, Turcomans, Uzbeks, Hazaras, Balochs, Aimaqs, and others. Whether or not an Afghan nation shall continue to exist over and above these ethnicities shall depend, as it has depended since the middle of the 18th century, upon the character of hegemony on the level of the state.

Thus, when we speak of these nations we are referring not so much to some set of supposedly permanent and primordial facts of ethnicity or language or race or religion, or of some idealized spiritual ethos. We refer, rather, as we must, to the mundane world of territorial boundaries, armies, markets, systems of taxation and governance, bodies of legislation, artefacts of ideology, facts and rights of residence, and so forth. That is to say: force, legality, hegemony. In other words, it is a characteristic of the capitalist era that nations and states tend to converge; that a nation is either created by or finds its material form of existence in a state; and that consolidated nations arise only where a hegemonic bloc is able, simultaneously, to fashion a nationalist and populist ideology as the principal of its own legitimation, as well as to construct a state that fixes the boundaries of what eventually becomes a nation. No wonder, then, that precisely those class forces that are most prominent in the organization of the peripheral state are also the ones most prominent in articulating that whole set of ideological positions that appear in left-wing literature under the rubric of 'the national question'. It is no exaggeration to say, I think, that every nationalist movement in our region, whether of the assimilative or of the separatist kind, whether anti-colonial and revolutionary or ethnocentric and chauvanist, is led primarily by personnel that originates in segments of the intermediate classes. This personnel is sometimes allied with fractions of capital and landed property, sometimes not; some might make a revolutionary choice, as many have done in the Palestine Resistance, while others may settle down to be outright reactionaries, as did Mulla Barazani among the Kurds, when he eventually became a mere plaything in the hands of the Irani monarchy and the CIA. Neither their ideological outlooks nor their alliances are pre-ordained by their class origins. But their strategic location in the whole range of national-ist politics is at any rate beyond question.

Conclusion

These matters can be discussed ad infinitum, and it is impossible to conclude with a neat summary of an argument so lengthy and complex. Our basic contention, nevertheless, is that in the concrete conditions prevailing in our region, the intermediate classes, led normally by the petty bourgeoisie, occupy a strategic space in the field of politics, and that the final outcome in most political conjunctures tends to be influenced decisively by the political choices made by these classes and by the fractions, within these classes, that gain paramountcy in the politics of these classes. Whether particular fractions shall make a revolutionary or a reactionary choice in a given conjuncture shall depend upon the specificity of fraction and conjuncture, and upon the general balance of class powers prevailing in society at large.

References

Abdel-Malek, Anour
1968   Egypt: Military Society. New York: Random House.
Abrahamian, Ervand
1982   Iran: Between Two Revolutions. Princeton: Princeton University Press.
Ahmad, Aijaz
1978   "Democracy and dictatorship in Pakistan." Journal of Contemporary Asia 8.
Ahmed, Feroz
1969   The Young Turks, London: Oxford University Press.
Alavi, Hamza
1965   "Peasants and revolution." In The Socialist Register. New York, Monthly Review Press. (Expanded version in Gough and Sharma (eds.), Imperialism and Revolution In South Asia. New York: Monthly Review Press.)
1971   "The crisis of nationalities and the State of Pakistan." Journal of Contemporary Asia 1, (3).
1972   "The state in post-colonial societies: Pakistan and Bangladesh." New Left Review (74).
Amin, Samir
1970   The Maghreb in the Modern World. London: Penguin.
Amjad, Rashid
1974   Industrial Concentration and Economic Power in Pakistan. Lahore: Punjab University Press.
Blair, Thomas L.
1970   The Land to Those Who Work It: Algeria's Experiment in Workers' Management. New York: Doubleday.
Cleg, Ian
1971   Workers' Self-Management in Algeria. New York: Monthly Review Press.
Dastarac, Alexandre and M. Levant
1980   "What went wrong in Afghanistan." MERIP Reports (89).
Devlin, John
1976   The Ba´ath Party: A History From its Origins to 1966. Palo Alto, CA: Stanford University Press.
Dodwell, Henry
1931   The Founder of Modern Egypt, A Study of Muhammad Ali Pasha. Cambridge: Cambridge University Press.
Gramsci, Antonio
1971   The Prison Notebooks. New York: International Publishers.
1978   Selections from Political Writings, 1921–1926. New York: International Publishers

Gregorian, Vartan
1969   The Emergence of Modern Afghanistan. Palo Alto, CA: Stanford University Press.
Halliday, Fred
1978   "Revolution in Afghanistan." New Left Review (112).
1979   Iran: Dictatorship and Development. London: Penguin.
Hambrachi, Arslan
1966   Algeria: The Revolution that Failed. London: Pall Mall.
Hussein, Mahmoud
1974   Class Conflict in Egypt: 1945–1970. New York: Monthly Review Press.
Inalric, Hilal
1973   The Ottoman Empire: The Classical Age, 1300–1600. New York.
Issawi, Charles (ed).
1966   The Economic History of the Middle East 1800–1914. Chicago: University of Chicago
        Press.
Kayder, Caglar
1979   "The political economy of Turkey's democracy." New Left Review 115.
Keddie, Nikkie R.
1981   Roots of Revolution: An Interpretative History of Modern Iran. New Haven: Yale
        University Press.
Lewis, Bernard
1961   The Emergence of Modern Turkey. London: Oxford University Press.
Merdin, Sherif
1962   The Genesis of Yound Ottoman Thought. Princeton, NJ: Princeton University Press.
Marx, K. and F. Engels
1968   Selected Works. New York: İnternational Publishers.
Mortimer, Edward
1982   Faith and Power: The Politics of Islam. New York: Random House.
Olson, Robert
1983   The Ba´ath and Syria: 1947–1982. Princeton: Kingston Press.
Petran, Tabitha
1972   Syria. New York: Praegar.
Philby, H. St. John
1968   Saudi Arabia. Beirut: Librairi du Liban.
Saul, John S.
1979   "The state in postcolonial societies." In The State and Revolution in East Africa. New
        York: Monthly Review Press.
Shaw, Stanford
1977   History of the Ottoman Empire and Modern Turkey (2 vols.). Cambridge: Cambridge
        University Press.
Wilbur, Donald N. (ed)
1962   Afghanistan. New York: Taplinger.
Wolfe, Eric R.
1969   Peasant Wars of the Twentieth Century. New York: Harper & Row.

CHAPTER THREE

Novella Zett Keith and Nelson W. Keith: The Rise of the Middle Class in Jamaica

In the theoretical formulations relating to the Third World the middle class does not stand out prominently among the dynamic forces influencing socio-economic change. Although development social scientists of the modernization school did assign prominence to technocrats, the "educated class," and the "middle class military" as modernizers (Nun, 1967; Johnson, 1958; Alba, 1968), the critical tradition was for long influenced by the perceptions of such Third World writers as Fanon, C. L. R. James, Aimée Cesaire: the middle class in the Third World was a close analogue of its metropolitan counterpart, a class of devoted consumers fully and irredeemably wedded to the capitalist ethos. Its occasional outbursts of radical rhetoric tended to resonate mainly at the ideological level; one could not count on the class to initiate the needed program of change for post-colonial societies.[1]

There exists, on the other hand, a growing body of writings on the "exceptional" form of the state in the periphery, a form arising from the perceived dislocation between the economic and political "moments." Briefly, the state acquires an increased measure of relative autonomy from the economically dominant classes and becomes an instrument of class creation for those social agents that control key structures within the state apparatus. These agents are alternatively conceptualized as a "higher bureaucracy," "bureaucratic class," "bureaucratic bourgeoisie," or "state bourgeoisie."[2] This development is not taken to signify a profound alteration of social relations, though in certain writings it forms the basis of the "non-capitalist path" (Nyerere, 1968; Solodnikov, 1973); rather, it is most often seen as a variant: state capitalism. The analytical approaches taken to these phenomena carry all the signs of theoretical flux, yet there are some constancies to draw one's attention: the invariable presence in strategic places of intermediate elements or classes—the petty bourgeoisie, the "intelligentsia," the middle class. We begin to perceive the workings of distinct social mechanisms in the periphery, propelling these actors to a prominence unlike any experienced in the center.

The new role of the middle class does not emerge from any particularities in its *economic* location, which is not in itself likely to lead to "revolutionary" overtures. The realms within which the class functions are linked to the reproduction of capitalist relations and are not directly articulated with the pivotal process of production upon which class conflict and fundamental social change are based: The middle class, as so-called unproductive workers, reproduce the conditions for effective capital accumulation (Marx, 1952: 148–97). We must recall, however, that the reproduction of capitalist relations in the periphery requires a multiplicity of mediations without counterpart in the center. The class or fraction of a class that figures prominently in these mediations is likely to play a correspondingly prominent role in the social formation, as the political moment acquires ascendancy over the economic. One of the contentions underlying this chapter is that the Jamaican class structure, not unlike other Third World structures, possesses a middle class not fitting the stereotype. Certain fractions of the class emerge as nodal fractions in the social formation, in a way that is quite atypical of the evolution of the middle class in capitalist formations of the center.

From a global perspective, the fundamental differences between the two limbs of the class revolve around the patterns of capital accumulation in each bloc. While it is true, as Samir Amin (1972) convincingly argues, that capitalist accumulation envelopes the center and the periphery in a single, coherent, and dominant mode of production, the processes of articulation of the two systems of economics give rise to differences in class relations. The dominant impulse in these patterns arises from the historical process upon which depends the continuing economic growth of the central economies: a process that, in the current phase, makes of the periphery the providers of consumption goods (Department II) and of the center the producers of capital goods (Department I). [3]In the periphery this impulse meets and becomes articulated with pre- and non-capitalist modes of production. Thus the two blocs are created, termed peripheral capitalism and central capitalism, each characterized by its own variant of social and productive relations.

The more important repercussions of this division of labor on social class relations in the Third World may be schematically stated as follows:

(1) The systematic retardation of peripheral capitalist development has led to relatively weak capitalist and working classes.
(2) The peculiar structure of these economies and the enlarged interventionist

and welfare functions discharged by the state have resulted in a rapid and continuous growth of the middle class.

(3) The middle class has successfully penetrated certain sections of the state apparatus—the political, in particular—thereby enabling its more powerful elements to play a decisive role in political governance and direction of the economy.

There are indeed other factors, largely of a cultural and historical nature, contributing to the peculiarity of the middle class in the periphery. Our brief excursus on the distinctions between the two patterns of capital accumulation—which has already revealed important differences—must be taken to the other levels of class relations that assume greater importance to the extent that the economic moment is weak.

What our research forces progressively to our attention is the discrepant role of the peripheral bourgeoisie. Uneven development—an invariable feature of the capitalist mode of production—ensures the chronic weakness of this class vis-à-vis its metropolitan counterpart and a comparable weakness with respect to the peripheral middle class. If there can be no vacuum in power relations, then such discrepancies translate into a distinctive feature of class relations: The dominant class is not the hegemonic class; this is to say, that while the capitalist class dominates at the economic level, it does not do so at the levels of the political and ideological structures. Unlike the ruling class structure of the modern capitalist social formation—in which the dominant class tends to be the hegemonic class—that of the periphery exhibits a certain permeability allowing for access from without.

What are the internal weaknesses contributing to the overall fragility of the peripheral bourgeoisie? The main difficulty stems from inter-fractional dissonances exposing the class as a whole to countervailing ideological postures. Of the fractions comprising Third World bourgeoisies, two have been stressed in much of the literature on development: a comprador fraction and a "national" fraction. The former fraction is tied exclusively to foreign capital and imperialist penetration. It draws its life-blood from a parasitic relationship with foreign capital and owes its continued existence to its ability to protect foreign interests and priorities locally. In a nutshell, the stewardship entails the continuing role of foreign capital in production for export and its control of import-substituting industries geared to imported capital and inputs.

The national capitalist fraction, on the other hand, represents elements of the bourgeoisie that would soon see a decline in the dominance of foreign capital based on its own program of economic development. Here the stress is on the growth and development of indigenous industries, with an inferior role to be played by foreign capital. It advocates the restriction of imports that could be locally produced, favors national control of local resources, argues for the progressive use of local raw materials, and so on. It is quite clear that these positions are antagonistic. The advance of one fraction is almost at the direct expense of the other.

The fractionalization of the peripheral bourgeoisie presents yet more complexities when a closer focus is brought to bear on the "national" bourgeoisie. The term designates a cohesive economic and political unit that, in fact, may be embryonic, its existence signalled only as a tendency within the process of capital accumulation. In many peripheral social formations, the groupings of disparate origins that would coalesce to form a "national" fraction of capital—arising from pre-capitalist and capitalist modes of production—need the agency of the state to accomplish the project of class formation (Taylor, 1979; Foster-Carter, 1978).

We discover, therefore, that the necessity of presenting a united front, a fairly uniform ideology, is dogged by intrinsic weaknesses of a structural nature, derived from the place of the class within global capital accumulation. Of course, the situation is quite different in the central capitalist formation. While inter-fractional disputes exist within the bourgeoisie, these are resolvable against the background of a unified ideology. The level of capitalist development in these formations results in a pattern of interlocking economic sectors that, though prone to conflict, are oriented to complementarity in the longer run. In the "Third World" complementarity is replaced by mutual exclusiveness. The economies, even in the case of the "semi-periphery," are riddled with these warring fractions. In turn, the fractions must take their differences for resolution to state apparatuses made stronger and more independent partly as a result of this absence of unity.

If the cohesion of the capitalist class is fragmented from within, the class is further weakened by fissures in the fabric of hegemony, the result of forces emerging from below. In the periphery, contradictions between dominant and subordinate classes are often compounded by ethnic or racial divisions as well as by too close an identification of certain fractions of the local capitalist class with the ex-colonial power. The petty bourgeoisie or the middle class acquires a degree of legitimacy in the eyes of subordinate classes through its leadership role in the independence struggle, and it is through these forces that the capitalist class must often rule.

The Bureaucratic Middle Class

The rise of the middle class (or petty bourgeoisie—this term is often used to include the former)[4] in the Third World has received some attention in the last decade, as suggested above, coincident with the inclination of the class to use its position within the state apparatus to arrogate economic power to itself. The history of the economic development of the Third World clearly shows that, whichever mode of economic strategy is undertaken, its implementation is followed by immense expansion of the state apparatuses, an expansion to be explained by the manner of articulation of Third World economies to overall capitalist development. The process of "blocking" that results from the highly selective and uneven division of labor between center and periphery leads to a compulsory adoption of Keynesian economics. In turn, as economic activity revolves less around forms of production geared to generating employment, the state is called upon more and more to provide employment and to ward off economic stagnation. Usually this is achieved by the progressive enlargement of the bureaucracy through the provision of "patronage" employment (Leys, 1974; Sandbrook, 1975; Taylor, 1979).

The growth of the state apparatus is not in itself sufficient cause for the arrogation of power by a fraction of the middle class. The most plausible explanation for the clearly bourgeois mindset of the fraction and its emancipation from an essentially supervisory role is provided by the role of ideology. There is a distinction between mental and manual labor that serves to put the "proper" distance between the middle class and the subordinate classes. The quest for education is perhaps the most potent drive in ex-colonial countries: Education is truly a new means of production. The middle class of the periphery absorbs the dominant ideology but is, unlike its metropolitan counterpart, not subject to the hegemonic control of the dominant class. We find this difference to be significant in at least two respects. First, the resulting socialization, when unhampered by ruling class constraint, is aggressively self-serving. There is an almost inherent tendency for lawyers, accountants, economists, business administrators, and so on to break loose on their own behalf if constraints are token or weak. If a portion of their professional education stressed the benefits of achievement, history and aspects of their training also contribute to a strong conviction that certain things belong to them as a matter of right. Second, the strategic location of the fraction within the state apparatuses allows for a combination of opportunity for the exercise of decisive power and the mindset to provide the rationalization: The strategic fraction of the class is justified on all counts to be creative on its own behalf and is scarcely plagued by ambivalences directed at its bourgeois or proletarian status.

If the process of capital accumulation on a world scale etches a structurally determined political role for the bureaucratic middle class, there are other factors contributing to its entrenchment. As is well known, peripheral social formations are most often characterized by the articulated co-existence of the capitalist mode of production with pre- or non-capitalist modes. The result of this articulation is a greater complexity of the class structure—much greater than that encountered under central capitalism—with differing socio-economic priorities, differing consciousness, and unpredictable political ideologies (Foster-Carter, 1978; Taylor, 1979; Post, 1978). It follows from a structural viewpoint that the majority of these classes function outside of capitalist market relations: peasants, petty-bourgeoisie, semi-proletariat, and lumpens are the main classes whose interests must be mediated within the context of the capitalist mode of production.

In these circumstances the part to be played by the state in redressing a balance between largely discrepant class interests is simply enormous. This mediatory role of the bureaucratic middle class within the state, amplified by the ascendancy of the middle class as a whole and compounded by the structural weakness of the bourgeoisie, provides the fraction with a pronounced "relative autonomy." This relative autonomy keeps the bureaucratic fraction anchored to the main principles of capitalism but affords them significant power—as when, for example, it is realized that the key to maintaining stable politics among such volatile elements as the lumpens and certain sections of the peasantry remains in the hands of the bureaucratic middle class. In short, the politics of coalition aided in significant measure by the politics of scarcity serve to entrench the power of the bureaucratic middle class. Being a class not likely to miss a political trick, it has seized every opportunity to cement its new-found power by forming alliances with elements from the subaltern classes.

The stress placed on the influence of the structural factors upon the particular nature of the middle class does not tell the full story. There are also cultural and historical factors that should not be ignored. History and culture are especially important to the development of the Jamaican middle class. As we shall see, color and race effectively ushered in the first intermediate class (the "coloreds") into political prominence. The stigma linked to these factors worked against the plantocracy in the post-emancipation years and well beyond. The lack of political legitimacy of the planter class was linked to its incapacity to generalize the capitalist ideology to an ex-slave population familiar with the crudest barbarities of racism. The middle class (the "coloreds")—middle in color and midway the distance between planter and freedman—came to occupy a structurally necessary role for continuing capital accumulation.

We see then that the middle class in the Third World contrasts with its metropolitan counterpart in quite remarkable ways. It is against this background of "anomalies" that we shall now proceed with our historical account.

The Jamaican Setting

In 1974 the governing People's National Party (PNP) in Jamaica instituted a change-oriented program flanked by "democratic socialist" principles. Briefly, the agenda consisted of four major and related facets: (1) state ownership or at least substantial state involvement and control in certain key sectors of the economy (bauxite and aluminum, construction, some manufacturing, import-export activities); (2) reorganization of agriculture through the institution of worker cooperatives in the sugar industry, state and cooperative farms, and a program of land-lease aimed at improving the efficiency of small farmers and modestly redistributing land; (3) mobilization of "human resources" reflected in worker participation programs, adult education, citizen participation, youth service projects and other similar initiatives; and (4) initiatives in the international arena designed to address the inequalities among nations (Jamaican Government, 1973, 1974, 1975). In this last respect, Jamaica was the moving force behind the formation of the International Bauxite Association (IBA), a producers' cartel; it played a leadership role in the movement of non-aligned nations and the demands put forth by this group for a "North-South" dialogue; and it emphasized Third World solidarity and cooperation. These programs, the PNP government claimed, were designed to create an economy "fundamentally under national control and responsive to national ends" (Jamaica Daily Gleaner, 10/27/1969; Jamaican Government, 1972a). The aim was to exchange dependency for inner-directed development (Nelson Keith, 1981).

In class terms, the change agenda followed the lines of a national-popularist alliance, one, that is, that would pit the "popular" sectors and the national bourgeoisie (such that there was) against foreign and allied interests represented locally by the comprador bourgeoisie. The importers and the merchants bore the first brunt of the attack on peripheral capitalism. Commercial interests were clearly warned that they would be subjected to severe retrenchment. The monopoly exercised in the importation and distribution of commodities would be removed; the main purveyors of the sector, salesmen, were told in no uncertain terms that their days were numbered (Jamaican Government, 1972b: 99). The functions of distribution and importation would eventually be assumed by the State Trading Corporation. For its part, the attack on foreign capital took the form of a unilateral abrogation of existing contracts with the Canadian and U.S.-owned bauxite and aluminum corporations and renegotiation indicating the government's intention to play a significant role in the future development of the industry (Reid, 1977).

Was the major impulse behind this agenda a progressive fraction of the capitalist class—an industrial fraction coming into its own? Although the PNP did initially have the support of interests that could be so identified, our research has indicated that industrial and commercial capitalist interests were too closely meshed to sustain for long an attacK on the latter interests. Throughout the post-war period (1946–1968) the distributive sector had persistently jostled agriculture and manufacturing as the principal contributor to the Gross National Product (Jefferson, 1972: 43–44). And yet this does not fully convey the extent of control of the commercial fraction over the economy. Indirect control came by way of the central place occupied by distributive trades *vis-à-vis* other sectors of the economy. The manufacturing sector relied on imported inputs to the order of some 40 percent of production requirements, clearly a boon to the distributive sector and an index of dependence (Ayub, 1981: 60–61). As further evidence, one should note a marked propensity of the banking sector to favor commercial undertakings and the progress of consumerism, a sign of a seeming alliance between these two interests. Only in 1968 did loans to the manufacturing sector for the first time reach the level of loans to the distributive trades (21 percent of outstanding amounts); in the same year, term lending comprised almost 20 percent of the total outlay of commercial credit and was described as a veritable hire-purchase boom (Jefferson, 1972: 243; Girvan, 1971: 208). Jamaican capitalism, in spite of real and visible fractional conflicts, continued to be dominated by commercial capital. One must look elsewhere for the dominant force behind the proposed change. As there was no significant movement from below, the attention, accordingly, shifts to the middle class.

It is our contention that the program offered as "democratic socialism" in the 1970s represents a comprehensive developmental model sponsored by a fraction of the middle class—the bureaucratic-entrepreneurial fraction— that was rendered powerful largely by its position within the state apparatus. Through this program of enhanced state direction and control of the economy, a particular mediation of crisis was attempted that would, if successful, result in the transformation of the fraction into a state bourgeoisie (Novella Keith, 1981).

The rise of the middle class, both in power and numbers, was the result of a series of events already foreshadowed in the immediate post-emancipation period (1833–65) and finding their fullest expression to date in the politics of "democratic socialism." These events, as our conceptual sketch on the middle class in the periphery indicates, were such as to reveal the special twist in social relations that conferred on the class an important mediatory role and propelled it toward a bona fide bourgeois status. We will examine below in some detail the historical emergence of the Jamaican middle class from its roots in the post-emancipation "colored sector," following with a sketch of the more recent period, designed to convey the continuity of this movement up to the present.

The "Coloreds" in the Post-Emancipation Era

Economic Transformation and Class Relations

Sugar and slavery were the twin offsprings of mercantilism. The demise of this system, swept aside by Britain's industrial revolution and the consequent espousal of free trade in the 19th century, was catastrophic for the sugar planter and devastating for his metropolitan ally, the merchant class. Within the space of some twenty years, merchants and planters were dealt a double blow: they were forcefully cut loose from their bulwarks, a captive labor force and a protected market, as the tide swung in favor of the industrial bourgeoisie. Slavery was abolished in Jamaica in 1833, with apprenticeship ending in 1838. The preferential tariffs favoring colonial sugar were dismantled between 1846 and 1854: The principles of free trade required of the colony a reorganization of production along "rational" lines, with the rewards going preponderantly to the cheapest producers in the market (Ragatz, 1928; Green, 1976; Hall, 1959). Produced within the monopolistic structure, West Indian sugar was quite unable to compete, as Table 3.1 reveals.

It should be appreciated that the realities of international economics would impose themselves through the mediation of the social forces within the social formation. The crisis in productive relations brought about by pressures originating within the center became intricately interwoven with a

TABLE 3.1   Sugar Prices, British West Indies, Cuba, Brazil, 1841-1846

Year	British West Indies (per cwt.)		Cuba		Brazil	
	s.	d.	s.	d.	s.	d.
1841	39	8	21	6	20	9
1842	36	11	20	1	18	3
1843	33	9	21	2	17	2
1844	33	8	21	8	17	0
1845	32	11	26	4	20	5
1846	34	5	24	6	19	11

SOURCES: *British Parliamentary Papers* 1847-1848 (Vol. 58, p 442); *British Parliamentary Papers* 1866 (Vol. 66, p. 193), cited in Green (1976: 231).

pattern of class relations that would impress their own consequences on the decline of the old form of production and the success of its replacement.

The crucial requirement of the post-emancipation era was the creation of a dependable, industrious labor force that would sell its labor power to the plantations for a "reasonable" wage; in other words, the successful separation of capital and labor. There is ample evidence that all proponents contemplated such an outcome for abolition. On the eve of full emancipation, in 1836, Lord Glenelg forwarded to all Governors in the British West Indies a dispatch dealing with the anticipated withdrawal of free labor from the estates:

> How far it may be possible to check this apparently natural course . . . effectually, it is not easy to determine; but by diminishing the facilities of obtaining land, it may certainly be impeded. . . . [I]t is of great importance in the mean time that the evil should not be aggravated by the inconsiderate neglect, or the incautious distribution of those lands which are at the disposal of the Crown. . . . In order to prevent this, it will be necessary to prevent the occupation of any Crown lands by persons not possessing a proprietary title to them; and to fix such a price upon all Crown lands as may place them out of the reach of persons without capital [British Government, 1836b: 10].

Nor did the altered circumstances of the planter class in later years deter the Crown from pursuit of this objective. In 1865, year of the infamous Morant Bay rebellion that inaugurated an authoritarian form of government (Crown colony government), stipendiary magistrates addressed a petition to the Queen on behalf of the peasantry. Would Her Majesty take cognizance of the "rapidly approaching importance" of the peasantry and thereby direct land reform compatible with these realities? The reply: "Her Majesty will regard with interest and satisfaction their advancement through their own merits and efforts in rendering the plantation productive, thereby enabling the planters to pay them higher wages for the same hours of work than are received by the best field labourers in England" (Augier and Gordon, 1962: 178).

Yet there were considerable difficulties in the way of this transformation. The legacy of prosperity had left the planters with the institutional framework of internal self-rule—an elected Legislative Assembly and a customary interdiction of the Governor's formal veto power—coupled with a stubborn insistence on their right to absolute rule of their "property." Already during the 1820s they had fiercely resisted, and then ably circumvented, imperial directives for improved slave codes and other requests which impinged upon their domain. In the 1830s, the planters still represented a powerful force in the metropolis; 85 percent of the plantations in Jamaica were owned by absentees who, joined to the other Caribbean plantation owners and the big merchant houses in the West India Lobby, exerted considerable influence in Imperial political circles (Green, 1976: 385–387; Hall, 1971). The legal battle against the abolitionists had been lost but the pattern of class relations to emerge from abolition was yet to be forged. The years of apprenticeship (1833–1838) were especially crucial in this respect. What strictures would the planters impose on the newly freed slaves, as a way of maintaining the spirit, if not the law, of the old social relations, and with what possibly disastrous consequences? The "savageries" of the Haitian revolution (1791–1804) were still within living memory, kept in the forefront of imagination by the long history of slave rebellions in Jamaica, the latest of which had occurred in 1831 (Ragatz, 1928: 443).

The extremely antagonistic character of class relations was not the only tendency needing mediation. If the separation of capital and labor was to succeed, the freedmen would have to be transformed into wage laborers rather than freeholders. In Jamaica, the relative abundance of "mountain" land and the old practice of giving slaves their own "provision plots," made the establishment of a secondary peasant economy a real possibility; already there was a thriving internal market in "ground provisions," the starchy foods that comprised the staple diet (Olivier, 1936: 134–135). And the very success of the plantation economy, with its concomitant displacement of the early "small settlers," had ensured for a number of the free black and the growing free colored population a place as small artisans and freeholders (Sheridan, 1970: 216; M. Campbell, 1976: 45). Furthermore, the slaves had found some protectors in the despised Baptist missionaries, who strongly encouraged the establishment of post-abolition Free Villages (Lowenthal, 1972: 60–61). There was, therefore, the possibility that the planters would attempt to stem the tide through draconian measures, reacting not only out of a stubborn conservatism, but from a real threat posed by the withdrawal of labor from the plantations and the emergence of a peasant economy.[5]

The above highlight the profound and lasting contradictions of the period. We must assign a crucially important role to the interplay of antagonistic classes within the ambit of the capitalist transformation of agriculture that was sponsored by the Colonial Office and the tensions between this project and an emerging peasant economy, which grew as a result of the economic weakness of the planter class and further undermined its ability to achieve the desired transformation. This set of conflicting class relations was accompanied by other tensions stemming from the opposed interests of the dominant classes in the periphery and the center, represented by the planter class and the Colonial Office respectively. While united in the projected transformation of the freedmen into a compliant labor force, these two were considerably at odds on the issue of the concomitant transformation of the planter class into a capitalist class, navigating on its own the rough seas of competitive, non-protected economic relations. This contradiction was especially in evidence during the twenty-year period that spanned the abolition of slavery and the dismantling of protective tariffs.

The following excerpt of correspondence between the Governor and the Colonial Office captures the urgency of the historical moment:

> I have no hesitation in declaring to your Lordship that nothing is wanting to the success of free labour in Jamaica, but just and fair dealing towards the labourers. Necessity, the great controller of temper and human interests, may yet induce this desirable end; but at present, mismanagement and discontent have greatly suspended industry, and placed the ordinary agriculture of the island in considerable confusion [Bell and Morrell, 1968: 408].

The dispatch carried its share of self-serving optimism, in also dismissing the possibility of any outbreak of resistance. Nonetheless, this mid-century message conveyed more powerfully than ever a structural necessity glimpsed upon emancipation: The new circumstances required the alteration of the structures of domination. The possibility of authoritarian colonial rule was openly advanced as early as 1839, when strong sentiments were expressed that Britain should abolish all West Indian Assemblies and concentrate power in her own hands. Yet against such an eventuality stood poised the West India interests in Britain, still powerful enough to cause a governmental crisis surrounding this issue (Morrell, 1969: 383; Heuman, 1981). Societal transformation required greater subtlety; caution counselled a strategy of careful manipulation of all parties. At both extremes of the crisis were two irreconcilable classes, in between was the answer to effect the necessary compromise—the intermediate colored sector.

The Colored Middle Sector
as the Mediating Agent

By the 1830s there were in Jamaica some 30,000 free "coloreds" out of a population of 371,000; the white contingent stood at some 15,000 and included—but not as a group of equal status—a significant Jewish presence of some 5000 (Eisner, 1961: 127). The product of liaisons between white men and black women—there was always a scarcity of white women in Jamaica and these liaisons were the order of the day—the coloreds comprised a quasi-caste: a strange, alienated breed, belonging to neither world. The economic location of the group was varied. As calculated in 1825, there were some 400 coloreds among the "very rich," 5,500 were in "fair circumstances," while the rest were "absolutely poor." At the top were the highly educated owners of plantations and the professionals, followed by substantial numbers of artisans, small merchants, shopkeepers, and cultivators (Tikasingh, 1968: 14–16; Heuman, 1981: 6). In spite of the great economic differentiation, the coloreds were united by social and political ostracism that affected them all equally: Legal "disabilities" had progressively, as their numbers and wealth tended to grow, stripped them of the rights of citizens. They could not be employed in public office or sit in the legislature; they could not vote, give evidence against whites, and, after 1761, inherit more than £1200 worth of property other than by passage of a private bill (Heuman, 1981: 6; Brathwaite, 1971). Nonetheless, there was a continued, considerable concentration of wealth in their hands, particularly notable after 1815, when economic decline had caused the departure of some 50 percent of the white population.

With increased wealth and consequence, the coloreds could not long be kept from political involvement. In the 1820s, their requests for political rights, through petitions to the Jamaican Assembly and the Colonial Office, became more pressing. These were met by resistance on the part of the planters: Understanding the inherent ambiguity in the position of the coloreds, they oscillated between acceptance and suspicion. Race, color and the dominance of the European culture propelled the middle sector to mimesis. Yet the history of domination had left its mark: How could a people treated "as the Egyptians had treated the Israelites" be transformed into an ally? (Edwards, 1966: 23) The Jamaican Assembly repeatedly turned down motions to grant the coloreds full citizenship.

Support for the coloreds was forthcoming, however, from a more powerful source: the Imperial government. The attempts of the Jamaican Assembly to shore up its weak position by granting the rights of citizenship to another discriminated group, the Jews, were linked by the Colonial Office to the granting of political rights to the coloreds. All disabilities were removed for the two intermediate groups in 1830–1831 (Hurwitz and Hurwitz, 1965). The way was clear for the insertion of the middle sector into the center of the political sphere.

By the late 1830s, it became evident that the growing political presence of the coloreds would attempt to organize itself in a concerted way: Under the tutelage of the Marquis of Sligo, the coloreds spearheaded a "liberal clique," the Town Party, whose prime purpose was to frustrate the obstructionist policies of the planter class (M. Campbell, 1976: 235; Morrell, 1966: 150). The recalcitrance of the latter, as expected, was felt on two fronts: through overly repressive policies toward the freedmen and concerted efforts to stem the movement toward free trade. When more direct means of attack in the Imperial Parliament failed, resistance took the form of obstruction of government; in the famous "retrenchment" battles of the 1840s, the planting interest repeatedly set about to delay passage of revenue bills, cut salaries of government officials and other employees, and so threaten the stability of the colony. The plan, directed by the West India interests in Britain, was to embarrass the Whig government over its management of colonial problems and so cause the downfall of the proponents of free trade (Heuman, 1981: 142–143; British Government, 1849). The coloreds, whose destiny was closely bound to that of Jamaica, would resist the planters' reckless initiatives, supporting the Governor in his fight against retrenchment. Although never more than a substantial minority in the Jamaican Assembly, the Town Party was able to defeat repeatedly the Country Party (the planters) on this issue.[6]

An added bonus to the potential contribution of the coloreds was to be had in the realm of ideology. In a class structure that continued to be quite repressive to the black ex-slaves, who could best propagandize the general interests of capital? The prime candidates would hardly be the slave-master class! The Colonial Office was quick to exploit the potentialities of the colored group. In 1840, recommendations were tabled to have educated coloreds appointed to "Superior Offices" to provide "impressive examples" to their "brethren." Not long after, and thanks to the pressure exerted by the Town Party, select members from their ranks were appointed to such posts as Attorney-General (M. Campbell, 1976: 210, 236).

The important conclusion to be derived from the above is that support for the advancement of the coloreds by the Colonial Office was prompted by self interest rather than paternalism. The strategy was quite simple, as revealed by the following Colonial Office communique: "The plantocracy . . . might see evil in the transfer of their power to a lower order, and might be inclined to cooperate with the Government in order to guard against apprehended encroachment from the Popular Party."[7] The planter class was being graced with a graphic demonstration of the dangers to be faced away from the protective mantle of the Imperial Parliament. And yet, would the intricate manipulations be kept within the desired bounds? What were the inclinations of these newly emergent intermediate sectors and how would they respond to increased political participation?

Middle Sector Mediation
and Economic Innovation

The answer to the above question is intimately connected to matters of race and class and the economic transformation that weakened the local dominant class. Could the contradictions between planters and freedmen and between planters and the industrial bourgeoisie in Britain provide the opening for an alternative economic transformation, spearheaded by an alliance of the coloreds with the peasantry? History indicates that the coloreds were not a revolutionary force; nonetheless, they were a force to be reckoned with in its own right and not merely as an appendage of the Crown. The scenario that was acted out in mid-nineteenth century would set the pattern for future social relations in Jamaica and the role of the middle class. At the heart of the pattern is a disassociation from the weakened economic structure and the attempt to supplant the dominant class by championing economic innovation: a pattern weak and burdened by ambiguity in its first appearance, but becoming strengthened progressively as the weakness of the dominant class became systemic, and revealing its full potential (albeit still stifled) with the emergence of "democratic socialism" in the 1970s.

During the crisis years following the 1846 Sugar Act, the Town Party demonstrated its disassociation from the plantation economy in a number of ways, particularly by refusing fiscal support for the importation of indentured labor from the East Indies, which was to supplement the recalcitrant labor force of the freedmen. The crisis solidified the ties of the "party," as unity was achieved through opposition to the interests of the planters. Questioned, finally, was the wisdom that equated the health of the plantation with that of the colony, while the Town Party was increasingly drawn to supporting interests rooted in the economic activities of the "small settlers" and defined as national in scope (British Government, 1852: 187). Unfair taxation, labelled "class legislation," was often though not always successfully resisted. The support of the coloreds for the creation of educational facilities was constant. These were not only to be facilities for professional education, clearly the boon of the middle class; they should provide technical and industrial training, to "encourage craft and cottage industries which relied on local materials" (Heuman, 1981: 140; Green, 1976: 363–364). The "small settlers" responded in kind: During the 1840s and early 1850s the votes of the small freeholders were responsible for swinging elections in favor of colored representatives, at the expense of the planter class (Heuman, 1981: 122–123). The politics of color and nationalism gave indication that a gradual transformation was under way; the economic weakness of the planter class appeared to make way for political demise.

In order to appreciate the extent of the threatened change, we must briefly refer to the transformation of the economy around mid-century. Between 1844 and 1854, fully 314 plantations, or 49 percent of the complement, were abandoned. Of the coffee estates, 65 percent were abandoned (Green, 1976; Hall, 1959). Sugar production suffered a vast decline, as the tonnage produced in these years was, on the average, only one-third that of the years 1814–1823 (Sheridan, 1970: 41; Green, 1976: 246). The decline of the planters was matched by the growth of small freeholds and the wealth of locally-based merchants. The number of freeholds estimated to have been only 2000 in 1838, increased to some 23,000 by 1845 (Hall, 1959: 160–162; British Government, 1840, 1845: 332). The new class configuration in the countryside contributed to a changing pattern of agricultural production and concomitant changes in relations of exchange in agriculture. It has been estimated that the value of "small settler" output for 1850 stood at £113,500 for sugar, coffee, arrowroot (the traditional export crops) and at £1,019,300 for other domestic food production—nearly one-third of the Gross Domestic Product for that year (Eisner, 1961: 46, 53, 56). Overall, the repercussions on the class structure were considerable. The value accrued to local merchants' from the peasants' output is thought to have been considerable, as was the merchants' income from the local distributive sector. A comparison of the national income figures for 1832 and 1850 reveals a shift in the composition of the merchants' income toward greater reliance on the peasant sector. It stands to reason that, whereas the planters had relied on British merchant houses for their export and import needs (indeed, the planter and merchant were often one and the same), the effect of the reorganization of the agricultural sector would favor local merchants. Between 1832 and 1850 mercantile income from local distribution of consumer goods is estimated to have increased by approximately 50 percent. During the same years, the contribution of planters to national income declined to one-sixth of the original figure, so that in 1850 the merchants' contribution was double that of the planters (Eisner, 1961: 28, 46; Hall, 1959: 227–229).

The delicate web of social relations that the Colonial Office was bent on spinning was threatened with destruction. The colored sector had been vastly useful in mediating class antagonisms that would have interfered with the transition to wage labor and rationalized capitalist agriculture: It had tempered the planters' most vicious attacks on the freedmen and their resistance to the dismantling of the mercantilist system. Could the trend be discouraged before it produced irreparable damage? Writing of the general political climate of the early 1850s, W. P. Morrell (1966: 261) captures the tensions in their unequivocality: It was said that the peasantry and "the vivacious, capricious coloured race were showing themselves eager for consequence and power." The Imperial government and the planter class shared a determination to prevent transfer of political power to colored and black elements. Yet, without firm intervention, such a turn of events appeared inevitable (Heuman, 1981: 148).

We noted above that the colored sector was not inclined to become a revolutionary force. By temperment and socialization, they could not bring themselves to think expansively of the freedmen; their attitude was one primed by racial and class superiority, though they acknowledged and utilized the growing political power of the freedmen. Yet the sector was anything but the harmless ape of white culture. The rigidities of the caste-like system of which it had been a part were slowly dissolving. Class alliances supported by an alternative view of social and production relations began to emerge. One writer even observes that the politics of the sector had betrayed a "socialist" inflection, a transformation consistent with the changing features of the social formation.[8] While the colored sector was not the unrelenting champion of the peasantry, it became quite evident that the interests of the two were being driven towards each other by objective factors. The time had come to nip a potentially dangerous political development in the bud.

The process of dismantling began. The position of the Jamaican governor, Sir Charles Grey, was unequivocal: The return of a colored majority in the Assembly in 1854 would be a "fearsome misfortune" (British Government, 1854). True to form, the colored middle sector betrayed by its actions the ambiguities of its position: The Assembly, which had provided it with a measure of power, was threatened by the too rapid ascendancy of brown and black forces. Should the group insist on measures to strengthen representative government, and so enter into an unequivocal alliance with the "lower orders"? Or should the limited gains achieved so far be maintained by acquiescing in measures restraining the rise of these social forces? The coloreds were divided: A measure to restrict the electorate was passed in 1859, reducing the small freeholder vote by two-thirds.[9] By 1860, the numbers of colored and black representatives in the Assembly were reduced to 14 out of 47. By 1864, only 1,903 persons out of a population of 441,264 were qualified to vote (British Government, 1864).

The result of this systematic destruction of the middle sector and peasantry by a coalition of the Colonial Office and the planters eventuated in the Morant Bay rebellion of 1865. Frustration translated into carnage and anti-white sentiments. The actual events flowing from the rebellion need not bother us here. It is enough to state that the attacked classes, especially the peasants, vented their simmering anger at a weak and impotent planter class. In the end, this class, largely through the solicitude of the infamous Governor Eyre, surrendered their representative form of government in exchange for Crown colony status. Government would be conducted from the Imperial Parliament, the Assembly voluntarily assuming an advising role.[10]

The Meaning of Crown Colony Government

What are the important points to be adduced from the above account? We may start with the consequences flowing from Crown colony government: The tide of "middle class" governance was halted. The history of the period is replete with indications that, had the colored middle sector been allowed to sustain its drive to power, qualitatively different political and economic forms would have emerged. The plantation would, in all probability, have vanished and been replaced by a peasant-oriented economy. As for the middle sector, it is perhaps a bit cavalier to suggest that here was a new bourgeoisie denied its full development. And yet there is considerable support for this interpretation (Knox, 1965).

All too often historians have tended to focus undue attention on the flair for mimesis of which the middle class was indefensibly guilty. It is not unusual also to have them castigated for a lack of entrepreneurial acumen; in this period, the charge was based, for the most part, on the failure more enthusiastically to purchase bankrupt and abandoned sugar estates. It would seem, however, that the sector was sufficiently perceptive to realize that the days of the plantation were numbered and that other forms of economic organization were necessary. The spread of entrepreneurial activities away from plantation agriculture was, for the times, quite impressive. As Douglas Hall (1959: 33) has shown, conscientious efforts were made to launch small scale industries, mining operations, the production of silk and the like. That these floundered was due in large part to the lack of Imperial encouragement, the scarcity of capital, and the continuing preferential treatment accorded to plantation agriculture (Brathwaite, 1971: 89–95; Post, 1978: 36–37).

Here the colored sector might have been denied the opportunity to entrench their *economic* interests. They could not, however, have been denied their *political* role. It is a structurally determined role made necessary by the vagaries of class, color, and the particularities of history. The nature of slavery gave this imperative feature to the functions of the colored sector. Slavery had created a gulf between the planter and his ex-slave that needed mediations that only the middle sector could effect. It follows, therefore, that the reverses suffered through the imposition of Crown colony government were temporary. At some point in the development of social relations—in this case, a labor rebellion in the 1930s—the political functions would once again be called into action as the way of promoting capital accumulation.

Crown colony government also signalled an important shift in the relation of economic and political structures that would have significant repercussions in the future evolution of social and economic relations in the colony. What emerges with this form of the state is a dislocation between the political and the economic "moment." In other words, though threatened in its dominance in the economic sphere, the dominant class was nonetheless able to retain a measure of power through intervention at the political level, mediated in this case by the metropolitan bourgeoisie. In the ideal-typical case where political and ideological dominance are functions of a strong economic base, the class—or fraction of a class—which emerges to political dominance does so with the resolution of contradictions in the old mode of production. Of course, the old contradictions do not disappear but linger in the period of transition. Ultimately, however, contradictions specific to this mode of production are transformed as the new mode alters social relations according to its own inherent tendencies.

In the case of Jamaica, and, generally, peripheral social formations, however, intervention at the political level shores up the weak mode of production (capitalist plantation agriculture)—including its contradictions—while the emerging mode of production (peasant production, in this case) and its inherent contradictions become articulated with the first. The resultant social formation is characterized by an overriding presence of contradictions within and between differently organized productive activities. Indeed, this seems to provide one of the defining characteristics of peripheral social formations. In Jamaica, it was not the inherent superiority of capitalism, as measured by a progressive use of the forces of production, that resolved the contradictions. The mode of production that won the day was a backward kind of capitalism, artificially supported by metropolitan intervention at the political level (Post, 1978).

The colored sector, denied its "rightful place" by Crown colony government, would nonetheless continue to grow and demand access to political power. Turned into a sizable middle class by the industrialization drive of the 1950s, it would again be catapulted by the logic of capital accumulation into its ambiguous posture: advocacy of nationalism, mild versions of socialism and "inner-directed" development. We shall now briefly examine the contours of intervention by the middle class in the modern period.

The Bridge to the Present

The 1938 Labor Rebellion
and the Middle Class

We have to wait until the 1930s for a convergence of socio-economic factors and political activity that would again propel the middle class into center stage. The significant event was a labor rebellion of major proportions, occurring in much of the Caribbean in 1937–1938 and giving notice of an imperative need for changes in economic and political structures in response to the renewed political consciousness of subordinate and intermediate classes.

The rebellion was the logical culmination of a systematic denial of the needs of the peasantry and agro-proletariat, related, in turn, to the long-standing governmental support for large-scale capitalist agriculture over other economic alternatives—a preference dating back to the post-abolition period.[11] Yet, while enjoying constant government support, the agrarian-mercantile capitalist class did not succeed in securing a strong economic base until well into the twentieth century. An almost total collapse of the sugar industry in the latter part of the nineteenth century provided an important stimulus for the emergence of a substantial class of peasants and small landowners. This was also connected to the development of banana cultivation, an export crop requiring considerably smaller investments than sugar production. Nonetheless, by the 1930s, these opportunities were being foreclosed, substantially as the result of the consolidation of export-oriented estate agriculture.[12]

The census undertaken in 1943 was to give some indication of the magnitude of the distress facing the population: at this time, 25.6 percent of the experienced labor force was officially unemployed and the average worker was occupied only 60 percent of the time. Fully 70 percent of the labor force was in the category of casual laborers. Approximately 50,000 would-be entrants in the labor force were also unemployed. It was further estimated that 30,000 farming families owning less than 10 acres each could only achieve a marginal level of subsistence (Cumper, 1956: 59–60).

It is little wonder that the "rebels" of 1938 clamored for land and opportunities for wage labor of a regular rather than casual nature (Phelps, 1960; Post, 1978). Yet there were indications of a deeper understanding of the workings of oppression, as revealed by a popular song of the marchers, sung to the tune of a well-known ditty:

> White man ha' de money
> and Black man ha' de labor

For all their apparent simplicity, these words speak of circumstances in which the dichotomy of capital versus labor, systemically imposed by the capitalist mode of production, was compounded by antagonisms rooted in the historical experience of slavery. "Massa" had become the white capitalist. Race and class were now joined, creating the potential for a formidable ideological challenge to the system of exploitation. Political organization was clearly the key to the kind of changes to be demanded; it is at this point that the middle class could simply be denied no longer its structurally determined political role.

The period of Crown colony government had seen the rise of a middle class, spawned from the earlier and more amorphous colored sector. Contributing to the development of the class were certain gains in education. Between 1890 and 1929 there was a tripling of the number of secondary school places. While still woefully inadequate, these jumped from 878 to 2677. The literacy rate, as measured by the ability to read *and* write, had increased steadily from 32 percent of the population in 1891 to 52 percent in 1921. While education, the cachet par excellence of the middle class, was making these small but significant advances, employment opportunities also increased. The numbers of teachers, civil servants, technicians and clerks in commercial employment experienced a continuous growth from 1861 to 1921, increasing from some 2700 to nearly 15,000.[13]

And yet the class was stifled. At the time of the rebellion, many members of the class were in self-imposed exile in metropolitan centers, as opportunities to achieve the desired social position in the socio-political context of Jamaica were largely foreclosed. An important source of power and privilege, the civil service, was increasingly the preserve of Britons and representatives of the local white families, especially after the closing of recruitment by competitive examination in 1911. Representative Government Associations, supported largely by the small middle class, clamored during the 1920s for constitutional reform to give more power to the now largely black and colored legislature, but were generally ignored, even after a measure of support provided by the findings of a Commission of Enquiry (the "Wood Commission") in 1923 (Proctor, 1973; Roberts, 1955).

In this context, it is little wonder that the politics espoused by middle class organizations in the late 1930s and 1940s had a distinctly nationalist and radical edge. Under the leadership of Norman W. Manley, a distinguished barrister, the People's National Party created a vision of the middle class as the defenders of the rights of the unemployed, the "small settlers," the workers, and, in general, the "oppressed," couched in the guise of an abiding interest in the welfare of the nation: The conflict-ridden backward capitalism which characterized Jamaica would be replaced by a society of small producers, artisans and small capitalists who would eschew British and foreign rule and govern themselves. A distinctly Fabian form of socialism was advocated (PNP, 1939; O'Meally, 1938; Nettleford, 1971).

Clearly, the middle class was not ready to enter into the service of capital but was offering, instead, its own project for the future of Jamaica—a project in which the echoes of the 1850s were unmistakeable. According to this agenda, the state, under the tutelage of the middle class, would preside over the desired transformation. In such circumstances, could the middle class, from the perspective of the dominant class structure, act as the mediating agent? Surely the socialist ideology and nationalist rhetoric of the PNP threatened to have a radicalizing effect on the masses, providing a most undesirable vehicle for their as yet incomplete understanding of class dynamics.

We must quickly add, however, that the convergence of subordinate and intermediate classes under the banner of "socialist" principles was impeded by serious obstacles. Chief among them was the fact that the prospective alliance was not immediately and enthusiastically embraced by the subordinate classes, who heaped upon the educated brown middle class almost as much vituperation and suspicion as they reserved for the planter class. By culture and aspirations they were seen as a colonized elite, one which self-consciously described itself as "their betters." The disaffection between the two groups received ample confirmation on occasion of the first elections based on universal suffrage, held in 1944. The victory went neither to the capitalist party (the Democratic Party of Jamaica), which was roundly defeated, nor to the middle class party (the PNP), but to a motley "mass" party headed by Alexander Bustamante, the Jamaica Labour Party (JLP). Yet this outcome was not acceptable in terms of finding a suitable channel for the institutionalization of mass protest, for Bustamante was reckoned by the British as a "rabble rouser," one not to be trusted. Disaffection and an evolving class consciousness combined to place the leadership of subordinate classes in less than desirable hands! Further, in spite of the divergencies mentioned above, objective circumstances appeared to support the eventual strengthening of the PNP project. Already the second elections held in 1949 had recorded an increase of support for the PNP from 25 percent to 49 percent of the electorate, mostly as the result of labor organizing by the PNP "left" (Munroe, 1972, 1977).

There was a second barrier to the "socialist" alliance of subordinate and intermediate classes, however, one that redounded to the advantage of the dominant class structure. It was simply that socialism, even in its mild Fabian form, caused considerable discomfort among significant numbers of the middle class itself. The advent of universal suffrage (itself part of the accommodation to the crisis of 1938) called for a restructuring of the system of domination: The electoral results amply demonstrated the necessity of appropriate mediation between the antagonistic classes. The answer was the displacement of the politico-ideological posture of the PNP from the alliance with the subordinate classes; the roots of its antagonism to the dominant class must be addressed, and these were found in the exclusion of the middle class from power.

The tack was to allow entry of the middle class into the power bloc and to encourage its participation in politico-economic reconstruction from within. The "radical moment" of the political practice of the class receded and by 1952 the swing was completed by the abject removal of the Party's left wing. The solution to the crisis announced by the labor rebellion entailed the shifting of the demands for change onto the plane of constitutional reform and industrialization through foreign investment. This plan left capitalist agriculture free to consolidate and enlarge its holdings at the expense of the peasantry,[14] and otherwise created a nice "fit" between the requirements of domination within Jamaica and the current requirements of international capital. What remained of the earlier "socialism" of the PNP was the idea of state planning, statutory boards, increased social measures, and the drive for industrial development—all activities that would serve to enlarge and strengthen the middle class (Nettleford, 1971: 196–199; PNP, 1955; Jamaican Government, 1949: 154, 201).

Evolution of a Strategic Fraction
of the Middle Class

We have given some emphasis to the details above because they reveal the broad contours of the social relations that propelled the middle class away from mimesis and toward a role that did not fit their image as the servants of capital—that of politico-economic innovators. It is equally observed, nonetheless, that much of the class did aptly fit the latter description and continued to do so into the 1950s and 1960s. We must differentiate, in particular, between certain members of the class strategically located within the politico-ideological apparatus—politicians, trade unionists, journalists and other professionals—and other segments of the salaried middle class. The latter, as Manfred Halpern (1968: 196, 198) perceptively suggests, are those interested "only in safe careers." These individuals are largely politically passive and lack economic inventiveness; they are mainly elements of the executive, technical and clerical detachments "that [have] neither deep conviction nor understanding." In Jamaican parlance, they are the mainstay of the "been-to's," their distinguishing trait a penchant for vivid renderings of their frequent visits abroad, undertaken mostly to satisfy a passionate interest in consumption.

It is with the first group that we are primarily concerned—a group that we have provisionally named the "bureaucratic-entrepreneurial" fraction—for it is among them that the "anomalous" tendencies of the class find their most pronounced expression.[15] On account of its newness the phenomenon is not easily grasped in all its complexities; some distinguishing characteristics have nonetheless emerged, which provide revealing insights into the workings of the fraction. Before offering any details, we wish to stress that the basis for the emergence of the fraction lies in the interplay between proximity to economic and political power and the shape itself of politico-economic structures that allowed the translation of proximity into participation and, later, attempted dominance.

It is well to reiterate that closeness to economic and political power is one of the defining characteristics of the middle class in the center as well as the periphery, at least for the upper stratum of the class; in itself, it does not lead to a qualitative altering of the status of the class *vis-à-vis* the capitalist class, a fact already alluded to in our earlier discussion on the "technocracy." Proximity may, of course, lead to a relatively more favorable sharing of the surplus, and this was amply evident in Jamaica in the 1960s, when the middle class figured in statistics showing a high-degree of skewness in income distribution. At this time, 5 percent of the population in the highest income group received 31 percent of the national income; as the highest occupational group—taken to include the capitalist class and the upper stratum of the middle class—comprised 5 percent of the classified labor force (see Table 3.2), the sharing of the middle class in the reward structure is evident (Morris and Adelman, 1971: 27). A talent for "crawling and worming" had paid huge dividends! (James, 1970: 193). Nonetheless, this phenomenon would not in itself have any particular significance for us, unless, that is (as we shall indicate below), it entailed more than quantitative growth: a changed contour of class relations.

The special advantages of proximity to power resulted from a peculiar quality of political and economic structures, which made the dividing line between classes at this level a porous membrane more so than an impenetrable barrier. The middle class, as we have seen, emerged as the mediator of antagonisms between two irreconcilable and relatively weak class-racial groups. In mediating these antagonisms the class was able at times to transcend its service role to the capitalist class, elaborating and attempting to act, instead, on its own agenda for change. Broadly speaking, this "self-reliant" strain of economic and political practice has tended to emerge at times of severe crises of capital accumulation—crises that, let us not forget, do invariably have a political component. This pattern was to resurface forcefully during the 1970s, when the responsibility of mediating a crisis of accumulation fell to the People's National Party. It was foreshadowed, however, during the earlier period.

Let us examine first the characteristics of the *economic* structure that allowed for middle class participation. The opportunities for forays into private enterprise came by two routes: the vastly enhanced role of public spending as the economy assumed distinctly Keynesian features, and the comprador relationship to foreign capital. It should be recalled that by the early 1950s an industrialization program was instituted that proposed to rely heavily on government incentives to "attract" capital and, in so doing, issued an open invitation to foreign investors. Import-substitution and export-promotion were to be the central features of the governmental program. In addition to tax advantages, duty-free imports and other such incentives, the government directly underwrote the development of the infrastructure and the provision of sources of "risk" capital. Para-statal bodies such as the Industrial and the Agricultural Development Corporations, the Small Business Loans Board, and the Jamaica Development Bank were created for these purposes.[16] In the process, government spending increased significantly, both absolutely and in relation to the Gross Domestic Product, so that by 1968 public expenditure stood at 20.7 percent of the G.D.P., up from 13.8 percent in 1952. It is important to note that the increase was not funded through taxation, which remained quite low, but through government borrowing, 44 percent of which came from foreign sources.[17] It is safe to infer a continuing middle class bias from these data, speaking as they do of the increased role of the state in the economy.

If we are to understand the beneficial results of these practices to the bureaucratic-entrepreneurial fraction of the middle class, we must further comment on the "Millsian" quality of the circle of top policy makers, party officials, bureaucrats and professionals. Among these representatives of the class, access to those yielding power and influence is within easy reach, and the exchange of "favors" is the order of the day. These relationships are a frequent occurrence in social formations of the periphery; sometimes framed in a "clientelistic" mode of analysis, they owe their existence less to personal networks (e.g., attendance to elite boarding schools) than to the absence of structures insulating the officials or bureaucrats at hand from other well-placed members of the fraction. The fact is that the trade union official of today often becomes the senator or the government bank manager of tomorrow (Sandbrook, 1975: chap. 6). It is the preponderance of political channels as means to power and wealth, in the context of the expansion of the state apparatus, that ensures the continuance of these patterns.

These outlines of the politico-economic structure should provide sufficient indication of an abundance of opportunities to participate in entrepreneurial ventures. Import-substitution, access to information and to loan capital, government contracts, tax breaks, all provided a fertile ground. Not to be discounted are the opportunities created by the provision of services to foreign capital. Participation in the business venture at hand, in lieu of fee, was not an uncommon practice, especially for members of the legal profession.

Although quantitative research establishing the extent to which the entrepreneurial activities of the class had evolved has not been undertaken, the entrenchment of the bureaucratic-entrepreneurial fraction in production relations has been more than suggestively borne out by investment data from the public sector. Disclosures by the Jamaica Development Bank (JDB), the Agricultural Credit Board, the Small Business Loans Board and other such institutions leave little doubt as to the objective trends, indicating a substantial use of available loan funds by well-placed members of the fraction. Real estate, tourism, and middle-sized manufacturing ventures provided ample opportunities for such incursions.[18] At the same time, one should stress that participation in such economic activities remained an important but nonetheless secondary involvement, an offshoot of the original and still central professional or political activity of the fraction. Indeed, it is for this reason that one cannot suggest a simple transformation to bourgeois status and it may be appropriate, depending on circumstances, to refer to this capital as "parasitic capital" (Bonnie Campbell, 1978).

This important distinction would become more significant as the crisis of accumulation reached substantial proportions. The crisis had, of necessity, an underlying economic basis of which only brief mention need be made here. Most importantly, in the last half of the 1960s Jamaica was faced with the end of the phase of "easy" import substitution, the end of expansion of its important bauxite industry, and a crisis in export agriculture. The balance of payments, always a critical indicator for a small open economy such as Jamaica, was quite revealing. Deficits on current account hovered between £10 and £19 million in the 1956-66 period but increased drastically to £26.6 million in 1967 and £42.7 million in 1968 (Jefferson, 1972; Girvan, 1971; Palmer, 1979). They reflected, equally, a persistent failure, in spite of inducements, to develop significant non-traditional export industries; and they were mirrored by a growing public indebtedness that resulted from the compounded effects of the low effective rate of taxation and the increasing demands for government intervention on the political and economic levels.[19]

The political forces interacting with the crisis are best characterized as follows: a capitalist class whose traditional weakness was compounded by internal fissures; fragmented subordinate classes, with large petty bourgeois and lumpen components, which were not revolutionary but were sufficiently "restless" to threaten stability and thus the "investment climate"; a fraction of the middle class whose political and economic ascendance were founded on its structural role as mediator of antagonisms in the furtherance of capital accumulation. Together, they pointed to the logic of the attempted solutions out of the impasse.

First, the middle class. Although during the 1950s and 1960s the PNP had progressively grown to resemble the Jamaica Labour Party in membership and actual programs, the Party had nonetheless retained a distinctly middle class ideology. The clues point in the direction of the everpresent importance assigned to education and anything bearing the trappings of the "intelligentsia." This orientation was translated into a political vision marked by broadened parameters, often informed by social-scientific positions (especially those of dependency theory, espoused by university-trained intellectuals), proffering all-encompassing solutions to social ills.[20] Two points are worth mentioning in this respect. A study of Jamaican leaders undertaken between 1958 and 1962 revealed a stronger emphasis on egalitarianism and planning for "progress" within the PNP than the JLP (Bell, 1964). Later, these were translated into a renewal of "socialism," which resurfaced in the party's platform during elections in 1964, and was transformed by 1969 into "economic nationalism." The reformist orientation here was unmistakeable, although we must be careful not to equate the party with the class or even the bureaucratic-entrepreneurial fraction. There were, as we shall see below, clear comprador strains within the class that would, when put to the test, reject the party's agenda for change. Nonetheless, these utterances and orientation found ready audiences in the early 1970s.

Whereas the peasantry and working class had been the principal forces to spark the political crisis of 1938, their role in the late 1960s and 1970s was subordinate to that of certain fractions of the capitalist and middle classes. Changes of considerable magnitude had occurred in the structure of the economy, and thus the labor force, as Table 3.2 indicates; yet these did not add to a surge of direct and well-articulated demands for change from "below." It is true that the working class comprised some 25 percent of the labor force (44 percent of the employed labor force in 1974, by some estimates!) (Nelson, 1974; Gonsalves, 1976) and was substantially organized: Labor unions claimed a total membership ranging between 251,000 (1964) and 327,000 (1974), with "paid-up" members around 145,000 (1964, 1966) and strikes were a frequent occurrence, especially between 1969 and 1972 (Gonsalves, 1976). Yet the close association between the two major unions and the two political parties diminished the unions' potential role as instruments of class interests, making them prone, instead, to political manipulation. Further, with nearly one-third of the employed labor force classified as "self-employed, independent," there remained a strong—and unorganized—petty bourgeois presence among the subordinate classes. The picture would not be complete without reference to the large numbers of un- and under-employed and lumpens, which comprised some 30 percent of the labor force.

Such structural divisions within the subordinate classes did not augur well for the prospects of an organized assault upon the system. Rather, there was indirect and unorganized pressure in the form of wildcat strikes (which were apparently increasing), poor "labor-management" relations, mounting crime and violence, and the growth of a more secular and radical contingent within the Rastafarian sects (especially among young urban lumpens and middle class youth). This period was also marked by a resurgence of "leftist" activities, principally in and around the university, which, though primarily intellectual, were beginning to make contact with the working class. (Beckford and Witter, 1980; Girvan, 1968; Lacey, 1977).

Thus, while the subordinate classes showed unmistakeable signs of systemic strain in need of mediation, the dominant influences in the necessary politico-economic restructuring would originate from a divided power bloc. Within the capitalist class, a fledgling industrial faction appeared

TABLE 3.2   Classifiable Labor Force by Occupation, 1943, 1960, and 1972

Occupation Group	1943	1960	1972
Professional, technical administrative, managerial	14,477[a] (2.9%)	31,174 (5.0%)	45,401 (6.3%)
Clerical and sales	8,918 (1.8%)	69.629 (11.5%)	86,034 (11.9%)
Service	70,568[b] (14.1%)	103,263 (17.1%)	118,186 (16.4%)
Self-employed and independent	99,829[c] (20.0%)	*	222,650 (30.8%)
Craftsmen, production	126,082 (25.3%)	126,568 (20.9%)	126,617 (17.5%)
Unskilled, manual, and unspecified	178,818 (35.9%)	276,189 (44.5%)	123,622 (17.1%)
Total	498,692 (100.0%)	606,823 (100.0%)	722,612 (100.0%)

SOURCES: Cumper (n.d.); *Population and Vital Statistics,* Dept of Statistics, Jamaica (1973); *The Labour Force, 1972,* Dept. of Statistics, Jamaica (1973).
*Category not included for 1960.
a. Includes 7889 professionals, 1244 managers, 1788 employers outside agriculture and 3476 foremen, overseers, inspectors.
b. All servants.
c. Includes 1900 farmers employing some labor and 74,784 own account agricultural workers.

eager to restructure the relationship to foreign capital and its local comprador alliances. These would hail the initiatives of the new government vis à vis the bauxite industry and even praise the announced policies of democratic socialism, prompting a renowned political analyst to comment:

> If the business community were united in feeling that Business is threatened by the Government, then it could have some impact on the voters. But it should be obvious to any observer that there are certain firms, business executives and others who are so heavily and openly committed to the party in power, that they certainly do not see the Government as a threat [Sunday Gleaner, 7/28/1974].

The logic of this alliance is discerned upon examination of the structure of the capitalist class in the post-war period. On the surface, the Jamaican economy was substantially controlled by a tightly-knit group of "21 families" with interests across the entire spectrum of productive activities. Pioneering studies by Stanley Reid and Peter Phillips concluded that the Jamaican capitalist class was characterized by "a marriage of interests rather than conflict." There was evidence, further, of links between "old wealth" and the corporate economy. Reid noted that "concentration of a landownership provided some supportive framework for the development of the corporate economy" (Reid, 1976: 44; Phillips, 1976). Yet fissures appear when one shifts the focus from interlocks and intermarriage to the dynamics of capital itself. We refer to its competitive tendencies that assumed the guise of an incipient national capital attempting to remove some of the fetters attendant to peripheral "industrialization" by joining forces with the state.

We discussed earlier the preponderant influence of commercial capital in the Jamaican economy. The distributive sector, in fact, continued to make the largest contribution to the Gross Domestic Product (19 percent in 1970). However, stimulated by incentive legislation, there developed in the post-war period large and diversified corporate groups with interests in all sectors of the economy (the "21 families"): import-export, manufacturing (import-substitution), real estate development and construction, insurance and finance, tourism, and so on. The growth of concentration can be observed by noting that Industrial Commercial Developments (I.C.D.), one of the largest corporations on the Jamaican Stock Exchange, had revenues of J$55 million and declared pre-tax profits of J$1.5 million in 1974 (I.C.D. Annual Report, 1974). The connections with foreign capital were substantial. And yet, also evident was the propensity of capital to expand and seek new outlets through mergers (Reid, 1976: 68–69); the inception of CARICOM (the Caribbean Common Market) in 1968 provided a regional market and a limited degree of new investment opportunities (Chernick, 1978).

Such growth would naturally revive competitive tendencies as the limits of an all-too-circumscribed economic arena were approached. It is here that the role of the state would come into play. According to the Industrial Development Programme proposed by the PNP, the public sector would directly intervene in these areas of the economy considered critical "from a growth inducing point of view," with an eye to eliminating "the problem of sector under-investment and the irrational allocation of resources" (Jamaican Government, 1975: 3). The greater ability of the state to mobilize resources (e.g., through inter-government loans) would permit the exploration of ventures beyond the reach of private capital alone. Further, the risks which innovative undertakings usually entail would be socialized, as the development plan marked a special role for government in "trail blazing" ventures and the location of new markets. Here the state would muster its political and ideological strength, seeking to find new partners and opportunities through the call for Third World cooperation. Once the road was paved, private capital would be invited to participate and establish appropriate linkages. Two examples of such undertakings envisioned in the development plan were the highly capital-intensive vertically integrated production of aluminium and its derivatives and a petro-chemical complex, the Luana project, with an estimated cost of $132 million (Jamaican Government, 1975).

The more heavily comprador elements of the capitalist class, represented by the Chamber of Commerce and a portion of the membership of the Jamaica Manufacturers Association, expressed serious reservations about the project (Interviews, 1977). The perceived threat was real, as the required transformation represented nothing short of a refashioning of the relationship to foreign capital and a restructuring of the economy to reduce dependence. In the projected alteration of production priorities there was little room for "finishing touch" industries, monopolies grown sluggish in the protective hold of import-substitution, and trade and industries directed exclusively to the small internal market for "luxury" commodities. There was, consequently, a marked preference among these elements for a model more in line with current patterns of accumulation: the export-led industrialization that characterized South Korea, Taiwan, and other "Third World miracles" and that was championed by international organizations such as the World Bank (I.B.R.D., 1974). To ensure compliance with its agenda, the government initiated a policy of import and foreign currency restrictions and established the State Trading Corporation (STC) as a major government importing agency.[21]

The "national popularist" alliance, born under the wing of the PNP, had proposed an alternative to the prevailing patterns of capital accumulation and had taken the first steps down the road. A familiar scenario, albeit with important differences, was once again repeating itself. To the model attuned to and thus supported by metropolitan capital—capitalist plantations, industrialization by invitation, export-led industrialization—was counterposed an alternative, championed by an intermediate social grouping. By the 1970s the bureaucratic-entrepreneurial fraction had acquired sufficient power to begin translating its agenda for change into reality: State power would finally carry the reward of control over the economy. But the ambitious task would prove to be beyond reach. Besides the expected obstacles posed by international capital and its allies there stood others, potentially even more devastating, as they revealed the precariousness of the attempted "national popularist" alliance. Not only were relations with "national" capital and labor threatened by divergent interests—the internal integrity of the middle class fraction was similarly affected. Indeed, for the middle class, the economic advancement experienced in the 1960s militated against the execution of the "socialist" plan.

A fraction of a class consists, as noted above, of an intra-class division based on the differential combination of means of production and labor power. The emergence of "democratic socialism" therefore appears to announce a new fraction in formation, one that would make use of the political power of the class to combine labor and the means of production in a new way—that is, under the tutelage of the state. The transformation would entail relinquishing the junior partnership with capital and, potentially, the political alliance with labor. The assumption of overall responsibility for fostering capital accumulation and thus the joining of economic and political power would necessitate the control and, if necessary, the curbing, of both capital and labor. As for the middle class, the new fraction, as an embryonic "state bourgeoisie," would tend to come into conflict with other fractions having closer links to the "free enterprise" economy. The bureaucratic-entrepreneurial fraction, out of which this new tendency emerged, had distinguished itself by its inroads into "private" rather than "public" economic activities. It had benefited directly by the policies of import substitution and the relationship to foreign capital. Thus an attack against the system fashioned in the post-war period could not be directed merely at "a few" foreign and comprador elements but would affect ultimately significant segments of the middle class itself.

The tone of the conflict is captured in its essence by the comments of a minister of government, whose substantial indebtedness for investment purposes (J$1.8 million) was adjudged by a journalist to fall short of socialist principles:

> Let me first point out loud and clear that the People's National Party is not a communist party and does not subscribe to, or aspire to ideologies or life style proclaimed or portrayed by Mao Tse Tung. If the People's National Party were a communist party, or in fact proposed to be, I will (sic) not be a member of that Party. I certainly do not plan to wear Mao's two cotton uniforms if I can avoid it [Kenneth McNeill, Letter to the Editor, Jamaican Weekly Gleaner, 3/8/1977].

Given such unambiguous attachments, it should not come as a surprise that the fledgling state fraction (represented now not by the entire party, but largely by its "left" wing) quickly found itself isolated and under attack from all sides.

A brief review of key events should adequately portray its bleak position. The capitalist class, though still divided, exhibited a new "united front" through the Private Sector Organization of Jamaica (PSOJ), created in 1976. It supported the actions of the International Monetary Fund, that, called upon for assistance with foreign exchange difficulties in 1977 and 1978, insisted on the usual formula for "setting the Jamaican economy in order": reduced government spending for social and economic programs, wage controls, and currency devaluations, all for the stated purpose of stimulating the productivity of the private sector. Even before the imposition of these strictures, the government had found it necessary to curb the militancyy of labor: the requirements of furthering capital accumulation had led to the passage of the Labour Relations and Industrial Disputes Act in 1975, to which were added stringent amendements in 1978 (Josephs, 1977; Ross, 1975). As these structural imperatives propelled the government into an unambiguous position on the matter of the antagonism of capital and labor, fledgling socialist organizations gained some strength, stimulated by the crisis as well as the ideological discourse generated by the PNP agenda for change. Particularly noteworthy were the rise of socialist unions (Gonsalves, 1976) and a Marxist-Leninist political party, the Workers Party of Jamaica (WPJ—previously the Workers Liberation League) headed by Dr. Trevor Munroe.

Having gained an understanding of the circumstances through which the middle class in Jamaica came to play its significant politico-economic role, what can we expect for the future? It is unclear, even at this writing, what facets of the "inner-directed" agenda may remain as part of the economic program. In the disarray of the late 1970s, the economy came to a standstill and a JLP government was returned to office after elections held in 1980 on a platform apparently favoring a return to the *status quo ante*. Yet, in practice, this is hardly possible. The factors that led to the ascendance of the middle class fraction remain as central aspects of the social structure; and while they are most clearly articulated by one political party—the PNP—they constitute the background against which the policies of any government must be formulated. It was, after all, a JLP government that provoked the wrath of the capitalist class in the late 1960s, turning it toward the PNP, by attempting to reform tax laws and otherwise legislate in areas previously left untouched (Senior, 1972, Yorke, 1971).

For the moment, the export-led model enjoys the ascendance. A team representing the capitalist class (comprised of the Presidents of the Chamber of Commerce, the Manufacturers Association and the Private Sector Organization) had returned from a visit to South Korea in 1978 with great praises for the "refreshing" way they "went about the business of developing their country" (Daily Gleaner, 12/4/1978). And currently Jamaica is the centerpiece of the Reagan administration's Caribbean Basin Plan. Yet few investments have actually materialized.

The rise to power of the middle class has been checked and Jamaica has been reestablished within the fold of international capitalism without success for the sought restructuring of the relationship. Yet this victory leaves social relations in a balance more precarious than ever, for the intricate pattern of mediations forged over the last century and a half has been seriously damaged. The choices for class alliances are now more clearly drawn. How long can an unabashedly pro-capitalist stance as is favored by the present government be maintained, without changes in the form of the state? If the mediatory role of the middle class was indeed, as we have maintained, structurally determined, then the passage of the bureaucratic-entrepreneurial fraction openly into the capitalist camp might very well be the harbinger of more open confrontations between the opposed classes.

Notes

1. See for example the writings of the "dependency" school: Bodenheimer (1971), Frank (1971), Dos Santos (1970), and Cockcroft, Frank, and Johnson (1972).

2. See Shivji (1976), Cowen and Kinyanjui (1977), Leys (1974). For a useful review of some of the literature and a contribution in its own right see Ziemann and Langendorfer (1977).

3. Arghiri Emmanuel (1972: ch. 1 and 2) treats "center" and "periphery" within capital accumulation on a world scale. The Department I/Department II schema with the differential (and complementary) profit margins generated within each sphere of production *in a single economy* can be applied to the center/periphery orbit. Department I applies to the advanced capitalist economies, Department II to the periphery. As the combined forms of production make for a general rate of profit and therefore common values of all commodities involved in production (including labor), the labor theory of value is taken to apply to the overall production process—linking the social classes of both poles to a common process of accumulation. Also see Amin (1977: 117–136, 181–252).

4. The conceptualization of these intermediate social classes is often found wanting, as quite distinct groupings tend to be included under the catchall umbrella of the petty bourgeoisie. We shall employ the term "middle class" to include all salaried workers and free professionals who mediate between the capitalist class on the one hand and the proletariat, peasantry, sub- and lumpen proletariat on the other: those, that is, who dominate as well as are dominated, oppress as well as are oppressed. See Carchedi (1977).

5. The fear was well founded. The Vagrancy Act, passed in 1833, was unbelievably restrictive. See British Government (1836), Hall (1959).

6. Heuman (1981: 142). The representation of coloreds and blacks in the Jamaican Assembly was as follows: 1838–1844 (8); 1844–1849 (unknown increase over earlier figure); 1849–1854 (20—of which 3 black); 1854–1860 (17); 1860–1863 (14) (Heuman, 1981: 131, 138, 140).

7. Metcalfe to Russell, 12 February 1841 and 21 September 1841, in Bell and Morrell (1968: 416). The "Popular Party" and the "Town Party" were one and the same.

8. Heuman (1981: Appendix A, pp. 197–98) criticizes Mavis Campbell's (1976) conclusions that the behavior of the coloreds was largely prompted by the "aping" of white culture. According to Heuman, the behavior represented a "new radicalism."

9. Heuman (1981: 131, 149–150). Freeholders comprised some 60 percent of the electorate in 1858 but only some 30 percent in 1860. During this time and until the advent of uneversal suffrage in 1944 the electorate was always quite small.

10. For a brief review see Morrell (1969: 399–432). On the events following the Morant Bay rebellion and forming the background of the 1938 labor rebellion see Ken Post (1978).

11. By the last decades of the century the sugar industry contributed only 15 percent of Jamaica's total export trade and was failing. Government support for peasant production continued to be envisaged as a solution of last resort. Beginning in 1901, the Crown subsidized a steamship line to market bananas, a crop that would eventually supplant sugar. (British Government, 1898; Olivier, 1936).

12. By the late 1890s peasants cultivated 17 percent of sugar acreage, 74 percent of coffee acreage, 45 percent each of banana, coconut, and cocoa acreate. (Eisner, 1961: 79; British

Government, 1898: Appendix, 136–143). Estates again began to expand after 1911 (Cumper, 1956: 270–271).

13. Eisner (1961: 332–337, 165–166). A discussion also in Post (1978: 92–94). The number of secondary school places in 1929 represented only 2 percent of schoolchildren; 15,000 teachers, etc. in 1921 represented 4.3 percent of the workforce.

14. For the institutionalization of labor's demands see Harrod (1972: 208–249). By 1954 sugar estates owned 37 percent of all cultivated acreage (45 percent in 1968) (Smith, 1976: 38; Brewster, 1972).

15. The term "fraction" refers to an intra-class division based on a differential combination of labor power and means of production: e.g. commercial fraction, industrial fraction, and so on.

16. Ayub (1981). Non-traditional manufactured exports (e.g. other than sugar, bananas, etc.) have remained negligible: 8 percent (gross value) of total exports in 1968 (Jefferson, 1972: 138–139). Most of the expansion of these exports in later years was directed to the Caribbean Common Market (CARICOM) area (Ayub, 1981: Chap. 6).

17. Absolute increase between 1952–68 was more than 500 percent (Jefferson 1972: 236–251). On taxation: the actual corporate rate (1959–1968) was around 22 percent while the nominal tax rate was 40 percent (Jefferson, 1972: 228). Between 1973 and 1976 public expenditure rose from 21.2 percent of G.D.P. to 35.2 percent of G.D.P. (Economic and Social Survey, Jamaica, 1976, 1976). The majority of jobs created during the latter period (1972–1976) were in Government administration (Jamaica Newsletter, Jan.-Feb. 1979: 5).

18. One of the authors, Nelson Keith, is a former attorney, involved in the sphere of real estate development in Jamaica. He notes that he "is able not to disavow allegations tying powerful middle class interests with those of foreign capital. Frequent rumors involving major political figures in governments of the late 1960s and the present, in such areas as the construction sector and tourism have frequently been bandied about in circumstances challenging law suits in libel, yet such court actions are conspicuous by their absence!" (1981: 417, n. 112). The contention is supported by interviews with officials of the Jamaica Development Bank, August 1977 (anonymity requested). In 1977 a short list of disclosures by some lending institutions revealed, among others, an indebtedness of J$2.2 million by 7 fairly influential PNP members (*Jamaican Weekly Gleaner*, March 8, 1977: 12).

19. See note 17. Public expenditure classified under "development expenditure" increased from less than 10 percent of total in the early 1950s to more than 25 percent on the average during 1962–1967 (Jefferson, 1972: 252). An example of "political/social" expenditure: Jamaica has no unemployment insurance. There is a tradition of government provision of work at Christmas time that governments would eliminate at their peril.

20. See the work of the New World Group (New World Quarterly; Girvan and Jefferson, 1972) and the writings of Girvan (1968, 1971) and Beckford (1972). Girvan became the Director of the National Planning Agency during the last PNP Government (1972–1981); Beckford was a frequent government adviser on agriculture. On the party's programs see PNP (1966) and "Text of address of president of PNP, Mr. Michael Manley . . ." reproduced in Jamaican Daily Gleaner, October 27, 1969: 23.

21. See Ayub (1982: Table 3–1 and pp. 33–35) for quantitative restrictions on imports. Prohibited imports included consumer commodities previously found in abundance, the list growing with time. By 1977, the President of the Chamber of Commerce was bitterly complaining about negative effects on the commercial community: see speech by Avis Henriques to Montego Bay Rotary Club (Jamaican Weekly Gleaner, March 8, 1977: 16).

References

Alba, Victor
1968   Politics and the Labor Movement in Latin America. Stanford: Stanford University Press.

Amin, Samir
1976   Unequal Development. New York: Monthly Review Press.
1977   Imperialism and Unequal Development. New York: Monthly Review Press.

Augier, F. R. and S. C. Gordon
1962   Sources of West Indian History. London: Longmans, Green.

Ayub, Mahmood Ali
1981   Made in Jamaica; The Development of the Manufacturing Sector. World Bank Occasional Paper No. 31. Baltimore: Johns Hopkins University Press.

Beckford, George
1972   Persistent Poverty: Underdevelopment in Plantation Economies of the Third World. New York: Oxford University Press.

Beckford, George and Michael Witter
1980   Small Garden . . . Bitter Weed: Struggle and Change in Jamaica. London: Zed Press.

Bell, Kenneth and W. P. Morrell (eds.)
1968   Select Documents on British Policy 1830–1860. Oxford: Clarendon Press.

Bell, Wendell
1964   Jamaican Leaders: Political Attitudes in a New Nation. Berkeley: University of California Press.

Bodenheimer, Susanne J.
1971   The Ideology of Developmentalism; The American Paradigm Surrogate in Latin American Studies. Beverly Hills, CA: Sage.

Brathwaite, Edward
1971   The Development of Creole Society in Jamaica, 1770–1820. London: Oxford University Press.

Brewster, Havelock
1972   "Jamaica's life or death: the sugar industry." In Norman Girvan and Owen Jefferson (eds.) Readings in the Political Economy of the Caribbean. Kingston: New World Publications.

British Government
1836a Report from the Select Committee on Negro Apprenticeship in the Colonies, Appendix 3, "Observations on Jamaican Acts." British Parliamentary Papers, 1836, 1, pp. 427–431.
1836b Papers Relating to the Abolition of Slavery, Part 3: Jamaica. British Parliamentary Papers, 1836, 48.
1840   Colonial Office 137/250 Metcalfe to Russell, December 14, 1840.
1845   "Copies of the Last Census of the Population." British Parliamentary Papers 1845, 31.
1849   "Debate in Council on the Rejection of the Retrenchment Bill, February 8, 1849." In C. E. Grey to Earl Grey, February 19, 1848, Appendix. British Parliamentary Papers 1849, 37, pp. 244–265.
1852   C. E. Grey to Pakington, August 23, 1852. British Parliamentary Papers 1852–1853, 67.
1854   Colonial Office 137/324, Barkly to Grey, October 19, 1954.
1864   Colonial Office 137/385, Eyre to Newcastle, December 19, 1864.
1898   Norman Commission Report. British Parliamentary Papers 1898, 50.

Campbell, Bonnie
1978 "Ivory Coast." In John Dunn (ed.) West African States: Failure and Promise. New York: Cambridge University Press.
Campbell, Mavis C.
1976 The Dynamics of Change in a Slave Society; A Sociopolitical History of the Free Coloreds of Jamaica, 1800–1865. Rutherford, NJ: Fairleigh Dickinson University Press.
Carchedi, Guglielmo
1977 On the Economic Identification of Social Classes. London: Routledge & Kegan Paul.
Chernick, Sidney
1978 The Commonwealth Caribbean; The Integration Experience. Baltimore: Johns Hopkins University Press.
Cockcroft, James, Andre G. Frank, and Dale L. Johnson
1972 Dependence and Underdevelopment: Latin America's Political Economy. New York: Doubleday.
Cowen, M. and K. Kinyanjui
1977 Some Problems of Capital and Class in Kenya. Occasional Paper No. 16. Nairobi: Institute for Development Studies.
Cumper, George E.
1956 "Population movements in Jamaica, 1830–1950." Social and Economic Studies 5, 3: 261–280.
n.d. The Social Structure of Jamaica. Kingston: University College of the West Indies.
Dos Santos, Theotonio
1970 "The structure of dependence." American Economic Review 60 (May): 231–236.
Edwards, Bryan
1966 The History of the West Indies, Vol. 2. New York: Arno Press.
Eisner, Gisela
1961 Jamaica, 1830–1930: A Study in Economic Growth. Manchester: Manchester University Press.
Evans, Peter
1979 Dependent Development: The Alliance of Multinational, State and Local Capital in Brazil. Princeton: Princeton University Press.
Emmanuel, Arghiri
1972 Unequal Exchange: A Study of the Imperialism of Trade. New York: Monthly Review Press.
Fanon, Frantz
1966 The Wretched of the Earth. New York: Grove Press.
Frank, Andre Gunder
1971 Capitalism and Underdevelopment in Latin America. London: Penguin.
Foster-Carter, Aidan
1978 "The modes of production controversy." New Left Review 107 (Jan.-Feb.): 47–77.
Girvan, Norman
1968 "After Rodney: the politics of student protest in Jamaica." New World Quarterly, High Season.
1971 Foreign Capital and Economic Underdevelopment in Jamaica. Mona, Jamaica: Institute of Social and Economic Research.
Gonsalves, Ralph
1976 "The trade union movement in Jamaica: its growth and some resultant problems." In Carl Stone and Aggrey Brown (eds.) Essays in Power and Change in Jamaica. Mona,

Jamaica: Department of Government and Extra-Mural Centre, University of the West Indies.

Green, William

1976   British Slave Emancipation: The Sugar Colonies and the Great Experiment 1830–1865. Oxford: Clarendon Press.

Hall, Douglas

1959   Free Jamaica 1838–1865: An Economic History. New Haven, CT: Yale University Press.

1971   A Brief History of the West India Committee. Barbados: Caribbean Universities Press

Halpern, Manfred

1968   "The new middle class." In Harvey G. Kebschull (ed.) Politics in Transitional Societies. New York: Appleton-Century-Crofts.

Harrod, Jeffrey

1972   Trade Union Foreign Policy: A Study of British and American Trade Union Activities in Jamaica. Garden City, NY: Doubleday.

Heuman, Gad J.

1981   Between Black and White: Race, Politics and the Free Coloreds in Jamaica, 1792–1865. Westport, CT: Greenwood Press.

Hurwitz, Samuel J. and Edith Hurwitz

1965   "The new world sets an example for the old: the Jews of Jamaica and political rights 1661–1831." American Jewish Historical Quarterly 55, 1:37–56.

International Bank for Reconstruction and Development

1974   "Current Economic Position and Prospects of Jamaica Vol. I." Report #257 a-JM. (mimeo)

Jamaican Government

1949   Jamaica Hansard, Proceedings of the House of Representatives of Jamaica, 1949, 1.

1972a   Address of the Hon. Michael Manley, Prime Minister and Minister of External Affairs of Jamaica, at the 27th Session of the UN General Assembly, October 2, 1972. Kingston: Agency for Public Information. (mimeo)

1972b   "Statement by Michael Manley on New Economic Policy, House of Representatives, November 9, 1972." Jamaica Hansard 1 no. 2.

1973   "Green Paper on Agricultural Development Strategy." Reprinted in Jamaica Daily News, November 23, 1973 –December 4, 1973.

1974   Democratic Socialism for Jamaica—The Government Policy for National Development. Kingston: Agency for Public Information.

1975   Green Paper on Industrial Development Programme—Jamaica, 1975–1980. Kingston: Government Printer.

1977a   "The IMF Agreement." Ministry Paper No. 28. Kingston: Ministry of Finance, File No. 406/02 (April 21).

1977b   "Incomes Policy 1977." Ministry Paper No. 13. Kingston: Ministry of Finance (April 21).

James, C. L. R.

1970   "The West Indian middle classes." In Trevor Munroe and Rupert Lewis (eds.) Readings in Government and Politics of the West Indies. Kingston: New World Publications.

Jefferson, Owen

1972   The Post-War Economic Development of Jamaica. Mona, Jamaica: Institute of Social and Economic Research.

Johnson, John

1958   Political Change in Latin America; The Emergence of the Middle Sectors. Stanford: Stanford University Press.

Josephs, Keith
1977   "Struggle for fundamental labour reforms." Socialism! 4, 3: 13–25.
Keith, Nelson W.
1981   A Developmental Strategy in Historico-Structural Perspective: Dependency Theory, Dependency Management and the Bauxite Policies in Jamaica. Ph.D. thesis, Rutgers University.
Keith, Novella
1981   Democratic Socialism in Jamaica: Politics of Reform, Transition to Socialism or "Third Way" of Development? Ph.D. thesis, Rutgers University.
Knox, Graham
1965   "Political change in Jamaica (1866–1906) and local reaction to the policies of the Crown Colony Government." In F. M. Andic and T. G. Mathews (eds.) The Caribbean in Transition. Rio Piedras, Puerto Rico: Institute of Caribbean Studies.
Lacey, Terry
1977   Violence and Politics in Jamaica, 1960–1970. London: Frank Cass.
Leys, Colin
1974   Underdevelopment in Kenya: The Political Economy of Neo-Colonialism. 1964–1971. Berkeley: University of California Press.
Long, Norman
1975   "Structural dependency, modes of production and economic brokerage in rural Peru." In Ivar Oxaal et al. (eds.) Beyond the Sociology of Development. London: Routledge & Kegan Paul.
Lowenthal, David
1972   West Indian Societies. New York: Oxford University Press.
Morrell, W. P.
1966   British Colonial Policy in the Age of Peel and Russell. London: Frank Cass.
1969   British Colonial Policy in the Mid-Victorian Age. Oxford: Clarendon Press.
Morris, C. T. and Adelman, I.
1971   "An anatomy of income distribution patterns in developing nations." Development Digest (October).
Munroe, Trevor
1972   The Politics of Constitutional Decolonization: Jamaica 1944–1962. Mona, Jamaica: Institute of Social and Economic Studies.
1977   "The Marxist 'Left' in Jamaica 1940–1972." Working Paper No. 15. Mona, Jamaica: Institute of Social and Economic Research.
Nelson, Cecil
1974   "The class structure of Jamaican society." Socialism! 1, 1.
Nettleford, Rex
1971   Norman Washington Manley: Manley and the New Jamaica. New York: Africana Publishers.
Nun, Jose
1967   "The middle class military coup." In C. Veliz (ed.) The Politics of Conformity in Latin America. London: Oxford University Press.
Nyerere, Julius
1968   Ujamaa: Essays on Socialism. New York: Oxford University Press.
Olivier, Lord
1936   Jamaica, the Blessed Island. London: Faber and Faber.
O'Meally, Jaime
1938   "Why we demand self-government." New York: Jamaica Progressive League.

Palmer, Ransford
1979   Caribbean Dependence on the United States Economy. New York: Praeger.
People's National Party
1939   Outline of Policy and Programme of the People's National Party. Kingston: People's National Party.
1955   PNP Plan for Progress. Kingston: People's National Party.
1966   A Plan for Action Today. Kingston: People's National Party.
Phelps, O. W.
1960   "The rise of the labour movement in Jamaica." Social and Economic Studies 9, 4:417–468.
Phillips, Peter
1976   "Capitalist elites in Jamaica." In Carl Stone and Aggrey Brown (eds.) Essays in Power and Change in Jamaica. Jamaica: Department of Government and Extra-Mural Centre, University of the West Indies.
Post, Ken W.
1978   Arise Ye Starvelings: The Jamaican Labour Rebellion of 1938 and its Aftermath. Boston: Martinus Nijoff.
Proctor, Jesse Harris
1973   "British West Indian Society and Government in Transition 1920–60." In David Lowenthal and Lambros Comitas (eds.) The Aftermath of Sovereignty. Garden City, NY: Anchor Books.
Ragatz, Lowell J.
1928   The Fall of the Planter Class in the British Caribbean, 1763–1833. New York: Octagon Press.
Reid, Stanley
1976   "An introductory approach to the concentration of power in the Jamaican corporate economy and notes on its origin." In Carl Stone and Aggrey Brown (eds.) Essays in Power and Change in Jamaica. Jamaica: Department of Government and Extra-Mural Centre, University of the West Indies.
1977   Strategy and Policy Issues in Resource Bargaining: A Case Study of the Jamaican Bauxite-Alumina Industry Since 1974. Jamaica: Department of Management Studies, University of the West Indies.
Roberts, W. Adolphe
1955   Jamaica: The Portrait of an Island. New York: Coward-McCann.
Ross, Shala
1975   "Stage set for bourgeois anti-worker law." Socialism! 2, 3:8–14.
Sandbrook, Richard
1975   Proletarians and African Capitalism: The Kenyan Case, 1960–1972. New York: Cambridge University Press.
Senior, Olive
1972   The Message Is Change: A Perspective on the 1972 General Elections. Kingston: Kingston Publishers.
Sheridan, Richard
1970   The Development of Plantations to 1750. Barbados: Caribbean Universities Press.
Shivji, Issa
1976   Class Struggles in Tanzania. New York: Monthly Review Press.
Smith, Shirley
1976   Industrial Growth, Employment Opportunity and Migration within and from Jamaica, 1943–1970. Ph.D. thesis, University of Pennsylvania.

Solodnikov, V. G.
1973   The Present Stage of Non-Capitalist Development in Asia and Africa. Budapest: Center
       for Afro-Asian Research of the Hungarian Academy of Sciences.
Stone, Carl
1974   Electoral Politics and Public Opinion in Jamaica. Mona, Jamaica: Institute of Social and
       Economic Research.
Taylor, John
1979   From Modernization to Modes of Production. Atlantic Highlands, NJ: Humanities
       Press.
Tikasingh, Gerad
1968   A Method for Estimating the Free Coloured Population of Jamaica. Master's thesis,
       University of the West Indies.
Yorke, Stephen
1971   "Employers associations and the Income Tax (Amendment) Act of 1970." In Trevor
       Munroe and Rupert Lewis (eds.) Readings in Government and Politics of the West
       Indies. Kingston: New World Publications.
Ziemann, W. and M. Langendorfer
1977   "The State in Peripheral Societies," Socialist Register.

Cecilia A. Karch: Class Formation

and Class and Race Relations

in the West Indies

This chapter analyzes the dynamic between changing forms of international capitalism, the historical formation of classes, and contemporary class and race relations in the Commonwealth Caribbean. The development of peripheral capitalism in the Caribbean with its legacy of a slave mode of production and plantation economy has evolved class/race relations of a particular form that are manifested in present social structures and party politics.

The chapter analyzes the manner in which late nineteenth-early twentieth century international developments significantly altered class/race relations of the slave period. New class antagonisms and alignments occurred in the wake of these changes. International developments and local antagonisms among fractions of the dominant classes of the islands resulted in the emergence of a new commercial, agro-export bourgeoisie that successfully unsurped power from the old plantocracy. Other social classes were also affected: Conditions continued to worsen for the agroproletariat and peasantry and an urban working class emerged. However, it is the birth and historical development of salaried black middle groups and a black petty bourgeoisie which is given particular attention due to their important sociopolitical role from the 1930s onward.

The Legacy of
the Plantation System

Wherever the plantation system has spread it has monopolized capital, land, and labor and dominated all relations of production. The plantation system not only produces its own class structure, it inhibits the viable formation of alternate class structures within its sphere of influence. Conversely, when the plantation system declines, changes, or is broken up, its reorganization facilitates the formation of alternate class structures. Relations of production in plantation societies vary world-wide, according to different articulations with the international market, degree of dependency on metropolitan countries and ecological factors. The plantation economies are found primarily in the tropics and principally in formerly colonial dependencies. While relations of production in plantation economies are inextricably bound up with the history of colonialism and imperial rivalries, these relations are also specific, governed by unique historical factors of internal development.

In the Caribbean, the plantation system was established in the 17th and 18th centuries. The West Indies became "colonies of exploitation" whose indigenous peoples were exterminated and labor requirements were satisfied by the massive importation of African slaves. Early mercantile capitalism in the metropole was interlocked with the slave mode of production in the New World. The all-pervasive nature of the plantation system in the West Indies was characterized by a virtual monopoly over the means of livelihood for the inhabitants of the territory: monocrop production, a rigid, oligarchic internal power structure, and nearly total dependence on external trade with little self-sufficiency (Beckford, 1972).

Under the slave mode of production the West Indian colonies were structurally part of an overseas economy in which they were simply the locus of production. The dynamic for economic development resided outside the plantation, not within. This is the main reason why throughout the eighteenth and nineteenth centuries the majority of plantation owners were absentee, residing in the metropole. The change from slavery to the capitalist plantation system was also initiated from abroad. Under the impulse of developments in England (the shift from mercantile to industrial capitalism), the Post-Emancipation period in the West Indies witnessed the introduction of the corporate plantation, the creation of an agro-proletariat, and a formation and marginalization of a peasantry.

In the late nineteenth century the West Indies, in common with colonies throughout the world, became fully integrated into international capitalism in its monopoly and imperialist stage, primarily through the emergence and dominance of monopoly plantation corporations. The preeminence of the multi-national plantation radically altered colonial societies to fit its requirements. In the Caribbean, the long established plantation system facilitated the introduction of monopoly capitalist plantation enterprises. Consequently local social formations were better able to adjust to the changing conditions than were pre-capitalist economies in South East Asia or Africa.

Slave plantation society had evolved certain distinctive features that were tenaciously maintained in the transformation to modern capitalist relations of production. The caste system based on African slavery of the earlier plantation era formed the basis for the emergent class system where color was rigidly correlated with occupation, power, and status. Strict control of the labor supply managed along color lines were maintained, with the majority of the population dependent on the plantation for survival well into the twentieth century.

Limited social mobility occurred for some, largely white-black mixed ancestry "colored" persons, in the post-Emancipation period. Continued development of the modern capitalist plantation economy gave colored persons main entry at the point that the system required more skilled workers, professionals, and white collar workers such as accountants and clerks, than could be supplied by the resident white population. However, this restricted social mobility was predicted on the assimilation of the culture and values of the dominant local white plantocracy and the colonial power. By the turn of the century distinctions manifesting themselves in education, language, residence, religious beliefs and practices, and other ideological components, buttressed class divisions—and all were associated with race.

In sum, changes in the post-Emancipation period were wrought by the shift from slavery to wage labor. These in turn, were predicated on the transition of metropolitan industrial capitalism, which introduced the corporate plantation into West Indian colonies. However, given the tenacity of the plantation system as a total institution, many of the characteristics of the slave period, particularly patterns of domination and subordination based on color/race, culture, and the correlation between class and race were integrated with emerging capitalist social relations. This created unique social relations that are slowly being transformed in the present conjuncture. In fact, analysis of these unique characteristics is essential to understanding the present dynamic of Caribbean societies. Thus the point of departure in analyzing social classes, class relations, and the state in the West Indies must be the social structure of the plantation economy and the dynamic of race/color.

Class/Color Dynamic

It has been argued by many social scientists in the region (R. T. Smith, 1967; Harris, 1964; M. G. Smith, 1965; Brathwaite, 1953) that the racial characteristics that determined caste lines under the slave mode of production in plantation societies are still in existence. These authors argue that race/color is still the primary demarcation between superordinate/subordinate classes. With Emancipation and the diversification of the plantation economy, some modifications in the class structure occurred, but race remained the most salient factor in social relations. While not disagreeing with this analysis I hope to demonstrate the manner in which race/color often confuses a class analysis and in practice has more often than not defeated social movements that operate solely from *either* a color perspective *or* a class perspective. For, in fact, color consciousness has often been the motor of class consciousness (e.g., Garveyism).

Slavery as a mode of production linked to the plantation system was an institution of labor exploitation that established hierarchical relationships of a caste nature. The white oligarchy in all the islands established and sought to maintain a social system predicated on race/color. However, changing conditions of capitalism, the international sugar crisis from late nineteenth century to World War I, and the world Depression of the 1930s necessitated changes in the proprietary plantation system of the West Indies. Everywhere there was a reduction in the number of estates and their amalgamation in the hands of fewer owners. Estate ownership came to be dominated by corporations, many of them metropolitan plantation enterprises, such as Bookers and Tate and Lyle; many of the local corporate plantations were owned by merchants who bought into the plantation sector, forming in the process an agro-commercial bourgeoisie, the new ruling class of the region. Throughout this period of plantation transformation the local dominant interests and the colonial power sought to implement a policy of containment against the aspirations and assertions of the black masses and their predominantly colored middle class leaders.

Under the slave mode of production people of mixed parentage were differentiated from the mass of the black population because of their white ancestry. Privileges were extended in proportion to their whiteness so that over time they formed strata of Afro-creole freedmen intermediate between the two primary classes, masters and slaves. Depending on the specifics of island social formations, these mixed middle classes were of greater or lesser importance.

In Jamaica their importance grew steadily as a result of the absentee nature of the plantation system. "By 1838 a large brown skin middle class has emerged in Jamaica. The mulattoes owned some 50,000 slaves before Emancipation and substantial pimento and coffee holdings. By 1832 they were represented in the Jamaica Assembly and by 1837 eight of the 45 members of the Assembly were from this colored class" (Forsythe, 1975:25).

Conversely, in Barbados where the plantocracy was resident and nearly all of the land was alienated, mulattoes who were freedmen gradually displaced resident whites in the skilled trades, but they were effectively barred from plantation ownership and commerce. There were only three colored families who owned plantations during the slave period. Unlike Jamaica, the freedmen population was small, only 6 percent of the population in the 1830s, and they were divided nearly equally between black and colored (46.6 percent black and 53.3 percent colored) (Handler and Lio, 1974:217). Shade gradations have consequently had less ideological and political importance and been less integral to class consciousness in Barbados than in Jamaica.

In Trinidad, the plantation system developed late in the slave period. In 1838 on the eve of Emancipation only 43,265 acres out of a total acreage of 208,379 was cultivated; and unlike Barbados, the greatest proportion of land was Crown lands. Even as late as 1860 only 1/20th of the total acreage was under cultivation. Trinidad supported a free coloured population which outnumbered the whites. Within this population was a significant number of colored proprietors, a situation that exacerbated antagonistic fractionalism within the plantocracy that was also divided ethnically among whites— French creoles, the British and those of Spanish descent. In addition, the free colored were petty-bourgeois. They owned retail shops, dry goods stores, and were accountants and tradesmen. They also worked as clerks for merchants and lawyers. Even before slavery ended there was a high level of education among the colored population. By 1838, this section of the population was represented in the Legislative Council by Jean Baptiste Philip.

Everywhere, however, the white oligarchy enacted measures to prevent mobility of the colored middle classes that could challenge the hegemony of the white slave-owning class. It would be a mistake to assume that social class was paramount and phenotypical characteristics and genetics (race) were of tangential importance in Caribbean stratification systems. The majority of colored people were not large property and slave owners; they were petty-bourgeois shopkeepers and artisans. During the slave mode of production the mixed groupings were far more dependent than were traditional petty-bourgeois groupings in the metropole; they were, in effect, the *creation* of the slave-owning class and their class position was determined by the needs and caprice of the dominant white class.

Paternalism as a means of domination was predicated on subservience and proximity to white civilization, i.e., rejection by coloreds of all things African and the espousal of European ideology and culture. Thus genetics, phenotype and ideology influenced class positioning and the "brown middle class" was comprised of groupings of shopkeepers, artisans, some property and slave owners, and a few professionals under obligation to deny the African and act European. These groupings in a fully developed metropolitan capitalist context would have different places in economic relations, but in the West Indies both under slavery and in the post-Emancipation period (while the social formations were being transformed into peripheral capitalist formations) the intermediate position of the colored groupings in the race/color stratification system placed them in the same class. As Poulantzas has theoretically stated:

> If certain groupings which at first sight seem to occupy different places in economic relations can be considered as belonging to the same class, this is because these places, although they are different, nevertheless have the same effects at the political and ideological level [1975:205].

It is important to remember that although Abolition served to transform the relations of production from slave to wage labor, it was a change in the basis of exploiting labor; the plantation system and its international linkages remained intact.

Racist values and institutions were the bedrock of the superstructure, and "after the abolition of slavery racism *continued* to serve an essential function in the overall growth and development of the international capitalist order in the Americas" (Girvan, 1975:13). The colored middle class position was determined not only by the class polarization between the agro-commercial bourgeoisie and the agro-proletariat/peasantry in the 100 years after Emancipation, but also by race/color. The much discussed self-hatred and insecurity of the colored middle-class of that period and their ambiguity and contradictions vis-à-vis the two primary classes can only be understood within the context of the ideological significance of race. Divisions in West Indian social formations between the lighter shades who had better class advantages and the darker population, who suffered greater discrimination caused color consciousness to supercede class consciousness.

Color was instrumental in placing people into classes, so much so, that over time class and color were *perceived* as coterminous. The needs of a developing capitalist society short of whites to perform functionary roles meant that "we are all unequal, but some are more unequal than others," that is, the expanding social formation accomodated limited mobility for a select grouping. Nevertheless, all persons of color were limited in their economic advancement because inferiority was defined in physical as well as in cultural terms: "No matter how culturally white an African might become, he remained a 'Negro' and consequently, by definition a slave and therefore, permanently the subject of unmitigated exploitation and the source of primitive capitalist accumulation" (Girvan, 1975:8).

The Corporate Plantation Economy and the Intermediate Classes

From mid-nineteenth century petty-bourgeois groupings and professional strata grew steadily in the West Indies. The middle classes of the region, due to restrictions on landowning, were urban dwellers. The growth of intermediate social elements was the result of the expansion of the commercial sector and wage labor. The civil service in the British West Indies became a selective reward system. It provided limited opportunities for mobility to pacify aspirations of the West Indian middle classes. The significance of the colored and black intermediate groups, and their role in emerging class relations and in the nationalist movement varied from island to island. Here I will briefly describe the process up to 1945 in Barbados, Jamaica, and Trinidad, focusing primarily on the years of working class revolt, the 1930s and 1940s.

Barbados

In the Post-Emancipation period Afro-Barbadians owned 25.1 percent of all housing property in Bridgetown of an annual value of 30 pounds sterling and over. Here, as elsewhere in the region, the majority of the petty bourgeoisie were colored. In 1891 they comprised 43.9 percent of the urban population. However, economic and social advancement for people of African descent, whether colored or black, was more limited then in the other islands.

Barbados supported a large white population and racial descrimination and strict occupational lines were easier to maintain. Both the commercial and the production sectors, firmly in white hands practiced discriminatory methods of limiting the number of Afro-Barbadians allowed into the class, largely by refusing important business contacts and credit. Nonetheless, small-scale commercial and artisanal shops emerged. Those colored and a few blacks who inherited money often went abroad to study theology, medicine, and law, rather than attempt to buck the system and try to break into commerce or sugar production. The core of the intermediate classes were comprised of shopkeepers, skilled artisans such as blacksmiths and butchers, and a salaried sector of teachers. Leadership in the Afro-Barbadian community was drawn from the educated, who were often more literate than whites. These black and colored professionals were largely an unpropertied group. Only a few were able to obtain the right to vote or hold office, consequently they were unable to wield significant economic or political power to advance themselves or the mass of the unfranchised population.

The white petty bourgeoisie and white collar employees were more privileged and had more options. The bulk of the clerks, bookkeepers and shop assistants of Bridgetown were white. In Barbados these occupations carried high status. The emergence and consolidation of the corporate plantation economy from 1870 to the outbreak of World War II benefited the white strata relatively greater than any other sector of the population. Whites also dominated the professional classes out of proportion to their numbers; and, of course, they monopolized the overseer and managerial positions in estates and sugar factories. Until the mid-twentieth century they were overrepresented in government service, transport and communications (Karch, 1977).

Changes in production and the expansion of commerce affected social relations and were expressed in a power struggle within the colonial juridical and political superstructure. The commercial bourgeoisie gravitated toward the British doctrines of positivism and liberalism. In this they often had allies among the educated Afro-Barbadian middle classes. The plantocracy, on the other hand, was on the defensive protecting its interests against economic and political changes. Planter and commercial interest were often in conflict with one another. However, the racial factor intervened. Legislation that would have granted greater racial equality and/or black political power was consistently vetoed by both the plantocracy and the merchant class. This reflected more than anything else the powerlessness of Afro-Barbadian intermediate groups.

It was the world-wide depression of the 1930s that propelled the Afro-Barbadian middle classes into political leadership. Unemployment among the "middle classes was abnormally high" according to the Deane Commission appointed after the riots of 1937. The closure of traditional emigration outlets in the 1920s and 1930s, exacerbating a precarious economic position, was an important factor in their growing political militancy. However, dependency on the paternalism of the oligarchy and identification with the concept of Empire blunted the national revolutionary consciousness of the middle groups. The class as a class did not support working class revolt against the system. It was a minority of middle class individuals who became political leaders and spokesmen for the black majority. The meteoric rise of middle class leaders was predicated on the support of the black working class, who provided the massive unrest that propelled them into the forefront of the anti-colonial and trade union struggle.

When leadership emerged from the ranks of the working-class it was suppressed. Thus a radical working class movement that would have challenged the system was subverted. The nationalist movement forced the political system to become more representative of the racial composition of the population and removed some of the worst exploitative features of the system significantly transforming the social formation (Marks, 1966).

The 1937 riots were a watershed, as they were throughout the West Indies. The riots served to bring the black working class and the predominately colored middle-classes into an alliance that took the form of the

Progressive League, later to become the Barbados Labour Party. The League had two primary wings, one political, the other industrial. The later was organized as the Barbados Workers Union in 1941. Organized as a general union, intra-class and industrial versus craft rivalries did not emerge to blunt the focus of black class struggle. The Barbados Workers Union's alliance with the Labour Party gave the party not only a mass base, but once elected, the party began to draw up legislation that gave, for the first time in three hundred years, economic and political rights to the black working class.

However, Grantley Adams, the leader of the party, and the rest of the executive, believed firmly in the superiority of British party politics and the Westminister model of government. Under an oligarchic system such as Barbados's, such political practice could do little to redress the social relations of production and control over the economy which were the sources of black oppression. The Labour Party focused on decolonization rather than economic transformation and social reform: "When the political fight is won, economic ills will disappear," Adams stated.

Thus, class relations were modified, but hardly revolutionized. Meanwhile, the agro-commercial bourgeoisie was in the process of consolidating its hold on the economy. They dominated in the production and commercial sectors and set policy by directing the statutory boards. The corporate plantation economy that had its inception in the last quarter of the nineteenth century was consolidated. Faced with growing class militancy, the agro-commercial bourgeoisie was forced to bargain with the trade union movement. Many of the most exploitative factors of class-race relations were modified; but they were not transformed (Karch, 1979:252).

Jamaica

Post-Emancipation Jamaica was characterized by both absentee plantation ownership and abandoned plantations. Metropolitan capital in the hands of British merchant houses led to the corporatization of most Jamaican plantations. The existence of large tracts of abandoned land and the availability of mountainous Crown Land encouraged the development of a sizeable peasantry in the 1840s–1850s. However, from mid-century onward corporate capitalist production in bananas and sugar prevented the peasantry from expanding into a vibrant landowning class, and in fact, despite holding small plots, the Jamaican peasant was dependent in good part on wage labor. Continuing crisis in sugar in the twentieth century forced nearly 70,000 people to migrate to Kingston between 1921–1943 creating the shanty towns of the city, while 10,000 emigrated annually, primarily to Cuba, in the same period.

For the colored middle classes, the absence of a strong local white oligarchy as in Barbados, allowed for greater social mobility and political participation. As we have seen, several coloreds sat in the Assembly prior to Emancipation and their numbers increased throughout the late nineteenth and early twentieth centuries. Colored Jamaicans were particularly active in reform movements throughout the period. However, the race/color dynamic operated in Jamaica, as elsewhere in the region. Mobility was contained; the majority of the agro-commercial bourgeoisie was white.

Despite the discontent and oft-times open rebellion, such as Morant Bay in 1865, the severe constraints of the colonial state prohibited the emergence of black leadership from the masses, mobilized in their own self-interest, until the rise of Marcus Garvey in the 1920s. Garvey, however, as organizer of the first international mass movement of black people in the Diaspora, was persecuted and ultimately had to flee Jamaica. Garvey's movement is highly significant as the embryo of modern political movements in Jamaica and as a catharsis in the development of racial pride that became a corner-stone of the labor movement and the anti-colonial struggle.

As in Barbados, the crisis of world capitalism in the 1930s closed the door to immigration to Cuba, the United States, and elsewhere, and this coupled with rising prices, unemployment, and depressed wages led to spontaneous rebellion. "Between May 23rd and 31st, 1938 the social order was shaken by a full scale rising of the black masses" (Munroe, 1972:21).

Similar to Barbados, the initial reaction of both the local white ruling class and the brown middle classes was repressive. However, the Jamaican middle classes had for some time been involved in political struggle against the colonial state largely through the medium of the Jamaican Union of Teachers (JUT) and the Jamaican Agricultural Society (JAS). In fact, since its inception in 1894 the JUT "acted as the focal point for a special Jamaican struggle against colonialism. The nationalism of the JUT and the JAS was a class nationalism of the petty-bourgeoisie" (Lewis, 1968:172). The Afro-Jamaican middle classes by 1910 had five coloreds and one black repre-sentative out of fourteen elected members on the Legislative Council. There are few places in the West Indies where the middle classes could be said to have been more successful and upwardly mobile than in Jamaica. Conse-quently, the term "brown middle class" has more meaning and has been a focal point of class struggle in Jamaica since the 1940s, culminating today in the Rastafari movement's protest against "brown man rule." In the early twentieth century the JUT, JAS, and the Jamaican Progressive League desired home rule, not independence, and reform, not major changes, in the internal social structure.

Garvey's political organization of the black masses, his effective service as councilman, and the liberating ideology of African pride were influential factors in the 1938 uprising that prompted sections of the colored middle-class to join with, and ultimately take over, the fledgling nationalist and labor movements. Two political parties, the Jamaican Labour Party (JLP) and the Peoples National Party (PNP) were formed and led by two cousins Alexander Bustamente and Norman Washington Manley, respectively. Between 1939 and 1944 the movements became more militant as it became apparent that the colonial power had no intention of instituting a meaningful political and social reform program.

This necessitated building bridges across color/class lines as the only effective means of forcing the colonial power to "concede" democratic government. Bustamente ("Busta"), whose demagogy was reminiscent of Butler's appeal in Trinidad was the most successful. By January 1944 the Bustamente Industrial Trade Union had some 37,000 members. Attempts to form a coalition between Busta and Manley had failed by 1942. Reasons for failure are color associations and ideological cleavages as perceived by the black masses. Munroe states that primary importance must be attached to the "historical alienation of brown from black which the brief upheaval of 1938 had done nothing to heal" (1972:123).

In fact, Munroe argues, the role of the brown intermediate classes in the 1938 struggle, the ambivalent or hostile attitude of many PNP supporters, and the role of some middle class persons as special constabulary, actually widened the gap between black and brown sections. Reference was made in the *Jamaica Labour Weekly* to Manley's "long association with the oppressors of the poor."

The PNP was a coalition of the urban middle group's with some working class support. The party was ideologically divided, united only under the nationalist umbrella. There was a strong left-wing element within the movement under the leadership of the "four H's" (Ken Hill, Richard Hart, Frank Hill, Arthur Henry) in the Trade Union Council. Their success as organizers was crucial in expanding the base of the party. However, the alliance between the left-wing and the professional sections of the party was an uneasy one. Both the ruling class and the majority of the colored middle class were totally opposed to the Socialism of the TUC. The additional animosity of Bustamente, the acknowledged Moses of the black masses, hindered the party as well, forcing it to pursue a middle course which ultimately, for the purpose of electoral expediency, resulted in the expulsion of the left-wing. Thus the PNP was in the precarious position of being strongly opposed by the agrocommercial bourgeoise, yet unable to win over the black masses.

The JLP, on the other hand, was a one person party under the total control of Bustamente. Busta ran the party "in the interest of the masses." In fact, there was less representation of working class blacks in the JLP than in the

PNP. According to Eaton (1975:24), the black majority were relatively unconcerned with the mechanics of party politics. Their trust and support for Bustamente stemmed from his embracement of "their cause" in respect to higher wages, and his ability to lambast their brown and white enemies. Thus for the mass of the black agro-proletariat, "it was a question of voting for the nominee of the man who was a trusted friend, who understood their needs, had been willing to stand for them, and who could be expected to look after them and promote their welfare" (Eaton, 1975:24).

The white ruling class preferred Bustamente and the JLP to Manley and the PNP because the PNP was seen as the party of the educated middle classes promoting a program that promised to destroy existing colonial social relations, with the personnel able to do it. The PNP was seen as threatening existing class relations and power arrangements, while Bustamente was viewed as a rabble-rouser who could be controlled. Bustamente was loud in his denunciations of self-government and socialism/communism; therefore, Bustamente was the lesser of two evils.

The 1944 elections, Jamaica's first election under universal suffrage, signalled the waning of overt political influence on the part of the white ruling class and the coming to power of the colored middle class. The success of Bustamente as a charasmatic leader of a populist party did not increase the political power of the masses. By the 1950s the JLP was essentially a conservative party whose executive was comprised of doctors and lawyers. The PNP was led by a group of colored intellectuals and professionals, predominantly Fabian socialists. The left-wing was expelled from the Trade Union Council. By 1955 the two party system was firmly controlled by moderate and conservative middle class leadership.

Trinidad

In Trinidad the race/class dialectic elucidates a more complex dynamic as the divisions between white, colored, and black are modified by the greater division between Afro- and Indo-Trinidadians. After 1838 the labor shortage on the island was exacerbated because of the abundance of land available for freehold. The freedmen of Trinidad were at an advantage in the incipient class struggle that emerged with the abolition of the slave mode of production. Unlike Barbados, where the freedmen could not escape from the plantation (over 90 percent of the land was alienated), the Trinidadian freedman, like his Jamaican counterpart, had an alternative to wage work. Moreover, wages on Trinidadian plantations were the highest in the West Indies and were coupled with perquisites such as free housing, provision grounds, fish, and rum. The aim of the planters in giving perquisites was to provide themselves with an ample and reliable labor force that would stay on the estates.

Despite all these inducements, Trinidadian blacks abandoned the plantation, both to work their own plots, thus developing into a rudimentary peasantry, and to migrate to urban areas. By 1859 less than 5,000 Afro-Trinidadians were working on estates.

Planter response to this situation was massive immigration. Initially, this was supplied by Free Africans and West Indians, notably Barbadians, the latter attracted to Trinidad by high wages. Bounties were levied to encourage labor recruitment. The search was so successful in draining labor from the other islands that pressure was eventually put on the Colonial Office to place an embargo on inter-island bounties. In the 1840–1850s substantial immigration from Portuguese Madeira and China was also encouraged. Although the introduction of these new ethnic groups contributed to the ethnic stratification of the island and became important to class relations, it did not solve the requirements of the expanding plantation system as the immigrants rapidly abandoned plantation labor. The Portuguese and Chinese became upwardly mobile as petty-bourgeois shopkeepers in both urban and rural areas. Given the struggle between agro-capital and plantation labor, with the planter class having no intention of altering existing relations of production, the system might have collapsed without the introduction of indentured East Indian labor.

Imperial interests in the metropole were willing to give in to planter demands for cheap labor forstalling further conflict between the former and the demands of the emerging agro-proletariat and the colored middle class for greater politico-economic power. Labor from India was considered inexhaustible. British colonial hegemony over the sub-continent facilitated labor manipulation from one territory to the next. Between 1845 and 1917, 143,939 Indians were contracted to Trinidad under the "new system of slavery."[1]

Indian indentured laborers were strictly confined to the plantations to which they were assigned. Absence from the plantation without a pass was a criminal offense and resulted not only in imprisonment but forfeiture of wages. The result of these neo-slavery relations was the creation of the two fractions of the working-class of the colony: Afro and Indo-Trinidadians were separated spacially, culturally, and racially, in addition to occupational segregation. This cleavage remains today the most divisive factor in Trinidadian society.

The gulf between Afro- and Indo-Trinidadians explains only one facet of social relations, for the broader Caribbean dynamic of class/color permeated colonial Trinidad as well. The local ruling class of the island was divided ethnically primarily between Spanish and French Creoles (who with British dominance in sugar became professionals and cocoa planters), and the dominant British fraction, who were the most prominent commission agents, sugar estate owners and colonial functionaries. Racism against the colored intermediate class was virulent, although at first sight more subtle because of their large numbers.

From the mid-nineteenth century when British merchant houses bought into the plantation sector and rationalized it, most of the old colored, Spanish, and French Creole families lost their estates, and by the end of the nineteenth century they were to be found primarily in the professions. Color/race boundaries were quite pronounced. Not only was this colored middle class separated from the white ruling class but also from the black working class, many of whom were either of Free African or Afro-West Indian descent. Recognized and recognizing themselves as a distinct social group, the colored middle class rarely interacted with the black masses. J. J. Thomas, prominent colored barrister in a letter to the newspaper *NEW ERA* stated that "racism was not only a matter of oppressing whites and oppressed blacks: race prejudice and discrimination were practiced by all sectors, and the colored and black middle class were the most shade conscious of all" (Brereton, 1972:336).

Economic expansion and the development of Port-of-Spain as a commercial center between 1870 and 1937 allowed for upward mobility for a select group of educated blacks, most of whom through hard work and sacrifice had achieved scholarship places in the elite colleges of the island. The latter socialized and inter-married with the old colored creole fractions. As elsewhere in the region the core of the Afro-Trinidadian middle groups was made up of schoolmasters, civil servants, and clerical workers. Color/shade gradations, while important, were counterpoised with class distinctions that separated them from the Afro-Trinidadian working-class comprised of domestics, artisans and unskilled workers in the expanding oil industry. Thus while the middle strata were barred from white society, their education, wealth, and class position made them endogamous groupings and mitigated against interaction with working-class blacks. In this period there is little contact with Indo-Trinidadians who remain closed off from the larger society in barracks on the plantations or as itinerant merchants, small shopkeepers and smallholders primarily in South and Central Trinidad. The small minority of East Indians who were accumulating wealth and becoming petty-bourgeois were tied to the Indian community as communal leaders; not to the colored and black middle classes.

Politically, the colonial state apparatus was far more authoritarian and repressive than in Barbados. Trinidad had no experience of a self-governing legislative body; instead the Governor of the colony exercised despotic power. There was a nominated Legislative Council with official and unofficial members, "the latter represented the special electoral colleges of sugar, cocoa, commerce and the professions" (Lewis, 1968:199) Sugar interests dominated Trinidad politically and economically.

A reform movement was launched in the last quarter of the nineteenth century. Limited to the educated section of the community, members of the French creole fraction and the colored and black middle classes united against the sugar interests and the colonial government over the taxation levied to support Indian indenture and to fight for greater representation in government. The battle was fought on two fronts: (1) in public with mass meetings and in the Afro-Trinidadian middle class press, and (2) privately in the Legislative Council.

The vanguard of the movement was the colored newspapers of the middle class community. As the movement gained a mass base and became more radical, culminating in the Water Riots of 1903, the French Creoles abandoned their stance on all the issues. Class and race considerations superseded their desire for a greater share of power; they would not share that power with the Afro-Trinidadian middle classes.

The race/color inequalities in Trinidadian society made mass organization more difficult to achieve than in the other islands. These divisions blunted both class consciousness and Trinidadian nationalism. They also buttressed the colonial power's consensus that Trinidad of all the British West Indian islands was least suited for representative government.

Because of their class position in commerce and their fair skin, the immigrant Chinese, Syrian and Portuguese tended to become upwardly mobile and today they are established segments within the dominant class. They still perceive themselves and are perceived by Afro and Indo Trinidadians to be "off-white." The former immigrant groups, as ethnic segments, never identified with the various progressive movements which accelerated after the First World War. Captain Cipriani, of Corsican descent with French Creole connections, who led the masses in a first working-class anti-colonial movement is an individual exception.

Unlike Jamaica and Barbados, the middle classes remained relatively quiescent throughout the struggle for constitutional reform in the 1920s and during the working class revolt of the 1930s. Their moment arrived after the Second World War with the development of the People's National Movement (PNM) under Dr. Eric Williams. Working-class revolt in the 1930s was the culmination of poor wages in the recently discovered oil fields, the experiences of politically conscious members of the West Indian regiment in the War and the end of indenture coupled with worsening depression in the sugar belt. Both Indo- and Afro-Trinidadians as individuals were active in the early struggle and there were attempts to unite the two sections common struggle, particularly through the medium of the Trinidad Labour Party in the 1920s. However, Indo- and Afro-Trinidadians were divided on the issue of constitutional reform. Indo-Trinidadians feared that elective representation would deny them their share of seats in the Legislative Council due to the massive illiteracy of this section of the population. They did not trust progressive Afro-Trinidadians to speak for them and their interests. Nevertheless, when constitutional reform came to Trinidad in 1925 two of the three "Socialists" elected to the Council were Indian: Teelucksingh and Roodal.

Despite constitutional reform in 1925, defacto power still resided with the governor and his appointees to the Council. In effect, the representatives of the people were a buffer between the agro-commercial bourgeoisie and the Afro- and Indo-Trinidadian masses. They were expected to give "the people's" stamp of approval to the Imperial government's programs. In consequence, as agitation and repression increased in the 1930s in the oil fields and sugar belt, class revolt bypassed the elected representatives and the Trinidad Labour Party.

Of the two acknowledged leaders of the revolt one was black (Uriah Butler) and one was Indian (AdrianCola Rienzi), who together formed the British Empire Workers and Citizen Home Rule Party in 1936. Butler, a Grenadian, worked in Roodal's oilfields in La Brea. He was pastor of the Butlerite Moravian Baptist Church. This religious organization and his Biblical exhortations were central to the messianic appeal of his leadership. The organization was centered in La Brea where 40 percent of the population were Grenadians.

Rienzi was a lawyer who returned to Trinidad from the United Kingdom in 1929 after involvement there in radical causes. He was primarily concerned with mobilizing the masses, both Afro- and Indo-Trinidadian along popular front lines. It was Rienzi who in 1937 formed the Oil Workers Trade Union (OWTU), overwhelmingly an Afro-Trinidadian union. OWTU has been the vanguard of the worker's movement from its inception. Rienzi was also active in the sugar belt and played a major role in the sugar strikes of 1937 that, along with Butler's strike in the oil fields, led to working class revolt in every sector of the economy and a massive general strike that had repercussions throughout the Caribbean.

Working-class revolt led to the growth of trade unionism and nationalist movements in Jamaica and Barbados, but in Trinidad racial divisions could not be transcended. Rienzi and Butler fell out in a leadership struggle that personified the deeper divisions between blacks and East Indians. The combination of Butler's oratorical and Rienzi's organizational skills would have made for the most viable working-class movement in the region. As it was, unity was dissipated.

"The period 1938–56 witnessed the nadir of Trinidadian life" (Lewis, 1968:99). The vacuum created by proletarian disunity was manifested in vapid politics lacking organized political parties with a mass base. Rampant individualism, corruption, racialism, and leaders whose primary goal was the spoils of office were a reflection of the divisions within the working class and the inability of the Afro- and Indo-Trinidadian to join together to form a national movement.

Political Independence, Race/Color, and the Issue of the National Bourgeoisie

The end of World War II marked the beginning of "constitutional decol-onization" in Jamaica, Barbados, and Trinidad. As we have shown, the anti-colonial struggle was fought by the black masses who lacked organiza-tional skills, and whose leaders were, in the main, repressed and supplanted by individuals from the colored and black middle classes. Considering their intermediate position in the antagonistic relations between the colonial ruling class and the black agro-proletariat, the predominately colored mid-dle classes stood to gain socially and politically by filling the organizational and leadership vacuum amongst the agro-proletariat.

In all these islands, decolonization proceeded piecemeal, in a manner that has retained much of the inegalitarian social relations of the corporate plantation period. Despite the recent promotion of peripheral capitalism based on import substitution and the introduction of foreign capital in "screw-driver industries," which has created new class formations, the color-class dynamic of the plantation system remains the most salient characteristic of present day Caribbean societies.

Peripheral capitalist development has meant, however, upward mobility for the black petty-bourgeoisie, with a few individuals and families even entering into the commercial bourgeoisie, and most importantly their assumption of state power as a governing group. Yet, as we shall see, the local bourgeoisie remains largely white and seated within interlocking directorates of corporations formed principally in the period of corporate commercial capitalism, 1870–1945.

The local bourgeoisies with their base in import-export operations were largely in favor of the expansion of foreign capital in the 1950s and 1960s, which quickly made inroads in bauxite, oil, manufacturing, tourism, and commercial banking. There was some opposition in Jamaica and Trinidad to import-substitutive industries which would disrupt the traditional pattern of commerce. However, the majority of local corporations quickly adapted to the expansion of transnational capitalism in the 1960s and '70s and have taken advantage of governmental incentives. Conglomerates such as Barba-dos Shipping and Trading (BST) in Barbados, Neal and Massy, and Alstons-McEanerney in Trinidad and the Issa, Matelon, and Ashenheim conglomer-ates in Jamaica have expanded their operations to include manufacturing, tourism, insurance and finance.

The political parties of the region have objectively functioned to limit the political power of the black working class by making the party dominant over workers' movements. The nationalism of the PNP-JLP in Jamaica, the BLP-DLP in Barbados and the PNM in Trinidad is a class nationalism of the petty-bourgeoisie. Their programs in the 1950s and 1960s were generally populist and espoused a variant of national capitalism under the assumed "enlightened" guidance of international capitalism. The middle classes have, since the War, attempted to form and maintain political parties with a wide populist base that cuts across class/color/race, under the banner of nationalism. In the 1950s and '60s they even attempted to deny the class basis of society. But the Black Power revolts of the late 1960s- early 1970s forced political parties to either adopt democratic socialist principles that also recognize the racial dynamic and/or institute repressive measures to stem unrest.

In effect, the intermediate classes as the governing group of the islands still perform the same function that they did under the plantation system. They remain a buffer grouping between the predominantly white bourgeoisie and the mainly black masses. Structurally, then, their class location within the social division of labor, can be seen in terms of their relationship to the two primary classes. Color/race is of greater or lesser importance depending on the specificity of each island social forma- tion. The racial characteristics of each social formation intertwine with and complicate class struggles. In the context of local class and race struggles, the induced reproduction of international capitalist relations into the Commonwealth Caribbean has been largely responsible for the reorganization of social formations. But this occurs within island states that suffer the legacy of the plantation system with its social relations of slavery.

Barbados

Unlike a few countries in Latin America in the Caribbean, a local urban industrial bourgeoisie and other newly formed social interests have rarely challenged traditional oligarchies. Throughout the West Indies the local bourgeoisie has retained an agro-commercial base. In Barbados particular- ly, the local bourgeoisie evolved from a base in import-export operations. Entrepreneurs in commerce bought into and consolidated the estate and distribution sectors in the late nineteenth and early twentieth centuries. During that highly competitive era the newer commercial interests merged with and at other times wrested power from the plantocracy, transforming both fractions into a new, consolidated ruling class, the agro-commercial bourgeoisie (Karch, 1977, 1979).

In Barbados, during the First and Second Development Decades the agro-commercial bourgeoisie expanded, in cooperation with foreign capital, into the new manufacturing and tourist sectors, blocking the emergence of a new industrial class fraction to challenge their hegemony. Agricultural, commercial, and industrial interests are found in the same economic groupings. The main base, however, is *not* manufacturing, but agro-commercial. The issue of nationalization that has been of ideological and economic significance to the decolonizing world, is not very important in Barbados. The development programs of the island have espoused direct foreign investment primarily in tourism and manufacturing, yet local ownership retains a high percentage of these operations.

During the tourist boom of the 1960s, some 42 percent of the tourist industry was estimated to be controlled by foreign interests, 40 percent was considered to be locally owned, and the balance of 20 percent made up of jointly owned enterprises (B. Watson, 1974:19–20). In manufacturing, the bulk of traditional industries established prior to the First Development Decade are locally owned. This includes bakeries, brick-making, beverages, iron works, and so on. Industries established by incentive legislation naturally have a high component of foreign ownership. But here again, the local capitalist class has been able to retain an interest, particularly in the garment industry, one of the most important in the sector. The same holds for the building and construction industries. Agriculture is 100 percent locally owned.

Yet, no discussion of the local bourgeoisie is adequate unless it analyses the dynamic of class/race factors. In Barbados the hegemonic fraction, the agro-commercial bourgeoisie is white, the governing fraction is black and colored. The Afro-Barbadian governing fraction has not felt compelled to wrest control of the major sectors of the economy from the white agro-commercial bourgeoisie, and in fact, they have encouraged private capitalist investment that is predominantely white. Government planners believed that local black capital via special incentives to small businessmen could work in conjunction with foreign capital to produce a black manufacturing class; this has not occurred. There has been an increase in black ownership of small businesses but it neither challenges nor is independent of the white agro-commercial bourgeosie.

Public ownership of the primary means of production has been a continuing ideological theme, particularly of the sugar industry, which carries with it the stigma of slavery. Although often an election slogan, neither party has seen fit to implement policy that would challenge white economic dominance and risk disruption of the economy. It is the international sugar economy and the dependent position of Barbados within this nexus which is forcing greater accommodation between the white agro-commercial bourgeoisie and the black governing fraction. In this period of crisis the state is assuming greater control over the plantation sector, including ownership of estates. An incipient state bourgeoisie, predominantly black is in formation, but it remains unclear what form this class's relationship to the agro-commercial bourgeoisie will take.

The white agro-commercial bourgeoisie is politically weak and can only maintain itself by compromise and accommodation. When the economy is in a slump and unemployment rises, they become the natural targets. It is only by deflecting the blame onto government policies that they are able to circumvent direct attack. But again, it is a tenuous position, as they are often the focal point of culpability for the political parties led by blacks who are accountable to a black constituency. In the final analysis class issues are racial issues and will remain so long as the dominant property owning class is the white minority.

Jamaica

Since independence, greater numbers of individual blacks have become upwardly mobile in Jamaica, but the social policies formulated by the JLP and PNP governments have not resulted in a radical restructuring of the social formation ameliorating the class/color stratification system.

The local bourgeoisie has further entrenched itself with the dependent development of the last decades and its strong ties to metropolitan capital. Levels of growth in Jamaica in the 1960s were in the region of 7 percent per annum, among the highest of underdeveloped countries. There was a five-fold increase between 1950–1961 in the value of manufacturing in the gross domestic product; sharp increases also took place in construction and distribution. Rapid capitalist expansion consolidated the wealth and power of the commercial fraction who invested heavily in manufacturing and construction (Phillips, 1977:8). The development programs of the government since 1962 reflect the political power of this class.[2] By 1970 undistributed corporate profit accounted for 70 percent of Gross Domestic Savings; only 0.4 percent of all businesses made this contribution and they are controlled by 21 families, all white and linked by corporate and family ties.

The corporate fraction makes policy by serving on statuatory boards and forming alliances with both political parties. Thus, although the corporate fraction abandoned contesting the polls directly, they have reconsolidated themselves by indirect control over the state apparatus. The agro-commercial bourgeoisie in Jamaica has been transformed into a commercial-manufacturing bourgeoisie and has *increased* its economic power since the advent of self-government.

The victory of the PNP in 1972 and again in 1976 after ten years in opposition and the rebirth of the ideology of "democratic socialism" has been unable to stem or usurp the power of the white Jamaican bourgeoisie. The middle class Jamaican governing group found itself in the buffer position of trying to placate wide mass opposition and to institute a reformist restructuring of the society. The Manley government faced the intransigence of the mainly white ruling class and intense mass dissatisfaction arising from racial oppression, psychological alienation, massive unemployment and deplorable social conditions. From the perspective of both the rural agro-proletariat and the shanty-town dwellers of Kingston, political independence has not improved the objective living conditions of the majority of dispossessed blacks nor has it given them a voice in government.

The organized labor movement is firmly linked to the two political parties and the workers themselves are divided by this subordination. Sporadic violence between JLP and PNP (BITU and NWU) members is entrenched in the Jamaican political system. Attempts to unify the working class outside the dominant labor-movement/political-party lines have met with repression.

This affiliation of the labor movement to middle class political parties has incurred the dissatisfaction, and often the wrath, of the black masses. In a study by Carl Stone (1975:74) over 60 percent of both skilled and unskilled labor "expressed a preference for new non-party unions, over the dominant party affiliated NWU and BITU trade unions."

Support for the two parties is dependent on clientelism, Stone (1980:208) argues that the Jamaican state demonstrates corporatist tendencies similar to Mexico with clientelism the dominant structure that links private interests with the state. Union leaders operate as brokers for the two political parties dispensing patronage to the faithful. Reflecting mass dissatisfaction with the system that has emerged in the post-colonial period, 10 percent of skilled labor and 24 percent of unskilled labor expressed the view that "violence was the only effective path through which the poor could obtain a more improved social condition in the society" (Stone, 1975:79).

However, violence, cynicism, alienation and a tremendous growth in urban crime have not been the only channels through which the black masses of Jamaica have expressed their alienation and class discontent. The rise of "black power" and the Rastafarian movement in the 1960s reflected the fact that race/color remained a primary component of class struggle in Jamaica. The growing popularity and spread of Rastafarianism throughout the Caribbean testify to its saliency. The struggle for "roots" and the determination of one's identity manifested by Rastafarianism expresses the challenge of black national liberation against the entire social formation, both at the base of economic exploitation and at the superstructural level in terms of values and ideology.

Although the Rastafari movement has never developed a coherent political strategy, the enormous identification with its religious, ethnic, and cultural aspects were capitalized on in developing an ideology to challenge the power structure. The Black Power movement of the 1960s–1970s sought to mobilize the black masses through appeals to race, class, and the anti-imperialist struggle. The racial consciousness articulated by Rastafarianism, combined with the growing discontent with post-independence economic development as articulated by intellectuals at the University of the West Indies, threatened to become a serious challenge to the state and the white and colored bourgeoisie state functionaries. Even though the coalition disintegrated both from internal dissention and state repression, its ramifications are still being felt in Jamaica today.

Michael Manley (Joshua) and the PNP coopted much of the symbolism of Black Power and Rastafarianism in both the 1972 and 1976 elections. The PNP government sought to check potential black revolutionary movements by adopting an anti-imperialist stance in foreign policy, expressing solidarity with liberation struggles in Africa, reproachment with Cuba, by elevating Marcus Garvey to a national hero, and by bringing cultural hero Bob Marley onto the political stage. The "democratic socialism" of the present PNP is similar to and in fact the legacy of the "democratic socialism" of Norman Manley in the 1940s.

PNP policies led to hostility from the local bourgeoisie and imperialist interests (World Bank, IMF, adverse press reports abroad, attempts at destabilization supported from abroad). Manley inherited the same problems as his father suffered in the early days of party politics. The PNP in 1976 remained a divided party with a small militant left-wing and a large moderate sector. Fear grew among the middle classes in particular that Manley's democratic socialism coupled with racial militancy, Rastafarianism, and lumpen violence would usher in social chaos culminating in armed struggle.

After 1976 the PNP under Manley found itself in an unhealthy broker-middle position, defending itself against attacks and destablization attempts on the part of the local dominant class in alliance with metropolitan interests, serious ideological divisions within the party itself, as well as sporadic manifestations of organized violence on the part of lumpen groupings.

The PNP defeat at the polls in the 1981 elections was the result of a well orchestrated campaign. The JLP made little secret of its links with metropolitan corporate interests and the American government. The economic situation, largely but not solely a result of IMF sanctions and distabilization, had deteriorated drastically. The most violent campaign in Jamaican history was argued ideologically on the issue of "deliverance" by capitalism or socialism. Millions of Jamaicans felt that democratic socialism and the PNP had failed. Hundreds of people died during the campaign as gun men of both parties ruled the streets. The ideological position of both parties has hardened—JLP solidly right wing, pro-capitalist and pro-American, the PNP social democratic with a significant Marxist faction. There is also a growing Marxist-Leninist party affiliated with several radical unions. The class struggle in Jamaica intensified with the 1981 elections, and as economic "deliverance" fails to materialize greater repression and internal control can be expected as popular discontent resurfaces.

Jamaican society remains highly polarized between white and black with the colored intermediate classes, represented by the state functionaries and political leadership, playing an accommodationist role to local business and foreign interests and alternately wooing and repressing the black masses who elect them to office.

Trinidad

Presently, the island republic of Trinidad-Tobago is considered to be the capitalist success story of the Caribbean. The discovery of petroleum resources at the turn of the century led to the development of a mineral export economy that over time replaced sugar and cocoa monoculture. Trinidad also experienced U.S. occupation during the Second World War under a 1941 agreement that did not end until 1967. In the 1950s Trinidad awakened to nationalism under the leadership of Dr. Eric Williams and the People's National Movement (PNM). Petroleum, the U.S. occupation, and PNM policies have been the most significant factors in the development of a strong peripheral capitalism on the island.[3]

In the late 1950s and especially after independence (1962) a strategy of diversification based on the Puerto Rican model, Operation Bootstrap, was adopted in Trinidad. By the end of the First Development Decade, Trinidad-Tobago was the most industrialized nation in the Commonwealth Caribbean.

The economy is predicated primarily on revenues earned from foreign corporations in the petroleum and import-substitution sectors. However, especially since 1970, the government has made numerous purchases and minority share acquisitions that have given it ownership of a substantial portion of the economy. Government acquisitions include sugar, sectors of the oil industry, banking, communications, motor car assembly, and the manufacture of beverage and spirits. Revenues from oil have placed Trinidad-Tobago in the enviable position of being the only island state in the Commonwealth Caribbean to possess considerable foreign exchange reserves. In fact, the Government has become a money lender, providing in the recent past loans to Jamaica, Barbados, and Guyana.

However, Trinidad is plagued by a host of social problems, some in—herited from the colonial past and others the product of uneven industrial development superimposed on a land tenure system of the plantation period.

Trinidad remains a racially divided society. When Eric Williams returned to Trinidad and formed the PNM he promised it would be "a political party of men and women of honesty and incorruptibility, of all races, colours, classes and creeds with a coherent and sensible programme of economic, social and political reform aimed at the development of the country as a whole" (Lewis, 1968:212). The zeal and dynamism of Williams and the PNM represented a breath of fresh air in a Trinidad "working for the Yankee dollar"; a Trinidad characterized by political opportunism, racial/ color divisions and corruption—charges that are still levied today. Perhaps, the PNM's greatest success has been the forging of a Trinidadian identity and culture; but it remains to this day an Afro-Trinidadian culture and identity.

The present class structure of Trinidad demonstrates a familiar race/ color/class dynamic with the important addition of the class positions of East Indians. Similar to Jamaica, the economic development programs of the last twenty years have consolidated the power of the predominately white local bourgeoisie. Forming conglomerates, the local corporations, whose base before the War was primarily agro-commercial, have extended themselves into manufacturing, primarily of an import substitution kind, which has grown at record high rates largely because of the expansion of petrochemical economy since 1973.

Yet, the local bourgeoisie of Trinidad remains a comprador class. Texaco, Amoco, Tesoro, W. R. Grace, Unilever and the banking capital of Barclay's and Royal Bank dominate the economy. The local manufacturing sector provides the appropriate linkages whereby the penetration of international capital can be conducted under local auspices. Neal and Massy, McEanerney-Alstons, Gordon Grant, H. E. Robinson are all old commercial enterprises that have expanded their economic base. The Alston's group, for example, has seen its total assets expanded from $TT 17m in 1962 to nearly three times as much in 1975, approximately $50m covering some five completely owned enterprises in the manufacture of building products, general marketing, freight and stevedoring services, polyelrene production, marine engineering and shipbuilding along with distribution of industrial equipment (Gomes, n.d.:354).

However, the state of Trinidad-Tobago has also embarked on a number of joint ventures with domestic private capital and with foreign private capital. Expansion of the state sector in over 40 state enterprises introduces a new contradiction between the traditional primary class contradictions and racial cleavages in the society.

This rapid expansion has facilitated the growth of the petty-bourgeoisie in the island. The majority of the intermediate classes in Trinidad has historically been black and colored, with important sections of the minority ethnic groups: Chinese, Portuguese, and Syrian. The PNM ruling party has expressed the aspirations and ideology of the Afro-Trinidian petty-bourgeoisie. The opposition parties in Trinidad have been primarily Indo-Trinidadian parties.

In fact, the racial cleavage divided the nationalist movement from its very beginnings in 1956. Williams was identified as pro-black and anti-Indian. Each of the dominant groups feared the results of the other taking power. Those past election years were violent ones: "The intensity with which the 1961 election was fought was just short of riotous proportions, which attests to the fact that the political manifestations of racial cleavage runs very deep in Trinidadian society" (Bahadoorsingh, 1971:55). All subsequent elections, including the 1981 elections, have been fought largely on race; and the results by constituency demonstrate that the majority of the electorate go to the polls and vote along racial lines.

Much of the animosity not only is the result of historical cleavages between Afro- and Indo-Trinidadians and their inability to form a united working class nationalist movement in the 1930s and '40s, but also is due to the fact that while the private capitalist class remains primarily white, the expanding state dominated by 25 years of PNM rule has formed the mobility of Afro-Trinidadian intermediate classes. Taking state power in Trinidad-Tobago today is more than serving as a governing group, it is controlling a significant percentage of capital accumulation and dispersal of patronage.

There has been considerable upward mobility of Indo-Trinidadians since the War. It was primarily Indians who profited from the U.S. occupation establishing transport and construction firms that capitalized on the massive infrastructure programs. Indo-Trinidadians had already gained a foothold in the retail and distribution sectors before the War. The general expansion had the effect of increasing consumer demands from which chains such as Kirpalani's benefited.

While Creoles fear "Indian expansion," Indo-Trinidadians feel that they have not been given their share in the expansion of the public sector, nor do they have equal political influence in government. The primary beneficiaries of public sector expansion have been the urban working class and civil servants, the Creole PNM constituency. This meant the establishment of a solid base of 'political patronage' for the PNM. In the period 1956–1962 the foundations were laid for the expansion of the civil service from which emerged a black bureaucratic grouping.

This demonstrates a significantly different dynamic of class/race than occurs in the rest of the Commonwealth Caribbean, with the exception of Guyana. The state under the PNM has fulfilled the function of promoting both a local bourgeoisie, which is predominately white and the heir of commercial capital under colonialism, and an important black bureaucratic-technocratic grouping. The latter grouping is based in management of the 34 fully owned state companies, 15 more enterprises of majority state participation, and 16 firms with decided state interest. All are operated by predominately Afro-Trinidadian administrators and technicians. New intra-class rivalries have appeared which are heightened by the racial factor. Increasing state activity is eliciting both conflict and accommodation from traditional white bourgeoisie and the "nouveau" bourgeois Indo-Trinidadians who are wary of Afro-Trinidadian domination.

Trinidadian politics reflects the race and class divisions. The formal opposition party, the United Labour Front (ULF) is a working-class based party but the majority of its members are Indo-Trinidadians and the party is perceived by Trinidadians to be an "Indian party." Consequently, in racially divided Trinidad this party under the Westminster based constituency system of "first-past-the-post" is able to win seats only in the Central and South of the island where the majority of the population is Indian. In the last election this party formed an Alliance with two smaller parties; one representing Afro-Trinidadian Tobago interests, the Democratic Action Congress (DAC), and the other Afro-Trinidadian intellectuals under the leadership of former U.W.I. lecturer and economist Lloyd Best. The Alliance is a left-leaning party opposed to the state clientelism of the PNM.

The newest political party to emerge in the last five years, the Organization for National Reconstruction, is the least sectarian in memberships of the three major political parties. It is a populist party drawing support nationwide from every ethnic/racial grouping and across class lines. However, the party is supported (some would argue formed) by a significant sector of the corporate bourgeoisie and by middle class professionals opposed to corruption and inefficiency in the regime. In fact, leadership of the party is vested in a former PNM Attorney General Karl Hudson Phillips. This support the PNM uses skillfully to portray the party as the political organ of "red" (fair skin) and white people who would turn the clock back and reimpose an inequalitarian social system of the corporate plantation period. To the black masses a vote for ONR became a vote for a return to white rule.

The PNM party machine is very effective in mobilizing what the party euphemistically calls the "grass roots." The normal 30 percent electoral support, which is enough in a multi-party system to ensure victory, comes from the solid support of the Afro-Trinidadian and other West Indian proletariat residing in Trinidad, who continue to identify the PNM as the party which declared "Massa Day Done." Their support is also contingent on patronage. The largesse is widely spread via "Special Works," a billion dollar welfare project that provides steady income of several days a month work for the unemployed. This program has successfully stemmed the revolutionary discontent of the early 1970s, but has seriously eroded the task of nation-building as it has not been used to train the marginally employed, unskilled workers, and the unemployed; it is merely a welfare program. Should the petrodollar economy slow down, the mass discontent of 1970 could well reemerge as "Special Works" cannot transform social relations. What is known as the "February Revolution" of 1970 was a crisis of legitimacy for the state and was the result of continued impoverishment, lack of housing, archaic land use patterns based on the plantation system and repressive and anti-union legislation. Black Power in 1970 Trinidad represented mass opposition to foreign domination, to the direction of dependent capitalist development and to the continued ownership of the means of production, distribution, and exchange by a local white bourgeoisie. The February Revolution was thwarted largely because the social movement could not transcend racial divisions nor was it organized as a revolutionary party. Despite explicit calls for Afro-Indo solidarity on the part of the National Joint Action Committee (NJAC), the majority of Indo-Trinidadians did not support NJAC and the Black Power Movement. The crisis reached its culmination with a call for a general strike and the mutiny of the army. Stability was restored with the declaration of a state of emergency, martial law, and preventive detention. A para-military campaign was waged by the government against guerillas through 1973. Once again, the racial divisions that characterize Trinidadian society were significant in saving the regime.

The 1981 elections proved conclusively that Trinidadian society still remains dangerously divided along race/color lines. This polarization ensures the continuity of a virtual one party (PNM) state for years to come. The party, however, is a minority party and thus its continued success is also dependent on the continuous flow of petrodollars. Divide and rule politics resting on a dependent export economy characterize Trinidad of the 1980s, as has been the case for so long. The growth of state activity and the institutionalization of a predominantly Afro-Trinidadian one party state ensures that social relations and class conflict in Trinidad will continue to be inextricably bound up with race/color even as social groupings and classes assume modern capitalist forms.

Conclusion

In the Commonwealth Caribbean the history of class struggle since the end of the slave period has been compounded by race/color divisions in the various islands. The primary dynamic has been the struggle of the descendants of slaves and indentured servants to usurp control from a European ruling class. The base of this struggle has been the agro-proletariat and peasantry. However, the role of intermediate classes—petty bourgeois "brown" and "black" middle classes—has been a pivotal one due to their position between the polarized bourgeoisie and the agro-proletariat, and the ideological significance of race. What is termed the "brown middle class" in the Commonwealth Caribbean is more than an ascriptive term.

Unlike the petty-bourgeoisie of the metropolitan world, this class, because of the historically racist structure of Caribbean social formations, has vacillated between supporting the white bourgeoisie and uniting with the Afro- and Indo-West Indian proletariat, while seeking to wrest governmental power from that bourgeoisie. The period 1860–1960 was characterized by intense struggle on the part of individuals from the middle classes to reform the political apparatus. Middle class leaders were social democrats who felt that only by gaining admittance into the formal political structure, by expanding the franchise, would they be able to achieve a redistribution of resources.

In the 1960s de-colonization was gradual and reformist, administered by the middle class in a manner that did not disrupt the inherited system of unequal wealth and economic power. Development programs facilitated further penetration of foreign capital and expansion of private domestic capital, while the ideology of the Cold War and the restraining influence of the metropolitan powers curtailed socialist links and aspirations.

Class conflict has heightened since independence. The dominant fraction of the bourgeoisie remains predominantly white and linked with foreign capital. The state apparatus is manned by a governing fraction drawn from the black and colored middle classes. Conflict is endemic, for on the one hand, the state functionaries have been the executors of policies that serve the interests of the white bourgeoisie; while on the other hand, as the political leaders of the Afro- and Indo-West Indian majority, their mandate is to institute the redistribution of wealth and power to that majority. Additionally, particularly where, as in Trinidad, we see the emergence of a state bourgeoisie, this class begins to preserve and seek to address its own class interests that place it in conflict situations at different times with both the private capital bourgeoisie and the working classes. Growing confrontation in the state sector over wages expresses one aspect of this tendency. Thus, despite the fact that they perform objective functions on behalf of the white bourgeoisie, as the primary struggle between capitalists and workers has always been seen ideologically in racial, as well as in class terms, their accountability and source of political power lies with the masses. Hence the problem posed by the Black Power movements in the early 1970s. As a result, class struggle in the West Indies assumes diverse manifestations and will continue to intertwine with race/color divisions for many years to come.

Notes

1. The arrival of indentured labor served to depress local wages for blacks, brought difficulties to smallholders in competition with plantation production, and ushered in a new period of repression and coercion for the Afro-Trinidadian worker. 238,909 East Indians were sent to British Guiana, 36,412 to Jamaica, with smaller numbers to the Windwards. The daily wage in Trinidad was better in 1838 than in 1938 (Millette 1978:29).

2. "In deciding on a policy for industrial development, the government made a firm commitment, entrusting the task to the private sector and limiting the role of the public sector to the provision of infrastructure and the development of a climate favorable to enterprise in which risk-taking would be less hazardous" (Jefferson, 1972).

3. "The PNM should be chary of 18th century political labels and categories, especially those of an emotive appeal which have no relevance for the 20th century world, let alone the West Indian environment. In every case, the test must be which [economic strategy] is best designed to improve the living conditions and promote the development of the people as a whole. Placed against this background, nationalization, private enterprise, public and private capitalism become mere techniques to be used at one time or another for a larger end, and not merely as ends in themselves. The PNM's sole aim is the removal of the political and economic barriers to the full development of the West Indian personality" (Ryan, 1966:223).

References

Bahadoorsingh, Krishna
1971 "The racial factor in Trinidad Politics." Pp. 53–60 in Trevor Munroe and Rupert Lewis (eds.) Readings in Government and Politics in the West Indies. Jamaica: University of the West Indies.
Beckford, George
1972 Persistent Poverty. New York: Oxford University Press.
Brathwaite, Lloyd
1953 "Social Stratification in Trinidad." Social and Economic Studies 2 (October).
Brereton, Bridget
1972 "A social history of Trinidad 1870–1900." Ph.D. thesis, University of the West Indies.
Eaton, George
1975 *Alexander Bustamente and Modern Jamaica.* Kingston: Kingston Publishers.
Forsythe, Dennis
1975 "Race, colour and class in the British West Indies." Pp. 16–42 in A. W. Singham (ed.) *The Commonwealth Caribbean Into the Seventies.* Occasional Paper Series No. 10. Montreal: Centre for Developing Area Studies, McGill University.
Girvan, Norman
1975 *Aspects of the Political Economy of Race in the Caribbean and in the Americas.* Working Paper No. 7. Jamaica: Institute for Social and Economic Research.
Gomes, P. I.
n.d. "Trinidad and Tobago under black elite rule, 1962–76." Ph.D. thesis (draft).
Handler, Jerome and Arnold Lio
1974 "Barbados." Pp. 214–257 in D. W. Cohen and J. P. Greene (eds.) Neither Slave Nor Free. Baltimore: Johns Hopkins University Press.
Harris, Marvin
1964 Patterns of Race in the Americas. Westport, CT: Greenwood.

Jefferson, Owen
1972   *Post-War Economic Development of Jamaica*. Jamaica: Institute for Social and Economic Research.

Karch, Cecilia
1977   Changes in Barbadian Social Structure, 1960–1937. Cave Hill, Barbados: Institute of Social and Economic Research.
1979   The Transformation and Consolidation of the Corporate Plantation Economy in Barbados, 1960–1977. Ph.D. dissertation, Rutgers University.

Lewis, Gordon K.
1968   *The Growth of the Modern West Indies*. New York: Monthly Review Press.

Marxs, F. X.
1966   *The History of the Barbados Workers Union*. Bridgetown: Barbados Workers' Union.

Munroe, Trevor
1972   *The Politics of Constitutional Decolonization in Jamaica*. Jamaica: Institute for Social and Economic Research.

Phillips, Peter
1977   "Jamaican elites: 1938 to present." Pp. 1–14 in A. Brown and C. Stone (eds.) *Essays on Power and Change in Jamaica*. Kingston: Jamaica Publishing.

Poulantzas, Nicos
1975   *Classes in Contemporary Capitalism*. London: New Left Books.

Ryan, Selwyn
1966   The Transition to Nationhood in Trinidad-Tobago. Ph.D. thesis, Cornell University.

Smith, M. G.
1965   *The Plural Society in the British West Indies*. Berkeley: University of California Press.

Smith, R. T.
1967   "Social stratification, cultural pluralism, and integration in West Indian societies." Pp. 236–258 in S. Lewis and T. G. Mathews (eds.) *Caribbean Integration*. Rio Piedras: University of Puerto Rico.

Stone, Carl
1975   "Urban social movements in post-war Jamaica." Pp. 71–93 in A. W. Singham (ed.) *The Commonwealth Caribbean Into The Seventies*. Occasional Paper Series No. 10. Montreal: Centre for Developing Area Studies, McGill University.

Stone, Carl
1980   Democracy and Clientelism in Jamaica. New Brunswick, NJ: Transaction Books.

Watson, Beverly
1974   *Supplementary Notes on Foreign Investment in the Commonwealth Caribbean*. Jamaica: Institute for Social and Economic Research.

Watson, Hilbourne
1975   "Leadership and imperialism in the commonwealth Caribbean." Pp. 43–67 in A. W. Singham (ed.) *The Commonwealth Caribbean Into the Seventies*. Occasional Paper Series No. 10. Montreal: Centre for Developing Area Studies, McGill University.

PART ONE

Muhammad Shahidullah: Class Formation and Class Relations in Bangladesh

The purpose of this chapter is to trace the historical process of class formation in the region that is now Bangladesh. The analysis of class formation is developed in order to provide an explanation of the class relations that in turn provided the context for (1) the British colonization of Bengal, which had the main effects of obstructing autonomous development, deforming the system of commodity production that in fact grew out of the pre-colonial modes, and of giving rise to a new class structure which itself inhibited further development; (2) the assimilation of East Bengal, after 1947, to the newly constituted Pakistani state as an underdeveloped periphery subservient to the dominant class represented in that state; and (3) the emergence of the state of Bangladesh in 1971.

Particular attention is given to the historical formation of intermediate classes. A native "administrative class" cultivated by the British, together with the landlords of the region, as an instrument of colonial rule was formed in the measure that the British destroyed indigenous merchants and artisans and subjected the peasantry to increased oppression. The administrative class, divided between Hindus and Moslems, later turned upon their masters, as well as upon the Hindu landlords of East Bengal. In the post-colonial period this class was considerably expanded into a "new middle class," which, together with a rural petty bourgeoisie that had replaced the land-owners and in the presence of a weak Bengali bourgeoisie, became after 1971 the dominant class of Bangladesh.

Our point of departure in this analysis is the articulation/disarticulation dynamic of the modes of production in this region during the pre-colonial, colonial and post-colonial stages. Class realities of any given country of the Third World cannot be grasped in their historical specificity without a prior analysis of the mode(s) of production specific to that social formation.

However, that analysis cannot be undertaken without taking into account the penetration of the indigenous economies by a relatively higher mode of production—namely the capitalist mode—over the course of centuries. The contemporary class structure, and the complexities in relations among the different classes, as well as the intricate articulations among different elements of the indigenous modes of production, are very much rooted in the manner and extent to which these relations and articulations were altered by the penetration of, and subordination to, the system of capitalist production.

The Pre-Capitalist Mode of Production in Bengal: Potentialities of Capitalist Transformation

In the pre-colonial society of Bengal, agriculture was the dominant form of production. The whole society was organized and centered around surplus drawn from the peasant producers as land revenue. Lands were traditionally owned by the peasant producers but the land lords (Zamindars) had the hereditary rights to claim a portion of the produce as land revenue. The King or the state again had the customary and juridical right to receive a certain amount of the collected land revenue from the landlords. On the basis of the surplus produced in agriculture arose several estates of landlordism, along with a corresponding state (Habib, 1963, 1969).

In the pre-colonial towns, production was primarily cotton and silk goods. Weavers were the earliest petty commodity producers in Bengal. There were also gold, silver and black smiths, potters, painters, carpenters and sankharis. In the towns these artisans and craftsmen lived in guild-like communities (Karim, 1964).

Now a question arises as to the general nature of agricultural and artisanal processes of production in pre-colonial Bengal: Was the mode of production distinctly an Asiatic mode or simply a variant of feudalism? According to Marx's view, Indian societies were organized under the Asiatic mode of production characterized by the absence of private property in land, self-sufficient village communities with a unity of manufacture and agriculture and despotism based on hydraulic necessity. But there is some doubt that the specific mode that developed in Bengal should be considered specifically "Asiatic", it was nearer to, yet distinct from, a feudal mode. Marx and Engels define property under feudalism in this way:

> The chief form of property during the feudal epoch consisted on the one hand of landed property with serf labour chained to it, and on the other, of the labour of the individual with small capital commanding the labour of journeymen.

The organization of both was determined by the restricted conditions of production—the small scale—and primitive cultivation of the land and the craft type of industry [Marx and Engels, 1977:46].

The pre-colonial society of Bengal was characterized by agricultural and craft processes of production, although their nature varied from that of feudal Europe. Bengal peasants were not serfs; everywhere they were under certain defined economic obligations which were independent of their control and which took the form of services to be paid either in cash or in kind (Dobb, 1970). In Western European feudalism, particularly in England, the manor was the unit of production. There was no manorialism in Bengal in the proper sense of the term. The unit of production was an individual peasant family. Since the unit of production was different, the organization of landowning classes was also different. The Bengal peasants were not like English villeins who had to render agricultural services to their lords. The Bengal peasants were more like the free tenants of English manors. In medieval England the free tenants "held their tenements from father to son as if there were a specific agreement between them and the lord, performing certain services and paying certain rents; and this class was the most important of all" (Gwatkin et al., 1922:479). Agricultural lands in Bengal were formally owned by the peasants. Relations of production were expressed in terms of the assessment and the collection of land revenue by a class with hereditary tributary rights. The intensity of class struggle was different from that of Europe because of the different organization of production, but Bengal villages were never without conflict with landlords. In the English manorial organization, the officials and servants of the lords comprised a separate estate. In Bengal, the delegates and the intermediaries of the lords who collected revenue can be said to have formed a separate estate, though they were not connected with the processes of production in the way the officials and servants of the manorial organizations were. The system of vassalage in Bengal was represented by the Mansabdars and Jaigirdars who were assigned lands by the state in return for military services. The system of vassalage developed significantly during Mughal rule in Bengal. But the Bengal vassals could not create underlords with any kind of economic or political power.

One of the dominant characteristics of Western European feudalism was its decentralization of economic and political power. This feature is also relevant to pre-colonial Bengal. Bengal, until the advent of the British, had hardly been ruled by any centralized authority, though several attempts had been made for that purpose at different periods of its history. Owing to its geographical location, Bengal, particularly East Bengal, remained isolated from the main stream of development in power and politics during the centuries of Muslim rule. The despotic states that were established in India at different periods before the onset of British colonialism could not bring the Bengal landlords under complete subjugation (Raychaudhuri, 1969).

The main socio-economic features of pre-colonial Bengal were thus: the existence of a system of economic obligations and coercions over peasants, the presence of a group of petty commodity producers in guild-like communities, the system of vassalage introduced by the Muslim rulers, and the relative autonomy of the Bengal landlords from the ruling despotic states (Desai, 1969).

Two sets of class relations can be identified. The primary set was comprised of the local landlords, their administrative intermediaries, the peasants and the petty commodity producers. Here the dominant contradiction was between the landlords and the peasant producers. The secondary set of relations was comprised of the local landlords and the administrative officials and intermediaries who represented the dominance of the state or the king. Here the contradiction was between the two fractions of the ruling class—one which generated from within and the other which was imposed from outside (Mughal ruling class). All these classes (estates) were dependent on agricultural surplus. Their mutual relations and antagonisms were determined in terms of their share in the amount of agricultural surplus.

If feudalism is defined as a social system in which the direct producers are kept under specific economic obligations by a ruling class, then the pattern of relations existing in pre-colonial Bengal can possibly be described as feudal relations. What is, however, more significant is that pre-colonial social relations in Bengal were undergoing a process of disintegration during the eighteenth century. The hypothesis of "unchangingness" of the Asiatic mode of production advanced by Marx, Weber and other Western historians suffers limitations.

In the sphere of agricultural production, while the introduction of money rent by the Mughals had some obvious effects, the most important disintegrating element was the increasing pressure for land revenue on the peasant producers. The element of disintegration in this sphere of production was both external and internal in nature. The pressure of the Mughal state on the local landlords, which began to develop since the beginning of the eighteenth century, was external to the system of production. But it led to the development of internal coersion and repression by local landlords on the peasant producers. The increasing pressure for revenue created a political crisis between local landlords and the Mughal state while also causing differentiation to creep into the process of production—a situation which took place in Europe in the fourteenth and fifteenth centuries. While there began to emerge a rich group of peasants interested in large-scale cultivation through employing wage labor (Khudkhast peasants), another group of peasants, having lost their lands and other means of production, was subject to a process of proletarianization (Shahidullah, 1977).

In artisanal production, on the other hand, the forces of transition were represented by the gradual penetration of merchant capital into the process of production. In silk and cotton goods this was a consequence of increasing demand on the world market. Reorganization of production under the impact of merchant capital was known in Bengal as the system of "Dadni." Evidence indicates that the Dadni system caused a process of differentiation to take place within petty commodity production. A sector of the weavers, who could not do any specialized work, became separated from their means of production and ended up as wage laborers, while another sector, under the impact of the growing demand for their products, was accumulating capital for further investment in large-scale manufacturing through employing wage laborers.

These processes of differentiation, in my view, represented in precolonial Bengal the elements of transition from pre-capitalist to incipient forms of capitalist accumulation and class relations. But it was in this period of disintegration of the pre-capitalist mode of production, and crisis of state power which developed on its basis, that Bengal fell under colonialism.

Class Formation and Class Relations
in Colonial Bengal

The transition from one mode of production to another is basically a transformation in class relations. This transformation is as much political as it is economic. The transition is tied to the emergence of new forms and methods of production, while the forward movement of emerging economic forms depend on articulation to the political level. During the period of transition, political power "is itself an economic power" (Marx & Engels, 1972). The indigenous classes in Bengal, having been subordinated to colonialism, failed to grapple with the basic element of transition, namely political power.

Through British colonialism Bengal was gradually integrated into the world capitalist system. Since then a new history of the development of underdevelopment has been produced. The dynamic of class formation and class relations in Bengal began to be structured by and subordinated to the dynamic of English capitalism.

From 1765 to 1858, exclusive political control over Bengal was in the hands of the East India Company. During this period of almost a century, the British parliament had virtually no control over the activities of the East India Company in Bengal. The capitalist mode of production had not yet become dominant in eighteenth century England, which was still in a period of the primitive accumulation of capital. The bourgeoisie of the East India Company, a mercantile class corresponding to the economic stage of primitive accumulation, set about a process of plunder and the drainage of resources in Bengal (Dutt, 1950, 1943; Bauchamp, 1934). Of all the steps that were taken for this purpose, two were most significant: (1) juridic changes in the structure of agrarian property and hence in the process of revenue collection and (2) the establishment of complete political control over inland and foreign trade in Bengal. An enormous amount of wealth was drained off through the extraction of land revenues and through the monopoly over the exports of Bengal's goods and manufactures, yet the most significant impact of the early colonial policies of the mercantile bourgeoisie was on class formation and class relations in Bengal.

The landlords who formed the traditional ruling class of Bengal had no hereditary rights over the ownership of lands that were held in perpetuity by the peasant producers. With the promulgation of the act of Permanent Settlement in 1793, the colonial bourgeoise declared that the landlords were the proprietors of the lands in their respective jurisdiction. As a result of this change in one of the principle aspects of production relations—the form of ownership—the old landed oligarchy soon disintegrated and a new one began to develop (Islam, 1972).

> The original class of Zamindars . . . soon melted away under the pressure of
> the Company, in order to be replaced by mercantile speculators who now hold
> all the land of Bengal, with the exception of estates returned under the direct
> management the Government [Marx and Engels, 1972:78].

After the Settlement Act many who were formerly revenue collectors, merchants or native agents of the Company began to buy lands and became landlords. "In Bengal the total 'number of landlords which did not exceed 100 in the beginning of Hastings administration in 1772, rose in the course of the century to 154,200' " (Maddison, 1971:46) A host of intermediaries between the landlords and the actual peasants developed through the process of subinfeudation of lands. Noting this phenomenon, Marx remarks of the Bengali landlords: "Not content to be placed with regard to the British Government in the situation of middle men, they have created in their turn a class of 'hereditary' middlemen called patnidars, who created again their subpatnidars, etc., so that a perfect scale of hierarchy of middlemen has sprung up, which presses with its entire weight on the unfortunate cultivator" (Marx and Engels, 1972:78). Another author indicates that in the district of Jessore alone in slightly more than half a century, 317 estates (1793) multiplied into 4550 estates (1858) (Palit, 1975:15).

The formation of this new landed class in response to the needs of the primitive accumulation of capital by the British mercantile bourgeoisie led to the blockage of any indigenous process of transition in Bengal's agriculture. The khudkhast cultivation began to disintegrate, while peasant pauper-ization accelerated (Palit, 1975).

The attainment of British political control over trade led to the destruction of urban petty commodity producers, particularly the weavers. Marx observed:

> The monopolies of salt, opium, betel and other commodities, were inexhaust-able mines of wealth. The employees themselves fixed the price and plun-dered at will the unhappy Hindus. The Governor-General took part in this private traffic. . . . Great fortunes sprang up like mushrooms in a day; primitive accumulation went on without the advance of a shilling [Marx and Engels, 1972:294].

Along with the oppression of the artisans, there was a process of liquidation of the native mercantile bourgeoisie through discriminatory trade and tax policies. By the end of the eighteenth century, in the absence of political support "the big merchants were completely wiped out in Bengal and elsewhere" (Mukherjee, 1958). A significant amount of merchant capital, retreating from commerce under colonial pressure, was invested instead in buying Zamindari estates.

The net effect of the political control by the British mercantile bourgeoisie, in addition to the amount of wealth that was drained off, was the destruction of the possibilities of the growth of a new capitalistic class structure and the development possibilities resulting from the gradual ero-sion of the mode of production indigenous to the area. Instead the British formed a new landed class subservient to the foreign mercantile bourgeoisie, they pauperized and firmly subordinated the peasantry to pre-capitalist forms of class oppression, and they subordinated and restructured artisanal production toward the ends of export, destroying part of the indigenous mercantile bourgeoisie and converting others into landlords.

By the end of the eighteenth century, the industrial revolution was already under way in England. While the merchants of Bengal were becom-ing landlords under the rule of the Company, their counterparts in England were transforming themselves into industrial capitalists and moving toward the capture of state power. The monopoly of the East India Company came to an end in 1858. From 1858 to 1947, Bengal remained under the control of the British Crown. English Free-trade capitalism began to penetrate into Bengal in new dimensions. "The whole character of the trade was changed" (Marx, 1972:51). A process of unequal exchange in trade and a stage of new disarticulation in production set in.

While England was changing from mercantile to industrial capitalism, the system of landlordism created by earlier British colonialism in Bengal became increasingly commercial. Pre-capitalist relations of production were reinforced in the interest of jute production for the world market. Corresponding to the changing demand of the metropolitan bourgeoisie for agricultural raw materials, a class of sub-infeudatory landlords called the "Jotders" was formed. While the extraction of agricultural surplus by the landlords was in the form of money rent, the Jotders were interested in rent-in-kind, i.e. at least a half share of the produced crop which they provided to the British merchants.

The introduction of free-trade capitalism in the sphere of commerce and industry, on the other hand, not only destroyed the indigenous basis of the once highly developed guild production that had survived the rule of the East India Company, but also led to a gradual concentration and consolidation of economic power by the locally resident metropolitian bourgeoisie (Bagchi, 1972). The volume of foreign trade increased, the number of joint stock companies rose (in 1902–1903, there were 407 joint stock companies in Bengal), industrial factories started to develop and the number of banking offices became larger. In 1947, there were 243 banking offices in Bengal (Misra, 1961:232). These were accompanied by the growth and development of the railway and postal system, English education, and various legal and political reform measures. The basic strategy was to make Bengal more responsive to the demand of the industrial capitalism of England. It was in response to these new developments that a new agro-commercial bourgeoisie, petty bourgeoisie, and an administrative class began to develop in Bengal establishing new forms of class relations.

The agro-commercial bourgeoisie developed in colonial Bengal as a fraction of the landed class and was centered primarily around the trade of jute. The demand for raw jute began to increase after the establishment of jute manufacturing industries at Dundee (Gadgil, 1971). With the continuing production of jute, rice, tea, coconut, and other commercial crops for export, a sector of the landed class and the Jotders turned to merchant activity, becoming in effect an agro-commercial bourgeoisie.[1]

The increasing trading activities in Bengal by the colonial bourgeoisie provided also the basis for the formation of a petty bourgeoisie class. This class was comprised of the Sayodagars, Mahajans, Goswamis, Paikers, Dokandars, Baparis, Dalals and rural money lenders. In this group one can also include those associated with the retinues of the colonial administrative offices and the Zamindari estates (Peons, Chawkidars, Dafadars, Naibs, Tashildars, Gomosthas, and so on) and all the traditional rural and urban artisans and professional groups (Dhopa, Napit, Kamar, Kumar, Sutar, Tati, and so on). While the origin of this "old" petty bourgeoisie class was rooted in the pre-colonial period, the advent of colonialism led to the enlargement of the class (excepting the weavers). The activities of people engaged in the internal exchange of goods and commodities was in particular greatly increased.

In terms of class formation, the most significant event in colonial Bengal, particularly after 1858, was the development of a "new" petty bourgeoisie of salaried middle strata, an "administrative class" as distinct from the "old" petty bourgeoisie described above. English education was introduced by the colonial state to create a native administrative class and a group of white collar workers. In Calcutta the Hindu College was established in 1816 and the Mohammedan College in 1823. The Serampur College was opened in 1818 under the supervision of the distinguished missionary William Carey. The University of Calcutta came into being in 1857; Dacca University in 1920. By 1885 there were twenty-five colleges in Bengal (McCully, 1940). These educational institutions trained an administrative class—bureaucrats, lawyers, doctors, journalists, engineers, teachers, literary persons and the like. While in the West, the growth of the salaried middle class was the result of indigenous economic and technological changes, in Bengal this class was entirely the by product of the administrative needs of the colonial power.

In sum, British colonialism destroyed the possibilities of a transition out of the indigenous pre-capitalist mode of production, while it also impelled the development of new class formations comprising the landed class, a petty bourgeoisie, and a salaried administrative class in colonial Bengal.

Class Relations, Class Contradictions, and Class Alliances

The big landlords, Jotders and various intermediaries formed a distinct class of owners of the dominant means of production. In the first half of the nineteenth century associations of the landlords (The Zamindars Association of Calcutta, 1838; The British Indian Society, 1839; The British Indian Association, 1851) were established and published various journals *(The Reformer, Bengal Herald, Bengal Harkuru)*. There remained, however, a fractionalization within the landed class. The dominant fraction, based particularly in East Bengal, was comprised of Hindus. The weaker fraction was the Muslim. But in terms of their class interests, both these fractions collaborated with the colonial state and the colonial planters who began to enter Bengal after 1835 establishing Indigo and Tea plantations (Palit, 1975).

The dominant contradiction in the sphere of agricultural production was between the local landlords and Jotders and the peasants. Peasant "rights" had not been precisely defined in the act of the Permanent Settlement and therefore a reckless expropriation of the agricultural surplus continued throughout the whole colonial period. The peasants not only paid the stipulated amount of revenue but also various surcharges (Palit, 1975). The position of the sharecroppers became worse than that of the tenants. While agriculture became increasingly commercially oriented, the forms of exploitation and oppression of the peasantry remained largely pre-capitalist in character. The development of commercial agriculture, concentration of lands in few hands, and the increase in peasant pauperization were not associated with any great trend towards the development of modern capitalist farming. The surplus labor of the peasants was extracted through the collection of money-rents and rents-in-kind, of which the metropolitan bourgeoisie was the ultimate beneficiary. The local landed class, without any significant improvement in the productive forces, could reproduce the relations facilitating high levels of surplus extraction because their economic basis was rooted in the system of colonialism. The interest of the local landed class and the dominant British elements had been mutually aligned within the framework of the colonial state (Rajat and Ratna, 1973).

The contradiction between the landed class and the peasant producers was expressed in different rebellions at different stages of the development of the colonial rule (Faraidi Movement, 1818; Sirajgonj Movement, 1872–73; the Blue Mutiny, 1859–62; Tebhaga Movement, 1946–47). But in the presence of a strong colonial state, those movements attained very little success. The agricultural reforms of 1859, 1883, 1885, 1928, and 1934 (Bhuiyan, 1978) did extend rights of occupancy to some categories of peasants, but within the structure of landlordism those concessions did fail to bring any significant change in the forces and relations of production in agriculture.

The native agro-commercial bourgeoisie developed only in association with and subservience to foreign merchants. No significant challenge to the dominance of the metropolitan bourgeoisie and thereby to colonialism came from the agro-commercial bourgeoisie because of their "comprador" character and their inextricable links with landlordism.

Different working class movements gathered strength particularly after the Russian Revolution and the subsequent formation of the Indian Communist Party in 1921 under the leadership of M. N. Roy and Muzaffar Ahamed. The rise of plantations in the nineteenth century, the growth of jute industries, the growing number of landless peasants, and the stripping of the artisans from their hereditary occupations contributed to the growth of the working class and of workers' movements centering around Calcutta. But since the working class was relatively small and weak and while politics was dominated by landed interests and the administrative class, there developed no significant challenge to colonialism from this source.

The administrative class that developed in colonial Bengal was not a unified class. The dominant group was comprised of Hindus and the weaker sector of Muslims. For both these sectors, money for education came mostly from lands. The nature of this class has been correctly summarized by Broomfield who called them the "Bhadralock elite" (gentlemen elite). They were

> a socially privileged and consequently superior group, economically dependent upon landed rents and professional and clerical employment; keeping its distance from the masses by its acceptence of high caste proscriptions and command of education [Broomfield, 1968:213].

The rise of this class and the accompanying growth in the cultivation of science, art, literature, philosophy, and history has sometimes been described as a period of the "Renaissance of Bengal" in the nineteenth and early twentieth centuries. But this was a different Renaissance than the European. In Europe, the Renaissance was a period of challenge to feudal lords, kings, and nobles. It was an age of challenge to the authority of the Church. It was a time of the development of national bourgeoisies and nation states. But in Bengal, the administrative class (with few individual exceptions) did not rise to challenge the authority of the landed class and the domination of British colonialism. Their origins and interests were too locked up with those of the landed class and they were too dependent on the colonial state. The same was the case for the "old" petty bourgeoisie.

The entire class structure in Bengal was built around the system of landlordism and colonialism. The landed class and the administrative class, the two relatively highly developed classes, together with a nascent agro-commercial bourgeoisie allied with the colonial state because it was through the perpetuation of the colonial state that these classes could continue to maintain their relatively privileged class positions. The colonial state cultivated the native landed and administrative classes as support classes.

One of the most intriguing questions in the history of colonial Bengal is the reasons for the deep divisions among the Hindus and the Muslims and the consequent separation of Bengal, with the East becoming Muslim East Pakistan, at the end of the colonial rule in 1947. Historically this division is rooted into the process of Islamization in the region. Significant numbers of people of Bengal were converted to Islam from Hinduism and Buddhism through the Turkish conquest in the beginning of the thirteenth century. Through the conquest and conversion, the ideology of Islam was superimposed on basic production processes of the society during the five centuries of Muslim rule before the British. The process of Islamization, however, did not bring any significant change in the structure of pre-capitalist class relations (Omar, 1967:36). Rather it consolidated those relations by developing a tiny group of "aristocrats" from among the Muslims who are said to have migrated to the region either as official bureaucrats of the Muslim rulers, as preachers of Islam or as traders (Karim, 1964). The process of Islamization, in effect, began to create a fractionalization in the upper hierarchy of the society in terms of more control over land revenue, but brought no change to the economic position of the mass of peasants who converted to Islam, possibly in the hope of loosening exploitation.[2]

The division within the dominant class created by Islamization in the pre-colonial period became widened in the colonial time mainly through the effects of English education (Omar, 1967:45) The Muslim aristocrats and the religious figures remained almost for a century hostile to the British cólonial state and its various modernizing steps, particularly to English education. The development of various revivalist movements during the nineteenth century (Faraidi Movement, 1818; Tariquat-I-Muhammadyah Movement, 1818) are indications of an attitude of ideological hostility to British rule. By the time the Muslims began to get an English education, the Hindus were firmly entrenched into the administrative services of the colonial state and took up the leading positions in different technical and intellectual persuits, particularly in Bengal.

The religious divisions within the local support classes of British colonialism began to widen after the beginning of the twentieth century. This became evidenced in politics after the Curzonian partition of Bengal in 1905 (Cronin, 1975). Being faced with some problems of administration and having thought of getting the support of the weaker sectors of the Muslim landed class of Eastern Bengal in a situation of increasing demand for political power by the dominant fractions of the landed and administrative classes, Lord Curzon, the then Governor of Bengal, decided to make Eastern Bengal, including Assam, a separate province of administration. The partition had been overwhelmingly supported by the Muslim landed and administrative classes of Eastern Bengal in particular and the Muslim peasants in general.

> The partition and the opportunities which it suggested, served to unite the Muslim population against a common enemy. The small educated and professional class saw the opportunity for patronage and the support of government in the competition with the Hindu bhadralock, while the peasantry saw a new chance to assert themselves against their Hindu landlords [Cronin, 1975:101].

But the partition was opposed by the Hindu landed and administrative classes because it went against their interests. In 1911, with the increasing growth of radicalism among the members of these classes expressed in the Swadeshi Movement and Terrorist Movement, the colonial state decided to withdraw its scheme for the partition of of Bengal. Bengal remained united.

But the divisions between the Hindu and Muslim landed and administrative classes kept on widening. The politics of Bengal from the second decade of the twentieth century to the end of colonialism in 1947 was guided primarily by the competing, but not always sharply conflicting, politico-economic interests of these two sectors of the landed and administrative classes.

A political party, the All India Congress, was established in 1885 with a view to representing the interests of the landed class, agro-commercial bourgeoisie, and the administrative class. But considering the Congress was dominated by Hindus, the Muslims built another political organization, the All India Muslim League, in 1906. Immediately after its formation the League sought an explicit alliance with the colonial state. The first and foremost resolution of the party was "To promote, among the Musalmans of India, feeling of loyalty to the British Government." (Pirzada, 1969:6) The members who represented Eastern Bengal in the constitution-making body all belonged to the landed class. There were six members from Western Bengal: two were landed aristocrats and four belonged to the administrative class (Pirzada, 1969).

Thus by the beginning of the present century, the religiously divided support classes of British colonialism became politically organized. A tripartite political tug-of-war began to develop within the colonial power bloc between these two sectors and the metropolitan bourgeoisie. (Here it should be remembered that the struggle in Bengal was a part of an overall struggle in India.)

After the annulment of the partition of Bengal in 1911, the Muslims became hostile to the colonial state. They came to an alliance with the Hindus (Khilafat Movement, Lucknow Pact, Non Co-operation Movement) in order to put pressure on the colonial government for granting more political rights to them—to grant a fully responsible government in India. But the colonial state at that time was not willing to completely yield to the demands of its restive support classes. The Montagu-Chelmsford reforms of 1921 introduced a system of dyarchy which maintained that some issues and subjects were to be administered directly by the governors appointed by the British Crown. After that a series of steps were taken by the colonial state (Simon Commission, Communal Award Plan of 1932, The Cripps Mission of 1942, The Wavel Plan and the Simla Conference of 1945, The Cabinet Mission Plan of 1946) to come to an agreement with other contenders of the power bloc about the political future of India.

Meanwhile, the uneasy alliance between Hindus and Muslims at the higher level of politics began to fall apart, partly under the impact of the Khilafat Movement which in rural areas, particularly in Eastern Bengal, became a movement not only against the British but also against the Hindu landed class. The breakup of the alliance culminated in the declarations of

Nehru Report in 1938 and Lahore Resolution in 1940. The Nehru Report demanded a fully responsible system of government in which the majority would be sovereign. The Lahore Resolution demanded separate states for the Muslims. The colonial state was, by and large, in favour of the proposal for a unified state in India. This led to a crisis in the power bloc. The political crisis developed into a communal crisis. The struggle between the two fractions of the landed and administrative classes appeared as struggle between the Hindus and Muslims. The colonial state eventually conceded to the demand of the weaker fraction for a separate state—the state of Pakistan (Mountbatten Plan, June 3, 1947). Accordingly, Bengal became divided. The Muslim majority region of Eastern Bengal joined with Pakistan. The direct rule of the metropolitan bourgeoisie through the colonial state came to an end.

From 1905 to 1947, the politics of Eastern Bengal, now the nation of Bangladesh, was dominated mainly by the landed class, themselves a formation of British colonialism. Under the sway of landlords and colonialism, political divisions developed along religious lines. Islam was used as a means for political mobilization. The Muslim peasants and working class people supported the Muslim landed class because they thought that by joining with them and ultimately by joining with the state of Pakistan they could get rid of the domination of the Hindu landed class and the Hindu agro-commercial bourgeoisie. For the impoverished peasantry it was a fact of class struggle. But the Muslim landed class was not identified as an object of the struggle. The Muslim landed class in alliance with the Muslim peasants and the working class fought against the Hindu landed class. The transition from Eastern Bengal to East Pakistan was thus merely a transition of political power from one fraction to another of the same landed class. The process of colonialism together with the historical forces created through the process of Islamization obstructed the development of a nationalist and revolutionary struggle against colonialism and the backward social structure that the British had shaped.

Class Formation and Class Relations During the Rule of the Post-Colonial State of Pakistan (1947–1970)

It is because of the peculiar historical circumstances created by colonialism (class configurations, underdeveloped productive forces, colonial cultural framework and so on) that Pakistan, immediately after its formation, began to follow the capitalistic path of development. While in the era of colonialism dependency relations were sustained and recreated through the economic and political control of the metropolitan bourgeoisie, during the post-colonial period those relations were sustained and reproduced by the activities and policies of a post-colonial state that rested upon pre-existing class formations.

Since the process of the primitive accumulation of capital had been blocked by colonialism, the most baffling problem faced by the post-colonial state of Pakistan in the initial years was the intense scarcity of capital. This scarcity of capital, in combination with the nature of the class forces guiding the state, led to new forms of dependence on metropolitan capital. During the Cold War in the 1950s, Pakistan entered into an alliance with American capital and since then, in spite of all crises in political management during the last three decades, it has remained unchanged. During the fifteen year period from 1952 to 1967, Pakistan received a total of $3.5 billion from the United States and more than one billion more from the World Bank, the United Kingdom and Canada (Brecher and Abbas, 1972:62–81).

In addition to the influx of foreign capital, Pakistan also started to mobilize domestic sources of capital from agriculture, particularly through the export of jute and jute goods. East Pakistan had a monopoly on the production of jute. So from the beginning, the post-colonial state of Pakistan began to control the the production and marketing of jute and jute goods in East Pakistan through various legal and institutional steps (Jute Ordinance, 1949, replaced by the Jute Act of 1956; Jute Marketing Corporation, 1957; Provincial Jute Dealers Registration Law of 1949; Central Jute Act of 1956; Jute Ordinance, 1962; Jute Research Institute). During the year 1948–1949, Pakistan exported jute worth 1,195.6 million rupees and in 1963–1964, jute worth 1,065 million rupees was exported. This capital from jute, which was extracted by exploiting the peasant producers of East Pakistan through the overvaluation of the domestic currency, the various export control mechanisms, and a terms of trade unfavorable to agriculture was then used to import machines for manufacturing industries located in West Pakistan (Nations, 1971). By attracting capital from foreign investors, foreign loans and a high level of exploitation of peasant producers, particularly the jute producers of East Pakistan, Pakistan embarked on a project of state managed capitalist development. My main purpose here is to examine how and to what extent the class structure of East Pakistan changed under the policies of the post-colonial state of Pakistan. In other words, the purpose is to show how the post colonial state sustained and recreated the antagonistic relations within the social formation of East Pakistan and relations of dependence between East and West Pakistan—and how this led to the development of another political crisis in this region resulting in the establishment of Bangladesh in 1971.

Agrarian Production and the
Rural Petty Bourgeoisie

Since the main source of capital accumulation from East Pakistan was agriculture, the Pakistani state made efforts to develop controls over agricultural lands and producers. This was accomplished by the abolition of the system of landlordism in 1950. The agricultural surplus in the form of land revenue, which previously went to the local landlords and the colonial bourgeoisie, now began to be appropriated by the state. During the year 1947–1955, the annual rate of extraction was 31.2 million rupees. In 1964–1965, during the full operation of the State Acquisition and Tenancy Act, revenue extraction increased to 150 million rupees.

With the removal of the Hindu landed class there remained no significant class to act as a base for political control and political management in rural East Pakistan.[3] The weaker fraction of the Muslim landed class whose position had also been changed with the abolition of landlordism, was not large or strong enough to exert controls over the rural areas. The Pakistani state, faced with the necessity of assuring the smooth carrying out of the process of agrarian surplus extraction and containing rural radicalism, devised a program, with the assistance of American experts on agrarian modernization, called the "Village Agricultural, Industrial Development Program" (Village-AID) in 1953. The purpose was to develop a class of rural elite capable of providing leadership for agrarian modernization while maintaining a controlling link between the peasants and the state. This program was, however, abondoned in 1960 and the system of "Basic Democracies" was introduced. The Basic Democracies consisted of rural elected representatives. Through the local and divisional councils they were linked to the state. The representatives were drawn from a class of rural petty bourgeoisie. Most of the members of this class were landowners, small businessmen, or persons related to Zamindari estates before the abolition of landlordism. While the controls over agricultural revenue had been taken over by the state, political, economic, and ideological controls over the agricultural producers were exerted by this class of rural petty bourgeoisie (Tepper, 1976).

By the 1960s, West Pakistan had achieved a considerable success in industrialization. The immediate need of an incipient West Pakistani bourgeoisie, whose formation was being facilitated by state policies, was that of developing the rural infrastructural arrangements in East Pakistan for an effective movement of agricultural raw material from villages to cities and of manufactured goods from cities to villages and to raise the aggregate output. It was in response to these structural needs of the rising West Pakistani bourgeoisie that the state began to develop a series of modernizing program in East Pakistan's agriculture. The Water and Power Development Authority and the Academy for Rural Development were established in 1959 and the Agricultural Development Corporation and Agricultural Development Bank of Pakistan in 1961 and 1962. The Rural Works Program, Thana Irrigation Program, the Integrated Rural Development Program and various other programs for agrarian modernization were initiated in the decade of 1960s. The ceiling on landholding was increased from 100 to 375 bighs (from about 33 acres to 125 acres). In the period from 1950–1955, agriculture received only 6 percent of the total development expenditure of the state. During the third Five Year Plan period (1965–1970), agriculture received 12 percent of the total state development expenditure.

Despite the abolition of landlordism, the deliberate development of a class of rural petty bourgeoisie and the introduction of various institutional and technical innovations by the state, East Pakistan's agriculture failed to develop along capitalist lines (Bhuiyan, 1978; Abdullah, 1976; Alamgir, 1978; Jahangir, 1977; Westergaard, 1978; Rahman, 1974; Hartmann and Boyce, 1979; Omar, 1978). The above measures shifted the source of their exploitation from landlords to the state and helped integrate East Pakistani peasants into the world capitalist system. The rural petty bourgeoisie of East Pakistan, instead of turning into capitalist farmers like most of their counterparts in West Pakistan (Burki, 1976; Alavi, 1976), remained as political intermediaries between the state and the peasants.

Industrial Production and the Development of a Dependent Bourgeoisie in East Pakistan

Pakistan's strategy for developing capitalism in industry was both through the encouragement of private investment and the investment of state capital. The main strategy was to build industries with the help of the state capital and then gradually to turn them over to private capitalists through a process of disinvestment. Profits generated by the state enterprises were added to state funds from jute exports and foreign loans to build more new industries which were again put into a process of disinvestment. The investment of private capital was also facilitated by providing infrastructural opportunities by the state. The state thus set in a process of formation of a bourgeoisie, particularly in West Pakistan, through bureaucratic control, management and development planning, depending heavily on foreign assistence (International Labor Review, 1948; ECAFE Report, 1951; United Nations Department of Economic and Social Affairs Report, 1961).

By 1960, under the guidance of the state, Pakistan "witnessed a significant pace of industrialization. While national income rose by 37 percent, the percentage share contributed by manufacturing doubled, and agriculture's share correspondingly declined" (Power, 1969: 9).[4] Through the investment of private capital and enjoyment of advantages of the state's policy of disinvestment, a class of industrial bourgeoisie became firmly entrenched into the structure of capitalism in Pakistan by the 1960s.

But this class did not develop as a unified class in Pakistan. The dominant fraction of this class was composed of the financial-industrial houses of West Pakistan—the Adamjee, Dawood, Valika, Colony, Fancy, Bawany Crescent, Beco, Wazir Ali, Amins, Nishat, Hoti, Fateh, Isphahani, and Karim. Most of the members of this fraction belonged to the communities of Memons, Dawaood, Bhoras, Panjabi Sheikh, Chinioto, and Khoja Ismaili who migrated from India to West Pakistan (mainly in Karachi, Lahore and Lyallpur) in 1947 (Amjad, 1974). The Bengali bourgeoisie of East Pakistan comprised the weaker fraction. They had developed also by accumulating capital through the export-import business and under the control, management and planning of the state bureaucracy, particularly in the mid-1960s (Papanek, 1969).

One of the dominant characteristics of the Bengali bourgeoisie was its dependence on the state bureaucracy. The West Pakistani fraction of the bourgeoisie was also dependent but they could assert influence at the political level, particularly during the Ayub period (1958–1969). But the weaker fraction of the East Pakistani bourgeoisie had virtually no political influence. The West Pakistani bourgeoisie controlled the major segments of industrial assets in the private sector of East Pakistan (Bawani, Amins, Isphahani, and Karim had their entire holdings in East Pakistan; 50.3 percent of Dawood's and 51 percent of Adamjee's total net assets were located in East Pakistan). Yet the East Pakistani bourgeoisie hardly came into any conflict with them. They were subservient both to the state bureaucracy and to the dominant fraction of the West Pakistani bourgeoisie.[5]

The New Middle Class

Having embarked on a plan for industrialization through state control, Pakistan faced the need for trained manpower in order to run the emerging public corporations, banking institutions, research organizations, and various industrial establishments. So, a number of schools, colleges, universities, research institutions, and training centers were established in East Pakistan during the decades of the 1950s and the 1960s. Having been educated and trained in these institutions and also abroad under the sponsorship of various foreign agencies, the size and the dimension of the new middle class of East Pakistan—the basis of which was formed under British colonialism as an administrative class—was considerably extended. The main fraction of this class, which maintained its "administrative" character, was comprised of state functionaries and military officials who multiplied in numbers with the expansion of state activities. The resources for the development of this class, by and large, came from both rural and urban landed property. Many came from the rural petty bourgeois who financed their education and later, because of their access to political power, began to make themselves into a small commercial bourgeoisie through control over a substantial amount of urban landed property, particularly after the mid-'60s.

Because of their structural relations with the state and landed property, the new middle class supported the power of West Pakistani state over East Pakistan. During the Ayub period (1958–1969) a significant sector of the intellectuals of East Pakistan had been mobilized for the "Islamization" of Bengali culture.

The Old Petty Bourgeoisie

The old petty bourgeoisie seemed to have undergone no significant change during the Pakistani period. Few traders or small producers developed into commercial or industrial entrepreneurs. Since their centers of activities were located mostly in rural Bazara and Mufassal towns, they had hardly any access to the bureaucracy for export-import licenses and other state-directed commercial and industrial advantages. The only change in this class was an extension in its size and the removal of Hindu dominance. But such a dominance had partly been taken over, particularly in the major cities, by non-Bengali people who migrated from India to East Pakistan in 1947, mainly by the Khoja Ismailis. As a non-Bengali immigrant group, they had limited access to the governmental bureaucracy in getting various commercial advantages.

The Working Class

The size of the working class, though small to this day, had been substantially increased during the period of Pakistani rule. In 1965, there were 35,989 workers employed in cotton textile industries in East Pakistan; in 1970, there were 59,500. In 1965, there were 78,077 workers in Jute industries; in 1970, 163,000. Similar growth had also been achieved in other industrial sectors (Statistical Year Book of Bangladesh, 1975). The main part of this working class had been recruited from the rural landless peasants.

The Lumpen Proletariat

During the rule of Pakistan, there also developed in East Pakistan's urban areas, particularly in Dacca, a class of lumpen proletariat comprised of the Rickshaw pullers, Kulis, Thelawalas, Feriwalas, slum-dwellers, servants, beggars and other people related to lower categories of urban services. The main group was comprised of the Rickshawalas and the slum-dwellers. Most of the members of this class belong to the category of displaced rural landless peasants removed from their ancestral homesteads.

Class Relations and the Crisis of Dependent Development in East Pakistan

The post-colonial class structure in East Pakistan then was comprised of the rural petty bourgeoisie, a small and weak mainly commercial bourgeoisie, the old petty bourgeoisie, the new middle class, the working class, the peasantry, and the lumpen proletariat. The disintegration of the colonial landed class and the formation of these classes were the results of the process of state-managed, foreign-supported development on one hand and the process of capital accumulation by the industrial bourgeoisie of West Pakistan on the other. The surplus generated by the economy was appropriated and the interests of all the classes of East Pakistan were subordinated to the Pakistani state and the West Pakistani industrial bourgeoisie. Nevertheless, for a time an alliance developed between the rural petty bourgeoisie, the bourgeoisie and the new middle class of East Pakistan and the state managers and the industrial bourgeoisie of West Pakistan. The state managed this alliance in the interest of the private capital of West Pakistan and in relation to Pakistan's growing place in international capitalism.

The modernization and dependent capitalist development policies pursued by the Pakistani state in East Pakistan resulted in the appropriation of agricultural surplus and the elimination of Hindu and Muslim landed classes, blockage of private capital accumulation through bureaucratic control, the disintegration of East's indigenous industrial structure developed mainly by the Hindu bourgeoisie (Papanek, 1969:123) and the formation of a dependent class structure.[6]

With the various subordinate classes of East Pakistan acting as support classes to a state representing interests of the West Pakistani industrial bourgeoisie, the dominant contradiction in East Pakistan appeared as a contradiction between the state on the one hand and the peasants, working class, and the lumpen proletariat on the other hand. However, this contradiction began to be politically expressed in East Pakistan under the leadership of sectors of the new middle and petty bourgeois classes. The abolition of the system of landlordism in East Pakistan in 1950 yielded an increased importance to rural and urban petty bourgeoisies and new middle classes. Sectors of these classes became increasingly critical of the role of the Pakistani state. The formation of East Pakistan Student League in 1948; The Youth League in 1948; the Awami League in 1949; the language movement of 1952; the formation of the Krishak Sramic Party (Peasant and Labour Party) in 1952; the United Front in 1953; the defeat of the Muslim League party in the general election of 1954; the formation of the National Awami Party (leftist) in 1957—these were all indications of the growing power of the petty bourgeois and middle classes and their challenge to the Pakistani state, particularly in the pre-Ayub period (1947–1958). During the Ayub period (1958–1969), however, other sectors of these classes turned into supporters of the Pakistani state because of some improvement in the availability of consumer goods, extension of educational opportunities, development of urban housing facilities, and the opportunities to get into the bureaucracy and other state-sector employments. Thus, the new middle and petty bourgeois classes were politically divided over the central issue of the subordination of East Bengal to West Pakistani interests.

When the Army seized state power, politics was banned in Pakistan for four years (1958–1962). Politics was again introduced in 1962. The Awami League then became the vanguard not only of sectors of the petty bourgeois and new middle classes but also of the peasants, working class, and the lumpen proletariats of East Pakistan. The power basis of the Awami League considerably weakened when Ayub won over a large section of the intermediate elements by distributing various opportunities. From the mid-1960s, the Awami League therefore began to organize the working class and the peasants. Through the formulation of the six-points program in 1966, the Awami League brought a crisis in the relations between East and West Pakistan. A new class alliance came into force in East Pakistan (1969–1970) between the Awami League leadership on the one hand and the peasants, working class, and the lumpen proletariats on the other. The basic demand of the Awami League was autonomy for East Pakistan with control over foreign aid and trade. But the Pakistani state and the industrial bourgeoisie of West Pakistan could not rely on the political promises of limited autonomy by the Awami League probably because a substantial amount of its support came from the peasants and the working class. The Pakistani state, under control of the Army, let loose a reign of terror and repression in East Pakistan in 1971. But that only contributed to strengthening the Awami League leadership by eventually drawing the support from the Eastern bourgeoisie and the new middle class. This led to the disintegration of the state of Pakistan and the transformation of East Pakistan, under leadership of the Awami League, into a separate state—the state of Bangladesh. For the peasants, the working class and the lumpen proletariats it was a struggle against the Pakistani state and the classes which sustained it. But it was fought in alliance with and under the leadership of the petty bourgeois and new middle classes.

Bangladesh: Emerging Class Relations and Class Contradictions

The Awami League leadership, after it took over the state power in Bangladesh in 1971, developed a "radical tone" to its ideological pronouncements by declaring socialism as one of the main principles of organizing the state. The program of socialism, or "Mujibism" as it has sometimes been called, soon led to deep ideological divisions within the sectors of the new middle class who had earlier made alliances with the Pakistani state and the West Pakistani industrial bourgeoisie but later, during the political crisis, had supported for a time the Awami League movement. The rising Bengali bourgeoisie, particularly, turned sharply against socialist policies. In the absence of support from other sectors of the new middle class, especially the Army and the bureaucracy, the Awami League government plunged into a crisis. Since its rise to state power was sudden and its socialism was without a firm class foundation, the Awami League leadership did not have the capacity either to reach to a consensus through class alliances or to resolve the emerging contradictions through control mechanisms. The crisis culminated with the formation of the one párty system (BAKSAL) and the introduction of the Presidential form of government in 1975. Immediately after the formation of the BAKSAL, Mujib and his family were killed and the government of the Awami League was overthrown by a faction of the Army. The state of the Awami League had nationalized the major industries, fixed land ceiling on 100 bighs (about 33.3 acres), and dislodged the power of the traditional rural petty bourgeoisie, but those changes could not be institutionalized in the absence of support from the various contending sectors of the new middle class (Robinson and Griffin, 1974).

By the end of 1975, through a series of reconciliations and realignment of factions, the Army became entrenched in the arena of political power. A new power bloc came into force, comprised of some sectors of the Army, the civil bureaucracy, the bourgeoisie and the intelligentsia. The basic economic strategy of this new power bloc represented by the Bangladesh National Party (BNP), which continues to rule even after the assasination of Ziaur Rahman, has been to stimulate and subsidize private capital.

In the sphere of agriculture, attempts are being made to increase production through almost the same processes of development as adopted by the

Pakistani state. Rural development attempts are being made through a program called "Swanirvar" (self reliance), which is dependent on foreign assistance. The Integrated Rural Development Program, the Food For Works Program and other rural development programs have been developing a huge agrarian bureaucracy without bringing any basic change in rural social life.

In the sphere of industry, the state is trying to strengthen the basis of the indigenous Bengali bourgeoisie by providing bank loans, infrastructural opportunities, and various bureaucratic privileges. The state does not favor direct economic intervention as did the state of Pakistan in its initial period of industrialization. To reactivate the private sector, the state has taken various measures to disinvest most of the industries nationalized by the Awami League government. Attempts have been made to raise the ceiling of private sector investment, reduce the scope of various state corporations, liberalize credit facilities, and permit collaboration with foreign capital.

To what extent the present power bloc of the Bangladesh National Party will be successful in modernizing the country cannot be evaluated in any precise terms. However, a few problems that are likely to develop as a result of the state's present economic policies can be noted.

The process of modernization in agriculture will improve the conditions of the rich peasants but also remove poor peasants from ownership of lands and increase share-cropping for the rich peasants, without any significant movement toward large-scale capitalist farming. The new rural institutional innovations in the form "Gram Sarkar" will develop a rural governmental bureaucracy like the Basic Democracy of the Ayub period.

The liberalization policies of the state regarding the promotion of the private sector will strengthen and expand the basis of the commercial bourgeoisie. A significant part of the foreign capital which is being loaned to this class and the capital coming from private individuals working abroad is being invested in commercial and real estate business rather than in productive industrial enterprises. Private and transnational capital lack confidence in Bangladesh's political future.

The assasinations of Seikh Mujibur Rahman in 1975 and Ziaur Rahman in 1981 indicate some deep conflicts among the various fractions of the new Bengali middle class. Under the rule of the present power bloc with the hegemonic presence of the Army two situations will develop in Bangladesh. On the one hand the political and ideological fractionalizations within the middle class will be widened. This will increasingly generate small-scale political instabilities. On the other hand, the peasants, the working class, and the lumpenproletariat who comprise about 90 percent of the total population will be increasingly alienated from the state power and its developmental programs. This will generate potentialities for large-scale political movements against the present power bloc, particularly against its hegemonic fraction—the Army.

Conclusion

Before its insertion into world capitalism through colonialism, the region which is now called Bangladesh was undergoing a process of indigenous transformation in class structure along capitalistic lines under the impact of differentiations in peasant and petty commodity modes of production. The development of colonialism led to a blockage of those processes of transition by contributing to the formation of a new class structure dominated by a landed class, a comprador agro-commercial bourgeoisie, and an administrative class. These were, however, not unified classes. The dominant fractions were comprised of the Hindus and the weaker fractions of the Muslims. The reasons for this religious division, though partly embedded into the historical process of Islamization in this region, are mainly rooted in the process of colonization and colonial class formation. Since the formation and interests of these classes was linked to landlordism, no significant challenge to colonialism came from these classes. Within the alliance between the colonial state and these classes, however, there developed an internal struggle between the dominant and the weaker fractions centering around the problem of political power. The struggle between the Hindus and the Muslims of these classes eventually led to the transformation of the region of Eastern Bengal into East Pakistan. The Muslim peasants and the working class entered into an alliance with the Muslim landed interests to overthrow the dominance of the Hindu landowners.

During the post-colonial period, a new form of domination again developed in East Pakistan. This was partly because of the weak position of the Eastern Muslim landed and the new middle classes, but mainly because of the control of the state by the West Pakistani industrial bourgeoisie and the military-bureaucratic authority. The state of Pakistan managed a process of capitalist development and created a dependent class structure in East Pakistan which was comprised of the rural petty bourgeoisie, urban new middle class, and a weak industrial bourgeoisie. Within the alliance of these dependent classes of East Pakistan supporting the Pakistani state, there developed internal contradictions for more access to political power. This was articulated by some sectors of the middle class under the leadership of the Awami League. The resultant political struggle of the Awami League led to the disintegration of Pakistan and the creation of the state of Bangladesh when the peasants, the working class, and the lumpenproletariats were brought into an alliance to overthrow West Pakistani domination.

The Awami League government, after it took over the state power in 1971, could not develop a centralized political authority for mobilizing the peasants and the working class in favor of its programs. The transitional socialist state of the Awami League was soon smashed by bourgeois and petty bourgeois forces under the leadership of the Army. A new power bloc was formed in 1975 comprised of the small Bengali bourgeoisie, different fractions of the petty bourgeoisie, and the new middle class under the hegemony of the Army. The absence of any basic restructuring policies in economy and politics on the part of this power bloc means that the stage is set for a greater conflict with peasants, the working class, and the lumpen-proletariats. The removal of the Hindu landed class and the overthrow of the West Pakistani bourgeois hegemony set the possibilities, due to absence of any more religious or language issues, of developing internal polarization and contradictions along class lines. The present power bloc can perhaps perpetuate its control as long as it can satisfy the economic demands of the urban new middle class and the urban petty bourgeoisie. But under the constraints of the underdeveloped production forces and internal political tensions, the present power bloc cannot continue for long even through the use of repressive mechanisms. There will always be movements for revitalizing a democratic polity.

The historical development of class formations and class relations in Bangladesh suggests one very important theoretical consideration: In post-colonial societies, because of historical circumstances related to colonialism, there has arisen a complexity in class structure—a complexity wherein the new middle class has a dominant position. The classes relating to production, the bourgeoisie, the peasants, the working class could not historically achieve a strong position because from the beginning of colonialism the development of the production processes of these societies had been controlled and guided primarily in the interests of metropolitan capitalism. In the post-colonial period, it is the new middle class which superseded the administrative class of colonial times, that recreates the conditions of underdevelopment.

Notes

1. The industrial bourgeoisie formed in colonial India, particularly in Bengal, was not only subservient to the colonial bourgeoisie but also highly internally fractionalized. Bengal industries, particularly jute industries, were owned and controlled almost completely by the colonial bourgeoisie (Bagchi, 1972). The weaker sector of the industrial bourgeoisie was comprised mainly of non-Bengalis. There is no evidence, at least known to the author, of the existence of an East Bengali Muslim industrial house in Calcutta.

2. In 1950, out of a total of 2,237 large estates in East Bengal, 358 were owned by Muslims (Stepanek, 1978:95).

3. The partition of Bengal was followed by mass migration of the Hindus to India. By 1950, about two million Hindus migrated to West Bengal (Kabir, 1980).

4. By 1960 in the industrial state of Karachi there were 447 enterprises. Of these, 128 were textile mills; 101 engineering plants; 35 chemical and pharmaceutical industries; 18 oil and soap factories; 15 food processing plants; 14 plastic factors; 5 steel re-rolling mills; 8 paint and varnish factories; 10 leather and rubber industries; 5 cigarette plants. By 1959 in Hyderabad there were 25 industrial plants which included textile mills and engineering plants (UN Department of Economic and Social Affairs Report, 1961, 1962).

5. In 1971, about 66% of fixed assets in the jute manufacturing industry in East Pakistan was owned by the West Pakistani bourgeoisie (Ahamed, 1974).

6. "Over 14 years, from 1948 to 1961, East Pakistan's total balance of trade surplus was about 1,500 million rupees, a capital outflow which, together with foreign capital of about 3,900 million rupees, financed West Pakistan's cumulative deficit of 5,400 million rupees. In addition, East Pakistan had a deficit of about 3,500 million with West. If we assume that on the average Pakistan products are priced 40 percent above their equivalents in world markets, there is implied an additional transfer from East to West of about 1,000 million rupees. This gives a total transfer of about 2,500 million rupees for 14 years, or about 180 million rupees per year" (Power, 1969:19).

References

Abdullah, A.
1976   "Land reform and agrarian change in Bangladesh." The Bangladesh Development Studies 4, 1: 67–115

Abdullah, A. et al.
1976   "Agrarian structure and the IRDP-preliminary considerations." The Bangladesh Development Studies 4, 2: 209–266

Ahamed, Q. K.
1974   "Aspects of the management of nationalized industries in Bangladesh." The Bangladesh Development Studies 2, 3: 675–702.

Alamgir, M.
1978   Bangladesh-A Case of Below Poverty Level Equilibrium Trap. Dacca: Bangladesh Institute of Development Studies.

Alavi, H.
1976   "The rural elite and agricultural development in Pakistan." In Robert D. Stevens, Hamza Alavi, and Peter J. Bertocci (eds.) Rural Development in Bangladesh and Pakistan. Honolulu: University Press of Hawaii.

Bagchi, A. K.
1972   Private Investment in India 1900–1939. London: Cambridge University Press.

Beauchamp, J.
1934   British Imperialism in India. London.

Brecher, I. and S. A. Abbas
1972   Foreign Aid and Industrial Development in Pakistan. Cambridge: University Press.

Broomfield, J. H.
1968   Elite Conflict in a Plural Society: Twentieth Century Bengal. Berkeley: University of California Press.

Bhuiyan, M.
1978   Society and Economy of Bangladesh—Semi-Feudalism? Capitalist Underdevelopment? Dacca: Dhanshiri Prakashani.

Burki, S. J.
1976   "The development of Pakistan's agriculture: an interdisciplinary explanation." In

Robert D. Stevens, Hamza Alavi, and Peter J. Bertocci (eds.) Rural Development in Bangladesh and Pakistan. Honolulu: The University Press of Hawaii.

Cronin, R. P.

1975   "The government of Eastern Bengal and Assam and 'Class Rule' in Eastern Bengal, 1905–1912." In John R. Mclane (ed.) Bengal in The Nineteenth and Twentieth Centuries. East Lansing: Asian Studies Center, Michigan State University.

Desai, A. R.

1969   Rural Sociology of India. Bombay: Popular Prakashan.

Dobb, M.

1970   Studies in the Development of Capitalism. New York: International Publishers.

Dutt, R. C.

1950   The Economic History of India, Vol. I, II. London: Routledge & Kegan Paul.

Dutt, R. P.

1943   The Problem of India. New York: International Publishers.

ECAFE Report

1951   Mobilization of Domestic capital in certain countries of Asia and the Far East. Bangkok: Department of Economic Affairs.

Gadgil, D. R.

1971   The Industrial Evolution of India in Recent Times 1860–1939. Bombay: Oxford University Press.

Gwatkin, H. M. et al. (eds.)

1922   The Cambridge Medieval History, Vol. III New York: Macmillan.

Habib, I.

1963   The Agrarian System of Mughal India. London: Asia Publishing House.

Habib, I.

1969   "Potentialities of capitalist development in the economy of Mughal India." Journal of Economic History 29, 1: 32–78.

Hartmann, B. and J. Bouce

1979   Needless Hunger: Voices from a Bangladesh Village. Institute For Food and Development Policy, California.

International Labor Review

1948   "Industrial policy in Pakistan—government statement of April 1948." LVIII (July–Dec.). (Geneva)

1954   "Development planning in Pakistan." LXIX (Jan.–June). (Geneva)

Islam, S.

1972   "Changes in land control in Bengal under the early operation of the permanent settlement." Asiatic Society of Bangladesh 17, 3: 19–34.

Jahangir, B. K.

1977   Origin and the Development of Capitalism in Bangladesh. Dacca: Sahitta Sangsad. (Bengali)

Karim, A.

1964   Dacca—The Mughal Capital. Dacca: Asiatic Society of Pakistan.

Maddison, A.

1971   Class Structure and Economic Growth. London: George Allen & Unwin.

Marx, K. and F. Engels

1972   On Colonialism. New York: International Publishers.

1977   The German Ideology (C. J. Arthur, ed.). New York: International Publishers.

Mukherjee, R.

1957   The Dynamics of a Rural Society. Berlin: Akademic-Verlag.

1958   The Rise and Fall of the East India Company. Berlin.

McCully, B. T.
1940 English Education and the Origins of Indian Nationalism. New York: Columbia University Press.

Misra, B. B.
1961 The Indian Middle Class: Their Growth in Modern Times 1860–1939. London: Oxford University Press.

Nations, R.
1971 "The economic structure of Pakistan: class and colony." New Left Review, pp. 3–26.

Omar, B.
1967 The Crisis of Culture. Dacca: Granthana. (Bengali)

Power, J. H.
1969 "Industrialization in Pakistan: a case of frustrated take-off?" In A. R. Khan (ed.) Studies on the Strategy and Technique of Development Planning. Karachi: Din Muhammad Press.

Papanek, H.
1969 "Entreprenuers in East Pakistan." In Bengal Change and Continuity. South Asia Series Occasional Paper No. 16.

Pirzada, S. H. (ed.)
1969 Foundations of Pakistan: All India Muslim League Document 1906–1947. Karachi: National Publishing House.

Palit, C.
1975 Tension in Bengal Rural Society. Calcutta: Progress Publishers.

Rahman, A.
1974 The Development of Capitalism in Bangladesh Agriculture. Dacca.

Raychaudhury, T.
1969 Bengal Under Akbar and Jahangir. Delhi: Munshiram Manoharlal.

Tepper, E. L.
1976 "The administration of rural reforms: structural constraints and political dilemmas." In Robert D. Stevens et al. (eds.) Rural Development in Bangladesh and Pakistan. Honolulu: The University of Hawaii Press.

Robinson, E. A. G. and K. Griffin (eds.)
1974 The Economic Development of Bangladesh within a Socialist Framwork. New York: John Hiley.

Rajat, R. and R. Ratna
1973 "The dynamics of continuity in rural Bengal under the British imperialism: a study of quasi-stable equilibrium in underdeveloped societies in a changing world." Indian Economic and Social history Review 10, 2: 103–128.

Shahidullah, M.
1977 Modernization Versus Dependency in the context of Colonial Bengal. M. A. thesis, McMaster University.

Sobhan
1968 Basic Democracies, works Program and Rural Development in East Pakistan. Dacca: Bureau of Economics, Dacca University.

United Nations Department of Economic and Social Affairs Report
1961 Establishment of Industrial Estates in Underdeveloped Countries. New York: United Nations.

United Nations Department of Economic and Social Affairs Report
1962 Industrial Estates in Asia and the Far East. New York: United Nations.

Westergaard, K.
1978 "Mode of production in Bangladesh." Journal of Social Studies No. 2: 1–26.

Part Two: Class and State

Dale L. Johnson: The State as an Expression of Class Relations

In conventional political thinking the democratic state is thought to correspond organically to capitalism and the "totalitarian" state to socialism. Authoritarian states in capitalist societies are posed as anomalies. Thus, the classic fascist states of Italy, Germany, Spain, and Japan were seen as aberrations, particular regimes that emerged out of the crises of post World War I turmoil and the Great Depression. Modern political doctrine ("modernization theory") explains that the various dictatorships of the Third World are products of the *lack of* capitalist development and the social and political modernization that are presumed to be associated with development. The contrast between the assertions of conventional political theory and prevailing realities are stark: The great majority of capitalist societies are governed by dictatorship and as capitalist development proceeds in Asia, Africa, and Latin America the incidences of military rule abound.

Marxist analysts also have difficulty in adjusting to the rapidity and rudeness of changing forms of the state. By the 1970s most of the democracies of Latin America had collapsed. Yet a substantial Marxist literature continued to invoke assumptions of dictatorships as "exceptional forms of the state." Titles like *Fuerzas armadas y Estados de excepción en América Latina* (Carranza, 1976) attracted no particular attention in spite of the apparent normality of "Estados de excepción." The reality is that the form of the dependent type of capitalist state is characteristically one variety or another of dictatorship. Especially in the present phase of world capitalist development, dictatorship is not the exception, but the rule. Moreover, while Marxist classics in class analysis offer some general methodological guidelines for an historically grounded dialectics of class and the state, few if any of the constellations of class power undergirding authoritarian forms of dependent states bear any resemblance to the specific balance of class forces Marx analyzed in the Bonapartist regime or Engels in his study of Bismarck. Nor is there within the range of dictatorships in peripheral nations a state that seems to represent the "catastrophic equilibrium" of stalemated hegemony of which Gramsci wrote (although Argentina has been written about in this way by Juan Portantiero, 1974).

This chapter examines the forms of capitalist states, arguing that democracy, always a precarious achievement of popular struggles, is being eclipsed today on a world-scale by new types of dictatorships. Currents within the Marxist theory of the state are critically examined and a theoretical view of the state as "an institutional expression of class relations" is distilled from the literature. A case study, the Chilean military regime, provides a basis for understanding new authoritarian state forms in terms of the dialectic between localized class relations and internationalized structural forces.

Democracy and Dictatorship

There is much nonsense about dictatorship and even more about democracy. To begin, I formulate some very basic points. In these matters what may seem cynicism is simply political realism. As Atilio Borón notes:

> We are confronted, then, with a paradox that has given rise to no little confusion; the development of capitalism rests upon persistent violation of the institutional structure and political ideology which are held to be the most authentic product of the "genius" of capitalism. The stunning realization that economic liberalism requires and generates political despotism shattered the optimistic expectations of the fifties and early sixties [1981:45].

But we do not have to look to the Third World today for the association between economic freedom and political tyranny. Democratic forms of the state emerged out of the several centuries of social struggles in the development of Western capitalism. Democratic freedoms, universal rights, and liberal forms of political rule were first of all historical conquest of emerging European merchants and industrialists in their struggles for class supremacy against aristocracies and to modernize the old order. Once these classes established their political rule, grudging room was made for wider democratic forms. (Or more accurately, as their economic dominance was prudently given political recognition by monarchs and aristocrats in government office, the gates for broader democratic pressures were opened.) The *content* given these forms (mainly achieved in the twentieth century) represent social gains of peoples' struggles against the masters of their fate. Capitalists are not the authors of democratic rights and freedoms. Peasants, workers, and others denied democratic rights struggled for them. To this day it seems fairly evident that, given their preferences, businessmen would much rather run the entire society on the model of the modern corporation; that is, according to a system of hierarchical authority in which each person has a more or less fixed place and specialized role. And, were rulers allowed unconstrained rule, these fixed places would be much more governed by ascriptive standards of class origin, nationality, race, and sex than by universalistic criteria of achievement. Fortunately, the social struggles of peoples suffering diverse forms of class, national, racial, and sexual oppression have so far prevented advanced capitalism from degenerating into a modern-day feudalism in which corporate giants divide the land and serfs among themselves.

The democratic and social gains of historical struggles in Western democracies are constantly threatened. Only the weight of history and continuing struggle preserve them. The logic of the political rule of an economically dominant class in any established capitalist society, whether industrial or dependent and underdeveloped is not democracy, but some form of authoritarianism. This seems to me rather elementary, but many people still share the ideological notion that democracy and capitalism go together like bread and butter or sausage and sauerkraut. Just the opposite.

Of course, no class may easily impose its preferences for order, fixed hierarchy, and unchallenged supremacy. As dominant classes, bourgeoisies are accustomed to accomodate themselves to imperfect conditions. They simply try to administer—in particular through the medium of the state—a society of competition and conflict in which there are all manner of structural and oppositional constraints on their power. The bourgeoisies of Europe and North America have come to accept the need to work within the constraints the historic achievement of the democratic state represents—at least this seems the case under "normal" circumstances.

Under normal circumstances, democracy has, from the perspective of dominant classes, certain advantages. Democracy allows classes and groups in conflict to articulate their interests and political parties to aggregate them (to use the political science jargon). This provides information about the consciousness and movement of social forces, institutional channels for social struggle, and a higher level of legitimacy for the system. The economically dominant class and managers of the state can gain better perspectives on the nature and extent of constraints, on the correlation of social forces, and on possible courses of action. Democracy provides a more efficient framework for the ideological apparatus to function and problems of legitimacy are less acute when force and repression are less direct, extensive, and brutal. The system makes non-arbitrary and peaceful resolution of conflicts of interests among contending fractions of the dominant class possible. But if democracy has all these advantages, why are there only a small and dwindling number of democratic states in the world today?

Even in Europe and North America, the democratic state is a fragile institution. Here a broad statement can be made that has relevance beyond the democracies of the center countries: The continuation of democratic forms of the state assumes strong and confident national business classes, manageable crises, and a level of struggle by workers and other change forces sufficient to keep the authoritarian predispositions of the dominant class in check, but not so strong a level of class struggle as to threaten the prevailing order. These conditions have generally prevailed in the Western advanced capitalist countries since World War II. But this points to another generalization about the norm of political rule: Stable political democracy represents a mild and constrained, but effective form of class dictatorship. Under capitalism, political democracy comes at the price of a lack of social advance toward a new society. And when, with democratic freedoms, the relatively favorable conditions for political expression threaten social advances beyond prevailing institutional limits, dictatorship looms.

With these elementary generalizations in mind, we can begin to specify some of the broad historical conditions that make dictatorship, rather than democracy, the characteristic form of the state in peripheral countries. Of particular salience are the following conditions: Local business classes are weak, faction-ridden, and structurally subordinated to international capital; what I term "transitional" or "organic" crises that cannot be managed; and class struggles that cannot be contained within the limits of the existing order, threatening a transition to socialism.

Where Latin American, Asian, and African constitutional regimes do remain in power, there is not much substance to democratic forms. Weak political parties, fragile constitutions, fraudulent elections, and the absence or non-functioning of the attributes of democratic systems are not due, as the conventional view posits, to a lack of the social and political "modernization" that will come with the development that presumably flows from the full integration of dependent nations into the international economic order. On the contrary, the most "modern" form of political rule in the dependent periphery is a new form of military dictatorship, a new fascism that shows a different face than the European variety, but one that may be even more threatening to civilization.

These dictatorships are structurally rooted in the historical legacies of underdevelopment and dependent development and the present day articulations of local capitalisms with the international system. Politically at national levels, these new barbarisms are reflections of dependent, weak, vacillating and desperate local dominant classes and their inability to institutionalize and broaden political rule in the face of crises of various dimensions, profound social antagonisms, and lack of ideological hegemony.

These dictatorships are "modern" not only in the sophisticated management of repression. They bear little resemblance to the traditional authoritarian forms of the state of, say, the Somoza dynasty of Nicaragua, or the mythical rule of the patriarch in Gabriel Garcia Marquez's fascinating novel, *The Autumn of the Patriarch* (1977). The dictatorships of countries like Brazil, Chile, Argentina, Uruguay, and to a certain degree the Philippines, Indonesia, pre-1979 Iran, Pakistan and South Korea are sophisticated projects of hegemony. These projects involve: (1) explicit class alliances between international and local capitals; (2) the reconstitution of alliances of forces and power blocs on a national scale; (3) the implementation of development strategies consistent with changing forms of international dependence and with shifts in power and economic potential within the local dominant class; (4) the emergence of new ideological forms of domination, especially the doctrines of "national security" and "economic liberalism;" and (5) the restructuring of the state as an efficient institution of capital accumulation and repression of oppositional forces. These several dimensions of the hegemonic projects can be referred to in summary fashion as the "national security state."

I will shortly outline the main features of one such state, the Chilean. The following two chapters examine the forces that produce national security states in greater depth. It is first necessary to clarify elements of a theory of the capitalist state.

Elements of a Theory of the State

In spite of more than a decade of critical intellectual challenge,[1] conventional political theory remains as bogged down as it ever has been in mystifications and apologetics for the slick forms of political oppression in the advanced capitalist countries and the ever grosser forms in the dependent and underdeveloped countries. My colleagues at Rutgers University, Martin Oppenheimer and Jane Canning (1979), refer to the "clean form" of the "national security state" emerging in countries like West Germany and the United States and the "dirty form" in Latin America and Asia. There have been, however, some advances on the other side of the ideological divide, in the Marxist theory of the state. Recent work tries to avoid the oversimplifications of classical Marxism and transcend the purely critical ideological discourse that characterized Marxist writing on the state from the late 1960s to the mid-1970s.

The sharp debates over the theory of the state in recent literature have been organized around the "instrumentalist" and "structuralist" views on the state (or "influence" and "constraint" theories; see Offe, 1972). Other perspectives include the "Hegelian Marxist" and "state derivation theory." This literature variously and selectively draws upon the classic insights of Marx's conception of the capitalist state as "a committee for managing the common affairs of the whole bourgeoisie," his analysis of Bonapartism as "the religion of the bourgeoisie," Engels' insistence on the "relative autonomy" of the state, Lenin's views in *State and Revolution,* and Gramsci's concept of "hegemony."

While these divergent ideas have advanced thinking on the capitalist state considerably, the posing of many of the arguments in the often polemical terms of combative camps within Marxism has, I think, also served to confuse issues and, especially, to divert attention to ever higher levels of abstraction—with a consequent deemphasis on studies of concrete forms of the state and what might be general to them. Deductive reasoning is substituted for historical/empirical study. An inductive dimension to the construction of a theory of the state is sorely needed.

Since the terms of the debate have been by now so widely disseminated it would be superfluous to restate them. Instead, I focus on what can be distilled from the literature concerning the capitalist state that will be most useful in an analysis of authoritarian forms in peripheral societies.[2] In this respect, the first thing to note is that the literature, while posing questions of the capitalist state in general, is in actuality predominantly concerned with the democratic form (and authoritarian content) of the state in advanced capitalist countries. The book that initiated the great debate, Ralph Miliband's *The State in Capitalist Society* (1969), is in fact subtitled *An Analysis of the Western System of Power*. A theory of the state demands attention to the variety of state forms on a world scale.

Miliband's book represented the culmination of the debunking of pluralist theory of conventional political thought and the construction of an elementary Marxist theory of class, power, and the state, but one entirely based on and largely applicable to advanced capitalist democracies. Miliband extended his very substantial contribution in a later book (1977). In spite of the thunderous criticisms made of Miliband's "instrumentalism," there seems little to quarrel with in his essential posture: Control of the means of production and monopolization of economic power gives the capitalist class decisive political power over, above, and within the state. In Western democracies, the dominant interests organize influential policy-forming groups (e.g., the Trilateral Commission); representatives from the class often serve within governments in top positions; and different sectoral interests exercise strong pressure on any and all state apparatuses to act in terms of their interests. This is, quite simply, an empirical reality, confirmed and reconfirmed in numerous studies of "power structure" and by everyday observation. It is also undeniable that the approach has generated, with all its limitations (Mollenhopf, 1975, sums these limitations), an enormous body of worthwhile studies of structures of power and decision-making (in the United States led by William Domhoff, 1967, 1979, 1980).

The instrumental view, until recently widely held by persons within the British and North American context, surely has made a worthy contribution by debunking mainstream pluralist ideology, by accurately pointing to the class nature of the state, and by revealing the mechanisms of the exercise of political power. It is also rather simplistic. Nicos Poulantzas (1973, 1978), Offe (1972), Gold, Lo, and Wright (1975), Block (1977), the German state derivation theorists (Holloway and Picciotto, 1978), and others have correctly pointed to the limitations of an approach which largely confines itself to showing the correspondence between the formation of government policy, the content of state activities, and the interests of the ruling class. This conception is especially deficient when viewing instances within the Third World where local bourgeoisies often are quite divided and weak and where a sizeable proportion of the economy is controlled by foreign capital and national governments. Military juntas cannot be seen simply as instruments of a local bourgeoisie, nor of transnational capital. While in South American instances a reasonable case can be made that military regimes function as the political directorate of a coalition of local finance and industrial capital and transnational capital, in some African and Asian nations one can hardly locate an identifiable local bourgeoisie—but nonetheless clearly ascendent is a mature capitalist state. This state is firmly enmeshed in dependency relations within the international system and its policies eventually nurture an incipient local capitalist class. The chapter on Bangladesh and Ahmad's study in this volume document these generalizations.

Apart from the relative strength and weakness of the bourgeoisie, in general there are two fundamental factors that limit the degree to which an economically dominant social class, or particular constellations of interests within that class, can utilize the state instrumentally in pursuit of particular ends or a broad hegemony. One is the complex of constraints placed upon state activity by economic exigency, by structurally given boundaries, by an inevitable competition of capitals, and, periodically, by crisis. The other factor is the combative strength of the constellation of social forces in opposition.

The "structuralist" view of the state emphasizes the constraints, boundaries, and system-rooted instabilities of class political rule. Later I will argue that structuralists do not deal dynamically with class relations; but they are correct in beginning an analysis at the structural level. Poulantzas (1969, 1973, 1974, 1978) has addressed the question of the capitalist state more extensively than any other Marxist. His work has become synonomous with the structuralist concept of the state. This approach first of all rejects those instrumentalist, subjectivist,[3] or other currents within Marxism that consider the state either as a subject or as a thing. The state is not, according to Poulantzas, an entity separate from society, standing above it, and embodying an intrinsic rationality expressing the general will. He insists that the state is not a tool that can be manipulated at will by a ruling class, but an institution that holds a "relative autonomy" from class interests.

In the Poulantzian view, the state is the "factor of unity in a social formation." There are two fundamental postulates in Poulantzas's structuralist view of the state. The first is that the state embodies a broad social function: to preserve the social cohesion by seeing to the reproduction of the social formation. To accomplish this function the state must possess a "relative autonomy" from specific class interests. The second postulate, more clearly stated in his later writings, is that the state is a social relation, in a similar sense in which capital is a social relation. The relations between classes are "condensed" within the state; the state, by its nature as a class state, reproduces within itself the contradictions of class.

These are ideas of some complexity and his earlier theoretical elaborations have been severely criticized for being excessively abstract, pedantic or tendentious, static and ahistorical, to mention just the main deficiencies (Miliband, 1969, 1973; Laclau 1977; and many others). The theoretical problems with Marxist structuralism in general have been amply discussed elsewhere (Johnson, 1982). Poulantzas's conception of the state particularly suffers from its origins in Althusserian regional theory. Here I would agree with what I understand to be the main contribution of a variant of structuralist thinking, state derivation theory: "The political" is not a distinct region or specific and autonomous object of Marxist science. Rather, political phenomena must be seen in terms of the capital accumulation process and the varying forms of class relations that underly and respond to that process.

A considerable body of literature developed in the 1970s in the Federal Republic of Germany surrounding the problem of the state. Particularly noteworthy is the work of Claus Offe (1976; Offe and Range, 1975) and writing on the "derivation of the state" *(Staatsableitung)*. (Readily available in English are Holloway and Picciotto, 1978, and von Beyme, 1976.) Reacting against both instrumentalist conceptions of the state/ruling class nexus and the idea of the autonomy (in conventional theory) and relative autonomy of the state (in competing Marxist conceptions like those of Poulantzas, as well as the political theory of Habermas and Offe), the "derivationists" have attempted to abstract systematically the diverse functions of the state from the principles of capital accumulation and the contradictions of capitalism. Thus, for example, the repressive apparatus of the state derives from the social relations of exploitation, which require "that relations of force should be abstracted from the immediate process of production and located in an instance standing apart . . . thus constituting discrete 'political' and 'economic' spheres" (Holloway and Picciotto, 1978:24). Similarly, the rule of law does not derive from the activities of legislatures, laws only codify the norms of property and commodity relations prevailing in society.

In general, state derivation theory is more consistent with a traditional Marxist conception of base and superstructure than is Althusserian regional theory or the political theory of Habermas (1975) and Offe (1976). The structure and function of the state are logically derived from the logic of the system. Joachim Hirsch has stated this in its most extreme (non-Althusserian) structuralist form,

the basic social relations are always the historical product of objective laws which assert themselves through the actions of individuals. These laws have a determining effect for as long as the essential structural features of the capitalist form of society remain intact. This means that concrete social structures, the mutual relation of classes and the dominant form of the division of labor are essentially incapable of being subjected to conscious, planned—in this sense political—influence and transformation. The basic structures and laws of development of bourgeois societies are not capable of being 'regulated' politically. The conscious organization of social relations would require the abolition of the capital relation.

If, therefore, we assume that bourgeois society necessarily reproduces its structurally determining characteristics through the operation of objective laws which assert themselves behind the backs of individuals, then the social conditions for the constitution of the form of the bourgeois state can now be more clearly defined by logical derivation [in Holloway and Picciotto, 1978:61].

Hirsch, however, goes on to argue (with a considerable leap in his own logic) that the derivation of form (by which he means structure and function) necessarily requires, always within a general theory of capital accumulation and crisis, "an analysis of the concrete historical development of the capitalist reproduction process and of the changing conditions of capital valorization and class relations" (Holloway and Picciotto, 1978:66).

In my judgment, there is at best a considerable inconsistency between the statements of general theory, often restatements of Marx's "original principles" (such as the falling rate of profit tendency, Johnson, 1982) and the study of concrete historical development. Hirsch's concluding statement presents a superior guideline to his more abstract formulations of structural determinism:

A real materialist theory of the bourgeois state presupposes a discriminating and empirically substantial analysis not only of the process of accumulation and development of capital and of the movements of competition, but also of the concretely developing class structures and their changes. We must clarify—also empirically—what classes and class fractions—individual monopolies and monopoly groups, the different parts of the middle bourgeoisie, the "new" and "old" middle classes and the divisions of the proletariat—stand in which relations to the various parts of the state apparatus. In other words: *the class character of the state must be worked out in historical concreteness* [Holloway and Picciotto, 1978:107].

State derivation theory seems to reflect a problematic of advanced monopoly (or "late") capitalism, as well perhaps as a certain Germanic intellectual heritage: the problematic of the forms of legitimation and political domination. The historical and concrete grounding of the problematic of domination changes radically in the case of the Third World. While Habermas, Offe, and the derivationists offer penetrating insights into the political and cultural order of "late" capitalism, all seem to suffer from a certain formalism. It is very difficult to reconcile a predominant concern with the functions of the state, or with the conditions of social reproduction, or with cultural domination, with an historically grounded dialectic of capital accumulation, crisis, and class relations on the periphery. This is especially so in relation to authoritarian forms of dependent states, the most recent manifestations of which are qualitatively new developments in the history of international development. Theorizing about the functions of the state and the ideological forms of domination seem to settle into the background in a Chilean or Argentine context.

This much at least can be distilled from the different structuralist perspectives: The state is not a "thing," nor a simple instrument of a ruling class; nor is it a neutral entity above the classes. *The state is an institutional expression of class relations.* Goran Therborn, who takes a non-Althusserian structuralist viewpoint, states:

> What then does the ruling class do when it rules? Essentially, it ensures that its dominant positions in the economy, state apparatus and ideological superstructures are reproduced by the state in relation both to the other modes of production present within the social formation and to the international system of social formations. These reproductive state interventions are enmeshed in the structural dynamics of the mode of reproduction, but they also have to be secured in the thick of the class struggle [1978:242].

The placement of "class struggle" in the context of structural factors and movement is necessary to an adequate theory of the state.

If the state is seen in terms of class relations as well as structures and functions, there is also something to be said for the structuralists' insistence that the essentials of the state transcend whatever regimes succeed to power and whatever forms of authoritarianism or democracy are assumed by the state. The capitalist state evidences a set of generalized functions common to the many different forms. Despite great variations in conjunctional constraints, it is implied, the state does what it has to do no matter what government is in power, because the system of capitalism has its own logic and its own contradictions which must be addressed. State activities are hemmed in by structural constraints.

At a quite abstract level, the structuralists are probably right in that the state does what it has to do in terms of the logic of the system. But does not this just arrive full circle back at the generality of Marx's traditional dictum, the state as "the executive committee of the whole bourgeoisie," that initiated the whole structuralist critique of instrumentalism? Surely, and this is where structural determinism falls down by not rooting it in class analysis, what has to be done is subject to a range of political choices as to the manner of doing it. At the extreme this can mean a political outcome of fascist dictatorship or of democratic reform. The direction of choice is not just determined by the explicit basis of the structural constraints, but by the history, level, and direction of class and diverse forms of social struggle which come into play. Political outcomes occur within a conjunctural field of social struggle and constellations of social forces. While specific conjunctures are shaped by structural forces and longer-term historical trends in the development of capitalism, actual political outcomes are decided by the play of social forces. This understanding of the dialectics of structural determinism and class struggle was captured in some of the Marxist classics (e.g., *The Eighteenth Brumaire*)—but is little in evidence today. Thus, while the structuralists have succeeded in conceptualizing the state as an institutional expression of class relations, they have not been able, in their captivation with structure and function, to build upon this insightful conceptualization.

In spite of this insight and the many contributions of structural approaches to the state, there are still other limitations that go beyond the lack of a class dynamic. In keeping with the theoretical critique of a previous volume in this book series (Johnson, 1982), these perspectives, whether Poulantzian or state derivationist, to one or another degree, are variations on a "left-wing functionalism." Functional notions of change and development are always evolutionary, rather than dialectical or concretely historical. The functions performed by states and the structures constructed to facilitate these functions are not, as any form of evolutionary functionalism seems to imply, products of linear evolution that respond to functional necessities for "rational" forms of social organization, "laws of motion," or any other force abstracted from history by great thinkers—or by modern-day Marxists who attempt to integrate Marx's analysis of capital with the rationalism of Hegel or Weber and the functionalism of Parsons. To be sure, states must respond to events within the structural limits and constraints determined within a mode of production in transformation. In this sense, some functions are general to the capitalist state and predetermined by the movement of the mode of production. But there is nothing linearly evolutionary in this process, as transformations in the mode of production proceed unevenly, with rapid leaps, periods of stagnation, and in contradictory directions, as well as in response to the political interference, rooted in social struggle, that can retard or accelerate the process. Historically, the state expressing the class of struggles of society, has been the chief vehicle for political intervention in the economic process. And the structure, function, form, and activities of states are fundamentally products of the movement of social forces that emerge in dialectical interrelation with the economic process.

State and Class

We have then the following, very generalized, substantive conclusions about the nature of states in capitalist societies. Democracy is the exceptional form of the state and democratic forms are mainly historical achievements, constantly threatened, of people's struggles. Democracy assumes a dominant class that can manage periodic crises and contain the struggles of dominated classes with limited force. The legacy of colonialism and imperialism and continuing situations of dependency engender weak dominant classes, deep crises, sharp social struggles, and dictatorship in Asia, Africa, and Latin America. The most ferocious dictatorships are located in the most developed of the underdeveloped countries.

Theoretically, instrumentalist, structuralist, and derivationist theories of the state, while separately deficient in key respects, do offer certain conceptually necessary elements for analyses of states in capitalist societies. I have tried to distill these elements in the proposition that "the state is an institutional expression of class relations." As a guide to research, this proposition requires a proper appreciation of the dialectic of structural determinisms and the process of class struggle. The structural logic of capitalist development provides the general context for the assumption of particular functions and forms by the state, but it is always the historical course of class struggle that actualizes and concretizes these functions and forms.

This chapter concludes with an analysis of the Chilean military dictatorship that employs this theoretical departure. The approach is further developed in the succeeding two chapters, with a study of the state forms associated with crises of transition, the structure of local bourgeoisies, the social political roles of intermediate class formations, and the struggle for hegemony by the classes and social forces that constitute the social bases of militarized states. This analysis draws upon South American experience.

Dependency, Class, and Dictatorship:
Chile

Chile's military dictatorship is a specific outcome of a localized class war. It expresses a strategic conquest by one side, but a victory that can only be assured over the years by unrelenting repression. The short years of hope on the part of Chileans and millions everywhere incited by the democratic and socialist vision of the Popular Unity government (1970–1973), followed by the long years of misery under the heeled boot of reaction, are the human realities of this class war. The war is being fought by Chileans on Chilean terrain, but it has been highly structured by the historical legacy of externally conditioned dependency and underdevelopment and it is situated within a phase of international development today being generalized on a world scale.

The Chilean drama aroused great international interest and expectation, followed by dismay. Perhaps no historical experience has been so thoroughly analyzed as the events of 1970–1973 in this remote corner of the world (see my review essay on books in English, Johnson, 1982b). In interpreting these events, some authors attribute primary causality to the actions of the United States and transnational corporations against the Popular Unity government. The great majority of analysts, however, concern themselves primarily with Chilean internal forces and events. Scores of books and hundreds of articles give primacy to domestic politics. Indeed political factors unique to the Chilean situation are overwhelmingly present. These added up to a favorable conjuncture for socialism and democracy, fought for the peaceful way.

Under the Presidency of Eduardo Frei (1964–1970) the Christian Democratic "Revolución en Libertad" had disintegrated. Yet the idea of real social reform as an answer to the problems of injustice, poverty, and underdevelopment was widely generalized and legitimated. While the level of class struggle had sharply accelerated throughout the 1950s and 1960s, it did so without severely straining the nation's unique democratic political institutionality. The long-standing militance of the Chilean working class achieved new levels, strengthening the Communist and Socialist parties; and to this was added the increased pressures of peasants and farm laborers, unorganized workers, and slum-dwellers, all emergent social forces often guided by new political groupings to the left of the Communists and the moderate faction of the Socialist Party. The Chilean dominant class and its political representation on the traditional Right were placed squarely on the defensive. By 1970 the logic of the political moment greatly favored the "Chilean Road to Socialism."

Similarly, political factors are salient in the 1970–1973 period of the Popular Unity. The substantial literature almost entirely revolves around the "lessons of Chile." The "lessons" drawn are primarily political and often flow rather directly from the ideological stance of the analyst. Among those hostile to the military regime there are three main positions.

One interpretation faults the Popular Unity for its failure to compromise with the opposition forces, its wrongheaded economic policies, its failure to control the revolutionary left and to contain popular mobilization, adminis-trative ineptitude, and other strategic and tactical errors (see especially Tomic, 1979; Sigmund, 1977; and Alexander, 1978). This critique has two problems. First it blames the victim. It was the opposition, not the Popular Unity, that failed to compromise and the opposition that bears the responsi-bility for bringing down terror upon the nation. Second, it attempts to negate the important (but not determinative) role of transnational corporations and United States policy in bringing a popular and democratic government to a bloody end.

A second position is held by many persons associated with or very sympathetic to the Popular Unity and its strategy (excellent critical reflec-tions by architects of Popular Unity policies are contained in Gil, Lagos, and Landsberger, 1979). They stress inconsistencies between economic policies and political aims; the lack of programmatic agreement within the Popular Unity and the left opposition to government policies by revolutionary forces outside the governing coalition; administrative disorganization and inability to achieve a controlled process of socialist transition in the face of an instransigent and seditious opposition on the one hand and large-scale popular mobilization on the other hand; and failure to seize the political initiative in opportune moments. A range of other problems of tactics and political conduct are discussed in a substantial, critical literature (see espe-cially Boorstein, 1977).

But constructing socialism is more a question of strategy than of tactics and political choices made in the course of struggle. Left-wing critics of the Popular Unity are scornful of the entire strategy of "political-institu-tional gradualism" (Smirnow, 1981) or "historic compromise" (Palacios, 1979). Revolutions fail when strategies of class alliances are faulty. The Popular Unity sought a broad alliance of classes and social forces. Critics argue that this required policies that subverted the socialist ends of the government, placed brakes on popular mobilization, and forced accomodation with opposition forces and the military to the point that it dictated political timidity and made the government weaker and weaker. Crucial to Popular Unity strategy were the Chilean middle strata. Class analysis by strategists of the "Chilean Road" led them to envi-sion the winning over or at least neutralization of the great bulk of the petty privileged elements. A minority did move with events. By 1972, however, the great majority of the salaried middle strata and small business-men had become mobilized in a great counter-revolutionary wave of reaction.[4] While in retrospect the strategy of the "Chilean Road" can be recognized as seriously flawed, left-wing critics seem to underestimate the degree to which both strategy and tactics were highly constrained by the defined political situation, by the shifting balance of forces, and by the intelligence and capabilities of the counter-revolutionary strategists.

It is not my purpose here to evaluate these critiques (see Johnson, 1982b). The question addressed is the role of localized political factors in understanding the transformation of a democratic state to an authoritarian one. The emphasis in the vast literature on Chile on the political course of events preceding Salvador Allende's election to the Presidency and the dramatic political events of 1970–1973 all point toward the main underlying factor: Chile was experiencing a level of social struggle that by 1972 had reached proportions that could not be contained within the pre-existing limits of the nation's institutions. The extraordinary repression that followed the military intervention in September, 1973 brought the character of struggle as class war into sharp relief. A united military came down decidedly on the side of counter-revolutionary reaction: military forces attacked the Presidential Palace with rockets and guns, killing President Allende; one-sided gun battles erupted throughout the country; persons on the Left were killed by the thousands or rounded up, incarcerated, and sometimes tortured and executed; political parties of the Left were abolished and the activities of other political groups suspended; trade unions and workers' organizations were smashed; a gestapo-like secret police (DINA) was quickly institutionalized; heretofore vibrant democratic and constitutional traditions were voided. The Chilean state came to express a new, one-sided turn in class relations: a bloody and harsh dictatorship by the locally dominant class carried out by loyal military forces and supported by powerful foreign allies.

The state of the class struggle in Chile is thus the *proximate* cause of the militarized form of the country's capitalist state. In the terms theoretically explored earlier, the dramatic change in the form of the state is an expression of a qualitative change in underlying class relations. But there are *general determinants* of the proximate. Class relations are territorially situated, but they are also internationally conditioned. Few analysts of the Chilean circumstances have been able to identify adequately the general determinants and place them in dialectical interrelation with the proximate factors of localized class struggle. In less abstract language this means that the historical course of Chilean class struggle, while it carries its own internal dynamic, has been structured by the nation's long history of dependency and underdevelopment.

This history has been treated in general terms in the Chapter 1 discussion of international political economy and stages of capitalist development on the periphery. The specifics of the Chilean case can be briefly sketched. In the "stage of national development" (1930–1955) Chile had developed a considerable industrial base and internal market. An industrial bourgeoisie of some stature and its counterpart, an urban-industrial working class, were formed. The formerly powerful landowner/commercial oligarchy, a product of the prior stage of "the development of underdevelopment," was displaced from direct political power, and reformist forces, with a solid base in the middle strata and pushed by worker struggles, monopolized government office from 1938 to 1970, with only a brief conservative interlude from 1958–1964. The state became the guiding force in building a stronger national capitalism. But by the 1950s "import-substitution industrialization" had reached its limits. The conservative government of Alessandri (1958–1964) and the resurgent reformism of Christian Democracy under President Frei (1964–1970) both sought to gear Chile to a new articulation with the emerging world of transnational capital. In an attempt to stimulate growth and deepen the industrial base the Frei government, in particular, cultivated transnational capital investments in Chile. Frei did so, however, without reversing the state-interventionist, developmentalist model of state activity established during the prior decades of reform and national development. National industry continued to be protected by tariffs and there was a "Chileanization" of copper. During the 1960s more than 100 transnational corporations made sizeable investments in Chile (Johnson, 1972: chap. 1). The economy nevertheless continued to stagnate and inflation rates never fell below 25 percent. In the late 1960s there was a major recession.

The year 1970 was a conjuncture favorable to a qualitative leap in the Chilean reform process. The correlation of social forces had shifted greatly in favor of the Left and toward a deepening of the statist, developmentalist model of development. The Chilean state during 1970–1973 came to express a decided upturn in the combative strength of workers, peasants, and other oppressed groups, a shift of some sectors of the middle strata toward an alliance with these forces, and a relative decline in the power of the bourgeois class and its allies within the middle strata and petty bourgeoisie. This put enormous pressures on the country's democratic institutions and civil traditions. The bourgeois class as a whole, the petty bourgeoisie, and substantial sectors of the middle strata turned militantly to the right as the struggle unfolded. The policies of a socialist government occupying the executive of a capitalist state attempted to deal directly with the legacy of underdevelopment and dependency and the exhaustion of Chile's pre-existing mode of capital accumulation and stagnated development. The goal of the Popular Unity was to further strengthen the class power of the oppressed to effect a transition from capitalist underdevelopment to socialist development, but without shattering the pre-existing democratic institutionality. Jose Nun's assessment of the moment when Allende assumed the Presidency is apt: "A certain kind of capitalism had been exhausted and with it a certain kind of political system . . . the crisis was not unleashed by the Popular Unity. The Allende government was at once both an expression of that crisis and a bold effort to find a solution to it from the left" (1979:461).

The Popular Unity years were an intensified period of class struggle within a stagnant economy and exhausted political system—and this was the proximate cause of the military intervention. From the perspective of the class whose interests were fundamentally threatened (and its domestic and foreign allies) what was necessary was not just to smash the forces threatening real change and to completely subordinate the classes and groups exerting revolutionary pressures, but to supplant the exhausted, pre-existing forms of accumulation and development with a complete reorientation of Chilean political economy and its close integration into the latest phase of international capitalist development. In Chile (as in Argentina from 1976 and Uruguay from 1973), this meant the need to change the model of accumulation based on import-substitution manufacture, state intervention, and development of internal markets to an industrial-export system guided by principles of economic liberalism and directly tied to the internationalized economy of transnational corporations.[5] The policies to effect this complete reorientation of political economy required more than a temporary blow to the revolutionary forces; long-term suppression of democratic forms of the state are a prerequisite for a successful shift of the economic model.

The strategists within and behind the military junta see one key to development in exporting those products in which Chile has a "comparative advantage": copper, of course, but increasingly agricultural production from the nation's potentially productive Central Valley, wood and paper products from the vast forests of the South, and industrial exports in which transnational corporations will cooperate with local capital to take advantage of the cheap and controlled labor force created by repression of the working class. The great Asian success stories of South Korea and Taiwan and the dramatic increase in Brazil's industrial exports since 1968 by means of government facilitation of transnational corporate/local capital cooperation have not been lost on the Chilean junta and the local powers behind the barracks.

At the same time, the regime pursues another objective, the restructuring of national capital to eliminate "inefficient" business and to centralize and concentrate capital in the hands of big "economic groups" in a position to do business with transnational capital. This requires policies that, in practice, have not proved consistent with export promotion. Monetary and exchange rate policy drive up interest rates making banking very profitable but credit unavailable to productive enterprise, while capital is channeled into currency and other forms of speculation and imports become cheap and exports expensive. These contradictory objectives are pursued in relation to what is seen as the underlying economic imperative: a complete relinking of the Chilean to the world economy of the transnational corporation. What is constituent to this imperative is a reordering of *all* class relations in a dependent social order like that of Chile. The shift to a new mode of political economy, restructures the capitalist class itself, eliminating any possibility of a "national bourgeoisie" linked to local markets and to an interventionist state. Moreover, it requires the purging of the salaried middle strata and the petty bourgeoisie from the power block that was, of necessity, mobilized to destroy the old system. Policies adversely effecting their interests are pursued. The profound changes in class relations and the policies needed to effect the transition to a new political economy are simply incompatible with even limited forms of democratic rule. And the Chilean military plans an indefinite tenure.

The internationally conditioned and locally rooted economic imperative and its constituent class dynamics, in a word the "relations of dependency" as they shape and articulate with a dependent economy and local class struggles, are the ultimate (as distinct from the proximate) source of the abortion of the Chilean road to socialism.

This is not at all to lay aside the earlier emphasis on intensified class struggle, to resort to external causation of Chilean events, or to conspiratorial explanation. One can even agree with Sigmund (who entirely rejects dependency analysis) that the "invisible blockade," CIA covert activities, and other U.S. interventions "exacerbated and intensified an already desperate situation." But these were "not a central factor in the destruction of Chilean constitutionalism" (1977). What Sigmund entirely ignores, and what many of the other authors downgrade, is the degree to which Chilean political economy and class structure is an historical product of the nation's relations with international capitalism. Since this history is general to the region, this is why militarized states are not the exception, but the rule in Latin America.

A capsule history of the first years of the Chilean dictatorship should serve to document the main "lesson" of Chile: Dictatorship proximately located in intensified national class struggles, is structurally rooted in the articulation of a dependent economy and local class relations with international political economy.

The first year of the dictatorship was one of the restoration of the challenged hegemony of the bourgeois class as a whole. The forces of the Popular Unity were smashed; agrarian and industrial properties intervened or seized by workers were returned to private ownership; sympathizers of the Left were purged from the state bureaucracy and the educational system and replaced by military officers or civilians of acceptable ideological stance. Government economic policies did not excessively castigate any sector of the dominant class. The Armed Forces played the role of political representative of the bourgeoisie as a whole.

Having consolidated power, however, the regime soon began to move away from the kinds of policies that implied a project to establish a shared hegemony of all the fractions of the bourgeoisie and a pay-off to small businessmen and middle strata supporters of the counter-revolutionary project. The petty bourgeoisie and middle strata were first demobilized an then purged altogether from the class alliance that brought the regime to power.

Already by the end of 1974 prominent civilian and military architects of the military intervention began to react as strongly as circumstances permited to the direction taken by the junta. Orlando Saenz, President of the principal industrial trade association during the Allende government, grumbled and lobbied, while overtly fascist elements (I use the term in the strict European sense) within the petty bourgeoisie began to agitate. Officers representing political alternatives within the Armed Forces that offered a broader conception of the social base of the regime began to be retired or shuffled out of the way. Oscar Bonilla, a General with close ties to the Christian Democrats, was conveniently killed in a helicopter crash. General Torres de la Cruz and other genuinely fascist officers who proposed a political system of continual mobilization of the small business and middle class allies of the regime were purged. By the end of 1975, General Pinochet moved against a group of Army officers and a key Admiral that had presented a critical petition. The purging of the Armed Forces of elements not willing to fall strictly into line behind the project as given expression by President Pinochet reached its culmination in 1978 with the removal of the Air Force representative on the junta, General Leigh, and the forced retirement of a large number of Air Force officers backing him. Meanwhile, Pinochet's famed DINA (intelligence service) sent agents to Buenos Aires to assassinate the exiled constitutionalist General Carlos Prats. Civilian cabinet ministers came and went. The first "Super-minister" of Economy, Raúl Saez, opposed the "shock treatment" economic policy in formation for 1975 and lost his influence.

Chile's "shock treatment" began with Pinochet's investment of special powers in the hands of a civilian, Jorge Cauas, Minister of Finance. The shock treatment was publically presented as necessary to break runaway inflation by sharply restricting government spending, by removing price controls and letting the market find equilibrium, by restricting credit, by reducing real incomes of the waged workers and salaried employees, and by a series of other drastic measures. The Cauas Plan only modestly succeeded in reducing inflation, which finally became more or less controlled in 1979. But controlling inflation was only a secondary end of the shock treatment.

The economic policies of the Pinochet regime from April, 1975 were calculated to completely restructure the economy and to provide a long-term basis for a more stable social and political order that was to be organized under the hegemony of a particular fraction of the dominant class, the financial/industrial oligarchy, a series of economic groups in close alignment with transnational capital. The Cauas Plan succeeded in achieving a substantial redistribution of capital from the hands of weaker businesses into the hand of powerful financial interest groups (organized around banks and *Financieras*). What seemed to have occurred in the space of a few short years, due directly to the policies of the military government, was a telescoping of the process of centralization of capital common to capitalist development. The State Development Corporation sold off publicly-owned firms to private capital. By 1981, only 12 of more than 500 firms remained in the state sector, sold at bargain prices to the groups. Capital was siphoned into the financial system where it was absorbed in speculation and credit to the corporate creditworthy. Chile has deindustrialized. In 1982 GNP plummeted 12 percent and 810 companies went into bankruptcy. Agriculture increasingly produces crops for export rather than food for Chileans, while smaller farms are idled for lack of credit.

The financial interest groups (some with appropriate descriptive names like *las Piranas*) that had long given structure to the dominant sectors of Chilean capital achieved a renewed vitality, gobbling up more factories and businesses and establishing new links with foreign capital.

Acquisitions by interest group conglomerates has been in part financed by loans from foreign banks and international lending agencies. Chile had over $18 billion in foreign debt, in 1983 one of the highest per capita debts in the world. Through over-valuation of the peso, interest and repayment on foreign loans by Chilean banks can be made with dollars cheaply purchased from the Central Bank. Government policy on exchange rates has favored expansion of foreign banks operating in Chile and shifted financial resources to large domestic banks associated with the interest groups. Currency speculation, high interest rates, and the undermining of export potential are additional consequences of foreign exchange rate policy. Moreover, foreign debt payments consume a huge proportion of foreign exchange—in 1981, 80 percent of export earnings.

Chile's economic structure, already under the increasingly sway of large economic groups since the 1950s, became highly oligopolistic under the junta. Six major congomerates now control most of the economy.[6] The two largest groups, Cruzat-Larrain and Vial, control over 50 percent of all private capital (Kornbluh, 1982).

The restructuring of the Chilean capitalist class is significant. An industrial bourgeoisie of some stature (though not comparable to Argentine "national capital") had grown up under the stimulatory and protective wing of an interventionist state that dated back to the Popular Front of 1938. The Pinochet regime turned sharply away from 35 years of state encouragement of national industry. The Cauas Plan and its depressive economic effects were devasting for national capital tied to the domestic market.[7]

Since 1976 bankruptcies and take-overs by conglomerates of long-established national industries have been commonplace. In 1980, Jorge Cheyre, President of the important metallurgical trade association ASIMET and staunch supporter of the military intervention, was jailed for issuing checks with insufficient funds. "From his cell he denounced the 'usurious moneylenders' who had brought him to this, and explained that his company, Famasol, which produces domestic appliances, had been unable for some time to raise loans from commercial banks" (Latin America Weekly Report, 1980:7). The driving of national industries to bankruptcy or to merger into conglomerates intensified the conflicts between *blandos* (soft-liners) and *duros* (hardliners) within the government. "The *blando/duro* struggle is in part a conflict between the sectors forming or supporting the economic groups, including some government ministers, and the opposition to these clans" (Latin American Weekly Report, 1980:7). The *duros* are fascists in the classic European mold. They favor a more nationalist-corporatist model, more state intervention, and greater protection of national industry. The *blandos* are followers of "Chicago School" doctrines of monetarism and laissez faire.

The major impact was of course felt by Chilean workers. With their trade unions destroyed or under strict control, with their political representation abolished, and their leadership decapitated, they had no means to resist a drastic reduction in real wages. (This has variously been estimated at between 44 percent and 60 percent from 1972 to 1975 with a further reduction from an index of 100 in January 1975 to 77.5 in March 1976. From 1977 real wages more or less stabilized until the severe economic down turn of 1982.) Unemployment soared to levels never before reached in the country and unemployment, underemployment, and "marginality" remain at high levels to this day, with an official unemployment rate around 20 percent. Reduction in state spending of 44 percent in 1975 as compared to 1973 and the inflation and severe economic contraction that continued to 1978 hit the salaried middle strata hard. The economic crunch and reduced real incomes of the great majority drove many small businesses to ruin.

Of course, this vast restructuring of the economy and of Chilean class relations was not a smooth process. It required force and great policy firmness. Until 1982–1983 General Pinochet was firmly situated in power and he continues with surprising tenacity. Still, the extremely narrow social base of the regime and the internecine struggles within the dominant class and the military establishment—squabbles resting upon a cauldron of popular discontent checked mainly by fear—make political stability unpredictable.

Over the years the Pinochet project, backed by the big economic groups, enforced by the military regime's policies, and buttressed with billions in loans from international banks (but limited foreign investments) had to vie with a series of alternative projects. There was first a fascist insistence on a return to the heady days of 1973. They called for a reinvigorization of mass mobilization and the full articulation of nationalist-populist dictatorship, together with the corporative organization of society and the institutional participation of all classes in the state. Ample sectors of the petty bourgeoisie and the military supported this project, but it had only very limited backing among Chile's frightened bourgeoisie whose eyes were turned abroad for economic ties and political support. The Christian Democrats called for a return to civilian government, backed by military presence to keep the working class in line and the Left out of politics. They hoped to pursue less extreme repression and economic and social policies aimed at accomodation to the diverse "moderate" social forces in disarray in the harsh Chilean reality. Finally, there was a civilianizing plan by sectors of the traditional Right, a conservative version of the Christian Democratic project designed to restore a modicum of respectability to Chile's tarnished international image.

There are a number of reasons why the Pinochet project has triumphed. First, because the accumulation model and general development strategy corresponds to the structural logic of Chile's dependence within the latest phase of international capitalist development. Second, because, in its political as well as economic aspects, the Pinochet project rests firmly on the class interests and power of the predominant fraction of the local bourgeoisie, the oligarchy of finance capital. Third, because Pinochet's Junta has been able to act as a political directorate; the Junta achieved a certain independence from the conflicting class fractions, including finance capital, supporting the dictatorship, as well as from the officialdom of the Armed Forces. Fourth, because the spector of a working class and Left resurgence resides in the background as a deterrent to excessive internecine struggle within the bourgeoisie and the military. Fifth, because the Pinochet regime has been able to counterbalance or repress other political alternatives.

It should be added that alternatives to the regime are politically in abeyance, not wholly eliminated. The *blandos* lost ground in the depression of 1982–1983. Criticism by business interests adversely effected by the regime's policies and the crisis has been at a high level since 1982. By early 1984 no alternative project seemed to have gained ascendancy. However, large-scale street demonstrations, a growing popular resistance, and depressionary economic conditions have unleashed rumors of military actions to topple Pinochet.

Pinochet's policies and their rationales, together with the Junta's ideological exhortations have been frequently made explicit. As I have argued, the implicit but overriding imperative of the dictatorship is revealed in its efforts to reorient completely Chilean political economy and with it the class relations that provide the dynamic of Chilean society. These are some of the explicit guidelines adopted and pursued consistently today:

—The government rejects the long-standing entrepreneurial role of the state as inefficient. Public investments have been sharply curtailed and the government sold most state enterprise (copper excepted).
—Market regulation by the state is ruled out because it provokes disequilibrium in prices and prejudices optimum allocation of private investment.
—National industry has been dependent on the state, inefficient, and incapable of bringing about economic growth. The government has ceased "discriminatory favoritism" and state subsidies. Custom tariffs have been greatly reduced or abolished because protectionism impedes competition and efficiency. Medium and small industry must live within a new competitive system without state support, or die.
—The state is seen as an "orientor of development." There is support for export sectors where comparative advantages for long-term growth exist in agriculture, industry, and mining.

The implementation of these guidelines have completely reversed prior development strategies and severely impacted class relations. In general, the government's policies aim at bringing about an economic accord and political alignment between large financial/industrial economic groups, big exporting landowners (often linked by family or partnership with urban groups), and transnational capital. It is directed against smaller-scale national industry, small business, the salaried middle strata (except the highest managerial and technical levels who are handsomely paid), with the workers, peasants, and "marginal" peoples the chief victim. At bottom, the regime came to represent a narrow class of big business oligarchs who desperately search for a closer and closer integration with international capital.

The ideological pronouncements of the regime are also revealing of its project. Pinochet and company have embarked on a brave attempt to achieve a long-term and stable hegemony that cloaks itself in nineteenth century and "Chicago School" economic liberalism, twentieth century technocratic authoritarianism, and Pentagonese doctrines of "national security." These are the three main components of the Chilean hegemonic project.

The ideologues of the Chilean junta have evolved a sophisticated critique of the ideology of "developmentalism" and its theoretical grounding in Keynesian, post-Keynesian, and Marxian economics. For many decades the development strategies of Chile and many other countries were guided by broad conceptions inspired by the work of nationalist, developmentalist economists within the Economic Commission for Latin America. The new ideologues contend (I think correctly) that developmentalism in the economic sphere and its ideological twin in the political sphere, reformism (such as the Frei government's "Revolución en Libertad"), have been directly responsible for the political space in which socialist and revolutionary ideology could grow, finally achieving a strong foothold in the Popular Unity period.

As noted, the Pinochet regime has not confined itself to critiques of their adversaries' doctrines, but has indeed vigorously propounded its own ideological and theoretical principles. The most noteworthy is not the tired doctrines of "national security," but the wholesale promulgation of a nineteenth century economic liberalism, which by and large since the Keynesian revolution had been relegated to the obscurity of the University of Chicago. (André Gunder Frank, 1976, has analyzed the doctrines of the "Chicago Boys" and the effects of its implementation in Chile with extraordinary lucidity.)

The long-term stability and growth aimed for with these principles and policies requires having a sophisticated group of native capitalists ready to do business with international capital, a skilled and specialized labor force, low wages, the absence of strikes, social peace, low-priced and abundant natural resources, a healthy and stable economic policy, a favorable climate for foreign investment, and international backing.

My sense is that, in all these respects the Pinochet regime has been successful (except international support, mainly confined to billions in bank loans, see Moffitt and Letelier, 1976). But the principles and policies have not led to growth and stability.[8] Moreover, the resistance, even considering the extent and effectiveness of the repression, has been surprisingly ineffectual; this permitted the regime to loosen the repression somewhat. Both popular resistence and repression have increased since 1982, but it is evident that the dictatorship could endure for some time yet, even though the transnational corporations, fearing eventual instability, are not rushing to the banquet and American banks have reduced the flow of now risky credits.

But the long-term prospects for the construction of a new society on the ashes of one of the world's most obscene political phenomena of our time are good enough that many Chileans will likely, when political action does not mean suicide, stake their lives on it. One Chilean observer in reflecting on the tragedy of the Chilean experience noted "the sometimes pathetic dreams of which Chilean political mythology has been fabricated" (Tapia Videla, 1979). During the Popular Unity years millions of Chileans dreamed of a new society, democratically and peacefully constructed. The myth of the "peaceful way" has been rudely laid to rest. "A raw mythology now spews from the barrels of guns: Chile's problems are not underdevelopment, foreign dependency, social injustice, and an oppressive social order; Chile's problem, indeed the nation's sickness, is Marxism" (Johnson, 1982b). For the oppressed classes and the Left the next time around there will be no "pathetic dreams" and less "political mythology" to cloud strategy. And the Chilean middle strata and petty bourgeoisie, having now experienced the horror they helped to bring about, are not as likely to be the impediment they were during the nation's great and tragic years of democratic socialism.

I have been concerned here to state the elements of a theory of the state and to outline some of the main features of a specific case of an authoritarian state. But Chile is but one case. The next two chapters ground a theory of the state in a deeper analysis of class relations, examine the antecedents to the "national security state" in South American cases, and develop the concept of "hegemonic projects." The militarized states of Chile, Argentina, Uruguay, and Brazil (resurgent with variations in several Asian countries) fundamentally represent failing efforts to establish the class hegemony of an alliance of narrow segments of local bourgeoisies and transnational capital.

Notes

1. Critiques of conventional political theory are too numerous to cite. Ralph Miliband (1969) should be given credit for initiating the devastating criticism of "pluralist theory"; Andre Gunder Frank pioneered the challenge to "modernization theory" with his famous article "The Sociology of Development and the Underdevelopment of Sociology" (1972); José Ocampo and I wrote an early critique (1972) that adapted Frank's approach to specific questions of the state.

2. Analyses that explicitly try to link trends in the theory of the state in Western Marxism to studies of peripheral states are few. Petras concludes: "By providing a concrete historical explanation of the formation of the state and the classes which dominate it, we avoid the abstract, a historical deductive approaches of Poulantzas and the overly narrow empiricist arguments of Miliband" (1976:24).

3. The "instrumentalist" or "influence" theory has also been referred to as the "subjectivist" approach (Therborn, 1978).

4. The class analysis underlying Popular Unity strategy was explicitly stated by MAPU, one of the parties to the Popular Unity coalition (translated in Johnson, 1972: chap. 10). Petras (1975) and Smirnow (1981) both provide excellent accounts of the political behavior of the middle strata.

5. There is always the risk of imputing too much determination to the "general determinants" of international political economy. The cautions well-stated by Atilio Borón should be heeded: The form of South American dictatorships "corresponds to the profound reorganization of the productive apparatus imposed by the new mode of capitalist accumulation, above all in conjunctures marked by a significant advance in the class struggle. We should be careful, however, not to carry this argument too far, reducing the new forms of bourgeois domination to mere effects of a mechanical, unilinear determination of the political superstructure by the economic base. For it is only 'in the last instance' that these economic determinants are actually effective. In reality, a host of social, political, ideological and cultural mediations shape the specific mode and degree to which the structural elements of the social formation condition the forms of the State and the political process" (1981:61).

6. There is a fairly recent study of Chilean economic groups which I have been unable to secure: Fernando Dahse, *Mapa de extreme riqueza* (Santiago, 1979).

7. The Argentine military have outdone the Chilean in every respect, including the extent of repression. Under the Argentine dictatorship, the policies of the Superminister Martinez de Hoz seriously undermined the country's nationally-based industrial establishment, concentrating

and centralizing capital at the level of the local finance capital/transnational corporate complex. This is discussed more extensively in the following chapters.

8. Chile's economy plunged into depression in 1982. Industrial production declined sharply, construction fell by 50 percent over 1981, unemployment soared to new heights, GNP fell precipitously. Even though the regime has greatly favored finance capital and foreign bank credit poured in, the economy has such deep problems that even banks controled by economic groups are in trouble. In the face of this General Pinochet appointed in August, 1982 a new superminister of finance and economy, Rolf Lüders. This person had long been associated with the Vial economic group, one of Chile's largest oligarchic clans. This reveals the persistence of "Chicago School" policies, as well as the subservience of the dictatorship to narrow interests. It was rumored, however, that Lüders was not Pinochet's first choice. "The General would have preferred to bring into the government members of the 'traditional right' grouped around former President Jorge Alessandri. This group has been highly critical of the government's management of both the economy and the slow transition to civilian rule, and had apparently demanded political concessions from the President in return for entering the government which Pinochet, however, was not willing to grant (Latin America Weekly Repart, 1982:2).

Lüders is a principle stockholder in the Chilean Mortgage Bank (BHC) headed by Javier Vial, architect of Chile's largest interest group. In 1970, BHC acting as a holding company, controlled 42 companies, a mutual funds, and assets of $426 million. During the military years the original BHC group split into two schools of *piranas* and by 1978 controlled 195 companies valued at $4.3 billion. The groups directors and executives flowed in and out of cabinet posts; the clans bought up state firms at undervalued prices and floated in a sea of easy foreign credits. (Congress cut off credits to Chile from U.S. government agencies because of human rights violations, but American banks simply stepped in with billions). What resulted was bigger conglomerates, but not new productive investments. Incredibly, this occured even with access to formerly government controlled pension funds. In 1980, the regime "reformed" the social security and retirement system, creating privately administered Administradores de Fondos Previsionales (AFP), free of government supervision. Seventy percent of AFP assets (estimated at $2 annually, 13 percent of GNP) became controlled by two groups, Vial and Cruzat-Larrain (Volk, 1983:9). The speculative, empire-building, free-borrowing, and unproductive activities of the economic groups, in the depths of general economic decline, led to a general collapse of banking in 1983. The Pinochet regime even felt compeled to send government administrators into the Vial groups banks, BHC and Banco de Chile. The cabinet was again reshuffled, but Pinochet and his fundamental policies continue—since mid-1983 in the context of masses of people on the streets squared off against the dictorship's army and police forces.

References

Alexander, Robert J.
1978 The Tragedy of Chile. Westport, CT: Greenwood Press.
von Beyme, Klaus (ed.)
1976 German Political Studies. Beverly Hills, CA: Sage.
Block, Fred
1977 "The ruling class does not rule: notes on the Marxist theory of the state." Socialist Review 33 (May–June): 6–28.
Boorstein, Edward
1977 Allendés Chile. New York: International Publishers.
Borón, Atilio
1981 "Latin America: between Hobbes and Friedman." New Left Review 130 (November–December): 45–66.
Carranza, M. A.
1978 Fuerzas armadas y Estado de excepción en América Latina. Mexico: Siglo XXI.

Chilcote, Ronald H. and Dale L. Johnson (eds.)
1983   Theories of Development: Mode of Production or Dependency? Beverly Hills, CA: Sage.

Domhoff, William G.
1967   Who Rules America? Englewood Cliffs, NJ: Prentice Hall.
1979   The Powers that Be: Processes of Ruling Class Domination in America. New York: Random House.
1980   Power Structure Research (ed.). Beverly Hills, CA: Sage.

Frank, André Gunder
1975   "An open letter about Chile to Arnold Harberger and Milton Creedman." Review of Radical Political Economics 7 (Summer):61–76.

Garcia Marquez, Gabriel
1977   The Autumn of the Patriarch. New York: Avon.

Gil, Federico G., Ricardo Lagos Escobar, and Henry A. Landsberger (eds.)
1979   Chile at the Turning Point: Lessons of the Socialist Years, 1970–1973. Philadelphia: Institute for the Study of Human Issues.

Gold, David A., Clarence Y. H. Lo, and Erik Olin Wright
1975   "Recent developments in Marxist theories of the capitalist state." Monthly Review, Part I (October) and Part II (November).

Habermas, Jurgen
1975   Legitimation Crisis. Boston: Beacon Press.

Hirsch, Joachim
1978   "The state apparatus and social reproduction: elements of a theory of the bourgeois state." Pp. 57–107 in John Holloway and Sol Picciotto (eds.) State and Capital. Austin: University of Texas Press.

Holloway, John and Sol Picciotto (eds.)
1978   State and Capital. Austin: University of Texas Press.

Johnson, Dale L.
1972   The Chilean Road to Socialism (ed.). New York: Doubleday.
1982a   Class and Social Development: A New Theory of the Middle Classes (ed.). Beverly Hills, CA: Sage.
1982b   "Chile: before and during." Science and Society 46 (Winter): 461–475
1983   "Class analysis and dependency." Chapter 7 in Ronald H. Chilcote and Dale L. Johnson (eds.) Theories of Development: Mode of Production or Dependency? Beverly Hills, CA: Sage.

Kornbluh, Peter R.
1982   "Chilean economy: not a leaf moves." NACLA Report on the Americas 16 (July–August): 42–45.

Laclau, Ernesto
1977   Politics and Ideology in Marxist Theory. London: New Left Books.

Latin America Weekly Report
1980   "'Usury' squeezes industry into the hands of the clans." Latin America Weekly Report WR-80-22 (June 6):7
1982   "Finance Ministry falls to BHC man." WR-82-35 (September 10):2.

Miliband, Ralph
1969   The State in Capitalist Society: An Analysis of the Western System of Power. New York: Basic Books.
1970   "The capitalist state—reply to Nicos Poulantzas." New Left Review 59 (Jan.–Feb.).
1973   "Poulantzas and the capitalist state." New Left Review 82.
1977   Marxism and Politics. London: Oxford University Press.

Moffitt, Michael and Isabel Letelier
1978   Human Rights, Economic Aid and Private Banks: The Case of Chile. Washington, DC: Institute for Policy Studies.

Mollenhopf, John
1975   "Theories of the state and power structure research." Insurgent Sociologist 5 (Spring): 245–264.

Nun, Jose
1979   "Observations on the nature of authoritarian regimes." Pp 461–468 in Federico G. Gil, Ricardo Lagos Escobar, and Henry A. Landsberger (eds.) Chile at the Turning Point: Lessons of the Socialist Years, 1970–1973. Philadelphia: Institute for the Study of Human Issues.

Ocampo, José A. and Dale L. Johnson
1972   "The concept of political development." Chapter 13 in James D. Cockcroft, André Gunder Frank, and Dale L. Johnson (eds.) Dependence and Underdevelopment. New York: Doubleday.

Offe, Claus
1972   "Political authority and class structure—an analysis of late capitalist societies." International Journal of Sociology 2, 1.
1976   "Structural problems of the capitalist state." In Klaus von Beyme (ed.) German Political Studies. Beverly Hills, CA: Sage.

Offe, Claus and Volker Range
1975   "Theses on the theory of the state." New German Critique 6 (Fall).

Oppenheimer, Martin and Jane C. Canning
1979   "The national security state." Berkeley Journal of Sociology 23: 3–33.

Palacios, Jorge
1979   Chile: An Attempt at "Historic Compromise." Chicago: Banner Press.

Petras, James and Morris Monley
1975   United States and Chile. New York: Monthly Review Press.
1976   "Class and politics in the periphery and the transition to socialism." Review of Radical Political Economics 8 (Summer): 20–36.

Portantiero, Juan C.
1974   "Dominant classes and political crisis in Argentina today." Latin American Perspectives 1 (Fall):93–120.

Poulantzas, Nicos
1969   "The problem of the capitalist state." New Left Review 58 (Nov.–Dec.):67–78.
1973   Political Power and Social Classes. London: New Left Books.
1974   Fascism and Dictatorship. London: New Left Books.
1976   "The capitalist state: a reply to Miliband and Laclau." New Left Review (Jan.–Feb.):63–83.
1978   State Power, Socialism. London: New Left Books.

Sigmund, Paul E.
1977   The Overthrow of Allende and the Politics of Chile, 1964–1976. Pittsburgh: University of Pittsburgh Press.

Smirnow, Gabriel
1981   The Revolution Disarmed: Chile 1979–1973. New York: Monthly Review Press.

Tapia Videla, Jorge I.
1979   "The endless search for a Chile that never was." Latin American Research Review 14(3): 280–291.

Therborn, Göran
1978   What Does the Ruling Class Do When it Rules? London: New Left Books.

Tomic, Rodomiro
1979   Some Clarifications of Certain Historical Facts." Pp 187–191 in Federico G. Gil, Ricardo Lagos, and Henry A. Landsberger (eds.) Chile at the Turning Point. Philadelphia: Institute for the Study of Human Issues.
Volk, Steven
1983   "The lessons and legacy of a dark decade." NACLA Report on The Americas 17 (September–October): 2–14.

Dale L. Johnson: Class Roots of Dictatorship in South America: Local Bourgeoisies and Transnational Capital

The most notable feature of the Latin American experience in recent years is military dictatorship. The method of class analysis—when dependency relations are placed in proper focus—bares the roots of this devastating political phenomenon. An explanation of military dictatorship as the "characteristic" rather than "exceptional" form of the state in the more advanced nations of Latin America (and other parts of the Third World) resides, in the first instance, in an analysis of the internationalized process of capital accumulation as it articulates with local economies and social structures. This process is one in which the movement of transnational forces of production carries dramatically changing class formations and sharply conflictive class relations. And these relations shape and limit the accumulation process in ways that distort development and turn it sharply from human need and social ends. Specifically, in the stage of dependent development in the Southern Cone of South America, the transnationalized accumulation process—as a "general determinant" of development processes (Johnson, 1983)—has transformed the structure and given a new, dependent face to the local dominant class; has qualitatively changed the relations between different fractions of this class; has eclipsed or subordinated important social interests tied to the old order of classic underdevelopment; has formed or yielded a considerable maturity to newer classes and social forces; and has brought about a crisis of transition from one stage of development to another stage. These factors have given an explosive quality to the struggles of classes and the various social and institutional forces in the region, especially in the Southern Cone. And these social struggles of the 1960s and 1970s in the Southern Cone have transformed crises of transition from one developmental stage ("national development") to another stage ("dependent development") into conjunctures of *organic crises,* out of which have come the especially brutal dictatorships of Argentina, Chile, and Uruguay. ("Stages of development" are explained in Chapter 1.) All these regimes depend on a high level of repression to achieve and maintain state power. Each has failed to establish workable development strategies (Brazil is somewhat of an exception) or to achieve a wide or solid social base of political support within civil society. Ambitious projects seeking a broad hegemony have failed. Nevertheless, only the Argentine dictatorship has collapsed. While the Brazilian military government is withering away, the Chilean and Uruguayan dictatorships have endured more than a decade.

In seeking to explain the dynamics of militarized states and illusive hegemony, I consider first the transformation of the local bourgeoisies and intra-class relations, to then turn in the next chapter to questions of the full gamut of class relations and their political outcomes.

Transnationalization of Capital Accumulation and the Local Bourgeoisie

The local bourgeoisies of the Southern Cone are composed of distinct fractions. The fraction that now exercises an economic predominance is constituted by a series of interrelated but competing "interest groups" (usually family based) of finance capitalists. This fraction of the broader capitalist class has its historical roots in the oligarchic formations of the late nineteenth and early twentieth century stage of the development of underdevelopment; today it scrambles to associate itself with transnational capital and to translate its economic predominance into a broader hegemony. While finance capital together with transnational corporations are the most important grouping, other interests are present. There is a fraction of "national capital" located largely in the consumer goods industry that prospered during the stage of national development. National business today is struggling for survival in the face of concentrated transnational and local finance capital and the policies of military governments bent on restructuring capital and giving a new direction to the development process. There is also a managerial bourgeoisie of growing significance: The managers of subsidiaries of transnational corporations are often of local origin; finance capital employs a substantial group of professional managers; and there is a strata of technocrats located in the state productive and administrative apparatuses. Finally, there are groupings of traditional landowners, commercial agriculturalists, and other producers of primary products.

The character of the local bourgeoisie and the relations between the various fractions have changed radically over the last two decades, carrying significant political consequences. The changing intra-class relations are associated with the capital accumulation process in the stage of dependent development.

Over the last three decades in the Cone of South America, the accumulation of capital has proceeded mainly on three bases: in new industries in response to the movement of transnational productive forces and international markets for non-traditional exports; through conquest by modern capital (foreign and domestic) of traditional forms of production and in the opening-up of new sectors in consumer durables and intermediate products; and through the medium of state activity. These avenues of accumulation occur hand-in-hand with a pronounced bi-polarization of the social-economic structure. On the one hand there is an accelerating rate of concentration and centralization of capital both on a world scale of transnational capital and within peripheral nations; on the other hand there is an extensive process of dislocation of people from traditional forms of production and subsistence and greatly increased subordination of labor to modern capital. Labor subordination takes two forms; an expansive class of waged laborers whose organization, bargaining power, and real incomes are reduced and an astounding pauperization (some use the term "marginalization" or "immiseration") of substantial sectors of the population.

The new avenues of capital accumulation nevertheless have not reduced the traditional feature of underdevelopment: dependence upon exports of primary commodities. Deficits in the balance of payments and gigantic foreign debts of the countries embarked on dependent development are consequences of increased need for imports to sustain the process. Continued reliance on or even accelerated production of primary exports is therefore imperative. The social and political significance of this continued reliance upon primary export production will be explored shortly.

The impulses toward outward expansion of the transnational corporation from Western centers and the penetration and economic impact of transnational capital in Third World economies has been amply studied. Since our focus is class formation and class relations—questions not at all satisfactorily addressed in the available literature—suffice simply to state a well-documented generalization on the economics of the "new dependency" (dos Santos, 1968, 1970). Since the 1950s transnational corporations have become the principal source of the movement of the forces of production in the international economy, extending even into remote locations on the periphery. And this movement of productive forces has a decidedly transformative impact on local economies and class relations. The penetration of transnational capital has proceeded further in the Southern Cone than elsewhere in the Third World (save Mexico; there are also rapidly increasing investments in the Philippines, Taiwan, South Korea, and India). And the effects have been correspondingly greater there than elsewhere. At the same time, an internal situation cushions the movement of transnational capital in South America. The higher level in the development of the productive forces, achieved in the prior stage of national development, and the formation of substantial and more solidified working, intermediate, and capitalist classes in the Southern Cone, articulates with the internationalized productive forces. The interpenetrations of internationalized forces and relatively developed and modernized local economic and social structures both facilitate the movement of these forces and bring about a new stage of development, "dependent development." It has also produced in Argentina, Uruguay, and Chile, organic crises and military dictatorship. With important qualifications, the same may be said of Brazil.

Dependent development in which transnational corporations control, in cooperation with local finance capital and dependent states, the principal productive forces generates a "modern sector" composed of intermediate industrial goods, durable consumer goods for the local market, manufactures for export, and banking and complementary service activities. This undermines the competitive bases, both in terms of markets and the competition of capitals, of long-established business of national character. In the Southern Cone, the economic sectors that had previously constituted the main productive forces and that had prospered and matured during the stage of national development began to exhibit a *contradictory complementarity* in relation to movement within the new, transnationalized sectors. The contradictory aspect is that, to varying degrees and at different rhythms in the different countries, modern capital progressively assumes a concentrated and centralized form and reorganizes under its sway the traditional sectors of production of national capital. These sectors include the small and medium sized industrial firms serving local markets, the simple commodity production of the petty bourgeoisie and, to varying degrees, a commercial agricultural sector that had historically preserved "pre-capitalist" forms of social relations in the countryside. In terms of class relations, this contradictory process produces antagonisms between established national fractions of capital and the transnational and local finance capital partnership. But this is also a process that defines a new, complementary role for national capital. To the degree that traditional, competitive national sectors are either forced into bankruptcy or reorganized, under the structural force of the accumulation process, into complementary production and commercial relations with modern capital, the bases of intra-bourgeois class antagonisms change from competition to subordination of one type of capital by another. It becomes less a question of competition of old industrial and new finance capital than of dependency of traditional business upon transnationalized, monopoly capital for its continued existence.

The Local Bourgeoisie and
Its Predominant Fraction

In summary, the modern sector of primary accumulation is constituted by subsidiaries of transnational corporations, local economic groups of finance capital operating in association with transnationals, and large state enterprises, some of which are joint ventures with private foreign and/or local finance capital. State enterprises are highly significant in Brazil, but military governments in Argentina and Chile have turned important state firms over to private interests. There is a continuing dependence on primary export commodities, so that big ranchers, coffee barons, plantation owners, and mine owners retain a place, though declining in centrality, in the social structure and political order. Large-scale urban enterprises are monopolistic, while small and medium-size national capital struggles for survival in highly competitive sectors or works out complementary relations with the modern sector. Within the local bourgeoisie, the finance capital fraction is unequivocally dominant in the Southern Cone.

The concentration of capital and the extension of monopoly into competitive sectors of the economy, even into commercial agriculture as "agribusiness" displaces the *latifundia,* is organized by highly centralized finance capital; that is, by a specifically constituted class of locally-based financiers. They operate out of banks, extending control through diverse sectors. The state is impelled to oversee the process. Transnational capital, while the most dynamic productive force, must depend upon local partners and on governments working to assure a favorable private investment climate to smooth its way into national economies.

The salient features of the formation of a local bourgeoisie during the stage of dependent development, its structure and internal fractionalization, can be inferred from the various studies of changing economic structures and investment trends and shifts. A first approximation to the structure of the bourgeoisie can be gleaned from examination of the source of capital and its size and location. There are large-scale private national and foreign as well as state firms in the monopoly sector and these are distinct from medium-sized and smaller-scale business in the competitive sector. The various capitals are also differentiated sectorally, by type of activity. This differentiation retains some significance in the study of the formation of the bourgeoisie since the historical divisions of capital within prior stages of development still persist to some degree in the stage of dependent development.

To a certain degree, however, the sectoral divisions within local capital have declined in importance in the stage of dependent development as a consequence of the reorganization of the heart of the local bourgeoisie into groupings of finance capitalists with multi-sectoral investments, the insertion of transnational capital into predominant positions in the most dynamic sectors, and the reduction of smaller-scale, competitive industrial and merchant capital to activities in contradictory complementarity to monopoly capital or to a precarious existence in the competitive sector. Moreover, there has also been a relegation of landowners (except for Argentina's cattlemen/bankers) to a more subordinated position in the economy and power structure.

The character of finance capital is also defined by its internal organization. The "interest group" organization of corporate activity that is emphasized in the literature implies a modern version of the "oligarchic clans" of old.[1] The centralization of capital is in fact effected by big capitalists grouped into extended family units or into a limited grouping of *socios* operating out of financial institutions. Each interest group extends its operations into controlling large-scale and medium-sized firms in diverse economic sectors. They operate much as a conglomerate in the advanced industrial countries: a controlling administrative center extends horizontally, not so much for purposes of operational control as such, as for access to financial resources that can be utilized to continue the process of centralization of economic power.

There is of course competition between economic groups. This is a competition of capitals, not market competition. As each attempts to extend control over diverse activities, it competes for terrain to penetrate and scrambles for access to association with transnational corporations, international credits, and the favors of the state.

Finance capital is today indisputably the dominant fraction of the local bourgeoisie in the South American countries under consideration. For the most part these interests have their historical origins in the fusion of merchant and commercial agricultural capitals, producing close-knit oligarchic formations, that began during the transition from the stage of classic underdevelopment to the stage of national development.[2]

The historical origins of the finance capital fraction contradict any pretensions of combative, independent national existence. Today's Buenos Aires banker-industrialist is the gentleman rancher of yesterday's *pampa;* the big businessman of São Paulo began as a coffee baron; the boards of directors of Santiago banks are composed of former export-import merchants and *latifundistas*. Modern finance capital is the direct descendant of the traditional oligarchies of the stage of nineteenth century development of underdevelopment. This oligarchy was a class that prospered and perpetuated its local dominance by relating directly to the mono-export economy of the period, subordinating itself firmly within the relations of dependence that historically developed what we now call underdevelopment. Its feuding factions of the nineteenth century had fused together its economic interests and socially coalesced by the early twentieth century. It is a class that survived the traumas of the crisis of the 1930s and two world wars and began its process of regeneration on a new economic foundation during the stage of national development. Given the origins of finance capital, it is hardly surprising that they in no way resemble a "national bourgeoisie." The South American businessmen of today, like their oligarchic forebears (whose family names and traditions of intermarriages they maintain), willingly mesh themselves within the relations of dependence that today assume a new form. They seek a local hegemony by associating themselves with a very strong ally, transnational industrial and banking capital.

The formation of local finance capital must be viewed, then, in relation to its historical origins and to its current prop. The contradiction is that as the economic predominance of local finance capital is achieved, it becomes more and more dependent, a local appendage of international capital and beholden to a state that pursues policies in relation to the structural logic of that dependence.

Presented above is a structural glimpse of the nature of the South American bourgeoisie in the recent stage of dependent development. Analyzed below is the historical process that resulted in a fractionalized capitalist class—and military dictatorship.

Traditional Oligarchies and
the Formation of National Capital
and Intermediate Groups

Analysts of the historical development of capitalism often theoretically counterpose the retrograde dominant class interests of the *ancién regime* to progressive industrial and competitive capital. In South America, the structural roots of those business sectors said to compose the "national bourgeoisie" reside in "traditional industries" producing for internal consumption in a competitive market (textiles and apparel, leather and shoes, food processing, most other non-durable consumer goods, and some sectors of the metal and small tools industries), in the wholesale trade and larger retail outlets, and in medium-sized, capitalized farming. These are the sectors that prospered during the stage of national development in South America. In the more recent period they have gone bankrupt, been taken over by finance capital, or subordinated in the trajectory of transnationalized capital accumulation. The space remaining for national capital today is limited to the interstices of economies dominated by transnational and local finance capital.

The demise of national capital is a history of frustrated national capitalism. In South America the only historical parallel to European development might be the "revolution from above" of Bismarkian Germany (Engels, 1969–1970; Moore, 1966), where a sector of the traditional dominant class "modernized," leaving little space for an emergent industrial bourgeoisie to shape a more progressive and democratic future.[3] Capitalist development in which the dominant class interests of the *ancién regime* are not destroyed or subordinated by profound reform experiences does seem to result in highly authoritarian regimes.

The literature analyzing Latin American twentieth century historical development has often posed questions drawn from the presumed opposition of classically underdeveloped, "pre-capitalist," agrarian, mono-export economic order with a national capitalist industrial order emerging in the Depression and War period. Much of the writing (prior to the mid-1960s challenge of dependency theory to evolutionary and modernization theory) assumed, with only cursory historical or empirical examination, an opposition between social interests situated in the distinct pre-capitalist ("traditional") and capitalist ("modern") sectors of a "dual society." In its most sophisticated exposition (e.g., structural history or evolutionary Marxist as opposed to simplistic modernization theory), this stance, generalized from European social history, postulated the central antagonism as between industrial interests striving for a new order and the traditional agrarian-merchantile classes bent on preserving backwardness.

Without any doubt the nineteenth century formation in Latin America of agrarian-mercantile dominant classes and the policies of the oligarchic states controlled by these interests proved inimical to industrial progress. There are but limited exceptions to this in the region. In the late nineteenth and early twentieth centuries, Argentina and Uruguay experienced a considerable development of internal commerce and some industrial growth. This development was a spin-off of the relative success of beef exports to European markets. Railroad networks from the interior to the ports were built (with largely British capital) and there was processing of chilled and frozen beef and leather products (largely local capital) and investments in flour and sugar mills; additionally, construction, textile, and food processing industries were established to house, cloth, and feed burgeoning urban populations of the early twentieth century. In both countries, traditional agrarian-mercantile oligarchies were forced to share political power with reform political forces based on newly formed intermediate class interests. Government policy then became supportive, although selectively and modestly so, of commercial and industrial development. Moreover, the social and political policies of reform governments prior to 1930 facilitated the emergence and strengthening of new social forces—salaried middle strata, workers, and smaller businessmen—well in advance of their "natural" formation through the economic process. Large-scale immigration from Europe, including many persons with industrial and business experience, became an important factor in national development.

In viewing the social structure of classic underdevelopment, "traditional oligarchies" should not be confused with "feudal aristrocrats"; nor should the reform forces active in the period be confused with a "progressive" or "national" bourgeoisie.

In Argentina, for example, the cattle barons of Buenos Aires Province were not Prussian *junkers* or feudal barons; they constituted a preeminently capitalist class. The reform forces emanated from the petty bourgeoisie and salaried middle strata, not from an industrial bourgeoisie. Merging with the cattle barons were the big merchants. The Buenos Aires export-import merchants—tied-up with British commercial capital—became closely linked by family and business ties to the ranchers. This is a very different situation than in the transition to capitalism in Europe where merchants were a separate class from landowners and where the "middle class" was largely synonymous with emerging industrial interests. The Argentine agrarian-mercantile oligarchy, with its class interests tied to primary export production, the source of classic underdevelopment, behaved rationally in accumulating capital from the rich natural and exportable resources of the *pampa*. They did seek additional sources of investment as opportunities were presented within the limiting, dependent structure of classic underdevelopment; and they were not adverse to permitting some leeway for enterprising Italian, German, Lebanese, and Jewish immigrants to establish businesses—in all other respects the immigrant bourgeoisie was excluded or ignored. The industrial development pursued or permitted by oligarchic interests helped to maintain political stability, though at the cost of modest social reform, and later permitted a better overall adjustment to world depression and war.

Building on the limited industrial base built-up in prior decades, Argentina and Uruguay, together with Brazil, Chile, and Mexico, initiated a process of incipient industrialization in the circumstances of the Great Depression and World War II. In analyzing the transition from classic underdevelopment to national development the question, once again, is the degree to which, in actual historical experience, emerging industrial systems are antagonistic with the socio-economic order of classic underdevelopment; that is to say, how has the contradiction between the forces of production, pushing toward capitalist development, and the relations of production, with the power of entrenched oligarchies tending to preserve pre-existing forms, concretely developed in the region? The question is best addressed through examination of the structurally determined antagonisms that lead to social struggle between representatives of the different orders in concrete cases.

In viewing concrete cases it is apparent that there are many national variations within the Latin American region—and the rest of the Third World is quite distinct from Latin America. Further, there are *no direct parallels* with Western European historical development (other than that noted above with Bismarkian Germany). The *general* pattern in Latin America seems to be that the inarticulations and contradictions between emerging industrial and traditional agricultural-mineral export economies and the social force they produce have not been of sufficient severity as to either retard irretrievably or transform irreversibly Latin American economies and societies. This is one reason why one can still refer to the substantially industrialized societies of Argentina, Brazil, Chile, Mexico, and Uruguay as "underdeveloped."

The specific patterns need to be accounted for without losing sight of the generalizations that are necessary to understand regional and global processes of development and underdevelopment. In Latin America there are rather clear examples of how, under given historical circumstances, class interests associated with classic underdevelopment can initiate, at least in the face of crises of that system, modernization efforts. Conversely, social interests assumed to be associated with the emergence of an industrial order have only weakly supported, or sometimes put themselves in opposition to, state policies fomenting industrial development and social-political modernization.

Argentina and Chile are both examples of how traditional oligarchies modernized themselves to some extent while laying the groundwork for the transition from classic underdevelopment to incipient industrialization, limiting or suppressing the formation of a "national" industrial bourgeoisie in the process. (The situation in Brazil, Uruguay, and Mexico was somewhat different as these nations had populist, reform, or revolutionary states during the 1930s that facilitated industrialization.) Both the Peronist state (1946–1955) and the Popular Front and subsequent Radical Party governments in Chile (1938–1952)—representing interests more favorably inclined toward an industrial order—furthered the industrialization process initiated by their respective oligarchies during the 1930s. Only in Mexico, however, were these oligarchies eliminated from the historical scene.

From the standpoint of understanding the forces behind industrial development, Argentina, the most industrialized country in the third world, is the most interesting.

Facing the collapse of the export economy and frightened by political assertions of reformist social forces, the Argentine oligarchy engineered a military *coup* in 1930. This conservative restoration, with heavy-handed military backing, lasted until the next military coup in 1943, responding to the interests of dissident social forces and featuring Colonel Juan Peron.

Argentine government policies during the 1930s favored industrialization. These policies were initiated and effectively promoted by the dominant fraction of the oligarchy. This narrow grouping was the *invernadores*, cattle fatteners and chilled beef exporters of the Buenos Aires area, as opposed to the *criadores*, the ranchers of the interior. Industrial interests, especially as represented by the Unión Industrial Argentina, of course supported protective tariffs and other state measures favoring industrial development. However, their support did not originate from a position of power as a new class with a vision of an industrial future for the nation; all but the largest of industrial interests were but passive beneficiaries of a new development strategy initiated by the oligarchy and carried out by their allies in the state apparatus. The major political party of the era, the Unión Cívica Radical (UCR) displaced by the military coup of 1930 and representing sectors of the middle strata, petty bourgeoisie, some marginal landowners, and a few business interests, consistently opposed this development strategy. They were joined in opposition by the subordinate fraction of the traditional oligarchy, the cattle ranchers of the interior.

How can the anomaly of export oligarchy support for and presumably more visionary social interests in opposition to industrialization policies be accounted for? Perhaps because the social forces represented by the UCR were themselves products of the social structure of classic underdevelopment. In prior decades they had gained enough political power to liberalize and modernize the political and social order, to the degree that the Argentine state prior to 1930 could no longer be characterized as strictly oligarchic. However, during the 1930s their consciousness did not seem to be able to transcend a defense of the old order to formulate a more radical alternative to the limited industrial system sought by a traditional oligarchy bent on modernization without fundamental change or sharing power with other class forces. Clearly this middle class party did not speak for emerging industrial interests. The Argentine historical sociologists Murmis and Portantiero (1971) suggest one reason, the urban middle groups were structurally more "consumers" than "producers" for whom industrialization meant more expensive locally produced goods of inferior quality to the imports they were accustomed to.

The landed interests of the interior, adamant in opposition to any industrialization, also opposed the Buenos Aires cattlemen and export merchants because the latter used their leverage over and within the state (as dominant fractions of divided oligarchies have always done in Latin American states) to shift the burden of depression-era export losses to other cattlemen and to the society at large. This was accomplished by treaties favoring export of the chilled beef they controlled, as opposed to the frozen meat exported by interior ranchers. Treaties during the Depression stabilized chilled beef exports at 300,000 tons per year, while frozen beef exports dropped from pre-Depression highs of 209,000 tons to 56,000 tons. This was perhaps the last of a century-long intra-class struggle between Buenos Aires beef and export interests and interior ranchers and farmers, as the rise of the Buenos Aires finance capital groups from their base in the *invernadores* and export merchants, and the later integration of the interior cities into the industrial economy, left interior landed interests as simply one of many lesser vested interest groups.

The development strategy of the 1930s was essentially for the state—largely through control of tariffs, exchange rates, export and import policies, and government initiatives—to induce import-substitution industrial production. This was a considerable success. Industrial developments boomed. Oligarchic families began to diversify their investments from cattle lands, beef exports, and export-import houses to finance and industry. Small shops established by immigrant entrepreneurs grew into large factories. The working class expanded, incorporating both former artisans and migrating peasants and farm workers. Small businessmen and salaried middle elements greatly increased in number and importance.

The character of the two major sectors of today's Argentine dominant class were formed during this period of incipient industrialization, finance capital, and the industrial bourgeoisie. The most enterprising among the cattle ranchers and beef exporters seized the opportunity to transform themselves—yet without ever loosing their links to agro-export agriculture—into a modern class of finance capitalists. For example, Bunge and Born, today one of Argentina's largest conglomerates, began to diversify out of pampas cattle and Patagonian sheep even before the 1930s crisis. In 1897 the association between two leading agricultural families had led to the establishment of a large flour mill and in 1926 a textile plant was opened. They built several chemical plants in the 1930s. Later they became formally associated with the German company Farbwerke Hoechst in the chemical industry, producing everything from acids to paints and packaging. Bunge became President of the industrial trade association, the Unión Industrial Argentina, during the 1930s. The conglomerate has since diversified and expanded investments and take-overs. By 1970 Bunge and Born controlled five of the firms on the list of the top 100 corporations in Argentina. Bunge and Born functions as an international holding company and as such has large investments in Brazil and extensive links to European and North American corporations. The conglomerate figures among the world's leading grain trading houses.

As industrial growth boomed in the 1930s and 1940s, many big cattlemen joined Señores Bunge and Born in exchanging riding togs and leisure hours at the Jockey Club for hectic rounds of meetings of the Boards of Directors of banks and major firms in all sectors. The evolution of the core of the Argentine oligarchy into groupings of finance capitalists took place without the class ever loosing its tap roots in export agriculture. Moreover, big ranchers who did not modernize remained a powerful fraction of the dominant class, at least until the mid-1960s.

However, during the period the oligarchs did not monopolize industrial development. Argentina, more than anywhere else in Latin America, has a class of industrial and commercial interests that are non-oligarchic in origin. These businessmen are, in great proportion, immigrants (Italians, Germans, Jews, Lebanese and so on) or their descendants, who came with capital and business expertise during the late nineteenth and first decades of the twentieth century, before the oligarchy and the post-World War II transnational corporations had moved decisively into industrial and commercial terrain. This ethnically-divided group evidenced little cohesiveness or self-consciousness as an industrial bourgeoisie, characteristics that various studies indicate persisted at least into the 1960s.[4]

The blockage of beef exports to Europe during World War II and the unavailability of imports spurred a good deal of import-substitution industrialization in Buenos Aires and to a lesser extent in the interior cities. The bulk of this was undertaken by immigrant entrepreneurs, while oligarchic capital more often went into finance and industry related to agriculture, such as sugar refining in the North and flour mills in Buenos Aires. The latter interests were influential in promoting the principle industrial trade association, which in part explains why the Unión Industrial Argentina did not become a vehicle for expressing the interests of a "national bourgeoisie"—until, in the 1970s, it was too late.

The national development occuring in the Depression and World War II led to significant changes in the social structure and to the strengthening of dissident social forces. After the 1943 military coup, Juan Peron forged a coalition of classes and diverse social interests in an attempt to build a strong and viable system of national capitalism. The state took on entrepreneurial functions, buying out British infrastructural investments and establishing large state firms in vital industries. Oligarchic interests were excluded from the direct exercise of state power, and part of their revenue was appropriated through state controls over agricultural exports. However, their general interests as an economically dominant social class were never fundamentally threatened, though their strident opposition to Juan and Eva Peron made it appear so. The Perons' organized workers and the *descamisados* ("shirtless ones") as a power base to effect a novel form of social power, the populist state. The attempt to build a viable national capitalism foundered in the face of the post-War strength and expansion of international capital, the lack of development of an assertive "national bourgeoisie" that could live with militantly Peronist workers and oppose the old oligarchy, and Peron's failure to use the power of workers (for which there was favorable opportunity) to break the dominant position on the land and in the banks and industries of the oligarchy. In 1955, these interests, with their military allies and with substantial middle strata and petty bourgeois support, over-threw Peron.

The policies of the post-Peron military government, and with some variation those of subsequent civilian governments, responded first to the interests of the big ranchers, including those that had not yet expanded into urban business activity. Under Peron, revenues from agricultural exports that were controlled through establishment of a state export commission, were used to divert capital away from that sector, passing through the hands of the state and into industry and other national development projects. This policy was totally reversed through diverse government measures and export revenues reverted into the hands of big agro-export interests. The same interests benefited from shifting foreign transactions back into the private sector and liberalizing trade. This constituted a return to the pre-Peron state policies of the 1930s, with one exception—government encouragement of direct foreign investment. The most significant part of this reversion was the decision to subordinate the interests of national capital that had begun to mature under the aegis of the populist state and the weakened links of external dependency in the war and post-war periods. In every avenue there was closure to the Peronist attempt to construct a system of national capitalism. The late 1950s civilian government opened the doors to transnational capital with two new foreign investment laws in 1959 and 1961. The Illia government of 1964 placed some restrictions on transfer of profits abroad, but the effect of this was nullified by the military dictatorship that assumed power in 1966.

The thrust of the development strategy of the class interests in command of the state apparatus from 1955 to 1966 was to promote primary exports while depending on foreign capital to develop the industrial and other sectors of a modern economy. However, finance capital increasingly joined forces with transnational capital with joint investments, licensing arrangements, and interlocking directorates between foreign and Argentine corporations. Predominance within the local capitalist class shifted directly to finance capital and government policies so supportive of export agriculture while leaving industry to foreigners became anachronistic. The Armed Forces staging the 1966 intervention subordinated fractional differences within the dominant class, favoring the interests of the financial bourgeoisie in association with foreign capital; the junta under General Onganía suppressed the interests of national capital, the petty bourgeoisie, and middle strata, and forcibly repressed the unions, the working class, and the organized Left. In 1968 and 1969 there were serious worker insurrections in all the industrial centers and real expressions of discontent by national capital. Great political instability finally led to military withdrawal from government and the return of Peron in 1973—and finally to the return of the military in 1976, this time with the unparalled ruthlessness of the national security state.

Transnational Capital, State Enterprise, and the Managerial-Technocratic Bourgeoisie

The primary economic feature of the dependent development of recent decades is an accelerated rate of centralization and concentration of capital. Centralization refers to patterns of horizontal control of production. In South America this has taken the primary form of economic groups of finance capital acting as conglomerates, as analyzed above. Concentration refers to monopolization or oligopolization and to vertical integration of firms within particular sectors of production. Economic concentration is associated with the increased predominance of foreign corporations, state firms, and local finance capital. For example, in Argentina in 1955 the largest 150 firms controlled 20 percent of industrial production; by 1969 this had increased to 32 percent. In the latter year 60 percent of the 150 largest firms were subsidiaries of foreign corporations (some with Argentine private and state participation), while 22 percent were owned by Argentine private capital (13 of these firms were linked to transnational corporations through minority equity participation and/or patent and licensing arrangements), and 18 percent were large state enterprises. While medium-sized and smaller-scale competitive capital lost considerable ground during the period, it nonetheless still accounted for about 40 percent of industrial production and employed 57 percent of the industrial labor force in the late 1960s.

Of the top 30 firms in Argentina in 1970, 10 were state enterprises (mainly oil, steel, and infra-structural), 14 were foreign (motor vehicles, oil, chemicals, tires, and tobacco), and six Argentine private capital (food processing, steel, footwear, and cellulose).

In some instances there is considerable interpenetration between foreign, local finance capital, and state capital. The example of Bunge and Born is cited above. The Brazilian Matarazzo group has a very similar evolution to Bunge and Born. Another Argentine example is Celulosa Argentina, one of the largest private Argentine firms. This company shares ownership of another large Argentine company, Electroclor, with ICI, the British chemical firm. Electroclor in turn (in the late 1960s) had a 10 percent share of

Petroquimico Bahia Blanco, then a new, largely state-owned firm. A large share of Celulosa Argentina is controlled by the private financial interests behind Fabril Financiera, a holding company which is also involved with Dunlop-Pirelli of the United Kingdom and Italy.

The close relation between transnational corporations, local finance capital, and state capital is more pronounced in Brazil than in Argentina. Peter Evan's excellent study *Dependent Development* is appropriately subtitled "The Alliance of Multinational, State, and Local Capital in Brazil." Evans's thesis is that "The dominant class in the semi-periphery is seen as composed of three interdependent partners who have a common interest in capital accumulation and in the subordination of the mass population, but whose interests are also contradictory" (1979:52). His empirical study reveals much more complementarity of interest than contradiction and conflict within the "triple alliance." Evans suggests that the relation between foreign and local capital has encompassed both denationalization and 'simultaneous and differentiated expansion' " (1979:103).

Evans studied the concentration of capital in different sectors of the economy:

—Sectors with local predominance include leather products, printing and publishing, apparel and footwear, wood products, paper, nonmetallic minerals.
—Other sectors have local predominance with significant foreign participation: food and beverages, textiles, metal fabrication.
—Foreign firms are predominant but local capital significantly participates in chemicals, machinery, electrical machinery.
—Extensive foreign control exists in tobacco, rubber products, pharmaceuticals, and transportation equipment.
—State enterprises predominate in transportation, power, steel, mining, and other key areas.

Those industries controlled by national capital are relatively stagnant and their importance in terms of the value added in manufacturing is less than 20%. Subsidiaries of transnational corporations tend to be in highly dynamic sectors requiring large investments and high technology. Return on capital in these sectors is higher than in others. Sectors where foreign and local capital are mixed (in joint ventures in some cases, in competition in others) produce the bulk of the value added. It is in these sectors of mixed participation where Brazilian finance capital (termed *grupos multibilionarios* in Brazil) become increasingly associated with transnational capital. Evans provides some detail on the mode and extent of the incorporation of seven local groups into "the structure of international capital." About one-third of foreign investment in the 1960s was joint ventures with Brazilian capital.

Unlike many nations in Latin America, Argentina does not have a long history of foreign investment that completely dominated the export economy. Still, nineteenth and early twentieth century British investments were substantial, the bulk of it located in railroads. British merchants were also resident in Buenos Aires export-import businesses and there were a variety of other British and American companies.

Foreign investment began to decline under the effects of the depression. Between 1931 and 1945 British investments fell from $4,294 million to $2,271. Peron then bought out most of the remainder, leaving only $402 million in British capital in 1955. U.S. investments declined from $1,436 in 1931 to $558 in 1955. Total foreign investment decreased from $7,640 million to $1,860 million during the same years.

During Peron's last years (1951–1955) new foreign investment amounted to only $16 million. After the 1955 military coup, coinciding with the maturation of the transnational corporation, foreign investment began a spectacular spiral upwards, to over $250 million in new investments in 1956–1958. In the next two years transnational capital invested more than a half billion dollars in Argentina. Between 1960 and 1971 the rate slowed down, but the total reached $811 in new investments.

The flow of foreign capital during the initial years of dependent development was by no means one way. Profit and dividend transfers abroad during the 1960 decade ranged from $30 million (1963) to $108 million (1969), for an average of about $85 million annually. In addition, interest payments on foreign capital's external debt averaged $68 million annually. The total public and private foreign debt during the decade of the 1960s more than doubled to nearly $6 billion and service on the debt became a considerable drain on foreign exchange. Added to this transfer of capital abroad were payments for foreign licenses and royalties.

In total, net direct foreign investment between 1955 and 1972 reached $1,313.2 million: This investment increased the participation of transnational corporations in Argentine production from 8% to 40%. The Ongania regime's Economic Minister from 1966, Krieger Vasena (an Argentine director of 12 transnational corporations), issued a new banking law that facilitated the rapid establishment of a strong foreign presence in the financial sector. Transnational banks acquired 19 Argentine banks between 1967 and 1969, achieving control of about one-fifth of all bank transactions. The total of foreign capital invested in Brazil is triple that of Argentina, $3.6 in 1974. By 1973, Brazil had become the sixth largest market for subsidiaries of American corporations.

United States corporations accounted for about two-thirds of the foreign investment in Argentina during this period. In 1973, the U.S. corporate share of all foreign investments in Argentina was 56.5%, or $1.3 billion.

U.S. capital is concentrated in the chemical, plastics, metallurgical, electrical appliance, and auto industries. These sectors are all heavily concentrated.

Growing economic concentration and the influx of foreign capital, with state policies favoring these trends, led to difficult times for smaller and medium-sized Argentine firms, even though national capital continued to control substantial amounts of production. While foreign investment boomed, the economy as a whole stagnated. During the apex of the foreign investment boom the rate of bankruptcies increased sharply: from 67 per month in 1960 to 107 in 1961 and 153 in 1962. In 1968, there were a total of 1,647 bankruptcies and in 1970 2,982, involving peso values of 324.7 million and 1.15 billion, respectively. Large foreign firms or local finance capital moved in to take the markets previously enjoyed by bankrupt firms.

Acquisition of Argentine companies by transnational and Argentine finance capital also proceeded apace with the growing degree of economic concentration. Fifty-three Argentine firms of substantial size, many pressed by economic circumstances, were acquired by transnational corporations between 1963 and 1971; nine of these acquisitions were among the very largest owned by Argentine national capital.

In the space of two decades the Argentine economy had become very heavily penetrated by transnational capital, mostly in monopoly form as indicated in these key sectors of the economy in the late 1960s:

Fertilizers: 1 foreign firm controlled 100% of production
Petrochemicals: 5 foreign firms controlled 100% of production
Tires: 3 foreign firms controlled 83% of production
Non-ferrous metals: 2 foreign firms controlled 85% of production
Engines: 2 foreign firms controlled 60% of production
Compressed gases: 2 foreign firms controlled 60% of production
Paints: 4 foreign firms controlled 70% of production

Of course, the real degree of monopolization of markets is not necessarily revealed in statistics on concentration in an oligoplistic structure; there is considerable product specialization such that a single firm may have a large proportion or all of the market for that product, while competing with other firms in other product lines.

In rhythm with economic concentration was increasing inequality in income distribution. The share of salaries and wages in the national income gradually declined from a high of 45.6 percent in 1954 to 35.2 percent in 1972. The upper 10% of income recipients increased their share of the national income at the expense of all other income groups. This too affected the situation of national capital, as markets for ordinary consumer goods became more constricted with declining mass purchasing power. In Brazil, dependent development also has had a pronounced effect on income distribution. In 1960 the richest one percent and five percent had 11.7 percent and 27.3 percent of national income, respectively; by 1970 their proportions had increased to 17.8 percent and 36.3 percent; the poorest 80 percent of income earners lost 8.7 percent of their share of national income over the decade.

The state controls 10 of the top 30 enterprises in Argentina. These are transportation and utility companies, except for YPF, the state oil company, SOMISA, the largest steel works, and Siam di Tella (sold by Argentina private interests in 1965 to IKA-Renault and acquired by the state in 1972; a one-time producer of motor vehicles, the company now produces mainly electrical appliances). The state has established a number of other enterprises that do not figure among the largest, but are located in strategic sectors. State enterprises have accumulated a considerable indebtedness to international financial institutions, U.S. government agencies, and foreign banks.

In South America, as in the rest of the Third World, the state has historically assumed an ever-widening array of functions, and these tend to increase in number and significance with capitalist development. The entrepreneurial functions of government have been much less circumscribed in the dependent countries than in Western cases. In the typical view of capitalists, government should not directly accumulate capital and invest it in the production process, except in those areas essential to development but unprofitable to private enterprise (such as transportation facilities); to do so diminishes the private accumulation of capital and places the state in competition with private capital.

The limits to the entrepreneurial role of the state, however, appear to be quite wide, for in many Third World nations the state has in fact historically evolved as the most successful of national entrepreneurs. It is not unusual for the government's share of total investment to exceed substantially that of private capital and for the state to compete with private capital in the production of producers and consumers goods. (State enterprises are often monopolies in particular sectors, and thus not usually in direct market competition as such, but state enterprises are often in a strong position in the competition of capitals.)

The entrepreneurial functions and managerial prerogatives of the state have been greater in Brazil than elsewhere in South America. The Brazilian state performs its entrepreneurial role at two levels, direct investments in large-scale infra-structural and industrial developments and in being the pivotal actor in making the triple alliance function.

Brazilian state firms have grown even faster than transnational corporation operations. In 1973 government enterprises accounted for 39 percent of total production, with the strongest presence in public utilities (84 percent of all assets), mining (63 percent), banking and finance (38 percent), services (36 percent), and industry (19 percent).

The technocrats and military managers of the Brazilian state have spearheaded rather impressive projects of joint ventures between government enterprise, transnational corporations, and local business (almost exclusively finance capital). Evans notes:

> The new partnerships between the state and the multinationals also have implications for the future position of local capital. The setting up of a joint venture provides a context for bringing in the 'national bourgeoisie' as a third partner. The creation of 'tri-pé' or 'tripod' ventures reinforces the tendency toward alliances between the local elite groups and the multinationals. It also gives local capital another way of expanding the sphere in which it can operate. The creation of partnerships does not abolish the previous division of labor, either between local and foreign or between state and private capital. In fact, joint ventures tend to take place in sectors that lie on the 'buffer zones' between the territories of different kinds of capital. Alliances blur the boundaries, while at the same time fostering a new, more tightly knit kind of integration among the different kinds of capital [1979:227].

Evans studied such tri-pé ventures in petrochemicals, mining, pharmaceuticals, and apparel.

Dependent development and its accompanying "modernization" also form two new groupings of increasing significance: a managerial bourgeoisie and a techno-bureaucracy. The managerial grouping is attached to firms in the monopoly sector of transnational corporations and large-scale private capital; persons associated with certain law firms that specialize in connecting transnational investors to local influentials and government agencies are also part of this new fraction of the local bourgeoisie. The technocrats are situated in the state apparatuses; in the main civilians even under highly militarized states, this group grows in importance with the addition of each new state function. Since local finance capital is not the dominant force in capital accumulation and since transnational capital is foreign to the national environment, both must cultivate ties and seek favors from the techno-bureaucracy.

There are too few studies of these formations to do more than note their growing number and importance. Davis and Goodman (1972) provide a descriptive study of management practices in Latin America. Jonas and Dixon (1979) are the only analysts to posit links between the formation of managerial and technocratic groups and transformations of the social structure and political order with dependent development. Newfarmer (1977) studied interlocking directorates between competing foreign and domestic firms in the Brazilian electrical industry. Evans (1979) discusses the Brazilian "state bourgeoisie" and Moreira Alves (1974–1975) presents an interesting analysis of Brazilian technocrats under the military government. My own study of Chilean industrial managers, together with similar 1960s studies in other countries (cited in Johnson, 1966–1967, 1967–1968), are out of date with recent developments, in which managers have achieved an undoubtably more central place.

It should be noted that Latin America has produced a large proportion of the world's leading economists and theorists of development and underdevelopment. The UN's Economic Commission for Latin America, for many years the leading agency in development policy in the region, is staffed by highly esteemed professionals, many of whom are nationalist and "developmentalist" in orientation. With the overthrow of reformist and populist states in Latin America, the juntas of militarized states all moved quickly to replace civilian nationalistic technocrats with military officers or civilians of conservative views as managers of state enterprises and administrators of government agencies; military authorities dismantled or completely reoriented state development corporations staffed with progressive development economists, and restructured the relations between state, local, and foreign capital, converting the technocrats into an instrument of the process of denationalization. The technocrats have changed faces and ideology, but they remain a key and growing sector.

Coffee Barons, Ranchers, and Latifundistas

The place of landowners in the structure of the dominant class and their relations with the finance capital/transnational capital alliance raises some theoretical difficulties that have not been resolved in the literature. There are also empirical uncertainties in the rapidly changing structure. Historically, the development of the capitalist mode of production in the periphery has been a highly uneven process, sometimes conceptualized as a process of "dissolution and conservation" of pre-existing modes of production, which are typically agrarian in character. In my view, uneven development in Latin America is not a question of pre-capitalist modes of production in articulation with the capitalist mode; it has never been one of transition from feudalism to capitalism and certainly not of feudal landlords versus a nascent industrial bourgeoisie. (These questions are addressed in Chilcote and Johnson, 1983, and in Johnson, 1981). Uneven development is more aptly seen as a telescoping of the forms of dependent development upon the historically evolved structures of nineteenth and early twentieth century classic underdevelopment and the national development of the 1930s and

1940s. Since the 1950s, the newest forms of monopoly capitalism character-istic of the imperial center have been transplanted upon indigenous struc-tures—economic, social, and political structures—that retain some of the salient characteristics of prior stages of capitalist development and underde-velopment.

Dependence upon primary production is a salient feature from prior stages retained during the stage of dependent development. For this reason, primary producers, as a fraction of the dominant class, continue to have some, though diminishing, importance.

There is considerable national variation in the place of agriculturalists and landlords in Latin America economies, social structures, and political systems. In Mexico, Bolivia, and Peru traditional landed "aristrocrats" *(latifundistas)* have been all but eliminated as a consequence of agrarian reforms. (In Chile agrarian reform was for the most part reversed by the post-1973 military government.) Venezuela's mild agrarian reform was less important than petroleum wealth and industrial development in undermining the power of traditional *latifundistas* of the plains and the plantation-owners of the coast. In Brazil and Colombia coffee barons and tropical plantation owners remain important sectors of national business classes, as do the ranchers and big farmers of Argentina and Uruguay. However, throughout the region, leading families of these traditional rural sectors have long since either been relegated to the position of country gentlemen, become modern capitalist farmers, or shifted their main interests to urban financial and commercial activities. Through agribusiness or urban activities they became associated with either modern finance capital or competitive national cap-ital. Zeitlin and Ratcliff's study of the structure of the Chilean dominant class (1975) is particularly good on the family and business interlocks between landlords and urban capitalists. Sergio Bagú notes "the big interest groups have become intertwined by way of investments and family ties. There are industrialist-landlords in all countries and ranchers with interests in urban firms." (1975:44).

In much of the region, elements that remain primarily engaged in com-mercial agriculture constitute subordinate parts, usually very ideologically reactionary, of prevailing national power blocs. They have some political weight and are taken into account by those who effectively wield power, but their interests do not determine the development strategies adopted by the predominant business sectors and governments.

The Argentine ranchers remain a more fundamental element of the dominant class than elsewhere in the region. While perhaps overstating the case, Sergio Bagú indicates that "the old oligarchy conserves very well delineated cultural and group limits." Further, "the old landowning and cattle oligarchy of the Argentine *pampa húmeda* is, without any doubt, the only one of the continent that has not been shaken by the misfortunes of history: very rich and presently prospering" (1975:43).

With respect to rural interests in Uruguay, Bagú says: "The landowning oligarchy specializing in the production of wool, with beef a secondary activity and a colateral participation in cereal, continues to stand on its feet as an economic sector. As a social class it is today considerably linked with commercial and financial interests" (1975:43). The agriculture of Uruguay, since the late nineteenth century oriented to agro-export is richly blessed by nature, but functions extensively with both elemental technology and low labor requirements. The nation of European immigrants was never saddled with traditional productive structures and aristocratic class cultures. By the turn of the century, export revenues were financing modernizing reform and considerable urban commercial and industrial development. These were sponsored by a democratic state in which a vast petty bourgeoisie and important salaried middle strata were an integral part of the social basis of the power bloc led by urban export-import merchants and commercial agriculturalists turning into a class of urban businessmen.

Before the relatively recent consolidation of centralized states in Latin American countries, regionally-based class interests fought, often violently, among themselves. Regional power of landowners is mainly ancient history. In the United States and to a perhaps lesser degree in the more administratively centralized nations of Europe, smaller-scale capital in the competitive sector tends to dominate state and local government, while monopoly capital exercises its instrumental power through the national government. The extreme centralization of economic activities in a principal city and the administrative consolidation of national states in Latin America in recent decades have made it difficult for regional competitive capital or landowners to exercise any appreciable political prerogatives through the medium of provincial or municipal governments. Historically provinces were the private fiefdoms of regional *caciques* or *gamonales*. There are still some residues of this structure, but influence is exercised over matters that do not have great significance to national economic and political affairs. The traditional forms of domination over agricultural laborers, peasants, and the impoverished peoples of smaller towns once exercised directly by provincial dominant classes have shifted to modern forms implemented by the armed forces, national police, and judiciaries subject to national government control.

Primary production in agriculture and mining, the highly conflictive relations of production within these spheres, and the links between primary producers and other sectors nevertheless remain significant. In Latin America today the primary export sector, corresponding to the imperatives of the nineteenth and early twentieth century international division of labor is still the life blood of the economy. For example, while subsidiaries of transnational corporations and the Brazilian firms export increasing amounts of manufactured goods, the economy is very dependent on coffee, mineral, and other primary exports. (Even the anachronistic plantations of the Northeast, once utilizing slave labor, still survive with a combination of landlord/peon relations and waged labor with less than subsistence wages.) Primary export dependency is even more exaggerated in Uruguay, Argentina, and Chile. While industrial sectors are now the principal locus of capital accumulation, this accumulation heavily depends upon the availability of foreign exchange earned through pursuing primary exports.[5] In class terms, continuing dependence on primary exports means that the locally predominant fraction, finance capital, must either control that production, or facilitate the investment of transnational agribusiness or mining corporations, or make a favored space for interests involved in traditional primary exports. To the degree that finance capital retains or reasserts control over primary exports, with which it has historic links in any case, or invites foreign agribusiness and mining investors, it becomes locked into the long established structural patterns of classical underdevelopment. To the degree that a separate fraction of primary producers is protected both the intra-class division of landlords and capitalists and the sharply conflictive landlord and agricultural worker or mine-owner and miner social relation is preserved.

In practice, especially after the establishment of military governments, all three of these avenues of preservation of the old features of underdevelopment have been cemented. The Pinochet regime in Chile, as noted in chapter 6, aims at development policies designed to restructure capital away from traditional consumer goods industry and toward forestry, a revitalization of export agriculture, and copper. The old doctrine of comparative advantages has been dusted off and applied to the new international circumstances: Chilean private and foreign capital, with state incentives, guarantees, or participation, enter into a partnership taking advantage of an internal supply of cheap labor created through the repressive policies of the regime, a favorable investment climate, abundant natural resources, and the backing of foreign banks to again emphasize an export economy. This development strategy, after a decade of effort, has not worked and is not likely to work in the 1980s, but in the process the dominant class is remolded and all class relations reach extremes of antagonism. These relations are for the time being kept from exploding by the effective institutionalization of the state repressive apparatus.

Notes

1. There is a considerable empirical literature on "economic groups," especially on Chile, Argentina, Brazil, and Peru. This dates back to the early 1960s and the classic study of Lagos (1961); the most solid empirical study is Zeitlin and Ratcliff (1975); and the most recent is Cordero and Santin (1982).

2. The dominant sector of Mexican capital developed somewhat later than in South America and in a much more direct relationship to the state; nor does it possess the political power of the oligarches of Argentina, Brazil, Chile, and Uruguay.

3. The parallel with Bismarkian Germany is more one of pattern than substance, as Latin American modes of production and class structures bore little resemblence to those of late nineteenth century Germany. The Mexican revolution which more or less eliminated traditional dominant class power is a Latin American exception to this pattern. See also analyses of the Peruvian Revolution in Chapters 1 and 9.

4. However, Argentine industrialists have been much more assertive (especially since the 1960s) than in Chile or Brazil. In Chile, immigrant industrialists were the main figures in national development, but were not in any way constituted as a self-conscious class (Johnson, 1967–1968, 1968–1969). (For more extensive analysis of Chilean industrialists and references to the studies of Latin American industrial bourgeoisies, see Johnson, 1966). In the writing on Argentine history I have found Murmis and Portantiero (1971) particularly helpful. Also, useful was *Latin American Perspectives* (1974, 1982).

5. Though industrial exports were increasing, especially in Brazil and Mexico, accumulation depends on foreign exchange earned through primary exports—and of course foreign investments and international credits. Much "foreign" investment is actually generated from local sources. Moreover, since the net flow of foreign investment (capital inflow minus outflow of profit remissions, royalties, and other service charges) is not very great or even negative (depending on the country and time period), the accumulation process depends upon foreign loans. The foreign debt becomes astronomical and the nation ever more firmly locked into debt trap dependency.

References

Bagú, Sergio
1975   "Las clases sociales del subdesarrollo." Pp. 9–52 in Sergio Bagu et al., Problemas del subdesarrollo Latinoamericano. Mexico: Nuestro Tiempo.
Chilcote, Ronald H. and Dale L. Johnson (eds.)
1983   Theories of Development: Mode of Production or Dependency? Beverly Hills, CA: Sage.
Comblin, José
1979   The Church and the National Security State. Maryknoll, NY: Orbis Books.
Cordero, Salvador and Rafael Santín
1982   Los grupos industriales: una nueva organización económica en México. Mexico: Cuadernos del CES, El Colegio de Mexico.
Davis, Stanley M. and Louis Wolf Goodman
1970   Workers and Managers in Latin America. Lexington, MA: D. C. Heath.
dos Santos, Teotonio
1968   El nuevo caracter de la dependencia. Santiago, Chile: Universidad de Chile, Cuadernos del Centro de Estudios Socio-Económicos, No. 10.
1970   "The structure of dependence." American Economic Review 60 (May): 231–236.

Dreifus, René Armand
1980   1964: A conquista do Estado. Acão política, poder e golpe de classe. Rio de Janeiro: Editora vozes.
Engels, Frederick
1969–70   The Role of Force in History. Volume 3 of Marx, Karl and Frederick Engels, Selected Works. Moscow: Progress Publishers.
Evans, Peter
1979   Dependent Development. The Alliance of Multinational, State, and Local Capital in Brazil. Princeton, NJ: Princeton University Press.
Jessop, Bob
1983   "Accumulation strategies, state forms, and hegemonic projects." Kapitalistate 10/11: 89–112.
Johnson, Dale L.
1966   Industry and Industrialists in Chile. Ph.D. dissertation, Stanford University.
1967–1968   Industrialization, Social Mobility, and Class Formation in Chile. Monograph Series Studies in Comparative International Development 3, No. 7. St. Louis: Washington University.
1968–1969   The "National" and "Progressive" Bourgeoise in Chile. Monograph Series Studies in Comparative International Development 4, No. 4. St. Louis: Washington University.
1981   "Economism and determinism in dependency theory." Latin American Perspectives 30/31 (Summer/Fall): 108–117.
1983   "Class analysis and dependency," pp. 231–255 in Ronald H. Chilcote and Dale L. Johnson (eds.) Theories of Development: Mode of Production or Dependency? Beverly Hills, CA: Sage.
Jonas, Suzanne and Marlene Dixon
1979   "Proletarianization and class alliances in the Americas." Synthesis 3 (Fall): 1–13.
Latin American Perspectives
1974   "Argentina: Peronism and crisis." Special issue, Vol. 1 (Fall).
1982   "Argentina in Crisis." Special issue, Vol. 9 (Fall).
Lagos, Ricardo
1961   La concentración del poder económico. Santiago, Chile: Editorial del Pacífico.
McDonough, Peter
1981   Power and Ideology in Brazil. Princeton, NJ: Princeton University Press.
Moore, Barrington, Jr.
1966   Social Origins of Dictatorship and Democracy. Lords and Peasants in the Making of the Modern World. Boston: Beacon Press.
Moreira Alves, Marcio
1974–75   "The political economy of the Brazilian technocracy." Berkeley Journal of Sociology 19:109–124.
Murmis, Miguel and Juan Carlos Portantiero
1971   Esudios sobre los orígenes del Peronismo. Buenos Aires: Siglo 21.
Newfarmer, Richard S.
1977   Multinational conglomerates and the economics of dependent development: A Case Study of the International Electrical Oligopoly and Brazil's Electrical Industry. Ph.D. dissertation, University of Wisconsin, Madison.
Zeitlin, Maurice and Richard Ratcliff
1975   "Research methods for the analysis of the internal structure of dominant classes: the case of landlords and capitalists in Chile." Latin American Research Review 10 (No. 3): 5–57.

CHAPTER EIGHT

Dale L. Johnson: Local Bourgeoisies, Intermediate Strata, and Hegemony in South America

Dominant classes in Latin America are sharply divided. There is no "national bourgeoisie" that can establish hegemony with the consent or pacific acquiescence of the citizenry. A vacuum in class power in civil society creates an objective need for decisive state power. And this becomes imperative as dependent development structurally polarizes the social order between concentrated and centralized capital and a maturing working class and as the same process dispossesses millions of people of their traditional subsistence without providing industrial employment. The intermediate classes have their place in this polarization and in creating a behemoth of state power. That same behemoth now consumes their aspirations.

Examined first is the significance of the divisions within the local bourgeoisie; this is followed by an analysis of the broader class formations, those in demise as well as those in ascendence, and the antagonisms and struggles that have presented conjunctures of "organic crisis." Concluding the chapter is an analysis of the main features of the "national security states" that have emerged in these conjunctures in South America and the prospects for democratization of dictatorship.

The Significance of Fractional Conflicts

The formation of a dominant (or any other) class cannot be understood solely in terms of the structure of the economy, the direction of the accumulation process, and the preservation-dissolution of pre-existing forms from prior development stages. Studies of the concentration and centralization of capital, of the sources and avenues of accumulation, and of the sectoral development of the economy provide empirical knowledge of the economic roots of a dominant class. A dialectics of class relates economic roots to social branches, the economic process to the changing social relations associated with that process. Capital accumulation is a process of unfolding class relationships. (This is examined theoretically in Johnson, 1982: chaps. 1–3.)

There is a methodological problem in relying too extensively upon the empirical studies of sectoral economic concentration, interlocking directorates between banks and industries, family and business links between urban capitalists and landlords, and so on. These studies have informed the prior chapter's analysis of the local bourgeoisie and its fractions. The conclusions are evident: In each of the nations of the Southern Cone the economic roots of a class of high finance capital is empirically demonstrable. Since the 1950s, monopoly firms have come to concentrate production and dominate markets in the main economic sectors; centralization of capital has proceeded apace under the away of banks financial institutions; industrial capital in intermediate and durable consumer goods has become the principal locus of capital accumulation. Various studies have revealed the central place in this process of a reduced group of big capitalists associating themselves with foreign capital.

Nevertheless, the empirical studies of Latin American dominant classes are almost always static in conception and they often exaggerate the strength of finance capital and ignore the implication of structural trends for intrabourgeois class relations. For this reason, I have tried, in the prior chapter and in the pages that follow, to pursue a somewhat more historical method geared toward understanding the basis of recent intra-class conflict. Succinctly stated, analysis indicates that while modernized local finance capital, which has deep historical roots in traditional oligarchies, aspires toward an economic predominance, subordinating national capital to his end, it does so in alliance with transnational capital, which in effect becomes a senior partner (though operating from a distance) and while also preserving an uneasy relation or intermingling with the traditional primary export interests.

To explore further the social branches: The process of capital accumulation in the stage of dependent development has two major structural concomitants, both having to do with changes in intra-bourgeois class relations. First, it progressively undermines the basis for the emergence of any class formation approximating a "national bourgeoisie." Second, it creates a disjuncture between the existing social bases and modes of exercising state power and the qualitative shifts in relations between fractions of the capitalist class.

The character of the dominant class, especially its status as a "national bourgeoisie," is still much debated. Events seem to me to moot the debate. Local finance capital finds its association with transnational capital highly advantageous, while smaller-scale, competitive national capital is gradually eliminated or subordinated into internal relations of dependence as concen-

trated and centralized capital gains ground. Within the limits of the interstices remaining to national capital, businessmen can hardly aspire to the
status of "national bourgeoisie."

There is then, in the face of recent relations of dependence and new forms
of capital accumulation, a "denationalization of the national bourgeoisie"
(Johnson, 1973a, 1973b; Cockcroft, Frank, and Johnson, 1972). But this is
not the only factor in understanding the character of the local bourgeoisie.

The trend toward strengthening of the finance capital fraction and
weakening of smaller-scale capital flows with the logic of the accumulation
process. But this logic benefits some interests and adversely effects others.
The political logic is therefore that the structural trend is promoted by some
interests and resisted by others. Class fractionalization has a structural
source in historical patterns of economic development and a social-political
source. The relations of classes in the new conditions presented by economic
development lead to new directions in class struggle. In terms of intracapi-
talist class struggles, the finance capital fraction has, in recent years, moved
energetically in the political sphere to translate its increased economic
predominance, shared with transnational capital, into a new hegemony in
the form of "modern" military dictatorship. At the same time, the exclusion
from the privileged association with transnational capital, competitive disadvantages engendered by the concentration and centralization of capital,
and government policies favoring the finance capital/transnational capital
alliance, would seem to present an objective basis for the emergence of a
nationalist fraction of the bourgeoisie. Whether a bourgeois nationalism
emerges from the disadvantaged sector to resist the structural trend and its
political concomitants, however, depends on the course of the class struggle. In actual experience to date, only in Argentina, especially during the
early and middle 1970s, did a fraction of the local bourgeoisie transform
itself into a "national bourgeoisie" of sorts. This was due largely to the
specific character of the political struggle there, quite distinct from the
neighboring countries of South America, that permitted a self-conscious,
nationalist fraction of the bourgeoisie to organize itself in the form of a class
organization, the General Economic Confederation, and to forge a political
alliance with the trade union movement and Peronist elements. This alliance
fell apart after Peron's death (1974) and this sector of the bourgeoisie was
sharply subordinated politically and devastated economically through government policies after the 1976 military intervention. This devastation,
however, was one of the factors in bringing about the collapse of the
Argentine dictatorship in 1983.

Thus the local bourgeoisie as a whole, having lost any basis for becoming
a "national bourgeoisie," is also a sharply divided class: Finance capital
comes into conflict with declining groupings of national industrial entre-

preneurs and landowners and the different economic groups of finance capital compete among themselves to extend their conglomerations. This provides another "structural effect" that, in the crisis of transition, has a considerable implication for the state.

The intra-bourgeois fractional conflicts create an objective need for the state to intervene, either to protect threatened national capital, or to attempt to achieve a balance of competing interests within the anarchy of the competition of capitals, or to implement policies that facilitate the structural imperatives of dependent development. The democratic, reform, and populist states of the Southern Cone in the 1950s and 1960s (and the Peronist government of 1973–1976), because of their multi-class social bases formed in the stage of national development, proved incapable of responding effectively to the objective need for decisive state intervention. These states did not prove competent either (a) to protect national industry and vigorously pursue strategies of continuing to build a system of national capitalism, or (b) to achieve an amalgam of a state-directed national capitalism and dependent development, or (c) to follow the logic of the direction of capital accumulation and class relations under the new forms of dependency relations. In Latin America, Peru attempted strategy (a) between 1968–1974—it collapsed; Chile under the Christian Democrats tried strategy (b)—this led to a socialist government; only Mexico has been able to pursue strategy (c) without resorting to dictatorship.

Thus, the process of internal accumulation under the imperatives of changing relations of dependency and the new strains within intrabourgeois class relations in the transition to dependent development demanded qualitative changes in the class character and policies of the state. *A bourgeoisie that associates with transnational capital in order to gain local predominance, weakens itself as an instrument of the nation. A vacuum in class power is created in which the behemoth of state power thrives. A dependent and divided local bourgeoisie needs a strong, decisive state.* This is one of the most important ingredients in the final recipe for military dictatorship. Once firmly established, each of the dictatorships moved decisively to restructure the relations between the fractions of capital and to subordinate or terrorize the other classes, in strict accordance with the structural logic of dependent development.

In some respects, this analysis of the structural effects of intra-bourgeois class relations approximates, as theoretically posed in chapter 6, a structuralist statement. The movement of transnational forces of production and the internal concentration of production and centralization of control carry structural effects that the state, as the institution of reproduction of the capitalist order, must intervene to confront: The state "does what it has to do" in terms of the system as a whole. I have tried to take the level of analysis somewhat further than a purely structuralist stance, along the lines suggested by state derivation theory, in that the capital accumulation process is viewed as a socially contradictory process, involving changing bases for antagonistic class relations. Dependent development reorganizes the bourgeoisie and brings about qualitative changes in intra-class struggles. The finance capital/transnational capital alliance comes out on top in this struggle and the character of the local bourgeoisie as a whole changes from anything resembling a "national bourgeoisie" to a "dependent bourgeoisie." Since each of the military governments of the Southern Cone moved decisively to impose policies consistent with the interests of this alliance and in keeping with the new character of the local bourgeoisie, the analysis implicitly moves away from a structuralist stance and toward a more "instrumentalist" conception. This also needs to be taken a good deal further, for the range of ruthless measures adopted by militarized states cannot be accounted for instrumentally as the outcome of foreign economic penetration, an alliance of foreign and local capital, and intra-class struggles within the local dominant class. The emergence of the national security state can only be understood root and branch in terms of the process of dependent development and the full gamut of unfolding class relations in the conjunctures of the crisis of the 1960s and 1970s.

The Broader Spectrum of Class Relations

The emergence and consolidation of the alliance between the dominant finance capital fraction of the local, dependent bourgeoisie and transnational capital has always to be seen in relation to the other class formations within the national societies of the Southern Cone. In keeping with the perspective of uneven development, these class formations are of two types: those that are tied to the old order of preceding development stages and those that, while in incipient formation in prior periods, are primarily products of the economic and social transformations of the recent period of dependent development. The former include national capitalists in the competitive sector, the petty bourgeoisie, and landowners and agricultural laborers engaged in traditional export production. The latter formations include the managerial bourgeoisie and technocratic staff, the working class, the salaried middle class, a vast "surplus population" or "marginal underclass" (Johnson, 1972), and various social or institutional forces such as students, intellectuals, the church, and the military.

Discussed in the previous chapter were national capital, the managerial and technocratic elements, and landowners; accordingly we turn to a brief sketch of the subaltern classes and institutional forces, followed by an analysis of the old petty bourgeoisie and the new salaried intermediate classes; the concluding section analyzes how the struggles of these contending forces came together in crisis conjunctures, with an outcome of military dictatorship.

Workers, Masses, and Institutional Forces

During the 1950s and 1960s in the Southern Cone, the industrial working classes achieved a considerable advance in size and strength—together with and in opposition to foreign and domestic monopoly capital that had attached to itself a large contingent of professionalized managers. The political maturity and class assertions of workers strongly reverberated in South American political scenes.

The main thrust of accumulation under dependent development is industrialization—steel, energy, cars, electrical appliances, chemicals, manufactures and semi-processed goods for export. Modern industry imposes a modernized labor process of imported technology and organizational forms and substantially augments a working class already in formation in the period of national development. The working class—though in the 1960s only about 15 percent of the labor force in Brazil, 20 percent in Chile and Uruguay, and 25 percent in Argentina—had begun to reach maturity. Militant trade unionism and support for the most radical populism and Marxist parties among growing sectors of workers were the order of the day. The gradual extension of capital into the countryside displaced millions to the cities and converted the bulk of the remaining peasantry into a rural semi-proletariat; urban slums mushroomed and agricultural unions and rural social movements exploded.

The "dissolution" effects of uneven, dependent development have been greater than the "conservation" effects, including great dislocations in the countryside and towns. The way of life of millions of people was totally disrupted. An astounding, massive marginalization and immiseration of millions of peasants and workers—the creation of a vast "surplus population" or "underclass"—took place. Migration from the countryside, high birth rates, and the inability of new capital intensive industry to absorb the exploding supply of labor swelled the underclasses of large and small cities. The specter of possible mobilization of the impoverished masses (or "marginals" as they came to be called)[1] for fundamental change haunted the consciousness of all the privileged classes.

An array of new social forces distinct from the classes came sharply into play in the 1960s. As part of programs of national development, reform and populist governments had created an expanding system of higher education. University training became a way for the offspring of the traditional petty bourgeoisie in decline to find a new place in society and for the growing salaried middle class to seek its intergenerational reproduction. These students organized and exerted pressure for reform and, as the 1960s progressed, for revolutionary change. Youthful sectors drawn largely from the more privileged classes carried out guerrilla operations—in Uruguay the Tupamaros and in Argentina the ERP (Revolutionary Army of the People). Both were liquidated by the military in the 1970s. Artists and writers developed a new, critical culture that flourished in the turmoil and expectations of the 1960s. Marxism became the principle mode of analysis among intellectuals. Latin America, with Chile becoming its principle seat, became a world center of creative cultural and intellectual advance. The great struggles and issues of the day divided the Church. A radical theology of liberation revitalized Catholicism everywhere and in Latin America mobilized large numbers of Christians for socialism. And, finally, the military, trained and equipped by the United States, became a consolidated, national institution.

The main roots of military dictatorship are located in the relation between the finance capital/transnational capital alliance and the classes and institutional forces that are products of dependent development. And within these volatile relations, the antagonism between modern capital and an industrial working class, for the first time in Latin American history, came to define the central place in the movement of events. Unhappily, there is no space for an analysis (see Johnson, 1983), beyond the summary description above, of the working class, nor of the underclass and insitutional forces whose assertions added greatly to the clamor for change. (On the place of the working class see Spalding, 1977, and *Latin American Perspectives*, 1976.) But the salaried intermediate class—because it came to play such a decisive role in the polarized camps of the finance capital/transnational capital and modern working class in the conjunctural events leading up to the military coups of the 1960s and 1970s—deserves a more analytic treatment. This class became a principle prop in new projects of an illusive hegemony forged by the alliance of local and international centers of power. It is also this class, within the context of the central capital/labor antagonism in the harsh conditions of military dictatorship, that will likely play an important role in the disintegration and collapse of these regimes.

Intermediate Classes, Old and New

The petty bourgeoisies and salaried middle classes are principal social bases for the different forms states have assumed in Latin America. During the earlier historical stage of national development, these social forces were instrumental in the collapse of oligarchic states and the establishment of democratic-reform and populist states. As the region entered the stage of dependent development more complex social structures were formed and sharpened social struggles ensued. New, self-interested and assertive social strata in the middle ranges proliferated as a consequence of industrialization, urbanization, and other change processes; new stratification hierarchies were induced, giving greater social privilege to intermediate groups; institutions were extended into vast bureaucratic complexes, forming a large social category of authoritative functionaries; new forms of consciousness and ideology were forged; as the capitalist and working classes and masses structurally polarized and internally fragmented, the mediating role of intermediate forces came fully into prominence. The Southern Cone countries in particular entered into crisis. As the different classes and class fractions clashed in deeper conflict, the intermediate groups came to occupy central places in both the political strategies of the reform and revolutionary forces and in the hegemonic projects of the reactionary forces. In great majorities, the intermediate classes moved in support of military dictatorship of counterrevolutionary character.

In the recent period, however, directions of economic and social development and the extreme polarization of power relations have subordinated these groupings. In the stagnant economies of South America in the 1980s their numbers are no longer significantly increasing, their employment and income situation deteriorates, and their places in bureaucratic hierarchies are more circumscribed. The military stewards have demobilized their political energies and pay scant attention to either their particular interests or their frustrated political ambitions as arbiters of the polarized social order.

Intermediate classes are conventionally divided into "old" and "new" segments, the independent producers and small businessmen of the classic petty bourgeoisie and the new middle class of salaried professionals, technicians, and administrative employees.

The petty bourgeoisie in South America can be given the same treatment here that history has accorded this class everywhere where modern forms of capitalist development have taken root—it is reduced to a question of passing significance.

Perhaps this is somewhat of an overstatement since there is still a substantial commercial petty bourgeoisie in South America as well as a group of independent professional practicioners. But small producers are by and large dispossessed of productive property or forced into marginal positions in commerce. Only the expanding service sector provides opportunities for petty entrepreneurship. Many artisans and shopkeepers shift their activities to services, so that much of what remains of the petty bourgeoisie is transformed into a class serving the consumption needs of the socially privileged and affluent groups created by dependent development. But in the main as small workshops and businesses fold, the only thing proprietors have left to sell is their labor power.

At the same time, the social-political effects of the passing of the petty bourgeoisie are quite profound. The petty bourgeoisie valiantly struggles (as it has everywhere throughout world history) for its survival. In the end they lose, but not without leaving indelible marks on the crisis conjunctures that are mainly defined, not by their struggles, but by the transition to new forms of capital accumulation, by the increasingly antagonistic relations of classes and social forces formed or maturing in the process of dependent development, and by the disjuncture between the class alliances undergirding reform and populist states and the changed economic circumstances and shifting balance of social forces.

The process of historical demise of the old petty bourgeoisies and the formation of new salaried intermediate groups in South America is broadly parallel to that in the industrial countries. Both industrialization and "modernization" in the social/cultural sphere proliferate salaried middle elements. Development in South America since the 1930s has required technical and administrative labor and generated an increasing surplus to support these employees at levels above the subsistence of the great majority. They came to constitute the principal market for the industrial production provided first by national capital and later by foreign and local monopoly capital. To sustain these markets and further the growth of the industrial and associated service economy, their numbers, as a proportion of the population gradually increase, along with their levels of real income. During the stage of dependent development one of the main features of industrialization is its relative capital intensity. This requires technical labor. Through improving technical capacity and adopting large-scale and modern industrial organization, the need for directly productive workers, however, relatively decreases. As technology makes labor more productive and markets remain constrained to the more affluent consumers, the process produces the opposite of productive labor; advertising agents, salesmen, and servicing and other "unproductive" personnel become a significant part of the intermediate class.[2]

In the social-cultural and civic spheres the secularization and expansion of the educational system, the rationalization and extension of the state apparatuses, and the demise of popular culture and the production of mass culture, all open up intermediate places in the class structure.

As dependent development unfolds the intermediate classes formed are increasingly subject to contradictory structural forces affecting their social position. On the one hand, the middle groups become integrated into the structure of privilege. On the other hand, these privileges easily become eroded.

The middle groups live at or above the socially defined minimum standard of living, in vivid contrast to the working class and surplus population. In the distribution of stratification attributes, such as higher education and occupational prestige, they are relatively privileged. The roles they perform within institutions—their jobs and their civic participation—are socially rewarded, relatively secure, and instrinsically more personally rewarding than the roles ascribed to the less fortunate. Their lives are less disrupted by change processes. They adopt a certain culture and life style—consumerism, careerism and status striving, competitiveness, a keen awareness of their unique individuality and collective privilege. They expect their children's futures to be more or less assured by social inheritance of social privilege. The youth are accorded a certain latitude of freedom to dissent and, within the limits of the social structure, to become. Middle class women may be less subjugated as women than working class women.

The general tendency has been for dependent development to widen the social gap between the salaried middle and the working classes. Work situations, income levels, and styles of life are quite distinct; the two classes live in separate residential areas; the socialization processes that affect the culture and consciousness of the two classes are very different. However, as dependent development advances, there seems to be a growing gap between the higher level professional and administrative groupings and the lower level technicians and employees. As in the industrial countries, the work of the lower strata of "white collar" employees becomes more like that of industrial workers as the labor process is rationalized and routinized. They scramble with workers for the short-supply of minimally adequate housing. As time goes on, the class situation of the lower segments deteriorates.

Moreover, in the recent periods of dictatorship and economic decline (Brazil) or collapse (Argentina and Chile), the privileged class situation of the entire intermediate class comes under pressure. The military authorities repress or ignore their social and political ambitions. Of greater long-term consequence is the inexorable tendency of dependent development to propel the social order more sharply into two poles, those who possess property and control and those whose only property is their marketable labor power. What remains of the petty bourgeoisie is further eroded, some forced into the working class, others moving horizontally into a salaried middle class whose ranks are now more difficult to breach. Free professionals take regimented, salaried jobs in bureaucratic institutions; administrative and technical work is rationalized, routinized, and where military authority permits, trade-unionized, as if it were workers' work. There is a dialectic operating: as dependent development creates a more complex social structure—proliferating new social strata, inducing new stratification hierarchies, extending institutions into vast bureaucratic complexes, facilitating new forms of consciousness, forging new ideologies, and fractionalizing the social classes—it also increasingly reduces the social structure to its basic class polarization. With strong-armed states overseeing this polarization there is less need for the mediating roles of intermediate groups. This does not mean that, once politically subordinated and once the conditions of "proletarianization" of the middle ranks has advanced sufficiently, they will join the workers and downtrodden mass in consciousness, ideology, and political movement; only that the position of the intermediate class becomes more structurally ambivalent and, as the process of dependent development under military-technocratic management continues, increasingly so.

The emergence phase of military dictatorship is then characterized by these features of the social structure: formation of a substantial salaried intermediate class; a relative demise of classes associated with prior stages of development, rural classes, national capital, and the petty bourgeoisie; a growing polarization between modern monopoly capital, foreign and domestic, and a modern working class and vast surplus population; social and institutional forces, students, intellectuals, religious groups, become politically mobilized.

In the absence of a "leading class" that can through the state translate its economic predominance into the exercise of hegemony over the civil society, other social forces emerge to act as surrogates for the political rule of capital. In the stage of national development and reform or populist states in South America this place was filled by an alliance of diverse class forces in which sectors of the intermediate classes were prominent. In the stage of dependent development, they lost their allegiance to democracy and reform; but in time they too were subordinated as the military became the political directorate of the local finance capital/transnational capital alliance. Military forces moved not simply to displace civilian rule, but to establish, in the difficult search for a true hegemony, an entirely new form of the state.

Goosestepping Toward Hegemony:
The National Security State

The first "National Security State" was established in Brazil in 1964 with the military overthrow of the government of President Goulart. The military intervention was preceded by strong opposition to the reformist and nationalist policies of the government and large-scale populist mobilizations of workers and peasants and slum-dwellers. In the context of economic difficulties and high inflation, strong pressures from the United States and transnational corporations, and, most importantly, the exhaustion of national development depending on import-substitution industrialization and state intervention, the capitalist class as a whole, backed by mobilizations of sizeable segments of the middle class, gave clear indication that it was time for the military to move. By 1968, a year of fierce repression and consolidation of policy direction, the main features of the region's first National Security State were firmly established.

Meanwhile, in 1966, the Argentine military made its first attempt at achieving such a state, only to collapse a few years later under the pressure of worker insurrections, a resurgence of Peronism, popular mobilization for reform, and revolutionary agitation. The military came back with a vengeance in 1976 to establish a dictatorship whose murderous policies surpassed that of the more notorious Chilean regime and was rivaled only in Guatemala and El Salvador (countries where states more and more take on the "modern" features of the national security state). In 1973, the democratic states of Uruguay and Chile were mortally lanced by bayonets.

These regimes were established in what I term "conjunctures of organic crisis." This crisis is quite distinct from the depressionary busts usually connoted by the term, though in each South American instance there have been deep structural problems of the economy. Organic crisis comes about in the transition from one stage of development to another, when shifts in avenues of capital accumulation are also associated with intra-class conflicts within the dominant class and sharpened broader class struggle. The character of regimes are results of particular "hegemonic projects" (a concept developed in Johnson, 1982: chaps. 2, 6; see also Jessop, 1983). And they have, or will, collapse, or at least decline greatly in effectiveness, as economic conditions, accelerated social struggle, and the contradictory nature of the projects prevent the establishment of a true hegemony.

Where these projects have been implemented in South America (Brazil, Argentina, Chile, and Uruguay), the broad features of the state are threefold: (1) The repressive apparatus comes to subsume or overshadow all other facets of state activity. The form of this repression greatly resembles that of classic European fascism, which has caused many observers to apply the term "fascist" to regimes that are best seen as responses to an entirely different set of historical circumstances than that of Europe in the 1930s. (2) The state relentlessly pursues particular policies of national economic development. These policies bear little resemblence to the corporativism, nationalism, and statism of classic fascism. In crucial respects, they are the opposite: The regime aims toward disorganizing interest groups and classes; economic policies are geared to exterior markets, investment sources, and credits and emphasize the principles of classic liberalism. (Brazil more statist policies are somewhat of an exception.) (3) Attempts at legitimation revolve mainly around pronouncements of threatened national security. Since, once the opposition is crushed and the regime consolidated, the mass base of the National Security State is demobilized, these pronouncements tend to resound like official proclamations. While the torture, death squads, censorship, and other ruthless repressions are fascist in style, there is no Nazi or Falangist party, no marching brown shirts, to actively carry the message to the support classes of the dictatorship—largely the salaried middle class, the petty bourgeoisie, and the entire business community.

The Repressive Apparatus. The most notable ingredient of the hegemonic project is the forceful application of new formulae of political rule. (1) A military institutionality replaces civilian forms of state administration to such a degree that it touches all the interstiches of daily life: states of siege, military tribunals—the subordination of the whole of civil society to bureaucratic management and military discipline. (2) Military dictatorship is not a dictatorship of a military man (General Pinochet is a strong dictator, but not a Somoza) but of the Armed Forces as an institution—the Junta— that professes a long-term stewardship of society. (3) A secret police apparatus is developed not only to terrorize the people, but also to deter opposition forces within the classes and groups dispossed in general to support the regime and within the military. Clandestine, right-wing terrorist groups are organized to carry out extra-official torture and assasination. This has resulted in thousands and thousands of "disappeared" persons in several countries (at least 30,000 in Argentina during 1976–1980). (4) Government is technocratic rule backed by the threat or actuality of repression. The normal play of political parties and interest groups is recessed indefinitely or placed under strict control; even popular mobilization in support of the dictatorship is suppressed.

These are the features we have elsewhere referred to as the "dirty" form of the national security state, as distinct from the "clean" form latent in such countries as the United States and the Federal Republic of Germany (Oppenheimer and Canning, 1979).

Development Strategy. South American generals, industrialists, and bankers share an overriding obsession: Economic growth is imperative for the long-term stability of free enterprise and the values of Western Civilization as manifested at the level of the nation. The concept of development is ideologically paired with the notion of national security. More development means greater security, and greater security is a prerequisite for development. There is some variation among countries in specifics and successes of the development strategy. In Brazil, the tradition of state intervention was maintained, while in Chile, Argentina, and Uruguay there was an astounding turn toward the principles of classic economic liberalism. Brazil enjoyed a considerable economic growth for over a decade before sliding into a relative stagnation. The Argentine military humbly withdrew from government in 1983 with an economy in total chaos, while the Chilean and Uruguayan economies have continued in chronic crisis. In all cases, development strategies have been adopted that are congruent with the interests of the local finance capital/transnational corporate alliance and in line with the logic of the structural dependence of the country in the international political economy. For these reasons it is completely erroneous to impute a specific autonomy, apart from the classes in struggle, to the military as a social force. At most, military officialdom becomes the political directorate of a particular class alliance. Similarly, since development strategies are so strictly subordinated within relations of dependency and the interests that benefit are so narrow it is highly misleading to characterize national security states as "developmentalist," in any meaningful sense of the term.

The salient features of strategies of dependent development have been specifically examined in a previous chapter in the case of Chile and need not detain us further here.[3]

Legitimation. In the years preceding military intervention in South America it became clear to all that existing systems lacked legitimacy in the minds of substantial sectors of the population. The rhetoric of reform permeated the political culture and revolutionary sentiments had penetrated beyond Marxist intellectuals and rebellious youth into sectors of the popular classes. Perhaps even greater numbers of people simply acquiesced to the status quo without giving it any particular allegiance. Such precarious hegemony that had previously held disintegrated. There was no class that could *lead* in Gramsci's sense. A genuine "national bourgeoisie" simply did not mature sufficiently in the stage of national development and the potential of national capital began to decline with dependent development. Rightist political parties representing the interests of local finance and transnational capital had very reduced electoral support and economically powerful groups had difficulty in influencing political developments.

A viable project of hegemony therefore had to seek strenuously to strengthen the local capitalist class through forceful political controls and economic development and to gain greater allegiance among significant sectors of the citizenry, feats which in Latin America only Mexico has begun to approach with some success.

The ideology of legitimation proceeds mainly from representations of the dictatorship as the "savior of the country." Secondarily, legitimation is propounded in the ideology of the depoliticization of the state administration and technocratic efficiency and in a nationalism that is directed, not toward mobilization of popular support, but toward defining the "unpatriotic." The ideology of national security, propounded through strict control of the "ideological state apparatuses," justifies dictatorship as the only manner of maintaining the country united against internal and external enemies, preserving "Western Christian Civilization." This is also an imported manifestation of the doctrine of "hemispheric security" propounded in official quarters in the United States.

National security ideology is rooted in geopolitics and in strategy, both viewed as sciences. For General Agosto Pinochet, a former professor of geopolitics, these sciences examine "the influence of geographical and historical factors on the life and evolution of the states, in order to arrive at political conclusions. It serves as a guide for statesmen in managing both internal and external politics and directs the military in preparing the National Defense and in working out strategy" (quoted in Comblin, 1979:67). Comblin (1979) has examined the geopolitical concepts of the generals in some detail. What it comes down to is a state of permanent war against the enemies of the state; in practice this means the anniliation of internal "subversives" and "communists," as defined by military authorities.

The government and the management of institutions is reserved for the most capable elites, with the demagogy of politicians and elections that brought the country to ruin displaced by hierarchical, centralized authority. Schools, the media, government ministries are geared to serve the missions of security, saving democracy from the menace of communist totalitarianism, and the long-term strategy of national salvation through order and progress.

The Democratization of Dictatorship

The only aspect of the project that can be considered successful has been the repression of the immediate enemies of the national security state. The democratization of dictatorship will eventually ensue. Whether this will be a limited, "guided" democracy or a socialist democracy depends upon international circumstances, but even more saliently, upon the ability of domestic forces of opposition to dictatorship to achieve an effective alliance and to pursue relentlessly a project of change. In these alliances and projects intermediate classes, while important actors, will not hold the center stage they did in the emergence of the national security state. Let us hope (but not expect) that this time around they will bang their pots and pans against dictatorship, while tolerating the birth of a new order of human rights, democracy, and development.

In the consolidation phase of the national security state the local bourgeoisie/transnational capital alliance delivers its hegemonic pretensions to the military, which acts as its political directorate, and surrenders to the structural logic of dependent development. National security states all have one thing in common once consolidated: The junta ruling in the name of the dominant alliance and pursuing policies consistent with these class interests is not able to maintain the effective class alliance that brought it to power. A process of disintegration ensues. In Chile, Argentina, and Uruguay organic crises are deep and pervasive. Times are tougher in Brazil and there are great pressures for a real democratic opening. The strategy of dependent development pursued requires the regimes to turn not only upon the working class and peasantry but upon their previous support classes as well. As necessary or convenient, the regimes even unleash official and unofficial violence against former supporters. The ideology of national security is revealed to increasing sectors of the population as a sham and the regimes are more or less delegitimized, remaining in power mainly by repression and fear.

This opens up the possibility of a broad alliance of classes in which successful popular insurrection in the manner of Iran is not impossible (the outcome would be completely different). Broad-based insurrectionary alliances, however, are not likely, since the basic class antagonisms are at a much higher level in South America than in Iran. In such circumstances an alliance between the working class and popular masses, the petty bourgeoisie, the middle strata and lesser business interests is extremely fragile and the threat of working class hegemony and a transition to socialism much more real, as demonstrated in Argentina in the early 1970s. The reestablishment of some form of pseudo-democratic state that is bound to be weak and unstable seems the most likely possibility over the next several years in countries of the Southern Cone.

The future of the dependent capitalist state everywhere, and especially in the more developed and less democratic countries of Asia as well as Latin America, is chronic instability, oscillation back and forth between authoritarian regimes bent on preventive counter-revolution and dependent development and pseudo-democratic states that, in the face of mounting internal struggle and internationally induced crisis, move backward to barbarous repression or forward to socialism. At best, the military-managed controlled civilianized democratic states will represent perhaps a necessary breathing spell while the full force of the dialectic between authoritarian reaction and revolution works itself out.

Notes

1. There is a considerable controversy about the concept of "marginality." For conceptual clarification see Johnson (1972) and for a recent discussion see Cockcroft (1983) and Quijano (1983).

2. The distinction between productive and unproductive labor has very limited usefulness in analyzing class formation. See Johnson (1982: chap. 2).

3. On the theoretical aspects of the congruence between development strategies and hegemonic projects see Jessop (1983). Brazilian development strategies and official ideology are expertly analyzed by Evans (1979), McDonough (1981), and Dreifus (1980).

References

Cockcroft, James D.
1983   "Immiseration, not marginalization: the case of Mexico." Latin American Perspectives 37/38 (Spring/Summer): 86–107.

Cockcroft, James D., André Gunder Frank, and Dale L. Johnson
1972 Dependence and Underdevelopment. Latin America's Political Economy. New York: Doubleday.

Combin, José
1971 The Church and the National Security State. Maryknoll, NY: Orbis Press.

Dreifus, René Armand
1980 1964: a conquista do Estado. Acão política, poder e golpe de classe. Rio de Janeiro: Editora Vozes.

Evans, Peter
1979 Dependent Development: The Alliance of Multinational, State, and Local Capital in Brazil. Princeton, NJ: Princeton University Press.

Jessop, Bob
1983 "Accumulation strategies, state forms, and hegemonic projects." Kapitalistate 10/11: 89–112.

Johnson, Dale L.
1972 "On oppressed classes." Chapter 7 in James D. Cockcroft, André Gunder Frank, and Dale L. Johnson, Dependence and Underdevelopment. Latin America's Political Economy. New York: Doubleday.
1973a The Sociology of Change and Reaction in Latin America. Indianapolis: Bobbs-Merrill.
1973b The Chilean Road to Socialism. New York: Doubleday.
1982 Class and Social Development: A New Theory of the Middle Classes. Beverly Hills, CA: Sage.
1983 "Class formation and struggle in Latin America." Latin American Perspectives 37/38 (Spring/Summer): 2–18.

Latin American Perspectives
1976 "Imperialism and the working class in Latin America." Special issue 3 (Winter).

McDonough, Peter
1981 Power and Ideology in Brazil. Princeton, NJ: Princeton University Press.

Oppenheimer, Martin and Jane Canning
1978- "The national security state: repression within capitalism." Berkeley Journal of Sociology
79   23: 3-33.

Quijano, Aníbal
1983 "Imperialism and marginality in Latin America." Latin American Perspectives 37/38 (Spring/Summer): 76–85.

Spalding, Horbart A.
1977 Organized Labor in Latin America: Historical Case Studies of Workers in Dependent Societies. New York: New York University Press.

Part Three: Classes in the Socialist Transition

CHAPTER NINE

Thomas Bamat: Peru's Plan Inca: The Rise and Fall of a Populist Project

In October 1968 General Juan Velasco and the "Revolutionary Government of the Armed Forces" put an end to the formally democratic government of Fernando Belaunde in Peru. "Plan Inca," the project of radical social reform prepared by Velasco and the Colonels who plotted the coup with him, remained a secret document. But it outlined the basic measures that the Velasco forces would later enact: the nationalization of some foreign enterprise, a sweeping agrarian reform, more decided State control in the local economy and social reforms which were to draw worldwide attention to the Peruvian political process.[1]

In October 1977 General Francisco Morales—who succeeded Velasco as President in August of 1975—and the Commission of the Armed Forces and Police he directed officially announced a timetable for a return of civilian government to Peru by 1980. "Plan Túpac Amaru," the project for ending the reforms and transferring government, had been public for ten months. It outlined political measures that the Morales government then strove to enact: the "adjustment" and termination of the structural reforms, their "institutionalization" in a new Constitution, and a return to elections.

Two Generals, two Plans and two Octobers mark alpha and omega points of a period of Peruvian history that envelops far more than the vicissitudes of military versus civilian rule. They mark conjunctures in which the continued dependence of Peru on foreign capital was best symbolized first by the transnational corporation IPC (International Petroleum Company) and then increasingly by the demands of the IMF (International Monetary Fund). More importantly they delimit a period of historic social transformations within Peru itself: the demise of the landowning sectors of the bourgeoisie and a reordering of dominant class power, the establishment of a new political role for the military and sustained but uneven growth in the organizational capacity of working class and popular forces.

At present the interests of monopoly capital and the austere economic measures imposed through the International Monetary Fund reign supreme in Peru. They exact an overwhelming toll, including acute increases in infant mortality, on peasants, laborers and the urban poor in particular. The process of returning to democratic forms starkly contrasts with simultaneous repression and restriction on political freedoms.

In 1968 when Velasco and his supporters initiated their reform project the correlation of forces was far different. The dominant classes were more heterogeneous, less politically adept and more weakly organized. The same was true of peasants, laborers and the Left. "Petty bourgeois populism" borne on the assertion of the expanding middle elements of Peruvian society could prosper for a time in such a conjuncture, and did.

What is striking when one examines the "Peruvian revolution" is how a project of radical reform that emerged historically from the middle sectors and petty bourgeoisie and that sought economic development with a conciliation between the interests of social classes, led almost inevitably to the consolidation of class power by an urban-industrial bourgeoisie linked to foreign capital and the brutal subjugation of popular interests.

To make sense of this apparent contradiction is the aim of this essay. Here I will look beyond the intentions of the social actors that took the center of Peru's political stage in 1968—and of those who have replaced them there—to both the structural constraints on the reform project and the development of the forces that eventually doomed it. Prior to that, however, it is necessary to examine the historical context from which Plan Inca emerged in the first place.

Antecedents of a Populist Coup

In the 1960s, Peru, like most dependent social formations, was inserted within capitalism's international division of labor essentially as a producer of mineral and agricultural commodities. Among them were copper, iron, zinc, oil, fishmeal, sugar, and cotton. Local industrial manufacturing was growing significantly for the first time, however, under the impetus of recent and rising foreign investments.

In the decade following the end of the Second World War a new mode of capital penetration into Latin America had evolved. Foreign investors modified the agro-mineral fixation of the pre-War period. Productive capital flowed into industrial manufacturing. Transnational enterprises jumped national tariff barriers and began production geared principally to internal markets. It was in countries with an already developed industrial base and relatively larger markets that the phenomenon occurred first: Mexico, Brazil, Argentina. But by the beginning of the 1960s the tendency had made itself felt in countries like Peru.

In Peru, U.S. direct investment in manufacturing grew from $15 million in 1950 to $35 million in 1960, to $96 million by 1968. Between 1960 and 1969, the manufacturing share of total U.S. investment grew from 7.8

percent to 13.4 percent. Of the some 242 transnational enterprises operating in Peru shortly after the 1968 coup, 164 had entered the country since 1960 and only 35 prior to 1950 (Anaya, 1974:23, 39). This influx of capital had important effects not only on the Peruvian economy in general, but on the character of its dominant classes.

Indeed, successive periods in the accumulation of capital on a world scale and within Peru had added greater complexity to the composition of the local dominant classes since well before the 1960s. To the comprador bourgeoisie linked to the old enclaves of foreign capital, and to a semi-feudal landowning class in the remote highlands, were added modern fractions of a capitalist class engaged directly in production: agroexporters rooted in the coastal plantations (sugar and cotton) and the initial elements of an industrial bourgeoisie. There also were groups engaged in the fishing sector and in small mining, and important investments in commerce and banking intimately related to the capitalist agricultural plantations.

Peru's bloc of dominant classes in the 1960s, then, included a politically weak, semi-feudal class of highland landowners and a highly diversified capitalist class—a bourgeoisie with that defensive interpenetration of agrarian, commercial, financial, service, and industrial interests that Cardoso (1969:164) calls a normal adaptive measure in the development of capitalism in a country suffering dependence and undergoing some import-substituting industrialization.

The explicitly capitalist sector of the dominant classes was not clearly divisible into class fractions along the lines of the distinct forms in which capital expresses itself in the process of its reproduction (i.e., productive capital, commercial capital, interest-bearing capital, and profit from ground-rent), but it did lend itself to certain differentiations of political and economic interests, particularly with regard to industrialization. I will attempt to characterize them briefly but clearly here, since they have a direct bearing on the political developments leading up to the 1968 coup.

An Emergent Industrial Sector

The bourgeoisie of the 1960s was an unambiguously capitalist class deriving its profits from the exploitation of wage labor. Its interests ranged from massive agricultural plantations to insurance and banking, to industries producing consumer and intermediate commodities (foodstuffs, textiles, furniture, wood, cement, non-ferrous metals) as well as some capital goods.[2] The range of investments was matched by an interwoven pattern of ownership and control: Each of the various families, oligarchic clans or "financial groups" held a wide spectrum of investments.

Several of the major writers on the dominant classes in Peru have demonstrated the interwoven nature of economic interests by selecting the holdings of a few exemplary families (see, for example, Favre, 1969:83–87; Astiz, 1969:54–55; Malpica, 1968: Bourricaud, 1969). Each shows the "fact" that the capital and power of the old bourgeoisie—with the possible exception of the Prado family—was based on agriculture for export but spread out over commerce, finance, construction, mining and manufacturing. The implication, even when it is not made as straightforwardly as in Favre (1969:87–88), is that there were no internal contradictions in the interests of the Peruvian capitalist class.

Despite this intermingling of dominant class investment, there is considerable concrete evidence that an identifiable industrial sector of the bourgeoisie was *emergent* during the 1960s. The industrialists did not "engineer" the 1968 military coup to impose their interests over more traditional agrocommercial and banking sectors of the bourgeoisie—an argument put forth by Dore and Weeks (1976:66)—but they were coming into their own.

Empirical data on the juridicial property of enterprises, overlapping directorates and "sources" of capital in works such as the above detect the shared economic interests of the dominant classes. They do *not* detect the relative weights of investment in one branch of the economy or another, or the formation of groups with growing interests in industrial manufacturing and projects for increasing investments in that branch of the economy. It is not with property data but rather that gleaned from the terrain of projects, ideologies and policy conflicts that one can perceive the presence of an emerging industrial sector of capital in Peru during the 1960s.

A survey by Fritz Wils (1975), for example, reveals some interesting points. Few of the industrialists he interviewed prior to the 1968 coup had a political vision that transcended the gates of their factory, but Wils did discover a group with what he called an awareness of "structural problems and the need for structural solutions." These industrialists were not the potentially more nationalistic small and medium "independents" but those in subsidiaries of transnational corporations and in the large national enterprise complexes that he called the "consortia" (1975:170). They were organized and assumed leading roles in the National Society of Industries (SNI) at the end of Belaunde's presidency. Many of their number also pertained to Action for Development (APD), an organization in Lima that conducted study groups and seminars and proposed reforms to modernize capitalism and "rationalize" the institutions of the state so as to promote industrial growth.

The reforms this group proposed were not drastic. They were essentially financial and administrative, and did not suggest agrarian reform or pitched conflict with the agroexporters. Modernizing capitalism and rationalizing the State were necessary for furthering industrial development but the emerging industrialists were tied to more traditional interests. While they exhibited growing independence from the latter, they were not in a position to wage a frontal attack on more traditional sectors of their class (see Wils, 1975:181). They were not ready for "Plan Inca."

Ferner (1977) presents further evidence for this kind of position. Peruvian industrialists were relatively weak, he argues, in part because industrialization had reflected the dynamism of the export sectors. But the editorials in the National Society of Industries' monthly *Industria Peruana* in 1967–1968 demonstrate that the industrialists had a "specific program" related to the development of their economic sector and it was "distinct from the strategy adopted by other bourgeois factions, in particular the export sectors" (1977:59).[3]

There were numerous issues that divided industrial interests from those of Peruvian capital located more definitively in other sectors of economic activity. They were generally linked to different concrete foreign capitals and there was competition for credit (Dore and Weeks, 1976:62–63). Furthermore, while the emerging industrialists hoped to export in the future they were still largely tied to the internal market for the realization of value. This established a distinct set of interests around the exchange rate of the local currency. If manufacturers were to continue growing they needed more energetic promotional policies from the State.

At the level of class practices and ideological discourse there were visible expressions of these differing interests. Parliament, which was controlled during the Belaunde years by the traditional agroexporters, was the site of some intense conflicts. A heated polemic broke out in parliament in 1966 around government promotion of agriculture and livestock, with a simultaneous plan to reduce protective tariffs accorded to local manufacturing in the 1959 Industrial Promotion Law. Industrial interests lost that one. (see García, 1975:32). In mid-1968, however, the traditional interests concentrated around the UNO party (National Odriist Union) in parliament failed in their efforts to prevent the Executive branch of government and the Minister of Economy and Commerce, Manuel Ulloa, from assuming emergency decree powers and initiating a move toward greater "modernization" and industrialization of Peruvian capitalism. These and other issues surfaced in the local press. *El Comercio* defended an industrialist position while *La Prensa* advocated the more traditionalist one.

One of the clearest expressions of the emerging industrialists' development concerns just prior to the military coup was a speech delivered by President Raffo of the SNI at the Center for High Military Studies (CAEM). Raffo listed a whole series of limits on industrial growth which Peru would have to overcome: an economic structure dependent on the export of primary commodities and the importation of manufactured goods, a lack of sufficient capital, technology and credits; a permanent inflationary tendency; a small internal market; and the lack of adequate protective legislation for industry.[4]

Unlike writers such as Favre (1969) or Espinoza and Osorio (1972), then, I maintain that there *was* a contradiction between the agroexporters and more industrial sectors of the bourgeoisie. It was present objectively in multiple concrete restrictions on the expansion of Peruvian manufacturing and on capital accumulation, and it was becoming visible empirically in terms of very real but limited intra-bourgeois conflicts.

The key point, however, is this: The contradiction was not expressed *predominantly* in the 1960s in terms of intrabourgeois conflict. It emerged more explicitly in collisions between moderate and more radical reform projects borne by Peru's "new petty bourgeoisie" or salaried middle strata, and the traditional bourgeoisie's project of dominance-as-usual. It arose ideologically and politically not so much from the industrialists themselves as from technocrats, professionals, politicians—and eventually military officers. Plan Inca was the heir to decades of petty bourgeois populism. A government that would promote sweeping agrarian reform and a far stronger State was not the dream of the emergent industrial bourgeoisie—though it gained from it eventually—but the brainchild of "petty-bourgeois" reformers.

The Rise and Role of the Salaried Middle Strata

In the 1920s and 1930s Peru had entered a process of social change that shook the bases of economic production, the relations between countryside and city, the social distribution of education and knowledge, and the modes of class domination within the country. These changes brought an end to a century of "oligarchic" rule based on armed violence and a certain popular passivity. The previously uncontested dominance of foreign capital and the large landowners now faced popular challenge.

The most important initial change in the class structure associated with this process was not among either the dominant or the laboring classes. It was the rise of an urban petty bourgeoisie.

Beginning about 1920, the first of a series of rural migrations toward the capital city of Lima began. By the 1950s the migrating population would be composed mostly of poor peasants, but the first wave was of small landowners and merchants. This rural petty bourgeoisie abandoned the provinces and the countryside because of the decreasing possibilities of earning a livelihood there and for the promises of the urban center. The large foreign agricultural and mining enterprises (Grace, Cerro) had been consolidating their landholdings along the northern coast and in the central highlands and the semifeudal *gamonales* had been extending their landholdings elsewhere. This displaced not only smallholders in several sections of the country but also small merchants since commercial transactions tended to be swallowed up in the same consolidation process (Lizarzaburu, 1976:6ff.).

Once established in Lima the new urban stratum secured professional and technical training for the succeeding generation. But the occupational structure, given the limited development of the productive forces, the nature of foreign domination and the division of labor, provided limited opportunities for employment and upward mobility. The new urban petty bourgeoisie expressed its consequent unrest in a highly critical posture vis-à-vis imperialism and the traditional "oligarchy."

The ranks of the urban newcomers were augmented with the advent of foreign immigrants as well. They arrived as early as the turn of the century and their sons and daughters were added to the expanding middle strata dedicated to urban commerce, the liberal and technical professions, and an inflated State bureaucracy.

Political expressions of the new urban social sectors were reformist and even revolutionary tendencies and movements, beginning with APRA and the Communist Party in the 1930s and later including the Popular Action, Christian Democrat and Social Progressive parties of the 1950s. Moderate forces from the reform parties filled posts in Peru's growing State bureaucracy and with the Presidency of Belaunde in 1963 it was they who assumed immediate control of the Executive machinery of the State.

By the 1950s the dominant classes were devoid of clear internal leadership and experiencing a precipitous decline in national "legitimacy." The bourgeoisie had neither a political party of its own nor the allegiance of a corps of "organic intellectuals" capable of rationalizing and justifying the old forms of class domination. The industrial working class was small but growing in size and organization. Strikes, for example, would reach historically high proportions in the 1960s.[5] Peasants had emerged as an effective political force for the first time during the 1950s and continued to press for land reforms. The basis of organized opposition to the traditional dominant classes was potentially very large, and it was growing.

In this context sectors of the middle strata or "new petty bourgeoisie" played a highly ambiguous but crucial role as a political pivot between the dominant and the exploited classes. "Moderate" sectors of the petty bourgeoisie functioned as articulators of ideology, strategists for limited social change, and filters in the struggle for power. They were not a passive clientele of the dominant classes but an active force, particularly in the 1960s. They had schooling, plans, political parties, and initiative. Their development projects sought the promotion of a modern industrial sector of the bourgeoisie and provided many emerging industrialists with a political and ideological home.

The new petty bourgeoisie in Peru occupied part of a political void created by the decline of the agroexporters. Its discourse reverberated through the political and ideological fields, but the new petty bourgeoisie remained a social sector thoroughly dependent on the reproduction of capital. It was incapable of occupying a position of real class leadership in the power bloc.

Three Projects for Development

Cotler (1971:100–104) has asserted that there were essentially three projects or models of capitalist growth dominating the wider ideological/political field during the Belaunde regime and that each had a tradition stretching back to the Thirties. All three sought foreign capital and technology as a means of stimulating growth and modernization, but they differed in the kinds of controls that would be placed on foreign capital, the aim of accumulation, the place of the State and the participation of the popular masses. Two of the three had strong support from the new petty bourgeoisie.

The classic liberal project of the agroexporting bourgeoisie, expressed through the National Society of Agriculture (SNA) and voiced by *La Prensa,* posited no limits on foreign capital but rather stimulants, "confidence" and "security." Economic growth was to center on the external market and external circuits of capital. The State's economic interventions would be limited to providing infrastructure for economic development (roads, communication networks) and limited social services. The popular sectors were to be left marginal to the wealth produced and strongly discouraged from expressing themselves politically. In the 1960s, the Odriists (UNO) promoted such a project in the legislature and their alliance with APRA helped block any agrarian reform. But this traditional project opposed to basic changes had relatively little support among the influential middle sectors in or outside of government. When APRA abandoned the UNO in 1968 and pacted with the right wing of Popular Action, this project was thoroughly undermined.

The first of the two projects advanced by sectors of the new petty bourgeoisie was one of radical reform. This essentially had been the project of APRA in the 1930s and was inherited, with certain modifications, by the more radical wing of Popular Action (AP), by Christian Democrats and by the Social Progressive Movement in the 1950s and 1960s when APRA openly moved to the right.[6] The project included State controls and planning functions, agrarian reform and industrialization aimed at the expansion of the internal market, and "popular participation." The major transformation in this populist project, comparing its expression in the '30s with that of the

'60s, was that in the latter period the middle strata leadership of the populist alliance operated in a technocratic mode more than via the pressure of the popular base itself (Cotler, 1971:114–115).

The final project and the second with significant middle strata or new petty-bourgeois support was "intermediate" in terms of the projects already mentioned. It sought a strengthening of the State but not so much to control foreign capital or address social inequalities as simply to foster the growth of industry and a local urban-industrial bourgeoisie. Defended by *El Comercio,* the right wing of AP, emerging industrialists and more conservative elements in the new petty bourgeoisie, it sought to restrict popular political participation to its "safest" expressions. By mid-1968 this project had enlisted the support of APRA.

Each of these three projects had a "place" in the Belaunde regime of 1963–1968. The liberal agroexporting project dominated the nation's legislative center of power. The latter two projects vied for favor within the Popular Action Party of Belaunde itself, and occupied the chambers of Cabinet policymaking with varying force in different periods.

Lizarzaburu (1976) affirms that within Popular Action there were three factions contending for leadership during the 1960s. These were the "radicals," the "centrists" and the right-wing "carlists."[7] In four distinct moments from 1963 to 1968 first the radicals, then the centrists, then the radicals again, and finally the "carlists" controlled the executive branch of government.

The radicals espoused the populist project described above and the carlists what was referred to as the "intermediate" model, fostering above all the development of industry. The Belaunde regime was inaugurated with the "hundred days" of the radicals but its initiatives were blocked by the traditional interests in the legislature. The regime closed with the one-hundred twenty days of the "carlists," under the leadership of Economy and Commerce Minister Manuel Ulloa. The efforts of the latter to confront the economic crisis into which Peru entered in 1967, and to resolve the stalemate in the relation of political forces by enlisting APRA's support for a project of dependent industrialization, was blocked by political scandal[8] and then by the presence of Army tanks in the Plaza de Armas.

It is my position that the military leaders who seized the State machinery in October of 1968 and imposed Plan Inca essentially chose to *reinstate and carry through the populist development project of petty bourgeois "radicals."* As Cotler notes (1971:128), the military's initial plan was a "typical version of development as proposed by the Economic Commission for Latin America (CEPAL)." It was not far either from those of such reformist middle sector organizations as the Christian Democrats or the radical wing of Popular Action.

Plan Inca was meant to promote industrial expansion via agrarian reform and stronger State action. Simultaneously it was to advance the interests of Peruvian peasants and workers. The aim of its immediate authors was to weaken Peru's dependence on foreign capital, stimulate economic growth and—with the possible exception of the big landowners—reconcile the class interests of all Peruvians.

This nationalist and populist reform project could thrive and weather adversity in a conjuncture marked by a politically weak and disorganized dominant class, and popular and working class forces that were only beginning to coalesce. Before long, however, it would come undone and reveal the depth of the internal inconsistencies that marked it from the beginning.

The Character of the Reforms

It is impossible within the confines of this article to explain fully *why* a group of leading Peruvian military officers made populist politics its own; certainly that has not been common in Latin America of late. Nor is there space to explain any more than the essentials of the nature and extent of the multiple social reforms that were enacted in Peru after 1968 and reversed by 1977.

When the forces of General Velasco ousted the Belaunde regime from government in 1968 they affirmed that the new military junta would embody the interests of the nation as a whole against both foreign domination and the traditional local oligarchy. Their "Statute of the Revolutionary Government" indicated that the government would promote industrial development, a more equitable distribution of wealth and income, national unity, greater relative independence from foreign control and honest government.[9] In the years that followed state policy promoted agrarian reform, a series of new industrial laws, a remarkable expansion of the economic functions of the State and a partial reordering of the relationships with foreign capital and the U.S. government.

Agrarian reform was one of the first major changes. It began in June of 1969 and ended officially when the phase of land expropriations was declared complete by the Morales government in June of 1976. An estimated 47% of all usable agricultural, grazing and forest land of the country was affected (Caballero, 1977:146). Seven million hectares were adjudicated but only about one-third of the families engaged in the agricultural and livestock sectors of the economy benefited directly and only one-fourth of the rural labor force was assured a relatively permanent source of work (Harding, 1975:220; Caballero, 1977:149). While the benefits for the Peruvian peasantry were limited—and a source of mounting political tensions—the costs to the big capitalist and pre-capitalist landowners was considerable. As class forces, though not as individuals, they were eliminated from power at the national level.

The agrarian reform stimulated the development of smaller private land-owning in the countryside and also gave rise to new technical and bureau-cratic middle strata employed by the state, which in many respects replaced the traditional large landowners in the social relations of production. In agriculture, as in other areas of the reform process, there was a tendency for areas of state capitalism to develop (see Caballero, 1977:151).

One of the basic aims of "Plan Inca" and of the Agrarian Reform Law was to transfer local capital into industrial manufacturing. Payment scales for expropriated lands accorded higher compensation to those who were willing to invest in industry. In fact the concession was generally ignored by the former landowners, who had little confidence in the new government (see García-Sayan, 1977:209ff). In addition to the sudden enactment of agrarian reform the government began to reorder the industrial sector, and a lack of "business confidence" soon created more widespread problems for the new government. -

Industrial reform began with the General Law of Industries and the Industrial Community Law in 1970. Among the reforms were restrictions on foreign ownership and profits in industry, State ownership of the "basic industries" (steel, cement, paper, petrochemicals) and assurances of em-ployment stability for workers.[10] The two most controversial measures, however, were the formation of "industrial communities" and the 1974 proposal for developing a "Social Property" sector as the dominant one in the national economy.

The "industrial communities" scheme was aimed directly at class con-ciliation by creating shared class interests in expanded industrial develop-ment and high productivity. The "industrial community" was to represent the full-time workers in each firm, and administer their slowly increasing share in the ownership of the firm up to a possible maximum of 50%. At least one representative of the community was to sit on each firm's board of directors and the number was to increase in conjunction with the number of shares the community held.

Growth of the Communities in the manufacturing sector was rapid from 1970–1972, rising from the 594 formed in 1970 to 3,146 by the end of 1972, then leveling off. In the same period the number of actual workers in the Communities jumped from 63,634 to nearly 200,000.[11] But the effective participation of workers in ownership and management of the enterprises was a process that would have taken decades, even if the Law had not been reversed in 1977 (Knight, 1975:371). In the end, bourgeois opposition to the measure resulted in its virtual elimination.[12]

A similar fate awaited the Social Property Law of 1974. Originally it stipulated that social property enterprises were to be owned by the totality of the workers in a given sector. Moreover, while social property would coexist with state enterprises, a reformed private sector and the purely private sector, it would become the *preponderant sector of national economic life*. The enactment of such a scheme might have been a qualitative leap—the initiation of a break with the capitalist system—but the Law emerged just as the bottom was falling out of the reform project as a whole. By the time that Plan Túpac Amaru was announced in 1977, the social property sector's "priority" for the future had been redefined essentially to that of absorbing some of the unemployed into labor-intensive enterprises.

Among the overall effects of government industrial policy during the Velasco years were a growing tension between the regime and the bourgeoisie, the reluctance of both local and foreign capital to invest in manufacturing, an expansion in the number of industries owned wholly or partially by the state and a heightening of conflict between workers and capitalists. Government policies seemed to produce not class conciliation, but rather a growth in class consciousness and organization among both workers and capitalists.

Those measures which were most objectionable to local and foreign capitalists were reversed in 1976 and 1977 under the Morales government. Industrialists emerged victorious on a number of fronts: the redefinition of Social Property's role, reversal of the most threatening aspects of the Industrial Community, the reduction of the State capitalist area of the economy and of the public portion of investment, the right to dismiss hundreds of militant workers (following the General Strike of July 19, 1977), improved access to military and civilian bureaucratic policymakers, and the promise of a return to non-military government.

An expansion in the economic functions of the State was foreshadowed in Plan Inca, but the reluctance of private capital to invest in the Peruvian "experiment" contributed to the enhancement of that tendency. As already mentioned, there was the growth of a huge area of state capitalism in agriculture and a marked growth of state enterprises in industry. In addition, the state took over much of the banking system; established giant State enterprises in the fields of mining and petroleum (Petroperú, Centromín, Mineroperú) through the expropriation of foreign businesses; magnified the role of centralized planning; established controls on foreign commerce; took over the fishing industry and increased the public percentage of total gross investment from 36 percent to 52 percent in just four years (1970–1974).[13]

The percentages of State ownership and State investment began to decline in 1975, but a good indicator of the extremes they reached in the "modern" area of the Peruvian economy is data compiled by Fitzgerald on the percentages of output (value added) which pertained to the State, foreign capital and local non-State entities in 1968, and then in 1974. While the data indicate only the shifts in formal, juridical ownership of property (and thus are misleading about the social relations of production, particularly in agriculture) they do give an impressive overall picture of the expansion of the "public sector" by 1974 (see Table 9.1).

Like the expansion of the economic functions of the State, the challenges to the dominance of foreign capital clearly ebbed after 1974. The reordering of Peru's relations with foreign capital and the U.S. government began with the State takeover of the International Petroleum Company (an Exxon affiliate) in the days immediately following the 1968 coup. Restrictions on foreign capital via the Andean Pact and the General Law of Industries, additional nationalizations and the uncertain political climate created by the process of reforms further contributed to a hostile climate between the regime and the U.S. in the first years of military rule. There was an embargo threat, postponement of investment projects and a refusal to extend soft credits or to renegotiate Peru's foreign debt.

A turning point came with the bilateral Mercado-Greene agreements between Peru and the United States in 1974. They established "mutually satisfactory" compensation for expropriated U.S. firms and opened the door for significant new investments, especially in the mining sector, as well as new credits. A steady unblocking of investment and credit is demonstrated in the following key items from the Peruvian balance of payments for the early 1970s (see Table 9.2).

One of the express objectives of Plan Inca was to lessen dependence on foreign capital. The opposite has occurred. As is evident in Table 9.1, there was a reduction in the foreign ownership of the means of production in the Peruvian economy. Yet the state did not nationalize the most profitable and dynamic industries, and the nation's tax structure was left intact. The social reforms and the expansion of the public sector of the economy, including a sharp rise in arms purchases, had no adequate sources of internal

TABLE 9.1   Pattern of Formal Enterprise Ownership
(percentages of value added)

| | 1968 | | | 1974 | | |
	State	Domestic	Foreign	State	Domestic	Foreign
Agriculture	0	75	25	0	100	0
Mining	0	15	85	40	15	45
Industry	3	43	54	35	33	32
Banking	25	25	50	66	31	3
Fishing	0	48	52	100	0	0
Total	18	48	34	42	45	13

SOURCE: Fitzgerald (1976:36, 116-117).[14]
NOTE: See Fitzgerald for additional data and explanation of method. Included are enterprises with at least six employees. I have elaborated the data, rearranged the categories slightly, but maintained his basic schema. "Cooperatives" were categorized here as "domestic," though for theoretical reasons "state" would be more correct.

TABLE 9.2   Net Foreign Investments and Loans to Peru, 1971-1975
             (millions of U.S. $)

	1971	1972	1973	1974	1975
Net direct private investment	−42	−5	52	94	316
Net public sector loans	14	120	282	620	806

SOURCE: Banco Continental, *Peru in Figures* '76 (1977).

financing. The result was massive foreign borrowing and the development of a foreign debt that grew from U.S. $700 million in 1968 to an estimated $4,400 million by early 1977. By 1975 that figure already represented 218 percent the value of Peruvian exports and 29 percent of its GDP.[14]

What might appear to indicate a reduction of foreign dependency then, the state's replacement of foreign capital in the ownership of numerous enterprises, actually contributed to a debilitating need for massive loans. The most visible locus of dependence quickly shifted to international banking, and by 1976 and 1977 a consortium of private banks and the International Monetary Fund were tightly monitoring the government's administration of an austere political economy. Given the devastating human cost of such economic policies, the French daily *Le Monde* declared Peru "the I.M.F.'s Vietnam."[15]

How does one account for such outcomes when the project initiated under the code name Inca in 1968 had such different goals? Plans for radical social reform and economic development with a conciliation between the interests of social classes led not to a harmonious "third way" between capitalism and socialism, but to a consolidation of the class interests of the bourgeoisie and the brutal subjugation of popular interests.

The apparent explanation may seem simple: Velasco and his followers were replaced by General Morales in a peaceful coup in 1975 and a new military-engineered project and vision took over. A simple personnel change interpretation fails to do justice to the Peruvian reality, however. To make sense of the rise and fall of Plan Inca it is essential to examine two key factors: the global structural constraints on the reform project itself and the development of conflicting social forces in Peru. That is my aim in the final section of this article.

The Undoing of Plan Inca

Peru in 1968 was far from being in a revolutionary or even pre-revolutionary conjuncture, though it was ripe for social change. The dominant classes, particularly the landowning and commercial sectors within them, were losing economic and political power and ideological legitimacy within the country. Even the emerging industrialists were poorly organized and relatively devoid of structural and historical vision.

In such a conjuncture an urban, educated new petty bourgeoisie opposed to the old order could promote projects for national development and relatively greater independence from foreign control. Its projects stressed the need for industrial growth and rational efficiency and, to greater and lesser degrees, incorporated the interests of peasants and workers in land, a more equitable distribution of wealth and political power. But there was no organized basis in 1968 for a challenge to the capitalist system itself. Property and control of the means of production and the overall logic of profit and capital accumulation were not questioned by many in Peru.

In its way, Plan Inca expressed this reality. Its program for government action followed the contours of the historical project of capitalist development inherited from APRA in the 1930s and the more radical sectors of the new petty bourgeoisie in the 1960s. The populist reform project of Velasco and the Colonels submitted itself to the logic of world capitalism and the class relations inherent in it.

In the years following the 1968 coup, the reform project was developed and adapted in the context of acute social conflict and changing circumstance. Plans such as the Industrial Communities were almost certainly not present in detail in the original "Plan Inca" document. But Industrial Communities and even Social Property priority were never immediate or very serious threats to the working of the capitalist mode of production. State ideologues declared Peru anti-imperialist and "neither capitalist nor communist," but the Velasco regime was willing to make generous concessions to foreign capital and never failed to reproduce the elements of the predominance of capitalist relations of production and exchange: the exploitation of wage labor, strict management control over the labor process, a traditional division of manual and mental labor, universal market exchange, and the generalized use of money in the sphere of circulation.[16]

What were the concrete implications of submitting to the logic of capitalism? For one thing it meant that the framers of Plan Inca had to look to private capital, both foreign and local, as the key to the modernization and industrialization of the country. The Velasco regime expected the support of local industrialists for the project it launched in 1968. It also hoped that the nationalization of the International Petroleum Company would be perceived as an "exceptional case" and that other reforms would not lead to a cut-off in foreign investments, particularly in industrial manufacturing. But the withdrawal of private investments came just the same.

In mining, by far the predominant historical locus of foreign investment, there was obvious stagnation until 1973 and virtually all the increases thereafter pertained to a single investment project: the United States' South-

ern Peru Copper Company's *Cuajone* project.[17] In industry there was a lack
of new enterprises, and even the levels of reinvestment in existing firms
reached abysmal lows in 1970 and 1971 following the Industrial Reform
Law. The ratio of fixed asset investments to "profits" (value added less
remunerations), which had averaged 17 percent from 1963 through 1967,
fell to 9 percent in those two years, and still had not recovered fully when
Velasco left office in 1975.[18]

Submitting the reform process to the logic of capitalist social relations
also guaranteed the continued exploitation and alienation of the working
class and much of the peasantry. These direct producers, even under
the rubrics of agrarian reform and "industrial communities," had little
or no effective control over the labor process and experienced little or
no lasting improvement in their real incomes, though their expectations
were heightened by the reformist climate.[19] General unrest, strikes, and
land seizures were common under the Velasco regime and both peasant
and working class organizations pressured the regime for more radical
measures.

Despite opposition and adversities the Velasco regime did not abandon
its social reforms. Sectors within the government even attempted to radical-
ize the process. When private investment was withheld, the "public" sector
expanded, and the social property scheme of 1973–1974 represented, if only
on paper, a potential break with the dominance of capitalist social relations.
But the government never established a coherent plan for abandoning
capitalism. That had not been a goal of Plan Inca. To the contrary, the fiscal
policies of the Velasco regime were evidence of ambiguous reformism and
short-sightedness. They failed to provide the State with the resources required for continuing or deepening the process of change, and the growth of
the State debt guaranteed ever greater dependence on international banking
capital and its "sound" economic policies.

The nationalization of private enterprises did not create an important
basis for State revenues. Compensation was paid to all affected firms,
including the originally unrenumerated IPC. Furthermore the State did not
take over the firms which had the highest profits or those located in the most
dynamic branches of industry (Dore and Weeks, 1976:68; Dore, 1977:79;
Weeks, 1977:138–139). In one case in particular, that of the fishing industry, it nationalized enterprises riddled with debt and facing continued
crisis due to ecological factors. A number of state enterprises operated
at a loss.

A potential source of increased revenues for the Government might have
been new taxes on wealth and profits, but the regime left intact a regressive
tax system that favored the wealthiest and the corporations and put most of
the burden on the middle strata (Fitzgerald, 1976:43-45). There was a

consistent rise in enterprise profits as a share of national income during the Velasco years. But while profits rose from 15.5 percent in 1968 to 23.6 percent in 1974,[20] taxes on enterprise profits actually fell (see Table 9.3). The personal component of direct taxes grew more rapidly than the corporate one because exemptions were given to private enterprises in the unfulfilled hope of stimulating greater private investment.

These factors, added to massive arms expenditures and the well-known corruption in State enterprises like EPSA, led to a spectacular growth of the national debt. Heavy domestic borrowing was followed by heavy foreign borrowing. As percentages of the GDP domestic borrowing rose from 1.3 percent to 8 percent between 1969 and 1971, while net foreign borrowing rose from 1.8 percent in 1972 to 6.0 percent by 1974 and continued to grow thereafter (see Fitzgerald, 1976:54–55). The foreign debt was estimated at nearly U.S. $5 billion by late 1977. Pressures for an austere "orthodox" political economy emanating from the International Monetary Fund became hard for government policymakers to resist.

The constraints on the process of change were not limited to the inherent contradictions of the reform project, however. They were spelled out in the burgeoning conflict of social forces as the Velasco regime sought the creation of a broad, stable base of support for its reforms and failed to come up with it.

The make-shift nature of the reform project and its internal inconsistencies—particularly the lack of "independent" resources with which to finance social change—had their roots in the ambiguous and heterogeneous tendencies present within the Government from the beginning. Petty bourgeoisie populism thrived in a conjuncture marked by the disarticulation of both dominant-class and popular social forces. But as the reform process evolved, contradictory interests took shape in the form of organized class forces, and groups within the salaried middle sectors tended to define their politics too along sharper class lines.

The bourgeoisie, despite a wide variety of tactics, developed considerable coherence in its opposition to the increasingly statist and radical reforms, particularly via its class organizations: the Society of Industries, the Chambers of Commerce, Mining Society, ADEX. Even in the early

TABLE 9.3   Ratio of Peruvian Profit Tax to Net Enterprise Profits, 1967-1974 (percentages)

1967	1968	1969	1970	1971	1972	1973	1974
25.5	25.8	26.2	26.5	21.6	22.7	18.6	20.2

SOURCE: Banco Central de Reserva, *Cuentas Nacionales del Peru,* 1960-1974 (Lima, 1976:16).

period of reforms marked by the initiative of radical military officers and petty bourgeois technocrats, capital secured a process of social reproduction favorable to its most basic interests. Discrepancies within the military and private capital's weight in state power centers assured indemnization for expropriated owners of land and enterprises, allowed for the subterfuge of the rights of industrial communities, slowed the pace of agrarian reform, prevented an urban reform and labor communities in the commercial sphere, maintained the basic structure of production and consumption priorities intact, and avoided a progressive tax reform. By the time General Morales had replaced Velasco in the Presidency the bourgeoisie was capable of rolling back even many of the reforms that *had* been achieved.

The popular classes too became better organized and more militant after 1968. There was a steady radicalization both in the organizations more independent of the state apparatuses (the parties of the far Left, the Peasant Confederation CCP, the teachers' SUTEP, labor unions) and in the very organizations created by the State to mobilize a social base for its project (the Labor Communities' CONACI, the Peasant CNA). The latter organizations, for example, moved increasingly from populist to class politics.

Class polarization and growing militance left the governing alliance of military officers and allied sectors of the petty bourgeoisie relatively isolated. To add to their dilemma leftist regimes in Bolivia (1971) and Chile (1973) were toppled and the effects of the global recession began to be felt locally in 1974 and 1975. As Pásara (1976:16) has put it: the reform project played its last cards *without* achieving class conciliation; it "failed to recruit either the bourgeoisie or the people—and in an increasingly deteriorating economic context."

The growing polarization of social forces in Peru was expressed within the regime itself in condensed and institutionally mediated fashion. From 1974 onward four major tendencies were at play within the military government. In 1974–1975 the strongest of these was a state capitalist, corporatist and quasifascist tendency known in Peru as "The Mission." Led by generals like Fishing Minister Tantaleán and Interior Minister Richter, it held a right-wing statist position closely representing the interests neither of the popular classes nor of the private bourgeoisie but rather those of military and new petty-bourgeois interests developed in the course of the project itself. It established close personal links to a physically ailing and increasingly authoritarian Velasco in 1974–1975, but was eliminated by the August 1975 Morales coup, leaving three tendencies intact.

These three were the private capital, right-wing tendency which Admiral Vargas Caballero had represented until being forced from the Government in May of 1974; a "pragmatic" centrist position which President Morales himself later came to exemplify most clearly; and a radical-populist tendency led by generals such as Fernández Maldonado and Leonidas Rodríguez who had helped to draft Plan Inca in the first place. In short, a right-center-left spectrum expressed in condensed fashion through the prism of military rule the social forces in conflict in the Peruvian social formation.

Pásara (1976:17) contends that there was an alliance of all three of these tendencies against "the Mission" in the 1975 coup, but this is dubious. Information provided by both General Rodríguez himself and Velasco's press secretary Augusto Zimmerman lead me to believe that the August 1975 coup was planned by the Center and the populist officers only.[21] An evolving conservative alliance within the Morales regime came later.

The Morales coup of 1975 brought an end to rule by General Velasco alone and broadened the participation of the conservative Navy and Air Force in the commanding heights of government. It placed a technocrat rather than a man of deep ideological convictions in the presidency. And in a conjuncture of severe economic problems and mounting class strife, it produced a center-right alliance within the military. The purge of the radical populist officers began with Leonidas Rodríguez in late 1975, and was complete by mid-1976. An evident right-turn in economic policy began in March of 1976 and continued through the official promulgation of Plan Túpac Amaru in October of 1977.

The radical populist tendency was the one which housed the authors of Plan Inca, but they were left powerless to respond to growing reaction within the government. General Velasco was gone, they had no project to present in the new conjuncture, and full and open support of growing popular struggle was impossible for governing military officers to accept. Plan Inca was spent.

Populism and state capitalist tendencies gave way in Peru to selective repression, falling wages, the reversal of numerous reforms, and a "reprivatization" of the central axis of the economy. The defiance of the IPC was replaced by submission to the IMF. Finally, in 1977, the "Revolutionary Government of the Armed Forces" announced its readiness to call elections for a Constituent Assembly and to prepare the return to "civilian rule" which was to come in 1980. The political climate in the country today is marked by sharper class conflicts. The moment when romantic "petty-bourgeois populism" could propser in Peru is past.

Notes

1. Plan Inca as penned by Velasco and the Colonels in 1968 was far from a comprehensive project of government. Policy evolved over time and in the context of social struggle. The basic orientation of the action, however, appears to have been there from the beginning.

2. In 1967, industrial value added was divided as follows: Industries producing mostly consumer goods: 55 percent Industries producing mostly intermediate goods: 34 percent Industries producing mostly capital goods: 11 percent (Espinoza and Osorio, 1972:25).

3. The May, 1968 editorial on the devaluation of the local currency as a history-making brake on economic development, is a good example.

4. "If Industry Doesn't Progress There Will Be no Social Development," *Industria Peruana* (June 1968:6–8). The speech was delivered on April 22, 1968.

5. The number of man-hours lost in officially recognized strikes in 1966 was a record that would not be surpassed until the far more volatile year of 1973 (*Las Huelgas en el Peru*, Lima: Ministerio de Trabajo, 1973).

6. The logic of APRA's growing conservatism is beyond the scope of this article. Opportunism among its leadership was certainly not an insignificant factor (see Villanueva, 1977).

7. So named only because a number of its leaders happened to be named Carlos.

8. This centered on a missing page in a contract the Peruvian government had accorded to the International Petroleum Company (IPC), a subsidiary of Exxon. The page supposedly revealed the degree to which national interests had been surrendered to foreign capital.

9. See COAP, *La Revolución Nacional Peruana* (1972:11–15) for the "Manifesto of the Revolutionary Government," issued October 2, 1968.

10. The measure dealing with this was the Labor Stability Law of November 10, 1970.

11. Ministerio de Industrias y Turismo, *Estadística de Comunidades Industriales*, Lima, 1974.

12. In the New Industrial Community Law of 1977, workers lost their right to voting participation on boards of directors, and enterprise shares were to be distributed to workers *individually*, breaking the potential for any collective control.

13. For investment data, see *The Andean Report* (May 1977:99).

14. "Why the Banks Bailed out Peru", *Business Week*, (March 21, 1977:117) for the 1977 estimate, Banco Continental for the 1975 data.

15. See *The Andean Report*, Lima (December 1977:222). The same report notes that in negotiations for a hoped-for U.S. Treasury loan, the Peruvian delegation "offered to set up a monitoring system under which the United States could check that (Peruvian) Treasury, or any other, funds would not be siphoned off to pay for Russian arms" (p. 221). Such was the degree of dependence at the time.

16. On this point see Bettelheim (1973) and Quijano (1972).

17. See Sociedad de Minería, *Perú Minero (1974:*283) for data from 1968–1973.

18. Ratio developed on the basis of data for value added, remunerations and fixed assets investments taken from the Ministerio de Industrias y Turismo, *Estadística Industrial*, various years. See Bamat (1978:231).

19. Real wages in the capital city of Lima did grow about 33 percent from 1970 to 1973, but have plummeted from that time since. See DESCO, *Informative Político* #51 (December 1976:36) for data from 1968–1976. On income distribution, see Webb (1975).

20. Data from Banco Central de Reserva, *Cuentas Nacionales*, various years.

21. Discussions with Rodríguez at Louvain-la-Neuve, Belgium, November 19, 1977 and with Zimmerman in Lima, Peru, July 2, 1977.

References

Anaya Franco, Eduardo
1974   Imperialismo, industrialización y transferencia de tecnologia en el Perú. Lima: Editorial Horizonte.

Andean Report
1977   Lima (various issues).
Astiz, Carlos A.
1969   Pressure Groups and Power Elites in Peruvian Politics. Ithica, NY: Cornell University Press.
Bamat, Thomas
1977   "Relative state autonomy and capitalism in Brazil and Peru." The Insurgent Sociologist VII (Spring): 74–84.
1978   From Plan Inca to Plan Tupac Amaru: The Recomposition of the Peruvian Power Bloc, 1968–1977. Ph.D. thesis; Rutgers University.
Banco Central de Reserva del Perú
1968   Cuentas Nacionales, 1950–1967. Lima.
1976   Cuentas Nacionales, 1968–1974. Lima.
Bettelheim, Charles
1973   "State property and socialism." Economy and Society II, 4: 395–420.
Bourricaud, Francois
1969   "Notas acerca de la Oligarquía Peruana"; "La Clase Dirigente Peruana: Oligarcas e Industriales." Pp. 13–44 and 119–135 in Matos Mar (ed.) La Oligarquía en el Perú. Buenos Aires: Amorrortu.
Business Week
1977   "Why the banks bailed out Peru." (March 21): 117–118.
Caballero, Jose María
1977   "Sobre el carácter de la reforma agraria peruana." Latin American Perspectives IV (Summer): 146–159.
Cardoso, Fernando Henrique
1969   "Hegemonía burguesa e independencia económica: raizes estructurais de crise política Brasileira." Pp. 154–85 in Mudancas Sociais na America Latina. São Paulo: Difusao Europeia do Livro.
COAP (Comité de Asesoramiento de la Presidencia de la República)
1972   La Revolución Nacional Peruana. Lima: COAP.
Cotler, Julio
1971   "Crisis política y populismo militar." Pp. 87–174 in Fuenzalida Vollmar et al., Perú Hoy. Mexico: Siglo Veintiuno.
DESCO (Centro de Estudios y promoción del Desarrollo)
1976–1977   Informativo Político (monthly: various issues). Lima.
Dore, Elizabeth
1977   "Crisis and accumulation in the Peruvian mining industry 1968–1974." Latin American Perspectives IV (Summer): 77–102.
Dore, Elizabeth and John Weeks
1976   "The intensification of the assault against the working class in 'revolutionary' Peru." Latin American Perspectives III (Spring): 55–83.
1977   "Class alliances and class struggle in Peru." Latin American Perspectives IV (Summer): 4–17.
Espinoza, Humberto y Jorge Osorio
1972   El poder económico en la industria. Lima: Universidad Nacional Federico Villareal.
Favre, Henri
1969   "El desarrollo y las formas del poder oligárquico en el Perú" and "Misteriosa Oligarquía: Observaciones a las tesis de Francois Bourricaud y Jorge Bravo Bresani." Pp. 71–115 and 136–148 in Matos Mar (ed.) La Oligarquía en el Perú. Buenos Aires: Amorrortu.

Ferner, Anthony
1977   "La evolución de la burguesía industrial en el Perú: intereses y facciones." (Carlos Indacochea, trans.). Lima: Universidad Católica.
Fitzgerald, E.V.K.
1976   The State and Economic Development: Peru since 1968. Cambridge: Cambridge University Press
García de Romana, Alberto
1975   "Comportamiento gremial y político de los empresarios industriales, 1968–73." Lima: Universidad Católica, Taller de Estudios Urbano-Industriales. (mimeo)
García-Sayan, Diego
1977   "La reforma agraria hoy." Pp. 137–216 in DESCO, Estado y Politica Agraria. Lima: DESCO.
Harding, Colin
1975   "Land reform and social conflict in Peru." Pp. 220–253 in Abraham F. Lowenthal (ed.) The Peruvian Experiment: Continuity and Change under Military Rule. Princeton: Princeton University Press.
Knight, Peter T.
1975   "New forms of economic organization in Peru: toward workers' self-management." Pp. 350–401 in Abraham F. Lowenthal (ed.) The Peruvian Experiment: Continuity and Change Under Military Rule. Princeton: Princeton University Press.
Lizarzaburn, Pedro
1976   "La caída del régimen belaundista: un análisis político o la tragicomedia de los hombres de la renovación." Lima: CISEPA, Universidad Católica. (mimeo)
Malpica, Carlos
1968   Los Dueños del Perú. Lima: Ediciones Ensayos Sociales.
Ministerio de Industrias y Turismo
1963–75   Estadística Industrial (various issues). Lima: MIT.
1974   Estadística de Comunidades Industriales. Lima: MIT.
Ministerio de Trabajo
1973   Las Huelgas en el Perú. Lima: Min. de Trabajo.
Pásara, Luis
1976   "El Viraje: por qué, cómo y cuánto." Marka (May 6): 15–18.
Quijano, Aníbal
1972   "Imperialismo y capitalismo de Estado." Socieded y Politica 1: 5–18.
Sociedad de Industrias (S de I)
1968–77   Industria Peruana (various issues). Lima: S de I.
Sociedad Nacional de Minería
1974   Peru Minero 1974. Lima: SNMyP.
Villanueva, Victor
1977   "The petty-bourgeois ideology of the Peruvian Aprista Party." Latin American Perspectives IV (Summer): 57–76.
Webb, Richard
1975   "Government policy and the distribution of income in Peru, 1963–1973." Pp. 79–127 in Abraham F. Lowenthal (ed.) The Peruvian Experiment: Continuity and Change under Military Rule. Princeton: Princeton University Press.
Weeks, John
1977   "Backwardness, foreign capital and accumulation in the manufacturing sector of Peru, 1954–1975." Latin American Perspectives IV (Summer): 124–145.
Wils, Fritz
1975   Industrialists, Industrialization and the Nation State in Peru. The Hague: Institute of Social Studies.

Alan Stoleroff: State Capitalism and Class Formation in the Soviet Union

Until recently Marxists generally conceived of the social formations typified by the Soviet Union as transitional in some manner. It was assumed that the political revolutions beginning in October 1917 were the take-off point of a transition between capitalism and socialism. This chapter will attempt to demonstrate the inadequacy of such a perspective on the basis of a Marxist analysis of class.

A transitional social formation is defined as one in which a radical rupture has occurred in the specific combination of economic, political, and ideological structures which constitute the capitalist mode of production. According to Marxist-Leninist theory, this rupture occurs when state power is "seized" through the intermediary of a revolutionary party which has an organic relation to the dominated classes. The political relations which ensure the reproduction of the capitalist relations of production are thus altered, opening the way for a socialist transition.

The assumption that the Soviet Union is such a transitional social formation is based on the reduction of economic relations to the juridical relations of property ownership and the false identification of a proletarian revolution with the seizure of power by a political power (the Communist Party). The further assumption that the Soviet Union is a "socialist" society is based upon the myth that classes are abolished with the elimination of individual private property.

A socialist transition need not be the only possible outcome of an ideologically anti-capitalist political revolution even if it coincides with a working class and popular revolutionary movement. A political revolution typically conceals its real social character—which can only be known through historical analysis—and appropriates for itself the myth of a social transformation. This is particularly the case when the principal actors (the Communist Parties) play their roles in the name of a class (the proletariat). Following a political revolution, a new combination of political and ideological structures may emerge which reproduces the general subordination of

AUTHOR'S NOTE: This chapter is the result of discussion with and criticism of earlier drafts by Charles Bettelheim, Bernard Chavance, Norman Finkelstein, Dale Johnson, and Tcheka Patricio.

the direct producers. This chapter will argue that in the Soviet Union a new system has emerged in which the juridical form of state property and a bureaucratic-party dictatorship are determinant in the expanding reproduction of a division of labor that contains the basic functions and relations of a capitalist division of labor. The system in the Soviet Union is best identified as a form of state capitalism. What requires study is the process by which classes and the relations between them are reconstituted in modified forms following the construction of a new state.[1]

The process of class formation in the Soviet Union will be analyzed with respect to the Marxist theory of class and class struggle. First, classes are constituted within the relations of production, that is, by the functions the various agents of production fulfill in the reproduction of the social division of labor. The relations of production must in no way be reduced to the legal-juridical relations of property ownership. Second, by their very existence, classes struggle and engage in specific practices. Practices (economic, political, ideological, cultural) analytically correspond to class relations. The classes which are the object of this study have their basis in a capitalist-style division of labor, the system of state property and in the historical development of a system dependent on the organization of a party/class domination.

An analysis of class formation in Soviet-type societies must confront the state ideology of these societies. An evident problem consists of the fact that this ideology is itself a form of Marxism. In the Soviet Union the dominant ideology rests on the notion that socialism has been achieved; antagonistic classes have been eliminated because ownership of the means of production has been "socialized" through state property. Stalin announced once and for all in his famous speech to the 17th Congress of the C.P.S.U. that:

> The facts show that we have already laid the foundations of a socialist society in the U.S.S.R., and it only remains for us to erect the superstructures—a task which undoubtedly is much easier than that of laying the foundations of a socialist society [1972b:257].

According to Soviet ideology, the superstructures which Stalin spoke of were consolidated by the ratification of the 1936 Constitution. The legitimacy of this new Constitution was explicitly premised on the assertion that exploiting classes and class antagonisms had disappeared forever once the superiority of state forms of property had been achieved.[2]

In Soviet ideology, state ownership of the means of production is positively identified with social ownership and social appropriation of the means and results of production. For a critical Marxist theory, the notion that classes can be abolished and socialism established by forced collectivization and by modification of the legal relations of property is an abomination.

While serving as the basis of the ruling ideology in Soviet-type social formations, Marxism has also served a critical function in relation to these societies. Since as early as 1917 such varied authors as Kautsky, Luxemburg, Trotsky, Korsch, Mattick, Marcuse, Djilas, Sweezy, and Bettelheim—not to mention Mao Tse-tung—have criticized the Soviet project precisely on the basis of what they considered to be either a critical or "correct" Marxism, in opposition to the Marxism in power.

There is also an extensive body of literature (Oppenheimer, n.d.) on Soviet-type social formations whose theoretical roots can best be traced to the early sociological theorists of bureaucracy (Weber) and elites (Michels). The basic proposition of these theories is that in societies typified by the Soviet Union a new "class" has emerged which is characterized by its monopolization of political power. This approach remains insufficient in that it merely describes the political life of such societies, abstracting the observations from an analysis of economic class forces whose interests are reflected in the policies, practices, and structure of the state. Thus the concept "class" is not given its deserved materialist content. An unspecified "bureaucracy" often figures predominantly in these analyses, with no theoretical precision on the relation between bureaucracy and class in a system of state property.

Djilas (1957) descriptively identifies this new "class" by way of its bureaucratic, political character. He does not produce a rigorous analysis of the place of the new state in the expanded reproduction of the capitalist mode of production. This lack of rigor and the fact that this Yugoslavian ex-Communist's semi-self-criticism was heralded by the right in a period when the Soviet "model of socialism" was still prestigious among Marxists has often led this work to be unfortunately classified within bureaucracy and elite theory. Nevertheless, Djilas correctly identifies institutional relationships which constitute the ruling class of societies typified by the Soviet Union: the "political bureaucracy," the State, the Party and social relations which "resemble state capitalism" (1957:38, 35).

Trotsky's theory of the "bureaucratic deformation" of the Soviet state is well known and until recently provided the primary "left" critique of Soviet experience. It states that the ruling strata of Soviet society form a parasitic caste whose appearance is the result of the uniquely "Stalinist" bureaucratic degeneration of the Soviet revolution. This caste utilizes its political and social position to maintain its own material privileges in opposition to the workers. Nevertheless, Trotsky and his disciples insist on characterizing the Soviet state as a "workers' " state due to the absence of the juridical form of private ownership of the means of production. They refuse to acknowledge the class nature of bureaucracy because its existence is tied with state ownership of the means of production (Trotsky, 1937). Mandel (1968, 1978) shows himself to be trapped in a theoretical framework which locates the defining characteristics of class one-sidedly in legal-juridical property relations. The assumption in his thought is that state property equals the property of the workers. This is why he refers to a "new" mode of production rather than a modified form of the capitalist mode of production, i.e. state capitalism (1968:563, 565).

Official Soviet ideology, Stalinism, *and* Trotskyism have in common the "economistic" distortion of Marxism derived from the Second International. This economistic distortion locates the motor force of history in general, and of the transition to socialism in particular, one-sidedly in the development of the productive forces. Economism negates the proposition that the class struggle is the motor force of historical transformation and that the key to the transition to socialism (i.e., the abolition of classes) is located precisely in the transformation of the social relations or production, that is, a fundamental change in the position of the direct producers.

In *The Revolution Betrayed,* Trotsky reduces the survival and re-emergence of vast inequality, social stratification, state repression, bureaucracy, hierarchical relations in the enterprises, and so on in the Soviet Union of the 1930s to the retarded development of the forces of production and the subsequent scarcity of consumer goods. He derives from this that the main indicator in the progress of the transition to socialism is to be found in the relations or norms of distribution. Such a view is stated explicitly by Mandel (1968:572). He concludes that on the basis of state property the capitalist mode of production can no longer exist; he refers to the sources of inequality that are the "norms of distribution" by using the mystical notion of survivals of capitalist relations of production.

Paul Sweezy (1980) has developed an analysis which acknowledges that Soviet-type societies are class societies while explicitly rejecting the "Bettelheimian" theory that these are state capitalist formations. While recognizing the existence of a ruling class and a proletariat, Sweezy does not accept the notion that this ruling class constitutes a "state bourgeoisie." His argument rests on his characterization of *capitalism:*

> The economic foundation of capitalism has three determining characteristics: (1) ownership of the means of production by private capitalists; (2) separation of the total social capital into many competing or potentially competing units; and (3) production of the great bulk of commodities (both goods and services) by workers who, owning no means of production of their own, are obliged to sell their labor power to capitalists in order to acquire the means of subsistence [1980:139–140].

According to Sweezy the first two of these capitalist characteristics have been eliminated in Soviet-type societies—the first by state ownership and

control; the second by his claim that the enterprises are not really autonomous and "form parts of a hierarchical structure of decision-making and
control which reaches its peak in the top political organs of the state"
(1980:140). On the first point Sweezy overlooks the real content of state
ownership. The modification of the juridical form of existence of capital is
not its elimination as capital. On the second point Sweezy apparently can not
appreciate the objective autonomy and competition imposed upon the individual enterprises by the continuing existence of commodity production due
to his "fetishization" of the effectiveness of planning. The autonomy of
enterprise operation is obviously limited by the imposing central economic
authority. Yet forms of competition do in fact exist, manifested in the
"profitability criterion," which can potentially even end in the closing of
unprofitable enterprises (Bettelheim, 1975; Nove, 1968; Wilczynski, 1970,
1972, 1973).

A major problem for Sweezy and others is the confusion of an analysis of
the economic system (the forms of regulation of capital and its movement
within particular formations) with the mode of production (determined by an
articulation of the social relations of production with the character of the
productive forces). Many of the so-called "laws" of capital purported to
have been demonstrated by Marx in *Capital* are not immutable, that is, at
least not in their manifestation. For instance, the crises of accumulation of
state capital in the Soviet Union do not take the same form as for private
monopoly capital; the primary form is a constant crisis of shortage (of raw
materials, labor power, goods on the market, and so forth) combined with
over-accumulation in some branches and under-accumulation in others
(Lafort and Leborgne, 1979). The superstructure does have a major effect on
the economy. The centralized, bureaucratic economic direction alters the
"spontaneous" working out of the laws of capital in ways other than the
traditional crisis of overproduction that manifests itself in monopoly capitalism. In fact, to recognize that the advanced capitalist countries are re-
experiencing crises of overproduction does not mean the form of capitalist
crisis has not changed; the emergence of "stagflation" is a sign of the
evolution of capital, in part influenced by the forms of economic intervention of the modern state. The Soviet-type state capitalist formations may
experience contrasting economic dynamics precisely because of the form of
state and society that has evolved.

Methodological Considerations

For the most part, Western and Soviet academic work is uninterested in
the question of class as understood by critical Marxism. It is held that
"classes" in the Marxist sense can not exist because of the absence of private

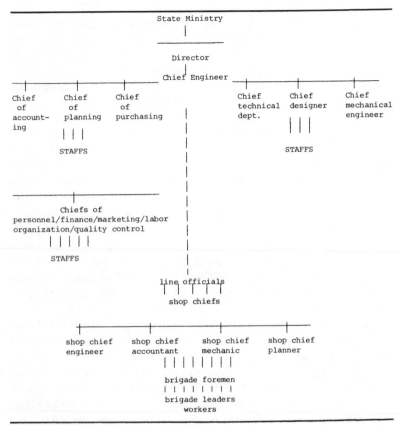

Figure 10.1

ownership of the means of production. This notion is reinforced by the official statistical categories of the Soviet census which are elaborated upon the same theoretical (or rather ideological) basis. Soviet statistics acknowledge the existence of only two classes: (1) workers and white-collar employees (i.e., manual and non-manual workers), and (2) kolkhoz peasants (i.e., collective farmers). These categories are derived from the two legal categories of "socialist" property: state property and collective property.

Such a categorization of Soviet social structure is ideologically derived, that is, it tends to conceal actual class differentiation. For example, there is no clear breakdown within these groupings between workers or white-collar employees who exercise either functions of labor or functions of management and supervision within Soviet productive enterprises. Soviet sociologists have at most split the non-manual category into the intelligentsia and ordinary white-collar employees. Thus there are no separate, accurate, and exclusive statistics for enterprise directors or management personnel; these are often lumped together in subsidiary statistics as administrative employees. Likewise, statistics regarding the distribution of functions within the state bureaucracy are practically non-existent. This latter problem creates a difficulty even for analysis of social inequality in that income, perquisites, and so on of the highest grades of state functionaries are diffused throughout broader, less specific strata or are not reported at all.

There is a vast Soviet and non-Soviet literature which characterizes the Soviet social structure as "stratified" according to income, political and cultural attributes, and so on while maintaining the non-existence of distinct and antagonistic social classes. Such studies begin with the assumption that the Marxist theory of social class is uniquely grounded in legal property relations and that therefore the only possible class contradictions in the Soviet Union are those of a non-antagonistic character between "workers" and collective peasantry. This not only renders the category "workers" meaningless but for political ends exaggerates the difference in class position between the expropriated factory proletariat and the effectively expropriated agricultural producer on the "collective" farm. Such an approach is employed to direct research onto the terrain of the non-Marxian analytic variables of social stratification along the lines of Weberian sociology. Having necessarily found that various stratification trends do exist, they conclude that Soviet society is stratified along various variables but is not class stratified—of course, the methodology has confirmed the initial hypothesis (see, for example, Lane and O'Dell, 1978). Such an approach obscures the eclectic blending of two fundamentally opposed paradigms of sociological analysis. The Marxist theory of social class is grounded in an historical analysis of the divisions among the agents of production according to the real relations of production. Obviously, inter-class and intra-class stratifications along numerous sociological variables gives specificity to different class systems but such stratification is not the determinant of social class. Rather, stratification is determined by the historical relations between classes in a concrete social formation.

A deeper problem exists when Marxists attempt to utilize social stratification as the method of class analysis for social formations typified by the Soviet Union. Essentially they revert to a method of empiricism or a theory of "power elites." Marxists have clearly recognized this problem in their analysis of the evolution of the corporate structure of modern capitalism when they have criticized such notions as the "managerial revolution." Studies of this problem have explicitly recognized that the use of empirical analysis of legal ownership of portions of stock could serve merely to point out the weaknesses of bourgeois sociology on its own terrain (Zeitlin, 1974). Class relations in any social formation can only be grasped through substantive analysis of the real relations of production, on which legal property relations are a superstructure. Marxists have also implicitly recognized this problem in their studies of the role of the state in dependent social formation. They have developed a concept of a bureaucratic bourgeoisie whose function as a bourgeoisie is determined not by legal private ownership but by the relation of this stratum to the state, which exercises a particular function in the expanded reproduction of capital.

The nature of class and the relations between classes in the Soviet Union cannot be sufficiently comprehended by reference to the system of economic relations alone. State capital, which is a form of collective capital, does not provide for the reproduction of social classes in the same manner as individual capital. The sociological means of organization and recruitment to these classes can not be conceived of in terms similar to property rights or lack of property rights. For example, inheritance is not an inter-generational means of passing on class membership.

It is evident that the Communist Party apparatus is the unique institution of organization and recruitment of the functionaries of the Soviet state and economy. This empirical observation is not without significance for the problem of class formation. Through its selective mechanisms (the *nomenklatura* for example), the party constitutes an institution—in itself the dominant apparatus of the state—for the reproduction of the functionaries of social capital at all levels. The dominant political institution of Soviet society fulfills a class-reproductive function in Soviet society. Thus the discussion of class formation in this society must refer to an articulation of the system of economic and political relations.

The political level, of course, does not in and of itself constitute social classes. It is at the economic level—the social division of labor—that class positions are produced. But in the Soviet Union the political system organizes the agents of production. The economic system is articulated with a political system of party domination. Though party domination in the U.S.S.R. has a history and an autonomy, it is only in conjunction with the specific form of the capitalist division of labor which exists in this society that it becomes a fundamental determinant of class.

The Soviet social formation is recent and a new type of society, the consequence of a prolonged destruction of the social structure of Czarism by civil war, economic ruin and reconstruction, and various campaigns of state terror from which no social stratum escaped without significant mutation. While the capitalist social relations of production have been reproduced throughout Soviet post-revolutionary evolution, the social sources of recruitment of the agents of capital and labor—and the agents themselves—were profoundly transformed. Classes have specific histories, the continuity of which is inseparable from their formation. Classes do not simply exist as a function of economic structure, though without the economic determinant of real property relations and functions within a given division of labor, class can not be comprehended. In this sense, though we may observe the non-disintegration of certain social strata which existed under the Czarist regime (for example, the "bourgeois specialists"), the classes of contemporary Soviet society are new classes. We are, so to speak, dealing with new wine in old bottles.

Classes and Property

In a well-known statement, Lenin said that classes are determined

> by the place they occupy in a historically determined system of social production, by their relation (in most cases fixed in law) to the means of production, by their role in the social organization of labor, and, consequently, by the mode of acquisition and the dimensions of the share of social wealth of which they dispose [1977:16].

It is significant that Lenin relegated the legal-juridical relations, the law, to parenthesis. A modification of the juridical form of property relations alone would leave intact the "places occupied," "relations," "roles" and the "mode of acquisition" founded upon the separation of the direct producers from the means of production.

In the competitive and monopoly stages of capitalism, the social division of labor is fixed by the legal-juridical form of individual private ownership of the means of production. Individual private property empowers a class of capitalists to appropriate the surplus-labor of the direct producers in the form of surplus-value. But capital (as Marx made clear) implies a social relation (not a thing) and is not to be equated with legal-juridical private property relations (Balibar, 1977). With state capitalism, the legal-juridical form of state property fixed by law the social divisions of labor and empowers the state to appropriate the surplus-labor of the direct producers. The elimination of private property displaces the mediation between the direct producers and the means of production to the state.

The Marxist theory of the abolition of classes posits the elimination of individual, collective, and state property. Such a revolution can only be achieved through the producers' democratic control over the means and results of labor, i.e., their "reunification" with the means of production. (This is intended logically and not as a statement of political preference.) Put dialectically, this implies the elimination of property altogether in that property itself signifies the alienation of labor. Complimantarily, this signifies the disappearance of commodity production, the system of wage-labor, and the economic categories of capital. State property may be a prerequisite or a necessary aspect of this process—if the direct producers likewise dominate the state—but, it may not be sufficient. The notion of a transition to socialism as a statization of property and production is handed down from the Second International's conception of socialism as the progressive and necessary result of state capitalism, itself conceived of as "organized" capitalism (Chavance, 1980; Mattick, 1978). But whether or not state property is a necessary transitional step in this process, the emergence of the "free association" of the producers requires the negation of property as such. The negation of state property and reciprocally the "withering away" of the state are aspects of the abolition of classes. (Whether or not Marx and Engels' theory is utopian is not the question here and does not affect the Marxist analysis of capital and class.)

The juridical form of state ownership does not eliminate the intervention of non-laborers as "owners" of the means of production, as purchasers of labor-power and as disposers of the product. In state capitalist formations the state exercises precisely these functions. In social formations typified by the Soviet Union, non-laborers, i.e., the agents of the state and managerial bureaucracies, do intervene in the process of production in such a manner.

Capital, Division of Labor, and Wage-Labor

The economic categories that Marx analyzes in *Capital* are derived from and reflect actual social relationships. These categories attest to the existence of capitalist commodity relations and will continue to assert themselves unless the social relations of which they are reflective are themselves transformed. To the extent that any of these contradictory social relations continue to manifest themselves in the course of social production, the power of capital continued to exert itself; therefore, these categories will likewise manifest their power. If the categories profit, prices and wages continue to appear in Soviet-type formations, their continued existence should not be explained as mere "residues" or ideological "survivals." They are not old forms asserting themselves with new contents. Rather they continued to arise because of the existence of capitalist commodity relations.[3] If the categories exist so do the social relations of which they are a product. If labor-power is exchanged against money this signifies the existence of wage-labor and capital. The existence of wage-labor and capital signifies the existence of antagonistic classes.[4]

Marx's exposition of the social division of labor within the factory implies two complementary social relations: (1) social production, i.e., the cooperation of numbers of detail workers toward one productive end and (2) a hierarchical relation of subjugation which consists of the authority of capital, the functionaries of capital, and the "hierarchic gradation of the workmen themselves." This second aspect of division of labor within the factory is referred to broadly by Bettelheim (1974) as a division between the tasks of direction (i.e., tasks or functions of capital) and tasks of execution (i.e., tasks or function of labor). This social division of labor should be understood as an inseparable form of the existence of capital. It is precisely this that Marx is referring to when he speaks of capital as a social relation or of the individual capitalist as the personification of capital. The capitalist personifies the authority required to organize the labor process in a capitalist manner—that is, in a manner appropriate to the production of surplus-value. The specialized jobs of management and supervisor emerge, necessarily with the control of labor by capital or functions of capital (1967, I:331). The capitalist division of labor involves the intervention of non-laborers who are the agents of capital in a labor-process set in motion by direct producers who dispose of their labor-power as a commodity. Its existence is not contingent upon the form of property.

Capitalist social relations are characterized by a double separation: the separation of the direct producers from the means of production (i.e., from direct disposal, control or appropriation of the means of production) and the separation of the productive units one from the other (i.e., commodity production relations; see Bettelheim, 1975:77–85; Marx, 1967, III:877–884). In Soviet-type systems, state property merely disguises production relations that oppose the private character of economic property to the social character of the productive forces.

The wage form signifies the commodity character of labor-power. The wage form is THE expression of the separation of the direct producers from their means of production. In other words, the "re-unification" of the direct producers with their means of production can not take place under the wage form. Thus if in Soviet-type formations labor-power is exchanged against money as wages, this signifies the existence of the wage-labor system.

Nor is the existence of labor-power as a commodity dependent upon a juridically endowed private capitalist on the other side of the relationship. There are two possible conceptions of the location of the sale/purchase of labor-power in Soviet-type formations. There is first the state in the role of global capitalist as juridically it is the holder of capital. There is secondly the individual productive units, where the sale and contract of labor-power actually take place.

The commodity nature of labor-power means on the one hand the exist-ence of capital and on the other the existence of mediating relations between the direct producers and the means of production. These mediating relations take the form of the agents and institutions which organize them. The effect of state property is the displacement of these mediating relations from the private bourgeoisie to the institution of the state (the "home" of collective capital) and the class of agents which occupy directing places in the division of labor. At the same time, state property in and of itself does not displace the relation between capital and labor within the enterprise and at the point of production. In the Soviet Union, the surface form of this mediation has changed at the point of production as a legacy of the initial revolutionary period. The present day bureaucratic workers commissions or assemblies are the mutated form of the revolutionary factory committees. The labor-contracting and social managing "trade unions" that today are organs of the state and the asphixiated forms of the defensive proletarian organizations. Moreover, the capitalist division of labor is highly visible. The separation of the direct producers from the means of production principally takes the concrete form of a complete and radical separation of the direct producers from the state and from enterprise control.

The class nature of the Soviet state is obscured and mystified by the original seizure of power by a party acting in the name of the proletariat. This state reflects the reproduction of wage-labor and a division of labor that opposes workers to the class of agents in the bureaucracy and the enterprises that intervene in production as disposers of the means of production and as appropriators of the product, that is, a state bourgeoisie.

The Proletariat

The proletariat is that class, which divorced from control over the state and the means of production, is subjected to the conditions of exploitation through its position in the social division of labor.

The formation of the proletariat in the Soviet Union has its origins in the regime of the private-owning bourgeoisie. A sizeable and organized proletariat was in existence at the time of the October Revolution. This proletariat was then already one of the most highly concentrated in the world due to the high concentration of industry in Russia.

In 1913, some 8,600,000 workers and handicraftsmen (including seasonal workers) were then occupied in large and small-scale industry within Czarist Russia, of which some 3,500,000 was the annual average number of wage workers. After the revolution, the working class, along with family dependents, increased in percentage from 14.6 percent in 1928 (the year production finally approached the level of 1913) to 44.2 percent in 1959. The number of workers in the Soviet Union in 1959 amounted to 46,146,000 or 46.5 percent of the occupied population. Adding the Soviet category "employees" with workers, the 1964 total was 73,200,000 (Smirnov, 1966:26–27). In 1977, workers alone made up 61.6 percent of the active population (Berton-Hogge, 1978:3). What is not apparent in these statistics are the changes in the structure of the working class since the 1920s.

First, there is the inclusion in these statistics of those members of the active labor force employed on state farms but not of those employed on collective farms who are conceived of as peasantry. It is questionable whether there is other than ideological significance in the Soviet distinction between the class position of state farm workers and collective farm workers. The distinction is not based upon the division of labor but on legal forms of property. Certainly, the "collective peasantry" does not relate to the land in the manner typical of peasant production. Of much greater importance in the rural reality is the allotment of a small plot of land and private ownership of livestock for private production and sale on the market—but this right is not restricted to the members of the collective farms. Moreover, at least a portion of the income of the kholkhoznik as well as the state farm member is paid in the form of wages, with the difference that the wages of the kholkhoz member are much more directly tied to the productivity of the cooperative as a whole (Lavigne, 1974:120).

A second characteristic of the Soviet working class is its concentration in large enterprise. In 1963 almost 75 percent of manufacturing workers were engaged in establishments employing over 500 workers. The percentage of workers employed in establishments of over 1,000 workers was 56.5 in 1950 and 61.2 in 1958. This rate of concentration is substantially higher than in the United States for the corresponding period (Smirnov, 1966:29).

In the Soviet Union, the process of structuration of the labor force has great similarities with that of the monopoly capitalist countries. The growth of the service sector has been increasingly significant and within this sector there has been a similar development of a capitalist division of labor (Lane and O'Dell, 1978:10–18). Soviet statistics refer to this group as "those engaged in nonmanual service work (primarily non-specialists—employees)." This stratum is estimated as making up 11% of the labor force in 1966–1967. A characteristic of this stratum is that it is not engaged in the "management of the people" (Gordon and Klopov, 1973:29).

The analysis of the proletariat in the Soviet Union requires study of the historical transformations of the Soviet state and the Communist Party. In the conditions of the revolutionary upheavals the proletariat underwent successive transformations that can be divided into two historical phases. The first concerns the period of the upswing of revolution which corresponded to an unprecedented mobilization and organization of this class. The result was the formation of a new state power. The new state power following the October Revolution had its basis of support in the organizations of independent political power of the urban masses—the Soviets. The Soviet institution served to give this new state power an apparent class character. The state that emerged from the Soviets was the consequence of the growing hegemony of a particular type of party—the Communist Party.

The proletariat underwent significant modification with the political revolution of 1917. It entered a process of becoming the ruling class of Soviet society as in this conjuncture state power appeared to be held by it through the intermediary of the Communist Party which acted explicitly in its name. This class made up the backbone of the revolutionary army and secured the existence of Soviet power in the civil war. But this process also engendered a dispersal of this class. A significant portion of the working class was killed in the civil war and many workers dispersed to the countryside in search of food.

The second phase of the proletariat's development was the consequence of the growing rupture between the new state apparatus and the working masses. This rupture corresponded to a new and radical separation of the direct producers from the political means of control over the disposition of the means of production.

In his last writings Lenin had already drawn attention to the bureaucratization of the state apparatus, the incorporation into it of the cadres of the old regime and the authoritarian and despotic practices towards the masses which had become typical (Bettelheim, 1976; Narkiewicz, 1970). However, the qualitative transformation of this state from a transitional political power influenced by the masses into a political power dominated by a despotic state bureaucracy corresponded to the breakdown of the worker-peasant alliance and the destruction within the Communist Part of any vestiges of democracy in the post-NEP period. Trotsky characterized this period as a "Thermidorian reaction."

The working class was reconstituted following the consolidation of state power and the stabilization of the economy. Two developments in this process, beyond economic stabilization, go hand in hand: the promulgation of labor codes and the expropriation of the peasantry.

The source of recruitment of the Soviet proletariat was for the most part from the peasantry throughout the NEP period and even more so through the rapid industrialization of the first Five Year Plan. "In the first Five Year Plan period (1928–1932), 8,500,000 out of the 12,500,000 new employees in industry were former peasants. Up to World War II, the main source for the organized enlistment of manpower was from the countryside" (Osipov, 1966:39). The expropriation of the Soviet peasantry, the forced collectivization which uprooted millions of middle and poor peasants, supplied the growing industries with a vast source of recruits.

These new proletarians of peasant origin were not particularly well suited for the factory discipline to which they were rapidly subjected. Many of these new workers had been accustomed to take on seasonal industrial labor in the past and continued to leave industry and return to the countryside. Absenteeism, lateness, and indisciplines were all serious problems to planners who demanded the creation of a stable, disciplined work force (Broderson, 1966:59–92).

The introduction of the first five-year plan "required" the strict factory-disciplining of a labor force of peasant origin which had been proletarianized overnight. The fluidity of labor was a serious obstacle to the realization of the plan. In order to surmount this obstacle, state direction of labor was put into effect in combination with severe negative incentives. These sanctions were applied to all forms of state provided services and benefits, including housing, unemployment insurance, disability compensation, and so on. (Deutscher, 1950:75–120). Perhaps the most important of these negative incentives was fear of the forced labor camp. "The fear of the forced labour camp came now to play the role that the fear of unemployment had played under capitalism—it maintained labour discipline. This stage, however, was reached only in the latter part of the thirties, when mass deportation of political suspects, too, became a normal practice" (Deutscher, 1950:92).

"Positive" incentives took the form of the generalization of piece-rate wages and "Stakhnovite" production campaigns. In *Capital,* Marx refers to piece-rate wages as the ideal form of payment (1967, I:556). By the late 1930s piece-rates were the norm of payment whenever it was technically feasible (Conquest, 1967:55–58). The result of "Stakhovism" was not only an intensification of manual labor to an extreme for such workers, but was also the condemnation of large groups of workers to activities of preparatory work for the Stakhnovites. Such a relationship between a mass of unskilled, preparatory workers and the skilled worker now relieved of preparatory and clean-up work greatly divided and fragmented the working class.

In the late 1920s the state apparatuses concerned with the organization of labor underwent rapid transformations to accomplish the task of proletarianizing the peasantry and disciplining the working class. As Stalin said, "We must no longer count on a spontaneous influx of manpower. This means that we must pass from the 'policy' of waiting for the spontaneous influx to the policy of organized recruitment of workers for industry" (cited in Conquest, 1967:24). A series of laws and agencies of a system of "organized recruitment" of workers from the countryside to industry was developed. This recruitment policy was combined with the introduction of a series of particularly repressive labor codes. Uncontrolled labor turnover was dealt with by exclusion from employment benefits. Absenteeism and lateness were penalized with jail sentences including deportation to forced labor camps. There was the introduction of a domestic passport for the purpose of controlling the movement of labor. By 1938, every worker was required to be in possession of a workbook without which subsequent employment was made very difficult. All these restrictions upon labor were instituted before the threat of war, which only multiplied the severity of the labor codes.

These developments were associated as well with the transformation of the trade unions and the introduction of particular forms of material incentives to reward the most productive workers through emulation campaigns. Clearly, the introduction of such practices was a manifestation of the radical separation and break which had occurred between the state power and the mass of workers.

Following the purges of the late 1920s, the trade unions were deprived of any specifically trade union function. By the end of the 1930s, these institutions became trade unions in name only. Between 1933–1935 the practice of employing workers by "collective agreements" between trade unions and management was phased out. Trade unions began to take on little more than production propaganda and social insurance functions (Brown, 1966; Sorenson, 1969).

The introduction of these measures coincided with an ideological assault, led by Stalin himself, against "petty-bourgeois egalitarianism" or "levelling" as it was often called. As a result of the introduction of piece-rate wages, the rewards to "Stakhnovite" workers (who Deutscher referred to as a virtual aristocracy of Soviet labor [1950]) and other forms of material incentives and disincentives, great patterns of wage differentiation occurred within the Soviet working class. At the same time the differentiation between managerial and worker incomes and privileges widened significantly. This was bound to lead to discontent among the mass of workers as well as disillusionment among those whose political inspiration came from the October Revolution. But in accordance with the norms which were dominant in the Soviet industrialization process, these material incentives and the subsequent inter-class and intra-class inequality played a central role. It was necessary for the forces in charge of the state and economy to smash any obstacles to this development. Social and economic inequality became legitimated and enshrined within Soviet state ideology.

The so-called excesses and mistakes of the Stalin period were in fact the means by which the state bourgeoisie in formation waged class war against the workers and peasants.

The State Bourgeoisie

In social formations typified by the Soviet Union, the state disposes of the means of production and appropriates the product. The state serves as the location for the constitution of a new ruling class on the basis of the legal-juridical relation of state ownership of the means of production. More precisely, the Party serves as the vehicle of the reconstitution of the bourgeoisie as a state bourgeoisie.

The concept of state bourgeoisie refers to that social class constituted by the agents of production who fulfill the commanding and controlling functions over the production process as a whole. As property ownership is centralized in the state, control of social capital is centralized in the state apparatus. Nevertheless, individual enterprises exist as separate units of production. There are thus two sites of particular importance in which the contradictions of class formation become crystallized. The first is the state and the second is the productive enterprise. Both the state apparatuses and the enterprise managements tend to engender bureaucracies, that is, social groupings which occupy directing functions. As these state and managerial bureaucracies are self-reproducing, the process of class formation is crystallized in the contradictory relations between the bureaucracy and the direct producers.

Clearly, the characteristics of the state bourgeois are subject to what Lenin called the modifications which classes undergo following political revolution. The socio-economic power of the state bourgeoisie is derived from its control over the means of production through the conduit of its relation to the state, i.e., its power rests upon the juridical form of state property. It is not the result of a relationship equatable with private individual ownership but rather of the functions which the state apparatuses and their functionaries perform in the social division of labor. The income of this class does not directly appear in the form of profit of enterprise; its appropriation of the social surplus product is concealed under the form of a salary (this is of course not the case for that portion of income obtained from bonuses whose source is enterprise profit). Any society requires appropriation of the surplus product for the achievement of socially necessary ends. That the appropriation of the social surplus should constitute an element of class formation is not due to the obvious fact that the direct producers can not retrieve the entire social surplus if the conditions for expanded reproduction are to be secured. It is due to the functions and nature of this appropriation by a class that exercises specialized functions in relation to the accumulation of capital. The Soviet state bourgeoisie had to struggle, at great social cost, to wrest control of these functions and achieve its class supremacy.

The core of the state bourgeoisie is in the state apparatus—the party leadership, state leadership, state ministries, planning apparatuses. It is these bodies which exercise control over the means of production and the use of the social product independently of the direct producers. They are, of course, subject to the constraints of the class struggle, which through decades of class war they have, in recent years and for now, been able to contain.

The state bourgeoisie consists of two fractions whose division is similar to the division between private owners of capital (such as banks, stockholders) and functionaries of industrial capital (managers). The leading apparatuses of the Communist Party form a special structure that historically constituted and now reproduces the state bourgeoisie as a class. This is accomplished through the party's now more or less uncontested institutional power over the state apparatus (therefore of state capital) and its power of selection of the agents of state capital. This commanding and organizing structure of the party expresses the power of the state bourgeoisie while it also imposes its domination on the fractions of this class. In fact, the party machine is practically identical with the supreme apparatuses of the state. Where they are not identical, the party leads through parallel structures (Lowit, 1977). The agents of party and state "own" the state, which owns the social capital divided into enterprise units and determine the short and long term use of the means of production. The agents of these apparatuses compose a definite class who members are interchangeable. It is this fact which gives the appearance in Soviet-type formations that politics "dominates" or "replaces" economics as the leading dynamic in the use of the means of production (Sweezy, 1980:147). More precisely, it is political structures that determine the economic agents, whose economic practices are identified with the state.

The members of this class and their characteristics are not well known. More is known about the institutions which are invested with state economic power and their relations with the productive enterprises: the Communist Party Politbureau, the party's Secretariat, the republican governments, the Gosplan, the Gosstroi, the State Committee for Material Supplies, the State Committee for Science and Technique, the All-union and Union-republican economic ministries, and the like (Lane, 1976:127; Nove, 1968:110). These are all state institutions effectively charged with short and long term disposal over the use of the means of production that determine the trend of capital accumulation.

These institutions should not be confused with the productive enterprises themselves. Though the productive enterprises have obtained ambiguous degrees of autonomy in operation, particularly since the later 1960s, the state planning process continues to integrate the individual productive units into a centralized economic apparatus where effective control over the social means of production rests with the ministries. In fact, ministries have a tendency to establish forms of "autarchic empires" of vertical industrial organization in order to assure the successful achievement of goals of the particular industry. Often the ministry will invest its capital in new enterprises, functionally outside of the purview of the ministry itself, in order to ensure the supply of raw materials or means of production. Further, there is good reason to believe that the restraints, if not the failure, of the Soviet economic reforms of the 1960s is due to the resistance of the bureaucracies of the centralized ministries who see their power threatened by increased autonomy of the productive enterprises (Nove, 1979:155–165).

Nevertheless a second dependent and subordinate fraction of this class can be located in the distinct stratum of factory or enterprise directors. These agents exercise immediate functions of direction over the direct producers in the enterprises themselves. The position of this fraction has changed over time, in correspondence with a struggle with the dominant party/state elements. From an intermediate group in the social division of labor, this fraction has become an integral component of the state bourgeoisie.

The origin of this second, subordinate fraction is in the organization of enterprises on the basis of one-man management in which full authority in the enterprise rests with the Director. This fraction had its source of recruitment in both (1) the "red" specialists of proletarian or party origin who were assigned to these tasks by the state and (2) the "bourgeois" specialists left over from the old regime (often former owners of an enterprise), who were called upon by the state to exercise this function (Bailes, 1978; Bienstock, Schwarz, and Yugow, 1944; Granick, 1954; Berliner, 1957; Azrael, 1966). The power and importance of enterprise management was held in check and violently subordinated to the dominant fraction during the Stalin period. This subordination corresponded to the extremely centralized, command economy of that period. The function of the managers then was essentially that of carrying out the will of the state planning apparatuses at the enterprise level. As such they had not yet exercised autonomy to any extent in the disposal of the means of production. At that stage they constituted an intermediate stratum.

As early as 1936, 97 per cent of plant managers, 82 per cent of chiefs of construction, 40 per cent of chief engineers were Communists. These percentages increased further. . . . In plants, Party apparatus and general plant administration have become more and more homogenous, both socially and psychologically. The roots of the friction between plant managers and Party secretaries in plants have died out [Bienstock, Schwarz, and Yugow, 1944:30].

Following the Second World War, managers began to exercise more control and autonomy of decision-making at the enterprise level. The reforms of the post-Stalin period very much correspond to a rise in the importance of this fraction. This can be seen in the formalization and legalization of a greater degree of control in the economic process by these managers. They have been granted larger powers of decision-making regarding the disposition of the means of production, the utilization of enterprise profit, the utilization of labor-power and even the establishment of prices.

That managers have become a self-perpetuating stratum occupying class functions in the division of labor is evidenced by the findings of Soviet researchers. Shkaratan found in a sample survey of enterprises and cities that "the average overall length of employment in all groups and in all cities ranges from 11.5 to 14 years' except, naturally, among the group of executives of labor collectives, whose average length of employment ranges from 18 to 20 years." He also found that "56.6% of executives have been employed for more than 20 years. . . . the promotion of young people to executive positions does not occur with sufficient frequency" (Yanowitch and Fisher, 1973:71). When we combined the stability of the positions of the agents of managerial functions with the significant social privileges that devolve from this position (Matthews, 1978) we find that there exists a cohesive group with a definite material interest in maintaining and not breaking down the existing division of labor. Another Soviet sociologist has therefore concluded that "insofar as they comprise a distinct stratum specially employed in performing managerial functions, there are essential differences between them and other strata of working people (including personnel in mental work who do not perform administrative and managerial functions)" It is significant that Shkaratan states his agreement with this conclusion on the basis of his own research (Yanowitch and Fisher, 1973:67).

The Party serves to constitute the state bourgeoisie and its two predominant fractions into a ruling class in relation to state power. Here the essential thing to look at is not the numbers or percentage of members of various social groupings in the Communist Party, though such an analysis sheds an interesting light on the class character of the Party. The various social groups of Soviet society are "represented" in the Party but there are some visible trends in membership by social category. There is firstly very low membership rates among the mass of the unskilled proletariat, whereas approximately 54 percent of management personnel are members of the Party (Lane and O'Dell, 1978:26). The largest social grouping proportionately in Party membership in the Soviet Union is the official statistical category called "employees" who made up approximately 45.9 percent of Party membership in 1967. However, as Matthews points out, the "weight of the 'employee' element conceals, in fact, the dominance of the intelligentsia. Managers and specialists, who in 1967 made up, at a generous estimate, 14 per cent of the total labour force, occupied a third of the places in the Party" (1972:218).

The important thing to glean from these statistics is that due to their dominant position in the social division of labor these management and bureaucratic strata occupy a dominant political position as well. There is an extremely high correlation between elements who occupy decision-making positions in the state political apparatuses, the state planning apparatuses and the productive enterprises and the elements who hold leading and responsible positions in the Communist Party apparatus. There is every empirical indication to suggest that these strata effectively utilize their political positions to direct Soviet development in accordance with their class interests. In other words, the analysis of the structure of the social division of labor does not stand alone as an explanation for the nature of state policy towards social control and economic planning. In reality the development of such policy can not be abstracted from the development of class consciousness.

An interesting indication of the class consciousness of this social class emerges incidently from a Soviet study of the attitudes of various social groups regarding "ownership of socialist property"—in other words, their attitudes toward STATE property:

> Mukhachev and Borovik again found variations in the attitudes of different groups of workers when they tried to study general "ownership relations" towards the factory. They asked the question (in sixteen lathebuilding factories), "Do you consider yourself to be one of the proprietors (khozyaev) of socialist production?" 47.2 per cent said yes; 22.5 per cent, no; 22.1 per cent did not know and 8.2 per cent did not answer. Those who actually participated in the various institutions of control of the production process had the more positive attitudes towards socialist property [Lane and O'Dell, 1978:43–44].

Lane and O'Dell are here adopting uncritically the Soviet usage of the term worker, which includes the management personnel. It is apparent from this study that it is precisely the latter who are most conscious of their interest in relation to the existing form of property relation. Consciousness generally reflects the social position and material interest of the social group; clearly, the very unequal patterns of material rewards and remuneration "in Soviet society, where managers receive disproportionate bonuses for the performance of "socialist" property, is reflected in consciousness.

The Party serves as well as the elaborator and transmitter of the dominant ideology. Thus there is a definite link between the class function of the Party at this level and the official ideology surrounding the notions of state property as the "property of the whole people" and the "socialist mode of production." Here we are confronted with the role of the function of social control and cohesiveness in a society divided into antagonistic social classes. The dominant ideology, which in any social formation is the ideology of the ruling class, is an expression of a state bourgeoisie whose social role is legitimated by its position in a system of property relationships dominated by the form of state property. Official ideology places the motor force of history in the development of the forces of production and negates the continuation of the class struggle and is naturally suited to such a legitimating function.

Intermediate Positions

An analysis of position intermediate between the proletariat and the state bourgeoisie in the Soviet Union must distinguish between two sources of class formation. Firstly, there is the strictly economic source, that of function within a capitalist division of labor and the labor process. There is secondly a source specific to Sovietytype formations which derives from the bureaucratic system of social and political control. This system can in no way be abstracted from the determination of the specificity of the state capitalist formations and their class relations.

In the Soviet social formation the various social positions intermediate between the state bourgeoisie and the proletariat do not include the traditional petty bourgeoisie to any significant extent as private property exists only marginally in the area of small handicrafts. The economically deprived intermediate groupings are those within the social division of labor that fulfill a combined function. This has been defined by Carchedi (1975) as the control function of capital and the function of the "collective laborer." There are on the other hand rapidly increasing numbers of functionaries, technical experts, and "mental" workers who, following Carchedi, are "both exploiter (or oppressor) and exploited (or oppressed)" (1975:51). Due to their heterogeneous composition and apparent contradictory character it is difficult to conceive of these groupings as constituting a coherent and unified middle class. In a state capitalist social formation, where capital is not privately owned, and where the bourgeoisie is constituted through functions and positions within the state, the contradictory character of intermediate strata is probably more in evidence than in the advanced monopoly capitalist countries.

Within the typical Soviet firm there are numerous and diverse intermediate position between the enterprise director and the workers at the point of production. The following chart provides a schematic idea of the social division of labor within a typical Soviet factory. The managerial system of "one-man" management makes it not arbitrary to locate a class boundary determined by function and disposition over the means of production between the Director and Chief Engineer on the one hand and the subordinate department chiefs and their staffs on the other. This latter category occupies functions intermediate between the enterprise directions and the immediate producers. These are typically functions which combine productive and non-productive activities.

The categories of occupations, such as technicians, engineers, specialists, etc., appear to be undergoing "proletarianization" to the extent that these occupations have been separated from their managerial function.

The process of proletarianization of occupations outside the sphere of material production has important implications for the development of intermediary classes and strata. In Soviet statistics these strata are lumped together in the category of intelligentsia or "specialists." Their relationship to property ownership is similar to that of the working class in that they do not control property as does the state bourgeoisie and their form of payment is salaried. To the extent that these strata of specialists are not occupied in functions of management of people, they have also experienced a significant proletarianization of their relation to the labor process. Gordon and Klopov estimate that approximately 43% of such "specialists" are employed in the sector of material production or linked to material production. (The interesting thing to know would be how the other 57 percent of those lumped into the category of "specialists" are employed in the social division of labor.) They go on to state:

> The overwhelming majority of specialists engaged in material production work within the framework of large collectives, and are subordinated to their discipline, organization and interests. . . . Moreover, the technological revolution is bringing with it an increase in a group of specialists whose work is in no way connected with the management of people and in degree of breakdown differs little from the labor of workers [1973:30–31].

They then summarize this development in the following way:

> Thus, in socialist society as in developed capitalist countries, there is taking place, although on a different socio-economic base, a universal process of consolidation of hired laborers into a single class [1973:32].

The point, however, of this paper is precisely that this process which is "universal" is not actually occurring on a fundamentally "different socio-economic base" but rather on one characterized by a capitalist social division of labor. As Braverman (1974) so effectively pointed out, this process is not one which is neutral or inherent in regards to economic and social development, but is rather one which is subject to the class norms of capital accumulation. The socio-economic difference is a difference in legal property relations. But this change in legal property relations has not abolished the social division of labor dividing the agents of production according to functions of direction and functions of execution or labor. There continues to exist in the social formations in question various specialized agents who occupy specialized functions of control over the disposal of the means of production and the management of people. These agents are delegated control functions by the state bourgeoisie and form precisely a social class, or more precisely, fractions of an intermediate class which is separated from the direct producers.

The dubious and ambiguous statistical and sociological category of "intelligentsia" used by the Soviets tends to overlap with out concept of intermediate class (Churchward, 1973). But this category is both too broad and unrigorous for class analysis. Too often literature minimizes or even negates the antagonistic class functions of strata who have in common certain levels of education and the appearance that their occupations concern "mental labor."

In a particularly important though apologetic essay Volkov points out the radical distinction between those employed in mental labor who exercise the function of a "production-technical intelligentsia" and those occupied in the exercise of management functions. He states:

> Quantitatively, this group makes up a large portion of the general mass of those engaged in mental labor, and with the development of our society its numerical strength in absolute terms not only is not decreasing but is growing. In 1941 the group numbered 5,515,000; in 1958—5,579,000; and in 1960—5,753,000 [1973:53].

It is possible to understand the absolute growth of this strata as arising from a two-fold process. On the one hand, there are those elements in this still broad category of mental/administrative labor who exercise a significant control over the disposition of the means of production and who constitute a fraction of the state bourgeoisie—largely the enterprise directors. On the other hand, there are those growing elements, similar to what is referred to in the United States as "middle managers" who occupy an intermediate position between the state functionaries and enterprise directors and who carry out a will determined from above. It is clear from a further discussion in Volkov's essay that the category which he has enumerated contains such disparate elements in relation to the social division of labor as shop superintendents, directors of factories, personnel in plant management and higher organs of economic management as well as persons employed in state organs of administrative-political management not directly related to production.

Also within the intermediate class are the political functionaries, or employees at a level of intermediate responsibility of apparently political organizations, who, though their proclaimed social function is strictly that of political and social control, play a determinant and necessary role in the reproduction of social classes and their relations. Though we have said that political determinants do not "replace" economic determinants in these social formations, it is correct to stipulate that the political structures, relations and institutions are integrally and organically co-determinants of a very specific form of capitalism—one in which the political level is inseparable from the economic. Since the Soviet state expresses an elaborately hierarchized class dictatorship, the functionaries of this state are quite numerous and constitute an important fraction of an intermediate class that is encharged with reproducing the conditions of the dictatorship.

Both party and state are the source of existence of these intermediate strata. The statistical and occupational categories referred to here are so-called "government employees (juridical personnel, inspectors and so on)" (Semyonov, 1966:132), trade union officials in the apparatus and within the enterprises, secretaries and responsible members of local Party and Komsomol organizations, and so on.

Conclusion

The capitalist division of labor does not disappear with the appointment of a "communist" manager by the "socialist" state to the tasks of enterprise direction. Bourgeois political practices do not cease because the agents of a new state apparatus may have been recruited from either the working class or a "proletarian" party. As long as the social and political relations of capital are not attacked in an all-sided way—by the workers' increased domination of production, of the state apparatus and of society in general—the capitalist relations of production will be modified, reproduced and reinforced within a new context.

In Marx's theory, the transition to socialism requires a class dictatorship of the proletariat actualized in a new revolutionary state power dominated by the masses. By itself a revolutionary party (or parties) can not serve as the instrumentality of this class dictatorship. That in the course of real history parties have attempted to substitute themselves for a class is largely the political basis for the development of state capitalism (Mattick, 1978). Socialism, i.e., the abolition of classes, can only be an act of liberation of the workers themselves (as Marx said from the time of the *Manifesto*) or it cannot be.

Marxism and Marxism-Leninism conceive of the seizure of power by the "proletariat" as the nodal point of the revolutionary process. But as Marx and Lenin proposed, the proletariat can not merely take hold of the old state machinery and wield it for its own purposes; it must be "smashed." Yet the state, like capital, is not a thing; it is a complex political-social relation. The theoretical conclusion must then be that the state can not be simply "smashed" by an act of violence as if it were a thing or a definite group of people. The political and social relations upon which the state arises must be radically transformed. Thus, the seizure of power does not guarantee that a revolution will not be subsequently frozen and that the previous political-social relations will not be reconsolidated—even if in new forms. A political revolution may itself be the brake on a social revolution if its objective effect is to centralize political and economic power in a new state apparatus which becomes progressively separated from the masses.

Notes

1. It is interesting to keep in mind that Lenin originally formulated a similar proposition: "Classes have remained, but in the era of the dictatorship of the proletariat EVERY class has undergone a change, and the relations between classes have also changed. The class struggle does not disappear under the dictatorship of the proletariat; it merely assumes different forms" (1975:11).

2. A typical statement of the position of Soviet theory is the following: "The establishment of social ownership in all branches of the national economy completes the transition from capitalism to socialism. Socialism now develops on the basis of large-scale industry and highly mechanized collective farming" (Dutt, n.d.: 694). Any Soviet textbook on political economy will provide similar examples. Stalin's last major work, *Economic Problems of Socialism in the U.S.S.R.* (the content of which remains a pillar of Soviet ideology), is replete with statements to the effect that "the system of wage labor and exploitation has been abolished." In spite of his recognition that commodity production continues to exist (though it is now conceived of as "socialist" commodity production!) and his further recognition that consumer goods remain commodities, Stalin was confident enough to state: "The working class is not only not bereft of power and means of production, but, on the contrary, is in possession of the power and controls the means of production. Talk of labor power being a commodity, and of 'hiring' of workers sounds rather absurd now, under our system" (1972:17). Not only have exploiting classes and class antagonisms been eliminated, but so have the distinctions between mental and physical labor! Is it really such a big step from Stalin to the post-Krushchevian notion that the Soviet Union is already on the path of "communist construction."

3. Bettelheim, in *Economic Calculation and Forms of Property,* traces the existence of the value-form (prices, money) in the formation of economic plans in Soviet-type social formations to the actual continued existence of commodity production. Stalin, as well as contemporary Soviet writers, explained the continues existence of the value-form in three ways: (1) as ideological residue of the old form, (2) due to the contradiction between state and collective forms of property, and (3) due to the insertion of "socialist" economies in the international capitalist market. These do not account for economic relations between state owned enterprises taking the value-form. Bettelheim discovers its basis in the commodity relations in reality between the units of production, the real independent character of the production processes carried out in the enterprises. This is one aspect of the "double separation" which characterizes the capitalist mode of production.

4. "Capitalist production, therefore, of itself reproduces the separation between labour-power and the means of labour. It thereby reproduces and perpetuates the condition for exploiting the labourer" (Marx, 1967, I:577). He continues: "Capitalist production, therefore, under its aspect of a continuous connected process, of a process of reproduction, produces not only commodities, not only surplus-value, but it also produces the capitalist relation; on the one side the capitalist, on the other the wage-labourer" (Marx, 1967, I:578).

References

Azrael, Jeremy H.
1966   Managerial Power and Soviet Politics. Cambridge: Harvard University Press.
Bailes, Kendall F.
1978   Technology and Society Under Lenin and Stalin. Princeton: Princeton University Press.
Balibar, Etienne
1977   On the Dictatorship of the Proletariat. London: New Left Books.
Berliner, Joseph J.
1957   Factory and Manager in the U.S.S.R. Cambridge: Harvard University Press.
Berton-Hogge, R.
1977–78   "Les Ouvriers en URSS: Etude d'un Mode de Vie", Problemes Politiques et
        Sociaux, 54 (Dec.–Feb.):63–67.
Bettelheim, Charles
1974   Cultural Revolution and Industrial Organization in China. New York: Monthly Review
        Press.
1975   Economic Calculation and Forms of Property. New York: Monthly Review Press.
1976   Class Struggles in the U.S.S.R., Vol. I. New York: Monthly Review Press.
1978   Class Struggles in the U.S.S.R., Vol. II. New York: Monthly Review Press.
Bienstock, G., S. Scwarz, and A. Yugow
1944   Management in Russian Industry and Agriculture. London: Oxford University Press.
Braverman, Harry
1974   Labor and Monopoly Capital. New York: Monthly Review Press.
Broderson, Arvid
1966   The Soviet Worker. New York: Random House.
Brown, Emily Clark
1966   Soviet Trade Unions and Labor Relations. Cambridge: Harvard University Press.
Carchedi, Guglielmo
1975   "On the economic identification of the new middle classes." Economy and Society 4
        (February): 1–86.
Chavance, Bernard
1980   Le Capital Socialiste. Paris: Le Sycomore.
Churchward, L. G.
1973   The Soviet Intelligentsia. London: Routledge & Kegan Paul.
Conquest, Robert (ed.)
1967   Industrial Workers in the U.S.S.R. New York: Praeger.
Deutscher, Isaac
1973   Soviet Trade Unions. Westport, CT: Hyperion Press.
Djilas, Molvan
1957   The New Class. New York: Praeger.
Dutt, Clemens
n.d.   Fundamentals of Marxism-Leninism. Moscow: Foreign Languages Publishing House.
Gordon, L. A. and E. V. Klopov
1973   "Some problems of the social structure of the Soviet working class." In M. Yanowitch
        and W. A. Fisher (eds.) Social Stratification and Mobility in the U.S.S.R. White Plains,
        NY: International Arts and Sciences Press.
Granick, David
1954   Management of the Industrial Firm in the U.S.S.R. New York: Columbia University
        Press.

Lafort, Jean and Danielle Leborgne
1979   L'accumulation de capital et les crises dans l'U.R.S.S. contemporaine. Paris: CEP-
       REMAP.
Lane, David
1976   The Socialist Industrial State. London: Allen & Unwin.
Lane, David and Felicity O'Dell
1978   The Soviet Industrial Worker. Oxford: Martin Robertson.
Lavigne, Marie
1974   The Socialist Economies of the Soviet Union and Europe. White Plains, NY: Interna-
       tional Arts & Sciences Press.
Lenin, V. I.
1975   Politics and Economics in the Era of the Dictatorship of the Proletariat. Peking: Foreign
       Languages Press.
1977   The Great Beginning. Peking: Foreign Languages Press.
Lowit, Thomas
1979   "Y'a-t-il des états en Europe de l'Est?" Revue Francaise de Sociologie 20 (April–June):
       431–466.
Mandel, Ernest
1968   Marxist Economic Theory, Vol. II. New York: Monthly Review Press.
1978   "On the nature of the Soviet state." New Left Review 108 (March–April): 23–47.
Marx, Karl
1967   Capital. Vols. I, II, III. New York: International Publishers.
Matthews, Mervyn
1972   Class and Society in Soviet Russia. New York: Walker and Company.
1978   Privilege in the Soviet Union. London: Allen & Unwin.
Mattick, Paul
1978   Anti-Bolshevik Communism. New York: St. Martin's Press.
Narkiewicz, Olga A.
1970   The Making of the Soviet State Apparatus. Manchester: Manchester University Press.
Nove, Alec
1968   The Soviet Economy. New York: Praeger.
1979   Political Economy and Soviet Socialism. London: Allen & Unwin.
Oppenheimer, Martin
n.d.   "The development of the theory of the 'new class.' " (unpublished)
Osipov, A. P.
1966   "Redistribution of labour and changes in its occupational composition." In G. V.
       Osipov (ed.) Industry and Labour in the U.S.S.R. London: Tavistock.
Richman, Barry
1967   Management Development and Education in the Soviet Union. East Lansing: Michigan
       State University.
Semyonov, V. S.
1966   "Soviet intellectuals and white-collar workers." In G. V. Osipov (ed.) Industry and
       Labour in the U.S.S.R. London: Tavistock.
Shkaratan, O. I.
1973   "Social groups in the working class of a developed socialist society." In M. Yanowitch
       and W. A. Fisher (eds.) Social Stratification and Mobility in the U.S.S.R. White Plains,
       NY: International Arts & Sciences Press.
Smirnov, G. L.
1966   "The rate of growth of the Soviet working class and changes in its composition with
       respect to occupation and skill." In G. V. Osipov (ed.) Industry and Labour in the
       U.S.S.R. London: Tavistock.

Sorenson, Jay. B.
1969   The Life and Death of Soviet Trade Unionism 1917–1928. New York: Atherton Press.
Stalin, J. V.
1972   Economic Problems of Socialism in the U.S.S.R. Peking: Foreign Languages Press.
1972b The Essential Stalin (Bruce Franklin, ed.). Garden City, NY: Anchor.
Sweezy, Paul
1980   Post-Revolutionary Society. New York: Monthly Review Press.
Trotsky, Leon
1937   The Revolution Betrayed. Garden City, NY: Doubleday.
Volkov, Iu. E.
1973   "Social structure and the functions of management." In M. Yanowitch and W. A. Fisher
       (eds.) Social Stratification and Mobility in the U.S.S.R. White Plains, NY: Internation-
       al Arts & Sciences Press.
Wilczynski, J.
1970   The Economics of Socialism. London: Allen & Unwin.
1972   Socialist Economic Development. New York: Praeger.
1973   Profit, Risk and Incentives under Socialist Economic Planning. London: Macmillan.
Yanowitch, Murray and Wesley A. Fisher (eds.)
1973   Social Stratification and Mobility in the U.S.S.R. White Plains, NY: International Arts
       & Sciences Press.
Zeitlin, Maurice
1974   "Corporate ownership and control: the large corporation and the capitalist class."
       American Journal of Sociology 79 (March): 1173–1119.

About the Authors

Aijaz Ahmad, a native of Pakistan, is a professor of English and sociology at Rutgers University. He has published widely in the areas of Asian studies and international development. He is currently working on a book on Islam and politics.

Thomas Bamat's contribution stems from his dissertation research in Peru. He completed his Ph.D. at Rutgers in 1978 and is currently working with the Maryknoll Order's international projects in Ecuador.

Dale Johnson, editor of this volume and of the book series *Class, State, & Development,* is a professor of sociology at Rutgers University. He is currently involved in research on regional development of the Chesapeake Bay region.

Cecilia Karch, formerly of the Rutgers University Sociology Department, taught history and sociology at the University of the West Indies, Trinidad, and is currently consulting on projects of Caribbean development from her base in Barbados.

Nelson Keith completed his Ph.D. in 1980 in sociology at Rutgers with a dissertation on Jamaican political economy. He is currently teaching at Temple University and doing consulting work.

Novella Zett Keith is a professor of sociology at Stockton State College, New Jersey. She completed her degree in sociology at Rutgers in 1980 with a dissertation on Jamaican social structure and politics.

Mohammed Shahidullah is a professor of sociology at Rajshahi University, Bangladesh. He did his doctoral studies at Rutgers and the University of Pittsburgh.

Alan Stoleroff, currently doing research in Portugal, completed his dissertation on regional deindustrialization in northern France in 1983.

DATE DUE

DEMCO 38-297

A NORTON CRITICAL EDITION

MODERN DRAMA

AUTHORITATIVE TEXTS OF

THE WILD DUCK · THREE SISTERS
THE DEVIL'S DISCIPLE · A DREAM PLAY
DESIRE UNDER THE ELMS · HENRY IV

BACKGROUNDS AND CRITICISM

Edited by

ANTHONY CAPUTI
CORNELL UNIVERSITY

W · W · NORTON & COMPANY · INC · *New York*

Library of Congress Catalog Card No. 65-23037

W. W. NORTON & COMPANY, INC.
also publishes

THE NORTON ANTHOLOGY OF ENGLISH LITERATURE
edited by M. H. Abrams et al.

THE NORTON ANTHOLOGY OF POETRY
edited by Arthur M. Eastman et al.

WORLD MASTERPIECES
edited by Maynard Mack et al.

THE NORTON READER
edited by Arthur M. Eastman et al.

THE NORTON FACSIMILE OF
THE FIRST FOLIO OF SHAKESPEARE
prepared by Charlton Hinman
and the NORTON CRITICAL EDITIONS

ISBN 0 393 04278 2 Cloth Edition
ISBN 0 393 09665 5 Paper Edition
PRINTED IN THE UNITED STATES OF AMERICA
9 0

Contents

Foreword

Modern drama, as any list of recent publications will tell you, is an anthologist's heaven. Its wealth of playwrights and plays, its great variety of modes and styles, and its inevitable lack of hierarchical categories and time-sanctioned judgments permit excesses of ingenuity and whimsy unknown in other periods of dramatic history. That this should be so is understandable. Modern drama is still too much with us for any anthologist to be absolutely certain that this play is not important while that one is, or that this playwright is an innovator of the order of Sophocles while that one is distinctly a third-rate hack. Because it is all so relevant to *us*, and because it is still a living drama, whose meaning is obscure because its story is incomplete, we cannot view it as we view, rightly or wrongly, the Ages of Pericles or Elizabeth I. With few reliable guidelines and a superabundance of playwrights, critics, theatre historians, and amateur experts all hotly disputing the major and minor classifications, we continue to look and to read and to attempt discriminations, conscious that, though our efforts may be tentative, we have no choice but to make them.

Yet seventy years of study and criticism have not been entirely in vain; modern drama has been with us long enough to permit at least a number of preliminary distinctions and discriminations about its broad movement and about the playwrights who furnish the outline for that movement. Slowly but steadily a body of opinion has clarified itself, which, though it scarcely tells all and predicts almost nothing, has furnished a matrix for inquiry and understanding that most scholars and critics accept without protest. The trick for them, and perhaps even more notably for teachers of drama, is to accept and use this way of describing modern drama so that its provisional orderliness illuminates the richness of the subject but does not blind readers and students to its ambiguity and complexity.

It has been my purpose in this collection to do substantially that: to represent the broad outline of modern drama in the work of those playwrights who, critics and scholars agree, best describe it. For each playwright I have tried to choose a play both distinguished in its own right and exemplary of the peculiar thrust exerted by the playwright on the shaping of modern dramatic tradition. In each case, moreover, I have chosen plays which in my personal experience have proven themselves both accessible and of deep and enduring interest to students. The supporting materials by the playwrights and the essays by diverse hands comprise a mixture of well-known pieces, little-known pieces, and new work; they have been selected to assist, to provoke, to extend, and to enrich in various ways and to various ends.

Certain of the essays, in fact, declare more explicitly than the plays themselves what has been the second, though no less important, governing principle in the selection of materials for this book. Since no collection of modern plays can avoid being an anthology of documents illustrative of what social critics solemnly call the modern condition, I have deliberately attempted here to represent plays and supporting writings which supply material for that study even as they establish the facts of literary and dramatic history. In my opinion, modern drama embodies the peculiar tension, discord, hilarity, and hysteria of the twentieth-century with an integrity, or call it all-at-onceness, impossible in its sister-genres; in the unusual fullness of the dramatic image we approach the special quality of contemporary life most fairly. Certainly among the playwrights represented here are several who have been accorded major roles in the forging of modern sensibility. It is hoped, in any case, that instructors and students will find in these materials the wherewithal to illuminate modern drama in any and all of the ways that identify its singular literary and cultural importance.

ANTHONY CAPUTI

On Reading Modern Plays

Reading modern plays shares with the reading of plays from any historical period the problem of texts not primarily designed to be read. Plays are not, after all, poems or novels: they do not communicate initially and essentially by words, but by actions, by way of actors doing and saying things, by way of a complex fusion of visual and auditory resources of which the words spoken are only one. Reading the plays of any period, then, is inevitably a highly creative process by which the reader tries to construct from the verbal text as much as possible of the dynamic imagery of actors moving and speaking within a particular theatrical space. Reading modern plays differs from this general activity only to the extent that modern drama works through the languages of dramatic action peculiar to our time.

Of the psychological process by which readers transvalue the words on the page into scenes and series of scenes in the theatres of the mind we know very little. We read, and with the help of imagination and knowledge the images form, breathe, and develop the power to move us. Criticism can be useful to us to the extent that it trains the imagination and supplies the knowledge necessary to it, but criticism does not so much explain the creative process of reading as it stimulates and directs it. It is always partial and imperfect because it imposes a critical activity on a creative one; it is valuable because it realizes, by this in some respects false imposition, a heightened and enriched order of reading.

In reading plays, then, it is necessary to begin by accepting the premises of criticism: that a play is a rationally ordered whole; that its parts are related to each other and that all its parts are related to the whole according to rational principles; that the whole, therefore, is susceptible to rational analysis. These premises are useful, even when accompanied by an awareness that playwrights undoubtedly often work by methods other than rational ones, because only by accepting them can the reader assemble or reassemble the structure of a dramatic action with some assurance that it is a structure and not a chaos, a totality governed by a purpose and not a chance hotchpotch of parts; only then can the reader bring consistency and system to his activity. Having accepted these premises, in any case, the reader is then in a position to read the play as a system of mutually illuminating artistic decisions, a structure of choices made by the playwright out of the deliberate purpose of fashioning a particular dramatic action, one endowed with the power to move us this way rather than that, to encourage us to think this rather than that. By moving back and forth from the words or facts of the play to this gradually widening structure of decisions he will construct not merely an explanation for the facts, but a line of artistic reasoning that, theoretically, sharpens and enriches his perception of the dramatic action even as it explains it. It is futile to point out that the artistic reasoning devolved may have little to do with the actual process by which the playwright designed the work; it has served its purpose if it activates the play and causes it to release its power in a fashion consistent with the most honest and rigorous thought that the reader can bring to bear.

Reading plays, therefore, can be seen as a process by which the words or facts of the play are converted into animate images, which, in turn, are focussed, related to each other, and organized as a totality by reference to a pervasive artistic rationale. As a process it is emphatically exploratory: it never exhausts itself, and it always involves a back-and-forth movement between particular question rooted in fact and controlling rationale. To a large extent it consists in asking proper questions. In *Oedipus Rex* why has Sophocles chosen to conclude his play, not with Oedipus' lamentation after he has gouged out his eyes, but with his scene with his daughters as he prepares to go into exile? In *Hamlet* why has Shakespeare decided to have Ophelia report Hamlet's visit to her bedroom rather than have them play the scene? In *Desire Under the Elms* why has Eugene O'Neill given Ephraim Cabot so many speeches about religion and knowledge? Each of these questions can be formulated in terms of perfectly obvious indications in the verbal text, yet each is at the same time a part of a whole battery of questions which, as they are answered, lead to a progressively fuller conception of what the peculiar nature of this or that dramatic action is.

In the interests of bringing some clarity and system to an activity which can never be pellucid we might identify three distinct kinds or orders of artistic decision in the making of plays. First there is that order of decision which concerns the material out of which the dramatic action is fashioned. Why, it is important to ask, has the playwright chosen to make an action out of this particular story? What is there in its outline, what is there about its characters, what is there about the relationships among its characters that make these materials suitable to his purposes? Why in *Oedipus Rex* the story of Oedipus and not that of Creon? Why in *Hamlet* the story of a prince who cannot carry out what he sees to be a just revenge? Why in *A Dream Play* the story of the Daughter of Indra's visit to earth and her painful education in human experience? These are not questions that can be answered in isolation, of course; they must be considered with others and must be related to others. Why does Ophelia have this particular character rather than another? Why in the *Three Sisters* has Chekhov given Andrey this particular combination of strengths and weaknesses and not another? Because these questions concern the basic materials of the play, the substance from which it is formed, the artistic decisions involved might usefully be called substantial decisions.

Somewhat less general and far-reaching is a second order of decision which concerns the primary shaping of the play. In other words, once the materials or substance have been selected (and it bears repeating that we are constructing a temporal sequence that is useful to the critic-reader but that may have very little to do with the actual composition of the play), what decisions best explain the fundamental shape imposed on these materials? Why has Sophocles chosen to begin his play where he has rather than earlier or later in the story? Why has he represented this scene and reported that one? Why has Shakespeare chosen to treat the events of *Hamlet* in this particular scale and with these proportions? Why has so much time been given to Hamlet's internal debate and, relatively speaking, so little to his love affair with Ophelia? Why has Pirandello decided not to reveal Henry IV's "cure" to the audience until toward the end of Act II and not earlier? Because these questions probe decisions which, we assume, conferred a primary shape on the play, because they determined, that is, what was to be represented, in what order the various events were to be represented, and in what scale and proportion they were to be represented, the decisions might be called representational decisions.

Finally, there is a third order of decision which concerns the peculiar focus accorded to a dramatic action. Beyond the decisions that explain why these particular materials have been selected and why they have been shaped to present this basic dramatic image, there is a host of more limited decisions that sharpen particular qualities, highlight particular issues, embolden particular elements, in other words, that focus the action and its peculiar power. Why has Sophocles emphasized blindness in *Oedipus Rex*? Why has Shakespeare encouraged us to compare Hamlet, Laertes, and Fortinbras by putting them in analogous positions? Why has Ibsen entitled his play *The Wild Duck*? This order of decision comprehends all those details of technique which, though they rarely do more than confer a peculiar finish on a play, usually proceed from its fundamental controlling intentions. For convenience they might be called focussing decisions, though the term scarcely does justice to their variety.

Taken together, these artistic decisions constitute a structure or system which criticism creates for the purpose of assisting the reader in his creation, or more properly re-creation, of the artistic totality of the play. As he reads, he probes to construct, isolates to combine, reasons to use his imagination the more effectively. In reading plays his aim is to set on the imaginary stage of his mind the most authoritative, most complete version of the dramatic imagery of actors moving and speaking in a particular theatrical space that he can derive from the words on the page.

This way of reading plays, of course, is never quite the same for all plays, and it is notably different for plays from different traditions. Each of the decisions that goes into the making of a play is inevitably conditioned by the special theatrical bias, the special dramatic style, and the special ambience of social, political, and religious values of the historical period in which the play was written. Sophocles could not write a Shakespearean play just as Shakespeare could not write a Sophoclean play: each approached the act of creating for the theatre having been formed as a playwright by the physical theatres, the modes of presentation, the theatrical conventions, and the norms of dramatic composition of his time. If the reader of plays is to deal fairly with the works of different historical periods, accordingly, he must incorporate into the creative process of reading as much knowledge as he can recover of the cultural and dramatic history that he honestly feels contributed to the shaping of the play. His re-creation of the play by way of his construction of the system of its governing artistic decisions must be filtered through and qualified by this knowledge. Needless to say, the task is always rendered more difficult by gaps in our knowledge: to the extent that we do not know everything about the physical stage in Shakespeare's age, about the style of playing practised by his actor-colleagues, and about the specific cultural context in which his plays were written and produced—to that extent, it is probably fair to say, we can never know any Shakespearean play definitively. But we do the best we can with the knowledge that the effort is eminently worth making and that printed texts are as close as we are ever likely to come to many of the dramatic masterpieces of our tradition.

Reading modern plays is in many respects a vastly less complicated matter. Although the process of transvaluing the words on the page into the imagery of actors in motion is much the same, we do not have to read deeply in linguistic history to understand the words, in stage history to understand the modes of production, or in cultural history to understand the forces that drive our dramatists. Because the plays derive from our tradition, or from a tradition very close to our own, we come to them with a readiness that we must labor long to duplicate for great plays of the past.

Yet the advantages offered by modern plays must not be exaggerated, for their accessibility is deceptive. To begin with, modern drama embraces tremendous diversity. Unlike their predecessors, modern playwrights range freely over dramatic history, adapting the resources of diverse traditions to their purposes and experimenting with an abandon that makes for unparalleled variety. As readers and theatre-goers, we are, unfortunately, ill-prepared for that variety. Typically, we have been introduced to drama by way of films, television plays, and a limited number of experiences in the theatre, with the result that we have grown accustomed to plays in the realistic style of Arthur Miller's *All My Sons* or Tennessee Williams' *Night of the Iguana.* Such works present us with relatively familiar actions and worlds and for the most part give little difficulty; moreover, because of them we have been prompted to think, mistakenly, that the realistic mode of presentation is the fundamental language of the theatre. It is small wonder, then, that even the most sophisticated are frequently bewildered and baffled by that extensive part of modern drama that is non-realistic, by the radical departures from illusionism to be met in the surrealists, expressionists, and, lately, in the dramatists of the Theatre of the Absurd. The orientation toward theatre that the deeply ingrained tradition of realism encourages us to, with some gains for us, surely, as far as realistic plays go, impedes in us a readiness to deal with that important part of modern drama written in non-realistic modes.

Moreover, it is possible to argue that our familiarity with realism also entails disadvantages for reading and seeing plays of that kind. Because realism as a way of approaching experience, as a way of looking at the world and thinking about it, is so profoundly embedded in twentieth century experience, we seldom stop to think that as a movement in art, letters, and, in general, in cultural history it too was the result of a complicated historical process: it had its beginnings, it had its pioneers, and it underwent various modifications; it was part of that changing fabric of values that steadily conditioned playwrights to formulate new artistic intentions and to search for new solutions to their artistic problems. To see realism and the particular works that derive from it fairly, we must see it with a perspective that familiarity makes difficult for us.

If the problems of reading realistic plays are more deceptive, however, they are no more difficult than those involved in reading other kinds of modern plays. With every modern play the reader must develop and maintain a perspective on the modern world, on everything that has prompted the playwright to formulate this rather than that artistic purpose, that has led him to this rather than to that system of artistic decisions. Reading modern plays, accordingly, requires an awareness of the historical process by which our world became what it is, as well as of the manifold shifts in subject matter, forms, and intention by which modern drama became what it is. It requires, in other words, a study as extensive as possible of the history of modern sensibility, of, roughly, the hundred years of moral and psychological crises that have brought us to mid-twentieth century.

Fortunately, modern drama provides abundant evidence for such a study, and, in fact, it is hoped that the plays and essays included in this collection will lend themselves to that purpose. Because of the complexity of the subject, however, no collection of the scope of this one could be adequately illustrative, just as no essay of the scope of the present one could be definitive in its analysis. The intention is to illustrate broadly the principal directions of modern drama and the main currents in experience in the modern era that have prompted dramatists to take these directions.

Some time ago John Gassner provided a highly useful distinction for breaking down the multiplicity of forms to be met in modern drama in his *Form and Idea in Modern Theatre*, where he proposed that all roughly contemporary dramatic practice can be generally comprehended under the headings "realism" and "theatricalism." By realism in the theatre, of course, he meant that practice of creating or attempting to create illusions of real life on the stage. To understand this important stream in modern theatrical practice, however, we must first see that realism, more broadly considered, was a far-reaching movement in art, politics, religion, and literature that emerged in the last half of the nineteenth century to produce an essentially new, modern way of looking at the world. It might be said, very generally, that with the waning of the closed, orderly world that had been the basis of medieval and much of Renaissance civilization, realism provided a way of conceiving of a new one, more particularly a new way of apprehending and thinking about experience, of making sense of it or of trying to make sense of it.

This distinctive way of approaching the external world can be traced, of course, to many sources, but preeminent among its historical causes was the rise of science and of scientific habits of thought. In the work of Descartes and his fellow pioneers in the seventeenth century the foundations for modern science and for its distinctive approach to truth were laid. Descartes' *Discourse on Method* (1637) is important not only for its emphasis on method, but also for its emphasis on material evidence and the importance of individual experience. After Descartes, again very broadly speaking, truth was to be derived from what was knowable in sensuous terms, both from what could be measured (the material world) and from what could be experienced (the individual life). The result was a new way of relating man to his physical surroundings and a new interest in the particular, material world, the consequences of which for traditional beliefs and material and technological developments are too commonplace to rehearse.

By the nineteenth century, of course, the world was quite different from that of Descartes: it was a world with an urban emphasis, with vastly improved technical and industrial means, and with the habit of formulating its problems and of contriving solutions for them in this new way. It is useful to remember that this was the century of Charles Darwin, Karl Marx, Herbert Spencer, and John Stuart Mill, all men prone to look to material fact for their evidence. This was a century, moreover, dominated by that natural son of science, the idea of progress, the belief that physical nature and human nature could be mastered in man's best interests, a belief, it should be added, that at that time, as in our own, was supported by unprecedented changes and ostensible improvements in all quarters of life.

The world of letters responded to this movement with most alacrity, not in the theatre or in poetry, but in that form that owes most to this way of approaching experience, the novel. In the theatre the progress of realism was slow and discontinuous, and, indeed, the complete story of its emergence in the nineteenth century is too chaotic to tell here. We see signs of its emergence in the popularity of the Well-made Play, an ingeniously designed dramatic structure that put a premium on probability of a rather superficial sort, and the sporadic attention to authentic backgrounds and costumes in scattered productions in England and France. But all this did little more than prepare the scene for Emile Zola and the vigorous efforts made toward the end of the century to produce a revolution in the theatre. Zola, already known through his novels as a champion of that specialized form of realism called naturalism, is chiefly to be credited with articulating the theory of dramatic realism. In his "Preface" to *Thérèse Raquin* (1873) he claimed that "the experimental and scientific spirit of the century [would] enter the domain of the drama," that he had "invented a new formula, namely that there must be no more formulas." Once Zola had prepared the way, it was inevitable that an artist from the theatre should come forward to take up his challenge, and one soon did in the improbable figure of an employee of the Paris Gas Co., André Antoine. With the opening on March 30, 1887 of Antoine's Théâtre Libre, as Mordecai Gorelik puts it, "the Baroque ideal of theatrical splendor [went] down forever, having outlived its usefulness"[1] and the tradition of dramatic realism was put on a secure footing. Although always a small, experimental theatre, the Théâtre Libre brought realism to the fore and by way of its productions established its method, encouraged playwrights to practise it and introduced the work of some

---

1. *New Theatres for Old* (New York, 1957), p. 79.

of them, and prompted the foundation of a number of similarly dedicated "free" theatres in other European capitals.

The importance of these theatres cannot be too greatly stressed. They meant the establishment of standards of play-writing and of play production that constitute the nucleus of the realistic tradition in the theatre. At the center of this activity was the purpose to present an objective, analytic picture of the world, to present a slice of life that candidly exposed what were confidently taken to be the "facts" of experience. To carry out this aim, special techniques were devised. The tradition of elocutionary acting was quickly outmoded by an acting style that emphasized life-like appearance and behavior, a style most clearly seen in the work of Constantin Stanislavsky at the Moscow Art Theatre and in his present-day American disciples, the "Method" actors. The convention of painted scenery and selected properties was replaced by the ideal of exact reproduction in stage settings: the stage set became an environment bearing a meaningful relation to the action it contained. On such a stage the stage curtain became a fourth wall, an entry to a magic world of illusion, and the ideal of illusionism—the aim to create and sustain the illusion that what is being seen is a segment of overseen reality—became supreme.

Since 1890 dramatic realism has provided the fundamental idiom for the theatre in the west. We have seen it undergo many modifications, and we have seen it watered down in such a way that illusion has often been contrived for illusion's sake and the exploratory and critical emphasis of its pioneers has been blurred in favor of a kind of superficial snapshot-taking, as if a snapshot were in itself explanatory. To do justice, then, to the fervor and dedication with which the movement was launched and to its important practitioneers, we must keep firmly in view the seriousness of its basic aims and the passion with which its pioneers sought to lay surfaces bare so as to divest fact of its incrustations and penetrate to something on which solid structures could be built.

HENRIK IBSEN (1828-1906) has sometimes been called the Father of Modern Drama probably because he was the first important playwright to realize in practice the profound possibilities of dramatic realism. Yet, though a bias for social criticism is to be found in even his earliest work, it was not until Ibsen left Norway that he entered upon the period of social problem plays in which he perfected the realistic prose form for which he subsequently became famous. These are the plays in which he primarily focussed on society and in which he usually found more solidity and honesty in a vigorous individual conscience than in society's rules. This work includes plays like *The League of Youth, Pillars of Society, A Doll's House, Ghosts,* and *An Enemy of the People,* plays that have been called "dramas of retrospective analysis" because they begin in the midst of a crisis and move forward in time while looking back to reconstruct and reinterpret the past in terms of present conditions.

By easy stages this work led Ibsen to an increasing interest in the possibility that perhaps, after all, absolute truth could not be found anywhere, that all truth was relative; and to accommodate this more intricate and elusive subject, he modified the earlier formula to allow for elaborate character analysis. In his next plays, which include *The Wild Duck, Rosmersholm,* and *Hedda Gabler,* he was prompted to an increasing use of metaphoric and symbolistic devices; with them he marked out new possibilities for realistic drama both in his combination of realistic and poetic technique and in the new subjects that he continuously explored. Yet despite his technical penchant toward the end of his career for symbol and metaphor, he remained in a very important sense a realist to the core. His approach to the human condition, his way of assembling evidence, and his assumptions about how it should be regarded and how conclusions should be derived from it, were essentially those of a scientific, critical temperament. He differed from and surpassed those of like temperament chiefly in the rigorous honesty which prompted him to admit that this approach to experience frequently enabled him to raise questions which he could not answer.

In Russia, meantime, ANTON CHEKHOV (1860-1904) was taking the resources of realism in another direction. A doctor by profession, Chekhov won quick success as a writer of short stories, but at first had considerable difficulty as a playwright. His early failures were chiefly the result of the elusive dramatic form he gradually perfected, a form that superficially resembles the work of Ibsen, but that was sufficiently different to require a special style of playing that no company in Russia could provide until the Moscow Art Theatre succeeded with the famous production of *The Sea Gull* in 1898.

Chekhov's plays are certainly nothing if not realistic: what could be truer to life than his depiction of households milling about aimlessly and talking about apparently nothing? But the usual charge that in his plays nothing happens is a misleading exaggeration. Characteristically, Chekhov designed actions in which very little in the way of outward incident is represented, but in which his characters are revealed between the big events of their lives, as they are waiting to go into dinner or while they are sitting around after dinner musing about the past and their wasted youths. Chekhov was difficult for his contemporaries because of this new emphasis: he typically chose to de-emphasize incident in the interests of tracing character and the motions of character through the ebb and flow of trivial conversation. In this way he was able in plays like *Uncle Vanya, Three Sisters,* and *The Cherry Orchard* to animate profound strains of vitality in his characters and to throw into relief, not the usual linear development of the action from event to event, but a kind of spatial pattern, inward into the characters rooted in their situation and outward into the implications of the relatively unchanging situation. Moreover, he was able to manage through the imagery of characters doing very little and, though talking a great deal, saying very little a delicate stage-poetry of tremendous power. Although critics might say that in Chekhov's plays nothing happens, none, or at least few, would argue that they are about nothing: somehow he makes the "nothing" of his actions a nothing that has to do with everything.

GEORGE BERNARD SHAW (1856-1950), meanwhile, saw still other dramatic possibilities in the program of realism. Although profoundly influenced by Ibsen at the outset, Shaw quickly fashioned from the resources of realism a dramatic form that gave the fullest possible expression to his critical cast of mind and then continued to modify this form during a long life and career. In his early plays, among which are some of his best known, plays like *Arms and the Man* and *The Devil's Disciple*, he characteristically devised an action that superficially looked like a conventional melodrama, or military romance, or domestic comedy, and then proceeded to undermine it from within in such a way as to upend the traditional assumptions on which the form was based and the traditional attitudes held by most of the characters contained by it. Shaw's aim was to call values into question, to challenge orthodoxies, to explode unexamined assumptions, and in this way to liberate society from obsolescence so that foundations for a new society could be laid. He was frankly didactic, with the artistic consequence that his plays are replete with witty and incisive discussions of issues of all kinds, discussions that gradually grew longer as Shaw grew older until he coined the phrase "the discussion play." But he was always, at bottom, a comic artist, one who saw the limitations of even his most intelligent, most Shavian characters, and the inevitable comedy of the human mind applying itself to the intractable energy of life.

In the work of Shaw, Chekhov, and Ibsen, at any rate, the principal directions of realism were marked out and its principal structural formulae were set forth. Subsequent playwrights in this tradition were to combine, modify, and neglect these precedents in more ways than can be quickly summarized, but they were never—and still are not—entirely free of them. With the work of these pioneers the basic tradition of modern drama was established.

Yet even during the early, most zealous years of the realistic movement, the forces of reaction were already at work. From the beginning certain men of letters and men of the theatre had challenged the realist program, and they struck at the very heart of its theory by arguing that the outer world of facts and things, the backgrounds so laboriously re-created, the environments so methodically analyzed, count for nothing. Reality, in their view, was not to be found by studying the material world, but by knowing the inner world, how we feel about the facts, the things and the backgrounds. Mordecai Gorelik has summarized their rebellion in a striking paragraph:

> Do not bring on the stage your carcass of reality. . . . Do not exhibit your vanloads of bricabrac, your butcher shops with real meat, your restaurant walls of cement and tile, your streets paved with real cobblestones. These collections of materials do not tell us the nature of the world; rather they confess your inability to define the nature of the world. If you really wish to give us an illusion of life, you must seize upon the essence of life. Forget the body; give us the soul.[2]

This passage crystallizes the cry of a diverse group of dissenters that from the turn of the century to the present can usefully be gathered under the heading of "theatricalists." The theatricalist movement can be conveniently traced to the production at Paul Fort's Théâtre de l'Art in Paris in 1896 of Alfred Jarry's grotesque play *Ubu-roi*.

Theatricalism in all its historical manifestations, including, among others, Surrealism, Expressionism, and Absurdist Theatre, insists on a radically different use of the theatre from that of realism and derives from a vastly different set of assumptions. Its anti-illusionistic bias is tied firmly to the belief that the realists have betrayed the essence of theatre by using it to create illusions. By banishing or attempting to banish stage conventions, those shared understandings between performers and spectators by which both accept that a play is a highly artificial and special kind of image of life, the realists have tried to make the theatre like life. But the theatre is not and should not be like life, the theatricalists insist; it has its own highly specialized and extravagantly colorful and dynamic resources, which an exaggerated attention to the creation of realistic surfaces nullifies.

Much of the initial impulse and fundamental theory for the theatricalists derived from the Symbolist movement in letters at the end of the nineteenth century. Very simply stated, the aim of the Symbolists was to produce in their work analogues to states of being, in poetry, for example, to create verbal analogues to highly complex states of mind and spirit, to use language as sound is used in music to represent a way of feeling about the world. In the theatre a key figure in this movement was Richard Wagner (1813-83). Wagner's ambition was to synthesize the arts of poetry, drama, and music in his operas so that the result—the total imagery of music, words, and action—could move an audience to states of feeling and awareness inaccessible by mere reason. The total imagery of Wagner's theatre, unified, as it was, by musical principles, was to communicate as only art in its highest reaches can. Translated into theatrical terms, this led to Jean Cocteau's famous distinction between poetry *of* the theatre, that poetry that results from an imaginative use of theatrical resources, and poetry *in* the theatre, mere verse in the theatre.

It was probably inevitable that the leaders of this movement would be, particularly in the early years, scene designers and directors. Building on its premise that the imagery of the theatre should make for a peculiar unity, a special language of expression, men like Gordon Craig, Georg Fuchs, and Adolph Appia produced a revolution in scene design, stage lighting, and theatre esthetics. Different phases and aspects of the movement go by different names—"the New Stagecraft," "Presentational Staging," "Surrealism," "Expressionism," etc.—but essentially all were governed by the purpose of using theatrical imagery to represent inward conditions. With the theory, moreover, came a new group of theatres: Paul Fort's Théâtre de l'Art was established in 1891, the Munich Artists' Theatre in 1908, and Jacque Copeau's Théâtre du Vieux Colombier in 1913. Russia, where very important work in the realistic mode was being done at the Moscow Art Theatre, saw the most extreme theatricalist experimentation in the work of defectors from that theatre.

But developments in theatrical technique alone do not provide a sufficient background for understanding theatricalism any more than they do for understanding realism. The leaders in both movements were deeply interested in the theatre, it is true, but they were also interested in the world and in themselves and in what was happening to the world and themselves. Both theatricalism and realism represent important responses or reactions to the world of the nineteenth century with which the leaders of these respective movements quite consciously saw themselves to be breaking, and both identify shifts in thought and feeling that constitute the basis for modernism. With the work of Ibsen, Chekhov, Shaw, August Strindberg, and Jarry a new outlook was emerging, a new conception of man, a new idea of his powers and limitations, a new image of his world and of his relations to it.

Basic to this outlook was the profound sense that the past was discontinuous with the present, that an unbridgeable abyss separated modern man from his forbears. Although many of the developments in science and thought that are summoned to account for this abyss had emerged in the nineteenth century, the character and quality of life in that century seems not to have been deeply affected by them. Despite and, indeed, in part because of men like Darwin and Marx, a sovereign optimism was firmly imbedded in much nineteenth-century activity—public, private, and artistic. The Victorians, for example, grandly committed to their high mission in life, still felt that human character was a thing human beings could do something about and that it was the highest of human responsibilities to cultivate it. But as the evidence began to come in to suggest that the millenium was not going to appear as quickly as some had thought it would, as new ideas began to have implications for human beings that no one had foreseen, as institutions of all kinds began to teeter under the pressure of these ideas, as industrialization and urbanization began to produce a variety of inner and outer horrors that no one had predicted, and as society scrambled away from the world it had known and in directions that it realized it knew less and less about, a new insecurity was born. Conditioned in the twentieth century by two world wars, a great depression, a general intensification of the malaise that has followed from the increasingly dehumanized mechanization of society, this insecurity has compounded until at its worst men have come to feel estranged from all but material values, to feel themselves involved in and even committed to a world they do not understand or want.

Joseph Wood Krutch has argued in *"Modernism" in the Modern Theatre* that the essential effect of all these developments was that man's fate was taken out of his hands. Darwin not only deprived man of his divine birthright; he also posited a view of development and change that made adaptation and not moral will the chief determinant in life. Marx insisted that not only man and other organisms were subject to laws that had nothing to do with man's highest ideals for himself, but institutions and societies as well were so governed—societies by a law of class warfare that was working itself out whatever men as individuals might wish. Add to this the accumulating findings of the new disciplines of anthropology and sociology, findings that made perfectly clear that men in other places had built societies in quite different ways from ours, and it becomes clear why man became such a diminished creature. Truth had become a relative thing, not an absolute and unchanging reality; at best it was a statement that satisfied an individual or a group at a certain time and in a certain place. Man had become a baffled creature, as Matthew Arnold puts it, "Wandering between two worlds, one dead,/ The other powerless to be born."

Of the many convulsions in thought and feeling that led to what is called modernism, however, probably none has had more profound effects on the world of letters and the theatre than the new psychology. Traditionally man had been viewed as a fallen but essentially rational creature; each man was presumed to have a distinctive moral character propelled by a moral will that was an expression of that character. But under the onslaughts of the new psychology man gradually became less and less a rational creature and more and more an irrational one, a creature determined by heredity and environment, a bundle of drives, instincts, and non-rational predispositions. One of the consequences of this change was that much that tradition had claimed as evidence of man's greatness and dignity became evidence of personal adjustments or maladjustments. Honor, heroism, cowardice, self-sacrifice, sin, and even love began to be reinterpreted as the peculiar products of particular environments. Perhaps most devastating of all, the traditional concept of character, that belief according to which we all have a reasonably integrated, unique identity with a history and continuity of its own, began to dissolve as the idea grew that man, any man, is substantially an anthology of roles to be played. Beset by an erosive sense of relativity in all things, twentieth-century man capitulated to the sense of estrangement, isolation, fragmentation, and incoherence so readily discovered in contemporary experience.

It is not surprising that playwrights primarily interested in this malaise of spirit should be drawn to theatricalist forms and should be in the fore of theatricalist experimentation. Most of the celebrated "isms" of the twentieth century trace to attempts to discover and represent the quality and character of modern experience and only secondarily to an attempt to comment on it; they break into discrete submovements largely because each emphasizes different clusters of qualities and favors different aspects of that experience. Dadaism sought to surprise and disturb by means of ostensibly anarchic combinations of elements, in sculpture, for example, to shock the observer by means of its fur-lined coffeecups and disengaged toiletseats into a kind of defiant integrity of response. More important historically, Surrealism sought to represent the processes of thought and feeling as they are actually experienced in the chaos that is the inner life of modern man—disjointed, grotesque, vaguely nightmarish, and sometimes extremely comic. Both movements were curiously infertile in the theatre in that they produced few plays of any consequence, but very important in that they vitalized the theatricalist tradition by marking out more daring, more sensational possibilities than had yet been tried. Expressionism, on the other hand, both influenced theatre practice and produced a considerable number of important plays. Originally a term intended as the opposite of Impressionism, it emphasized states of feeling and, as a movement in the theatre, took shape in the hands of German writers after the debacle of World War I. Feeling betrayed by civilized ideals—by the social and political rules and customs that suddenly had become obsolete for them, these writers argued that the only reality worth talking about, worth worrying about, worth beginning with in any attempt to build a world was the reality of how they felt; and all they knew for sure was their own terror, disgust, and bewilderment. They developed a mode of dramatic composition and production, accordingly, that communicated as full a sense as possible of their sense of outrage, a cry and a shriek almost always qualified by leftist political implications, and by way of the work of playwrights like Georg Kaiser and Ernest Toller and of directors like Erwin Piscator they soon made their influence felt throughout the world of western theatre.

Actually, much of this work and many of the "isms" that were lovingly articulated and passionately defended had been strangely and brilliantly anticipated by AUGUST STRINDBERG (1849-1912). Strindberg wrote his first plays in the realist mode, and in *The Father* and *Miss Julie* achieved powerful studies of anguish. But the method of dramatic realism was never entirely adequate to his interest in the eternal ambiguity of character and human relationships or to his predilection to render a nigh hallucinatory sense of the world. With *The Dance of Death* and *To Damascus*, accordingly, he developed new dramatic forms, partly symbolic, partly allegorical, partly fantastic—forms that allowed him to represent fragments of character in different incarnations of the same character, to move freely through space and time, to crystalize in dramatic terms the insubstantiality, irrationality, and torment of experience. In these plays and plays like *A Dream Play* and *The Spook Sonata* he anticipated much that was to become basic to surrealist and expressionist theory and practice. Out of the anguish of his personal life, in fact, he succeeded in clarifying possibilities for theatricalism that very few of his followers have been able to realize as fully as he had.

LUIGI PIRANDELLO (1867-1936) was, strictly speaking, neither a realist nor a theatricalist: he wrote plays in both traditions and he excelled in both; yet perhaps more than any modern playwright he relentlessly searched the personal problem of instability and lostness. Already successful as a short-story writer, Pirandello achieved his first mature representation of this crisis in modern sensibility in *Liolà* and *It is So (If You Think It Is)*, straightforward realistic plays. Thereafter, though he continued to work in the realistic idiom, he turned more and more frequently to theatricalist methods as he became more deeply involved in questions of being, appearance, and reality. Many have felt that his sense of the world is most fully and effectively rendered in the theatricalist works that use the theatre as a central metaphor, works like *Six Characters in Search of an Author*, *Tonight We Improvise*, and *Each in His Own Way*. Some have argued that his *Henry IV* is not only his best play, but one of the most important plays of the century. But whatever the dramatic method, Pirandello's plays are important for their representation of the chimeric quality that penetrates the experience of twentieth-century man as his world has become less and less a place with firm reference points and more and more a hall of mirrors. His triumphant combination of the horror, the grotesqueness, the irony, and the hilarity of this condition laid the foundation for much of the work to follow him.

In America, which had not lagged far behind Europe in theatrical developments but where theatre was largely derivative through the first two decades of the twentieth century, the first playwright to respond to the invitations of realism and theatricalism with work of an important order was EUGENE O'NEILL (1888-1953). O'Neill's career as a playwright is a saga of experimentation in dramatic modes. After a beginning that featured realistic forms, he turned to Expressionism in *Emperor Jones* and *The Hairy Ape* and then to a number of personalized theatricalist forms. But he never abandoned realism entirely: he returned to it in mid-career in plays like *Desire Under the Elms* and then again in such late plays as *Long Day's Journey Into Night* and *A Touch of the Poet*. O'Neill's work as a playwright represents an intensely personal search for coherence in what was always for him the chaos of twentieth-century experience. Profoundly influenced by psychoanalytic thought, he typically probed the inner life of his characters, seeking at levels of only partial consciousness and in the mysterious bonds and tensions of family life a structure or frame of reference lacking in the public world. With his decisive emergence and that of the group of directors, scene designers, actors, and playwrights who were his contemporaries in the early 1920's, American drama was at last put on a firm footing, and depths of dramatic energy and imagination were actuated that quickly led to an important dramatic literature.

Since 1920 the American theatre has been an important part of the western tradition, always acutely sensitive to developments elsewhere, sometimes in the fore of experimentation and accomplishment. Here, as elsewhere, the streams of realism and theatricalism have continued to flourish, yielding from time to time such exciting subspecies as Bertold Brecht's Epic Theatre, the Social Theatre of the 1930's, and, recently, the Theatre of the Absurd. But the basic premises of these traditions have not changed; the so-called new departures in theatrical and dramatic idiom are really only variations, if occasionally important and exciting ones, on the methods for using theatrical imagery worked out by the pioneers of realism and theatricalism.

Reading modern plays, accordingly, requires above all a readiness to adjust the imagination to a variety of ways of assembling, combining, and animating theatrical resources, a readiness to convert the words of the text into the particular realist or theatricalist unity intended. Clearly the more one can bring to this act of creative imagination of an understanding of the assumptions and backgrounds of the several dramatic idioms to be encountered, the closer one will approach to the expressive totality that each of these plays is. Unfortunately, the problems both of comprehension and judgment for the reader of modern plays are complicated by the fact that most traditional critical categories and terminology are of very little help. Before 1850 much of the dramatic writing of consequence could be usefully referred to the categories of tragedy or comedy; but since, and particularly in the twentieth century, the words have little utility. Whatever one might say in favor of the possibility of tragic expression in our era, it is entirely clear that much of our serious dramatic writing cannot be called tragedy, if the term is to have a reasonably precise meaning. In our century serious drama has splintered into a spectrum of forms, some vastly different from others in method as well as effect, but all sharing in common the purpose to confront the gravest, most distressing problems of our time. The reader of modern plays must take these new directions into account for what they are. And the problem is no less complex for comedy. Although a great deal has been written that is loosely called comedy, the term as it applies to works of the past can scarcely comprehend the multiplicity of forms and effects designated by it in our time. All modern drama, it might be argued, is most fairly approached with an openness of outlook that allows the individual work to define its own character and quality.

The Texts of the Plays

HENRIK IBSEN

The Wild Duck†

Play in Five Acts

Characters

HAAKON WERLE, *businessman, industrialist, etc.*
GREGERS WERLE, *his son*
OLD EKDAL
HJALMAR EKDAL, *his son, a photographer*
GINA EKDAL, *Hjalmar's wife*
HEDVIG, *their fourteen-year-old daughter*
MRS. SÖRBY, *housekeeper to Haakon Werle*
RELLING, *a doctor*
MOLVIK, *a one-time theological student*
PETTERSEN, *Haakon Werle's servant*
GRAABERG, *the book-keeper*
JENSEN, *a hired waiter*
A fat gentleman
A balding gentleman
A short-sighted gentleman
Six other gentlemen, Haakon Werle's guests
Several hired servants

The first act is at the home of Haakon Werle, and the four following acts at Hjalmar Ekdal's

Act One

At HAAKON WERLE's *house. The study, expensively and comfortably appointed, with bookcases and upholstered furniture; in the middle of the room a desk with papers and documents; the room is softly lit by green-shaded lamps. Folding doors at the back of the room are standing open, and the curtains are drawn back. The sitting-room, spacious and elegant, can be seen within, brilliantly lit by lamps and candelabra. In the study, right front, a baize-covered door*

† From *The Oxford Ibsen*, Volume VI, re-translated by James Walter McFarlane. © Oxford University Press 1960. Reprinted by permission.

leads to the offices. Left front, a fireplace with a glowing coal fire; and further back, a double door into the dining-room.

PETTERSEN, WERLE'S *servant, in livery, and* JENSEN, *the hired waiter in black, are putting the study in order. In the sitting-room, two or three other hired servants are busy arranging the room and lighting candles. A buzz of conversation can be heard from the dining-room, and the laughter of many voices; somebody taps a knife on a glass; silence follows and a toast is proposed; cheers, and again the buzz of conversation.*

PETTERSEN [*lights a lamp on the mantelpiece and puts on the shade*]. Aye, just listen to them, Jensen. There's the old man at it now, off on a long toast to Mrs. Sörby.

JENSEN [*moving an armchair forward*]. Is it right what people say— that there's something between them?

PETTERSEN. God knows.

JENSEN. 'Cos he's been a bit of a lad in his day, hasn't he?

PETTERSEN. Maybe.

JENSEN. They say he's giving this dinner for his son.

PETTERSEN. Yes. His son came home yesterday.

JENSEN. I never knew old Werle had a son.

PETTERSEN. Oh, he's got a son, all right. But you could never get him to leave the works up at Höidal. In all the years I've worked in this house, he's never once been to town.

A HIRED WAITER [*at the door into the sitting-room*]. Here, Pettersen, there's an old fellow here who . . .

PETTERSEN [*muttering*]. Oh damn. Who wants to come here at *this* time!

[OLD EKDAL *appears in the sitting-room from the right. He is wearing a shabby greatcoat with a high collar, and woollen mittens. He is carrying in his hand a stick and a fur cap, and under his arm a brown-paper parcel. He is wearing a dirty auburn wig and has a little grey moustache.*]

PETTERSEN [*goes towards him*]. Good Lord! What are *you* doing in here?

EKDAL [*in the doorway*]. I just *have* to get into the office, Pettersen.

PETTERSEN. The office shut an hour ago, and . . .

EKDAL. That's what they told me round at the gates, old man. But Graaberg's still in there. Be a good sort, Pettersen, and let me in *this* way. [*He points to the baize door.*] I've been this way before.

PETTERSEN. All right, then, you might as well. [*Opens the door.*] But mind you don't forget to go the proper way out. We've got company.

EKDAL. I can see that . . . hm! Thanks Pettersen, old man. Good old friend. Thanks! [*Mutters to himself.*] Silly old fool! [*He goes into the office;* PETTERSEN *shuts the door after him.*]

JENSEN. Does *he* work in the office as well.

PETTERSEN. No, they just farm some of the copying out to him at rush times. Not but what he hasn't been somebody in his time, Old Ekdal.

JENSEN. Yes, he seemed to have something about him.

PETTERSEN. You're right there. What would you say if I told you that he'd been a lieutenant!

JENSEN. Get away—him a lieutenant!

PETTERSEN. So help me, he was. But then he switched over to the timber business or whatever it was. Supposed to have done the dirty on Old Werle once, or so they say. They were both in on the Höidal works together, you see. Oh, I know Old Ekdal well enough, I do! Many's the time we have had a nip and a bottle of beer together down at Ma Eriksen's.

JENSEN. I don't suppose he's got much money to throw about, has he?

PETTERSEN. Good Lord, man, it's me that does the paying, believe you me. I think people ought to show a bit of respect to those who have known better days.

JENSEN. Did he go bankrupt, then?

PETTERSEN. No, it was worse than that. He was given hard labour.

JENSEN. Hard labour?

PETTERSEN. Or imprisonment, anyway—[*Listens.*] Hush! They are leaving the table now.

> [*A couple of servants open the dining-room doors from within.* MRS. SÖRBY *comes out, in conversation with two gentlemen, followed gradually by all the other guests and* HAAKON WERLE. HJALMAR EKDAL *and* GREGERS WERLE *come last.*]

MRS. SÖRBY [*to the servant, in passing*]. Pettersen, will you have coffee served in the music room, please.

PETTERSEN. Very good, Mrs. Sörby.

> [*She and the two gentlemen go into the sitting-room and out of it to the right.* PETTERSEN *and* JENSEN *go out the same way.*]

A FAT GUEST [*to a* BALDING GUEST]. Whew! What a dinner! Took a bit of getting through!

THE BALDING GUEST. Oh, if you put your mind to it, it's incredible what you can manage in three hours.

THE FAT GUEST. Yes, but afterwards, my dear sir, afterwards!

A THIRD GUEST. I hear they are serving coffee and liqueurs in the music room.

THE FAT GUEST. Splendid! And perhaps Mrs. Sörby will play something for us.

THE BALDING GUEST [*in a low voice*]. As long as she doesn't try playing anything *on* us.

THE FAT GUEST. Oh, I hardly think so. Bertha isn't the sort to go back on her old friends. [*They laugh and go into the sitting-room.*]

WERLE [*in a low, irritable voice*]. I don't think anybody noticed, Gregers.

GREGERS [*looks at him*]. Noticed what?

WERLE. Didn't you notice either?

GREGERS. What was there for me to notice?

WERLE. There were thirteen of us at table.

GREGERS. Really? Were there thirteen?

WERLE [*with a glance towards* HJALMAR EKDAL]. There are twelve of us as a rule.[*To the rest.*] Come along in here gentlemen. [*He and the rest of the guests, except* HJALMAR *and* GREGERS, *go out at the back to the right.*]

HJALMAR [*who has heard what was said*]. You shouldn't have sent me that invitation, Gregers.

GREGERS. What! They say the party's for me. Am I not allowed to invite my best and only friend. . . .

HJALMAR. But I don't think your father is very pleased. I never come near the house any other time.

GREGERS. So I hear. But I had to see you and have a talk, because I dare say I'll be leaving again soon.—Yes, here we are, two old school friends, and drifted far, far apart, haven't we? We can't have seen each other now for sixteen or seventeen years.

HJALMAR. Is it as long as all that?

GREGERS. It is indeed. Well now, how are you getting along? You are looking well. You've put on a bit of weight, I might almost call you stout.

HJALMAR. Well, I don't know that I would call it stout exactly; but I dare say I look a bit more of a man now than I did then.

GREGERS. Yes, you do. Outwardly you don't seem to have suffered much harm.

HJALMAR [*in a rather gloomy voice*]. Ah, but inwardly, Gregers. It's different there, I can tell you. Of course, you know about the terrible things that have happened to me and my family since we last saw each other.

GREGERS [*softer*]. How are things now with your father?

HJALMAR. My dear fellow, don't let's talk about *that*. My poor unfortunate father is of course living in with me. He has nobody else in the whole world to turn to. But it's so desperately hard for me to talk about all this, you know.—Tell me instead how you have been getting on up at the works.

GREGERS. Delightfully lonely, that's how I've been. Plenty of opportunity to think about all sorts of things. Come over here; let's make ourselves comfortable. [*He sits down in an armchair by the fire and draws* HJALMAR *down into another beside him.*]

HJALMAR [*with feeling*]. Thank you all the same, Gregers, for asking me to your father's dinner-party. For now I can see that you don't hold anything against me any more.

GREGERS [*in surprise*]. What made you think I had anything against you?

HJALMAR. You did have the first few years.

GREGERS. What first few years?

HJALMAR. After the big crash came. And it was only natural you should. It was only by a hair's breadth that your own father missed being dragged into all that . . . that dreadful affair.

GREGERS. And you think I should have held that against you? Whoever gave you that idea?

HJALMAR. I know you *did*, Gregers. Your father told me himself.

GREGERS [*amazed*]. My father! Indeed. Hm! Was that the reason I never heard from you . . . not a single word?

HJALMAR. Yes.

GREGERS. Not even when you went and became a photographer?

HJALMAR. Your father said there was no point in writing to you about anything.

GREGERS [*absently*]. Well, well . . . perhaps he was right. But now Hjalmar, tell me . . . are you reasonably satisfied with things as they are now?

HJALMAR [*with a gentle sigh*]. Oh yes, I think so, pretty well. Can't really complain. As you might expect, it was a bit strange for me, in a way, to begin with. The circumstances I found myself in were so completely changed, of course; but then everything else was completely changed as well. The terrible calamity to Father . . . the shame and the disgrace, Gregers. . . .

GREGERS [*feelingly*]. Yes, indeed, indeed.

HJALMAR. I couldn't possibly think of continuing my studies; there wasn't a penny left, if anything just the opposite, in fact. There were debts. Mostly to your father, I think.

GREGERS. Hm!

HJALMAR. Well, I thought it best to make a clean break, you know . . . leave all of the old life and its ways behind. Your father in particular advised me to do that. And since he had put himself out to be so helpful to me . . .

GREGERS. My father?

HJALMAR. Yes, surely you know that? Where could I have found the money to learn photography and set up a studio and establish myself? That sort of thing costs money, I can tell you.

GREGERS. And my father paid for all that?

HJALMAR. Yes, Gregers, didn't you know? I understood from him he had written and told you.

GREGERS. Not a word that it was *him*. He must have forgotten. We have never exchanged anything but business letters. So it was my father, was it!

HJALMAR. Yes, it was him all right. He never wanted anybody to know. But it *was* him. And it was him, too, who made it possible for me to get married. But maybe you didn't know anything about that either?

GREGERS. No, I certainly didn't. [*Clapping him on the arm.*] But my dear Hjalmar, I can't tell you how delighted I am to hear all this . . . yet a bit worried as well. Perhaps I *have* been rather unjust to my father about certain things. For this does reveal a certain kindness of heart, doesn't it? Almost in a way as though he had a conscience. . . .

HJALMAR. Conscience!

GREGERS. Well, well, whatever you care to call it then. No, I can't tell you how glad I am to hear this about my father.—So you are married, then, Hjalmar! That's more than I'm ever likely to be. Well then, I hope you find married life suits you?

HJALMAR. Yes, I do. She's as good and capable a wife as ever a man could wish for. Nor is she altogether without education.

GREGERS [*a little surprised*]. No, I don't suppose she is.

HJALMAR. Life is a great teacher, you see. Contact with me every day . . . and then we have pretty regular visits from one or two most intelligent people. You wouldn't know Gina again, I assure you.

GREGERS. Gina?

HJALMAR. Yes, my dear Gregers, don't you remember she was called Gina?

GREGERS. Who was called Gina? I haven't the slightest idea what . . .

HJALMAR. But don't you remember her being in service in this house for a time.

GREGERS [*looks at him*]. Is it Gina Hansen?

HJALMAR. Yes, of course it's Gina Hansen.

GREGERS. . . . who kept house for us in the last year of Mother's illness?

HJALMAR. That's right. But my dear friend, I know for certain your father wrote and told you I had got married.

GREGERS [*who has risen*]. Yes, he did actually; but he didn't say . . . [*Walks up and down.*] But wait a minute . . . perhaps after all he did . . . now that I think about it. But my father always writes me such short letters. [*Sits on the arm of the chair.*] Listen, Hjalmar, tell me—this is really rather amusing—how did you happen to meet Gina . . . meet your wife?

HJALMAR. Oh, it was quite straightforward. Gina didn't stay very long here in the house. There was a lot of upset here at the time, what with your mother's illness. . . . Gina couldn't put up with it all, so she gave notice and left. That was the year before your mother died . . . or it might have been the same year.

GREGERS. It was the same year. I was up at the works at the time. But what about afterwards?

HJALMAR. Well, Gina went to live at home with her mother, a Mrs. Hansen, a very capable and hard-working woman who ran a little café. She also had a room to let, as well, a really nice, comfortable room.

GREGERS. And you, I take it, were lucky enough to land it?

HJALMAR. Yes. Actually it was your father who put me on to it. And it was *there*, you see, that I really got to know Gina.

GREGERS. So you got engaged?

HJALMAR. Yes. You know how it is with young people, they very soon get attached to each other. Hm. . . .

GREGERS [*rises and walks about*]. Tell me . . . when you got engaged . . . was it then that my father got you to . . . I mean, was it then that you began to take up photography?

HJALMAR. That's right. Because I was very keen on settling down to something, and the quicker the better. And both your father and I felt that this idea of photography was the best. And Gina thought the same. Besides, there was another reason as well, you see; it just so happened that Gina had taken up retouching.

GREGERS. That fitted in extraordinarily well.

HJALMAR. [*pleased, rises*]. Yes, didn't it Gregers! It *did* fit in extraordinarily well, don't you think?

GREGERS. Yes it did, I must say. My father seems almost to have acted the part of Providence for you.

HJALMAR [*moved*]. He did not forsake his old friend's son in the hour of need. For he *is* good-hearted, you see.

MRS. SÖRBY [*enters, arm in arm with* HAAKON WERLE]. Now, my dear Mr. Werle, please don't argue. You mustn't stay in there any longer staring at all those lights. It's not good for you.

WERLE [*letting go her arm and running his hand over his eyes*]. I rather believe you are right.

[PETTERSEN *and* JENSEN, *the hired waiter, enter with trays.*]

MRS. SÖRBY [*to the guests in the other room*]. Punch is served, gentlemen; if anybody wants any, he'll have to come in here and get it.

THE FAT GUEST [*walks over to* MRS. SÖRBY]. But, I say, is it true you have abolished our precious freedom to smoke?

MRS. SÖRBY. Yes, my dear sir. Here, in Mr. Werle's private domain, it is forbidden.

THE BALDING GUEST. And when did you introduce this harsh clause into our smoking regulations, Mrs. Sörby?

MRS. SÖRBY. After the previous dinner-party, my dear sir. For there were certain people who over-stepped the mark.

THE BALDING GUEST. And is one not allowed to overstep the mark just the tiniest bit, Bertha? Seriously?

MRS. SÖRBY. Not in any circumstances, Mr. Balle.

[*Most of the guests are now assembled in* WERLE'S *room; the servants hand round punch.*]

WERLE [*to* HJALMAR, *who is standing over at table*]. What are *you* standing there looking at, Ekdal?

HJALMAR. It's just an album, Mr. Werle.

THE BALDING GUEST [*strolling about*]. Ah! Photographs! That's obviously something for you.

THE FAT GUEST [*in an armchair*]. Haven't you brought along any of your own?

HJALMAR. No, I haven't.

THE FAT GUEST. You should have done. It's good for the digestion to sit and look at pictures.

THE BALDING GUEST. And it always adds something to the general entertainment, don't you know!

A SHORT-SIGHTED GUEST. All contributions gratefully received.

MRS. SÖRBY. What they mean is that, if you are invited out, you are expected to work for your supper, Mr. Ekdal.

THE FAT GUEST. And *that*, where the food is good, is just sheer pleasure, of course!

THE BALDING GUEST. Good Lord, if it's a matter of keeping body and soul together, I must say . . .

MRS. SÖRBY. You are right there!

[*They continue laughing and joking.*]

GREGERS [*quietly*]. You must join in, Hjalmar.

HJALMAR [*with a shrug*]. What do you expect me to say?

THE FAT GUEST. Don't you think, Mr. Werle, that Tokay can be regarded as relatively kind to the stomach?

WERLE [*by the fireplace*]. I can certainly vouch for the Tokay you had today, at any rate; it was one of the very finest vintages. Of course you must have seen that yourself.

THE FAT GUEST. Yes, it had a wonderfully delicate bouquet.

HJALMAR [*uncertainly*]. Does the vintage make any difference?

THE FAT GUEST [*laughing*]. By Heavens, that's good!

WERLE [*smiling*]. There's obviously not much point in putting good wine in front of *you*.

THE BALDING GUEST. It's the same with Tokay as with photographs, Mr. Ekdal. There has to be sunlight. Or am I wrong?

HJALMAR. No, indeed. Sunlight certainly plays a part.

MRS. SÖRBY. Well then it's exactly the same with you court officials. You have got to have a place in the sun as well, as the saying goes.

THE BALDING GUEST. Come, come, that joke's a bit ancient.

THE SHORT-SIGHTED GUEST. Mrs. Sörby is showing her paces. . . .

THE FAT GUEST. . . . And at our expense. [*Threateningly.*] Bertha! Bertha!

MRS. SÖRBY. Well, but it's perfectly true that the different vintages can vary enormously. The old vintages are the best.

THE SHORT-SIGHTED GUEST. Do you reckon *me* among the old ones?

MRS. SÖRBY. Oh, far from it.

THE BALDING GUEST. Listen to her! But what about *me* then, my dear Mrs. Sörby.

THE FAT GUEST. Yes, and me! What vintages do you class us among?

MRS. SÖRBY. I count you among the sweet vintages, gentlemen.

[*She sips a glass of punch; the guests laugh and joke with her.*]

WERLE. Mrs. Sörby always finds a way out . . . when she wants to. But you are not drinking, gentlemen. Pettersen, would you mind . . . ! Gregers, I think we might take a glass together. [GREGERS *does not move.*] Won't you join us, Ekdal? I didn't get a chance of drinking to you at table.

[GRAABERG, *the book-keeper, looks through the baize door.*]

GRAABERG. Excuse me, Mr. Werle, but I can't get out.

WERLE. What, you locked in again?

GRAABERG. Yes, and Flakstad's gone off with the keys. . . .

WERLE. Well, you had better come through this way.

GRAABERG. But there's somebody else as well. . . .

WERLE. Come on, come on, both of you. Don't be shy.

[GRAABERG *and* OLD EKDAL *come out of the office.*]

WERLE [*involuntarily*]. Ah!

[*The laughter and chatter of the guests die away.* HJALMAR *starts up at the sight of his father, puts down his glass and turns towards the fireplace.*]

EKDAL [*without looking up, making a series of little bows to each side as he walks, mumbling*]. Excuse me. Came the wrong way. The gate's locked . . . gate's locked. Excuse me.

[*He and* GRAABERG *go out at the back, right.*]

WERLE [*with clenched teeth*]. Damn that Graaberg.

GREGERS [*staring open-mouthed, to* HJALMAR]. Surely that was never . . . !

THE FAT GUEST. What was that? Who was it?

GREGERS. Oh, nobody. Just the book-keeper and another man.

THE SHORT-SIGHTED GUEST [*to* HJALMAR]. Did you know the man?

HJALMAR. I don't know . . . I didn't notice. . . .

THE FAT GUEST [*rises*]. What the devil's wrong? [*He walks over to some of the others who are talking in lowered voices.*]

MRS. SÖRBY [*whispers to the servant*]. Slip him something outside, something really good.

PETTERSEN [*nodding*]. Certainly. [*Goes out.*]

GREGERS [*in a low, shocked, voice to* HJALMAR]. Then it really *was* him.

HJALMAR. Yes.

GREGERS. And yet you stood here and denied that you knew him!

HJALMAR [*in an urgent whisper*]. How could I . . . ?

GREGERS. . . . acknowledge your own father?

HJALMAR [*bitterly*]. Oh, if you were in my shoes, you . . .

[*The conversation among the guests, which has been conducted in low voices, now changes over to a forced conviviality.*]

THE BALDING GUEST [*approaching* HJALMAR *and* GREGERS *in friendly fashion*]. Ah! Standing here and reviving old student memories, eh? Don't you smoke, Mr. Ekdal? Want a light? Oh, no! That's right, we mustn't . . .

HJALMAR. No, thank you! I don't want . . .

THE FAT GUEST. Couldn't you recite us a nice piece of poetry, Mr. Ekdal? There was a time once when you used to do that so prettily.

HJALMAR. I'm afraid I can't remember any.

THE FAT GUEST. Oh, what a pity. Well, Balle, what do you think we had better do now?

[*The two guests walk across the room and out into another room.*]

HJALMAR [*gloomily*]. Gregers—I must go. When once a man has felt the crushing blows of fate, you know. . . . Say goodbye to your father for me.

GREGERS. Yes, of course. Are you going straight home?

HJALMAR. Yes. Why ?

GREGERS. Nothing . . . just that I might drop in afterwards.

HJALMAR. No, don't do that. Not at my home. My house is a sad place, Gregers . . . especially after a brilliant banquet like this. We can always meet somewhere in town.

MRS. SÖRBY [*comes across and speaks in a low voice*]. Are you leaving, Mr. Ekdal?

HJALMAR. Yes.

MRS. SÖRBY. Give my regards to Gina.

HJALMAR. Thank you.

MRS. SÖRBY. And tell her I'll look in one of these days.

HJALMAR. Thanks, I will. [*To* GREGERS.] Stay here. I want to slip out unnoticed. [*He sidles across the room, into the next room, and out to the right.*]

MRS. SÖRBY [*softly, to the servant who has returned*]. Well, did the old fellow get anything?

PETTERSEN. Yes, I slipped him a bottle of brandy.

MRS. SÖRBY. Oh, you might have found him something a bit better than that.

PETTERSEN. Not at all, Mrs. Sörby. Brandy is the best thing he knows.

THE FAT GUEST [*in the doorway, with a sheet of music in his hands*]. Do you think we might play something together, Mrs. Sörby?

MRS. SÖRBY. Yes, let's do that.

THE GUESTS. Bravo, bravo!

[*She and all the guests go through the room and out to the right.* GREGERS *remains standing by the fire.* HAAKON WERLE *is searching for something in the writing-desk and seems to want* GREGERS *to leave. As the latter does not move,* WERLE *crosses to the doorway.*]

GREGERS. Just a moment, Father.

WERLE [*stops*]. What is it?

GREGERS. I want a word with you.

WERLE. Can't it wait till we are alone?

GREGERS. No, it can't. Because we might very easily never find ourselves alone.

WERLE [*approaching him*]. What do you mean by *that?*

[*During what follows, a piano is distantly heard from the music room.*]

GREGERS. How could people here let that family go to the dogs like that?

WERLE. I presume you mean the Ekdals?

GREGERS. Yes, I mean the Ekdals. Lieutenant Ekdal was such a close friend of yours once.

WERLE. Yes, he was a bit too close, I'm afraid. And I wasn't allowed to forget it either for years afterwards. He's the one I have to thank for the fact that *my* reputation also suffered.

GREGERS [*quietly*]. Was *he* in fact the only guilty one?

WERLE. Who else do you imagine there could be?

GREGERS. Well, the two of you were both in on the big timber deal together . . . weren't you?

WERLE. But was it not Ekdal who drew up the survey map of the area, that dubious map? He was the one who felled all that illegal timber on state land. It was he who was responsible for running the whole thing up there. I had no idea what Lieutenant Ekdal was up to.

GREGERS. Lieutenant Ekdal didn't seem to have much idea himself what he was up to.

WERLE. That might well be. But the fact remains he was found guilty and I was acquitted.

GREGERS. Yes, I know well enough there was no proof.

WERLE. Acquittal is acquittal. Why do you go raking up all these old and dreadful stories that turned my hair grey before its time? Are these the things you have been brooding about all these years up there? I can tell you one thing, Gregers: here in town all these stories have been forgotten long ago, as far as they concern *me*.

GREGERS. And the poor Ekdals?

WERLE. What do you really expect me to do for these people? When Ekdal was let out, he was a broken man, past helping. Some people in this world only need to get a couple of slugs in them and they go plunging right down to the depths, and they never come up again. You can take my word for it, Gregers, I have gone just as far as I ever could, short of laying myself open to all sorts of suspicion and gossip. . . .

GREGERS. Suspicion? Yes, indeed.

WERLE. I've put Ekdal on doing some copying for the office, and I pay him far, far more for his work than it is worth. . . .

GREGERS [*without looking at him*]. Hm! I don't doubt *that*.

WERLE. You smile? Perhaps you think I'm not telling you the truth? I admit there's nothing in my books to account for it; I never enter expenses of that kind.

GREGERS [*smiles coldly*]. No, there are some expenses better not accounted for.

WERLE [*startled*]. What do you mean by *that*?

GREGERS [*summoning up his courage*]. Have you accounted for what it cost to have Hjalmar Ekdal taught photography?

WERLE. I . . . Why should that be accounted for?

GREGERS. I know now that it was you who paid for it. And now I also know it was you who saw him so nicely settled.

WERLE. Well, and you still want to say I've done nothing for the Ekdals! Those people have involved me in quite enough expense, I can tell you.

GREGERS. Have you entered any of those expenses?

WERLE. What are you asking me about *that* for?

GREGERS. Oh, there are good reasons. Listen, tell me . . . that time you were ready to take such a warm interest in your old friend's son . . . wasn't that just when he was about to get married?

WERLE. Come now . . . how the devil do you expect me, after all these years . . . ?

GREGERS. You wrote me a letter at the time—a business letter, of course, and in the postscript it said, quite briefly, that Hjalmar Ekdal had married a Miss Hansen.

WERLE. Yes, and that was quite right. That's what she was called.

GREGERS. But what you didn't say was that Miss Hansen was Gina Hansen, our housekeeper as was.

WERLE [*with a scornful, but forced laugh*]. No, because it never struck me you were particularly interested in our one-time housekeeper.

GREGERS. No more I was. But . . . [*Lowers his voice.*] . . . there were others in this house who *were* particularly interested in her.

WERLE. What do you mean by *that*? [*Flaring up.*] You are not referring to me, I hope!

GREGERS [*quietly, but firmly*]. Yes, I am referring to you.

WERLE. You have the impertinence to . . . ! How dare you . . . ! And as for this . . . the photographer, the ungrateful . . . how dare he have the nerve to make accusations of this kind!

GREGERS. Hjalmar has never said a single word about this. I don't think he has the slightest suspicion of anything of the kind.

WERLE. Where have you got it from, then? Who could have said a thing like that?

GREGERS. My poor, unhappy mother said it. And that was the last time I saw her.

WERLE. Your mother! Yes, I might have known. The two of you were always pretty thick. She was the one who set you against me from the start.

GREGERS. No, it was all the things she had to put up with, till in the end she gave way and went completely to pieces.

WERLE. Oh, she hadn't anything to put up with at all, no more than plenty of other people, anyway. But what can you do with people that are sick and overwrought? That's something *I* found out. And then along you come harbouring suspicions like this, raking up all sorts of old rumours and nasty gossip about your own father. Listen now, Gregers, I honestly think that at your age you might find something a bit more useful to do.

GREGERS. Yes, perhaps the time has come.

WERLE. Then perhaps you wouldn't take things quite so seriously as you tend to do now. What's the point in you sitting up there at the works, year in and year out, slaving away like any ordinary clerk and not taking a penny more than the standard wage. It's sheer stupidity.

GREGERS. Oh, if only I were quite sure about that.

WERLE. I think I understand you. You want to be independent, don't want to be under any obligation to me. But now is just the opportunity for you to get your independence, be your own master.

GREGERS. Really? And in what way?

WERLE. When I wrote to you saying it was essential you came to town at once . . . hm . . .

GREGERS. Yes, what is it actually you wanted me for? I have been waiting all day to hear.

WERLE. I propose offering you a partnership in the firm.

GREGERS. Me? In your firm? As a partner?

WERLE. Yes. There would be no need for us always to be on top of each other. I thought you might take over the business here in town, and I should move up to the works.

GREGERS. *You* would?

WERLE. Yes. I haven't the capacity for work I once had, you know. And I have to watch my eyes, Gregers, they have started getting a bit weak.

GREGERS. They have always been that way.

WERLE. Not as bad as they are now. And besides—circumstances might make it desirable for me to live up there—at any rate for a time.

GREGERS. I had never imagined anything like that.

WERLE. Listen now, Gregers. There are many things where we don't exactly hit it off. But all the same we are father and son. I think we should be able to reach some kind of understanding between us.

GREGERS. To outward appearances, I suppose you mean?

WERLE. Well, at least that would be something. Think it over, Gregers. Don't you think something like that could be done? Eh?

GREGERS [*looking at him coldly*]. There's something behind all this.

WERLE. What do you mean?

GREGERS. There must be something you want to use me for.

WERLE. When two people are as closely connected as we are, one always has some use for the other, surely.

GREGERS. Yes, that's what they say.

WERLE. I should like to have you at home now for a while. I'm a lonely man, Gregers; I've always felt lonely, all my life; but especially now that I'm getting on a bit in years. I need somebody near me.

GREGERS. You've got Mrs. Sörby.

WERLE. Yes, I have. And she's become pretty nearly indispensable. She's bright, she's easy-going, she livens the place up. And that I can do with pretty badly.

GREGERS. Quite. But in that case you have got what you want.

WERLE. Yes, but I'm afraid it won't last. With a woman in a situation like this, it's so easy for the world to put a false interpretation on things. Indeed, you might say it doesn't do the man very much good, either.

GREGERS. Oh, when a man gives the sort of dinner-parties you give, he can risk a fair amount.

WERLE. Yes, but what about her, Gregers? I'm afraid she won't put up with it much longer. And even if she did—even if she disregarded all the gossip and the back-biting and things like that, out of devotion to me . . . ? Wouldn't you think, then, Gregers, you with your strong sense of justice . . .

GREGERS [*interrupts him*]. Without beating about the bush, tell me one thing. Are you thinking of marrying her?

WERLE. And if I were, what then?

GREGERS. Yes. That's what I'm asking, too. What then?

WERLE. Would you be so completely dead set against it?

GREGERS. No, not at all. By no means.

WERLE. I didn't know whether, perhaps out of respect for the memory of your late mother . . .

GREGERS. I am not neurotic.

WERLE. Well, whether you are or not, you have taken a great weight off my mind. I am delighted I can count on your support in this matter.

GREGERS [*looks steadily at him*]. Now I see what you want to use me for.

WERLE. Use you for? What an expression!

GREGERS. Oh, let's not be too particular in our choice of words—not when we are alone, at any rate. [*Laughs shortly.*] So that's it! That's why I damn' well had to turn up here in town in person. A bit of family life had to be organized in the house all for Mrs. Sörby's sake. A little tableau: father and son! That's something new, that is.

WERLE. How dare you speak like that!

GREGERS. When has there ever been any family life here? Never as long as I can remember! But now, if you please, there's a sudden need for something in that line. Think of the good impression it must create when it is known how the son hurried home—on wings of devotion—to his ageing father's wedding feast. What will be left then of all the stories about the things the poor dead wife had to put up with. Not a whisper! Her own son kills them all stone dead.

WERLE. Gregers, I don't think there's any man in the world you hate as much as me.

GREGERS [*quietly*]. I have seen you at too close quarters.

WERLE. You have seen me with your mother's eyes. [*Drops his voice a little.*] But you mustn't forget that those eyes were . . . clouded, now and again.

GREGERS [*trembling*]. I understand what you are getting at. But who bears the blame for my mother's unhappy disability. It's you, and all these . . . ! The last of them was this female who was palmed off on Hjalmar Ekdal when you no longer . . . ugh!

WERLE [*shrugging his shoulders*]. Word for word, as though I were listening to your mother.

GREGERS [*without paying any attention to him*]. . . . and now there he sits, so tremendously trusting and innocent, in the midst of deceit, living under the same roof with a woman like that and not knowing that what he calls his home is built on a lie. [*Comes a step nearer.*] When I look back on everything you've done, it's as if I looked out over a battlefield strewn with shattered lives.

WERLE. I almost think the gulf between us is too wide.

GREGERS [*with a stiff bow*]. So I have observed; I shall therefore take my hat and go.

WERLE. Go? Leave the house?

GREGERS. For now at last I see an objective I can live for.

WERLE. What sort of objective is that?

GREGERS. You would only laugh if I told you.

WERLE. Laughter doesn't come so easily to a lonely man, Gregers.

GREGERS [*pointing out to the back*]. Look, Father, your guests are playing Blind Man's Buff with Mrs. Sörby. Good night and good-bye.

> [*He goes out at the back to the right. Laughter and banter are heard from the guests, who come into view in the outer room.*]

WERLE [*muttering scornfully after* GREGERS]. Huh! Poor fellow. And he says he's not neurotic!

Act Two

HJALMAR EKDAL'S *studio. The room, which is quite large, is recognizably an attic. On the right is a pitched roof with big skylights, half covered by a blue curtain. In the corner, top right, is the entrance-hall door; downstage, on the same side, a door leads into the living-room. Similarly there are two doors on the left wall, and between them an iron stove. On the rear wall are broad double sliding doors. The studio is cheaply but pleasantly furnished. Between the doors on the right, off the wall a little, stands a sofa, with a table and some chairs; on the table, a lighted lamp, shaded; in the corner by the stove, an old armchair. Various pieces of photographic apparatus and equipment are disposed about the room. On the rear wall, left of the double doors, is a bookcase containing a few books, some boxes and bottles of chemicals, various kinds of instruments, tools and other objects. Photographs and one or two little things like brushes, paper and so on are lying on the table.*

GINA EKDAL *is sitting at the table, sewing.* HEDVIG *is sitting reading a book on the sofa, shading her eyes with her hands, her thumbs in her ears.*

GINA [*after glancing several times at her, as though secretly worried*]. Hedvig!

> [HEDVIG *does not hear.*]

GINA [*louder*]. Hedvig!

HEDVIG [*takes her hands away and looks up*]. Yes, Mother?

GINA. Hedvig dear, you mustn't sit reading any longer.

HEDVIG. Oh, but Mother, can't I read a little bit more? Just a little!

GINA. No, no, you must put the book away now. Your father doesn't like it; he never reads himself in the evenings.

HEDVIG [*shuts the book*]. No, Daddy isn't such a great one for reading.

GINA [*putting her sewing down and taking a pencil and a little notebook on the table*]. Can you remember what we paid for the butter today?

HEDVIG. It was one crown sixty-five.

GINA. That's right. [*Makes a note.*] The amount of butter we go through in this house! And then there was the salami and the cheese . . . let me see. . . . [*Notes it down.*] Then there was the ham . . . hm. . . . [*Adds it up.*] Yes, that already comes to . . .

HEDVIG. And then there was the beer.

GINA. Yes, that's right. [*Notes it down.*] It soon mounts up. But there's nothing you can do about it.

HEDVIG. But then Daddy was going to be out, so there was no need to cook a dinner just for the two of us.

GINA. Yes, that was lucky. And then there was that eight crowns fifty I got for the photographs as well.

HEDVIG. Fancy! Was it as much as that?

GINA. Eight crowns fifty exactly.

> [*Silence.* GINA *takes up her sewing again.* HEDVIG *takes paper and pencil and begins to draw, shading her eyes with her left hand.*]

HEDVIG. Isn't it lovely to think of Daddy being at a big dinner-party at Mr. Werle's!

GINA. You can't really say he's at Mr. Werle's. It was the son who asked him. [*After a pause.*] We've got nothing to do with Mr. Werle.

HEDVIG. I'm so terribly looking forward to Daddy coming home. Because he promised he'd ask Mrs. Sörby for something nice for me.

GINA. Aye, there's plenty of good things going in *that* house, believe you me.

HEDVIG [*goes on drawing*]. I think I might even be a little bit hungry.

> [OLD EKDAL, *with the bundle of papers under his arm and another parcel in his coat pocket, enters by the hall door.*]

GINA. You're very late home today, Grandfather.

EKDAL. They had shut the office. Had to wait in Graaberg's room. And then I came out through . . . hm:

HEDVIG. Did they give you any more copying to do, Grandfather?

EKDAL. All this lot. Just look!

GINA. That was nice.

HEDVIG. And you've got another parcel in your pocket as well.

EKDAL. Eh? Nonsense! That isn't anything. [*Stands his walking stick in the corner.*] This will keep me busy for a long time, Gina, this will. [*Draws one of the sliding doors in the rear wall a little to one side.*] Hush! [*Peeps into the room for a moment or two and then carefully shuts the door again.*] Heh! heh! The whole lot's asleep. And *she's* gone to sleep in the basket. Heh! heh!

HEDVIG. Are you sure she'll not be cold in that basket, Grandfather?

EKDAL. Whatever gives you that idea! Cold? In all that straw? [*Walks over to the door, upper left.*] Are there any matches?

GINA. The matches are on the chest of drawers.

> [EKDAL *goes into his room.*]

HEDVIG. It was jolly good, Grandfather getting all that copying to do.

GINA. Yes, poor old soul; now he can earn himself a bit of pocket-money.

HEDVIG. And besides, he'll not be able to sit all morning down at that horrid Ma Eriksen's place.

GINA. Yes, that's another thing.

> [*Short silence.*]

HEDVIG. Do you think they'll still be having their dinner?

GINA. Lord knows. I dare say they could be.

HEDVIG. Think of all the lovely things Daddy will be getting to eat! I'm sure he'll be in a good mood when he comes home. Don't you think so, Mother?

GINA. Yes, I do. But just think, if only we could tell him we'd managed to let the room.

HEDVIG. But that's not necessary tonight.

GINA. Oh, it would come in very handy, you know. It's just standing there doing nothing.

HEDVIG. No, what I meant was we don't need it tonight because Daddy will be in a good temper anyway. It's better if we leave the business about the room for some other time.

GINA [*looks across at her*]. Do you like having something nice to tell your father when he comes home at night?

HEDVIG. Yes, because it makes things a bit more cheerful.

GINA [*thoughtfully*]. Oh yes, there's something in that.

[OLD EKDAL *comes in again and makes for the door, front left.*]

GINA [*half turning on her chair*]. Do you want something in the kitchen, Grandfather?

EKDAL. Yes, I do. Don't get up. [*Goes out.*]

GINA. I hope he isn't messing about with the fire in there! [*Waits a moment.*] Just go and see what he's up to, Hedvig.

[EKDAL *comes in again with a little jug of hot water.*]

HEDVIG. Have you been getting some hot water, Grandfather?

EKDAL. Yes, I have. I want it for something. I've got some writing to do, and the ink's gone all thick like porridge . . . heh!

GINA. But you ought to have your supper first, Grandfather. It's all set.

EKDAL. I can't be bothered with any supper, Gina. I'm terribly busy, I tell you. I don't want anybody coming into my room. Nobody at all . . . hm!

[*He goes into his room.* GINA *and* HEDVIG *look at each other.*]

GINA [*in a low voice*]. Where do you suppose he got the money from?

HEDVIG. He must have got it from Graaberg.

GINA. No, never. Graaberg always sends the money to me.

HEDVIG. Then he must have got a bottle on tick[1] somewhere.

GINA. Nobody will give him anything on tick, poor old soul.

[HJALMAR EKDAL, *wearing a topcoat and a grey felt hat, enters right.*]

GINA [*throws down her sewing and gets up*]. Why, Hjalmar! Are you back already!

HEDVIG [*at the same time jumping up*]. Fancy coming now, Daddy!

HJALMAR [*putting down his hat*]. Well, most of them were coming away.

HEDVIG. So early?

---

1. Translator's Britishism meaning "on credit."

HJALMAR. Yes, it was a dinner party, you know.

    [*About to take off his topcoat.*]

GINA. Let me help you.

HEDVIG. And me.

    [*They help him off with his coat,* GINA *hangs it up on the rear wall.*]

HEDVIG. Were there many there, Daddy?

HJALMAR. Oh no, not many. There were about twelve or fourteen of us when we sat down.

GINA. And did you manage to talk to them all?

HJALMAR. Oh yes, a little. But it was Gregers who monopolized me in the main.

GINA. Is Gregers still as awful as ever.

HJALMAR. Well, he's not particularly good-looking. Hasn't the old man come home?

HEDVIG. Yes, Grandfather's in there writing.

HJALMAR. Did he say anything?

GINA. No, what about?

HJALMAR. Didn't he say anything about . . . ? I thought I heard he'd been to see Graaberg. I'll look in on him for a minute.

GINA. No, no, it's hardly worth . . .

HJALMAR. Why not? Did he say he didn't want me to go in?

GINA. He didn't want *anybody* going in tonight. . . .

HEDVIG [*making signs*]. Sst! sst!

GINA [*does not notice*]. . . . he's been and got himself some hot water. . . .

HJALMAR. Ah! Is he sitting there . . . ?

GINA. Yes, that's just what he is doing.

HJALMAR. Ah, well . . . my poor, white-haired, old father . . . ! Yes, let him get what little pleasure he can out of life.

    [OLD EKDAL, *in a dressing-gown, his pipe lit, comes in from his room.*]

EKDAL. You back? I thought it was you I heard talking.

HJALMAR. I've just this minute come.

EKDAL. You didn't see me, did you?

HJALMAR. No, but they said you'd gone through. And I thought I'd walk home with you.

EKDAL. Hm! Nice of you, Hjalmar! Who were all the people there?

HJALMAR. Oh, all sorts. There was Mr. Flor, he's something at Court, and Mr. Balle and Mr. Kaspersen and Mr. . . . What's-his-name. . . . I can't remember . . . all of them people in Court circles. . . .

EKDAL [*nods*]. Do you hear *that*, Gina? He's been mixing with high society.

GINA. Yes, things are pretty posh in that house now.

HEDVIG. Did any of them sing, Daddy? Or give a recitation?

HJALMAR. No, they just burbled on. They wanted to get me to recite to them, but I wasn't having any.

EKDAL. You weren't having any, eh?

GINA. You could easily have done it, if you wanted to.

HJALMAR. No. You haven't to be at everybody's beck and call. [*Walking up and down.*] I'm not, anyway.

EKDAL. No, no. You don't catch Hjalmar as easily as that.

HJALMAR. I don't see why *I* should be expected to provide the entertainment when I happen to have an evening out. Let the others put themselves out a little. That sort does nothing but go from one house to the next, eating and drinking, day in and day out. Let them jolly well do something in return for all the good food they get.

GINA. But I hope you didn't tell them that?

HJALMAR [*hums*]. Hm . . . hm . . . hm. They were told quite a number of things. . . .

EKDAL. What! All those Court people!

HJALMAR. That doesn't make them any different. [*Casually.*] After that we had a little argument about the Tokay.

EKDAL. Tokay, eh? That's a good wine, that!

HJALMAR [*pauses*]. It *can* be. But, you know, the different vintages are not always equally good; it all depends on how much sunshine the grapes have had.

GINA. Why, Hjalmar, the things you know!

EKDAL. And that's what they started arguing about?

HJALMAR. They tried it on; but then they were given to understand that it was exactly the same with Court officials. It was pointed out that not all *their* vintages were equally good either.

GINA. Really, the things you think of!

EKDAL. Heh, heh! So they had to put that in their pipes and smoke it!

HJALMAR. They got it, straight to their faces!

EKDAL. There you are, Gina. He let them have it straight to their faces, these people at Court.

GINA. Well, fancy! Straight to their faces!

HJALMAR. Yes, but I don't want it talked about. It's not the sort of thing to pass on. And it was all taken in good part, of course. They were nice, pleasant people. Why should I want to hurt them? No!

EKDAL. But straight to their faces . . .

HEDVIG [*ingratiatingly*]. What fun it is to see you in evening dress. You look so nice in evening dress, Daddy!

HJALMAR. Yes, I do, don't I! And this one is really an impeccable fit. Almost as though it had been made for me . . . a bit tight under the arms, perhaps. Help me off, Hedvig. [*Takes the coat off.*] I'll put my jacket on instead. Where have you put my jacket, Gina?

GINA. Here it is.

[*Brings the jacket and helps him on with it.*]

HJALMAR. There we are! Don't forget to let Molvik have the coat back first thing tomorrow morning.

GINA [*puts it aside*]. We'll see to that all right.

HJALMAR [*stretching himself*]. Ah, that feels a bit more like home. And I think it's rather more my line to wear a few casual things like this about the house. Don't you think so, Hedvig?

HEDVIG. Yes, Daddy, I do!

HJALMAR. And if I pull out my tie like this so that the ends can flap about. . . . Look! Eh?

HEDVIG. Yes, it goes well with your moustache and your curly hair.

HJALMAR. I wouldn't exactly call it curly; more wavy, you might say.

HEDVIG. Yes, because it has such soft curls.

HJALMAR. Waves, actually.

HEDVIG [*after a pause, tugs at his coat*]. Daddy!

HJALMAR. Well, what is it?

HEDVIG. Oh, you know as well as I do.

HJALMAR. No, honestly I don't.

HEDVIG [*laughing and crying*]. Oh yes you do, Daddy. You mustn't tease me any longer.

HJALMAR. But what is it?

HEDVIG [*shaking him*]. Oh, stop it now and come on, Daddy. You remember all those nice things you promised me.

HJALMAR. Oh, there now! Fancy me forgetting!

HEDVIG. Now you are just making fun of me, Daddy. Oh, it's horrid of you! Where have you put them?

HJALMAR. But just a minute! I've got something else for you, Hedvig.

[*Walks across and feels in the pockets of the coat.*]

HEDVIG [*jumping and clapping her hands*]. Oh, Mother, Mother!

GINA. Look, you see! Just give him time. . . .

HJALMAR [*with a piece of paper*]. Look, here it is.

HEDVIG. This thing? It's just a piece of paper.

HJALMAR. That's the menu, Hedvig, the complete menu. There it says 'Bill of fare', that means menu.

HEDVIG. Haven't you got anything else?

HJALMAR. I forgot the rest, I tell you. But believe me—it's no great treat having to eat all those things. Go and sit over at the table now, and read what it says on the card, and afterwards I'll tell you what the different courses taste like. There you are, Hedvig.

HEDVIG [*swallows her tears*]. Thanks.

[*She sits down, but does not read;* GINA *makes a sign to her, which* HJALMAR *notices.*]

HJALMAR [*pacing up and down*]. It's incredible all the things a man is supposed to think about; he's only to forget the slightest thing, and straight away all he gets is a lot of sour looks. Well, that's another thing you get used to. [*Pauses near the stove, beside the old man.*] Have you peeped in this evening, Father?

EKDAL. Yes, you bet I have. She's gone in the basket.

HJALMAR. Has she really? In the basket! She must be getting used to it.

EKDAL. Yes, I told you she would. But now, you know, there are still a few other things. . . .

HJALMAR. One or two improvements, you mean.

EKDAL. They've *got* to be done, you know.

HJALMAR. Yes, let's have a little chat about these improvements, Father. Come on, we'll sit on the sofa.

EKDAL. Yes, fine. Hm! Think I'll just fill my pipe first. . . . Must clean it out as well. Hm!
  [*He goes into his room.*]

GINA [*smiles to* HJALMAR]. Cleaning his pipe!

HJALMAR. Well, well, Gina, just let him be . . . he's just a poor, old wreck of a man. . . . Yes, those improvements. . . . We'd best get them done tomorrow.

GINA. You'll not have any time tomorrow, Hjalmar.

HEDVIG [*breaking in*]. Yes he will, Mother!

GINA. . . . Don't forget those prints that need retouching; they've been asked for ever so many times.

HJALMAR. What! Those prints again? They'll be ready all right. Have there been any new orders?

GINA. No, worse luck. Tomorrow I've nothing but those two sittings, you know.

HJALMAR. Is that all? Oh well, if you are not ready to put yourself out, then . . .

GINA. But what more am I supposed to do? I'm putting as many adverts in the papers as we can afford, I reckon.

HJALMAR. Oh, the papers, the papers. You can see what use *that* is. And I suppose nobody's been to look at the room either?

GINA. No, not yet.

HJALMAR. Just what you might expect. If people don't show any initiative . . . well! We must pull ourselves together, Gina!

HEDVIG [*going over to him*]. Wouldn't you like me to fetch you your flute, Daddy?

HJALMAR. No, no flute, thank you. *I* don't need any of life's little pleasures! [*Paces about.*] Oh yes, I'll be working tomorrow all right, don't you fret. Working till I'm fit to drop. . . .

GINA. But, my dear Hjalmar, I didn't mean it that way.

HEDVIG. Daddy, what about bringing you a bottle of beer?

HJALMAR. No, certainly not. There's no need to bring out anything for me. . . . [*Pauses.*] Beer? Was it beer you said?

HEDVIG [*gaily*]. Yes, Daddy. Nice cool beer.

HJALMAR. Well . . . if you really want to, you might bring a bottle.

GINA. Yes, go on. It'll cheer things up a bit.
  [HEDVIG *runs over towards the kitchen door.*]

HJALMAR [*stops her by the stove, looks at her, takes her head in his hands and draws her to him*]. Hedvig! Hedvig!

HEDVIG [*smiling through her tears*]. Daddy dear!

HJALMAR. No, don't call me that. There I've been sitting indulging myself at the rich man's table . . . stuffing myself at the festive board . . . ! And I couldn't even . . .

GINA [*sitting at the table*]. Oh, don't talk so silly, Hjalmar.

HJALMAR. It's true. But you mustn't think too badly of me. You know I love you, all the same.

HEDVIG [*throws her arms around him*]. And we love you so much, too, Daddy!

HJALMAR. And even if I am a bit unreasonable now and again, well . . . heavens above! You mustn't forget I'm a man beset by a whole host of troubles. Well, now! [*Dries his eyes.*] This is not the moment for beer. Bring me my flute.

[HEDVIG *runs to the shelves and gets it.*]

HJALMAR. Thanks! There we are. With flute in hand, and both of you close to me . . . ah!

[HEDVIG *sits down at the table beside* GINA; HJALMAR *walks up and down and begins resolutely on a rendering of a Bohemian folk dance, but in a slow elegiac tempo with much 'feeling'.*]

HJALMAR [*breaks off the tune, holds out his left hand to* GINA *and says with emotion*]. What though we have to pinch and scrape in this place, Gina! It's still our home. And this I will say: it is good to be here.

[*He starts to play again; at once there is a knock at the door.*]

GINA [*gets up*]. Hush, Hjalmar! I think somebody's coming.

HJALMAR [*placing the flute back on the shelf*]. Isn't that just like it!

[GINA *walks over and opens the door.*]

GREGERS WERLE [*outside in the passage*]. Excuse me, but . . .

GINA [*shrinking back*]. Oh!

GREGERS. . . . doesn't Mr. Ekdal the photographer live here?

GINA. Yes, he does.

HJALMAR [*walks over to the door*]. Gregers! Is that you again! Come along in.

GREGERS [*comes in*]. I told you I'd be looking in, didn't I?

HJALMAR. But tonight . . . ? Have you left the party?

GREGERS. Both the party and my father's house. Good evening, Mrs. Ekdal. I'm not sure if you recognize me again?

GINA. Oh yes. It's not difficult to recognize you again, Mr. Werle.

GREGERS. No, they say I take after my mother, and I expect you remember her ail right.

HJALMAR. Did you say you've left the house?

GREGERS. Yes, I've moved to a hotel.

HJALMAR. Have you now! Well, now that you're here, you might as well take your things off and sit down.

GREGERS. Thanks.

[*Takes off his topcoat. He has changed into plain grey country tweeds.*]

HJALMAR. Here, on the sofa. Make yourself comfortable.

[GREGERS *sits down on the sofa*, HJALMAR *on a chair at the table.*]

GREGERS [*looking round*]. So this is your place, Hjalmar. This is where you live.

HJALMAR. This, as you see, is the studio. . . .

GINA. But it's a bit more roomy here, so we like being in here best.

HJALMAR. We had a nicer place before; but there's one great advantage about this flat, and that's all the extra space. . . .

GINA. And we've also got another room on the other side of the passage, and we can let that.

GREGERS [*to* HJALMAR]. Well, well . . . so you've got lodgers as well?

HJALMAR. No, not yet. It's not as easily done as all that, you know. It needs initiative. [*To* HEDVIG.] Now what about that beer!

[HEDVIG *nods and goes out to the kitchen.*]

GREGERS. So that's your daughter?

HJALMAR. Yes, that's Hedvig.

GREGERS. And she's an only child?

HJALMAR. She's the only one, yes. She's our greatest joy in life, and . . . [*Drops his voice.*] . . . she's also our deepest sorrow, Gregers.

GREGERS. What do you mean?

HJALMAR. Yes, Gregers. She is in grave danger of losing her sight.

GREGERS. Going blind!

HJALMAR. Yes. So far there's only been the first signs, and things might still be all right for quite some time yet. But the doctor has warned us. It's inevitable.

GREGERS. How terribly sad. How did she get like that?

HJALMAR [*sighs*]. Apparently, it's hereditary.

GREGERS [*with a start*]. Hereditary!

GINA. Hjalmar's mother also had poor sight.

HJALMAR. Yes, that's what Father says. I can't remember her myself.

GREGERS. The poor child. And how does she take it?

HJALMAR. Oh, can't you see we haven't the heart to tell her. She doesn't suspect anything. Happy and carefree, just like a little singing bird, there she goes fluttering into a life of eternal night. [*Overcome.*] Oh, it's quite heart-breaking for me, Gregers!

[HEDVIG *enters carrying a tray with beer and glasses which she puts on the table.*]

HJALMAR [*strokes her head*]. Thank you, Hedvig.

[HEDVIG *puts her arms round his neck and whispers in his ear.*]

HJALMAR. No, no sandwiches just now. [*Looks across.*] Unless perhaps Gregers would like some?

GREGERS [*declining*]. No, no thank you.

HJALMAR [*still sadly*]. Well, perhaps you might fetch a few, after all. If you've a crust, that would be all right. But mind you see there's plenty of butter on.

[HEDVIG *nods happily and goes out again into the kitchen.*]

GREGERS [*who has been following her with his eyes*]. She looks strong and healthy enough to me in other respects.

GINA. Yes, there's nothing much else wrong with her, thank God.

GREGERS. She's going to be like you in time, Mrs. Ekdal. How old might she be now?

GINA. Hedvig is just fourteen; it's her birthday the day after tomorrow.

GREGERS. She's a big girl for her age.

GINA. Yes, she's just shot up this last year.

GREGERS. It makes you realize your own age when you see all the young people growing up. How long is it you've been married now?

GINA. We've been married now . . . yes, close on fifteen years.

GREGERS. Fancy, is it so long?

GINA [*suddenly attentive, watching him*]. Yes, that's what it is all right.

HJALMAR. Yes, it must be all that. Fifteen years all but a few months. [*Changing the subject.*] It must have seemed a long time for *you*, Gregers, sitting up there at the works.

GREGERS. It seemed long at the time. But looking back now, I hardly know where it's all gone to.

[OLD EKDAL *comes out of his room, without his pipe, but wearing his old officer's cap; his gait is a bit unsteady.*]

EKDAL. Now then, Hjalmar, now we can sit down and talk about that . . . er . . . what was it again?

HJALMAR [*goes across to him*]. Father, there's somebody here, Gregers Werle . . . I don't know if you remember him.

EKDAL [*looks at* GREGERS, *who has risen*]. Werle? Is that the son? What does he want with me?

HJALMAR. Nothing. It's me he's come to see.

EKDAL. Ah! So there isn't anything the matter?

HJALMAR. No, nothing at all.

EKDAL [*waving his arms*]. Not that I care, you know; I'm not frightened, but . . .

GREGERS [*walks over to him*]. All I wanted was to bring greetings from your old hunting grounds, Lieutenant Ekdal.

EKDAL. Hunting grounds?

GREGERS. Yes, up there by the Höidal works.

EKDAL. Oh, there! They knew me well enough up there at one time.

GREGERS. You were a great one for shooting in those days.

EKDAL. Yes, I dare say you're right there. You are looking at my uniform. I don't have to ask anybody if I can wear it here in the house. So long as I don't go out in the street with it on . . .

[HEDVIG *brings in a plate of sandwiches which she puts on the table.*]

HJALMAR. Sit down now, Father, and have a glass of beer. Help yourself, Gregers.

[EKDAL *staggers mumbling over to the sofa.* GREGERS *sits on the chair nearest him,* HJALMAR *on the other side of* GREGERS. GINA *sits sewing a little way from the table;* HEDVIG *stands beside her father.*]

GREGERS. Can you remember, Lieutenant Ekdal, how Hjalmar and I used to come up in the summer and at Christmas to visit you?

EKDAL. Did you? No, no, no, I can't remember that. But I was a pretty crack shot, although I say it myself. I've even shot bears . . . nine of them, no less.

GREGERS [*looks sympathetically at him*]. And have you given up shooting now?

EKDAL. Oh no, I wouldn't say *that*, my dear sir. Still manage a bit of shooting now and again. Not *that* sort, of course. Because the forest, you know . . . the forest . . . the forest . . . ! [*Drinks.*] Is the forest in good shape up there now?

GREGERS. Not as fine as it was in your day. There's been a lot of felling.

EKDAL. Felling, eh? [*Lowers his voice, as if afraid.*] That's a dangerous business, that. That brings trouble. The forests avenge themselves.

HJALMAR [*fills up his glass*]. A little more, Father?

GREGERS. How is it possible for a man so fond of the outdoor life as you are to live cooped up here in town, hemmed in by these four walls?

EKDAL [*gives a short laugh and glances at* HJALMAR]. Oh, it's not bad here. Not bad at all.

GREGERS. But what about all those things that came to be so much a part of you at one time? The cool, caressing breezes, the open-air life in the forest and on the moors, among the beasts and the birds. . . .

EKDAL [*smiling*]. Hjalmar, shall we show him?

HJALMAR [*quickly, and a little embarrassed*]. Oh, no, no, Father. Not tonight.

GREGERS. What does he want to show me?

HJALMAR. Oh, it's only a sort of . . . You can see it another time.

GREGERS [*continues talking to the old man*]. Now what I had in mind, Lieutenant Ekdal, was that you ought to come back with me up to the works; I'll be returning there very soon. You could quite easily get copying to do up there as well. And there's really nothing here to keep you amused or liven things up for you.

EKDAL [*staring at him in astonishment*]. Me? Nothing here for me . . . ?

GREGERS. Oh yes, you have Hjalmar. But then he's got his own family. And a man like yourself who's always felt the call of the wild . . .

EKDAL [*strikes the table*]. Hjalmar, he *must* see it now.

HJALMAR. But, Father, is it worth it? It's dark. . . .

EKDAL. Nonsense! It's moonlight. [*Gets up.*] I tell you he *must* see it. Let me past. Come on and help me, Hjalmar!

HEDVIG. Oh yes, go on, Daddy.

HJALMAR [*gets up*]. Very well.

GREGERS [*to* GINA]. What is it?

GINA. Oh, you mustn't expect anything very special.

[EKDAL *and* HJALMAR *have gone to the back wall, and each pushes one of the sliding doors to one side;* HEDVIG *helps* OLD EKDAL; GREGERS *remains standing by the sofa;* GINA *sits unperturbed, sewing. Through the door can be seen a long irregularly shaped loft, with recesses and a couple of free-standing stove-pipes. There are skylights through which bright moonlight shines on some parts of the loft, leaving the rest in deep shadow.*]

EKDAL [*to* GREGERS]. You'd best come right over.

GREGERS [*walks over to them.*] But what *is* it, then?

EKDAL. Look and see. Hm!

HJALMAR [*rather embarrassed*]. All this belongs to Father, you understand.

GREGERS [*beside the door, looks into the loft*]. So you keep poultry, Lieutenant Ekdal!

EKDAL. I'll say we keep poultry. They've gone to roost now. But you should just see *this* poultry in daylight!

HEDVIG. And then there's . . .

EKDAL. Hush! hush! Don't say anything yet.

GREGERS. You've got pigeons as well, I see.

EKDAL. Oh yes! Sure, we have pigeons! They have their nesting boxes up under the eaves. Pigeons like best being up high, you know.

HJALMAR. They're not all ordinary pigeons, though.

EKDAL. Ordinary! No, I should just say not! We've got some tumblers, and we've also a pair of pouters. But come over here! Can you see that hutch over there by the wall?

GREGERS. Yes. What do you use that for?

EKDAL. That's where the rabbits sleep at night, my dear fellow.

GREGERS. Well! So you've got rabbits as well?

EKDAL. Yes, I should damn' well think we have got rabbits! He's asking if we've got rabbits, Hjalmar! Ha! But *now* we really do come to something! *Now* it comes! Out of the way, Hedvig! Come and stand here, that's right; now look down there. Can you see a basket with straw in?

GREGERS. Yes, I can. And I can see a bird sitting in the basket.

EKDAL. Ha! 'A bird!'

GREGERS. Isn't it a duck?

EKDAL [*hurt*]. Yes, obviously it's a duck.

HJALMAR. But what *kind* of duck do you think it is?

HEDVIG. It isn't an ordinary duck. . . .

EKDAL. Hush!

GREGERS. And it isn't one of those foreign breeds either.

EKDAL. No, Mr. . . . Werle; that's no foreign breed; that's a wild duck.

GREGERS. No, is it really? A wild duck?

EKDAL. Yes, that's just what it is. That 'bird' as you call it . . . that's a wild duck. Our wild duck, my dear sir.

HEDVIG. *My* wild duck. Because it belongs to *me*.

GREGERS. And can it really live up here in the loft? Does it get on all right here?

EKDAL. Of course she's got a trough of water to splash about in, you understand.

HJALMAR. Clean water every other day.

GINA [*turning to* HJALMAR]. Hjalmar, my dear, it's getting absolutely freezing in here now.

EKDAL. Hm, let's shut it up then. It's not good to disturb them when they're settled for the night, either. Go on, Hedvig, help!

[HJALMAR *and* HEDVIG *push the doors of the loft closed.*]

EKDAL. You can come and see her properly another time. [*Sits in the armchair by the stove.*] Oh, very remarkable birds, wild ducks are, I can tell you.

GREGERS. But how did you manage to catch it, Lieutenant Ekdal?

EKDAL. It wasn't me who caught it. There's a certain gentleman here in town whom we can thank for that.

GREGERS [*with a slight start*]. That gentleman wouldn't happen to be my father, would it?

EKDAL. You've got it! Precisely! Your father! Hm!

HJALMAR. Funny your guessing *that*, Gregers.

GREGERS. You told me before that you owed such a lot to my father, and so I thought . . .

GINA. But we didn't get the duck from Mr. Werle personally. . . .

EKDAL. It's Haakon Werle we have to thank for her just the same, Gina. [*To* GREGERS.] You see, he was out in a boat, and he let fly at her. But his sight isn't so good now, your father's isn't. Hm! So she was only winged.

GREGERS. Aha! She got a slug or two in her, did she!

HJALMAR. Yes, two or three maybe.

HEDVIG. It was in the wing, so she couldn't fly.

GREGERS. And then she dived right down to the bottom, eh!

EKDAL [*sleepily, his voice thick*]. She did that. Always do that, wild ducks do. Go plunging right to the bottom . . . as deep as they can get, my dear sir . . . hold on with their beaks to the weeds and stuff—and all the other mess you find down there. Then they never come up again.

GREGERS. But, Lieutenant Ekdal, *your* wild duck came up again.

EKDAL. He had such an absurdly clever dog, your father. . . . And that dog, he dived in and fetched the duck up again.

GREGERS [*turning to* HJALMAR]. And then you got it?

HJALMAR. Not straight away. First it was taken to your father's, but it didn't seem to thrive there; so Pettersen was told to do away with it. . . .

EKDAL [*half asleep*]. Ha! Pettersen! That old fool. . . .

HJALMAR [*in a lower voice*]. That was the way we got it, you see, with Father knowing Pettersen; when he heard all the business about the wild duck, he managed to get it turned over to him.

GREGERS. And now it's thriving perfectly well in the loft.

HJALMAR. Yes, incredibly so. It's got quite fat. Well, it's been so long there now it's forgotten what real wild life is like. And that's all that counts.

GREGERS. I'm sure you are right, Hjalmar. So long as it never catches sight of sea and sky. . . . But I mustn't stay any longer. I think your father's asleep.

HJALMAR. Oh, don't you worry about that. . . .

GREGERS. But, by the way . . . didn't you say you had a room to let . . . a vacant room?

HJALMAR. Yes, what of it? Perhaps you know somebody . . . ?

GREGERS. Can I have the room?

HJALMAR. You?

GINA. What, *you*, Mr. Werle . . . ?

GREGERS. Can I have the room? I'd move in first thing tomorrow morning.

HJALMAR. Yes, with the greatest pleasure. . . .

GINA. Oh, but Mr. Werle, that's not the sort of room for the likes of you, really.

HJALMAR. But, Gina, what are you saying?

GINA. Well, I mean, that room isn't big enough or light enough, and . . .

GREGERS. I'm not fussy about that, Mrs. Ekdal.

HJALMAR. Myself I'd have said it was rather a nice room; and not badly furnished either.

GINA. But don't forget about those two living underneath.

GREGERS. Who are they?

GINA. Oh, one of them's been a private tutor . . .

HJALMAR. That's Mr. Molvik.

GINA. . . . and then there's a doctor called Relling.

GREGERS. Relling? I know him slightly; he was in practice up in Höidal for a while.

GINA. They're a right pair of wasters, them two. As often as not they're off on a binge in the evenings, and they don't come back till late at night, and then they're not always quite . . .

GREGERS. You soon get used to things like that. I hope I shall be like the wild duck and . . .

GINA. Well, I think you'd better sleep on it first, all the same.

GREGERS. I don't think you're very keen on having me in the house, Mrs. Ekdal.

GINA. Heavens, whatever gives you that idea?

HJALMAR. Yes, really you are behaving very strangely, Gina. [*To* GREGERS.] But tell me, does this mean you are thinking of staying on in town for the time being?

GREGERS [*putting on his topcoat*]. Yes, now I'm thinking of staying.

HJALMAR. But not at your father's? What do you intend doing with yourself?

GREGERS. Ah, if only I knew *that*, my dear Hjalmar . . . it wouldn't be so bad. But when you are burdened with a name like 'Gregers' . . . !'Gregers!' And followed by 'Werle'![2] Have you ever heard anything so hideous?

HJALMAR. Oh, I don't know. . . .

GREGERS. Ugh! I feel I would want to spit at anybody with a name like that. But when once you have the burden of being 'Gregers . . . Werle' in this life, as I have . . .

HJALMAR [*laughs*]. Ha! ha! And if you weren't 'Gregers Werle', what would you want to be?

GREGERS. If I had the choice, I should like most of all to be a clever dog.

GINA. A dog!

HEDVIG [*involuntarily*]. Oh, no!

GREGERS. Yes, a really absurdly clever dog; the sort that goes in after

2. Gregers is referring to the sound of the names.

wild ducks when they dive down and bite on to the weeds and tangle in the mud.

HJALMAR. You know, Gregers . . . I don't understand a word of what you are saying.

GREGERS. Oh, well, I dare say there's nothing much to it, anyway. Well then, first thing tomorrow . . . and I'll move in. [*To* GINA.] I'll not cause you much bother; I'll do for myself. [*To* HJALMAR.] We'll talk about the rest tomorrow. Good night, Mrs. Ekdal. [*Nods to* HEDVIG.] Good night!

GINA. Good night, Mr. Werle.

HEDVIG. Good night.

HJALMAR [*who has lit a candle*]. Just a minute, I'll bring a light. It's sure to be dark on the stairs.

[GREGERS *and* HJALMAR *leave by the hall door.*]

GINA [*staring vacantly, her sewing on her lap*]. Wasn't that funny, him talking about wanting to be a dog?

HEDVIG. I'll tell you what, Mother . . . I think he meant something else.

GINA. What else could he mean?

HEDVIG. I don't know. But all the time it was just as though he meant something different from what he was saying.

GINA. Do you think so? It was certainly very funny.

HJALMAR [*comes back*]. The lamp was still on. [*Snuffs the candle and puts it down.*] Ah, at last a man can get a bite to eat. [*Begins to eat a sandwich.*] There you are, you see, Gina . . . see what you can do with a bit of initiative. . . .

GINA. What do you mean 'initiative'?

HJALMAR. Well, wasn't it lucky getting the room let at last. And then imagine! . . . to somebody like Gregers . . . an old friend.

GINA. Really, I don't know what to say, I don't.

HEDVIG. Oh Mother, it'll be lovely, you'll see.

HJALMAR. You are funny, you know. First you were keen on getting it let, and now you don't like it.

GINA. Oh, yes, Hjalmar. If only it had been somebody else. . . . But what do you suppose Mr. Werle's going to-say?

HJALMAR. Old Werle? It's no concern of his.

GINA. But you can see they've fallen out about something again, what with him moving out of the house. You know what those two are like with each other.

HJALMAR. Yes, that may be, but . . .

GINA. And now perhaps Mr. Werle will think you are behind it all. . . .

HJALMAR. Let him think! Good God, I admit Mr. Werle's done a great deal for me. But that doesn't mean I've got to go on for ever doing what he wants me to do.

GINA. But, Hjalmar dear, it might also affect Grandfather. Perhaps he'll lose the little bit of money he makes working for Graaberg.

HJALMAR. I could almost wish he would! Isn't it rather humiliating for a man like me to see his grey-haired father being treated like an outcast? But soon we shall know what time in its fullness will bring, I should think. [*Helps himself to another sandwich.*] As truly as I have a mission in life, so shall I fulfil it!

HEDVIG. Oh yes, Daddy, do!

GINA. Hush! Mind you don't wake him.

HJALMAR [*in a lower voice*]. I *will* fulfil it, I tell you. The day will come, when . . . And that's why it's a good thing we managed to let the room; it gives me a bit more independence. And *that's* something a man with a mission in life must have. [*Over by the armchair, greatly moved.*] My poor white-haired old father! Trust in your Hjalmar! He has broad shoulders . . . strong shoulders, anyway. One fine day you'll wake up and . . . [*To* GINA.] You believe that, don't you?

GINA [*getting up*]. Of course I believe it. But let's see about getting him to bed first.

HJALMAR. Yes, let's.

[*They lift the old man carefully.*]

Act Three

HJALMAR EKDAL'S *studio. It is morning; the daylight comes through the big window in the sloping roof; the curtain is drawn back.*

HJALMAR *is sitting at the table busy retouching a photograph; several other pictures are lying in front of him. After a while* GINA *comes in by the hall door, in her hat and coat, carrying on her arm a covered basket.*

HJALMAR. Is that you back already, Gina?

GINA. Oh, yes. Have to look slippy.[3] [*She puts the basket on a chair and takes off her things.*]

HJALMAR. Did you look in on Gregers?

GINA. Yes, I did. And a bonny sight it is in there. He's no sooner here but what he's got the whole room in a right rare state.

HJALMAR. Oh?

GINA. Yes, he wanted to manage for himself, he said. Decided to light the fire, so what did he do but screw the damper down so the whole room was filled with smoke. Ugh, the stink! Just like . . .

HJALMAR. Oh dear!

GINA. But you haven't heard the best bit. Because then he wanted to put it out, so he just took a whole jug of water off the washstand and poured it all into the stove, and now there's the most awful wet mess all over the floor.

HJALMAR. What a nuisance!

GINA. I've got the woman downstairs to come and clean up after him—the pig. But the place won't be fit to go into again until this afternoon.

HJALMAR. What's he doing with himself in the meantime?

GINA. He was going out for a bit, he said.

HJALMAR. I looked in on him as well for a minute. Just after you'd gone out.

3. Translator's Britishism meaning "nimble," "spry."

GINA. So I heard. And you've asked him to lunch.

HJALMAR. Just for a bit of a bite of something, you know. Seeing it's his first day . . . we can't really get out of it. You've always got something in the house.

GINA. I'd better see what I can find.

HJALMAR. But let's not be too stingy about it. Because I think Relling and Molvik are also coming up. I happened to run into Relling on the stairs, you see, so I more or less had to . . .

GINA. So we're going to have them two an' all.

HJALMAR. Good Lord . . . one or two more or less . . . that's surely neither here nor there.

OLD EKDAL [*opens his door and looks out*]. I say, Hjalmar . . . ! [*Notices* GINA.] Oh . . . ah . . .

GINA. Is there something you want, Grandfather?

EKDAL. Oh no, it doesn't matter. Hm! [*Goes in again.*]

GINA [*takes the basket*]. Just keep an eye on him and see he doesn't go out.

HJALMAR. Yes, yes, I will. . . . I say, Gina, a little bit of herring salad would be nice. Because Relling and Molvik were out on the tiles[4] last night.

GINA. As long as they don't land on me before . . .

HJALMAR. No, of course they won't. Take your time.

GINA. Yes, all right. And in the meantime you can get a bit of work done.

HJALMAR. I *am* working! I'm working as hard as I can.

GINA. Because then it means you'll have *that* off your hands, you see. [*She takes the basket and goes out to the kitchen.* HJALMAR *sits a while working on the photograph with a brush, with obvious distaste and reluctance.*]

EKDAL [*peeps out, looks round the studio and says in a low voice*]. Busy, Hjalmar?

HJALMAR. Yes, can't you see I'm sitting here slaving away at these portraits. . . .

EKDAL. Oh well, of course, if you're all *that* busy. . . . Hm! [*Goes in again: the door remains standing open.*]

HJALMAR [*continues for a while in silence; then he puts down his brush and walks over to the door*]. Are you busy, Father?

EKDAL [*from within, grumbling*]. If *you're* so busy, then *I'm* busy too. Hm!

HJALMAR. All right. [*Goes back to his work.*]

EKDAL [*after a short pause, appears again at his door*]. Hm! Look, Hjalmar, I'm not *really* as busy as all that.

HJALMAR. I thought you were busy with your copying.

EKDAL. Oh, hell! Surely Graaberg can wait a day or two, can't he? I don't suppose it's a matter of life and death.

HJALMAR. No, and besides you're no slave.

EKDAL. Then there was that thing, you know, for in there . . .

4. Translator's Britishism meaning "on the loose," "on the town."

HJALMAR. Yes, precisely. Do you want to go in? Shall I open up for you?

EKDAL. That's maybe not such a bad idea.

HJALMAR [*getting up*]. And then we'd have *that* off our hands.

EKDAL. Exactly. It has to be ready for first thing tomorrow morning. It is tomorrow, isn't it? Eh?

HJALMAR. Yes, it's tomorrow all right.

[HJALMAR *and* EKDAL *take a door each and push; the morning sun is shining in through the skylights; a few pigeons are flying about, others sit cooing on the rafters; occasionally, hens can be heard cackling from further back in the loft.*]

HJALMAR. Well, you'd better get on with it now, Father.

EKDAL [*goes in*]. Aren't you coming?

HJALMAR. Yes, do you know . . . I rather think . . . [*Sees* GINA *at the kitchen door.*] Who me? No, I haven't time. I have to work. But what about our little gadget . . . ? [*He pulls a string and inside a curtain falls, the bottom part of which consists of a strip of old sail cloth, and the upper part of a piece of fishing net stretched taut. As a result the floor of the loft is no longer visible.*]

HJALMAR [*walks over to the table.*] There now! Perhaps I can get on in peace for a while now.

GINA. Is he fiddling about in there again?

HJALMAR. Would you rather see him running off to Ma Eriksen's? [*Sits down.*] Do you want something? You said . . .

GINA. I just wanted to ask if you thought we could lay the table in *here*?

HJALMAR. Yes. I take it we haven't got anybody booked for as early as that.

GINA. No, the only people I'm expecting are that couple that wanted to be taken together.

HJALMAR. Why the devil couldn't they have been taken together some other day!

GINA. Now, Hjalmar my dear, I booked them specially for after dinner when you are having your sleep.

HJALMAR. Oh well, that's all right then. Yes, we'll eat in here.

GINA. All right. But there's no hurry about laying the table. There's nothing to stop you from using it for a good while yet.

HJALMAR. Surely you can see I'm using the table just about as hard as I can go.

GINA. And then you'll be free later, won't you? [*Goes out into the kitchen again. Short pause.*]

EKDAL [*appears at the loft door, behind the net*]. Hjalmar!

HJALMAR. Well?

EKDAL. I'm afraid we'll have to move the water trough after all.

HJALMAR. Yes, that's just what I've been saying all along.

EKDAL. Hm, hm, hm!

[*Moves away from the door again.* HJALMAR *does a little work, glances over at the loft and half gets up.* HEDVIG *comes in from the kitchen.*]

HJALMAR [*sits down again quickly*]. What do you want?

HEDVIG. I just wanted to be beside you, Daddy.

HJALMAR [*after a moment*]. What do you want to come sniffing round like this for? Are you supposed to be keeping an eye on me, or something?

HEDVIG. No, of course not.

HJALMAR. What's your mother up to now out there?

HEDVIG. Oh, she's right in the middle of making herring salad. [*Walks over to the table.*] Isn't there anything I could help you with, Daddy?

HJALMAR. No, no. I'd best see to it all myself . . . as long as my strength lasts. There's no need, Hedvig; provided your father manages to keep his health. . . .

HEDVIG. Oh, no, Daddy! You mustn't say horrid things like that. [*She wanders round, stops by the opening and looks into the loft.*]

HJALMAR. What's he doing, Hedvig?

HEDVIG. Looks like a new way up to the water trough.

HJALMAR. He'll never manage *that* by himself, never in this world! Yet here am I condemned to sit here . . . !

HEDVIG [*goes across to him*]. Let *me* have the brush, Daddy. I *can* do it, you know.

HJALMAR. Nonsense. You'll just ruin your eyes.

HEDVIG. Really I shan't. Come on, give me the brush.

HJALMAR [*gets up*]. Well, I don't suppose it'd take more than a minute or two.

HEDVIG. Pooh! What if it did! [*Takes the brush.*] There now. [*Sits down.*] And here's one I can copy from.

HJALMAR. But don't ruin your eyes! D'you hear? I'm not taking any responsibility; you have to take the responsibility yourself. Understand?

HEDVIG [*retouching*]. Yes, yes, I will.

HJALMAR. You are a clever little girl, Hedvig. Just for a couple of minutes, then. [*He slips past the edge of the curtaining into the loft.* HEDVIG *sits at her work.* HJALMAR *and* EKDAL *can be heard discussing things inside.*]

HJALMAR [*appears behind the netting*]. Oh, Hedvig, hand me those pincers off the shelf, will you? And the chisel as well. [*Turns to face into the loft.*] Now I just want you to see something, Father, Just give me the chance to show you what I mean first. [HEDVIG *fetches the tools he wanted from the shelf and hands them in to him.*]

HJALMAR. Thanks. Yes, it was a good thing I came, you know. [*Moves away from the opening; hammering and talking are heard within.* HEDVIG *stands there watching them. A moment later there is a knock on the hall door which she does not notice.* GREGERS WERLE *comes in and stands near the door; he is bare-headed and without a topcoat.*]

GREGERS. Hm?

HEDVIG [*turns and walks over to him*]. Good morning! Please come in.

GREGERS. Thanks. [*Looks over at the loft.*] Sounds as though you've got workmen in the house.

HEDVIG. No, it's only Daddy and Grandfather. I'll go and tell them.

GREGERS. No, no, don't do that. I'll just wait a minute or two instead. [*He sits down on the sofa.*]

HEDVIG. Everything's in such a mess. . . . [*Begins to clear away the photographs.*]

GREGERS. Oh, just leave it. Are these photographs waiting to be finished?

HEDVIG. Yes, it's just a little job I was helping Daddy with.

GREGERS. Please don't let me disturb you.

HEDVIG. All right. [*She arranges the things around her again and settles down to work; GREGERS watches her in silence.*]

GREGERS. Did the wild duck sleep well last night?

HEDVIG. Yes, thank you, I think so.

GREGERS [*turning towards the loft*]. It looks quite different in daylight from what it did last night by moonlight.

HEDVIG. Yes, it can change such a lot. In the mornings it looks different from in the afternoons; and when it's raining it looks different from when it's fine.

GREGERS. Have you noticed that?

HEDVIG. Yes, you can't help seeing it.

GREGERS. Do you like being in there too beside the wild duck.

HEDVIG. Yes, when it can be managed. . . .

GREGERS. But I dare say you haven't a great deal of spare time. You have to go to school, haven't you?

HEDVIG. No, I don't go now any more. Daddy is afraid I'll spoil my eyes.

GREGERS. So he probably helps you with your lessons himself.

HEDVIG. Daddy's promised to do some lessons with me, but he hasn't been able to find the time just yet.

GREGERS. But isn't there anybody else who could help you a little?

HEDVIG. Yes, there's Mr. Molvik; but he's not always quite . . . not properly . . . er . . .

GREGERS. You mean, he's drunk?

HEDVIG. Yes, he is.

GREGERS. Well then, you've got time for all sorts of things. And inside there, it must just be like a world of its own, I should think?

HEDVIG. Yes, all of its own. And such a lot of strange things, too.

GREGERS. Really?

HEDVIG. Yes, big cupboards with books in, and a lot of the books have pictures.

GREGERS. Aha!

HEDVIG. And then there's an old cabinet with drawers and compartments in, and a big clock with figures that are supposed to pop in and out. But the clock doesn't go any more.

GREGERS. So time stands still in there . . . beside the wild duck.

HEDVIG. Yes. And then there are old paint boxes and things like that. And all the books.

GREGERS. And do you read these books?

HEDVIG. Oh yes, when I can manage it. But most of them are in English, and I don't understand that. But then I look at the pictures. There's a great big book called *Harryson's History of London*—it must be easily a hundred years old—and that has an enormous number of pictures in. In the front there's a picture of Death with an hour glass, and a girl. I think that's awful. But then there's also all the other pictures of churches and palaces and streets and big ships sailing on the sea.

GREGERS. But tell me, where did you get all these rare things from?

HEDVIG. Oh, an old sea captain used to live here once, and he brought them back with him. They used to call him 'the Flying Dutchman'.5 That was funny, because he *wasn't* a Dutchman at all.

GREGERS. Wasn't he?

HEDVIG. No. But then in the end he never came back; and all these things were just left here.

GREGERS. Listen now, tell me—when you sit in there looking at the pictures, don't you ever feel you want to get out into the big wide world itself and see something of it?

HEDVIG. Not me! I'm always going to stay at home and help my father and mother.

GREGERS. Touching up photographs?

HEDVIG. No, not just that. Best of all I'd like to learn how to engrave pictures like those in the English books.

GREGERS. Hm! What does your father say to that?

HEDVIG. I don't think Daddy likes it; Daddy's funny that way. Just think, he keeps on at me about learning basket-weaving and wicker-work! But I can't see there can be anything much in *that*.

GREGERS. Oh, no! I don't think so either.

HEDVIG. But Daddy's right when he says if I'd learnt basket-work, I could have made the new basket for the wild duck.

GREGERS. Yes, you could; and you would have been the proper person to do it.

HEDVIG. Because it's my wild duck.

GREGERS. Of course, it is.

HEDVIG. Yes, it belongs to *me*. But Daddy and Grandfather can have the loan of it as often as they like.

GREGERS. Indeed, and what do they do with it?

HEDVIG. Oh, they look after it, and build things for it, and things like that.

GREGERS. I suppose they do; because the wild duck is the most important of all the things in there.

HEDVIG. Yes, she is; because she's a *real* wild bird. It's such a shame, poor thing, she hasn't anybody to keep her company.

---

5. A specter-ship or its captain; believed to haunt the waters about the Cape of Good Hope. There are various legends to explain why its captain is condemned to sail around the cape forever and never make port.

GREGERS. No family, like the rabbits.

HEDVIG. No. There's plenty of hens too, and they have grown up together from being chickens. But she's completely cut off from her friends. And then everything about the wild duck is so mysterious. Nobody really knows her; and nobody knows where she's from either.

GREGERS. And the fact that she's been down in the briny deep.

HEDVIG [*glances quickly at him, suppresses a smile and asks*]. What makes you say 'the briny deep'?

GREGERS. What do you expect me to say?

HEDVIG. You could say 'the bottom of the sea' or 'the sea bed'.

GREGERS. But can't I just as well say 'the briny deep'?

HEDVIG. Yes. But it sounds so strange when I hear other people say 'briny deep'.

GREGERS. Why is that? Tell me.

HEDVIG. No, I don't want to. It's just silly.

GREGERS. Oh, I'm sure it isn't. Tell me why you smiled?

HEDVIG. It's because every time I catch myself wondering about things in there—suddenly, you know without thinking—it always strikes me that the whole room and everything in it should be called 'the briny deep'. But that's just silly.

GREGERS. No, you mustn't say that .

HEDVIG. Yes, of course, because it's really only a loft.

GREGERS [*looking hard at her*]. Are you so certain?

HEDVIG [*astonished*]. That it's a loft?

GREGERS. Yes. Do you know for sure?

> [HEDVIG *looks at him, open-mouthed and silent.* GINA *enters from the kitchen with a tablecloth.*]

GREGERS [*gets up*]. I'm afraid I've come too early.

GINA. Oh, well, I suppose you've got to be somewhere. Anyway, it will soon be ready. Clear the table, Hedvig.

> [HEDVIG *clears up; she and* GINA *lay the table during the following dialogue.* GREGERS *sits down in the easy-chair and glances through an album.*]

GREGERS. I hear you can do retouching, Mrs. Ekdal.

GINA [*with a sidelong glance*]. Yes, I can that.

GREGERS. That was very lucky.

GINA. What do you mean, 'lucky'?

GREGERS. After Hjalmar took up photography, I mean.

HEDVIG. Mother can do photography too.

GINA. Oh yes, I've managed to pick *that* up, all right.

GREGERS. I dare say you're the one that runs the business.

GINA. Yes, when Hjalmar hasn't the time himself. . . .

GREGERS. I imagine his time's pretty well taken up with his old father.

GINA. Yes. And besides it's no job for a man like Hjalmar taking pictures all day long.

GREGERS. I quite agree. But once he's gone in for that kind of thing . . .

GINA. Hjalmar's not like any of your ordinary photographers, Mr. Werle, I can tell you.

GREGERS. Quite. But all the same . . .
> [*A shot is fired inside the loft.*]

GREGERS [*starts up*]. What's that!

GINA. Huh! They're shooting again!

GREGERS. Do they shoot, too?

HEDVIG. They go out hunting.

GREGERS. They what! [*Walks over to the loft door.*] Are you hunting, Hjalmar?

HJALMAR [*behind the netting*]. You here? I didn't know. I was so busy. . . . [*To* HEDVIG.] Why didn't you tell us? [*Comes into the studio.*]

GREGERS. Do you go shooting in the loft?

HJALMAR [*shows him a double-barrelled pistol*]. Oh, only with this.

GINA. Yes, and the two of you will finish up by having an accident one of these fine days with that gun.

HJALMAR [*irritated*]. How many times do I have to tell you a weapon like this is called a pistol.

GINA. Well, I can't see that's much better myself.

GREGERS. So you've taken up hunting too, Hjalmar?

HJALMAR. Just a bit of rabbit shooting, now and again. Mostly for Father's sake, you know.

GINA. Funny creatures, men! Always have to have something to deviate themselves with.

HJALMAR [*angrily*]. That's right, yes. We always have to have something to divert ourselves with.

GINA. Yes, *that's* what I said.

HJALMAR. Oh, well! [*To* GREGERS.] Yes, you see, we are lucky the loft is so placed that nobody can hear us when we shoot. [*Places the pistol on the top shelf.*] Don't touch the pistol, Hedvig! One of the barrels is loaded, don't forget.

GREGERS [*looks in through the netting*]. I see you've also got a sporting gun.

HJALMAR. That's Father's old gun. You can't fire it any more, there's something wrong with the lock. But it's fun to have it all the same, because we can take it to pieces and clean it every now and then and grease it and put it together again. . . . Of course, it's mainly my father who tinkers about with these things.

HEDVIG [*over beside* GREGERS]. Now you can see the wild duck properly.

GREGERS. I'm just looking at it now. She seems to be dragging one wing a bit, I think.

HJALMAR. Well, that's not surprising; after all, she's been wounded.

GREGERS. And she's trailing one foot too. Or am I mistaken?

HJALMAR. Perhaps ever so slightly.

HEDVIG. Well, that was the foot the dog bit.

HJALMAR. Otherwise there's absolutely nothing wrong with her; and that's really rather remarkable when you consider she's had a load of shot in her and been chewed about by a dog. . . .

GREGERS [*with a glance at* HEDVIG]. . . . and been down in the briny deep . . . for so long.

HEDVIG [*smiles*]. Yes.

GINA [*arranging the table*]. That blessed wild duck! All the carrying-on there is about that bird!

HJALMAR. Hm! . . . Will lunch soon be ready?

GINA. Any minute now. Hedvig, you must come and help me now.

[GINA *and* HEDVIG *go out into the kitchen.*]

HJALMAR [*in an undertone*]. I don't think there's any point in standing and watching Father. He doesn't like it.

[GREGERS *walks away from the loft door.*]

HJALMAR. And I'd better shut it up before the others arrive. [*Waving his hands to chase the birds away.*] Shoo! Shoo! Get away. [*Speaking as he draws up the curtaining, and pulls the doors together.*] These gadgets here are my own invention. Really it's great fun having something like this to look after, and mending it when it gets broken. And besides it's absolutely necessary, you know, because Gina doesn't like having the rabbits and hens in the studio.

GREGERS. Of course not. And I suppose it's your wife who has the running of it?

HJALMAR. The routine jobs I generally leave to her; then I can retire to the living-room and give my attention to more important things.

GREGERS. What sort of things, actually, Hjalmar?

HJALMAR. I'm surprised you haven't asked me about *that* before. Or perhaps you haven't heard about the invention?

GREGERS. Invention? No.

HJALMAR. Really? Haven't you? Oh, of course, being stuck out there in the wilds, up in the forest. . . .

GREGERS. So you've made an invention!

HJALMAR. Haven't quite managed it yet, but I'm busy on it. When I decided to devote myself to photography, you don't suppose it was with the idea of doing nothing but take pictures of anybody who happened to come along?

GREGERS. No, no, your wife's just been saying the same thing.

HJALMAR. I swore that if I was going to dedicate my powers to this calling, I would raise it to the level where it was both an art and a science. So I decided to make this remarkable invention.

GREGERS. And what does the invention consist of? What's the purpose of it?

HJALMAR. Ah, my dear Gregers, you mustn't ask for details yet. It all takes time, you know. And you mustn't think it's vanity that's urging me on. I'm not thinking of myself in the least. Oh no, night and day I see before me what must be my life's work.

GREGERS. What life's work?

HJALMAR. Have you forgotten that dear old, silver-haired man?

GREGERS. Your poor old father? Yes, but what can you in fact do for him?

HJALMAR. I can restore his own self-respect by raising once more the name of Ekdal to a place of honour and dignity.

GREGERS. So that is your life's work, then?

HJALMAR. Yes, I will rescue this poor castaway, shipwrecked as he was from the moment the storm broke over him. During that terrible inquiry he was no longer himself. That pistol over there, Gregers . . . the one we use to shoot rabbits with . . . it has played its role in the tragedy of the House of Ekdal.

GREGERS. The pistol? Really?

HJALMAR. When judgement had been pronounced and he was about to be sent to prison . . . he had the pistol in his hand. . . .

GREGERS. He had the . . . ?

HJALMAR. Yes, but he didn't dare. He was a coward. He was already so demoralized, so broken in spirit by then. Oh, can you imagine it? Him a soldier, a man who had shot no less than nine bears, who was descended from two lieutenant-colonels . . . not both at the same time of course. . . . Can you imagine it, Gregers?

GREGERS. Yes, I can imagine it very well.

HJALMAR. I can't. But then the pistol figured a second time in our family history. When they had taken him away, and he sat there under lock and key—oh, that was a terrible time for me, I can tell you. I kept the blinds lowered at both windows. When I looked out and saw the sun shining the same as usual, I couldn't understand it. I saw people walking about the streets, laughing and talking about things of no importance. I couldn't understand it. I felt that all creation ought to have come to a standstill, like an eclipse.

GREGERS. I felt just the same when Mother died.

HJALMAR. It was in such a moment that Hjalmar Ekdal held the pistol to his own breast.

GREGERS. You too thought of . . . !

HJALMAR. Yes.

GREGERS. But you didn't shoot?

HJALMAR. No. At the crucial moment I won a great victory over myself. I went on living. But as you can quite understand, it takes some courage to choose life on *those* terms.

GREGERS. Well, it depends how you look at it.

HJALMAR. No, my dear fellow, there's no doubt about it. But it was all for the best, because soon now I shall have my invention ready. And Dr. Relling thinks—as I do too—that Father will then be able to wear his uniform again. I ask for no other reward than that.

GREGERS. So *that's* how it is with the uniform he . . . ?

HJALMAR. Yes, *that's* what he longs and yearns for more than anything else. You have no idea how my heart bleeds for him. Every time we have a little family party—like Gina's and my wedding anniversary, or whatever it might be—in comes the old chap dressed in his lieutenant's uniform of happy memory. But if there's so much as a knock on the front door—because he daren't show himself in front of strangers—away he's off into his room again as fast as his poor old legs will carry him. It's heart-breaking for a son to have to see things like that, Gregers.

GREGERS. Roughly, when do you think the invention will be ready?

HJALMAR. Good Lord, you mustn't ask me about details like dates.

An invention is something you can never be completely master of. It's largely a matter of inspiration . . . of intuition . . . and it's pretty nearly impossible to predict when that will come.

GREGERS. But it's making good progress?

HJALMAR. Certainly it's making good progress. Not a day goes by but what I do something on the invention; I'm absorbed in it. Every day after dinner I shut myself up in the living-room, where I can concentrate in peace. But it's no good people trying to rush me, that's no good. Relling says the same.

GREGERS. And you don't feel all these things going on in the loft take you away from your work . . . distract you too much?

HJALMAR. No, no. On the contrary. You mustn't get that idea at all. I can't always go on poring over the same old exhausting problems. I've got to have something else as well to keep me occupied. Inspiration, revelation, you know—when it comes, it comes, that's all.

GREGERS. My dear Hjalmar, I almost believe you've a bit of the wild duck about you.

HJALMAR. The wild duck? How do you make that out?

GREGERS. You have gone plunging down and bitten fast to the weeds.

HJALMAR. You are referring, I suppose, to the blow that crippled my father and very nearly killed him . . . and me too?

GREGERS. Not primarily to that. I wouldn't say you're lamed exactly; but you've landed up in a poison swamp, Hjalmar; you've picked up some insidious disease, and you've gone down to die in the dark.

HJALMAR. Me? Die in the dark? Look, Gregers, you really must stop this kind of talk.

GREGERS. But don't upset yourself. I'll see we get you up again. For now, you see, I too know what my life's work is to be. I found out yesterday.

HJALMAR. That's all very well; but will you please keep *me* out of it. I can assure you that, apart from feeling naturally rather depressed, I am as well as any man could wish.

GREGERS. The very fact that you are, also comes from the poison.

HJALMAR. Please now, my dear Gregers, let's have no more of this talk about diseases and poisons; I'm just not used to that kind of conversation; in my house people never talk to me about unpleasant things.

GREGERS. That's something I can well believe.

HJALMAR. No, it isn't good for me. And this place *doesn't* smell like a swamp, as you keep saying. I know it's only the humble home of a poor photographer of modest means . . . and the place is not very grand. But I am an inventor, you know . . . and a breadwinner too. That's what keeps me above all these petty things.—Ah! Here they are with the lunch!

> [GINA *and* HEDVIG *carry in bottles of beer, a decanter of brandy, glasses and other things for the table; at the same time,* RELLING *and* MOLVIK *enter from the hallway; both are without hats or topcoats;* MOLVIK *is dressed in black.*]

GINA [*putting the things on the table*]. Trust them two to be here in time.

RELLING. Molvik got the idea he could smell herring salad, and then there was no holding him. Good morning for the second time, Ekdal.

HJALMAR. Gregers, may I introduce Mr. Molvik, and Doctor . . . ah, but of course you know Relling?

GREGERS. Yes, slightly.

RELLING. Oh, it's Mr. Werle, junior. Yes, we came up against each other once or twice up at the Höidal works. You've just moved in?

GREGERS. I moved in this morning.

RELLING. Molvik and I live just underneath, so if ever you need a doctor or a parson, you don't have far to go.

GREGERS. Thanks, it could happen. Yesterday there were thirteen of us at table.

HJALMAR. Oh, let's not get on to that horrid business again!

RELLING. You needn't worry, Ekdal, it's not going to affect you.

HJALMAR. I hope not, if only for my family's sake. But now let's sit down, and eat, drink and be merry.

GREGERS. Shouldn't we wait for your father?

HJALMAR. No, he'll have his in his room afterwards. Come along!
    [*The men sit down at the table, and eat and drink.* GINA *and* HEDVIG *go in and out, waiting on them.*]

RELLING. Molvik was filthy drunk last night, Mrs. Ekdal.

GINA. What, again last night?

RELLING. Didn't you hear him when I brought him home during the night?

GINA. No, can't say I did.

RELLING. Just as well. Because last night Molvik was pretty dreadful.

GINA. Is this true, Mr. Molvik?

MOLVIK. Let us draw a veil over the events of last night. Such things bear no relation to my better self.

RELLING. It just comes over him like a sort of revelation, and then there's nothing for it but to take him out on a binge. Mr. Molvik, you see, is a demonic.

GREGERS. A demonic?

RELLING. Molvik is a demonic, yes.

GREGERS. Hm!

RELLING. And demonic natures are not made for the straight and narrow; they've got to kick over the traces now and then. . . . So you still manage to stick it up there at those nasty, filthy works?

GREGERS. I have until now.

RELLING. And did you get anywhere with that 'claim' you were always coming out with?

GREGERS. Claim? [*Understands him.*] Oh, that!

HJALMAR. What's all this about 'claims', Gregers?

GREGERS. Oh, it's nothing.

RELLING. Ah, but there *was* something. He used to go the rounds of all the labourers' cottages serving up what he called 'the claim of the ideal'.

GREGERS. I was young then.

RELLING. You're right there; you were very young. And this 'claim of the ideal'—you never got anybody to honour it as long as *I* was there.

GREGERS. Nor afterwards, either.

RELLING. Well, I suppose you've had the sense to mark the price down a bit.

GREGERS. Never when I'm dealing with a man who *is* a man.

HJALMAR. Well, that strikes me as being pretty reasonable.—Butter please, Gina.

RELLING. And a slice of pork for Molvik.

MOLVIK. Ugh, not pork!

[*There is a knock on the loft door.*]

HJALMAR. Open up, Hedvig. Father wants to be let out.

[HEDVIG *goes and opens the door a little;* OLD EKDAL *enters carrying a fresh rabbit skin; she shuts the door after him.*]

EKDAL. Good morning, gentlemen! Had some good hunting today. Bagged a big 'un.

HJALMAR. Have you gone and skinned it without *me* . . . !

EKDAL. Salted it, too. It's good tender meat, rabbit-meat. And sweet. Tastes like sugar. Enjoy your lunch, gentlemen!

[*Goes into his room.*]

MOLVIK [*rising*]. Excuse me . . . I can't . . . I must run downstairs at once. . . .

RELLING. Have some soda-water, man!

MOLVIK [*hurrying*]. Ugh! Ugh!

[*Leaves by the hall door.*]

RELLING [*to* HJALMAR]. Let's drink to the grand old sportsman.

HJALMAR [*touching glasses with him*]. Yes, to the sportsman, standing on the brink of the grave.

RELLING. To the grey-haired. . . . [*Drinks.*] But tell me, is it grey hair he has, or is it white?

HJALMAR. Actually, it's somewhere in between. As a matter of fact, he hasn't got all that much hair left.

RELLING. Ah well, people still manage to get by with a wig. Yes, Ekdal, you're really a very lucky man, devoting your life to this splendid mission.

HJALMAR. And I *do* devote myself to it, too, I can tell you.

RELLING. And then you've also got your clever little wife to look after you, pottering about in her slippers all nice and cuddlesome, and making the place all cosy.

HJALMAR. Yes, Gina. . . . [*Nods to her.*] You are a great helpmate to have on life's way, my dear.

GINA. Oh, I wish you wouldn't sit there weighing me up and down.

RELLING. Then what about your Hedvig, eh, Ekdal?

HJALMAR [*moved*]. The child, yes! More than anything else, the child. Come to me, Hedvig. [*Strokes her hair.*] What day is it tomorrow?

HEDVIG. Oh, no, you mustn't say anything, Daddy!

HJALMAR. It's like a knife plunged into my heart when I think how little there will be. Just a small party there in the loft. . . .

HEDVIG. Oh, but that will be simply lovely!

RELLING. Just you wait till this amazing invention sees the light of day, Hedvig.

HJALMAR. Ah yes, then you'll see! Hedvig, I've decided I must make your future secure. You shall not want for anything as long as you live. I shall insist on your having . . . something or other. That shall be the humble inventor's only reward.

HEDVIG [*with her arm round his neck, whispers*]. Oh, my dear, dear Daddy!

RELLING [*to* GREGERS]. Well now, don't you think *this* makes a nice change, to sit at a well-filled table in a happy family circle.

HJALMAR. Yes, I really appreciate these meal-times.

GREGERS. Personally I don't thrive in a poisoned atmosphere.

RELLING. Poisoned atmosphere?

HJALMAR. Oh, let's not have that nonsense all over again!

GINA. God knows there aren't any bad smells in here, Mr. Werle. I give the place a good airing every blessed day.

GREGERS [*rising from the table*]. No amount of airing will get rid of the stench *I* mean!

HJALMAR. Stench!

GINA. Well, what do you think of that, Hjalmar!

RELLING. Excuse me . . . I suppose *you* couldn't be the one who has brought the stench in, from the mines up there?

GREGERS. It's just like you to call what I bring into this house a stench.

RELLING [*walks across to him*]. Listen, Mr. Werle, junior! I strongly suspect you are still carrying this 'claim of the ideal' about with you in full, in your back pocket.

GREGERS. I carry it in my breast.

RELLING. Well, carry the thing where the devil you like; but I wouldn't advise you to try and cash in on it here as long as *I'm* about the place.

GREGERS. And if I do?

RELLING. Then you'll find yourself going head-first down the stairs. Now you know.

HJALMAR [*getting up*]. I say, Relling!

GREGERS. Yes, you just try throwing me out and . . .

GINA [*coming between them*]. You mustn't do that, Mr. Relling. But *this* I will say, Mr. Werle—anybody who can make such an awful mess as the one in your stove has no right coming to me and talking about smells.

[*There is a knock at the hall door.*]

HEDVIG. Mother, somebody's knocking.

HJALMAR. Oh, really! There's just no end to all these comings and goings.

GINA. Let me go. [*Walks over and opens the door, starts, shudders and draws back.*] Oh!

[HAAKON WERLE, *wearing a fur coat, takes a step into the room.*]

WERLE. I beg your pardon, but I believe my son is supposed to be living here.

GINA [*gulping*]. Yes.

HJALMAR [*coming forward*]. Won't you be so good, Mr. Werle, as
to . . .

WERLE. Thanks. All I want is to speak to my son.

GREGERS. Yes, what is it? Here I am.

WERLE. I wish to speak to you in your room.

GREGERS. In my room . . . very well.

[*He turns to go.*]

GINA. Good Lord, no! It's in no state for . . .

WERLE. Well, out in the passage, then; I wish to speak to you
privately.

HJALMAR. You can do that here, Mr. Werle. Relling can come into
the living-room.

[HJALMAR *and* RELLING *go out right;* GINA *leads* HEDVIG *out
into the kitchen.*]

GREGERS [*after a short pause*]. Well, now we are alone.

WERLE. You passed a number of remarks last night. . . . And since
you've now moved in on the Ekdals, I can only assume that you
have in mind something against me.

GREGERS. What I have in mind is to open Hjalmar Ekdal's eyes. He
shall see the situation as it is . . . that's all.

WERLE. Is *this* the life's work you were talking about yesterday?

GREGERS. Yes. You haven't left me any other.

WERLE. Is it my fault, then, if your ideas are all mixed up, Gregers?

GREGERS. You've messed up my whole life. I'm not thinking of all
the business with Mother. . . . But it's thanks to you that I now suffer the torment of a desperately guilty conscience.

WERLE. Aha! So it's your conscience that's a bit queer, eh?

GREGERS. I should have stood up to you at the time the trap was laid
for Lieutenant Ekdal. I should have warned him. For I had a pretty good idea how things would turn out in the end.

WERLE. Yes, you really should have spoken out then.

GREGERS. I didn't dare. I was scared . . . too much of a coward. I
can't tell you how frightened of you I was then and for a long
time after, too.

WERLE. It would seem that that fear is past now.

GREGERS. Fortunately it is. The wrong that's been done to Old
Ekdal, both by me and by . . . others, can never be put right. But
what I can do now is free Hjalmar from all the lies and deceit
that are causing his ruination.

WERLE. Do you think *that's* likely to do any good?

GREGERS. I'm convinced it will.

WERLE. Do you really think Hjalmar Ekdal is the sort of man who
would thank you for that kind of favour?

GREGERS. Yes. He *is* that sort.

WERLE. Hm! We'll see.

GREGERS. And besides, if I'm to go on living, I must find something
to cure my sick conscience.

WERLE. It will never recover. From being a child, you've always had a sickly conscience. It's a heritage from your mother, Gregers . . . one thing she did leave you.

GREGERS [*with a contemptuous smile*]. That must have been a bitter pill to swallow when you found you had miscalculated, after expecting her to bring you a fortune.

WERLE. Let us keep to the point.—Are you set on this scheme of putting Ekdal on what you imagine to be the right track?

GREGERS. Yes, I'm quite set on it.

WERLE. Well, in that case I might have saved myself a journey. For I suppose it's no use asking you now if you'll come home again?

GREGERS. No.

WERLE. And you won't come into the firm either?

GREGERS. No.

WERLE. Very well. But as I now intend to marry again, the estate will be divided between us.

GREGERS [*quickly*]. No. I don't want that.

WERLE. You don't want that?

GREGERS. No. My conscience won't let me.

WERLE [*after a pause*]. Are you going back up to the works again?

GREGERS. No. I regard myself as having left your service.

WERLE. But what will you do now?

GREGERS. I shall fulfil my mission, that's all.

WERLE. But what about afterwards? What are you going to live on?

GREGERS. I've saved a bit out of my pay.

WERLE. But how long will *that* last!

GREGERS. I think it will last my time out.

WERLE. What do you mean by that?

GREGERS. I'm not answering any more questions.

WERLE. Goodbye, then, Gregers.

GREGERS. Goodbye.

[HAAKON WERLE *goes.*]

HJALMAR [*peeps in*]. Has he gone?

GREGERS. Yes.

[HJALMAR *and* RELLING *enter;* GINA *and* HEDVIG *come in from the kitchen.*]

RELLING. That's put paid to *that* lunch.

GREGERS. Put your things on, Hjalmar. You are coming for a long walk with me.

HJALMAR. Yes, with pleasure. What did your father want? Anything to do with me?

GREGERS. Just come with me. We must have a little talk. I'll go and get my coat.

[*He goes out by the hall door.*]

GINA. I wouldn't go out with him if I was you, Hjalmar.

RELLING. No. don't do it, old man; stay where you are.

HJALMAR [*takes his hat and topcoat*]. What, when an old friend feels the need to open up his heart to me . . . !

RELLING. Damn it, man! Can't you see the man's mad, barmy, off his head!

GINA. There you are! Now just you be told! His mother sometimes used to have bouts just the same as that.

HJALMAR. All the more reason for him to need a friend's watchful eye. [*To* GINA.] See that dinner's ready in good time, won't you? Goodbye for now.

[*He leaves by the hall door.*]

RELLING. What a pity the man didn't get to hell out of it down one of those mines at Höidal.

GINA. Good Lord! Why d'you say that?

RELLING [*muttering*]. Oh, I've got my reasons.

GINA. D'you think young Werle is really mad?

RELLING. No, worse luck! He's no madder than most. But one kind of ailment he is suffering from, all the same.

GINA. What's wrong with him, then?

RELLING. I'll tell you, Mrs. Ekdal. He's an acute case of inflamed scruples.

GINA. Inflamed scruples?

HEDVIG. Is that a sort of illness?

RELLING. Yes. It's a national illness. But it only occurs sporadically. [*Nods to* GINA.] Thanks for lunch!

[*He goes out by the hall door.*]

GINA [*walking restlessly about the room*]. Ugh, that Gregers Werle. He's always been a queer fish.

HEDVIG [*stands by the table and looks inquiringly at her.*] I think this is all very strange.

Act Four

HJALMAR EKDAL'S *studio. A photograph has obviously just been taken; a camera covered with a cloth, a stand, a few chairs, a what-not and similar things are standing about the floor. Late afternoon light, with the sun about to set; after a little while it begins to get dark.*

GINA *is standing at the open door, in her hand a little container and a wet photographic plate; she is speaking to somebody outside.*

GINA. Yes, absolutely certain. I always keep my promises. The first dozen will be ready for Monday. Good afternoon, good afternoon!

[*Somebody can be heard going downstairs.* GINA *shuts the door, puts the plate into the container and puts that in the shrouded camera.*]

HEDVIG [*enters from the kitchen*]. Have they gone now?

GINA [*tidying up*]. Yes, thank heavens. I've got rid of them at last.

HEDVIG. I wonder why Daddy hasn't come back yet?

GINA. Are you sure he's not down at Relling's?

HEDVIG. No, he's not there. I slipped down the back stairs just now and asked.

GINA. And his dinner's standing here getting cold.

HEDVIG. Yes, fancy! And Daddy's generally home for his dinner on the dot.

GINA. Oh, don't fret, he'll be here soon.

HEDVIG. Oh, I do wish he'd come; because everything seems so strange now.

GINA [*calls out*]. There he is!

> [HJALMAR EKDAL *comes in through the hall door.*]

HEDVIG [*going to meet him*]. Daddy! We've been waiting and waiting for you.

GINA [*glancing across*]. There's a long time you've been, Hjalmar.

HJALMAR [*without looking at her*]. Yes, I have, rather.

> [*He takes off his topcoat;* GINA *and* HEDVIG *go to help him; he waves them away.*]

GINA. Have you had something to eat with Gregers Werle?

HJALMAR [*hangs up his coat*]. No.

GINA [*going towards the kitchen door*]. Then I'll bring your dinner in for you.

HJALMAR. No, don't bother about any dinner. I don't want anything to eat now.

HEDVIG [*going closer*]. Aren't you feeling well, Daddy?

HJALMAR. Feeling well? Oh yes, not so bad. We went for a rather tiring walk, Gregers and I.

GINA. You shouldn't have, Hjalmar; you're not used to it.

HJALMAR. Huh! There are many things a man's got to get used to in this world. [*Walks up and down.*] Has anybody been here while I've been out?

GINA. Only that engaged couple.

HJALMAR. No new orders?

GINA. No, not today.

HEDVIG. There'll be some more tomorrow all right, Daddy, you'll see.

HJALMAR. I hope you're right. Because tomorrow I'm going to get down to things in real earnest.

HEDVIG. Tomorrow! You haven't forgotten what day it is tomorrow?

HJALMAR. Oh, that's right. . . . Well, the day after, then. After this I'm doing everything myself; I want to do the work all on my own.

GINA. But, Hjalmar, what's the good of *that*? You'll only make your life a misery. I can still manage the photographing; and then you can get on with the invention.

HEDVIG. And then there's the wild duck, Daddy . . . and all the hens and rabbits. . . .

HJALMAR. Don't speak to me about all that nonsense! I'm never going to set foot in that loft again after today.

HEDVIG. But Daddy, you promised me there'd be a party tomorrow. . . .

HJALMAR. Hm, that's right. . . . Well, starting the day after tomorrow, then. That damned wild duck, I'd like to wring its neck.

HEDVIG [*with a scream*]. The wild duck!

GINA. Well, I never did!

HEDVIG [*shaking him*]. But Daddy . . . it's *my* wild duck!

HJALMAR. That's the only thing that's stopping me. I haven't the heart. . . . For your sake, Hedvig, I haven't the heart. But deep down inside me I ought to. I can't see why I should have any creature under my roof that's been in *that* man's hands.

GINA. But, good Lord, just because it was that rogue Pettersen Grandfather got it off, that's no . . .

HJALMAR [*walking about*]. There are certain demands . . . what should I call them? Let us say, demands of the ideal . . . certain claims that a man can't disregard without doing violence to his own soul.

HEDVIG [*following him about*]. But think of the wild duck . . . the poor little wild duck!

HJALMAR [*halts*]. I've told you I'm not going to touch it . . . for your sake. Not a hair of its . . . well, as I said, I'm not going to touch it. There are things of much greater importance to be undertaken. But it's time you had your evening walk, Hedvig; it's nicely dusk for you now.

HEDVIG. No, I can't be bothered to go out now.

HJALMAR. Yes, go on. You seem to be blinking a lot. It's not good for you, all these fumes in here. The air's thick here, under this roof.

HEDVIG. All right, I'll run down the back stairs and go for a little walk. Where's my hat and coat? Oh, they're in my room. But mind, Daddy . . . you mustn't do anything to the wild duck while I'm out.

HJALMAR. Not a feather of its head shall be touched. [*Hugging her.*] You and I, Hedvig . . . we two! Now, run along, my dear.

[HEDVIG *waves to her parents and goes out through the kitchen.*]

HJALMAR [*walks up and down without looking up*]. Gina.

GINA. Yes?

HJALMAR. As from tomorrow—or the day after, let us say—I think I would like to keep the household accounts myself.

GINA. You want to keep the accounts as well?

HJALMAR. Yes, or keep a check on what comes in, at any rate.

GINA. Oh, *that's* not a big job, so help me.

HJALMAR. Ah, I'm not so sure of *that*; you seem to make the money stretch a remarkably long way. [*Halts and looks at her.*] How does that happen?

GINA. It's because Hedvig and me don't need very much.

HJALMAR. Is it true Father gets paid pretty lavishly for the copying he does for Mr. Werle?

GINA. I don't know that it's *so* lavish. I don't know what the rates are for things like that.

HJALMAR. Well, roughly what does he get? Tell me!

GINA. It varies; roughly the cost of his board, and a bit extra for pocket money.

HJALMAR. The cost of his board! You never told me that before!

GINA. Well, really I couldn't. You liked to think he got everything from you.

HJALMAR. And instead he gets it all from Werle!

GINA. Oh well, he's not likely to miss it.

HJALMAR. Light the lamp!

GINA [*lights it*]. Besides, we don't really know if it actually comes from him. It might easily be Graaberg. . . .

HJALMAR. Why are you trying to shift things on to Graaberg?

GINA. Well, I don't know. I just thought . . .

HJALMAR. Huh!

GINA. It wasn't me that got Grandfather his copying to do. It was Berta, that time she was here.

HJALMAR. Your voice seems to be trembling.

GINA [*putting on the shade*]. Is it?

HJALMAR. And your hands are shaking. Aren't they?

GINA [*firmly*]. Tell me straight, Hjalmar. What's he gone and told you about me?

HJALMAR. Is it true . . . *can* it really be true . . . that there was something between you and Old Werle when you were in service there?

GINA. It's not true. Not then, there wasn't. Mr. Werle pestered me plenty, that I will say. And his wife thought there was something in it. What a fuss she kicked up! She just went for me, played merry hell, she did. So I left.

HJALMAR. But then afterwards?

GINA. Well, then I went home. And my mother . . . she wasn't quite what you thought she was, Hjalmar. She kept on at me, about one thing and another. . . . Because Werle was a widower by then.

HJALMAR. Well, what then?

GINA. Well, you might as well know it. He wouldn't be satisfied till he'd had his way.

HJALMAR [*clasping his hands together*]. Is this the mother of my child! How could you keep a thing like that hidden from me!

GINA. Yes, it was wrong of me. I should have told you long ago.

HJALMAR. You should have told me at the time—then I'd have known what sort of woman you were.

GINA. But would you have married me just the same?

HJALMAR. However can you think that?

GINA. There you are! That's why I didn't dare say anything at the time. Because I'd come to like you so very much, you know. I couldn't go and make my whole life a misery. . . .

HJALMAR [*walking about*]. Is this my Hedvig's mother! To think that everything I see around me here . . . [*Kicks a chair.*] My entire home, all of it I owe to your previous lover. Ah, that lecherous old Werle!

GINA. Do you regret the fourteen or fifteen years we have lived together?

HJALMAR [*standing in front of her*]. Tell me this. Haven't you— every day, every hour—regretted this web of deceit you've spun around me like a spider? Answer me that! Haven't you in fact been suffering agonies of worry and remorse?

GINA. Oh, my dear Hjalmar, really I've had far too many other things to think of, what with running the house and everything. . . .

HJALMAR. And this past of yours, do you never give it a thought now?

GINA. No. God knows, I'd pretty nearly forgotten all that old business.

HJALMAR. Oh, how can you stand there so calm and unconcerned! That's what I find so absolutely outrageous. Imagine—not the slightest sign of regret.

GINA. But tell me now, Hjalmar—where would you have been now if you hadn't had somebody like me for a wife?

HJALMAR. Like you!

GINA. Yes, because I've always been as you might say a bit more down-to-earth and business-like than you. Well, that's understandable—I'm a year or two older, after all.

HJALMAR. Where would I have been?

GINA. You were in a pretty bad way all round when you first met me. You can hardly deny that.

HJALMAR. You call that being in a bad way? Oh, you don't under-stand what it means when a man is weighed down with worry and despair—especially a man with my fiery temperament.

GINA. Well, well, have it as you will. I don't want to make too much of a song and dance about it, either, because you turned out to be a right good husband once you'd got your own house and home.—And we'd made things so nice and cosy, and Hedvig and me were just starting to manage a little bit extra for ourselves in the way of food and clothes.

HJALMAR. Yes, in this swamp of deceit.

GINA. Ugh! That horrible man! What did he have to go and shove his nose in here for!

HJALMAR. I too used to think our home was a good place. What a mistake that was. Now where am I going to find the stimulus I need to make my invention a reality? Perhaps it will die with me; and your past, Gina, will be what's killed it.

GINA [*close to tears*]. Oh Hjalmar, you mustn't say things like that. When all my days I've spent only doing what I thought was best for you.

HJALMAR. I ask you—what about the breadwinner's dream now? When I used to lie in there on the sofa turning the invention over in my mind, I vaguely knew it would drain the very last bit of my strength. I had the feeling that the day I held the patent in my hands, would mark my own . . . last hour. And it was my dream that you should be left comfortably settled, to take your place as the widow of the one-time inventor.

GINA [*drying her tears*]. No, Hjalmar you *mustn't* talk like that. God forbid I should ever live to see the day I'm left a widow!

HJALMAR. Oh, it's all the same either way. Everything's over and done with now. Everything!

[GREGERS WERLE *cautiously opens the hall door and looks in.*]

GREGERS. May I come in?

HJALMAR. Yes, come in.

GREGERS [*advances, his face beaming with joy and holds out his hands to them*]. Well now, my dear people . . . ![*Looks from one to the other and whispers to* HJALMAR.] Haven't you done it yet, then?

HJALMAR [*aloud*]. I *have* done it.

GREGERS. You *have*?

HJALMAR. I have experienced the bitterest moment of my life.

GREGERS. But also the most sublime, I should think.

HJALMAR. Well, we've got it off our chests, anyway.

GINA. May God forgive you, Mr. Werle.

GREGERS [*greatly astonished*]. But I don't understand.

HJALMAR. What don't you understand?

GREGERS. Now that you have laid bare your souls—this exchange on which you can now build a completely new mode of life—a way of living together in truth, free of all deception. . . .

HJALMAR. Yes, I know; I know all that.

GREGERS. I was absolutely convinced when I came in through that door that I should be greeted by the light of radiant understanding on the faces of husband and wife alike. And all I see is this dull, gloomy, miserable . . .

GINA. Very well then. [*She takes the shade off the lamp.*]

GREGERS. You're not trying to understand me, Mrs. Ekdal. Well, well; in your case perhaps with time . . . But *you* now, Hjalmar? Surely this passage of arms has brought you to some higher resolve.

HJALMAR. Yes, of course it has. That is . . . in a sort of way.

GREGERS. For there is surely no joy in life comparable with that of forgiving one who has sinned, and of raising her up again in love.

HJALMAR. Do you think a man so easily gets over the bitter draught I have just drunk?

GREGERS. No! No *ordinary* man, I dare say. But a man like you . . . !

HJALMAR. Yes, I know, I know. But you mustn't rush me, Gregers. It takes time you know.

GREGERS. There's a *lot* of the wild duck about you, Hjalmar.

[*RELLING has come in by the entrance door.*]

RELLING. What's this now! Is the wild duck on the go again?

HJALMAR. The poor maimed victim of Mr. Werle's sport, yes.

RELLING. Mr. Werle? Is it *him* you're talking about?

HJALMAR. Him and . . . the rest of us.

RELLING [*to GREGERS under his breadth*]. God damn you!

HJALMAR. What do you say?

RELLING. I was merely expressing the pious wish that this quack here would pack himself off where he belongs. If he stops here, he's just as likely to be the ruination of the pair of you.

GREGERS. Neither of them is being ruined, Mr. Relling. I needn't say anything about Hjalmar; him we know. But she too, deep down within her, surely has something trustworthy, something sincere. . . .

GINA [*near to tears*]. Then you should have just let me be as I was.

RELLING [*to GREGERS*]. Would it be impertinent if I asked what exactly it is you want in this house?

GREGERS. I want to lay the foundation of a true marriage.

RELLING. Don't you think the Ekdals' marriage is good enough as it is?

GREGERS. It's probably as good a marriage as most, I regret to say. But it has never been a *true* marriage.

HJALMAR. You've never given much attention to the claims of the ideal, Relling.

RELLING. Don't talk rubbish, my lad! Mr. Werle, just let me ask you how many—at a rough guess—how many true marriages you have seen in your life?

GREGERS. I hardly think I've seen a single one.

RELLING. Nor have I.

GREGERS. But I've seen innumerable marriages of the opposite kind. And I've had the chance of seeing at close quarters the havoc a marriage like that can wreak on both parties.

HJALMAR. The whole moral basis of a man's life can crumble beneath his feet—*that* is the terrible thing.

RELLING. Well, I've never actually been married myself, so I can't really judge these things. But one thing I do know: that the *child* is also part of the marriage. And you should leave the child in peace.

HJALMAR. Ah, Hedvig! My poor Hedvig!

RELLING. Yes, you'd better just see that you keep Hedvig out of all this. You are both grown people; God knows you can please yourself how much you want to muck up your own personal affairs. But I'm telling you this: just you be careful the way you treat Hedvig, or else you'll perhaps end up by doing her serious harm.

HJALMAR. Harm?

RELLING. Yes, or else she'll do herself some harm—and maybe others with her.

GINA. But how can you tell a thing like that, Mr. Relling?

HJALMAR. There's no immediate danger for her eyes, is there?

RELLING. None of this has got anything to do with her eyes. But Hedvig is at a difficult age. She might get hold of all sorts of funny ideas.

GINA. Why, that's just what she does do! I don't like the way she's started playing with the fire out in the kitchen. She calls it playing houses on fire. Many a time I'm frightened she *will* set the house on fire.

RELLING. There you are, you see. I knew it.

GREGERS [*to* RELLING]. But how do you explain a thing like that?

RELLING [*disdainfully*]. She's reached the age of puberty, my dear sir.

HJALMAR. As long as the child has *me* . . . ! As long as I can keep body and soul together . . . !

[*There is a knock at the door.*]

GINA. Hush, Hjalmar! There's somebody in the hall. [*Calls.*] Come in.

[MRS. SÖRBY, *in outdoor clothes, comes in.*]

MRS. SÖRBY. Good evening!

GINA [*walks over to her*]. Why, Berta, it's you!

MRS. SÖRBY. Yes, it's me. But perhaps I've come at an awkward time?

HJALMAR. Not at all. A messenger from *that* house . . . !

MRS. SÖRBY [*to* GINA]. To be quite honest, I hoped I'd find the menfolk out at this time of day; I just thought I'd pop in for a little chat and say goodbye.

GINA. Oh? Are you leaving?

MRS. SÖRBY. Yes, first thing tomorrow morning . . . up to Höidal. Mr. Werle left this afternoon. [*Casually to* GREGERS.] He sends his regards.

GINA. Well fancy!

HJALMAR. Mr. Werle's gone, d'you say? And you are going to follow him?

MRS. SÖRBY. Yes. What have you got to say to *that* Mr. Ekdal?

HJALMAR. Watch out, that's all I've got to say.

GREGERS. Let me explain. My father and Mrs. Sörby are going to be married.

HJALMAR. Going to be married!

GINA. Oh, Berta! At last!

RELLING [*with a tremor in his voice*]. Surely this is never true?

MRS. SÖRBY. Yes, my dear Mr. Relling, it's perfectly true.

RELLING. You want to marry again?

MRS. SÖRBY. Yes, that's what it amounts to. Mr. Werle got a special licence, and we'll just have a quiet wedding up at Höidal.

GREGERS. Then I must wish you every happiness, like a good stepson.

MRS. SÖRBY. Thank you, if you really mean it. I can only hope it's going to bring happiness both for me and Mr. Werle.

RELLING. You are safe in hoping that. Mr. Werle never gets drunk— as far as I know, at any rate. And I don't suppose he's in the habit of knocking his wives about either, like our late lamented horse doctor.

MRS. SÖRBY. Oh, let Sörby rest in peace, now. He had his good points too, like everybody else.

RELLING. Mr. Werle has some even better points, I dare say.

MRS. SÖRBY. At any rate he hasn't gone and squandered what was best in him. Any man who does *that* must take the consequences.

RELLING. Tonight I am going to go out with Molvik.

MRS. SÖRBY. You shouldn't, Mr. Relling; please don't—for my sake.

RELLING. There's nothing else for it. [*To* HJALMAR.] You can come too, if you want.

GINA. No thank you. Hjalmar's not going out with you to *them* kind of places.

HJALMAR [*angrily in an undertone*]. Oh, shut up!

RELLING. Goodbye, Mrs.——Werle.

[*He goes out through the hall door.*]

GREGERS [*to* MRS. SÖRBY]. It seems as though you and Dr. Relling know each other pretty well.

MRS. SÖRBY. Yes, we've known each other for years. Once upon a time it looked as if we might have made something of it, the two of us.

GREGERS. Just as well for you that you didn't.

MRS. SÖRBY. Yes, you might well say that. But I've always taken care not to act on impulse. A woman can't just throw herself away, either.

GREGERS. And you're not the least bit afraid I might drop my father a hint about this old affair?

MRS. SÖRBY. You may take it I've already told him myself.

GREGERS. Indeed?

MRS. SÖRBY. Your father knows every conceivable thing that anybody could truthfully think of saying about me. I've told him everything. It was the very first thing I did, when he began to make his intentions plain.

GREGERS. Then I think you must be more than usually frank.

MRS. SÖRBY. Frank is something I've always been. It's the best policy for us women.

HJALMAR. What do you say to that, Gina?

GINA. Oh, we women are so different—some one way, and some another.

MRS. SÖRBY. Well, Gina, I think it's wisest to do things the way I've done them now. And for his part, Mr. Werle hasn't tried to hide anything either. And that's mainly what's brought us together. Now he can sit and talk to me quite openly, just like a child. The whole of his youth and the best years of his manhood, all he heard was a lot of sermonizing about his sins—a healthy and vigorous man like him. And many's the time, from what I've heard, those sermons were about entirely imaginary offences.

GINA. Yes, it's true enough what you say.

GREGERS. If you ladies are going to start on *that* topic, it would no doubt be best if I went.

MRS. SÖRBY. There's no need to go on that account. I won't say another word. But I wanted to make it quite clear to you that nothing's been hushed up and everything's been above board. It might seem as though this is a great piece of luck for me; and so it is, in one way. But at the same time I don't think I'm taking more than I'm giving. I'll never let him down. And I can look after him and take care of him, as nobody else can, now that he'll soon be helpless.

HJALMAR. Be helpless?

GREGERS [*to* MRS. SÖRBY]. Yes, yes. Don't talk about it here.

MRS. SÖRBY. There's no point in hiding it any longer, however much he would like to. He's going blind.

HJALMAR [*with a start*]. Going blind? That's very strange. He's going blind too?

GINA. Lots of people in the same position.

MRS. SÖRBY. And you can imagine what that means for a businessman. Well, I shall try to use my eyes for him as best I can. But now I mustn't stay any longer; I've got so many things to see to at the moment.—Oh yes, something I had to tell you, Mr. Ekdal: if there was anything Mr. Werle could do for you, would you please just approach Graaberg about it.

GREGERS. An offer Hjalmar Ekdal will certainly decline.

MRS. SÖRBY. Indeed? I don't seem to remember him in the past . . .

GINA. No, Berta! Hjalmar doesn't have to take anything from Mr. Werle now.

HJALMAR [*slowly and weightily*]. Give my regards to your future husband and tell him from me that in the near future I intend to call on Graaberg . . .

GREGERS. What! You mean that!

HJALMAR. . . . As I was saying, to call on Graaberg and ask for a statement of the amount I owe his employer. I will pay this debt of honour—ha! ha! debt of honour, that's good! But enough of that. I will repay everything, with five per cent interest.

GINA. But, Hjalmar dear, heaven knows we haven't any money to do that.

HJALMAR. Tell your *fiancé* I am working away steadily at my invention. Tell him the thing that sustains me in this exhausting task is the desire to be rid of a painful burden of debt. That is why I am working on the invention. All the proceeds from it will go towards discharging those obligations imposed on me by your future husband's pecuniary outlay.

MRS. SÖRBY. Something's happened in this house.

HJALMAR. Yes, it has.

MRS. SÖRBY. Very well, goodbye, then! I still had a few things I'd have liked to talk to you about, Gina, but they'd better wait now till another time. Goodbye!

[HJALMAR *and* GREGERS *bow silently.* GINA *accompanies* MRS. SÖRBY *to the door.*]

HJALMAR. Not across the threshold, Gina!

[MRS. SÖRBY *goes;* GINA *shuts the door after her.*]

HJALMAR. There now, Gregers. Now I've got that load of debt off my shoulders.

GREGERS. Soon you will, anyway.

HJALMAR. I think it must be said that my behaviour was most correct.

GREGERS. You are the man I always took you for.

HJALMAR. In certain cases it is impossible to disregard the claim of the ideal. As head of a family there's nothing I can do but grin and bear it. Believe me it's no joke for a man without private means to have to pay off a debt from many years ago, on which, as it were, the dust of oblivion had already settled. But that makes no difference—I have certain human rights, too, that crave satisfaction.

GREGERS [*placing a hand on his shoulder*]. My dear Hjalmar, wasn't it a good thing I came?

HJALMAR. Yes.

GREGERS. So you saw quite clearly how things were—wasn't that a good thing?

HJALMAR [*a little impatiently*]. Yes, of course it was a good thing. But there is one thing that offends my sense of justice.

GREGERS. And what is that?

HJALMAR. The fact that . . . Well, I don't really know if I ought to speak so freely about your father.

GREGERS. Don't mind me at all.

HJALMAR. Well then. . . . You see, what I think is so distressing is the fact that it's now not me who is founding a true marriage, but him.

GREGERS. How can you say that!

HJALMAR. But it's true. Your father and Mrs. Sörby are entering upon a marriage based on full confidence, based on complete and unqualified frankness on both sides; they are not keeping anything back; there's no deception underneath it all. If I might so put it, it's an agreement for the mutual forgiveness of sin.

GREGERS. What of it?

HJALMAR. Well, *there* it all is. But from what you said, you had to go through all this difficult business before you could found a true marriage.

GREGERS. But that's something quite different, Hjalmar. Surely you're not going to compare either yourself or her with those two . . . ? You see what I mean, don't you?

HJALMAR. But I can't get over the fact that there's something in all this that offends my sense of justice. It looks for all the world as though there were no justice at all in things.

GINA. Good gracious, Hjalmar! You mustn't say things like that.

GREGERS. Hm, let's not get ourselves involved in questions like that.

HJALMAR. Yet, on the other hand, I might almost claim to see the guiding finger of fate. He is going blind.

GINA. Oh, perhaps it's not so certain.

HJALMAR. There's no doubt about it. At least we *ought* not to doubt it, for that is precisely what makes it a just retribution. He at one time has blinded a trusting fellow creature. . . .

GREGERS. He has, I regret to say, blinded many.

HJALMAR. And now comes this mysterious implacable power and demands the man's own eyes.

GINA. Ugh, how can you say such awful things! You make me feel scared.

HJALMAR. It profits a man occasionally to immerse himself in the darker things of life.

[HEDVIG, *in her hat and coat, comes in through the hall door, happy and breathless.*]

GINA. You back again already?

HEDVIG. Yes, I didn't want to go any farther. And it was just as well, because I met somebody at the door.

HJALMAR. That must have been Mrs. Sörby.

HEDVIG. Yes.

HJALMAR [*walking up and down*]. I'd like to think you'd seen her for the last time.

[*Silence.* HEDVIG *looks shyly from one to the other as though trying to estimate their mood.*]

HEDVIG [*going over to* HJALMAR, *coaxingly*]. Daddy!

HJALMAR. Well—what is it, Hedvig?

HEDVIG. Mrs. Sörby had something for me.

HJALMAR [*halts*]. For you?

HEDVIG. Yes. It's something for tomorrow.

GINA. Berta has always had some little thing for your birthday.

HJALMAR. What is it?

HEDVIG. Oh, you mustn't know what it is yet. Mother has to bring it to me in bed first thing in the morning.

HJALMAR. Oh, all this secrecy, and me being kept in the dark!

HEDVIG [*hastily*]. But you can see it if you like. A big letter.
[*She takes a letter out of her coat pocket.*]

HJALMAR. A letter, too?

HEDVIG. There's only the letter. I suppose the rest is to come later. But just imagine, a letter! I've never had a letter before. And it says 'Miss' on the front. [*Reads.*] 'Miss Hedvig Ekdal.' Fancy, that's me.

HJALMAR. Let me see the letter.

HEDVIG [*hands it to him*]. There, you see.

HJALMAR. That's old Mr. Werle's writing.

GINA. Are you sure, Hjalmar?

HJALMAR. Look yourself.

GINA. Oh, you don't think I would know, do you?

HJALMAR. Hedvig, may I open the letter . . . and read it?

HEDVIG. Yes, of course you may, if you want to.

GINA. Please, not tonight, Hjalmar. You know it's meant for to-morrow.

HEDVIG [*softly*]. Oh, please let him read it! It's sure to be something nice. And then Daddy will be pleased and we'll all be happy again.

HJALMAR. I may open it, then?

HEDVIG. Yes, Daddy, please do. It will be fun to find out what it is.

HJALMAR. Very well. [*He opens the letter, reads it, and seems a little taken aback.*] What's this . . . ?

GINA. What does it say?

HEDVIG. Yes, Daddy, do tell us.

HJALMAR. Be quiet. [*Reads it through again; he has turned pale, but controls himself.*] It is a deed of gift, Hedvig.

HEDVIG. Well, fancy that! What am I getting?

HJALMAR. Read it yourself.
[HEDVIG *walks over to the lamp and reads for a moment or two.*]

HJALMAR [*in an undertone, clenching his hands*]. The eyes, the eyes . . . and now this letter.

HEDVIG [*interrupts her reading*]. Yes, but it looks to me as though it's Grandfather who is getting it.

HJALMAR [*takes the letter from her*]. Gina—can you understand this?

GINA. I don't know the first thing about it. Tell me what it is.

HJALMAR. Mr. Werle writes to Hedvig to say that her old grand-father needn't bother about doing any more copying, and that in future he can draw one hundred crowns a month straight from the office. . . .

GREGERS. Aha!

HEDVIG. A hundred crowns, Mother. I read that bit.

GINA. That will be nice for Grandfather.

HJALMAR. . . . a hundred crowns, for as long as he needs it. That means, of course, until he's passed away.

GINA. Well, that's him provided for, poor old soul.

HJALMAR. That's not all. You didn't read far enough, Hedvig. After that, it's to come to you.

HEDVIG. To me? All that?

HJALMAR. You are assured a like amount for the rest of your life, he writes. Do you hear that, Gina?

GINA. Yes, I heard.

HEDVIG. Fancy—all that money I'm going to get! [*Shakes him.*] Daddy, Daddy, aren't you glad?

HJALMAR [*moving away from her*]. Glad! [*Walks up and down.*] Oh, this puts quite a new perspective on things! It opens my eyes to all sorts of possibilities. It's Hedvig. She's the one he's being so generous to!

GINA. Yes, because she's the one who's having the birthday. . . .

HEDVIG. You shall have it, all the same, Daddy. You know I'll give all the money to you and Mother.

HJALMAR. To your mother, yes. That's just it.

GREGERS. Hjalmar, this is a trap that's being set for you.

HJALMAR. Could it be another trap, do you think?

GREGERS. When he was here this morning, he said: 'Hjalmar Ekdal is not the man you take him to be.'

HJALMAR. Not the man . . . !

GREGERS. 'Just wait, you'll see,' he said.

HJALMAR. See that I'd let myself be bought off for a price . . . !

HEDVIG. Mother, what is all this about?

GINA. Go and take your things off.

[*Near to tears,* HEDVIG *goes out by the kitchen door.*].

GREGERS. Yes, Hjalmar. Now we'll see who's right, him or me.

HJALMAR [*slowly tears the document in two, and places the pieces on the table*]. There's my answer.

GREGERS. As I expected.

HJALMAR [*goes over to* GINA *who is standing by the stove and says in a low voice*]. Now let's have no more pretence. If this affair was over and done with when you . . . 'got fond' of me as you put it . . . why did he go and arrange things so that we could afford to get married?

GINA. I suppose he thought he'd be able to come and go here as he liked.

HJALMAR. Is that all? Wasn't he afraid of a certain possibility.

GINA. I don't know what you mean.

HJALMAR. I want to know if . . . your child has a right to live under my roof.

GINA [*drawing herself up, her eyes flashing*]. You ask me that!

HJALMAR. I want a straight answer. Is Hedvig mine . . . or . . . ? Well!

GINA [*looking at him coldly and defiantly*]. I don't know.

HJALMAR [*trembling slightly*]. You don't know!

GINA. How should *I* know? A person like *me*. . . .

HJALMAR [*quietly turning away from her*]. This house is no place for me any more.

GREGERS. Think well what you are doing, Hjalmar!

HJALMAR [*putting on his topcoat*]. There's no need to think here, not for a man like me.

GREGERS. Yes there is. There's a tremendous lot to think about. The three of you must remain together if you, Hjalmar, are to win through to that sublime mood of magnanimity and forgiveness.

HJALMAR. I don't *want* to. Never, never! My hat! [*Takes his hat*]. My home has collapsed in ruins about my ears! [*Bursts into tears.*] Gregers, I have no child!

HEDVIG [*who has opened the kitchen door*]. What are you saying? [*Crosses to him.*] Daddy! Daddy!

GINA. There, there.

HJALMAR. Don't come near me, Hedvig! Go away! I can't bear to look at you. Oh, those eyes . . . ! Goodbye.

[*He makes for the door.*]

HEDVIG [*clings tight to him and screams*]. No! No! Don't leave me.

GINA [*shouts*]. Look at the child, Hjalmar! Look at her!

HJALMAR. I will not! I cannot! Let me go. I must get away from all this.

[*He tears himself free of Hedvig and goes out by the hall door.*]

HEDVIG [*with despair in her eyes*]. He's leaving us, Mother! He's leaving us. He's never coming back any more!

GINA. Don't cry, Hedvig. Your father's coming back all right.

HEDVIG [*throws herself sobbing on the sofa*]. No, no, he's never coming back to us again.

GREGERS. You do believe I meant it all for the best, Mrs. Ekdal?

GINA. Yes, I dare say you did. But may God forgive you, all the same.

HEDVIG [*lying on the sofa*]. Oh, I just feel as though I want to die! What have I done? Mother, you must get him to come home again!

GINA. Yes, yes. Be quiet now, and I'll just go out and see if I can see him. [*Puts on her outdoor things.*] He might have gone into Relling's. But you mustn't lie there crying, now. Promise?

HEDVIG [*sobbing convulsively*]. Yes, I'll stop crying. As long as Daddy comes back.

GREGERS [*to* GINA, *who is about to leave*]. Wouldn't it perhaps be better to let him fight his bitter fight to the end.

GINA. Oh, he can do that afterwards. The first thing is to get the child quietened down.

[*She goes out through the hall door.*]

HEDVIG [*sits up and dries her eyes*]. Now you must tell me what's the matter. Why doesn't Daddy want me any more?

GREGERS. You mustn't ask *that* until you've grown up into a big girl.

HEDVIG [*sobbing*]. But I can't go on feeling as awful and miserable as this all the time till I'm grown-up.—I know what it is.—Perhaps I'm not really Daddy's.

GREGERS [*uneasily*]. How could *that* be?

HEDVIG. Mother could have found me, maybe. And now perhaps Daddy's found out. I've read about things like that.

GREGERS. Well, but even so . . .

HEDVIG. Then I think he might have been just as fond of me. Even more. After all, we got the wild duck sent to us as a present, and I'm awfully fond of that.

GREGERS [*leading her off the subject*]. Yes, the wild duck, that's right. Let's talk a bit about the wild duck, Hedvig.

HEDVIG. Poor little wild duck! He can't bear the sight of it, either. D'you know he wanted to wring its neck.

GREGERS. Oh, I'm sure he wouldn't do that.

HEDVIG. No, but that's what he said. And I thought it was rather horrid of Daddy to say that. Because I say a prayer for the wild duck every night, and I ask for it to be delivered from death and all evil.

GREGERS [*looking at her*]. Do you always say your prayers?

HEDVIG. Yes.

GREGERS. Who taught you that?

HEDVIG. I taught myself. It was once when Daddy was very ill, and had to have leeches on his neck. And he said he was at death's door.

GREGERS. Well?

HEDVIG. So I said a prayer for him, after I'd gone to bed. And I've done it ever since.

GREGERS. And now you pray for the wild duck as well?

HEDVIG. I thought I'd better include the wild duck, too. She was so poorly to begin with.

GREGERS. Do you say your prayers in the morning, too?

HEDVIG. Oh no, I don't.

GREGERS. Why don't you say your prayers in the morning as well?

HEDVIG. Well, it's light in the mornings; there's nothing to be afraid of any more.

GREGERS. And the wild duck you are so terribly fond of—your father wants to wring its neck.

HEDVIG. No, he said if *he* had his way, he'd do it. But he said he'd spare it for my sake. That was sweet of him.

GREGERS [*coming closer*]. Supposing you offered to sacrifice the wild duck for *his* sake?

HEDVIG [*rising*]. The wild duck!

GREGERS. Suppose you were ready to sacrifice for him the most precious thing you had in the world?

HEDVIG. Do you think *that* would help?

GREGERS. Try it, Hedvig.

HEDVIG [*quietly, with shining eyes*]. Yes, I will try it.

GREGERS. Have you the proper strength of mind, do you think?

HEDVIG. I'll ask Grandfather to shoot the wild duck for me.

GREGERS. Yes, do that. But not a word to your mother about this!

HEDVIG. Why not?

GREGERS. She doesn't understand us.

HEDVIG. The wild duck. I'll try it first thing tomorrow morning.
    [GINA *enters through the hall door.*]

HEDVIG [*goes to meet her*]. Did you find him, Mother?

GINA. No, but I heard he'd called and gone out with Relling.

GREGERS. Are you sure?

GINA. Yes, the caretaker's wife said so. Molvik was with them too, she said.

GREGERS. At a time like this, when his soul desperately needs solitude to win through . . . !

GINA [*takes her things off*]. Yes, men are funny, they are that. God alone knows where Relling has dragged him off to! I rushed over to Ma Eriksen's, but they weren't there.

HEDVIG [*fighting her tears*]. Oh! What if he never comes back home again!

GREGERS. He will come back. I shall take a message to him in the morning, and you'll see he'll come. Sleep well and rest assured about *that*, Hedvig. Good night. [*Goes out through the hall door.*]

HEDVIG [*throws her arms round* GINA'S *neck, sobbing*]. Mother! Mother!

GINA [*pats her on the back and sighs*]. Ah yes. Relling was right. This is what happens when you get these stupid idiots coming round with their fancy demands.

Act Five

HJALMAR EKDAL'S *studio, in the cold grey light of morning; wet snow is lying on the large panes of the skylight.* GINA, *wearing an overall, comes in from the kitchen carrying a brush and a duster and walks over towards the living-room door. At that moment,* HEDVIG *rushes in from the hall.*

GINA [*stops*]. Well?

HEDVIG. Yes, Mother, I think he's very likely in with Relling . . .

GINA. You see, now!

HEDVIG. . . . because the caretaker's wife said she heard two other people come in with Relling last night.

GINA. I fancied as much.

HEDVIG. But that doesn't help very much if he won't come back here.

GINA. At least I can pop down and talk to him.

[OLD EKDAL, *in dressing-gown and slippers and smoking a pipe, appears at the door of his room.*]

EKDAL. Hjalmar! Isn't Hjalmar at home?

GINA. No, he's gone out.

EKDAL. So early? When it's snowing as heavily as this? Oh well, all right, I can go this morning by myself.

[*He pulls the loft door aside;* HEDVIG *helps him; he goes in and she shuts the door behind him.*]

HEDVIG [*in an undertone*]. Oh, Mother, what will poor Grandfather say when he hears Daddy's going to leave us.

GINA. Oh, rubbish! Grandfather mustn't hear anything about it. What a godsend he wasn't around yesterday when all that business was going on.

HEDVIG. Yes, but . . .

[GREGERS *enters through the hall door*.]

GREGERS. Well? Found any trace of him?

GINA. As like as not, he's down there in with Relling, they say.

GREGERS. In with Relling! Has he really been out with those fellows?

GINA. He has that.

GREGERS. But how *could* he? When he desperately needed solitude and a chance to collect himself. . . .

GINA. Ah, you might well say that.

[RELLING *enters from the hall*.]

HEDVIG [*crosses to him*]. Is Daddy in with you?

GINA [*at the same time*]. Is he there?

RELLING. Indeed he is.

HEDVIG. And you never told us!

RELLING. Yes, I'm a bea . . . east. But I had to see to that other bea . . . east first, the demonic one, I mean, of course. And then I fell right off to sleep, so I . . .

GINA. What's Hjalmar got to say today?

RELLING. He doesn't say anything.

GINA. Hasn't he said anything at all?

RELLING. Not a blessed word.

GREGERS. Ah no, I understand that so well.

GINA. What's he doing with himself, then?

RELLING. He's lying on the sofa, snoring.

GINA. Is he? Yes, Hjalmar's pretty good at snoring.

HEDVIG. Is he asleep? Can he really sleep?

RELLING. It certainly looks like it.

GREGERS. Quite understandable! Torn as he was by the conflict in his soul. . . .

GINA. And him not used to late nights.

HEDVIG. Perhaps it's best for him to get some sleep, Mother.

GINA. That's what I'm thinking too. There's no point then in waking him up too soon. Thanks, Mr. Relling. Now I'd better get the house tidied up a bit first . . . then . . . come and help me, Hedvig.

[GINA *and* HEDVIG *go into the living-room*.]

GREGERS [*turns to* RELLING]. Have you any views on the spiritual turmoil going on in Hjalmar Ekdal?

RELLING. I'm damned if I can see any spiritual turmoil going on in him.

GREGERS. What! At a crisis like this, when his whole life has been put on a completely new basis . . . ? How do you suppose a personality like Hjalmar's . . . ?

RELLING. Personality? Him! If he ever showed any signs of anything as abnormal as a personality, it was all thoroughly cleared out of him, root and branch, when he was still a lad—that I can assure you.

GREGERS. That would seem very strange . . . after being brought up with such affectionate care, as he was.

RELLING. By those two crazy, hysterical maiden aunts of his, you mean?

GREGERS. Let me tell you they were women who never shut their eyes to the claim of the ideal.—Ah, I suppose you are just trying to be funny again.

RELLING. No, I'm in no mood for that. Besides, I know all about it. The amount of rhetoric he's brought up about these two 'soul-mothers' of his! But I don't think he has much to thank them for. Ekdal's misfortune is that in his own little circle he's always been considered a shining light. . . .

GREGERS. And don't you think he is? Deep down within, I mean.

RELLING. *I've* never seen any sign of it. Whether his father thought that—that might well be. The dear Lieutenant has always been a bit of a blockhead, all his life.

GREGERS. He's always been a man with the spirit of a child. *That's* what you don't understand.

RELLING. All right, all right! But when our dear, sweet little Hjalmar began as a student of sorts, he was immediately regarded by his fellow-students too as a man with a brilliant future. He was handsome, too, quite captivating—pink and white—the sort the girls all fall for. And because he was the sentimental sort, and there was something appealing in his voice, and because he learned the knack of reciting other people's poetry and other people's ideas . . .

GREGERS [*indignantly*]. Is this Hjalmar Ekdal you are talking about?

RELLING. It is, with your permission. For that's the inside view of this little demi-god you are grovelling to.

GREGERS. I wouldn't have said I was so completely blind as all that.

RELLING. Oh yes, you are. Pretty well, anyway. You see, *you* are a sick man, too.

GREGERS. You are right there.

RELLING. Well then. In your case there are complications. First there are these troublesome inflamed scruples. But then there's something much worse: you are subject to serious fits of hero-worship. You've always got to go round finding something to admire that's not really any of your business.

GREGERS. I must indeed look for something beyond my own self.

RELLING. But then you go and make such tremendous blunders about these wonderful beings you imagine you see and hear around you. Now you are at it again, coming to another labourer's cottage with that claim of the ideal. There just aren't any solvent people living here.

GREGERS. If you haven't any higher opinion of Hjalmar Ekdal than that, I wonder you find any pleasure at all in being everlastingly in his company·

RELLING. Good God, I'm supposed to be a doctor of sorts, aren't I, though I'm ashamed to say it? I have to do something in the way of looking after the sick who are living in the same house as me, poor things.

GREGERS. Really! Is Hjalmar Ekdal sick too?

RELLING. Pretty nearly everybody's sick, unfortunately.

GREGERS. And what treatment are you giving Hjalmar?

RELLING. The usual. I try to keep his life-lie going.

GREGERS. Life ... lie? I don't think I quite caught ... ?

RELLING. That's right. That's what I said: the life-lie. You see, the life-lie is the stimulating principle.

GREGERS. May I ask what sort of a life-lie Hjalmar has been inoculated with?

RELLING. I'm afraid not; I don't give secrets like that away to quacks. You would just be in a position to mess him up even worse for me. But it's a tried and tested method; I have used it on Molvik as well. I have made him a 'demonic'. That's the particular cure I had to apply to him.

GREGERS. Isn't he demonic?

RELLING. What the devil do you think being demonic means? It's just a bit of silly nonsense I thought up to keep him alive. If I hadn't done that, the poor devil would have succumbed to mortification and despair years ago. Same with the old Lieutenant there. But he's managed to find his own course of treatment.

GREGERS. Lieutenant Ekdal? What about him?

RELLING. Well, what do you think? Him, the great bear-hunter, shooting rabbits there in the loft? There isn't a happier sportsman in the world than that old man when he gets a chance of raking round in there among all the rubbish. He's collected up four or five withered old Christmas trees, and there's no difference for him between them and the whole tremendous living forest of Höidal. The cocks and the hens are the game birds in the tree tops; and the rabbits hopping about the floor, they are the bears that this intrepid he-man goes in pursuit of.

GREGERS. Poor old, unhappy Lieutenant Ekdal. He certainly has had to relinquish a lot of his youthful ideals.

RELLING. While I remember, Mr. Werle junior—don't use this fancy word 'ideals'; we've got a plain word that's good enough: 'lies'.

GREGERS. Are you trying to say the two things are related?

RELLING. Yes, not unlike typhus and putrid fever.

GREGERS. Dr. Relling, I shall not rest until I have rescued Hjalmar Ekdal from your clutches!

RELLING. So much the worse for *him*. Take the life-lie away from the average man and straight away you take away his happiness. [*To* HEDVIG, *who comes in from the living-room.*] Well, now my little wild duck mother, I'll pop down now and see whether that father of yours is still lying there thinking about his wonderful invention.

[*He goes out through the hall door.*]

GREGERS [*approaches* HEDVIG]. I can see from your face nothing's been done.

HEDVIG. What? Oh, the wild duck. No.

GREGERS. Your courage failed you, I imagine, when it came to the point.

HEDVIG. No it isn't that. But when I woke up early this morning and remembered what we'd talked about, it seemed so strange.

GREGERS. Strange?

HEDVIG. Yes, I don't know. . . . Last night when I first heard it, it seemed such a lovely idea; but when I thought about it again after I had slept on it, it didn't seem much of an idea.

GREGERS. Ah no. You could hardly be expected to grow up here without being the worse for it in some way.

HEDVIG. Oh, what do I care about that. If only Daddy would come. . . .

GREGERS. Ah, if only you'd had your eyes opened to what really makes life worth while! If you had the genuine, joyous, courageous spirit of self-sacrifice, then you would see how quickly he would come back to you. But I still have faith in you, Hedvig.

> [*He goes out through the hall door.* HEDVIG *wanders about the room; she is about to go into the kitchen when there is a knocking from within the loft.* HEDVIG *goes over and opens the door slightly.* OLD EKDAL *comes out; he pushes the door to again.*]

EKDAL. Huh! It's not much fun having to go for your morning walk by yourself.

HEDVIG. Didn't you fancy going shooting, Grandfather?

EKDAL. It's not the weather for it today. So dark you can hardly see anything.

HEDVIG. Don't you ever feel like shooting anything else but rabbits?

EKDAL. Aren't the rabbits good enough, then, eh?

HEDVIG. I mean, what about the wild duck?

EKDAL. Ha! ha! Are you frightened I'll go and shoot your wild duck. Not for the world, my dear! I'd never do that!

HEDVIG. No, I dare say you couldn't. It's supposed to be very difficult to shoot wild duck.

EKDAL. Couldn't I? I should jolly well think I could.

HEDVIG. How would you set about it, Grandfather? I don't mean with *my* wild duck, but with others.

EKDAL. I'd try to make sure I shot them in the breast, you know. That's the best place. And then you have to shoot them *against* the lie of the feathers, you see—never with the feathers.

HEDVIG. Do they die then, Grandfather?

EKDAL. I'll say they do . . . if you shoot them properly. Well, I'd better go and tidy myself up. Hm . . . you see . . . hm!

> [*He goes into his room.* HEDVIG *waits a moment, glances towards the living-room door, walks across to the bookcase and, standing on tiptoe, she takes the double-barrelled pistol down off the shelf and looks at it.* GINA *with her brush and duster, enters from the living-room.* HEDVIG *quickly replaces the pistol without being noticed.*]

GINA. Don't go upsetting your father's things, Hedvig.

HEDVIG [*moving away from the bookcase*]. I was just tidying up a bit.

GINA. Go into the kitchen instead and see if the coffee is still hot. I'll take a tray of something down with me when I go and see him.

> [HEDVIG *goes out.* GINA *begins dusting up the studio. A moment later the passage door is hesitantly opened and* HJALMAR EKDAL *looks in. He has his topcoat on, but no hat; he is un-*

washed, his hair is ruffled and untidy; he looks heavy and dull about the eyes.]

GINA [*stops what she is doing, her broom in her hand and looks at him*]. Oh, Hjalmar . . . so you've come back?

HJALMAR [*enters and answers in a dull voice*]. I've come . . . but I'm leaving again at once.

GINA. Yes, yes, I suppose that's all right. But good Lord, there's a sight you look!

HJALMAR. A sight?

GINA. Just look at your good winter coat! Not much use for anything now.

HEDVIG [*at the kitchen door*]. Mother, shall I . . . ? [*Sees* HJALMAR, *screams with joy and runs across to him.*] Oh, Daddy! Daddy!

HJALMAR [*turns aside and waves her away*]. Go away, go away! [*To* GINA.] Take her away from me, I tell you!

GINA [*in a low voice*]. Go into the living-room, Hedvig.

[HEDVIG *goes in silently.*]

HJALMAR [*busying himself pulling out the table drawer*]. I must have my books with me. Where are my books?

GINA. What books?

HJALMAR. My scientific works, of course—the technical periodicals I use for my invention.

GINA [*looks in the bookcase*]. Are these them, without any backs on?

HJALMAR. Of course they are.

GINA [*putting a pile of unbound books on the table*]. Shouldn't I get Hedvig to cut the pages for you?

HJALMAR. I don't need any cutting doing.

[*Short silence.*]

GINA. So you haven't changed your mind about moving out and leaving us, Hjalmar.

HJALMAR [*rummaging among the books*]. I should have thought that was pretty evident.

GINA. Ah, well.

HJALMAR [*angrily*]. I can't stay on here having a knife twisted in my heart every hour of the day.

GINA. God forgive you for thinking I could be that bad.

HJALMAR. Prove to me that . . . !

GINA. Strikes me *you're* the one that should think about proving.

HJALMAR. With a past like yours? There are certain claims . . . I might almost be tempted to call them claims of the ideal. . . .

GINA. What about Grandfather? What's to be done with *him*, poor old fellow?

HJALMAR. I know my duty. The helpless old man will come along with me. I shall go to town and make the necessary arrangements. . . . Hm! [*Hesistates.*] Has anybody seen my hat on the stairs?

GINA. No, have you lost your hat?

HJALMAR. There's no doubt I had it on when I got back last night. But I couldn't find it again today.

GINA. Lord! Wherever did you land up with them two old soaks?

HJALMAR. Oh, don't ask questions about things that don't matter. Do you think I'm in a mood to remember details?

GINA. As long as you haven't caught cold, Hjalmar.
[*She goes out into the kitchen.*]

HJALMAR [*talking angrily to himself in an undertone as he empties the table drawer*]. You are a blackguard, Relling. Nothing but a scoundrel, a shameless rake. If only I could get somebody to do you in!
[*He puts some old letters to one side, finds the torn document of the day before, picks it up and looks at the pieces. As* GINA *comes in he quickly puts them down again.*]

GINA [*puts a breakfast tray on the table*]. Just a drop of something to warm you up, if you can fancy it. And some bread and butter and some cold meat.

HJALMAR [*glances at the tray*]. Meat? Never again under this roof! I don't care if I haven't had a bite for nearly twenty-four hours.— My notes! The start of my autobiography! Where's my diary and all my important papers? [*He opens the living-room door, but draws back.*] There she is again.

GINA. Heavens above, the child has to be somewhere!

HJALMAR. Come out.
[*He stands back; and* HEDVIG, *terrified, comes into the studio.*]

HJALMAR [*his hand on the door handle, speaks to* GINA]. As I spend these last moments in what was once my home, I wish to remain undisturbed by those who have no business to be here. . . .

HEDVIG [*runs across to her mother and asks in a low trembling voice*]. Does he mean me?

GINA. Stay in the kitchen, Hedvig. Or no—go into your own room instead. [*Speaking to* HJALMAR, *as she goes in to where he is.*] Just a minute, Hjalmar. Don't upset everything in that chest of drawers. *I* know where everything is.
[HEDVIG *stands motionless for a moment, frightened and confused; she bites her lip to stop herself from crying, and clenches and unclenches her hands.*]

HEDVIG [*softly*]. The wild duck!
[*She creeps across and takes the pistol from the shelf, opens the loft door a little way, slips in and pulls the door behind her.* HJALMAR *and* GINA *begin to argue in the living-room.*]

HJALMAR [*comes out carrying some exercise books and old sheets of paper, which he puts on the table*]. Oh, that old valise isn't much use. There are thousands of things I've got to hump away with me.

GINA [*follows with the valise*]. Well, leave the other things for the time being; just take a shirt and a pair of pants with you now.

HJALMAR. Phew! All these exhausting preparations!
[*He takes off his topcoat and throws it on the sofa.*]

GINA. Your coffee's getting cold.

HJALMAR. Hm!
[*He takes a mouthful without thinking, and then another.*]

GINA [*dusting the backs of the chairs*]. Your worst job now will be finding another loft big enough for the rabbits.

HJALMAR. What! Have I to drag all those rabbits along with me as well?

GINA. Yes, you know Grandfather couldn't live without his rabbits.

HJALMAR. He'll damn' well have to get used to the idea. There are more important matters in life than rabbits among the things *I'm* having to do without.

GINA [*dusting the bookcase*]. Shall I put your flute in your valise?

HJALMAR. No. I don't want any flute. But give me the pistol.

GINA. You want to take that pistol!

HJALMAR. Yes. My loaded pistol.

GINA [*looks for it*]. It's gone. He must have taken it in with him.

HJALMAR. Is he in the loft?

GINA. Oh, he's bound to be.

HJALMAR. Hm. Poor lonely old fellow.

[*He takes a piece of bread and butter, eats it, and drinks up the coffee.*]

GINA. If only we hadn't let that room, you could have moved in there.

HJALMAR. Me live under the same roof as . . . ! Never! Never!

GINA. But couldn't you shake down for a day or two in the living-room? You could be all on your own there.

HJALMAR. Never within these walls!

GINA. Well, what about going in with Relling and Molvik?

HJALMAR. I don't want to hear their names. Just thinking of them is enough to put me off my food, nearly. . . . Ah no! I must out into the storm and the snow . . . go from house to house seeking shelter for my father and myself.

GINA. But, Hjalmar, you haven't any hat. You've lost your hat, remember?

HJALMAR. Oh, the scum. Can't trust them with anything! I'll have to get myself a hat on the way. [*He takes another piece of bread.*] The necessary arrangements will have to be made. I've no desire to go risking my life as well.

[*He looks for something on the tray.*]

GINA. What are you looking for?

HJALMAR. Butter.

GINA. I'll get some straight away. [*Goes out into the kitchen.*]

HJALMAR [*calls after her*]. Oh, you needn't bother. I can just as well eat it dry.

GINA [*brings a butter dish*]. There you are, now. Supposed to be freshly churned.

[*She pours him a fresh cup of coffee; he sits down on the sofa, spreads more butter on the bread, eats and drinks in silence for a moment or two.*]

HJALMAR. Would I, without being disturbed by anybody—anybody at all—be able to move into the living-room for a day or two?

GINA. Yes, you could very nicely, and for as long as you wanted to.

HJALMAR. Because I can't see much likelihood of moving all Father's things out very fast.

GINA. There's something else as well. You'll have to tell him first about not wanting to live here with the rest of us any longer.

HJALMAR [*pushes his coffee cup away*]. Yes, that's another thing. All these complicated arrangements to be revised. I must consider things first, I must have a breathing space. I can't take all these burdens on in one single day.

GINA. No, and when it's such awful weather, too, on top of everything.

HJALMAR [*fingers Werle's letter*]. I see this paper's lying about here still.

GINA. Yes, I haven't touched it.

HJALMAR. Not that this bit of paper's got anything to do with me . . .

GINA. Well, I've got no use for it.

HJALMAR. . . . but there's not much point in letting it get destroyed, all the same. In all the upset when I move, it could so easily . . .

GINA. I'll take care of it, Hjalmar.

HJALMAR. After all, this letter belongs in the first place to Father; and it will have to be for him to decide whether he wants to make use of it or not.

GINA [*sighs*]. Yes, poor old Father.

HJALMAR. Might as well be on the safe side. . . . Where will I find the paste?

GINA [*goes to the bookcase*]. Here's the paste pot.

HJALMAR. And a brush?

GINA. Here's the brush as well.

[*She brings him the things.*]

HJALMAR [*taking the scissors*]. Just needs a strip of paper along the back. . . . [*He cuts and pastes.*] Far be it from me to lay hands on anybody else's property, least of all on a penniless old man's. And not on . . . the other person's, either, for that matter. . . . There we are. It can stay there for the present. And when it's dry, put it away. I don't want to see that document ever again. Never!

[GREGERS WERLE *comes in from the hall.*]

GREGERS [*a little surprised*]. What! You here, Hjalmar?

HJALMAR [*gets up quickly*]. I had sunk down from exhaustion.

GREGERS. I see you've had some breakfast.

HJALMAR. The body too makes known its claims on us at times.

GREGERS. What have you decided to do?

HJALMAR. For a man such as me there is but one way open. I am in the process of collecting together the more important of my possessions. But it takes time, you understand.

GINA [*a little impatiently*]. Shall I get the room ready for you, or shall I pack the valise?

HJALMAR [*with an irritated glance at* GREGERS]. Pack . . . and get the room ready.

GINA [*takes the valise*]. All right, I'll put the shirt and the other things in, then.

[*She goes into the living-room and shuts the door behind her.*]

GREGERS [*after a short silence*]. I would never have thought that it would end like this. Is it really essential that you should leave house and home?

HJALMAR [*walking about restlessly*]. What do you expect me to do, then?—I am not made for unhappiness, Gregers. Everything around me has got to be nice and secure and peaceful.

GREGERS. But can't that be done? Try. To my mind you've got a firm foundation to build on . . . just begin at the beginning. Remember you've got your invention to live for, too.

HJALMAR. Oh, shut up about the invention. That's probably pretty far away.

GREGERS. Really?

HJALMAR. Good Lord, what in fact do you expect me to invent? Practically everything's been invented by other people already. It gets more and more difficult every day.

GREGERS. After you've put such a lot of work into it!

HJALMAR. It was that devil Relling who put me up to it.

GREGERS. Relling?

HJALMAR. Yes, he was the one who first suggested I was capable of making some special invention in photography.

GREGERS. Aha! . . . It was Relling!

HJALMAR. It's a thing that's made me intensely happy. Not so much because of the invention itself, as because Hedvig believed in it— believed in it with all the passion of a child. . . . What I mean is that I, like a fool, went and imagined that she believed in it.

GREGERS. Do you really suppose Hedvig went out of her way to deceive you!

HJALMAR. I'm ready to think anything now. Hedvig's the stumbling block now. She'll finish up by taking all the sunshine out of my life.

GREGERS. Hedvig! D'you mean Hedvig! How could *she* ever do anything like that?

HJALMAR [*without answering*]. I can't tell you how I loved that child. I can't tell you how happy I felt every time I came home to my modest room and she would come running across to me, with her poor sweet, strained little eyes. Oh, gullible fool that I was! I was so inexpressibly fond of her . . . And I deluded myself into imagining she was equally fond of me, too.

GREGERS. Can you say that *that* was merely a delusion?

HJALMAR. How should I know? I cannot get anything out of Gina. And anyway she has absolutely no understanding of the element of idealism in this situation. But I feel the need to unburden myself to you Gregers. There's this terrible uncertainty—perhaps Hedvig never really loved me at all.

GREGERS. That is something that you might very well get proof of. [*Listens.*] What's that? I thought I heard the wild duck cry.

HJALMAR. It's the wild duck quacking. Father is in the loft.

GREGERS. Is he! [*Joy lights up his face.*] What I was saying is that you might well have proof that poor misunderstood Hedvig does love you!

HJALMAR. Oh, what proof can she give me! I can hardly place any reliance on anything she says.

GREGERS. I'm sure there's nothing deceitful about Hedvig.

HJALMAR. Oh, Gregers, that's just what isn't so certain. Who knows what Gina and that Mrs. Sörby have sat here whispering and gossiping about? And Hedvig's got long ears. Perhaps that deed of gift wasn't so unexpected. I fancy I noticed something of the sort.

GREGERS. What's this that's got into you?

HJALMAR. I have had my eyes opened. You just watch—you'll see this deed of gift is only a beginning. Mrs. Sörby has always been specially fond of Hedvig, and now she has the power to do whatever she wants for the child. They can take her away from me any time they like.

GREGERS. Hedvig will never, never leave *you*.

HJALMAR. Don't you be so sure. What if they stand there with full hands beckoning to her . . . ? Oh, and I can't tell you how much I loved her! How it would have given me supreme happiness just to have taken her by the hand and led her along, as one leads a child that is afraid of the dark through a great empty room! I'm now convinced that the bitter truth is that the poor photographer up in his attic flat never really meant anything to her at all. All she did in her cunning was to take care that she kept on good terms with him until the right moment came.

GREGERS. You don't really believe that yourself, Hjalmar.

HJALMAR. That's the terrible thing, of course. I just don't know what to believe . . . and I'll never know. But surely you don't doubt it's as I say? Ha! ha! You rely too much on people's idealism, my dear Gregers! Suppose the others came along, their hands full, and they called to the child: 'Come away from him. With us, life is at your feet. . . .'

GREGERS [*quickly*]. Well, what then, d'you think?

HJALMAR. If I then asked her: 'Hedvig, are you willing to give up this life for my sake?' [*Laughs scornfully.*] Oh, yes! I must say. You would soon hear the sort of answer I would get!

[*A pistol shot is heard within the loft.*]

GREGERS [*shouts with joy*]. Hjalmar!

HJALMAR. Look at that, now. He has to go shooting!

GINA. Oh, Hjalmar, I think Grandfather's banging away there in the loft by himself.

HJALMAR. I'll look in.

GREGERS [*quickly, excitedly*]. Wait a minute! Do you know what that was?

HJALMAR. Of course I know what it was.

GREGERS. No, you don't. But *I* do. That was the proof!

HJALMAR. What proof?

GREGERS. That was the child's sacrifice. She's got your father to shoot the wild duck.

HJALMAR. Shoot the wild duck!

GINA. Well . . . !

HJALMAR. What's *that* for?

GREGERS. She wanted to sacrifice the most precious thing she had in the world, for your sake. Then, she thought, you couldn't help loving her again.

HJALMAR [*softly, with emotion*]. Oh, that child!

GINA. The things she thinks of!

GREGERS. All she wanted was for you to love her again, Hjalmar; she didn't think she could live without that.

GINA [*fighting back her tears*]. There you see, Hjalmar.

HJALMAR. Gina, where is she?

GINA [*sniffing*]. Poor little thing, she's sitting out in the kitchen, I expect.

HJALMAR [*crosses, and throws open the kitchen door*]. Hedvig, come out! Come to me! [*Looks round.*] No, she's not here.

GINA. Then she must be in her own room.

HJALMAR [*from outside*]. No, she isn't here either. [*Comes in.*] She must have gone out.

GINA. Well, you wouldn't have her anywhere in the house.

HJALMAR. Oh, if only she'd come back home again soon . . . so that I can tell her properly. . . . Everything's going to be all right, Gregers. Now I really believe we can begin life all over again.

GREGERS [*quietly*]. I knew it—knew that redemption would come through the child.

> [OLD EKDAL *appears at the door of his room, dressed in full uniform and busy trying to buckle on his sword.*]

HJALMAR [*astonished*]. Father! Are you there!

GINA. Were you shooting in your room, Father?

EKDAL [*indignantly, coming into the room*]. What d'you mean by going shooting alone, Hjalmar?

HJALMAR [*tense, bewildered*]. Wasn't it you who fired that shot in the loft?

EKDAL. Me? A shot? Huh!

GREGERS [*calls to* HJALMAR]. She's shot the wild duck herself!

HJALMAR. What's all this! [*He rushes to the door of the loft, pulls it to one side, looks in and screams.*] Hedvig!

GINA [*running to the door*]. Dear God, what's the matter!

HJALMAR [*goes in*]. She's lying on the floor!

GREGERS. Hedvig! On the floor!

> [He goes in to HJALMAR.]

GINA [*at the same time*]. Hedvig! [*She goes into the loft.*] Oh no! No!

EKDAL. Aha! *She's* gone off shooting too, eh?

> [HJALMAR, GINA, *and* GREGERS *carry* HEDVIG *into the studio; her right hand hangs down, her fingers still gripping the pistol.*]

HJALMAR [*desperately*]. The pistol's gone off. She's been shot. Call for help! Help!

GINA [*runs into the hall and shouts down*]. Relling! Relling! Dr. Relling! Come up as fast as you can!

> [HJALMAR *and* GREGERS *lay* HEDVIG *down on the sofa.*]

EKDAL [*quietly*]. The forest's revenge!

HJALMAR [*beside her on his knees*]. She'll come round soon. She'll come round. . . . Yes, yes.

GINA [*who has come in again*]. Where's she been shot? I can't see anything. . . .

[RELLING *hurries in, followed closely by* MOLVIK; *the latter has neither waistcoat nor collar, and his coat is flying open*.]

RELLING. What's going on here?

GINA. They say Hedvig has shot herself.

HJALMAR. Come here and help!

RELLING. Shot herself! [*He shifts the table to one side, and begins examining her*.]

HJALMAR [*looking anxiously up at him*]. It can't be anything serious, eh, Relling? She's hardly bleeding. Surely it can't be serious?

RELLING. How did this happen?

HJALMAR. Oh, how do I know . . . !

GINA. She wanted to shoot the wild duck.

RELLING. The wild duck?

HJALMAR. The pistol must have gone off.

RELLING. Hm! Indeed!

EKDAL. The forest's revenge. Still I'm not frightened.

[*He goes into the loft and shuts himself in*.]

HJALMAR. Well, Relling . . . why don't you say something?

RELLING. The bullet hit her in the breast.

HJALMAR. Yes, but she'll be coming round.

RELLING. Can't you see Hedvig is dead?

GINA [*bursts into tears*]. Oh my little one!

GREGERS [*huskily*]. In the briny deep . . .

HJALMAR [*springing up*]. No, no, she *must* live! Oh, for God's sake, Relling . . . just for a moment, just long enough for me to tell her how infinitely I loved her all the time!

RELLING. She was hit in the heart. Internal haemorrhage. She died instantaneously.

HJALMAR. And I drove her away from me like some animal. And in terror she crept into the loft and died, for love of me. [*Sobbing*.] I can never make it up to her again! Never be able to tell her . . . ! [*He clenches his hands and cries to heaven*.] Oh, God on high . . . if Thou *art* there! Why hast Thou done this to me?

GINA. Hush, hush, you mustn't say such terrible things. We had no right to keep her, I dare say.

MOLVIK. The child is not dead; it sleeps.

RELLING. Rubbish!

HJALMAR [*more composed, goes over to the sofa and looks down on* HEDVIG *with folded arms*]. There she lies, stiff and still.

RELLING [*trying to free the pistol*]. It's so tight, so tight.

GINA. Please, Relling, don't force her little fingers. Leave the pistol there.

HJALMAR. She shall take it with her.

GINA. Yes, let her. But she mustn't lie out here for everybody to see. She shall go into her own little room, she shall. Help me with her, Hjalmar.

[HJALMAR *and* GINA *take* HEDVIG *between them.*]

HJALMAR [*as they carry her out*]. Oh, Gina, can you bear this?

GINA. We must help one another. For *now* she's as much yours as mine, isn't she?

MOLVIK [*stretches out his arms and mutters*]. Praised be the Lord. Earth to earth . . . earth to earth. . . .

RELLING [*whispers*]. Shut up, man! You are drunk!

[HJALMAR *and* GINA *carry the body out by the kitchen door.* RELLING *shuts it after them.* MOLVIK *sneaks out into the hall.*]

RELLING [*crosses to* GREGERS]. Nobody's ever going to persuade me this was an accident.

GREGERS [*who has stood horror-stricken, his face twitching*]. Nobody can say how this dreadful thing happened.

RELLING. There was a powderburn on her dress. She must have pressed the pistol right against her breast and fired.

GREGERS. Hedvig has not died in vain. Didn't you see how grief brought out what was noblest in him?

RELLING. Most people feel some nobility when they stand grieving in the presence of death. But how long do you suppose this glory will last in *his* case?

GREGERS. Surely it will continue and flourish for the rest of his life!

RELLING. Give him nine months and little Hedvig will be nothing more than the theme of a pretty little party piece.

GREGERS. You dare say that about Hjalmar Ekdal!

RELLING. We can discuss it again when the first grass starts showing on her grave. Then he'll bring it all up, all about 'the child so untimely torn from a loving father's heart'. Then you'll see him wallowing deeper and deeper in sentimentality and self-pity. Just you watch!

GREGERS. If *you* are right and *I* am wrong, life will no longer be worth living.

RELLING. Oh, life wouldn't be too bad if only these blessed people who come canvassing their ideals round everybody's door would leave us poor souls in peace.

GREGERS [*staring into space*]. In that case I am glad my destiny is what it is.

RELLING. If I may ask—what is your destiny?

GREGERS [*turning to leave*]. To be thirteenth at table.

RELLING. The devil it is!

ANTON CHEKHOV

Three Sisters[†]

A Drama in Four Acts

Characters in the Play

PROZOROV, *Andrey Serghyeevich*
NATASHA (*Natalia Ivanovna*), *his fiancée, afterwards his wife*
OLGA (*Olga Serghyeevna, Olia*) ⎫
MASHA (*Maria Serghyeevna*) ⎬ *his sisters*
IRENA (*Irena Serghyeevna*) ⎭
KOOLYGHIN, *Fiodor Ilyich, master at the High School for boys, husband of Masha*
VERSHININ, *Alexandr Ignatyevich, Lieutenant-Colonel, Battery Commander*
TOOZENBACH, *Nikolai Lvovich, Baron, Lieutenant in the Army*
SOLIONY, *Vassily Vassilich, Captain*
CHEBUTYKIN, *Ivan Romanych, Army Doctor*
FEDOTIK, *Aleksey Petrovich, Second Lieutenant*
RODÈ, *Vladimir Karlovich, Second Lieutenant*
FERAPONT (*Ferapont Spiridonych*), *an old porter from the County Office*
ANFISA, *the Prozorovs' former nurse, an old woman of 80*

The action takes place in a county town

Act One

[*A drawing-room in the Prozorovs' house; it is separated from a large ballroom*[1] *at the back by a row of columns. It is midday; there is cheerful sunshine outside. In the ballroom the table is being laid for lunch.* OLGA, *wearing the regulation dark-blue dress of a secondary*

† Translated by Elizaveta Fen., 1900. Reprinted by permission of the publisher, Penguin Books, Ltd. After this translation was made, an important manuscript text of the play was found in Moscow in 1953; A. R. Vladimirskaya has studied it, and Ronald Hingley has reproduced her findings in Appendix III of *The Oxford Chekhov* (London, 1964), III, 307-12. In my notes I have represented the more significant of the variant readings; I follow Hingley in referring to the text as the Moscow manuscript.
1. A large room, sparsely furnished, used for receptions and dances in Russian houses. [*Translator's note.*]

school mistress, is correcting her pupils' work, standing or walking about as she does so. MASHA, *in a black dress, is sitting reading a book, her hat on her lap.* IRENA, *in white, stands lost in thought.*]

OLGA. It's exactly a year ago that Father died, isn't it? This very day, the fifth of May—your Saint's day, Irena. I remember it was very cold and it was snowing. I felt then as if I should never survive his death; and you had fainted and were lying quite still, as if you were dead. And now—a year's gone by, and we talk about it so easily. You're wearing white, and your face is positively radiant. . . .

[*A clock strikes twelve.*]

The clock struck twelve then, too. [*A pause.*] I remember when Father was being taken to the cemetery there was a military band, and a salute with rifle fire. That was because he was a general, in command of a brigade. And yet there weren't many people at the funeral. Of course, it was raining hard, raining and snowing.

IRENA. Need we bring up all these memories?

[*Baron* TOOZENBACH, CHEBUTYKIN *and* SOLIONY *appear behind the columns by the table in the ballroom.*]

OLGA. It's so warm to-day that we can keep the windows wide open, and yet there aren't any leaves showing on the birch trees. Father was made a brigadier eleven years ago, and then he left Moscow and took us with him. I remember so well how everything in Moscow was in blossom by now, everything was soaked in sunlight and warmth. Eleven years have gone by, yet I remember everything about it, as if we'd only left yesterday. Oh, Heavens! When I woke up this morning and saw this flood of sunshine, all this spring sunshine, I felt so moved and so happy! I felt such a longing to get back home to Moscow!

CHEBUTYKIN [*to* TOOZENBACH]. The devil you have!

TOOZENBACH. It's nonsense, I agree.

MASHA [*absorbed in her book, whistles a tune under her breath*].

OLGA. Masha, do stop whistling! How can you? [*A pause.*] I suppose I must get this continual headache because I have to go to school every day and go on teaching right into the evening. I seem to have the thoughts of someone quite old. Honestly, I've been feeling as if my strength and youth were running out of me drop by drop, day after day. Day after day, all these four years that I've been working at the school. . . . I just have one longing and it seems to grow stronger and stronger. . . .

IRENA. If only we could go back to Moscow! Sell the house, finish with our life here, and go back to Moscow.

OLGA. Yes, Moscow! As soon as we possibly can.

[CHEBUTYKIN *and* TOOZENBACH *laugh.*]

IRENA. I suppose Andrey will soon get a professorship. He isn't likely to go on living here. The only problem is our poor Masha.

OLGA. Masha can come and stay the whole summer with us every year in Moscow.

MASHA [*whistles a tune under her breath*].

IRENA. Everything will settle itself, with God's help. [*Looks through the window.*] What lovely weather it is to-day! Really, I don't know why there's such joy in my heart. I remembered this morning that it was my Saint's day,[2] and suddenly I felt so happy, and I thought of the time when we were children, and Mother was still alive. And then such wonderful thoughts came to me, such wonderful stirring thoughts!

OLGA. You're so lovely to-day, you really do look most attractive. Masha looks pretty to-day, too. Andrey could be good-looking, but he's grown so stout. It doesn't suit him. As for me, I've just aged and grown a lot thinner. I suppose it's through getting so irritated with the girls at school. But to-day I'm at home, I'm free, and my headache's gone, and I feel much younger than I did yesterday. I'm only twenty-eight, after all. . . . I suppose everything that God wills must be right and good, but I can't help thinking sometimes that if I'd got married and stayed at home, it would have been a better thing for me. [*A pause.*] I would have been very fond of my husband.

TOOZENBACH [*to* SOLIONY]. Really, you talk such a lot of nonsense, I'm tired of listening to you. [*Comes into the drawing-room.*] I forgot to tell you: Vershinin, our new battery commander, is going to call on you to-day. [*Sits down by the piano.*]

OLGA. I'm very glad to hear it.

IRENA. Is he old?

TOOZENBACH. No, not particularly. Forty, forty-five at the most. [*Plays quietly.*] He seems a nice fellow. Certainly not a fool. His only weakness is that he talks too much.

IRENA. Is he interesting?

TOOZENBACH. He's all right, only he's got a wife, a mother-in-law and two little girls. What's more, she's his second wife. He calls on everybody and tells them that he's got a wife and two little girls. He'll tell you about it, too. I'm sure of that. His wife seems to be a bit soft in the head. She wears a long plait like a girl, she is always philosophizing and talking in high-flown language, and then she often tries to commit suicide, apparently just to annoy her husband. I would have run away from a wife like that years ago, but he puts up with it, and just grumbles about it.

SOLIONY [*enters the drawing-room with* CHEBUTYKIN]. Now I can only lift sixty pounds with one hand, but with two I can lift two hundred pounds, or even two hundred and forty. So I conclude from that that two men are not just twice as strong as one, but three times as strong, if not more.

CHEBUTYKIN [*reads the paper as he comes in*]. Here's a recipe for falling hair . . . two ounces of naphthaline, half-a-bottle of methyllated spirit . . . dissolve and apply once a day. . . . [*Writes it down in a notebook.*] Must make a note of it. [*To* SOLIONY.] Well, as I was trying to explain to you, you cork the bottle and pass a glass tube through the cork. Then you take a pinch of ordinary powdered alum, and . . .

2. The Feast Day of the saint after whom she was named; a day celebrated like a birthday in many European countries.

IRENA. Ivan Romanych, dear Ivan Romanych!

CHEBUTYKIN. What is it, my child, what is it?

IRENA. Tell me, why is it I'm so happy to-day? Just as if I were sailing along in a boat with big white sails, and above me the wide, blue sky, and in the sky great white birds floating around?

CHEBUTYKIN [*kisses both her hands, tenderly*]. My little white bird!

IRENA. You know, when I woke up this morning, and after I'd got up and washed, I suddenly felt as if everything in the world had become clear to me, and I knew the way I ought to live. I know it all now, my dear Ivan Romanych. Man must work by the sweat of his brow whatever his class, and that should make up the whole meaning and purpose of his life and happiness and contentment. Oh, how good it must be to be a workman, getting up with the sun and breaking stones by the roadside—or a shepherd—or a schoolmaster teaching the children—or an engine-driver on the railway. Good Heavens! it's better to be a mere ox or horse, and work, than the sort of young woman who wakes up at twelve, and drinks her coffee in bed, and then takes two hours dressing. . . . How dreadful! You know how you long for a cool drink in hot weather? Well, that's the way I long for work. And if I don't get up early from now on and really work, you can refuse to be friends with me any more, Ivan Romanych.

CHEBUTYKIN [*tenderly*]. So I will, so I will. . . .

OLGA. Father taught us to get up at seven o'clock and so Irena always wakes up at seven—but then she stays in bed till at least nine, thinking about something or other. And with such a serious expression on her face, too! [*Laughs.*]

IRENA. You think it's strange when I look serious because you always think of me as a little girl. I'm twenty, you know!

TOOZENBACH. All this longing for work. . . . Heavens! how well I can understand it! I've never done a stroke of work in my life. I was born in Petersburg, an unfriendly, idle city—born into a family where work and worries were simply unknown. I remember a valet pulling off my boots for me when I came home from the cadet school. . . . I grumbled at the way he did it, and my mother looked on in admiration. She was quite surprised when other people looked at me in any other way. I was so carefully protected from work! But I doubt whether they succeeded in protecting me for good and all—yes, I doubt it very much! The time's come: there's a terrific thunder-cloud advancing upon us, a mighty storm is coming to freshen us up! Yes, it's coming all right, it's quite near already, and it's going to blow away all this idleness and indifference, and prejudice against work, this rot of boredom that our society is suffering from. I'm going to work, and in twenty-five or thirty years' time every man and woman will be working. Every one of us!

CHEBUTYKIN. I'm not going to work.

TOOZENBACH. You don't count.

SOLIONY. In twenty-five years' time you won't be alive, thank goodness. In a couple of years you'll die from a stroke—or I'll lose my temper with you and put a bullet in your head, my good fellow. [*Take a scent bottle from his pocket and sprinkles the scent over his chest and hands.*]

CHEBUTYKIN [*laughs*]. It's quite true that I never have done any work. Not a stroke since I left the university. I haven't even read a book, only newspapers. [*Takes another newspaper out of his pocket.*] For instance, here. . . . I know from the paper that there was a person called Dobroliubov, but what he wrote about I've not the faintest idea. . . . God alone knows. . . .

[*Someone knocks on the floor from downstairs.*]

There! They're calling me to come down: there's someone come to see me. I'll be back in a moment. . . . [*Goes out hurriedly, stroking his beard.*]

IRENA. He's up to one of his little games.

TOOZENBACH. Yes. He looked very solemn as he left. He's obviously going to give you a present.

IRENA. I do dislike that sort of thing. . . .

OLGA. Yes, isn't it dreadful? He's always doing something silly.

MASHA. 'A green oak grows by a curving shore, And round that oak hangs a golden chain'³ . . . [*Gets up as she sings under her breath.*]

OLGA. You're sad to-day, Masha.

MASHA [*puts on her hat, singing*].

OLGA. Where are you going?

MASHA. Home.

IRENA. What a strange thing to do.

TOOZENBACH. What! Going away from your sister's party?

MASHA. What does it matter? I'll be back this evening. Good-bye, my darling. [*Kisses* IRENA.] And once again—I wish you all the happiness in the world. In the old days when Father was alive we used to have thirty or forty officers at our parties. What gay parties we had! And to-day—what have we got to-day? A man and a half, and the place is as quiet as a tomb. I'm going home. I'm depressed to-day, I'm sad, so don't listen to me. [*Laughs through her tears.*] We'll have a talk later, but good-bye for now, my dear. I'll go somewhere or other. . . .

IRENA [*displeased*]. Really, you are a . . .

OLGA [*tearfully*]. I understand you, Masha.

SOLIONY. If a man starts philosophizing, you call that philosophy, or possibly just sophistry, but if a woman or a couple of women start philosophizing you call that . . . what would you call it, now? Ask me another!

MASHA. What are you talking about? You are a disconcerting person!

SOLIONY. Nothing.

'He had no time to say "Oh, oh!"
Before that bear had struck him low' . . .⁴

[*A pause.*]

MASHA [*to* OLGA, *crossly*]. Do stop snivelling!

[*Enter* ANFISA *and* FERAPONT, *the latter carrying a large cake.*]

3. From the Introduction to N. Pushkin's poem *Russlan and Ludmila*. 4. From I. A. Krylov's fable *The Peasant and The Laborer*.

ANFISA. Come along, my dear, this way. Come in, your boots are quite clean. [*To* IRENA.] A cake from Protopopov, at the Council Office.

IRENA. Thank you. Tell him I'm very grateful to him. [*Takes the cake.*]

FERAPONT. What's that?

IRENA [*louder*]. Tell him I sent my thanks.

OLGA. Nanny, will you give him a piece of cake? Go along, Ferapont, they'll give you some cake.

FERAPONT. What's that?

ANFISA. Come along with me, Ferapont Spiridonych, my dear. Come along. [*Goes out with* FERAPONT.]

MASHA. I don't like that Protopopov fellow, Mihail Potapych, or Ivanych, or whatever it is. It's best not to invite him here.

IRENA. I haven't invited him.

MASHA. Thank goodness.

[*Enter* CHEBUTYKIN, *followed by a soldier carrying a silver samovar. Murmurs of astonishment and displeasure.*]

OLGA [*covering her face with her hands*]. A samovar! But this is dreadful![5] [*Goes through to the ballroom and stands by the table.*]

IRENA. My dear Ivan Romanych, what are you thinking about?

TOOZENBACH [*laughs*]. Didn't I tell you?

MASHA. Ivan Romanych, you really ought to be ashamed of yourself!

CHEBUTYKIN. My dear, sweet girls, I've no one in the world but you. You're dearer to me than anything in the world! I'm nearly sixty, I'm an old man, a lonely, utterly unimportant old man. The only thing that's worth anything in me is my love for you, and if it weren't for you, really I would have been dead long ago. [*To* IRENA.] My dear, my sweet little girl, haven't I known you since the very day you were born? Didn't I carry you about in my arms? . . . didn't I love your dear mother?

IRENA. But why do you get such expensive presents?

CHEBUTYKIN [*tearfully and crossly*]. Expensive presents! . . . Get along with you! [*To the orderly.*] Put the samovar over there. [*Mimics* IRENA.] Expensive presents!

[*The orderly takes the samovar to the ballroom.*]

ANFISA [*crosses the drawing-room*]. My dears, there's a strange colonel just arrived. He's taken off his coat and he's coming up now. Irenushka, do be nice and polite to him, won't you? [*In the door way.*] And it's high time we had lunch, too. . . . Oh, dear! [*Goes out.*]

TOOZENBACH. It's Vershinin, I suppose.

[*Enter* VERSHININ.]

TOOZENBACH. Lieutenant-Colonel Vershinin!

VERSHININ [*to* MASHA *and* IRENA]. Allow me to introduce myself— Lieutenant-Colonel Vershinin. I'm so glad, so very glad to be here at last. How you've changed! Dear, dear, how you've changed!

IRENA. Please, do sit down. We're very pleased to see you, I'm sure.

5. "Dreadful" because in Russia a silver samovar is the traditional gift for a twenty-fifth wedding anniversary.

VERSHININ [*gayly*]. I'm so glad to see you, so glad! But there were three of you, weren't there?—three sisters. I remember there were three little girls. I don't remember their faces, but I knew your father, Colonel Prozorov, and I remember he had three little girls. Oh, yes, I saw them myself. I remember them quite well. How time flies! Dear, dear, how it flies!

TOOZENBACH. Alexandr Ignatyevich comes from Moscow.

IRENA. From Moscow? You come from Moscow?

VERSHININ. Yes, from Moscow. Your father was a battery commander there, and I was an officer in the same brigade. [*To* MASHA.] I seem to remember your face a little.

MASHA. I don't remember you at all.

IRENA. Olia, Olia! [*Calls towards the ballroom.*] Olia, do come!

  [OLGA *enters from the ballroom.*]

IRENA. It seems that Lieutenant-Colonel Vershinin comes from Moscow.

VERSHININ. You must be Olga Serghyeevna, the eldest. And you are Maria. . . . And you are Irena, the youngest. . . .

OLGA. You come from Moscow?

VERSHININ. Yes. I studied in Moscow and entered the service there. I stayed there quite a long time, but then I was put in charge of a battery here—so I moved out here, you see. I don't really remember you, you know, I only remember that there were three sisters. I remember your father, though, I remember him very well. All I need to do is to close my eyes and I can see him standing there as if he were alive. I used to visit you in Moscow.

OLGA. I thought I remembered everybody, and yet . . .

VERSHININ. My Christian names are Alexandr Ignatyevich.

IRENA. Alexandr Ignatyevich, and you come from Moscow! Well, what a surprise!

OLGA. We're going to live there, you know.

IRENA. We hope to be there by the autumn. It's our home town, we were born there. . . . In Staraya Basmannaya Street.

  [*Both laugh happily.*]

MASHA. Fancy meeting a fellow townsman so unexpectedly! [*Eagerly.*] I remember now. Do you remember, Olga, there was someone they used to call 'the lovesick Major'? You were a Lieutenant then, weren't you, and you were in love with someone or other, and everyone used to tease you about it. They called you 'Major' for some reason or other.

VERSHININ [*laughs*]. That's it, that's it. . . . 'The lovesick Major', that's what they called me.

MASHA. In those days you only had a moustache. . . . Oh, dear, how much older you look! [*Tearfully.*] How much older!

VERSHININ. Yes, I was still a young man in the days when they called me 'the lovesick Major'. I was in love then. It's different now.

OLGA. But you haven't got a single grey hair! You've aged, yes, but you're certainly not an old man.

VERSHININ. Nevertheless, I'm turned forty-two. Is it long since you left Moscow?

IRENA. Eleven years. Now what are you crying for, Masha, you funny girl? . . . [*Tearfully.*] You'll make me cry, too.

MASHA. I'm not crying. What was the street you lived in?

VERSHININ. In the Staraya Basmannaya.

OLGA. We did, too.

VERSHININ. At one time I lived in the Niemietzkaya Street. I used to walk from there to the Krasny Barracks, and I remember there was such a gloomy bridge I had to cross. I used to hear the noise of the water rushing under it. I remember how lonely and sad I felt there. [*A pause.*] But what a magnificently wide river you have here! It's a marvellous river!

OLGA. Yes, but this is a cold place. It's cold here, and there are too many mosquitoes.

VERSHININ. Really? I should have said you had a really good healthy climate here, a real Russian climate. Forest, river . . . birch-trees, too. The dear, unpretentious birchtrees—I love them more than any of the other trees. It's nice living here. But there's one rather strange thing, the station is fifteen miles from the town. And no one knows why.

SOLIONY. I know why it is.

[*Everyone looks at him.*]

Because if the station were nearer, it wouldn't be so far away, and as it is so far away, it can't be nearer.

[*An awkward silence.*]

TOOZENBACH. You like your little joke, Vassily Vassilich.

OLGA. I'm sure I remember you now. I know I do.

VERSHININ. I knew your mother.

CHEBUTYKIN. She was a good woman, God bless her memory!

IRENA. Mamma was buried in Moscow.

OLGA. At the convent of Novo-Dievichye.[6]

MASHA. You know, I'm even beginning to forget what she looked like. I suppose people will lose all memory of us in just the same way. We'll be forgotten.

VERSHININ. Yes, we shall all be forgotten. Such is our fate, and we can't do anything about it. And all the things that seem serious, important and full of meaning to us now will be forgotten one day—or anyway they won't seem important any more.

[*A pause.*]

It's strange to think that we're utterly unable to tell what will be regarded as great and important in the future and what will be thought of as just paltry and ridiculous. Didn't the great discoveries of Copernicus—or of Columbus, if you like—appear useless and unimportant to begin with?—whereas some rubbish, written up by an eccentric fool, was regarded as a revelation of great truth? It may well be that in time to come the life we live to-day will seem strange and uncomfortable and stupid and not too clean, either, and perhaps even wicked. . . .[7]

TOOZENBACH. Who can tell? It's just as possible that future genera-

6. The new monastery of the Virgin, the most famous in Moscow.

7. The Moscow ms. has "and perhaps even terribly wicked."

tions will think that we lived our lives on a very high plane and remember us with respect. After all, we no longer have tortures and public executions and invasions, though there's still a great deal of suffering!

SOLIONY [*in a high-pitched voice as if calling to chickens*]. Cluck, cluck, cluck! There's nothing our good Baron loves as much as a nice bit of philosophizing.

TOOZENBACH. Vassily Vassilich, will you kindly leave me alone? [*Moves to another chair.*] It's becoming tiresome.

SOLIONY [*as before*]. Cluck, cluck, cluck! . . .

TOOZENBACH [*to* VERSHININ]. The suffering that we see around us— and there's so much of it—itself proves that our society has at least achieved a level of morality which is higher. . . .

VERSHININ. Yes, yes, of course.

CHEBUTYKIN. You said just now, Baron, that our age will be called great; but people are small all the same. . . . [*Gets up.*] Look how small I am.

[*A violin is played off stage.*]

MASHA. That's Andrey playing the violin; he's our brother, you know.

IRENA. We've got quite a clever brother. . . . We're expecting him to be a professor. Papa was a military man, but Andrey chose an academic career.

OLGA. We've been teasing him to-day. We think he's in love, just a little.

IRENA. With a girl who lives down here. She'll be calling in to-day most likely.

MASHA. The way she dresses herself is awful! It's not that her clothes are just ugly and old-fashioned, they're simply pathetic. She'll put on some weird-looking, bright yellow skirt with a crude sort of fringe affair, and then a red blouse to go with it. And her cheeks look as though they've been scrubbed, they're so shiny! Andrey's not in love with her—I can't believe it; after all, he has got some taste. I think he's just playing the fool, just to annoy us. I heard yesterday that she's going to get married to Protopopov, the chairman of the local council. I thought it was an excellent idea. [*Calls through the side door.*] Andrey, come here, will you? Just for a moment, dear.

[*Enter* ANDREY.]

OLGA. This is my brother, Andrey Serghyeevich.

VERSHININ. Vershinin.

ANDREY. Prozorov. [*Wipes the perspiration from his face*]. I believe you've been appointed battery commander here?

OLGA. What do you think, dear? Alexandr Ignatyevich comes from Moscow.

ANDREY. Do you, really? Congratulations! You'll get no peace from my sisters now.

VERSHININ. I'm afraid your sisters must be getting tired of me already.

IRENA. Just look, Andrey gave me this little picture frame to-day. [*Shows him the frame.*] He made it himself.

VERSHININ [*looks at the frame, not knowing what to say*]. Yes, it's . . . it's very nice indeed. . . .

IRENA. Do you see that little frame over the piano? He made that one, too.

[ANDREY *waves his hand impatiently and walks off.*]

OLGA. He's awfully clever, and he plays the violin, and he makes all sorts of things, too. In fact, he's very gifted all round. Andrey, please, don't go. He's got such a bad habit—always going off like this. Come here!

[MASHA *and* IRENA *take him by the arms and lead him back, laughing.*]

MASHA. Now just you come here!

ANDREY. Do leave me alone, please do!

MASHA. You are a silly! They used to call Alexandr Ignatyevich 'the lovesick Major', and he didn't get annoyed.

VERSHININ. Not in the least.

MASHA. I feel like calling you a 'lovesick fiddler'.

IRENA. Or a 'lovesick professor'.

OLGA. He's fallen in love! Our Andriusha's in love!

IRENA [*clapping her hands*]. Three cheers for Andriusha! Andriusha's in love!

CHEBUTYKIN [*comes up behind* ANDREY *and puts his arms round his waist*]. 'Nature created us for love alone.' . . . [*Laughs loudly, still holding his paper in his hand.*]

ANDREY. That's enough of it, that's enough. . . . [*Wipes his face.*] I couldn't get to sleep all night, and I'm not feeling too grand just now. I read till four o'clock, and then I went to bed, but nothing happened. I kept thinking about one thing and another . . . and it gets light so early; the sun just pours into my room. I'd like to translate a book from the English while I'm here during the summer.

VERSHININ. You read English, then?

ANDREY. Yes. My father—God bless his memory—used to simply wear us out with learning. It sounds silly, I know, but I must confess that since he died I've begun to grow stout, as if I'd been physically relieved of the strain. I've grown quite stout in a year. Yes, thanks to Father, my sisters and I know French and German and English, and Irena here knows Italian, too. But what an effort it all cost us!

MASHA. Knowing three languages in a town like this is an unnecessary luxury. In fact, not even a luxury, but just a sort of useless encumbrance . . . it's rather like having a sixth finger on your hand. We know a lot of stuff that's just useless.

VERSHININ. Really! [*Laughs.*] You know a lot of stuff that's useless! It seems to me that there's no place on earth, however dull and depressing it may be, where intelligence and education can be useless. Let us suppose that among the hundred thousand people in this town, all of them, no doubt, very backward and uncultured, there are just three people like yourselves. Obviously, you can't hope to triumph over all the mass of ignorance around you; as your life goes by, you'll have to keep giving in little by little until you get lost in the crowd, in the hundred thousand. Life will swallow you up, but you'll not quite disappear, you'll make some impression on it. After you've gone, perhaps six more people like you will turn up, then twelve, and so on, until in the end most people will have become like you. So in two or three hundred years life on this old earth of ours will have become marvellously beautiful. Man longs for a life like that, and if it isn't here yet, he must imagine it, wait for it, dream about it, prepare for it, he must know and see more than his father and his grandfather did. [*Laughs.*] And you're complaining because you know a lot of stuff that's useless.

MASHA [*takes off her hat*]. I'll be staying to lunch.

IRENA [*with a sigh*]. Really, someone should have written all that down.

[ANDREY *has left the room, unnoticed.*]

TOOZENBACH. You say that in time to come life will be marvellously beautiful. That's probably true. But in order to share in it now, at a distance so to speak, we must prepare for it and work for it.

VERSHININ [*gets up*]. Yes. . . . What a lot of flowers you've got here! [*Looks round.*] And what a marvellous house! I do envy you! All my life I seem to have been pigging it in small flats, with two chairs and a sofa and a stove which always smokes. It's the flowers that I've missed in my life, flowers like these! . . . [*Rubs his hands.*] Oh, well, never mind!

TOOZENBACH. Yes, we must work. I suppose you're thinking I'm a sentimental German. But I assure you I'm not—I'm Russian. I don't speak a word of German. My father was brought up in the Greek Orthodox faith. [*A pause.*]

VERSHININ [*walks up and down the room*]. You know, I often wonder what it would be like if you could start your life over again—deliberately, I mean, consciously. . . . Suppose you could put aside the life you'd lived already, as though it was just a sort of rough draft, and then start another one like a fair copy. If that happened, I think the thing you'd want most of all would be not to repeat yourself. You'd try at least to create a new environment for yourself, a flat like this one, for instance, with some flowers and plenty of light. . . . I have a wife, you know, and two little girls; and my wife's not very well, and all that. . . . Well, if I had to start my life all over again, I wouldn't marry. . . . No, no!

[*Enter* KOOLYGHIN, *in the uniform of a teacher.*]

KOOLYGHIN [*approaches* IRENA]. Congratulations, dear sister—from the bottom of my heart, congratulations on your Saint's day. I wish you good health and everything a girl of your age ought to have! And allow me to present you with this little book. . . . [*Hands her a book.*] It's the history of our school covering the whole fifty years of its existence. I wrote it myself. Quite a trifle, of course—I wrote it in my spare time when I had nothing better to do—but I hope you'll read it nevertheless. Good morning to you all! [*To* VERSHININ.] Allow me to introduce myself. Koolyghin's the name;

I'm a master at the secondary school here. And a town councillor. [*To* IRENA.] You'll find a list in the book of all the pupils who have completed their studies at our school during the last fifty years. *Feci quod potui, faciant meliora potentes.*[8] [*Kisses* MASHA.]

IRENA. But you gave me this book last Easter!

KOOLYGHIN [*laughs*]. Did I really? In that case, give it me back—or no, better give it to the Colonel. Please do take it, Colonel. Maybe you'll read it some time when you've nothing better to do.

VERSHININ. Thank you very much. [*Prepares to leave.*] I'm so very glad to have made your acquaintance. . . .

OLGA. You aren't going, are you? . . . Really, you mustn't.

IRENA. But you'll stay and have lunch with us! Please do.

OLGA. Please do.

VERSHININ [*bows*]. I see I've intruded on your Saint's day party. I didn't know. Forgive me for not offering you my congratulations. [*Goes into the ballroom with* OLGA.]

KOOLYGHIN. To-day is Sunday, my friends, a day of rest; let us rest and enjoy it, each according to his age and position in life! We shall have to roll up the carpets and put them away till the winter. . . . We must remember to put some naphthaline on them, or Persian powder. . . . The Romans enjoyed good health because they knew how to work *and* how to rest. They had *mens sana in corpore sano.*[9] Their life had a definite shape, a form. . . . The director of the school says that the most important thing about life is form. . . . A thing that loses its form is finished—that's just as true of our ordinary, everyday lives. [*Takes* MASHA *by the waist and laughs.*] Masha loves me. My wife loves me. Yes, and the curtains will have to be put away with the carpets, too. . . . I'm cheerful to-day, I'm in quite excellent spirits. . . . Masha, we're invited to the director's at four o'clock to-day. A country walk has been arranged for the teachers and their families.

MASHA. I'm not going.

KOOLYGHIN [*distressed*]. Masha, darling, why not?

MASHA. I'll tell you later. . . . [*Crossly.*] All right, I'll come, only leave me alone now. . . . [*Walks off.*]

KOOLYGHIN. And after the walk we shall all spend the evening at the director's house. In spite of weak health, that man is certainly sparing no pains to be sociable. A first-rate, thoroughly enlightened man! A most excellent person! After the conference yesterday he said to me: 'I'm tired, Fiodor Ilyich. I'm tired!' [*Looks at the clock, then at his watch.*] Your clock is seven minutes fast. Yes, 'I'm tired,' he said.

[*The sound of the violin is heard off stage.*]

OLGA. Will you all come and sit down, please! Lunch is ready. There's a pie.

KOOLYGHIN. Ah, Olga, my dear girl! Last night I worked up to eleven o'clock, and I felt tired, but to-day I'm quite happy. [*Goes to the table in the ballroom.*] My dear Olga!

8. "I did what I could, let those who are more able do better." 9. "A sound mind in a sound body."

CHEBUTYKIN [*puts the newspaper in his pocket and combs his beard*].
A pie? Excellent!

MASHA [*sternly to* CHEBUTYKIN]. Remember, you mustn't take anything to drink to-day. Do you hear? It's bad for you.

CHEBUTYKIN. Never mind. I've got over that weakness long ago! I
haven't done any heavy drinking for two years. [*Impatiently.*]
Anyway, my dear, what does it matter?

MASHA. All the same, don't you dare to drink anything. Mind you
don't now! [*Crossly, but taking care that her husband does not
hear.*] So now I've got to spend another of these damnably boring
evenings at the director's!

TOOZENBACH. I wouldn't go if I were you, and that's that.

CHEBUTYKIN. Don't you go, my dear.

MASHA. Don't go, indeed! Oh, what a damnable life! It's intolerable. . . . [*Goes into the ballroom.*]

CHEBUTYKIN [*follows her*]. Well, well! . . .

SOLIONY [*as he passes* TOOZENBACH *on the way to the ballroom*].
Cluck, cluck, cluck!

TOOZENBACH. Do stop it, Vassily Vassilich. I've really had enough
of it. . . .

SOLIONY. Cluck, cluck, cluck! . . .

KOOLYGHIN [*gaily*]. Your health, Colonel! I'm a schoolmaster . . .
and I'm quite one of the family here, as it were. I'm Masha's husband. She's got a sweet nature, such a very sweet nature!

VERSHININ. I think I'll have a little of this dark vodka. [*Drinks.*] Your
health! [*To* OLGA.] I do feel so happy with you people!

[*Only* IRENA *and* TOOZENBACH *remain in the drawing-room.*]

IRENA. Masha's a bit out of humour to-day. You know, she got married when she was eighteen, and then her husband seemed the
cleverest man in the world to her. It's different now. He's the
kindest of men, but not the cleverest.

OLGA [*impatiently*]. Andrey, will you please come?

ANDREY [*off stage*]. Just coming. [*Enters and goes to the table.*]

TOOZENBACH. What are you thinking about?

IRENA. Oh, nothing special. You know, I don't like this man Soliony,
I'm quite afraid of him. Whenever he opens his mouth he says
something silly.

TOOZENBACH. He's a strange fellow. I'm sorry for him, even though
he irritates me. In fact, I feel more sorry for him than irritated. I
think he's shy. When he's alone with me, he can be quite sensible and friendly, but in company he's offensive and bullying.
Don't go over there just yet, let them get settled down at the
table. Let me stay beside you for a bit. Tell me what you're thinking about. [*A pause.*] You're twenty . . . and I'm not thirty yet myself. What years and years we still have ahead of us, a whole long
succession of years, all full of my love for you! . . .

IRENA. Don't talk to me about love, Nikolai Lvovich.

TOOZENBACH [*not listening*]. Oh, I long so passionately for life, I
long to work and strive so much, and all this longing is somehow
mingled with my love for you, Irena. And just because you happen

to be beautiful, life appears beautiful to me! What are you think-ing about?

IRENA. You say that life is beautiful. Maybe it is—but what if it only seems to be beautiful? Our lives, I mean the lives of us three sisters, haven't been beautiful up to now. The truth is that life has been stifling us, like weeds in a garden. I'm afraid I'm crying. . . . So unnecessary. . . . [*Quickly dries her eyes and smiles.*] We must work, work! The reason we feel depressed and take such a gloomy view of life is that we've never known what it is to make a real effort. We're the children of parents who despised work. . . .

[*Enter* NATALIA IVANOVNA. *She is wearing a pink dress with a green belt.*]

NATASHA. They've gone in to lunch already. . . . I'm late. . . . [*Glances at herself in a mirror, adjusts her dress.*] My hair seems to be all right. . . . [*Catches sight of* IRENA.] My dear Irena Serghyeevna, congratulations! [*Gives her a vigorous and prolonged kiss.*] You've got such a lot of visitors. . . . I feel quite shy. . . . How do you do, Baron?

OLGA [*enters the drawing-room*]. Oh, there you are, Natalia Ivanovna! How are you, my dear?

[*They kiss each other.*]

NATASHA. Congratulations! You've such a lot of people here, I feel dreadfully shy. . . .

OLGA. It's all right, they're all old friends. [*Alarmed, dropping her voice.*] You've got a green belt on! My dear, that's surely a mis-take!

NATASHA. Why, is it a bad omen, or what?

OLGA. No, but it just doesn't go with your dress . . . it looks so strange. . . .

NATASHA [*tearfully*]. Really? But it isn't really green, you know, it's a sort of dull colour. . . . [*Follows* OLGA *to the ballroom.*]

[*All are now seated at the table; the drawing-room is empty.*]

KOOLYGHIN. Irena, you know, I do wish you'd find yourself a good husband. In my view it's high time you got married.

CHEBUTYKIN. You ought to get yourself a nice little husband, too, Natalia Ivanovna.

KOOLYGHIN. Natalia Ivanovna already has a husband in view.

MASHA [*strikes her plate with her fork*].[1] A glass of wine for me, please! Three cheers for our jolly old life! We keep our end up, we do!

KOOLYGHIN. Masha, you won't get more than five out of ten for good conduct!

VERSHININ. I say, this liqueur's very nice. What is it made of?

SOLIONY. Black beetles!

IRENA. Ugh! ugh! How disgusting!

OLGA. We're having roast turkey for dinner to-night, and then apple tart. Thank goodness, I'll be here all day to-day . . . this evening, too. You must all come this evening.

---

1. This piece of business is omitted in the Moscow ms.

VERSHININ. May I come in the evening, too?

IRENA. Yes, please do.

NATASHA. They don't stand on ceremony here.

CHEBUTYKIN. 'Nature created us for love alone.' . . . [*Laughs.*]

ANDREY [*crossly*]. Will you stop it, please? Aren't you tired of it yet?

> [FEDOTIK *and* RODÈ *come in with a large basket of flowers.*]

FEDOTIK. Just look here, they're having lunch already!

RODÈ [*in a loud voice*]. Having their lunch? So they are, they're having lunch already.

FEDOTIK. Wait half a minute. [*Takes a snapshot.*] One! Just one minute more! . . . [*Takes another snapshot.*] Two! All over now.

> [*They pick up the basket and go into the ballroom where they are greeted uproariously.*]

RODÈ [*loudly*]. Congratulations, Irena Serghyeevna! I wish you all the best, everything you'd wish for yourself! Gorgeous weather to-day, absolutely marvellous. I've been out walking the whole morning with the boys. You do know that I teach gym at the high school, don't you? . . .

FEDOTIK. You may move now, Irena Serghyeevna, that is, if you want to. [*Takes a snapshot.*] You do look attractive to-day. [*Takes a top out of his pocket.*] By the way, look at this top. It's got a wonderful hum.

IRENA. What a sweet little thing!

MASHA. 'A green oak grows by a curving shore, And round that oak hangs a golden chain.' . . . A green chain around that oak. . . . [*Peevishly.*] Why do I keep on saying that? Those lines have been worrying me all day long!

KOOLYGHIN. Do you know, we're thirteen at table?

RODÈ [*loudly*]. You don't really believe in these old superstitions, do you? [*Laughter.*]

KOOLYGHIN. When thirteen people sit down to table, it means that some of them are in love. Is it you, by any chance, Ivan Romanych?

CHEBUTYKIN. Oh, I'm just an old sinner. . . . But what I can't make out is why Natalia Ivanovna looks so embarrassed.

> [*Loud laughter.* NATASHA *runs out into the drawing-room,* ANDREY *follows her.*]

ANDREY. Please, Natasha, don't take any notice of them! Stop . . . wait a moment. . . . Please!

NATASHA. I feel so ashamed. . . . I don't know what's the matter with me, and they're all laughing at me. It's awful of me to leave the table like that, but I couldn't help it. . . . I just couldn't. . . . [*Covers her face with her hands.*]

ANDREY. My dear girl, please, please don't get upset. Honestly, they don't mean any harm, they're just teasing. My dear, sweet girl, they're really good-natured folks, they all are, and they're fond of us both. Come over to the window, they can't see us there. . . . [*Looks round.*]

NATASHA. You see, I'm not used to being with a lot of people.

ANDREY. Oh, how young you are, Natasha, how wonderfully, beautifully young! My dear, sweet girl, don't get so upset! Do believe me, believe me. . . . I'm so happy, so full of love, of joy. . . . No, they can't see us here! They can't see us! How did I come to love you, when was it? . . . I don't understand anything. My precious, my sweet, my innocent girl, please—I want you to marry me! I love you, I love you as I've never loved anybody. . . . [*Kisses her.*]

[*Enter two officers and, seeing* NATASHA *and* ANDREY *kissing, stand and stare in amazement.*]

CURTAIN

Act Two

The scene is the same as in Act I
[*It is eight o'clock in the evening. The faint sound of an accordion is heard coming from the street.*

The stage is unlit. Enter NATALIA IVANOVNA *in a dressing-gown, carrying a candle. She crosses the stage and stops by the door leading to* ANDREY'S *room.*]

NATASHA. What are you doing, Andriusha? Reading? It's all right, I only wanted to know. . . . [*Goes to another door, opens it, looks inside and shuts it again.*] No one's left a light anywhere. . . .

ANDREY [*enters with a book in his hand*]. What is it, Natasha?

NATASHA. I was just going round to see if anyone had left a light anywhere. It's carnival week, and the servants are so excited about it . . . anything might happen! You've got to watch them. Last night about twelve o'clock I happened to go into the dining-room, and—would you believe it?—there was a candle alight on the table. I've not found out who lit it. [*Puts the candle down.*] What time is it?

ANDREY [*glances at his watch*]. Quarter past eight.

NATASHA. And Olga and Irena still out. They aren't back from work yet, poor things! Olga's still at some teachers' conference, and Irena's at the post office. [*Sighs.*] This morning I said to Irena: 'Do take care of yourself, my dear.' But she won't listen. Did you say it was a quarter past eight? I'm afraid Bobik is not at all well. Why does he get so cold? Yesterday he had a temperature, but to-day he feels quite cold when you touch him. . . . I'm so afraid!

ANDREY. It's all right, Natasha. The boy's well enough.

NATASHA. Still, I think he ought to have a special diet. I'm so anxious about him. By the way, they tell me that some carnival party's supposed to be coming here soon after nine. I'd rather they didn't come, Andriusha.

ANDREY. Well, I really don't know what I can do. They've been asked to come.

NATASHA. This morning the dear little fellow woke up and looked at me, and then suddenly he smiled. He recognized me, you see. 'Good morning, Bobik,' I said, 'good morning, darling precious!' And then he laughed. Babies understand everything, you know, they understand us perfectly well. Anyway, Andriusha, I'll tell the servants not to let that carnival party in.

ANDREY [*irresolutely*]. Well . . . it's really for my sisters to decide, isn't it? It's their house, after all.

NATASHA. Yes, it's their house as well. I'll tell them, too. . . . They're so kind. . . . [*Walks off.*] I've ordered sour milk for supper. The doctor says you ought to eat nothing but sour milk, or you'll never get any thinner. [*Stops.*] Bobik feels so cold. I'm afraid his room is too cold for him. He ought to move into a warmer room, at least until the warm weather comes. Irena's room, for instance—that's just a perfect room for a baby: it's dry, and it gets the sun all day long. We must tell her: perhaps she'd share Olga's room for a bit. . . . In any case, she's never at home during the day, she only sleeps there. . . . [*A pause.*] Andriusha, why don't you say anything?

ANDREY. I was just day-dreaming. . . . There's nothing to say, anyway. . . .

NATASHA. Well. . . . What was it I was going to tell you? Oh, yes! Ferapont from the Council Office wants to see you about something.

ANDREY [*Yawns*]. Tell him to come up.

[NATASHA *goes out.* ANDREY, *bending over the candle which she has left behind, begins to read his book. Enter* FERAPONT *in an old shabby overcoat, his collar turned up, his ears muffled in a scarf.*]

ANDREY. Hullo, old chap! What did you want to see me about?

FERAPONT. The chairman's sent you the register and a letter or something. Here they are. [*Hands him the book and the letter.*]

ANDREY. Thanks. That's all right. Incidentally, why have you come so late? It's gone eight already.

FERAPONT. What's that?

ANDREY [*raising his voice*]. I said, why have you come so late? It's gone eight already.

FERAPONT. That's right. It was still daylight when I came first, but they wouldn't let me see you. The master's engaged, they said. Well, if you're engaged, you're engaged. I'm not in a hurry. [*Thinking that* ANDREY *has said something.*] What's that?

ANDREY. Nothing. [*Turns over the pages of the register.*] To-morrow's Friday, there's no meeting, but I'll go to the office just the same . . . do some work. I'm so bored at home! . . . [*A pause.*] Yes, my dear old fellow, how things do change, what a fraud life is! So strange! To-day I picked up this book, just out of boredom, because I hadn't anything to do. It's a copy of some lectures I attended at the University. . . . Good Heavens! Just think—I'm secretary of the local council now, and Protopopov's chairman, and the most I can ever hope for is to become a member of the council myself! I—a member of the local council! I, who dream every night that I'm a professor in Moscow University, a famous academician, the pride of all Russia!

FERAPONT. I'm sorry, I can't tell you. I don't hear very well.

ANDREY. If you could hear properly I don't think I'd be talking to you like this. I must talk to someone, but my wife doesn't seem to understand me, and as for my sisters . . . I'm afraid of them for some reason or other, I'm afraid of them laughing at me and pulling my leg. . . . I don't drink and I don't like going to pubs, but my word! how I'd enjoy an hour or so at Tyestov's, or the Great Moscow Restaurant! Yes, my dear fellow, I would indeed!

FERAPONT. The other day at the office a contractor was telling me about some business men who were eating pancakes in Moscow. One of them ate forty pancakes and died. It was either forty or fifty, I can't remember exactly.

ANDREY. You can sit in some huge restaurant in Moscow without knowing anyone, and no one knowing you; yet somehow you don't feel that you don't belong there. . . . Whereas here you know everybody, and everybody knows you, and yet you don't feel you belong here, you feel you don't belong at all. . . . You're lonely and you feel a stranger.

FERAPONT. What's that? [*A pause.*] It was the same man that told me—of course, he may have been lying—he said that there's an enormous rope stretched right across Moscow.

ANDREY. Whatever for?

FERAPONT. I'm sorry, I can't tell you. That's what he said.

ANDREY. What nonsense! [*Reads the book.*] Have you ever been to Moscow?

FERAPONT [*after a pause*]. No. It wasn't God's wish. [*A pause.*] Shall I go now?

ANDREY. Yes, you may go. Good-bye.

    [FERAPONT *goes out.*]

Good-bye. [*Reading.*] Come in the morning to take some letters. . . . You can go now. [*A pause.*] He's gone.

    [*A bell rings.*]

Yes, that's how it is. . . . [*Stretches and slowly goes to his room.*] [*Singing is heard off stage; a nurse is putting a baby to sleep. Enter* MASHA *and* VERSHININ. *While they talk together, a maid lights a lamp and candles in the ballroom.*]

MASHA. I don't know. [*A pause.*] I don't know. Habit's very important, of course. For instance, after Father died, for a long time we couldn't get accustomed to the idea that we hadn't any orderlies to wait on us. But, habit apart, I think it's quite right what I was saying. Perhaps it's different in other places, but in this town the military certainly do seem to be the nicest and most generous and best-mannered people.

VERSHININ. I'm thirsty. I could do with a nice glass of tea.

MASHA [*glances at her watch*]. They'll bring it in presently. You see, they married me off when I was eighteen. I was afraid of my husband because he was a school-master, and I had only just left school myself. He seemed terribly learned then, very clever and important. Now it's quite different, unfortunately.

VERSHININ. Yes. . . . I see. . . .

MASHA. I don't say anything against my husband—I'm used to him now—but there are such a lot of vulgar and unpleasant and offensive people among the other civilians. Vulgarity upsets me, it makes me feel insulted, I actually suffer when I meet someone who lacks refinement and gentle manners, and courtesy. When I'm with the other teachers, my husband's friends, I just suffer.

VERSHININ. Yes, of course. But I should have thought that in a town like this the civilians and the army people were equally uninteresting. There's nothing to choose between them. If you talk to any educated person here, civilian or military, he'll generally tell you that he's just worn out. It's either his wife, or his house, or his estate, or his horse, or something. . . . We Russians are capable of such elevated thoughts—then why do we have such low ideals in practical life? Why is it, why?

MASHA. Why?

VERSHININ. Yes, why does his wife wear him out, why do his children wear him out? And what about *him* wearing out his wife and children?

MASHA. You're a bit low-spirited to-day, aren't you?

VERSHININ. Perhaps. I haven't had any dinner to-day. I've had nothing to eat since morning. One of my daughters is a bit off colour, and when the children are ill, I get so worried. I feel utterly conscience-stricken at having given them a mother like theirs. Oh, if only you could have seen her this morning! What a despicable woman! We started quarrelling at seven o'clock, and at nine I just walked out and slammed the door. [*A pause.*] I never talk about these things in the ordinary way. It's a strange thing, but you're the only person I feel I dare complain to. [*Kisses her hand.*] Don't be angry with me. I've nobody, nobody but you. . . . [*A pause.*]

MASHA. What a noise the wind's making in the stove! Just before Father died the wind howled in the chimney just like that.

VERSHININ. Are you superstitious?

MASHA. Yes.

VERSHININ. How strange. [*Kisses her hand.*] You really are a wonderful creature, a marvellous creature! Wonderful, marvellous! It's quite dark here, but I can see your eyes shining.

MASHA [*moves to another chair*]. There's more light over here.

VERSHININ. I love you, I love you, I love you. . . . I love your eyes, I love your movements. . . . I dream about them. A wonderful, marvellous being!

MASHA [*laughing softly*]. When you talk to me like that, somehow I can't help laughing, although I'm afraid at the same time. Don't say it again, please. [*Half-audibly.*] Well, no . . . go on. I don't mind. . . . [*Covers her face with her hands.*] I don't mind. . . . Someone's coming. . . . Let's talk about something else. . . .

[*Enter* IRENA *and* TOOZENBACH *through the ballroom.*]

TOOZENBACH. I have a triple-barrelled name—Baron Toozenbach-Krone-Alschauer—but actually I'm a Russian. I was baptized in the Greek-Orthodox faith, just like yourself. I haven't really got any German characteristics, except maybe the obstinate patient way I keep on pestering you. Look how I bring you home every evening.

IRENA. How tired I am!

TOOZENBACH. And I'll go on fetching you from the post office and bringing you home every evening for the next twenty years—unless you send me away. . . . [*Noticing* MASHA *and* VERSHININ, *with pleasure.*] Oh, it's you! How are you?

IRENA. Well, here I am, home at last! [*To* MASHA.] A woman came into the post office just before I left. She wanted to send a wire to her brother in Saratov to tell him her son had just died, but she couldn't remember the address. So we had to send the wire without an address, just to Saratov. She was crying and I was rude to her, for no reason at all. 'I've no time to waste,' I told her. So stupid of me. We're having the carnival crowd to-day, aren't we?

MASHA. Yes.

IRENA [*sits down*]. How nice it is to rest! I am tired!

TOOZENBACH [*smiling*]. When you come back from work, you look so young, so pathetic, somehow. . . . [*A pause.*]

IRENA. I'm tired. No, I don't like working at the post office, I don't like it at all.

MASHA. You've got thinner. . . . [*Whistles.*] You look younger, too, and your face looks quite boyish.

TOOZENBACH. It's the way she does her hair.

IRENA. I must look for another job. This one doesn't suit me. It hasn't got what I always longed for and dreamed about. It's the sort of work you do without inspiration, without even thinking.

[*Someone knocks at the floor from below.*]

That's the Doctor knocking. [*To* TOOZENBACH.] Will you answer him, dear? . . . I can't. . . . I'm so tired.

TOOZENBACH [*knocks on the floor*].

IRENA. He'll be up in a moment. We must do something about all this. Andrey and the Doctor went to the club last night and lost at cards again. They say Andrey lost two hundred roubles.

MASHA [*with indifference*]. Well, what are we to do about it?

IRENA. He lost a fortnight ago, and he lost in December, too. I wish to goodness he'd lose everything we've got, and soon, too, and then perhaps we'd move out of this place. Good Heavens, I dream of Moscow every night. Sometimes I feel as if I were going mad. [*Laughs.*] We're going to Moscow in June. How many months are there till June? . . . February, March, April, May . . . nearly half-a-year!

MASHA. We must take care that Natasha doesn't get to know about him losing at cards.

IRENA. I don't think she cares.

[*Enter* CHEBUTYKIN. *He has been resting on his bed since dinner and has only just got up. He combs his beard, then sits down at the table and takes out a newspaper.*]

MASHA. There he is. Has he paid his rent yet?

IRENA [*laughs*]. No. Not a penny for the last eight months. I suppose he's forgotten.

MASHA [*laughs*]. How solemn he looks sitting there!
  [*They all laugh. A pause.*]
IRENA. Why don't you say something, Alexandr Ignatyevich?
VERSHININ. I don't know. I'm just longing for some tea. I'd give my
  life for a glass of tea! I've had nothing to eat since morning. . . .
CHEBUTYKIN. Irena Serghyeevna!
IRENA. What is it?
CHEBUTYKIN. Please come here. V*enez ici!*
  [IRENA *goes over to him and sits down at the table.*]
  I can't do without you.
  [IRENA *lays out the cards for a game of patience.*]
VERSHININ. Well, if we can't have any tea, let's do a bit of philosophiz-
  ing, anyway.
TOOZENBACH. Yes, let's. What about?
VERSHININ. What about? Well . . . let's try to imagine what life will
  be like after we're dead, say in two or three hundred years.
TOOZENBACH. All right, then. . . . After we're dead, people will fly
  about in balloons, the cut of their coats will be different, the sixth
  sense will be discovered, and possibly even developed and used, for
  all I know. . . . But I believe life itself will remain the same; it will
  still be difficult and full of mystery and full of happiness. And in a
  thousand years' time people will still be sighing and complaining: 'How hard this business of living is!'—and yet they'll still be
  scared of death and unwilling to die, just as they are now.
VERSHININ [*after a moment's thought*]. Well, you know . . . how shall
  I put it? I think everything in the world is bound to change gradually—in fact, it's changing before our very eyes. In two or three
  hundred years, or maybe a thousand years—it doesn't matter how
  long exactly—life will be different. It will be happy. Of course,
  we shan't be able to enjoy that future life, but all the same, what
  we're living for now is to create it, we work and . . . yes, we suffer
  in order to create it. That's the goal of our life, and you might
  say that's the only happiness we shall ever achieve.
MASHA [*laughs quietly*].
TOOZENBACH. Why are you laughing?
MASHA. I don't know. I've been laughing all day to-day.
VERSHININ [*to* TOOZENBACH]. I went to the same cadet school as you
  did but I never went on to the Military Academy. I read a great
  deal, of course, but I never know what books I ought to choose,
  and probably I read a lot of stuff that's not worth anything. But
  the longer I live the more I seem to long for knowledge. My hair's
  going grey and I'm getting on in years, and yet how little I know,
  how little! All the same, I think I do know one thing which is not
  only true but also most important. I'm sure of it. Oh, if only I
  could convince you that there's not going to be any happiness for
  our own generation, that there mustn't be and won't be. . . .
  We've just got to work and work. All the happiness is reserved
  for our descendants, our remote descendants. [*A pause.*] Anyway,
  if I'm not to be happy, then at least my children's children will
  be.

[FEDOTIK *and* RODÈ *enter the ballroom; they sit down and sing quietly, one of them playing on a guitar.*]

TOOZENBACH. So you won't even allow us to dream of happiness! But what if I *am* happy?

VERSHININ. You're not.

TOOZENBACH [*flinging up his hands and laughing*]. We don't understand one another, that's obvious. How can I convince you?

MASHA [*laughs quietly*].

TOOZENBACH [*holds up a finger to her*]. Show a finger to her and she'll laugh! [*To* VERSHININ.] And life will be just the same as ever not merely in a couple of hundred years' time, but in a million years. Life doesn't change, it always goes on the same; it follows its own laws, which don't concern us, which we can't discover anyway. Think of the birds that migrate in the autumn, the cranes, for instance: they just fly on and on. It doesn't matter what sort of thoughts they've got in their heads, great thoughts or little thoughts, they just fly on and on, not knowing where or why. And they'll go on flying no matter how many philosophers they happen to have flying with them. Let them philosophize as much as they like, as long as they go on flying.

MASHA. Isn't there some meaning?

TOOZENBACH. Meaning? . . . Look out there, it's snowing. What's the meaning of that? [*A pause.*]

MASHA. I think a human being has got to have some faith, or at least he's got to seek faith. Otherwise his life will be empty, empty. . . . How can you live and not know why the cranes fly, why children are born, why the stars shine in the sky! . . . You must either know why you live, or else . . . nothing matters . . . everything's just wild grass. . . . [*A pause.*]

VERSHININ. All the same, I'm sorry my youth's over.

MASHA. 'It's a bore to be alive in this world, friends,' that's what Gogol[2] says.

TOOZENBACH. And I feel like saying: it's hopeless arguing with you, friends! I give you up.

CHEBUTYKIN [*reads out of the paper*]. Balsac's marriage took place at Berdichev.[3]

IRENA [*sings softly to herself*].

CHEBUTYKIN. Must write this down in my notebook. [*Writes.*] Balsac's marriage took place at Berdichev. [*Reads on.*]

IRENA [*playing patience, pensively*]. Balsac's marriage took place at Berdichev.

TOOZENBACH. Well, I've thrown in my hand. Did you know that I'd sent in my resignation, Maria Serghyeevna?

MASHA. Yes, I heard about it. I don't see anything good in it, either. I don't like civilians.

TOOZENBACH. Never mind. [*Gets up.*] What sort of a soldier do I make, anyway? I'm not even good-looking. Well, what does it

2. Russian novelist and play wright (1809-52).
3. A town in Western Russia well known for its almost exclusively Jewish population [*Translator's note*]. A notoriously ugly, run-down place.

matter? I'll work. I'd like to do such a hard day's work that when I came home in the evening I'd fall on my bed exhausted and go to sleep at once. [*Goes to the ballroom.*] I should think working men sleep well at nights!

FEDOTIK [*to* IRENA]. I've got you some coloured crayons at Pyzhikov's, in Moscow Street. And this little penknife, too. . . .

IRENA. You still treat me as if I were a little girl. I wish you'd remember I'm grown up now. [*Takes the crayons and the penknife, joyfully.*] They're awfully nice!

FEDOTIK. Look, I bought a knife for myself, too. You see, it's got another blade here, and then another . . . this thing's for cleaning your ears, and these are nail-scissors, and this is for cleaning your nails. . . .

RODÈ [*in a loud voice*]. Doctor, how old are you?

CHEBUTYKIN. I? Thirty-two.

    [*Laughter*]

FEDOTIK. I'll show you another kind of patience. [*Sets out the cards.*]
    [*The samovar is brought in, and* ANFISA *attends to it. Shortly afterwards* NATASHA *comes in and begins to fuss around the table.*]

SOLIONY [*enters, bows to the company and sits down at the table*].

VERSHININ. What a wind, though!

MASHA. Yes. I'm tired of winter. I've almost forgotten what summer is like.

IRENA [*playing patience*]. It's coming out. We'll get to Moscow!

FEDOTIK. No, it's not coming out. You see, the eight has to go on the two of spades. [*Laughs.*] That means you won't go to Moscow.

CHEBUTYKIN [*reads the paper*]. Tzitzikar.[4] Smallpox is raging. . . .

ANFISA [*goes up to* MASHA]. Masha, the tea's ready, dear. [*To* VERSHININ.] Will you please come to the table, your Excellency? Forgive me, your name's slipped my memory. . . .

MASHA. Bring it here, Nanny. I'm not coming over there.

IRENA. Nanny!

ANFISA. Comi-ing!

NATASHA [*to* SOLIONY]. You know, even tiny babies understand what we say perfectly well! 'Good morning, Bobik,' I said to him only to-day, 'Good morning, my precious!'—and then he looked at me in such a special sort of way. You may say it's only a mother's imagination, but it isn't, I do assure you. No, no! He really is an extraordinary child!

SOLIONY. If that child were mine, I'd cook him up in a frying pan and eat him. [*Picks up his glass, goes into the drawing-room and sits down in a corner.*]

NATASHA [*covers her face with her hands*]. What a rude, ill-mannered person!

MASHA. People who don't even notice whether it's summer or winter are lucky! I think I'd be indifferent to the weather if I were living in Moscow.

VERSHININ. I've just been reading the diary of some French cabinet

4. A resort town famed for its beauty.

minister—he wrote it in prison. He got sent to prison in connection with the Panama affair. He writes with such a passionate delight about the birds he can see through the prison window—the birds he never even noticed when he was a cabinet minister. Of course, now he's released he won't notice them any more. . . . And in the same way, you won't notice Moscow once you live there again. We're not happy and we can't be happy: we only want happiness.

TOOZENBACH [picks up a box from the table]. I say, where are all the chocolates?

IRENA. Soliony's eaten them.

TOOZENBACH. All of them?

ANFISA [serving VERSHININ with tea]. Here's a letter for you, Sir.

VERSHININ. For me? [Takes the letter.] From my daughter. [Reads it.] Yes, of course. . . . Forgive me, Maria Serghyeevna, I'll just leave quietly. I won't have any tea. [Gets up, agitated.] Always the same thing. . . .

MASHA. What is it? Secret?

VERSHININ [in a low voice]. My wife's taken poison again. I must go. I'll get away without them seeing me. All this is so dreadfully unpleasant. [Kisses MASHA's hand.] My dear, good, sweet girl. . . . I'll go out this way, quietly. . . . [Goes out.]

ANFISA. Where's he off to? And I've just brought him some tea! What a queer fellow!

MASHA [flaring up]. Leave me alone! Why do you keep worrying me? Why don't you leave me in peace? [Goes to the table, cup in hand.] I'm sick and tired of you, silly old woman!

ANFISA. Why. . . . I didn't mean to offend you, dear.

ANDREY'S VOICE [off stage]. Anfisa!

ANFISA [mimics him]. Anfisa! Sitting there in his den! . . . [Goes out.]

MASHA [by the table in the ballroom, crossly]. Do let me sit down somewhere! [Jumbles up the cards laid out on the table.] You take up the whole table with your cards! Why don't you get on with your tea?

IRENA. How bad-tempered you are, Masha!

MASHA. Well, if I'm bad-tempered, don't talk to me, then. Don't touch me!

CHEBUTYKIN [laughs]. Don't touch her! . . . Take care you don't touch her!

MASHA. You may be sixty, but you're always gabbling some damn nonsense or other, just like a child. . . .

NATASHA [sighs]. My dear Masha, need you use such expressions? You know, with your good looks you'd be thought so charming, even by the best people—yes, I honestly mean it—if only you wouldn't use these expressions of yours! Je vous prie, pardonnez moi, Marie, mais vous avez des manières un peu grossières.[5]

TOOZENBACH [with suppressed laughter]. Pass me. . . . I say, will you please pass me. . . . Is that cognac over there, or what? . . .

5. "I beg you, pardon me, Marie, but your manners are a bit coarse."

NATASHA. Il parait que mon Bobik déjà ne dort pas.[6] . . . I think he's awake. He's not been too well to-day. I must go and see him . . . excuse me. [*Goes out.*]

IRENA. I say, where has Alexandr Ignatyevich gone to?

MASHA. He's gone home. His wife's done something queer again.

TOOZENBACH [*goes over to* SOLIONY *with a decanter of cognac*]. You always sit alone brooding over something or other—though what it's all about nobody knows. Well, let's make it up. Let's have a cognac together. [*They drink.*] I suppose I'll have to play the piano all night to-night—a lot of rubbishy tunes, of course. . . . Never mind!

SOLIONY. Why did you say 'let's make it up'? We haven't quarrelled.

TOOZENBACH. You always give me the feeling that there's something wrong between us. You're a strange character, no doubt about it.

SOLIONY [*recites*]. 'I am strange, but who's not so? Don't be angry, Aleko!'[7]

TOOZENBACH. What's Aleko got to do with it? . . . [*A pause.*]

SOLIONY. When I'm alone with somebody I'm all right, I'm just like other people. But in company, I get depressed and shy, and . . . I talk all sorts of nonsense. All the same, I'm a good deal more honest and well-intentioned than plenty of others. I can prove I am.

TOOZENBACH. You often make me angry because you keep on pestering me when we're in company—but all the same, I do like you for some reason. . . . I'm going to get drunk to-night, whatever happens! Let's have another drink!

SOLIONY. Yes, let's [*A pause.*] I've never had anything against you personally, Baron. But my temperament's rather like Lermontov's.[8] [*In a low voice.*] I even look a little like Lermontov, I've been told. . . . [*Takes a scent bottle from his pocket and sprinkles some scent on his hands.*]

TOOZENBACH. I have sent in my resignation! Finished! I've been considering it for five years, and now I've made up my mind at last. I'm going to work.

SOLIONY [*recites*]. 'Don't be angry, Aleko. . . . Away, away with all your dreams!'

[*During the conversation* ANDREY *enters quietly with a book in his hand and sits down by the candle.*]

TOOZENBACH. I'm going to work!

CHEBUTYKIN [*comes into the drawing-room with* IRENA]. And the food they treated me to was the genuine Caucasian stuff; onion soup, followed by chehartma—that's a meat dish, you know.

SOLIONY. Cheremsha isn't meat at all; it's a plant, something like an onion.

CHEBUTYKIN. No-o, my dear friend. Chehartma isn't an onion, its roast mutton.

---

6. "It seems that my Bobik already isn't asleep." As unidiomatic in French as it is in English.
7. From M. J. Lermontov's poem *The Gypsies*.

8. Russian poet (1814-41). In his comments on the play Chekhov was firm on the point that Soliony does not really resemble Lermontov. The resemblance exists only in his mind.

SOLIONY. I tell you cheremsha is a kind of onion.

CHEBUTYKIN. Well, why should I argue about it with you? You've never been to the Caucasus and you've never tasted chehartma.

SOLIONY. I haven't tasted it because I can't stand the smell of it. Cheremsha stinks just like garlic.

ANDREY [*imploringly*]. Do stop it, friends! Please stop it!

TOOZENBACH. When's the carnival crowd coming along?

IRENA. They promised to be here by nine—that means any moment now.

TOOZENBACH [*embraces* ANDREY *and sings*]. 'Ah, my beautiful porch, my lovely new porch, my . . .[9]

ANDREY [*dances and sings*]. 'My new porch all made of maple-wood. . . .'

CHEBUTYKIN [*dances*]. 'With fancy carving over the door. . . .'
[*Laughter.*]

TOOZENBACH [*kisses* ANDREY]. Let's have a drink, the devil take it! Andriusha, let's drink to eternal friendship. I'll come with you when you go back to Moscow University.

SOLIONY. Which university? There are two universities in Moscow.

ANDREY. There's only one.

SOLIONY. I tell you there are two.

ANDREY. Never mind, make it three. The more the merrier.

SOLIONY. There are two universities in Moscow.
[*Murmurs of protest and cries of 'Hush!'*]
There are two universities in Moscow, an old one and a new one. But if you don't want to listen to what I'm saying, if my conversation irritates you, I can keep silent. In fact I can go to another room. . . . [*Goes out through one of the doors.*]

TOOZENBACH. Bravo, bravo! [*Laughs.*] Let's get started, my friends, I'll play for you. What a funny creature that Soliony is! . . . [*Sits down at the piano and plays a waltz.*]

MASHA [*dances alone*]. The Baron is drunk, the Baron is drunk, the Baron is drunk. . . .
[*Enter* NATASHA.]

NATASHA [*to* CHEBUTYKIN]. Ivan Romanych! [*Speaks to him, then goes out quietly.* CHEBUTYKIN *touches* TOOZENBACH *on the shoulder and whispers to him.*]

IRENA. What is it?

CHEBUTYKIN. It's time we were going. Good-night.

IRENA. But really. . . . What about the carnival party?

ANDREY [*embarrassed*]. The carnival party's not coming. You see, my dear, Natasha says that Bobik isn't very well, and so . . . Anyway, I don't know . . . and I certainly don't care. . . .

IRENA [*shrugs her shoulders*]. Bobik's not very well! . . .

MASHA. Never mind, we'll keep our end up! If they turn us out, out we must go! [*To* IRENA.] It isn't Bobik who's not well, it's her. . . . There! . . . [*Taps her forehead with her finger.*] Petty little bourgeois housewife!

---

9. A traditional Russian dance-song. [*Translator's note.*]

[ANDREY *goes to his room on the right.* CHEBUTYKIN *follows him. The guests say good-bye in the ballroom.*]

FEDOTIK. What a pity! I'd been hoping to spend the evening here, but of course, if the baby's ill. . . . I'll bring him some toys to-morrow.

RODÈ [*in a loud voice*]. I had a good long sleep after lunch to-day on purpose, I thought I'd be dancing all night. I mean to say, it's only just nine o'clock.

MASHA. Let's go outside and talk it over. We can decide what to do then.

[*Voices are heard saying 'Good-bye! God bless you!' and* TOOZENBACH *is heard laughing gaily. Everyone goes out.* ANFISA *and a maid clear the table and put out the lights. The nurse sings to the baby off-stage. Enter* ANDREY, *wearing an overcoat and hat, followed by* CHEBUTYKIN. *They move quiet-ly.*]

CHEBUTYKIN. I've never found time to get married, somehow . . . partly because my life's just flashed past me like lightning, and partly because I was always madly in love with your mother and she was married. . . .

ANDREY. One shouldn't marry. One shouldn't marry because it's so boring.

CHEBUTYKIN. That may be so, but what about loneliness? You can philosophize as much as you like, dear boy, but loneliness is a dreadful thing. Although, really . . . well, it doesn't matter a damn, of course! . . .

ANDREY. Let's get along quickly.

CHEBUTYKIN. What's the hurry? There's plenty of time.

ANDREY. I'm afraid my wife may try to stop me.

CHEBUTYKIN. Ah!

ANDREY. I won't play cards to-night, I'll just sit and watch. I'm not feeling too well. . . . What ought I to do for this breathlessness, Ivan Romanych?

CHEBUTYKIN. Why ask me, dear boy? I can't remember—I simply don't know.

ANDREY. Let's go through the kitchen.

[*They go out. A bell rings. The ring is repeated, then voices and laughter are heard.*]

IRENA [*coming in*]. What's that?

ANFISA [*in a whisper*]. The carnival party.

[*The bell rings again.*]

IRENA. Tell them there's no one at home, Nanny. Apologize to them.

[ANFISA *goes out.* IRENA *walks up and down the room, lost in thought. She seems agitated. Enter* SOLIONY.]

SOLIONY [*puzzled*]. There's no one here. . . . Where is everybody?

IRENA. They've gone home.

SOLIONY. How strange! Then you're alone here?

IRENA. Yes, alone. [*A pause.*] Well . . . good-night.

SOLIONY. I know I behaved tactlessly just now, I lost control of my-self. But you're different from the others, you stand out high above them—you're pure, you can see where the truth lies. . . . You're the only person in the world who can possibly understand me. I love you. . . . I love you with a deep, infinite . . .

IRENA. Do please go away. Good-night!

SOLIONY. I can't live without you. [*Follows her.*] Oh, it's such a delight just to look at you! [*With tears.*] Oh, my happiness! Your glorious, marvellous, entrancing eyes—eyes like no other woman's I've ever seen. . . .

IRENA [*coldly*]. Please stop it, Vassily Vassilich!

SOLIONY. I've never spoken to you of my love before . . . it makes me feel as if I were living on a different planet. . . . [*Rubs his forehead.*] Never mind! I can't force you to love me, obviously. But I don't intend to have any rivals—successful rivals, I mean. . . . No, no! I swear to you by everything I hold sacred that if there's anyone else, I'll kill him. Oh, how wonderful you are!

[*Enter* NATASHA *carrying a candle.*]

NATASHA [*pokes her head into one room, then into another, but passes the door leading to her husband's room*]. Andrey's reading in there. Better let him read. Forgive me, Vassily Vassilich, I didn't know you were here. I'm afraid I'm not properly dressed.

SOLIONY. I don't care. Good-bye. [*Goes out.*]

NATASHA. You must be tired, my poor dear girl. [*Kisses* IRENA.] You ought to go to bed earlier.

IRENA. Is Bobik asleep?

NATASHA. Yes, he's asleep. But he's not sleeping peacefully. By the way, my dear, I've been meaning to speak to you for some time but there's always been something . . . either you're not here, or I'm too busy. . . . You see, I think that Bobik's nursery is so cold and damp. . . . And your room is just ideal for a baby. Darling, do you think you could move into Olga's room?

IRENA [*not understanding her*]. Where to?

[*The sound of bells is heard outside, as a 'troika' is driven up to the house.*]

NATASHA. You can share a room with Olia for the time being, and Bobik can have your room. He is such a darling! This morning I said to him: 'Bobik, you're my very own! My very own!' And he just gazed at me with his dear little eyes.

[*The door bell rings.*]

That must be Olga. How late she is!

[*A maid comes up to* NATASHA *and whispers in her ear.*]

NATASHA. Protopopov! What a funny fellow! Protopopov's come to ask me to go for a drive with him. In a troika! [*Laughs.*] Aren't these men strange creatures! . . .

[*The door bell rings again.*]

Someone's ringing. Shall I go for a short drive? Just for a quarter of an hour? [*To the maid.*] Tell him I'll be down in a minute.

[*The door bell rings.*]

That's the bell again. I suppose it's Olga. [*Goes out.*]

[*The maid runs out;* IRENA *sits lost in thought. Enter* KOOLY-GHIN *and* OLGA, *followed by* VERSHININ.]

KOOLYGHIN. Well! What's the meaning of this? You said you were going to have a party.

VERSHININ. It's a strange thing. I left here about half an hour ago, and they were expecting a carnival party then.

IRENA. They've all gone.

KOOLYGHIN. Masha's gone, too? Where has she gone to? And why is Protopopov waiting outside in a troika? Who's he waiting for?

IRENA. Please don't ask me questions. I'm tired.

KOOLYGHIN. You . . . spoilt child!

OLGA. The conference has only just ended. I'm quite worn out. The headmistress is ill and I'm deputizing for her. My head's aching, oh, my head, my head. . . . [*Sits down.*] Andrey lost two hundred roubles at cards last night. The whole town's talking about it. . . .

KOOLYGHIN. Yes, the conference exhausted me, too. [*Sits down.*]

VERSHININ. So now my wife's taken it into her head to try to frighten me. She tried to poison herself. However, everything's all right now, so I can relax, thank goodness. . . . So we've got to go away? Well, good-night to you, all the best. Fiodor Illych, would you care to come along with me somewhere or other? I can't stay at home tonight, I really can't. . . . Do come!

KOOLYGHIN. I'm tired. I don't think I'll come. [*Gets up.*] I'm tired. Has my wife gone home?

IRENA. I think so.

KOOLYGHIN [*kisses* IRENA's *hand*]. Good-night. We can rest to-morrow and the day after to-morrow, two whole days! Well, I wish you all the best. [*Going out.*] How I long for some tea! I reckoned on spending the evening in congenial company, but—o, *fallacem hominum spem!*[1] Always use the accusative case in exclamations.

VERSHININ. Well; it looks as if I'll have to go somewhere by myself. [*Goes out with* KOOLYGHIN, *whistling.*]

OLGA. My head aches, oh, my head. . . . Andrey lost at cards . . . the whole town's talking. . . . I'll go and lie down. [*Going out.*] To-morrow I'm free. Heavens, what a joy! To-morrow I'm free, and the day after to-morrow I'm free. . . . My head's aching, oh, my poor head. . . .

IRENA [*alone*]. They've all gone. No one's left.
   [*Someone is playing an accordion in the street. The nurse sings in the next room.*]

NATASHA [*crosses the ballroom, wearing a fur coat and a cap. She is followed by the maid*]. I'll be back in half an hour. I'm just going for a little drive. [*Goes out.*]

IRENA [*alone, with intense longing*]. Moscow! Moscow! Moscow!

CURTAIN

Act Three

[A *bedroom now shared by* OLGA *and* IRENA. *There are two beds, one on the right, the other on the left, each screened off from the*

1. "Oh, the futile hopes of men."

centre of the room. It is past two o'clock in the morning. Off-stage the alarm is being sounded on account of a fire which has been raging for some time.[2] The inmates of the house have not yet been to bed. MASHA *is lying on a couch, dressed, as usual, in black.* OLGA *and* ANFISA *come in.*]

ANFISA. Now they're sitting down there, under the stairs. . . . I keep telling them to come upstairs, that they shouldn't sit down there, but they just cry. 'We don't know where our Papa is,' they say, 'perhaps he's got burned in the fire.' What an idea! And there are people in the yard, too . . . half-dressed. . . .

OLGA [*takes a dress out of a wardrobe*]. Take this grey frock, Nanny. . . . And this one. . . . This blouse, too. . . . And this skirt. Oh, Heavens! what is happening! Apparently the whole of the Kirsanovsky Street's been burnt down. . . . Take this . . . and this, too. . . . [*Throws the clothes into* ANFISA's *arms*.] The poor Vershinins had a fright. Their house only just escaped being burnt down. They'll have to spend the night here . . . we musn't let them go home. Poor Fedotik's lost everything, he's got nothing left. . . .

ANFISA. I'd better call Ferapont, Oliushka, I can't carry all this.

OLGA [*rings*]. No one takes any notice when I ring. [*Calls through the door.*] Is anyone there? Will someone come up, please!

[*A window, red with the glow of the fire, can be seen through the open door. The sound of a passing fire engine is heard.*]

How dreadful it all is! And how tired of it I am!

[*Enter* FERAPONT.]

Take this downstairs please. . . . The Kolotilin girls are sitting under the stairs . . . give it to them. And this, too. . . .

FERAPONT. Very good, Madam. Moscow was burned down in 1812 just the same. Mercy on us! . . . Yes, the French were surprised all right.

OLGA. Go along now, take this down.

FERAPONT. Very good. [*Goes out.*]

OLGA. Give it all away, Nanny dear. We won't keep anything, give it all away. . . . I'm so tired, I can hardly keep on my feet. We musn't let the Vershinins go home. The little girls can sleep in the drawing-room, and Alexandr Ignatyevich can share the downstairs room with the Baron. Fedotik can go in with the Baron, too, or maybe he'd better sleep in the ballroom. The doctor's gone and got drunk—you'd think he'd done it on purpose; he's so hopelessly drunk that we can't let anyone go into his room. Vershinin's wife will have to go into the drawing-room too.

ANFISA [*wearily*]. Don't send me away, Oliushka, darling! Don't send me away!

OLGA. What nonsense you're talking, Nanny! No one's sending you away.

ANFISA [*leans her head against* OLGA's *breast*]. My dearest girl! I do work, you know, I work as hard as I can. . . . I suppose now I'm

2. Chekhov insisted that Act III was to be very quiet, that all the noise was to be in the distance. He himself directed the sound-effects.

getting weaker, I'll be told to go. But where can I go? Where? I'm eighty years old. I'm over eighty-one!

OLGA. You sit down for a while, Nanny. . . . You're tired, you poor dear. . . . [*Makes her sit down.*] Just rest a bit. You've turned quite pale.

[*Enter* NATASHA.]

NATASHA. They're saying we ought to start a subscription in aid of the victims of the fire. You know—form a society or something for the purpose. Well, why not? It's an excellent idea! In any case it's up to us to help the poor as best we can. Bobik and Sofochka are fast asleep as if nothing had happened. We've got such a crowd of people in the house; the place seems full of people whichever way you turn. There's 'flu about in the town. . . . I'm so afraid the children might catch it.

OLGA [*without listening to her*]. You can't see the fire from this room; it's quiet in here.

NATASHA. Yes. . . . I suppose my hair is all over the place. [*Stands in front of the mirror.*] They say I've got stouter, but it's not true! I'm not a bit stouter. Masha's asleep . . . she's tired, poor girl. . . . [*To* ANFISA, *coldly.*] How dare you sit down in my presence? Get up! Get out of here!

[ANFISA *goes out. A pause.*]

I can't understand why you keep that old woman in the house.

OLGA [*taken aback*]. Forgive me for saying it, but I can't understand how you . . .

NATASHA. She's quite useless here. She's just a peasant woman, her right place is in the country. You're spoiling her. I do like order in the home, I don't like having useless people about. [*Strokes* OLGA's *cheek.*] You're tired, my poor dear! Our headmistress is is tired! You know, when my Sofochka grows up and goes to school, I'll be frightened of you.

OLGA. I'm not going to be a headmistress.

NATASHA. You'll be asked to, Olechka. It's settled.

OLGA. I'll refuse. I couldn't do it. . . . I wouldn't be strong enough. [*Drinks water.*] You spoke so harshly to Nanny just now. . . . You must forgive me for saying so, but I just can't stand that sort of thing . . . it made me feel quite faint. . . .

NATASHA [*agitated*]. Forgive me, Olia, forgive me. I didn't mean to upset you.

[MASHA *gets up, picks up a pillow and goes out in a huff.*]

OLGA. Please try to understand me, dear. . . . It may be that we've been brought up in a peculiar way, but anyway I just can't bear it. When people are treated like that, it gets me down, I feel quite ill. . . . I simply get unnerved. . . .

NATASHA. Forgive me, dear, forgive me! . . . [*Kisses her.*]

OLGA. Any cruel or tactless remark, even the slightest discourtesy, upsets me. . . .

NATASHA. It's quite true, I know I often say things which would be better left unsaid—but you must agree with me, dear, that she'd be better in the country somewhere.

OLGA. She's been with us for thirty years.

NATASHA. But she can't do any work now, can she? Either I don't understand you, or you don't want to understand me. She can't work, she just sleeps or sits about.

OLGA. Well, let her sit about.

NATASHA [*in surprise*]. What do you mean, let her sit about! Surely she is a servant! [*Tearfully.*] No, I don't understand you, Olia! I have a nurse for the children and a wet nurse and we share a maid and a cook. Whatever do we want this old woman for? What for?

[*The alarm is sounded again.*]

OLGA. I've aged ten years to-night.

NATASHA. We must sort things out, Olia.[3] You're working at your school, and I'm working at home. You're teaching and I'm running the house. And when I say anything about the servants, I know what I'm talking about. . . . That old thief, that old witch must get out of this house to-morrow! . . . [*Stamps her feet.*] How dare you vex me so? How dare you? [*Recovering her self-control.*] Really, if you don't move downstairs, we'll always be quarrelling. This is quite dreadful!

[*Enter* KOOLYGHIN.]

KOOLYGHIN. Where's Masha? It's time we went home. They say the fire's getting less fierce. [*Stretches.*] Only one block got burnt down, but to begin with it looked as if the whole town was going to be set on fire by that wind. [*Sits down.*] I'm so tired, Olechka, my dear. You know, I've often thought that if I hadn't married Masha, I'd have married you, Olechka. You're so kind. I'm worn out. [*Listens.*]

OLGA. What is it?

KOOLYGHIN. The doctor's got drunk just as if he'd done it on purpose. Hopelessly drunk. . . . As if he'd done it on purpose. [*Gets up.*] I think he's coming up here. . . . Can you hear him? Yes, he's coming up. [*Laughs.*] What a fellow, really! . . . I'm going to hide myself. [*Goes to the wardrobe and stands between it and the wall.*] What a scoundrel!

OLGA. He's been off drinking for two years, and now suddenly he goes and gets drunk. . . . [*Walks with* NATASHA *towards the back of the room.*]

[CHEBUTYKIN *enters; walking firmly and soberly he crosses the room, stops, looks round, then goes to the wash-stand and begins to wash his hands.*]

CHEBUTYKIN [*glumly*]. The devil take them all . . . all the lot of them! They think I can treat anything just because I'm a doctor, but I know positively nothing at all. I've forgotten everything I used to know. I remember nothing, positively nothing.

[OLGA *and* NATASHA *leave the room without his noticing.*]

The devil take them! Last Wednesday I attended a woman at Zasyp. She died, and it's all my fault that she did die. Yes. . . . I used to know a thing or two twenty-five years ago, but now I don't remember anything. Not a thing! Perhaps I'm not a man at

---

3. Moscow ms.: "We must sort things out once and for all, Olia."

all, but I just imagine that I've got hands and feet and a head. Perhaps I don't exist at all, and I only imagine that I'm walking about and eating and sleeping. [*Weeps.*] Oh, if only I could simply stop existing! [*Stops crying, glumly.*] God knows. . . . The other day they were talking about Shakespeare and Voltaire at the club. . . . I haven't read either, never read a single line of either, but I tried to make out by my expression that I had. The others did the same. How petty it all is! How despicable! And then suddenly I thought of the woman I killed on Wednesday. It all came back to me, and I felt such a swine, so sick of myself that I went and got drunk. . . .

[*Enter* IRENA, VERSHININ *and* TOOZENBACH. TOOZENBACH *is wearing a fashionable new civilian suit.*]

IRENA. Let's sit down here for a while. No one will come in here.

VERSHININ. The whole town would have been burnt down but for the soldiers. They're a fine lot of fellows! [*Rubs his hands with pleasure.*] Excellent fellows! Yes, they're a fine lot!

KOOLYGHIN [*approaches them*]. What's the time?

TOOZENBACH. It's gone three. It's beginning to get light.

IRENA. Everyone's sitting in the ballroom and nobody thinks of leaving. That man Soliony there, too. . . . [*To* CHEBUTYKIN.] You ought to go to bed, Doctor.

CHEBUTYKIN. I'm all right. . . . Thanks. . . . [*Combs his beard.*]

KOOLYGHIN [*laughs*]. Half seas over,[4] Ivan Romanych! [*Slaps him on the shoulder.*] You're a fine one! *In vino veritas,*[5] as they used to say in Rome.

TOOZENBACH. Everyone keeps asking me to arrange a concert in aid of the victims of the fire.

IRENA. Well, who'd you get to perform in it?

TOOZENBACH. It could be done if we wanted to. Maria Serghyeevna plays the piano wonderfully well, in my opinion.

KOOLYGHIN. Yes, wonderfully well!

IRENA. She's forgotten how to. She hasn't played for three years. . . . or maybe it's four.

TOOZENBACH. Nobody understands music in this town, not a single person. But I do—I really do—and I assure you quite definitely that Maria Serghyeevna plays magnificently. She's almost a genius for it.

KOOLYGHIN. You're right, Baron. I'm very fond of Masha. She's such a nice girl.

TOOZENBACH. Fancy being able to play so exquisitely, and yet having nobody, nobody at all, to appreciate it!

KOOLYGHIN [*sighs*]. Yes. . . . But would it be quite proper for her to play in a concert? [*A pause.*] I don't know anything about these matters, my friends. Perhaps it'll be perfectly all right. But you know, although our director is a good man, a very good man indeed, and most intelligent, I know that he does hold certain views. . . . Of course, this doesn't really concern him, but I'll have a word with him about it, all the same, if you like.

---

4. Britishism meaning almost drunk.   5. "In wine there is truth."

CHEBUTYKIN [*picks up a china clock and examines it*].

VERSHININ. I've got my clothes in such a mess helping to put out the fire, I must look like nothing on earth. [*A pause.*] I believe they were saying yesterday that our brigade might be transferred to somewhere a long way away. Some said it was to be Poland, and some said it was Cheeta, in Siberia.

TOOZENBACH. I heard that, too. Well, the town will seem quite deserted.

IRENA. We'll go away, too!

CHEBUTYKIN [*drops the clock and breaks it*]. Smashed to smithereens!
[*A pause. Everyone looks upset and embarrassed.*]

KOOLYGHIN [*picks up the pieces*]. Fancy breaking such a valuable thing! Ah, Ivan Romanych, Ivan Romanych! You'll get a bad mark for that!

IRENA. It was my mother's clock.

CHEBUTYKIN. Well, supposing it was. If it was your mother's, then it was your mother's. Perhaps I didn't smash it. Perhaps it only appears that I did. Perhaps it only appears to us that we exist, whereas in reality we don't exist at all. I don't know anything, no one knows anything. [*Stops at the door.*] Why are you staring at me? Natasha's having a nice little affair with Protopopov, and you don't see it. You sit here seeing nothing, and meanwhile Natasha's having a nice little affair with Protopopov. . . . [*Sings.*] Would you like a date?[6] . . . [*Goes out.*]

VERSHININ. So. . . . [*Laughs.*] How odd it all is, really! [*A pause.*] When the fire started, I ran home as fast as I could. When I got near, I could see that our house was all right and out of danger, but the two little girls were standing there, in the doorway in their night clothes. Their mother wasn't there. People were rushing about, horses, dogs . . . and in the kiddies' faces I saw a frightened, anxious, appealing look, I don't know what! . . . My heart sank when I saw their faces. My God, I thought, what will these children have to go through in the course of their poor lives? And they may live a long time, too! I picked them up and ran back here with them, and all the time I was running, I was thinking the same thing: what will they have to go through?
[*The alarm is sounded. A pause.*]
When I got here, my wife was here already . . . angry, shouting!
[*Enter* MASHA *carrying a pillow; she sits down on the couch.*]

VERSHININ. And when my little girls were standing in the doorway with nothing on but their night clothes, and the street was red with the glow of the fire and full of terrifying noises, it struck me that the same sort of thing used to happen years ago, when armies used to make sudden raids on towns, and plunder them and set them on fire. . . . Anyway, is there any essential difference between things as they were and as they are now? And before very long, say, in another two or three hundred years, people may be looking at our present life just as we look at the past now, with horror

6. Chekhov identified this as a line from a contemporary operetta, the name of which he could not recall.

and scorn. Our own times may seem uncouth to them, boring and frightfully uncomfortable and strange. . . . Oh, what a great life it'll be then, what a life! [*Laughs.*] Forgive me, I'm philosophizing my head off again . . . but may I go on, please? I'm bursting to philosophize just at the moment. I'm in the mood for it. [*A pause.*] You seem as if you've all gone to sleep. As I was saying: what a great life it will be in the future! Just try to imagine it. . . . At the present time there are only three people of your intellectual calibre in the whole of this town, but future generations will be more productive of people like you. They'll go on producing more and more of the same sort until at last the time will come when everything will be just as you'd wish it yourselves. People will live their lives in your way, and then even you may be outmoded, and a new lot will come along who will be even better than you are. . . . [*Laughs.*] I'm in quite a special mood to-day. I feel full of a tremendous urge to live. . . . [*Sings.*]

'To Love all ages are in fee,
    The passion's good for you and me.' . . .[7] [*Laughs.*]

MASHA [*sings*]. Tara-tara-tara. . . .

VERSHININ. Tum-tum. . . .

MASHA. Tara-tara . . .

VERSHININ. Tum-tum, tum-tum. . . . [*Laughs.*]
    [*Enter* FEDOTIK.]

FEDOTIK [*dancing about*]. Burnt, burnt! Everything I've got burnt!
    [*All laugh.*]

IRENA. It's hardly a joking matter. Has everything really been burnt?

FEDOTIK [*laughs*]. Everything, completely. I've got nothing left. My guitar's burnt, my photographs are burnt, all my letters are burnt. Even the little note-book I was going to give you has been burnt.
    [*Enter* SOLIONY.]

IRENA. No, please go away, Vassily Vassilich. You can't come in here.

SOLIONY. Can't I? Why can the Baron come in here if I can't?

VERSHININ. We really must go, all of us. What's the fire doing?

SOLIONY. It's dying down, they say. Well, I must say it's a peculiar thing that the Baron can come in here, and I can't. [*Takes a scent bottle from his pocket and sprinkles himself with scent.*]

VERSHININ. Tara-tara.

MASHA. Tum-tum, tum-tum.

VERSHININ [*laughs, to* SOLIONY]. Let's go to the ballroom.

SOLIONY. Very well, we'll make a note of this. 'I hardly need to make my moral yet more clear: That might be teasing geese, I fear!'[8] [*Looks at* TOOZENBACH.] Cluck, cluck, cluck! [*Goes out with* VERSHININ *and* FEDOTIK.]

IRENA. That Soliony has smoked the room out. . . . [*Puzzled.*] The Baron's asleep. Baron! Baron!

TOOZENBACH [*waking out of his doze*]. I must be tired. The brickworks. . . . No, I'm not talking in my sleep. I really do intend to

---

7. From P. I. Tchaikovsky's operatic version of Pushkin's *Eugene Onegin.*

8. From I. A. Krylov's fable *Geese.* [*Translator's note.*]

go to the brick-works and start working there quite soon. I've had a talk with the manager. [*To* IRENA, *tenderly.*] You are so pale, so beautiful, so fascinating . . . Your pallor seems to light up the darkness around you, as if it were luminous, somehow. . . . You're sad, you're dissatisfied with the life you have to live. . . . Oh, come away with me, let's go away and work together!

MASHA. Nikolai Lvovich, I wish you'd go away.

TOOZENBACH [*laughs*]. Oh, you're here, are you? I didn't see you. [*Kisses* IRENA's *hand.*] Good-bye, I'm going. You know, as I look at you now, I keep thinking of the day—it was a long time ago, your Saint's day—when you talked to us about the joy of work. . . . You were so gay and high-spirited then. . . . And what a happy life I saw ahead of me! Where is it all now? [*Kisses her hand.*] There are tears in your eyes. You should go to bed, it's beginning to get light . . . it's almost morning. . . . Oh, if only I could give my life for you!

MASHA. Nikolai Lvovich, please go away! Really now. . . .

TOOZENBACH. I'm going. [*Goes out.*]

MASHA [*lies down*]. Are you asleep, Fiodor?

KOOLYGHIN. Eh?

MASHA. Why don't you go home?

KOOLYGHIN. My darling Masha, my sweet, my precious Masha. . . .

IRENA. She's tired. Let her rest a while, Fyedia.

KOOLYGHIN. I'll go in a moment. My wife, my dear, good wife! . . . How I love you! . . . only you!

MASHA [*crossly*]. Amo, amas, amat, amamus, amatis, amant![9]

KOOLYGHIN [*laughs*]. Really, she's an amazing woman!—I've been married to you for seven years, but I feel as if we were only married yesterday. Yes, on my word of honour, I do! You really are amazing! Oh, I'm so happy, happy, happy!

MASHA. And I'm so bored, bored, bored! [*Sits up.*] I can't get it out of my head. . . . It's simply disgustng. It's like having a nail driven into my head. No, I can't keep silent about it any more. It's about Andrey. . . . He's actually mortgaged this house to a bank, and his wife's got hold of all the money—and yet the house doesn't belong to him, it belongs to all four of us! Surely, he must realize that, if he's got any honesty.

KOOLYGHIN. Why bring all this up, Masha? Why bother about it now? Andriusha owes money all round. . . . Leave him alone.

MASHA. Anyway, it's disgusting. [*Lies down.*]

KOOLYGHIN. Well, we aren't poor, Masha. I've got work, I teach at the county school, I give private lessons in my spare time. . . . I'm just a plain, honest man. . . . *Omnia mea mecum porto,*[1] as they say.

MASHA. I don't ask for anything, but I'm just disgusted by injustice. [*A pause.*] Why don't you go home, Fiodor?

KOOLYGHIN [*kisses her*]. You're tired. Just rest here for a while. . . . I'll go home and wait for you. . . . Go to sleep. [*Goes to the door.*] I'm happy, happy, happy! [*Goes out.*]

9. He conjugates the verb "to love." 1. "Everything I have I carry with me."

IRENA. The truth is that Andrey is getting to be shallow-minded. He's ageing and since he's been living with that woman he's lost all the inspiration he used to have! Not long ago he was working for a professorship, and yet yesterday he boasted of having at last been elected a member of the County Council. Fancy him a member, with Protopopov as chairman! They say the whole town's laughing at him, he's the only one who doesn't know anything or see anything. And now, you see, everyone's at the fire, while he's just sitting in his room, not taking the slightest notice of it. Just playing his violin. [*Agitated.*] Oh, how dreadful it is, how dreadful, how dreadful! I can't bear it any longer, I can't, I really can't! . . .

[*Enter* OLGA. *She starts arranging things on her bedside table.*]

IRENA [*sobs loudly*]. You must turn me out of here! Turn me out; I can't stand it any more!

OLGA [*alarmed*]. What is it? What is it, darling?

IRENA [*sobbing*]. Where. . . . Where has it all gone to? Where is it? Oh, God! I've forgotten. . . . I've forgotten everything . . . there's nothing but a muddle in my head. . . . I don't remember what the Italian for 'window' is, or for 'ceiling'. . . . Every day I'm forgetting more and more, and life's slipping by, and it will never, never come back. . . . We shall never go to Moscow. . . . I can see that we shall never go. . . .

OLGA. Don't, my dear, don't. . . .

IRENA [*trying to control herself*]. Oh, I'm so miserable! . . . I can't work, I won't work! I've had enough of it, enough! . . . First I worked on the telegraph, now I'm in the County Council office, and I hate and despise everything they give me to do there. . . . I'm twenty-three years old, I've been working all this time, and I feel as if my brain's dried up. I know I've got thinner and uglier and older, and I find no kind of satisfaction in anything, none at all. And the time's passing . . . and I feel as if I'm moving away from any hope of a genuine, fine life, I'm moving further and further away and sinking into a kind of abyss. I feel in despair, and I don't know why I'm still alive, why I haven't killed myself. . . .

OLGA. Don't cry, my dear child, don't cry. . . . It hurts me.

IRENA. I'm not crying any more. That's enough of it. Look, I'm not crying now. Enough of it, enough! . . .

OLGA. Darling, let me tell you something. . . . I just want to speak as your sister, as your friend. . . . That is, if you want my advice. . . . Why don't you marry the Baron?

IRENA [*weeps quietly*].

OLGA. After all, you do respect him, you think a lot of him. . . . It's true, he's not good-looking, but he's such a decent, clean-minded sort of man. . . . After all, one doesn't marry for love, but to fulfil a duty. At least, I think so, and I'd marry even if I weren't in love. I'd marry anyone that proposed to me, as long as he was a decent man. I'd even marry an old man.

IRENA. I've been waiting all this time, imagining that we'd be moving to Moscow, and I'd meet the man I'm meant for there. I've dreamt about him and I've loved him in my dreams. . . . But it's all turned out to be nonsense . . . nonsense. . . .

OLGA [*embracing her*]. My darling sweetheart, I understand everything perfectly. When the Baron resigned his commission and came to see us in his civilian clothes, I thought he looked so plain that I actually started to cry. . . . He asked me why I was crying. . . . How could I tell him? But, of course, if it were God's will that he should marry you, I'd feel perfectly happy about it. That's quite a different matter, quite different!

[NATASHA, *carrying a candle, comes out of the door on the right, crosses the stage and goes out through the door on the left without saying anything.*]

MASHA [*sits up*]. She goes about looking as if she'd started the fire.

OLGA. You're silly, Masha. You're the stupidest person in our family. Forgive me for saying so.

[*A pause.*]

MASHA. My dear sisters, I've got something to confess to you. I must get some relief, I feel the need of it in my heart. I'll confess it to you two alone, and then never again, never to anybody! I'll tell you in a minute. [*In a low voice.*] It's a secret, but you'll have to know everything. I can't keep silent any more. [*A pause.*] I'm in love, in love. . . . I love that man. . . . You saw him here just now. . . . Well, what's the good? . . . I love Vershinin. . . .

OLGA [*goes behind her screen*]. Don't say it. I don't want to hear it.

MASHA. Well, what's to be done? [*Holding her head.*] I thought he was queer at first, then I started to pity him . . . then I began to love him . . . love everything about him—his voice, his talk, his misfortunes, his two little girls. . . .

OLGA. Nevertheless, I don't want to hear it. You can say any nonsense you like, I'm not listening.

MASHA. Oh, you're stupid, Olia![2] If I love him, well—that's my fate! That's my destiny. . . . He loves me, too. It's all rather frightening, isn't it? Not a good thing, is it? [*Takes* IRENA *by the hand and draws her to her.*] Oh, my dear! . . . How are we going to live through the rest of our lives? What's going to become of us? When you read a novel, everything in it seems so old and obvious, but when you fall in love yourself, you suddenly discover that you don't really know anything, and you've got to make your own decisions. . . . My dear sisters, my dear sisters! . . . I've confessed it all to you, and now I'll keep quiet. . . . I'll be like that madman in the story by Gogol—silence . . . silence! . . .

[*Enter* ANDREY *followed by* FERAPONT.]

ANDREY [*crossly*]. What do you want? I don't understand you.

FERAPONT [*stopping in the doorway, impatiently*]. I've asked you about ten times already, Andrey Serghyeevich.

ANDREY. In the first place, you're not to call me Andrey Serghyeevich—call me 'Your Honour'.

FERAPONT. The firemen are asking Your Honour if they may drive

2. Moscow ms.: "Oh, you're funny, Olia."

through your garden to get to the river. They've been going a long way round all this time—it's a terrible business!

ANDREY. All right. Tell them it's all right.

[FERAPONT *goes out.*]

They keep on plaguing me. Where's Olga?

[OLGA *comes from behind the screen.*]

I wanted to see you. Will you give me the key to the cupboard? I've lost mine. You know the key I mean, the small one you've got. . . .

[OLGA *silently hands him the key.* IRENA *goes behind the screen on her side of the room.*]

ANDREY. What a terrific fire! It's going down though. That Ferapont annoyed me, the devil take him! Silly thing he made me say. . . . Telling him to call me 'Your Honour'! . . . [*A pause.*] Why don't you say anything, Olia? [*A pause.*] It's about time you stopped this nonsense . . . sulking like this for no reason whatever. . . . You here, Masha? And Irena's here, too. That's excellent! We can talk it over then, frankly and once for all. What have you got against me? What is it?

OLGA. Drop it now, Andriusha. Let's talk it over to-morrow. [*Agitated.*] What a dreadful night!

ANDREY [*in great embarrassment*]. Don't get upset. I'm asking you quite calmly, what have you got against me? Tell me frankly.

VERSHININ'S VOICE [*off stage*]. Tum-tum-tum!

MASHA [*in a loud voice, getting up*]. Tara-tara-tara! [*To* OLGA.] Goodbye, Olia, God bless you! [*Goes behind the screen and kisses* IRENA.] Sleep well. . . . Good-bye, Andrey, I should leave them now, they're tired . . . talk it over to-morrow. . . . [*Goes out.*]

OLGA. Really, Andriusha, let's leave it till to-morrow. . . . [*Goes behind the screen on her side of the room.*] It's time to go to bed.

ANDREY. I only want to say one thing, then I'll go. In a moment. . . . First of all, you've got something against my wife, against Natasha. I've always been conscious of it from the day we got married. Natasha is a fine woman, she's honest and straightforward and high-principled. . . . That's my opinion. I love and respect my wife. You understand that I respect her, and I expect others to respect her, too. I repeat: she's an honest, high-principled woman, and all your grievances against her—if you don't mind my saying so—are just imagination, and nothing more. . . . [*A pause.*] Secondly, you seem to be annoyed with me for not making myself a professor, and not doing any academic work. But I'm working in the Council Office, I'm a member of the County Council, and I feel my service there is just as fine and valuable as any academic work I might do. I'm a member of the County Council, and if you want to know, I'm proud of it! [*A pause.*] Thirdly . . . there's something else I must tell you. . . . I know I mortgaged the house without asking your permission. . . . That was wrong, I admit it, and I ask you to forgive me. . . . I was driven to it by my debts. . . . I'm in debt for about thirty-five thousand roubles. I don't play cards any more, I've given it up long ago. . . . The only thing I can say to justify myself is that you girls get an annuity, while I don't get anything . . . no income, I mean. . . . [*A pause.*]

KOOLYGHIN [*calling through the door*]. Is Masha there? She's not there? [*Alarmed.*] Where can she be then? It's very strange. . . . [*Goes away.*]

ANDREY. So you won't listen? Natasha is a good, honest woman, I tell you. [*Walks up and down the stage, then stops.*] When I married her, I thought we were going to be happy, I thought we should all be happy. . . . But . . . oh, my God! . . . [*Weeps.*] My dear sisters, my dear, good sisters, don't believe what I've been saying, don't believe it. . . . [*Goes out.*]

KOOLYGHIN [*through the door, agitated*]. Where's Masha? Isn't Masha here? Extraordinary! [*Goes away.*]

[*The alarm is heard again. The stage is empty.*]

IRENA [*speaking from behind the screen*]. Olia! Who's that knocking on the floor?

OLGA. It's the doctor, Ivan Romanych. He's drunk.

IRENA. It's been one thing after another all night. [*A pause.*] Olia! [*Peeps out from behind the screen.*] Have you heard? The troops are being moved from the district . . . they're being sent somewhere a long way off.

OLGA. That's only a rumour.

IRENA. We'll be left quite alone then. . . . Olia!

OLGA. Well?

IRENA. Olia, darling, I do respect the Baron. . . . I think a lot of him, he's a very good man. . . . I'll marry him, Olia, I'll agree to marry him, if only we can go to Moscow! Let's go, please do let's go! There's nowhere in all the world like Moscow. Let's go, Olia! Let's go!

CURTAIN

Act Four

[*The old garden belonging to the Prozorovs' house. A river is seen at the end of a long avenue of fir-trees, and on the far bank of the river a forest. On the right of the stage there is a verandah with a table on which champagne bottles and glasses have been left. It is midday. From time to time people from the street pass through the garden to get to the river. Five or six soldiers march through quickly.*

CHEBUTYKIN, *radiating a mood of benevolence which does not leave him throughout the act, is sitting in a chair in the garden. He is wearing his army cap and is holding a walking stick, as if ready to be called away at any moment.* KOOLYGHIN, *with a decoration round his neck and with his moustache shaved off,* TOOZENBACH *and* IRENA *are standing on the verandah saying good-bye to* FEDOTIK *and* RODÈ, *who are coming down the steps. Both officers are in marching uniform.*]

TOOZENBACH [*embracing* FEDOTIK]. You're a good fellow, Fedotik;

we've been good friends! [*Embraces* RODÈ.] Once more, then. . . . Good-bye, my dear friends!

IRENA. Au revoir!

FEDOTIK. It's not 'au revoir'. It's good-bye. We shall never meet again!

KOOLYGHIN. Who knows? [*Wipes his eyes, smiling.*] There! you've made me cry.

IRENA. We'll meet some time.

FEDOTIK. Perhaps in ten or fifteen years' time. But then we'll hardly know one another. . . . We shall just meet and say: 'How are you?' coldly. . . . [*Takes a snapshot.*] Wait a moment. . . . Just one more, for the last time.

RODÈ [*embraces* TOOZENBACH]. We're not likely to meet again. . . . [*Kisses* IRENA's *hand.*] Thank you for everything . . . everything!

FEDOTIK [*annoyed*]. Do just wait a second!

TOOZENBACH. We'll meet again if we're fated to meet. Do write to us. Be sure to write.

RODÈ [*glancing round the garden*]. Good-bye, trees! [*Shouts.*] Heigh-ho! [*A pause.*] Good-bye, echo!

KOOLYGHIN. I wouldn't be surprised if you got married out there, in Poland. . . . You'll get a Polish wife, and she'll put her arms round you and say: Kohane![3] [*Laughs.*]

FEDOTIK [*glances at his watch*]. There's less than an hour to go. Soliony is the only one from our battery who's going down the river on the barge. All the others are marching with the division. Three batteries are leaving to-day by road and three more to-morrow—then the town will be quite peaceful.

TOOZENBACH. Yes, and dreadfully dull, too.

RODÈ By the way, where's Maria Serghyeevna?

KOOLYGHIN. She's somewhere in the garden.

FEDOTIK. We must say good-bye to her.

RODÈ. Good-bye. I really must go, or I'll burst into tears. [*Quickly embraces* TOOZENBACH *and* KOOLYGHIN, *kisses* IRENA's *hand.*] Life's been very pleasant here. . . .

FEDOTIK [*to* KOOLYGHIN]. Here's something for a souvenir for you—a note-book with a pencil. . . . We'll go down to the river through here. [*They go off, glancing back.*]

RODÈ [*shouts*]. Heigh-ho!

KOOLYGHIN [*shouts*]. Good-bye!

> [*At the back of the stage* FEDOTIK *and* RODÈ *meet* MASHA, *and say good-bye to her; she goes off with them.*]

IRENA. They've gone. . . . [*Sits down on the bottom step of the verandah.*]

CHEBUTYKIN. They forgot to say good-bye to me.

IRENA. Well, what about you?

CHEBUTYKIN. That's true, I forgot, too. Never mind, I'll be seeing them again quite soon. I'll be leaving to-morrow. Yes . . . only one more day. And then, in a year's time I'll be retiring. I'll come back here and finish the rest of my life near you. There's just one more

---

3. A Polish word meaning "beloved." [*Translator's note.*]

year to go and then I get my pension. . . . [*Puts a newspaper in his pocket and takes out another.*] I'll come back here and lead a reformed life. I'll be a nice, quiet, well-behaved little man.

IRENA. Yes, it's really time you reformed, my dear friend. You ought to live a different sort of life, somehow.

CHEBUTYKIN. Yes. . . . I think so, too. [*Sings quietly.*] Tarara-boom-di-ay. . . . I'm sitting on a tomb-di-ay. . . .

KOOLYGHIN. Ivan Romanych is incorrigible! Incorrigible!

CHEBUTYKIN. Yes, you ought to have taken me in hand. You'd have reformed me!

IRENA. Fiodor's shaved his moustache off. I can't bear to look at him.

KOOLYGHIN. Why not?

CHEBUTYKIN. If I could just tell you what your face looks like now—but I daren't.

KOOLYGHIN. Well! Such are the conventions of life! *Modus vivendi,*[4] you know. The director shaved his moustache off, so I shaved mine off when they gave me an inspectorship. No one likes it, but personally I'm quite indifferent. I'm content. Whether I've got a moustache or not, it's all the same to me. [*Sits down.*]

ANDREY [*passes across the back of the stage pushing a pram with a child asleep in it*].

IRENA. Ivan Romanych, my dear friend, I'm awfully worried about something. You were out in the town garden last night—tell me what happened there?

CHEBUTYKIN. What happened? Nothing. Just a trifling thing. [*Reads his paper.*] It doesn't matter anyway.

KOOLYGHIN. They say that Soliony and the Baron met in the town garden outside the theatre last night and . . .

TOOZENBACH. Don't, please! What's the good? . . . [*Waves his hand at him deprecatingly and goes into the house.*]

KOOLYGHIN. It was outside the theatre. . . . Soliony started badgering the Baron, and he lost patience and said something that offended him.

CHEBUTYKIN. I don't know anything about it. Its' all nonsense.

KOOLYGHIN. A school-master once wrote 'nonsense' in Russian over a pupil's essay, and the pupil puzzled over it, thinking it was a Latin word. [*Laughs.*] Frightfully funny, you know! They say that Soliony's in love with Irena and that he got to hate the Baron more and more. . . . Well, that's understandable. Irena's a very nice girl. She's a bit like Masha, she tends to get wrapped up in her own thoughts. [*To* IRENA.] But your disposition is more easy-going than Masha's. And yet Masha has a very nice disposition, too. I love her, I love my Masha.

[*From the back of the stage comes a shout: 'Heigh-ho!'*]

IRENA [*starts*]. Anything seems to startle me to-day. [*A pause.*] I've got everything ready, too. I'm sending my luggage off after lunch. The Baron and I are going to get married to-morrow, and directly afterwards we've moving to the brick-works, and the day after

4. "Manner of living."

to-morrow I'm starting work at the school. So our new life will begin, God willing! When I was sitting for my teacher's diploma, I suddenly started crying for sheer joy, with a sort of feeling of blessedness. . . . [*A pause.*] The carrier will be coming for my luggage in a minute. . . .

KOOLYGHIN. That's all very well, but somehow I can't feel that it's meant to be serious. All ideas and theories, but nothing really serious. Anyway, I wish you luck from the bottom of my heart.

CHEBUTYKIN [*moved*]. My dearest girl, my precious child! You've gone on so far ahead of me, I'll never catch you up now. I've got left behind like a bird which has grown too old and can't keep up with the rest of the flock. Fly away, my dears, fly away, and God be with you! [*A pause.*] It's a pity you've shaved your moustache off, Fiodor Illyich.

KOOLYGHIN. Don't keep on about it, please! [*Sighs.*] Well, the soldiers will be leaving to-day, and everything will go back to what it was before. Anyway, whatever they say, Masha is a good, loyal wife. Yes, I love her dearly and I'm thankful for what God has given me. Fate treats people so differently. For instance, there's an excise clerk here called Kozyrev. He was at school with me and he was expelled in his fifth year because he just couldn't grasp the *ut consecutivum*.[5] He's dreadfully hard up now, and in bad health, too, and whenever I meet him, I just say to him: 'Hullo, *ut consecutivum!*' 'Yes', he replies, 'that's just the trouble —*consecutivum*' . . . and he starts coughing. Whereas I—I've been lucky all my life. I'm happy, I've actually been awarded the order of Saint Stanislav, second class—and now I'm teaching the children the same old *ut consecutivum*. Of course, I'm clever, cleverer than plenty of other people, but happiness does not consist of merely being clever. . . .

[*In the house someone plays 'The Maiden's Prayer'.*]

IRENA. To-morrow night I shan't have to listen to the 'Maiden's Prayer'. I shan't have to meet Protopopov. . . . [*A pause.*] By the way, he's in the sitting-room. He's come again.

KOOLYGHIN. Hasn't our headmistress arrived yet?

IRENA. No, we've sent for her. If you only knew how difficult it is for me to live here by myself, without Olia! She lives at the school now; she's the headmistress and she's busy the whole day. And I'm here alone, bored, with nothing to do, and I hate the very room I live in. So I've just made up my mind—if I'm really not going to be able to live in Moscow, that's that. It's my fate, that's all. Nothing can be done about it. It's God's will, everything that happens, and that's the truth. Nikolai Lvovich proposed to me. . . . Well, I thought it over, and I made up my mind. He's such a nice man, it's really extraordinary how nice he is. . . . And then suddenly I felt as though my soul had grown wings, I felt more cheerful and so relieved somehow that I wanted to work again. Just to start work! . . . Only something happened yesterday, and now I feel as though something mysterious is hanging over me. . . .

5. "And so it follows."

CHEBUTYKIN. Nonsense!

NATASHA [*speaking through the window*]. Our headmistress!

KOOLYGHIN. Our headmistress has arrived! Let's go indoors.
[*Goes indoors with* IRENA.]

CHEBUTYKIN [*reads his paper and sings quietly to himself*]. Tarara-
boom-di-ay. . . . I'm sitting on a tomb-di-ay. . . .
[MASHA *walks up to him;* ANDREY *passes across the back of
the stage pushing the pram.*]

MASHA. You look very comfortable sitting here. . . .

CHEBUTYKIN. Well, why not? Anything happening?

MASHA [*sits down*]. No, nothing. [*A pause.*] Tell me something. Were
you in love with my mother?

CHEBUTYKIN. Yes, very much in love.

MASHA. Did she love you?

CHEBUTYKIN [*after a pause*]. I can't remember now.

MASHA. Is my man here? Our cook Marfa always used to call her
policeman 'my man'. Is he here?

CHEBUTYKIN. Not yet.

MASHA. When you have to take your happiness in snatches, in little
bits, as I do, and then lose it, as I've lost it, you gradually get
hardened and bad-tempered. [*Points at her breast.*] Something's
boiling over inside me, here. [*Looking at* ANDREY, *who again crosses the stage with the pram.*] There's Andrey, our dear brother. . . .
All our hopes are gone. It's the same as when thousands of people
haul a huge bell up into a tower. Untold labour and money is
spent on it, and then suddenly it falls and gets smashed. Suddenly,
without rhyme or reason. It was the same with Andrey. . . .

ANDREY. When are they going to settle down in the house? They're
making such a row.

CHEBUTYKIN. They will soon. [*Looks at his watch.*] This is an old-
fashioned watch: it strikes. . . . [*Winds his watch which then
strikes.*] The first, second and fifth batteries will be leaving punctually at one o'clock. [*A pause.*] And I shall leave to-morrow.

ANDREY. For good?

CHEBUTYKIN. I don't know. I may return in about a year. Although,
God knows . . . it's all the same. . . .
[*The sounds of a harp and a violin are heard.*]

ANDREY. The town will seem quite empty. Life will be snuffed out
like a candle. [*A pause.*] Something happened yesterday outside
the theatre; everybody's talking about it. I'm the only one that
doesn't seem to know about it.

CHEBUTYKIN. It was nothing. A lot of nonsense. Soliony started
badgering the Baron, or something. The Baron lost his temper
and insulted him, and in the end Soliony had to challenge him to
a duel. [*Looks at his watch.*] I think it's time to go. . . . At half-
past twelve, in the forest over there, on the other side of the
river. . . . Bang-bang! [*Laughs.*] Soliony imagines he's like Lermontov. He actually writes poems. But, joking apart, this is his third
duel.

MASHA. Whose third duel?

CHEBUTYKIN. Soliony's.

MASHA. What about the Baron?

CHEBUTYKIN. Well, what about him? [A *pause.*]

MASHA. My thoughts are all in a muddle. . . . But what I mean to say is that they shouldn't be allowed to fight. He might wound the Baron or even kill him.

CHEBUTYKIN. The Baron's a good enough fellow, but what does it really matter if there's one Baron more or less in the world? Well, let it be! It's all the same.

> [*The shouts of 'Ah-oo!' and 'Heigh-ho!' are heard from beyond the garden.*]

That's Skvortsov, the second, shouting from the boat. He can wait.

ANDREY. I think it's simply immoral to fight a duel, or even to be present at one as a doctor.

CHEBUTYKIN. That's only how it seems. . . . We don't exist, nothing exists, it only seems to us that we do. . . . And what difference does it make?

MASHA. Talk, talk, nothing but talk all day long! . . . [*Starts to go.*] Having to live in this awful climate with the snow threatening to fall at any moment, and then on the top of it having to listen to all this sort of talk. . . . [*Stops.*] I won't go into the house, I can't bear going in there. . . . Will you let me know when Vershinin comes? . . . [*Walks off along the avenue.*] Look, the birds are beginning to fly away already! [*Looks up.*] Swans or geese. . . . Dear birds, happy birds. . . . [*Goes off.*]

ANDREY. Our house will seem quite deserted. The officers will go, you'll go, my sister will get married, and I'll be left alone in the house.

CHEBUTYKIN. What about your wife?

> [*Enter* FERAPONT *with some papers.*]

ANDREY. My wife is my wife. She's a good, decent sort of woman . . . she's really very kind, too, but there's something about her which pulls her down to the level of an animal . . . a sort of mean, blind, thick-skinned animal—anyway, not a human being. I'm telling you this as a friend, the only person I can talk openly to. I love Natasha, it's true. But at times she appears to me so utterly vulgar, that I feel quite bewildered by it, and then I can't understand why, for what reasons I love her—or, anyway, did love her. . . .

CHEBUTYKIN [*gets up*]. Well, dear boy, I'm going away to-morrow and it may be we shall never see each other again. So I'll give you a bit of advice. Put on your hat, take a walking stick, and go away. . . . Go away, and don't ever look back. And the further you go, the better.

> [SOLIONY *passes across the back of the stage accompanied by two officers. Seeing* CHEBUTYKIN, *he turns towards him, while the officers walk on.*]

SOLIONY. It's time, Doctor. Half past twelve already. [*Shakes hands with* ANDREY.]

CHEBUTYKIN. In a moment. Oh, I'm tired of you all. [*To* ANDREY.]

Andriusha, if anyone asks for me, tell them I'll be back presently. [*Sighs.*] Oh-ho-ho!

SOLIONY. 'He had no time to say "Oh, oh!"
      Before that bear had struck him low.' . . .
[*Walks off with him.*] What are you groaning about, old man?

CHEBUTYKIN. Oh, well!

SOLIONY. How do you feel?

CHEBUTYKIN [*crossly*]. Like a last year's bird's-nest.

SOLIONY. You needn't be so agitated about it, old boy. I shan't indulge in anything much, I'll just scorch his wings a little, like a woodcock's. [*Takes out a scent bottle and sprinkles scent over his hands.*] I've used up a whole bottle to-day, but my hands still smell. They smell like a corpse. [*A pause.*] Yes. . . . Do you remember that poem of Lermontov's?
      'And he, rebellious, seeks a storm,
        As if in storms there were tranquillity.' . . .

CHEBUTYKIN. Yes.
      'He had no time to say "Oh, oh!"
      Before that bear had struck him low.'
[*Goes out with* SOLIONY.]
[*Shouts of* 'Heigh-ho!' 'Ah-oo!' *are heard. Enter* ANDREY *and* FERAPONT.]

FERAPONT. Will you sign these papers, please?

ANDREY [*with irritation*]. Leave me alone! Leave me alone, for Heaven's sake. [*Goes off with the pram.*]

FERAPONT. Well, what am I supposed to do with the papers then? They are meant to be signed, aren't they? [*Goes to back of stage.*]
[*Enter* IRENA *and* TOOZENBACH, *the latter wearing a straw hat.* KOOLYGHIN *crosses the stage, calling:* 'Ah-oo! Masha! Ah-oo!']

TOOZENBACH. I think he's the only person in the whole town who's glad that the army is leaving.

IRENA. That's quite understandable, really. [*A pause.*] The town will look quite empty.

TOOZENBACH. My dear, I'll be back in a moment.

IRENA. Where are you going?

TOOZENBACH. I must slip back to the town, and then . . . I want to see some of my colleagues off.

IRENA. It's not true. . . . Nikolai, why are you so absent-minded to-day? [*A pause.*] What happened outside the theatre last night?

TOOZENBACH [*with a movement of impatience*]. I'll be back in an hour. . . . I'll be back with you again. [*Kisses her hands.*] My treasure! . . . [*Gazes into her eyes.*] It's five years since I first began to love you, and still I can't get used to it, and you seem more beautiful every day. What wonderful, lovely hair! What marvellous eyes! I'll take you away to-morrow. We'll work, we'll be rich, my dreams will come to life again. And you'll be happy! But—there's only one 'but', only one—you don't love me!

IRENA. I can't help that! I'll be your wife, I'll be loyal and obedient to you, but I can't love you. . . . What's to be done? [*Weeps.*] I've never loved anyone in my life. Oh, I've had such dreams about being in love! I've been dreaming about it for ever so long, day and night . . . but somehow my soul seems like an expensive piano which someone has locked up and the key's got lost. [*A pause.*] Your eyes are so restless.

TOOZENBACH. I was awake all night. Not that there's anything to be afraid of in my life, nothing threatening. . . . Only the thought of that lost key torments me and keeps me awake. Say something to me. . . . [*A pause.*] Say something![6]

IRENA. What? What am I to say? What?

TOOZENBACH. Anything.

IRENA. Don't, my dear, don't. . . . [*A pause.*]

TOOZENBACH. Such trifles, such silly little things sometimes become so important suddenly, for no apparent reason! You laugh at them, just as you always have done, you still regard them as trifles, and yet you suddenly find they're in control, and you haven't the power to stop them. But don't let us talk about all that! Really, I feel quite elated. I feel as if I was seeing those fir-trees and maples and birches for the first time in my life. They all seem to be looking at me with a sort of inquisitive look and waiting for something. What beautiful trees—and how beautiful, when you think of it, life ought to be with trees like these!

[*Shouts of 'Ah-oo! Heigh-ho!' are heard.*]

I must go, it's time. . . . Look at that dead tree, it's all dried-up, but it's still swaying in the wind along with the others. And in the same way, it seems to me that, if I die, I shall still have a share in life somehow or other. Goodbye, my dear. . . . [*Kisses her hands.*] Your papers, the ones you gave me, are on my desk, under the calendar.

IRENA. I'm coming with you.

TOOZENBACH [*alarmed*]. No, no! [*Goes off quickly, then stops in the avenue.*] Irena!

IRENA. What?

TOOZENBACH [*not knowing what to say*]. I didn't have any coffee this morning. Will you tell them to get some ready for me? [*Goes off quickly.*]

[IRENA *stands, lost in thought, then goes to the back of the stage and sits down on a swing. Enter* ANDREY *with the pram;* FERAPONT *appears.*]

FERAPONT. Andrey Serghyeech, the papers aren't mine, you know, they're the office papers. I didn't make them up.

ANDREY. Oh, where has all my past life gone to?—the time when I was young and gay and clever, when I used to have fine dreams and great thoughts, and the present and the future were bright with hope? Why do we become so dull and commonplace and uninteresting almost before we've begun to live? Why do we get lazy, indifferent, useless, unhappy? . . . This town's been in existence for two hundred years; a hundred thousand people live in it, but there's not one who's any different from all the others!

6. Moscow ms.: adds these lines:
IRENA. But what? What? Everything around us is so mysterious, the old trees stand there so silently. [*Lays her head on his chest.*]
TOOZENBACH. Say something to me.

There's never been a scholar or an artist or a saint in this place, never a single man sufficiently outstanding to make you feel passionately that you wanted to emulate him. People here do nothing but eat, drink and sleep. . . . Then they die and some more take their places, and they eat, drink and sleep, too—and just to introduce a bit of variety into their lives, so as to avoid getting completely stupid with boredom, they indulge in their disgusting gossip and vodka and gambling and law-suits. The wives deceive their husbands, and the husbands lie to their wives, and pretend they don't see anything and don't hear anything. . . . And all this overwhelming vulgarity and pettiness crushes the children and puts out any spark they might have in them, so that they, too, become miserable, half-dead creatures, just like one another and just like their parents! . . . [*To* FERAPONT, *crossly.*] What do you want?

FERAPONT. What? Here are the papers to sign.

ANDREY. What a nuisance you are!

FERAPONT [*hands him the papers*]. The porter at the finance department told me just now . . . he said last winter they had two hundred degrees of frost in Petersburg.

ANDREY. I hate the life I live at present, but oh! the sense of elation when I think of the future! Then I feel so light-hearted, such a sense of release! I seem to see light ahead, light and freedom. I see myself free, and my children, too—free from idleness, free from *kvass*,[7] free from eternal meals of goose and cabbage, free from after-dinner naps, free from all this degrading parasitism! . . .

FERAPONT. They say two thousand people were frozen to death. They say everyone was scared stiff. It was either in Petersburg or in Moscow, I can't remember exactly.

ANDREY [*with sudden emotion, tenderly*]. My dear sisters, my dear good sisters! [*Tearfully.*] Masha, my dear sister! . . .

NATASHA [*through the window*]. Who's that talking so loudly there? Is that you, Andriusha? You'll wake Sofochka. *Il ne faut pas faire du bruit, la Sophie est dormie déjà. Vous êtes un ours.*[8] [*Getting angry.*] If you want to talk, give the pram to someone else. Ferapont, take the pram from the master.

FERAPONT. Yes, Madam. [*Takes the pram.*]

ANDREY [*shamefacedly*]. I was talking quietly.

NATASHA [*in the window, caressing her small son*]. Bobik! Naughty Bobik! Aren't you a naughty boy!

ANDREY [*glancing through the papers*]. All right, I'll go through them and sign them if they need it. You can take them back to the office later. [*Goes into the house, reading the papers.*]

[FERAPONT *wheels the pram into the garden.*]

NATASHA [*in the window*].What's Mummy's name, Bobik? You darling! And who's that lady? Auntie Olia. Say: 'Hullo, Auntie Olia.'

[*Two street musicians, a man and a girl, enter and begin to play on a violin and a harp;* VERSHININ, OLGA *and* ANFISA

---

7. A thin sour beer made from rye or barley.

8. "You must not make any noise, Sophie is asleep already. You're a bear."

come out of the house and listen in silence for a few moments;
then IRENA *approaches them.*]

OLGA. Our garden's like a public road; everybody goes through it. Nanny, give something to the musicians.

ANFISA [*giving them money*]. Go along now, God bless you, good people!

[*The musicians bow and go away.*]

Poor, homeless folk! Whoever would go dragging round the streets playing tunes if he had enough to eat? [*To* IRENA.] How are you, Irenushka? [*Kisses her.*] Ah, my child, what a life I'm having! Such comfort! In a large flat at the school with Oliushka—and no rent to pay, either! The Lord's been kind to me in my old age. I've never had such a comfortable time in my life, old sinner that I am! A big flat, and no rent to pay, and a whole room to myself, with my own bed. All free. Sometimes when I wake up in the night I begin to think, and then—Oh, Lord! Oh, Holy Mother of God!—there's no one happier in the world than me!

VERSHININ [*glances at his watch*]. We shall be starting in a moment, Olga Serghyeevna. It's time I went. [*A pause.*] I wish you all the happiness in the world . . . everything. . . . Where's Maria Seerghyeevna?

IRENA. She's somewhere in the garden. I'll go and look for her.

VERSHININ. That's kind of you. I really must hurry.

ANFISA. I'll come and help to look for her. [*Calls out.*] Mashenka, ah-oo!

[*Goes with* IRENA *towards the far end of the garden.*]

Ah-oo! Ah-oo!

VERSHININ. Everything comes to an end. Well, here we are—and now it's going to be 'good-bye'. [*Looks at his watch.*] The city gave us a sort of farewell lunch. There was champagne, and the mayor made a speech, and I ate and listened, but in spirit I was with you here. . . . [*Glances round the garden.*] I've grown so . . . so accustomed to you.

OLGA. Shall we meet again some day, I wonder?

VERSHININ. Most likely not! [*A pause.*] My wife and the two little girls will be staying on here for a month or two. Please, if anything happens, if they need anything. . . .

OLGA. Yes, yes, of course. You needn't worry about that. [*A pause.*] To-morrow there won't be a single officer or soldier in the town. . . . All that will be just a memory, and, of course, a new life will begin for us here. . . . [*A pause.*] Nothing ever happens as we'd like it to. I didn't want to be a headmistress, and yet now I am one. It means we shan't be going to live in Moscow. . . .

VERSHININ. Well. . . . Thank you for everything. Forgive me if ever I've done anything. . . . I've talked a lot too much, far too much. . . . Forgive me for that, don't think too unkindly of me.

OLGA [*wipes her eyes*]. Now . . . why is Masha so long coming?

VERSHININ. What else can I tell you now it's time to say 'good-bye'? What shall I philosophize about now? . . . [*Laughs.*] Yes, life is difficult. It seems quite hopeless for a lot of us, just a kind of impasse. . . . And yet you must admit that it is gradually getting easier and brighter, and it's clear that the time isn't far off when the light will spread everywhere. [*Looks at his watch.*] Time, it's time for me to go. . . . In the old days the human race was always making war, its entire existence was taken up with campaigns, advances, retreats, victories. . . . But now all that's out of date, and in its place there's a huge vacuum, clamouring to be filled. Humanity is passionately seeking something to fill it with and, of course, it will find something some day. Oh! If only it would happen soon! [*A pause.*] If only we could educate the industrious people and make the educated people industrious. . . . [*Looks at his watch.*] I really must go. . . .

OLGA. Here she comes!

[*Enter* MASHA.]

VERSHININ. I've come to say good-bye. . . .

[OLGA *walks off and stands a little to one side so as not to interfere with their leave-taking.*]

MASHA [*looking into his face*]. Good-bye! . . . [*A long kiss.*]

OLGA. That'll do, that'll do.

MASHA [*sobs loudly*].

VERSHININ. Write to me. . . . Don't forget me! Let me go . . . it's time. Olga Serghyeevna, please take her away . . . I must go . . . I'm late already. . . . [*Deeply moved, kisses* OLGA's *hands, then embraces* MASHA *once again, and goes out quickly.*]

OLGA. That'll do, Masha! Don't, my dear, don't. . . .

[*Enter* KOOLYGHIN.]

KOOLYGHIN [*embarrassed*]. Never mind, let her cry, let her. . . . My dear Masha, my dear, sweet Masha. . . . You're my wife, and I'm happy in spite of everything. . . . I'm not complaining, I've no reproach to make—not a single one. . . . Olga here is my witness. . . . We'll start our life over again in the same old way, and you won't hear a word from me . . . not a hint. . . .

MASHA [*suppressing her sobs*]. 'A green oak grows by a curving shore, And round that oak hangs a golden chain.' . . . 'A golden chain round that oak.' . . . Oh, I'm going mad. . . . By a curving shore . . . a green oak. . . .

OLGA. Calm yourself, Masha, calm yourself. . . . Give her some water.

MASHA. I'm not crying any more. . . .

KOOLYGHIN. She's not crying any more . . . she's a good girl.

[*The hollow sound of a gun-shot is heard in the distance.*]

MASHA. 'A green oak grows by a curving shore, And round that oak hangs a golden chain.' . . . A green cat . . . a green oak . . . I've got it all mixed up. . . . [*Drinks water.*] My life's messed up. . . . I don't want anything now. . . . I'll calm down in a moment. . . . It doesn't matter. . . . What *is* 'the curving shore'? Why does it keep coming into my head all the time? My thoughts are all mixed up.

[*Enter* IRENA.]

OLGA. Calm down, Masha. That's right . . . good girl! . . . Let's go indoors.

MASHA [*irritably*]. I'm not going in there! [*Sobs, but immediately checks herself.*] I don't go into that house now, and I'm not going to. . . .

IRENA. Let's sit down together for a moment, and not talk about anything. I'm going away to-morrow, you know. . . . [*A pause.*]

KOOLYGHIN. Yesterday I took away a false beard and a moustache from a boy in the third form. I've got them here. [*Puts them on.*] Do I look like our German teacher? . . . [*Laughs.*] I do, don't I? The boys are funny.

MASHA. It's true, you do look like that German of yours.

OLGA [*laughs*]. Yes, he does.

[MASHA *cries.*]

IRENA. That's enough, Masha!

KOOLYGHIN. Very much like him, I think!

[*Enter* NATASHA.]

NATASHA [*to the maid*]. What? Oh, yes. Mr. Protopov is going to keep an eye on Sofochka, and Andrey Serghyeevich is going to take Bobik out in the pram. What a lot of work these children make! . . . [*To* IRENA.] Irena, you're really leaving to-morrow? What a pity! Do stay just another week, won't you? [*Catching sight of* KOOLYGHIN, *shrieks; he laughs and takes off the false beard and moustache.*] Get away with you! How you scared me! [*To* IRENA.] I've grown so accustomed to you being here. . . . You mustn't think it's going to be easy for me to be without you. I'll get Andrey and his old violin to move into your room: he can saw away at it as much as he likes there. And then we'll move Sofochka into his room. She's such a wonderful child, really! Such a lovely little girl! This morning she looked at me with such a sweet expression, and then she said: 'Ma-mma!'

KOOLYGHIN. It's quite true, she is a beautiful child.

NATASHA. So to-morrow I'll be alone here. [*Sighs.*] I'll have this fir-tree avenue cut down first, then that maple tree over there. It looks so awful in the evenings.[9] . . . [*To* IRENA.] My dear, that belt you're wearing doesn't suit you at all. Not at all good taste. You want something brighter to go with that dress. . . . I'll tell them to put flowers all round here, lots of flowers, so that we get plenty of scent from them. . . . [*Sternly.*] Why is there a fork lying on this seat? [*Going into the house, to the maid.*] Why is that fork left on the seat there? [*Shouts.*] Don't answer me back!

KOOLYGHIN. There she goes again!

[*A band plays a military march off-stage; all listen.*]

OLGA. They're going.

[*Enter* CHEBUTYKIN.]

MASHA. The soldiers are going. Well. . . . Happy journey to them! [*To her husband.*] We must go home. . . . Where's my hat and cape? . . .

KOOLYGHIN. I took them indoors. I'll bring them at once.

OLGA. Yes, we can go home now. It's time.

CHEBUTYKIN. Olga Serghyeevna!

---

9. Moscow ms.: "It is so frightful and looks so awful in the evenings."

OLGA. What is it? [*A pause.*] What?

CHEBUTYKIN. Nothing. . . . I don't know quite how to tell you. . . . [*Whispers into her ear.*]

OLGA [*frightened*]. It can't be true!

CHEBUTYKIN. Yes . . . a bad business. . . . I'm so tired . . . quite worn out. . . . I don't want to say another word. . . . [*With annoyance.*] Anyway, nothing matters! . . .

MASHA. What's happened?

OLGA [*puts her arms round* IRENA]. What a dreadful day! . . . I don't know how to tell you, dear. . . .

IRENA. What is it? Tell me quickly, what is it? For Heaven's sake! . . . [*Cries.*]

CHEBUTYKIN. The Baron's just been killed in a duel.

IRENA [*cries quietly*]. I knew it, I knew it. . . .

CHEBUTYKIN [*goes to the back of the stage and sits down*]. I'm tired. . . . [*Takes a newspaper out of his pocket.*] Let them cry for a bit. . . . [*Sings quietly to himself.*] Tarara-boom-di-ay, I'm sitting on a tomb-di-ay. . . . What difference does it make? . . .

[*The three sisters stand huddled together.*]

MASHA. Oh, listen to that band! They're leaving us . . . one of them's gone for good . . . for ever! We're left alone . . . to start our lives all over again. We must go on living . . . we must go on living. . . .

IRENA [*puts her head on* OLGA's *breast*]. Some day people will know why such things happen, and what the purpose of all this suffering is. . . . Then there won't be any more riddles. . . . Meanwhile we must go on living . . . and working. Yes, we must just go on working! To-morrow I'll go away alone and teach in a school somewhere; I'll give my life to people who need it. . . . It's autumn now, winter will soon be here, and the snow will cover everything . . . but I'll go on working and working! . . .

OLGA [*puts her arms round both her sisters*]. How cheerfully and jauntily that band's playing—really I feel as if I wanted to live! Merciful God! The years will pass, and we shall all be gone for good and quite forgotten. . . . Our faces and our voices will be forgotten and people won't even know that there were once three of us here. . . . But our sufferings may mean happiness for the people who come after us. . . . There'll be a time when peace and happiness reign in the world, and then we shall be remembered kindly and blessed. No, my dear sisters, life isn't finished for us yet! We're going to live! The band is playing so cheerfully and joyfully—maybe, if we wait a little longer, we shall find out why we live, why we suffer. . . . Oh, if we only knew, if only we knew!

[*The music grows fainter and fainter.* KOOLYGHIN, *smiling happily, brings out the hat and the cape.* ANDREY *enters; he is pushing the pram with* BOBIK *sitting in it.*]

CHEBUTYKIN [*sings quietly to himself*]. Tarara-boom-di-ay. . . . I'm sitting on a tomb-di-ay. . . . [*Reads the paper.*] What does it matter? Nothing matters!

OLGA. If only we knew, if only we knew! . . .

CURTAIN

GEORGE BERNARD SHAW

The Devil's Disciple[†]

A Melodrama

Act I

At the most wretched hour between a black night and a wintry morning in the year 1777, Mrs Dudgeon, of New Hampshire, is sitting up in the kitchen and general dwelling room of her farm house on the outskirts of the town of Websterbridge. She is not a prepossessing woman. No woman looks her best after sitting up all night; and Mrs Dudgeon's face, even at its best, is grimly trenched by the channels into which the barren forms and observances of a dead Puritanism can pen a bitter temper and a fierce pride. She is an elderly matron who has worked hard and got nothing by it except dominion and detestation in her sordid home, and an unquestioned reputation for piety and respectability among her neighbors, to whom drink and debauchery are still so much more tempting than religion and rectitude, that they conceive goodness simply as self-denial. This conception is easily extended to others-denial, and finally generalized as covering anything disagreeable. So Mrs Dudgeon, being exceedingly disagreeable, is held to be exceedingly good. Short of flat felony, she enjoys complete license except for amiable weaknesses of any sort, and is consequently, without knowing it, the most licentious woman in the parish on the strength of never having broken the seventh commandment or missed a Sunday at the Presbyterian church.

The year 1777 is the one in which the passions roused by the breaking-off of the American colonies from England, more by their own weight than their own will, boiled up to shooting point, the shooting being idealized to the English mind as suppression of rebellion and maintenance of British dominion, and to the American as defence of liberty, resistance to tyranny, and self-sacrifice on the altar of the Rights of Man. Into the merits of these idealizations it is not here necessary to inquire: suffice it to say, without prejudice, that they have convinced both Americans and English that the most highminded course for them to pursue is to kill as many of one another as possible, and that military operations to that end are in full swing, morally supported by confident requests from the clergy of both sides for the blessing of God on their arms.

[†] From *Three Plays For Puritans.*

Under such circumstances many other women besides this disagreeable Mrs Dudgeon find themselves sitting up all night waiting for news. Like her, too, they fall asleep towards morning at the risk of nodding themselves into the kitchen fire. Mrs Dudgeon sleeps with a shawl over her head, and her feet on a broad fender of iron laths, the step of the domestic altar of the fireplace, with its huge hobs and boiler, and its hinged arm above the smoky mantelshelf for roasting. The plain kitchen table is opposite the fire, at her elbow, with a candle on it in a tin sconce. Her chair, like all the others in the room, is uncushioned and unpainted; but as it has a round railed back and a seat conventionally moulded to the sitter's curves, it is comparatively a chair of state. The room has three doors, one on the same side as the fireplace, near the corner, leading to the best bedroom; one, at the opposite end of the opposite wall, leading to the scullery and washhouse; and the housedoor, with its latch, heavy lock, and clumsy wooden bar, in the front wall, between the window in its middle and the corner next the bedroom door. Between the door and the window a rack of pegs suggests to the deductive observer that the men of the house are all away, as there are no hats or coats on them. On the other side of the window the clock hangs on a nail, with its white wooden dial, black iron weights, and brass pendulum. Between the clock and the corner, a big cupboard, locked, stands on a dwarf dresser full of common crockery.

On the side opposite the fireplace, between the door and the corner, a shamelessly ugly black horsehair sofa stands against the wall. An inspection of its stridulous surface shews that Mrs Dudgeon is not alone. A girl of sixteen or seventeen has fallen asleep on it. She is a wild, timid looking creature with black hair and tanned skin. Her frock, a scanty garment, is rent, weatherstained, berrystained, and by no means scrupulously clean. It hangs on her with a freedom which, taken with her brown legs and bare feet, suggests no great stock of underclothing.

Suddenly there comes a tapping at the door, not loud enough to wake the sleepers. Then knocking, which disturbs Mrs Dudgeon a little. Finally the latch is tried, whereupon she springs up at once.

MRS DUDGEON [*threateningly*] Well, why dont you open the door? [*She sees that the girl is asleep, and immediately raises a clamor of heartfelt vexation*]. Well, dear, dear me! Now this is—[*shaking her*] wake up, wake up: do you hear?

THE GIRL [*sitting up*] What is it?

MRS DUDGEON. Wake up; and be ashamed of yourself, you unfeeling sinful girl, falling asleep like that, and your father hardly cold in his grave.

THE GIRL [*half asleep still*] I didn't mean to. I dropped off—

MRS DUDGEON [*cutting her short*] Oh yes, youve plenty of excuses, I daresay. Dropped off! [*Fiercely, as the knocking recommences*] Why dont you get up and let your uncle in? after me waiting up all night for him! [*She pushes her rudely off the sofa*]. There:

I'll open the door: much good you are to wait up. Go and mend that fire a bit.

> *The girl, cowed and wretched, goes to the fire and puts a log on. Mrs Dudgeon unbars the door and opens it, letting into the stuffy kitchen a little of the freshness and a great deal of the chill of the dawn, also her second son Christy, a fattish, stupid, fairhaired, roundfaced man of about 22, muffled in a plaid shawl and grey overcoat. He hurries, shivering, to the fire, leaving Mrs Dudgeon to shut the door.*

CHRISTY [*at the fire*] F—f—f! but it is cold. [*Seeing the girl, and staring lumpishly at her*] Why, who are you?

THE GIRL [*shyly*] Essie.

MRS DUDGEON. Oh, you may well ask. [*To Essie*] Go to your room, child, and lie down, since you havnt feeling enough to keep you awake. Your history isnt fit for your own ears to hear.

ESSIE. I—

MRS DUDGEON [*peremptorily*] Dont answer me, Miss; but shew your obedience by doing what I tell you. [*Essie, almost in tears, crosses the room to the door near the sofa*]. And dont forget your prayers. [*Essie goes out*]. She'd have gone to bed last night just as if nothing had happened if I'd let her.

CHRISTY [*phlegmatically*] Well, she cant be expected to feel Uncle Peter's death like one of the family.

MRS DUDGEON. What are you talking about, child? Isnt she his daughter—the punishment of his wickedness and shame? [*She assaults her chair by sitting down*].

CHRISTY [*staring*] Uncle Peter's daughter!

MRS DUDGEON. Why else should she be here? D'ye think Ive not had enough trouble and care put upon me bringing up my own girls, let alone you and your good-for-nothing brother, without having your uncle's bastards—

CHRISTY [*interrupting her with an apprehensive glance at the door by which Essie went out*] Sh! She may hear you.

MRS DUDGEON [*raising her voice*] Let her hear me. People who fear God dont fear to give the devil's work its right name. [*Christy, soullessly indifferent to the strife of Good and Evil, stares at the fire, warming himself*]. Well, how long are you going to stare there like a stuck pig? What news have you for me?

CHRISTY [*taking off his hat and shawl and going to the rack to hang them up*] The minister is to break the news to you. He'll be here presently.

MRS DUDGEON. Break what news?

CHRISTY [*standing on tiptoe, from boyish habit, to hang his hat up, though he is quite tall enough to reach the peg, and speaking with callous placidity, considering the nature of the announcement*] Father's dead too.

MRS DUDGEON [*stupent*] Your father!

CHRISTY [*sulkily, coming back to the fire and warming himself again, attending much more to the fire than to his mother*] Well, it's not my fault. When we got to Nevinstown we found him ill in bed. He didnt know us at first. The minister sat up with him and sent me away. He died in the night.

MRS DUDGEON [*bursting into dry angry tears*] Well, I do think this is hard on me—very hard on me. His brother, that was a disgrace to us all his life, gets hanged on the public gallows as a rebel; and your father, instead of staying at home where his duty was, with his own family, goes after him and dies, leaving everything on my shoulders. After sending this girl to me to take care of, too! [*She plucks her shawl vexedly over her ears*]. It's sinful, so it is: downright sinful.

CHRISTY [*with a slow, bovine cheerfulness, after a pause*] I think it's going to be a fine morning, after all.

MRS DUDGEON [*railing at him*] A fine morning! And your father newly dead! Wheres your feelings, child?

CHRISTY [*obstinately*] Well, I didnt mean any harm. I suppose a man may make a remark about the weather even if his father's dead.

MRS DUDGEON [*bitterly*] A nice comfort my children are to me! One son a fool, and the other a lost sinner thats left his home to live with smugglers and gypsies and villains, the scum of the earth!
     Someone knocks.

CHRISTY [*without moving*] That's the minister.

MRS DUDGEON [*sharply*] Well, arnt you going to let Mr Anderson in?
     Christy goes sheepishly to the door. Mrs Dudgeon buries her face in her hands, as it is her duty as a widow to be overcome with grief. Christy opens the door, and admits the minister, Anthony Anderson, a shrewd, genial, ready Presbyterian divine of about 50, with something of the authority of his profession in his bearing. But it is an altogether secular authority, sweetened by a conciliatory, sensible manner not at all suggestive of a quite thorough-going other-worldliness. He is a strong, healthy man too, with a thick sanguine neck; and his keen, cheerful mouth cuts into somewhat fleshy corners. No doubt an excellent parson, but still a man capable of making the most of this world, and perhaps a little apologetically conscious of getting on better with it than a sound Presbyterian ought.

ANDERSON [*to Christy, at the door, looking at Mrs Dudgeon whilst he takes off his cloak*] Have you told her?

CHRISTY. She made me. [*He shuts the door; yawns; and loafs across to the sofa, where he sits down and presently drops off to sleep*].
     Anderson looks compassionately at Mrs Dudgeon. Then he hangs his cloak and hat on the rack. Mrs Dudgeon dries her eyes and looks up at him.

ANDERSON. Sister: the Lord has laid his hand very heavily upon you.

MRS DUDGEON [*with intensely recalcitrant resignation*] It's His will, I suppose; and I must bow to it. But I do think it hard. What call had Timothy to go to Springtown, and remind everybody that he belonged to a man that was being hanged?—and [*spitefully*] that deserved it, if ever a man did.

ANDERSON [*gently*] They were brothers, Mrs Dudgeon.

MRS DUDGEON. Timothy never acknowledged him as his brother after we were married: he had too much respect for me to insult me with such a brother. Would such a selfish wretch as Peter have come thirty miles to see Timothy hanged, do you think? Not thirty yards, not he. However, I must bear my cross as best I may: least said is soonest mended.

ANDERSON [*very grave, coming down to the fire to stand with his back to it*] Your eldest son was present at the execution, Mrs Dudgeon.

MRS DUDGEON [*disagreeably surprised*] Richard?

ANDERSON [*nodding*] Yes.

MRS DUDGEON [*vindictively*] Let it be a warning to him. He may end that way himself, the wicked, dissolute, godless—[*she suddenly stops; her voice fails; and she asks, with evident dread*] Did Timothy see him?

ANDERSON. Yes.

MRS DUDGEON [*holding her breath*] Well?

ANDERSON. He only saw him in the crowd: they did not speak. [*Mrs Dudgeon, greatly relieved, exhales the pent up breath and sits at her ease again*]. Your husband was greatly touched and impressed by his brother's awful death. [*Mrs Dudgeon sneers. Anderson breaks off to demand with some indignation*] Well, wasnt it only natural, Mrs Dudgeon? He softened towards his prodigal son in that moment. He sent for him to come to see him.

MRS DUDGEON [*her alarm renewed*] Sent for Richard!

ANDERSON. Yes; but Richard would not come. He sent his father a message; but I'm sorry to say it was a wicked message—an awful message.

MRS DUDGEON. What was it?

ANDERSON. That he would stand by his wicked uncle and stand against his good parents, in this world and the next.

MRS DUDGEON [*implacably*] He will be punished for it. He will be punished for it—in both worlds.

ANDERSON. That is not in our hands, Mrs Dudgeon.

MRS DUDGEON. Did I say it was, Mr Anderson? We are told that the wicked shall be punished. Why should we do our duty and keep God's law if there is to be no difference made between us and those who follow their own likings and dislikings, and make a jest of us and of their Maker's word?

ANDERSON. Well, Richard's earthly father has been merciful to him; and his heavenly judge is the father of us all.

MRS DUDGEON [*forgetting herself*] Richard's earthly father was a soft-headed—

ANDERSON [*shocked*] Oh!

MRS DUDGEON [*with a touch of shame*] Well, I am Richard's mother. If I am against him who has any right to be for him? [*Trying to conciliate him*] Wont you sit down, Mr. Anderson? I should have asked you before; but I'm so troubled.

ANDERSON. Thank you. [*He takes a chair from beside the fireplace, and turns it so that he can sit comfortably at the fire. When he is seated he adds, in the tone of a man who knows that he is opening a difficult subject*] Has Christy told you about the new will?

MRS DUDGEON [*all her fears returning*] The new will! Did Timothy—? [*She breaks off, gasping, unable to complete the question*].

ANDERSON. Yes. In his last hours he changed his mind.

MRS DUDGEON [*white with intense rage*] And you let him rob me?

ANDERSON. I had no power to prevent him giving what was his to his own son.

MRS DUDGEON. He had nothing of his own. His money was the money I brought him as my marriage portion. It was for me to deal with my own money and my own son. He dare not have done it if I had been with him; and well he knew it. That was why he stole away like a thief to take advantage of the law to rob me by making a new will behind my back. The more shame on you, Mr Anderson,—you, a minister of the gospel—to act as his accomplice in such a crime.

ANDERSON [*rising*] I will take no offence at what you say in the first bitterness of your grief.

MRS DUDGEON [*contemptuously*] Grief!

ANDERSON. Well, of your disappointment, if you can find it in your heart to think that the better word.

MRS DUDGEON. My heart! My heart! And since when, pray, have you begun to hold up our hearts as trustworthy guides for us?

ANDERSON [*rather guiltily*] I—er—

MRS DUDGEON [*vehemently*] Dont lie, Mr Anderson. We are told that the heart of man is deceitful above all things, and desperately wicked. My heart belonged, not to Timothy, but to that poor wretched brother of his that has just ended his days with a rope round his neck—aye, to Peter Dudgeon. You know it: old Eli Hawkins, the man to whose pulpit you succeeded, though you are not worthy to loose his shoe latchet, told it you when he gave over our souls into your charge. He warned me and strengthened me against my heart, and made me marry a Godfearing man—as he thought. What else but that discipline has made me the woman I am? And you, you, who followed your heart in your marriage, you talk to me of what I find in my heart. Go home to your pretty wife, man; and leave me to my prayers. [*She turns from him and leans with her elbows on the table, brooding over her wrongs and taking no further notice of him*].

ANDERSON [*willing enough to escape*] The Lord forbid that I should come between you and the source of all comfort! [*He goes to the rack for his coat and hat*].

MRS DUDGEON [*without looking at him*] The Lord will know what to forbid and what to allow without your help.

ANDERSON And whom to forgive, I hope—Eli Hawkins and myself, if we have ever set up our preaching against His law. [*He fastens his cloak, and is now ready to go*]. Just one word—on necessary business, Mrs Dudgeon. There is the reading of the will to be gone through; and Richard has a right to be present. He is in the town; but he has the grace to say that he does not want to force himself in here.

MRS DUDGEON. He shall come here. Does he expect us to leave his father's house for his convenience? Let them all come, and come quickly, and go quickly. They shall not make the will an excuse to shirk half their day's work. I shall be ready, never fear.

ANDERSON [*coming back a step or two*] Mrs Dudgeon: I used to have some little influence with you. When did I lose it?

MRS DUDGEON [*still without turning to him*] When you married for love. Now youre answered.

ANDERSON. Yes: I am answered. [*He goes out, musing*].

MRS DUDGEON [*to herself, thinking of her husband*] Thief! Thief!! [*She shakes herself angrily out of her chair; throws back the shawl from her head; and sets to work to prepare the room for the reading of the will, beginning by replacing Anderson's chair against the wall, and pushing back her own to the window. Then she calls, in her hard, driving, wrathful way*] Christy. [*No answer: he is fast asleep*]. Christy. [*She shakes him roughly*]. Get up out of that; and be ashamed of yourself—sleeping, and your father dead! [*She returns to the table; puts the candle on the mantelshelf; and takes from the table drawer a red table cloth which she spreads*].

CHRISTY [*rising reluctantly*] Well, do you suppose we are never going to sleep until we are out of mourning?

MRS DUDGEON. I want none of your sulks. Here: help me to set this table. [*They place the table in the middle of the room, with Christy's end towards the fireplace and Mrs Dudgeon's towards the sofa. Christy drops the table as soon as possible, and goes to the fire, leaving his mother to make the final adjustments of its position*]. We shall have the minister back here with the lawyer and all the family to read the will before you have done toasting yourself. Go and wake that girl; and then light the stove in the shed; you cant have your breakfast here. And mind you wash yourself, and make yourself fit to receive the company. [*She punctuates these orders by going to the cupboard; unlocking it; and producing a decanter of wine, which has no doubt stood there untouched since the last state occasion in the family, and some glasses, which she sets on the table. Also two green ware plates, on one of which she puts a barnbrack*[1] *with a knife beside it. On the other she shakes some biscuits out of a tin, putting back one or two, and counting the rest*]. Now mind: there are ten biscuits there: let there be ten there when I come back after dressing myself. And keep your fingers off the raisins in that cake. And tell Essie the same. I suppose I can trust you to bring in the case of stuffed birds without breaking the glass? [*She replaces the tin in the cupboard, which she locks, pocketing the key carefully*].

CHRISTY [*lingering at the fire*] Youd better put the inkstand instead, for the lawyer.

MRS DUDGEON. Thats no answer to make to me, sir. Go and do as

---

1. A cake or loaf containing currants.

youre told. [*Christy turns sullenly to obey*]. Stop: take down that shutter before you go, and let the daylight in: you cant expect me to do all the heavy work of the house with a great lout like you idling about.

> *Christy takes the window bar out of its clamps, and puts it aside; then opens the shutter, shewing the grey morning. Mrs Dudgeon takes the sconce² from the mantelshelf; blows out the candle; extinguishes the snuff by pinching it with her fingers, first licking them for the purpose; and replaces the sconce on the shelf.*

CHRISTY [*looking through the window*] Here's the minister's wife.

MRS DUDGEON [*displeased*] What! Is she coming here?

CHRISTY. Yes.

MRS DUDGEON. What does she want troubling me at this hour, before I am properly dressed to receive people?

CHRISTY. Youd better ask her.

MRS DUDGEON [*threateningly*] Youd better keep a civil tongue in your head. [*He goes sulkily towards the door. She comes after him plying him with instructions*]. Tell that girl to come to me as soon as she's had her breakfast. And tell her to make herself fit to be seen before the people. [*Christy goes out and slams the door in her face*]. Nice manners, that! [*Someone knocks at the house door: she turns and cries inhospitably*] Come in. [*Judith Anderson, the minister's wife, comes in. Judith is more than twenty years younger than her husband, though she will never be as young as he in vitality. She is pretty and proper and ladylike, and has been admired and petted into an opinion of herself sufficiently favorable to give her a self-assurance which serves her instead of strength. She has a pretty taste in dress, and in her face the pretty lines of a sentimental character formed by dreams. Even her little self-complacency is pretty, like a child's vanity. Rather a pathetic creature to any sympathetic observer who knows how rough a place the world is. One feels, on the whole, that Anderson might have chosen worse, and that she, needing protection, could not have chosen better*]. Oh, it's you, is it, Mrs Anderson?

JUDITH [*very politely—almost patronizingly*] Yes. Can I do anything for you, Mrs Dudgeon? Can I help to get the place ready before they come to read the will?

MRS DUDGEON [*stiffly*] Thank you, Mrs Anderson, my house is always ready for anyone to come into.

MRS ANDERSON [*with complacent amiability*] Yes, indeed it is. Perhaps you had rather I did not intrude on you just now.

MRS DUDGEON. Oh, one more or less will make no difference this morning, Mrs Anderson. Now that youre here, youd better stay. If you wouldnt mind shutting the door! [*Judith smiles, implying "How stupid of me!" and shuts it with an exasperating air of doing something pretty and becoming*]. Thats better. I must go and tidy myself a bit. I suppose you dont mind stopping here to receive anyone that comes until I'm ready.

2. A candlestick with a handle.

JUDITH [*graciously giving her leave*] Oh yes, certainly. Leave that to me, Mrs Dudgeon; and take your time. [*She hangs her cloak and bonnet on the rack*].

MRS DUDGEON [*half sneering*] I thought that would be more in your way than getting the house ready. [*Essie comes back*]. Oh, here you are! [*Severely*] Come here: let me see you. [*Essie timidly goes to her. Mrs. Dudgeon takes her roughly by the arm and pulls her round to inspect the results of her attempt to clean and tidy herself—results which shew little practice and less conviction*]. Mm! Thats what you call doing your hair properly, I suppose. It's easy to see what you are, and how you were brought up. [*She throws her arm away, and goes on, peremptorily*] Now you listen to me and do as youre told. You sit down there in the corner by the fire; and when the company comes dont dare to speak until youre spoken to. [*Essie creeps away to the fireplace*]. Your father's people had better see you and know youre there: theyre as much bound to keep you from starvation as I am. At any rate they might help. But let me have no chattering and making free with them, as if you were their equal. Do you hear?

ESSIE. Yes.

MRS DUDGEON. Well, then go and do as youre told. [*Essie sits down miserably on the corner of the fender furthest from the door*]. Never mind her, Mrs Anderson: you know who she is and what she is. If she gives you any trouble, just tell me; and I'll settle accounts with her. [*Mrs Dudgeon goes into the bedroom, shutting the door sharply behind her as if even it had to be made do its duty with a ruthless hand*].

JUDITH [*patronizing Essie, and arranging the cake and wine on the table more becomingly*] You must not mind if your aunt is strict with you. She is a very good woman, and desires your good too.

ESSIE [*in listless misery*] Yes.

JUDITH [*annoyed with Essie for her failure to be consoled and edified, and to appreciate the kindly condescension of the remark*] You are not going to be sullen, I hope, Essie.

ESSIE. No.

JUDITH. Thats a good girl! [*She places a couple of chairs at the table with their backs to the window, with a pleasant sense of being a more thoughtful housekeeper than Mrs Dudgeon*]. Do you know any of your father's relatives?

ESSIE. No. They wouldnt have anything to do with him: they were too religious. Father used to talk about Dick Dudgeon; but I never saw him.

JUDITH [*ostentatiously shocked*] Dick Dudgeon! Essie: do you wish to be a really respectable and grateful girl, and to make a place for yourself here by steady good conduct?

ESSIE [*very half-heartedly*] Yes.

JUDITH. Then you must never mention the name of Richard Dudgeon —never even think about him. He is a bad man.

ESSIE. What has he done?

JUDITH. You must not ask questions about him, Essie. You are too young to know what it is to be a bad man. But he is a smuggler; and he lives with gypsies; and he has no love for his mother and his family; and he wrestles and plays games on Sunday instead of going to church. Never let him into your presence, if you can help it, Essie; and try to keep yourself and all womanhood unspotted by contact with such men.

ESSIE. Yes.

JUDITH [*again displeased*] I am afraid you say Yes and No without thinking very deeply.

ESSIE. Yes. At least I mean—

JUDITH [*severely*] What do you mean?

ESSIE [*almost crying*] Only—my father was a smuggler; and— [*Someone knocks*].

JUDITH. They are beginning to come. Now remember your aunt's directions, Essie; and be a good girl. [*Christy comes back with the stand of stuffed birds under a glass case, and an inkstand, which he places on the table*]. Good morning, Mr Dudgeon. Will you open the door, please: the people have come.

CHRISTY. Good morning. [*He opens the house door*].

The morning is now fairly bright and warm; and Anderson, who is the first to enter, has left his cloak at home. He is accompanied by Lawyer Hawkins, a brisk, middleaged man in brown riding gaiters and yellow breeches, looking as much squire as solicitor. He and Anderson are allowed precedence as representing the learned professions. After them comes the family, headed by the senior uncle, William Dudgeon, a large, shapeless man, bottle-nose and evidently no ascetic at table. His clothes are not the clothes, nor his anxious wife the wife, of a prosperous man. The junior uncle, Titus Dudgeon, is a wiry little terrier of a man, with an immense and visibly purse-proud wife, both free from the cares of the William household.

Hawkins at once goes briskly to the table and takes the chair nearest the sofa, Christy having left the inkstand there. He puts his hat on the floor beside him, and produces the will. Uncle William comes to the fire and stands on the hearth warming his coat tails, leaving Mrs Williams derelict near the door. Uncle Titus, who is the lady's man of the family, rescues her by giving her his disengaged arm and bringing her to the sofa, where he sits down warmly between his own lady and his brother's. Anderson hangs up his hat and waits for a word with Judith.

JUDITH. She will be here in a moment. Ask them to wait. [*She taps at the bedroom door. Receiving an answer from within, she opens it and passes through*].

ANDERSON [*taking his place at the table at the opposite end to Hawkins*] Our poor afflicted sister will be with us in a moment. Are we all here?

CHRISTY [*at the house door, which he has just shut*] All except Dick.

The callousness with which Christy names the reprobate jars on the moral sense of the family. Uncle William shakes his head slowly and repeatedly. Mrs Titus catches her breath convulsively through her nose. Her husband speaks.

UNCLE TITUS. Well, I hope he will have the grace not to come. I hope so.

> *The Dudgeons all murmur assent, except Christy, who goes to the window and posts himself there, looking out. Hawkins smiles secretively as if he knew something that would change their tune if they knew it. Anderson is uneasy: the love of solemn family councils, especially funeral ones, is not in his nature. Judith appears at the bedroom door.*

JUDITH [*with gentle impressiveness*] Friends, Mrs. Dudgeon. [*She takes the chair from beside the fireplace; and places it for Mrs Dudgeon, who comes from the bedroom in black, with a clean handkerchief to her eyes. All rise, except Essie. Mrs Titus and Mrs William produce equally clean handkerchiefs and weep. It is an affecting moment*].

UNCLE WILLIAM. Would it comfort you, sister, if we were to offer up a prayer?

UNCLE TITUS. Or sing a hymn?

ANDERSON [*rather hastily*] I have been with our sister this morning already, friends. In our hearts we ask a blessing.

ALL [*except Essie*] Amen.

> *They all sit down, except Judith, who stands behind Mrs Dudgeon's chair.*

JUDITH [*to Essie*] Essie: did you say Amen?

ESSIE [*scaredly*] No.

JUDITH. Then say it, like a good girl.

ESSIE. Amen.

UNCLE WILLIAM [*encouragingly*] Thats right: thats right. We know who you are; but we are willing to be kind to you if you are a good girl and deserve it. We are all equal before the Throne.

> *This republican sentiment does not please the women, who are convinced that the Throne is precisely the place where their superiority, often questioned in this world, will be recognized and rewarded.*

CHRISTY [*at the window*] Here's Dick.

> *Anderson and Hawkins look round sociably. Essie, with a gleam of interest breaking through her misery, looks up. Christy grins and gapes expectantly at the door. The rest are petrified with the intensity of their sense of Virtue menaced with outrage by the approach of flaunting Vice. The reprobate appears in the doorway, graced beyond his alleged merits by the morning sunlight. He is certainly the best looking member of the family; but his expression is reckless and sardonic, his manner defiant and satirical, his dress picturesquely careless. Only, his forehead and mouth betray an extraordinary steadfastness; and his eyes are the eyes of a fanatic.*

RICHARD [*on the threshold, taking off his hat*] Ladies and gentlemen: your servant, your very humble servant. [*With this comprehensive insult, he throws his hat to Christy with a suddenness that makes him jump like a negligent wicket keeper, and comes into the middle of the room, where he turns and deliberately surveys the company].* How happy you all look! how glad to see me! [*He turns towards Mrs Dudgeon's chair; and his lip rolls up horribly from his dog tooth as he meets her look of undisguised hatred].* Well, mother: keeping up appearances as usual? thats right, thats right. [*Judith pointedly moves away from his neighborhood to the other side of the kitchen, holding her skirt instinctively as if to save it from contamination. Uncle Titus promptly marks his approval of her action by rising from the sofa, and placing a chair for her to sit down upon].* What! Uncle William! I havnt seen you since you gave up drinking. [*Poor Uncle William, shamed, would protest; but Richard claps him heartily on his shoulder, adding*] you have given it up, havnt you? [*releasing him with a playful push*] of course you have: quite right too: you overdid it. [*He turns away from Uncle William and makes for the sofa].* And now, where is that upright horsedealer Uncle Titus? Uncle Titus: come forth. [*He comes upon him holding the chair as Judith sits down].* As usual, looking after the ladies!

UNCLE TITUS [*indignantly*] Be ashamed of yourself, sir—

RICHARD [*interrupting him and shaking his hand in spite of him*] I am: I am; but I am proud of my uncle—proud of all my relatives— [*again surveying them*] who could look at them and not be proud and joyful? [*Uncle Titus, overborne, resumes his seat on the sofa. Richard turns to the table].* Ah, Mr Anderson, still at the good work, still shepherding them. Keep them up to the mark, minister, keep them up to the mark. Come! [*with a spring he seats himself on the table and takes up the decanter*] clink a glass with me, Pastor, for the sake of old times.

ANDERSON. You know, I think, Mr Dudgeon, that I do not drink before dinner.

RICHARD. You will, some day, Pastor: Uncle William used to drink before breakfast. Come: it will give your sermons unction. [*He smells the wine and makes a wry face].* But do not begin on my mother's company sherry. I stole some when I was six years old; and I have been a temperate man ever since. [*He puts the decanter down and changes the subject].* So I hear you are married, Pastor, and that your wife has a most ungodly allowance of good looks.

ANDERSON [*quietly indicating Judith*] Sir: you are in the presence of my wife. [*Judith rises and stands with stony propriety].*

RICHARD [*quickly slipping down from the table with instinctive good manners*] Your servant, madam: no offence. [*He looks at her earnestly].* You deserve your reputation; but I'm sorry to see by your expression that youre a good woman. [*She looks shocked, and sits down amid a murmur of indignant sympathy from his relatives. Anderson, sensible enough to know that these demonstrations can only gratify and encourage a man who is deliberately trying to provoke them, remains perfectly goodhumored].* All the same, Pastor, I respect you more than I did before. By the way, did I hear, or did I not, that our late lamented Uncle Peter, though unmarried, was a father?

UNCLE TITUS. He had only one irregular child, sir.

RICHARD. Only one! He thinks one a mere trifle! I blush for you, Uncle Titus.

ANDERSON. Mr Dudgeon: you are in the presence of your mother and her grief.

RICHARD. It touches me profoundly, Pastor. By the way, what has become of the irregular child?

ANDERSON [*pointing to Essie*] There, sir, listening to you.

RICHARD [*shocked into sincerity*] What! Why the devil didnt you tell me that before? Children suffer enough in this house without— [*He hurries remorsefully to Essie*]. Come, little cousin! never mind me: it was not meant to hurt you. [*She looks up gratefully at him. Her tearstained face affects him violently; and he bursts out, in a transport of wrath*] Who has been making her cry? Who has been ill-treating her? By God—

MRS DUDGEON [*rising and confronting him*] Silence your blasphemous tongue. I will bear no more of this. Leave my house.

RICHARD. How do you know it's your house until the will is read? [*They look at one another for a moment with intense hatred; and then she sinks, checkmated, into her chair. Richard goes boldly up past Anderson to the window, where he takes the railed chair in his hand*]. Ladies and gentlemen: as the eldest son of my late father, and the unworthy head of this household, I bid you welcome. By your leave, Minister Anderson: by your leave, Lawyer Hawkins. The head of the table for the head of the family. [*He places the chair at the table between the minister and the attorney; sits down between them; and addresses the assembly with a presidential air*]. We meet on a melancholy occasion: a father dead! an uncle actually hanged, and probably damned. [*He shakes his head deploringly. The relatives freeze with horror*]. Thats right: pull your longest faces [*his voice suddenly sweetens gravely as his glance lights on Essie*] provided only there is hope in the eyes of the child. [*Briskly*] Now then, Lawyer Hawkins: business, business. Get on with the will, man.

TITUS. Do not let yourself be ordered or hurried, Mr Hawkins.

HAWKINS [*very politely and willingly*] Mr Dudgeon means no offence, I feel sure. I will not keep you one second, Mr Dudgeon. Just while I get my glasses—[*he fumbles for them. The Dudgeons look at one another with misgiving*].

RICHARD. Aha! They notice your civility, Mr Hawkins. They are prepared for the worst. A glass of wine to clear your voice before you begin. [*He pours out one for him and hands it; then pours one for himself*].

HAWKINS. Thank you, Mr Dudgeon. Your good health, sir.

RICHARD. Yours, sir. [*With the glass half way to his lips, he checks himself, giving a dubious glance at the wine, and adds, with quaint intensity*] Will anyone oblige me with a glass of water?

Essie, who has been hanging on his every word and movement, rises stealthily and slips out behind Mrs Dudgeon through the bedroom door, returning presently with a jug and going out of the house as quietly as possible.

HAWKINS. The will is not exactly in proper legal phraseology.

RICHARD. No: my father died without the consolations of the law.

HAWKINS. Good again, Mr Dudgeon, good again. [*Preparing to read*] Are you ready, sir?

RICHARD. Ready, aye ready. For what we are about to receive, may the Lord make us truly thankful. Go ahead.

HAWKINS [*reading*] "This is the last will and testament of me Timothy Dudgeon on my deathbed at Nevinstown on the road from Springtown to Websterbridge on this twenty-fourth day of September, one thousand seven hundred and seventy-seven. I hereby revoke all former wills made by me and declare that I am of sound mind and know well what I am doing and that this is my real will according to my own wish and affections."

RICHARD [*glancing at his mother*] Aha!

HAWKINS [*shaking his head*] Bad phraseology, sir, wrong phraseology. "I give and bequeath a hundred pounds to my younger son Christopher Dudgeon, fifty pounds to be paid to him on the day of his marriage to Sarah Wilkins if she will have him, and ten pounds on the birth of each of his children up to the number of five."

RICHARD. How if she wont have him?

CHRISTY. She will if I have fifty pounds.

RICHARD. Good, my brother. Proceed.

HAWKINS. "I give and bequeath to my wife Annie Dudgeon, born Annie Primrose"—you see he did not know the law, Mr Dudgeon: your mother was not born Annie: she was christened so—"an annuity of fifty-two pounds a year for life [*Mrs Dudgeon, with all eyes on her, holds herself convulsively rigid*] to be paid out of the interest on her own money"—there's a way to put it, Mr Dudgeon! Her own money!

MRS DUDGEON. A very good way to put God's truth. It was every penny my own. Fifty-two pounds a year!

HAWKINS. "And I recommend her for her goodneess and piety to the forgiving care of her children, having stood between them and her as far as I could to the best of my ability."

MRS DUDGEON. And this is my reward! [*Raging inwardly*] You know what I think, Mr Anderson: you know the word I gave to it.

ANDERSON. It cannot be helped, Mrs Dudgeon. We must take what comes to us. [*To Hawkins*]. Go on, sir.

HAWKINS. "I give and bequeath my house at Websterbridge with the land belonging to it and all the rest of my property soever to my eldest son and heir, Richard Dudgeon."

RICHARD. Oho! The fatted calf, Minister, the fatted calf.

HAWKINS. "On these conditions—"

RICHARD. The devil! Are there conditions?

HAWKINS. "To wit: first, that he shall not let my brother Peter's natural child starve or be driven by want to an evil life."

RICHARD [*emphatically, striking his fist on the table*] Agreed.

> *Mrs Dudgeon, turning to look malignantly at Essie, misses her and looks quickly round to see where she has moved to; then, seeing that she has left the room without leave, closes her lips vengefully.*

HAWKINS. "Second, that he shall be a good friend to my old horse Jim"—[*again shaking his head*] he should have written James, sir.

RICHARD. James shall live in clover. Go on.

HAWKINS.—"and keep my deaf farm labourer Prodger Feston in his service."

RICHARD. Prodger Feston shall get drunk every Saturday.

HAWKINS. "Third, that he make Christy a present on his marriage out of the ornaments in the best room."

RICHARD [*holding up the stuffed birds*] Here you are, Christy.

CHRISTY [*disappointed*] I'd rather have the china peacocks.

RICHARD. You shall have both. [*Christy is greatly pleased*]. Go on.

HAWKINS. "Fourthly and lastly, that he try to live at peace with his mother as far as she will consent to it."

RICHARD [*dubiously*] Hm! Anything more, Mr Hawkins?

HAWKINS [*solemnly*] "Finally I give and bequeath my soul into my Maker's hands, humbly asking forgiveness for all my sins and mistakes, and hoping that He will so guide my son that it may not be said that I have done wrong in trusting to him rather than to others in the perplexity of my last hour in this strange place."

ANDERSON. Amen.

THE UNCLES AND AUNTS. Amen.

RICHARD. My mother does not say Amen.

MRS DUDGEON [*rising, unable to give up her property without a struggle*] Mr Hawkins: is that a proper will? Remember, I have his rightful, legal will, drawn up by yourself, leaving all to me.

HAWKINS. This is a very wrongly and irregularly worded will, Mrs Dudgeon; though [*turning politely to Richard*] it contains in my judgment an excellent disposal of his property.

ANDERSON [*interposing before Mrs Dudgeon can retort*] That is not what you are asked, Mr Hawkins. Is it a legal will?

HAWKINS. The courts will sustain it against the other.

ANDERSON. But why, if the other is more lawfully worded?

HAWKINS. Because, sir, the courts will sustain the claim of a man—and that man the eldest son—against any woman, if they can. I warned you, Mrs Dudgeon, when you got me to draw that other will, that it was not a wise will, and that though you might make him sign it, he would never be easy until he revoked it. But you wouldnt take advice; and now Mr Richard is cock of the walk. [*He takes his hat from the floor; rises; and begins pocketing his papers and spectacles*].

> *This is the signal for the breaking-up of the party. Anderson takes his hat from the rack and joins Uncle William at the fire. Titus fetches Judith her things from the rack. The three on the sofa rise and chat with Hawkins. Mrs Dudgeon, now an intruder in her own house, stands inert, crushed by the*

weight of the law on women, accepting it, as she has been trained to accept all monstrous calamities, as proofs of the greatness of the power that inflicts them, and of her own wormlike insignificance. For at this time, remember, Mary Wollstonecraft[3] is as yet only a girl of eighteen, and her Vindication of the Rights of Women is still fourteen years off. Mrs Dudgeon is rescued from her apathy by Essie, who comes back with the jug full of water. She is taking it to Richard when Mrs Dudgeon stops her.

MRS DUDGEON [*threatening her*] Where have you been? [*Essie, appalled, tries to answer, but cannot*]. How dare you go out by yourself after the orders I gave you?

ESSIE. He asked for a drink—[*she stops, her tongue cleaving to her palate with terror*].

JUDITH [*with gentler severity*] Who asked for a drink? [*Essie, speechless, points to Richard*].

RICHARD. What! I!

JUDITH [*shocked*] Oh Essie, Essie!

RICHARD. I believe I did. [*He takes a glass and holds it to Essie to be filled. Her hand shakes*]. What! afraid of me?

ESSIE [*quickly*] No. I—[*She pours out the water*].

RICHARD [*tasting it*] Ah, youve been up the street to the market gate spring to get that. [*He takes a draught*]. Delicious! Thank you. [*Unfortunately, at this moment he chances to catch sight of Judith's face, which expresses the most prudish disapproval of his evident attraction for Essie, who is devouring him with her grateful eyes. His mocking expression returns instantly. He puts down the glass; deliberately winds his arm round Essie's shoulders; and brings her into the middle of the company. Mrs Dudgeon being in Essie's way as they come past the table, he says*] By your leave, mother [*and compels her to make way for them*]. What do they call you? Bessie?

ESSIE. Essie.

RICHARD. Essie, to be sure. Are you a good girl, Essie?

ESSIE [*greatly disappointed that he, of all people, should begin at her in this way*] Yes. [*She looks doubtfully at Judith*]. I think so. I mean I—I hope so.

RICHARD. Essie: did you ever hear of a person called the devil?

ANDERSON [*revolted*] Shame on you, sir, with a mere child—

RICHARD. By your leave, Minister: I do not interfere with your sermons: do not you interrupt mine. [*To Essie*] Do you know what they call me, Essie?

ESSIE. Dick.

RICHARD [*amused: patting her on the shoulder*] Yes, Dick; but something else too. They call me the Devil's Disciple.

ESSIE. Why do you let them?

RICHARD [*seriously*] Because it's true. I was brought up in the other service; but I knew from the first that the Devil was my natural

---

3. An English author; the wife of the reformer William Godwin. Her chief work was her *Vindication of the Rights of Woman* (1792).

master and captain and friend. I saw that he was in the right, and that the world cringed to his conqueror only through fear. I prayed secretly to him; and he comforted me, and saved me from having my spirit broken in this house of children's tears. I promised him my soul, and swore an oath that I would stand up for him in this world and stand by him in the next. [*Solemnly*] That promise and that oath made a man of me. From this day this house is his home; and no child shall cry in it: this hearth is his altar; and no soul shall ever cower over it in the dark evenings and be afraid. Now [*turning forcibly on the rest*] which of you good men will take this child and rescue her from the house of the devil?

JUDITH [*coming to Essie and throwing a protecting arm about her*] I will. You should be burnt alive.

ESSIE. But I dont want to. [*She shrinks back, leaving Richard and Judith face to face*].

RICHARD [*to Judith*] Actually doesnt want to, most virtuous lady!

UNCLE TITUS. Have a care, Richard Dudgeon. The law—

RICHARD [*turning threateningly on him*] Have a care, you. In an hour from this there will be no law here but martial law. I passed the soldiers within six miles on my way here: before noon Major Swindon's gallows for rebels will be up in the market place.

ANDERSON [*calmly*] What have we to fear from that, sir?

RICHARD. More than you think. He hanged the wrong man at Springtown: he thought Uncle Peter was respectable, because the Dudgeons had a good name. But his next example will be the best man in the town to whom he can bring home a rebellious word. Well, we're all rebels; and you know it.

ALL THE MEN [*except Anderson*] No, no, no!

RICHARD. Yes, you are. You havnt damned King George up hill and down dale as I have; but youve prayed for his defeat; and you, Anthony Anderson, have conducted the service, and sold your family bible to buy a pair of pistols. They maynt hang me, perhaps; because the moral effect of the Devil's Disciple dancing on nothing wouldnt help them. But a minister! [*Judith, dismayed, clings to Anderson*] or a lawyer! [*Hawkins smiles like a man able to take care of himself*] or an upright horsedealer! [*Uncle Titus snarls at him in rage and terror*] or a reformed drunkard! [*Uncle William, utterly unnerved, moans and wobbles with fear*] eh? Would that shew that King George meant business—ha?

ANDERSON [*perfectly self-possessed*] Come, my dear: he is only trying to frighten you. There is no danger. [*He takes her out of the house. The rest crowd to the door to follow him, except Essie, who remains near Richard*].

RICHARD [*boisterously derisive*] Now then: how many of you will stay with me; run up the American flag on the devil's house; and make a fight for freedom? [*They scramble out, Christy among them, hustling one another in their haste*] Ha ha! Long live the devil! [*To Mrs Dudgeon, who is following them*] What, mother! Are you off too?

MRS DUDGEON [*deadly pale, with her hand on her heart as if she had *received a deathblow*] My curse on you! My dying curse! [*She goes out*].

RICHARD [*calling after her*] It will bring me luck. Ha ha ha!

ESSIE [*anxiously*] Maynt I stay?

RICHARD [*turning to her*] What! Have they forgotten to save your soul in their anxiety about their own bodies? Oh yes: you may stay. [*He turns excitedly away again and shakes his fist after them. His left fist, also clenched, hangs down. Essie seizes it and kisses it, her tears falling on it. He starts and looks at it*]. Tears! The devil's baptism! [*She falls on her knees, sobbing. He stoops goodnaturedly to raise her, saying*] Oh yes, you may cry that way, Essie, if you like.

Act II

Minister Anderson's house is in the main street of Websterbridge, not far from the town hall. To the eye of the eighteenth century New Englander, it is much grander than the plain farmhouse of the Dudgeons; but it is so plain itself that a modern house agent would let both at about the same rent. The chief dwelling room has the same sort of kitchen fireplace, with boiler, toaster hanging on the bars, movable iron griddle socketed to the hob, hook above for roasting, and broad fender, on which stand a kettle and a plate of buttered toast. The door, between the fireplace and the corner, has neither panels, fingerplates nor handles: it is made of plain boards, and fastens with a latch. The table is a kitchen table, with a treacle colored cover of American cloth,[4] chapped at the corners by draping. The tea service on it consists of two thick cups and saucers of the plainest ware, with milk jug and bowl to match, each large enough to contain nearly a quart, on a black japanned tray, and, in the middle of the table, a wooden trencher with a big loaf upon it, and a square half pound block of butter in a crock. The big oak press facing the fire from the opposite side of the room, is for use and storage, not for ornament; and the minister's house coat hangs on a peg from its door, shewing that he is out; for when he is in, it is his best coat that hangs there. His big riding boots stand beside the press, evidently in their usual place, and rather proud of themselves. In fact, the evolution of the minister's kitchen, dining room and drawing room into three separate apartments has not yet taken place; and so, from the point of view of our pampered period, he is no better off than the Dudgeons.

But there is a difference, for all that. To begin with, Mrs Anderson is a pleasanter person to live with than Mrs Dudgeon. To which Mrs Dudgeon would at once reply, with reason, that Mrs Anderson has no children to look after; no poultry, pigs nor cattle; a steady and sufficient income not directly dependent on harvests and prices at fairs; an affectionate husband who is a tower of strength to her: in short, that life is as easy at the minister's house as it is hard at the farm. This is true; but to explain a fact is not to alter it; and how-

4. Heavy, enameled oilcloth.

*ever little credit Mrs Anderson may deserve for making her home
happier, she has certainly succeeded in doing it. The outward and
visible signs of her superior social pretensions are, a drugget[5] on the
floor, a plaster ceiling between the timbers, and chairs which, though
not upholstered, are stained and polished. The fine arts are represented by a mezzotint portrait of some Presbyterian divine, a copper-
plate of Raphael's St Paul preaching at Athens, a rococo presentation clock on the mantelshelf, flanked by a couple of miniatures, a
pair of crockery dogs with baskets in their mouths, and, at the corners, two large cowrie[6] shells. A pretty feature of the room is the low
wide latticed window, nearly its whole width, with little red curtains
running on a rod half way up it to serve as a blind. There is no sofa;
but one of the seats, standing near the press, has a railed back and is
long enough to accommodate two people easily. On the whole, it is
rather the sort of room that the nineteenth century has ended in
struggling to get back to under the leadership of Mr Philip Webb and
his disciples in domestic architecture, though no genteel clergyman
would have tolerated it fifty years ago.*

*The evening has closed in; and the room is dark except for the
cosy firelight and the dim oil lamps seen through the window in the
wet street, where there is a quiet, steady, warm, windless downpour of
rain. As the town clocks strikes the quarter, Judith comes in with a
couple of candles in earthenware candlesticks, and sets them on the
table. Her self-conscious airs of the morning are gone: she is anxious
and frightened. She goes to the window and peers into the street.
The first thing she sees there is her husband, hurrying home through
the rain. She gives a little gasp of relief, not very far removed from a
sob, and turns to the door. Anderson comes in, wrapped in a very
wet cloak.*

JUDITH [*running to him*] Oh, here you are at last, at last! [*She attempts to embrace him*].

ANDERSON [*keeping her off*] Take care, my love: I'm wet. Wait till
I get my cloak off. [*He places a chair with its back to the fire; hangs
his cloak on it to dry; shakes the rain from his hat and puts it on
the fender; and at last turns with his hands outstretched to Judith*].
Now! [*She flies into his arms*]. I am not late, am I? The town
clock struck the quarter as I came in at the front door. And the
town clock is always fast.

JUDITH. I'm sure it's slow this evening. I'm so glad youre back.

ANDERSON [*taking her more closely in his arms*] Anxious, my dear?

JUDITH. A little.

ANDERSON. Why, youve been crying.

JUDITH. Only a little. Never mind: it's all over now. [*A bugle call
is heard in the distance. She starts in terror and retreats to the
long seat, listening.*] Whats that?

ANDERSON [*following her tenderly to the seat and making her sit
down with him*] Only King George, my dear. He's returning to
barracks, or having his roll called, or getting ready for tea, or boot-

5. A rug.
6. Shiny seashells shaped to have a large   inner chamber; frequently used for decoration.

ing or saddling or something. Soldiers dont ring the bell or call over the banisters when they want anything: they send a boy out with a bugle to disturb the whole town.

JUDITH. Do you think there is really any danger?

ANDERSON. Not the least in the world.

JUDITH. You say that to comfort me, not because you believe it.

ANDERSON. My dear: in this world there is always danger for those who are afraid of it. Theres a danger that the house will catch fire in the night; but we shant sleep any the less soundly for that.

JUDITH. Yes, I know what you always say; and youre quite right. Oh, quite right: I know it. But—I suppose I'm not brave: thats all. My heart shrinks every time I think of the soldiers.

ANDERSON. Never mind that, dear: bravery is none the worse for costing a little pain.

JUDITH. Yes, I suppose so. [*Embracing him again*] Oh how brave you are, my dear! [*With tears in her eyes*] Well, I'll be brave too: you shant be ashamed of your wife.

ANDERSON. Thats right. Now you make me happy. Well, well! [*He rises and goes cheerily to the fire to dry his shoes*]. I called on Richard Dudgeon on my way back; but he wasnt in.

JUDITH [*rising in consternation*] You called on that man!

ANDERSON [*reassuring her*] Oh, nothing happened, dearie. He was out.

JUDITH [*almost in tears, as if the visit were a personal humiliation to her*] But why did you go there?

ANDERSON [*gravely*] Well, it is all the talk that Major Swindon is going to do what he did in Springtcwn—make an example of some notorious rebel, as he calls us. He pounced on Peter Dudgeon as the worst character there; and it is the general belief that he will pounce on Richard as the worst here.

JUDITH. But Richard said—

ANDERSON [*goodhumoredly cutting her short*] Pooh! Richard said! He said what he thought would frighten you and frighten me, my dear. He said what perhaps (God forgive him!) he would like to believe. It's a terrible thing to think of what death must mean for a man like that. I felt that I must warn him. I left a message for him.

JUDITH [*querulously*] What message?

ANDERSON. Only that I should be glad to see him for a moment on a matter of importance to himself, and that if he would look in here when he was passing he would be welcome.

JUDITH [*aghast*] You asked that man to come here!

ANDERSON. I did.

JUDITH [*sinking on the seat and clasping her hands*] I hope he wont come! Oh, I pray that he may not come!

ANDERSON. Why? Dont you want him to be warned?

JUDITH. He must know his danger. Oh, Tony, is it wrong to hate a blasphemer and a villain? I do hate him. I cant get him out of my mind: I know he will bring harm with him. He insulted you: he insulted me: he insulted his mother.

ANDERSON [*quaintly*] Well, dear, let's forgive him; and then it wont matter.

JUDITH. Oh, I know it's wrong to hate anybody; but—

ANDERSON [*going over to her with humorous tenderness*] Come, dear, youre not so wicked as you think. The worst sin towards our fellow creatures is not to hate them, but to be indifferent to them; thats the essence of inhumanity. After all, my dear, if you watch people carefully, youll be surprised to find how like hate is to love. [*She starts, strangely touched—even appalled. He is amused at her*]. Yes: I'm quite in earnest. Think of how some of our married friends worry one another, tax one another, are jealous of one another, cant bear to let one another out of sight for a day, are more like jailers and slave-owners than lovers. Think of those very same people with their enemies, scrupulous, lofty, self-respecting, determined to be independent of one another, careful of how they speak of one another—pooh! havent you often thought that if they only knew it, they were better friends to their enemies than to their own husbands and wives? Come: depend on it, my dear, you are really fonder of Richard than you are of me, if you only knew it. Eh!

JUDITH Oh, dont say that: dont say that, Tony, even in jest. You dont know what a horrible feeling it gives me.

ANDERSON [*laughing*] Well, well: never mind, pet. He's a bad man; and you hate him as he deserves. And youre going to make the tea, arnt you?

JUDITH [*remorsefully*] Oh yes, I forgot. Ive been keeping you waiting all this time. [*She goes to the fire and puts on the kettle*].

ANDERSON [*going to the press and taking his coat off*] Have you stitched up the shoulder of my old coat?

JUDITH. Yes, dear. [*She goes to the table, and sets about putting the tea into the teapot from the caddy*].

ANDERSON [*as he changes his coat for the older one hanging on the press, and replaces it by the one he has just taken off*] Did anyone call when I was out?

JUDITH. No, only—[*Someone knocks at the door. With a start which betrays her intense nervousness, she retreats to the further end of the table with the tea caddy and spoon in her hands exclaiming*] Who's that?

ANDERSON [*going to her and patting her encouragingly on the shoulder*] All right, pet, all right. He wont eat you, whoever he is. [*She tries to smile, and nearly makes herself cry. He goes to the door and opens it. Richard is there, without overcoat or cloak*]. You might have raised the latch and come in, Mr Dudgeon. Nobody stands on much ceremony with us. [*Hospitably*] Come in. [*Richard comes in carelessly and stands at the table, looking round the room with a slight pucker of his nose at the mezzotinted divine on the wall. Judith keeps her eyes on the tea caddy*]. Is it still raining? [*He shuts the door*].

RICHARD. Raining like the very [*his eye catches Judith's as she looks quickly and haughtily up*]—I beg your pardon; but [*shewing that his coat is wet*] you see—!

ANDERSON. Take it off, sir; and let it hang before the fire a while:

my wife will excuse your shirtsleeves. Judith: put in another spoonful of tea for Mr Dudgeon.

RICHARD [*eyeing him cynically*] The magic of property, Pastor! Are even you civil to me now that I have succeeded to my father's estate?

> *Judith throws down the spoon indignantly.*

ANDERSON [*quite unruffled, and helping Richard off with his coat*] I think, sir, that since you accept my hospitality, you cannot have so bad an opinion of it. Sit down. [*With the coat in his hand, he points to the railed seat. Richard, in his shirtsleeves, looks at him half quarrelsomely for a moment; then, with a nod, acknowledges that the minister has got the better of him, and sits down on the seat. Anderson pushes his cloak into a heap on the seat of the chair at the fire, and hangs Richard's coat on the back in its place*].

RICHARD. I come, sir, on your own invitation. You left word you had something important to tell me.

ANDERSON. I have a warning which it is my duty to give you.

RICHARD [*quickly rising*] You want to preach to me. Excuse me: I prefer a walk in the rain [*he makes for his coat*].

ANDERSON [*stopping him*] Dont be alarmed, sir: I am no great preacher. You are quite safe. [*Richard smiles in spite of himself. His glance softens: he even makes a gesture of excuse. Anderson, seeing that he has tamed him, now addresses him earnestly*]. Mr Dudgeon: you are in danger in this town.

RICHARD. What danger?

ANDERSON. Your uncle's danger. Major Swindon's gallows.

RICHARD. It is you who are in danger. I warned you—

ANDERSON [*interrupting him goodhumoredly but authoritatively*] Yes, yes, Mr Dudgeon; but they do not think so in the town. And even if I were in danger, I have duties here which I must not forsake. But you are a free man. Why should you run any risk?

RICHARD. Do you think I should be any great loss, Minister?

ANDERSON. I think that a man's life is worth saving, whoever it belongs to. [*Richard makes him an ironical bow. Anderson returns the bow humorously*]. Come: youll have a cup of tea, to prevent you catching cold?

RICHARD. I observe that Mrs Anderson is not quite so pressing as you are, Pastor.

JUDITH [*almost stifled with resentment, which she has been expecting her husband to share and express for her at every insult of Richard's*] You are welcome for my husband's sake. [*She brings the teapot to the fireplace and sets it on the hob*].

RICHARD. I know I am not welcome for my own, madam. [*He rises*]. But I think I will not break bread here, Minister.

ANDERSON [*cheerily*] Give me a good reason for that.

RICHARD. Because there is something in you that I respect, and that makes me desire to have you for my enemy.

ANDERSON. Thats well said. On those terms, sir, I will accept your enmity or any man's. Judith: Mr Dudgeon will stay to tea. Sit down: it will take a few minutes to draw by the fire. [*Richard glances at him with a troubled face; then sits down with his head bent, to hide a convulsive swelling of his throat].* I was just saying to my wife, Mr Dudgeon, that enmity—[*She grasps his hand and looks imploringly at him, doing both with an intensity that checks him at once*]. Well, well, I mustnt tell you, I see; but it was nothing that need leave us worse friend—enemies, I mean. Judith is a great enemy of yours.

RICHARD. If all my enemies were like Mrs Anderson, I should be the best Christian in America.

ANDERSON [*gratified, patting her hand*] You hear that, Judith? Mr Dudgeon knows how to turn a compliment.

The latch is lifted from without.

JUDITH [*starting*] Who is that?

Christy comes in.

CHRISTY [*stopping and staring at Richard*] Oh, are you here?

RICHARD. Yes. Begone, you fool: Mrs Anderson doesnt want the whole family to tea at once.

CHRISTY [*coming further in*] Mother's very ill.

RICHARD. Well, does she want to see me?

CHRISTY. No.

RICHARD. I thought not.

CHRISTY. She wants to see the minister—at once.

JUDITH [*to Anderson*] Oh, not before youve had some tea.

ANDERSON. I shall enjoy it more when I come back, dear. [*He is about to take up his cloak*].

CHRISTY. The rain's over.

ANDERSON [*dropping the cloak and picking up his hat from the fender*] Where is your mother, Christy?

CHRISTY. At Uncle Titus's.

ANDERSON. Have you fetched the doctor?

CHRISTY. No: she didn't tell me to.

ANDERSON. Go on there at once: I'll overtake you on his doorstep. [*Christy turns to go*]. Wait a moment. Your brother must be anxious to know the particulars.

RICHARD. Psha! not I: he doesnt know; and I dont care. [*Violently*] Be off, you oaf. [*Christy runs out. Richards adds, a little shame-facedly*] We shall know soon enough.

ANDERSON. Well, perhaps you will let me bring you the news myself. Judith: will you give Mr Dudgeon his tea, and keep him here until I return.

JUDITH [*white and trembling*] Must I—

ANDERSON [*taking her hands and interrupting her to cover her agitation*] My dear: I can depend on you?

JUDITH [*with a piteous effort to be worthy of his trust*] Yes.

ANDERSON [*pressing her hand against his cheek*] You will not mind two old people like us, Mr Dudgeon. [*Going*] I shall not say good evening: you will be here when I come back. [*He goes out*].

They watch him pass the window, and then look at each other dumbly, quite disconcerted. Richard, noting the quiver of her lips, is the first to pull himself together.

RICHARD. Mrs Anderson: I am perfectly aware of the nature of your sentiments towards me. I shall not intrude on you. Good evening. [*Again he starts for the fireplace to get his coat*].

JUDITH [*getting between him and the coat*] No, no. Dont go: please don't go.

RICHARD [*roughly*] Why? You dont want me here.

JUDITH. Yes, I—[*Wringing her hands in despair*] Oh, if I tell you the truth, you will use it to torment me.

RICHARD [*indignantly*] Torment! What right have you to say that? Do you expect me to stay after that?

JUDITH. I want you to stay; but [*suddenly raging at him like an angry child*] it is not because I like you.

RICHARD. Indeed!

JUDITH. Yes: I had rather you did go than mistake me about that. I hate and dread you; and my husband knows it. If you are not here when he comes back, he will believe that I disobeyed him and drove you away.

RICHARD [*ironically*] Whereas, of course, you have really been so kind and hospitable and charming to me that I only want to go away out of mere contrariness, eh?

    Judith, unable to bear it, sinks on the chair and bursts into tears.

RICHARD. Stop, stop, stop, I tell you. Dont do that. [*Putting his hand to his breast as if to a wound*] He wrung my heart by being a man. Need you tear it by being a woman? Has he not raised you above my insults, like himself? [*She stops crying, and recovers herself somewhat, looking at him with a scared curiosity*]. There: thats right. [*Sympathetically*] Youre better now, arnt you? [*He puts his hand encouragingly on her shoulder. She instantly rises haughtily, and stares at him defiantly. He at once drops into his usual sardonic tone*]. Ah, thats better. You are yourself again: so is Richard. Well, shall we go to tea like a quiet respectable couple, and wait for your husband's return?

JUDITH [*rather ashamed of herself*] If you please. I—I am sorry to have been so foolish. [*She stoops to take up the plate of toast from the fender*].

RICHARD. I am sorry, for your sake, that I am—what I am. Allow me. [*He takes the plate from her and goes with it to the table*].

JUDITH [*following with the teapot*] Will you sit down? [*He sits down at the end of the table nearest the press. There is a plate and knife laid there. The other plate is laid near it: but Judith stays at the opposite end of the table, next the fire, and takes her place there, drawing the tray towards her*]. Do you take sugar?

RICHARD. No: but plenty of milk. Let me give you some toast. [*He puts some on the second plate, and hands it to her, with the knife. The action shews quickly how well he knows that she has avoided her usual place so as to be as far from him as possible*].

JUDITH [*consciously*] Thanks. [*She gives him his tea*]. Wont you help yourself?

RICHARD. Thanks. [*He puts a piece of toast on his own plate; and she pours out tea for herself*].

JUDITH [*observing that he tastes nothing*] Dont you like it? You are not eating anything.

RICHARD. Neither are you.

JUDITH [*nervously*] I never care much for my tea. Please dont mind me.

RICHARD [*looking dreamily round*] I am thinking. It is all so strange to me. I can see the beauty and peace of this home: I think I have never been more at rest in my life than at this moment; and yet I know quite well I could never live here. It's not in my nature, I suppose, to be domesticated. But it's very beautiful: it's almost holy. [*He muses a moment, and then laughs softly*].

JUDITH [*quickly*] Why do you laugh?

RICHARD. I was thinking that if any stranger came in here now, he would take us for man and wife.

JUDITH [*taking offence*] You mean, I suppose, that you are more my age than he is.

RICHARD [*staring at this unexpected turn*] I never thought of such a thing. [*Sardonic again*]. I see there is another side to domestic joy.

JUDITH [*angrily*] I would rather have a husband whom everybody respects than—than—

RICHARD. Than the devil's disciple. You are right; but I daresay your love helps him to be a good man, just as your hate helps me to be a bad one.

JUDITH. My husband has been very good to you. He has forgiven you for insulting him, and is trying to save you. Can you not forgive him for being so much better than you are? How dare you belittle him by putting yourself in his place?

RICHARD. Did I?

JUDITH. Yes, you did. You said that if anybody came in they would take us for man and—[*She stops, terrorstricken, as a squad of soldiers tramps past the window*]. The English soldiers! Oh, what do they—

RICHARD [*listening*] Sh!

A VOICE [*oustide*] Halt! Four outside: two in with me.

Judith half rises, listening and looking with dilated eyes at Richard, who takes up his cup prosaically, and is drinking his tea when the latch goes up with a sharp click, and an English sergeant walks into the room with two privates, who post themselves at the door. He comes promptly to the table between them.

THE SERGEANT. Sorry to disturb you, mum. Duty! Anthony Anderson: I arrest you in King George's name as a rebel.

JUDITH [*pointing at Richard*] But that is not—[*He looks up quickly at her, with a face of iron. She stops her mouth hastily with the hand she has raised to indicate him, and stands staring affrightedly*].

THE SERGEANT. Come, parson: put your coat on and come along.

RICHARD. Yes: I'll come. [*He rises and takes a step towards his own coat; then recollects himself, and with his back to the sergeant, moves his gaze slowly round the room without turning his head until he sees Anderson's black coat hanging up on the press. He goes composedly to it; takes it down; and puts it on. The idea of himself as a parson tickles him: he looks down at the black sleeve on his arm, and then smiles slyly at Judith, whose white face shews him that what she is painfully struggling to grasp is not the humor of the situation but its horror. He turns to the sergeant, who is approaching him with a pair of handcuffs hidden behind him, and says lightly]* Did you ever arrest a man of my cloth before, Sergeant?

THE SERGEANT *[instinctively respectful, half to the black coat, half to Richard's good breeding]* Well, no sir. At least, only an army chaplain. *[Shewing the handcuffs]*. I'm sorry sir; but duty—

RICHARD. Just so, Sergeant. Well, I'm not ashamed of them: thank you kindly for the apology. *[He holds out his hands]*.

SERGEANT *[not availing himself of the offer]* One gentleman to another, sir. Wouldnt you like to say a word to your missis, sir, before you go?

RICHARD *[smiling]* Oh, we shall meet again before—eh? *[meaning "before you hang me"]*.

SERGEANT *[loudly, with ostentatious cheerfulness]* Oh, of course, of course. No call for the lady to distress herself. Still—*[in a lower voice, intended for Richard alone]* your last chance, sir.

> *They look at one another significantly for a moment. Then Richard exhales a deep breath and turns towards Judith.*

RICHARD *[very distinctly]* My love. *[She looks at him, pitiably pale, and tries to answer, but cannot—tries also to come to him, but cannot trust herself to stand without the support of the table]*. This gallant gentleman is good enough to allow us a moment of leavetaking. *[The sergeant retires delicately and joins his men near the door]*. He is trying to spare you the truth; but you had better know it. Are you listening to me? *[She signifies assent]*. Do you understand that I am going to my death? *[She signifies that she understands]*. Remember, you must find our friend who was with us just now. Do you understand? *[She signifies yes]*. See that you get him safely out of harm's way. Don't for your life let him know of my danger; but if he finds it out, tell him that he cannot save me: they would hang him; and they would not spare me. And tell him that I am steadfast in my religion as he is in his, and that he may depend on me to the death. *[He turns to go, and meets the eye of the sergeant, who looks a litle suspicious. He considers a moment, and then, turning roguishly to Judith with something of a smile breaking through his earnestness, says]* And now, my dear, I am afraid the sergeant will not believe that you love me like a wife unless you give one kiss before I go.

> *He approaches her and holds out his arms. She quits the table and almost falls into them.*

JUDITH *[the words choking her]* I ought to—it's murder—

RICHARD. No: only a kiss *[softly to her]* for his sake.

JUDITH. I cant. You must—

RICHARD [*folding her in his arms with an impulse of compassion for her distress*] My poor girl!

> *Judith, with a sudden effort, throws her arms round him; kisses him; and swoons away, dropping from his arms to the ground as if the kiss had killed her.*

RICHARD [*going quickly to the sergeant*] Now, Sergeant: quick, before she comes to. The handcuffs. [*He puts out his hands*].

SERGEANT [*pocketing them*] Never mind, sir: I'll trust you. Youre a game one. You ought to a bin a soldier, sir. Between them two, please. [*The soldiers place themselves one before Richard and one behind him. The sergeant opens the door*].

RICHARD [*taking a last look round him*] Goodbye, wife: goodbye, home. Muffle the drums, and quick march!

> *The sergeant signs to the leading soldier to march. They file out quickly.* * * * * * * * * * * *When Anderson returns from Mrs Dudgeon's, he is astonished to find the room apparently empty and almost in darkness except for the glow from the fire; for one of the candles has burnt out, and the other is at its last flicker.*

ANDERSON. Why, what on earth—— [*Calling*] Judith, Judith! [*He listens: there is no answer*]. Hm! [*He goes to the cupboard; takes a candle from the drawer; lights it at the flicker of the expiring one on the table; and looks wonderingly at the untasted meal by its light. Then he sticks it in the candlestick; takes off his hat; and scratches his head, much puzzled. This action causes him to look at the floor for the first time; and there he sees Judith lying motionless with her eyes closed. He runs to her and stoops beside her, lifting her head*]. Judith.

JUDITH [*waking; for her swoon has passed into the sleep of exhaustion after suffering*] Yes. Did you call? Whats the matter?

ANDERSON. Ive just come in and found you lying here with the candles burnt out and the tea poured out and cold. What has happened?

JUDITH [*still astray*] I dont know. Have I been asleep? I suppose— [*She stops blankly*]. I dont know.

ANDERSON [*groaning*] Heaven forgive me, I left you alone with that scoundrel. [*Judith remembers. With an agonized cry, she clutches his shoulders and drags herself to her feet as he rises with her. He clasps her tenderly in his arms*]. My poor pet!

JUDITH [*frantically clinging to him*] What shall I do? Oh my God, what shall I do?

ANDERSON. Never mind, never mind, my dearest dear: it was my fault. Come: youre safe now; and youre not hurt, are you? [*He takes his arms from her to see whether she can stand*]. There: thats right, thats right. If only you are not hurt, nothing else matters.

JUDITH. No, no, no: I'm not hurt.

ANDERSON. Thank Heaven for that! Come now: [*leading her to the railed seat and making her sit down beside him*] sit down and rest: you can tell me about it to-morrow. Or [*misunderstanding her dis-*

tress] you shall not tell me at all if it worries you. There, there! [*Cheerfully*] I'll make you some fresh tea: that will set you up again. [*He goes to the table, and empties the teapot in the slop bowl*].

JUDITH [*in a strained tone*] Tony.

ANDERSON. Yes, dear?

JUDITH. Do you think we are only in a dream now?

ANDERSON [*glancing round at her for a moment with a pang of anxiety, though he goes on steadily and cheerfully putting fresh tea into the pot*] Perhaps so, pet. But you may as well dream a cup of tea when youre about it.

JUDITH. Oh stop, stop. You dont know—[*Distracted, she buries her face in her knotted hands*].

ANDERSON [*breaking down and coming to her*] My dear, what is it? I cant bear it any longer: you must tell me. It was all my fault: I was mad to trust him.

JUDITH. No: dont say that. You mustnt say that. He—oh no, no: I cant. Tony: dont speak to me. Take my hands—both my hands. [*He takes them, wondering*]. Make me think of you, not of him. There's danger, frightful danger; but it is your danger; and I cant keep thinking of it: I cant, I cant: my mind goes back to his danger. He must be saved—no: you must be saved: you, you, you. [*She springs up as if to do something or go somewhere, exclaiming*] Oh, Heaven help me!

ANDERSON [*keeping his seat and holding her hands with resolute composure*] Calmly, calmly, my pet. Youre quite distracted.

JUDITH. I may well be. I dont know what to do. I dont know what to do. [*Tearing her hands away*]. I must save him. [*Anderson rises in alarm as she runs wildly to the door. It is opened in her face by Essie, who hurries in full of anxiety. The surprise is so disagreeable to Judith that it brings her to her senses. Her tone is sharp and angry as she demands*] What do you want?

ESSIE. I was to come to you.

ANDERSON. Who told you to?

ESSIE [*staring at him, as if his presence astonished her*] Are you here?

JUDITH. Of course. Dont be foolish, child.

ANDERSON. Gently, dearest: youll frighten her. [*Going between them*]. Come here, Essie. [*She comes to him*]. Who sent you?

ESSIE. Dick. He sent me word by a soldier. I was to come here at once and do whatever Mrs Anderson told me.

ANDERSON [*enlightened*] A soldier! Ah, I see it all now! They have arrested Richard. [*Judith makes a gesture of despair*].

ESSIE. No. I asked the soldier. Dick's safe. But the soldier said you had been taken.

ANDERSON. I! [*Bewildered, he turns to Judith for an explanation*].

JUDITH [*coaxingly*] Allright, dear: I understand. [*To Essie*] Thank you, Essie, for coming; but I don't need you now. You may go home.

ESSIE [*suspicious*] Are you sure Dick has not been touched? Perhaps he told the soldier to say it was the minister. [*Anxiously*] Mrs Anderson: do you think it can have been that?

ANDERSON. Tell her the truth if it is so, Judith. She will learn it from the first neighbor she meets in the street. [*Judith turns away and covers her eyes with her hands*].

ESSIE [*wailing*] But what will they do to him? Oh, what will they do to him? Will they hang him? [*Judith shudders convulsively, and throws herself into the chair in which Richard sat at the tea table*].

ANDERSON [*patting Essie's shoulder and trying to comfort her*] I hope not. I hope not. Perhaps if youre very quiet and patient, we may be able to help him in some way.

ESSIE. Yes—help him—yes, yes, yes. I'll be good.

ANDERSON. I must go to him at once, Judith.

JUDITH [*springing up*] Oh no. You must go away—far away, to some place of safety.

ANDERSON. Pooh!

JUDITH [*passionately*] Do you want to kill me? Do you think I can bear to live for days and days with every knock at the door—every footstep—giving me a spasm of terror? to lie awake for nights and nights in an agony of dread, listening for them to come and arrest you?

ANDERSON. Do you think it would be better to know that I had run away from my post at the first sign of danger?

JUDITH [*bitterly*] Oh, you wont go. I know it. Youll stay; and I shall go mad.

ANDERSON. My dear, your duty—

JUDITH [*fiercely*] What do I care about my duty?

ANDERSON [*shocked*] Judith!

JUDITH. I am doing my duty. I am clinging to my duty. My duty is to get you away, to save you, to leave him to his fate [*Essie utters a cry of distress and sinks on the chair at the fire, sobbing silently*]. My instinct is the same as hers—to save him above all things, though it would be so much better for him to die! so much greater! But I know you will take your own way as he took it. I have no power. [*She sits down sullenly on the railed seat*] I'm only a woman: I can do nothing but sit here and suffer. Only, tell him I tried to save you—that I did my best to save you.

ANDERSON. My dear, I am afraid he will be thinking more of his own danger than of mine.

JUDITH. Stop; or I shall hate you.

ANDERSON [*remonstrating*] Come, come, come! How am I to leave you if you talk like this? You are quite out of your senses. [*He turns to Essie*] Essie.

ESSIE [*eagerly rising and drying her eyes*] Yes?

ANDERSON. Just wait outside a moment, like a good girl: Mrs Anderson is not well. [*Essie looks doubtful*]. Never fear: I'll come to you presently; and I'll go to Dick.

ESSIE. You are sure you will go to him? [*Whispering*]. You wont let her prevent you?

ANDERSON [*smiling*] No, no: it's all right. All right. [*She goes*]. Thats a good girl. [*He closes the door, and returns to Judith*].

JUDITH [*seated—rigid*] You are going to your death.

ANDERSON [*quaintly*] Then I shall go in my best coat, dear. [*He turns to the press, beginning to take off his coat*]. Where—? [*He stares at the empty nail for a moment; then looks quickly round to the fire; strides across to it; and lifts Richard's coat*]. Why, my dear, it seems that he has gone in my best coat.

JUDITH [*still motionless*] Yes.

ANDERSON. Did the soldiers make a mistake?

JUDITH. Yes: they made a mistake.

ANDERSON. He might have told them. Poor fellow, he was too upset, I suppose.

JUDITH. Yes: he might have told them. So might I.

ANDERSON. Well, it's all very puzzling—almost funny. It's curious how these little things strike us even in the most—[*He breaks off and begins putting on Richard's coat*]. I'd better take him his own coat. I know what he'll say—[*imitating Richard's sardonic manner*] "Anxious about my soul, Pastor, and also about your best coat." Eh?

JUDITH. Yes, that is just what he will say to you. [*Vacantly*] It doesnt matter: I shall never see either of you again.

ANDERSON [*rallying her*] Oh pooh, pooh, pooh! [*He sits down beside her*]. Is this how you keep your promise that I shant be ashamed of my brave wife?

JUDITH. No: this is how I break it. I cannot keep my promises to him: why should I keep my promises to you?

ANDERSON. Dont speak so strangely, my love. It sounds insincere to me. [*She looks unutterable reproach at him*]. Yes, dear, nonsense is always insincere; and my dearest is talking nonsense. Just nonsense. [*Her face darkens into dumb obstinacy. She stares straight before her, and does not look at him again, absorbed in Richard's fate. He scans her face; sees that his rallying has produced no effect; and gives it up, making no further effort to conceal his anxiety*]. I wish I knew what has frightened you so. Was there a struggle? Did he fight?

JUDITH. No. He smiled.

ANDERSON. Did he realize his danger, do you think?

JUDITH. He realized yours.

ANDERSON. Mine!

JUDITH [*monotonously*] He said "See that you get him safely out of harm's way." I promised: I cant keep my promise. He said, "Dont for your life let him know of my danger." Ive told you of it. He said that if you found it out, you could not save him—that they will hang him and not spare you.

ANDERSON [*rising in generous indignation*] And you think that I will let a man with that much good in him die like a dog, when a few words might make him die like a Christian. I'm ashamed of you, Judith.

JUDITH. He will be steadfast in his religion as you are in yours; and you may depend on him to the death. He said so.

ANDERSON. God forgive him! What else did he say?

JUDITH. He said goodbye.

ANDERSON [*fidgeting nervously to and fro in great concern*] Poor fellow, poor fellow! You said goodbye to him in all kindness and charity, Judith, I hope.

JUDITH. I kissed him.

ANDERSON. What! Judith!

JUDITH. Are you angry?

ANDERSON. No, no. You were right: you were right. Poor fellow, poor fellow! [*Greatly distressed*] To be hanged like that at his age! And then did they take him away?

JUDITH [*wearily*] Then you were here: thats the next thing I remember. I suppose I fainted. Now bid me goodbye, Tony. Perhaps I shall faint again. I wish I could die.

ANDERSON. No, no my dear: you must pull yourself together and be sensible. I am in no danger—not the least in the world.

JUDITH [*solemnly*] You are going to your death, Tony—your sure death, if God will let innocent men be murdered. They will not let you see him: they will arrest you the moment you give your name. It was for you the soldiers came.

ANDERSON [*thunderstruck*] For me!!! [*His fists clinch; his neck thickens; his face reddens; the fleshy purses under his eyes become injected with hot blood; the man of peace vanishes, transfigured into a choleric and formidable man of war. Still, she does not come out of her absorption to look at him: her eyes are steadfast with a mechanical reflection of Richard's steadfastness*].

JUDITH. He took your place: he is dying to save you. That is why he went in your coat. That is why I kissed him.

ANDERSON [*exploding*] Blood an'owns![7] [*His voice is rough and dominant, his gesture full of brute energy*]. Here! Essie, Essie!

ESSIE [*running in*] Yes.

ANDERSON [*impetuously*] Off with you as hard as you can run, to the inn. Tell them to saddle the fastest and strongest horse they have [*Judith rises breathless, and stares at him incredulously*]—the chestnut mare, if she's fresh—without a moment's delay. Go into the stable yard and tell the black man there that I'll give him a silver dollar if the horse is waiting for me when I come, and that I am close on your heels. Away with you. [*His energy sends Essie flying from the room. He pounces on his riding boots; rushes with them to the chair at the fire; and begins pulling them on*].

JUDITH [*unable to believe such a thing of him*] You are not going to him!

ANDERSON [*busy with the boots*] Going to him! What good would that do? [*Growling to himself as he gets the first boot on with a wrench*] I'll go to them, so I will. [*To Judith peremptorily*] Get me the pistols: I want them, And money, money: I want money—all the money in the house. [*He stoops over the other boot, grumbling*] A great satisfaction it would be to him to have my company on the gallows. [*He pulls on the boot*].

JUDITH. You are deserting him, then?

7. *I.e.*, God's blood and wounds!

ANDERSON. Hold your tongue, woman; and get me the pistols. [*She goes to the press and takes from it a leather belt with two pistols, a powder horn, and a bag of bullets attached to it. She throws it on the table. Then she unlocks a drawer in the press and takes out a purse. Anderson grabs the belt and buckles it on, saying*] If they took him for me in my coat, perhaps theyll take me for him in his. [*Hitching the belt into its place*] Do I look like him?

JUDITH [*turning with the purse in her hand*] Horribly unlike him.

ANDERSON [*snatching the purse from her and emptying it on the table*] Hm! We shall see.

JUDITH [*sitting down helplessly*] Is it of any use to pray, do you think, Tony?

ANDERSON [*counting the money*] Pray! Can we pray Swindon's rope off Richard's neck?

JUDITH. God may soften Major Swindon's heart.

ANDERSON [*contemptuously—pocketing a handful of money*] Let him, then. I am not God; and I must go to work another way. [*Judith gasps at the blasphemy. He throws the purse on the table*]. Keep that. Ive taken 25 dollars.

JUDITH. Have you forgotten even that you are a minister?

ANDERSON. Minister be—faugh! My hat: wheres my hat? [*He snatches up hat and cloak, and puts both on in hot haste*] Now listen, you. If you can get a word with him by pretending youre his wife, tell him to hold his tongue until morning: that will give me all the start I need.

JUDITH [*solemnly*] You may depend on him to the death.

ANDERSON. Youre a fool, a fool, Judith. [*For a moment checking the torrent of his haste, and speaking with something of his old quiet and impressive conviction*] You dont know the man youre married to. [*Essie returns. He swoops at her at once*]. Well: is the horse ready?

ESSIE [*breathless*] It will be ready when you come.

ANDERSON. Good. [*He makes for the door*].

JUDITH [*rising and stretching out her arms after him involuntarily*] Wont you say goodbye?

ANDERSON. And waste another half minute! Psha! [*He rushes out like an avalanche*].

ESSIE [*hurrying to Judith*] He has gone to save Richard, hasnt he?

JUDITH. To save Richard! No: Richard has saved him. He has gone to save himself. Richard must die.

> Essie screams with terror and falls on her knees, hiding her face. Judith, without heeding her, looks rigidly straight in front of her, at the vision of Richard, dying.

Act III

Early next morning the sergeant, at the British headquarters in the Town Hall, unlocks the door of a little empty panelled waiting room, and invites Judith to enter. She has had a bad night, probably a rather delirious one; for even in the reality of the raw morning, her fixed gaze comes back at moments when her attention is not strongly held.

The sergeant considers that her feelings do her credit, and is sympathetic in an encouraging military way. Being a fine figure of a man, vain of his uniform and of his rank, he feels specially qualified, in a respectful way, to console her.

SERGEANT. You can have a quiet word with him here, mum.

JUDITH. Shall I have long to wait?

SERGEANT. No, mum, not a minute. We kep him in the Bridewell for the night; and he's just been brought over here for the court martial. Dont fret, mum: he slep like a child, and has made a rare good breakfast.

JUDITH [*incredulously*] He is in good spirits!

SERGEANT. Tip top, mum. The chaplain looked in to see him last night; and he won seventeen shillings off him at spoil five. He spent it among us like the gentleman he is. Duty's duty, mum, of course; but youre among friends here. [*The tramp of a couple of soldiers is heard approaching*]. There: I think he's coming. [*Richard comes in, without a sign of care or captivity in his bearing. The sergeant nods to the two soldiers, and shews them the key of the room in his hand. They withdraw*]. Your good lady, sir.

RICHARD [*going to her*] What! My wife. My adored one. [*He takes her hand and kisses it with a perverse, raffish gallantry*]. How long do you allow a brokenhearted husband for leave-taking, Sergeant?

SERGEANT. As long as we can, sir. We shall not disturb you till the court sits.

RICHARD. But it has struck the hour.

SERGEANT. So it has, sir; but there's a delay. General Burgoyne's just arrived—Gentlemanly Johnny we call him, sir—and he wont have done finding fault with everything this side of half past. I know him, sir: I served with him in Portugal. You may count on twenty minutes, sir; and by your leave I wont waste any more of them. [*He goes out, locking the door. Richard immediately drops his raffish manner and turns to Judith with considerate sincerity*].

RICHARD. Mrs Anderson: this visit is very kind of you. And how are you after last night? I had to leave you before you recovered; but I sent word to Essie to go and look after you. Did she understand the message?

JUDITH [*breathless and urgent*] Oh, dont think of me: I havnt come here to talk about myself. Are they going to—to—[*meaning "to hang you"*]?

RICHARD [*whimsically*] At noon, punctually. At least, that was when they disposed of Uncle Peter. [*She shudders*]. Is your husband safe? Is he on the wing?

JUDITH. He is no longer my husband.

RICHARD [*opening his eyes wide*] Eh?

JUDITH. I disobeyed you. I told him everything. I expected him to come here and save you. I wanted him to come here and save you. He ran away instead.

RICHARD. Well, thats what I meant him to do. What good would his staying have done? Theyd only have hanged us both.

JUDITH [*with reproachful earnestness*] Richard Dudgeon: on your honour, what would you have done in his place?

RICHARD. Exactly what he has done, of course.

JUDITH. Oh, why will you not be simple with me—honest and straightforward? If you are so selfish as that, why did you let them take you last night?

RICHARD [*gaily*] Upon my life, Mrs Anderson, I dont know. Ive been asking myself that question ever since; and I can find no manner of reason for acting as I did.

JUDITH. You know you did it for his sake, believing he was a more worthy man than yourself.

RICHARD [*laughing*] Oho! No: thats a very pretty reason, I must say; but I'm not so modest as that. No: it wasnt for his sake.

JUDITH [*after a pause, during which she looks shamefacedly at him, blushing painfully*] Was it for my sake?

RICHARD [*gallantly*] Well, you had a hand in it. It must have been a little for your sake. You let them take me, at all events.

JUDITH. Oh, do you think I have not been telling myself that all night? Your death will be at my door. [*Impulsively, she gives him her hand, and adds, with intense earnestness*] If I could save you as you saved him, I would do it, no matter how cruel the death was.

RICHARD [*holding her hand and smiling, but keeping her almost at arms length*] I am very sure I shouldnt let you.

JUDITH. Dont you see that I can save you?

RICHARD. How? By changing clothes with me, eh?

JUDITH [*disengaging her hand to touch his lips with it*] Dont [*meaning "Dont jest"*]. No: by telling the Court who you really are.

RICHARD [*frowning*] No use: they wouldnt spare me; and it would spoil half his chance of escaping. They are determined to cow us by making an example of somebody on that gallows today. Well, let us cow them by showing that we can stand by one another to the death. That is the only force that can send Burgoyne back across the Atlantic and make America a nation.

JUDITH [*impatiently*] Oh, what does all that matter?

RICHARD [*laughing*] True: what does it matter? what does anything matter? You see, men have these strange notions, Mrs Anderson; and women see the folly of them.

JUDITH. Women have to lose those they love through them.

RICHARD. They can easily get fresh lovers.

JUDITH [*revolted*] Oh! [*Vehemently*] Do you realize that you are going to kill yourself?

RICHARD. The only man I have any right to kill, Mrs Anderson. Dont be concerned: no woman will lose her lover through my death. [*Smiling*] Bless you, nobody cares for me. Have you heard that my mother is dead?

JUDITH. Dead!

RICHARD. Of heart disease—in the night. Her last word to me was her curse: I dont think I could have borne her blessing. My other relatives will not grieve much on my account. Essie will cry for a day or two; but I have provided for her: I made my own will last night.

JUDITH [*stonily, after a moment's silence*] And I!

RICHARD [*surprised*] You?

JUDITH. Yes, I. Am I not to care at all?

RICHARD [*gaily and bluntly*] Not a scrap. Oh, you expressed your feelings towards me very frankly yesterday. What happened may have softened you for the moment; but believe me, Mrs Anderson, you dont like a bone in my skin or a hair on my head. I shall be as good a riddance at 12 today as I should have been at 12 yesterday.

JUDITH [*her voice trembling*] What can I do to shew you that you are mistaken.

RICHARD. Dont trouble. I'll give you credit for liking me a little better than you did. All I say is that my death will not break your heart.

JUDITH [*almost in a whisper*] How do you know? [*She puts her hands on his shoulders and looks intently at him*].

RICHARD [*amazed—divining the truth*] Mrs Anderson! [*The bell of the town clock strikes the quarter. He collects himself, and removes her hands, saying rather coldly*] Excuse me: they will be here for me presently. It is too late.

JUDITH. It is not too late. Call me as witness: they will never kill you when they know how heroically you have acted.

RICHARD [*with some scorn*] Indeed! But if I dont go through with it, where will the heroism be? I shall simply have tricked them; and theyll hang me for that like a dog. Serve me right too!

JUDITH [*wildly*] Oh, I believe you want to die.

RICHARD [*obstinately*] No I dont.

JUDITH. Then why not try to save yourself? I implore you—listen. You said just now that you saved him for my sake—yes [*clutching him as he recoils with a gesture of denial*] a little for my sake. Well, save yourself for my sake. And I will go with you to the end of the world.

RICHARD [*taking her by the wrists and holding her a little way from him, looking steadily at her*] Judith.

JUDITH [*breathless—delighted at the name*] Yes.

RICHARD. If I said—to please you—that I did what I did ever so little for your sake, I lied as men always lie to women. You know how much I have lived with worthless men—aye, and worthless women too. Well, they could all rise to some sort of goodness and kindness when they were in love [*the word love comes from him with true Puritan scorn*]. That has taught me to set very little store by the goodness that only comes out red hot. What I did last night, I did in cold blood, caring not half so much for your husband, or [*ruthlessly*] for you [*she droops, stricken*] as I do for myself. I had no motive and no interest: all I can tell you is that when it came to the point whether I would take my neck out of the noose and put another man's into it, I could not do it. I dont know why not: I see myself as a fool for my pains; but I could not and I cannot. I have been brought up standing by the law of my own nature;

and I may not go against it, gallows or no gallows. [*She has slow-ly raised her head and is now looking full at him*]. I should have done the same for any other man in the town, or any other man's wife. [*Releasing her*] Do you understand that?

JUDITH. Yes: you mean that you do not love me.

RICHARD [*revolted—with fierce contempt*] Is that all it means to you?

JUDITH. What more—what worse—can it mean to me? [*The sergeant knocks. The blow on the door jars on her heart*]. Oh, one moment more. [*She throws herself on her knees*]. I pray to you—

RICHARD. Hush! [*Calling*] Come in. [*The sergeant unlocks the door and opens it. The guard is with him*].

SERGEANT [*coming in*] Time's up, sir.

RICHARD. Quite ready, Sergeant. Now, my dear. [*He attempts to raise her*].

JUDITH [*clinging to him*] Only one thing more—I entreat, I implore you. Let me be present in the court. I have seen Major Swindon: he said I should be allowed if you asked it. You will ask it. It is my last request: I shall never ask you anything again. [*She clasps his knee*]. I beg and pray it of you.

RICHARD. If I do, will you be silent?

JUDITH. Yes.

RICHARD. You will keep faith?

JUDITH. I will keep—[*She breaks down, sobbing*].

RICHARD [*taking her arm to lift her*] Just—her other arm, Sergeant.
They go out, she sobbing convulsively, supported by the two men.

Meanwhile, the Council Chamber is ready for the court martial. It is a large, lofty room, with a chair of state in the middle under a tall canopy with a gilt crown, and maroon curtains with the royal monogram G. R. In front of the chair is a table, also draped in maroon, with a bell, a heavy inkstand, and writing materials on it. Several chairs are set at the table. The door is at the right hand of the occupant of the chair of state when it has an occupant: at present it is empty. Major Swindon, a pale, sandy-haired, very conscientious looking man of about 45, sits at the end of the table with his back to the door, writing. He is alone until the sergeant announces the General in a subdued manner which suggests that Gentle-manly Johnny has been making his presence felt rather heavi-ly.

SERGEANT. The General, sir.
Swindon rises hastily. The general comes in: the sergeant goes out. General Burgoyne is 55, and very well preserved. He is a man of fashion, gallant enough to have made a distinguished marriage by an elopement, witty enough to write successful comedies, aristocratically-connected enough to have had op-portunities of high military distinction. His eyes, large, bril-liant, apprehensive, and intelligent, are his most remarkable feature: without them his fine nose and small mouth would

suggest rather more fastidiousness and less force than go to the making of a first rate general. Just now the eyes are angry and tragic, and the mouth and nostrils tense.

BURGOYNE. Major Swindon, I presume.

SWINDON. Yes. General Burgoyne, if I mistake not. [*They bow to one another ceremoniously*]. I am glad to have the support of your presence this morning. It is not particularly lively business, hanging this poor devil of a minister.

BURGOYNE [*throwing himself into Swindon's chair*] No, sir, it is not. It is making too much of the fellow to execute him: what more could you have done if he had been a member of the Church of England? Martyrdom, sir, is what these people like: it is the only way in which a man can become famous without ability. However, you have committed us to hanging him; and the sooner he is hanged the better.

SWINDON. We have arranged it for 12 clock. Nothing remains to be done except to try him.

BURGOYNE [*looking at him with suppressed anger*] Nothing—except to save your own necks, perhaps. Have you heard the news from Springtown?

SWINDON. Nothing special. The latest reports are satisfactory.

BURGOYNE [*rising in amazement*] Satisfactory, sir! Satisfactory!! [*He stares at him for a moment, and then adds, with grim intensity*] I am glad you take that view of them.

SWINDON [*puzzled*] Do I understand that in your opinion—

BURGOYNE. I do not express my opinion. I never stoop to that habit of profane language which unfortunately coarsens our profession. If I did, sir, perhaps I should be able to express my opinion of the news from Springtown—the news which you [*severely*] have apparently not heard. How soon do you get news from your supports here?—in the course of a month, eh?

SWINDON [*turning sulky*] I suppose the reports have been taken to you, sir, instead of to me. Is there anything serious?

BURGOYNE [*taking a report from his pocket and holding it up*] Springtown's in the hands of the rebels. [*He throws the report on the table*].

SWINDON [*aghast*] Since yesterday!

BURGOYNE. Since two o'clock this morning. Perhaps we shall be in their hands before two o'clock tomorrow morning. Have you thought of that?

SWINDON [*confidently*] As to that, General, the British soldier will give a good account of himself.

BURGOYNE [*bitterly*] And therefore, I suppose, sir, the British officer need not know his business: the British soldier will get him out of his blunders with the bayonet. In future, sir, I must ask you to be a little less generous with the blood of your men, and a little more generous with your own brains.

SWINDON. I am sorry I cannot pretend to your intellectual eminence, sir. I can only do my best, and rely on the devotion of my countrymen.

BURGOYNE [*suddenly becoming suavely sarcastic*] May I ask are you writing a melodrama, Major Swindon?

SWINDON [*flushing*] No, sir.

BURGOYNE.What a pity! What a pity! [*Dropping his sarcastic tone and facing him suddenly and seriously*] Do you at all realize, sir, that we have nothing standing between us and destruction but our own bluff and the sheepishness of these colonists? They are men of the same English stock as ourselves: six to one of us [*repeating it emphatically*] six to one, sir; and nearly half our troops are Hessians, Brunswickers, German dragoons, and Indians with scalping knives. These are the countrymen on whose devotion you rely! Suppose the colonists find a leader! Suppose the news from Springtown should turn out to mean that they have already found a leader! What shall we do then? Eh?

SWINDON [*sullenly*] Our duty, sir, I presume.

BURGOYNE [*again sarcastic—giving him up as a fool*]. Quite so, quite so. Thank you, Major Swindon, thank you. Now youve settled the question, sir—thrown a flood of light on the situation. What a comfort to me to feel that I have at my side so devoted and able an officer to support me in this emergency! I think, sir, it will probably relieve both our feelings if we proceed to hang this dissenter without further delay [*he strikes the bell*] especially as I am debarred by my principles from the customary military vent for my feelings. [*The sergeant appears*]. Bring your man in.

SERGEANT. Yes, sir.

BURGOYNE. And mention to any officer you may meet that the court cannot wait any longer for him.

SWINDON [*keeping his temper with difficulty*] The staff is perfectly ready, sir. They have been waiting your convenience for fully half an hour. Perfectly ready, sir.

BURGOYNE [*blandly*] So am I. [*Several officers come in and take their seats. One of them sits at the end of the table furthest from the door, and acts throughout as clerk of the court, making notes of the proceedings. The uniforms are those of the 9th, 20th, 21st, 24th, 47th, 53rd, and 62nd British Infantry. One officer is a Major General of the Royal Artillery. There are also German officers of the Hessian Rifles, and of German dragoon and Brunswicker regiments*]. Oh, good morning, gentlemen. Sorry to disturb you, I am sure. Very good of you to spare us a few moments.

SWINDON. Will you preside, sir?

BURGOYNE [*becoming additionally polished, lofty, sarcastic, and urbane now that he is in public*] No, sir: I feel my own deficiencies too keenly to presume so far. If you will kindly allow, I will sit at the feet of Gamaliel.[8] [*He takes the chair at the end of the table next the door, and motions Swindon to the chair of state, waiting for him to be seated before sitting down himself*].

SWINDON [*greatly annoyed*] As you please, sir, I am only trying to do my duty under excessively trying circumstances. [*He takes his place in the chair of state*].

8. A lawmaker and teacher; he was the teacher of the Apostle Paul.

Burgoyne, relaxing his studied demeanor for the moment, sits down and begins to read the report with knitted brows and careworn looks, reflecting on his desperate situation and Swindon's uselessness. Richard is brought in. Judith walks beside him. Two soldiers precede and two follow him, with the sergeant in command. They cross the room to the wall opposite the door; but when Richard has just passed before the chair of state the sergeant stops him with a touch on the arm, and posts himself behind him, at his elbow. Judith stands timidly at the wall. The four soldiers place themselves in a squad near her.

BURGOYNE [*looking up and seeing Judith*] Who is that woman?

SERGEANT. Prisoner's wife, sir.

SWINDON [*nervously*] She begged me to allow her to be present; and I thought—

BURGOYNE [*completing the sentence for him ironically*] You thought it would be a pleasure for her. Quite so, quite so. [*Blandly*] Give the lady a chair; and make her thoroughly comfortable.

The sergeant fetches a chair and places it near Richard.

JUDITH. Thank you, sir. [*She sits down after an awestricken curtsy to Burgoyne, which he acknowledges by a dignified bend of his head*].

SWINDON [*to Richard, sharply*] Your name, sir?

RICHARD [*affable, but obstinate*] Come: you dont mean to say that youve brought me here without knowing who I am?

SWINDON. As a matter of form, sir, give your name.

RICHARD. As a matter of form then, my name is Anthony Anderson, Presbyterian minister in this town.

BURGOYNE [*interested*] Indeed! Pray, Mr Anderson, what do you gentlemen believe?

RICHARD. I shall be happy to explain if time is allowed me. I cannot undertake to complete your conversion in less than a fortnight.

SWINDON [*snubbing him*] We are not here to discuss your views.

BURGOYNE [*with an elaborate bow to the unfortunate Swindon*] I stand rebuked.

SWINDON [*embarrassed*] Oh, not you, I as—

BURGOYNE. Dont mention it. [*To Richard, very politely*] Any political views, Mr Anderson?

RICHARD. I understand that that is just what we are here to find out.

SWINDON [*severely*] Do you mean to deny that you are a rebel?

RICHARD. I am an American, sir.

SWINDON. What do you expect me to think of that speech, Mr Anderson?

RICHARD. I never expect a soldier to think, sir.

Burogyne is boundlessly delighted by this retort, which almost reconciles him to the loss of America.

SWINDON [*whitening with anger*] I advise you not to be insolent, prisoner.

RICHARD. You cant help yourself, General. When you make up your mind to hang a man, you put yourself at a disadvantage with him.

Why should I be civil to you? I may as well be hanged for a sheep as a lamb.

SWINDON. You have no right to assume that the court has made up its mind without a fair trial. And you will please not address me as General. I am Major Swindon.

RICHARD. A thousand pardons. I thought I had the honor of addressing Gentlemanly Johnny.

> *Sensation among the officers. The sergeant has a narrow escape from a guffaw.*

BURGOYNE [*with extreme suavity*] I believe I am Gentlemanly Johnny, sir, at your service. My more intimate friends call me General Burgoyne. [*Richard bows with perfect politeness*]. You will understand, sir, I hope, since you seem to be a gentleman and a man of some spirit in spite of your calling, that if we should have the misfortune to hang you, we shall do so as a mere matter of political necessity and military duty, without any personal ill-feeling.

RICHARD. Oh, quite so. That makes all the difference in the world, of course.

> *They all smile in spite of themselves; and some of the younger officers burst out laughing.*

JUDITH [*her dread and horror deepening at every one of these jests and compliments*] How can you?

RICHARD. You promised to be silent.

BURGOYNE [*to Judith, with studied courtesy*] Believe me, Madam, your husband is placing us under the greatest obligation by taking this very disagreeable business so thoroughly in the spirit of a gentleman. Sergeant: give Mr Anderson a chair. [*The sergeant does so. Richard sits down*]. Now, Major Swindon: we are waiting for you.

SWINDON. You are aware, I presume, Mr Anderson, of your obligations as a subject of His Majesty King George the Third.

RICHARD. I am aware, sir, that His Majesty King George the Third is about to hang me because I object to Lord North's robbing me.

SWINDON. That is a treasonable speech, sir.

RICHARD [*briefly*] Yes. I meant it to be.

BURGOYNE [*strongly deprecating this line of defence, but still polite*] Dont you think, Mr Anderson, that this is rather—if you will excuse the word—a vulgar line to take? Why should you cry out robbery because of a stamp duty and a tea duty and so forth? After all, it is the essence of your position as a gentleman that you pay with a good grace.

RICHARD. It is not the money, General. But to be swindled by a pigheaded lunatic like King George—

SWINDON [*scandalized*] Chut, sir—silence!

SERGEANT [*in stentorian tones, greatly shocked*] Silence!

BURGOYNE [*unruffled*] Ah, that is another point of view. My position does not allow of my going into that, except in private. But [*shrugging his shoulders*] of course, Mr Anderson, if you are determined to be hanged [*Judith flinches*] there's nothing more to be said. An unusual taste! however [*with a final shrug*]—!

SWINDON [*to Burgoyne*] Shall we call witnesses?

RICHARD. What need is there of witnesses? If the townspeople here had listened to me, you would have found the streets barricaded, the houses loopholed, and the people in arms to hold the town against you to the last man. But you arrived, unfortunately, before we had got out of the talking stage; and then it was too late.

SWINDON [*severely*] Well, sir, we shall teach you and your townspeople a lesson they will not forget. Have you anything more to say?

RICHARD. I think you might have the decency to treat me as a prisoner of war, and shoot me like a man instead of hanging me like a dog.

BURGOYNE [*sympathetically*] Now there, Mr Anderson, you talk like a civilian, if you will excuse my saying so. Have you any idea of the average marksmanship of the army of His Majesty King George the Third? If we make you up a firing party, what will happen? Half of them will miss you: the rest will make a mess of the business and leave you to the provo-marshal's pistol. Whereas we can hang you in a perfectly workmanlike and agreeable way. [*Kindly*] Let me persuade you to be hanged, Mr Anderson?

JUDITH [*sick with horror*] My God!

RICHARD [*to Judith*] Your promise! [*To Burgoyne*] Thank you, General: that view of the case did not occur to me before. To oblige you, I withdraw my objection to the rope. Hang me, by all means.

BURGOYNE [*smoothly*] Will 12 o'clock suit you, Mr Anderson?

RICHARD. I shall be at your disposal then, General.

BURGOYNE [*rising*] Nothing more to be said, gentlemen. [*They all rise*].

JUDITH [*rushing to the table*] Oh, you are not going to murder a man like that, without a proper trial—without thinking of what you are doing—without—[*she cannot find words*].

RICHARD. Is this how you keep your promise?

JUDITH. If I am not to speak, you must. Defend yourself: save yourself: tell them the truth.

RICHARD [*worriedly*] I have told them truth enough to hang me ten times over. If you say another word you will risk other lives; but you will not save mine.

BURGOYNE. My good lady, our only desire is to save unpleasantness. What satisfaction would it give you to have a solemn fuss made, with my friend Swindon in a black cap and so forth? I am sure we are greatly indebted to the admirable tact and gentlemanly feeling shewn by your husband.

JUDITH [*throwing the words in his face*] Oh, you are mad. Is it nothing to you what wicked thing you do if only you do it like a gentleman? Is it nothing to you whether you are a murderer or not, if only you murder in a red coat? [*Desperately*] You shall not hang him: that man is not my husband.

The officers look at one another, and whisper: some of the Germans asking their neighbors to explain what the woman had said. Burgoyne, who has been visibly shaken by Judith's reproach, recovers himself promptly at this new development. Richard meanwhile raises his voice above the buzz.

RICHARD. I appeal to you, gentlemen, to put an end to this. She will not believe that she cannot save me. Break up the court.

BURGOYNE [*in a voice so quiet and firm that it restores silence at once*] One moment, Mr Anderson. One moment, gentlemen. [*He resumes his seat. Swindon and the officers follow his example*]. Let me understand you clearly, madam. Do you mean that this gentleman is not your husband, or merely—I wish to put this with all delicacy—that you are not his wife?

JUDITH. I dont know what you mean. I say that he is not my husband —that my husband has escaped. This man took his place to save him. Ask anyone in the town—send out into the street for the first person you find there, and bring him in as a witness. He will tell you that the prisoner is not Anthony Anderson.

BURGOYNE [*quietly, as before*] Sergeant.

SERGEANT. Yes, sir.

BURGOYNE. Go out into the street and bring in the first townsman you see there.

SERGEANT [*making for the door*] Yes sir.

BURGOYNE [*as the sergeant passes*] The first clean, sober townsman you see.

SERGEANT. Yes sir. [*He goes out*].

BURGOYNE. Sit down, Mr Anderson—if I may call you so for the present. [*Richard sits down*]. Sit down, madam, whilst we wait. Give the lady a newspaper.

RICHARD [*indignantly*] Shame!

BURGOYNE [*keenly, with a half smile*] If you are not her husband, sir, the case is not a serious one—for her. [*Richard bites his lip, silenced*].

JUDITH [*to Richard, as she returns to her seat*] I couldnt help it. [*He shakes his head. She sits down*].

BURGOYNE. You will understand of course, Mr Anderson, that you must not build on this little incident. We are bound to make an example of somebody.

RICHARD. I quite understand. I suppose there's no use in my explaining.

BURGOYNE. I think we should prefer independent testimony, if you dont mind.

> The sergeant, with a packet of papers in his hand, returns conducting Christy, who is much scared.

SERGEANT [*giving Burgoyne the packet*] Dispatches, sir. Delivered by a corporal of the 33rd. Dead beat with hard riding, sir.

> Burgoyne opens the dispatches, and presently becomes absorbed in them. They are so serious as to take his attention completely from the court martial.

THE SERGEANT [*to Christy*] Now then. Attention; and take your hat off. [*He puts himself in charge of Christy, who stands on Burgoyne's side of the court*].

RICHARD [*in his usual bullying tone to Christy*] Dont be frightened, you fool: youre only wanted as a witness. Theyre not going to hang you.

SWINDON. What's your name?

CHRISTY. Christy.

RICHARD [*impatiently*] Christopher Dudgeon, you blatant idiot. Give your full name.

SWINDON. Be silent, prisoner. You must not prompt the witness.

RICHARD. Very well. But I warn you you'll get nothing out of him unless you shake it out of him. He has been too well brought up by a pious mother to have any sense or manhood left in him.

BURGOYNE [*springing up and speaking to the sergeant in a startling voice*] Where is the man who brought these?

SERGEANT. In the guard-room, sir.

> *Burgoyne goes out with a haste that sets the officers exchanging looks.*

SWINDON [*to Christy*] Do you know Anthony Anderson, the Presbyterian minister?

CHRISTY. Of course I do [*implying that Swindon must be an ass not to know it*].

SWINDON. Is he here?

CHRISTY [*staring round*] I dont know.

SWINDON. Do you see him?

CHRISTY. No.

SWINDON. You seem to know the prisoner?

CHRISTY. Do you mean Dick?

SWINDON. Which is Dick?

CHRISTY [*pointing to Richard*] Him.

SWINDON. What is his name?

CHRISTY. Dick.

RICHARD. Answer properly, you jumping jackass. What do they know about Dick?

CHRISTY. Well, you are Dick, aint you? What am I to say?

SWINDON. Address me, sir; and do you, prisoner, be silent. Tell us who the prisoner is.

CHRISTY. He's my brother Dick—Richard—Richard Dudgeon.

SWINDON. Your brother!

CHRISTY. Yes.

SWINDON. You are sure he is not Anderson.

CHRISTY. Who?

RICHARD [*exasperatedly*] Me, me, me, you—

SWINDON. Silence, sir.

SERGEANT [*shouting*] Silence.

RICHARD [*impatiently*] Yah! [*To Christy*] He wants to know am I Minister Anderson. Tell him, and stop grinning like a zany.

CHRISTY [*grinning more than ever*] You Pastor Anderson! [*To Swindon*] Why, Mr Anderson's a minister—a very good man; and Dick's a bad character: the respectable people wont speak to him. He's the bad brother: I'm the good one. [*The officers laugh outright. The soldiers grin*].

SWINDON. Who arrested this man?

SERGEANT. I did, sir. I found him in the minister's house, sitting at tea with the lady with his coat off, quite at home. If he isnt married to her, he ought to be.

SWINDON. Did he answer to the minister's name?

SERGEANT. Yes, sir but not to a minister's nature. You ask the chaplain, sir.

SWINDON [*to Richard, threateningly*] So, sir you have attempted to cheat us. And your name is Richard Dudgeon?

RICHARD. Youve found it out at last, have you?

SWINDON. Dudgeon is a name well known to us, eh?

RICHARD. Yes: Peter Dudgeon, whom you murdered, was my uncle.

SWINDON. Hm! [*He compresses his lips, and looks at Richard with vindictive gravity*].

CHRISTY. Are they going to hang you, Dick?

RICHARD. Yes. Get out: theyve done with you.

CHRISTY. And I may keep the china peacocks?

RICHARD [*jumping up*] Get out. Get out, you blithering baboon, you. [*Christy flies, panicstricken*].

SWINDON [*rising—all rise*] Since you have taken the minister's place, Richard Dudgeon, you shall go through with it. The execution will take place at 12 o'clock as arranged; and unless Anderson surrenders before then, you shall take his place on the gallows. Sergeant: take your man out.

JUDITH [*distracted*] No, no—

SWINDON [*fiercely, dreading a renewal of her entreaties*] Take that woman away.

RICHARD [*springing across the table with a tiger-like bound, and seizing Swindon by the throat*] You infernal scoundrel—

> *The sergeant rushes to the rescue from one side, the soldiers from the other. They seize Richard and drag him back to his place. Swindon, who has been thrown supine on the table, rises, arranging his stock.[9] He is about to speak, when he is anticipated by Burgoyne, who has just appeared at the door with two papers in his hand: a white letter and a blue dispatch.*

BURGOYNE [*advancing to the table, elaborately cool*] What is this? Whats happening? Mr Anderson: I'm astonished at you.

RICHARD. I am sorry I disturbed you, General. I merely wanted to strangle your understrapper there. [*Breaking out violently at Swindon*] Why do you raise the devil in me by bullying the woman like that? You oatmeal faced dog, I'd twist your cursed head off with the greatest satisfaction. [*He puts out his hands to the sergeant*] Here: handcuff me, will you; or I'll not undertake to keep my fingers off him.

> *The sergeant takes out a pair of handcuffs and looks to Burgoyne for instructions.*

BURGOYNE. Have you addressed profane language to the lady, Major Swindon?

SWINDON [*very angry*] No, sir, certainly not. That question should

9. A close-fitting band for the neck.

not have been put to me. I ordered the woman to be removed, as she was disorderly; and the fellow sprang at me. Put away those handcuffs. I am perfectly able to take care of myself.

RICHARD. Now you talk like a man, I have no quarrel with you.

BURGOYNE. Mr Anderson—

SWINDON. His name is Dudgeon, sir, Richard Dudgeon. He is an impostor.

BURGOYNE [*brusquely*] Nonsense, sir: you hanged Dudgeon at Springtown.

RICHARD. It was my uncle, General.

BURGOYNE. Oh, your uncle. [*To Swindon, handsomely*] I beg your pardon, Major Swindon. [*Swindon acknowledges the apology stiffly. Burgoyne turns to Richard*]. We are somewhat unfortunate in our relations with your family. Well, Mr Dudgeon, what I wanted to ask you is this. Who is [*reading the name from the letter*] William Maindeck Parshotter?

RICHARD. He is the Mayor of Springtown.

BURGOYNE. Is William—Maindeck and so on—a man of his word?

RICHARD. Is he selling you anything?

BURGOYNE. No.

RICHARD. Then you may depend on him.

BURGOYNE. Thank you, Mr—'m Dudgeon. By the way, since you are not Mr Anderson, do we still—eh, Major Swindon? [*meaning "do we still hang him?"*]

RICHARD. The arrangements are unaltered, General.

BURGOYNE. Ah, indeed. I am sorry. Good morning, Mr Dudgeon. Good morning, madam.

RICHARD [*interrupting Judith almost fiercely as she is about to make some wild appeal, and taking her arm resolutely*] Not one word more. Come.

> She looks imploringly at him, but is overborne by his determination. They are marched out by the four soldiers: the sergeant very sulky, walking between Swindon and Richard, whom he watches as if he were a dangerous animal.

BURGOYNE. Gentlemen: we need not detain you. Major Swindon: a word with you. [*The officers go out. Burgoyne waits with unruffled serenity until the last of them disappears. Then he becomes very grave, and addresses Swindon for the first time without his title*]. Swindon: do you know what this is [*shewing him the letter*]?

SWINDON. What?

BURGOYNE. A demand for a safe-conduct for an officer of their militia to come here and arrange terms with us.

SWINDON. Oh, they are giving in.

BURGOYNE. They add that they are sending the man who raised Springtown last night and drove us out; so that we may know that we are dealing with an officer of importance.

SWINDON. Pooh!

BURGOYNE. He will be fully empowered to arrange the terms of— guess what.

SWINDON. Their surrender, I hope.

BURGOYNE. No: our evacuation of the town. They offer us just six hours to clear out.

SWINDON. What monstrous impudence!

BURGOYNE. What shall we do, eh?

SWINDON. March on Springtown and strike a decisive blow at once.

BURGOYNE [*quietly*] Hm! [*Turning to the door*] Come to the adjutant's office.

SWINDON. What for?

BURGOYNE. To write out that safe-conduct. [*He puts his hand to the door knob to open it*].

SWINDON [*who has not budged*] General Burgoyne.

BURGOYNE [*returning*] Sir?

SWINDON. It is my duty to tell you, sir, that I do not consider the threats of a mob of rebellious tradesmen a sufficient reason for our giving way.

BURGOYNE [*imperturbable*] Suppose I resign my command to you, what will you do?

SWINDON. I will undertake to do what we have marched south from Quebec to do, and what General Howe has marched north from New York to do: effect a junction at Albany and wipe out the rebel army with our united forces.

BURGOYNE [*enigmatically*] And will you wipe out our enemies in London, too?

SWINDON. In London! What enemies?

BURGOYNE [*forcibly*] Jobbery and snobbery, incompetence and Red Tape. [*He holds up the dispatch and adds, with despair in his face and voice*] I have just learnt, sir, that General Howe is still in New York.

SWINDON. [*thunderstruck*] Good God! He has disobeyed orders!

BURGOYNE [*with sardonic calm*] He has received no orders, sir. Some gentleman in London forgot to dispatch them: he was leaving town for his holiday, I believe. To avoid upsetting his arrangements, England will lose her American colonies; and in a few days you and I will be at Saratoga with 5,000 men to face 18,000 rebels in an impregnable position.

SWINDON. [*appalled*] Impossible!

BURGOYNE [*coldly*] I beg your pardon?

SWINDON. I cant believe it! What will History say?

BURGOYNE. History, sir, will tell lies, as usual. Come: we must send the safe-conduct. [*He goes out*].

SWINDON [*following distractedly*] My God, my God! We shall be wiped out.

> *As noon approaches there is excitement in the market place. The gallows which hangs there permanently for the terror of evildoers, with such minor advertizers and examples of crime as the pillory, the whipping post, and the stocks, has a new rope attached, with the noose hitched up to one of the uprights, out of reach of the boys. Its ladder, too, has been brought out and placed in position by the town beadle, who*

stands by to guard it from unauthorized climbing. The Web-sterbridge townsfolk are present in force, and in high spirits; for the news has spread that it is the devil's disciple and not the minister that King George and his terrible general are about to hang: consequently the execution can be enjoyed without any misgiving as to its righteousness, or to the cowardice of allowing it to take place without a struggle. There is even some fear of a disappointment as midday approaches and the arrival of the beadle with the ladder remains the only sign of preparation. But at last reassuring shouts of Here they come: Here they are, are heard; and a company of soldiers with fixed bayonets, half British infantry, half Hessians, tramp quickly into the middle of the market place, driving the crowd to the sides.

THE SERGEANT. Halt. Front. Dress. [*The soldiers change their column into a square enclosing the gallows, their petty officers, energetical-ly led by the sergeant, hustling the persons who find themselves in-side the square out at the corners*]. Now then! Out of it with you: out of it. Some o youll get strung up yourselves presently. Form that square there, will you, you damned Hoosians. No use talkin German to them: talk to their toes with the butt ends of your muskets: theyll understand that. Get out of it, will you. [*He comes upon Judith, standing near the gallows*]. Now then: youve no call here.

JUDITH. May I not stay? What harm am I doing?

SERGEANT. I want none of your argufying. You ought to be ashamed of yourself, running to see a man hanged thats not your husband. And he's no better than yourself. I told my major he was a gentle-man; and then he goes and tries to strangle him, and calls his bless-ed Majesty a lunatic. So out of it with you, double quick.

JUDITH. Will you take these two silver dollars and let me stay?

The sergeant, without an instant's hesitation, looks quickly and furtively round as he shoots the money dexterously into his pocket. Then he raises his voice in virtuous indignation.

THE SERGEANT. Me take mony in the execution of my duty! Certain-ly not. Now I'll tell you what I'll do, to teach you to corrupt the King's officer. I'll put you under arrest until the execution's over. You just stand there; and dont let me see you as much as move from that spot until youre let. [*With a swift wink at her he points to the corner of the square behind the gallows on his right, and turns noisily away, shouting*] Now then, dress up and keep em back, will you.

Cries of Hush and Silence are heard among the townfolk; and the sound of a military band, playing the Dead March from Saul, is heard. The crowd becomes quiet at once; and the sergeant and petty officers, hurrying to the back of the square, with a few whispered orders and some stealthy hustling cause it to open and admit the funeral procession, which is protected from the crowd by a double file of soldiers. First come Burgoyne and Swindon, who, on entering the square, glance with distaste at the gallows, and avoid passing under it by wheeling a little to the right and stationing themselves on that side. Then Mr Brudenell,[1] the chaplain, in his surplice, with his prayer book open in his hand, walking beside Richard, who is moody and disorderly. He walks doggedly through the gallows framework, and posts himself a little in front of it. Behind him comes the executioner, a stalwart soldier in his shirtsleeves. Following him, two soldiers haul a light military waggon. Finally comes the band, which posts itself at the back of the square, and finishes the Dead March. Judith, watching Richard painfully, steals down to the gallows, and stands leaning against its right-post. During the conversation which follows, the two soldiers place the cart under the gallows, and stand by the shafts, which point backwards. The executioner takes a set of steps from the cart and places it ready for the prisoner to mount. Then he climbs the tall ladder which stands against the gallows, and cuts the string by which the rope is hitched up; so that the noose drops dangling over the cart, into which he steps as he descends.

RICHARD [*with suppressed impatience, to Brudenell*] Look here, sir: this is no place for a man of your profession. Hadnt you better go away?

SWINDON. I appeal to you, prisoner, if you have any sense of decency left, to listen to the ministrations of the chaplain, and pay due heed to the solemnity of the occasion.

THE CHAPLAIN [*gently reproving Richard*] Try to control yourself, and submit to the divine will. [*He lifts his book to proceed with the service*].

RICHARD. Answer for your own will, sir, and those of your accomplices here [*indicating Burgoyne and Swindon*]: I see little divinity about them or you. You talk to me of Christianity when you are in the act of hanging your enemies. Was there ever such blasphemous nonsense! [*To Swindon, more rudely*] Youve got up the solemnity of the occasion, as you call it, to impress the people with your own dignity—Handel's music and a clergyman to make murder look like piety! Do you suppose *I* am going to help you? Youve asked me to choose the rope because you dont know your own trade well enough to shoot me properly. Well, hang away and have done with it.

SWINDON [*to the chaplain*] Can you do nothing with him, Mr Brudenell?

CHAPLAIN. I will try, sir. [*Beginning to read*] Man that is born of woman hath—

RICHARD [*fixing his eyes on him*] "Thou shalt not kill."
    The book drops in Brudenell's hands.

CHAPLAIN [*confessing his embarrassment*] What am I to say, Mr Dudgeon?

---

1. According to Shaw's Notes to the play, Brudenell, like Burgoyne, was a real person.

RICHARD. Let me alone, man, cant you?

BURGOYNE [*with extreme urbanity*] I think, Mr Brudenell, that as the usual professional observations seem to strike Mr Dudgeon as incongruous under the circumstances, you had better omit them until—er—until Mr Dudgeon can no longer be inconvenienced by them. [*Brudenell, with a shrug, shuts his book and retires behind the gallows*]. You seem in a hurry, Mr Dudgeon.

RICHARD [*with the horror of death upon him*] Do you think this is a pleasant sort of thing to be kept waiting for? Youve made up your mind to commit murder: well, do it and have done with it.

BURGOYNE. Mr Dudgeon: we are only doing this—

RICHARD. Because youre paid to do it.

SWINDON. You insolent—[*he swallows his rage*].

BURGOYNE [*with much charm of manner*] Ah, I am really sorry that you should think that, Mr Dudgeon. If you knew what my commission cost me, and what my pay is, you would think better of me. I should be glad to part from you on friendly terms.

RICHARD. Hark ye, General Burgoyne. If you think that I like being hanged, youre mistaken. I dont like it; and I dont mean to pretend that I do. And if you think I'm obliged to you for hanging me in a gentlemanly way, youre wrong there too. I take the whole business in devilish bad part; and the only satisfaction I have in it is that youll feel a good deal meaner than I'll look when it's over. [*He turns away, and is striding to the cart when Judith advances and interposes with her arms stretched out to him. Richard, feeling that a very little will upset his self-possession, shrinks from her, crying*] What are you doing here? This is no place for you. [*She makes a gesture as if to touch him. He recoils impatiently*] No: go away, go away: youll unnerve me. Take her away, will you.

JUDITH. Wont you bid me goodbye?

RICHARD [*allowing her to take his hand*] Oh goodbye, goodbye. Now go—go—quickly. [*She clings to his hand—will not be put off with so cold a last farewell—at last, as he tries to disengage himself, throws herself on his breast in agony*].

SWINDON [*angrily to the sergeant, who, alarmed at Judith's movement, has come from the back of the square to pull her back, and stopped irresolutely on finding that he is too late*] How is this? Why is she inside the lines?

SERGEANT [*guiltily*] I dunno, sir. She's that artful—cant keep her away.

BURGOYNE. You were bribed.

SERGEANT [*protesting*] No, sir—

SWINDON [*severely*] Fall back. [*He obeys*].

RICHARD [*imploringly to those around him, and finally to Burgoyne, as the least stolid of them*] Take her away. Do you think I want a woman near me now?

BURGOYNE [*going to Judith and taking her hand*] Here, madam: you had better keep inside the lines; but stand here behind us; and dont look.

Richard, with a great sobbing sigh of relief as she releases him and turns to Burgoyne, flies for refuge to the cart and mounts into it. The executioner takes off his coat and pinions him.

JUDITH [*resisting Burgoyne quietly and drawing her hand away*] No: I must stay. I wont look. [*She goes to the right of the gallows. She tries to look at Richard, but turns away with a frightful shudder, and falls on her knees in prayer. Brudenell comes towards her from the back of the square*].

BURGOYNE [*nodding approvingly as she kneels*] Ah, quite so. Do not disturb her, Mr Brudenell: that will do very nicely. [*Brudenell nods also, and withdraws a little, watching her sympathetically. Burgoyne resumes his former position, and takes out a handsome gold chronometer*]. Now then, are those preparations made? We must not detain Mr Dudgeon.

By this time Richard's hands are bound behind him; and the noose is round his neck. The two soldiers take the shafts of the waggon, ready to pull it away. The executioner, standing in the cart behind Richard, makes a sign to the sergeant.

SERGEANT [*to Burgoyne*] Ready, sir.

BURGOYNE. Have you anything more to say, Mr Dudgeon? It wants two minutes of twelve still.

RICHARD [*in the strong voice of a man who has conquered the bitterness of death*] Your watch is two minutes slow by the town clock, which I can see from here, General. [*The town clock strikes the first stroke of twelve. Involuntarily the people flinch at the sound, and a subdued groan breaks from them*]. Amen! my life for the world's future!

ANDERSON [*shouting as he rushes into the market place*] Amen; and stop the execution. [*He bursts through the line of soldiers opposite Burgoyne, and rushes, panting, to the gallows*]. I am Anthony Anderson, the man you want.

The crowd, intensely excited, listens with all its ears. Judith, half rising, stares at him; then lifts her hands like one whose dearest prayer has been granted.

SWINDON. Indeed. Then you are just in time to take your place on the gallows. Arrest him.

At a sign from the sergeant, two soldiers come forward to seize Anderson.

ANDERSON [*thrusting a paper under Swindon's nose*] There's my safe-conduct, sir.

SWINDON [*taken aback*] Safe-conduct! Are you—!

ANDERSON [*emphatically*] I am. [*The two soldiers take him by the elbows*]. Tell these men to take their hands off me.

SWINDON [*to the men*] Let him go.

SERGEANT. Fall back.

The two men return to their places. The townfolk raise a cheer; and begin to exchange exultant looks, with a presentiment of triumph as they see their Pastor speaking with their enemies in the gate.[2]

2. "Gate" in the archaic sense of street or thoroughfare.

ANDERSON [*exhaling a deep breath of relief, and dabbing his perspiring brow with his handkerchief*] Thank God, I was in time!

BURGOYNE [*calm as ever, and still watch in hand*] Ample time, sir. Plenty of time. I should never dream of hanging any gentleman by an American clock. [*He puts up his watch*].

ANDERSON. Yes: we are some minutes ahead of you already, General. Now tell them to take the rope from the neck of that American citizen.

BURGOYNE [*to the executioner in the cart—very politely*] Kindly undo Mr Dudgeon.

> The executioner takes the rope from Richard's neck, unties his hands, and helps him on with his coat.

JUDITH [*stealing timidly to Anderson*] Tony.

ANDERSON [*putting his arm round her shoulders and bantering her affectionately*] Well, what do you think of your husband now, eh?—eh??—eh???

JUDITH. I am ashamed—[*she hides her face against his breast*].

BURGOYNE [*to Swindon*] You look disappointed, Major Swindon.

SWINDON. You look defeated, General Burgoyne.

BURGOYNE. I am, sir; and I am humane enough to be glad of it. [*Richard jumps down from the cart, Brudenell offering his hand to help him, and runs to Anderson, whose left hand he shakes heartily, the right being occupied by Judith*]. By the way, Mr Anderson, I do not quite understand. The safe-conduct was for a commander of the militia. I understand you are a—[*He looks as pointedly as his good manners permit at the riding boots, the pistols, and Richard's coat, and adds*]—a clergyman.

ANDERSON [*between Judith and Richard*] Sir: it is in the hour of trial that a man finds his true profession. This foolish young man [*placing his hand on Richard's shoulder*] boasted himself the Devil's Disciple; but when the hour of trial came to him, he found that it was his destiny to suffer and be faithful to the death. I thought myself a decent minister of the gospel of peace; but when the hour of trial came to me, I found that it was my destiny to be a man of action, and that my place was amid the thunder of the captains and the shouting. So I am starting life at fifty as Captain Anthony Anderson of the Springtown militia; and the Devil's Disciple here will start presently as the Reverend Richard Dudgeon, and wag his pow[3] in my old pulpit, and give good advice to this silly sentimental little wife of mine [*putting his other hand on her shoulder. She steals a glance at Richard to see how the prospect pleases him*]. Your mother told me, Richard, that I should never have chosen Judith if I'd been born for the ministry. I am afraid she was right; so, by your leave, you may keep my coat and I'll keep yours.

RICHARD. Minister—I should say Captain. I have behaved like a fool.

JUDITH. Like a hero.

RICHARD. Much the same thing, perhaps. [*With some bitterness towards himself*] But no: if I had been any good, I should have

3. Head.

done for you what you did for me, instead of making a vain sacrifice.

ANDERSON. Not vain, my boy. It takes all sorts to make a world—saints as well as soldiers. [*Turning to Burgoyne*] And now, General, time presses; and America is in a hurry. Have you realized that though you may occupy towns and win battles, you cannot conquer a nation?

BURGOYNE. My good sir, without a Conquest you cannot have an aristocracy. Come and settle the matter at my quarters.

ANDERSON. At your service, sir. [*To Richard*] See Judith home for me, will you, my boy. [*He hands her over to him*]. Now, General. [*He goes busily up the market place towards the Town Hall, leaving Judith and Richard together. Burgoyne follows him a step or two; then checks himself and turns to Richard*].

BURGOYNE. Oh, by the way, Mr Dudgeon, I shall be glad to see you at lunch at half-past one. [*He pauses a moment and adds, with politely veiled slyness*] Bring Mrs Anderson, if she will be so good. [*To Swindon, who is fuming*] Take it quietly, Major Swindon: your friend the British soldier can stand up to anything except the British War Office. [*He follows Anderson*].

SERGEANT [*to Swindon*] What orders, sir?

SWINDON [*savagely*] Orders! What use are orders now! There's no army. Back to quarters; and be d—[*He turns on his heel and goes*].

SERGEANT [*pugnacious and patriotic, repudiating the idea of defeat*] 'Tention. Now then: cock up your chins, and shew em you dont care a damn for em. Slope arms! Fours! Wheel! Quick march!

> *The drums mark time with a tremendous bang; the band strikes up British Grenadiers; and the Sergeant, Brudenell, and the English troops march off defiantly to their quarters. The townsfolk press in behind, and follow them up the market, jeering at them; and the town band, a very primitive affair, brings up the rear, playing Yankee Doodle. Essie, who comes in with them, runs to Richard.*

ESSIE. Oh, Dick!

RICHARD [*good-humoredly, but wilfully*] Now, now: come, come! I dont mind being hanged; but I will not be cried over.

ESSIE. No, I promise. I'll be good. [*She tries to restrain her tears, but cannot*]. I—I want to see where the soldiers are going to. [*She goes a little way up the market, pretending to look after the crowd*].

JUDITH. Promise me you will never tell him.

RICHARD. Dont be afraid.

> *They shake hands on it.*

ESSIE [*calling to them*] Theyre coming back. They want you.

> *Jubilation in the market. The townsfolk surge back again in wild enthusiasm with their band, and hoist Richard on their shoulders, cheering him.*

AUGUST STRINDBERG

A Dream Play†

Dramatis Personæ

(*The voice of*) FATHER INDRA
INDRA'S DAUGHTER
THE GLAZIER
THE OFFICER
THE FATHER
THE MOTHER
LINA
THE DOORKEEPER
THE BILLSTICKER
THE PROMPTER
THE POLICEMAN
THE LAWYER
THE DEAN OF PHILOSOPHY
THE DEAN OF THEOLOGY
THE DEAN OF MEDICINE
THE DEAN OF LAW
THE CHANCELLOR
KRISTIN
THE QUARANTINE MASTER
THE ELDERLY FOP
THE COQUETTE
THE FRIEND
THE POET
HE
SHE (*doubles with Victoria's voice*)
THE PENSIONER
UGLY EDITH
EDITH'S MOTHER
THE NAVAL OFFICER
ALICE

† From August Strindberg, *Six Plays of Strindberg*, translated by Elizabeth Sprigge. Copyright 1955 by Elizabeth Sprigge.

THE SCHOOLMASTER
NILS
THE HUSBAND
THE WIFE
THE BLIND MAN
1ST COAL HEAVER
2ND COAL HEAVER
THE GENTLEMAN
THE LADY
SINGERS AND DANCERS (*Members of the Opera Company*)
CLERKS, GRADUATES, MAIDS, SCHOOLBOYS, CHILDREN, CREW,
RIGHTEOUS PEOPLE.

Prologue

An impression of clouds, crumbling cliffs, ruins of castles and for-
tresses.
The constellations Leo, Virgo and Libra are seen, with the planet
Jupiter shining brightly among them.
On the highest cloud-peak stands THE DAUGHTER OF INDRA. INDRA'S
VOICE[1] *is heard from above.*

INDRA'S VOICE. Where art thou, Daughter?
DAUGHTER. Here, Father, here!
INDRA'S VOICE. Thou hast strayed, my child.
  Take heed, thou sinkest.
  How cam'st thou here?
DAUGHTER. Borne on a cloud, I followed the lightning's
  blazing trail from the ethereal heights.
  But the cloud sank, and still is falling.
  Tell me, great Father Indra, to what region
  am I come? The air's so dense, so hard to breathe.
INDRA'S VOICE. Leaving the second world thou camest to the
  third.
  From Cucra, Star of the Morning.
  Far art thou come and enterest
  Earth's atmosphere. Mark there
  The Sun's Seventh House that's called the Scales.
  The Morning Star is at the autumn weighing,
  When day and night are equal.
DAUGHTER. Thou speak'st of Earth. Is that the dark
  and heavy world the moon lights up?
INDRA'S VOICE. It is the darkest and the heaviest
  of all the spheres that swing in space.
DAUGHTER. Does not the sun shine there?
INDRA'S VOICE. It shines, but not unceasingly.
DAUGHTER. Now the clouds part, and I can see . . .

1. In the Vedic religion Indra is the air; a great warrior, he is preeminently
dominant god of the middle realm or known as the thunder-god.

INDRA'S VOICE. What see'st thou, child?

DAUGHTER. I see . . . that Earth is fair . . . It has green woods,
blue waters, white mountains, yellow fields.

INDRA'S VOICE. Yes, it is fair, as all that Brahma[2] shaped,
yet in the dawn of time
was fairer still. Then came a change,
a shifting of the orbit, maybe of more.
Revolt followed by crime which had to be suppressed.

DAUGHTER. Now I hear sounds arising . . .
What kind of creatures dwell down there?

INDRA'S VOICE. Go down and see. The Creator's children I would not
decry,
but it's their language that thou hearest.

DAUGHTER. It sounds as if . . . it has no cheerful ring.

INDRA'S VOICE. So I believe. Their mother-tongue
is called Complaint. Truly a discontented,
thankless race is this of Earth.

DAUGHTER. Ah, say not so! Now I hear shouts of joy,
and blare and boom. I see the lightning flash.
Now bells are pealing and the fires are lit.
A thousand thousand voices rise,
singing their praise and thanks to heaven.
[Pause.]
Thy judgment is too hard on them, my Father.

INDRA. Descend and see, and hear, then come again
and tell me if their lamentations
and complaint are justified.

DAUGHTER. So be it. I descend. Come with me, Father!

INDRA. No. I cannot breathe their air.

DAUGHTER. Now the cloud sinks. It's growing dense. I suffocate!
This is not air, but smoke and water that I breathe,
so heavy that it drags me down and down.
And now I clearly feel its reeling!
This third is surely not the highest world.

INDRA. Neither the highest, truly, nor the lowest.
It is called Dust, and whirls with all the rest,
And so at times its people, struck with dizziness,
live on the borderline of folly and insanity . . .
Courage, my child, for this is but a test!

DAUGHTER. [On her knees as the cloud descends.]
I am sinking!

[*The curtain rises on* THE GROWING CASTLE.
*The background shows a forest of giant hollyhocks in bloom:
white, pink, crimson, sulphur-yellow and violet. Above this
rises the gilded roof of a castle with a flower-bud crowning its
summit. Under the walls of the castle lie heaps of straw and
stable-muck.*

2. In the Vedic religion the personalized god derived from impersonal, self-exist- ent Being; the creator or evolver.

On each side of the stage are stylised representations of interiors, architecture and landscape which remain unchanged throughout the play.

The GLAZIER *and the* DAUGHTER *enter together.*]

DAUGHTER. The castle keeps on growing up out of the earth. Do you see how it has grown since last year?

GLAZIER. [*To himself*] I've never seen that castle before—and I've never heard of a castle growing ... but ... [*To the* DAUGHTER *with conviction*] Yes, it's grown six feet, but that's because they've manured it. And if you look carefully, you'll see it's put out a wing on the sunny side.

DAUGHTER. Ought it not to blossom soon? We are already halfway through the summer.

GLAZIER. Don't you see the flower up there?

DAUGHTER. [*Joyfully*] Yes, I see it. Father, tell me something. Why do flowers grow out of dirt?

GLAZIER. They don't like the dirt, so they shoot up as fast as they can into the light—to blossom and to die.

DAUGHTER. Do you know who lives in the castle?

GLAZIER. I used to know, but I've forgotten.

DAUGHTER. I believe there is a prisoner inside, waiting for me to set him free.

GLAZIER. What will you get if you do?

DAUGHTER. One does not bargain about what one has to do. Let us go into the castle.

GLAZIER. Very well, we will.

[*They go towards the background which slowly vanishes to the sides, disclosing a simple bare room with a table and a few chairs. A screen cuts the stage in two—the other half unlighted.* A YOUNG OFFICER *in an unconventional modern uniform sits rocking his chair and striking the table with his sword.*

The DAUGHTER *and the* GLAZIER *enter.*

She goes up to the OFFICER *and gently takes the sword from his hands.*]

DAUGHTER. No, no, you mustn't do that.

OFFICER. Please, Agnes, let me keep my sword.

DAUGHTER. But you are cutting the table to pieces. [*To the* GLAZIER] Father, you go down to the harness room and put in that window pane, and we will meet later.

[*Exit* GLAZIER]

DAUGHTER. You are a prisoner in your own room. I have come to set you free.

OFFICER. I have been waiting for this, but I wasn't sure you would want to.

DAUGHTER. The castle is strong—it has seven walls—but it shall be done. Do you want to be set free—or not?

OFFICER. To tell the truth, I don't know. Either way I'll suffer. Every joy has to be paid for twice over with sorrow. It's wretched here, but I'd have to endure three times the agony for the joys of freedom . . . Agnes, I'll bear it, if only I may see you.

DAUGHTER. What do you see in me?

OFFICER. The beautiful, which is the harmony of the universe. There are lines in your form which I have only found in the movement of the stars, in the melody of strings, in the vibrations of light. You are a child of heaven.

DAUGHTER. So are you.

OFFICER. Then why do I have to groom horses, clean stables and have the muck removed?

DAUGHTER. So that you may long to get away.

OFFICER. I do. But it's so hard to pull oneself out of it all.

DAUGHTER. It is one's duty to seek freedom in the light.

OFFICER. Duty? Life has not done its duty by me.

DAUGHTER. You feel wronged by life?

OFFICER. Yes. It has been unjust. . . .

[*Voices are now heard from behind the dividing screen, which is drawn aside as the lights go up on the other set: a homely living-room. The* OFFICER *and the* DAUGHTER *stand watching, gestures and expression held. The* MOTHER, *an invalid, sits at a table. In front of her is a lighted candle, which from time to time she trims with snuffers. On the table are piles of new underclothing, which she is marking with a quill pen. Beyond is a brown cupboard*
The FATHER *brings her a silk shawl.*]

FATHER. [*Gently*] I have brought you this.

MOTHER. What use is a silk shawl to me, my dear, when I am going to die so soon?

FATHER. You believe what the doctor says?

MOTHER. What he says too, but most of all I believe the voice that speaks within me.

FATHER. [*Sorrowfully*] Then it really is grave . . . And you are thinking of your children, first and last.

MOTHER. They were my life, my justification, my happiness, and my sorrow.

FATHER. Kristina, forgive me . . . for everything.

MOTHER. For what? Ah, my dear, forgive *me!* We have both hurt each other. Why, we don't know. We could not do otherwise . . . However, here is the children's new linen. See that they change twice a week—on Wednesdays and Sundays, and that Louisa washes them—all over . . . Are you going out?

FATHER. I have to go to the school at eleven.

MOTHER. Before you go ask Alfred to come.

FATHER. [*Pointing to the* OFFICER] But, dear heart, he is here.

MOTHER. My sight must be going too . . . Yes, it's getting so dark. [*Snuffs candle*] Alfred, come!

[*The* FATHER *goes o it through the middle of the wall, nodding goodbye. The* OFFICER *moves forward to the* MOTHER.]

MOTHER. Who is that girl?

OFFICER. [*Whispering*] That's Agnes.

MOTHER. Oh, is it Agnes? Do you know what they are saying? That she is the daughter of the God Indra, who begged to come down to Earth so as to know what it is really like for human beings. But don't say anything.

OFFICER. She *is* a child of the Gods.

MOTHER. [*Raising her voice*] Alfred, my son, I shall soon be leaving you and your brothers and sisters. I want to say one thing—for you to remember all your life.

OFFICER [*Sadly*] What is it, Mother?

MOTHER. Only one thing: never quarrel with God.

OFFICER. What do you mean, Mother?

MOTHER. You must not go on feeling you have been wronged by life.

OFFICER. But I've been treated so unjustly.

MOTHER. You're still harping on the time you were unjustly punished for taking that money which was afterwards found.

OFFICER. Yes. That piece of injustice gave a twist to the whole of my life.

MOTHER. I see. Well now, you just go over to that cupboard . . .

OFFICER. [*Ashamed*] So you know about that. The . . .

MOTHER. "The Swiss Family Robinson" which . . .

OFFICER. Don't say any more . . .

MOTHER. Which your brother was punished for . . . when it was *you* who had torn it to pieces and hidden it.

OFFICER. Think of that cupboard still being there after twenty years. We have moved so many times—and my mother died ten years ago.

MOTHER. Yes. What of it? You are always questioning everything, and so spoiling the best of life for yourself . . . Ah, here's Lina!

    [*Enter* LINA.]

LINA. Thank you very much all the same, Ma'am, but I can't go to the christening.

MOTHER. Why not, child?

LINA. I've got nothing to wear.

MOTHER. You can borrow this shawl of mine.

LINA. Oh no, Ma'am, you're very kind, but that would never do.

MOTHER. I can't see why not. I shan't be going to any more parties.

OFFICER. What will Father say? After all, it's a present from him.

MOTHER. What small minds!

FATHER. [*Putting his head in*] Are you going to lend my present to the maid?

MOTHER. Don't talk like that! Remember I was in service once myself. Why should you hurt an innocent girl?

FATHER. Why should you hurt me, your husband?

MOTHER. Ah, this life! If you do something good, someone else is sure to think it bad; if you are kind to one person, you're sure to harm another. Ah, this life!

    [*She snuffs the candle so that it goes out. The room grows dark and the screen is drawn forward again.*]

DAUGHTER. Human beings are to be pitied.

OFFICER. Do you think so?

DAUGHTER. Yes, life is hard. But love conquers everything. Come and see.

> [*They withdraw and the background disappears. The* OFFICER *vanishes and the* DAUGHTER *comes forward alone. The new scene shows an old derelict wall. In the middle of the wall a gate opens on an alley leading to a green plot where a giant blue monkshood is growing. To the left of the gate is the door-window of the Stage Doorkeeper's lodge. The Stage Door-keeper is sitting with a grey shawl over her head and shoulders, crocheting a star-patterned coverlet. On the right is an announcement-board which the* BILLSTICKER *is washing. Near him is a fishnet with a green handle and a green fish box. Further right the cupboard from the previous set has become a door with an air-hole shaped like a four-leafed clover. To the left is a small lime tree with a coal-black stem and a few pale green leaves.*
> *The* DAUGHTER *goes up to the* DOORKEEPER.]

DAUGHTER. Isn't the star coverlet finished yet?

DOORKEEPER. No, my dear. Twenty-six years is nothing for such a piece of work.

DAUGHTER. And your sweetheart never came back?

DOORKEEPER. No, but it wasn't his fault. He *had* to take himself off, poor fellow. That was thirty years ago.

DAUGHTER. [*To* BILLSTICKER] She was in the ballet, wasn't she? Here —at the Opera.

BILLSTICKER. She was the prima ballerina, but when *he* went away, it seems he took her dancing with him . . . so she never got any more parts.

DAUGHTER. All complain—with their eyes, and with their voices too.

BILLSTICKER. I haven't much to complain of—not now I've got my net and a green fish box.

DAUGHTER. Does that make you happy?

BILLSTICKER. Yes, very happy. That was my dream when I was little, and now it's come true. I'm all of fifty now, you know.

DAUGHTER. Fifty years for a fishnet and a box!

BILLSTICKER. A *green* box, a *green* one . . .

DAUGHTER. [*To* DOORKEEPER] Let me have that shawl now, and I'll sit here and watch the children of men. But you must stand behind and tell me about them.

> [*The* DAUGHTER *puts on the shawl and sits down by the gate.*]

DOORKEEPER. This is the last day of the Opera season. They hear now if they've been engaged for the next.

DAUGHTER. And those who have not?

DOORKEEPER. Lord Jesus, what a scene! I always pull my shawl over my head.

DAUGHTER. Poor things!

DOORKEEPER. Look, here's one coming. She's not been engaged. See how she's crying!

> [*The* SINGER *rushes in from the right and goes through the*

gate with her handkerchief to her eyes. She pauses a moment in the alley beyond and leans her head against the wall, then goes quickly out.]

DAUGHTER. Human beings are to be pitied.

DOORKEEPER. But here comes one who seems happy enough.

[*The* OFFICER *comes down the alley, wearing a frock-coat and top hat. He carries a bouquet of roses and looks radiantly happy.*]

DOORKEEPER. He's going to marry Miss Victoria.

OFFICER. [*Downstage, looks up and sings*] Victoria!

DOORKEEPER. The young lady will be down in a minute.

WOMAN'S VOICE. [*From above, sings*] I am here!

OFFICER. [*Pacing*] Well, I am waiting.

DAUGHTER. Don't you know me?

OFFICER. No, I know only one woman—Victoria! Seven years I have come here to wait for her—at noon when the sun reaches the chimneys, and in the evening as darkness falls. Look at the paving. See? Worn by the steps of the faithful lover? Hurrah! She is mine. [*Sings*] Victoria! [*No answer.*] Well, she's dressing now. [*To the* BILLSTICKER] Ah, a fishnet I see! Everyone here at the Opera is crazy about fishnets—or rather about fish. Dumb fish—because they cannot sing . . . What does a thing like that cost?

BILLSTICKER. It's rather dear.

OFFICER. [*Sings*] Victoria! . . . [*Shakes the lime tree*] Look, it's budding again! For the eighth time. [*Sings*] Victoria! . . . Now, she's doing her hair . . . [*To* DAUGHTER] Madam, kindly allow me to go up and fetch my bride.

DOORKEEPER. Nobody's to go on the stage.

OFFICER. Seven years I've walked up and down here. Seven times three hundred and sixty-five I make two thousand five hundred and fifty-five. [*Stops and pokes the door with the clover-shaped hole.*] Then this door I've seen two thousand five hundred and fifty-five times and I still don't know where it leads to. And this clover leaf to let in the light. Who does it let the light in for? Is anyone inside? Does anybody live there?

DOORKEEPER. I don't know. I've never seen it open.

OFFICER. It looks like a larder door I saw when I was four years old, when I went out one Sunday afternoon with the maid—to see another family and other maids. But I only got as far as the kitchen, where I sat between the water barrel and the salt tub. I've seen so many kitchens in my time, and the larders are always in the passage, with round holes and a clover leaf in the door. But the Opera can't have a larder as it hasn't got a kitchen. [*Sings*] Victoria! [*To* DAUGHTER] Excuse me, Madam, she can't leave by any other way, can she?

DOORKEEPER. No, there is no other way.

OFFICER. Good. Then I'm bound to meet her.

[*Members of the Opera Company swarm out of the building, scrutinised by the* OFFICER. *They go out by the gate.*]

She's sure to come. [*To* DAUGHTER] Madam, that blue monkshood out there—I saw it when I was a child. Is it the same one? I remember it in a rectory garden when I was seven—with two doves, blue doves, under the hood. Then a bee came and went into the hood, and I thought: "Now I've got you," so I grabbed the flower, but the bee stung through it, and I burst into tears. However, the rector's wife came and put moist earth on it—and then we had wild strawberries and milk for supper . . . I believe it's growing dark already. Where are you off to, Billsticker?

BILLSTICKER. Home to my supper.

[*Exit with fishnet and box.*]

OFFICER. [*Rubbing his eyes*] Supper? At this time of day? . . . [*To* DAUGHTER] Excuse me, may I just step inside a moment and telephone to the Growing Castle?

DAUGHTER. What do you want to say to them?

OFFICER. I want to tell the glazier to put in the double windows. It will be winter soon and I'm so dreadfully cold.

[*The* OFFICER *goes in the* DOORKEEPER's *Lodge.*]

DAUGHTER. Who is Miss Victoria?

DOORKEEPER. She is his love.

DAUGHTER. A true answer. What she is to us or others doesn't matter to him. Only what she is to *him*, that's what she *is*.

[*It grows dark suddenly.*]

DOORKEEPER. [*Lighting the lantern*] Dusk falls quickly today.

DAUGHTER. To the gods a year is as a minute.

DOORKEEPER. While to human beings a minute may be as long as a year.

[*The* OFFICER *comes out again. He looks shabbier, and the roses are withered.*]

OFFICER. Hasn't she come yet?

DOORKEEPER. No.

OFFICER. She's sure to come. She'll come. [*Paces up and down*] But all the same . . . perhaps it would be wiser to cancel that luncheon . . . as it's now evening. Yes, that's what I'll do. [*Goes in and telephones.*]

DOORKEEPER. [*To* DAUGHTER] May I have my shawl now?

DAUGHTER. No, my friend. You rest and I'll take your place, because I want to know about human beings and life—to find out if it really is as hard as they say.

DOORKEEPER. But you don't get any sleep on this job. Never any sleep, night or day.

DAUGHTER. No sleep at night?

DOORKEEPER. Well, if you can get any with the bell wire on your arm, because the night watchmen go up on the stage and are changed every three hours . . .

DAUGHTER. That must be torture.

DOORKEEPER. So you think, but we others are glad enough to get such a job. If you knew how much I'm envied.

DAUGHTER. Envied? Does one envy the tortured?

DOORKEEPER. Yes. But I'll tell you what's worse than night-watching and drudgery and draughts and cold and damp. That's having to listen, as I do, to all their tales of woe. They all come to me. Why? Perhaps they read in my wrinkles the runes of suffering, and that makes them talk. In that shawl, my dear, thirty years of torment's hidden—my own and others.

DAUGHTER. That's why it is so heavy and stings like nettles.

DOORKEEPER. Wear it if you like. When it gets too heavy, call me and I'll come and relieve you of it.

DAUGHTER. Goodbye. What you can bear, surely I can.

DOORKEEPER. We shall see. But be kind to my young friends and put up with their complaining.

[*The* DOORKEEPER *disappears down the alley. The stage is blacked out. When light returns, the lime tree is bare, the blue monkshood withered, and the green plot at the end of the alley has turned brown.*

The OFFICER *enters. His hair is grey and he has a grey beard. His clothes are ragged; his collar soiled and limp. He still carries the bouquet of roses, but the petals have dropped.*]

OFFICER. [*Wandering round*] By all the signs, summer is over and autumn at hand. I can tell that by the lime tree—and the monkshood. [*Pacing*] But autumn is *my* spring, for then the theatre opens again. And then she is bound to come. [*To* DAUGHTER] Dear lady, may I sit on this chair for a while?

DAUGHTER. Do, my friend. I can stand.

OFFICER. [*Sitting*] If only I could sleep a little it would be better.

[*He falls asleep for a moment, then starts up and begins walking again. He stops by the clover-leaf door and pokes it.*]

OFFICER. This door—it gives me no peace. What is there behind it? Something must be. [*Soft ballet music is heard from above.*] Ah, the rehearsals have begun! [*The lights come and go like a lighthouse beam.*] What's this? [*Speaking in time with the flashes.*] Light and darkness; light and darkness.

DAUGHTER. [*With the same timing*] Day and night; day and night. A merciful providence wants to shorten your waiting. And so the days fly, chasing the nights.

[*The light is now constant. The* BILLSTICKER *enters with his net and his implements.*]

OFFICER. Here's the Billsticker with his net. How was the fishing?

BILLSTICKER. Not too bad. The summer was hot and a bit long . . . the net was all right, but not quite what I had in mind.

OFFICER. "Not quite what I had in mind." Excellently put. Nothing ever is as one imagined it—because one's mind goes further than the act, goes beyond the object. [*He walks up and down striking the bouquet against the walls until the last leaves fall.*]

BILLSTICKER. Hasn't she come down yet?

OFFICER. No, not yet, but she'll come soon. Do you know what's behind that door, Billsticker?

BILLSTICKER. No, I've never seen it open.

OFFICER. I'm going to telephone to a locksmith to come and open it. [*Goes into the Lodge. The* BILLSTICKER *pastes up a poster and moves away.*]

DAUGHTER. What was wrong with the fishnet?

BILLSTICKER. Wrong? Well, there wasn't anything wrong exactly. But it wasn't what I'd had in mind, and so I didn't enjoy it *quite* as much . . .

DAUGHTER. How did you imagine the net?

BILLSTICKER. How? I can't quite tell you . . .

DAUGHTER. Let me tell you. In your imagination it was different— green but not *that* green.

BILLSTICKER. You understand, Madam. You understand everything. That's why they all come to you with their troubles. Now if you'd only listen to me, just this once . . .

DAUGHTER. But I will, gladly. Come in here and pour out your heart. [*She goes into the Lodge. The* BILLSTICKER *stays outside and talks to her through the window.*

> *The stage is blacked out again, then gradually the lights go up. The lime tree is in leaf; the monkshood in bloom; the sun shines on the greenery at the end of the alley. The* BILL- STICKER *is still at the window and the* DAUGHTER *can be seen inside.*
>
> *The* OFFICER *enters from the Lodge. He is old and white-haired; his clothes and shoes are in rags. He carries the stems of the bouquet. He totters backwards and forwards slowly like a very old man, and reads the poster. A* BALLET GIRL *comes out of the Theatre.*]

OFFICER. Has Miss Victoria gone?

BALLET GIRL. No, she hasn't.

OFFICER. Then I'll wait. Will she come soon?

BALLET GIRL. [*Gravely*] Yes, she's sure to.

OFFICER. Don't go—then you'll be able to see what's behind that door. I've sent for the locksmith.

BALLET GIRL. That will be really interesting to see this door opened. The door and the Growing Castle. Do you know the Growing Castle?

OFFICER. Do I? Wasn't I imprisoned there?

BALLET GIRL. Really, was that you? But why did they have so many horses there?

OFFICER. It was a stable castle, you see.

BALLET GIRL. [*Distressed*] How silly of me not to have thought of that.

> [*Moves towards the Lodge. A* CHORUS GIRL *comes out of the Theatre.*]

OFFICER. Has Miss Victoria gone?

CHORUS GIRL. [*Gravely*] No, she hasn't gone. She never goes.

OFFICER. That's because she loves me. No, you mustn't go before the locksmith comes. He's going to open this door.

CHORUS GIRL. Oh, is the door going to be opened? Really? What fun! I just want to ask the Doorkeeper something.

> [*She joins the* BILLSTICKER *at the window. The* PROMPTER *comes out of the Theatre.*]

OFFICER. Has Miss Victoria gone?

PROMPTER. Not so far as I know.

OFFICER. There you are! Didn't I say she was waiting for me? No, don't go. The door's going to be opened.

PROMPTER. Which door?

OFFICER. Is there more than one door?

PROMPTER. Oh, I see—the one with the clover-leaf! Of course I'll stay. I just want to have a few words with the Doorkeeper.

[*He joins the group at the window. They all speak in turn to the* DAUGHTER. *The* GLAZIER *comes through the gate.*]

OFFICER. Are you the locksmith?

GLAZIER. No, the locksmith had company. But a glazier's just as good.

OFFICER. Yes, indeed . . . indeed. But . . . er . . . have you brought your diamond with you?

GLAZIER. Of course. A glazier without a diamond—what good would that be?

OFFICER. None. Let's get to work then. [*He claps his hands. All group themselves in a circle round the door.* MALE CHORUS *in costumes of Die Meistersinger, and* GIRL DANCERS *from Aïda come out of the theatre and join them.*] Locksmith—or Glazier—do your duty! [*The* GLAZIER *goes towards the door holding out his diamond.*] A moment such as this does not recur often in a lifetime. Therefore, my good friends, I beg you to reflect seriously upon . . .

[*During the last words the* POLICEMAN *has entered by the gate.*]

POLICEMAN. In the name of the law I forbid the opening of this door.

OFFICER. Oh God, what a fuss there is whenever one wants to do anything new and great! Well—we shall take proceedings . . . To the lawyer then, and we will see if the law holds good. To the lawyer!

[*Without any lowering of the curtain the scene changes to the* LAWYER'S *office. The gate has now become the gate in an office railing stretching across the stage. The* DOORKEEPER'S *Lodge is a recess for the* LAWYER'S *desk, the lime tree, leafless, a coat-and-hat stand. The announcement-board is covered with proclamations and Court decrees and the clover-door is a document cupboard.*

The LAWYER *in frock coat and white tie is sitting on the left inside the railing of the gate, at this high desk covered with papers. His appearance bears witness to unspeakable suffering. His face is chalk-white, furrowed and purple-shadowed. He is hideous; his face mirrors all the crime and vice with which, through his profession, he has been involved.*

Of his two clerks one has only one arm; the other a single eye.

The people, who had gathered to witness the opening of the door, are now clients waiting to see the LAWYER, *and look as if they have always been there.*]

[The DAUGHTER, *wearing the shawl, and the* OFFICER *are in front. The* OFFICER *looks curiously at the cupboard door and from time to time pokes it.*

The LAWYER *goes up to the* DAUGHTER.]

LAWYER. If you let me have that shawl, my dear, I'll hang it here until the stove is lighted and then I'll burn it with all its griefs and miseries.

DAUGHTER. Not yet, my friend. I must let it get quite full first, and I want above all to gather *your* sufferings up in it, the crimes you have absorbed from others, the vices, swindles, slanders, libel . . .

LAWYER. My child, your shawl would not be big enough. Look at these walls! Isn't the wall-paper stained as if by every kind of sin? Look at these documents in which I write records of evil! Look at me! . . . Nobody who comes here ever smiles. Nothing but vile looks, bared teeth, clenched fists, and all of them squirt their malice, their envy, their suspicions over me. Look, my hands are black and can never be clean! See how cracked they are and bleeding! I can never wear my clothes for more than a few days because they stink of other people's crimes. Sometimes I have the place fumigated with sulphur, but that doesn't help. I sleep in the next room and dream of nothing but crime. I have a murder case in Court now—that's bad enough—but do you know what's worst of all? Separating husbands and wives. Then earth and heaven seem to cry aloud, to cry treason against primal power, the source of good, against love! And then, do you know, after reams of paper have been filled with mutual accusations, if some kindly person takes one or other of the couple aside and asks them in a friendly sort of way the simple question—"What have you really got against your husband—or your wife?"—then he, or she, stands speechless. They don't know. Oh, once it was something to do with a salad, another time about some word. Usually it's about nothing at all. But the suffering, the agony! All this I have to bear. Look at me! Do you think, marked as I am by crime, I can ever win a woman's love? Or that anyone wants to be the friend of a man who has to enforce payment of all the debts of the town? It's misery to be human.

DAUGHTER. Human life is pitiable!

LAWYER. It is indeed. And what people live on is a mystery to me. They marry with an income of two thousand crowns when they need four. They borrow, to be sure, they all borrow, and so scrape along somehow by the skin of their teeth until they die. Then the estate is always insolvent. Who has to pay up in the end? Tell me that.

DAUGHTER. He who feeds the birds.

LAWYER. Well, if He who feeds the birds would come down to earth and see the plight of the unfortunate children of men, perhaps He would have some compassion . . .

DAUGHTER. Human life is pitiful.

LAWYER. Yes, that's the truth. [*To the* OFFICER] What do you want?

OFFICER. I only want to ask if Miss Victoria has gone.

LAWYER. No, she hasn't. You can rest assured of that. Why do you keep poking my cupboard?

OFFICER. I thought the door was so very like . . .

LAWYER. Oh, no, no, no!

[*Church bells ring.*]

OFFICER. Is there a funeral in the town?

LAWYER. No, it's Graduation—the conferring of Doctors' degrees. I myself am about to receive the degree of Doctor of Law. Perhaps you would like to graduate and receive a laurel wreath?

OFFICER. Why not? It would be a little distraction.

LAWYER. Then perhaps we should proceed at once to the solemn rites. But you must go and change.

[*Exit* OFFICER.

The stage is blacked out and changes to the interior of the Church.

The barrier now serves as the chancel rail. The announcement-board shows the numbers of the hymns. The lime-tree hatstand has become a candelabra, the Lawyer's desk is the Chancellor's lectern, and the Clover-door leads to the vestry. The Chorus from Die Meistersinger are ushers with wands. The dancers carry the laurel wreaths. The rest of the people are the congregation.

The new background shows only a gigantic organ, with a mirror over the keyboard.

Music is heard. At the sides stand the four Deans of the Faculties—Philosophy, Theology, Medicine and Law. For a moment there is no movement, then:

The USHERS *come forward from the right.*[3]

The DANCERS *follow, holding laurel wreaths in their outstretched hands.*

Three GRADUATES *come in from the left, are crowned in turn by the* DANCERS *and go out to the right.*

The LAWYER *advances to receive his wreath.*

The DANCERS *turn away, refusing to crown him, and go out. The* LAWYER, *greatly agitated, leans against a pillar.*

Everyone disappears. The LAWYER *is alone.*

The DAUGHTER *enters with a white shawl over her head and shoulders.*]

DAUGHTER. Look, I have washed the shawl. But what are you doing here? Didn't you get your laurels?

LAWYER. No. I was discredited.

DAUGHTER. Why? Because you have defended the poor, said a good word for the sinner, eased the burden of the guilty, obtained reprieve for the condemned? Woe to mankind! Men are not angels, but pitiable creatures.

---

3. This scene follows exactly the normal ceremony in a Swedish university when Doctors' degrees are conferred. As each Graduate has the wreath put on his head, a gun outside is fired. The Chancellor and the Faculties bow. Then the new doctor bows to them. One of the Graduates should be the Officer and another the Schoolmaster of the later scene. [*Translator's note.*]

LAWYER. Do not judge men harshly. It is my business to plead for them.

DAUGHTER. [*Leaning against the organ*] Why do they strike their friends in the face?

LAWYER. They know no better.

DAUGHTER. Let us enlighten them—you and I together. Will you?

LAWYER. There can be no enlightenment for them. Oh that the gods in heaven might hear our woe!

DAUGHTER. It shall reach the throne. [*Sits at the organ.*] Do you know what I see in this mirror? The world as it should be. For as it is it's wrong way up.

LAWYER. How did it come to be wrong way up?

DAUGHTER. When the copy was made.

LAWYER. Ah! You yourself have said it—the copy! I always felt this must be a poor copy, and when I began to remember its origin nothing satisfied me. Then they said I was cynical and had a jaundiced eye, and so forth.

DAUGHTER. It is a mad world. Consider these four Faculties. Organized society subsidizes all four: Theology, the doctrine of Divinity, continually attacked and ridiculed by Philosophy claiming wisdom for itself; and Medicine always giving the lie to Philosophy and discounting Theology as one of the sciences, calling it superstition. And there they sit together on the Council, whose function is to teach young men respect for the University. Yes, it's a madhouse. And woe to him who first recovers his senses!

LAWYER. The first to discover it are the theologians. For their preliminary studies they take Philosophy, which teaches them that Theology is nonsense, and then they learn from Theology that Philosophy is nonsense. Madness.

DAUGHTER. Then there's Law, serving all but its servants.

LAWYER. Justice, to the just unjust. Right so often wrong.

DAUGHTER. Thus you have made it, O Children of Men! Child, come! You shall have a wreath from me . . . one more fitting. [*She puts a crown of thorns on his head.*] Now I will play to you. [*She sits at the organ and plays a Kyrie, but instead of the organ, voices are heard singing. The last note of each phrase is sustained.*]

CHILDREN'S VOICES. Lord! Lord!

WOMEN'S VOICES. Be merciful!

MEN'S VOICES (*Tenor*). Deliver us for Thy mercy's sake.

MEN'S VOICES (*Bass.*) Save Thy children, O Lord, and be not wrathful against us.

ALL. Be merciful! Hear us! Have compassion for mortals. Are we so far from Thee? Out of the depths we call. Grace, Lord! Let not the burden be to heavy for Thy children. Hear us! Hear us!

[*The stage darkens as the* DAUGHTER *rises and approaches the* LAWYER.

By means of lighting the organ is changed to the wall of a grotto. The sea seeps in between basalt pillars with a harmony of waves and wind.]

LAWYER. Where are we?

DAUGHTER. What do you hear?

LAWYER. I hear drops falling.

DAUGHTER. Those are the tears of mankind weeping. What more do you hear?

LAWYER. A sighing . . . a moaning . . . a wailing.

DAUGHTER. The lamentation of mortals has reached so far, no further. But why this endless lamentation? Is there no joy in life?

LAWYER. Yes. The sweetest which is also the bitterest—love! Marriage and a home. The highest and the lowest.

DAUGHTER. Let me put it to the test.

LAWYER. With me?

DAUGHTER. With you. You know the rocks, the stumbling stones. Let us avoid them.

LAWYER. I am poor.

DAUGHTER. Does that matter if we love one another? And a little beauty costs nothing.

LAWYER. My antipathies may be your sympathies.

DAUGHTER. They can be balanced.

LAWYER. Supposing we tire?

DAUGHTER. Children will come, bringing ever new interests.

LAWYER. You? You will take me, poor, ugly, despised, discredited?

DAUGHTER. Yes, Let us join our destinies.

LAWYER. So be it.

> [*The scene changes to a very simple room adjoining the* LAW-YER's *office. On the right is a large curtained double bed, close to it a window with double panes; on the left a stove and kitchen utensils.*
> *At the back an open door leads to the office, where a number of poor people can be seen awaiting admission.* KRISTIN, *the maid, is pasting strips of paper along the edges of the inner window.*
> *The* DAUGHTER, *pale and worn, is at the stove.*]

KRISTIN. I paste, I paste.

DAUGHTER. You are shutting out the air. I am suffocating.

KRISTIN. Now there's only one small crack left.

DAUGHTER. Air, air! I cannot breathe.

KRISTIN. I paste, I paste.

LAWYER. [*From the office*] That's right, Kristin. Warmth is precious.
> [KRISTIN *pastes the last crack.*]

DAUGHTER. Oh, it's as if you are glueing up my mouth!

LAWYER. [*Coming to the doorway with a document in his hand*] Is the child asleep?

DAUGHTER. Yes, at last.

LAWYER. [*Mildly*] That screaming frightens away my clients.

DAUGHTER. [*Gently*] What can be done about it?

LAWYER. Nothing.

DAUGHTER. We must take a bigger flat.

LAWYER. We have no money.

DAUGHTER. May I open the window, please? This bad air is choking me.

LAWYER. Then the warmth would escape, and we should freeze.

DAUGHTER. It's horrible! Can't we at least scrub the place?

LAWYER. You can't scrub—neither can I, and Kristin must go on pasting. She must paste up the whole house, every crack in floor and walls and ceiling.

[*Exit* KRISTIN, *delighted.*]

DAUGHTER. I was prepared for poverty, not dirt.

LAWYER. Poverty is always rather dirty.

DAUGHTER. This is worse than I dreamt.

LAWYER. We haven't had the worst. There's still food in the pot.

DAUGHTER. But what food!

LAWYER. Cabbage is cheap, nourishing and good.

DAUGHTER. For those who like cabbage. To me it's repulsive.

LAWYER. Why didn't you say so?

DAUGHTER. Because I loved you. I wanted to sacrifice my taste.

LAWYER. Now I must sacrifice my taste for cabbage. Sacrifices must be mutual.

DAUGHTER. Then what shall we eat? Fish? But you hate fish.

LAWYER. And it's dear.

DAUGHTER. This is harder than I believed.

LAWYER. [*Gently*] You see how hard it is. And the child which should be our bond and blessing is our undoing.

DAUGHTER. Dearest! I am dying in this air, in this room with its backyard view, with babies screaming through endless sleepless hours, and those people out there wailing and quarrelling and accusing . . . Here I can only die.

LAWYER. Poor little flower, without light, without air.

DAUGHTER. And you say there are others worse off.

LAWYER. I am one of the envied of the neighbourhood.

DAUGHTER. None of it would matter, if only I could have some beauty in our home.

LAWYER. I know what you're thinking of—a plant, a heliotrope to be exact; but that costs as much as six quarts of milk or half a bushel of potatoes.

DAUGHTER. I would gladly go without food to have my flower.

LAWYER. There is one kind of beauty that costs nothing. Not to have it in his home is sheer torture for a man with any sense of beauty.

DAUGHTER. What is that?

LAWYER. If I tell you, you will lose your temper.

DAUGHTER. We agreed never to lose our tempers.

LAWYER. We agreed. Yes. All will be well, Agnes, if we can avoid those sharp hard tones. You know them—no, not yet.

DAUGHTER. We shall never hear those.

LAWYER. Never, if it depends on me.

DAUGHTER. Now tell me.

LAWYER. Well, when I come into a house, first I look to see how the curtains are hung. [*Goes to the window and adjusts the curtain.*] If they hang like a bit of string or rag, I soon leave. Then I glance at the chairs. If they are in their places, I stay. [*Puts a chair straight against the wall.*] Next I look at the candlesticks. If the candles are crooked, then the whole house is askew. [*Straightens a candle on the bureau.*] That you see, my dear, is the beauty which costs nothing.

DAUGHTER. [*Bowing her head*] Not that sharp tone, Axel!

LAWYER. It wasn't sharp.

DAUGHTER. Yes it was.

LAWYER. The devil take it!

DAUGHTER. What kind of language is that?

LAWYER. Forgive me, Agnes. But I have suffered as much from your untidiness as you do from the dirt. And I haven't dared straighten things myself, because you would have been offended and thought I was reproaching you. Oh, shall we stop this?

DAUGHTER. It is terribly hard to be married, harder than anything. I think one has to be an angel.

LAWYER. I think one has.

DAUGHTER. I am beginning to hate you after all this.

LAWYER. Alas for us then! But let us prevent hatred. I promise never to mention untidiness again, athough it is torture to me.

DAUGHTER. And I will eat cabbage, although that is torment to me.

LAWYER. And so—life together is a torment. One's pleasure is the other's pain.

DAUGHTER. Human beings are pitiful.

LAWYER. You see that now?

DAUGHTER. Yes. But in God's name let us avoid the rocks, now that we know them so well.

LAWYER. Let us do that. We are tolerant, enlightened people. Of course we can make allowances and forgive.

DAUGHTER. Of course we can smile at trifles.

LAWYER. We, only we can do it. Do you know, I read in the paper this morning . . . By the way, where is the paper?

DAUGHTER. [*Embarrassed*] Which paper?

LAWYER. [*Harshly*] Do I take more than one newspaper?

DAUGHTER. Smile—and don't speak harshly! I lit the fire with your newspaper.

LAWYER. [*Violently*] The devil you did!

DAUGHTER. Please smile. I burnt it because it mocked what to me is holy.

LAWYER. What to me is unholy! Huh! [*Striking his hands together. beside himself.*] I'll smile, I'll smile till my back teeth show. I'll be tolerant and swallow my opinions and say yes to everything and cant and cringe. So you've burnt my paper, have you? [*Pulls the bed curtains.*] Very well. Now I'm gong to tidy up until you lose your temper . . . Agnes, this is quite impossible!

DAUGHTER. Indeed it is.

LAWYER. Yet we must stay together. Not for our vows' sake, but for the child's.

DAUGHTER. That's true—for the child's sake. Yes, yes, we must go on.

LAWYER. And now I must attend to my clients. Listen to them muttering. They can't wait to tear one another to pieces, to get each other fined and imprisoned. Benighted souls!

[*Enter* KRISTIN *with pasting materials.*]

DAUGHTER. Wretched, wretched beings! And all this pasting! [*She bows her head in dumb despair.*]

KRISTIN. I paste, I paste!

[*The* LAWYER *standing by the door, nervously fingers the handle.*]

DAUGHTER. Oh how that handle squeaks! It is as if you were twisting my heart-strings.

LAWYER. I twist, I twist!

DAUGHTER. Don't!

LAWYER. I twist . . .

DAUGHTER. No!

LAWYER. I . . .

[*The* OFFICER—*now middle-aged—takes hold of the handle from inside the office.*]

OFFICER. May I?

LAWYER. [*Letting go of the handle*] Certainly. As you have got your degree.

OFFICER. [*Entering*] The whole of life is now mine. All paths are open to me. I have set foot on Parnassus, the laurels are won. Immortality, fame, all are mine!

LAWYER. What are you going to live on?

OFFICER. Live on?

LAWYER. You'll need a roof surely, and clothes and food?

OFFICER. Those are always to be had, as long as there's someone who cares for you.

LAWYER. Fancy that now, fancy that! Paste, Kristin, paste! Until they cannot breathe. [*Goes out backwards, nodding.*]

KRISTIN. I paste, I paste! Until they cannot breathe.

OFFICER. Will you come now?

DAUGHTER. Oh quickly! But where to?

OFFICER. To Fairhaven, where it is summer and the sun is shining. Youth is there, children and flowers, singing and dancing, feasting and merrymaking.

[*Exit* KRISTIN.]

DAUGHTER. I would like to go there.

OFFICER. Come!

LAWYER. [*Entering*] Now I shall return to my first hell. This one was the second—and worst. The sweetest hell is the worst. Look, she's left hairpins all over the floor again! [*Picks one up.*]

OFFICER. So he has discovered the hairpins too.

LAWYER. Too? Look at this one. There are two prongs but one pin. Two and yet one. If I straighten it out, it becomes one single piece. If I bend it, it is two, without ceasing to be one. In other words the two are one. But if I break it—like this [*Breaks it in half,*] then the two are two. [*He throws away the pieces.*]

OFFICER. So much he has seen. But before one can break it, the prongs must diverge. If they converge, it holds.

LAWYER. And if they are parallel, they never meet. Then it neither holds nor breaks.

OFFICER. The hairpin is the most perfect of all created things. A straight line which is yet two parallel lines.

LAWYER. A lock that closes when open.

OFFICER. Closes open—a plait of hair loosed while bound.

LAWYER. Like this door. When I close it, I open the way out, for you, Agnes.

[*Goes out, closing the door.*]

DAUGHTER. And now?

[*The scene changes. The bed with its hangings is transformed into a tent, the stove remaining. The new background shows a beautiful wooded shore, with beflagged landing stages and white boats, some with sails set. Among the trees are little Italianesque villas, pavilions, kiosks and marble statues.*

In the middle distance is a strait.

The foreground presents a sharp contrast with the background. Burnt hillsides, black and white tree stumps as after a forest fire, red heather, red pigsties and outhouses. On the right is an open-air establishment for remedial exercises, where people are being treated on machines resembling instruments of torture.

On the left is part of the Quarantine Station; open sheds with furnaces, boilers and pipes.

The DAUGHTER *and the* OFFICER *are standing as at the end of the previous scene.*

The QUARANTINE MASTER, *dressed as a blackamoor, comes along the shore.*]

OFFICER. [*Going up and shaking hands with the* QUARANTINE MASTER] What? You here, old Gasbags?[4]

Q. MASTER. Yes, I'm here.

OFFICER. Is this place Fairhaven?

Q. MASTER. No, that's over there. [*Points across the strait.*] This is Foulstrand.

OFFICER. Then we've come wrong.

Q. MASTER. We! Aren't you going to introduce me?

OFFICER. It wouldn't do. [*Low*] That is the Daughter of Indra.

Q. MASTER. Of Indra? I thought it must be Varuna[5] himself. Well, aren't you surprised to find me black in the face?

OFFICER. My dear fellow, I am over fifty, at which age one ceases to be surprised. I assumed at once that you were going to a fancy dress ball this afternoon.

Q. MASTER. Quite correct. I hope you'll come with me.

OFFICER. Certainly, for there doesn't seem to be any attraction in this place. What kind of people live here?

Q. MASTER. The sick live here, and the healthy over there.

OFFICER. But surely only the poor here?

Q. MASTER. No, my boy, here you have the rich. [*Indicates the gymnasium.*] Look at that man on the rack. He's eaten too much

4. Original "Ordström," meaning "Stream of Words." [*Translator's note.*]

5. In the Vedic religion a celestial god; the chief upholder of physical and moral order, he judges and punishes.

pâté-de-foie-gras with truffles, and drunk so much Burgundy that his feet are knotted.

OFFICER. Knotted?

Q. MASTER. He's got knotted feet, and that one lying on the guillotine has drunk so much brandy that his backbone's got to be mangled.

OFFICER. That's not very pleasant either.

Q. MASTER. What's more here on this side live all those who have some misery to hide. Look at this one coming now, for instance.

[*An elderly fop is wheeled on to the stage in a bath chair, accompanied by a gaunt and hideous coquette of sixty, dressed in the latest fashion and attended by the "Friend," a man of forty.*]

OFFICER. It's the Major! Our schoolfellow.

Q. MASTER. Don Juan! You see, he's still in love with the spectre at his side. He doesn't see that she has grown old, that she is ugly, faithless, cruel.

OFFICER. There's true love for you. I never would have thought that flighty fellow had it in him to love so deeply and ardently.

Q. MASTER. That's a nice way of looking at it.

OFFICER. I've been in love myself—with Victoria. As a matter of fact I still pace up and down the alley, waiting for her.

Q. MASTER. So you're the fellow who waits in the alley?

OFFICER. I am he.

Q. MASTER. Well, have you got that door open yet?

OFFICER. No, we're still fighting the case. The Billsticker is out with the fishnet, you see, which delays the taking of evidence. Meanwhile, the Glazier has put in windowpanes at the castle, which has grown half a story. It has been an unusually good year this year—warm and damp.

Q. MASTER. [*Pointing to the sheds*] But you've certainly had nothing like the heat of my place there.

OFFICER. What's the temperature of your furnaces then?

Q. MASTER. When we're disinfecting cholera suspects, we keep them at sixty degrees.

OFFICER. But is there cholera about again?

Q. MASTER. Didn't you know?

OFFICER. Of course I know. But I so often forget what I know.

Q. MASTER. And I so often wish I could forget—especially myself. That's why I go in for masquerades, fancy dress, theatricals.

OFFICER. Why. What's the matter with you?

Q. MASTER. If I talk, they say I'm bragging. If I hold my tongue they call me a hypocrite.

OFFICER. Is that why you blacked your face?

Q. MASTER. Yes. A shade blacker than I am.

OFFICER. Who's this coming?

Q. MASTER. Oh, he's a poet! He's going to have his mud bath.

[*The* POET *enters, looking at the sky and carrying a pail of mud.*]

OFFICER. But, good heavens, he ought to bathe in light and air!

Q. MASTER. No, he lives so much in the higher spheres that he gets homesick for the mud. It hardens his skin to wallow in the mire, just as it does with pigs. After his bath he doesn't feel the gadflies stinging.

OFFICER. What a strange world of contradictions!

POET. [*Ecstatically*] Out of clay the god Ptah[6] fashioned man on a potter's wheel, a lathe [*Mockingly*] or some other damned thing . . . [*Ecstatically*] Out of clay the sculptor fashions his more or less immortal masterpieces [*Mockingly*] which are usually only rubbish. [*Ecstatically*] Out of clay are formed these objects, so domestically essential bearing the generic name of pots and pans. [*Mockingly*] Not that it matters in the least to me what they're called. [*Ecstatically*] Such is clay! When clay is fluid, it is called mud. *C'est mon affaire!*[7] [*Calls.*] Lina!

[*Enter* LINA *with a bucket.*]

POET. Lina, show yourself to Miss Agnes. She knew you ten years ago when you were a young, happy, and, let me add, pretty girl. [*To* DAUGHTER] Look at her now! Five children, drudgery, squalling, hunger, blows. See how beauty has perished, how joy has vanished in the fulfillment of duties which should give the inner contentment which shows in the harmonious lines of a face, in the tranquil shinging of the eyes . . .

Q. MASTER. [*Putting a hand to the* POET's *lips*] Shut up! Shut up!

POET. That's what they all say. But if you are silent, they tell you to talk. How inconsistent people are!

[*Distant dance music is heard.*]

DAUGHTER. [*Going up to* LINA] Tell me your troubles.

LINA. No, I daren't. I'd catch it all the worse if I did.

DAUGHTER. Who is so cruel?

LINA. I daren't talk about it. I'll be beaten.

POET. May be, but I shall talk about it even if the Blackamoor knocks my teeth out. I shall talk about all the injustice there is here. Agnes, Daughter of the Gods, do you hear that music up on the hill? Well, that's a dance for Lina's sister, who has come home from town—where she went astray, you understand. Now they are killing the fatted calf, while Lina, who stayed at home, has to carry the swill pail and feed the pigs.

DAUGHTER. There is rejoicing in that home because the wanderer has forsaken the path of evil, not only because she has come home. Remember that.

POET. Then give a ball and a supper every evening for this blameless servant who has never gone astray. Do that for her—they never do. On the contrary, when Lina is free, she has to go to prayer meetings where she's reprimanded for not being perfect. Is that justice?

DAUGHTER. Your questions are difficult to answer, because there are so many unknown factors.

---

6. In Egyptian mythology he was the creative force or divine builder.

7. "Leave it to me."

POET. The Caliph, Harun the Just,[8] was of the same opinion. Sitting quietly on his exalted throne he could never see how those below were faring. Presently complaints reached his lofty ear, so one fine day he stepped down in disguise and walked unobserved among the crowd to watch the workings of justice.

DAUGHTER. You do not think I am Harun the Just, do you?

OFFICER. Let's change the subject. Here are newcomers.

[*A white boat, shaped like a dragon, glides into the Strait. It has a light blue silken sail on a gilded yard, and a golden mast with a rose-red pennon. At the helm, with their arms round each other's waists, sit* HE *and* SHE.]

There you see perfect happiness, utter bliss, the ecstasy of young love.

[*The light grows stronger.* HE *stands up in the boat and sings.*]

HE.   Hail fairest bay!
                     Where I passed youth's spring tide,
                     where I dreamed its first roses,
                     I come now again,
                     no longer alone.
                     Forests and havens,
                     heaven and sea,
                     greet her!
                     My love, my bride,
                     my sun, my life!

[*The flags on Fairhaven dip in salute. White handkerchiefs wave from villas and shores. The music of harps and violins sound over the strait.*]

POET. See how light streams from them! And sound rings across the water! Eros![9]

OFFICER. It is Victoria.

Q. MASTER. Well, if it is . . .

OFFICER. It is his Victoria. I have my own, and mine no one will ever see. Now hoist the quarantine flag while I haul in the catch.

[*The* QUARANTINE MASTER *waves a yellow flag. The* OFFICER *pulls on a line which causes the boat to turn in towards Foulstrand.*]

Hold hard there!

[HE *and* SHE *become aware of the dreadful landscape and show their horror.*]

Q. MASTER. Yes, yes, it's hard lines, but everyone has to land here, everyone coming from infectious areas.

POET. Think of being able to speak like that—to behave like that when you see two human beings joined in love. Do not touch them! Do not lay hands on love—that is high treason. Alas, alas! All that is most lovely will now be dragged down, down into the mud.

---

8. Harun-al-Raschid, a highly successful and influential Caliph of Bagdad (A.D. 786-809); he is best known for the romantic tales told about him in the *Arabian Nights,* among which are stories of his expeditions among his people incognito.

9. In Greek mythology the god of love.

[HE *and* SHE *come ashore, shamed and sad.*]

HE. What is it? What have we done?[1]

Q. MASTER. You don't have to do anything in order to meet with life's little discomforts.

SHE. How brief are joy and happiness!

HE. How long must we stay here?

Q. MASTER. Forty days and forty nights.

SHE. We would rather throw ourselves into the sea.

HE. Live here—among burnt hills and pigsties?

POET. Love can overcome everything, even sulphur fumes and carbolic acid.[2]

[*The* QUARANTINE MASTER *goes into a shed. Blue sulphurous vapour pours out.*]

Q. MASTER [*Coming out*]. I'm burning the sulphur. Will you kindly step inside.

SHE. Oh, my blue dress will lose its colour!

Q. MASTER. And turn white. Your red roses will turn white too.

HE. So will your cheeks, in forty days.

SHE. [*To the* OFFICER] That will please you.

OFFICER. No, it won't. True, your happiness was the source of my misery, but . . . that's no matter. [HE *and* SHE *go into the shed.*] [*To* DAUGHTER.] I've got my degree now, and a job as tutor over there. [*Indicates Fairhaven.*] Heigho! And in the fall I'll get a post in a school, teaching the boys the same lessons I learnt myself, all through my childhood, all through my youth. Teach them the same lessons I learnt all through my manhood and finally all through my old age. The same lessons! What is twice two? How many times does two go into four without remainder? Until I get a pension and have nothing to do but wait for meals and the newspapers, until in the end I'm carried out to the crematorium and burnt to ashes.

[*To* QUARANTINE MASTER *as he comes out of the shed.*] Have you no pensioners here? To be a pensioner is the worst fate after twice two is four, going to school again when one's taken one's degree, asking the same questions until one dies . . .

[*An elderly man walks past with his hands behind his back.*] Look, there goes a pensioner waiting for his life to ebb. A captain, probably, who failed to become a Major, or a Clerk to the Court who was never promoted. Many are called, but few are chosen. He's just walking about, waiting for breakfast.

PENSIONER. No, for the paper, the morning paper!

OFFICER. And he is only fifty-four. He may go on for another twenty-five years, waiting for meals and the newspaper. Isn't that dreadful?

PENSIONER. What is not dreadful? Tell me that. Tell me that.

OFFICER. Yes. Let him tell you who can.

[*Exit* PENSIONER.]

---

1. Literally "woe to us." [*Translator's note.*]
2. The poet does not speak again and is not mentioned until the end of the later quayside scene, so perhaps here he goes out. [*Translator's note.*]

Now I shall teach boys twice two is four. How many times does two go into four without remainder? [*He clutches his head in despair.*]

[*Enter* HE *and* SHE *from the shed. Her dress and roses are white, her face pale. His clothes are also bleached.*]

And Victoria whom I loved, for whom I desired the greatest happiness on earth, she has her happiness now, the greatest happiness she can know, while I suffer, suffer, suffer!

SHE. Do you think I can be happy, seeing your suffering? How can you believe that? Perhaps it comforts you to know that I shall be a prisoner here for forty days and forty nights. Tell me, does it comfort you?

OFFICER. Yes and no. I cannot have pleasure while you have pain. Oh!

HE. And do you think my happiness can be built on your agony?

OFFICER. We are all to be pitied—all of us.

[*All lift their hands to heaven. A discordant cry of anguish breaks from their lips.*]

ALL. Oh!

DAUGHTER. O God, hear them! Life is evil! Mankind is to be pitied.

ALL. [*As before*] Oh!

[*The stage is blacked out and the scene changes.*

The whole landscape is in winter dress with snow on the ground and on the leafless trees. Foulstrand is in the background, in shadow.

The strait is still in the middle distance. On the near side is a landing stage with white boats and flags flying from flagstaffs. In the strait a white warship, a brig with gunports, is anchored.

The foreground presents Fairhaven, in full light.

On the right is a corner of the Assembly Rooms with open windows through which are seen couples dancing. On a box outside stand three MAIDS, *their arms round each other's waists, watching the dancing.*

On the steps is a bench on which UGLY EDITH *is sitting, bareheaded and sorrowful, with long dishevelled hair, before an open piano.*

On the left is a yellow wooden house outside which two children in summer dresses are playing ball.

The DAUGHTER *and* OFFICER *enter.*]

DAUGHTER. Here is peace and happiness. Holiday time. Work over, every day a festival, everyone in holiday attire. Music and dancing even in the morning. [*To the* MAIDS.] Why don't you go in and dance, my dears?

SERVANTS. Us?

OFFICER. But they are servants.

DAUGHTER. True. But why is Edith sitting there instead of dancing?

[EDITH *buries her face in her hands.*]

OFFICER. Don't ask her! She has been sitting there for three hours without being invited to dance. [*He goes into the yellow house.*]

DAUGHTER. What cruel pleasure!

> [*The* MOTHER, *in a décolleté dress, comes out of the Assembly Rooms and goes up to* EDITH.]

MOTHER. Why don't you go in as I told you?

EDITH. Because . . . because I can't be my own partner. I know I'm ugly and no one wants to dance with me, but I can avoid being reminded of it. [*She begins to play Bach's Toccata con Fuga, No. 10.*]

> [*The waltz at the ball is heard too, first faintly, then growing louder as if in competition with the Toccata. Gradually* EDITH *overcomes it and reduces it to silence. Dance couples appear in the doorway, and everyone stands reverently listening.*
>
> A NAVAL OFFICER *seizes* ALICE, *one of the guests, by the waist.*]

N. OFFICER. Come, quick! [*He leads her down to the landing stage.*

> EDITH *breaks off, rises and watches them in despair. She remains standing as if turned to stone.*
>
> *The front wall of the yellow house vanishes. Boys are sitting on forms, among them the* OFFICER *looking uncomfortable and worried. In front of them stands the* SCHOOLMASTER, *wearing spectacles and holding chalk and a cane.*]

SCHOOLMASTER. [*To the* OFFICER] Now, my boy, can you tell me what twice two is?

> [*The* OFFICER *remains seated, painfully searching his memory without finding an answer.*]

You must stand up when you are asked a question.

OFFICER. [*Rising anxiously*] Twice two . . . let me see . . . That makes two twos.

S. MASTER. Aha! So you have not prepared your lesson.

OFFICER. [*Embarrassed*] Yes, I have, but . . . I know what it is, but I can't say it.

S. MASTER. You're quibbling. You know the answer, do you? But you can't say it. Perhaps I can assist you. [*Pulls the* OFFICER'S *hair.*]

OFFICER. Oh, this is dreadful, really dreadful!

S. MASTER. Yes, it is dreadful that such a big boy should have no ambition.

OFFICER. [*Agonised*] A *big* boy. Yes I certainly am big, much bigger than these others. I am grown up. I have left school . . . [*As if waking*] I have even graduated. Why am I sitting here then? Haven't I got my degree?

S. MASTER. Certainly. But you have got to stay here and mature. Do you see? You must mature. Isn't that so?

OFFICER. [*Clasping his head*] Yes, that's so, one must mature . . . Twice two—is two, and this I will demonstrate by analogy, the highest form of proof. Listen! Once one is one, therefore twice two is two. For that which applies to the one must also apply to the other.

S. MASTER. The proof is perfectly in accord with the laws of logic, but the answer is wrong.

OFFICER. What is in accord with the laws of logic cannot be wrong.

Let us put it to the test. One into one goes once, therefore two into two goes twice.

s. master. Quite correct according to analogy. But what then is once three?

officer. It is three.

s. master. Consequently twice three is also three.

officer. [*Pondering*] No, that can't be right . . . It can't be, for if so . . . [*Sits down in despair.*] No, I am not mature yet . . .

s. master. No, you are not mature by a long way.

officer. Then how long shall I have to stay here?

s. master. How long? Here? You believe that time and space exist? Assuming time does exist, you ought to be able to say what time is. What is time?

officer. Time . . . [*Considers.*] I can't say, although I know what it is, Ergo, I may know what twice two is without being able to say it. Can you yourself say what time is?

s. master. Certainly I can.

all the boys. Tell us then!

s. master. Time? . . . Let me see. [*Stands motionless with his finger to his nose.*] While we speak, time flies. Consequently time is something which flies while I am speaking.

boy. [*Rising*] You're speaking now, sir, and while you're speaking, I fly. Consequently I am time. [*Flies.*]

s. master. That is quite correct according to the laws of logic.

officer. Then the laws of logic are absurd, for Nils, though he did fly, can't be time.

s. master. That is also quite correct according to the laws of logic, although it is absurd.

officer. Then logic is absurd.

s. master. It really looks like it. But if logic is absurd, then the whole world is absurd . . . and I'll be damned if I stay here and teach you absurdities! If anyone will stand us a drink, we'll go and bathe.

officer. That's a *posterus prius*,[3] a world back to front, for it's customary to bathe first and have one's drink afterwards. You old fossil!

s. master. Don't be so conceited, Doctor.

officer. Captain, if you please. I am an officer, and I don't understand why I should sit here among a lot of schoolboys and be insulted.

s. master. [*Wagging his finger*] We must mature!

[*Enter* quarantine master.]

q. master. The quarantine period has begun.

officer. So there you are. Fancy this fellow making me sit here on a form, when I've taken my degree.

q. master. Well, why don't you go away?

officer. Go away? That's easier said than done.

s. master. So I should think. Try!

officer. [*To* quarantine master] Save me! Save me from his eyes!

3. "What follows comes first."

Q. MASTER. Come on then! Come and help us dance. We must dance before the plague breaks out. We must.

OFFICER. Will the ship sail then?

Q. MASTER. The ship will sail first. A lot of tears will be shed of course.

OFFICER. Always tears; when she comes in and when she sails. Let's go.

[*They go out. The* SCHOOLMASTER *continues to give his lesson in mime.*

The MAIDS, *who were standing at the window of the ballroom, walk sadly down to the quay.* EDITH, *until then motionless beside the piano, follows them.*]

DAUGHTER. [*To* OFFICER] Isn't there one happy person in this paradise?

OFFICER. Yes, here comes a newly wed couple. Listen to them.

[*The* NEWLY WED COUPLE *enter.*]

HUSBAND. [*To* WIFE] My happiness is so complete that I wish to die.

WIFE. But why to die?

HUSBAND. In the midst of happiness grows a seed of unhappiness. Happiness consumes itself like a flame. It cannot burn for ever, it must go out, and the presentiment of its end destroys it at its very peak.

WIFE. Let us die together, now at once.

HUSBAND. Die! Yes, let us die. For I fear happiness, the deceiver.

[*They go towards the sea and disappear.*]

DAUGHTER. [*To the* OFFICER] Life is evil. Human beings are to be pitied!

OFFICER. Look who's coming now. This is the most envied mortal in the place. [*The* BLIND MAN *is led in.*] He is the owner of these hundreds of Italian villas. He owns all these bays and creeks and shores and woods, the fish in the water, the birds in the air and the game in the woods. These thousands of people are his tenants, and the sun rises over his sea and sets over his lands.

DAUGHTER. And does he complain too?

OFFICER. Yes, with good cause, as he cannot see.

Q. MASTER. He is blind.

DAUGHTER. The most envied of all!

OFFICER. Now he's going to see the ship sail with his son aboard.

BLIND MAN. I do not see, but I hear. I hear the fluke of the anchor tearing the clay bed, just as when the hook is dragged out of a fish and the heart comes up too through the gullet. My son, my only child, is going to journey to strange lands across the great sea. Only my thoughts can go with him . . . Now I hear the chain clanking . . . and there's something flapping and lashing like washing on a clothes line . . . Wet handkerchiefs perhaps . . . And I hear a sound of sighing . . . or sobbing . . . like people crying . . . Maybe the plash of small waves against the hull, or maybe the girls on the quay, the abandoned, the inconsolable. I once asked a child why the sea was salt, and the child, whose father was on a long voyage, replied at once: "The sea is salt because sailors cry so much." "But why do sailors cry so much?" "Well," he said, "because they keep going away . . . And so they're always drying their handkerchiefs up on the masts." "And why do people cry when they're sad?" I asked. "Oh," said he, "that's because the eye window must be washed sometimes, so we can see better."

[*The brig has set sail and glided away. The girls on the quay alternately wave their handkerchiefs and dry their eyes. Now on the topmast is hoisted the signal "*YES,*" a red ball on a white ground.* ALICE *waves a triumphant reply.*]

DAUGHTER. [*To* OFFICER] What does that flag mean?

OFFICER. It means "yes." It is the lieutenant's "yes" in red, red as heart's blood, written on the blue cloth of the sky.

DAUGHTER. Then what is "no" like?

OFFICER. Blue as tainted blood in blue veins. Look how elated Alice is.

DAUGHTER. And how Edith is weeping.

BLIND MAN. Meeting and parting, parting and meeting. That's life. I met his mother, then she went away. My son was left; now he has gone.

DAUGHTER. But he will come back.

BLIND MAN. Who is speaking to me? I have heard that voice before. In my dreams, in boyhood when summer holidays began, in early married life when my child was born. Whenever life smiled, I heard that voice, like the whisper of the South wind, like the sounds of a heavenly harp, like the angels' greeting, as I imagine it, on Christmas Eve.

[*The* LAWYER *enters, goes up to the* BLIND MAN *and whispers.*]

Really?

LAWYER. Yes, it's a fact. [*Goes across to the* DAUGHTER.] You have seen most things now, but you have not yet experienced the worst thing of all.

DAUGHTER. What can that be?

LAWYER. Repetitions, reiterations. Going back. Doing one's lessons again . . . Come!

DAUGHTER. Where to?

LAWYER. To your duties.

DAUGHTER. What are they?

LAWYER. Everything you abominate. Everything you least want to do, and yet must. They are to abstain and renounce, to go without, to leave behind. They are everything that is disagreeable, repulsive, painful.

DAUGHTER. Are there no pleasant duties?

LAWYER. They become pleasant when they are done.

DAUGHTER. When they no longer exist. So duty is altogether unpleasant. What then can one enjoy?

LAWYER. What one enjoys is sin.

DAUGHTER. Sin?

LAWYER. Which is punished. Yes. If I enjoy myself one day, one evening, the next day I have a bad conscience and go through the torments of hell.

DAUGHTER. How strange!

LAWYER. I wake in the morning with a headache, and then the repetition begins, but it is a distorted repetition, so that everything which was charming and witty and beautiful the night before appears in memory ugly, stupid, repulsive. Pleasure stinks, and enjoyment falls to pieces. What people call success is always a step towards the next failure. The successes in my life have been my downfall. Men have an instinctive dread of another's good fortune. They feel it's unjust that fate should favour any one man, so try to restore the balance by rolling boulders across his path. To have talent is to be in danger of one's life—one may so easily starve to death. However, you must go back to your duties, or I shall take proceedings against you, and we shall go through all three Courts, first, second, third.

DAUGHTER. Go back? To the stove and the cabbage and the baby clothes?

LAWYER. Yes. And it's washing day—the big wash when all the handkerchiefs have to be done.

DAUGHTER. Oh, must I do that again?

LAWYER. The whole of life is only repetition. Look at the schoolmaster there. Yesterday he took his doctor's degree, was crowned with laurels, scaled Parnassus, was embraced by the monarch. Today he is back at school, asking what twice two is . . . and that's what he will go on doing until he dies. But come now, back to your home.

DAUGHTER. I would rather die.

LAWYER. Die? One can't do that. To begin with taking one's own life is so dishonourable that even one's corpse is dishonoured. And to add to that one is damned, for it is a mortal sin.

DAUGHTER. It is not easy to be human.

ALL. Hear, hear!

DAUGHTER. I will not go back with you to humiliation and dirt. I shall return to the place from which I came. But first the door must be opened, so that I may know the secret. I wish the door to be opened.

[*Enter the* POET.]

LAWYER. Then you must retrace your steps, go back the way you came, and put up with all the horrors of a lawsuit; the repetitions, the redraftings, the reiterations.

DAUGHTER. So be it. But first I shall seek solitude in the wilderness to find myself. We shall meet again. [*To the* POET.] Come with me.

[A *distant cry of lamentation rises.*]

VOICES. Oh! oh! oh!

DAUGHTER. What was that?

LAWYER. The doomed at Foulstrand.

DAUGHTER. Why do they wail so today?

LAWYER. Because here the sun is shining, here is music and dance and youth. This makes them suffer more.

DAUGHTER. We must set them free.

LAWYER. Try! Once a deliverer came, but he was hanged upon a cross.

DAUGHTER. By whom?

LAWYER. By all the righteous.

DAUGHTER. Who are they?

LAWYER. Don't you know the righteous? Well, you will.

DAUGHTER. Was it they who refused you your degree?

LAWYER. Yes.

DAUGHTER. Then I do know them.

> [*The scene changes to a Mediterranean resort. In the background are villas, a Casino with a terrace, and a blue strip of sea. In the foreground is a white wall over which hang branches of orange trees in fruit. Below this to one side a huge heap of coal and two wheel barrows.*[4]
>
> The DAUGHTER *and the* LAWYER *come on to the terrace.*]

DAUGHTER. This is paradise.

1ST. COAL HEAVER. This is hell.

2ND. C. H. A hundred and twenty in the shade.

1ST. C. H. Shall we get into the sea?

2ND. C. H. Then the police'd come: "You mustn't bathe here!"

1ST. C. H. Can't we have a bit of fruit off that tree?

2ND. C. H. No. The police would come.

1ST. C. H. One can't work in this heat. I'm going to chuck it.

2ND. C. H. Then the police will come and take you up. [*Pause*] Besides, you'll have nothing to eat.

1ST. C. H. Nothing to eat! We, who do the most work, get the least food. And the rich, who do nothing, get it all. Might one not, without taking liberties with the truth, call this unjust? What has the Daughter of the Gods up there to say about it?

DAUGHTER. I have no answer. But, tell me, what have you done to get so black and have so hard a lot?

1ST. C. H. What have we done? Got ourselves born of poor and pretty bad parents. Been sentenced a couple of times maybe.

DAUGHTER. Sentenced?

1ST. C. H. Yes. The ones that don't get caught sit up there in the Casino eating eight course dinners with wine.

DAUGHTER. [*to* LAWYER] Can this be true?

LAWYER. More or less, yes.

DAUGHTER. Do you mean that everyone at some time or other deserves imprisonment?

LAWYER. Yes.

DAUGHTER. Even you?

LAWYER. Yes.

DAUGHTER. Is it true those poor men aren't allowed to bathe in that sea?

LAWYER. No, not even with their clothes on. Only those who try to

4. The coalheavers' scene was added after the play's completion.

drown themselves avoid paying. And they are more than likely to get beaten up at the police station.

DAUGHTER. Can't they go and bathe outside the town—in the country?

LAWYER. There is no country. It's all fenced in.

DAUGHTER. I mean where it is open and free.

LAWYER. Nothing is free. Everything is owned.

DAUGHTER. Even the sea, the vast, wide . . . ?

LAWYER. Everything. You can't go out in a boat, nor can you land, without it all being booked and paid for. It's marvellous.

DAUGHTER. This is not paradise.

LAWYER. I promise you that.

DAUGHTER. Why don't people do anything to improve conditions?

LAWYER. They certainly do. But all reformers end in prison or the madhouse.

DAUGHTER. Who puts them in prison?

LAWYER. All the righteous, all the respectable.

DAUGHTER. Who puts them in the madhouse?

LAWYER. Their own despair when they see the hopelessness of the struggle.

DAUGHTER. Has it occurred to anyone that there may be unknown reasons for this state of things?

LAWYER. Yes, the well-off always think that is so.

DAUGHTER. That there is nothing wrong with things as they are?

1ST. C. H. And yet we are the foundation of society. If there's no coal, the kitchen stove goes out and the fire on the hearth too. The machines in the factory stop working; the lights in streets and shops and homes all go out. Darkness and cold descend on you. That's why we sweat like hell carrying filthy coal. What do you give us in return?

LAWYER. [*To* DAUGHTER] Help them. [*Pause*] I know things can't be exactly the same for everybody, but why should there be such inequality?

[*The* GENTLEMAN *and the* LADY *cross the terrace.*]

LADY. Are you coming to play cards?

GENTLEMAN. No, I must go for a little walk to get an appetite for dinner.

[*Exeunt*]

1ST. C. H. To *get* an appetite!

2ND. C. H. To *get* . . . !

[*Children enter. When they catch sight of the black workers they scream with terror and run off.*]

1ST. C. H. They scream when they see us. They scream!

2ND. C. H. Curse it! We'd better get out the scaffolds soon and execute this rotten body.

1ST. C. H. Curse it, I say too!

LAWYER. [*To* DAUGHTER] It's all wrong. It's not the people who are so bad, but . . .

DAUGHTER. But?

LAWYER. The system.

DAUGHTER. [*Hiding her face in her hands*] This is not paradise.

1ST. C. H. No. This is hell, pure hell.

> [*The scene changes to the earlier set of Fingal's Cave.*[5]
> *Long green billows roll gently into the cave. A red bell-buoy
> rocks upon the waves, but gives no sound until later. Music
> of the winds. Music of the waves.*
> *The* DAUGHTER *is with the* POET.]

POET. Where have you brought me?

DAUGHTER. Far from the murmur and wailing of the children of
men. To this grotto at the ends of the oceans to which we give
the name *Indra's Ear*, for here, it is said, the King of Heaven listens to the lamentations of mortals.

POET. Why here?

DAUGHTER. Do you not see that this cave is shaped like a shell? Yes,
you see it. Do you not know that your ear is shaped like a shell?
You know, but you have given it no thought. [*She picks up a shell.*]
As a child, did you never hold a shell to your ear and listen to the
whisper of your heart's blood, to the humming of thoughts in
your brain, to the parting of a thousand little worn-out tissues in
the fabric of your body? All this you can hear in a small shell.
Think then what may be heard in this great one.

POET. [*Listening*] I hear nothing but the sighing of the wind.

DAUGHTER. Then I will be its interpreter. Listen to the lamentation
of the winds. [*She speaks to soft music.*]

> Born under heaven's clouds,
> chased were we by Indra's fires
> down to the crust of earth.
> The mould of acres soiled our feet,
> we had to bear
> the dust of roads and city smoke,
> the kitchen's reek and fumes of wine.
> Out to these spacious seas we blew,
> to air our lungs,
> to shake our wings
> and bathe our feet.
> Indra, Lord of Heaven,
> hear us!
> Listen to our sighing!
> Earth is not clean,
> life is not just,
> men are not evil
> nor are they good.
> They live as best they may
> from one day to another,
> Sons of dust in dust they walk,
> born of the dust,
> dust they become.

---

5. An extremely large grotto on the
island of Staffa, off the coast of Scot-
land. Fingal is an Irish folk-hero, a
legendary defender of the oppressed.

Feet they have to trudge,
no wings.
Dust-soiled they grow.
Is the fault theirs
or Thine?

POET. So I heard once . . .

DAUGHTER. Hush! The winds are still singing.

[*Continues to soft music.*]
We, the winds, the sons of air,
bear man's lamentation.
Thou hast heard us
on autumn eves in the chimney stack,
in the stove-pipe's vent,
in the window cracks,
as the rain wept on the tiles.
Or on winter nights,
mid the pine-wood's snows,
or on the stormy ocean,
has heard the moaning and the whine,
of rope and sail.
That is us, the winds,
the sons of air,
who from human breasts
we pierced ourselves,
these sounds of suffering learnt.
In sickroom, on the battlefield,
and most where the newborn lie,
screaming, complaining,
of the pain of being alive.
It is we, we, the winds
who whine and whistle,
woe! woe! woe!

POET. It seems to me that once before . . .

DAUGHTER. Hush! The waves are singing.

[*Speaks to soft music.*]
It is we, we the waves,
that rock the winds
to rest.
Green cradling waves,
wet are we and salt.
Like flames of fire,
wet flames we are.
Quenching, burning,
cleansing, bathing,
generating, multiplying.
We, we the waves,
that rock the winds
to rest.

False waves and faithless. Everything on earth that is not burned is drowned by those waves. Look there! [*She points to the wreck-age.*] Look what the sea has stolen and destroyed! All that remains of those sunken ships is their figureheads . . . and the names—Justice, Friendship, Golden Peace, and Hope. That's all that's left of hope, treacherous hope. Spars, rowlocks, bailers. And see! The lifebuoy which saved itself, letting those in need perish.

POET. [*Searching the wreckage*] Here is the name of the ship Justice. This is the ship which sailed from Fairhaven with the Blind Man's son on board. So she sank. And Alice's sweetheart was in her too, Edith's hopeless love.

DAUGHTER. The blind man? Fairhaven? Surely that I dreamt. Alice's sweetheart, ugly Edith, Foulstrand and the quarantine, the sulphur and carbolic, graduation in the church, the lawyer's office, the alley and Victoria. The Growing Castle and the Officer . . . These things I dreamt.

POET. Of these things I once made poetry.

DAUGHTER. You know then what poetry is?

POET. I know what dreams are. What is poetry?

DAUGHTER. Not reality, but more than reality. Not dreams, but waking dreams.

POET. Yet the children of men believe that poets merely play—invent and fabricate.

DAUGHTER. It is just as well, my friend, or else the world would be laid waste from lack of endeavour. All men would lie upon their backs, gazing at the heavens; no hand would be lifted to plough or spade, or plane or axe.

POET. Do you speak thus, Daughter of Indra? You, who are half of heaven?

DAUGHTER. You are right to reproach me. I have lived too long down here, and like you have bathed in mud. My thoughts can no longer fly. Clay is on their wings and soil about their feet. And I myself [*She raises her arms.*] I am sinking, sinking! Help me, Father God of Heaven! [*Silence.*] No longer can I hear His answer. The ether no longer carries the sound of His lips to the shell of my ear . . . the silver thread has snapped. Alas, I am earthbound!

POET. Do you mean then soon—to go?

DAUGHTER. As soon as I have burnt this earthly matter, for the waters of the ocean cannot cleanse me. Why do you ask?

POET. I have a prayer—a petition.

DAUGHTER. A petition?

POET. A petition from mankind to the ruler of the universe, drawn up by a dreamer.

DAUGHTER. Who is to present it?

POET. Indra's Daughter.

DAUGHTER. Can you speak the words?

POET. I can.

DAUGHTER. Speak them then.

POET. It is better that you should.

DAUGHTER. Where shall I read them?

POET. In my thoughts—or here. [*He gives her a scroll.*]

DAUGHTER. So be it. I will speak them. [*She takes the scroll but does not read.*]

> "Why with anguish are you born?
> Why do you hurt your mother so,
> Child of man, when bringing her
> the joy of motherhood,
> joy beyond all other joys?
> Why wake to life,
> why greet the light
> with a cry of fury and of pain,
> Child of man, when to be glad
> should be the gift of life?
> Why are we born like animals?
> We who stem from God and man,
> whose souls are longing to be clothed
> in other than this blood and filth.
> Must God's own image cut its teeth?"

[*Speaking her own thoughts*]

Silence! No more! The work may not condemn the master. Life's riddle still remains unsolved.

[*Continuing the* POET's *bitter words*]

> "And then the journey's course begins,
> over thistles, thorns and stones.
> If it should touch a beaten track,
> comes at once the cry: 'Keep off!'
> Pluck a flower, straight you'll find
> the bloom you picked to be another's.
> If cornfields lie across our path
> and you must pursue your way,
> trampling on another's crops,
> others then will trample yours
> that your loss may equal theirs.
> Every pleasure you enjoy
> brings to all your sorrow,
> yet your sorrow gives no gladness.
> So sorrow, sorrow upon sorrow
> on your way—until you're dead
> and then, alas, give others bread.

[*Her own thought.*]

> Is it thus, O son of dust,
> You seek to win the ear of God?

POET. How may son of dust find words,
  so pure, so light, so luminous,
  that they can rise up from the earth?
  Child of the Gods, translate for me,
  this lamentation into speech
  fit for Immortal ears.

DAUGHTER. I will.

POET. [*Pointing*] What is floating there—a buoy?

DAUGHTER. Yes.

POET. It is like a lung with a windpipe.

DAUGHTER. It is the watchman of the sea. When danger is abroad it sings.

POET. It seems to me that the sea is rising, and the waves beginning to . . .

DAUGHTER. You are not mistaken.

POET. Alas, what do I see? A ship—on the rocks.

DAUGHTER. What ship can it be?

POET. I believe it is the ghost-ship.

DAUGHTER. What is that?

POET. The Flying Dutchman.[6]

DAUGHTER. He? Why is he punished so cruelly, and why does he not come ashore?

POET. Because he had seven unfaithful wives.

DAUGHTER. Shall he be punished for that?

POET. Yes. All righteous men condemned him.

DAUGHTER. Incomprehensible world! How can he be freed from this curse?

POET. Freed? One would beware of freeing him.

DAUGHTER. Why?

POET. Because . . . No, that is not the Dutchman. It is an ordinary ship in distress. Then why does the buoy not sound? Look how the sea is rising! The waves are towering, and soon we shall be imprisoned in this cave. Now the ship's bell is ringing. Soon there will be another figurehead in here. Cry out buoy! Watchman, do your duty!

> [*The buoy sounds a four-part chord in fifths and sixths, like foghorns.*]

The crew is waving to us . . . but we ourselves perish.

DAUGHTER. Do you not want to be set free?

POET. Yes, yes I do! But not now . . . and not by water!

THE CREW. [*Singing four-part*] Christ Kyrie!

POET. They are calling and the sea is calling. But no one hears.

CREW. [*Singing as before*] Christ Kyrie!

DAUGHTER. Who is it coming there?

POET. Walking upon the water! Only One walks upon the water. It is not Peter, the rock, for he sank like a stone.

> [*A white light appears over the sea.*]

CREW. [*As before*] Christ Kyrie!

DAUGHTER. Is it He?

POET. It is He, the crucified.

DAUGHTER. Why, tell me why He was crucified.

POET. Because He wished to set men free.

DAUGHTER. Who—I have forgotten—who crucified Him?

> [*The cave grows darker.*]

POET. All righteous men.

DAUGHTER. This incomprehensible world!

POET. The sea is rising. Darkness is falling on us. The storm is growing wilder.

6. See note on p. 35.

[*The* CREW *shriek.*]

The crew are screaming with horror because they have seen their Saviour . . . and now . . . they are throwing themselves overboard in terror of the Redeemer.

[*The* CREW *shriek again.*]

Now they are screaming because they are going to die. They were born screaming and they die screaming.

[*The mounting waves threaten to drown them in the cave. The light begins to change.*]

DAUGHTER. If I were sure it was a ship . . .

POET. Indeed, I do not think it is a ship. It's a two storied house, with trees round it . . . and a telephone tower—a tower reaching to the skies. It's the modern Tower of Babel, sending up its wires to communicate with those above.

DAUGHTER. Child, man's thought needs no wires for its flight. The prayers of the devout penetrate all worlds. That is surely no Tower of Babel! If you wish to storm the heavens, storm them with your prayers.

POET. No, it's not a house . . . not a telephone tower. Do you see?

DAUGHTER. What do you see?

[*During the following speech, the scene changes to the alley of the Opera House.*]

POET. I see a snow-covered heath . . . a parade ground. The winter sun is shining behind a church on the hill, so that the tower casts its long shadow on the snow. Now a troop of soldiers comes marching over the heath. They march on the tower and up the spire . . . Now they are on the cross, and I seem to know that the first to tread on the weathercock must die . . . They are drawing near it. It's the Corporal at their head who . . . Ah! A cloud is sailing over the heath, across the sun . . . Now everything has gone. The moisture of the cloud has put out the fire of the sun. The sunlight created a shadowy image of the tower, but the shadow of the cloud smothered the image of the tower.

[*It is springtime. The tree and the monkshood are in bud. The* STAGE DOORKEEPER *sits in her old place. The* DAUGHTER *enters, followed by the* POET.]

DAUGHTER. [*To* DOORKEEPER] Has the Chancellor arrived yet?

DOORKEEPER. No.

DAUGHTER. Nor the Deans?

DOORKEEPER. No.

DAUGHTER. You must send for them at once. The door is going to be opened.

DOORKEEPER. It is so urgent?

DAUGHTER. Yes. It's thought that the answer to the riddle of the universe is locked up in there. So send for the Chancellor and the Deans of the four Faculties. [*The* DOORKEEPER *blows a whistle.*] And don't forget the Glazier and his diamond, or nothing can be done.

[*The personnel of the Opera pour from the building as in the earlier scene.*]

The OFFICER [*Young again, in morning coat and top hat, comes through the gate, carrying a bouquet of roses and looking radiantly happy.*]

OFFICER. [*Singing*] Victoria!

DOORKEEPER. The young lady will be down in a minute.

OFFICER. Good. The carriage is waiting, the table is laid, the champagne is on the ice . . . Let me embrace you, Madam. [*Embraces the* DOORKEEPER.] Victoria!

WOMAN'S VOICE. [*From above, singing.*] I am here.

OFFICER. [*Pacing*] Well, I am waiting.

POET. I seem to have lived through all this before.

DAUGHTER. I too.

POET. Perhaps I dreamt it.

DAUGHTER. Or made a poem of it.

POET. Or made a poem.

DAUGHTER. You know then what poetry is.

POET. I know what dreaming is.

DAUGHTER. I feel that once before, somewhere else, we said these words.

POET. Then soon you will know what reality is.

DAUGHTER. Or dreaming.

POET. Or poetry.

[*Enter the* CHANCELLOR *and the* DEANS OF THEOLOGY, PHILOSOPHY, MEDICINE *and* LAW, *followed by the* GLAZIER, *and a group of* RIGHTEOUS PEOPLE.]

CHANCELLOR. It's all a question of the door, you understand. What does the Dean of Theology think about it?

DEAN OF THEOLOGY. I don't think—I believe. Credo.

DEAN OF PHILOSOPHY. I think.

DEAN OF MEDICINE. I know.

DEAN OF LAW. I doubt—until I have heard the evidence and witnesses.

CHANCELLOR. Now they will quarrel again. Well then, first what does Theology believe?

THEOLOGY. I believe that this door ought not to be opened, as it conceals dangerous truths.

PHILOSOPHY. The truth is never dangerous.

MEDICINE. What is truth?

LAW. Whatever can be proved by two witnesses.

THEOLOGY. Anything can be proved by two false witnesses—if you're a pettifogger.

PHILOSOPHY. Truth is wisdom, and wisdom and knowledge are philosophy itself. Philosophy is the science of sciences, the knowledge of knowledge. All other sciences are its servants.

MEDICINE. The only science is natural science. Philosophy is not science. It is mere empty speculation.

THEOLOGY. Bravo!

PHILOSOPHY. [*To* DEAN OF THEOLOGY.] You say bravo. And what, may I ask, are you? The arch enemy of knowldege, the antithesis of science. You are ignorance and darkness.

MEDICINE. Bravo!

THEOLOGY. [*To* DEAN OF MEDICINE.] And you say bravo—you who can't see further than the end of your own nose in a magnifying glass. You who believe in nothing but your deceptive senses—in your eyes, for instance, which may be long-sighted, short-sighted, blind, purblind, squinting, one-eyed, colour-blind, red-blind, green-blind . . .

MEDICINE. Blockhead!

THEOLOGY. Ass!

    [*They fight.*]

CHANCELLOR. Enough! Birds of a feather shouldn't peck each other's eyes out.

PHILOSOPHY. Had I to choose between these two, Theology and Medicine, I should choose—neither.

LAW. And if I had to sit in judgment over you three, I should condemn—every one of you . . . You can't agree upon a single point, and never have been able to. Let's get back to the matter in hand. What's your opinion, Chancellor, of this door and the opening of it?

CHANCELLOR. Opinion? I don't have opinions. I am merely appointed by the Government to see you don't break each other's arms and legs in the Senate in the course of educating the young. Opinions? No, I take good care not to have any. I had a few once, but they were soon exploded. Opinions always are exploded—by opponents, of course. Perhaps we had better have the door opened now, even at the risk of it concealing dangerous truths.

LAW. What is truth? What is the truth?

THEOLOGY. I am the Truth and the Life . . .

PHILOSOPHY. I am the knowledge of knowledge.

MEDICINE. I am exact knowledge . . .

LAW. I doubt.

    [*They fight.*]

DAUGHTER. Shame on you, teachers of youth!

LAW. Chancellor, as delegate of the Government and head of the teaching staff, denounce this woman. She has cried "shame on you" which is contumely, and she has ironically referred to you as "teachers of youth," which is slander.

DAUGHTER. Poor youth!

LAW. She pities youth, and that's tantamount to accusing us. Chancellor, denounce her!

DAUGHTER. Yes, I accuse you—all of you—of sowing the seeds of doubt and dissension in the minds of the young.

LAW. Listen to her! She herself is raising doubts in the young as to our authority, yet she is accusing us of raising doubts. I appeal to all righteous men. Is this not a criminal offence?

ALL THE RIGHTEOUS. Yes, it is criminal.

LAW. The righteous have condemned you. Go in peace with your gains. Otherwise . . .

DAUGHTER. My gains? Otherwise what?

LAW. Otherwise you will be stoned.

POET. Or crucified.

DAUGHTER [*To the* POET]. I am going. Come with me and learn the answer to the riddle.

POET. Which riddle?

DAUGHTER. What does he mean by my "gains"?

POET. Probably nothing at all. That's what we call idle chatter. He was just chattering.

DAUGHTER. But that hurt me more than anything else.

POET. That's why he said it. Human beings are like that.

[*The* GLAZIER *opens the door and looks inside.*]

ALL THE RIGHTEOUS. Hurrah! The door is open.

[*The* DEANS *look inside.*]

CHANCELLOR. What was concealed behind that door?

GLAZIER. I can't see anything.

CHANCELLOR. He can't see anything. Well, I'm not surprised. Deans! What was concealed behind that door?

THEOLOGY. Nothing. That is the solution of the riddle of the universe. Out of nothing in the beginning God created heaven and earth.

PHILOSOPHY. Out of nothing comes nothing.

MEDICINE. Bosh! That is nothing.

LAW. I doubt everything. And there's some swindle here. I appeal to all righteous men.

DAUGHTER. [*To* POET]. Who are these righteous?

POET. Let him tell you who can. All the righteous are often just one person. Today they are me and mine, tomorrow you and yours. One is nominated for the post, or rather, one nominates oneself.

ALL THE RIGHTEOUS. We have been swindled.

CHANCELLOR. Who has swindled you?

ALL THE RIGHTEOUS. The Daughter!

CHANCELLOR. Will the Daughter kindly inform us what her idea was in having the door opened.

DAUGHTER. No, my friends. If I told you, you would not believe it.

MEDICINE. But there's nothing there.

DAUGHTER. What you say is correct. But you have not understood it.

MEDICINE. What she says is bosh.

ALL. Bosh!

DAUGHTER. [*To* POET.] They are to be pitied.

POET. Do you mean that seriously?

DAUGHTER. Very seriously.

POET. Do you think the righteous are to be pitied too?

DAUGHTER. They most of all perhaps.

POET. And the four Faculties?

DAUGHTER. They too, and not least. Four heads and four minds with a single body. Who created such a monster?

ALL. She does not answer.

CHANCELLOR. Then stone her!

DAUGHTER. This is the answer.

CHANCELLOR. Listen! She is answering.

ALL. Stone her! She is answering.

[*Enter* LAWYER.]

DAUGHTER. If she answers, or if she does not answer, stone her! [*To* POET.] Come, you Seer, and I will answer the riddle, but far from here, out in the wilderness, where none can hear us, none can see us. For . . .

[*The* LAWYER *interrupts by taking hold of her arm.*]

LAWYER. Have you forgotten your duties?

DAUGHTER. God knows I have not. But I have higher duties.

LAWYER. But your child?

DAUGHTER. My child? Yes?

LAWYER. Your child is calling you.

DAUGHTER. My child! Alas, I am earthbound! And this anguish in my breast, this agony, what is it?

LAWYER. Don't you know?

DAUGHTER. No.

LAWYER. It is the pangs of conscience.

DAUGHTER. The pangs of conscience?

LAWYER. Yes. They come after every neglected duty, after every pleasure, however innocent—if there is such a thing as an innocent pleasure, which is doubtful. And they also come every time one causes pain to one's neighbour.

DAUGHTER. Is there no remedy?

LAWYER. Yes, but only one. To do one's duty instantly.

DAUGHTER. You look like a devil when you say the word "duty." But when one has, as I, two duties?

LAWYER. Fulfil first one and then the other.

DAUGHTER. The higher first. Therefore, you look after my child, and I will do my duty.

LAWYER. Your child is unhappy without you. Can you let another suffer on your account?

DAUGHTER. There is conflict in my soul. It is pulled this way and that until it is torn in two.

LAWYER. These, you see, are life's little trials.

DAUGHTER. Oh, how they tear one!

POET. You would have nothing to do with me, if you knew what misery I have caused through following my vocation—yes, my vocation, which is the highest duty of all.

DAUGHTER. What do you mean?

POET. I had a father, whose hopes were centered in me, his only son. I was to have carried on his business, but I ran away from the Commercial College. Worry brought my father to his grave. My mother wanted me to be religious. I couldn't be religious. She disowned me. I had a friend who helped me when I was desperate, but that friend turned out to be a tyrant to the very people whose cause I upheld. So to save my soul I had to strike down my friend and benefactor. Since that time I have had no peace. I am considered base, contemptible, the scum of the earth. Nor do I get any comfort from my conscience when it tells me I did right, for the next moment it assures me I did wrong. That is the way of life.

DAUGHTER. Come with me, out into the wilderness.

LAWYER. Your child!

DAUGHTER. [*Indicating all present.*] These are my children. Each one of them is good, but as soon as they are together they fight and turn into devils. Farewell!

> [*Blackout. When the lights go up the scene has changed to outside the Castle.*
>
> *The set is the same as the earlier one, except that now the ground is covered with blue monkshood, aconite and other flowers. The chrysanthemum bud at the top of the tower is on the point of bursting. The Castle windows are lit with candles. In the foreground is a fire.*]

DAUGHTER. The hour is at hand when with the aid of fire I shall ascend again into the ether. This is what you call death and approach with so much fear.

POET. Fear of the unknown.

DAUGHTER. Which yet you know.

POET. Who knows it?

DAUGHTER. Mankind. Why do you not believe your prophets?

POET. Prophets have never been believed. Why is that? If they truly speak with the voice of God, why then do men not believe? His power to convince should be irresistible.

DAUGHTER. Have you always doubted?

POET. No, I have had faith many times, but after a while it drifted away, like a dream when one awakens.

DAUGHTER. To be mortal is not easy.

POET. You understand this now?

DAUGHTER. Yes.

POET. Tell me, did not Indra once send his son down to earth to hear man's complaint?

DAUGHTER. He did. And how was he received?

POET. How did he fulfil his mission?—to answer with a question.

DAUGHTER. To answer with another—was not the state of mankind bettered by his visit to the earth? Answer truly.

POET. Bettered? Yes, a little. Now, instead of further questions, will you tell me the answer to the riddle?

DAUGHTER. What purpose would that serve? You would not believe me.

POET. I shall believe you, for I know who you are.

DAUGHTER. Then I will tell you. In the dawn of time, before your sun gave light, Brahma, the divine primal force let himself be seduced by Maya, the World Mother, that he might propagate. This mingling of the divine element with the earthly was the Fall from heaven. This world, its life and its inhabitants are therefore only a mirage, a reflection, a dream image.

POET. My dream!

DAUGHTER. A true dream. But, in order to be freed from the earthly element, the descendants of Brahma sought renunciation and suffering. And so you have suffering as the deliverer. But this yearning for suffering comes into conflict with the longing for joy, for love. Now you understand what love is; supreme joy in the greatest suffering, the sweetest is the most bitter. Do you understand now what woman is? Woman, through whom sin and death entered into life.

POET. I understand. And the outcome?

DAUGHTER. What you yourself know. Conflict between the pain of joy and the joy of pain, between the anguish of the penitent and the pleasure of the sensual.

POET. And the conflict?

DAUGHTER. The conflict of opposites generates power, as fire and water create the force of steam.

POET. But peace? Rest?

DAUGHTER. Hush! You must ask no more, nor may I answer. The altar is decked for the sacrifice, the flowers keep vigil, the candles are lighted, the white sheet hangs in the window, the threshold is strewn with pine.[7]

POET. How calmly you speak! As if suffering did not exist for you.

DAUGHTER. Not exist? I suffered all your sufferings a hundred fold because my sensibilities were finer.

POET. Tell me your sorrows.

DAUGHTER. Poet, could you tell your own with utter truth? Could your words ever once convey your thoughts?

POET. You are right. No. To myself I have always seemed a deaf mute, and while the crowd was acclaiming my song, to me it seemed a jangle. And so, you see, I was always ashamed when men paid me homage.

DAUGHTER. And yet you wish me to speak? Look into my eyes.

POET. I cannot endure your gaze.

DAUGHTER. How then will you endure my words, if I speak in my own language?

POET. Even so, before you go, tell me from what you suffered most down here.

DAUGHTER. From living. From feeling my vision dimmed by having eyes, my hearing dulled by having ears, and my thought, my airy, luminous thought, bound down in a labyrinth of fat. You have seen a brain. What twisting channels, what creeping ways!

POET. Yes, and that is why the minds of the righteous are twisted.

DAUGHTER. Cruel, always cruel, each one of you.

POET. How can we be otherwise?

DAUGHTER. Now first I shake the dust from my feet, the earth, the clay. [*She takes off her shoes and puts them in the fire.*
   One after another the following characters come in, put their contributions on the fire, cross the stage and go out, while the POET *and the* DAUGHTER *stand watching.*]

DOORKEEPER. Perhaps I may burn my shawl too?

OFFICER. And I my roses, of which only the thorns are left.

BILLSTICKER. The posters can go, but my fishnet never.

GLAZIER. Farewell to the diamond that opened the door.

LAWYER. The report of the proceedings in the High Court touching the Pope's beard or the diminishing water supply in the sources of the Ganges.

---

7. Signs of mourning in Sweden. [*Translator's note.*]

QUARANTINE MASTER. A small contribution in the shape of the black mask which turned me into a blackamoor against my will.

VICTORIA [SHE]. My beauty—my sorrow.

EDITH. My ugliness—my sorrow.

BLINDMAN. [*Putting his hand in the fire.*] I give my hand which is my sight.

> [DON JUAN *is pushed in in the bathchair, accompanied by the* COQUETTE *and the* FRIEND].

DON JUAN. Make haste, make haste! Life is short.

POET. I have read that when a life is nearing its end, everything and everyone pass by in a single stream. Is this the end?

DAUGHTER. For me, yes. Farewell!

POET. Say a parting word!

DAUGHTER. No, I cannot. Do you think your language can express our thoughts?

> [*Enter the* DEAN OF THEOLOGY, *raging.*]

THEOLOGY. I am disowned by God; I am persecuted by men; I am abandoned by the Government, and scorned by my colleagues. How can I have faith when no one else has faith? How can I defend a God who does not defend His own people? It's all bosh!

> [*He throws a book on the fire and goes out. The* POET *snatches the book from the flames.*]

POET. Do you know what this is? A Book of Martyrs, a calendar with a martyr for each day of the year.

DAUGHTER. A martyr?

POET. Yes, one who was tortured and put to death for his faith. Tell me why. Do you believe all who are tortured suffer, all who are put to death feel pain? Surely suffering is redemption and death deliverance.

> [KRISTIN *enters with her paste and strips of paper.*]

KRISTIN. I paste, I paste, till there is nothing left to paste.

POET. If heaven itself cracked open, you would try to paste it up. Go away!

KRISTIN. Are there no inner windows in the Castle?

POET. No, none there.

KRISTIN. I'll go then, I'll go.

> [*Exit.*
> As the DAUGHTER *speaks her last lines the flames rise until the Castle is on fire.*]

DAUGHTER. The parting time has come; the end draws near.
> Farewell, you child of man, dreamer,
> poet, who knows best the way to live.
> Above the earth on wings you hover,
> plunging at times to graze the dust,
> but not to be submerged.
> Now I am going, now the hour has come
> to leave both friend and place,
> how sharp the loss of all I loved,
> how deep regret for all destroyed!
> Ah, now I know the whole of living's pain!

This then it is to be a human being—
ever to miss the thing one never prized
and feel remorse for what one never did,
to yearn to go, yet long to stay.
And so the human heart is split in two,
emotions by wild horses torn—
conflict, discord and uncertainty.
Farewell! Tell all on earth I shall remember them.
Where I am going, and in your name
   carry their lamentations to the throne.
Farewell!

[*She goes into the Castle. Music is heard. The background is
lighted up by the burning Castle, and now shows a wall of
human faces, questioning, mourning, despairing. While the
Castle is burning, the flower-bud on the roof bursts into a
giant chrysanthemum.*]

EUGENE O'NEILL

Desire Under the Elms[†]

Characters

EPHRAIM CABOT
SIMEON ⎫
PETER ⎬ *His sons*
EBEN ⎭
ABBIE PUTNAM
Young Girl, Two Farmers, The Fiddler, A Sheriff,
and other folk from the neighboring farms.

The action of the entire play takes places in, and immediately out-side of, the Cabot farmhouse in New England, in the year 1850. The south end of the house faces front to a stone wall with a wooden gate at center opening on a country road. The house is in good condi-tion but in need of paint. Its walls are a sickly grayish, the green of the shutters faded. Two enormous elms are on each side of the house. They bend their trailing branches down over the roof. They appear to protect and at the same time subdue. There is a sinister maternity in their aspect, a crushing, jealous absorption. They have developed from their intimate contact with the life of man in the house an appalling humaneness. They brood oppressively over the house. They are like exhausted women resting their sagging breasts and hands and hair on its roof, and when it rains their tears trickle down monotonously and rot on the shingles.

There is a path running from the gate around the right corner of the house to the front door. A narrow porch is on this side. The end wall facing us has two windows in its upper story, two larger ones on the floor below. The two upper are those of the father's bedroom and that of the brothers. On the left, ground floor, is the kitchen—on the right, the parlor, the shades of which are always drawn down.

Part One
Scene One

Exterior of the farmhouse. It is sunset of a day at the beginning of summer in the year 1850. There is no wind and everything is still. The sky above the roof is suffused with deep colors, the green of the elms glows, but the house is in shadow, seeming pale and washed out by contrast.

A door opens and EBEN CABOT *comes to the end of the porch and stands looking down the road to the right. He has a large bell in his hand and this he swings mechanically, awakening a deafening clangor. Then he puts his hands on his hips and stares up at the sky. He sighs with a puzzled awe and blurts out with halting appreciation.*

EBEN   God! Purty! (*His eyes fall and he stares about him frowningly. He is twenty-five, tall and sinewy. His face is well-formed, good-looking, but its expression is resentful and defensive. His defiant, dark eyes remind one of a wild animal's in captivity. Each day is a cage in which he finds himself trapped but inwardly unsubdued. There is a fierce repressed vitality about him. He has black hair, mustache, a thin curly trace of beard. He is dressed in rough farm clothes.*

   He spits on the ground with intense disgust, turns and goes back into the house.

   SIMEON *and* PETER *come in from their work in the fields. They are tall men, much older than their half-brother [*SIMEON *is thirty-nine and* PETER *thirty-seven], built on a squarer, simpler model, fleshier in body, more bovine and homelier in face, shrewder and more practical. Their shoulders stoop a bit from years of farm work. They clump heavily along in their clumsy thick-soled boots caked with earth. Their clothes, their faces, hands, bare arms and throats are earth-stained. They smell of earth. They stand together for a moment in front of the house and, as if with the one impulse, stare dumbly up at the sky, leaning on their hoes. Their faces have a compressed, unresigned expression. As they look upward, this softens*).

SIMEON   (*grudgingly*) Purty.

PETER   Ay-eh.

SIMEON   (*suddenly*) Eighteen years ago.

PETER   What?

SIMEON   Jenn. My woman. She died.

PETER   I'd fergot.

SIMEON   I rec'lect—now an' agin. Makes it lonesome. She'd hair long's a hoss' tail—an' yaller like gold!

PETER   Waal—she's gone. (*This with indifferent finality—then after a pause*) They's gold in the West, Sim.

SIMEON   (*still under the influence of sunset—vaguely*) In the sky!

PETER   Waal—in a manner o' speakin'—thar's the promise. (*Growing excited*) Gold in the sky—in the West—Golden Gate—California!—Goldest West!—fields o' gold!

SIMEON   (*excited in his turn*) Fortunes layin' just atop o' the ground waitin' t' be picked! Solomon's mines, they says! (*For a moment they continue looking up at the sky—then their eyes drop*).

PETER   (*with sardonic bitterness*) Here—it's stones atop o' the ground—stones atop o' stones—makin' stone walls—year atop o' year—him 'n' yew 'n' me 'n' then Eben—makin' stone walls fur him to fence us in!

SIMEON   We've wuked. Give our strength. Give our years. Plowed 'em under in the ground,—(*he stamps rebelliously*)—rottin'—makin' soil for his crops! (*A pause*) Waal—the farm pays good for hereabouts.

PETER   If we plowed in Californi-a, they'd be lumps o' gold in the furrow!

SIMEON   Californi-a's t'other side o' earth, a'most. We got t' calc'late—

PETER   (*after a pause*) 'Twould be hard fur me, too, to give up what we've 'arned here by our sweat. (*A pause.* EBEN *sticks his head out of the dining-room window, listening*).

SIMEON   Ay-eh. (*A pause*) Mebbe—he'll die soon.

PETER   (*doubtfully*) Mebbe.

SIMEON   Mebbe—fur all we knows—he's dead now.

PETER   Ye'd need proof.

SIMEON   He's been gone two months—with no word.

PETER   Left us in the fields an evenin' like this. Hitched up an' druv off into the West. That's plum onnateral. He hain't never been off this farm 'ceptin' t' the village in thirty year or more, not since he married Eben's maw. (*A pause. Shrewdly*) I calc'late we might git him declared crazy by the court.

SIMEON   He skinned 'em too slick. He got the best o' all on 'em. They'd never b'lieve him crazy. (*A pause*) We got t' wait—till he's under ground.

EBEN   (*with a sardonic chuckle*) Honor thy father! (*They turn, startled, and stare at him. He grins, then scowls*) I pray he's died. (*They stare at him. He continues matter-of-factly*) Supper's ready.

SIMEON *and* PETER   (*together*) Ay-eh.

EBEN   (*gazing up at the sky*) Sun's downin' purty.

SIMEON *and* PETER   (*together*) Ay-eh. They's gold in the West.

EBEN   Ay-eh. (*Pointing*) Yonder atop o' the hill pasture, ye mean?

SIMEON *and* PETER   (*together*) In Californi-a!

EBEN   Hunh? (*Stares at them indifferently for a second, then drawls*) Waal—supper's gittin' cold. (*He turns back into kitchen*).

SIMEON   (*startled—smacks his lips*) I air hungry!

PETER   (*sniffing*) I smells bacon!

SIMEON   (*with hungry appreciation*) Bacon's good!

PETER   (*in same tone*) Bacon's bacon! (*They turn, shouldering each other, their bodies bumping and rubbing together as they hurry clumsily to their food, like two friendly oxen toward their evening meal. They disappear around the right corner of house and can be heard entering the door*).

CURTAIN

Scene Two

The color fades from the sky. Twilight begins. The interior of the kitchen is now visible. A pine table is at center, a cookstove in the right rear corner, four rough wooden chairs, a tallow candle on the table. In the middle of the rear wall is fastened a big advertizing post-er with a ship in full sail and the word "California" in big letters. Kitchen utensils hang from nails. Everything is neat and in order but the atmosphere is of a men's camp kitchen rather than that of a home.

Places for three are laid. EBEN *takes boiled potatoes and bacon from the stove and puts them on the table, also a loaf of bread and a crock of water.* SIMEON *and* PETER *shoulder in, slump down in their chairs without a word.* EBEN *joins them. The three eat in silence for a moment, the two elder as naturally unrestrained as beasts of the field,* EBEN *picking at his food without appetite, glancing at them with a tolerant dislike.*

SIMEON (*suddenly turns to* EBEN) Looky here! Ye'd oughtn't t' said that, Eben.

PETER 'Twa'n't righteous.

EBEN What?

SIMEON Ye prayed he'd died.

EBEN Waal—don't yew pray it? (*A pause*).

PETER He's our Paw.

EBEN (*violently*) Not mine!

SIMEON (*dryly*) Ye'd not let no one else say that about yer Maw! Ha! (*He gives one abrupt sardonic guffaw.* PETER *grins*).

EBEN (*very pale*) I meant—I hain't his'n—I hain't like him—he hain't me!

PETER (*dryly*) Wait till ye've growed his age!

EBEN (*intensely*) I'm Maw—every drop o' blood! (*A pause. They stare at him with indifferent curiosity*).

PETER (*reminiscently*) She was good t' Sim 'n' me. A good step-maw's curse.

SIMEON She was good t' everyone.

EBEN (*greatly moved, gets to his feet and makes an awkward bow to each of them—stammering*) I be thankful t' ye. I'm her—her heir. (*He sits down in confusion*).

PETER (*after a pause—judicially*) She was good even t' him.

EBEN (*fiercely*) An' fur thanks he killed her!

SIMEON (*after a pause*) No one never kills nobody. It's allus some thin'. That's the murderer.

EBEN Didn't he slave Maw t' death?

PETER He's slaved himself t' death. He's slaved Sim 'n' me 'n' yew t' death—on'y none o' us hain't died—yit.

SIMEON It's somethin'—drivin' him—t' drive us!

EBEN (*vengefully*) Waal—I hold him t' jedgment! (*Then scornfully*) Somethin'! What's somethin'?

SIMEON Dunno.

EBEN (*sardonically*) What's drivin' yew to Californi-a, mebbe? (*They look at him in surprise*) Oh, I've heerd ye! (*Then, after a pause*) But ye'll never go t' the gold fields!

PETER (*assertively*) Mebbe!

EBEN Whar'll ye git the money?

PETER We kin walk. It's an a'mighty ways—Californi-a—but if yew was t' put all the steps we've walked on this farm end t' end we'd be in the moon!

EBEN The Injuns'll skulp ye on the plains.

SIMEON (*with grim humor*) We'll mebbe make 'em pay a hair fur a hair!

EBEN (*decisively*) But t'aint that. Ye won't never go because ye'll wait here fur yer share o' the farm, thinkin' allus he'll die soon.

SIMEON (*after a pause*) We've a right.

PETER Two-thirds belong t' us.

EBEN (*jumping to his feet*) Ye've no right! She wa'n't yewr Maw! It was her farm! Didn't he steal it from her? She's dead. It's my farm.

SIMEON (*sardonically*) Tell that t' Paw—when he comes! I'll bet ye a dollar he'll laugh—fur once in his life. Ha! (*He laughs himself in one single mirthless bark*).

PETER (*amused in turn, echoes his brother*) Ha!

SIMEON (*after a pause*) What've ye got held agin us, Eben? Year arter year it's skulked in yer eye—somethin'.

PETER Ay-eh.

EBEN Ay-eh. They's somethin'. (*Suddenly exploding*) Why didn't ye never stand between him 'n' my Maw when he was slavin' her to her grave—t' pay her back fur the kindness she done t' yew? (*There is a long pause. They stare at him in surprise*).

SIMEON Waal—the stock's got t' be watered.

PETER 'R they was woodin' t' do.

SIMEON 'R plowin'.

PETER 'R hayin'.

SIMEON 'R spreadin' manure.

PETER 'R weedin'.

SIMEON 'R prunin'.

PETER 'R milkin'.

EBEN (*breaking in harshly*) An' makin' walls—stone atop o' stone— makin' walls till yer heart's a stone ye heft up out o' the way o' growth onto a stone wall t' wall in yer heart!

SIMEON (*matter-of-factly*) We never had no time t' meddle.

PETER (*to* EBEN) Yew was fifteen afore yer Maw died—an' big fur yer age. Why didn't ye never do nothin'?

EBEN (*harshly*) They was chores t' do, wa'n't they? (*A pause—then slowly*) It was on'y arter she died I come to think o' it. Me cookin'—doin' her work—that made me know her, suffer her sufferin' —she'd come back t' help—come back t' bile potatoes—come back t' fry bacon—come back t' bake biscuits— come back all cramped up t' shake the fire, an' carry ashes, her eyes weepin' an' bloody with smoke an' cinders same's they used t' be. She still comes back—stands by the stove thar in the evenin'—she can't find it nateral sleepin' an' restin' in peace. She can't git used t' bein' free —even in her grave.

SIMEON She never complained none.

EBEN She'd got too tired. She'd got too used t' bein' too tired. That was what he done. (*With vengeful passion*) An' sooner'r later, I'll meddle. I'll say the thin's I didn't say then t' him! I'll yell 'em at the top o' my lungs. I'll see t' it my Maw gits some rest an' sleep in her grave! (*He sits down again, relapsing into a brooding silence. They look at him with a queer indifferent curiosity*).

PETER (*after a pause*) Whar in tarnation d'ye s'pose he went, Sim?

SIMEON Dunno. He druv off in the buggy, all spick an' span, with the mare all breshed an' shiny, druv off clackin' his tongue an' wavin' his whip. I remember it right well. I was finishin' plowin', it was spring an' May an' sunset, an' gold in the West, an' he druv off into it. I yells "Whar ye goin', Paw?" an' he hauls up by the stone wall a jiffy. His old snake's eyes was glitterin' in the sun like he'd been drinkin' a jugful an' he says with a mule's grin: "Don't ye run away till I come back!"

PETER Wonder if he knowed we was wantin' fur Californi-a?

SIMEON Mebbe. I didn't say nothin' and he says, lookin' kinder queer an' sick: "I been hearin' the hens cluckin' an' the roosters crowin' all the durn day. I been listenin' t' the cows lowin' an' everythin' else kickin' up till I can't stand it no more. It's spring an' I'm feelin' damned," he says. "Damned like an old bare hickory tree fit on'y fur burnin'," he says. An' then I calc'late I must've looked a mite hopeful, fur he adds real spry and vicious: "But dont git no fool idee I'm dead. I've sworn t' live a hundred an' I'll do it, if on'y t' spite yer sinful greed! An' now I'm ridin' out t' learn God's message t' me in the spring, like the prophets done. An' yew git back t' yer plowin'," he says. An' he druv off singin' a hymn. I thought he was drunk—'r I'd stopped him goin'.

EBEN (*scornfully*) No, ye wouldn't! Ye're scared o' him. He's stronger—inside—than both o' ye put together!

PETER (*sardonically*) An' yew—be yew Samson?

EBEN I'm gittin' stronger. I kin feel it growin' in me—growin' an' growin'—till it'll bust out—! (*He gets up and puts on his coat and a hat. They watch him, gradually breaking into grins. EBEN avoids their eyes sheepishly*) I'm goin' out fur a spell—up the road.

PETER T' the village?

SIMEON T' see Minnie?

EBEN (*defiantly*) Ay-eh?

PETER (*jeeringly*) The Scarlet Woman!

SIMEON Lust—that's what's growin' in ye!

EBEN Waal—she's purty!

PETER She's been purty fur twenty year!

SIMEON A new coat o' paint'll make a heifer out of forty.

EBEN She hain't forty!

PETER If she hain't, she's teeterin' on the edge.

EBEN (*desperately*) What d'yew know—

PETER All they is . . . Sim knew her—an' then me arter—

SIMEON An' Paw kin tell yew somethin' too! He was fust!

EBEN D'ye mean t' say he . . . ?

SIMEON (*with a grin*) Ay-eh! We air his heirs in everythin'!

EBEN (*intensely*) That's more to it! That grows on it! It'll bust soon! (*Then violently*) I'll go smash my fist in her face! (*He pulls open the door in rear violently*).

SIMEON (*with a wink at* PETER—*drawlingly*) Mebbe—but the night's wa'm—purty—by the time ye git thar mebbe ye'll kiss her instead!

PETER Sart'n he will! (*They both roar with coarse laughter.* EBEN *rushes out and slams the door—then the outside front door— comes around the corner of the house and stands still by the gate, staring up at the sky*).

SIMEON (*looking after him*) Like his Paw.

PETER Dead spit an' image!

SIMEON Dog'll eat dog!

PETER Ay-eh. (*Pause. With yearning*) Mebbe a year from now we'll be in Californi-a.

SIMEON Ay-eh. (*A pause. Both yawn*) Let's git t' bed. (*He blows out the candle. They go out door in rear.* EBEN *stretches his arms up to the sky—rebelliously*).

EBEN Waal—thar's a star, an' somewhar's they's him, an' here's me, an' thar's Min up the road—in the same night. What if I does kiss her? She's like t'night, she's soft 'n' wa'm, her eyes kin wink like a star, her mouth's wa'm, her arms're wa'm, she smells like a wa'm plowed field, she's purty . . . Ay-eh! By God A'mighty she's purty, an' I don't give a damn how many sins she's sinned afore mine or who she's sinned 'em with, my sin's as purty as any one of 'em! (*He strides off down the road to the left*).

CURTAIN

Scene Three

It is the pitch darkness just before dawn. EBEN *comes in from the left and goes around to the porch, feeling his way, chuckling bitterly and cursing half-aloud to himself.*

EBEN The cussed old miser! (*He can be heard going in the front door. There is a pause as he goes upstairs, then a loud knock on the bedroom door of the brothers*) Wake up!

SIMEON (*startedly*) Who's thar?

EBEN (*pushing open the door and coming in, a lighted candle in his hand. The bedroom of the brothers is revealed. Its ceiling is the sloping roof. They can stand upright only close to the center dividing wall of the upstairs.* SIMEON *and* PETER *are in a double bed, front.* EBEN's *cot is to the rear.* EBEN *has a mixture of silly grin and vicious scowl on his face*) I be!

PETER   (*angrily*) What in hell's-fire . . . ?

EBEN   I got news fur ye! Ha! (*He gives one abrupt sardonic guffaw*).

SIMEON   (*angrily*)   Couldn't ye hold it 'til we'd got our sleep?

EBEN   It's nigh sunup. (*Then explosively*) He's gone an' married agen!

SIMEON *and* PETER   (*explosively*) Paw?

EBEN   Got himself hitched to a female 'bout thirty-five—an' purty, they says . . .

SIMEON   (*aghast*) It's a durn lie!

PETER   Who says?

SIMEON   They been stringin' ye!

EBEN   Think I'm a dunce, do ye? The hull village says. The preacher from New Dover, he brung the news—told it t' our preacher— New Dover, that's whar the old loon got himself hitched—that's whar the woman lived—

PETER   (*no longer doubting—stunned*) Waal . . . !

SIMEON   (*the same*) Waal . . . !

EBEN   (*sitting down on a bed—with vicious hatred*) Ain't he a devil out o'hell? It's jest t' spite us—the damned old mule!

PETER   (*after a pause*) Everythin'll go t' her now.

SIMEON   Ay-eh. (*A pause—dully*) Waal—if it's done—

PETER   It's done us. (*Pause—then persuasively*) They's gold in the fields o' Californi-a, Sim. No good a-stayin' here now.

SIMEON   Jest what I was a-thinkin'. (*Then with decision*) S'well fust' last! Let's light out and git this mornin'.

PETER   Suits me.

EBEN   Ye must like walkin'.

SIMEON   (*sardonically*) If ye'd grow wings on us we'd fly thar!

EBEN   Ye'd like ridin' better—on a boat, wouldn't ye? (*Fumbles in his pocket and takes out a crumpled sheet of foolscap*) Waal, if ye sign this ye kin ride on a boat. I've had it writ out an' ready in case ye'd ever go. It says fur three hundred dollars t' each ye agree yewr shares o' the farm is sold t' me (*They look suspiciously at the paper. A pause*).

SIMEON   (*wonderingly*) But if he's hitched agen—

PETER   An' whar'd yew git that sum o' money, anyways?

EBEN (*cunningly*) I know whar it's hid. I been waitin'—Maw told me. She knew whar it lay fur years, but she was waitin' . . . It's her'n—the money he hoarded from her farm an' hid from Maw. It's my money by rights now.

PETER   Whar's it hid?

EBEN   (*cunningly*) Whar yew won't never find it without me. Maw spied on him—'r she'd never knowed. (*A pause. They look at him suspiciously, and he at them*) Waal, is it fa'r trade?

SIMEON   Dunno.

PETER   Dunno.

SIMEON   (*looking at window*) Sky's grayin'.

PETER   Ye better start the fire, Eben.

SIMEON An' fix some vittles.

EBEN Ay-eh. (*Then with a forced jocular heartiness*) I'll git ye a good one. If ye're startin' t' hoof it t' Californi-a ye'll need somethin' that'll stick t' yer ribs. (*He turns to the door, adding meaningly*) But ye kin ride on a boat if ye'll swap. (*He stops at the door and pauses. They stare at him*).

SIMEON (*suspiciously*) Whar was ye all night?

EBEN (*defiantly*) Up t' Min's. (*Then slowly*) Walkin' thar, fust I felt 's if I'd kiss her; then I got a-thinkin' o' what ye'd said o' him an' her an' I says, I'll bust her nose fur that! Then I got t' the village an' heerd the news an' I got madder 'n hell an' run all the way t' Min's not-knowin' what I'd do—(*He pauses—then sheepishly but more defiantly*) Waal—when I seen her, I didn't hit her—nor I didn't kiss her nuther—I begun t' beller like a calf an' cuss at the same time, I was so durn mad—an she got scared —an' I jest grabbed holt an' tuk her! (*Proudly*) Yes, sirree! I tuk her. She may've been his'n—an' your'n, too—but she's mine now!

SIMEON (*dryly*) In love, air yew?

EBEN (*with lofty scorn*) Love! I don't take no stock in sech slop!

PETER (*winking at* SIMEON) Mebbe Eben's aimin t' marry, too.

SIMEON Min'd make a true faithful he'pmeet! (*They snicker*).

EBEN What do I care fur her—'ceptin' she's round an' wa'm? The p'int is she was his'n—an' now she b'longs t' me! (*He goes to the door—then turns—rebelliously*) An' Min hain't sech a bad un. They's worse'n Min in the world, I'll bet ye! Wait'll we see this cow the Old Man's hitched t'! She'll beat Min, I got a notion! (*He starts to go out*).

SIMEON (*suddenly*) Mebbe ye'll try t' make her your'n, too?

PETER Ha! (*He gives a sardonic laugh of relish at this idea*).

EBEN (*spitting with disgust*) Her—here sleepin' with him—stealin' my Maw's farm! I'd as soon pet a skunk 'r kiss a snake! (*He goes out. The two stare after him suspiciously. A pause. They listen to his steps receding*).

PETER He's startin' the fire.

SIMEON I'd like t' ride t' Californi-a—but—

PETER Min might o' put some scheme in his head.

SIMEON Mebbe it's all a lie 'bout Paw marryin'. We'd best wait an' see the bride.

PETER An' don't sign nothin' till we does!

SIMEON Nor till we've tested it's good money! (*Then with a grin*) But if Paw's hitched we'd be sellin' Eben somethin' we'd never git nohow!

PETER We'll wait an' see. (*Then with sudden vindictive anger*) An' till he comes, let's yew 'n' me not wuk a lick, let Eben tend to thin's if he's a mind t', let's us jest sleep an' eat an' drink likker an' let the hull damned farm go t' blazes!

SIMEON (*excitedly*) By God, we've 'arned a rest! We'll play rich fur a change. I hain't a-going to stir outa bed till breakfast's ready.

PETER An' on the table!

SIMEON   (*after a pause—thoughtfully*) What d'ye calc'late she'll be like—our new Maw? Like Eben thinks?

PETER   More'n' likely.

SIMEON   (*vindictively*) Waal—I hope she's a she-devil that'll make him wish he was dead an' livin' in the pit o' hell fur comfort!

PETER   (*fervently*) Amen!

SIMEON   (*imitating his father's voice*) "I'm ridin' out t' learn God's message t' me in the spring like the prophets done," he says. I'll bet right then an' thar he knew plumb well he was goin' whorin', the stinkin' old hypocrite!

CURTAIN

Scene Four

Same as Scene Two—shows the interior of the kitchen with a lighted candle on table. It is gray dawn outside. SIMEON *and* PETER *are just finishing their breakfast.* EBEN *sits before his plate of untouched food, brooding frowningly.*

PETER   (*glancing at him rather irritably*) Lookin' glum don't help none.

SIMEON   (*sarcastically*) Sorrowin' over his lust o' the flesh!

PETER   (*with a grin*) Was she yer fust?

EBEN   (*angrily*) None o' yer business. (*A pause*) I was thinkin' o' him. I got a notion he's gittin' near—I kin feel him comin' on like yew kin feel malaria chill afore it takes ye.

PETER   It's too early yet.

SIMEON   Dunno. He'd like t' catch us nappin'—jest t' have somethin' t' hoss us 'round over.

PETER   (*mechanically gets to his feet.* SIMEON *does the same*) Waal —let's git t' wuk. (*They both plod mechanically toward the door before they realize. Then they stop short*).

SIMEON   (*grinning*) Ye're a cussed fool, Pete—and I be wuss! Let him see we hain't wukin'! We don't give a durn!

PETER   (*as they go back to the table*) Not a damned durn! It'll serve t' show him we're done with him. (*They sit down again.* EBEN *stares from one to the other with surprise*).

SIMEON   (*grins at him*) We're aimin' t' start bein' lilies o' the field.

PETER   Nary a toil 'r spin 'r lick o' wuk do we put in!

SIMEON   Ye're sole owner—till he comes—that's what ye wanted. Waal, ye got t' be sole hand, too.

PETER   The cows air bellerin'. Ye better hustle at the milkin'.

EBEN   (*with excited joy*) Ye mean ye'll sign the paper?

SIMEON   (*dryly*) Mebbe.

PETER   Mebbe.

SIMEON   We're considerin'. (*Peremptorily*) Ye better git t' wuk.

EBEN   (*with queer excitement*) It's Maw's farm agen! It's my farm! Them's my cows! I'll milk my durn fingers off fur cows o' mine! (*He goes out door in rear, they stare after him indifferently*).

SIMEON   Like his Paw.

PETER   Dead spit 'n' image!

SIMEON   Waal—let dog eat dog! (EBEN *comes out of front door and around the corner of the house. The sky is beginning to grow flushed with sunrise.* EBEN *stops by the gate and stares around him with glowing, possessive eyes. He takes in the whole farm with his embracing glance of desire*).

EBEN   It's purty! It's damned purty! It's mine! (*He suddenly throws his head back boldly and glares with hard, defiant eyes at the sky*) Mine, d'ye hear? Mine! (*He turns and walks quickly off left, rear, toward the barn. The two brothers light their pipes*).

SIMEON   (*putting his muddy boots up on the table, tilting back his chair, and puffing defiantly*) Waal—this air solid comfort—fur once.

PETER   Ay-eh. (*He follows suit. A pause. Unconsciously they both sign*).

SIMEON   (*suddenly*) He never was much o' a hand at milkin', Eben wa'n't.

PETER   (*with a snort*) His hands air like hoofs! (*A pause*).

SIMEON   Reach down the jug thar! Let's take a swaller. I'm feelin' kind o' low.

PETER   Good idee! (*He does so—gets two glasses—they pour out drinks of whisky*) Here's t' the gold in Californi-a!

SIMEON   An' luck t' find it! (*They drink—puff resolutely—sigh—take their feet down from the table*).

PETER   Likker don't 'pear t' sot right.

SIMEON   We hain't used t' it this early. (*A pause. They become very restless*).

PETER   Gittin' close in this kitchen.

SIMEON   (*with immense relief*) Let's git a breath o' air. (*They arise briskly and go out rear—appear around house and stop by the gate. They stare up at the sky with a numbed appreciation*).

PETER   Purty!

SIMEON   Ay-eh. Gold's t' the East now.

PETER   Sun's startin' with us fur the Golden West.

SIMEON   (*staring around the farm, his compressed face tightened, unable to conceal his emotion*) Waal—it's our last mornin'—mebbe.

PETER   (*the same*) Ay-eh.

SIMEON   (*stamps his foot on the earth and addresses it desperately*) Waal—ye've thirty year o' me buried in ye—spread out over ye—blood an' bone an' sweat—rotted away—fertilizin' ye—richin' yer soul—prime manure, by God, that's what I been t' ye!

PETER   Ay-eh! An' me!

SIMEON   An' yew, Peter. (*He sighs—then spits*) Waal—no use'n cryin' over spilt milk.

PETER   They's gold in the West—an' freedom, mebbe. We been slaves t' stone walls here.

SIMEON   (*defiantly*) We hain't nobody's slaves from this out—nor no thin's slaves nuther. (*A pause—restlessly*) Speakin' o' milk, wonder how Eben's managin'?

PETER   I s'pose he's managin'.

SIMEON Mebbe we'd ought t' help—this once.

PETER Mebbe. The cows knows us.

SIMEON An'likes us. They don't know him much.

PETER An' the hosses, an' pigs, an' chickens. They don't know him much.

SIMEON They knows us like brothers—an' likes us! (*Proudly*). Hain't we raised 'em t' be fust-rate, number one prize stock?

PETER We hain't—not no more.

SIMEON (*dully*) I was fergittin'. (*Then resignedly*) Waal, let's go help Eben a spell an' git waked up.

PETER Suits me. (*They are starting off down left, rear, for the barn when* EBEN *appears from there hurrying toward them, his face excited*).

EBEN (*breathlessly*) Waal—thar they be! The old mule an' the bride! I seen 'em from the barn down below at the turnin'.

PETER How could ye tell that far?

EBEN Hain't I as far-sight as he's near-sight? Don't I know the mare 'n'buggy, an' two people settin' in it? Who else . . . ? An' I tell ye I kin feel 'em a-comin', too! (*He squirms as if he had the itch*).

PETER (*beginning to be angry*) Waal—let him do his own unhitchin'!

SIMEON (*angry in his turn*) Let's hustle in an' git our bundles an' be a-goin' as he's a-comin'. I don't want never t' step inside the door agen arter he's back. (*They both start back around the corner of the house.* EBEN *follows them*).

EBEN (*anxiously*) Will ye sign it afore ye go?

PETER Let's see the color o' the old skinflint's money an' we'll sign. (*They disappear left. The two brothers clump upstairs to get their bundles.* EBEN *appears in the kitchen, runs to window, peers out, comes back and pulls up a strip of flooring in under stove, takes out a canvas bag and puts it on table, then sets the floorboard back in place. The two brothers appear a moment after. They carry old carpetbags*).

EBEN (*puts his hand on bag guardingly*) Have ye signed?

SIMEON (*shows paper in his hand*) Ay-eh. (*Greedily*) Be that the money?

EBEN (*opens bag and pours out pile of twenty-dollar gold pieces*) Twenty-dollar pieces—thirty of 'em. Count 'em. (*Peter does so, arranging them in stacks of five, biting one or two to test them*).

PETER Six hundred. (*He puts them in bag and puts it inside his shirt carefully*).

SIMEON (*handing paper to* EBEN) Har ye be.

EBEN (*after a glance, folds it carefully and hides it under his shirt—gratefully*) Thank yew.

PETER Thank yew fur the ride.

SIMEON We'll send ye a lump o' gold fur Christmas. (*A pause.* EBEN *stares at them and they at him*).

PETER (*awkwardly*) Waal—we're a-goin'.

SIMEON Comin' out t' the yard?

EBEN   No. I'm waitin' in here a spell. (*Another silence. The brothers edge awkwardly to door in rear—then turn and stand*).

SIMEON   Waal—good-by.

PETER   Good-by.

EBEN   Good-by. (*They go out. He sits down at the table, faces the stove and pulls out the paper. He looks from it to the stove. His face, lighted up by the shaft of sunlight from the window, has an expression of trance. His lips move. The two brothers come out to the gate*).

PETER   (*looking off toward barn*) Thar he be—unhitchin'.

SIMEON   (*with a chuckle*) I'll bet ye he's riled!

PETER   An' thar she be.

SIMEON   Let's wait 'n' see what our new Maw looks like.

PETER   (*with a grin*) An' give him our partin' cuss!

SIMEON   (*grinning*) I feel like raisin' fun. I feel light in my head an' feet.

PETER   Me, too. I feel like laffin' till I'd split up the middle.

SIMEON   Reckon it's the likker?

PETER   No. My feet feel itchin' t' walk an' walk—an' jump high over thin's—an'. . . .

SIMEON   Dance? (*A pause*).

PETER   (*puzzled*) It's plumb onnateral.

SIMEON   (*a light coming over his face*) I calc'late it's 'cause school's out. It's holiday. Fur once we're free!

PETER   (*dazedly*) Free?

SIMEON   The halter's broke—the harness is busted—the fence bars is down—the stone walls air crumblin' an' tumblin'! We'll be kickin' up an 'tearin' away down the road!

PETER   (*drawing a deep breath—oratorically*) Anybody that wants this stinkin' old rock-pile of a farm kin hev it. 'T ain't our'n, no sirree!

SIMEON   (*takes the gate off its hinges and puts it under his arm*) We harby 'bolishes shet gates, an' open gates, an' all gates, by thunder!

PETER   We'll take it with us fur luck an' let 'er sail free down some river.

SIMEON   (*as a sound of voices comes from left, rear*) Har they comes! (*The two brothers congeal into two stiff, grim-visaged statues.* EPHRAIM CABOT *and* ABBIE PUTNAM *come in.* CABOT *is seventy-five, tall and gaunt, with great, wiry, concentrated power, but stoop-shouldered from toil. His face is as hard as if it were hewn out of a boulder, yet there is a weakness in it, a petty pride in its own narrow strength. His eyes are small, close together, and extremely near-sighted, blinking continually in the effort to focus on objects, their stare having a straining, ingrowing quality. He is dressed in his dismal black Sunday suit.* ABBIE *is thirty-five, buxom, full of vitality. Her round face is pretty but marred by its rather gross sensuality. There is strength and obstinacy in her jaw, a hard determination in her eyes, and about her whole personality the same unsettled, untamed, desperate quality which is so apparent in* EBEN).

CABOT   (*as they enter—a queer strangled emotion in his dry cracking voice*) Har we be t' hum, Abbie.

ABBIE   (*with lust for the word*) Hum! (*Her eyes gloating on the house without seeming to see the two stiff figures at the gate*) It's purty—purty! I can't b'lieve it's r'ally mine.

CABOT   (*sharply*) Yewr'n? Mine! (*He stares at her penetratingly, she stares back. He adds relentingly*) Our'n—mebbe! It was lonesome too long. I was growin' old in the spring. A hum's got t' hev a woman.

ABBIE   (*her voice taking possession*) A woman's got t' hev a hum!

CABOT   (*nodding uncertainly*) Ay-eh. (*Then irritably*) Whar be they? Ain't thar nobody about—'r wukin'—'r nothin'?

ABBIE   (*sees the brothers. She returns their stare of cold appraising contempt with interest—slowly*) Thar's two men loafin' at the gate an' starin' at me like a couple o' strayed hogs.

CABOT   (*straining his eyes*) I kin see 'em—but I can't make out. . . .

SIMEON   It's Simeon.

PETER   It's Peter.

CABOT   (*exploding*) Why hain't ye wukin'?

SIMEON   (*dryly*) We're waitin' t' welcome ye hum—yew an' the bride!

CABOT   (*confusedly*) Huh? Waal—this be yer new Maw, boys. (*She stares at them and they at her*).

SIMEON   (*turns away and spits contemptuously*) I see her!

PETER   (*spits also*) An' I see her!

ABBIE   (*with the conqueror's conscious superiority*) I'll go in an' looks at *my* house. (*She goes slowly around to porch*).

SIMEON   (*with a snort*) Her house!

PETER   (*calls after her*) Ye'll find Eben inside. Ye better not tell him it's *yewr* house.

ABBIE   (*mouthing the name*) Eben. (*Then quietly*) I'll tell Eben.

CABOT   (*with a contemptuous sneer*) Ye needn't heed Eben. Eben's a dumb fool—like his Maw—soft an' simple!

SIMEON   (*with his sardonic burst of laughter*) Ha! Eben's a chip o' yew—spit 'n' image—hard 'n' bitter's a hickory tree! Dog'll eat dog. He'll eat ye yet, old man!

CABOT   (*commandingly*) Ye git t' wuk!

SIMEON   (*as* ABBIE *disappears in house—winks at* PETER *and says tauntingly*) So that thar's our new Maw, be it? Whar in hell did ye dig her up? (*He and* PETER *laugh*).

PETER   Ha! Ye'd better turn her in the pen with the other sows. (*They laugh uproariously, slapping their thighs*).

CABOT   (*so amazed at their effrontery that he stutters in confusion*) Simeon! Peter! What's come over ye? Air ye drunk?

SIMEON   We're free, old man—free o' yew an' the hull damned farm! (*They grow more and more hilarious and excited*).

PETER   An' we're startin' out fur the gold fields o' Californi-a!

SIMEON   Ye kin take this place an' burn it!

PETER   An bury it—fur all we cares!

SIMEON   We're free, old man! (*He cuts a caper*).

PETER   Free! (*He gives a kick in the air*).

SIMEON   (*in a frenzy*) Whoop!

PETER Whoop! (*They do an absurd Indian war dance about the old man who is petrified between rage and the fear that they are insane*).

SIMEON We're free as Injuns! Lucky we don't skulp ye!

PETER An' burn yer barn an' kill the stock!

SIMEON An' rape yer new woman! Whoop! (*He and* PETER *stop their dance, holding their sides, rocking with wild laughter*).

CABOT (*edging away*) Lust fur gold—fur the sinful, easy gold o' Californi-a! It's made ye mad!

SIMEON (*tauntingly*) Wouldn't ye like us to send ye back some sinful gold, ye old sinner?

PETER They's gold besides what's in Californi-a! (*He retreats back beyond the vision of the old man and takes the bag of money and flaunts it in the air above his head, laughing*).

SIMEON And sinfuller, too!

PETER We'll be voyagin' on the sea! Whoop! (*He leaps up and down*).

SIMEON Livin' free! Whoop! (*He leaps in turn*).

CABOT (*suddenly roaring with rage*) My cuss on ye!

SIMEON Take our'n in trade fur it! Whoop!

CABOT I'll hev ye both chained up in the asylum!

PETER Ye old skinflint! Good-by!

SIMEON Ye old blood sucker! Good-by!

CABOT Go afore I . . . !

PETER Whoop! (*He picks a stone from the road.* SIMEON *does the same*).

SIMEON Maw'll be in the parlor.

PETER Ay-eh! One! Two!

CABOT (*frightened*) What air ye . . . ?

PETER Three! (*They both throw, the stones, hitting the parlor window with a crash of glass, tearing the shade*).

SIMEON Whoop!

PETER Whoop!

CABOT (*in a fury now, rushing toward them*) If I kin lay hands on ye—I'll break yer bones fur ye! (*But they beat a capering retreat before him,* SIMEON *with the gate still under his arm.* CABOT *comes back, panting with impotent rage. Their voices as they go off take up the song of the gold-seekers to the old tune of "Oh, Susannah!"*)

> "I jumped aboard the Liza ship,
> And traveled on the sea,
> And every time I thought of home
> I wished it wasn't me!
> Oh! Californi-a,
> That's the land fur me!
> I'm off to Californi-a!
> With my wash bowl on my knee."

(*In the meantime, the window of the upper bedroom on right is raised and* ABBIE *sticks her head out. She looks down at* CABOT—*with a sigh of relief*).

ABBIE   Waal—that's the last o' them two, hain't it? (*He doesn't answer. Then in possessive tones*) This here's a nice bedroom, Ephraim. It's a r'al nice bed. Is it my room, Ephraim?

CABOT   (*grimly—without looking up*) Our'n! (*She cannot control a grimace of aversion and pulls back her head slowly and shuts the window. A sudden horrible thought seems to enter* CABOT'S *head*) They been up to somethin'! Mebbe—mebbe they've pizened the stock—'r somethin'! (*He almost runs off down toward the barn. A moment later the kitchen door is slowly pushed open and* ABBIE *enters. For a moment she stands looking at* EBEN. *He does not notice her at first. Her eyes take him in penetratingly with a calculating appraisal of his strength as against hers. But under this her desire is dimly awakened by his youth and good looks. Suddenly he becomes conscious of her presence and looks up. Their eyes meet. He leaps to his feet, glowering at her speechlessly*).

ABBIE   (*in her most seductive tones which she uses all through this scene*) Be you—Eben? I'm Abbie—(*She laughs*) I mean, I'm yer new Maw.

EBEN   (*viciously*) No, damn ye!

ABBIE   (*as if she hadn't heard—with a queer smile*) Yer Paw's spoke a lot o' yew. . . .

EBEN   Ha!

ABBIE   Ye mustn't mind him. He's an old man. (*A long pause. They stare at each other*) I don't want t' pretend playin' Maw t' ye, Eben. (*Admiringly*) Ye're too big an' too strong fur that. I want t' be frens with ye. Mebbe with me fur a fren ye'd find ye'd like livin' here better. I kin make it easy fur ye with him, mebbe. (*With a scornful sense of power*) I calc'late I kin git him t' do most anythin' fur me.

EBEN   (*with bitter scorn*) Ha! (*They stare again,* EBEN *obscurely moved, physically attracted to her—in forced stilted tones*) Yew kin go t' the devil!

ABBIE   (*calmly*) If cussin' me does ye good, cuss all ye've a mind t'. I'm all prepared t' have ye agin me—at fust. I don't blame ye nuther. I'd feel the same at any stranger comin' t' take my Maw's place. (*He shudders. She is watching him carefully*) Yew must've cared a lot fur yewr Maw, didn't ye? My Maw died afore I'd growed. I don't remember her none. (*A pause*) But yew won't hate me long, Eben. I'm not the wust in the world—an' yew an' me've got a lot in common. I kin tell that by lookin' at ye. Waal—I've had a hard life, too—oceans o' trouble an' nuthin' but wuk fur reward. I was a orphan early an' had t' wuk fur others in other folks' hums. Then I married an' he turned out a drunken spreer an' so he had to wuk fur others an' me too agen in other folks' hums, an' the baby died, an' my husband got sick an' died too, an' I was glad sayin' now I'm free fur once, on'y I diskivered right away all I was free fur was t' wuk agen in other folks' hums, doin' other folks' wuk till I'd most give up hope o' ever doin' my own wuk in my own hum, an' then your Paw come. . . . (CABOT *appears returning from the barn. He comes to the gate and looks down the road the brothers have gone. A faint strain of their retreating voices is heard: "Oh, Californi-a! That's the place for me." He stands glowering, his fist clenched, his face grim with rage).*

EBEN (*fighting against his growing attracion and sympathy—harshly*) An' bought yew—like a harlot! (*She is stung and flushes angrily. She has been sincerely moved by the recital of her troubles. He adds furiously*) An' the price he's payin' ye—this farm—was my Maw's, damn ye!—an' mine now!

ABBIE (*with a cool laugh of confidence*) Yewr'n? We'll see 'bout that! (*Then strongly*) Waal—what if I did need a hum? What else'd I marry an old man like him fur?

EBEN (*maliciously*) I'll tell him ye said that!

ABBIE (*smiling*) I'll say ye're lyin' a-purpose—an' he'll drive ye off the place!

EBEN Ye devil!

ABBIE (*defying him*) This be my farm—this be my hum—this be my kitchen—!

EBEN (*furiously, as if he were going to attack her*) Shut up, damn ye!

ABBIE (*walks up to him—a queer coarse expression of desire in her face and body—slowly*) An' upstairs—that be my bedroom—an' my bed! (*He stares into her eyes, terribly confused and torn. She adds softly*) I hain't bad nor mean—'ceptin' fur an enemy—but I got t' fight fur what's due me out o' life, if I ever 'spect t' git it. (*Then putting her hand on his arm—seductively*) Let's yew 'n' me be frens, Eben.

EBEN (*stupidly—as if hypnotized*) Ay-eh. (*Then furiously flinging off her arm*) No, ye durned old witch! I hate ye! (*He rushes out the door*).

ABBIE (*looks after him smiling satisfiedly—then half to herself, mouthing the word*) Eben's nice. (*She looks at the table, proudly*) I'll wash up *my* dishes now. (EBEN *appears outside, slamming the door behind him. He comes around corner, stops on seeing his father, and stands staring at him with hate*).

CABOT (*raising his arms to heaven in the fury he can no longer control*) Lord God o' Hosts, smite the undutiful sons with Thy wust cuss!

EBEN (*breaking in violently*) Yew 'n' yewr God! Allus cussin' folks —allus naggin' 'em!

CABOT (*oblivious to him—summoningly*) God o' the old! God o' the lonesome!

EBEN (*mockingly*) Naggin' His sheep t' sin! T' hell with yewr God! (CABOT *turns. He and* EBEN *glower at each other*).

CABOT (*harshly*) So it's yew. I might've knowed it. (*Shaking his finger threateningly at him*) Blasphemin' fool! (*Then quickly*) Why hain't ye t' wuk?

EBEN Why hain't yew? They've went. I can't wuk it all alone.

CABOT (*contemptuously*) Nor noways! I'm wuth ten o' ye yit, old's I be! Ye'll never be more'n half a man! (*Then, matter-of-factly*) Waal—let's git t' the barn. (*They go. A last faint note of the*

"*Californi-a*" *song is heard from the distance.* ABBIE *is washing her dishes*).

CURTAIN

Part Two
Scene One

The exterior of the farmhouse, as in Part One—a hot Sunday after-noon two months later. ABBIE, *dressed in her best, is discovered sitting in a rocker at the end of the porch. She rocks listlessly, ener-vated by the heat, staring in front of her with bored, half-closed eyes.*

EBEN *sticks his head out of his bedroom window. He looks around furtively and tries to see—or hear—if anyone is on the porch, but although he has been careful to make no noise,* ABBIE *has sensed his movement. She stops rocking, her face grows animated and eager, she waits attentively.* EBEN *seems to feel her presence, he scowls back his thoughts of her and spits with exaggerated disdain—then with-draws back into the room.* ABBIE *waits, holding her breath as she listens with passionate eagerness for every sound within the house.*

EBEN *comes out. Their eyes meet. His falter, he is confused, he turns away and slams the door resentfully. At this gesture,* ABBIE *laughs tantalizingly, amused but at the same time piqued and irritat-ed. He scowls, strides off the porch to the path and starts to walk past her to the road with a grand swagger of ignoring her existence. He is dressed in his store suit, spruced up, his face shines from soap and water.* ABBIE *leans forward on her chair, her eyes hard and angry now, and, as he passes her, gives a sneering, taunting chuckle.*

EBEN (*stung—turns on her furiously*) What air yew cacklin' 'bout?
ABBIE (*triumphant*) Yew!
EBEN What about me?
ABBIE Ye look all slicked up like a prize bull.
EBEN (*with a sneer*) Waal—ye hain't so durned purty yerself, be ye? (*They stare into each other's eyes, his held by hers in spite of himself, hers glowingly possessive. Their physical attraction be-comes a palpable force quivering in the hot air*).
ABBIE (*softly*) Ye don't mean that, Eben. Ye may think ye mean it, mebbe, but ye don't. Ye can't. It's agin nature, Eben. Ye been fightin' yer nature ever since the day I come—tryin' t' tell yer-self I hain't purty t'ye. (*She laughs a low humid laugh without taking her eyes from his. A pause—her body squirms desirously—she murmurs languorously*) Hain't the sun strong an' hot? Ye kin feel it burnin' into the earth—Nature—makin' thin's grow—bigger 'n' bigger—burnin' inside ye—makin' ye want t' grow—into somethin' else—till ye're jined with it—an' it's your'n—but it owns ye, too—an' makes ye grow bigger—like a tree—like them elums—(*She laughs again softly, holding his eyes. He takes*

a step toward her, compelled against his will) Nature'll beat ye, Eben. Ye might's well own up t' it fust 's last.

EBEN   (*trying to break from her spell—confusedly*) If Paw'd hear ye goin' on.... (*Resentfully*) But ye've made such a damned idjit out o' the old devil ...! (ABBIE *laughs*).

ABBIE   Waal—hain't it easier fur yew with him changed softer?

EBEN   (*defiantly*) No. I'm fightin' him—fightin' yew—fightin' fur Maw's rights t' her hum! (*This breaks her spell for him. He glowers at her*) An' I'm onto ye. Ye hain't foolin' me a mite. Ye're aimin' t' swaller up everythin' an' make it your'n. Waal, you'll find I'm a heap sight bigger hunk nor yew kin chew! (*He turns from her with a sneer*).

ABBIE   (*trying to regain her ascendancy—seductively*) Eben!

EBEN   Leave me be! (*He starts to walk away*).

ABBIE   (*more commandingly*) Eben!

EBEN   (*stops—resentfully*) What d'ye want?

ABBIE   (*trying to conceal a growing excitement*) Whar air ye goin'?

EBEN   (*with malicious nonchalance*) Oh—up the road a spell.

ABBIE   T' the village?

EBEN   (*airily*) Mebbe.

ABBIE   (*excitedly*) T' see that Min, I s'pose?

EBEN   Mebbe.

ABBIE   (*weakly*) What d'ye want t' waste time on her fur?

EBEN   (*revenging himself now—grinning at her*) Ye can't beat Nature, didn't ye say? (*He laughs and again starts to walk away*).

ABBIE   (*bursting out*)An ugly old hake![1]

EBEN   (*with a tantalizing sneer*) She's purtier'n yew be!

ABBIE   That every wuthless drunk in the country has....

EBEN   (*tauntingly*) Mebbe—but she's better'n yew. She owns up fa'r 'n' squar' t' her doin's.

ABBIE   (*furiously*) Don't ye dare compare....

EBEN   She don't go sneakin' an' stealin'—what's mine.

ABBIE   (*savagely seizing on his weak point*) Your'n? Yew mean—my farm?

EBEN   I mean the farm yew sold yerself fur like any other whore—my farm!

ABBIE   (*stung—fiercely*) Ye'll never live t' see the day when even a stinkin' weed on it'll belong t' ye! (*Then in a scream*) Git out o' my sight! Go on t' yer slut—disgracin' yer Paw 'n' me! I'll git yer Paw t' horsewhip ye off the place if I want t'! Ye're only livin' here cause I tolerate ye! Git along! I hate the sight o' ye! (*She stops panting and glaring at him*).

EBEN   (*returning her glance in kind*) An' I hate the sight o' yew! (*He turns and strides off up the road. She follows his retreating figure with concentrated hate. Old* CABOT *appears coming up from the barn. The hard, grim expression of his face has changed. He seems in some queer way softened, mellowed. His eyes have taken on a strange, incongruous dreamy quality. Yet there is not a hint*

---

1. A gossiping woman.

of physical weakness about him—rather he looks more robust and younger. ABBIE *sees him and turns away quickly with unconcealed aversion. He comes slowly up to her*).

CABOT (*mildly*) War yew an' Eben quarrelin' agen?

ABBIE (*shortly*) No.

CABOT Ye was talkin' a'mighty loud. (*He sits down on the edge of porch*).

ABBIE (*snappishly*) If ye heerd us they hain't no need askin' questions.

CABOT I didn't hear what ye said.

ABBIE (*relieved*) Waal—it wa'n't nothin' t' speak on.

CABOT (*after a pause*) Eben's queer.

ABBIE (*bitterly*) He's the dead spit 'n' image o' yew!

CABOT (*queerly interested*) D'ye think so, Abbie? (*After a pause, ruminatingly*) Me 'n' Eben's allus fit 'n' fit.² I never could b'ar him noways. He's so thunderin' soft—like his Maw.

ABBIE (*scornfully*) Ay-eh! 'Bout as soft as yew be!

CABOT (*as if he hadn't heard*) Mebbe I been too hard on him.

ABBIE (*jeeringly*) Waal—ye're gittin' soft now—soft as slop! That's what Eben was sayin'.

CABOT (*his face instantly grim and ominous*) Eben was sayin'? Waal, he'd best not do nothin' t' try me 'r he'll soon diskiver. . . . (*A pause. She keeps her face turned away. His gradually softens. He stares up at the sky*) Purty, hain't it?

ABBIE (*crossly*) I don't see nothin' purty.

CABOT The sky. Feels like a wa'm field up thar.

ABBIE (*sarcastically*) Air yew aimin' t' buy up over the farm too? (*She snickers contemptuously*).

CABOT (*strangely*) I'd like t' own my place up thar. (*A pause*) I'm gittin' old, Abbie. I'm gittin' ripe on the bough. (*A pause. She stares at him mystified. He goes on*) It's allus lonesome cold in the house—even when it's bilin' hot outside. Hain't yew noticed?

ABBIE No.

CABOT It's wa'm down t'the barn—nice smellin' an' warm—with the cows. (*A pause*) Cows is queer.

ABBIE Like yew?

CABOT Like Eben. (*A pause*) I'm gittin' t' feel resigned t' Eben—jest as I got t' feel 'bout his Maw. I'm gittin' t' learn to b'ar his softness—jest like her'n. I calc'late I c'd a'most take t' him—if he wa'n't sech a dumb fool! (*A pause*) I s'pose it's old age a'creepin' in my bones.

ABBIE (*indifferently*) Waal—ye hain't dead yet.

CABOT (*roused*) No, I hain't, yew bet—not by a hell of a sight!—I'm sound 'n' tough as hickory! (*Then moodily*) But arter three score and ten the Lord warns ye t' prepare. (*A pause*) That's why Eben's come in my head. Now that his cussed sinful brothers is gone their path t' hell, they's no one left but Eben.

ABBIE (*resentfully*) They's me, hain't they? (*Agitatedly*) What's all

---

2. Fighting, or at each other.

this sudden likin' ye've tuk to Eben? Why don't ye say nothin'
'bout me? Hain't I yer lawful wife?

CABOT (*simply*) Ay-eh. Ye be. (*A pause—he stares at her desirously
—his eyes grow avid—then with a sudden movement he seizes
her hands and squeezes them, declaiming in a queer camp-meeting
preacher's tempo*) Yew air my Rose o' Sharon! Behold, yew air
fair; yer eyes air doves; yer lips air like scarlet; yer two breasts air
like two fawns; yer navel be like a round goblet; yer belly be like a
heap o' wheat. . . . (*He covers her hand with kisses. She does not
seem to notice. She stares before her with hard angry eyes*).

ABBIE (*jerking her hands away—harshly*) So ye're plannin' t' leave
the farm t' Eben, air ye?

CABOT (*dazedly*) Leave . . . ? (*Then with resentful obstinacy*) I
hain't a-givin' it t' no one!

ABBIE (*remorselessly*) Ye can't take it with ye.

CABOT (*thinks a moment—then reluctantly*) No, I calc'late not.
(*After a pause—with a strange passion*) But if I could, I would,
by the Etarnal! 'R if I could, in my dyin' hour, I'd set it afire an'
watch it burn—this house an' every ear o' corn an' every tree down
t' the last blade o' hay! I'd sit an' know it was all a-dying with me
an' no one else'd ever own what was mine, what I'd made out o'
nothin' with my own sweat 'n' blood! (*A pause—then he adds
with a queer affection*) 'Ceptin' the cows. Them I'd turn free.

ABBIE (*harshly*) An' me?

CABOT (*with a queer smile*) Ye'd be turned free, too.

ABBIE (*furiously*) So that's the thanks I git fur marryin' ye—t'
have ye change kind to Eben who hates ye, an' talk o' turnin' me
out in the road.

CABOT (*hastily*) Abbie! Ye know I wa'n't. . . .

ABBIE (*vengefully*) Just let me tell ye a thing or two 'bout Eben!
Whar's he gone? T' see that harlot, Min! I tried fur t' stop him.
Disgracin' yew an' me—on the Sabbath, too!

CABOT (*rather guiltily*) He's a sinner—nateral-born. It's lust eatin'
his heart.

ABBIE (*enraged beyond endurance—wildly vindictive*) An' his lust
fur me! Kin ye find excuses fur that?

CABOT (*stares at her—after a dead pause*) Lust—fur yew?

ABBIE (*defiantly*) He was tryin t' make love t' me—when ye heerd
us quarrelin'.

CABOT (*stares at her—then a terrible expression of rage comes over
his face—he springs to his feet shaking all over*) By the A'mighty
God—I'll end him!

ABBIE (*frightened now for* EBEN) No! Don't ye!

CABOT (*violently*) I'll git the shotgun an' blow his soft brains t'
the top o' them elums!

ABBIE (*throwing her arms around him*) No, Ephraim!

CABOT (*pushing her away violently*) I will, by God!

ABBIE (*in a quieting tone*) Listen, Ephraim. 'Twa'n't nothin' bad
—on'y a boy's foolin'—'twa'n't meant serious—jest jokin' an'
teasin'. . . .

CABOT Then why did ye say—lust?

ABBIE It must hev sounded wusser'n I meant. An' I was mad at thinkin'—ye'd leave him the farm.

CABOT (*quieter but still grim and cruel*) Waal then, I'll horsewhip him off the place if that much'll content ye.

ABBIE (*reaching out and taking his hand*) No. Don't think o' me! Ye mustn't drive him off. 'Tain't sensible. Who'll ye get to help ye on the farm? They's no one hereabouts.

CABOT (*considers this—then nodding his appreciation*) Ye got a head on ye. (*Then irritably*) Waal, let him stay. (*He sits down on the edge of the porch. She sits beside him. He murmurs contemptuously*) I oughn't t' git riled so—at that 'ere fool calf. (*A pause*) But har's the p'int. What son o' mine'll keep on here t' the farm—when the Lord does call me? Simeon an' Peter air gone t' hell—an' Eben's follerin' 'em.

ABBIE They's me.

CABOT Ye're on'y a woman.

ABBIE I'm yewr wife.

CABOT That hain't me. A son is me—my blood—mine. Mine ought t' git mine. An' then it's still mine—even though I be six foot under. D'ye see?

ABBIE (*giving him a look of hatred*) Ay-eh. I see. (*She becomes very thoughtful, her face growing shrewd, her eyes studying* CABOT *craftily*).

CABOT I'm gittin' old—ripe on the bough. (*Then with a sudden forced reassurance*) Not but what I hain't a hard nut t' crack even yet—an' fur many a year t' come! By the Etarnal, I kin break most o' the young fellers' backs at any kind o' work any day o' the year!

ABBIE (*suddenly*) Mebbe the Lord'll give *us* a son.

CABOT (*turns and stares at her eagerly*) Ye mean—a son—t' me 'n' yew?

ABBIE (*with a cajoling smile*) Ye're a strong man yet, hain't ye? 'Tain't noways impossible, be it? We know that. Why d'ye stare so? Hain't ye never thought o' that afore? I been thinkin o' it all along. Ay-eh—an' I been prayin' it'd happen, too.

CABOT (*his face growing full of joyous pride and a sort of religious ecstasy*) Ye been prayin', Abbie?—fur a son?—t' us?

ABBIE Ay-eh. (*With a grim resolution*) I want a son now.

CABOT (*excitedly clutching both of her hands in his*) It'd be the blessin' o' God, Abbie—the blessin' o' God Almighty on me—in my old age—in my lonesomeness! They hain't nothin' I wouldn't do fur ye then, Abbie. Ye'd hev on'y t' ask it—anythin' ye'd a mind t'!

ABBIE (*interrupting*) Would ye will the farm t' me then—t' me an' it . . . ?

CABOT (*vehemently*) I'd do anythin' ye axed, I tell ye! I swar it! May I be everlastin' damned t' hell if I wouldn't! (*He sinks to his knees pulling her down with him. He trembles all over with the fervor of his hopes*) Pray t' the Lord agen, Abbie. It's the Sabbath!

I'll jine ye! Two prayers air better nor one "An' God hearkened unto Rachel"![3] An' God hearkened unto Abbie! Pray, Abbie! Pray fur him to hearken! (*He bows his head, mumbling. She pretends to do likewise but gives him a side glance of scorn and triumph*).

CURTAIN

Scene Two

About eight in the evening. The interior of the two bedrooms on the top floor is shown. EBEN *is sitting on the side of his bed in the room on the left. On account of the heat he has taken off everything but his undershirt and pants. His feet are bare. He faces front, brooding moodily, his chin propped on his hands, a desperate expression on his face.*

In the other room CABOT *and* ABBIE *are sitting side by side on the edge of their bed, an old four-poster with feather mattress. He is in his night shirt, she in her nightdress. He is still in the queer, excited mood into which the notion of a son has thrown him. Both rooms are lighted dimly and flickeringly by tallow candles.*

CABOT   The farm needs a son.

ABBIE   I need a son.

CABOT   Ay-eh. Sometimes ye air the farm an' sometimes the farm be yew. That's why I clove t' ye in my lonesomeness. (*A pause. He pounds his knee with his fist*) Me an' the farm has got t' beget a son!

ABBIE   Ye'd best go t' sleep. Ye're gittin' thin's all mixed.

CABOT   (*with an impatient gesture*) No, I hain't. My mind's clear's a well. Ye don't know me, that's it. (*He stares hopelessly at the floor*).

ABBIE   (*indifferently*) Mebbe. (*In the next room* EBEN *gets up and paces up and down distractedly.* ABBIE *hears him. Her eyes fasten on the intervening wall with concentrated attention.* EBEN *stops and stares. Their hot glances seem to meet through the wall. Unconsciously he stretches out his arms for her and she half rises. Then aware, he mutters a curse at himself and flings himself face downward on the bed, his clenched fists above his head, his face buried in the pillow.* ABBIE *relaxes with a faint sigh but her eyes remain fixed on the wall; she listens with all her attention for some movement from* EBEN).

CABOT   (*suddenly raises his head and looks at her—scornfully*) Will ye ever know me—'r will any man 'r woman? (*Shaking his head*) No. I calc'late 't wa'n't t' be. (*He turns away.* ABBIE *looks at the wall. Then, evidently unable to keep silent about his thoughts without looking at his wife, he puts out his hand and clutches her knee. She starts violently, looks at him, sees he is not watching her, concentrates again on the wall and pays no attention to what*

<hr>

3. Genesis xxx.

he says) Listen, Abbie. When I come here fifty odd year ago—I was jest twenty an' the strongest an' hardest ye ever seen—ten times as strong an' fifty times as hard as Eben. Waal—this place was nothin' but fields o'stones. Folks laughed when I tuk it. They couldn't know what I knowed. When ye kin make corn sprout out o' stones, God's livin' in yew! They wa'n't strong enuf fur that! They reckoned God was easy. They laughed. They don't laugh no more. Some died hereabouts. Some went West an' died. They're all under ground—fur follerin' arter an easy God. God hain't easy. (*He shakes his head slowly*) An' I growed hard. Folks kept allus sayin' he's a hard man like'twas sinful t' be hard, so's at last I said back at 'em: Waal then, by thunder, ye'll git me hard an' see how ye like it! (*Then suddenly*) But I give in t' weakness once. 'Twas arter I'd been here two year. I got weak—despairful—they was so many stones. They was a party leavin', givin' up, goin' West. I jined 'em. We tracked on 'n' on. We come t' broad medders, plains, whar the soil was black an' rich as gold. Nary a stone. Easy. Ye'd on'y to plow an' sow an' then set an' smoke yer pipe an' watch thin's grow; I could o' been a rich man—but somethin' in me fit me an' fit[4] me—the voice o' God sayin': "This hain't wuth nothin' t' Me. Git ye back t' hum!" I got afeerd o' that voice an' I lit out back t' hum here, leavin' my claim an' crops t' whoever'd a mind t' take em. Ay-eh. I actoolly give up what was rightful mine! God's hard, not easy! God's in the stones! Build my church on a rock—out o' stones an' I'll be in them! That's what He meant t' Peter! (*He sighs heavily—a pause*) Stones. I picked 'em up an' piled 'em into walls. Ye kin read the years o' my life in them walls, every day a hefted stone, climbin' over the hills up and down, fencin' in the fields that was mine, whar I'd made thin's grow out o' nothin'— like the will o'God, like the servant o' His hand. It wa'n't easy. It was hard an' He made me hard fur it. (*He pauses*) All the time I kept gittin' lonesomer. I tuk a wife. She bore Simeon an' Peter. She was a good woman. She wuked hard. We was married twenty year. She never knowed me. She helped but she never knowed what she was helpin'. I was allus lonesome. She died. After that it wa'n't so lonesome fur a spell. (*A pause*) I lost count o' the years. I had no time t' fool away countin' 'em. Sim an' Peter helped. The farm growed. It was all mine! When I thought o' that I didn't feel lonesome. (*A pause*) But ye can't hitch yer mind t' one thin' day an' night. I tuk another wife—Eben's Maw. Her folks was con-testin' me at law over my deeds t' the farm—my farm! That's why Eben keeps a-talkin' his fool talk o' this bein' his Maw's farm. She bore Eben. She was purty—but soft. She tried t' be hard. She couldn't. She never knowed me nor nothin'. It was lonesomer 'n hell with her. After a matter o' sixteen odd years, she died. (*A pause*) I lived with the boys. They hated me 'cause I was hard. I hated them 'cause they was soft. They coveted the farm without knowin' what it meant. It made me bitter 'n wormwood. It aged

4. "fought me and fought me."

me—them coveting what I'd made fur mine. Then this spring the call come—the voice o' God cryin' in my wilderness, in my lonesomeness—t' go out an' seek an' find! *(Turning to her with strange passion)* I sought ye an' I found ye! Yew air my Rose o' Sharon! Yer eyes air like. . . . *(She has turned a blank face, resentful eyes to his. He stares at her for a moment—then harshly)* Air ye any the wiser fur all I've told ye?

ABBIE *(confusedly)* Mebbe.

CABOT *(pushing her away from him—angrily)* Ye don't know nothin'—nor never will. If ye don't hev a son t' redeem ye. . . . *(This in a tone of cold threat)*.

ABBIE *(resentfully)* I've prayed, hain't I?

CABOT *(bitterly)* Pray agen—fur understandin'!

ABBIE *(a veiled threat in her tone)* Ye'll have a son out o' me, I promise ye.

CABOT How kin ye promise?

ABBIE I got second-sight mebbe. I kin foretell. *(She gives a queer smile)*.

CABOT I believe ye have. Ye give me the chills sometimes. *(He shivers)* It's cold in this house. It's oneasy. They's thin's pokin' about in the dark—in the corners. *(He pulls on his trousers, tucking in his night shirt, and pulls on his boots)*.

ABBIE *(surprised)* Whar air ye goin'?

CABOT *(queerly)* Down whar it's restful—whar it's warm down t' the barn. *(Bitterly)* I kin talk t' the cows. They know. They know the farm an' me. They'll give me peace. *(He turns to go out the door)*.

ABBIE *(a bit frightenedly)* Air ye ailin' tonight, Ephraim?

CABOT Growin'. Growin' ripe on the bough. *(He turns and goes, his boots clumping down the stairs. EBEN sits up with a start, listening. ABBIE is conscious of his movement and stares at the wall. CABOT comes out of the house around the corner and stands by the gate, blinking at the sky. He stretches up his hands in a tortured gesture)* God A'mighty, call from the dark! *(He listens as if expecting an answer. Then his arms drop, he shakes his head and plods off toward the barn. EBEN and ABBIE stare at each other through the wall. EBEN sighs heavily and ABBIE echoes it. Both become terribly nervous, uneasy. Finally ABBIE gets up and listens, her ear to the wall. He acts as if he saw every move she was making, he becomes resolutely still. She seems driven into a decision—goes out the door in rear determinedly. His eyes follow her. Then as the door of his room is opened softly, he turns away, waits in an attitude of strained fixity. ABBIE stands for a second staring at him, her eyes burning with desire. Then with a little cry she runs over and throws her arms about his neck, she pulls his head back and covers his mouth with kisses. At first, he submits dumbly; then he puts his arms about her neck and returns her kisses, but finally, suddenly aware of his hatred, he hurls her away from him, springing to his feet. They stand speechless and breathless, panting like two animals)*.

ABBIE (*at last—painfully*) Ye shouldn't, Eben—ye shouldn't—I'd make ye happy!

EBEN (*harshly*) I don't want t' be happy—from yew!

ABBIE (*helplessly*) Ye do, Eben! Ye do! Why d'ye lie?

EBEN (*viciously*) I don't take t'ye, I tell ye! I hate the sight o' ye!

ABBIE (*with an uncertain troubled laugh*) Waal, I kissed ye any-ways—an' ye kissed back—yer lips was burnin'—ye can't lie 'bout that! (*Intensely*) If ye don't care, why did ye kiss me back—why was yer lips burnin'?

EBEN (*wiping his mouth*) It was like pizen on 'em. (*Then taunting-ly*) When I kissed ye back, mebbe I thought 'twas someone else.

ABBIE (*wildly*) Min?

EBEN Mebbe.

ABBIE (*torturedly*) Did ye go t' see her? Did ye r'ally go? I thought ye mightn't. Is that why ye throwed me off jest now?

EBEN (*sneeringly*) What if it be?

ABBIE (*raging*) Then ye're a dog, Eben Cabot!

EBEN (*threateningly*) Ye can't talk that way t' me!

ABBIE (*with a shrill laugh*) Can't I? Did ye think I was in love with ye—a weak thin' like yew? Not much! I on'y wanted ye fur a purpose o' my own—an' I'll hev ye fur it yet 'cause I'm stronger'n yew be!

EBEN (*resentfully*) I knowed well it was on'y part o' yer plan t' swaller everythin'!

ABBIE (*tauntingly*) Mebbe!

EBEN (*furious*) Git out o' my room!

ABBIE This air my room an' ye're on'y hired help!

EBEN (*threateningly*) Git out afore I murder ye!

ABBIE (*quite confident now*) I hain't a mite afeerd. Ye want me, don't ye? Yes, ye do! An' yer Paw's son'll never kill what he wants! Look at yer eyes! They's lust fur me in 'em, burnin' 'em up! Look at yer lips now! They're tremblin' an' longin't t' kiss me, an' yer teeth t' bite! (*He is watching her now with a horrible fasci-nation. She laughs a crazy triumphant laugh*) I'm a-goin' t' make all o' this hum my hum! They's one rom hain't mine yet, but it's a-goin' t' be tonight. I'm a-goin' down now an' light up! (*She makes him a mocking bow*) Won't ye come courtin' me in the best parlor, Mister Cabot?

EBEN (*staring at her—horribly confused—dully*) Don't ye dare! It hain't been opened since Maw died an' was laid out thar! Don't ye . . . ! (*But her eyes are fixed on his so burningly that his will seems to wither before hers. He stands swaying toward her helplessly*).

ABBIE (*holding his eyes and putting all her will into her words as she backs out the door*) I'll expect ye afore long, Eben.

EBEN (*stares after her for a while, walking toward the door. A light appears in the parlor window. He murmurs*) In the parlor? (*This seems to arouse connotations for he comes back and puts on his white shirt, collar, half ties the tie mechanically, puts on coat, takes his hat, stands barefooted looking about him in bewilder-*

ment, mutters wonderingly) Maw! Whar air yew? (*Then goes slowly toward the door in rear*).

CURTAIN

Scene Three

A *few minutes later. The interior of the parlor is shown. A grim, repressed room like a tomb in which the family has been interred alive.* ABBIE *sits on the edge of the horsehair sofa. She has lighted all the candles and the room is revealed in all its preserved ugliness. A change has come over the woman. She looks awed and frightened now, ready to run away.*

The door is opened and EBEN *appears. His face wears an expression of obsessed confusion. He stands staring at her, his arms hanging disjointedly from his shoulders, his feet bare, his hat in his hand.*

ABBIE (*after a pause—with a nervous, formal politeness*) Won't ye set?

EBEN (*dully*) Ay-eh. (*Mechanically he places his hat carefully on the floor near the door and sits stiffly beside her on the edge of the sofa. A pause. They both remain rigid, looking straight ahead with eyes full of fear*).

ABBIE When I fust come in—in the dark—they seemed t' somethin' here.

EBEN (*simply*) Maw.

ABBIE I kin still feel—somethin'. . . .

EBEN It's Maw.

ABBIE At fust I was feered o' it. I wanted t' yell an' run. Now— since yew come—seems like it's growin' soft an' kind t' me. (*Addressing the air—queerly*) Thank yew.

EBEN Maw allus loved me.

ABBIE Mebbe it knows I love yew, too. Mebbe that makes it kind t' me.

EBEN (*dully*) I dunno. I should think she'd hate ye.

ABBIE (*with certainty*) No. I kin feel it don't—not no more.

EBEN Hate ye fur stealin' her place—here in her hum—settin' in her parlor whar she was laid—(*He suddenly stops, staring stupidly before him*).

ABBIE What is it, Eben?

EBEN (*in a whisper*) Seems like Maw didn't want me t' remind ye.

ABBIE (*excitedly*) I knowed, Eben! It's kind t' me! It don't b'ar me no grudges fur what I never knowed an' couldn't help!

EBEN Maw b'ars him a grudge.

ABBIE Waal, so does all o' us.

EBEN Ay-eh. (*With passion*) I does, by God!

ABBIE (*taking one of his hands in hers and patting it*) Thar. Don't git riled thinkin' o' him. Think o' yer Maw who's kind t' us. Tell me about yer Maw, Eben.

EBEN   They hain't nothin' much. She was kind. She was good.

ABBIE   (*putting one arm over his shoulder. He does not seem to notice—passionately*) I'll be kind an' good t' ye!

EBEN   Sometimes she used t' sing fur me.

ABBIE   I'll sing fur ye!

EBEN   This was her hum. This was her farm.

ABBIE   This is my hum! This is my farm!

EBEN   He married her t' steal 'em. She was soft an' easy. He couldn't 'preciate her.

ABBIE   He can't 'preciate me!

EBEN   He murdered her with his hardness.

ABBIE   He's murderin' me!

EBEN   She died. (*A pause*) Sometimes she used to sing fur me. (*He bursts into a fit of sobbing*).

ABBIE   (*both her arms round him—with wild passion*) I'll sing fur ye! I'll die fur ye! (*In spite of her overhelming desire for him, there is a sincere maternal love in her manner and voice—a horribly frank mixture of lust and mother love*) Don't cry, Eben! I'll take yer Maw's place! I'll be everythin' she was t' ye! Let me kiss ye, Eben! (*She pulls his head around. He makes a bewildered pretense of resistance. She is tender*) Don't be afeered! I'll kiss ye pure, Eben—same 's if I was a Maw t' ye—an' ye kin kiss me back 's if yew was my son—my boy—sayin' good-night t' me! Kiss me, Eben. (*They kiss in restrained fashion. Then suddenly wild passion overcomes her. She kisses him lustfully again and again and he flings his arms about her and returns her kisses. Suddenly, as in the bedroom, he frees himself from her violently and springs to his feet. He is trembling all over, in a strange state of terror.* ABBIE *strains her arms toward him with fierce pleading*) Don't ye leave me, Eben! Can't ye see it hain't enuf—lovin' ye like a Maw—can't ye see it's got t' be that an' more—much more—a hundred times more—fur me t' be happy—fur yew t' be happy?

EBEN   (*to the presence he feels in the room*) Maw! Maw! What d'ye want? What air ye tellin' me?

ABBIE   She's tellin' ye t' love me. She knows I love ye an' I'll be good t' ye. Can't ye feel it? Don't ye know? She's tellin' ye t' love me, Eben!

EBEN   Ay-eh. I feel—mebbe she—but—I can't figger out—why—when ye've stole her place—here in her hum—in the parlor whar she was—

ABBIE   (*fiercely*) She knows I love ye!

EBEN   (*his face suddenly lighting up with a fierce, triumphant grin*) I see it! I see why. It's her vengeance on him—so's she kin rest quiet in her grave!

ABBIE   (*wildly*) Vengeance o' God on the hull o' us! What d'we give a durn? I love ye, Eben! God knows I love ye! (*She stretches out her arms for him*).

EBEN   (*throws himself on his knees beside the sofa and grabs her*

in his arms—releasing all his pent-up passion) An' I love yew,
Abbie!—now I kin say it! I been dyin' fur want o' ye—every hour
since ye come! I love ye! (*Their lips meet in a fierce, bruising
kiss*).

CURTAIN

Scene Four

*Exterior of the farmhouse. It is just dawn. The front door at right
is opened and* EBEN *comes out and walks around to the gate. He is
dressed in his working clothes. He seems changed. His face wears a
bold and confident expression, he is grinning to himself with evident
satisfaction. As he gets near the gate, the window of the parlor is
heard opening and the shutters are flung back and* ABBIE *sticks her
head out. Her hair tumbles over her shoulders in disarray, her face
is flushed, she looks at* EBEN *with tender, languorous eyes and calls
softly.*

ABBIE   Eben. (*As he turns—playfully*) Jest one more kiss afore ye
go. I'm goin' to miss ye fearful all day.

EBEN   An' me yew, ye kin bet! (*He goes to her. They kiss several
times. He draws away, laughingly*) Thar. That's enuf, hain't it?
Ye won't hev none left fur next time.

ABBIE   I got a million o' 'em left fur yew! (*Then a bit anxiously*)
D'ye r'ally love me, Eben?

EBEN   (*emphatically*) I like ye better'n any gal I ever knowed!
That's gospel!

ABBIE   Likin' hain't lovin'.

EBEN   Waal then—I love ye. Now air yew satisfied?

ABBIE   Ay-eh, I be. (*She smiles at him adoringly*).

EBEN   I better git t' the barn. The old critter's liable t' suspicion an'
come sneakin' up.

ABBIE   (*with a confident laugh*) Let him! I kin allus pull the wool
over his eyes. I'm goin' t' leave the shutters open and let in the
sun 'n' air. This room's been dead long enuf. Now it's goin' t'
be my room!

EBEN   (*frowning*) Ay-eh.

ABBIE   (*hastily*) I meant—our room.

EBEN   Ay-eh.

ABBIE   We made it our'n last night, didn't we? We give it life—
our lovin' did. (*A pause*).

EBEN   (*with a strange look*) Maw's gone back t' her grave. She kin
sleep now.

ABBIE   May she rest in peace! (*Then tenderly rebuking*) Ye oughtn't
t' talk o' sad thin's—this mornin'.

EBEN   It jest come up in my mind o' itself.

ABBIE   Don't let it. (*He doesn't answer. She yawns*) Waal, I'm a-
goin' t' steal a wink o' sleep. I'll tell the Old Man I hain't feelin'
pert. Let him git his own vittles.

EBEN   I see him comin' from the barn. Ye better look smart an' git
upstairs.

ABBIE   Ay-eh. Good-by. Don't forget me. (*She throws him a kiss.
He grins—then squares his shoulders and awaits his father confidently.* CABOT *walks slowly up from the left, staring up at the sky
with a vague face*).

EBEN   (*jovially*) Mornin', Paw. Star-gazin' in daylight?

CABOT   Purty, hain't it?

EBEN   (*looking around him possessively*) It's a durned purty farm.

CABOT   I mean the sky.

EBEN   (*grinning*) How d'ye know? Them eyes o' your'n can't see
that fur. (*This tickles his humor and he slaps his thigh and laughs*)
Ho-ho! That's a good un!

CABOT   (*grimly sarcastic*) Ye're feelin' right chipper, hain't ye?
Whar'd ye steal the likker?

EBEN   (*good-naturedly*) 'Tain't likker. Jest life. (*Suddenly holding
out his hand—soberly*) Yew 'n' me is quits. Let's shake hands.

CABOT   (*suspiciously*) What's come over ye?

EBEN   Then don't. Mebbe it's jest as well. (*A moment's pause*)
What's come over me? (*Queerly*) Didn't ye feel her passin'—goin'
back t' her grave?

CABOT   (*dully*) Who?

EBEN   Maw. She kin rest now an' sleep content. She's quit with ye.

CABOT   (*confusedly*) I rested. I slept good—down with the cows.
They know how t' sleep. They're teachin' me.

EBEN   (*suddenly jovial again*) Good fur the cows! Waal—ye better
git t' work.

CABOT   (*grimly amused*) Air ye bossin' me, ye calf?

EBEN   (*beginning to laugh*) Ay-eh! I'm bossin' yew! Ha-ha-ha! See
how ye like it! Ha-ha-ha! I'm the prize rooster o' this roost. Ha-ha-
ha! (*He goes off toward the barn laughing*).

CABOT   (*looks after him with scornful pity*) Soft-headed. Like his
Maw. Dead spit 'n' image. No hope in him! (*He spits with con-
temptuous disgust*) A born fool! (*Then matter-of-factly*) Waal—
I'm gitin' peckish. (*He goes toward door*).

CURTAIN

Part Three
Scene One

A *night in late spring the following year. The kitchen and the two
bedrooms upstairs are shown. The two bedrooms are dimly lighted by
a tallow candle in each.* EBEN *is sitting on the side of the bed in his
room, his chin propped on his fists, his face a study of the struggle
he is making to understand his conflicting emotions. The noisy
laughter and music from below where a kitchen dance is in progress
annoy and distract him. He scowls at the floor.*

In the next room a cradle stands beside the double bed.

In the kitchen all is festivity. The stove has been taken down to give more room to the dancers. The chairs, with wooden benches added, have been pushed back against the walls. On these are seated, squeezed in tight against one another, farmers and their wives and their young folks of both sexes from the neighboring farms. They are all chattering and laughing loudly. They evidently have some secret joke in common. There is no end of winking, of nudging, of meaning nods of the head toward CABOT *who, in a state of extreme hilarious excitement increased by the amount he has drunk, is standing near the rear door where there is a small keg of whisky and serving drinks to all the men. In the left corner, front, dividing the attention with her husband,* ABBIE *is sitting in a rocking chair, a shawl wrapped about her shoulders. She is very pale, her face is thin and drawn, her eyes are fixed anxiously on the open door in rear as if waiting for someone.*

The musician is tuning up his fiddle, seated in the far right corner. He is a lanky young fellow with a long, weak face. His pale eyes blink incessantly and he grins about him slyly with a greedy malice.

ABBIE   (*suddenly turning to a young girl on her right*) Whar's Eben?

YOUNG GIRL   (*eyeing her scornfully*) I dunno, Mrs. Cabot. I hain't seen Eben in ages. (*Meaningly*) Seems like he's spent most o' his time t' hum since yew come.

ABBIE   (*vaguely*) I tuk his Maw's place.

YOUNG GIRL   Ay-eh. So I've heerd. (*She turns away to retail this bit of gossip to her mother sitting next to her.* ABBIE *turns to her left to a big stoutish middle-aged man whose flushed face and starting eyes show the amount of "likker" he has consumed*).

ABBIE   Ye hain't seen Eben, hev ye?

MAN   No, I hain't. (*Then he adds with a wink*) If yew hain't, who would?

ABBIE   He's the best dancer in the county. He'd ought t' come an' dance.

MAN   (*with a wink*) Mebbe he's doin' the dutiful an' walkin' the kid t' sleep. It's a boy, hain't it?

ABBIE   (*nodding vaguely*) Ay-eh—born two weeks back—purty's a picter.

MAN   They all is—t' their Maws. (*Then in a whisper, with a nudge and a leer*) Listen, Abbie—if ye ever git tired o' Eben, remember me! Don't fergit now! (*He looks at her uncomprehending face for a second—then grunts disgustedly*) Waal—guess I'll likker agin. (*He goes over and joins* CABOT *who is arguing noisily with an old farmer over cows. They all drink*).

ABBIE   (*this time appealing to nobody in particular*) Wonder what Eben's a-doin'? (*Her remark is repeated down the line with many a guffaw and titter until it reaches the fiddler. He fastens his blinking eyes on* ABBIE).

FIDDLER   (*raising his voice*) Bet I kin tell ye, Abbie, what Eben's doin'! He's down t' the church offerin' up prayers o' thanksgivin'. (*They all titter expectantly*).

A MAN   What fur? (*Another titter*).

FIDDLER 'Cause unto him a—(*He hesitates just long enough*) brother is born! (*A roar of laughter. They all look from* ABBIE *to* CABOT. *She is oblivious, staring at the door.* CABOT, *although he hasn't heard the words, is irritated by the laughter and steps forward, glaring about him. There is an immediate silence*).

CABOT What're ye all bleatin' about—like a flock o' goats? Why don't ye dance, damn ye? I axed ye here t' dance—t' eat, drink an' be merry—an' thar ye set cacklin' like a lot o' wet hens with the pip! Ye've swilled my likker an' guzzled my vittles like hogs, hain't ye? Then dance fur me, can't ye? That's fa'r an' squar', hain't it? (*A grumble of resentment goes around but they are all evidently in too much awe of him to express it openly*).

FIDDLER (*slyly*) We're waitin fur Eben. (*A suppressed laugh*).

CABOT (*with a fierce exultation*) T'hell with Eben! Eben's done fur now! I got a new son! (*His mood switching with drunken suddenness*) But ye needn't t' laugh at Eben, none o' ye! He's my blood, if he be a dumb fool. He's better nor any o' yew! He kin do a day's work a'most up t' what I kin—an' that'd put any o' yew pore critters t' shame!

FIDDLER An' he kin do a good night's work too! (*A roar of laughter*).

CABOT Laugh, ye damn fools! Ye're right jist the same, Fiddler. He kin work day an' night too, like I kin, if need be!

OLD FARMER (*from behind the keg where he is weaving drunkenly back and forth—with great simplicity*) They hain't many t' touch ye, Ephraim—a son at seventy-six. That's a hard man fur ye! I be on'y sixty-eight an' I couldn't do it. (*A roar of laughter in which* CABOT *joins uproariously*).

CABOT (*slapping him on the back*) I'm sorry fur ye, Hi. I'd never suspicion sech weakneesss from a boy like yew!

OLD FARMER An' I never reckoned yew had it in ye nuther, Ephraim. (*There is another laugh*).

CABOT (*suddenly grim*)I got a lot in me—a hell of a lot—folks don't know on. (*Turning to the fiddler*) Fiddle 'er up, durn ye! Give 'em somethin' t' dance t'! What air ye, an ornament? Hain't this a celebration? Then grease yer elbow an' go it!

FIDDLER (*seizes a drink which the* OLD FARMER *holds out to him and downs it*) Here goes! (*He starts to fiddle "Lady of the Lake."* Four young fellows and four girls form in two lines and dance a square dance. The FIDDLER shouts directions for the different movements, keeping his words in the rhythm of the music and interspersing them with jocular personal remarks to the dancers themselves. The people seated along the walls stamp their feet and clap their hands in unison. CABOT is especially active in this respect. Only ABBIE remains apathetic, staring at the door as if she were alone in a silent room*).

FIDDLER Swing your partner t' the right! That's it, Jim! Give her a b'ar hug! Her Haw hain't lookin'. (*Laughter*) Change partners! That suits ye, don't it, Essie, now ye got Reub afore ye? Look at her redden up, will ye? Waal, life is short an' so's love, as the feller says. (*Laughter*).

CABOT   (*excitedly, stamping his foot*) Go it, boys! Go it, gals!

FIDDLER   (*with a wink at the others*) Ye're the spryest seventy-six ever I sees, Ephraim! Now if ye'd on'y good eyesight . . . ! (*Suppressed laughter. He gives* CABOT *no chance to retort but roars*) Promenade! Ye're walkin' like a bride down the aisle, Sarah! Waal, while they's life they's allus hope, I've heerd tell. Swing your partner to the left! Gosh A'mighty, look at Johnny Cook high-steppin'! They hain't goin' t'be much strength left fur howin' in the corn lot t'morrow. (*Laughter*).

CABOT   Go it! Go it! (*Then suddenly, unable to restrain himself any longer, he prances into the midst of the dancers, scattering them, waving his arms about wildly*) Ye're all hoofs! Git out o' my road! Give me room! I'll show ye dancin'. Ye're all too soft! (*He pushes them roughly away. They crowd back toward the walls, muttering, looking at him resentfully*).

FIDDLER   (*jeeringly*) Go it, Ephraim! Go it! (*He starts "Pop Goes the Weasel," increasing the tempo with every verse until at the end he is fiddling crazily as fast as he can go*).

CABOT   (*starts to dance, which he does very well and with tremendous vigor. Then he begins to improvise, cuts incredibly grotesque capers, leaping up and cracking his heels togther, prancing around in a circle with body bent in an Indian war dance, then suddenly straightening up and kicking as high as he can with both legs. He is like a monkey on a string. And all the while he intersperses his antics with shouts and derisive comments*) Whoop! Here's dancin' fur ye! Whoop! See that! Seventy-six, if I'm a day! Hard as iron yet! Beatin' the young 'uns like I allus done! Look at me! I'd invite ye t' dance on my hundredth birthday-on'y ye'll all be dead by then. Ye're a sickly generation! Yer hearts air pink, not red! Yer veins is full o' mud an' water! I be the on'y man in the county! Whoop! See that! I'm a Injun! I've killed Injuns in the West afore ye was born—an' skulped 'em too! They's a arrer wound on my backside I c'd show ye! The hull tribe chased me. I outrun 'em all—with the arrer stuck in me! An' I tuk vengeance on 'em. Ten eyes fur an eye, that was my motter! Whoop! Look at me! I kin kick the ceilin' off the room! Whoop!

FIDDLER   (*stops playing—exhaustedly*) God A'mighty, I got enuf. Ye got the devil's strength in ye.

CABOT   (*delightedly*) Did I beat yew, too? Wa'al, ye played smart. Hev a swig. (*He pours whisky for himself and* FIDDLER. *They drink. The others watch* CABOT *silently with cold, hostile eyes. There is a dead pause. The* FIDDLER *rests.* CABOT *leans against the keg, panting, glaring around him confusedly. In the room above,* EBEN *gets to his feet and tiptoes out the door in rear, appearing a moment later in the other bedroom. He moves silently, even frightenedly, toward the cradle and stands there looking down at the baby. His face is as vague as his reactions are confused, but there is a trace of tenderness, of interested discovery. At the same moment that he reaches the cradle,* ABBIE *seems to sense something. She gets up weakly and goes to* CABOT).

ABBIE   I'm goin' up t' the baby.

CABOT   (*with real solicitation*) Air ye able fur the stairs? D'ye want
me t' help ye, Abbie?

ABBIE   No. I'm able. I'll be down agen soon.

CABOT   Don't ye git wore out! He needs ye, remember—our son
does! (*He grins affectionately, patting her on the back. She shrinks
from his touch*).

ABBIE   (*dully*) Don't—tech me. I'm goin'—up. (*She goes. CABOT
looks after her. A whisper goes around the room. CABOT turns. It
ceases. He wipes his forehead streaming with sweat. He is breathing pantingly*).

CABOT   I'm a-goin' out t' git fresh air. I'm feelin' a mite dizzy.
Fiddle up thar! Dance, all o'ye! Here's likker fur them as wants
it. Enjoy yerselves. I'll be back. (*He goes, closing the door behind
him*).

FIDDLER   (*sarcastically*) Don't hurry none on our account! (*A suppressed laugh. He imitates* ABBIE) Whar's Eben? (*More laughter*).

A WOMAN   (*loudly*) What's happened in this house is plain as the
nose on yer face! (*ABBIE appears in the doorway upstairs and stands
looking in surprise and adoration at* EBEN *who does not see her*).

A MAN   Ssshh! He's li-ble t' be listenin' at the door. That'd be like
him. (*Their voices die to an intensive whispering. Their faces are
concentrated on this gossip. A noise as of dead leaves in the wind
comes from the room.* CABOT *has come out from the porch and
stands by the gate, leaning on it, staring at the sky blinkingly.*
ABBIE *comes across the room silently.* EBEN *does not notice her
until quite near*).

EBEN   (*starting*) Abbie!

ABBIE   Ssshh! (*She throws her arms around him. They kiss—then
bend over the cradle together*) Ain't he purty?—dead spit 'n' image
o' yew!

EBEN   (*pleased*) Air he? I can't tell none.

ABBIE   E-zactly like!

EBEN   (*frowningly*) I don't like this. I don't like lettin' on what's
mine's his'n. I been doin' that all my life. I'm gittin t' the end o'
b'arin' it!

ABBIE   (*putting her finger on his lips*) We're doin' the best we kin.
We got t' wait. Somethin's bound t' happen. (*She puts her arms
around him*) I got t' go back.

EBEN   I'm goin' out. I can't b'ar it with the fiddle playin' an' the
laughin'.

ABBIE   Don't git feelin' low. I love ye, Eben. Kiss me. (*He kisses
her. They remain in each other's arms*).

CABOT   (*at the gate, confusedly*) Even the music can't drive it out—
somethin'. Ye kin feel it droppin' off the elums, climbin' up the
roof, sneakin' down the chimney, pokin' in the corners! They's no
peace in houses, they's no rest livin' with folks. Somethin's always
livin' with ye. (*With a deep sigh*) I'll go t' the barn an' rest a
spell. (*He goes wearily toward the barn*).

FIDDLER   (*tuning up*) Let's celebrate the old skunk gittin' fooled!

We kin have some fun now he's went. (*He starts to fiddle "Turkey in the Straw." There is real merriment now. The young folks get up to dance*).

CURTAIN

Scene Two

*A half-hour later—Exterior—*EBEN *is standing by the gate looking up at the sky, an expression of dumb pain bewildered by itself on his face.* CABOT *appears, returning from the barn, walking wearily, his eyes on the ground. He sees* EBEN *and his whole mood immediately changes. He becomes excited, a cruel, triumphant grin comes to his lips, he strides up and slaps* EBEN *on the back. From within comes the whining of the fiddle and the noise of stamping feet and laughing voices.*

CABOT   So har ye be!

EBEN   (*startled, stares at him with hatred for a moment—then dully*) Ay-eh.

CABOT   (*surveying him jeeringly*) Why hain't ye been in t' dance? They was all axin' fur ye.

EBEN   Let 'em ax!

CABOT   They's a hull passel o' purty gals.

EBEN   T' hell with 'em!

CABOT   Ye'd ought t' be marryin' one o' 'em soon.

EBEN   I hain't marryin' no one.

CABOT   Ye might 'arn a share o' a farm that way.

EBEN   (*with a sneer*) Like yew did, ye mean? I hain't that kind.

CABOT   (*stung*) Ye lie! 'Twas yer Maw's folks aimed t' steal my farm from me.

EBEN   Other folks don't say so. (*After a pause—defiantly*) An' I got a farm, anyways!

CABOT   (*derisively*) Whar?

EBEN   (*stamps a foot on the ground*) Har!

CABOT   (*throws his head back and laughs coarsely*) Ho-ho! Ye hev, hev ye? Waal, that's a good un!

EBEN   (*controlling himself—grimly*) Ye'll see!

CABOT   (*stares at him suspiciously, trying to make him out—a pause —then with scornful confidence*) Ay-eh. I'll see. So'll ye. It's ye that's blind—blind as a mole underground. (EBEN *suddenly laughs, one short sardonic bark: "Ha." A pause.* CABOT *peers at him with renewed suspicion*) Whar air ye hawin' 'bout? (EBEN *turns away without answering.* CABOT *grows angry*) God A'mighty, yew air a dumb dunce! They's nothin' in that thick skull o' your'n but noise—like a empty keg it be! (EBEN *doesn't seem to hear.* CABOT's *rage grows*) Yewr farm! God A'mighty! If we wa'n't a born donkey ye'd know ye'll never own stick nor stone on it, specially now arter him bein' born. It's his'n, I tell ye—his'n arter I die—but I'll live a hundred jest t' fool ye all—an' he'll be growed then—yewr age a'most! (EBEN *laughs again his sardonic "Ha."* *This drives* CABOT *into a fury*) Ha? Ye think ye kin git 'round that someways, do ye? Waal, it'll be her'n, too—Abbie's—ye won't git 'round her—she knows yer tricks—she'll be too much fur ye— she wants the farm her'n—she was afeerd o' ye—she told me ye was sneakin' 'round tryin' t' make love t' her t' git her on yer side ... ye ... ye mad fool, ye! (*He raises his clenched fists threateningly*).

EBEN (*is confronting him choking with rage*) Ye lie, ye old skunk! Abbie never said no sech thing!

CABOT (*suddenly triumphant when he sees how shaken* EBEN *is*) She did. An' I says, I'll blow his brains t' the top o' them elums— an' she says no, that hain't sense, who'll ye git t' help ye on the farm in his place—an' then she says yew'n me ought t' have a son—I know we kin, she says—an' I says, if we do, ye kin have anythin' I've got ye've a mind t'. An' she says, I wants Eben cut off so's this farm'll be mine when ye die! (*With terrible gloating*) An that's what's happened, hain't it? An' the farm's her'n! An' the dust o' the road—that's you'rn! Ha! Now who's hawin'?

EBEN (*has been listening, petrified with grief and rage—suddenly laughs wildly and brokenly*) Ha-ha-ha! So that's her sneakin' game —all along!—like I suspicioned at fust—t' swaller it all—an' me, too ... ! (*Madly*) I'll murder her! (*He springs toward the porch but* CABOT *is quicker and gets in between*).

CABOT No, ye don't!

EBEN Git out o' my road! (*He tries to throw* CABOT *aside. They grapple in what becomes immediately a murderous struggle. The old man's concentrated strength is too much for* EBEN. CABOT *gets one hand on his throat and presses him back across the stone well. At the same moment,* ABBIE *comes out on the porch. With a stifled cry she runs toward them*).

ABBIE Eben! Ephraim! (*She tugs at the hand on* EBEN's *throat*) Let go, Ephraim! Ye're chokin' him!

CABOT (*removes his hand and flings* EBEN *sideways full length on the grass, gasping and choking. With a cry,* ABBIE *kneels beside him, trying to take his head on her lap, but he pushes her away.* CABOT *stands looking down with fierce triumph*) Ye needn't t've fret, Abbie, I wa'n't aimin' t' kill him. He hain't wuth hangin' fur—not by a hell of a sight! (*More and more triumphantly*) Seventy-six an' him not thirty yit—an' look whar he be fur thinkin' his Paw was easy! No, by God, I hain't easy! An' him upstairs, I'll raise him t' be like me! (*He turns to leave them*) I'm goin' in an' dance!—sing an' celebrate! (*He walks to the porch—then turns with a great grin*) I don't calc'late it's left in him, but if he gits pesky, Abbie, ye jest sing out. I'll come a-runnin' an' by the Etarnal, I'll put him across my knee an' birch him! Ha-ha-ha! (*He goes into the house laughing. A moment later his loud "whoop" is heard*).

ABBIE (*tenderly*) Eben. Air ye hurt? (*She tries to kiss him but he pushes her violently away and struggles to a sitting position*).

EBEN (*gaspingly*) T' hell—with ye!

ABBIE (*not believing her ears*) It's me, Eben—Abbie—don't ye
know me?

EBEN (*glowering at her with hatred*) Ay-eh—I know ye—now! (*He
suddenly breaks down, sobbing weakly*).

ABBIE (*fearfully*) Eben—what's happened t' ye—why did ye look
at me 's if ye hated me?

EBEN (*violently, between sobs and gasps*) I do hate ye! Ye're a
whore—a damn trickin' whore!

ABBIE (*shrinking back horrified*) Eben! Ye don't know what ye're
sayin'!

EBEN (*scrambling to his feet and following her—accusingly*) Ye're
nothin' but a stinkin' passel o' lies! Ye've been lyin' t' me every
word ye spoke, day an' night, since we fust—done it. Ye've kept
sayin' ye loved me. . . .

ABBIE · (*frantically*) I do love ye (*She takes his hand but he flings
her away*).

EBEN (*unheeding*) Ye've made a fool o' me—a sick, dumb fool—
a-purpose! Ye've been on'y playin' yer sneakin', stealin' game all
along—gittin' me t' lie with ye so's ye'd hev a son he'd think was
his'n, an' makin' him promise he'd give ye the farm and let me
eat dust, if ye did git him a son! (*Staring at her with anguished,
bewildered eyes*)They must be a devil livin' in ye! T'ain't human
t' be as bad as that be!

ABBIE (*stunned—dully*) He told yew . . . ?

EBEN   Hain't it true? It hain't no good in yew lyin'.

ABBIE (*pleadingly*) Eben, listen—ye must listen—it was long ago
—afore we done nothin'—yew was scornin' me—goin' t' see Min—
when I was lovin' ye—an' I said it t' him t' git vengeance on ye!

EBEN (*unheedingly. With tortured passion*) I wish ye was dead!
I wish I was dead along with ye afore this come! (*Ragingly*) But
I'll git my vengeance too! I'll pray Maw t' come back t' help me—
t' put her cuss on yew an' him!

ABBIE (*brokenly*) Don't ye, Eben! Don't ye! (*She throws herself
on her knees before him, weeping*) I didn't mean t' do bad t' ye!
Fergive me, won't ye?

EBEN (*not seeming to hear her—fiercely*) I'll git squar' with the
old skunk—an' yew! I'll tell him the truth 'bout the son he's so
proud o'! Then I'll leave ye here t' pizen each other—with Maw
comin' out o' her grave at nights—an' I'll go t' the gold fields o'
Californi-a whar Sim an' Peter be!

ABBIE (*terrified*) Ye won't—leave me? Ye can't!

EBEN (*with fierce determination*) I'm a-goin', I tell ye! I'll git rich
thar an' come back an' fight him fur the farm he stole—an' I'll
kick ye both out in the road—t' beg an' sleep in the woods—an'
yer son along with ye—t' starve an' die! (*He is hysterical at the
end*).

ABBIE (*with a shudder—humbly*) He's yewr son, too, Eben.

EBEN (*torturedly*) I wish he never was born! I wish he'd die this
minit! I wish I'd never sot eyes on him! It's him—yew havin'
him—a-purpose t' steal—that's changed everythin'!

ABBIE   (*gently*) Did ye believe I loved ye—afore he come?

EBEN   Ay-eh—like a dumb ox!

ABBIE   An' ye don't believe no more?

EBEN   B'lieve a lyin' thief! Ha!

ABBIE   (*shudders—then humbly*) An' did ye r'ally love me afore?

EBEN   (*brokenly*) Ay-eh—an' ye was trickin' me!

ABBIE   An' ye don't love me now!

EBEN   (*violently*) I hate ye, I tell ye!

ABBIE   An' ye're truly goin' West—goin' t' leave me—all account o' him being born?

EBEN   I'm a-goin' in the mornin'—or may God strike me t' hell!

ABBIE   (*after a pause—with a dreadful cold intensity—slowly*) If that's what his comin 's done t' me—killin' yewr love—takin' yew away—my on'y joy—the on'y joy I ever knowed—like heaven t' me—purtier'n heaven—then I hate him, too, even if I be his Maw!

EBEN   (*bitterly*) Lies! Ye love him! He'll steal the farm fur ye! (*Brokenly*) But t'ain't the farm so much—not no more—it's yew foolin' me—gittin' me t' love ye—lyin' yew loved me—jest t' git a son t' steal!

ABBIE   (*distractedly*) He won't steal! I'd kill him fust! I do love ye! I'll prove t' ye . . . !

EBEN   (*harshly*) T'ain't no use lyin' no more. I'm deaf t' ye! (*He turns away*) I hain't seein' ye agen. Good-by!

ABBIE   (*pale with anguish*) Hain't ye even goin' t' kiss me—not once—arter all we loved?

EBEN   (*in a hard voice*) I hain't wantin' t' kiss ye never agen! I'm wantin' t' forgit I ever sot eyes on ye!

ABBIE   Eben!—ye mustn't—wait a spell—I want t' tell ye. . . .

EBEN   I'm a-goin' in t' git drunk. I'm a-goin' t' dance.

ABBIE   (*clinging to his arm—with passionate earnestness*) If I could make it—'s if he'd never come up between us—if I could prove t' ye I wa'n't schemin' t' steal from ye—so's everythin' could be jest the same with us, lovin' each other jest the same, kissin' an' happy the same's we've been happy afore he come—if I could do it— ye'd love me agen, wouldn't ye? Ye'd kiss me agen? Ye wouldn't never leave me, would ye?

EBEN   (*moved*) I calc'late not. (*Then shaking her hand off his arm —with a bitter smile*) But ye hain't God, be ye?

ABBIE   (*exultantly*) Remember ye've promised! (*Then with strange intensity*) Mebbe I kin take back one thin' God does!

EBEN   (*peering at her*) Ye're gittin' cracked, hain't ye? (*Then going towards door*) I'm a-goin' t' dance.

ABBIE   (*calls after him intensely*) I'll prove t' ye! I'll prove I love ye better'n. . . . (*He goes in the door, not seeming to hear. She remains standing where she is, looking after him—then she finishes desperately*) Better'n everythin' else in the world!

CURTAIN

Scene Three

Just before dawn in the morning—shows the kitchen and CABOT'S *bedroom. In the kitchen, by the light of a tallow candle on the table,* EBEN *is sitting, his chin propped on his hands, his drawn face blank and expressionless. His carpetbag is on the floor beside him. In the bedroom, dimly lighted by a small whale-oil lamp,* CABOT *lies asleep.* ABBIE *is bending over the cradle, listening, her face full of terror yet with an undercurrent of desperate triumph. Suddenly, she breaks down and sobs, appears about to throw herself on her knees beside the cradle; but the old man turns restlessly, groaning in his sleep, and she controls herself, and, shrinking away from the cradle with a gesture of horror, backs swiftly toward the door in rear and goes out. A moment later she comes into the kitchen and, running to* EBEN, *flings her arms about his neck and kisses him wildly. He hardens himself, he remains unmoved and cold, he keeps his eyes straight ahead.*

ABBIE (*hysterically*) I done it, Eben! I told ye I'd do it! I've proved I love ye—better'n everythin'—so's ye can't never doubt me no more!

EBEN (*dully*) Whatever ye done, it hain't no good now.

ABBIE (*wildly*) Don't ye say that! Kiss me, Eben, won't ye? I need ye t' kiss me arter what I done! I need ye t' say ye love me!

EBEN (*kisses her without emotion—dully*) That's fur goodby. I'm a-goin' soon.

ABBIE No! No! Ye won't go—not now!

EBEN (*going on with his own thoughts*) I been a-thinkin'—an' I hain't goin' t' tell Paw nothin'. I'll leave Maw t' take vengeance on ye. If I told him, the old skunk'd jest be stinkin' mean enuf to take it out on that baby. (*His voice showing emotion in spite of him*) An' I don't want nothin' bad t' happen t' him. He hain't t' blame fur yew. (*He adds with a certain queer pride*) An' he looks like me! An' by God, he's mine! An' some day I'll be a-comin' back an' . . . !

ABBIE (*too absorbed in her own thoughts to listen to him— pleadingly*) They's no cause fur ye t' go now—they's no sense— it's all the same's it was—they's nothin' come b'tween us now— arter what I done!

EBEN (*something in her voice arouses him. He stares at her a bit frightenedly*) Ye look mad, Abbie. What did ye do?

ABBIE I—I killed him, Eben.

EBEN (*amazed*) Ye killed him?

ABBIE (*dully*) Ay-eh.

EBEN (*recovering from his astonishment—savagely*) An' serves him right! But we got t' do somethin' quick t' make it look 's if the old skunk'd killed himself when he was drunk. We kin prove by 'em all how drunk he got.

ABBIE (*wildly*) No! No! Not him! (*Laughing distractedly*) But that's what I ought t' done, hain't it? I oughter killed him instead! Why didn't ye tell me?

EBEN   (*appalled*) Instead? What d'ye mean?

ABBIE   Not him.

EBEN   (*his face grown ghastly*) Not—not that baby!

ABBIE   (*dully*) Ay-eh?

EBEN   (*falls to his knees as if he'd been struck—his voice trembling with horror*) Oh, God A'mighty! A'mighty God! Maw, whar was ye, why didn't ye stop her?

ABBIE   (*simply*) She went back t' her grave that night we fust done it, remember? I hain't felt her about since. (*A pause.* EBEN *hides his head in his hands, trembling all over as if he had the ague. She goes on dully*) I left the piller over his little face. Then he killed himself. He stopped breathin'. (*She begins to weep softly*).

EBEN   (*rage beginning to mingle with grief*) He looked like me. He was mine, damn ye!

ABBIE   (*slowly and brokenly*) I didn't want t' do it. I hated myself fur doin' it. I loved him. He was so purty—dead spit 'n' image o' yew. But I loved yew more—an' yew was goin' away—far off whar I'd never see ye agen, never kiss ye, never feel ye pressed agin me agen—an' ye said ye hated me fur havin' him—ye said ye hated him an' wished he was dead—ye said if it hadn't been fur him comin' it'd be the same's afore between us.

EBEN   (*unable to endure this, springs to his feet in a fury, threatening her, his twiching fingers seeming to reach out for her throat*) Ye lie! I never said—I never dreamed ye'd—I'd cut off my head afore I'd hurt his finger!

ABBIE   (*piteously, sinking on her knees*) Eben, don't ye look at me like that—hatin' me—not after what I done fur ye—fur us—so's we could be happy agen—

EBEN   (*furiously now*) Shut up, or I'll kill ye! I see yer game now— the same old sneakin' trick—ye're aimin' t' blame me fur the murder ye done!

ABBIE   (*moaning—putting her hands over her ears*) Don't ye, Eben! Don't ye! (*She grasps his legs*).

EBEN   (*his mood suddenly changing to horror, shrinks away from her*) Don't ye tech me! Ye're pizen! How could ye—t' murder a pore little critter—Ye must've swapped yer soul t' hell! (*Suddenly raging*) Ha! I kin see why ye done it! Not the lies ye jest told— but 'cause ye wanted t' steal agen—steal the last thin' ye'd left me—my part o' him—no, the hull o' him—ye saw he looked like me—ye knowed he was all mine—an' ye couldn't b'ar it—I know ye! Ye killed him fur bein' mine! (*All this has driven him almost insane. He makes a rush past her for the door—then turns—shaking both fists at her, violently*) But I'll take vengeance now! I'll git the Sheriff! I'll tell him everythin'! Then I'll sing "I'm off to Californi-a!" an' go—gold—Golden Gate—gold sun—fields o' gold in the West! (*This last he half shouts, half croons incoherently, suddenly breaking off passionately*) I'm a-goin' fur the Sheriff t' come an' git ye! I want ye tuk away, locked up from me! I can't stand t' luk at ye! Murderer an' thief 'r not, ye still tempt me! I'll give ye up t' the Sheriff (*He turns and runs out, around the corner of house, panting and sobbing, and breaks into a swerving sprint down the road*).

ABBIE (*struggling to her feet, runs to the door, calling after him*) I love ye, Eben! I love ye! (*She stops at the door weakly, swaying, about to fall*) I don't care what ye do—if ye'll on'y love me agen— (*She falls limply to the floor in a faint*).

CURTAIN

Scene Four

About an hour later. Same as Scene Three. Shows the kitchen and CABOT's *bedroom. It is after dawn. The sky is brilliant with the sunrise. In the kitchen,* ABBIE *sits at the table, her body limp and exhausted, her head bowed down over her arms, her face hidden. Upstairs,* CABOT *is still asleep but awakens with a start. He looks toward the window and gives a snort of surprise and irritation—throws back the covers and begins hurriedly pulling on his clothes. Without looking behind him, he begins talking to* ABBIE *whom he supposes beside him.*

CABOT   Thunder 'n' lightin', Abbie! I hain't slept this late in fifty year! Looks 's if the sun was full riz a'most. Must've been the dancin' an' likker. Must be gittin' old. I hope Eben's t' wuk. Ye might've tuk the trouble t' rouse me, Abbie. (*He turns—sees no one there—surprised*) Waal—whar air she? Gittin' vittles. I calc'-late. (*He tiptoes to the cradle and peers down—proudly*) Mornin', sonny. Purty's a picture! Sleepin' sound. He don't beller all night like most o' 'em. (*He goes quietly out the door in rear—a few moments later enters kitchen—sees* ABBIE—*with satisfaction*) So thar ye be. Ye got any vittles cooked?

ABBIE   (*without moving*) No.

CABOT   (*coming to her, almost sympathetically*) Ye feelin' sick?

ABBIE   No.

CABOT   (*pats her on shoulder. She shudders*) Ye'd best lie down a spell. (*Half jocularly*) Yer son'll be needin' ye soon. He'd ought t' wake up with a gnashin' appetite, the sound way he's sleepin'.

ABBIE   (*shudders—then in a dead voice*) He hain't never goin' t' wake up.

CABOT   (*jokingly*) Takes after me this mornin'. I hain't slept so late in . . .

ABBIE   He's dead.

CABOT   (*stares at her—bewilderedly*) What. . . .

ABBIE   I killed him.

CABOT   (*stepping back from her—aghast*) Air ye drunk—'r crazy— 'r . . . !

ABBIE (*suddenly lifts her head and turns on him—wildly*) I killed
him, I tell ye! I smothered him. Go up an' see if ye don't b'lieve
me! (CABOT *stares at her a second, then bolts out the rear door—
can be heard bounding up the stairs—and rushes into the bedroom and over to the cradle.* ABBIE *has sunk back lifelessly into her
former position.* CABOT *puts his hand down on the body in the
crib. An expression of fear and horror comes over his face*).

CABOT (*shrinking away—tremblingly*) God A'mighty! God A'-
mighty. (*He stumbles out the door—in a short while returns to
the kitchen—comes to* ABBIE, *the stunned expression still on
his face—hoarsely*) Why did ye do it? Why? (*As she doesn't
answer, he grabs her violently by the shoulder and shakes her*) I
ax ye why ye done it! Ye'd better tell me 'r . . . !

ABBIE (*gives him a furious push which sends him staggering back
and springs to her feet—with wild rage and hatred*) Don't ye dare
tech me! What right hev ye t' question me 'bout him? He wa'n't
yewr son! Think I'd have a son by yew? I'd die fust! I hate the
sight o' ye an' allus did! It's yew I should've murdered, if I'd had
good sense! I hate ye! I love Eben. I did from the fust. An' he was
Eben's son—mine an' Eben's—not your'n!

CABOT (*stands looking a her dazedly—a pause—finding his words
with an effort—dully*) That was it—what I felt—pokin' round
the corners—while ye lied—holdin' yerself from me—sayin' ye'd
a'ready conceived—(*He lapses into crushed silence—then with a
strange emotion*) He's dead, sart'n. I felt his heart. Pore little
critter! (*He blinks back one tear, wiping his sleeve across his nose*).

ABBIE (*hysterically*) Don't ye! Don't ye! (*She sobs unrestrainedly*).

CABOT (*with a concentrated effort that stiffens his body into a
rigid line and hardens his face into a stony mask—through his
teeth to himself*) I got t' be—like a stone—a rock o' jedgment!
(*A pause. He gets complete control over himself—harshly*) If he
was Eben's, I be glad he air gone! An' mebbe I suspicioned it all
along. I felt they was somethin' onnateral—somewhars—the house
got so lonesome—an' cold—drivin' me down t' the barn—t' the
beasts o' the field. . . . Ay-eh. I must've suspicioned—somethin'.
Ye didn't fool me—not altogether, leastways—I'm too old a bird
—growin' ripe on the bough. . . . (*He becomes aware he is wandering, straightens again, looks at* ABBIE *with a cruel grin*) So ye'd
like t' hev murdered me 'stead o' him, would ye? Waal, I'll live to
a hundred! I'll live t' see ye hung! I'll deliver ye up t' the jedgment o' God an' the law! I'll git the Sheriff now. (*Starts for the
door*).

ABBIE (*dully*) Ye needn't. Eben's gone fur him.

CABOT (*amazed*) Eben—gone fur the Sheriff?

ABBIE Ay-eh.

CABOT T' inform agen ye?

ABBIE Ay-eh.

CABOT (*considers this—a pause—then in a hard voice*) Waal, I'm
thankful fur him savin' me the trouble. I'll git t' wuk. (*He goes
to the door—then turns—in a voice full of strange emotion*) He'd

ought t' been my son, Abbie. Ye'd ought t' loved me. I'm a man.
If ye'd loved me, I'd never told no Sheriff on ye no matter what
ye did, if they was t' brile me alive!

ABBIE   (*defensively*) They's more to it nor yew know, makes him
tell.

CABOT   (*dryly*) Fur yewr sake, I hope they be. (*He goes out—comes
around to the gate—stares up at the sky. His control relaxes. For
a moment he is old and weary. He murmurs despairingly*) God
A'mighty, I be lonesomer'n ever! (*He hears running footsteps from
the left, immediately is himself again.* EBEN *runs in, panting exhaustedly, wild-eyed and mad looking. He lurches through the
gate.* CABOT *grabs him by the shoulder.* EBEN *stares at him dumbly*)
Did ye tell the Sheriff?

EBEN   (*nodding stupidly*) Ay-eh.

CABOT   (*gives him a push away that sends him sprawling—laughing
with withering contempt*) Good fur ye! A prime chip o'yer Maw
ye be! (*He goes toward the barn, laughing harshly.* EBEN *scrambles
to his feet. Suddenly* CABOT *turns—grimly threatening*) Git off this
farm when the Sheriff takes her—or, by God, he'll have t' come
back an' git me fur murder, too! (*He stalks off.* EBEN *does not appear to have heard him. He runs to the door and comes into the
kitchen.* ABBIE *looks up with a cry of anguished joy.* EBEN *stumbles
over and throws himself on his knees beside her—sobbing brokenly*).

EBEN   Fergive me!

ABBIE   (*happily*) Eben! (*She kisses him and pulls his head over
against her breast*).

EBEN   I love ye! Fergive me!

ABBIE   (*ecstatically*) I'd fergive ye all the sins in hell fur sayin' that!
(*She kisses his head, pressing it to her with a fierce passion of possession*).

EBEN   (*brokenly*) But I told the Sheriff. He's comin' fur ye!

ABBIE   I kin b'ar what happens t' me—now!

EBEN   I woke him up. I told him. He says, wait 'til I git dressed. I
was waiting. I got to thinkin' o' yew. I got to thinkin' how I'd
loved ye. It hurt like somethin' was bustin' in my chest an' head.
I got t' cryin'. I knowed sudden I loved ye yet, an' allus would
love ye!

ABBIE   (*caressing his hair—tenderly*) My boy, hain't ye?

EBEN   I begun t' run back. I cut across the fields an' through the
woods. I thought ye might have time t' run away—with me—
an' . . .

ABBIE   (*shaking her head*) I got t' take my punishment—t' pay fur
my sin.

EBEN   Then I want t' share it with ye.

ABBIE   Ye didn't do nothin'.

EBEN   I put it in yer head. I wisht he was dead! I as much as urged
ye t' do it!

ABBIE   No. It was me alone!

EBEN   I'm as guilty as yew be! He was the child o' our sin.

ABBIE (*lifting her head as if defying God*) I don't repent that sin!
I hain't askin' God t' fergive that!

EBEN Nor me—but it led up t' the other—an' the murder ye did,
ye did 'count o' me—an' it's my murder, too. I'll tell the Sheriff—
an' if ye deny it, I'll say we planned it t'gether—an' they'll all
b'lieve me, fur they suspicion everythin' we've done, an' it'll seem
likely an' true to 'em. An' it is true—way down. I did help ye—
somehow.

ABBIE (*laying her head on his—sobbing*) No! I don't want yew t'
suffer!

EBEN I got t' pay fur my part o' the sin! An' I'd suffer wust leavin'
ye, goin' West, thinkin' o' ye day an' night, bein' out when yew
was in— (*Lowering his voice*) 'r bein' alive when yew was dead.
(*A pause*) I want t' share with ye, Abbie—prison 'r death 'r hell
'r anythin'! (*He looks into her eyes and forces a trembling smile*)
If I'm sharin' with ye, I won't feel lonesome, leastways.

ABBIE (*weakly*) Eben! I won't let ye! I can't let ye!

EBEN (*kissing her—tenderly*) Ye can't he'p yerself. I got ye beat
fur once!

ABBIE (*forcing a smile—adoringly*) I hain't beat—s'long's I got
ye!

EBEN (*hears the sound of feet outside*) Ssshh! Listen! They've come
t' take us!

ABBIE No, it's him. Don't give him no chance to fight ye, Eben.
Don't say nothin'—no matter what he says. An' I won't neither.
(*It is* CABOT. *He comes up from the barn in a great state of excite-
ment and strides into the house and then into the kitchen.* EBEN
is kneeling beside ABBIE, *his arm around her, hers around him.
They stare straight ahead*).

CABOT (*stares at them, his face hard. A long pause—vindictively*)
Ye make a slick pair o' murderin' turtle doves! Ye'd ought t' be
both hung on the same limb an' left thar t' swing in the breeze
an' rot—a warnin' t' old fools like me t' b'ar their lonesomeness
alone—an' fur young fools like ye t' hobble their lust. (*A pause.
The excitement returns to his face, his eyes snap, he looks a bit
crazy*) I couldn't work today. I couldn't take no interest. T' hell
with the farm! I'm leavin' it! I've turned the cows an' other stock
loose! I've druv 'em into the woods whar they kin be free! By
freein' 'em, I'm freein' myself! I'm quittin' here today! I'll set fire
t' house an' barn an' watch 'em burn, an' I'll leave yer Maw t'
haunt the ashes, an' I'll will the fields back t' God, so that nothin'
human kin never touch 'em! I'll be a-goin' to Californi-a—t' jine
Simeon an' Peter—true sons o' mine if they be dumb fools—an'
the Cabots'll find Solomon's Mines t'gether! (*He suddenly cuts a
mad caper*) Whoop! What was the song they sung? "Oh, Californi-a! That's the land fur me." (*He sings this—then gets on his
knees by the floor-board under which the money was hid*) An' I'll
sail thar on one o' the finest clippers I kin find! I've got the money!
Pity ye didn't know whar this was hidden so's ye could steal. . . .
(*He has pulled up the board. He stares—feels—stares again. A*

pause of dead silence. He slowly turns, slumping into a sitting position on the floor, his eyes like those of a dead fish, his face the sickly green of an attack of nausea. He swallows painfully several times—forces a weak smile at last) So—ye did steal it!

EBEN *(emotionlessly)* I swapped it t' Sim an' Peter fur their share o' the farm—t' pay their passage t' Californi-a.

CABOT *(with one sardonic)* Ha! *(He begins to recover. Gets slowly to his feet—strangely)* I calc'late God give it to 'em—not yew! God's hard, not easy! Mebbe they's easy gold in the West but it hain't God's gold. It hain't fur me. I kin hear His voice warnin' me agen t' be hard an' stay on my farm. I kin see his hand usin' Eben t' steal t' keep me from weakness. I kin feel I be in the palm o' His hand, His fingers guidin' me. *(A pause—then he mutters sadly)* It's a-goin' t' be lonesomer now than ever it war afore— an' I'm gittin' old, Lord—ripe on the bough. . . . *(Then stiffening)* Waal—what d'ye want? God's lonesome, hain't He? God's hard an' lonesome! *(A pause. The Sheriff with two men comes up the road from the left. They move cautiously to the door. The Sheriff knocks on it with the butt of his pistol).*

SHERIFF Open in the name o' the law! *(They start).*

CABOT They've come fur ye. *(He goes to the rear door)* Come in, Jim! *(The three men enter.* CABOT *meets them in doorway)* Jest a minit, Jim. I got 'em safe here. *(The Sheriff nods. He and his companions remain in the doorway).*

EBEN *(suddenly calls)* I lied this mornin', Jim. I helped her to do it. Ye kin take me, too.

ABBIE *(brokenly)* No!

CABOT Take 'em both. *(He comes forward—stares at* EBEN *with a trace of grudging admiration)* Purty good—fur yew! Waal, I got t' round up the stock. Good-by.

EBEN Good-by.

ABBIE Good-by. *(CABOT turns and strides past the men—comes out and around the corner of the house, his shoulders squared, his face stony, and stalks grimly toward the barn. In the meantime the Sheriff and men have come into the room).*

SHERIFF *(embarrassedly)* Wall—we'd best start.

ABBIE Wait. *(Turns to* EBEN*)* I love ye, Eben.

EBEN I love ye, Abbie. *(They kiss. The three men grin and shuffle embarrassedly.* EBEN *takes* ABBIE's *hand. They go out the door in rear, the men following, and come from the house, walking hand in hand to the gate.* EBEN *stops there and points to the sunrise sky)* Sun's a-rizin'. Purty, hain't it?

ABBIE Ay-eh. *(They both stand for a moment looking up raptly in attitudes strangely aloof and devout).*

SHERIFF *(looking around at the farm enviously—to his companion)* It's a jim-dandy farm, no denyin'. Wished I owned it!

CURTAIN

LUIGI PIRANDELLO

Henry IV†

A Tragedy in Three Acts

Characters

HENRY IV[1]
THE MARCHIONESS MATILDA SPINA
FRIDA, *her daughter*
CHARLES DI NOLLI, *the young Marquis*
BARON TITO BELCREDI
DOCTOR DIONYSIUS GENONI
HAROLD (FRANK)
LANDOLPH (LOLO)   }   *The four private counsellors (The*
ORDULPH (MOMO)   }   *names in brackets are nicknames)*
BERTHOLD (FINO)
JOHN, *the old waiter*
THE TWO VALETS IN COSTUME

A Solitary Villa in Italy in Our Own Time

Act I

Salon in the villa, furnished and decorated so as to look exactly like the throne room of Henry IV in the royal residence at Goslar.[2] Among the antique decorations there are two modern life-size portraits in oil

† From *Naked Masks: Five Plays* by Luigi Pirandello. Translated by Edward Storer. Edited by Eric Bentley. Copyright 1922, 1952, by E. P. Dutton & Co., Inc. Renewal, 1950, by Stefano, Fausto, and Lietta Pirandello. Dutton Paperback Edition. Reprinted by permission of E. P. Dutton & Co., Inc.
1. The German emperor Henry IV reigned from A.D. 1065 to 1106, for the first ten years under a series of regents. During his stormy reign he attempted to carry on the work of his predecessors by strengthening the empire against the German nobles and the Church. From his father, Henry III, he inherited the struggle with the nobles, led by Godfrey of Lorraine, who had profound ties with the papacy. With the election of Pope Gregory VII this struggle broadened to a bitter contention between the Church and the empire for supremacy. At one point, excommunicated and out of favor with his supporters, Henry had to humble himself before Gregory at Canossa; at others Henry excommunicated the Pope and elected an anti-Pope, Gregory again excommunicated him and supported an anti-king elected by the nobles, Henry marched on Rome, which he won and then lost, and Henry's sons betrayed him, first the eldest by deserting to the Pope, then the second by rebelling and setting himself up as an anti-king.

2. The permanent capital of Henry's kingdom.

painting. They are placed against the back wall, and mounted in a wooden stand that runs the whole length of the wall. (It is wide and protrudes, so that it is like a large bench.) One of the paintings is on the right; the other on the left of the throne, which is in the middle of the wall and divides the stand.

The Imperial chair and Baldachin.

The two portraits represent a lady and a gentleman, both young, dressed up in carnival costumes: one as "Henry IV," the other as the "Marchioness Matilda of Tuscany."[3] *Exits to right and left.*

When the curtain goes up, the two valets jump down, as if surprised, from the stand on which they have been lying, and go and take their positions, as rigid as statues, on either side below the throne with their halberds in their hands. Soon after, from the second exit, right, enter HAROLD, LANDOLPH, ORDULPH *and* BERTHOLD, *young men employed by the* MARQUIS CHARLES DI NOLLI *to play the part of "Secret Counsellors" at the court of "Henry IV." They are, therefore, dressed like German knights of the XIth century.* BERTHOLD, *nicknamed Fino, is just entering on his duties for the first time. His companions are telling him what he has to do and amusing themselves at his expense. The scene is to be played rapidly and vivaciously.*

LANDOLPH [*to* BERTHOLD *as if explaining*]. And this is the throne room.

HAROLD. At Goslar.

ORDULPH. Or at the castle in the Hartz,[4] if you prefer.

HAROLD. Or at Wurms.

LANDOLPH. According as to what's doing, it jumps about with us, now here, now there.

ORDULPH. In Saxony.

HAROLD. In Lombardy.

LANDOLPH. On the Rhine.

ONE OF THE VALETS [*without moving, just opening his lips*]. I say . . .

HAROLD [*turning round*]. What is it?

FIRST VALET [*like a statue*]. Is he coming in or not? [*He alludes to* HENRY IV.]

ORDULPH. No, no, he's asleep. You needn't worry.

SECOND VALET [*releasing his pose, taking a long breath and going to lie down again on the stand*]. You might have told us at once.

FIRST VALET [*going over to* HAROLD]. Have you got a match, please?

LANDOLPH. What? You can't smoke a pipe here, you know.

FIRST VALET [*while* HAROLD *offers him a light*]. No; a cigarette. [*Lights his cigarette and lies down again on the stand.*]

BERTHOLD [*who has been looking on in amazement, walking round the room, regarding the costumes of the others*]. I say . . . this

3. The "Great Countess" of Tuscany, she proved a fierce supporter of the papal party and a lifelong enemy to Henry. It was at her castle at Canossa that Henry humbled himself before Pope Gregory VII. At one point she gave refuge to Henry's second wife, Praxedis, who was suspected of infidelity; at another she urged Conrad, Henry's eldest son, to revolt.

4. One of Henry's devices for strengthening the monarchy was the construction of a series of castles.

room . . . these costumes . . . Which Henry IV is it? I don't quite get it. Is he Henry IV of France or not? [*At this* LANDOLPH, HAROLD, *and* ORDULPH, *burst out laughing.*]

LANDOLPH [*still laughing; and pointing to* BERTHOLD *as if inviting the others to make fun of him*]. Henry of France he says: ha! ha!

ORDULPH. He thought it was the king of France!

HAROLD. Henry IV of Germany, my boy: the Salian dynasty![5]

ORDULPH. The great and tragic Emperor!

LANDOLPH. He of Canossa. Every day we carry on here the terrible war between Church and State, by Jove.

ORDULPH. The Empire against the Papacy!

HAROLD. Anti-popes against the Pope!

LANDOLPH. Kings against anti-kings!

ORDULPH. War on the Saxons!

HAROLD. And all the rebels Princes!

LANDOLPH. Against the Emporer's own sons!

BERTHOLD [*covering his head with his hands to protect himself against this avalanche of information*]. I understand! I understand! Naturally, I didn't get the idea at first. I'm right then: these aren't costumes of the XVIth century?

HAROLD. XVIth century be hanged!

ORDULPH. We're somewhere between a thousand and eleven hundred.

LANDOLPH. Work it out for yourself: if we are before Canossa on the 25th of January, 1071 . . .[6]

BERTHOLD [*more confused than ever*]. Oh my God! What a mess I've made of it!

ORDULPH. Well, just slightly, if you supposed you were at the French court.

BERTHOLD. All that historical stuff I've swatted up!

LANDOLPH. My dear boy, it's four hundred years earlier.

BERTHOLD [*getting angry*]. Good Heavens! You ought to have told me it was Germany and not France. I can't tell you how many books I've read in the last fifteen days.

HAROLD. But I say, surely you knew that poor Tito was Adalbert of Bremen,[7] here?

BERTHOLD. Not a damned bit!

LANDOLPH. Well, don't you see how it is? When Tito died, the Marquis Di Nolli . . .

BERTHOLD. Oh, it was he, was it? He might have told me.

HAROLD. Perhaps he thought you knew.

LANDOLPH. He didn't want to engage anyone else in substitution. He thought the remaining three of us would do. But *he* began to cry out: "With Adalbert driven away . . .":[8] because, you see, he

---

5. Comprises a line of German emperors (A.D. 1024-1125), including Conrad II, Henry III, Henry IV, and Henry V.
6. Actually in 1077.
7. Archbishop Adalbert of Bremen was appointed by Henry III as a part of his plan to weaken the Saxon dukes. A formidable ally to both Henry III and Henry IV against the nobles, he served as Henry IV's regent for a few years before Henry came of age.
8. When Henry came of age in 1066, he was forced by Adalbert's enemies to dismiss him.

didn't imagine poor Tito was dead; but that, as Bishop Adalbert, the rival bishops of Cologne and Mayence had driven him off . . .

BERTHOLD [*taking his head in his hand*]. But I don't know a word of what you're talking about.

ORDULPH. So much the worse for you, my boy!

HAROLD. But the trouble is that not even we know who you are.

BERTHOLD. What? Not even you? You don't know who I'm supposed to be?

ORDULPH. Hum! "Berthold."

BERTHOLD. But which Berthold? And why Berthold?

LANDOLPH [*solemnly imitating* HENRY IV]. "They've driven Adalbert away from me. Well then, I want Berthold! I want Berthold!" That's what he said.

HAROLD. We three looked one another in the eyes: who's got to be Berthold?

ORDULPH. And so here you are, "Berthold," my dear fellow!

LANDOLPH. I'm afraid you will make a bit of a mess of it.

BERTHOLD [*indignant, getting ready to go*]. Ah, no! Thanks very much, but I'm off! I'm out of this!

HAROLD [*restraining him with the other two, amid laughter*]. Steady now! Don't get excited!

LANDOLPH. Cheer up, my dear fellow! We don't any of us know who we are really. He's Harold; he's Ordulph! I'm Landolph! That's the way he calls us. We've got used to it. But who are we? Names of the period! Yours, too, is a name of the period: Berthold! Only one of us, poor Tito, had got a really decent part, as you can read in history: that of the Bishop of Bremen. He was just like a real bishop. Tito did it awfully well, poor chap!

HAROLD. Look at the study he put into it!

LANDOLPH. Why, he even ordered his Majesty about, opposed his views, guided and counselled him. We're "secret counsellors"—in a manner of speaking only; because it is written in history that Henry IV was hated by the upper aristocracy for surrounding himself at court with young men of the bourgeoisie.

ORDULPH. Us, that is.

LANDOLPH. Yes, small devoted vassals, a bit dissolute and very gay . . .

BERTHOLD. So I've got to be gay as well?

HAROLD. I should say so! Same as we are!

ORDULPH. And it isn't too easy, you know.

LANDOLPH. It's a pity; because the way we're got up, we could do a fine historical reconstruction. There's any amount of material in the story of Henry IV. But, as a matter of fact, we do nothing. We have the form without the content. We're worse than the real secret counsellors of Henry IV; because certainly no one had given them a part to play—at any rate, they didn't feel they had a part to play. It was their life. They looked after their own interests at the expense of others, sold investitures and—what not! We stop here in this magnificent court—for what?—Just doing nothing. We're like so many puppets hung on the wall, waiting for someone to come and move us or make us talk.

HAROLD. Ah, no, old sport, not quite that! We've got to give the proper answer, you know. There's trouble if he asks you something and you don't chip in with the cue.

LANDOLPH. Yes. that's true.

BERTHOLD. Don't rub it in too hard! How the devil am I to give him the proper answer, if I've swatted up Henry IV of France, and now he turns out to be Henry IV of Germany? [*The other three laugh.*]

HAROLD. You'd better start and prepare yourself at once.

ORDULPH. We'll help you out.

HAROLD. We've got any amount of books on the subject. A brief run through the main points will do to begin with.

ORDULPH. At any rate, you must have got some sort of general idea.

HAROLD. Look here! [*Turns him around and shows him the portrait of the Marchioness Matilda on the wall.*] Who's that?

BERTHOLD [*looking at it*]. That? Well, the thing seems to me somewhat out of place, anyway: two modern paintings in the midst of all this respectable antiquity!

HAROLD. You're right! They weren't there in the beginning. There are two niches there behind the pictures. They were going to put up two statues in the style of the period. Then the places were covered with those canvases there.

LANDOLPH [*interrupting and continuing*]. They would certainly be out of place if they really were paintings!

BERTHOLD. What are they, if they aren't paintings?

LANDOLPH. Go and touch them! Pictures all right . . . but for him! [*Makes a mysterious gesture to the right, alluding to* HENRY IV.] . . . who never touches them! . . .

BERTHOLD. No? What are they for him?

LANDOLPH. Well, I'm only supposing, you know; but I imagine I'm about right. They're images such as . . . well—such as a mirror might throw back. Do you understand? That one there represents himself, as he is in this throne room, which is all in the style of the period. What's there to marvel at? If we put you before a mirror, won't you see yourself, alive, but dressed up in ancient costume? Well, it's as if there were two mirrors there, which cast back living images in the midst of a world which, as you well see, when you have lived with us, comes to life too.

BERTHOLD. I say, look here . . . I've no particular desire to go mad here.

HAROLD. Go mad, be hanged! You'll have a fine time!

BERTHOLD. Tell me this: how have you all managed to become so learned?

LANDOLPH. My dear fellow, you can't go back over 800 years of history without picking up a bit of experience.

HAROLD. Come on! Come on! You'll see how quickly you get into it!

ORDULPH. You'll learn wisdom, too, at this school.

BERTHOLD. Well, for Heaven's sake, help me a bit! Give me the main lines, anyway.

HAROLD. Leave it to us. We'll do it all between us.

LANDOLPH. We'll put your wires on you and fix you up like a first-class marionette. Come along! [THEY *take him by the arm to lead him away.*]

BERTHOLD [*stopping and looking at the portrait on the wall*]. Wait a minute! You haven't told me who that is. The Emperor's wife?

HAROLD. No! The Emperor's wife is Bertha of Susa, the sister of Amadeus II of Savoy.

ORDULPH. And the Emperor, who wants to be young with us, can't stand her, and wants to put her away.

LANDOLPH. That is his most ferocious enemy: Matilda, Marchioness of Tuscany.

BERTHOLD. Ah, I've got it: the one who gave hospitality to the Pope!

LANDOLPH. Exactly: at Canossa!

ORDULPH. Pope Gregory VII!

HAROLD. Our *bête noir!* Come on! come on! [*All four move toward the right to go out, when, from the left, the old servant* JOHN *enters in evening dress.*]

JOHN [*quickly, anxiously*]. Hss! Hss! Frank! Lolo!

HAROLD [*turning round*]. What is it?

BERTHOLD [*marvelling at seeing a man in modern clothes enter the throne room*]. Oh! I say, this is a bit too much, this chap here!

LANDOLPH. A man of the XXth century, here! Oh, go away! [THEY *run over to him, pretending to menace him and throw him out.*]

ORDULPH [*heroically*]. Messenger of Gregory VII, away!

HAROLD. Away! Away!

JOHN [*annoyed, defending himself*]. Oh, stop it! Stop it, I tell you!

ORDULPH. No, you can't set foot here!

HAROLD. Out with him!

LANDOLPH [*to* BERTHOLD]. Magic, you know! He's a demon conjured up by the Wizard of Rome! Out with your swords! [*Makes as if to draw a sword.*]

JOHN [*shouting*]. Stop it, will you? Don't play the fool with me! The Marquis has arrived with some friends . . .

LANDOLPH. Good! Good! Are there ladies too?

ORDULPH. Old or young?

JOHN. There are two gentlemen.

HAROLD. But the ladies, the ladies, who are they?

JOHN. The Marchioness and her daughter.

LANDOLPH [*surprised*]. What do you say?

ORDULPH. The Marchioness?

JOHN. The Marchioness! The Marchioness!

HAROLD. Who are the gentlemen?

JOHN. I don't know.

HAROLD [*to* BERTHOLD]. They're coming to bring us a message from the Pope, do you see?

ORDULPH. All messengers of Gregory VII! What fun!

JOHN. Will you let me speak, or not?

ORDULPH. Come on then!

JOHN. One of the two gentlemen is a doctor, I fancy.

LANDOLPH. Oh, I see, one of the usual doctors.

HAROLD. Bravo Berthold, you'll bring us luck!

LANDOLPH. You wait and see how we'll manage this doctor!

BERTHOLD. It looks as if I were going to get into a nice mess right away.

JOHN. If the gentlemen would allow me to speak . . . they want to come here into the throne room.

LANDOLPH [*surprised*]. What? She? The Marchioness here?

HAROLD. Then this is something quite different! No play-acting this time!

LANDOLPH. We'll have a real tragedy: that's what!

BERTHOLD [*curious*]. Why? Why?

ORDULPH [*pointing to the portrait*]. She is that person there, don't you understand?

LANDOLPH. The daughter is the fiancée of the Marquis. But what have they come for, I should like to know?

ORDULPH. If he sees her, there'll be trouble.

LANDOLPH. Perhaps he won't recognize her any more.

JOHN. You must keep him there, if he should wake up . . .

ORDULPH. Easier said than done, by Jove!

HAROLD. You know what he's like!

JOHN. —even by force, if necessary! Those are my orders. Go on! Go on!

HAROLD. Yes, because who knows if he hasn't already wakened up?

ORDULPH. Come on then!

LANDOLPH [*going towards* JOHN *with the others*]. You'll tell us later what it all means.

JOHN [*shouting after them*]. Close the door there, and hide the key! That other door too. [*Pointing to the other door on right.*]

JOHN [*to the* TWO VALETS]. Be off, you two! There! [*Pointing to exit right.*] Close the door after you, and hide the key!

> [*The* TWO VALETS *go out by the first door on right.* JOHN *moves over to the left to show in:* DONNA MATILDA SPINA, *the young* MARCHIONESS FRIDA, DR. DIONYSIUS GENONI, *the* BARON TITO BELCREDI *and the young* MARQUIS CHARLES DI NOLLI, *who, as master of the house, enters last.*
>
> DONNA MATILDA SPINA *is about 45, still handsome, although there are too patent signs of her attempts to remedy the ravages of time with make-up. Her head is thus rather like a Walkyrie.*[9] *This facial make-up contrasts with her beautiful sad mouth. A widow for many years, she now has as her friend the* BARON TITO BELCREDI, *whom neither she nor anyone else takes seriously—at least so it would appear.*
>
> *What* TITO BELCREDI *really is for her at bottom, he alone knows; and he is, therefore, entitled to laugh, if his friend feels the need of pretending not to know. He can always laugh at the jests which the beautiful Marchioness makes with the others at his expense. He is slim, prematurely gray, and younger than she is. His head is bird-like in shape. He would be a*

9. In Germanic mythology the divine female messengers of Odin who ride over battlefields gathering the spirits of dead heroes.

very vivacious person, if his ductile agility (which among other things makes him a redoubtable swordsman) were not enclosed in a sheath of Arab-like laziness, which is revealed in his strange, nasal drawn-out voice.

FRIDA, *the daughter of the Marchioness is* 19. *She is sad; because her imperious and too beautiful mother puts her in the shade, and provokes facile gossip against her daughter as well as against herself. Fortunately for her, she is engaged to the* MARQUIS CHARLES DI NOLLI.

CHARLES DI NOLLI *is a stiff young man, very indulgent towards others, but sure of himself for what he amounts to in the world. He is worried about all the responsibilities which he believes weigh on him. He is dressed in deep mourning for the recent death of his mother.*

DR. DIONYSIUS GENONI *has a bold rubicund Satyr-like face, prominent eyes, a pointed beard (which is silvery and shiny) and elegant manners. He is nearly bald. All enter in a state of perturbation, almost as if afraid, and all (except* DI NOLLI*) looking curiously about the room. At first, they speak sotto voce.*]

DI NOLLI [*to* JOHN]. Have you given the orders properly?

JOHN. Yes, my Lord; don't be anxious about that.

BELCREDI. Ah, magnificent! magnificent!

DOCTOR. How extremely interesting! Even in the surroundings his raving madness—is perfectly taken into account!

DONNA MATILDA [*glancing round for her portrait, discovers it, and goes up close to it*]. Ah! Here it is! [*Going back to admire it, while mixed emotions stir within her.*] Yes . . . yes . . . [*Calls her daughter* FRIDA.]

FRIDA. Ah, your portrait!

DONNA MATILDA. No, no . . . look again; it's you, not I, there!

DI NOLLI. Yes, it's quite true. I told you so. I . . .

DONNA MATILDA. But I would never have believed it! [*Shaking as if with a chill.*] What a strange feeling it gives one! [*Then looking at her daughter.*] Frida, what's the matter? [*She pulls her to her side, and slips an arm round her waist.*] Come: don't you see yourself in me there?

FRIDA. Well, I really . . .

DONNA MATILDA. Don't you think so? Don't you, really? [*Turning to* BELCREDI.] Look at it, Tito! Speak up, man!

BELCREDI [*without looking*]. Ah, no! I shan't look at it. For me, *a priori*,[1] certainly not!

DONNA MATILDA. Stupid! You think you are paying me a compliment! [*Turning to* DOCTOR GENONI.] What do you say, Doctor? Do say something, please!

DOCTOR [*makes a movement to go near to the picture*].

BELCREDI [*with his back turned, pretending to attract his attention secretly*].—Hss! No, Doctor! For the love of Heaven, have nothing to do with it!

---

1. "Given my assumptions."

DOCTOR [*getting bewildered and smiling*]. And why shouldn't I?

DONNA MATILDA. Don't listen to him! Come here! He's insufferable!

FRIDA. He acts the fool by profession, didn't you know that?

BELCREDI [*to the* DOCTOR, *seeing him go over*]. Look at your feet, Doctor! Mind where you're going!

DOCTOR. Why?

BELCREDI. Be careful you don't put your foot in it!

DOCTOR [*laughing feebly*]. No, no. After all, it seems to me there's no reason to be astonished at the fact that a daughter should resemble her mother!

BELCREDI. Hullo! Hullo! He's done it now; he's said it.

DONNA MATILDA [*with exaggerated anger, advancing towards* BELCREDI]. What's the matter? What has he said? What has he done?

DOCTOR [*candidly*]. Well, isn't it so?

BELCREDI [*answering the* MARCHIONESS]. I said there was nothing to be astounded at—and you are astounded! And why so, then, if the thing is so simple and natural for you now?

DONNA MATILDA [*still more angry*]. Fool! fool! It's just because it is so natural! Just because it isn't my daughter who is there. [*Pointing to the canvas.*] That is my portrait; and to find my daughter there instead of me fills me with astonishment, an astonishment which, I beg you to believe, is sincere. I forbid you to cast doubts on it.

FRIDA [*slowly and wearily*]. My God! It's always like this . . . rows over nothing . . .

BELCREDI [*also slowly, looking dejected, in accents of apology*]. I cast no doubt on anything! I noticed from the beginning that you haven't shared your mother's astonishment; or, if something did astonish you, it was because the likeness between you and the portrait seemed so strong.

DONNA MATILDA. Naturally! She cannot recognize herself in me as I was at her age; while I, there, can very well recognize myself in her as she is now!

DOCTOR. Quite right! Because a portrait is always there fixed in the twinkling of an eye: for the young lady something far away and without memories, while, for the Marchioness, it can bring back everything: movements, gestures, looks, smiles, a whole heap of things . . .

DONNA MATILDA. Exactly!

DOCTOR [*continuing, turning towards her*]. Naturally enough, you can live all these old sensations again in your daughter.

DONNA MATILDA. He always spoils every innocent pleasure for me, every touch I have of spontaneous sentiment! He does it merely to annoy me.

DOCTOR [*frightened at the disturbance he has caused, adopts a professorial tone*]. Likeness, dear Baron, is often the result of imponderable things. So one explains that . . .

BELCREDI [*interrupting the discourse*]. Somebody will soon be finding a likeness between you and me, my dear Professor!

DI NOLLI. Oh! let's finish with this, please! [*Points to the two doors on the right, as a warning that there is someone there who may be listening.*] We've wasted too much time as it is!

FRIDA. As one might expect when *he's* present. [*Alludes to* BELCREDI.]

DI NOLLI. Enough! The Doctor is here; and we have come for a very serious purpose which you all know is important for me.

DOCTOR. Yes, that is so! But now, first of all, let's try to get some points down exactly. Excuse me, Marchioness, will you tell me why your portrait is here? Did you present it to him then?

DONNA MATILDA. No, not at all. How could I have given it to him? I was just like Frida then—and not even engaged. I gave it to him three or four years after the accident. I gave it to him because his mother wished it so much . . . [*Points to* DI NOLLI.]

DOCTOR. She was his sister? [*Alludes to* HENRY IV.]

DI NOLLI. Yes, Doctor; and our coming here is a debt we pay to my mother who has been dead for more than a month. Instead of being here, she and I [*Indicating Frida.*] ought to be traveling together . . .

DOCTOR. . . . taking a cure of quite a different kind!

DI NOLLI. —Hum! Mother died in the firm conviction that her adored brother was just about to be cured.

DOCTOR. And can't you tell me, if you please, how she inferred this?

DI NOLLI. The conviction would appear to have derived from certain strange remarks which he made, a little before mother died.

DOCTOR. Oh, remarks! . . . Ah! . . . It would be extremely useful for me to have those remarks, word for word, if possible.

DI NOLLI. I can't remember them. I know that mother returned awfully upset from her last visit with him. On her death-bed, she made me promise that I would never neglect him, that I would have doctors see him, and examine him.

DOCTOR. Um! Um! Let me see! let me see! Sometimes very small reasons determine . . . and this portrait here then? . . .

DONNA MATILDA. For Heaven's sake, Doctor, don't attach excessive importance to this. It made an impression on me because I had not seen it for so many years!

DOCTOR. If you please, quietly, quietly . . .

DI NOLLI. —Well, yes, it must be about fifteen years ago.

DONNA MATILDA. More, more: eighteen!

DOCTOR. Forgive me, but you don't quite know what I'm trying to get at. I attach a very great importance to these two portraits . . . They were painted, naturally, prior to the famous—and most regrettable pageant, weren't they?

DONNA MATILDA. Of course!

DOCTOR. That is . . . when he was quite in his right mind—that's what I've been trying to say. Was it his suggestion that they should be painted?

DONNA MATILDA. Lots of the people who took part in the pageant had theirs done as a souvenir . . .

BELCREDI. I had mine done—as "Charles of Anjou!"[2]

---

2. Charles of Anjou (A.D. 1246-85) established the House of Anjou.

DONNA MATILDA. . . . as soon as the costumes were ready.

BELCREDI. As a matter of fact, it was proposed that the whole lot of us should be hung together in a gallery of the villa where the pageant took place. But in the end, everybody wanted to keep his own portrait.

DONNA MATILDA. And I gave him this portrait of me without very much regret . . . since his mother . . . [*Indicates* DI NOLLI.]

DOCTOR. You don't remember if it was he who asked for it?

DONNA MATILDA. Ah, that I don't remember . . . Maybe it was his sister, wanting to help out . . .

DOCTOR. One other thing: was it his idea, this pageant?

BELCREDI [*at once*]. No, no, it was mine!

DOCTOR. If you please . . .

DONNA MATILDA. Don't listen to him! It was poor Belassi's idea.

BELCREDI. Belassi! What had he got to do with it?

DONNA MATILDA. Count Belassi, who died, poor fellow, two or three months after . . .

BELCREDI. But if Belasi wasn't there when . . .

DI NOLLI. Excuse me, Doctor; but is it really necessary to establish whose the original idea was?

DOCTOR. It would help me, certainly!

BELCREDI. I tell you the idea was mine? There's nothing to be proud of in it, seeing what the result's been. Look here, Doctor, it was like this. One evening, in the first days of November, I was looking at an illustrated German review in the club. I was merely glancing at the pictures, because I can't read German. There was a picture of the Kaiser, at some University town where he had been a student . . . I don't remember which.

DOCTOR. Bonn, Bonn!

BELCREDI. —You are right: Bonn! He was on horseback, dressed up in one of those ancient German student guild-costumes, followed by a procession of noble students, also in costume. The picture gave me the idea. Already someone at the club had spoken of a pageant for the forthcoming carnival. So I had the notion that each of us should choose for this Tower of Babel pageant to represent some character: a king, an emperor, a prince, with his queen, empress, or lady, alongside of him—and all on horseback. The suggestion was at once accepted.

DONNA MATILDA. I had my invitation from Belassi.

BELCREDI. Well, he wasn't speaking the truth! That's all I can say, if he told you the idea was his. He wasn't even at the club the evening I made the suggestion, just as he [*Meaning* HENRY IV.] wasn't there either.

DOCTOR. So he chose the character of Henry IV?

DONNA MATILDA. Because I . . . thinking of my name, and not giving the choice any importance, said I would be the Marchioness Matilda of Tuscany.

DOCTOR. I . . . don't understand the relation between the two.

DONNA MATILDA. —Neither did I, to begin with, when he said that in that case he would be at my feet like Henry IV at Canossa. I had heard of Canossa of course; but to tell the truth, I'd forgotten most of the story; and I remember I received a curious impression when I had to get up my part, and found that I was the faithful and zealous friend of Pope Gregory VII in deadly enmity with the Emperor of Germany. Then I understood why, since I had chosen to represent his implacable enemy, he wanted to be near me in the pageant as Henry IV.

DOCTOR. Ah, perhaps because . . .

BELCREDI. —Good Heavens, Doctor, because he was then paying furious court to her! [*Indicates the* MARCHIONESS.] And she, naturally . . .

DONNA MATILDA. Naturally? Not naturally at all . . .

BELCREDI [*pointing to her*]. She shouldn't stand him . . .

DONNA MATILDA. —No, that isn't true! I didn't dislike him. Not at all! But for me, when a man begins to want to be taken seriously, well . . .

BELCREDI [*continuing for her*]. He gives you the clearest proof of his stupidity.

DONNA MATILDA. No, dear; not in this case; because he was never a fool like you.

BELCREDI. Anyway, I've never asked you to take me seriously.

DONNA MATILDA. Yes, I know. But with him one couldn't joke. [*Changing her tone and speaking to the* DOCTOR.] One of the many misfortunes which happen to us women, Doctor, is to see before us every now and again a pair of eyes glaring at us with a contained intense promise of eternal devotion. [*Bursts out laughing.*] There is nothing quite so funny. If men could only see themselves with that eternal look of fidelity in their faces! I've always thought it comic; then more even than now. But I want to make a confession—I can do so after twenty years or more. When I laughed at him then, it was partly out of fear. One might have almost believed a promise from those eyes of his. But it would have been very dangerous.

DOCTOR [*with lively interest*]. Ah! ah! This is most interesting! Very dangerous, you say?

DONNA MATILDA. Yes, because he was very different from the others. And then, I am . . . well . . . what shall I say? . . . a little impatient of all that is pondered, or tedious. But I was too young then, and a woman. I had the bit between my teeth. It would have required more courage than I felt I possessed. So I laughed at him too—with remorse, to spite myself, indeed; since I saw that my own laugh mingled with those of all the others—the other fools—who made fun of him.

BELCREDI. My own case, more or less!

DONNA MATILDA. You make people laugh at you, my dear, with your trick of always humiliating yourself. It was quite a different affair with him. There's a vast difference. And you—you know—people laugh in your face!

BELCREDI. Well, that's better than behind one's back!

DOCTOR. Let's get to the facts. He was then already somewhat exalted, if I understand rightly.

BELCREDI. Yes, but in a curious fashion, Doctor.

DOCTOR. How?

BELCREDI. Well, cold-bloodedly so to speak.

DONNA MATILDA. Not at all! It was like this, Doctor! He was a bit strange, certainly; but only because he was fond of life: eccentric, there!

BELCREDI. I don't say he simulated exaltation. On the contrary, he was often genuinely exalted. But I could swear, Doctor, that he saw himself at once in his own exaltation. Moreover, I'm certain it made him suffer. Sometimes he had the most comical fits of rage against himself.

DOCTOR. Yes?

DONNA MATILDA. That is true.

BELCREDI [*to* DONNA MATILDA]. And why? [*To the* DOCTOR.] Evidently, because that immediate lucidity that comes from acting, assuming a part, at once put him out of key with his own feelings, which seemed to him not exactly false, but like something he was obliged to give the value there and then of—what shall I say—of an act of intelligence, to make up for that sincere cordial warmth he felt lacking. So he improvised, exaggerated, let himself go, so as to distract and forget himself. He appeared inconstant, fatuous, and —yes—even ridiculous, sometimes.

DOCTOR. And may we say unsociable?

BELCREDI. No, not at all. He was famous for getting up things: *tableaux vivants*,[3] dances, theatrical performances for charity: all for the fun of the thing, of course. He was a jolly good actor, you know!

DI NOLLI. Madness has made a superb actor of him.

BELCREDI. —Why, so he was even in the old days. When the accident happened, after the horse fell . . .

DOCTOR. Hit the back of his head, didn't he?

DONNA MATILDA. Oh, it was horrible! He was beside me! I saw him between the horse's hoofs! It was rearing!

BELCREDI. None of us thought it was anything serious at first. There was a stop in the pageant, a bit of disorder. People wanted to know what had happened. But they'd already taken him off to the villa.

DONNA MATILDA. There wasn't the least sign of a wound, not a drop of blood.

BELCREDI. We thought he had merely fainted.

DONNA MATILDA. But two hours afterwards . . .

BELCREDI. He reappeared in the drawing-room of the villa . . . that is what I wanted to say . . .

DONNA MATILDA. My God! What a face he had. I saw the whole thing at once!

---

3. Famous scenes or pictures composed of live, costumed performers.

BELCREDI. No, no! that isn't true. Nobody saw it, Doctor, believe me!

DONNA MATILDA. Doubtless, because you were all like mad folk.

BELCREDI. Everybody was pretending to act his part for a joke. It was a regular Babel.

DONNA MATILDA. And you can imagine, Doctor, what terror struck into us when we understood that he, on the contrary, was playing his part in deadly earnest . . .

DOCTOR. Oh, he was there too, was he?

BELCREDI. Of course! He came straight into the midst of us. We thought he'd quite recovered, and was pretending, fooling, like all the rest of us . . . only doing it rather better; because, as I say, he knew how to act.

DONNA MATILDA. Some of them began to hit him with their whips and fans and sticks.

BELCREDI. And then—as a king, he was armed, of course—he drew out his sword and menaced two or three of us . . . It was a terrible moment, I can assure you!

DONNA MATILDA. I shall never forget that scene—all our masked faces hideous and terrified gazing at him, at that terrible mask of his face, which was no longer a mask, but madness, madness personified.

BELCREDI. He was Henry IV, Henry IV in person, in a moment of fury.

DONNA MATILDA. He'd got into it all the detail and minute preparation of a month's careful study. And it all burned and blazed there in the terrible obsession which lit his face.

DOCTOR. Yes, that is quite natural, of course. The momentary obsession of a dilettante became fixed, owing to the fall and the damage to the brain.

BELCREDI [*to* FRIDA *and* DI NOLLI]. You see the kind of jokes life can play on us. [*To* DI NOLLI.] You were four or five years old. [*To* FRIDA.] Your mother imagines you've taken her place there in that portrait; when, at the time, she had not the remotest idea that she would bring you into the world. My hair is already grey; and he—look at him—[*Points to portrait*]—ha! A smack on the head, and he never moves again: Henry IV for ever!

DOCTOR [*seeking to draw the attention of the others, looking learned and imposing*]. —Well, well, then it comes, we may say, to this . . . [*Suddenly the first exit to right, the one nearest footlights, opens, and* BERTHOLD *enters all excited.*]

BERTHOLD [*rushing in*]. I say! I say! [*Stops for a moment, arrested by the astonishment which his appearance has caused in the others.*]

FRIDA [*running away terrified*]. Oh dear! oh dear! it's he, it's . . .

DONNA MATILDA [*covering her face with her hands so as not to see*]. Is it, is it he?

DI NOLLI. No, no, what are you talking about? Be calm!

DOCTOR. Who is it then?

BELCREDI. One of our masqueraders.

DI NOLLI. He is one of the four youths we keep here to help him out in his madness . . .

BERTHOLD. I beg your pardon, Marquis . . .

DI NOLLI. Pardon be damned! I gave orders that the doors were to be closed, and that nobody should be allowed to enter.

BERTHOLD. Yes, sir, but I can't stand it any longer, and I ask you to let me go away this very minute.

DI NOLLI. Oh, you're the new valet, are you? You were supposed to begin this morning, weren't you?

BERTHOLD. Yes, sir, and I can't stand it, I can't bear it.

DONNA MATILDA [*to* DI NOLLI *excitedly*]. What? Then he's not so calm as you said?

BERTHOLD [*quickly*]. —No, no, my lady, it isn't he; it's my companions. You say "help him out with his madness," Marquis; but they don't do anything of the kind. They're the real madmen. I come here for the first time, and instead of helping me . . .

[LANDOLPH *and* HAROLD *come in from the same door, but hesitate on the threshold.*]

LANDOLPH. Excuse me?

HAROLD. May I come in, my Lord?

DI NOLLI. Come in! What's the matter? What are you all doing?

FRIDA. Oh God! I'm frightened! I'm going to run away. [*Makes towards exit at left.*]

DI NOLLI [*restraining her at once*]. No, no, Frida!

LANDOLPH. My Lord, this fool here . . . [*Indicates* BERTHOLD.]

BERTHOLD [*protesting*]. Ah, no thanks, my friends, no thanks! I'm not stopping here! I'm off!

LANDOLPH. What do you mean—you're not stopping here?

HAROLD. He's ruined everything, my Lord, running away in here!

LANDOLPH. He's made him quite mad. We can't keep him in there any longer. He's given orders that he's to be arrested; and he wants to "judge" him at once from the throne: What is to be done?

DI NOLLI. Shut the door, man! Shut the door! Go and close that door! [LANDOLPH *goes over to close it.*]

HAROLD. Ordulph, alone, won't be able to keep him there.

LANDOLPH. —My Lord, perhaps if we could announce the visitors at once, it would turn his thoughts. Have the gentlemen thought under what pretext they will present themselves to him?

DI NOLLI. —It's all been arranged! [*To the* DOCTOR.] If you, Doctor, think it well to see him at once. . . .

FRIDA. I'm not coming! I'm not coming! I'll keep out of this. You too, mother, for Heaven's sake, come away with me!

DOCTOR. —I say . . . I suppose he's not armed, is he?

DI NOLLI. —Nonsense! Of course not. [*To* FRIDA.] Frida, you know this is childish of you. You wanted to come!

FRIDA. I didn't at all. It was mother's idea.

DONNA MATILDA. And I'm quite ready to see him. What are we going to do?

BELCREDI. Must we absolutely dress up in some fashion or other?

LANDOLPH. —Absolutely essential, indispensable, sir. Alas! as you see . . . [*Shows his costume*], there'd be awful trouble if he saw you gentlemen in modern dress.

HAROLD. He would think it was some diabolical masquerade.

DI NOLLI. As these men seem to be in costume to you, so we appear to be in costume to him, in these modern clothes of ours.

LANDOLPH. It wouldn't matter so much if he wouldn't suppose it to be the work of his mortal enemy.

BELCREDI. Pope Gregory VII?

LANDOLPH. Precisely. He calls him "a pagan."

BELCREDI. The Pope a pagan? Not bad that!

LANDOLPH. —Yes, sir,—and a man who calls up the dead! He accuses him of all the diabolical arts. He's terribly afraid of him.

DOCTOR. Persecution mania!

HAROLD. He'd be simply furious.

DI NOLLI [*to* BELCREDI]. But there's no need for you to be there, you know. It's sufficient for the Doctor to see him.

DOCTOR. —What do you mean? . . . I? Alone?

DI NOLLI. —But they are there. [*Indicates the three young men.*]

DOCTOR. I don't mean that . . . I mean if the Marchioness . . .

DONNA MATILDA. Of course. I mean to see him too, naturally. I want to see him again.

FRIDA. Oh, why, mother, why? Do come away with me, I implore you!

DONNA MATILDA [*imperiously*]. Let me do as I wish! I came here for this purpose! [*To* LANDOLPH.] I shall be "Adelaide," the mother.

LANDOLPH. Excellent! The mother of the Empress Bertha. Good! It will be enough if her Ladyship wears the ducal crown and puts on a mantel that will hide her other clothes entirely. [*To* HAROLD.] Off you go, Harold!

HAROLD. Wait a moment! And this gentleman here? . . . [*Alludes to the* DOCTOR.]

DOCTOR. —Ah yes . . . we decided I was to be . . . the Bishop of Cluny, Hugh of Cluny!

HAROLD. The gentleman means the Abbot. Very good! Hugh of Cluny.[4]

LANDOLPH. —He's often been here before!

DOCTOR [*amazed*]. —What? Been here before?

LANDOLPH. —Don't be alarmed! I mean that it's an easily prepared disguise . . .

HAROLD. We've made use of it on other occasions, you see!

DOCTOR. But . . .

LANDOLPH. Oh, no there's no risk of his remembering. He pays more attention to the dress than to the person.

DONNA MATILDA. That's fortunate for me too then.

DI NOLLI. Frida, you and I'll get along. Come on, Tito!

BELCREDI. Ah no. If she [*Indicates the* MARCHIONESS.] stops here, so do I!

DONNA MATILDA. But I don't need you at all.

---

4. Henry's god-father, he interceded for Henry at Canossa.

BELCREDI. You may not need me, but I should like to see him again myself. Mayn't I?

LANDOLPH. Well, perhaps it would be better if there were three.

HAROLD. How is the gentleman to be dressed then?

BELCREDI. Oh, try and find some easy costume for me.

LANDOLPH [*to* HAROLD]. Hum! Yes . . . he'd better be from Cluny too.

BELCREDI. What do you mean—from Cluny?

LANDOLPH. A Benedictine's habit of the Abbey of Cluny. He can be in attendance on Monsignor. [*To* HAROLD.] Off you go! [*To* BERTHOLD.] And you too get away and keep out of sight all today. No, wait a bit! [*To* BERTHOLD.] You bring here the costumes he will give you. [*To* HAROLD.] You go at once and announce the visit of the "Duchess Adelaide" and "Monsignor Hugh of Cluny." Do you understand? [HAROLD *and* BERTHOLD *go off by the first door on the right.*]

DI NOLLI. We'll retire now. [*Goes off with* FRIDA, *left.*]

DOCTOR. Shall I be a *persona grata*[5] to him, as Hugh of Cluny?

LANDOLPH. Oh, rather! Don't worry about that! Monsignor has always been received here with great respect. You too, my Lady, he will be glad to see. He never forgets that it was owing to the intercession of you two that he was admitted to the Castle of Canossa and the presence of Gregory VII, who didn't want to receive him.

BELCREDI. And what do I do?

LANDOLPH. You stand a little apart, respectfully: that's all.

DONNA MATILDA [*irritated, nervous*]. You would do well to go away, you know.

BELCREDI [*slowly, spitefully*]. How upset you seem! . . .

DONNA MATILDA [*proudly*]. I am as I am. Leave me alone!
  [BERTHOLD *comes in with the costumes.*]

LANDOLPH [*seeing him enter*]. Ah, the costumes: here they are. This mantle is for the Marchioness . . .

DONNA MATILDA. Wait a minute! I'll take off my hat. [*Does so and gives it to* BERTHOLD.]

LANDOLPH. Put it down there! [*Then to the* MARCHIONESS, *while he offers to put the ducal crown on her head.*] Allow me!

DONNA MATILDA. Dear, dear! Isn't there a mirror here?

LANDOLPH. Yes, there's one there [*Points to the door on the left.*] If the Marchioness would rather put it on herself . . .

DONNA MATILDA. Yes, yes, that will be better. Give it to me! [*Takes up her hat and goes off with* BERTHOLD, *who carries the cloak and the crown.*]

BELCREDI. Well, I must say, I never thought I should be a Benedictine monk! By the way, this business must cost an awful lot of money.

THE DOCTOR. Like any other fantasy, naturally!

BELCREDI. Well, there's a fortune to go upon.

LANDOLPH. We have got there a whole wardrobe of costumes of the

5. "An acceptable person."

period, copied to perfection from old models. This is my special job. I get them from the best theatrical costumers. They cost lots of money. [DONNA MATILDA *re-enters, wearing mantle and crown.*]

BELCREDI [*at once, in admiration*]. Oh magnificent! Oh, truly regal!

DONNA MATILDA [*looking at* BELCREDI *and bursting out into laughter*]. Oh no, no! Take it off! You're impossible. You look like an ostrich dressed up as a monk.

BELCREDI. Well, how about the Doctor?

THE DOCTOR. I don't think I looked so bad, do I?

DONNA MATILDA. No; the Doctor's all right . . . but you are too funny for words.

THE DOCTOR. Do you have many receptions here then?

LANDOLPH. It depends. He often gives orders that such and such a person appear before him. Then we have to find someone who will take the part. Women too . . .

DONNA MATILDA [*hurt, but trying to hide the fact*]. Ah, women too?

LANDOLPH. Oh, yes; many at first.

BELCREDI [*laughing*]. Oh, that's great! In costume, like the Marchioness?

LANDOLPH. Oh well, you know, women of the kind that lend themselves to . . .

BELCREDI. Ah, I see! [*Perfidiously to the* MARCHIONESS.] Look out, you know he's becoming dangerous for you.

[*The second door on the right opens, and* HAROLD *appears making first of all a discreet sign that all conversation should cease.*]

HAROLD. His Majesty, the Emperor!

[*The* TWO VALETS *enter first, and go and stand on either side of the throne. Then* HENRY IV *comes in between* ORDULPH *and* HAROLD, *who keep a little in the rear respectfully.*

HENRY IV *is about 50 and very pale. The hair on the back of his head is already grey; over the temples and forehead it appears blond, owing to its having been tinted in an evident and puerile fashion. On his cheek bones he has two small, doll-like dabs of color, that stand out prominently against the rest of his tragic pallor. He is wearing a penitent's sack over his regal habit, as at Canossa. His eyes have a fixed look which is dreadful to see, and this expression is in strained contrast with the sackcloth.* ORDULPH *carries the Imperial crown;* HAROLD, *the sceptre with eagle, and the globe with the cross.*]

HENRY IV [*bowing first to* DONNA MATILDA *and afterwards to the* DOCTOR]. My lady . . . Monsignor . . . [*Then he looks at* BELCREDI *and seems about to greet him too; when, suddenly, he turns to* LANDOLPH, *who has approached him, and asks him sotto voce and with diffidence.*] Is that Peter Damiani?[6]

LANDOLPH. No, Sire. He is a monk from Cluny who is accompanying the Abbot.

---

6. The Cardinal-Bishop of Ostia, he led the party of churchmen who held a position between that of Henry and Pope Gregory. When Henry tried to divorce his first wife, Bertha, Peter Damiani forced him to take her back.

HENRY IV [*looks again at* BELCREDI *with increasing mistrust, and then noticing that he appears embarrassed and keeps glancing at* DONNA MATILDA *and the* DOCTOR, *stands upright and cries out*]. No, it's Peter Damiani! It's no use, father, your looking at the Duchess. [*Then turning quickly to* DONNA MATILDA *and the* DOCTOR *as though to ward off a danger.*] I swear it! I swear that my heart is changed towards your daughter. I confess that if he [*Indicates* BELCREDI.] hadn't come to forbid it in the name of Pope Alexander, I'd have repudiated her. Yes, yes, there were people ready to favour the repudiation: the Bishop of Mayence would have done it for a matter of one hundred and twenty farms. [*Looks at* LANDOLPH *a little perplexed and adds.*] But I mustn't speak ill of the bishops at this moment! [*More humbly to* BELCREDI.] I am grateful to you, believe me, I am grateful to you for the hindrance you put in my way!—God knows, my life's been all made of humiliations: my mother,[7] Adalbert, Tribur,[8] Goslar! And now this sackcloth you see me wearing! [*Changes tone suddenly and speaks like one who goes over his part in a parenthesis of astuteness.*] It doesn't matter: clarity of ideas, perspicacity, firmness and patience under adversity that's the thing. [*Then turning to all and speaking solemnly.*] I know how to make amends for the mistakes I have made; and I can humiliate myself even before you, Peter Damiani. [*Bows profoundly to him and remains curved. Then a suspicion is born in him which he is obliged to utter in menacing tones, almost against his will.*] Was it not perhaps you who started that obscene rumor that my holy mother had illicit relations with the Bishop of Augusta?

BELCREDI [*since* HENRY IV *has his finger pointed at him*]. No, no, it wasn't I . . .

HENRY IV [*straightening up*]. Not true, not true? Infamy! [*Looks at him and then adds.*] I didn't think you capable of it! [*Goes to the* DOCTOR *and plucks his sleeve, while winking at him knowingly.*] Always the same, Monsignor, those bishops, always the same!

HAROLD [*softly, whispering as if to help out the doctor*]. Yes, yes, the rapacious bishops!

THE DOCTOR [*to* HAROLD, *trying to keep it up*]. Ah, yes, those fellows . . . ah yes . . .

HENRY IV. Nothing satisfies them! I was a little boy, Monsignor . . . One passes the time, playing even, when, without knowing it, one is a king.—I was six years old; and they tore me away from my mother, and made use of me against her without my knowing anything about it . . . always profaning, always stealing, stealing! . . . One greedier than the other . . . Hanno worse than Stephen! Stephen worse than Hanno![9]

7. His mother served as his first regent, as Adalbert did as his last.
8. It was at Tribur in October of 1076 that Henry was forced to humble himself before the Saxon nobles and clergy and to accept their decision that he had to free himself from Pope Gregory's order of excommunication to retain his crown.

Shortly afterward Henry journeyed to Canossa.
9. Hanno was the Archbishop of Cologne, an ally to Godfrey of Lorraine; he served as Henry's regent between Henry's mother and Adalbert. Stephen is probably Pope Stephen IX, the brother of Godfrey of Lorraine.

LANDOLPH [*sotto voce, persuasively, to call his attention*]. Majesty!

HENRY IV [*turning round quickly*]. Ah yes . . . this isn't the moment to speak ill of the bishops. But this infamy against my mother, Monsignor, is too much. [*Looks at the* MARCHIONESS *and grows tender.*] And I can't even weep for her, Lady . . . I appeal to you who have a mother's heart! She came here to see me from her convent a month ago . . . They had told me she was dead! [*Sustained pause full of feeling. Then smiling sadly.*] I can't weep for her; because if you are here now, and I am like this [*Shows the sackcloth he is wearing.*] it means I am twenty-six years old!

HAROLD. And that she is therefore alive, Majesty! . . .

ORDULPH. Still in her convent!

HENRY IV [*looking at them*]. Ah yes! And I can postpone my grief to another time. [*Shows the* MARCHIONESS *almost with coquetry the tint he has given to his hair.*] Look! I am still fair . . . [*Then slowly as if in confidence.*] For you . . . there's no need! But little exterior details do help! A matter of time, Monsignor, do you understand me? [*Turns to the* MARCHIONESS *and notices her hair.*] Ah, but I see that you too, Duchess . . . Italian, eh? [*As much as to say "false"; but without any indignation, indeed rather with malicious admiration.*] Heaven forbid that I should show disgust or surprise! Nobody cares to recognize that obscure and fatal power which sets limits to our will. But I say, if one is born and one dies . . . Did you want to be born, Monsignor? I didn't! And in both cases, independently of our wills, so many things happen we would wish didn't happen, and to which we resign ourselves as best we can! . . .

DOCTOR [*merely to make a remark, while studying* HENRY IV *carefully*]. Alas! Yes, alas!

HENRY IV. It's like this: When we are not resigned, out come our desires. A woman wants to be a man . . . an old man would be young again. Desires, ridiculous fixed ideas of course—But reflect! Monsignor, those other desires are not less ridiculous: I mean, those desires where the will is kept within the limits of the possible. Not one of us can lie or pretend. We're all fixed in good faith in a certain concept of ourselves. However, Monsignor, while you keep yourself in order, holding on with both your hands to your holy habit, there slips down from your sleeves, there peels off from you like . . . like a serpent . . . something you don't notice: life, Monsignor! [*Turns to the* MARCHIONESS.] Has it never happened to you, my Lady, to find a different self in yourself? Have you always been the same? My God! One day . . . how was it, how was it you were able to commit this or that action? [*Fixes her so intently in the eyes as almost to make her blanch.*] Yes, that particular action, that very one: we understand each other! But don't be afraid: I shall reveal it to none. And you, Peter Damiani, how could you be a friend of that man? . . .

LANDOLPH. Majesty!

HENRY IV [*at once*]. No, I won't name him! [*Turning to* BELCREDI.] What did you think of him? But we all of us cling tight to our conceptions of ourselves, just as he who is growing old dyes his hair. What does it matter that this dyed hair of mine isn't a reality for you, if it *is*, to some extent, for me?—you, you, my Lady, certainly don't dye your hair to deceive the others, nor even yourself; but only to cheat your own image a little before the looking-glass. I do it for a joke! You do it seriously! But I assure you that you too, Madam, are in masquerade, though it be in all seriousness; and I am not speaking of the venerable crown on your brows or the ducal mantle. I am speaking only of the memory you wish to fix in yourself of your fair complexion one day when it pleased you—or of your dark complexion, if you were dark: the fading image of your youth! For you, Peter Damiani, on the contrary, the memory of what you have been, of what you have done, seems to you a recognition of past realities that remain within you like a dream. I'm in the same case too: with so many inexplicable memories—like dreams! Ah! . . . There's nothing to marvel at in it, Peter Damiani! Tomorrow it will be the same thing with our life of today! [*Suddenly getting excited and taking hold of his sackcloth.*] This sackcloth here . . . [*Beginning to take it off with a gesture of almost ferocious joy while the* THREE VALETS *run over to him, frightened, as if to prevent his doing so.*] Ah, my God! [*Draws back and throws off sackcloth.*] Tomorrow, at Bressanone, twenty-seven German and Lombard bishops will sign with me the act of deposition of Gregory VII! No Pope at all! Just a false monk!

ORDULPH [*with the other three*]. Majesty! Majesty! In God's name! . . .

HAROLD [*inviting him to put on the sackcloth again*]. Listen to what he says, Majesty!

LANDOLPH. Monsignor is here with the Duchess to intercede in your favor. [*Makes secret signs to the* DOCTOR *to say something at once.*]

DOCTOR [*foolishly*]. Ah yes . . . yes . . . we are here to intercede . . .

HENRY IV [*repenting at once, almost terrified, allowing the three to put on the sackcloth again, and pulling it down over him with his own hands*]. Pardon . . . yes . . . yes . . . pardon, Monsignor: forgive me, my Lady . . . I swear to you I feel the whole weight of the anathema. [*Bends himself, takes his face between his hands, as though waiting for something to crush him. Then changing tone, but without moving, says softly to* LANDOLPH, HAROLD *and* ORDULPH.] But I don't know why I cannot be humble before that man there! [*Indicates* BELCREDI.]

LANDOLPH [*sotto voce*]. But why, Majesty, do you insist on believing he is Peter Damiani, when he isn't, at all?

HENRY IV [*looking at him timorously*]. He isn't Peter Damiani?

HAROLD. No, no, he is a poor monk, Majesty.

HENRY IV [*sadly with a touch of exasperation*]. Ah! None of us can estimate what we do when we do it from instinct . . . You perhaps, Madam, can understand me better than the others, since you are a woman and a Duchess. This is a solemn and decisive moment. I could, you know, accept the assistance of the Lombard bishops, arrest the Pope, lock him up here in the castle, run to Rome and elect an anti-Pope; offer alliance to Robert Guiscard[1]—and Gregory VII would be lost! I resist the temptation; and, believe me, I am wise in doing so. I feel the atmosphere of our times and the majesty of one who knows how to be what he ought to be! a Pope! Do you feel inclined to laugh at me, seeing me like this? You would be foolish to do so; for you don't understand the political wisdom which makes this penitent's sack advisable. The parts may be changed tomorrow. What would you do then? Would you laugh to see the Pope a prisoner? No! It would come to the same thing: I dressed as a penitent, today; he, as prisoner tomorrow! But woe to him who doesn't know how to wear his mask, be he king or Pope!—Perhaps he is a bit too cruel! No! Yes, yes, maybe!— You remember, my Lady, how your daughter Bertha, for whom, I repeat, my feelings have changed [*Turns to* BELCREDI *and shouts to his face as if he were being contradicted by him.*]—Yes, changed on account of the affection and devotion she showed me in that terrible moment . . . [*Then once again to the* MARCHIONESS.] . . . you remember how she came with me, my Lady, followed me like a beggar and passed two nights out in the open, in the snow?[2] You are her mother! Doesn't this touch your mother's heart? Doesn't this urge you to pity, so that you will beg His Holiness for pardon, beg him to receive us?

DONNA MATILDA [*trembling, with feeble voice*]. Yes, yes, at once . . .

DOCTOR. It shall be done!

HENRY IV. And one thing more! [*Draws them in to listen to him.*] It isn't enough that he should receive me! You know he can do *everything—everything*. I tell you! He can even call up the dead. [*Touches his chest.*] Behold me! Do you see me? There is no magic art unknown to him. Well, Monsignor, my Lady, my torment is really this: that whether here or there [*Pointing to his portrait almost in fear.*] I can't free myself from this magic. I am a penitent now, you see; and I swear to you I shall remain so until he receives me. But you two, when the excommunication is taken off, must ask the Pope to do this thing he can so easily do: to take me away from that; [*Indicating the portrait again.*] and let me live wholly and freely my miserable life. A man can't always be twenty-six, my Lady. I ask this of you for your daughter's sake too; that I may love her as she deserves to be loved, well disposed as I am now, all tender towards her for her pity. There: it's all there! I am in your hands! [*Bows.*] My Lady! Monsignor!

[*He goes off, bowing grandly, through the door by which he entered, leaving everyone stupefied, and the* MARCHIONESS *so profoundly touched, that no sooner has he gone than she breaks out into sobs and sits down almost fainting.*]

CURTAIN

1. A powerful Norman prince and an ally of Pope Gregory's. When Henry took Rome and forced Pope Gregory to take refuge in the Castel San Angelo, Guiscard drove Henry out.
2. Henry stood in the outer courtyard at Canossa for three days before Pope Gregory agreed to see him.

Act II

Another room of the villa, adjoining the throne room. Its furniture is antique and severe. Principal exit at rear in the background. To the left, two windows looking on the garden. To the right, a door opening into the throne room.

Late afternoon of the same day.

DONNA MATILDA, *the* DOCTOR *and* BELCREDI *are on the stage engaged in conversation; but* DONNA MATILDA *stands to one side, evidently annoyed at what the other two are saying; although she cannot help listening, because, in her agitated state, everything interests her in spite of herself. The talk of the other two attracts her attention, because she instinctively feels the need for calm at the moment.*

BELCREDI. It may be as you say, Doctor, but that was my impression.

DOCTOR. I won't contradict you; but, believe me, it is only . . . an impression.

BELCREDI. Pardon me, but he even said so, and quite clearly [*Turning to the* MARCHIONESS.] Didn't he, Marchioness?

DONNA MATILDA [*turning round*]. What did he say? . . . [*Then not agreeing.*] Oh yes . . . but not for the reason you think!

DOCTOR. He was alluding to the costumes we had slipped on . . . Your cloak [*Indicating the* MARCHIONESS.] our Benedictine habits . . . But all this is childish!

DONNA MATILDA [*turning quickly, indignant*]. Childish? What do you mean, Doctor?

DOCTOR. From one point of view, it is—I beg you to let me say so, Marchioness! Yet, on the other hand, it is much more complicated than you can imagine.

DONNA MATILDA. To me, on the contrary, it is perfectly clear!

DOCTOR [*with a smile of pity of the competent person towards those who do not understand*]. We must take into account the peculiar psychology of madmen; which, you must know, enables us to be certain that they observe things and can, for instance, easily detect people who are disguised; can in fact recognize the disguise and yet believe in it; just as children do, for whom disguise is both play and reality. That is why I used the word childish. But the thing is extremely complicated, inasmuch as he must be perfectly aware of being an image to himself and for himself—that image there, in fact! [*Alluding to the portrait in the throne room, and pointing to the left.*]

BELCREDI. That's what he said!

DOCTOR. Very well then— An image before which other images, ours, have appeared: understand? Now he, in his acute and perfectly lucid delirium, was able to detect at once a difference between his image and ours: that is, he saw that ours were make-believes. So he suspected us; because all madmen are armed with a special diffidence. But that's all there is to it! Our make-believe, built up all round his, did not seem pitiful to him. While his seemed all the more tragic to us, in that he, as if in defiance—understand?—and induced by his suspicion, wanted to show us up merely as a joke. That was also partly the case with him, in coming before us with painted cheeks and hair, and saying he had done it on purpose for a jest.

DONNA MATILDA [*impatiently*]. No, it's not that, Doctor. It's not like that! It's not like that!

DOCTOR. Why isn't it, may I ask?

DONNA MATILDA [*with decision but trembling*]. I am perfectly certain he recognized me!

DOCTOR. It's not possible . . . it's not possible!

BELCREDI [*at the same time*]. Of course not!

DONNA MATILDA [*more than ever determined, almost convulsively*]. I tell you, he recognized me! When he came close up to speak to me—looking in my eyes, right into my eyes—he recognized me!

BELCREDI. But he was talking of your daughter!

DONNA MATILDA. That's not true! He was talking of me! Of me!

BELCREDI. Yes, perhaps, when he said . . .

DONNA MATILDA [*letting herself go*]. About my dyed hair! But didn't you notice that he added at once: "or the memory of your dark hair, if you were dark"? He remembered perfectly well that I was dark—then!

BELCREDI. Nonsense! nonsense!

DONNA MATILDA [*not listeng to him, turning to the* DOCTOR]. My hair, Doctor, is really dark—like my daughter's! That's why he spoke of her.

BELCREDI. But he doesn't even know your daughter! He's never seen her!

DONNA MATILDA. Exactly! Oh, you never understand anything! By my daughter, stupid, he meant me—as I was then!

BELCREDI. Oh, this is catching! This is catching, this madness!

DONNA MATILDA [*softly, with contempt*]. Fool!

BELCREDI. Excuse me, were you ever his wife? Your daughter is his wife—in his delirium: Bertha of Susa.

DONNA MATILDA. Exactly! Because I, no longer dark—as he remembered me—but *fair*, introduced myself as "Adelaide," the mother. My daughter doesn't exist for him: he's never seen her—you said so yourself! So how can he know whether she's fair or dark?

BELCREDI. But he said dark, speaking generally, just as anyone who wants to recall, whether fair or dark, a memory of youth in the color of the hair! And you, as usual, begin to imagine things! Doctor, you said I ought not to have come! It's she who ought not to have come!

DONNA MATILDA [*upset for a moment by* BELCREDI'S *remark, recovers herself. Then with a touch of anger, because doubtful*]. No, no . . . he spoke of me . . . He spoke all the time to me, with me, of me . . .

BELCREDI. That's not bad! He didn't leave me a moment's breathing space and you say he was talking all the time to you? Unless you think he was alluding to you too, when he was talking to Peter Damiani!

DONNA MATILDA [*defiantly, almost exceeding the limits of courteous discussion*]. Who knows? Can you tell me why, from the outset, he showed a strong dislike for you, for you alone? [*From the tone of the question, the expected answer must almost explicitly be: "because he understands you are my lover."* BELCREDI *feels this so well that he remains silent and can say nothing.*]

DOCTOR. The reason may also be found in the fact that only the visit of the Duchess Adelaide and the Abbot of Cluny was announced to him. Finding a third person present, who had not been announced, at once his suspicions . . .

BELCREDI. Yes, exactly! His suspicion made him see an enemy in me: Peter Damiani! But she's got it into her head, that he recognized her . . .

DONNA MATILDA. There's no doubt about it! I could see it from his eyes, doctor. You know, there's a way of looking that leaves no doubt whatever . . . Perhaps it was only for an instant, but I am sure!

DOCTOR. It is not impossible: a lucid moment . . .

DONNA MATILDA. Yes, perhaps . . . And then his speech seemed to me full of regret for his and my youth—for the horrible thing that happened to him, that has held him in that disguise from which he has never been able to free himself, and from which he longs to be free—he said so himself!

BELCREDI. Yes, so as to be able to make love to your daughter, or you, as you believe—having been touched by your pity.

DONNA MATILDA. Which is very great, I would ask you to believe.

BELCREDI. As one can see, Marchioness; so much so that a miracle-worker might expect a miracle from it!

DOCTOR. Will you let me speak? I don't work miracles, because I am a doctor and not a miracle-worker. I listened very intently to all he said; and I repeat that that certain analogical elasticity, common to all systematized delirium, is evidently with him much . . . what shall I say?—much relaxed! The elements, that is, of his delirium no longer hold together. It seems to me he has lost the equilibrium of his second personality and sudden recollections drag him—and this is very comforting—not from a state of incipient apathy, but rather from a morbid inclination to reflective melancholy, which shows a . . . a very considerable cerebral activity. Very comforting, I repeat! Now if, by this violent trick we've planned . . .

DONNA MATILDA [*turning to the window, in the tone of a sick person complaining*]. But how is it that the motor has not returned? It's three hours and a half since . . .

DOCTOR. What do you say?

DONNA MATILDA. The motor, Doctor! It's more than three hours and a half . . .

DOCTOR [*taking out his watch and looking at it*]. Yes, more than four hours, by this!

DONNA MATILDA. It could have reached here an hour ago at least! But, as usual . . .

BELCREDI. Perhaps they can't find the dress . . .

DONNA MATILDA. But I explained exactly where it was! [*Impatiently.*] And Frida . . . where is Frida?

BELCREDI [*looking out of the window*]. Perhaps she is in the garden with Charles . . .

DOCTOR. He'll talk her out of her fright.

BELCREDI. She's not afraid, Doctor; don't you believe it: the thing bores her rather . . .

DONNA MATILDA. Just don't ask anything of her! I know what she's like.

DOCTOR. Let's wait patiently. Anyhow, it will soon be over, and it has to be in the evening . . . It will only be the matter of a moment! If we can succeed in rousing him, as I was saying, and in breaking at one go the threads—already slack—which still bind him to this fiction of his, giving him back what he himself asks for—you remember, he said: "one cannot always be twenty-six years old, madam!" if we can give him freedom from this torment, which even *he* feels is a torment, then if he is able to recover at one bound the sensation of the distance of time . . .

BELCREDI [*quickly*]. He'll be cured! [*Then emphatically with irony.*] We'll pull him out of it all!

DOCTOR. Yes, we may hope to set him going again, like a watch which has stopped at a certain hour . . . just as if we had our watches in our hands and were waiting for that other watch to go again.—A shake—so—and let's hope it'll tell the time again after its long stop. [*At this point the* MARQUIS CHARLES DI NOLLI *enters from the principal entrance.*]

DONNA MATILDA. Oh, Charles! . . . And Frida? Where is she?

DI NOLLI. She'll be here in a moment.

DOCTOR. Has the motor arrived?

DI NOLLI. Yes.

DONNA MATILDA. Yes? Has the dress come?

DI NOLLI. It's been here some time.

DOCTOR. Good! Good!

DONNA MATILDA [*trembling*]. Where is she? Where's Frida?

DI NOLLI [*shrugging his shoulders and smiling sadly, like one lending himself unwillingly to an untimely joke*]. You'll see, you'll see! . . . [*Pointing towards the hall.*] Here she is! . . . [BERTHOLD *appears at the threshold of the hall, and announces with solemnity.*]

BERTHOLD. Her Highness the Countess Matilda of Canossa! [FRIDA *enters, magnificent and beautiful, arrayed in the robes of her mother as "Countless Matilda of Tuscany," so that she is a living copy of the portrait in the throne room.*]

FRIDA [*passing* BERTHOLD, *who is bowing, says to him with disdain*]. Of Tuscany, of Tuscany! Canossa is just one of my castles!

BELCREDI [*in admiration*]. Look! Look! She seems another person . . .

DONNA MATILDA. One would say it were I! Look!—Why, Frida, look! She's exactly my portrait, alive!

DOCTOR. Yes, yes . . . Perfect! Perfect! The portrait, to the life.

BELCREDI. Yes, there's no question about it. She *is* the portrait! Magnificent!

FRIDA. Don't make me laugh, or I shall burst! I say, mother, what a tiny waist you had? I had to squeeze so to get into this!

DONNA MATILDA [*arranging her dress a little*]. Wait! . . . Keep still! . . . These pleats . . . is it really so tight?

FRIDA. I'm suffocating! I implore you, to be quick! . . .

DOCTOR. But we must wait till it's evening!

FRIDA. No, no, I can't hold out till evening!

DONNA MATILDA. Why did you put it on so soon?

FRIDA. The moment I saw it, the temptation was irresistible . . .

DONNA MATILDA. At least you could have called me, or have had someone help you! It's still all crumpled.

FRIDA. So I saw, mother; but they are old creases; they won't come out.

DOCTOR. It doesn't matter, Marchioness! The illusion is perfect. [*Then coming nearer and asking her to come in front of her daughter, without hiding her.*] If you please, stay there, there . . . at a certain distance . . . now a little more forward . . .

BELCREDI. For the feeling of the distance of time . . .

DONNA MATILDA [*slightly turning to him*]. Twenty years after! A disaster! A tragedy!

BELCREDI. Now don't let's exaggerate!

DOCTOR [*embarrassed, trying to save the situation*]. No, no! I meant the dress . . . so as to see . . . You know . . .

BELCREDI [*laughing*]. Oh, as for the dress, Doctor, it isn't a matter of twenty years! It's eight hundred! An abyss! Do you really want to shove him across it [*Pointing first to* FRIDA *and then to* MARCHIONESS.] from there to here? But you'll have to pick him up in pieces with a basket! Just think now: for us it is a matter of twenty years, a couple of dresses, and a masquerade. But, if, as you say, Doctor, time has stopped for and around him: if he lives there [*Pointing to* FRIDA.] with her, eight hundred years ago . . . I repeat: the giddiness of the jump will be such, that finding himself suddenly among us . . . [*The* DOCTOR *shakes his head in dissent.*] You don't think so?

DOCTOR. No, because life, my dear baron, can take up its rhythms. This—our life—will at once become real also to him; and will pull him up directly, wresting from him suddenly the illusion, and showing him that the eight hundred years, as you say, are only twenty! It will be like one of those tricks, such as the leap into space, for instance, of the Masonic rite, which appears to be heaven knows how far, and is only a step down the stairs.

BELCREDI. Ah! An idea! Yes! Look at Frida and the Marchioness, doctor! Which is more advanced in time? We old people, Doctor! The young ones think they are more ahead; but it isn't true: we are more ahead, because time belongs to us more than to them.

DOCTOR. If the past didn't alienate us . . .

BELCREDI. It doesn't matter at all! How does it alienate us? They [*Pointing to* FRIDA *and* DI NOLLI.] have still to do what we have accomplished, Doctor: to grow old, doing the same foolish things, more or less, as we did . . . This is the illusion: that one comes forward through a door to life. It isn't so! As soon as one is born, one starts dying; therefore, he who started first is the most advanced of all. The youngest of us is father Adam! Look there: [*Pointing to* FRIDA.] eight hundred years younger than all of us— the Countess Matilda of Tuscany. [*He makes her a deep bow.*]

DI NOLLI. I say, Tito, don't start joking.

BELCREDI. Oh, you think I am joking? . . .

DI NOLLI. Of course, of course . . . all the time.

BELCREDI. Impossible! I've even dressed up as a Benedictine . . .

DI NOLLI. Yes, but for a serious purpose.

BELCREDI. Well, exactly. If it has been serious for the others . . . **for** Frida, now, for instance. [*Then turning to the* DOCTOR.] I swear, Doctor, I don't yet understand what you want to do.

DOCTOR [*annoyed*]. You'll see! Let me do as I wish . . . At present you see the Marchioness still dressed as . . .

BELCREDI. Oh, she also . . . has to masquerade?

DOCTOR. Of course! of course! In another dress that's in there ready to be used when it comes into his head he sees the Countess Matilda of Canossa before him.

FRIDA [*while talking quietly to* DI NOLLI *notices the doctor's mistake*]. Of Tuscany, of Tuscany!

DOCTOR. It's all the same!

BELCREDI. Oh, I see! He'll be faced by two of them . . .

DOCTOR. Two, precisely! And then . . .

FRIDA [*calling him aside*]. Come here, doctor! Listen!

DOCTOR. Here I am! [*Goes near the two young people and pretends to give some explanations to them.*]

BELCREDI [*softly to* DONNA MATILDA]. I say, this is getting rather strong, you know!

DONNA MATILDA [*looking him firmly in the face*]. What?

BELCREDI. Does it really interest you as much as all that—to make you willing to take part in . . . ? For a woman this is simply enormous! . . .

DONNA MATILDA. Yes, for an ordinary woman.

BELCREDI. Oh, no, my dear, for all women,—in a question like this! It's an abnegation.

DONNA MATILDA. I owe it to him.

BELCREDI. Don't lie! You know well enough it's not hurting you!

DONNA MATILDA. Well, then, where does the abnegation come in?

BELCREDI. Just enough to prevent you losing caste in other people's eyes—and just enough to offend me! . . .

DONNA MATILDA. But who is worrying about you now?

DI NOLLI [*coming forward*]. It's all right. It's all right. That's what we'll do! [*Turning toward* BERTHOLD.] Here you, go and call one of those fellows!

BERTHOLD. At once! [*Exit.*]

DONNA MATILDA. But first of all we've got to pretend that we are going away.

DI NOLLI. Exactly! I'll see to that . . . [*To* BELCREDI.] you don't mind staying here?

BELCREDI [*ironically*]. Oh, no, I don't mind, I don't mind! . . .

DI NOLLI. We must look out not to make him suspicious again, you know.

BELCREDI. Oh, Lord! *He* doesn't amount to anything!

DOCTOR. He must believe absolutely that we've gone away. [LANDOLPH *followed by* BERTHOLD *enters from the right.*]

LANDOLPH. May I come in?

DI NOLLI. Come in! Come in! I say—your name's Lolo, isn't it?

LANDOLPH. Lolo, or Landolph, just as you like!

DI NOLLI. Well, look here: the Doctor and the Marchioness are leaving, at once.

LANDOLPH. Very well. All we've got to say is that they have been able to obtain the permission for the reception from His Holiness. He's in there in his own apartments repenting of all he said—and in an awful state to have the pardon! Would you mind coming a minute? . . . If you would, just for a minute . . . put on the dress again . . .

DOCTOR. Why, of course, with pleasure . . .

LANDOLPH. Might I be allowed to make a suggestion? Why not add that the Marchioness of Tuscany has interceded with the Pope that he should be received?

DONNA MATILDA. You see, he has recognized me!

LANDOLPH. Forgive me . . . I don't know my history very well. I am sure you gentlemen know it much better! But I thought it was believed that Henry IV had a secret passion for the Marchioness of Tuscany.

DONNA MATILDA [*at once*]. Nothing of the kind! Nothing of the kind!

LANDOLPH. That's what I thought! But he says he's loved her . . . he's always saying it . . . And now he fears that her indignation for this secret love of his will work him harm with the Pope.

BELCREDI. We must let him understand that this aversion no longer exists.

LANDOLPH. Exactly! Of course!

DONNA MATILDA [*to* BELCREDI]. History says—I don't know whether you know it or not—that the Pope gave way to the supplications of the Marchioness Matilda and the Abbot of Cluny. And I may say, my dear Belcredi, that I intended to take advantage of this fact—at the time of the pageant—to show him my feelings were not so hostile to him as he supposed.

BELCREDI. You are most faithful to history, Marchioness . . .

LANDOLPH. Well then, the Marchioness could spare herself a double disguise and present herself with Monsignor [*Indicating the* DOCTOR.] as the Marchioness of Tuscany.

DOCTOR [*quickly, energetically*]. No, no! That won't do at all. It would ruin everything. The impression from the conformation must be a sudden one, give a shock! No, no, Marchioness, you will appear again as the Duchess Adelaide, the mother of the Empress. And then we'll go away. This is most necessary: that he should know we've gone away. Come on! Don't let's waste any more time! There's a lot to prepare.

[*Exeunt the* DOCTOR, DONNA MATILDA, *and* LANDOLPH, *right.*]

FRIDA. I am beginning to feel afraid again.

DI NOLLI. Again, Frida?

FRIDA. It would have been better if I had seen him before.

DI NOLLI. There's nothing to be frightened of, really.

FRIDA. He isn't furious, is he?

DI NOLLI. Of course not! he's quite calm.

BELCREDI [*with ironic sentimental affectation*]. Melancholy! Didn't you hear that he loves you?

FRIDA. Thanks! That's just why I am afraid.

BELCREDI. He won't do you any harm.

DI NOLLI. It'll only last a minute . . .

FRIDA. Yes, but there in the dark with him . . .

DI NOLLI. Only for a moment; and I will be near you, and all the others behind the door ready to run in. As soon as you see your mother, your part will be finished . . .

BELCREDI. I'm afraid of a different thing: that we're wasting our time . . .

DI NOLLI. Don't begin again! The remedy seems a sound one to me.

FRIDA. I think so too! I feel it! I'm all trembling!

BELCREDI. But, mad people, my dear friends—though they don't know it, alas—have this felicity which we don't take into account . . .

DI NOLLI [*interrupting, annoyed*]. What felicity? Nonsense!

BELCREDI [*forcefully*]. They don't reason!

DI NOLLI. What's reasoning got to do with it, anyway?

BELCREDI. Don't you call it reasoning that he will have to do—according to us—when he sees her [*Indicates* FRIDA.] and her mother? We've reasoned it all out, surely!

DI NOLLI. Nothing of the kind: no reasoning at all! We put before him a double image of his own fantasy, or fiction, as the doctor says.

BELCREDI [*suddenly*]. I say, I've never understood why they take degrees in medicine.

DI NOLLI [*amazed*]. Who?

BELCREDI. The alienists![3]

DI NOLLI. What ought they to take degrees in, then?

FRIDA. If they are alienists, in what else should they take degrees?

BELCREDI. In law, of course! All a matter of talk! The more they talk, the more highly they are considered. "Analogous elasticity," "the sensation of distance in time!" And the first thing they tell you is that they don't work miracles—when a miracle's just what is wanted! But they know that the more they say they are not miracle-workers, the more folk believe in their seriousness!

BERTHOLD [*who has been looking through the keyhole of the door on right*]. There they are! There they are! They're coming in here.

---

3. Those who make a specialty of diseases of the mind; a psychiatrist.

DI NOLLI. Are they?

BERTHOLD. He wants to come with them . . . Yes! . . . He's coming too!

DI NOLLI. Let's get away, then! Let's get away, at once! [*To* BER-THOLD.] You stop here!

BERTHOLD. Must I?

    [*Without answering him,* DI NOLLI, FRIDA, *and* BELCREDI *go out by the main exit, leaving* BERTHOLD *surprised. The door on the right opens, and* LANDOLPH *enters first, bowing. Then* DONNA MATILDA *comes in, with mantle and ducal crown as in the first act; also the* DOCTOR *as the* ABBOT OF CLUNY. HENRY IV *is among them in royal dress.* ORDULPH *and* HAROLD *enter last of all.*]

HENRY IV [*following up what he has been saying in the other room*]. And now I will ask you a question: how can I be astute, if you think me obstinate?

DOCTOR. No, no, not obstinate!

HENRY IV [*smiling, pleased*]. Then you think me really astute?

DOCTOR. No, no, neither obstinate, nor astute.

HENRY IV [*with benevolent irony*]. Monsignor, if obstinacy is not a vice which can go with astuteness, I hoped that in denying me the former, you would at least allow me a little of the latter. I can assure you I have great need of it. But if you want to keep it all for yourself . . .

DOCTOR. I? I? Do I seem astute to you?

HENRY IV. No. Monsignor! What do you say? Not in the least! Perhaps in this case, I may seem a little obstinate to you [*Cutting short to speak to* DONNA MATILDA.] With your permission: a word in confidence to the Duchess. [*Leads her aside and asks her very earnestly.*] Is your daughter really dear to you?

DONNA MATILDA [*dismayed*]. Why, yes, certainly . . .

HENRY IV. Do you wish me to compensate her with all my love, with all my devotion, for the grave wrongs I have done her—though you must not believe all the stories my enemies tell about my dis-soluteness!

DONNA MATILDA. No, no, I don't believe them. I never have believed such stories.

HENRY IV. Well, then are you willing?

DONNA MATILDA [*confused*]. What?

HENRY IV. That I return to love your daughter again? [*Looks at her and adds, in a mysterious tone of warning.*] You mustn't be a friend of the Marchioness of Tuscany!

DONNA MATILDA. I tell you again that she has begged and tried not less than ourselves to obtain your pardon . . .

HENRY IV [*softly, but excitedly*]. Don't tell me that! Don't say that to me! Don't you see the effect it has on me, my Lady?

DONNA MATILDA [*looks a him; then very softly as if in confidence*]. You love her still?

HENRY IV [*puzzled*]. Still? Still, you say? You know, then? But no-body knows! Nobody must know!

DONNA MATILDA. But perhaps she knows, if she has begged so hard for you!

HENRY IV [*looks at her and says*]. And you love your daughter? [*Brief pause. He turns to the* DOCTOR *with laughing accents.*] Ah, Monsignor, it's strange how little I think of my wife! It may be a sin, but I swear to you that I hardly feel her at all in my heart. What is stranger is that her own mother scarcely feels her in her heart. Confess, my Lady, that she amounts to very little for you. [*Turning to* DOCTOR.] She talks to me of that other woman, insistently, insistently, I don't know why! . . .

LANDOLPH [*humbly*]. Maybe, Majesty, it is to disabuse you of some ideas you have had about the Marchioness of Tuscany. [*Then, dismayed at having allowed himself this observation, adds.*] I mean just now, of course . . .

HENRY IV. You too maintain that she has been friendly to me?

LANDOLPH. Yes, at the moment, Majesty.

DONNA MATILDA. Exactly! Exactly! . . .

HENRY IV. I understand. That is to say, you don't believe I love her. I see! I see! Nobody's ever believed it, nobody's ever thought it. Better so, then! But enough, enough! [*Turns to the* DOCTOR *with changed expression.*] Monsignor, you see? The reasons the Pope has had for revoking the excommunication have got nothing at all to do with the reasons for which he excommunicated me originally. Tell Pope Gregory we shall meet again at Brixen. And you, Madame, should you chance to meet your daughter in the courtyard of the castle of your friend the Marchioness, ask her to visit me. We shall see if I succeed in keeping her close beside me as wife and Empress. Many women have presented themselves here already assuring me that they were she. And I thought to have her—yes, I tried sometimes—there's no shame in it, with one's wife!—But when they said they were Bertha, and they were from Susa, all of them—I can't think why—started laughing! [*Confidentially.*] Understand?—in bed—I undressed—so did she—yes, by God, undressed—a man and a woman—it's natural after all! Like that, we don't bother much about who we are. And one's dress is like a phantom that hovers always near one. Oh, Monsignor, phantoms in general are nothing more than trifling disorders of the spirit: images we cannot contain within the bounds of sleep. They reveal themselves even when we are awake, and they frighten us. I . . . ah . . . I am always afraid when, at night time, I see disordered images before me. Sometimes I am even afraid of my own blood pulsing loudly in my arteries in the silence of night, like the sound of a distant step in a lonely corridor! . . . But, forgive me! I have kept you standing too long already. I thank you, my Lady, I thank you, Monsignor. [DONNA MATILDA *and the* DOCTOR *go off bowing. As soon as they have gone,* HENRY IV *suddenly changes his tone.*] Buffoons, buffoons! One can play any tune on them! And that other fellow . . . Pietro Damiani! . . . Caught him out perfectly! He's afraid to appear before me again. [*Moves up and down excitedly while saying this; then sees* BER-

THOLD, *and points him out to the other three valets.*] Oh, look at this imbecile watching me with his mouth wide open! [*Shakes him.*] Don't you understand? Don't you see, idiot, how I treat them, how I play the fool with them, make them appear before me just as I wish? Miserable, frightened clowns that they are! And you [*Addressing the* VALETS.] are amazed that I tear off their ridiculous masks now, just as if it wasn't I who had made them mask themselves to satisfy this taste of mine for playing the madman!

LANDOLPH — HAROLD — ORDULPH [*bewildered, looking at one another*]. What? What does he say? What?

HENRY IV [*answers them imperiously*]. Enough! enough! Let's stop it. I'm tired of it. [*Then as if the thought left him no peace.*] By God! The impudence! To come here along with her lover! . . . And pretending to do it out of pity? So as not to infuriate a poor devil already out of the world, out of time, out of life! If it hadn't been supposed to be done out of pity, one can well imagine that fellow wouldn't have allowed it. Those people expect others to behave as they wish all the time. And, of course, there's nothing arrogant in that! Oh, no! Oh, no! It's merely their way of thinking, of feeling, of seeing. Everybody has his own way of thinking; you fellows, too. Yours is that of a flock of sheep—miserable, feeble, uncertain . . . But those others take advantage of this and make you accept their way of thinking; or, at least, they suppose they do; because, after all, what do they succeed in imposing on you? Words, words which anyone can interpret in his own manner! That's the way public opinion is formed! And it's a bad look out for a man who finds himself labelled one day with one of these words which everyone repeats; for example "madman," or "imbecile." Don't you think it is rather hard for a man to keep quiet, when he knows that there is a fellow going about trying to persuade everybody that he is as he sees him, trying to fix him in other people's opinion as a "madman"—according to him? Now I am talking seriously! Before I hurt my head, falling from my horse . . . [*Stops suddenly, noticing the dismay of the four young men.*] What's the matter with you? [*Imitates their amazed looks.*] What? Am I, or am I not, mad? Oh, yes! I'm mad all right! [*He becomes terrible.*] Well, then, by God, down on your knees, down on your knees! [*Makes them go down on their knees one by one.*] I order you to go down on your knees before me! And touch the ground three times with your foreheads! Down, down! That's the way you've got to be before madmen! [*Then annoyed with their facile humiliation.*] Get up, sheep! You obeyed me, didn't you? You might have put the strait jacket on me! . . . Crush a man with the weight of a word—it's nothing—a fly! all our life is crushed by the weight of words: the weight of the dead. Look at me here: can you really suppose that Henry IV is still alive? All the same, I speak, and order you live men about! Do you think it's a joke that the dead continue to live?—Yes, *here* it's a joke! But get out into the live world!—Ah, you say: what a beautiful sunrise—for us! All time is before us!—Dawn! We will do what we like with this day—.

Ah, yes! To Hell with tradition, the old conventions! Well, go on!
You will do nothing but repeat the old, old words, while you imagine you are living! [*Goes up to* BERTHOLD *who has now become
quite stupid*] You don't understand a word of this do you? What's
your name?

BERTHOLD. I? . . . What? . . . Berthold . . .

HENRY IV. Poor Berthold! What's your name here?

BERTHOLD. I . . . I . . . my name is Fino.

HENRY IV [*feeling the warning and critical glances of the others,
turns to them to reduce them to silence*]. Fino?

BERTHOLD. Fino Pagliuca, sire.

HENRY IV [*turning to* LANDOLPH]. I've heard you call each other by
your nick-names often enough! Your name is Lolo isn't it?

LANDOLPH. Yes, sire . . . [*Then with a sense of immense joy.*] Oh
Lord! Oh Lord! Then he is not mad . . .

HENRY IV [*brusquely*]. What?

LANDOLPH [*hesitating*]. No . . . I said . . .

HENRY IV. Not mad, any more. No. Don't you see? We're having a
joke on those that think I am mad! [*To* HAROLD.] I say, boy, your
name's Franco . . . [*To* ORDULPH] And yours . . .

ORDULPH. Momo.

HENRY IV. Momo, Momo . . . A nice name that!

LANDOLPH. So he isn't . . .

HENRY IV. What are you talking about? Of course not! Let's have
a jolly, good laugh! . . . [*Laughs.*] Ah! . . . Ah! . . . Ah! . . .

LANDOLPH — HAROLD — ORDULPH [*looking at each other half happy
and half dismayed*]. Then he's cured! . . . he's all right! . . .

HENRY IV. Silence! Silence! . . . [*To* BERTHOLD.] Why don't you
laugh? Are you offended? I didn't mean it especially for you. It's
convenient for everybody to insist that certain people are mad, so
they can be shut up. Do you know why? Because it's impossible to
hear them speak! What shall I say of these people who've just
gone away? That one is a whore, another a libertine, another a
swindler . . . don't you think so? You can't believe a word he says
. . . don't you think so?—By the way, they all listen to me terrified. And why are they terrified, if what I say isn't true? Of course,
you can't believe what madmen say—yet, at the same time, they
stand there with their eyes wide open with terror!—Why? Tell
me, tell me, why?—You see I'm quite calm now!

BERTHOLD. But perhaps, they think that . . .

HENRY IV. No, no, my dear fellow! Look me well in the eyes! . . . I
don't say that it's true—nothing is true, Berthold! But . . . look me
in the eyes!

BERTHOLD. Well . . .

HENRY IV. You see? You see? . . . You have terror in your own eyes
now because I seem mad to you! There's the proof of it! [*Laughs.*]

LANDOLPH [*coming forward in the name of the others, exasperated*].
What proof?

HENRY IV. Your being so dismayed because now I seem again mad
to you. You have thought me mad up to now, haven't you? You

feel that this dismay of yours can become terror too—something
to dash away the ground from under your feet and deprive you of
the air you breathe! Do you know what it means to find yourselves
face to face with a madman—with one who shakes the foundations of all you have built up in yourselves, your logic, the logic
of all your constructions? Madmen, lucky folk! construct without logic, or rather with a logic that flies like a feather. Voluble!
Voluble! Today like this and tomorrow—who knows? You say:
"This cannot be"; but for them everything can be. You
say: "This isn't true!" And why? Because it doesn't seem true to
you, or you, or you . . . [*Indicates the three of them in succession.*]
. . . and to a hundred thousand others! One must see what seems
true to these hundred thousand others who are not supposed to be
mad! What a magnificent spectacle they afford, when they reason!
What flowers of logic they scatter! I know that when I was a child,
I thought the moon in the pond was real. How many things I
thought real! I believed everything I was told—and I was happy!
Because it's a terrible thing if you don't hold on to that which
seems true to you today—to that which will seem true to you to-
morrow, even if it is the opposite of that which seemed true to
you yesterday. I would never wish you to think, as I have done,
on this horrible thing which really drives one mad: that if you
were beside another and looking into his eyes—as I one day looked
into somebody's eyes—you might as well be a beggar before a
door never to be opened to you; for he who does enter there will
never be you, but someone unknown to you with his own different
and impenetrable world . . . [*Long pause. Darkness gathers in the
room, increasing the sense of strangeness and consternation in
which the four young men are involved.* HENRY IV *remains aloof,
pondering on the misery which is not only his, but everybody's.
Then he pulls himself up, and says in an ordinary tone.*] It's getting
dark here . . .

ORDULPH. Shall I go for a lamp?

HENRY IV [*ironically*]. The lamp, yes the lamp! . . . Do you suppose I
don't know that as soon as I turn my back with my oil lamp to go to
bed, you turn on the electric light for yourselves, here, and even
there, in the throne room? I pretend not to see it!

ORDULPH. Well, then, shall I turn it on now?

HENRY IV. No, it would blind me! I want my lamp!

ORDULPH. It's ready here behind the door. [*Goes to the main exit,
opens the door, goes out for a moment, and returns with an ancient lamp which is held by a ring at the top.*]

HENRY IV. Ah, a little light! Sit there around the table, no, not like
that; in an elegant, easy, manner! . . . [*To* HAROLD.] Yes, you, like
that! [*Poses him.*] [*Then to* BERTHOLD.] You, so! . . . and I, here!
[*Sits opposite them.*] We could do with a little decorative moonlight. It's very useful for us, the moonlight. I feel a real necessity
for it, and pass a lot of time looking up at the moon from my window. Who would think, to look at her that she knows that eight
hundred years have passed, and that I, seated at the window, can-

not really be Henry IV gazing at the moon like any poor devil?
But, look, look! See what a magnificent night scene we have here:
the emperor surrounded by his faithful counsellors! . . . How do
you like it?

LANDOLPH [*softly to* HAROLD, *so as not to break the enchantment*].
And to think it wasn't true!

HENRY IV. True? What wasn't true?

LANDOLPH [*timidly as if to excuse himself*]. No . . . I mean . . . I
was saying this morning to him [*Indicates* BERTHOLD.]—he has
just entered on service here—I was saying: what a pity that dressed
like this and with so many beautiful costumes in the wardrobe . . .
and with a room like that . . . [*Indicates the throne room.*]

HENRY IV. Well? what's the pity?

LANDOLPH. Well . . . that we didn't know . . .

HENRY IV. That it was all done in jest, this comedy?

LANDOLPH. Because we thought that . . .

HAROLD [*coming to his assistance*]. Yes . . . that it was done seriously!

HENRY IV. What do you say? Doesn't it seem serious to you?

LANDOLPH. But if you say that . . .

HENRY IV. I say that—you are fools! You ought to have known how
to create a fantasy for yourselves, not to act it for me, or anyone
coming to see me; but naturally, simply, day by day, before nobody, feeling yourselves alive in the history of the eleventh century, here at the court of your emperor, Henry IV! You, Ordulph
[*Taking him by the arm.*], alive in the castle of Goslar, waking up
in the morning, getting out of bed, and entering straightway into
the dream, clothing yourself in the dream that would be no more
a dream, because you would have lived it, felt it all alive in you. You
would have drunk it in with the air you breathed; yet knowing all
the time that it was a dream, so you could better enjoy the privilege
afforded you of having to do nothing else but live this dream, this
far off and yet actual dream! And to think that at a distance of eight
centuries from this remote age of ours, so colored and so sepulchral,
the men of the twentieth century are torturing themselves in cease-
less anxiety to know how their fates and fortunes will work out!
Whereas you are already in history with me . . .

LANDOLPH. Yes, yes, very good!

HENRY IV. . . . . Everything determined, everything settled!

ORDULPH. Yes, yes!

HENRY IV. And sad as is my lot, hideous as some of the events are,
bitter the struggles and troublous the time—still all history! All
history that cannot change, understand? All fixed for ever! And
you could have admired at your ease how every effect followed
obediently its cause with perfect logic, how every event took place
precisely and coherently in each minute particular! The pleasure,
the pleasure of history, in fact, which is so great, was yours.

LANDOLPH. Beautiful, beautiful!

HENRY IV. Beautiful, but it's finished! Now that you know, I could
not do it any more! [*Takes his lamp to go to bed.*] Neither could
you, if up to now you haven't understood the reason of it! I am

sick of it now. [*Almost to himself with violent contained rage.*] By God, I'll make her sorry she came here! Dressed herself up as a mother-in-law for me . . . ! And he as an abbot . . . ! And they bring a doctor with them to study me . . . ! Who knows if they don't hope to cure me? . . . Clowns . . . ! I'd like to smack one of them at least in the face: yes, that one—a famous swordsman, they say! . . . He'll kill me . . . Well, we'll see, we'll see! . . . [*A knock at the door.*] Who is it?

THE VOICE OF JOHN. Deo Gratias!

HAROLD [*very pleased at the chance for another joke*]. Oh, it's John, it's old John, who comes every night to play the monk.

ORDULPH [*rubbing his hands*]. Yes, yes! Let's make him do it!

HENRY IV [*at once, severely*]. Fool, why? Just to play a joke on a poor old man who does it for love of me?

LANDOLPH [*to* ORDULPH]. It has to be as if it were true.

HENRY IV. Exactly, as if true! Because, only so, truth is not a jest [*Opens the door and admits* JOHN *dressed as a humble friar with a roll of parchment under his arm.*] Come in, come in, father! [*Then assuming a tone of tragic gravity and deep resentment.*] All the documents of my life and reign favorable to me were destroyed deliberately by my enemies. One only has escaped destruction, this, my life, written by a humble monk who is devoted to me. And you would laugh at him! [*Turns affectionately to* JOHN, *and invites him to sit down at the table.*] Sit down, father, sit down! Have the lamp near you! [*Puts the lamp near him.*] Write! Write!

JOHN [*opens the parchment and prepares to write from dictation*]. I am ready, your Majesty!

HENRY IV [*dictating*]. "The decree of peace proclaimed at Mayence helped the poor and the good, while it damaged the powerful and the bad. [*Curtain begins to fall.*] It brought wealth to the former, hunger and misery to the latter . . ."

CURTAIN

Act III

The throne room so dark that the wall at the bottom is hardly seen. The canvases of the two portraits have been taken away; and, within their frames, FRIDA, *dressed as the "Marchioness of Tuscany" and* CHARLES DI NOLLI, *as "Henry IV," have taken the exact positions of the portraits.*

For a moment, after the raising of curtain, the stage is empty. Then the door on the left opens; and HENRY IV, *holding the lamp by the ring on top of it, enters. He looks back to speak to the four young men, who, with* JOHN, *are presumedly in the adjoining hall, as at the end of the second act.*

HENRY IV. No, stay where you are, stay where you are. I shall manage all right by myself. Good night! [*Closes the door and walks,* very sad and tired, across the hall towards the second door on the right, which leads into his apartments.]

FRIDA [*as soon as she sees that he has just passed the throne, whispers from the niche like one who is on the point of fainting away with fright*]. Henry . . .

HENRY IV [*stopping at the voice, as if someone had stabbed him traitorously in the back, turns a terror-stricken face towards the wall at the bottom of the room; raising an arm instinctively, as if to defend himself and ward off a blow*]. Who is calling me? [*It is not a question, but an exclamation vibrating with terror, which does not expect a reply from the darkness and the terrible silence of the hall, which suddenly fills him with the suspicion that he is really mad.*]

FRIDA [*at his shudder of terror, is herself not less frightened at the part she is playing, and repeats a little more loudly*]. Henry! . . . [*But, although she wishes to act the part as they have given it to her, she stretches her head a little out of frame towards the other frame.*]

HENRY IV [*gives a dreadful cry; lets the lamp fall from his hands to cover his head with his arms, and makes a movement as if to run away*].

FRIDA [*jumping from the frame on to the stand and shouting like a mad woman*]. Henry! . . . Henry! . . . I'm afraid! . . . I'm terrified! . . .

[*And while* DI NOLLI *jumps in turn on to the stand and thence to the floor and runs to* FRIDA *who, on the verge of fainting, continues to cry out, the* DOCTOR, DONNA MATILDA, *also dressed as "Matilda of Tuscany,"* TITO BELCREDI. LANDOLPH, BERTHOLD *and* JOHN *enter the hall from the doors on the right and on the left. One of them turns on the light: a strange light coming from lamps hidden in the ceiling so that only the upper part of the stage is well lighted. The others without taking notice of* HENRY IV, *who looks on astonished by the unexpected inrush, after the moment of terror which still causes him to tremble, run anxiously to support and comfort the still shaking* FRIDA, *who is moaning in the arms of her fiancé. All are speaking at the same time.*]

DI NOLLI. No, no, Frida . . . Here I am . . . I am beside you!

DOCTOR [*coming with the others*]. Enough! Enough! There's nothing more to be done! . . .

DONNA MATILDA. He is cured, Frida. Look! He is cured! Don't you see?

DI NOLLI [*astonished*]. Cured?

BELCREDI. It was only for fun! Be calm!

FRIDA. No! I am afraid! I am afraid!

DONNA MATILDA. Afraid of what? Look at him! He was never mad at all! . . .

DI NOLLI. That isn't true! What are you saying? Cured?

DOCTOR. It appears so. I should say so . . .

BELCREDI. Yes, yes! They have told us so. [*Pointing to the four young men.*]

DONNA MATILDA. Yes, for a long time! He has confided in them, told them the truth!

DI NOLLI [*now more indignant than astonished*]. But what does it mean? If, up to a short time ago . . . ?

BELCREDI. Hum! He was acting, to take you in and also us, who in good faith . . .

DI NOLLI. Is it possible? To deceive his sister, also, right up to the time of her death?

HENRY IV [*remains apart, peering at one and now at the other under the accusation and the mockery of what all believe to be a cruel joke of his, which is now revealed. He has shown by the flashing of his eyes that he is meditating a revenge, which his violent contempt prevents him from defining clearly, as yet. Stung to the quick and with a clear idea of accepting the fiction they have insidiously worked up as true, he bursts forth at this point*]. Go on, I say! Go on!

DI NOLLI [*astonished at the cry*]. Go on! What do you mean?

HENRY IV. It isn't *your* sister only that is dead!

DI NOLLI. My sister? Yours, I say, whom you compelled up to the last moment, to present herself here as your mother Agnes!

HENRY IV. And was she not *your* mother?

DI NOLLI. My mother? Certainly my mother!

HENRY IV. But your mother is dead for me, *old and far away!* You have just got down now from there. [*Pointing to the frame from which he jumped down.*] And how do you know whether I have not wept her long in secret, dressed even as I am?

DONNA MATILDA [*dismayed, looking at the others*]. What does he say? [*Much impressed, observing him.*] Quietly! quietly, for Heaven's sake!

HENRY IV. What do I say? I ask all of you if Agnes was not the mother of Henry IV? [*Turns to* FRIDA *as if she were really the "Marchioness of Tuscany."*] You, Marchioness, it seems to me, ought to know.

FRIDA [*still frightened, draws closer to* DI NOLLI]. No, no, I don't know. Not I!

DOCTOR. It's the madness returning. . . . Quiet now, everybody!

BELCREDI [*indignant*]. Madness indeed, Doctor! He's acting again! . . .

HENRY IV [*suddenly*]. I? You have emptied those two frames over there, and he stands before my eyes as Henry IV . . .

BELCREDI. We've had enough of this joke now.

HENRY IV. Who said joke?

DOCTOR [*loudly to* BELCREDI]. Don't excite him, for the love of God!

BELCREDI [*without lending an ear to him, but speaking louder*]. But they have said so [*Pointing again to the four young men.*], they, they!

HENRY IV [*turning around and looking at them*]. You? Did you say it was all a joke?

LANDOLPH [*timid and embarrassed*]. No . . . really we said that you were cured.

BELCREDI. Look here! Enough of this! [*To* DONNA MATILDA.] Doesn't it seem to you that the sight of him, [*Pointing to* DI NOLLI.] Marchioness, and that of your daughter dressed so, is becoming an intolerable puerility?

DONNA MATILDA. Oh, be quiet! What does the dress matter, if he is cured?

HENRY IV. Cured, yes! I am cured! [*To* BELCREDI.] ah, but not to let it end this way all at once, as you suppose! [*Attacks him.*] Do you know that for twenty years nobody has ever dared to appear before me here like you and that gentleman? [*Pointing to the* DOCTOR.]

BELCREDI. Of course I know it. As a matter of fact, I too appeared before you this morning dressed . . .

HENRY IV. As a monk, yes!

BELCREDI. And you took me for Peter Damiani! And I didn't even laugh, believing, in fact, that . . .

HENRY IV. That I was mad! Does it make you laugh seeing her like that, now that I am cured? And yet you might have remembered that in my eyes her appearance now . . . [*Interrupts himself with a gesture of contempt.*] Ah! [*Suddenly turns to the* DOCTOR.] You are a doctor, aren't you?

DOCTOR. Yes.

HENRY IV. And you also took part in dressing her up as the Marchioness of Tuscany? To prepare a counterjoke for me here, eh?

DONNA MATILDA [*impetuously*]. No, no! What do you say? It was done for you! I did it for your sake.

DOCTOR [*quickly*]. To attempt, to try, not knowing . . .

HENRY IV [*cutting him short*. I understand. I say counter-joke, in his case [*Indicates* BELCREDI.] because he believes that I have been carrying on a jest . . .

BELCREDI. But excuse me, what do you mean? You say yourself you are cured.

HENRY IV. Let me speak! [*To the* DOCTOR.] Do you know, Doctor, that for a moment you ran the risk of making me mad again? By God, to make the portraits speak; to make them jump alive out of their frames . . .

DOCTOR. But you saw that all of us ran in at once, as soon as they told us . . .

HENRY IV. Certainly! [*Contemplates* FRIDA *and* DI NOLLI, *and then looks at the* MARCHIONESS, *and finally at his own costume.*] The combination is very beautiful . . . Two couples . . . Very good, very good, Doctor! For a madman, not bad! . . . [*With a slight wave of his hand to* BELCREDI.] It seems to him now to be a carnival out of season, eh? [*Turns to look at him.*] We'll get rid now of this masquerade costume of mine, so that I may come away with you. What do you say?

BELCREDI. With me? With us?

HENRY IV. Where shall we go? To the Club? In dress coats and with white ties? Or shall both of us go to the Marchioness' house?

BELCREDI. Wherever you like! Do you want to remain here still, to continue—alone—what was nothing but the unfortunate joke of a day of carnival? It is really incredible, incredible how you have been able to do all this, freed from the disaster that befell you!

HENRY IV. Yes, you see how it was! The fact is that falling from my horse and striking my head as I did, I was really mad for I know not how long . . .

DOCTOR. Ah! Did it last long?

HENRY IV [*very quickly to the* DOCTOR]. Yes, Doctor, a long time! I think it must have been about twelve years. [*Then suddenly turning to speak to* BELCREDI.] Thus I saw nothing, my dear fellow, of all that, after that day of carnival, happened for you but not for me: how things changed, how my friends deceived me, how my place was taken by another, and all the rest of it! And suppose my place had been taken in the heart of the woman I loved? . . . And how should I know who was dead or who had disappeared? . . . All this, you know, wasn't exactly a jest for me, as it seems to you . . .

BELCREDI. No, no! I don't mean that if you please. I mean after . . .

HENRY IV. Ah, yes? After? One day [*Stops and addresses the* DOCTOR.]—A most interesting case, Doctor! Study me well! Study me carefully! [*Trembles while speaking.*] All by itself, who knows how, one day the trouble here [*Touches his forehead.*] mended. Little by little, I open my eyes, and at first I don't know whether I am asleep or awake. Then I know I am awake. I touch this thing and that; I see clearly again . . . Ah!—then, as *he* says [*Alludes to* BELCREDI.] away, away with this masquerade, this incubus! Let's open the windows, breathe life once again! Away! Away! Let's run out! [*Suddenly pulling himself up.*] But where? And to do what? To show myself to all, secretly, as Henry IV, not like this, but arm in arm with you, among my dear friends?

BELCREDI. What are you saying?

DONNA MATILDA. Who could think it? It's not to be imagined. It was an accident.

HENRY IV. They all said I was mad before. [*To* BELCREDI.] And you know it! You were more ferocious than any one against those who tried to defend me.

BELCREDI. Oh, that was only a joke!

HENRY IV. Look at my hair! [*Shows him the hair on the nape of his neck.*]

BELCREDI. But mine is grey too!

HENRY IV. Yes, with this difference: that mine went grey here, as Henry IV, do you understand? And I never knew it! I perceived it all of a sudden, one day, when I opened my eyes; and I was terrified because I understood at once that not only had my hair gone grey, but that I was all grey, inside; that everything had fallen to pieces, that everything was finished; and I was going to arrive hungry as a wolf, at a banquet which had already been cleared away . . .

BELCREDI. Yes, but, what about the others? . . .

HENRY IV [*quickly*]. Ah, yes, I know! They couldn't wait until I was cured, not even those, who, behind my back, pricked my saddled horse till it bled. . . .

DI NOLLI [*agitated*]. What, what?

HENRY IV. Yes, treacherously, to make it rear and cause me to fall.

DONNA MATILDA [*quickly, in horror*]. This is the first time I knew that.

HENRY IV. That was also a joke, probably!

DONNA MATILDA. But who did it? Who was behind us, then?

HENRY IV. It doesn't matter who it was. All those that went on feasting and were ready to leave me their scrapings, Marchioness, of miserable pity, or some dirty remnant of remorse in the filthy plate! Thanks! [*Turning quickly to the* DOCTOR.] Now, Doctor, the case must be absolutely new in the history of madness; I preferred to remain mad—since I found everything ready and at my disposal for this new exquisite fantasy. I would live it—this madness of mine—with the most lucid consciousness; and thus revenge myself on the brutality of a stone which had dented my head. The solitude—this solitude—squalid and empty as it appeared to me when I opened my eyes again— I determined to deck it out with all the colors and splendors of that far off day of carnival, when you [*Looks at* DONNA MATILDA *and points* FRIDA *out to her.*]—when you, Marchioness, triumphed. So I would oblige all those who were around me to follow, by God, at my orders that famous pageant which had been—for you and not for me—the jest of a day. I would make it become—for ever—no more a joke but a reality, the reality of a real madness: here, all in masquerade, with throne room, and these my four secret counsellors: secret and, of course, traitors. [*He turns quickly towards them.*] I should like to know what you have gained by revealing the fact that I was cured! If I am cured, there's no longer any need of you, and you will be discharged! To give anyone one's confidence . . . that is really the act of a madman. But now I accuse you in my turn. [*Turning to othe others.*] Do you know? They thought [*Alludes to the* VALETS.] they could make fun of me too with you. [*Bursts out laughing. The others laugh, but shamefacedly, except* DONNA MATILDA.]

BELCREDI [*to* DI NOLLI]. Well, imagine that . . . That's not bad . . .

DI NOLLI [*to the* FOUR YOUNG MEN]. You?

HENRY IV. We must pardon them. This dress [*Plucking his dress*]. which is for me the evident, involuntary caricature of that other continuous, everlasting masquerade, of which we are the involuntary puppets [*Indicates* BELCREDI.], when, without knowing it, we mask ourselves with that which we appear to be . . . ah, that dress of theirs, this masquerade of theirs, of course, we must forgive it them, since they do not yet see it is identical with themselves . . . [*Turning again to* BELCREDI.] You know, it is quite easy to get accustomed to it. One walks about as a tragic character, just as if it were nothing . . . [*Imitates the tragic manner.*] in a room like this . . . Look here, doctor! I remember a priest, certainly Irish, a nice-looking priest, who was sleeping in the sun one November day, with his arm on the corner of the bench of a public garden.

He was lost in the golden delight of the mild sunny air which must have seemed for him almost summery. One may be sure that in that moment he did not know any more that he was a priest, or even where he was. He was dreaming . . . A little boy passed with a flower in his hand. He touched the priest with it here on the neck. I saw him open his laughing eyes, while all his mouth smiled with the beauty of his dream. He was forgetful of everything . . . But all at once, he pulled himself together, and stretched out his priest's cassock; and there came back to his eyes the same seriousness which you have seen in mine; because the Irish priests defend the seriousness of their Catholic faith with the same zeal with which I defend the sacred rights of hereditary monarchy! I am cured, gentlemen: because I can act the madman to perfection, here; and I do it very quietly, I'm only sorry for you that have to live your madness so agitatedly, without knowing it or seeing it.

BELCREDI. It comes to this, then, that it is we who are mad. That's what it is!

HENRY IV [*containing his irritation*]. But if you weren't mad, both you and she [*Indicating the* MARCHIONESS.] would you have come here to see me?

BELCREDI. To tell the truth, I came here believing that you were the madman.

HENRY IV [*suddenly indicating the* MARCHIONESS]. And she?

BELCREDI. Ah, as for her . . . I can't say. I see she is all fascinated by your words, by this *conscious* madness of yours. [*Turns to her.*] Dressed as you are [*Speaking to her.*], you could even remain here to live it out, Marchioness.

DONNA MATILDA. You are insolent!

HENRY IV [*conciliatingly*]. No, Marchioness, what he means to say is that the miracle would be complete, according to him, with you here, who—as the Marchioness of Tuscany, you well know,—could not be my friend, save, as at Canossa, to give me a little pity . . .

BELCREDI. Or even more than a little! She said so herself!

HENRY IV [*to the* MARCHIONESS, *continuing*]. And even, shall we say, a little remorse! . . .

BELCREDI. Yes, that too she has admitted.

DONNA MATILDA [*angry*]. Now look here . . .

HENRY IV [*quickly, to placate her*]. Don't bother about him! Don't mind him! Let him go on infuriating me—though the Doctor's told him not to. [*Turns to* BELCREDI.] But do you suppose I am going to trouble myself any more about what happened between us—the share you had in my misfortune with her [*Indicates the* MARCHIONESS *to him and pointing* BELCREDI *out to her.*] the part he has now in your life? This is my life! Quite a different thing from your life! Your life, the life in which you have grown old—I have not lived that life. [*To* DONNA MATILDA.] Was this what you wanted to show me with this sacrifice of yours, dressing yourself up like this, according to the Doctor's idea? Excellently done, Doctor! Oh, an excellent idea:—"As we were then, eh? and as we are now?" But I am not a madman according to your way of thinking, Doctor. I know very well that that man there [*Indicates* DI NOLLI.] cannot be me; because I am Henry IV, and have been, these twenty years, cast in this eternal masquerade. She has lived these years! [*Indicates the* MARCHIONESS.] She has enjoyed them and has become—look at her!—a woman I can no longer recognize. It is so that I knew her! [*Points to* FRIDA *and draws near her.*] This is the Marchioness I know, always this one! . . . You seem a lot of children to be so easily frightened by me . . . [*To* FRIDA.] And you're frightened too, little girl, aren't you, by the jest that they made you take part in—though they didn't understand it wouldn't be the jest they meant it to be, for me? Oh miracle of miracles! Prodigy of prodigies! The dream alive in you! More than alive in you! It was an image that wavered there and they've made you come to life! Oh, mine! You're mine, mine, mine, in my own right! [HE *holds her in his arms, laughing like a madman, while all stand still terrified. Then as they advance to tear* FRIDA *from his arms, he becomes furious, terrible and cries imperiously to his* VALETS.] Hold them! Hold them! I order you to hold them!

> [*The* FOUR YOUNG MEN *amazed, yet fascinated, move to execute his orders, automatically, and seize* DI NOLLI, *the* DOCTOR, *and* BELCREDI.]

BELCREDI [*freeing himself*]. Leave her alone! Leave her alone! You're no madman!

HENRY IV [*in a flash draws the sword from the side of* LANDOLPH, *who is close to him*]. I'm not mad, eh! Take that, you! . . . [*Drives sword into him. A cry of horror goes up. All rush over to assist* BELCREDI, *crying out together.*]

DI NOLLI. Has he wounded you?

BERTHOLD. Yes, yes, seriously!

DOCTOR. I told you so!

FRIDA. Oh God, oh God!

DI NOLLI. Frida, come here!

DONNA MATILDA. He's mad, mad!

DI NOLLI. Hold him!

BELCREDI [*while* THEY *take him away by the left exit,* HE *protests as he is borne out*]. No, no, you're not mad! You're not mad. He's not mad!

> [THEY *go out by the left amid cries and excitement. After a moment, one hears a still sharper, more piercing cry from* DONNA MATILDA, *and then, silence.*]

HENRY IV [*who has remained on the stage between* LANDOLPH, HAROLD *and* ORDULPH, *with his eyes almost starting out of his head, terrified by the life of his own masquerade which has driven him to crime.*] Now, yes . . . we'll have to [*Calls his* VALETS *around him as if to protect him.*] here we are . . . together . . . for ever!

CURTAIN

Backgrounds and Criticism

EMILE ZOLA

Preface to *Thérèse Raquin*† (1873)

It is by no means my intention to make my play a rallying standard. It has striking shortcomings, toward which no one is more severe than myself; if I were to criticize it, there would be only one thing I should not attack: the author's very obvious desire to bring the theatre into closer relation with the great movement toward truth and experimental science which has since the last century been on the increase in every manifestation of the human intellect. The movement was started by the new methods of science; thence, Naturalism revolutionized criticism and history, in submitting man and his works to a system of precise analysis, taking into account all circumstances, environment, and "organic cases." Then, in turn, art and letters were carried along with the current: painting became realistic—our landscape school killed the historical school—; the novel, that social and individual study with its extremely loose frame-work, after growing and growing, took up all the activities of man, absorbing little by little the various classifications made in the rhetorics of the past. These are all undeniable facts. We have now come to the birth of the true, that is the great, the only force of the century. Everything advances in a literary epoch. Whoever wishes to retreat or turn to one side, will be lost in the general dust. This is why I am absolutely convinced that in the near future the Naturalist movement will take its place in the realm of the drama, and bring with it the power of reality, the new life of modern art.

In the theater, every innovation is a delicate matter. Literary revolutions are slow in making themselves felt. And it is only logical that this should be the last citadel of falsehood: where the true belongs. The public as a whole resents having its habits changed, and the judgments which it passes have all the brutality of a death-sentence. But there comes a time when the public itself becomes an accomplice of the innovators; this is when, imbued with the new spirit, weary of the same stories repeated to it countless times, it feels an imperious desire for youth and originality.

I may be mistaken, but I believe that this is the situation of our public today. The historical drama is in its death-throes, unless something new comes to its assistance: that corpse needs new blood. It is said that the operetta and the dramatic fantasy have killed the

† From Barrett H. Clark, *European Theories of the Drama*, edited by Henry Popkin, New York, 1965. Pp. 377-79.

historical drama. This is not so: the historical drama is dying a natural death, of its own extravagances, lies, and platitudes. If comedy still maintains its place amid the general disintegration of the stage, it is because comedy clings closer to actual life, and is often true. I defy the last of the Romanticists to put upon the stage a heroic drama; at the sight of all the paraphernalia of armor, secret doors, poisoned wines and the rest, the audience would only shrug its shoulders. And melodrama, that bourgeois offspring of the romantic drama, is in the hearts of the people more dead than its predecessor; its false sentiment, its complications of stolen children and discovered documents, its impudent gasconnades, have finally rendered it despicable, so that any attempt to revive it proves abortive. The great works of 1830[1] will always remain advance-guard works, landmarks in a literary epoch, superb efforts which laid low the scaffoldings of the classics. But, now that everything is torn down, and swords and capes rendered useless, it is time to base our works on truth. To substitute the Romantic for the Classic tradition would be a refusal to take advantage of the liberty acquired by our forbears. There should no longer be any school, no more formulas, no standards of any sort; there is only life itself, an immense field where each may study and create as he likes.

I am attempting no justification of my own cause, I am merely expressing my profound conviction—upon which I particularly insist—that the experimental and scientific spirit of the century will enter the domain of the drama, and that in it lies its only possible salvation. Let the critics look about them and tell me from what direction help is to be expected, or a breath of life, to rehabilitate the drama? Of course, the past is dead. We must look to the future, and the future will have to do with the human problem studied in the frame-work of reality. We must cast aside fables of every sort, and delve into the living drama of the two-fold life of the character and its environment, bereft of every nursery tale, historical trapping, and the usual conventional stupidities. The decayed scaffoldings of the drama of yesterday will fall of their own accord. We must clear the ground. The well-known receipts for the tying and untying of an intrigue have served their time; now we must seek a simple and broad picture of men and things, such as Molière might write. Outside of a few scenic conventions, all that is now known as the "science of the theater" is merely a heap of clever tricks, a narrow tradition that serves to cramp the drama, a ready-made code of language and hackneyed situations, all known and planned out beforehand, which every original worker will scorn to use.

Naturalism is already stammering its first accents on the stage. I

1. The Romantic revolt in the French theatre led by Victor Hugo and Alex- andre Dumas [*Editor*].

shall not cite any particular work, but among the plays produced during these past two years, there are many that contain the germ of the movement whose approach I have prophesied. I am not taking into account plays by new authors, I refer especially to certain plays of dramatists who have grown old in the *métier,* who are clever enough to realize the new transformation that is taking place in our literature. The drama will either die, or become modern and realistic.

It is under the influence of these ideas that I have dramatized *Thérèse Raquin.* As I have said, there are in that novel a subject, characters and *milieu* constituting, to my mind, excellent elements for the tentative of which I have dreamed. I tried to make of it a purely human study, apart from every other interest, and go straight to the point; the action did not consist in any story invented for the occasion, but in the inner struggles of the characters; there was no logic of facts, but a logic of sensation and sentiment; and the dénouement was the mathematical result of the problem as proposed. I followed the novel step by step; I laid the play in the same room, dark and damp, in order not to lose relief or the sense of impending doom; I chose supernumerary fools, who were unnecessary from the point of view of strict technique, in order to place side by side with the fearful agony of my protagonists the drab life of every day; I tried continually to bring my setting into perfect accord with the occupations of my characters, in order that they might not *play,* but rather *live,* before the audience. I counted, I confess, and with good reason, on the intrinsic power of the drama to make up, in the minds of the audience, for the absence of intrigue and the usual details. The attempt was successful, and for that reason I am more hopeful for the plays I *shall* write than for *Thérèse Raquin.* I publish this play with vague regret, and with a mad desire to change whole scenes.

The critics were wild: they discussed the play with extreme violence. I have nothing to complain of, but rather thank them. I gained by hearing them praise the novel from which the play was taken, the novel which was so badly received by the press when it was first published. To-day the novel is good, and the drama is worthless. Let us hope that the play would be good were I able to extract something from it that the critics should declare bad. In criticism, you must be able to read between the lines. For instance, how could the old champions of 1830 be indulgent toward *Thérèse Raquin?* Supposing even that my merchant's wife were a queen and my murderer wore an apricot-colored cloak? And if at the last Thérèse and Laurent should take poison from a golden goblet filled to the brim with Syracusan wine? But that nasty little shop! And those lower middle-class shop-keepers that presume to participate in a drama of their own in their own house, with their oilcloth table-cover! It is certain that the last of the Romanticists, even if they found some talent in my play, would have denied it absolutely, with the beautiful injustice of literary passion. Then there were the critics whose beliefs were in direct opposition to my own; these very sincerely tried to persuade me that I was wrong to burrow in a place which was not their own. I read these critics carefully; they said some excellent things, and I shall do my best to profit by some of their utterances which particularly appealed to me. Finally, I have to thank those sympathetic critics, of my own age, those who share my hopes, because, sad to say, one rarely finds support among one's elders: one must grow along with one's own generation, be pushed ahead by the one that follows, and attain the idea and the manner of the time. * * *

ROBERT EDMOND JONES

Toward A New Stage†

What is called realism is usually a record of life at a low pitch and ebb viewed in the sunless light of day.
—WALTER DE LA MARE

In our fine arts not imitation but creation is the aim.
—EMERSON

Once again the air of Broadway is filled with the gloomy forebodings of the self-styled prophets of the theatre who are busy assuring us for the thousandth time that the theatre is dying. In the past we have not taken these prophecies of doom too seriously, for we have observed that the theatre is always dying and always being reborn, Phoenix-like, at the very moment when we have finished conducting the funeral service over its ashes. But this time there is a greater content of truth in what the prophets are telling us. The theatre we knew, the theatre we grew up in, has recently begun to show unmistakable symptoms of decline. It is dwindling and shrinking away, and presently it will be forgotten.

Let us look at this dying theatre for a moment. It is essentially a prose theatre, and of late it has become increasingly a theatre of journalism. The quality of legend is almost completely absent from contemporary plays. They appear to be uneasily conscious of the camera and the phonograph. There are brilliant exceptions to this

† From *The Dramatic Imagination* by Robert Edmond Jones, New York, 1941. Pp. 135-48. Copyright 1941 by Robert Edmond Jones. Reprinted with the permission of Theatre Arts Books, New York.

generalization—I need mention only *Green Pastures, Strange Interlude,* or Sophie Treadwell's exciting *Saxophone*[1]—but in the main the dramas of our time are as literal as if they had been dictated by the village iceman or by a parlor-maid peering through a keyhole.

It is this theatre that is dying. Motion pictures are draining the very life-blood from its veins.

Disquieting as this may be to the purveyors of show-business, there is a kind of cosmic logic in it. The theatre of our time grew up on a photographic basis and it would have continued to function contentedly on this basis for many years to come if motion pictures had not been invented. But nothing can be so photographic as a photograph, especially when that photograph moves and speaks. Motion pictures naturally attract to themselves everything that is factual, objective, explicit. Audiences are gradually coming to prefer realism on the screen to realism in the theatre. Almost insensibly Hollywood has brought an irresistible pressure to bear upon the realistic theatre and the picture-frame stage. Future generations may find it hard to believe that such things ever existed.

These statements are not to be construed as an adverse criticism of motion pictures. On the contrary: motion pictures have begun to take on a new life of their own, a life of pure thought, and they are becoming more alive every day. The fact is that in our time the theatre has become mixed, confused, a hybrid. A play can be made from almost any novel and a motion picture can be made from almost any play. What this means is that the theatre has not yet been brought to its own perfection. Literature is literature and theatre is theatre and motion pictures are motion pictures, but the theatre we know is all these things mixed together and scrambled. But now—fortunately, some of us believe—we may note an increasing tendency toward the separation of these various arts, each into its own characteristic form. Motion pictures are about to become a great liberating agent of drama. By draining the theatre of its literalness they are giving it back to imagination again.

Think of it! No more copybook dialogue; no more drug-store clerks drafted to impersonate themselves in real drug-stores transferred bodily to the stage, no more unsuccessful attempts to prove to us that we are riding the waves of the Atlantic Ocean with Columbus instead of sitting in a theatre, no more tasteful, well-furnished rooms with one wall missing. . . . A theatre set free for beauty and splendor and dreams—

1. Marc Connelly's *Green Pastures* (1930) and Eugene O'Neill's *Strange Interlude* (1928), the first a deliberately naive retelling of Bible stories and the second a probing psychological drama which attempted to dramatize the characters' unspoken thoughts, were boldly innovative dramatic experiments in their time. Sophie Treadwell's *Saxophone*, an experiment in "blues" drama, never received a New York production [*Editor*].

Of late years realism in the theatre has become more and more closely bound up with the idea of the "stage picture." But now it would seem that this idea is about to be done away with once and for all. The current conception of stage scenery as a more or less accurate representation of an actual scene—organized and simplified, to be sure, but still essentially a representation—is giving way to another conception of something far less actual and tangible. It is a truism of theatrical history that stage pictures become important only in periods of low dramatic vitality. Great dramas do not need to be illustrated or explained or embroidered. They need only to be brought to life on the stage. The reason we have had realistic stage "sets" for so long is that few of the dramas of our time have been vital enough to be able to dispense with them. That is the plain truth. Actually the best thing that could happen to our theatre at this moment would be for playwrights and actors and directors to be handed a bare stage on which no scenery could be placed, and then told that they must write and act and direct for this stage. In no time we should have the most exciting theatre in the world.

The task of the stage designer is to search for all sorts of new and direct and unhackneyed ways whereby he may establish the *sense of place*. The purpose of a stage setting, whatever its form, whether it be for tragedy, comedy, history, pastoral, pastoral-comical, historical-pastoral, tragical-historical, tragical-comical-historical-pastoral, scene individable or poem unlimited, is simply this: *to remind the audience of where the actors are supposed to be*. A true stage-setting is an invocation to the *genius loci*—a gesture "enforcing us to this place"—and nothing more. The theatre we know occupies itself with creating stage "illusion." What we are now interested in, however, is not illusion, but allusion, and allusion to the most magical beauty. *I seek less*, said Walt Whitman, *to display any theme or thought and more to bring you into the atmosphere of the theme or thought—there to pursue your own flight*. This is precisely the aim of stage designing, to bring the audience into the atmosphere of the theme or thought. Any device will be acceptable so long as it succeeds in carrying the audience along with it.

The loveliest and most poignant of all stage pictures are those that are seen in the mind's eye. All the elaborate mechanism of our modern stage cannot match for real evocation the line, *Tom's a-cold*. A mere indication of place can send our imaginations leaping. *We'll 'een to't like French falcons, fly at anything we see. . . .* It is this delighted exercise of imagination, this heady joy, that the theatre has lost and is about to find once more. Call upon this faculty—so strangely latent in all of us—and it responds at once, swift as Ariel to the summons of Prospero.

Shakespeare could set his stage with a phrase. Listen—

This castle hath a pleasant seat; the air
Nimbly and sweetly recommends itself
Unto our gentle senses. . . .

Listen again—

Now we bear the king
Toward Calais; grant him there; there seen,
Heave him away upon your wingèd thoughts
Athwart the sea. . . .

And here is William Butler Yeats' introduction to *The Only Jealousy of Emer*—

I call before the eyes a roof
With cross-beams darkened by smoke.
A fisher's net hangs from a beam,
A long oar lies against the wall.
I call up a poor fisher's house. . . .

And here is the speech of Hakuryo the Fisherman in the Japanese No drama, *Hagoromo*, so beautifully translated by Fenollosa—

I am come to shore. I disembark at Matsubara. It is just as they told me. A cloudless sky, a rain of flowers, strange fragrances all about me. These are no common things. Nor is this cloak that hangs upon the pine tree.

And finally—to take a more familiar example—here is a passage from Thornton Wilder's play, *Our Town*. The narrator is speaking—

This is our doctor's house—Doc Gibbs'. This is the back door.

Two arched trellises are pushed out, one by each proscenium pillar.

There's some scenery for those who think they have to have scenery.
There's a garden here. Corn . . . peas . . . beans . . . hollyhocks. . . .

These stage directions (for that is what they are; they direct us) evoke the *locale* and the mood of the particular drama in question with great ease and with great economy of means. How simple they are, and how telling, and how right! A few words, and the life-giving dramatic imagination answering the summons, fresh, innocent, immensely powerful, eagerly obedient.

In Shakespeare's day the written and the spoken word held a peculiar magic, as of something new-born. With this exciting new medium of dramatic expression at hand it was simple for a playwright to transport his audience from place to place by a spoken stage-direction,

In fair Verona, where we lay our scene . . .

or by a legend, THIS IS MASTER JONAH JACKDAWE'S HOUSE, or, PLAIN NEAR SALISBURY, painted on a signboard. A printed legend seen on our stage today would arouse only a momentary curiosity, or at most a pleasure akin to that of examining some antique stage trapping in a museum, a sword once handled by Burbage, a letter penned by Bernhardt. There is little to be gained by attempting to re-establish such purely literary indications of place in the theatre. But the spoken word still retains its power to enchant and transport an audience, and this power has recently been enhanced to an extraordinary and altogether unpredictable degree by the inventions of the sound amplifier and the radio transmitter. The technicians of the radio learned long ago to induce the necessary sense of place by means of spoken descriptions and so-called "sound-effects." These devices have caught the imagination of radio audiences. They are accepted without question and cause no surprise. We can hardly imagine a radio drama without them. It is odd that our playwrights and stage designers have not yet sensed the limitless potentialities of this new enhancement of the spoken word. A magical new medium of scenic evocation is waiting to be pressed into service. Imagine a Voice pervading a theatre from all directions at once, enveloping us, enfolding us, whispering to us of scenes "beautiful as pictures no man drew" . . .

Today we are more picture-minded than word-minded. But what we hear in the theatre must again take its place beside what we see in the theatre. If we are to enhance the spoken word by any means whatever we must first be sure that it is worth enhancing. Here is a direct challenge to our dramatists and our actors to clothe ideas in expressive speech and to give words once again their high original magic.

Imaginative minds have been at work in our theatre for years and they stand ready to create new scenic conventions at a moment's notice. We may look with profit at a few of the outstanding productions of these years. *The Cradle Will Rock*; A neutral-tinted cyclorama. A double row of chairs in which the members of the cast are seated in full view of the audience. An upright piano set slantwise near the footlights. The author enters, sits at the piano, plays a few bars of music, announces the various members of the cast, who bow in turn as their names are mentioned. Then he says simply, The first scene is laid in a night court. Two actors rise and speak the first lines. The play has begun. . . . *Julius Caesar:* The bare brick walls of the stage of the Mercury Theatre stained blood-red from floor to gridiron. The lighting equipment fully visible. A wide low platform set squarely in the center of the stage. A masterly handling of the crowds and some superb acting. . . . Stravinsky's *Oedipus Rex* presented by the League of Composers: The great stage of the Metropolitan Opera House a deep blue void out of which emerge the towering marionettes who symbolize the protagonists of the drama. Their speeches declaimed in song by blue-robed soloists and a blue-robed chorus grouped in a pyramid on the stage below them. . . . The procession of wet black umbrellas in the funeral scene of *Our Town.* The little toy Ark in *Green Pastures.* The Burning Bush in the same play, a tiny faded Christmas tree with a few colored electric light bulbs hanging on it. Best of all, and ever to be remembered, the March of the Pilgrims to the Promised Land on a treadmill retrieved from a musical comedy and put by the author to an exalted use of which its original inventor had never dreamed. And there are many others.

Audiences have found these productions thoroughly convincing. Their delighted acceptance of the imaginative conventions employed gives proof—if proof be needed—that the unrealistic idea has come into the theatre to stay. Whether the particular devices I have noted are to be adopted in future or not is a matter of no importance. We may take courage from them to move forward boldly and with confidence.

Newer and more imaginative scenic conventions will presently become firmly established in the theatre and representations of place will be superseded by evocations of the sense of place. Then the stage designer can turn his attention away from the problem of creating stage settings to the larger and far more engrossing problem of creating stages. For the primary concern of the stage designer is with stages, and not with stage settings. All our new devices for scenic evocation will be ineffective except in an exciting environment. The new drama and its new stage setting will require a new type of stage. What will this new stage be like?

First of all it will be presented frankly for what it is, a stage. I have never been able to understand why the stages of our theatres should invariably be so ugly. Theatre owners take great pains to make the auditoriums of their theatres glowing and cheerful and comfortable, but what we call a stage today is nothing more than a bare brick box fretted with radiator pipes. Why should this be so? One would think that a stage was something to be ashamed of, to be hidden away like an idiot child. Surely the first step toward creating a new stage is to make it an exciting thing in itself.

This stage will be simple, with the simplicity of the stages of the great theatres of the past. We shall turn again to the traditional, ancient stage, the platform, the *tréteau*, the boards that actors have trod from time out of mind. What we need in the theatre is a space for actors to act in, a space reserved for them where they may practice their immemorial art of holding the mirror up to nature. They will be able to move with ease to and from this space, they will be able to make their appropriate exits and entrances. We shall find a way to bathe these actors in expressive and dramatic light. And that is all.

I am looking forward to a theatre, a stage, a production, that will be exciting to the point of astonishment. Behind the proscenium will stand a structure of great beauty, existing in dignity, a Precinct set apart. It will be distinguished, austere, sparing in detail, rich in suggestion. It will carry with it a high mood of awe and eagerness. Like the great stages of the past, it will be an integral part of the structure of the theatre itself, fully visible at all times. Will this stage be too static, too inflexible, too "harshly frugal" for audiences to accept? Not at all. If it is beautiful and exciting and expressive we shall not tire of it. Moreover, its mood will be continually varied by changes of light.

Our new-old stage—this architectural structure sent through moods by light—will serve as never before to rivet our attention upon the actors' performance. It will remind us all over again that great drama is always presented to us in terms of action. In the ever-shifting tableaux of Shakespeare's plays, in the flow of the various scenes, he gives us an incessant visual excitement. Once we have arrived at an understanding of the inner pattern of any one of his plays and can externalize it on Shakespeare's own stage we discover an unsuspected visual brilliance arising directly from the variety of the action. It is the performance, not the setting, which charms us. The fixed stage becomes animated through the movement of the actors. All good actors will respond like thoroughbred race-horses to the challenge.

This fixed, impersonal, dynamic environment will be related to the particular drama in question by slight and subtle indications of place and mood—by ingenious arrangements of the necessary properties, by the groupings of the actors, by an evocative use of sound and light. Then the actors will be left free to proceed with the business of performance. In this connection we may again note a striking characteristic of radio drama. A stage setting remains on the stage throughout the action of any particular scene. But the setting of a radio drama is indicated at the beginning of the performance and then quietly dismissed. Radio audiences do not find it necessary to remain conscious of the setting during the action of the drama. They become absorbed in the performance at once. Why should not this be true of theatre audiences as well? Here is an idea that is filled with far-reaching suggestion for our stage designers. Can it be that the stage settings of today are too much with us, late and soon? Would not a setting be more effective if it were merely an indication of the atmosphere of the play offered to the audience for a moment at the beginning of the performance and then taken away again?

If we discard for a moment the idea of a setting as something that must act all through a play along with the actors and think of it instead as a brief ceremony of welcome, so to speak, a toast to introduce the speakers of the evening, all sorts of arresting and exciting visual compositions occur to us. Scenery takes wings, becomes once more a part of the eternal flight and fantasy of the theatre. Let us imagine a few of these "transitory shows of things." A curtain lifted at the back of the stage to reveal a momentary glimpse of a giant painting of the park on Sorin's estate—the First Act of *The Sea Gull*.[2] A delicate arrangement of screens and ironwork laced with moonlight for the setting of a modern drawing-room comedy, visible at the rise of the curtain, then gliding imperceptibly out of sight. A motion-picture screen lowered at the beginning of the performance of *He Who Gets Slapped*,[3] the life of the little circus given to the audience in a series of screen "wipe-outs." A group of actors arranged in a vividly expressive tableau at the rise of the curtain to evoke a battle-scene from *Richard III*, dissolving into the action of the play. And so on. Such ideas may seem far-fetched, but they are by no means so far-fetched as we might be inclined to believe.

No one seriously interested in the theatre can be anything but overjoyed at the encroachments of Hollywood upon Broadway. Hollywood is doing what the artists of our theatre have been trying to do for years. It is drawing realism out of the theatre as the legendary madstone—the Bezoar of the ancients—drew the madness from a lunatic patient. The only theatre worth saving, the only theatre worth having, is a theatre motion pictures cannot touch. When we succeed in eliminating from it every trace of the photographic attitude of mind, when we succeed in making a production that is the exact antithesis of a motion picture, a production that is everything a motion picture is not and nothing a motion picture is, the old lost magic will return once more. The realistic theatre, we may remember, is less than a hundred years old. But the theatre—great theatre, world theatre—is far older than that, so many centuries older that by comparison it makes our little candid-camera theatre seem like something that was thought up only the day before yesterday. We need not be impatient. A brilliant fresh theatre will presently appear.

2. By Anton Chekhov [*Editor*].
3. By Leonid Andreyev (1871–1919) [*Editor*].

ARTHUR MILLER
Tragedy and the Common Man†

In this age few tragedies are written. It has often been held that the lack is due to a paucity of heroes among us, or else that modern man has had the blood drawn out of his organs of belief by the skepticism of science, and the heroic attack on life cannot feed on an attitude of reserve and circumspection. For one reason or another, we are often held to be below tragedy—or tragedy above us. The inevitable conclusion is, of course, that the tragic mode is archaic, fit only for the very highly placed, the kings or the kingly, and where this admission is not made in so many words it is most often implied.

I believe that the common man is as apt a subject for tragedy in its highest sense as kings were. On the face of it this ought to be obvious in the light of modern psychiatry, which bases its analysis upon classic formulations, such as the Oedipus and Orestes complexes, for instances, which were enacted by royal beings, but which apply to everyone in similar emotional situations.

More simply, when the question of tragedy in art is not at issue, we never hesitate to attribute to the well-placed and the exalted the very same mental processes as the lowly. And finally, if the exaltation of tragic action were truly a property of the high-bred character alone, it is inconceivable that the mass of mankind should cherish tragedy above all other forms, let alone be capable of understanding it.

As a general rule, to which there may be exceptions unknown to me, I think the tragic feeling is evoked in us when we are in the presence of a character who is ready to lay down his life, if need be, to secure one thing—his sense of personal dignity. From Orestes to Hamlet, Medea to Macbeth, the underlying struggle is that of the individual attempting to gain his "rightful" position in his society.

Sometimes he is one who has been displaced from it, sometimes one who seeks to attain it for the first time, but the fateful wound from which the inevitable events spiral is the wound of indignity, and its dominant force is indignation. Tragedy, then, is the consequence of a man's total compulsion to evaluate himself justly.

In the sense of having been initiated by the hero himself, the tale always reveals what has been called his "tragic flaw," a failing that is not peculiar to grand or elevated characters. Nor is it necessarily a weakness. The flaw, or crack in the character, is really nothing—and need be nothing, but his inherent unwillingness to remain passive in the face of what he conceives to be a challenge to his

† From *The New York Times*, February 27, 1949, Sec. 2, pp. 1, 3. Copyright © 1949 by The New York Times Company.

Reprinted by permission of *The New York Times* and Ashley Famous Agency, Inc.

dignity, his image of his rightful status. Only the passive, only those who accept their lot without active retaliation, are "flawless." Most of us are in that category.

But there are among us today, as there always have been, those who act against the scheme of things that degrades them, and in the process of action everything we have accepted out of fear or insensitivity or ignorance is shaken before us and examined, and from this total onslaught by an individual against the seemingly stable cosmos surrounding us—from this total examination of the "unchangeable" environment—comes the terror and the fear that is classically associated with tragedy.

More important, from this total questioning of what has previously been unquestioned, we learn. And such a process is not beyond the common man. In revolutions around the world, these past thirty years, he has demonstrated again and again this inner dynamic of all tragedy.

Insistence upon the rank of the tragic hero, or the so-called nobility of his character, is really but a clinging to the outward forms of tragedy. If rank or nobility of character was indispensable, then it would follow that the problems of those with rank were the particular problems of tragedy. But surely the right of one monarch to capture the domain from another no longer raises our passions, nor are our concepts of justice what they were to the mind of an Elizabethan king.

The quality in such plays that does shake us, however, derives from the underlying fear of being displaced, the disaster inherent in being torn away from our chosen image of what and who we are in this world. Among us today this fear is as strong and perhaps stronger, than it ever was. In fact, it is the common man who knows this fear best.

Now, if it is true that tragedy is the consequence of a man's total compulsion to evaluate himself justly, his destruction in the attempt posits a wrong or an evil in his environment. And this is precisely the morality of tragedy and its lesson. The discovery of the moral law, which is what the enlightenment of tragedy consists of, is not the discovery of some abstract or metaphysical quantity.

The tragic right is a condition of life, a condition in which the human personality is able to flower and realize itself. The wrong is the condition which suppresses man, perverts the flowing out of his love and creative instinct. Tragedy enlightens—and it must, in that it points the heroic finger at the enemy of man's freedom. The thrust for freedom is the quality in tragedy which exalts. The revolutionary questioning of the stable environment is what terrifies. In no way is the common man debarred from such thoughts or such actions.

Seen in this light, our lack of tragedy may be partially accounted for by the turn which modern literature has taken toward the purely psychiatric view of life, or the purely sociological. If all our miseries, our indignities, are born and bred within our minds, then all action, let alone the heroic action, is obviously impossible.

And if society alone is responsible for the cramping of our lives, then the protagonist must needs be so pure and faultless as to force us to deny his validity as a character. From neither of these views can tragedy derive, simply because neither represents a balanced concept of life. Above all else, tragedy requires the finest appreciation by the writer of cause and effect.

No tragedy can therefore come about when its author fears to question absolutely everything, when he regards any institution, habit or custom as being either everlasting, immutable or inevitable. In the tragic view the need of man to wholly realize himself is the only fixed star, and whatever it is that hedges his nature and lowers it is ripe for attack and examination. Which is not to say that tragedy must preach revolution.

The Greeks could probe the very heavenly origin of their ways and return to confirm the rightness of laws. And Job could face God in anger, demanding his right and end in submission. But for a moment everything is in suspension, nothing is accepted, and in this stretching and tearing apart of the cosmos, in the very action of so doing, the character gains "size," the tragic stature which is spuriously attached to the royal or the highborn in our minds. The commonest of men may take on that stature to the extent of his willingness to throw all he has into the contest, the battle to secure his rightful place in his world.

There is a misconception of tragedy with which I have been struck in review after review, and in many conversations with writers and readers alike. It is the idea that tragedy is of necessity allied to pessimism. Even the dictionary says nothing more about the word than that it means a story with a sad or unhappy ending. This impression is so firmly fixed that I almost hesitate to claim that in truth tragedy implies more optimism in its author than does comedy, and that its final result ought to be the reinforcement of the onlooker's brightest opinions of the human animal.

For, if it is true to say that in essence the tragic hero is intent upon claiming his whole due as a personality, and if this struggle must be total and without reservation, then it automatically demonstrates the indestructible will of man to achieve his humanity.

The possibility of victory must be there in tragedy. Where pathos rules, where pathos is finally derived, a character has fought a battle he could not possibly have won. The pathetic is achieved when the protagonist is, by virtue of his witlessness, his insensitivity or the very air he gives off, incapable of grappling with a much superior force.

Pathos truly is the mode for the pessimist. But tragedy requires a nicer balance between what is possible and what is impossible. And it is curious, although edifying, that the plays we revere, century after century, are the tragedies. In them, and in them alone, lies the belief—optimistic, if you will, in the perfectibility of man.

It is time, I think, that we who are without kings, took up this bright thread of our history and followed it to the only place it can possibly lead in our time—the heart and spirit of the average man.

ANTONIN ARTAUD

No More Masterpieces†

One of the reasons for the asphyxiating atmosphere in which we live without possible escape or remedy—and in which we all share, even the most revolutionary among us—is our respect for what has been written, formulated, or painted, what has been given form, as if all expression were not at last exhausted, were not at a point where things must break apart if they are to start anew and begin fresh.

We must have done with this idea of masterpieces reserved for a self-styled elite and not understood by the general public; the mind has no such restricted districts as those so often used for clandestine sexual encounters.

Masterpieces of the past are good for the past: they are not good for us. We have the right to say what has been said and even what has not been said in a way that belongs to us, a way that is immediate and direct, corresponding to present modes of feeling, and understandable to everyone.

It is idiotic to reproach the masses for having no sense of the sublime, when the sublime is confused with one or another of its formal manifestations, which are moreover always defunct manifestations. And if for example a contemporary public does not understand *Oedipus Rex*, I shall make bold to say that it is the fault of *Oedipus Rex* and not of the public.

In *Oedipus Rex* there is the theme of incest and the idea that nature mocks at morality and that there are certain unspecified powers at large which we would do well to beware of, call them *destiny* or anything you choose.

† From *The Theater And Its Double* by Antonin Artaud, Translated from the French by Mary Caroline Richards, New York, 1958. Pp. 74-83. Published by Grove Press, Inc., copyright © 1958 by Grove Press, Inc. Reprinted by permission of the publishers.

There is in addition the presence of a plague epidemic which is a physical incarnation of these powers. But the whole in a manner and language that have lost all touch with the rude and epileptic rhythm of our time. Sophocles speaks grandly perhaps, but in a style that is no longer timely. His language is too refined for this age, it is as if he were speaking beside the point.

However, a public that shudders at train wrecks, that is familiar with earthquakes, plagues, revolutions, wars; that is sensitive to the disordered anguish of love, can be affected by all these grand notions and asks only to become aware of them, but on condition that it is addressed in its own language, and that its knowledge of these things does not come to it through adulterated trappings and speech that belong to extinct eras which will never live again.

Today as yesterday, the public is greedy for mystery: it asks only to become aware of the laws according to which destiny manifests itself, and to divine perhaps the secret of its apparitions.

Let us leave textual criticism to graduate students, formal criticism to esthetes, and recognize that what has been said is not still to be said; that an expression does not have the same value twice, does not live two lives; that all words, once spoken, are dead and function only at the moment when they are uttered, that a form, once it has served, cannot be used again and asks only to be replaced by another, and that the theater is the only place in the world where a gesture, once made, can never be made the same way twice.

If the public does not frequent our literary masterpieces, it is because those masterpieces are literary, that is to say, fixed; and fixed in forms that no longer respond to the needs of the time.

Far from blaming the public, we ought to blame the formal screen we interpose between ourselves and the public, and this new form of idolatry, the idolatry of fixed masterpieces which is one of the aspects of bourgeois conformism.

This conformism makes us confuse sublimity, ideas, and things with the forms they have taken in time and in our minds—in our snobbish, precious, aesthetic mentalities which the public does not understand.

How pointless in such matters to accuse the public of bad taste because it relishes insanities, so long as the public is not shown a valid spectacle; and I defy anyone to show me *here* a spectacle valid —valid in the supreme sense of the theater—since the last great romantic melodramas, i.e., since a hundred years ago.

The public, which takes the false for the true, has the sense of the true and always responds to it when it is manifested. However it is not upon the stage that the true is to be sought nowadays, but in the street; and if the crowd in the street is offered an occasion to show its human dignity, it will always do so.

If people are out of the habit of going to the theater, if we have all finally come to think of theater as an inferior art, a means of popular distraction, and to use it as an outlet for our worst instincts, it is because we have learned too well what the theater has been, namely, falsehood and illusion. It is because we have been accustomed for four hundred years, that is since the Renaissance, to a purely descriptive and narrative theater—storytelling psychology; it is because every possible ingenuity has been exerted in bringing to life on the stage plausible but detached beings, with the spectacle on one side, the public on the other—and because the public is no longer shown anything but the mirror of itself.

Shakespeare himself is responsible for this aberration and decline, this disinterested idea of the theater which wishes a theatrical performance to leave the public intact, without setting off one image that will shake the organism to its foundations and leave an ineffaceable scar.

If, in Shakespeare, a man is sometimes preoccupied with what transcends him, it is always in order to determine the ultimate consequences of this preoccupation within him, i.e., psychology.

Psychology, which works relentlessly to reduce the unknown to the known, to the quotidian and the ordinary, is the cause of the theater's abasement and its fearful loss of energy, which seems to me to have reached its lowest point. And I think both the theater and we ourselves have had enough of psychology.

I believe furthermore that we can all agree on this matter sufficiently so that there is no need to descend to the repugnant level of the modern and French theater to condemn the theater of psychology.

Stories about money, worry over money, social careerism, the pangs of love unspoiled by altruism, sexuality sugar-coated with an eroticism that has lost its mystery have nothing to do with the theater, even if they do belong to psychology. These torments, seductions, and lusts before which we are nothing but Peeping Toms gratifying our cravings, tend to go bad, and their rot turns to revolution: we must take this into account.

But this is not our most serious concern.

If Shakespeare and his imitators have gradually insinuated the idea of art for art's sake, with art on one side and life on the other, we can rest on this feeble and lazy idea only as long as the life outside endures. But there are too many signs that everything that used to sustain our lives no longer does so, that we are all mad, desperate, and sick. And I call for *us* to react.

This idea of a detached art, of poetry as a charm which exists only to distract our leisure, is a decadent idea and an unmistakable symptom of our power to castrate.

334 · *Antonin Artaud*

Our literary admiration for Rimbaud, Jarry, Lautréamont,[1] and a few others, which has driven two men to suicide, but turned into café gossip for the rest, belongs to this idea of literary poetry, of detached art, of neutral spiritual activity which creates nothing and produces nothing; and I can bear witness that at the very moment when that kind of personal poetry which involves only the man who creates it and only at the moment he creates it broke out in its most abusive fashion, the theater was scorned more than ever before by poets who have never had the sense of direct and concerted action, nor of efficacity, nor of danger.

We must get rid of our superstitious valuation of texts and *written* poetry. Written poetry is worth reading once, and then should be destroyed. Let the dead poets make way for others. Then we might even come to see that it is our veneration for what has already been created, however beautiful and valid it may be, that petrifies us, deadens our responses, and prevents us from making contact with that underlying power, call it thought-energy, the life force, the determinism of change, lunar menses, or anything you like. Beneath the poetry of the texts, there is the actual poetry, without form and without text. And just as the efficacity of masks in the magic practices of certain tribes is exhausted—and these masks are no longer good for anything except museums—so the poetic efficacity of a text is exhausted; yet the poetry and the efficacity of the theater are exhausted least quickly of all, since they permit the *action* of what is gesticulated and pronounced, and which is never made the same way twice.

It is a question of knowing what we want. If we are prepared for war, plague, famine, and slaughter we do not even need to say so, we have only to continue as we are; continue behaving like snobs, rushing en masse to hear such and such a singer, to see such and such an admirable performance which never transcends the realm of art (and even the Russian ballet at the height of its splendor never transcended the realm of art), to marvel at such and such an exhibition of painting in which exciting shapes explode here and there but at random and without any genuine consciousness of the forces they could rouse.

The empiricism, randomness, individualism, and anarchy must cease.

Enough of personal poems, benefitting those who create them much more than those who read them.

Once and for all, enough of this closed, egoistic, and personal art.

---

1. Arthur Rimbaud (1854–1891), Alfred Jarry (1873–1907), and Isidore Ducasse, Count of Lautréamont (1846–1870) were poets of the symbolist movement in France. All three lived unconventional, sensational lives [*Editor*].

Our spiritual anarchy and intellectual disorder is a function of the anarchy of everything else—or rather, everything else is a function of this anarchy.

I am not one of those who believe that civilization has to change in order for the theater to change; but I do believe that the theater, utilized in the highest and most difficult sense possible, has the power to influence the aspect and formation of things: and the encounter upon the stage of two passionate manifestations, two living centers, two nervous magnetisms is something as entire, true, even decisive, as, in life, the encounter of one epidermis with another in a timeless debauchery.

That is why I propose a theater of cruelty.—With this mania we all have for depreciating everything, as soon as I have said, "cruelty," everybody will at once take it to mean "blood." But *"theater of cruelty"* means a theater difficult and cruel for myself first of all. And, on the level of performance, it is not the cruelty we can exercise upon each other by hacking at each other's bodies, carving up our personal anatomies, or, like Assyrian emperors, sending parcels of human ears, noses, or neatly detached nostrils through the mail, but the much more terrible and necessary cruelty which things can exercise against us. We are not free. And the sky can still fall on our heads. And the theater has been created to teach us that first of all.

Either we will be capable of returning by present-day means to this superior idea of poetry and poetry-through-theater which underlies the Myths told by the great ancient tragedians, capable once more of entertaining a religious idea of the theater (without meditation, useless contemplation, and vague dreams), capable of attaining awareness and a possession of certain dominant forces, of certain notions that control all others, and (since ideas, when they are effective, carry their energy with them) capable of recovering within ourselves those energies which ultimately create order and increase the value of life, or else we might as well abandon ourselves now, without protest, and recognize that we are no longer good for anything but disorder, famine, blood, war, and epidemics.

Either we restore all the arts to a central attitude and necessity, finding an analogy between a gesture made in painting or the theater, and a gesture made by lava in a volcanic explosion, or we must stop painting, babbling, writing, or doing whatever it is we do.

I propose to bring back into the theater this elementary magical idea, taken up by modern psychoanalysis, which consists in effecting a patient's cure by making him assume the apparent and exterior attitudes of the desired condition.

I propose to renounce our empiricism of imagery, in which the unconscious furnishes images at random, and which the poet arranges at random too, calling them poetic and hence hermetic images, as if the kind of trance that poetry provides did not have its reverberations throughout the whole sensibility, in every nerve, and as if poetry were some vague force whose movements were invariable.

I propose to return through the theater to an idea of the physical knowledge of images and the means of inducing trances, as in Chinese medicine which knows, over the entire extent of the human anatomy, at what points to puncture in order to regulate the subtlest functions.

Those who have forgotten the communicative power and magical mimesis of a gesture, the theater can reinstruct, because a gesture carries its energy with it, and there are still human beings in the theater to manifest the force of the gesture made.

To create art is to deprive a gesture of its reverberation in the organism, whereas this reverberation, if the gesture is made in the conditions and with the force required, incites the organism and, through it, the entire individuality, to take attitudes in harmony with the gesture.

The theater is the only place in the world, the last general means we still possess of directly affecting the organism and, in periods of neurosis and petty sensuality like the one in which we are immersed, of attacking this sensuality by physical means it cannot withstand.

If music affects snakes, it is not on account of the spiritual notions it offers them, but because snakes are long and coil their length upon the earth, because their bodies touch the earth at almost every point; and because the musical vibrations which are communicated to the earth affect them like a very subtle, very long massage; and I propose to treat the spectators like the snakecharmer's subjects and conduct them *by means of their organisms* to an apprehension of the subtlest notions.

At first by crude means, which will gradually be refined. These immediate crude means will hold their attention at the start.

That is why in the "theater of cruelty" the spectator is in the center and the spectacle surrounds him.

In this spectacle the sonorisation is constant: sounds, noises, cries are chosen first for their vibratory quality, then for what they represent.

Among these gradually refined means light is interposed in its turn. Light which is not created merely to add color or to brighten, and which brings its power, influence, suggestions with it. And the light of a green cavern does not sensually dispose the organism like the light of a windy day.

After sound and light there is action, and the dynamism of action: here the theater, far from copying life, puts itself whenever possible in communication with pure forces. And whether you accept or deny them, there is nevertheless a way of speaking which gives the name of "forces" to whatever brings to birth images of energy in the unconscious, and gratuitous crime on the surface.

A violent and concentrated action is a kind of lyricism: it summons up supernatural images, a bloodstream of images, a bleeding spurt of images in the poet's head and in the spectator's as well.

Whatever the conflicts that haunt the mind of a given period, I defy any spectator to whom such violent scenes will have transferred their blood, who will have felt in himself the transit of a superior action, who will have seen the extraordinary and essential movements of his thought illuminated in extraordinary deeds—the violence and blood having been placed at the service of the violence of the thought—I defy that spectator to give himself up, once outside the theater, to ideas of war, riot, and blatant murder.

So expressed, this idea seems dangerous and sophomoric. It will be claimed that example breeds example, that if the attitude of cure induces cure, the attitude of murder will induce murder. Everything depends upon the manner and the purity with which the thing is done. There is a risk. But let it not be forgotten that though a theatrical gesture is violent, it is disinterested; and that the theater teaches precisely the uselessness of the action which, once done, is not to be done, and the superior use of the state unused by the action and which, *restored*, produces a purification.

I propose then a theater in which violent physical images crush and hypnotize the sensibility of the spectator seized by the theater as by a whirlwind of higher forces.

A theater which, abandoning psychology, recounts the extraordinary, stages natural conflicts, natural and subtle forces, and presents itself first of all as an exceptional power of redirection. A theater that induces trance, as the dances of Dervishes induce trance, and that addresses itself to the organism by precise instruments, by the same means as those of certain tribal music cures which we admire on records but are incapable of originating among ourselves.

There is a risk involved, but in the present circumstances I believe it is a risk worth running. I do not believe we have managed to revitalize the world we live in, and I do not believe it is worth the trouble of clinging to; but I do propose something to get us out of our marasmus, instead of continuing to complain about it, and about the boredom, inertia, and stupidity of everything.

Henrik Ibsen
and
The Wild Duck

HENRIK IBSEN

Letters and Speeches†

Letter to Georg Brandes[1]

Dresden, December 20, 1870

Dear Georg Brandes, You have been in my thoughts every day lately. I heard of your illness both from Councilor Hegel and from the Norwegian papers, but I did not write to you since I was afraid you might still be too weak to receive letters. Your kind note received yesterday has, however, quite reassured me. Many thanks for thinking of me!

You ask what you ought to undertake in the future. I can tell you: in the immediate future you must undertake nothing at all. You must give your mind a holiday for an indefinite period. You must lie still and grow strong. You see, these illnesses bring a blessing with them—the condition in which one comes out of them! A glorious time awaits you when you begin to regain your strength. I know this from personal experience. All evil thoughts had left me; I felt like eating only the lightest and most delicate foods—anything coarse, I thought, would taint me. It is an indescribable state of thankfulness and well-being.

And when you have grown strong and fit again, then what will you do? Why, then you will do what you must do. A nature such as yours has no choice.

I am not going to write you a long letter; that would not be good for you. And you had better not write to me for some time yet.

† From *Ibsen, Letters and Speeches*, edited by Evert Sprinchorn, New York, 1964. Pp. 105-7, 108, 109, 114-16, 226, 227, 337-38. Copyright © 1964 by Evert Sprinchorn. Reprinted by permission of the publishers, Hill & Wang, Inc.
1. A Danish literary critic (1842–1927) who was at this time ill with typhoid in Rome [*Editor*].

I was in Copenhagen last summer. You have many, many friends and adherents there; perhaps more than you realize. If you are away for a while, so much the better; one always gains something by being missed.

They have finally taken Rome away from us human beings and given it to the politicians.[2] Where shall we take refuge now? Rome was the one sanctuary in Europe, the only place that enjoyed true freedom—freedom from the tyranny of political freedom. I do not think I shall visit it again after what has happened. All that was delightful—the unsophisticatedness, the dirt—all that will disappear. For every statesman who crops up there, an artist will be ruined. And the glorious longing for liberty—that is at an end now. Yes—I for one must confess that the only thing I love about liberty is the struggle for it; I care nothing for the possession of it.

One morning some time ago my new work [on Julian the Apostate] became strikingly clear to me; and in my exuberance I dashed off a letter to you. But I never sent it. The mood did not last long, and when it was over, the letter was useless.

Moreover, the historic events of today are claiming a large share of my thoughts. The old illusory France has been smashed to bits, and as soon as the new, *de facto* Prussia is also smashed too, we shall enter the age of the future in one leap. How the old ideas will come tumbling about our ears! And it is high time they did. Up till now we have been living on nothing but crumbs from the revolutionary table of last century, and I think we have been chewing on that stuff long enough. The old terms must be invested with new meaning, and given new explanations. Liberty, equality, and fraternity are no longer what they were in the days of the late-lamented guillotine. This is what the politicians will not understand; and that is why I hate them. They want only their own special revolutions—external revolutions, political revolutions, etc. But that is only dabbling. What is really needed is a revolution of the human spirit. And in this *you* shall be one of those who take the lead. But the first thing to do is to get that fever out of your system.

Your devoted friend,
Henrik Ibsen

Letter to Georg Brandes

Dresden, February 17, 1871

Dear Brandes, I suspected that my long silence would make you angry. But I confidently trust that our relations are such that they will stand the strain. In fact, I have a decided feeling that a brisk correspondence would be much more dangerous to our friendship.

2. Rome had recently been annexed by the new Italian republic after a plebe- scite [*Editor*].

Once we have actually met, many things will assume another aspect; much will be cleared up on both sides. Until then I really run the danger of exhibiting myself to you through my casual remarks in quite a wrong light. You philosophers can prove black is white—and I have to desire to allow myself to be reduced, per correspondence, to a stone or a cock—even if it is possible to restore me after an oral explanation to the rank of a human being [a reference to Holberg's *Erasmus Montanus*]. In your previous letter you ironically admire my undisturbed mental equilibrium under the present conditions. There we have the stone! And now in your last friendly (?) note, you make me out a hater of liberty. The cock! The fact is that my mind is relatively calm because I regard France's present misfortune as the greatest good fortune that could befall her. As to liberty, I take it that our disagreement is a disagreement about words. I shall never agree to making liberty synonymous with political liberty. What you call liberty, I call liberties; and what I call the struggle for liberty is nothing but the steady, vital growth and pursuit of the very conception of liberty. He who possesses liberty as something already achieved possesses it dead and soulless; for the essence of the idea of liberty is that it continue to develop steadily as men pursue it and make it part of their being. Anyone who stops in the middle of the struggle and says, "Now I have it," shows that he has lost it. It is exactly this tendency to stop dead when a certain given amount of liberty has been acquired that is characteristic of the political state—and it is this that I said was not good.

Of course it is a benefit to possess the right to vote, the right of self-taxation, etc. But who benefits? The citizen, not the individual. Now, there is absolutely no logical necessity for the individual to be a citizen. On the contrary—the state is the curse of the individual. How did Prussia purchase its strength as a state? By absorbing the spirit of the individual into a political and geographical conception. The waiter makes the best soldier. Now, turn to the Jewish nation, the nobility of the human race. How has it managed to preserve itself—in its isolation, in its poetry—despite all the barbarity of the outside world? Because it had no state to burden it. Had the Jewish people remained in Palestine, it would long since have been ruined in the process of construction, like all the other nations. The state must be abolished! In that revolution I will take part. Undermine the idea of the state; make willingness and spiritual kinship the only essentials for union—and you have the beginning of a libberty that is of some value. Changing one form of government for another is merely a matter of toying with various degrees of the same thing—a little more or a little less. Folly, all of it.

Yes, dear friend, the great thing is not to allow oneself to be frightened by the venerableness of institutions. The state has its roots in time: it will reach its height in time. Greater things than it will fall; all religion will fall. Neither standards of morality nor of art are eternal. What is there that we are really obliged to hold on to? Who will vouch for it that two and two do not make five up on Jupiter?

I cannot and will not enlarge upon these points in a letter. My best thanks for your poem! It is not the last one you will write. The poet's calling proclaims itself in every line. You overestimate me, but I set that down to our friendship. But thank you, thank you! Keep me ever so in your thoughts. I shall not fail you! * * *

Yours sincerely,
Henrik Ibsen

Letter to Georg Brandes
Dresden, September 24, 1871

Dear Brandes, I always read your letters with strangely mixed feelings. They are more like poems than letters. What you write strikes me like a cry of distress from one who has been left the sole survivor in some great lifeless desert. And I cannot but rejoice, and thank you, that you direct this cry to me. But on the other hand, I begin to worry. I ask myself: "What will such a mood lead to?" And I have nothing to comfort myself with but the hope that it is only temporary. You seem to me to be passing through the same crisis that I passed through when I began to write *Brand*. I am convinced that you, too, will find the medicine that will drive the disease out of your system.

Energetic productivity is an excellent remedy. What I recommend for you is a thoroughgoing, full-blooded egoism, which will force you for a time to regard yourself and your work as the only things of consequence in this world, and everything else as simply nonexistent. Now, don't take this as evidence of something brutal in my nature! There is no way in which you can benefit society more than by coining the metal you have in yourself. I have never really had a very great feeling for solidarity. In fact, I have allowed it in my mental cargo only because it is a traditional article of belief. If one had the courage to throw it overboard altogether, one would be getting rid of the ballast that weighs most heavily on the personality. There are actually moments when the whole history of the world reminds one of a sinking ship; the only thing to do is to save oneself.

Nothing will come from special reforms. The whole human race is on the wrong track. That is the trouble. Is there really anything tenable in the present situation—with its unattainable ideals, etc.? All of human history reminds me of a cobbler who doesn't stick to his last but goes on the stage to act. And we have made a fiasco in both the roles of hero and lover. The only part in which we have shown a little talent is that of the naive comic; and with our more highly developed self-consciousness we shall no longer be fitted even for that. I do not believe that things are better in other countries. The masses, both at home and abroad, have absolutely no understanding of higher things.

And so I should raise a banner, should I? My dear friend, I would be putting on the same kind of performance Louis Napoleon did when he landed at Boulogne with an eagle on his head.[3] Later, when the hour of his destiny struck, he didn't need any eagle. In the course of my work on Julian, I have become a fatalist in a way; yet this play will be a kind of banner. But do not worry—this will not be a tendentious work. I explore the characters, their conflicting plans, the plot, and do not concern myself with the moral of the whole—always assuming, however, that by the moral of the story you do not mean its philosophy. You can take it for granted that the philosophy will burst forth as the final verdict on the struggle and on the victory. But this is too abstract to make much sense. You must look at the work itself.

Your last letter on this subject did not cause me any uneasiness. In the first place, I was prepared for such misgivings on your part; and in the second, I am not handling the subject in the way you assume.

I have received your book [probably *Criticisms and Portraits*], and all I can say is that I return to it again and again. It is incomprehensible to me, my dear, good Brandes, that you of all people can be despondent. Very few have received the call of the spirit as clearly and unmistakably as you have. What is the use of despairing? Have you any right to do so? But don't think I don't understand you perfectly.

. . . And now in conclusion accept my heartfelt thanks for your visit to Dresden. Those were festive hours for me. Best wishes for health, courage, happiness—everything good!

Yours sincerely,
Henrik Ibsen

Speech at the Banquet in Stockholm
Stockholm, September 24, 1887

Ladies and Gentlemen: I thank you most deeply for all the friendliness, for the welcoming spirit and the understanding that I have once again received proofs of here. It is a great joy to feel that one belongs to a greater country. But to reply fully to all the words of praise that I have just heard lies outside and beyond my power.

3. In 1840 Louis Napoleon, seeking to end his exile and to assume the throne of France, made a foolish and theatrical descent on Boulogne. He was captured, tried, and imprisoned [Translator's note].

There is, however, one point in particular that I should like to consider for a moment. It has been said that I, too, have contributed, and in a prominent way, to bringing about a new era in our countries. I believe, on the contrary, that the time in which we now live might with quite as good reason be described as a conclusion, and that something new is about to be born from it. For I believe that the teaching of natural science about evolution is also valid as regards the spiritual aspects of life. I believe that the time is not far off when political and social conceptions will cease to exist in their present forms, and that from both of them there will arise a unity, which for a while will contain within itself the conditions for the happiness of mankind. I believe that poetry, philosophy, and religion will be merged in a new category and become a new vital force, of which we who are living now can have no clear conception.

It has been said of me on different occasions that I am a pessimist. And so I am insofar as I do not believe in the everlastingness of human ideals. But I am also an optimist insofar as I firmly believe in the capacity for the propagation and development of ideals. Especially, to be more definite, I believe that the ideals of our time, while disintegrating, are tending toward what in my play *Emperor and Galilean* I designated "the third kingdom." Therefore, permit me to drink a toast to the future—to that which is to come. We are assembled here on a Saturday night. Following it, comes the day of rest, the holiday, the holy day—whichever you wish to call it. For my part I shall be content with my week's work, a lifelong week, if it can serve to prepare the spirit for tomorrow. But above all I shall be most content if it will serve to strengthen the spirit for that week of work that inevitably follows.

Thank you.

Speech at the Banquet of the Norwegian League for Women's Rights
Christiania, May 26, 1898

I am not a member of the Women's Rights League. Whatever I have written has been without any conscious thought of making propaganda. I have been more the poet and less the social philosopher than people generally seem inclined to believe. I thank you for the toast, but must disclaim the honor of having consciously worked for the women's rights movement. I am not even quite clear as to just what this women's rights movement really is. To me it has seemed a problem of mankind in general. And if you read my books carefully you will understand this. True enough, it is desirable to solve the woman problem, along with all the others; but that has not been the whole purpose. My task has been the *description of humanity*. To be sure, whenever such a description is felt to be reasonably true, the reader will read his own feelings and sentiments into the work of the poet. These are then attributed to the poet; but incorrectly so. Every reader remolds the work beautifully and neatly, each according to his own personality. Not only those who write but also those who read are poets. They are collaborators. They are often more poetical than the poet himself.

With these reservations, let me thank you for the toast you have given me. I do indeed recognize that women have an important task to perform in the particular directions this club is working along. I will express my thanks by proposing a toast to the League for Women's Rights, wishing it progress and success.

The task always before my mind has been to advance our country and to give our people a higher standard. To achieve this, two factors are important. It is for the *mothers*, by strenuous and sustained labor, to awaken a conscious feeling of *culture* and *discipline*. This feeling must be awakened before it will be possible to lift the people to a higher plane. It is the women who shall solve the human problem. As mothers they shall solve it. And only in that capacity can they solve it. Here lies a great task for woman. My thanks! And success to the League for Women's Rights!

ROBERT M. ADAMS

Ibsen on the Contrary†

A museum-culture, such as we live in, is forever digging up forgotten or semi-forgotten artifacts, dusting them off vigorously, giving them a new coat of varnish, oohing and aahing over them briefly, and then setting them on the top shelf of Case 17 in Room K to gather dust for another generation or two. That is where Ibsen is to be looked for these days—on a respectable eminence in a glassed case under half a century's dust. He was once a thunderstorm in the theater, and outside as well. A compatriot gently suggested during a friendly discussion that his work, though obviously great and certain to last a very long time, might not endure absolutely forever; Ibsen leaped from his chair in cold fury and flung it after the man's retreating head: "Rob me of eternity, and you rob me of everything!" Well, so far he has his eternity; but at the price of persisting, rather like a mummied head in an anthropological museum—shrunken, dried, *miniaturized*.

In fact, the flood of explanatory writing which, in the last decade

---

† Under the title "Henrik Ibsen: The Fifty-first Anniversary," an earlier version of this essay was first published in *The Hudson Review*, Vol. X, No. 3 (Autumn, 1957). It has been especially revised for this Norton Critical Edition.

of the nineteenth century and the first decade of the twentieth, set out to moderate Ibsen's strangeness and domesticate his art under the rubric of honest naturalism has done its work all too fully. The modern reader knows Ibsen, or thinks he knows him, too well by half. He is established in the public mind as an author of middle-class tragedies, a man who tried to transplant the art of Sophocles into the social milieu of William Dean Howells. It is hard to see why a first-class dramatic artist should want to undertake any such enterprise; therefore, Ibsen was not a first-class dramatic artist. The only flaw in this argument is its major premise. Ibsen in the great plays was not a simple bourgeois realist; the effect at which he was aiming was not Sophoclean, or in fact tragic, except in the most attenuated sense, a sense in which it hardly differs at all from the word "gloomy." Judged in its own terms, the effect at which he did aim is concentrated, rigorously economical, dramatically shattering. Above all, it is nothing so formal as trying to do in one social milieu what had already been done perfectly well in another.

If this argument is to be made within the scope of an article, we must not waste more than a paragraph on such fiddle-faddle as the notion that *Ghosts* is a play about venereal disease or that *A Doll's House* is a play about women's rights. On these terms, *King Lear* is a play about housing for the elderly and *Hamlet* a stage-debate over the reality of spooks. Veneral disease and its consequences are represented onstage in *Ghosts*; so, to all intents and purposes, is incest; but the theme of the play is inherited guilt, and the sexual pathology of the Alving family is an engine in the hands of that theme. *A Doll's House* represents a woman imbued with the idea of becoming a person, but it proposes nothing categorical about women becoming people; in fact, its real theme has nothing to do with the sexes. It is the irrepressible conflict of two different personalities which have founded themselves on two radically different estimates of reality. *Rosmersholm* describes the same conflict but assigns opposite roles to the sexes.

What, then, is the purpose of that bourgeois décor, lovingly detailed and meticulously accurate, which marks the plays of Ibsen's middle period? Miss Mary McCarthy (in *Partisan Review*, Winter, 1956) touches on one aspect when she says, approximately, that Ibsen's characters do little revealing things well and big dramatic ones badly. Precisely so. The bourgeois décor is a device of focus; by looking through it as well as at it, one sees, as through bifocal lenses, the immense moral differences that divide saint and satyr. In our nineteenth-century world they occur as the bank clerk's wife and the bank clerk; or perhaps as the country doctor and the small-town official. They are not, or do not at first seem, very far apart—husband and wife, brother and brother. Their gestures are not grandiose, they are limited, with the awkward charm of people who do not quite know who they are. But the audience can know exactly who they are. If you look at them under the ultra-violet light of Ibsen's satiric glance, their true characters will appear, like ancient writing on a palimpsest: Apollo under the frock coat; Hecate in a bustle; dog, swine, bull, crow, and boar behind the respectable features. Steady and impervious as they seem in their own eyes, the characters of Ibsen are in the eyes of the playwright and his chosen audience deliriously transparent; and the high comedy which attaches to Torvald Helmer or Hialmar Ekdal stems precisely from this combination (to which the inspiredly stupid seem most adaptable)—perfect bland solidity in themselves and absolute transparency in the eyes of others. Miss McCarthy talks of a shocking moment when Hialmar eats bread and butter in front of his hungry daughter; but that, though it might be someone else's shock, is not Ibsen's. Hedvig is not hungry; if she wanted to eat, there is not only bread and butter but herring salad for her. Actually she is not even present at the famous breakfast. But the point is elsewhere. Hialmer has a mighty mission to perform, and is on his way to perform it when he encounters that fatal bread and butter; and the joke is the person he reveals himself to be, even as he tries to talk himself into another identity. He is one of Natures's *noshers*[1]. . . . The telling little gesture reveals how unsuited he is to make a big one.

Like some other great writers who come to mind, Ibsen was not a man of many ideas or for that matter of wide technical virtuosity. Skeletally viewed, the plays from *Catiline* to *When We Dead Awaken* (and that covers half a century) all have a single underlying tension, are all efforts to work out the terms of a single dichotomy. Ibsen was trying all his life to find a stage-language for the sort of moral insights which appear at their clearest in the capering tetrameters and fantastic episodes of *Brand* and *Peer Gynt*. The saint and the satyr are clear to see in this diptych; and it is a commonplace that Ibsen repeated the characterizations many times. With varying accents and under different circumstances, Parson Manders, Peter Stockmann, Hialmar Ekdal, Torvald Helmer, Parson Strawman, Stensgård, and Rebecca West represent the spirit of Peer Gynt; with the same qualifications, Mrs. Alving, Thomas Stockmann, Gregers Werle, Nora Helmer, Falk, Rosmer, and Lona Hessel represent the spirit of Brand. Bourgeois realism is simply one, perhaps the most successful, of half a dozen different vehicles through which Ibsen tried to adjust his moral insights to the requirements of dramatic presentation. The so-called "middle-class dramas" all reverberate to the urgent note of a single conflict. The tension which explodes in the last act of *A Doll's House* is heard as a high, thin scream of

1. A Yiddish term for one who likes to snack.

agony throughout *Ghosts*. Shouted boisterously from the housetops in *An Enemy of the People*, it is magnificently inverted and buried in *The Wild Duck*, and raised to the cold, silver-gray tonality of tragic resignation and acceptance in *Rosmersholm*. In a familiar but handy jargon, it is the conflict between the ethical and the acquisitive personalities.

Ibsen's attitude toward this glacial schism in human nature, for which he found a terminology in Kierkegaard and an evidence in the slightest acts of everyday life, was ambiguous enough to satisfy the most passionate present-day pursuer of literary ambiguities. *Brand* is clearly a celebration of the heroic ethical personality as contrasted with the meeching conformity of the acquisitive, self-centered easygoers who find it comfortable to adjust all mottoes to the middle of the road. The respectable official and the bohemian artist are at one in repudiating the claim of the moral absolute; from this perspective one can glance forward to observe the artistic element which lies latent even in a clod like Torvald Helmer, a retoucher of life *par excellence*, a notary built precisely out of the debris of a poet. Against all this formless mish-mosh of the esthetic and acquisitive, these meager patchwork compromisers, Brand sets himself heart and soul. He will not have a God of Love, a muzzy-minded old forgiver of sins. But in the crashing chord of the last macaronic verse,

Han er *Deus Caritatis*! (He is the God of Love!)

God himself speaks to repudiate Brand. It is an ambiguous repudiation, to be sure; for in the very act of affirming His charity, the Lord wipes out the man who had questioned it; yet, though Brand is demolished, it cannot be said that any of the compromises against which he has struggled are reconstituted. Unresolved contradiction speaks here as clearly as in *Peer Gynt*, the hero of which is repeatedly exposed as an unscrupulous, acquisitive, esthetic rascal who in the pursuit of lies and acquisitions loses himself. Unpeeled, like an onion, he turns out to consist of wrappings without a center. Yet at the last moment, when he is completely lost, he is found, in the love of Solveig. Once again, it is an ambiguous reversal; the Button-Moulder is put off for a moment only by a symbol too glimmering and insubstantial to have much positive meaning. Both plays end in a tightly knotted sequence of reversals which defy logical restatement.

For the matter of that, the entire career proceeds on the basis of logical antitheses (the very last words of Ibsen's life were "On the contrary"). *The Wild Duck* caricatures the peddler of ethical truth whom *An Enemy of the People* glorifies; the crooked argument between Mrs. Sörby and Old Werle turns out to be the nearest thing to a true marriage anyone in *The Wild Duck* can achieve; Parson

Manders of *Ghosts* is a flatulent old fool, but he contains, even if he does not know, an ultimate truth about the fitness of the Alving household for freedom and happiness. The ethical way can and does destroy the esthetic; and vice-versa, too. Only a few rare and strongly assured souls can hope to survive the general disaster. A child could choose with more precision and decision than Ibsen ever displayed between the alternatives which he proposed to himself. A shopgirl could find more attractive alternatives to choose between. Any mealy-mouthed purveyor of platitudes could combine Ibsen's attitudes by watering them down to bring him safely within the confines of the great commonplace—"Truth without love is vain," or some such shuffling together of highsounding incompatibles. But the man himself defies these comfortable formulations; he was one of the great disquieters, and if he could not bring himself to a smug reconciliation of "love" and "truth," for example, it was because he knew better than the smug what these commitments imply. It was the sense that Ibsen was somehow in touch with moral categories larger and deeper than those commonly available to men that made him an international culture-hero to the late nineteenth century. He provided no answers, though his tone was always dogmatic; he asked, instead, terrible searching questions, at the top of his voice, with perfect scorn for anyone who did not know the answers, and only a little hesitation at his own ability to find them. As with Goethe, whom he resembles in so many ways, there is always an uneasy possibility that the inclusive-inconclusive Ibsen is a vast, vague Germanic fraud. The possibility cannot be talked out of existence, or exorcised with big names; yet if Ibsen was a mere windy trickster, it is odd that contemporaries as acute and diverse as James, Joyce, and Shaw should have been taken in by him.

But the inconclusive quality of Ibsen's philosophy, which is not in itself particularly novel or individual, has a special effect on the patterning of his dramas. At least until we come to those of the last period, starting with *Rosmersholm*, they are not arranged to provide an acting-out of guilt, a release, a lustration; they end with an assumption of new guilt, a full appreciation of one's total responsibility—and sometimes with a sharp repudiation of the audience itself for having been an audience assisting at an esthetic performance when it should have been acting and judging in an ethical one. After twenty years of struggle and failure, Ibsen's first international success was *Brand*; but he spoke of the play with disgust and disappointment (which it is hard not to think somewhat unreasonable), saying that he had written merely a play when he wanted to produce an action, a moral deed (Koht, *Life of Ibsen*, II, 27). The stage is not, perhaps, an inevitable place to express distaste for pretending

—or is it? Where and how else could a determined disquieter produce more disquiet?

The sardonic view which Ibsen takes of all his characters—of
Nora as well as Torvald Helmer, of Oswald as well as Helen Alving,
of Thomas as well as Peter Stockmann, of Dr. Relling and little
Hedvig Ekdal as well as of Gregers Werle and Hialmar—is one
major reason why the effect of his plays is not pronouncedly tragic.
Mockery alienates; and none of Ibsen's characters is quite exempt
from the corrosive effect of his mockery. There is, then, relatively
little identification; the audience does not transfer its feelings into
the protagonist; and hence, when the protagonist "falls," there is
almost no tragic release in the patterning of the plays. A *Doll's
House* ends by deliberately outraging the audience's dumb, hopeful, and generous character; the slamming of that door is as deliberate as the last, sneering chorus of *The Threepenny Opera*. *The Wild
Duck* ends, in total impasse, on an unresolved and ironic discord.
Even *Ghosts* (which provides a less obvious example) does not leave
the viewer "with calm of mind, all passion spent"; quite the contrary. It winds him up to a pitch, and leaves him there. The audience
has not seen the humbling of a pride which it shares with the protagonist; it has not even seen the unintended consequences of a
wrong decision brought instructively home to the person who made
it. Both these actions are well within the range of emotional patterning which we usually call "tragic." But the fate of Mrs. Alving,
while it has certain didactic overtones connected with failure to
make up one's mind, does not really purify the emotions or exemplify a general rule at all. After showing us clearly that to live in a
slavish and dishonest manner is contemptible, it shows with equal
clarity that to live freely and honestly is ruinous. Act II burns up the
orphanage, Act III burns up Oswald. It is a fate imagined by a man
who hated humanity for adopting shoddy consolations in place of
the truth that kills, a man whose fundamental idea was to "torpedo
the Ark." Ibsen's play strikes us with much the same sickening impact as the blow which stuns a bullock in an abattoir. Humanistically
speaking, the ending of *Ghosts* is altogether unhealthy; but then its
aim is not to render an image of man, no, nor of woman either, as
wise, healthy, and virtuous. It aims to nose out a corpse in the cargo,
it seeks to demonstrate to the entire human condition a sickness
unto death and beyond it.

The personal element so deeply buried in Ibsen's plays has sometimes come in for objections, both moral and artistic; but how they
can be made to bear against Ibsen without hoisting Dostoevsky and
Dante and Dickens as well is not clear. Conceivably there are potent
objections to be raised against the bitterly destructive uses to which

Ibsen turned his moral categories; but they are practical, not esthetic, objections. Like many late-nineteenth-century prophets, Ibsen thought the masks of moral idealism infinitely corrupting for the people who wore them; but he saw also that the mask-remover, the unmasker of masks, wears his own and specially deceptive disguise. The demand for truth as he presented it is infinite; it corrodes all false-faces and social forms. Now and then he saw that in particular circumstances his special appetite for guilt might be too much for pathetic humanity to bear; but as a rule this did not bother him much. It might even corrode out the inner life of his stage-characters, reducing Hedda Gabler, for instance, to a destructive monster, and Ulric Brendel to the mere animation of an open emptiness. Still, the ultimate demand and the helpless parody of a response were elements in the human condition as he saw it. A melancholy paradox, that Ibsen had no one to communicate this vision to except the shambling human race itself, and no way of communicating it except the ancient game of "Let's dress up and pretend."

There is of course something vulnerable about any man who preaches suicide but does not commit it, who professes his scorn for his art but continues to produce it. On this score, the allegory of *The Wild Duck* is quite as unsparing as Ibsen's worst enemies. But the paradox is larger than Ibsen's individual character. By refusing to turn back before the hard or even the impossible questions, he enlarged our definition of what a stage can be and perhaps even our sense of what a man can ask himself to become.

From the technical point of view, there is doubtless much more to be said against Ibsen's lurking presence in the dramas. Especially in the later series, something stiff and stolid tends to emerge from Ibsen's allegory. Independently of staging, without regard for pronouncedly "symbolic" interpretations, the thought sometimes gets too turgid for the action. *The Master Builder* is an example of this allegory which lays its dead hand over the drama's framework, and makes us feel constrained in the presence of something pompous. Hilda Wangel and her dream-kingdom of Appelsinia: it is all very mock-mystifying, and the more one knows about little Fraülein Bardach from Vienna and her frigid Berchtesgaden flirtation with Herr Doktor Ibsen, the more the whole play seems like a piece of put-together pseudo-profundity. Aside from this stiff, self-conscious quality, too, confessional allegory imposes major limitations on possible stage-effects; instead of a transparency and a solidity we get two side-by-side solidities. Still, it is impossible to write off the last dramas at a stroke. *Little Eyolf* may not, perhaps, be a stage action at all, but its low, devout melancholy, its endless twistings, turnings, and variations on the themes of human weakness and human guilt can be deeply moving.

Yet, to return to the main plays and the confessional, "symbolic" element as it undeniably occurs in these stage actions; at its best it provides a kind of indirect and satiric light which fills the simplest objects and most natural actions with luminous and perfect meaning. The Christmas tree and the letter stuck in a mailbox in *A Doll's House*; or the range and shading of sentiment about photography in *The Wild Duck*; or Engstrand's home for sailors in *Ghosts*; these things have a life of their own and then a life behind that life, a double existence that is the essence of Ibsen's art, and which they could never have if he were not writing "confessionally," on two levels. Whatever one calls the technique, "confessional," "allegorical," or "symbolist," it gives depth to a stage action, satiric indirectness to the author's point of view, and, at its best, immense vitality to the characters on the stage.

It is in terms like these that we ought to consider Ibsen, as Mr. Krutch (*Theatre Arts*, October, 1956) asks us to consider him, "a poet." The poetry is to be found, not in the flatulent and often obscure Germanic symbolism of the last plays (Miss McCarthy rightly calls it "corny"); not in fine writing, of which the best plays of the middle period are entirely and ruthlessly denuded; not in inventive frolics of wit and fancy, such as Ibsen showed himself capable of in *Peer Gynt*. It lies in an extraordinary gift of perfectly quiet, perfectly lucid double vision, hidden behind the polished façade of an amazingly supple and indirect dialogue. There is nothing more to it, really, than placing a blank short perspective next to an infinitely lengthened one, and making a counterpoint of the two. Some subtlety went into the writing of this counterpoint; it is rich in hints, innuendos, silences, avoidances, half-admissions. There is also something perfectly impeccable and cold about Ibsen's long vision, an austerity bespeaking long and almost inhuman discipline. But the essence of the effect is simplicity, not trickery; Ibsen's is an art of seeing into something and through it, not of raising hackles on the audience by promoting an intense reaction for or against it. Only contrast the Victorian-domestic treatment of adultery in a popeyed melodrama like James's *Portrait of a Lady* with the cool, understated handling of the same theme in *Rosmersholm*; it is the moral difference between *Sandford & Merton* and *Liaisons Dangereuses*. But, cold and remote as Ibsen's best perspectives often are, I do not think he uses them, even in *Hedda Gabler* (or at least never before then), to make dramatic conflicts an occasion of histrionic display. His view of life is bifocal and perhaps a little mad; but it is hardly ever stagy. Late photographs of Ibsen show a curious quality of the man's physical features; one eye focusses on the camera, the other looks fiercely through it, through the miserable photographer and the whole miserable nineteenth century, fastened on an infinite and perhaps a purely private perspective.

He was, in fact, a perfectly destructive author; the critics have shied away from saying it, and the explanatory writers of the early century thought it an impeachment to be repelled at all costs. But the long string of suicidal endings in the last plays (from *Rosmersholm* on, with the exception of *The Lady from the Sea*) tells its own story. Ibsen's satire of human beings was based on a discontent with the human condition itself. In his mind the very act of creation was a bringing of the soul to doom-judgment, a release of poisonous hatreds, a conditioned reflex keyed to personal torture. Modern opinion tends dimly to associate Ibsen as a late-nineteenth-century post-romantic with John Stuart Mill, Emile Zola, and chromos of "The Man With the Hoe" in dark wood frames. We shall probably be a good deal closer to the truth if we try for a while putting him with Jonathan Swift, Gustave Flaubert, and Franz Kafka as one of the great negative voices in literature. "Der Jasager und der Neinsager"[2]—it is an old dispute and a trite one; but it is not clear that the respectable party has yet established any inherent superiority or even temporary advantage. Let us hope it never will. If anything, we make too little of our sceptics; and, by trying to huddle all authors together under the same umbrella of a liberal-Christian democratic-individualist commonplace, render them perfectly innocuous and undistinctive.

In death as in life, Ibsen resists absorption. First and foremost he was a moralist, perhaps the last and certainly the hardest-minded of the stage-moralists. He was also a poet, but a poet who had to bury his poetry under the very prose of prose in order to make it live. He was a realist who thought nineteenth-century reality the most fantastic and improbable set of disguises ever devised by man. Finally, he took toward human existence as a whole a complex and austere viewpoint which is hard to communicate, difficult to appreciate, and impossible, really, to enjoy—which lays claim, in fact, to only one merit, that of embodying some part of a bitterly uncomfortable truth. Since our age has no concern whatever with truth, but only with adjustment, integration, motivation, and acceptance, Ibsen is evidently obsolete. Indeed, given all the handicaps which he chose or was furnished, it must always be more surprising that Ibsen once attained widespread popularity than that he has presently lost it.

Of course he is not, in a textbook phrase, the Father of Modern Drama. Such wholesale paternity would disgust him. Even Peer

2. "The yea-sayer and the nay-sayer."

Gynt was asked to father only one troll-brat—why must Ibsen be saddled with responsibility for Tennessee Williams? The *Streetcar*, that primordial Williams' play which is every year transposed into a different key under a different title, clearly derives from *Madame Bovary*—a novel which is also said, in its way, to be confessional. Perhaps Clifford Odets has a dramatic parent; if so, who can it be but Chekhov? Eugene O'Neill was begotten by Strindberg. And so it goes. If Ibsen has present-day successors, one of them is no doubt Arthur Miller. This is no more Ibsen's fault than it is to his credit. So long as we have a middle-class, we shall probably have dramas which discuss middle-class problems in a middle-class milieu. But if Ibsen's bourgeois décor and personal allegory lead somewhere near Arthur Miller, one must also add that his satiric vision and ethical insights point toward Bert Brecht. Brecht's epic theater is something other than Ibsen's ethical theatre largely because of Brecht's rueful, comic personality. But its core is the transformation of the audience from audience to something better, to the role of participant in the action or judge of it. The drama of Brecht invites us to sit in doom-judgment on a soul, a nation, a society, a condition of life; like Ibsen's drama it refuses the happy ending, in fact, the ending of any sort. Whatever its ultimate value, the theater of Brecht is certainly the largest and most impressive structure on the contemporary theatrical horizon.

And even if we insist upon visiting the sins of the sons on the fathers—an odd undertaking at any estimate—the chances are that Ibsen will not stagger under the burden. How many playwrights whose best work was done before 1890 are the fathers of anything or anyone these days? If Miss McCarthy is found beating Ibsen in the columns of *Partisan Review*, it can only be because he stands out among the windrows of dead and stacked dramatists as a figure still instinct with life, if not with health. He has long outlived the first generation of his offspring, Pinero and Jones, as well as his contemporaries, Scribe, Sardou, *et al.*; he is remembered now, when Christopher Fry is as dusty as Elmer Rice, and I make bold to think he will still be a subject of discussion when Ionesco and Beckett have taken their places among the fashionable obscure. No one will mistake him for a dramatist of the order of Sophocles or Shakespeare; but it will take a long perspective and some little purity of motive to account for him in the end.

R. ELLIS ROBERTS

[The Wild Duck]†

* * * In *The Wild Duck*, Ibsen dealt with a man who, unlike Horster,[1] could not distinguish between truths and the truth. Gregers Werle is a man who generalizes immediately: once anyone tells him a lie, he is a liar, a soldier for him would be a murderer, and also, I should think, the hangman. He has no notion of things in concrete at all; he deals solely with abstract virtues and vices, and so blunders immediately in his relations with human beings. I cannot for a moment believe that Ibsen thought Gregers was himself. He may have seen, even in his ironic way hoped, that people would take Gregers as a piece of self-portraiture; he may have actually intended to put Gregers forward as a caricature of his enemies' caricatures of himself; but taken in connection with his other plays, and his other characters, I see no reason to suppose that Gregers represents Ibsen any more than does Tesman or Borkman.[2] There is one slight piece of evidence—it is true little stress is laid on it—which Mr. Archer[3] quotes in defence of the identification of Ibsen and Gregers: namely, Gregers' watchword, "the claim of the ideal." It appears that Ibsen uses this phrase of himself in a letter to Mr. Gosse: but it is more important to see how he uses it in his plays. We have two people who are prominent in talking about the ideal: one is the fool Hialmar Tönnesen, in *The Pillars of Society*, the other the coward Manders, in *Ghosts*. In *Ghosts* the whole stress of one scene, nay, the whole stress of Mrs. Alving's problem is "Am I to support ideals or the truth?" and surely there is no doubt on which side the dramatist is. So when he produces a new play in which a character, who blunders from beginning to end, uses this same worn excuse, this dreary alternative to honest thinking, I can see no reason for supposing that the character represents the dramatist. To confuse "the ideal" with "the truth" is to mistake the whole meaning of Ibsen's work; he is perpetually protesting that truth and the ideal are always coming in contact, and that the only sound thing to do is to take refuge in reality. Of course all critics admit that Gregers' action is ill-advised; but too many have assumed that, in telling Hialmar Ekdal the truth, he is doing something analogous to what Mrs. Alving should have done, had she told her

---

† From R. Ellis Roberts, *Henrik Ibsen, A Critical Study*, London, 1912. Pp. 130-37. Copyright 1912. Reprinted by permission of the publisher, Martin Secker & Warburg, Ltd.
1. Captain Horster is a character in Ibsen's *The Enemy of the People* (1882) [*Editor*].

2. Tesman is a character in Ibsen's *Hedda Gabler* (1890); Borkman is from his *John Gabriel Borkman* (1896) [*Editor*].
3. William Archer(1856-1924), a drama critic at the turn of the century; an early champion and translator of Ibsen [*Editor*].

son and the world the truth about her husband. Really there is a huge difference between Hialmar's action and the action which Manders and Mrs. Alving should have taken. The difference does not lie merely in the fact that, in the case of *Ghosts*, the truth would have prevented a hideous course of cruelty, while in *The Wild Duck* the truth only brings unhappiness into a contented if rather foolish household. That is a difference, one that the Gregers of this world should consider. But the real difference is much deeper. In *Ghosts* the actual existence of the Alving family, the whole of the Alving "legend" is based on a lie: just as in *An Enemy of the People* the prosperity of the Baths is indissolubly bound with the falsehood believed about them. In *The Wild Duck* Gina's relations with Hialmar, and the affection of both of them for Hedvig, have nothing to do with old Werle's original act of deception. Though Hialmar is a shiftless fool, he is a perfectly happy fool, and his happiness is based on a real intercourse with his wife, and a real affection for his child. To tell him the truth would have, rightly, no sort of permanent effect on his family life, because his family life has never been nourished by the lie; it has an existence of its own. Nora's life,[4] Helen Alving's life, Consul Bornick's life[5] depended on the lie; each of them profited, each of them to some extent sold their souls for the lie. Now Hialmar and Gina gain nothing *real* from the lie; part of their material prosperity is due to it, but that does not affect their characters. The only person, indeed, who may be said to gain by the lie is old Werle: and he is not the kind of man to mind the truth, overmuch. He has lied as much from a sort of careless generosity as from any sinister motives of his own.

Thus Gregers' action is not only stupid; it is, at least from the standpoint of the other plays, wrong. How wrong it is he does not apparently suspect, even when he has to keep on whipping Hialmar up to remembering the situation, attempting to make him act an "heroic" part towards a woman for whom his feelings have not really suffered the slightest alteration, except that he feels a conventional recoil proper to his class at meeting with a conventional offence. But nothing of Hialmar is changed except his sentiments and his speeches; he keeps on trying to intoxicate himself into a fit of sorrowful anger with Gina, and Gregers endeavours to intoxicate him into a mood of ennoblement; and all the while, for the first time in his life, Hialmar's real nature is in danger of being tinged by deceit. Mere veracity has brought falsehood in its train; in the effort to keep step with Gregers' view of truth Hialmar begins to lose sight of real truth altogether, and it is only the sound of Hedvig's pistol that really shakes him out of his illusion.

---

4. Nora Helmer is in Ibsen's *A Doll's House* (1879) [*Editor*].

5. Consul Bornick is in Ibsen's *Pillars of Society* (1877) [*Editor*].

The Wild Duck is then not an attack, or even a satire, on the position Ibsen adopted in his previous plays; it is instead a restatement of the same conviction from a different standpoint. It continues the work of *An Enemy of the People*; there Ibsen attacked the majority of disciples who follow, without thinking, positions that only thought can excuse; here he attacks the mischievous crank who interprets any fresh movement. The cowards and the blackguards and the hypocrites are not the only enemies of truth; still more mischievous is the man who, before he has learnt to distinguish truth from falsehood, deems himself ready to be a prophet of the real.

The Wild Duck can, less almost than any of the plays of this period be reduced, as I have been trying to do, to a bare statement of a problem. There is not a character in it, from Hialmar and Gregers to Molvik, whom we should not recognize immediately, were we to meet them in some provincial town. Ibsen's astounding creative power had never been exhibited with such richness, such variety, and such complete mastery of his medium. It was a feeling of this, I believe that made him say of the play, "It occupies a place apart in my dramatic productions; its method of development is in many respects divergent from that of its predecessors." It is very noticeable that with the greater certainty of his plays, culminating in *Ghosts*, Ibsen had perceptibly narrowed his range; there is hardly a sentence in *Ghosts* that does not have a direct influence on the theme. I have felt that in *Ghosts* Ibsen produces an effect not unlike that of three navvies striking at the iron pin that dislodges our London pavingstones. First one character strikes, then another, then the third: but each strikes the same pin, and drives it further in the same direction. The sense of deliberate force and purpose in *Ghosts* becomes almost unbearable. In *The Wild Duck* this is altered; as before there is not a sentence which does not have its influence on the theme, but the influence is rarely direct. The play is just as intense, but it is far freer, far less arranged, far less under the direction of fate—and of the dramatist. *The Wild Duck* is, then, Ibsen's first play which is wholly "modern," not only in thought but in treatment. For anyone who has seen it, nay for one who has read it, the child's experiences come back, and life in the streets seems infinitely less real and actual than the bitter tragi-comedy of Gregers, Hedvig and Hialmar.

The Wild Duck is also noteworthy for being the first of Ibsen's prose plays in which symbolism plays a large part. It is true that in *Ghosts* there is a good deal of rather mysterious business about the uninsured condition of the Orphanage; but I think Ibsen only intended that the stress should be laid on this to throw a further light on Manders' character, to show that he is not able to face criticism even in a matter where he would have got a good deal of support.

Dismissing this, then, as in any case comparatively unimportant, the symbolism in *The Wild Duck* is a fresh characteristic of which none of Ibsen's plays in future were entirely to be deprived. In none, perhaps, has he used his symbols so skilfully. There is not a false note from beginning to end in all that difficult world of the garret, where the crazy old man is kept alive by memories that are almost hopes. What is so masterly in *The Wild Duck* is that all the symbolism falls absolutely into the play; we never suspect, as I do in *The Master-Builder*, that it is the dramatist's symbolism. It belongs intrinsically to Hedvig and her grandfather; and Gina, with an admirable rightness, serves to keep the symbolic world of the play far from the mistiness of Hauptmann,[6] or the allegorizing of Maeterlinck.[7] Ibsen's symbolism, here, at any rate, has the supreme quality that can alone successfully justify its use—it is a perfect language. What he expresses by the wild duck could not be expressed so perfectly by words: the symbolism of the play is a real channel of ideas, as true and as fresh as any of the old symbols that men get so used to that they sometimes take them for the reality. It has symbolism's ultimate beauty for being entirely appropriate to the characters and the circumstances, and it is not a little responsible for the fact that we leave this play with Hedvig's image fixed more definitely on our minds than that of any of the other characters. Hedvig, with her quick, loving temperament, with her alert child's mind, with her deep and passionate girl's nature is the truest and ablest portrait of a child in the whole of dramatic literature; and her perfection is very largely due to Ibsen's use of symbols.

M. C. BRADBROOK
[The Wild Duck]†

The old view of *The Wild Duck* was that it presented the obverse case of *A Doll's House* and *Ghosts*, and gave a timely warning against fanatic innovators. In this view the centre of the play lies in the mistakes of Gregers and the diagnosis of Relling, the only two characters capable of judgment or of moral decision. This is its "problem". As Shaw puts it:

6. Gerhart Hauptmann (1862–1946), a leading dramatist in the Realist movement in Germany who later turned to symbolic plays and neo-Romantic fantasies [*Editor*].
7. Maurice Maeterlinck (1862–1949), a Belgian playwright best known for his ultra-Romantic symbolic dramas [*Editor*].

† From M. C. Bradbrook, *Ibsen The Norwegian*, London, 1946. Pp. 102-7. Copyright 1946. Reprinted by permission of the publishers, Chatto and Windus, Ltd. Revised edition published 1966 by Chatto and Windus, Ltd., and Archon Books (Hamden, Conn.).

Now an interesting play cannot in the nature of things mean anything but a play in which problems of conduct and character of personal importance to the audience are raised and suggestively discussed.[1]

Three times Gregers the idealist crosses swords with Relling the psychologist and the play ends with their mutual defiance. The structure depends on Gregers' interventions; he is responsible not only for the breach between Gina and Hjalmer but also for the suggestion which drives Hedvig to her death. It may be that Gregers was a more interesting figure to contemporaries than he is today; but the fact is that although Gregers sets the play in motion, he is not the centre of interest. Ibsen himself seems to have shifted his ground as he wrote. We have indeed his own word that he did not think in terms of "problems," "Everything which I have written as a poet has had its origin in a frame of mind and situation in life. I never wrote because I had, as they say, 'found a good subject'", and in explanation of the artist's attitude to science: "What we, the uninitiated, do not possess as knowledge, we possess, I believe, to a certain degree, as intuition or instinct." He goes on to say that there is a kind of family likeness between scientists and artists of the same period, just as in portraits—he observes—there is a type characteristic of a given period, independent of any school of painters. Ibsen's own anticipation of psychological discoveries is itself a testimony to his theory; the most striking instance is *The Sea Woman*.

Ibsen would therefore in any case have repudiated the idea that in *The Wild Duck* he was being merely instructive. But it does appear that he began with the notion of a satiric comedy, rather in the mood of *An Enemy of the People*. The first act is out of key with what follows, although it is an excellent sketch of provincial good society in all its smug solidarity—a society which has made catspaws of the weak, as Ibsen had already depicted. Wehrle the elder is another Consul Bernick. In this society Gregers is playing the part of social reformer, and, as in all literature of the time, from *Aurora Leigh* to *Beauchamp's Career*, the way of the social reformer is thorny indeed. On the other hand, the social reformer is conscious of the nobility of his vocation, and is thus enabled to withstand all the fiery darts of the wicked and to hurl a pretty dart in turn. Miss Aurora Leigh—a notable social reformer—bids Lady Waldemar remember how

You sold that poisonous porridge called your soul,

and, beside her invective, Gregers's words to old Wehrle sound almost filial.[2] But the force of these scenes is almost entirely lost upon the reader of today.

1. *The Quintessence of Ibsenism.*
2. *Aurora Leigh* was written by Mrs. Browning in 1857.

In a sense, of course, Gregers is a permanent figure; he is the man who has found the entire solution to life in a creed, whether that of Marx or Freud, the Oxford Group or Yoga. He is Brand turned inside out.[3] He saw his mother as right and his father as wrong. He feels wronged by his father, and at the same time morbidly conscious of a duty towards Hjalmer, so he is driven to interference. In none of his highminded attempts does he pay any attention to the delicate human material he is handling—being what Hedda Gabler called "a specialist."[4] Nevertheless, Relling's brutalities are beside the mark. Gregers himself is mentally abnormal and, as he hints, physically a doomed man.

The play begins with his story; but the Ekdals run away with it. Ibsen said in a letter to his publisher, "The characters of *The Wild Duck* have endeared themselves to me," and by the characters, he clearly meant the Ekdals. Relling does his best to keep the play on a straight line with his sermon on the life-fantasy—in which he was anticipated by Francis Bacon;[5] but in the later acts Gregers is chiefly a "feed" to the Ekdals; he knits up an episode, or evokes a confidence from Hjalmer or Hedvig, but has little independent life.

The Ekdals gleam with vitality, even the sodden old Lieutenant. They are complex people who have simple minds. In the scene where old Ekdal decides to show Gregers the wild duck, they infect one another with excitement, until at last Hjalmer, who had begun by being rather ashamed of his hobby, joins in the chorus.

Lieut. Ekdal: That's where the rabbits go at night, old man!
Gregers: No, really? you've got rabbits too?
Lieut. Ekdal: Yes, you can well believe we've got rabbits. He's asking if we've got rabbits, Hjalmer! Aha! But now comes the great thing, look you! Now for it! Look out, Hedvig! Stand here: like that: now look in. Do you see a basket full of straw?
Gregers: Yes. And I see there's a bird in the basket.
Lieut. Ekdal: Aha—"a bird"!
Gregers: Isn't it a duck?
Lieut. Ekdal: Yes, you can bet it's a duck!
Hjalmer: But WHAT SORT of a duck, do you think?
Hedvig: It's not an ordinary duck——
Lieut. Ekdal: Sh! Sh!

In this second act, the charm and absurdity of the Ekdals are enhanced by their innocent self-deceptions. The old man pretending he wants his hot water only for his ink, Hjalmer crying "No beer at

3. The reforming hero of an earlier play by Ibsen [*Editor*].
4. In *Hedda Gabler* Hedda applies the term to her husband to suggest his narrowness within cultivated limits and to explain the tedium of his company [*Editor*].
5. "Doth any man doubt that if there were taken out of men's minds vain opinions, flattering hopes, false valuations, imaginations as one would, and the like, but it would leave the minds of a number of men poor shrunken things, full of melancholy and indisposition, and unpleasing to themselves." (*Essay:* "Of Truth")

a moment like this! Give me my flute!" are safe in the hands of their womenfolk, practising the ancient conspiratorial art of "managing father." What is humiliation for Nora becomes a game for Gina and Hedvig. It is a housecraft handed down from mother to daughter with the family recipes and ranging from maxims like "Feed the brute"—"Beer, father! lovely cool beer!" cries Hedvig—to that genuine faith in the Great Inventor which only the simple and childish could entertain, but which is the basis of Hjalmer's well-being. For he is a timid soul, easily snubbed, and needs the constant worship of his family to keep him in good heart. Hence his fretfulness at any suggestion of criticism; he feels betrayed from within the citadel.

Unsparingly as he is exposed, Hjalmer is not condemned. He, too, has endeared himself to Ibsen. He is not a Pecksniff or even a Skimpole[6]—rather he is a Micawber. When his preparation for heroic flight is punctured by Gina's "But what about all the rabbits?" he first cries despairingly. "What! have I got to take all the rabbits with me?" but almost at once wrests the alarming situation to his own advantage—"Father must get used to it. There are higher things than rabbits, which I have had to give up." His meanest act is when he gets Hedvig to finish his work so that he can potter in the attic, but salves his conscience by saying: "Don't hurt your eyes, do you hear? I'm not going to answer for it: you must decide for yourself, and so I warn you."

But his relish of the "patent contrivance" and his passionate concern about "a new path to the water-trough" are at least evidence of *livsglaeden*[7] if not of *arbeitsglaeden*.[8] He is so childish that he asks only for a part to play and an audience to applaud. Old Wehrle's cast-off mistress and her child are the perfect audience—docile, responsive, uncritical. His anger when he first suspects Hedvig not to be his is blind, savage and genuine.

> *Hjalmer:* My home's in ruins! (*Bursts into tears*) Gregers, I have no child now!
> *Hedvig:* What's that? Father! Father!
> *Gina:* Look at that, now!
> *Hjalmer:* Don't come near me, Hedvig! Go away . . . I can't bear to see her. Ah . . . her eyes . . . Goodbye.
> *Hedvig* (*screams*): No! No! Don't leave me!
> *Gina:* Look at the child, Hjalmer! Look at the child!
> *Hjalmer:* I won't! I can't! I'm going—away from all this.

But his later cruelty is false play-acting. "In these last minutes in my old home I wish to be free from—intruders!" "Does he mean

---

6. Characters in Dickens' *Martin Chuzzlewit* and *Bleak House*, respectively; both contemptible hypocrites [*Editor*].

7. "Joy of life" [*Editor*].
8. "Joy of work" [*Editor*].

me, mother?" asks Hedvig, trembling. In his last explanation to Gregers, Hjalmer admits his dependence on her love and hero-worship, a little too clearly to be completely in character. "There is that terrible doubt—perhaps Hedvig never really loved me . . ." and he makes up a fantasy of how Hedvig had all the time been really laughing at him and deceiving him. The appetite for proof of affection is begotten of anxiety, and in this confession, Hjalmer becomes pitiable, because he, too, is seen to be bankrupt, and broken. Selfish and parasitic as his love was, it sprang from and satisfied his deepest need.

Hjalmer is both a tragic and a comic figure: Hedvig, like Antigone and Cordelia, is the victim who redeems. She is a mere child, saying prayers for the wild duck "that it may be preserved from all harm," and making her deep-laid plans to keep father in good humour. But she is mysterious too: like the wild duck, no one knows "where she came from, or who her friends are"—it is essentially an open question whether she is Hjalmer's child or old Wehrle's; and she is subject to strange adolescent tides of feeling that rise "from the ocean depths." Hedvig's piteous limitations leave her exposed to catastrophe. She does believe in Hjalmer, as no one but a child could do. He is her God and when he betrays her, she is terror-stricken with all the final black despair of childhood. Gregers, in prompting her to kill the wild duck, uses the language of religion. It is to be a witness-bearing, a ritual sacrifice, to propitiate Hjalmer, the offended God. And so when Hjalmer presents his final "demand of the ideal" —"If I were to say, 'Hedvig, art willing to give up this *life* for me?'—thanks, you'd soon see the answer!" Hedvig puts the pistol to her own breast and fires. Yet it is unresolved whether she died in grief or as a sacrifice; from an adolescent impulse to self-destruction, or a childish desire for revenge—"I'll die and *then* you'll be sorry."

Her death is catastrophic, the only unambiguous event in the play; yet its causes are veiled. It is not related to the previous action by the kind of iron chain that draws on Osvald's death.[9] It is a shock yet inevitable. Gina, gathering the remnants of her poor tenderness, speaks the last word: "The child mustn't lie out here to be looked at. She shall go in her own little room, my pet."

The most mysterious and potent symbol of all is not a human character but the wild duck itself. Each of the characters has something in common with the wild duck's story, but that story reflects all the scattered lights of the play and focuses them in one. The potency and power of the wild duck is that of the ghost in *Hamlet,* or the witches in *Macbeth*: it unites and concentrates the implications which lie behind the action of individuals.

Relling's final gibe at Gregers belongs to another world—the

9. A character in Ibsen's *Ghosts* [*Editor*].

world of judgments, views and reason; the greatness of this play is that it moves upon so many levels simultaneously. Ibsen was no longer limited by his own chosen technique. The freedom and scope of *The Wild Duck* are a symptom of that increasing depth of humanity and generosity which was taking Ibsen further and further from the doctrinal and the propagandist. "Dramatic categories," he observed, "are elastic and must accommodate themselves to literary fact." The characters had endeared themselves to him and the dramatic category was modified accordingly, so that even the weakest is allowed to hint that he too has known "the ocean's depths."

Anton Chekhov

and

Three Sisters

ANTON CHEKHOV

Letters†

To Maria Kiseleva[1]

January 14, 1887, Moscow

***It is true that the world teems with "scoundrels—male and female." Human nature is imperfect and it would therefore be strange to observe only the righteous in this world. Certainly, to believe that literature bears the responsibility for digging up the "pearls" from the heap of muck would mean rejecting literature itself. Literature is called artistic when it depicts life as it actually is. Its aim is absolute and honest truth. To constrict its function to such a specialty as digging for "pearls" is as fatal for it as if you were to require Levitan[2] to draw a tree and omit the dirty bark and yellowing foliage. I agree that the "pearl" theory is a good thing, but surely a man of letters is not a pastry cook, nor an expert on cosmetics, nor an entertainer; he is a responsible person, under contract to his conscience and the consciousness of his duty; being in for a penny he has to be in for a pound, and no matter how distressing he finds it, he is in duty bound to battle with his fastidiousness and soil his imagination with the grime of life. He is like any ordinary reporter. What would you say if a reporter, out of a feeling of

† From *The Selected Letters of Anton Chekhov,* translated by Sidonie Lederer, edited by Lillian Hellman, New York, 1955. Pp. 19, 20, 54, 55, 133, 137-39. Copyright © 1955 by Lillian Hellman. Reprinted by permission of the publishers, Farrar, Straus & Giroux, Inc. From *Letters of Anton Tchehov to his Family and Friends,* translated by Constance Garnett, New York, 1920. Pp. 99, 100, 300, 318-20. Copyright © 1920, by The Macmillan Company; Copyright renewed 1948 by David Garnett. Reprinted by permission of the publishers, Chatto and Windus, Ltd., A. P. Watt & Co., and Willis Kingsley Wing.
1. Wife of a rich, cultured country gentleman from whom in the 1880's the Chekhovs rented a cottage [*Editor*].
2. Isaak Levitan (1861–1900), a landscape painter [*Editor*].

squeamishness or from the desire to give pleasure to his readers, would describe only honest city administrators, high-minded matrons and virtuous railroad magnates?

To chemists there is nothing unclean in this world. A man of letters should be as objective as a chemist; he has to renounce ordinary subjectivity and realize that manure piles play a very respectable role in a landscape and that evil passions are as inherent in life as good ones.***

Devotedly and respectfully,
A. *Chekhov*

To Alexei Suvorin[3]

May 30, 1888, Sumy

***You write that the talk about pessimism and Kisochka's[4] story in no way develop or solve the problem of pessimism. It seems to me that it is not up to writers to solve such questions as God, pessimism and so on. The job of the writer is to depict only who, how and under what circumstances people have spoken or thought about God or pessimism. The artist should not be a judge of his characters or of what they say, but only an objective observer. I heard a confused, indecisive talk by two Russians on pessimism and so must convey this conversation in the same form in which I heard it, but it is up to the jury, i.e., the readers, to give it an evaluation. My job is only to be talented, i.e., to be able to throw light upon some figures and speak their language. Shcheglov-Leontiev[5] finds fault with me for having ended my story with the sentence: "You can't appraise anything in this world!" In his opinion the artist-psychologist *must* analyze—that's why he's a psychologist. But I don't agree with him. It is high time for writing folk, especially artists, to admit you can't appraise anything in this world, as Socrates did in his day, and Voltaire. The crowd thinks it knows and understands everything: and the more stupid it is, the broader seems to be its scope. If the artist, in whom the crowd believes, dares to declare that he does not understand what he sees, that alone comprises deep knowledge in the domain of thought and a good step ahead . . .

What a letter I've concocted! I must end. Give my regards to Anna Ivanovna, Nastya and Borya. . . . Goodbye, keep well, and may God be good to you.

Your sincerely devoted
A. Chekhov

3. Editor of the *New Times*, a conservative newspaper in St. Petersburg [*Editor*].
4. A character in Chekhov's story *The Lights* [*Editor*].
5. Ivan Leontiev (1856–1911), a playwright and novelist [*Editor*].

To Alexei Suvorin
October 27, 1888, Moscow

***In conversation with my literary colleagues I always insist that it is not the artist's business to solve problems that require a specialist's knowledge. It is a bad thing if a writer tackles a subject he does not understand. We have specialists for dealing with special questions: it is their business to judge of the commune, of the future of capitalism, of the evils of drunkenness, of boots, of the diseases of women. An artist must only judge of what he understands, his field is just as limited as that of any other specialist—I repeat this and insist on it always. That in his sphere there are no questions, but only answers, can only be maintained by those who have never written and have had no experience of thinking in images. An artist observes, selects, guesses, combines—and this in itself presupposes a problem: unless he had set himself a problem from the very first there would be nothing to conjecture and nothing to select. To put it briefly, I will end by using the language of psychiatry: if one denies that creative work involves problems and purposes, one must admit that an artist creates without premeditation or intention, in a state of aberration; therefore, if an author boasted to me of having written a novel, without a preconceived design, under a sudden inspiration, I should call him mad.

You are right in demanding that an artist should take an intelligent attitude to his work, but you confuse two things: *solving a problem* and *stating a problem correctly*. It is only the second that is obligatory for the artist. In "Anna Karenin"[6] and "Evgeny Onyegin"[7] not a single problem is solved, but they satisfy you completely because all the problems are correctly stated in them. It is the business of the judge to put the right questions, but the answers must be given by the jury according to their own lights.***

A. Chekhov

To Alexei Suvorin
December 9, 1890, Moscow

***God's earth is good. It is only we on it who are bad. How little justice and humility we have, how poor our understanding of patriotism! A drunken, worn-out, good-for-nothing husband loves his wife and children, but what good is this love? The newspapers tell us we love our mighty land, but how does this love express itself? Instead of knowledge, there is insolence and boundless conceit, instead of labor, idleness and caddishness; there is no justice, the understanding of honor does not go beyond "the honor of the uniform," a uniform usually adorning our prisoners' dock. We must

6. Novel by Leo Tolstoy (1828–1910) [*Editor*].

7. Long poem by Alexander Pushkin (1799–1837) [*Editor*].

work, the hell with everything else. The important thing is that we must be just, and all the rest will be added unto us.

I want terribly to speak with you. My soul is in upheaval. I don't want to see anyone but you, because you are the only one I can talk to. The hell with Pleshcheyev.[8] And the hell with the actors, too.

I got your telegrams in deplorable condition, all of them torn . . . God keep you.

Yours,
A. Chekhov

To Anatol Koni[9]

January 26, 1891, St. Petersburg

Dear Sir,

I have not answered your letter in a hurry, as I am not leaving St. Petersburg before Saturday.

I shall attempt to describe in detail the situation of Sakhalin[1] children and adolescents. It is extraordinary. I saw hungry children, thirteen-year-old mistresses, girls of fifteen pregnant. Little girls enter upon prostitution at the age of twelve, sometimes before the coming of menstruation. The church and the school exist only on paper, the children are educated instead by their environment and convict atmosphere. By the way, I wrote down a conversation I had with a ten-year old boy. I was taking the census of the village of Upper Armudan; its inhabitants are to a man beggars, and notorious as reckless stoss players. I entered a hut: the parents were not at home, and on a bench sat a towheaded little fellow, round-shouldered, barefooted, in a brown study. We started talking:

I. What is your father's middle name?
He. I don't know.
I. How's that? You live with your father and don't know his name? You ought to be ashamed of yourself.
He. He isn't my real father.
I. What do you mean—not real?
He. He's living with Mom.
I. Does your mother have a husband or is she a widow?
He. A widow. She came here on account of her husband.
I. What do you mean by that?
He. She killed him.
I. Do you remember your father?
He. No. I'm illegitimate. She gave birth to me on Kara.

A prisoner, in foot shackles, who had murdered his wife, was with us on the Amur boat to Sakhalin. His poor half-orphaned daughter, a little girl of about six, was with him. I noticed that when the father went down from the upper to the lower deck, where

8. Alexei Pleshcheyev (1825–93), a prominent poet and essayist with whom Chekhov frequently differed [*Editor*].
9. A liberal lawyer and public official

(1844–1927) [*Editor*].
1. An island off the Pacific coast of Siberia used for criminals and political prisoners [*Editor*].

the toilet was, his guard and daughter followed; while the former sat in the toilet the armed soldier and the little girl stood at the door. When the prisoner climbed the staircase on his way back, the little girl clambered up and held on to his fetters. At night the little girl slept in a heap with the convicts and soldiers. Then I remember attending a funeral in Sakhalin. The wife of a transported criminal, who had left for Nikolayevsk, was being buried. Around the open grave stood four convicts as pallbearers—ex officio; the island treasurer and I in the capacity of Hamlet and Horatio, roamed about the cemetery; the dead woman's lodger, a Circassian, who had nothing else to do; and a peasant woman prisoner, who was here out of pity; she had brought along two children of the deceased—one an infant and the other little Alyosha, a boy of four dressed in a woman's jacket and blue pants with brightly colored patches on the knees. It was cold, raw, there was water in the grave, and the convicts stood around laughing. The sea was visible. Alyosha looked at the grave with curiosity; he wanted to wipe his chilly nose, but the long sleeves of the jacket got in the way. While the grave was being filled I asked him, "Where is your mother, Alyosha?"

He waved his arm like a gentleman who had lost at cards, laughed and said, "Buried!"

The prisoners laughed; the Circassian turned to us and asked what he was to do with the children, as he was not obliged to take care of them.

I did not come upon infectious diseases in Sakhalin, there was very little congenital syphilis, but I did see children blind, filthy, covered with rashes—all maladies symptomatic of neglect.

Of course I shall not solve the children's problem, and I don't know what should be done. But it seems to me you will not get anywhere with charity and leftovers from prison appropriations and other sums. To my way of thinking, it is harmful to approach this important problem by depending upon charity, which in Russia is a casual affair, or upon nonexistent funds. I should prefer to have the government be financially responsible.

My Moscow address is c/o Firgang, M. Dmitrovka Street.

Permit me to thank you for your cordiality and for your promise to visit me and to remain,

Your sincerely respectful and devoted,
A. Chekhov

To Alexei Suvorin
March 17, 1892, Melihovo.

* * * Ah, my dear fellow, if only you could take a holiday! Living in the country is inconvenient. The insufferable time of thaw and mud is beginning, but something marvellous and moving is taking

place in nature, the poetry and novelty of which makes up for all the discomforts of life. Every day there are surprises, one better than another. The starlings have returned, everywhere there is the gurgling of water, in places where the snow has thawed the grass is already green. The day drags on like eternity. One lives as though in Australia, somewhere at the ends of the earth; one's mood is calm, contemplative, and animal, in the sense that one does not regret yesterday or look forward to tomorrow. From here, far away, people seem very good, and that is natural, for in going away into the country we are not hiding from people but from our vanity, which in town among people is unjust and active beyond measure. Looking at the spring, I have a dreadful longing that there should be paradise in the other world. In fact, at moments I am so happy that I superstitiously pull myself up and remind myself of my creditors, who will one day drive me out of the Australia I have so happily won * * *

A. Chekhov

To Alexei Suvorin
November 25, 1892, Melihovo

It is easy to understand you, and there is no need for you to abuse yourself for obscurity of expression. You are a hard drinker, and I have regaled you with sweet lemonade, and you, after giving the lemonade its due, justly observe that there is no spirit in it. That is just what is lacking in our productions—the alcohol which could intoxicate and subjugate, and you state that very well. Why not? Putting aside "Ward No. 6"[2] and myself, let us discuss the matter in general, for that is more interesting. Let us discuss the general causes, if that won't bore you, and let us include the whole age. Tell me honestly, who of my contemporaries—that is, men between thirty and forty-five—have given the world one single drop of alcohol? Are not Korolenko, Nadson, and all the playwrights of to-day, lemonade? Have Ryepin's or Shishkin's pictures turned your head? Charming, talented, you are enthusiastic; but at the same time you can't forget that you want to smoke. Science and technical knowledge are passing through a great period now, but for our sort it is a flabby, stale, and dull time. We are stale and dull ourselves . . . The causes of this are not to be found in our stupidity, our lack of talent, or our insolence, as Burenin imagines, but in a disease which for the artist is worse than syphilis or sexual exhaustion. We lack "something," that is true, and that means that, lift the robe of our muse, and you will find within an empty void. Let me remind you that the writers, who we say are for all time or are simply good, and who intoxicate us, have one common and very important char-

2. A short story by Chekhov [*Editor*].

acteristic; they are going towards something and are summoning you towards it, too, and you feel not with your mind, but with your whole being, that they have some object, just like the ghost of Hamlet's father, who did not come and disturb the imagination for nothing. Some have more immediate objects—the abolition of serf-dom, the liberation of their country, politics, beauty, or simply vodka, like Denis Davydov; others have remote objects—God, life beyond the grave, the happiness of humanity, and so on. The best of them are realists and paint life as it is, but, through every line's being soaked in the consciousness of an object, you feel, besides life as it is, the life which ought to be, and that captivates you. And we? We! We paint life as it is, but beyond that—nothing at all. . . . Flog us and we can do no more! We have neither immediate nor remote aims, and in our soul there is a great empty space. We have no politics, we do not believe in revolution, we have no God, we are not afraid of ghosts, and I personally am not afraid even of death and blindness. One who wants nothing, hopes for nothing, and fears nothing, cannot be an artist. Whether it is a disease or not—what it is does not matter; but we ought to recognize that our position is worse than a governor's. I don't know how it will be with us in ten or twenty years—then circumstances may be different, but mean-while it would be rash to expect of us anything of real value, apart from the question whether we have talent or not. We write mechani-cally, merely obeying the long-established arrangement in accord-ance with which some men go into the government service, others into trade, others write. . . . Grigorovitch and you think I am clever. Yes, I am at least so far clever as not to conceal from myself my disease, and not to deceive myself, and not to cover up my own emptiness with other people's rags, such as the ideas of the sixties, and so on. I am not going to throw myself like Garshin over the banisters, but I am not going to flatter myself with hopes of a better future either. I am not to blame for my disease, and it's not for me to cure myself, for this disease, it must be supposed, has some good purpose hidden from us, and is not sent in vain. * * *

A. Chekhov

RONALD HINGLEY

[Chekhov's Comments on *Three Sisters*]†

'I've absolutely got to be present at rehearsals, I've got to! Four responsible female parts, four educated young women, I can't leave

† From *The Oxford Chekhov*, Volume III, translated and edited by Ronald Hingley, London, 1964. Pp. 313-16.

them to Stanislavsky,[1] with all my respect for his talent and under-standing. I must at least look in on rehearsals.' (*Letter to O. L. Knipper,*[2] *15 Sept. 1900.*)

'Do describe at least one rehearsal of *Three Sisters* for me. Doesn't anything need adding or taking away? Are you yourself acting well, darling? But do watch out. Don't look sad in any of the acts. You can look angry, that's all right, but not sad. People who have been unhappy for a long time, and grown used to it, don't get beyond whistling and are often wrapped up in their thoughts. So mind you look thoughtful fairly often on the stage during the conversations. Do you understand?" (*Letter to O. L. Knipper, 2 Jan. 1901.* Olga Knipper took the part of Masha in *Three Sisters.*)

'You write that Natasha, making her rounds of the house at night in Act Three, puts out the lights and looks for burglars under the furniture. But it seems better to me for her to cross the stage in a straight line without looking at anybody or anything, like Lady Mac-beth, with a candle. It's quicker and more frightening that way.' (*Letter to K. S. Stanislavsky, 2 Jan. 1901.*)

'Here are the answers to your questions:
'1. Irina doesn't know that Tuzenbakh is going off to fight a duel, but she guesses that some awkward incident occurred on the previ-ous day, an incident which may have important consequences, and bad ones at that. But when a woman guesses something she always says, "I knew it, I knew it."
'2. Chebutykin sings only the words, "Be so good as to accept one of these dates." These words come from an operetta which was once performed at the Hermitage Theatre. I don't remember what it was called. . . . Chebutykin mustn't sing anything else, other-wise his exit will take too long.
'Solyony really does think he looks like Lermontov, but of course he doesn't, it's absurd even to think of such a thing. . . . He must be made up to look like Lermontov. He has a great resemblance to Lermontov, but this resemblance exists only in Solyony's mind.' (*Letter to I. A. Tikhomirov, 14 Jan. 1901.*)

'That the end (of *Three Sisters*) reminds people of *Uncle Vanya* doesn't matter very much. After all, *Uncle Vanya* is my play and not someone else's, and it's thought to be a good thing to remind people of oneself in one's works.' (*Letter to K. S. Stanislavsky, 15 Jan. 1901.*)

---

1. Director of the Moscow Art Theatre, which produced most of Chekhov's plays.   2. Chekhov's wife was also an actress with the Moscow Art Theatre.

'Of course you can come in wearing a service-dress jacket in Act Three, that's quite all right. But why do you come into the drawing-room wearing a fur coat in Act Two? Why? Perhaps it does come off all right actually. Have it your own way.' (*Letter to A. L. Vishnevsky*, 17 *Jan*. 1901. Vichnevsky took the part of Vershinin in *Three Sisters*.)

'Of course Act Three must be conducted quietly on the stage to convey the feeling that people are tired and want to go to bed. What's all the noise about? The points at which the bells are to be rung off stage are shown.' (*Letter to O. L. Knipper*, 17 *Jan*. 1901. She had written to Chekhov on 11 Jan. 1901, saying that Stanislavsky, in a rehearsal of Act Three, had 'created a terrible hullabaloo on the stage with everyone running in all directions and getting excited'.)

'Well, how's *Three Sisters* getting on? Judging by your letters you're all talking outrageous rubbish. "Noise in Act Three"—but why noise? The noise is only in the distance—off stage, a vague, muffled noise—while everyone here on stage is tired and almost asleep. If you spoil Act Three you'll ruin the play and I shall be hissed off the stage in my old age. . . . Vershinin pronounces his "Ti tum ti tum ti" as a question, and you appear to answer it. And you think this is such an interesting trick that you bring out your "tum tum tum" as if it amuses you. . . . You bring out your "tum tum tum" and give a laugh, but not a loud one, just a little one. And while you're about it you don't want to look as you do in *Uncle Vanya* [Olga Knipper took the part of Sonya in *Uncle Vanya*]. You should look younger and more lively. Remember, you're fond of laughing and easily get angry. Anyway, I put my trust in you, darling, you're a good actress.

'I said at the time that it would be awkward to carry Tuzenbakh's body past on your stage, but Stanislavsky insisted he couldn't do without the body. I wrote to him that the body wasn't to be carried past. I don't know whether he got my letter.' (*Letter to O. L. Knipper*, 20 *Jan*. 1901.)

'Darling, Masha's repentance in Act Three isn't repentance at all, it's no more than a frank talk. Act it with feeling, but not desperately. Don't shout, put in some smiles, even if only a few, and in general act it so that people feel the tiredness of the night. And make them feel you're cleverer than your sisters—or at least that you think yourself cleverer. About your "tum tum tum", do as you like. You're a clever girl.' (*Letter to O. L. Knipper*, 21 *Jan*. 1901.)

'I've heard from you that you're leading Irina round by the arm in Act Three. Why is that? Is that consistent with your mood? You mustn't leave the sofa. Don't you think Irina can get about on her own?' (*Letter to O. L. Knipper, 24 Jan. 1901*.)

Stanislavsky on the first reading of *Three Sisters* to the Art Theatre Company:

Chekhov 'was convinced that he had written a gay comedy, but at the reading everyone took the play for a drama and wept as they listened to it. This made Chekhov think the play was incomprehensible and had failed.' (*K. S. Stanislavsky, 'My Life in Art', quoted in 'Chekhov i teatr', p. 260*.)

Stanislavsky also reports that Chekhov, on going abroad in the middle of rehearsals by the Moscow Art Theatre for the first performance of *Three Sisters*, left behind 'his military representative, a charming colonel whose job it was to see that no slackness occurred in matters relating to the uniform, bearing or habits of the officers, their way of life etc. Chekhov paid particular attention to this aspect of things, as rumours were going round the city that he had written a play directed against the army—which had aroused indignation, bad feeling and borebodings of alarm in military circles. In actual fact Chekhov was particularly anxious not to offend the services. He was well disposed to them, especially to the army, which according to him was carrying out a cultural mission by going into outlandish parts of the country and taking with it . . . knowledge, art, happiness and joy.' (*Ibid., pp. 261-2*.)

'On returning from abroad Chekhov was satisfied with us [with the Moscow Art Theatre performance of *Three Sisters*] *and only* regretted that during the fire [in Act Three] we didn't make the right noise when ringing the bell and sounding the military alarm signals. He was continually worrying about this and complaining to us about it. We invited him to rehearse the noises of the fire himself and put all the stage apparatus at his disposal for this purpose. Chekhov delightedly took on the part of producer and went at the thing with great enthusiasm, giving us a whole list of stuff which was supposed to be got ready for his noise experiment. I wasn't at the rehearsal as I was afraid of being in his way, so I don't know what happened there.' (*Ibid., p. 262*.)

"The thing which struck him most, a thing he couldn't put up with until his dying day, was the fact that his *Three Sisters*—and after that *The Cherry Orchard*—was a tragedy [тяжёлая драма— literally "a heavy drama"] of Russian life. He was sincerely convinced that it was a gay comedy, almost a farce. I can't remember that he ever defended any of his opinions with such feeling as he defended this one at the meeting where he first heard such a comment on his play.' (*K. S. Stanislavsky, 'A. P. Chekhov v Khudozhestvennom teatre', quoted in 'Chekhov i teatr', p. 278.*)

'Amidst all his agitation about the fate of his play, he was no little worried about how the alarm would be sounded in Act Three during the fire off stage. He wanted to demonstrate to us the jarring noise made by a provincial [church] bell. On every convenient occasion he would come up to one or other of us and try by use of his hands, by rhythm and gesticulation, to impress on us the mood evoked by this soul-searing provincial fire alarm.

'He attended almost all the rehearsals of his play, but only occasionally expressed his own opinion, cautiously and almost timidly. There was only one thing he insisted on with particular emphasis. Both in *Uncle Vanya* and here he was afraid of provincial life being exaggerated and caricatured, of his officers being turned into the usual heel-clickers with jingling spurs. He wanted us to play simple, charming, decent people, dressed in worn, untheatrical uniforms, without any theatrical military mannerisms, throwing back of shoulders, bluff remarks and the like.

' "That sort of thing just doesn't happen, you know," he insisted with great heat. "The services have changed, you know. They've become more cultured, you know, and many of them are even beginning to understand that their peacetime job is to carry culture with them into out-of-the-way spots." ' (*Idem, in 'Chekhov i teatr', p. 279.*)

'In the Theatre the play [*Three Sisters*] was read out in his presence. He was struggling with indignation and several times repeated, "But what I wrote was a farce." Later on he would say the same thing about *The Cherry Orchard* too, that he'd written a farce. In the last resort we just couldn't understand why he called the play a farce, when even in the manuscript *Three Sisters* was called a "drama". All the same, fifteen or twenty years afterwards various irresponsible persons would juggle with this phrase of his.

'When the actors, after listening to the play, asked him for explanations, he usually answered with phrases which explained very little—"Andrew wears slippers in this scene", or "Here he simply whistles." He was more exact on these matters in his letters.' (*V. I. Nemirovich-Danchenko, 'Iz proshlogo', quoted in 'Chekhov i teatr', p. 309.*)

'The first performances of *Three Sisters* took place . . . in Chekhov's absence. He first began to see the play at rehearsals in the autumn of the following season and made observations so detailed that he actually produced the scene of the fire in Act Three personally. He was dissatisfied with me [in the part of Andrew Pro-

zorov] at rehearsals, sent for me and went through Andrew's part with me in great detail with pauses and explanations. . . . He insisted that Andrew should be very excited in his last speech. "He must be just about ready to threaten the audience with his fists!" '
(V. V. *Luzhsky, from his recollections, quoted in 'Chekhov i teatr',* p. 353.)

WILLIAM GERHARDI
[The Effect of Chekhov's Work]†

I

There is an experience familiar to travellers. You sit at the train window, and the train shoots through the approaches of some big town, and you see tall squalid houses with the washing hanging out of the window, or perhaps a carpet being beaten in the yard; and your thoughts shoot back to those houses, carpets, linen, and the people living in their atmosphere. How strange, you think, that what is alien to you should be to them the very fibre of existence. And you become aware of the diversity of life, and of your hopeless handicap in keeping pace with it—life is too big, too quick, too varied—and of your puny, puny self.

The approach is from without (involving the particular thrill described); the experience, from within: it is we who live these hitherto unsuspected lives with the acuteness, with the privacy, indeed, of reminiscence. We say as we read Chekhov: 'How true to our own experience!' But we are living new, undiscovered lives. How is it? Because in truth there seems nothing that Chekhov does not know. And the test? The test is that the truth that there is nothing that *we* do not know does not occur to us till we are reading him, and then we say: 'How true to life.' Why? It may be that, accustomed to a cruder literature and cruder intercourse, we deemed irrational, irrelevant thought as in some manner 'illegitimate,' perverse—a sort of growth confined to our own eccentric self, and so kept it back on the subconscious threshold. How deceived we were as to its importance. For life is more complex, fluid and elusive, not than we had privately suspected (for potentially in a semi-conscious, inarticulate way, we are all of us profoundly subtle), but than we had expected to be told by others, much less to see in print. One of the chief delights of reading Chekhov is the discovery that our vaguely apprehended, half-suspected thoughts concerning the fluid-

† From William Gerhardi, *Anton Chekhov: A Critical Study,* London, 1923.

ness, complexity and elusiveness of life have been confirmed articulately and in print.

It is as if all along we had suspected that the private and unnoticed little things in life were the important ones; but had thought it necessary to present ourselves to our fellows in a stiff intellectual shirt-front. Chekhov has eased our joints with candour. To-day it is more difficult to pretend, more difficult to keep up an attitude of insincerity in literature, to affect a thing—even if your affectation be sincerity, a professed dislike of affectation! For this modern literature has the great Russian novelists to thank. The individual 'feel' of living must have been essentially the same for many ages back. It is impossible to credit that the inner, private life of our ancestors was quite as smooth and simple and direct as it was handed down to us in the fiction of their day, with its somewhat formal, as if 'dressed up' emotion. Where is the documentary evidence of their reactions to the subconscious side of life? Where is their complex inner life, which, if it were anything like our own, must have been strangely at variance with their smooth accounts of it? The older novelists, we suspect, reported life not as it was really lived, but as they thought it *should* be lived, or as they thought that others thought life was, or should be, lived. Perhaps the more rigid rules of life that held them caused them to distrust their inner sense in favour of the accepted forms and standards and conventions; bullied it, in fact, into timid acquiescence. For it is not till one's half-conscious suspicions are encouraged and confirmed by comparison with similar experiences of some one other than oneself that one is at all convinced that one's inner sense of things, discordant as it is with the accepted formal life of fact, is not an idiosyncrasy peculiar to oneself alone, but the real life experienced by every human being. And it is because there is in Chekhov's works that fluid undercurrent by which we recognize existence, because we see that he at least did not simplify life in order to round off his picture of it (the loose-end nature of it being just the picture he has set out to portray), and because in a complex version there are necessarily more points of affinity than in a simplified and stripped account of human life, that we recognize ourselves in mental and emotional experiences in point of fact unknown to us.

His is the art of creating convincing illusions of the life that is. And 'the life that is' is what *is* in the material sense of reality, *plus* all the romantic illusions and dreams, *plus* all the sneaking, private, half-conscious perceptions, suspicions, sensations that go side by side with the 'official,' barren life of fact. It is the wanton incompatibility of the reality of life with our romantic, smoother private visions of what life ought to be, and that, together, makes our life seem what it is, with its makeshifts, self-deception, contradiction, and emotional misunderstanding of individual and mutual sensibilities, which has seized him, and, because he saw beauty in it, has made him a creative artist.

How did he come to see beauty in it? Because, I think, he must have felt: now that is life; but somehow we expected, and go on expecting, in defiance of reality, that life ought to be more: we sense a kind of absolute beauty which is more like a song or a poem —'romantic'—and this is the comic pathos of our falling short of it. Why is there a decided sense of beauty about a child cherishing illusions? Why is there a pathetic beauty about the child losing those illusions? Why is there beauty in that tale of his about the little cobbler's boy (*Vanka Zshukov*), who, because he was homesick and ill-treated at the shop, wrote a letter to his grandfather in the village begging him to take him home at any cost, and after dropping the letter, addressed 'To grandfather in the country,' into the pillar-box, had happy dreams? Why? Unless it be that the inadequacy of what *is* throws the dream of that which ought to be into relief. We are born with a sense of paradise in us. Perhaps we do not go there, and it is only as though we had come from there.

> And this perpetual dissatisfaction with herself and everyone else, this series of crude mistakes which stand up like a mountain before one whenever one looks upon one's past, she would accept as her real life to which she was fated, and she would expect nothing better . . . Of course there was nothing better! Beautiful nature, dreams, music, told one story, but reality another. Evidently truth and happiness existed somewhere outside real life. (*At Home.*)

'Let me remind you,' he writes in a letter, 'that the writers who, we say, are for all time or are simply good, and who intoxicate us, have one common and very important characteristic: they are all going towards something and are summoning you towards it too, and you feel, not with your mind, but with your whole being, that they have some object . . . The best of them are realistic and paint life as it is, but, through every line's being soaked in the consciousness of an object, you feel, besides life as it is, the life which ought to be, and that captivates you.' This is the precise quality of Chekhov's own writing—not less so because, in a moment of depression, in his letter he laments the absence of these laudable characteristics from the writing of himself and his contemporaries. He, even more distinctly than his predecessors, makes us feel that he is going out and drawing us 'towards something' transcendental.

The sense of living is a several-fold experience consisting, as it were, of several layers of perception. We recognize life when we sense it. And the reason that so often we do not recognize life in the books that we read is, apart from any question of skill on the part of the writer, because one or more of the 'layers' of perception having been omitted by him, our sense of life is incomplete, impaired—not representative of life's flavour as we know it. Such writing, whatever its other merits, is less rich, if not less true. 'Romantic' fiction, therefore, expressing the smooth dreamy side of life divorced from most material reality; the so-called 'realistic' fiction employing real material facts with the smooth directness only possible in a romance, and, while ignoring the irrational dreamy side of life, flattering itself naïvely on being 'true to life' and 'realistic'; and, lastly, 'introspective' fiction, 'top-heavy' in so far as the detail of its means tends to exceed its own artistic end, are each necessarily poorer, *thinner* than the balanced combination of their elements. And it is this balance of the three elements that gives his work a life-like touch, removes him altogether from the musty flavour of tradition which attaches to the sedate profession of letters. When we read Chekhov we somehow forget all literary associations. It is as if, forsaking our various professions, we stepped aside to get a better view of life. And then it seems as if all other men of letters who lived on literature had done no more than step aside, henceforth to walk outside and beside life. Chekhov is indeed more than life in the sense that he is the quintessence of it. One forgets that it is books he is writing, that, like others, he must wield a pen, use words; the medium seems accidental. He is concerned with life, with the whole of life since the particular is unsatisfying, with the particular because the whole of life cannot be focused into vividness; and the particular which must needs exclude alternatives reminds him of what he is missing.

' "Why are thy songs so short?" a bird was once asked. "Is it because thou art short of breath?"

' "I have very many songs, and I should like to sing them all." '

This fragment from Daudet is jotted down in one of Chekhov's note-books. And certainly it is all but useless to classify his subject-matter. It encompasses all kinds of Russian life that one can think of; and it is the consummative variety of his works remembered as a whole that fills one with a mingled sense of wonder and of lost opportunities—a sense which springs from the realization of the vast variety of existence, impossible to experience since life is given but once, and stingily at that. It is in the essence of things that our appetite tends to increase in proportion to our knowledge of the things we miss, must needs go on doing so. But we do not propose to slacken our pace for all that, and readers of Chekhov may perhaps console themselves, because, to some extent at all events, literature like his may take the place of actual experience, without the physical exertion, sacrifices, inconvenience, and pain that is inseparable from the business of living; and when they die they may congratulate themselves on having lived a hundred lives—but paid for one!

Progression means a succession of lost opportunities. And this is where Chekhov grips us. The element that makes for his disquieting appeal is determined by this phenomenon. But to call him a pessimist is absurd. Nevertheless, this view of him is often held, not only by persons upon whom it is forced by the inevitable inadequacy of translations, but equally by those who read him in his native tongue. Perhaps progression as interpreted above would scarcely appear a cheerful proposition. It is a series of 'farewells,' sad, if you will, but yet inevitable, and beautiful because of their inherent quality of cosmic inevitability. The pessimistic attitude towards such phenomena would be one of whining at the failing in our common nature—an attitude extreme, crippled, and one-sided. Because it is unjust to life. For we are not even able to imagine the alternative of a transitory existence. To rebel against it, therefore, would be unjust. It would, as a practical proposition, be absurd. Chekhov, though the melancholy beauty of his plays and stories is the melancholy of a transitory world, cannot be called a pessimist, in the face of the ridiculous implication of such an attitude. A pessimistic attitude would mean that he had no sense of proportion; and it is perhaps the chief determining cause of his sensibility that he had, if ever a man had, a perfect sense of proportion. The optimistic attitude, on the other hand, being uncalled for by the delusive nature of happiness, is not altogether his either. For, says Colonel Vershinin in the *Three Sisters*: 'Recently I have been reading the diary of a certain French cabinet minister, written while he was in prison. With what rapture, what joy, he alludes to the birds he sees through the prison window, which he hadn't noticed while he was a minister. Now that he is released, of course, as before, he doesn't notice the birds. So you won't notice Moscow, when you come to live in it. We have no happiness, and there *is* none; we only long for it.' It is better to dream of paradise than to go there. For when you know you cease to care. Happiness, as we learn in retrospect, is when we feel we have a heaven in reserve. It was not apathy alone that kept the three sisters from embarking on the train to Moscow, but a suspicion deep down in their hearts that the climax coming at the end of the crescendo is generally somewhat disappointing. For lack of any further heaven in reserve. And this needs must be so, since there seems no existence outside motion. The stationary nature of happiness is a delusion. Faust wished he could say to a single moment: '*Verweile doch, du bist so schön!*'[1] It was an impossible demand; a contradiction in terms; a negation

---

1. "Yet linger, you are so beautiful."

of life, and with it of beauty. Chekhov was neither pessimist **nor** optimist. To him life is neither horrible nor happy, but unique, strange, fleeting, beautiful and awful.

And all the time, while life is passing, always you can feel in him that aching isolation of the individual soul. 'As I shall lie in the grave alone, so in fact I live alone,' is a thought jotted down in his note-book. His gay, companionable people laugh, but live alone. And mutely, by the mere fact of their presence upon earth, each seems to put a question.

> 'Yes, no one knows the real truth . . .' thought Laevski, look-ing wearily at the dark, restless sea. [*The Duel.*]
> 'It flings the boat back,' he thought; 'she makes two steps forward and one step back; but the boatmen are stubborn, they work the oars unceasingly, and are not afraid of the high waves. The boat goes on and on. Now she is out of sight, but in half an hour the boatmen will see the steamer lights distinctly, and within an hour they will be by the steamer ladder. So it is in life . . . In the search for truth man makes two steps forward and one step back. Suffering, mistakes, and weariness of life thrust them back, but the thirst for truth and stubborn will drive them on and on. And who knows? Perhaps they will reach the real truth at last.'

And it would seem as if the whole significance of life reposed on the validity of that 'perhaps.'

II

It is his sense of justice that is at the back of his discriminating faculty. In *Enemies* he writes:

> The doctor stood, leaning with one hand on the edge of the table, and looked at Abogin with that profound and somewhat cynical, ugly contempt only to be found in the eyes of sorrow and indigence when they are confronted with well-nourished comfort and elegance.

> . . . All the way home the doctor thought not of his wife, not of his Andrei, but of Abogin and the people in the house he had just left. His thoughts were unjust and inhumanly cruel. He con-demned Abogin and his wife and Papchinski and all who lived in rosy, subdued light among sweet perfumes, and all the way home he hated and despised them till his head ached. And a firm conviction concerning those people took shape in his mind.
> Time will pass and Kirilov's sorrow will pass, but that convic-tion, unjust and unworthy of the human heart, will not pass, but will remain in the doctor's mind to the grave.

In his note-book there is this delightful fragment, which is like a comical pendant to the idea expressed in *Enemies*:

The nobleman X. sold his estate to N. with all the furniture stock, etc., but he took away everything else, even the oven dampers, and after that N. hated all noblemen.

Human nature, he perceives, is sometimes subtle to an extraordinary degree, if analysed. And yet the experience which in literature we hail as remarkable is possibly familiar to us in real life. Solëni in the *Three Sisters* is said to be quite a good and sensible fellow provided he is alone with you, but in the company of other people he becomes unspeakably silly. He constantly comes up to Baron Tusenbach, with whom he is on very friendly terms when they are alone, and engages in significant but meaningless remarks, for no reason at all—or because he is shy and somewhat bored. A similar discernment shows in a jotting in one of Chekhov's note-books. X. and Z., who are good friends, begin, immediately they meet each other in the company of others, to chaff each other a little viciously—out of shyness. Possibly the idea which he first jotted down in his note-book as it occurred to him he subsequently realized in the *Three Sisters*. At any rate, it is very delightful. No doubt the average intelligent person is aware of making similar discoveries in the course of the routine of life (or it would not occur to him to applaud the thing when seen in print). But the average intelligence does not usually communicate these subtle observations to another, much less set them down in writing. In the average mind the discovery scarcely assumes the shape of words. It comes and goes, leaving no impression. And it is the expression of it that is a nerve-racking experience, or, as Mr. Arnold Bennett once put it: 'It is the *writing* which hastens death.'

At least one-half of Chekhov's attitude to life was humorous. Apart from his farces, his humour was of that high comedic quality: never quite divorced from a suspicion of tragedy. It is warm and human.

An example from his note-book:

N. tells how forty years ago X., a wonderful and extraordinary man, had saved the lives of five people, and N. feels it strange that every one listened with indifference, that the history of X. is already forgotten and uninteresting.

In the rough draft of the *Three Sisters* the schoolmaster, a self-sufficient bore, says: 'I'm a jolly fellow. I infect every one with my mood.' He is Màsha's husband. Irina, Màsha's sister, comments: 'Màsha's out of sorts to-day. She married when she was eighteen, when he seemed to her the wisest of men. And now it's different. He's the kindest man, but not the wisest.' And towards the end of the drama, when the sensitive, discriminating sisters are deeply moved and melancholy, the rather stupid optimistic schoolmaster holds forth: 'But I've been lucky all my life. I'm happy, and I even have the Stanislaus Cross, second grade. . . Of course, I'm a clever man, much cleverer than many, but happiness doesn't only lie in that.'

On Irina's birthday he gives her a present: 'It's the history of our High School during the last fifty years, written by myself. In this book you will find a list of all those who have taken the full course at our High School during these last fifty years.' The humour is indeed comi-tragic!

To take a few more examples from his note-books:

> He had nothing in his soul except recollections of his school-days as a cadet.
>
> He hoped to win two hundred thousand in a lottery, twice in succession, because two hundred thousand would not be enough for him.
>
> A certain captain taught his daughter the art of fortification.
>
> A schoolboy treats a lady to dinner in a restaurant. He has only one rouble twenty copecks. The bill comes to four roubles thirty copecks. He has no money and begins to cry. The proprietor boxes his ears. He was talking to the lady about Abyssinia.
>
> He learnt Swedish (Norwegian?) in order to study Ibsen, spent a lot of time and trouble, and suddenly realized that Ibsen was not important; he could not conceive what use he could now make of the Swedish language.
>
> A Government clerk gave his son a thrashing because he had only obtained five marks in all his subjects at school. It seemed to him not good enough. When he was told that he was in the wrong, that five is the highest mark obtainable, he thrashed his son again—out of vexation with himself.
>
> A young man collected a million stamps, lay down on them, and shot himself.
>
> 'Your fiancée is very pretty.' 'To me all women are alike.'
>
> An old man of eighty says to another old man of sixty: 'You ought to be ashamed, young man.'
>
> In the daytime conversations about the loose manners of the girls in secondary schools, in the evening a lecture on degeneration and the decline of everything, and at night, after all this, one longs to shoot oneself.

It has been said that some of the items jotted down in Chekhov's note-books are trashy. Well they might be, since they were meant to be put into the mouths of trashy people. When Chekhov wants to lapse into the minor key he selects material that borders on the humorous. Olga tells Irina that when the Baron left the army and came to them in plain clothes she began crying because he seemed so bad-looking. [*Three Sisters.*] He asked her why she was crying How could she tell him? Natàsha, Andrei's fiancée, who is reproved by Olga, and commented upon by Màsha, for the way she dresses, in her turn three years afterwards reproves Irina for her belt, which she describes as 'an error of taste.' From the timid fiancée, that she had been in the first act, Natàsha, when she marries Andrei, gradually, through a kind of peaceful penetration, becomes mistress of the household. She is just a little vulgar, but she does not see it, and actually reproves Màsha for her fresh and boisterous language, which to Natàsha's unsuspecting soul appears indelicate! She, whose genteel provincialism grates on the others, apes the manners of the nobility, and interjects in French (a practice condoned some thirty years before, but, by the time she has adopted it, already looked upon as a little vulgar by the nobility itself): '*Je vous prie, pardonnez-moi, Marie, mais vous avez manières un peu grossières.*' And the Baron, trying to restrain his laughter, mutters: 'Give me . . . give me . . . there's some cognac, I think.'

Her character is drawn in a masterly way, but so are all the characters in the *Three Sisters*; and it is interesting to note how by their separate attitude to her another shade of difference in the characters of the three sisters is revealed. The dialogue between Olga and Natàsha on the question of the servant is a marvellously illuminating piece of character drawing. Indeed, one suspects that Chekhov must have been aware that a mutual reluctance on the part of his characters to appreciate or understand each other's attitude or feeling inevitably enhances the sympathetic understanding and the sensibility of the audience. Thus, when the three sisters tell the Colonel of the wonders of the life in Moscow, whither they are longing to go back, the Colonel, who has just arrived from there, declares that their provincial town is far superior in climate and surroundings.

Or take this extract from the *Cherry Orchard*:

The servant-girl Dunyasha is dying to tell her young mistress, who has only just arrived from Paris, that she had been proposed to: 'I must tell you at once. I can't bear to wait a minute.'

ANYA (*tired*). At it again . . .
DUNAYASHA. The clerk Epihodov proposed to me after Easter.
ANYA. You're always at the same. (*Puts her hair straight.*) I've lost all my hairpins. (*She is very tired, even sways as she walks.*)
DUNAYASHA. I don't know what to think about it. He loves me, loves me so much!
ANYA. (*looks into her room; tenderly*). My room, my windows, just as if I'd never gone away. I'm at home!

Like Turgenev, he speaks of 'that eternal repose of "indifferent nature,"' of 'eternal reconciliation and of life everlasting':

At Oreanda they sat on a seat not far from the church, looked down at the sea, and were silent. Yalta was hardly visible through the morning mist; white clouds stood motionless on the mountain-top. The leaves did not stir on the trees, grasshoppers, chirruped, and the monotonous hollow sound of the sea, rising up from below, spoke of the peace, of the eternal sleep awaiting us. So it must have sounded when there was no Yalta, no Oreanda here, so it sounds now, and it will sound as indifferently and monotonously when we are all no more. And in this constancy, in this complete indifference to the life and death of each of us, there lies hid, perhaps, a pledge of our eternal salvation, of the unceasing movement of life upon earth, of unceasing progress toward perfection. Sitting beside a young woman who in the dawn seemed so lovely, soothed and spell-bound in these magical surroundings—the sea, mountains, clouds, the open sky—Gurov thought how in reality everything is beautiful in this world when one reflects: everything except what we think or do ourselves when we forget our human dignity and the higher aims of our existence. [*The Lady with the Dog.*]

His intuition draws him on towards the mystery of cosmic transitoriness, sensible behind the personal tragedy of loss:

That repellent horror which is thought of when we speak of death was absent from the room. In the numbness of everything, in the mother's attitude, in the indifference on the doctor's face, there was something that attracted and touched the heart, that subtle, almost elusive beauty of human sorrow which men will not for a long time learn to understand and describe, and which it seems only music can convey. There was a feeling of beauty, too, in the austere stillness. Kirilov and his wife were silent and not weeping, as though besides the bitterness of their loss they were conscious, too, of all the tragedy of their position; just as once their youth had passed away, so now together with this boy their right to have children had gone for ever to all eternity! [*Enemies.*]

And why this sense of tranquil beauty behind the bitterness of loss—as though there were some unknown justification in the seeming wantonness of it? A hidden harmony. What is it? And then in this fragment, found after his death, there is a hint that he is tapping with his pen the very source and justification of life's transitoriness —its simultaneous diversity:

Essentially all this is crude and meaningless, and romantic love appears as meaningless as an avalanche which involuntarily rolls down a mountain and overwhelms people. But when one listens to music, all this is—that some people lie in their graves and sleep, and that one woman is alive and, grey-haired, is now sitting in a box in the theatre, seems quiet and majestic, and the avalanche no longer meaningless, since in nature everything has a meaning. And everything is forgiven, and it would be strange not to forgive.

To him there is a meaning in the high indifference of nature to the ultimate importance of our ego; justification of all life in the balance of obliteration; mercy and stability in the ultimate release of the individual soul; and forgiveness in the thought that eventually no individual deed will matter individually. And by that indifference the very trivialities of life are balanced, and the stability transfigured with a meaning, 'since in nature everything has a meaning. And everything is forgiven, and it would be strange not to forgive.'

RONALD PEACOCK

[The Poet in the Theatre: Chekhov]†

Chekhov's is a refined art; and it is extraordinary how so delicate a writer has succeeded in the dramatic form which in the past had depended on much more elaborate and tense plots, events of greater violence, and more impetuous dynamic characters. He pays the scantest deference to the rules, satisfied if in a general way he can suggest movement and climax. It would be wrong to say that nothing happens; something is going on all the time, often something very large, from the psychological point of view. Uncle Vanya has lost his zest for life and we watch him lose the love that might have brought it back. A young poet sees his work coldly received by a successful writer, and the girl he loves seduced and abandoned by him. Three sisters struggle without success to find a meaning in their narrow provincial lives. A woman sees her property sold, her class and the values it stands for ousted by a new life that seems vulgar to her, and she is helpless. But such psychological happenings, as portrayed by Chekhov, are given a movement so slow that it almost negates itself and becomes simply a continuing condition. The fallings in love, the hysterics and nervous crises are symptomatic recurrences within this condition, marking the routine, not breaking it. Hence the remarkable effect of such violent actions as Chekhov does on occasion use—Treplev's suicide, Tusenbach's duel, Vanya's attempt at murder: they may, technically speaking, fulfil the function of a climax, bringing down a curtain, but they are felt to be less significant and less terrible than the state they interrupt. Such incidents in plays are usually the final catastrophe of a tense development and their effect is to inspire terror, and also to bring release through closing the development. Chekhov divests them of this kind of dramatic significance; they pass, and the condition remains. Their dramatic function is less in themselves than in throwing into relief a picture of permanent frustration.

† From Ronald Peacock, *The Poet in the Theatre*, New York, 1946. Pp. 94–104. Copyright 1946, © 1960 by Ronald Peacock. Reprinted by permission of the publishers, Hill & Wang, Inc.

Konstantin Treplev, in *The Sea Gull,* trying with some agony to find a style of writing, makes the following remark: "I come more and more to the conviction that it is not a question of new and old forms, but that what matters is that a man should write without thinking about forms at all, write because it springs freely from his soul." It is an observation that might safely be taken in reference to Chekhov himself, because its very generality is so characteristic of him. His treatment of life is to a great extent independent of definite forms sanctified by traditions; it is one reason why he is original. It doesn't matter to him very much whether he writes stories or plays; he handles each with a minimum regard for any theory or ideal of form. What he had to say he was able to transmit with a fair neglect of the architectonic element in the technique of the larger forms, of drama and nouvelle. The "form" in his work derives to a large extent from the visionary impression, the representative and epitomizing trait of character or speech or incident, and the smaller units of rhythm. He is, for instance, a master of the movement of impulsive feeling; when irritation and temper break out, or sentiment and love, or pity and sympathy, often in rapid alternation. He is at his finest in the creation of atmosphere and mood, particularly moods of suffering, frustration, and of aspiring thought. He is also expert at sketching in, with varying degrees of caricature, the drollery of subsidiary characters, small-scale line and colour that is less than foreground but more than background, delicate but vivid pieces in the pattern.

His extreme fineness of touch and subtle feeling for tone enable him to portray with a very acute sense of life characters who in many ways lack life, certainly energy and robustness. The people of *Uncle Vanya, Three Sisters* and *The Cherry Orchard* are some of them intelligent, some stupid, but nearly all ineffective; and those who are or have been active, like Astrov the hard-working doctor with his plans of work and development, or Olga the headmistress, feel that their strength is giving out and that failure is written over their struggle. Such vitality as is left to all these characters goes to feed a single slender flame of consciousness: that they are parched. Their souls have no energy, but they are still souls; their characters no aggressiveness, but they are still characters; their persons no will, but they are still aware of will, they know it is needed and they haven't got it. All the art of Chekhov, withdrawn from larger outline and concentrated on tremulous detail, goes into making this lifelessness, this paralysis vibrate.

He shows his people in their detachment from affairs. Their daily occupations, activities, and professional duties, when they have any are not overlooked, but they are important only as the broad foundation of monotonous or purposeless or hopeless disillusioned lives.

The immediate contrast is Ibsen's world, its people immersed in their businesses, their undertakings, their newspapers, their mayors and councils, their clergymen; the public arena, the social cross-currents providing a great stir of character and plot. Chekhov, in selecting his scene, virtually eliminates the buzz of practical affairs, and presenting his persons without the rigidities of the "well-made" play, he allows us to observe them within the inner chamber of their character. He descends upon them in their leisure moments and discovers them not as servants of a job or a duty or a purpose, propelled by practical reason or animal egoism, but as men and women who, however paralysed their wills may be, are conscious of their souls and seem to wait on some great transfiguration. Setting them free in this way from all conventional appearances of work and economic struggle, Chekhov shows an essence of spiritual character. Whatever their intellectual degree or moral rank, whether they are odd, or bored, or aspiring, or fluttered, or empty, or intensely suffering, these people are laid bare in their spiritual condition. It is upon this end that the artistic process of selection is bent. If a form is the emergence of an idea in terms of sensibility, Chekhov gets his form by isolating in the lives of his men and women the moments in which they are spiritually awake, when they hear a profound inner voice that detaches them from a lifeless material world and plunges them into a vital sensitiveness; when they suddenly become alive to questions, mysteries, meanings and the lack of them; when they become, in feeling, revolutionary. They hear echoes of worlds transcending their own, where love is requited, where there is less suffering, where men are happy; and they then have their characteristic impulse to do something to make the dream real, an impulse which in an odd sort of way is part of the dream itself. With such a purpose in his selection Chekhov is really testing his people for the nature of their souls. When they fail the test outright he satirizes them; those who are sensitive at all he portrays at the least with tenderness and at the most with tragic pathos, as in the case of the three sisters.

But to leave it at that does not do full justice to Chekhov's idea. For through his people he is testing life itself. In seeking, as we have suggested, the moment of pure spiritual awareness, he is raising in his own mind, in that of his characters, and in that of the spectator, the great problem of what constitutes the quality of life outside an immediate practical purpose. He is using a touchstone which is essentially that of all philosophy and all art; and he has made his dramatic form itself shape the question. How far are the values of life inseparable from the technique of living—from the economic struggle, the job to be done, the social adjustment, the simple moral victories? Is there a value that transcends all this, and what is it? What is the spirit, when it is free?

The magnitude of the question puts it amongst those that are valuable simply by being stated; they are signs at once of human endeavour and limitation. The curious mixture in Chekhov's plays of an ardent will to the remedy of "work"—they are always crying: 'We must work, we must work!—and of a deadening sense of futility is symptomatic. It indicates the mystery that lies between the knowledge that we can never attain perfection and the feeling that we must try.

Chekhov has always caused astonishment by the subtlety with which he seems to capture the movement of life itself; and one of the problems for criticism is to reconcile this extraordinary touch for "reality" with the poetic effect that is one of the most certain impressions left by his work. It is possible that his apparent closeness to reality, the very success of his nervous and sensitive response, has the paradoxical consequence of obscuring the extreme degree of selection that he exercises over his material; and his selection is all directed to revealing a delicate idealism of the inner life. Chekhov is a great idealist. His sentiment, his humour, his satire, his humanity, his form, his poetry, spring from this central fact.

By virtue of his idealism he has created people with all the potentiality of happiness and goodness. There are no rogues in Chekhov. There is no wickedness of character; the evil lies in the great shadow cast over life generally. Trigorin, who is the cause of unhappiness, is selfish, not vicious. Doctor Lvov, in the early play *Ivanov*, is a foolish meddler, but far from being bad he is a misguided idealist. Lopahin, the man who buys the Cherry Orchard, has the best intentions. To get a variety that makes his picture more natural, Chekhov uses absurd and ludicrous types in place of wilful or malevolent ones. His caricature, especially in *Three Sisters* where it is most mordant, is the vehicle of some of the bitterness that is in his picture. But it throws into relief the yearning of the central characters. There are, moreover, some very odd scenes. It is queer that people should sit talking about the future happiness of mankind whilst the town burns just outside. Yet in the midst of frustration, even of comicality, these people are for the most part noble. Flat, bored, sterile, helpless, they never cease to break out in impulses towards universal love, happiness, the ideal, beauty in nature and beauty in man. Irina's words "my soul is like a wonderful piano of which the key has been lost" might apply to most of Chekhov's characters; it epitomizes the whole scene of life. The pathos of *The Sea Gull*—a curious meditation on artistic types—lies in the fate of the two young sincere artists, Konstantin and Nina, at the hands of the showy successful ones, Madame Treplev, vain and self-centered, and Trigorin, the minor writer with a large established following. Something fragile—the spirit, an idealism, a yearning for poetry—is broken. There are no "moral problems" in Chekhov's work as in Ibsen and his disciples; but everywhere there is moral aspiration. The satirical strokes are an indirect indication of it, and the crisscross of unrequited loves, and also the expressive scenes of departure and farewell, the sadness of parting being the sadness of desolation and exclusion.

In the series of full-length plays Chekhov wrote there is a growing insistence on the social implications of the life he portrays. In the first, *Ivanov*, one notices little of it. The theme is clearly introduced in *The Sea Gull*, however; it is more unmistakable in *Uncle Vanya*, reaches a clearer form still in *Three Sisters*, until finally in *The Cherry Orchard*, where a self-made man buys the orchard from a hereditary proprietor in order to cut it down and develop the site for weekend bungalows, the action is provided by the supersession of one social class through another.

The social theme was a predominant one in the work of many of Chekhov's contemporaries. He is distinguished by an absolute subordination of particulars to a generalized "Stimmung,"[1] the character of which derives from the idealism we have spoken of. Hauptmann's social dramas, for instance, depend entirely on an interest, stimulated by philanthropy, in localized conditions: what it looks like amongst peasants who ruin themselves and their offspring by their craving for alcohol, or amongst impoverished weavers exploited and crushed by capitalist enterprise. Ibsen's social plays depend on localized problems; they show the domestic or the public crisis that arises where there is a conflict between moral beliefs held with conviction or obstinacy. Both these things—the portrayal of "conditions" and the analysis of particular principles—are absent in Chekhov. We sense certain currents in the atmosphere of his plays: criticism of a given state of society, the intellectual apprehension of the causes of change and the necessity of it, all the knowledge of what is going on, the moral judgement passed by a new idea upon an old order. But argument is avoided, whilst suffering is portrayed. Ideas are skilfully diffused amongst his characters and made to appear as part of the texture of life itself:

> VERSHININ. Yes. They will forget us. Such is our fate, there is no help for it. What seems to us serious, significant, very important, will one day be forgotten or will seem unimportant (*a pause*). And it's curious that we can't possibly tell what exactly will be considered great and important, and what will seem

1. "Mood" [*Editor*].

paltry and ridiculous. Did not the discoveries of Copernicus or Columbus, let us say, seem useless and ridiculous at first, while the nonsensical writings of some wiseacre seemed true? And it may be that our present life, which we accept so readily, will in time seem queer, uncomfortable, not sensible, not clean enough, perhaps even sinful. . . .

TUSENBACH. Who knows? Perhaps our age will be called a great one and remembered with respect. Now we have no torture-chamber, no executions, no invasions, but at the same time how much unhappiness there is!

SOLYONY (*in a high-pitched voice*). Chook, chook, chook. . . . It's bread and meat to the baron to talk about ideas.

TUSENBACH. Vassily Vassilyevitch, I ask you to let me alone . . . (*moves to another seat*). It gets boring, at last.

SOLYONY (*in a high-pitched voice*). Chook, chook, chook. . . .

TUSENBACH (*to* VERSHININ). The unhappiness which one observes now—there is so much of it—does indicate, however, that society has reached a certain moral level. . . .

VERSHININ. Yes, yes, of course.

TCHEBUTYKIN. You said just now, baron, that our age will be called great; but people are small all the same . . . (*gets up*). Look how small I am.

Chekhov's picture is of a social situation as a whole, but he builds it up from innumerable traits in individuals, and to this is due its intense liveliness. The subject, in one of its important aspects, is the the temper of a society, but within this main idea there is presented a world of everyday human hopes and ambitions, loves and hatreds, despairs and sadness, follies and discretions. The picture is indeed so generalized as to render any narrow interpretation of its social meaning false; there is a suggestion of timelessness that makes it a picture simply of human life. Of this *Three Sisters* is the best example, and if universality is the final test, it would rank as his greatest play. *The Cherry Orchard*, on the other hand, having the more explicit social theme, is the more skilful demonstration of how that theme can be treated imaginatively; it is more than illustration of social conditions or of an abstract idea, it is poetic statement.

The question arises in this connection as to how far Chekhov's plays reflect an actual state of society capable of documentation, or how far they express simply his own feelings about life. How true is his world to a historical reality, or how true is it simply to his personal view?

The answer would seem to be that he found a point where a dominant note of social life corresponded to a dominant feeling of his own; and his feeling was determined by a visionary sense of impending social change. He is able in consequence to be veracious about himself and about society at one and the same time. Because his own feeling is clear to his imagination the state of society is clear as well. His observation showed him the symptoms and his idealism gave him the right interpretation. This accounts for the extraordinary blend in his work of an objective picture and a lyrical emotion that comes from his own idealism. It is a blend that is extremely rare in drama, which as a form tends to the highest degree of impersonal statement, seen at its greatest depth and range in Shakespeare. At the hands of an idealist—Schiller is a very good example—the objective picture usually suffers through distortion or exaggeration.

If from the first production of *Ivanov* in 1887 at Moscow Chekhov's technique startled people by its strangeness, it was only what is constantly happening in the world of art. The form was new for a new subject. The characteristic playwriting method of the later nineteenth century is completely rejected. The "well-made" plot is replaced by "scenes" (Chekhov actually calls *Uncle Vanya* "scenes from country life") showing a group of associated persons and a sequence of incidents which are less important as part of a plot than as symptoms of a social condition and an emotional frame of mind. This "condition," to which almost everyone is subject, even servants, is more than a framework for a drama; it is itself the drama. A spiritual malaise experienced by society as a whole is shown as a crisis. Chekhov's form has the great virtue of being an organic one. He achieves with it a fineness of fibre that makes him unique amongst his contemporaries in the theatre. Here is some of the subtlety and poetry that Henry James wanted to find a place for in drama; some of the delicate spiritual response to life that Yeats missed so keenly in "realist" plays. Chekhov's artistic vitality lies in his bold adjustment of dramatic form to his vision and to the modern situation.

His limitation in handling the medium is that he only secures a part of what it can give. He was sceptical of rules and theories, and when he achieves as much as he does by following his inspiration, adverse criticism can easily appear to be niggling. Yet it would be over-zealous to take the success of his free manner as a plain demonstration that traditional experience in the form is valueless. There are some writers whose subject exactly suits the genius of the form or medium they choose, and others whom the absence of this correspondence forces to reply on a free use or variation of one of the traditional forms. Drama raises this problem more acutely than the novel because its conditions are so much stricter. What we must recognize is that a larger form like drama gives pleasure in itself, a pleasure which the audience shares with the dramatist and which is even present where the literary value is low. The "drama," the "dramatic," is at least part of the object in view, and the form naturally seeks an intensity of pleasure in proportion to the concentration of its means. All the greatest dramatists knew this, whatever their subject, their philosophy, their analysis of life; and at their best they combine a maximum of the ethos of their form with a maximum of life in their subject. Chekhov belongs to the group that adopt a form less for its own sake than for their own particular uses. His independence led him to neglect the utmost concentration of means, and he did not attain the degree of surrender to the dramatic medium that we observe in Racine, in Ibsen, or in Molière. In consequence he got less, from the form as such, in return. His originality is of the kind that is to a large extent achieved in spite of the authority of the medium. Shakespeare and Racine are great artists in a double sense: not only because a vision of life unfolds itself, but because their medium, too, unfolds its character and its powers. Chekhov is a great artist in the simple sense that he found the right terms for the presentation of his particular idea.

George Bernard Shaw
and
The Devil's Disciple

GEORGE BERNARD SHAW

Ideals and Idealists†

We have seen that as Man grows through the ages, he finds himself
bolder by the growth of his courage: that is, of his spirit (for so
the common people name it), and dares more and more to love and
trust instead of to fear and fight. But his courage has other effects:
he also raises himself from mere consciousness to knowledge by
daring more and more to face facts and tell himself the truth. For
in his infancy of helplessness and terror he could not face the inexorable; and facts being of all things the most inexorable, he masked
all the threatening ones as fast as he discovered them; so that now
every mask requires a hero to tear it off. The king of terrors, Death,
was the Arch-Inexorable: Man could not bear the dread of that. He
must persuade himself that Death can be propitiated, circumvented,
abolished. How he fixed the mask of personal immortality on the
face of Death for this purpose we all know. And he did the like
with all disagreeables as long as they remained inevitable. Otherwise he must have gone mad with terror of the grim shapes around
him, headed by the skeleton with the scythe and hour-glass. The
masks were his ideals, as he called them; and what, he would ask,
would life be without ideals? Thus he became an idealist, and remained so until he dared to begin pulling the masks off and looking
the spectres in the face—dared, that is, to be more and more a
realist. But all men are not equally brave; and the greatest terror
prevailed whenever some realist bolder than the rest laid hands on
a mask which they did not yet dare to do without.

† From George Bernard Shaw, *The Quintessence of Ibsenism*, London, 1891.
Pp. 19-30.

We have plenty of these masks around us still: some of them more fantastic than any of the Sandwich Islanders' masks in the British Museum. In our novels and romances especially we see the most beautiful of all the masks: those devised to disguise the brutalities of the sexual instinct in the earlier stages of its development and to soften the rigorous aspect of the iron laws by which Society regulates its gratification. When the social organism becomes bent on civilization, it has to force marriage and family life on the individual, because it can perpetuate itself in no other way whilst love is still known only by fitful glimpses, the basis of sexual relationship being in the main mere physical appetite. Under these circumstances men try to graft pleasure on necessity by desperately pretending that the institution forced upon them is a congenial one, making it a point of public decency to assume always that men spontaneously love their kindred better than their chance acquaintances, and that the woman once desired is always desired: also that the family is woman's proper sphere, and that no really womanly woman ever forms an attachment, or even knows what it means, until she is requested to do so by a man. Now if anyone's childhood has been embittered by the dislike of his mother and the ill-temper of his father; if his wife has ceased to care for him and he is heartily tired of his wife; if his brother is going to law with him over the division of the family property, and his son acting in studied defiance of his plans and wishes, it is hard for him to persuade himself that passion is eternal and that blood is thicker than water. Yet if he tells himself the truth, all his life seems a waste and a failure by the light of it. It comes then to this, that his neighbors must either agree with him that the whole system is a mistake, and discard it for a new one, which cannot possibly happen until social organization so far outgrows the institution that Society can perpetuate itself without it; or else they must keep him in countenance by resolutely making believe that all the illusions with which it has been masked are realities.

For the sake of precision, let us imagine a community of a thousand persons, organized for the perpetuation of the species on the basis of the British family as we know it at present. Seven hundred of them, we will suppose, find the British family arrangement quite good enough for them. Two hundred and ninety-nine find it a failure, but must put up with it since they are in a minority. The remaining person occupies a position to be explained presently. The 299 failures will not have the courage to face the fact that they are irremediable failures, since they cannot prevent the 700 satisfied ones from coercing them into conformity with the marriage law. They will accordingly try to persuade themselves that, whatever their own particular domestic arrangements may be, the family is a beautiful and holy natural institution. For the fox not only declares that the grapes he cannot get are sour: he also insists that the sloes he *can* get are sweet. Now observe what has happened. The family as it really is is a conventional arrangement, legally enforced, which the majority, because it happens to suit them, think good enough for the minority, whom it happens not to suit at all. The family as a beautiful and holy natural institution is only a fancy picture of what every family would have to be if everybody was to be suited, invented by the minority as a mask for the reality, which in its nakedness is intolerable to them. We call this sort of fancy picture an Ideal; and the policy of forcing individuals to act on the assumption that all ideals are real, and to recognize and accept such action as standard moral conduct, absolutely valid under all circumstances, contrary conduct or any advocacy of it being discountenanced and punished as immoral, may therefore be described as the policy of Idealism. Our 299 domestic failures are therefore become idealists as to marriage; and in proclaiming the ideal in fiction, poetry, pulpit and platform oratory, and serious private conversation, they will far outdo the 700 who comfortably accept marriage as a matter of course, never dreaming of calling it an "institution," much less a holy and beautiful one, and being pretty plainly of opinion that Idealism is a crackbrained fuss about nothing. The idealists, hurt by this, will retort by calling them Philistines. We then have our society classified as 700 Philistines and 299 idealists, leaving one man unclassified: the man strong enough to face the truth the idealists are shirking.

Such a man says of marriage, "This thing is a failure for many of us. It is insufferable that two human beings, having entered into relations which only warm affection can render tolerable, should be forced to maintain them after such affections have ceased to exist, or in spite of the fact that they have never arisen. The alleged natural attractions and repulsions upon which the family ideal is based do not exist; and it is historically false that the family was founded for the purpose of satisfying them. Let us provide otherwise for the social ends which the family subserves, and then abolish its compulsory character altogether." What will be the attitude of the rest to this outspoken man? The Philistines will simply think him mad. But the idealists will be terrified beyond measure at the proclamation of their hidden thought—at the presence of the traitor among the conspirators of silence—at the rending of the beautiful veil they and their poets have woven to hide the unbearable face of the truth. They will crucify him, burn him, violate their own ideals of family affection by taking his children away from him, ostracize him, brand him as immoral, profligate, filthy, and appeal against him to the despised Philistines, specially idealized for the occasion as Society. How far they will proceed against him depends on how far his courage exceeds theirs. At his worst, they call him cynic and paradoxer: at his best they do their utmost to ruin him, if not to take his life. Thus, purblindly courageous moralists like Mandeville and Larochefoucauld,[1] who merely state unpleasant facts without denying the validity of current ideals, and who indeed depend on those ideals to make their statements piquant, get off with nothing worse than this name of cynic, the free use of which is a familiar mark of the zealous idealist. But take the case of the man who has already served us as an example: Shelley. The idealists did not call Shelley a cynic: they called him a fiend until they invented a new illusion to enable them to enjoy the beauty of his lyrics, this illusion being nothing less than the pretence that since he was at bottom an idealist himself, his ideals must be identical with those of Tennyson and Longfellow, neither of whom ever wrote a line in which some highly respectable ideal was not implicit.[2]

Here the admission that Shelley, the realist, was an idealist too, seems to spoil the whole argument. And it certainly spoils its verbal consistency. For we unfortunately use this word ideal indifferently to denote both the institution which the ideal masks and the mask itself thereby producing desperate confusion of thought, since the institution may be an effete and poisonous one, whilst the mask may be, and indeed generally is, an image of what we would fain have in its place. If the existing facts, with their masks on, are to be called ideals, and the future possibilities which the masks depict are also to be called ideals—if, again, the man who is defending existing institutions by maintaining their identity with their masks is to be confounded under one name with the man who is striving to realize the future possibilities by tearing the mask and the thing masked asunder, then the position cannot be intelligibly described by mortal pen: you and I, reader, will be at cross purposes at every sentence unless you allow me to distinguish pioneers like Shelley and Ibsen as realists from the idealists of my imaginary community of one thousand. If you ask why I have not allotted the terms the other way, and called Shelley and Ibsen idealists and the conven-

1. Bernard Mandeville (c.1670–1733) was a satirist and philosopher, the author of *The Fable of the Bees* (1714). François de La Rochefoucauld (1613–1680) was a French moralist and writer of maxims [*Editor*].

2. The following are examples of the two stages of Shelley criticism: "We feel as if one of the darkest of the fiends had been clothed with a human body to enable him to gratify his enmity against the human race, and as if the supernatural atrocity of his hate were only heightened by his power to do injury. So strongly has this impression dwelt upon our minds that we absolutely asked a friend, who had seen this in-

dividual, to describe him to us—as if a cloven hoof, or horn, or flames from the mouth, must have marked the external appearance of so bitter an enemy of mankind" (*Literary Gazette, 19th May 1821*). "A beautiful and ineffectual angel, beating in the void his luminous wings in vain" (Matthew Arnold, in the Preface of his selection of poems by Byron, dated 1881).

The 1881 opinion is much sillier than the 1821 opinion. Further samples will be found in the articles of Henry Salt, one of the few writers on Shelley who understand his true position as a social pioneer.

tionalists realists, I reply that Ibsen himself, though he has not formally made the distinction, has so repeatedly harped on conventions and conventionalists as ideals and idealists that if I were now perversely to call them realities and realists, I should confuse readers of The Wild Duck and Rosmersholm more than I should help them. Doubtless I shall be reproached for puzzling people by thus limiting the meaning of the term ideal. But what, I ask, is that inevitable passing perplexity compared to the inextricable tangle I must produce if I follow the custom, and use the word indiscriminately in its two violently incompatible senses? If the term realist is objected to on account of some of its modern associations, I can only recommend you, if you must associate it with something else than my own description of its meaning (I do not deal in definitions), to associate it, not with Zola and Maupassant, but with Plato.

Now let us return to our community of 700 Philistines, 299 idealists, and 1 realist. The mere verbal ambiguity against which I have just provided is as nothing beside that which comes of any attempt to express the relations of these three sections, simple as they are, in terms of the ordinary systems of reason and duty. The idealist, higher in the ascent of evolution than the Philistine, yet hates the highest and strikes at him with a dread and rancor of which the easygoing Philistine is guiltless. The man who has risen above the danger and the fear that his acquisitiveness will lead him to theft, his temper to murder, and his affections to debauchery: this is he who is denounced as an arch-scoundrel and libertine, and thus confounded with the lowest because he is the highest. And it is not the ignorant and stupid who maintain this error, but the literate and the cultured. When the true prophet speaks, he is proved to be both rascal and idiot, not by those who have never read of how foolishly such learned demonstrations have come off in the past, but by those who have themselves written volumes on the crucifixions, the burnings, the stonings, the beheadings and hangings, the Siberia transportations, the calumny and ostracism which have been the lot of the pioneer as well as of the camp follower. It is from men of established literary reputation that we learn that William Blake was mad, that Shelley was spoiled by living in a low set, that Robert Owen was a man who did not know the world, that Ruskin was incapable of comprehending political economy, that Zola was a mere blackguard, and that Ibsen was "a Zola with a wooden leg." The great musician, accepted by the unskilled listener, is vilified by his fellow-musicians: it was the musical culture of Europe that pronounced Wagner the inferior of Mendelssohn and Meyerbeer. The great artist finds his foes among the painters, and not among the men in the street: it was the Royal Academy which placed forgotten nobodies above Burne Jones. It is not rational that it should be so; but it is so, for all that.

The realist at last loses patience with ideals altogether, and sees in them only something to blind us, something to numb us, something to murder self in us, something whereby, instead of resisting death, we can disarm it by committing suicide. The idealist, who has taken refuge with the ideals because he hates himself and is ashamed of himself, thinks that all this is so much the better. The realist, who has come to have a deep respect for himself and faith in the validity of his own will, thinks it so much the worse. To the one, human nature, naturally corrupt, is held back from ruinous excesses only by self-denying conformity to the ideals. To the other these ideals are only swaddling clothes which man has outgrown, and which insufferably impede his movements. No wonder the two cannot agree. The idealist says, "Realism means egotism; and egotism means depravity." The realist declares that when a man abnegates the will to live and be free in a world of the living and free, seeking only to conform to ideals for the sake of being, not himself, but "a good man," then he is morally dead and rotten, and must be left unheeded to abide his resurrection, if that by good luck arrive before his bodily death. Unfortunately, this is the sort of speech that nobody but a realist understands. It will be more amusing as well as more convincing to take an actual example of an idealist criticising a realist.

GEORGE BERNARD SHAW
On Diabolonian Ethics†

There is a foolish opinion prevalent that an author should allow his works to speak for themselves, and that he who appends and prefixes explanations to them is likely to be as bad an artist as the painter cited by Cervantes, who wrote under his picture This is a Cock, lest there should be any mistake about it. The pat retort to this thoughtless comparison is that the painter invariably does so label his picture. What is a Royal Academy catalogue but a series of statements that This is the Vale of Rest, This is The School of Athens, This is Chill October, This is The Prince of Wales, and so on? The reason most dramatists do not publish their plays with prefaces is that they cannot write them, the business of intellectually conscious philosopher and skilled critic being no part of the playwright's craft. Naturally, making a virtue of their incapacity, they either repudiate prefaces as shameful, or else, with a modest air,

† From George Bernard Shaw, "Preface" to *Three Plays for Puritans*, London, 1900. Pp. xxiv-xxix.

request some popular critic to supply one, as much as to say, Were I to tell the truth about myself I must needs seem vainglorious: were I to tell less than the truth I should do myself an injustice and deceive my readers. As to the critic thus called in from the outside, what can he do but imply that his friend's transcendent ability as a dramatist is surpassed only by his beautiful nature as a man? Now what I say is, why should I get another man to praise me when I can praise myself? I have no disabilities to plead: produce me your best critic, and I will criticize his head off. As to philosophy, I taught my critics the little they know in my Quintessence of Ibsenism; and now they turn their guns—the guns I loaded for them —on me, and proclaim that I write as if mankind had intellect without will, or heart, as they call it. Ingrates: who was it that directed your attention to the distinction between Will and Intellect? Not Schopenhauer, I think, but Shaw.

Again, they tell me that So-and-So, who does not write prefaces, is no chartalan. Well, I am. I first caught the ear of the British public on a cart in Hyde Park, to the blaring of brass bands, and this not at all as a reluctant sacrifice of my instinct of privacy to political necessity, but because, like all dramatists and mimes of genuine vocation, I am a natural-born mountebank. I am well aware that the ordinary British citizen requires a profession of shame from all mountebanks by way of homage to the sanctity of the ignoble private life to which he is condemned by his incapacity for public life. Thus Shakespear, after proclaiming that Not marble nor the gilded monuments of Princes should outlive his powerful rhyme, would apologise, in the approved taste, for making himself a motley to the view; and the British citizen has ever since quoted the apology and ignored the fanfare. When an actress writes her memoirs, she impresses on you in every chapter how cruelly it tried her feelings to exhibit her person to the public gaze; but she does not forget to decorate the book with a dozen portraits of herself. I really cannot respond to this demand for mock-modesty. I am ashamed neither of my work nor of the way it is done. I like explaining its merits to the huge majority who don't know good work from bad. It does them good; and it does me good, curing me of nervousness, laziness, and snobbishness. I write prefaces as Dryden did, and treatises as Wagner, because I *can*; and I would give half a dozen of Shakespear's plays for one of the prefaces he ought to have written. I leave the delicacies of retirement to those who are gentlemen first and literary workmen afterwards. The cart and trumpet for me.

This is all very well; but the trumpet is an instrument that grows on one; and sometimes my blasts have been so strident that even those who are most annoyed by them have mistaken the novelty of my shamelessness for novelty in my plays and opinions. Take, for instance, the first play in this volume, entitled The Devil's Disciple. It does not contain a single even passably novel incident. Every old patron of the Adelphi pit[1] would, were he not beglamored in a way presently to be explained, recognize the reading of the will, the oppressed orphan finding a protector, the arrest, the heroic sacrifice, the court martial, the scaffold, the reprieve at the last moment, as he recognizes beefsteak pudding on the bill of fare at his restaurant. Yet when the play was produced in 1897 in New York by Mr. Richard Mansfield, with a success that proves either that the melodrama was built on very safe old lines, or that the American public is composed exclusively of men of genius, the critics, though one said one thing and another another as to the play's merits, yet all agreed that it was novel—*original*, as they put it—to the verge of audacious eccentricity.

Now this, if it applies to the incidents, plot, construction, and general professional and technical qualities of the play, is nonsense; for the truth is, I am in these matters a very old-fashioned playwright. When a good deal of the same talk, both hostile and friendly, was provoked by my last volume of plays, Mr. Robert Buchanan, a dramatist who knows what I know and remembers what I remember of the history of the stage, pointed out that the stage tricks by which I gave the younger generation of playgoers an exquisite sense of quaint unexpectedness, had done duty years ago in Cool as a Cucumber, Used Up, and many forgotten farces and comedies of the Byron-Robertson school,[2] in which the imperturbably impudent comedian, afterwards shelved by the reaction to brainless sentimentality, was a stock figure. It is always so more or less: the novelties of one generation are only the resuscitated fashions of the generation before last.

But the stage tricks of The Devil's Disciple are not, like some of those of Arms and the Man, the forgotten ones of the sixties, but the hackneyed ones of our own time. Why, then were they not recognized? Partly, no doubt, because of my trumpet and cartwheel declamation. The critics were the victims of the long course of hypnotic suggestion by which G.B.S. the journalist manufactured an unconventional reputation for Bernard Shaw the author. In England as elsewhere the spontaneous recognition of really original work begins with a mere handful of people, and propagates itself so slowly that it has become a commonplace to say that genius, demanding bread, is given a stone after its possessor's death. The remedy for

1. The Adelphi was a well-known London theater in the nineteenth century, famous for its melodramas [*Editor*].
2. Henry James Byron (1834–84) was a highly successful writer of popular comedies, while Thomas William Robertson (1829–71), the founder of polite Realist drama in England, is usually thought to have worked to overthrow writers like him. Characteristically, Shaw links them on the grounds that both were successful and popular [*Editor*].

this is sedulous advertisement. Accordingly, I have advertised my-self so well that I find myself, whilst still in middle life, almost as legendary a person as the Flying Dutchman. Critics, like other peo-ple, see what they look for, not what is actually before them. In my plays they look for my legendary qualities, and find originality and brilliancy in my most hackneyed claptraps. Were I to republish Buckstone's Wreck Ashore as my latest comedy, it would be hailed as a masterpiece of perverse paradox and scintillating satire. Not, of course, by the really able critics—for example, you, my friend, now reading this sentence. The illusion that makes *you* think me so orig-inal is far subtler than that. The Devil's Disciple has, in truth, a genuine novelty in it. Only, that novelty is not any invention of my own, but simply the novelty of the advanced thought of my day. As such, it will assuredly lose its gloss with the lapse of time, and leave the Devil's Disciple exposed as the threadbare popular melo-drama it technically is.

Let me explain (for, as Mr. A. B. Walkley[3] has pointed out in his disquisitions on Frames of Mind, I am nothing if not explanatory). Dick Dudgeon, the devil's disciple, is a Puritan of the Puritans. He is brought up in a household where the Puritan religion has died, and become, in its corruption, an excuse for his mother's master passion of hatred in all its phases of cruelty and envy. This corruption has already been dramatized for us by Charles Dickens in his picture of the Clennam household in Little Dorrit: Mrs. Dudgeon being a replica of Mrs. Clennam with certain circumstan-tial variations, and perhaps a touch of the same author's Mrs. Gargery in Great Expectations. In such a home the young Puritan finds himself starved of religion, which is the most clamorous need of his nature. With all his mother's indomitable selffulness, but with Pity instead of Hatred as his master passion, he pities the devil; takes his side; and champions him, like a true Covenanter, against the world. He thus becomes, like all genuinely religious men, a repro-bate and an outcast. Once this is understood, the play becomes straightforwardly simple. The Diabolonian position is new to the London playgoer of today, but not to lovers of serious literature. From Prometheus to the Wagnerian Siegfried, some enemy of the gods, unterrified champion of those oppressed by them, has always towered among the heroes of the loftiest poetry. Our newest idol, the Overman,[4] celebrating the death of godhead, may be younger than the hills; but he is as old as the shepherds. Two and a half centuries ago our greatest English dramatizer of life, John Bunyan, ended one of his stories with the remark that there is a way to hell

3. Alfred Bingham Walkley (1855–1926) was an influential English drama critic [*Editor*].

4. Translation of "übermensch," Nietzs-che's superman [*Editor*].

even from the gates of heaven, and so led us to the equally true proposition that there is a way to heaven even from the gates of hell. A century ago William Blake was, like Dick Dudgeon, an avowed Diabolonian: he called his angels devils and his devils angels. His devil is a Redeemer. Let those who have praised my originality in conceiving Dick Dudgeon's strange religion read Blake's Marriage of Heaven and Hell; and I shall be fortunate if they do not rail at me for a plagiarist. But they need not go back to Blake and Bunyan. Have they not heard the recent fuss about Nietzsche and his Good and Evil Turned Inside Out? Mr. Robert Buchanan has actually written a long poem of which the Devil is the merciful hero, which poem was in my hands before a word of The Devil's Disciple was written. There never was a play more certain to be written than The Devil's Disciple at the end of the nineteenth century. The age was visibly pregnant with it.

I grieve to have to add that my old friends and colleagues the London critics for the most part shewed no sort of connoisseurship either in Puritanism or in Diabolonianism when the play was performed for a few weeks at a suburban theatre (Kennington) in October 1889 by Mr. Murray Carson. They took Mrs. Dudgeon at her own valuation as a religious woman because she was detestably disagreeable. And they took Dick as a blackguard, on her authority, because he was neither detestable nor disagreeable. But they presently found themselves in a dilemma. Why should a blackguard save another man's life, and that man no friend of his, at the risk of his own? Clearly, said the critic, because he is redeemed by love. All wicked heroes are, on the stage: that is the romantic metaphysic. Unfortunately for this explanation (which I do not profess to understand) it turned out in the third act that Dick was a Puritan in this respect also: a man impassioned only for saving grace, and not to be led or turned by wife or mother, Church or State, pride of life or lust of the flesh. In the lovely home of the courageous, affectionate, practical minister who marries a pretty wife twenty years younger than himelf, and turns soldier in an instant to save the man who has saved him, Dick looks round and understands the charm and the peace and the sanctity, but knows that such material comforts are not for him. When the woman nursed in that atmosphere falls in love with him and concludes (like the critics, who somehow always agree with my sentimental heroines) that he risked his life for her sake, he tells her the obvious truth that he would have done as much for any stranger—that the law of his own nature, and no interest nor lust whatsoever, forbade him to cry out that the hangman's noose should be taken off his neck only to be put on another man's.

But then, said the critics, where is the motive? *Why* did Dick save Anderson? On the stage, it appears, people do things for reasons.

Off the stage they don't: that is why your penny-in-the-slot heroes, who only work when you drop a motive into them, are so oppressively automatic and uninteresting. The saving of life at the risk of the saver's own is not a common thing; but modern populations are so vast that even the most uncommon things are recorded once a week or oftener. Not one of my critics but has seen a hundred times in his paper how some policeman or fireman or nursemaid has received a medal, or the compliments of a magistrate, or perhaps a public funeral, for risking his or her life to save another's. Has he ever seen it added that the saved was the husband of the woman the saver loved, or was that woman herself, or was even known to the saver as much as by sight? Never. When we want to read of the deeds that are done for love, whither do we turn? To the murder column; and there we are rarely disappointed.

Need I repeat that the theatre critic's professional routine so discourages any association between real life and the stage, that he soon loses the natural habit of referring to the one to explain the other? The critic who discovered a romantic motive for Dick's sacrifice was no mere literary dreamer, but a clever barrister. He pointed out that Dick Dudgeon clearly did adore Mrs. Anderson; that it was for her sake that he offered his life to save her beloved husband; and that his explicit denial of his passion was the splendid mendacity of a gentleman whose respect for a married woman, and duty to her absent husband, sealed his passion-palpitating lips. From the moment that this fatally plausible explanation was launched, my play became my critic's play, not mine. Thenceforth Dick Dudgeon every night confirmed the critic by stealing behind Judith, and mutely attesting his passion by surreptitiously imprinting a heartbroken kiss on a stray lock of her hair whilst he uttered the barren denial. As for me, I was just then wandering about the streets of Constantinople, unaware of all these doings. When I returned all was over. My personal relations with the critic and the actor forbade me to curse them. I had not even a chance of publicly forgiving them. They meant well by me; but if they ever write a play, may I be there to explain!

CHARLES A. CARPENTER

The Quintessence of Shaw's Ethical Position†

The controlling currents of idea and intention that run through all of a writer's works, whatever his subject, form, or strategy, are extremely hard to discern when the writer is as prolific and wide-

---

† Published for the first time, and printed here by permission of the author.

ranging as Bernard Shaw. What is his fundamental bent? What are the basic ingredients of his thought? What are the constant elements among the innumerable variables in his essays and plays? These questions have never been answered adequately, perhaps for the simple reason that few critics have elected to deal with the vast, word-encumbered realm of Shaw's motives, purposes, and doctrines. Those who have, moreover, too often describe its more curious and remote extremities, then acknowledge that its center must lie somewhere between—if indeed there is one at all. I believe there is. At one of the critics' favorite extremities, Shaw was an odd type of semi-mystic: an impassioned but distinctly unpoetic artist who claimed to be possessed by a "world betterment craze."[1] At another, he was a coldly cerebral (though unsystematic) philosopher: a leading advocate of the theory that a cosmic force is gradually turning life into a "vortex of pure thought." At dead center, however, Shaw was much less an artist or a philosopher than an intense rhetorician, a journalistic "battering ram."[2] No matter what guise he presented himself in, he was always trying to provoke men to behave in certain ways. This is why critics complain that his compulsions as an artist are not typically poetic and his edicts as a philosopher not sufficiently abstract. Both are conditioned by his predominant desire to influence human conduct. Eric Bentley briefly discussed Shaw's ethical preoccupations in 1947, but it is time they received the focus and clarification they require.[3]

Shaw's first book-length essay, *The Quintessence of Ibsenism*, contains the core of his ideas in relatively uncomplicated form. Despite its subject—and despite its definite values as an analysis of that subject—the book is still an uncamouflaged piece of Shavian propaganda. In a preface, Shaw speaks of it as "the living word of a man delivering a message to his own time." In the text, he even scolds Ibsen for deviating from the straight Shaw line. Not that he ignored the actual import of Ibsen's plays; rather he regularly looked for—and found—the message that tallied with his own.

Shaw once defended this practice, and his rationale offers an illuminating glimpse of his basic ethical convictions. In 1905, his newly authorized biographer, Archibald Henderson,[4] earnestly told him that he was determined to be just as well as accurate. Shaw replied:

---

1. Shaw says in his Postscript to Frank Harris' *Bernard Shaw* (New York, 1931; p. 428) that "a passion of pure political *Weltverbesserungswahn* (worldbetterment craze) ... is my own devouring malady."
2. Significantly, he once declared: "The theatre is my battering ram as much as the platform or the press." *Ellen Terry and Bernard Shaw: A Correspondence*, ed. Christopher St. John (New York, 1932), p. 110.
3. *Bernard Shaw, 1856–1950*, amended ed. (New York, 1947 and 1957), pp. 46–50.
4. Henderson, *George Bernard Shaw: Man of the Century* (New York, 1956), p. xxv.

> Be as accurate as you can; but as to being just, who are you that you should be just? . . . Write boldly according to your bent: say what you WANT to say and not what you think you ought to say or what is right or just or any such arid nonsense. You are not God Almighty; and nobody will expect justice from you or any other superhuman attribute. This affected, manufactured, artificial conscience of morality and justice and so on is of no use for the making of works of art: for that you must have the real conscience that gives a man courage to fulfil his will by saying what he likes. Accuracy only means discovering the relation of your will to facts instead of cooking the facts to save trouble.

Shaw follows his own advice so conspicuously in his study of Ibsen that it has earned the label The Quintessence of Shaw.

The thesis of *The Quintessence of Ibsenism*, and the main root of Shaw's ethical convictions, is that man must follow "not the abstract law but the living will." He must cast off the "artificial conscience" imposed upon him by moral codes and social institutions, and must replace it with a "real conscience" that springs from his own aspirations. Both the negative and positive sides of this dictum are fundamental elements in Shaw's thought from *My Dear Dorothea* (1878) to *Everybody's Political What's What?* (1944). Let us first consider the negative, or destructive, side.

Shaw's overriding purpose in life, as we have seen, was to promote "worldbetterment": the evolution of society and man. In *The Quintessence*, he argues that evolution is continually obstructed by "abstract law"—variously referred to as "institutions," "ideals of goodness," or simply "duty." He explains the relationship in a remark on the evolution of society: "social progress takes effect through the replacement of old institutions by new ones; and since every institution involves the recognition of the duty of conforming to it, progress must involve the repudiation of an established duty at every step." But *The Quintessence* as a whole calls for more than the destruction of individual institutions. Shaw seeks to destroy the very basis of the tendency to cherish ideals:—the normally unquestioned assumption that man should gear his conduct to some absolute or moral prescription. In his opinion, the assumption itself—"abstract law" in general—is the major deterrent to evolution. Moreover, Shaw rejects the possibility that ideal institutions may be developed. He is a world*betterer*, a meliorist, not an idealist in any sense. As such, he recognizes that the further improvement of society and man is feasible at any level of advancement, and he actively strives for that improvement.

The positive, constructive side of Shaw's ethical convictions is grounded in "the living will." Shaw says in *The Quintessence* that the human will is the immediate stimulant of progress. He defines the will, not mainly as a restraining force (our "will power"), but rather as the "prime motor" in all human action. To both Schopenhauer and Shaw, this faculty reflects a cosmic *Wille zu leben,* a force as real as gravity but discernable only through its effects. Shaw does not stop where Schopenhauer does, however, and his will to live is also a will to live better. He grafts onto Schopenhauer's "universal postulate" the idea of an ever-growing "social organism." Manifesting what M. H. Abrams terms "the genetic habit of mind," he regards Being as Becoming, and instinctively reads an upward movement into the process. The human will, according to this meliorist view, is the specific agent of a cosmic impulse to improve the world. On the personal plane, the will is "our old friend the soul or spirit of man," as Shaw expresses it; on the social plane, "all *valid human* institutions are constructed to fulfil man's will" (my italics). In sum, the gradual fulfillment of the human will constitutes the growth of the social organism, or, less obliquely, the evolution of life on earth.

But man cannot fulfil his will simply by following its promptings blindly. As Don Juan in *Man and Superman* points out, it needs something to steer it to its goal. Shaw declares that man's organ of thought, his brain, has the capacity to steer this force at once successfully and economically. In *The Quintessence* he remarks, "Only the other day our highest boast was that we were reasonable human beings. Today we laugh at that conceit, and see ourselves as wilful creatures. [But] ability to reason accurately is as desirable as ever; for by accurate reasoning only can we calculate our actions so as to do what we intend to do: that is, to fulfil our will." Even in Shaw's basically irrationalist conception, the intellect has an indispensable function in the process of evolution, and must therefore be developed as fully as possible. The will demands a change in life as it is, or gives birth to an image of a better life; the intellect ponders the why and the wherefore. As Shaw once explained it, reason does not determine the destination, but it searches for the shortest way.[5] The highly intellectual "philosophic man," according to Don Juan, is a man who "seeks in contemplation to discover the inner will of the world, in invention to discover the means of fulfilling that will, and in action to do that will by the so-discovered means."

To carry out its function in the evolutionary process effectively, the mind must first of all free itself, as we have seen. Many times in *The Quintessence* Shaw states that man must repudiate duty, which restricts the mind and thereby obstructs the fulfillment of the will; he must regard ideals as "only swaddling clothes which man has outgrown, and which insufferably impede his movement." At

5. *The Intelligent Woman's Guide to Socialism and Capitalism* (New York, 1928), p. 365.

best, he should try to attain the "vigilant openmindedness of Ibsen." But the intellect requires more than mere freedom from the pressures of abstract law. It also requires materials with which to formulate the higher modes of life that the will hints at and campaigns for. These materials are ideas. To Shaw, ideas are the stepping-stones of progress, since by means of them man visualizes the paths that his will may follow. Not only are they the materials that the mind creates, then deliberately works with as the hand works with tools; they also have lives of their own, independent of man, and thus "wills" of their own. As a result, ideas have peculiar powers of intruding themselves into the mind and implanting themselves there, with or without man's conscious consent.[6] Shaw defends his whole approach to Ibsen's plays by insisting that "the existence of a discoverable and perfectly definite thesis in a poet's work by no means depends on the completeness of his own intellectual consciousness of it." He even explains away the heretic atmosphere of Darwinian fatalism in the plays by maintaining that Ibsen's "prophetic belief in the spontaneous growth of the will made him a meliorist without reference to the operation of Natural Selection." Shaw's view of ideas as both usable materials and wilful entities is remarkably appropriate to his evolutionary doctrine.

To summarize, then, there are three basic elements in this doctrine. The human will, man's link with a cosmic force, functions to channel the evolutionary impulse; the intellect, a distinctively human faculty, looks for the most economical way to fulfil the will; and ideas, man-made articles which yet exist apart from man, are the alternative paths that the intellect considers in its search.

These elements were the fundamental ingredient in Shaw's ethical aims, the directives for human conduct which he was convinced would most effectively promote evolution. As such, moreover, they supplied the principal focus in his works as a playwright, which was, whatever else it may also have been, nothing if not ethical. Everywhere in this work, though with varying emphasis, Shaw strives first to eliminate the chief obstruction that the will encounters, man's sense of duty to established moral and social codes. Second, he attempts to strengthen and refine the human brain so that it will become as efficient an instrument of the will as possible. And third, he seeks to supply men's minds with ideas which might prove useful in the process of evolution. In short, he consistently aims to destroy ideals, to cultivate the intellect, and to implant ideas.

These three ethical convictions pervade Shaw's work from beginning to end. My purpose has been to single them out and put them

6. Particularly ideas in the form of jokes, Shaw says in a chapter he added to *The Quintessence of Ibsenism* in 1913. A "general law of the evolution of ideas" is that "every jest is an earnest in the womb of time."

in some sort of order, not to defend this assertion. Still, let us observe them in action through one highly significant piece of prose, Shaw's concluding statement about what he preferred to call the quintessence of Ibsenism. Ibsen's attack on ideals, he announces, is clear evidence that true religion is reviving after its suppression at the hands of Darwin. He continues:

(Ibsen) is on the side of the prophets in having devoted himself to shewing (*sic*) that the spirit or will of Man is constantly outgrowing the ideals, and that therefore thoughtless conformity to them is constantly producing results no less tragic than those which follow thoughtless violation of them. Thus the main effect of his plays is to keep before the public the importance of being always prepared to act immorally [that is, in opposition to currently accredited ideals]. . . . He protests against the ordinary assumption that there are certain moral institutions which justify all means used to maintain them, and insists that the supreme end shall be the inspired, eternal, ever growing one, not the external unchanging, artificial one; not the letter but the spirit; not the contract but the object of the contract; not the abstract law but the living will. And because the will to change our habits and thus defy morality arises before the intellect can reason out any racially benefficient purpose in the change, there is always an interval during which the individual can say no more than that he wants to behave immorally because he likes to, and because he will feel constrained and unhappy if he acts otherwise. For this reason it is enormously important that we should "mind our own business" and let other people do as they like unless we can prove some damage beyond the shock to our feelings and prejudices . . . The plain working truth is that it is not only good for people to be shocked occasionally, but absolutely necessary to the progress of society that they should be shocked pretty often. . . . The need for freedom of evolution is the sole basis of toleration, the sole valid argument against Inquisitions and Censorships, the sole reason for not burning heretics and sending every eccentric person to the madhouse. . . .

What Ibsen insists on is that there is no golden rule; that conduct must justify itself by its effect upon life and not by its conformity to any rule or ideal. And since life consists in the fulfilment of the will, which is constantly growing, and cannot be fulfilled today under the conditions which secured its fulfilment yesterday, he claims afresh the old Protestant right of private judgment in questions of conduct as against all institutions, the so-called Protestant Churches themselves included.

Here I must leave the matter, merely reminding those who may think that I have forgotten to reduce Ibsenism to a formula for them, that its quintessence is that there is no formula.

Strictly speaking, there is no formula for Shavianism either. But a rationale is discernible in that the entire Shavian canon is permeated by his emphasis on destroying ideals, cultivating the intellect, and implanting ideas as the principal means to the "supreme end" of evolution.

ERIC BENTLEY
[Melodrama and Education]†

The struggle between human vitality and artificial system which is the basis of Shavian comedy finds its chief manifestation in the struggle of the inner light of genuine conscience and healthy impulse against conventional ethics. The conventional ethics of modern life Shaw finds to be identical with those of stage melodrama.

Nothing is more significant than the statement that "all the world's a stage." The whole world *is* ruled by theatrical illusion. Between the Caesars, the emperors, the Christian heroes, the Grand Old Men, the kings, prophets, saints, heroes, and judges, of the newspapers and popular imagination, and the actual Juliuses, Napoleons, Gordons, Gladstones, and so on, there is the same difference as between Hamlet and Sir Henry Irving.[1] The case is not one of fanciful similitude, but of identity. The great critics are those who penetrate and understand the illusion: the great men are those who, as dramatists planning the development of nations, or as actors carrying out the drama, are behind the scenes of the world. . . .

Here we begin to see why the stage, and particularly the late-Victorian stage, was apt to Shaw's purposes. He ridiculed the unreality of Victorian melodrama by letting in a flood of "natural history.' But he found that the unreality was also real: the illusions of melodrama were precisely those which men fall victim to in "real" life. Hence the inversion of melodrama—a device found in Shaw from beginning to end—was not an arbitrary trick but an integral part of an interpretation of life.

We have seen it in use of two of his earliest plays; but there the basic conflict is between collectivism and individualism; only later is the conflict between vitality and system pervasive. The pattern of a new, definitely Shavian comedy is more clearly observable in the *Three Plays for Puritans* which cap the first decade of Shaw's work in the theatre: *The Devil's Disciple, Caesar and Cleopatra,* and

† From Eric Bentley, *Bernard Shaw,* New York, 1947. Pp. 108-11, 115-17. Copyright 1947, 1957, by New Directions. Reprinted with permission of the publisher, New Directions Publishing Corporation.

1. A famous nineteenth-century actor-manager; Shaw disliked Irving's spectacular productions, particularly of Shakespeare, and his strongly individualistic performances.

Captain Brassbound's Conversion. In each of the *Three Plays for Puritans* we see a protagonist who stands for vitality and natural history in the midst of a group who stand for system and melodrama. In each a second character—or antagonist—is educated, helped to grow up, if not actually " converted," by the protagonist. In fact this process of education is in each case the "inner" action of the play; the "outer" action consists of the noise and swagger of melodrama.

The first of the three plays—*The Devil's Disciple*—is also the crudest (though not the least popular, because the average audience enjoys in it the thing satirized—melodrama—a good deal more than the satire). Just because it is crude the play affords a clear instance of Shavian inversion. Every incident in the play—from the announcement of the legacy to the last-minute rescue at the scaffold —is a standard item of Victorian melodrama; so is every character from the dashing hero to the little orphan chee-ild Essie. When Shaw himself calls the play "threadbare melodrama" he means presumably that it is melodrama insufficiently Shavianized, insufficiently transformed into a satire upon melodrama. The dialogue of the first two acts might almost have been written by anybody—a thing one could not say of a single page of mature Shaw. The most fully Shavian passages of the play—those in which Burgoyne speaks —are inserted without the establishment of any very significant relationship between Burgoyne and the main story.

Shaw started, so he tells us, from a central situation: that of a young man's allowing himself to be led off to the gallows in someone else's place. This sacrificial act, derived perhaps from *A Tale of Two Cities*, is then interpreted unmelodramatically. Its noble motivation is removed: Dick is not giving up his life because he thinks more of the other man than of himself. More important, the *ig*noble motive is also removed. Dick is not in love with the man's wife and is not acting to impress her with his heroism. He acts out of spontaneous feeling and entirely without motive. We have noted that Shaw is sceptical about ideas because he believes in something that underlies them—feeling, vitality, conscience, natural virtue, for "it is quite useless to declare that all men are born free if you deny that they are born good." Good deeds are not performed for motives, but for their own sake. Though not all men who do only what they want to do are good men, no man who does what he does not want to do is a good man. Dick Dudgeon *wants* to sacrifice himself. His mother, whose whole life is self-sacrifice, is a bad woman because she thinks that virtue lies in self-denial, in the fact that she makes herself miserable.

The play abounds in outer action of the kind Shaw is often criticized for not having: physical, violent action, event, pursuit, crisis, escape. Yet, to be sure, lovers of soap opera and westerns would want to delete a good deal of his dialogue, since it is taken up to a large extent with the inner, psychological action. Now, although Shaw takes his outer actions from here, there, and everywhere, and achieves variety by sheer acquisitiveness, his inner actions follow one from another, are, in fate, a continuous working-out of one or two problems that have worried Shaw throughout his life. The inner action of *The Devil's Disciple*, for instance, is taken over from an earlier play, *Candida*. In both plays we see an apparently idyllic Christian home broken into by an eccentric outsider. In both plays the result of the encounter is that one of the three people is utterly disillusioned (Morell, Judith), one is "educated" in the sense of being able to see that his true nature is not what he thought it was (Marchbanks, Anderson), and one operates as a catalyst (Candida, Dick Dudgeon), effecting change without being changed, this last character being eponymous.[2] The duplication does not extend to psychology. In the earlier play the wife is the catalyst, in the later play the outsider. The protagonists are Candida and Dick Dudgeon, the antagonists Eugene Marchbanks and Judith, and the two parsons are, so to say, victims of the clash. There is no common moral, except that each man should act according to the law of his own nature. Judith learns that she is really a wife, and not an Isolde, Eugene learns that he can stand alone and is not a Tristan. As for the two parsons, Shaw uses both his favorite processes: one is disillusioned, the other converted.

* * *

Reviewing Shaw's first decade in the theatre, one can see that, taking up the materials of the theatre as he found them, and enriching them with thoughts and attitudes he had learnt from life and literature, Shaw created a new type of comedy. Compare any of his plays with the kind of play he is parodying or otherwise modifying and his own contribution to the drama will be evident. Were we to have entered a theatre in 1900 the things that would have struck us in a Shaw play, assuming that we were sympathetic enough to notice them, would have been—in order of their saliency—the endlessly witty and eloquent talk, the wideness of reference in the dialogue, the incredible liveliness of the characters, the swift tempo, the sudden and unexpected reverses (especially anticlimaxes), in a phrase, the unusual energy coupled with the unusual intellect. And the gist of the early reviews is that, though it wasn't drama, it was something as serious as it was entertaining, as brilliant as it was funny. The more intelligent reviewers began by gravely observing that it wasn't drama and ended by saying precisely the opposite.

2. Morell, Candida, and Marchbanks are all characters in Shaw's *Candida*. Morell is a clergyman, Candida his wife, and Marchbanks a young poet who falls in love with her.

Shaw is not a dramatist, says one, but a preacher and satirist—"incidentally, no doubt, he often gives us very good drama indeed." "The chief characteristics of Mr. Bernard Shaw's plays," says another, "are not precisely dramatic," yet he goes on to say of the new drama, "the special mode of its manifestation does belong to the stage." "As a conscientious critic," says a third, "I have pointed out that Mr. Shaw's abundance of ideas spoils his plays. I may add as a man," he somewhat disarmingly goes on, "that to me it is their great attraction."

It all boils down to the fact that Shaw's plays were good in an unfamiliar way. What was new about them? Though this question has been partly answered already it may be of interest to recall Shaw's own answer. He located the newness of Ibsen (and for "Ibsen," throughout *The Quintessence of Ibsenism*, we should read "Shaw") in two things: his naturalism and his use of discussion. The naturalism is arrived at primarily by the replacement of romance and melodrama by "natural history." This entails a vast extension of subject matter. Invariably naturalism has meant an extension of subject matter, so to say, downwards—towards the inclusion of low life and animal passions. Shaw made this extension in his Unpleasant Plays. A more characteristically Shavian extension of subject matter was the extension *upwards* in the Pleasant Plays and the *Three Plays for Puritans*, an extension towards the inclusion of the higher passions— the passion for beauty, for goodness, for control. Sardoodledom had removed from the theatre most of the serious interests of civilized men. Nobody did more than Shaw to bring them all back. And nobody brought them back more entertainingly.

MARTIN MEISEL
Rebels and Redcoats†

When Max Beerbohm passed judgment on *The Devil's Disciple* for *The Saturday Review*, he took the line of friendly bewilderment:

> "What scorn would Mr. Shaw have not poured down these columns on such a play? How he would have riddled the hero, the sympathetic scapegrace (called, of course, 'Dick') who, for all his wickedness, cannot bear to see a woman cry, and keeps a warm corner in his heart for the old horse Jim and the old servant Roger, and wishes to be hanged by the English in the place of another man, and tries to throttle the major for calling a lady a woman! What scathing analysis Mr. Shaw would have made of

† From Martin Meisel, *Shaw and the Nineteenth Century Theater*, Princeton, N.J., 1963. Pp. 194-206. Copyright 1963 by the Princeton University Press. Reprinted by permission of the publishers.

this fellow's character, declaring that he, 'G.B.S.,' refused to see anything noble in a man who, having lived the life of a wastrel and a blackguard, proposed to commit suicide by imposing on the credulity of a court-martial!"[1]

Though Beerbohm also reported that the end of the play "suddenly tumbled into wild frivolity," Shaw intended no such last-minute apology. When he had just written the play he reported to Ellen Terry that "this thing, with its heroic sacrifice, its impossible courtmartial, its execution . . . its sobbings and speeches and declamations, may possibly be the most monstrous piece of farcical absurdity that ever made an audience shriek with laughter. And yet I have honestly tried for dramatic effect."[2] In another spirit (incensed at the actor Richard Mansfield for preferring *The Devil's Disciple* to *Caesar*) Shaw declared that "The D's D is a melodrama, made up of all the stage Adelphi tricks—the reading of the will, the heroic sacrifice, the court martial, the execution, the reprieve at the last moment. Anybody could make a play that way."[3]

It is clear that *The Devil's Disciple* was meant to be taken wholeheartedly for what its subtitle proclaims it: "A Melodrama." The audience would feel on familiar ground when the attractive scapegrace appeared, chaffed his brother, the Comic Countryman, probed the hidden vices of the meanly respectable, and flushed with instinctive anger at the neglect of an orphan child. Yet, even in the first act, there were grounds for uneasiness in Dick's unfeeling treatment of his mother (a tender regard for a usually distant mother normally helped redeem a disreputable hero). The audience would find familiar dramatic values through the rest of the play: the hero was full of rousing dash; Judith Anderson, the heroine, was pretty and distressed; the situations were thrilling and suspenseful. Yet, the hero is subject to the same criticism that Lady Britomart levels at that other Devil's Disciple, Andrew Undershaft: he always does the right thing for the wrong reasons. Dick Dudgeon puts his head in a noose for his own sake, he claims, not for the sake of Judith or her husband. He flatly denies that he loves Judith or that he is moved by a spirit of heroic sacrifice.

Shaw never undercuts Dick's familiar predicaments; but the melodramatic crises are converted into crises in spiritual history. In the course of the play Richard finds his true vocation as a martyr-saint in the cause of humanity, while Anderson, the priest, finds his as a warrior. Other personages become allegorical challenges to the progress of the hero. Shaw wrote to Ellen Terry soon after completing the play: "Burgoyne is a gentleman; and that is the whole meaning

1. *Around Theatres* (New York, 1930), I, 51.
2. 30 Nov. 1896, *Ellen Terry and Bernard Shaw*, p. 97.
3. Letter to Mrs. Mansfield, 3 May 1899, in Henderson, *Man of the Century*, p. 473.

of that part of the play. It is not enough, for the instruction of this generation, that Richard should be superior to religion and morality as typified by his mother and his home, or to love as typified by Judith. He must also be superior to gentility: that is, to the whole ideal of modern society."[4] General Burgoyne is meant to appear to Dick's puritan spirit as Mr. Worldly Wise-man. The vigorous situations of the physical drama are meant to body forth the edifying situations of a spiritual contest.

For a contemporary theater-going audience, *The Devil's Disciple* would call up a number of specific associations. For example, melodramatists had long been accustomed to use a patriotic rebellion to justify a hero in wholehearted opposition to the symbols of orthodox authority. They did not favor the American revolution, perhaps because the rebellion was successful and the authority English, but nineteenth-century Ireland was a favorite setting for the perils of a fugitive from red-coated martial law.[5]

The best of the Irish Melodramas using a rebel and garrison situation is Boucicault's *Arrah-na-Pogue* (1864). Its close resemblance to *The Devil's Disciple* in a number of specific details simply emphasizes Shaw's transfer of the Irish sub-genre as a whole to America. Like Dick Dudgeon, Shaun the Post (Boucicault's own part, the "Irish Character Lead") makes a false confession to the authorities and is imprisoned in place of a hunted rebel, Beamish McCoul (the dashing Romantic Lead). As in *The Devil's Disciple*, there is a question of a heroic sacrifice for love. Shaun confesses for the sake of his own just-wed bride, whom he thinks has bestowed her love elsewhere, to save her from prison and the scandal of unchastity. His trial is a court-martial, similar to Dick Dudgeon's in conduct and appearance.[6] In both *Arrah-na-Pogue* and *The Devil's Disciple* the discourse is chiefly between the innocent accused and two officers, one gentlemanly and sympathetic, the other pompous and military-minded. Shaun's peasant wit in his responses is surprisingly close in language and idea to Dick's *diablerie*.

The association, in situation, character, and action, between Shaw's

---

4. 13 March 1897, *Ellen Terry and Bernard Shaw*, p. 124.

5. Examples are Samuel Lover's *Rory O'Moore* (1837), Edmund Falconer's *Peep o' Day* (1861), and Dion Boucicault's *Arrah-na-Pogue* (1864), *The Shaughraun* (1875), and *The Rapparee* (1870), See below, "Irish Romance." Not all plays presenting fugitive heroes at odds with military authority had Ireland for a background. Tom Taylor and Charles Reade's *Two Loves and a Life* (1854) is set in the Jacobite rebellion of 1745, and Tom Taylor's *A Sheep in Wolf's Clothing* (1857) uses Monmouth's Rebellion.

The latter play is similar to *The Devil's Disciple* in that it presents a rebel hiding from a Redcoat garrison with a pretense to be kept up on the part of the fugitive's wife. Anne Carew allows herself to be wooed by Colonel Percy Kirke in order to save her husband who is given out as dead. When her husband is discovered hiding in the house, rescue comes in the person of Lord Churchill, an embryonic Burgoyne, cool and gentlemanly, who softens the reign of terror.

6. See Allardyce Nicoll, *A History of English Drama 1660–1900* (Cambridge, 1959), V, 90-91.

rebel-and-redcoat play and revolutionary Irish Melodrama gave the deceptive comfort of a familiar setting to Dick Dudgeon's rebellious heterodoxies. But these were not the heterodoxies of the conventional gallant, if misguided, patriot-hero. The Devil's Disciple is a rebel, not against armies, rulers, or parties, but against ideas: against religion and morality, romantic love, and "the whole ideal of modern society."

The most recognizable situation in *The Devil's Disciple* presents Sydney Carton's heroic sacrifice for love from *A Tale of Two Cities*. The novel was notably dramatized by Tom Taylor in 1860 (with the help of Dickens himself) and by numerous lesser playwrights in the course of the century.[7] Tom Taylor's Sydney Carton is a Devil's Disciple with a puritan conscience, an impulse toward sacrificial martyrdom, and a sentimental fixation on another man's wife. On his first entrance, Carton announces himself:

> I'm an incurable idler. . . . For your offer of attentions—I don't think our tastes would suit. I'm fond of low company, late hours, loose haunts, and strong wine.
>
> DARN[AY]. Hardly the tastes, I fear, to make life either very pleasant or very profitable!
>
> CART[ON]. What the devil do you know about it?
>
> (*French A. E., pp.* 16-17)

But Carton cancels out this fine assertion of diabolical allegiance, for unlike Dick Dudgeon, he is altogether ashamed of himself and his way of life.

As in *The Devil's Disciple*, a high point in Tom Taylor's play is a trial scene, in which Darnay is condemned. Motivated entirely by love for Lucie Manette and by a sense of his own worthlessness, Carton drugs Darnay and takes his place. The trading of coats is a most important piece of business in the play, as it is in *The Devil's Disciple*. The last scenes also show some correspondences, the one play presenting Carton in a tumbril, the other Dudgeon on a cart with a rope on his neck. The plays are thus similar not only in their central action but even in their scenes and devices.

There is a telling resemblance between the rather famous poster for the Rev. Freeman Wills's later adaptation of Dickens' novel, *The Only Way* (1899), showing Martin Harvey as Sydney Carton at the guillotine and photographs of the last scene in the first London production of *The Devil's Disciple* (1907), directed by Shaw him-

7. See S. J. Adair Fitz-Gerald, *Dickens and the Drama* (London, 1910), pp. 269-85. Fitz-Gerald mentions eight different dramatic versions of the novel. He also treats the similarity of *A Tale* to Watts Phillips' play *The Dead Heart* (1859); Dumas *père's* play *Le* *Chevalier de la Maison Rouge* (1847), adapted as *Genevieve; or, The Reign of Terror* by Dion Boucicault (1853); and Bulwer-Lytton's romance *Zanoni*. All four works culminate in a similar self-sacrificing substitution during the reign of terror.

self (see Figures 11, 12). An earlier version of Wills's final tableau may be found in Watts Phillips' *The Dead Heart* (1859), revived by Irving and knowledgeably mentioned by Shaw.[8] Robert Landry (the "Dead Heart") was buried in the Bastille in the course of a romantic rivalry, and became a revolutionary power after his liberation. In the end he substitutes himself on the scaffold for the aristocratic son of the woman he has always loved:

> TABLEAU.—Back of stage opens and discovers a view of the guillotine, guarded by GENDARMES and SECTIONAIRES, surrounded by MOB. The tall old houses of quaint architecture are just touched by the light of early morning, which covers with a crimson glow the tower of Notre Dame. In the extreme background, upon scaffold, stands ROBERT LANDRY, prepared for the fatal axe. He extends his arms in direction of COUNTESS, as curtain slowly falls. (*French A.E.*, p. 58)

In reproducing this much-used scene, as in echoing the trial scene, the changing of coats, and the hero's diabolic pose, Shaw exploits the familiarity of the sacrifice for love in its standard theatrical embodiment. Shaw had Judith conceive of Dick Dudgeon's action in Sydney Carton terms in order to make his own point all the more vigorously: Dick Dudgeon is superior to the romantic love and the romantic self-hatred which provoke Sydney Carton and Robert Landry to the sacrifice.

In an undated letter to Hesketh Pearson, Shaw wrote of *The Devil's Disciple*, "The play was written round the scene of Dick's arrest, which has always been floating in my head as a situation for a play."[9] Scenes of arrest were frequently and naturally conjoined with a heroic substitution in both Melodrama and Melodramatic Farce, and some of these scenes are remarkably suggestive of *The Devil's Disciple* in making the presence of the wife or fiancée of the fugitive an essential part of the action. For example, in J. R. Planché's A *Peculiar Position* (1837—an adaptation of the *comédie vaudeville*, *La Frontière de Savoie* by Scribe and Bayard)—the Countess de Novara shuffles the passport of her fugitive husband with that of Champignon, a greengrocer, and then persuades Champignon to play the Count while her husband gets away. Champignon is arrested as the Count, and he puts on the Count's morning-gown to confirm his false identity. Similarly, Dick Dudgeon is arrested as the minister (because he is found in apparently intimate circumstances, at tea in his shirtsleeves, with the minister's wife in the minister's house), and he puts on the minister's characteristic coat to confirm his mistaken identity. Later, to lull the suspicions of the

8. *How to Become a Musical Critic*, p. 180.
9. Hesketh Pearson, *Bernard Shaw*, p. 200. See also Henderson, *Table-Talk of G. B. S.* (London, 1925), p. 75.

arresting sergeant, Dudgeon and Judith are obliged to show affection for each other. The same "peculiar position" provides most of the comedy in Planché's play.[1]

Conventionally, the man replaced on the scaffold contested the sacrifice, unless carefully reduced to impotence or unconsciousness by the skillful playwright. In *Arrah-na-Pogue*, Beamish McCoul gives himself up immediately, as soon as he hears of Shaun's arrest in his place. The conventional action similarly occurs in T. W. Robertson's adaption from Scribe and Legouvé, *The Ladies' Battle* (1851), where an amorous countess conceals a reputed Bonapartist leader in post-Empire France among her servants, and induces a hopelessly devoted lover to put on her livery and draw the searching police off the track. The plot succeeds and the real fugitive escapes; but when he learns that his substitute is to be summarily shot in his place, he returns to give himself up.

In *The Devil's Disciple*, when Judith finally tells her clerical husband that Dick Dudgeon has been arrested in his place, she fully expects him to hurry to English headquarters, and Dick himself had some apprehensions that this would be the minister's honorable action. Expecting and dreading the heroic gesture, Judith is sorely disillusioned when the clergyman jumps into his boots and rides away. Here Shaw is deliberately invoking a convention (articulated through Judith, who has all the audience's expectations); but his purpose is not merely to ridicule or, like Gilbert in *The Mikado* with his "Lord High Substitute," to burlesque this convention. The action at this point of *The Devil's Disciple* dramatizes Anderson's discovery of his true vocation. Surrender and self-sacrifice should come naturally to a Christian minister; instead, he finds his way in resistance and violence.

The last act of *The Devil's Disciple* is divided into three increasingly public scenes: the confrontation of Richard and Judith, where she offers her love and he rebuffs her; the court-martial; and the execution and delivery. Far from wishing the play to tumble into wild frivolity in the last act, Shaw was anxious to guard against it. He wrote Siegfried Trebitsch to instruct an Austrian Judith that she must weep at the end of the first scene "in a really heart-rending way; and all through the court martial she must not let the audience lose the sense of the horror with which she listens to the

---

1. More farcical versions of the arrest scene, utilizing some of the same elements, occur in J. M. Morton's *Your Life's in Danger* (1848), and in his *Steeple-Chase; or, In the Pigskin* (1865). The latter was a favorite play with J. L. Toole, who himself was a favorite in Dublin. Toole played Mr. Tittums, a hapless victim of error, and at one point, when a sheriff's officer is carrying him off to jail as another man, that other man's wife throws herself upon him to confirm the error and keep her husband safe. For another view of Shaw's use of *A Peculiar Position* and *The Ladies' Battle* (discussed below), see Stephen S. Stanton's introduction to *Camille and Other Plays*, New York, 1957, p. xxxviii.

deadly jesting of Burgoyne & Richard. All the rest is easy."[2] He was particularly concerned that productions exploit the proper melodramatic qualities of the scene of execution. He wrote Trebitsch that it was "very important to get the last scene well stage managed, with a big surging crowd."[3] And he complained to Mrs. Mansfield, who played Judith to her husband's Richard in New York:

> "I quite understand that the last scene is so arranged that nobody watches Judith, and that the spectacle of Richard Dudgeon making Sidney Carton faces keep the theatre palpitatingly indifferent to everything else. And that's just what I object to: it's all wrong: the audience ought to see everything—the frightful flying away of the minutes in conflict with the equally frightful deliberation of Burgoyne and the soldierlike smartness of the executioner: they ought to long for a delay instead of that silly eagerness to see whether the hanging will really come off or not and so on."[4]

The justice of Melodrama is providential; and therefore the greater the peril, and the more ingenious the circumstances of virtue's escape and vice's unmasking the greater the audience delight. When Sweet William, the simple, handsome, true-blue, universally loved and Billy Budd-like sailor in Douglas Jerrold's *Black-Ey'd Susan* (1829) is about to be hanged from the yard-arm for striking his captain, his situation seems altogether hopeless. The villain Doggrass has just been drowned fortuitously, with the paper which could save William's life fast in his pocket. Suspense grows as the execution approaches and the action plays up the pathos and hopelessness. Then, the hand of Providence shows itself: ever so naturally, but unexpectedly because the audience was too preoccupied to think ahead to the ritual of execution, William is saved. The ritual cannon sounds, and, conforming to popular lore, the body of Doggrass rises to the surface with pockets intact.

Even when the audience had become more sophisticated (and less talented authors could not contrive so ingenious a rescue), Shaw felt it was the writer's obligation in Melodrama to cultivate the sense of wonder and peril. Reviewing *The Girl I Left Behind Me* by Franklin Fyles and David Belasco (1895), Shaw points out:

> "The third act . . . is an adaptation of (Boucicault's) the Relief of Lucknow, which, as a dramatic situation, is so strong and familiar that it is hardly possible to spoil it, though the authors have done their best. The main difficulty is the foreknowledge of the hopelessly sophisticated audience that Mr. Terriss will rush in at the last moment, sword in hand, and rescue everybody. The authors' business was to carry us on from incident to incident so

---

2. MS postcard, 17 Feb. 1903.
3. MS postcard to Siegfried Trebitsch, 9 Aug. 1902. The last scene of *The Devil's Disciples* is as thoroughgoing a crowd-sensation scene as Shaw ever wrote.
4. Letter of 1 Jan. 1898, in Henderson, *Man of the Century*, p. 450.

convincingly and interestingly as to preoccupy us with the illusion of the situation sufficiently to put Mr. Terriss out of our heads." (*OTN*, I, 96)

To put Anderson and the Springtown messenger sufficiently out of our heads, Shaw arranges the last scene's marching and music, Judith's suffering, Dick's recapitulated rejection of religion, gentlemanliness, and love, and the final scare to the audience when it hears that the time for redemption has elapsed:

> BURGOYNE. Have you anything more to say, Mr. Dudgeon? It wants two minutes of twelve still.
>
> RICHARD (*in the strong voice of a man who has conquered the bitterness of death*) Your watch is two minutes slow by the town clock, which I can see from here, General. (*The town clock strikes the first stroke of twelve. Involuntarily the people flinch at the sound, and a subdued groan breaks from them.*)

Earlier, information has been planted that the town clock is always fast; and later, Burgoyne declares that he should never dream of hanging a gentleman by an American clock. But meanwhile, the audience has been given a turn.

The final catastrophe is averted, as it is so often in Melodrama, by Providence in the form of a legal technicality. As Sweet William escapes hanging because he was technically out of the Navy when he struck his captain, so both Dick and Anderson escape hanging because Dick was to be hanged only if Anderson failed to present himself by twelve noon, and Anderson came armed with Burgoyne's own safe-conduct. Moreover, the clock was fast.

The straightforward Melodrama of *The Devil's Disciple*, for which Shaw was so concerned in his letters and in his dramaturgy, is more than just an attractive container for the inner drama of ideas. Rather, in the economy of the play, the same familiar devices which serve the dramatic action serve the dramatic idea. Thus, the changing of coats, besides justifying Dick's arrest in the action, functions as an extended dramatic symbol of conversion. Initially there is simply an elaborate and exciting business with ironic overtones as the Devil's Disciple puts on the minister's coat under the eye of the sergeant. Then, when the Reverand Anthony Anderson learns what has happened, and "*the man of peace vanishes, transfigured into a choleric and formidable man of war*" (p. 45), he buckles a pistol belt over Dudgeon's coat, and significantly declares: "If they took him for me in my coat, perhaps theyll take me for him in his" (p. 46). Later, having rescued Richard with the cooperation of the British War Office, he tells Burgoyne:

> Sir: it is in the hour of trial that a man finds his true profession. This foolish young man . . . boasted himself the Devil's Disciple; but when the hour of trial came to him, he found that it was

his destiny to suffer and be faithful to the death. I thought myself a decent minister of the gospel of peace; but when the hour of trial came to me, I found that it was my destiny to be a man of action, and that my place was amid the thunder of the captains and the shouting. . . . Your mother told me, Richard, that I should never have chosen Judith if I'd been born for the ministry. I am afraid she was right; so, by your leave, you may keep my coat and I'll keep yours.

The exchange of coats is a visual metaphor for the twofold discovery and conversion which has taken place, for the accomplishment of a pair of spiritual destinies. In making this the true inner action of the play, Shaw has not departed a hairsbreadth from the understood ethos of Melodrama. In his "Art of Dramatic Composition," Dion Boucicault, perhaps the most accomplished melodramatist of the century, explained the providential wonders, technicalities, and coincidences of his art as follows:

"Life is profluent; all human actions are directed to some desired object, and Providence produces what, as they happen, we call accidents, but when past we perceive to be necessary results. And this should be the process of the fictitious providence of which a spectator is the witness, that he may be led to believe that he is watching the accomplishment of a destiny."[5]

5. *North American Review*, 126(1878),p. 45.

August Strindberg

and

A Dream Play

AUGUST STRINDBERG

Paradise Regained†

I reckon the summer and autumn of 1895—in spite of everything —among the happy resting places of my turbulent life. All my undertakings prospered, unknown friends brought food to me as the ravens did to Elijah. Money came to me of itself. I was able to buy books, natural-history specimens, and, among other things, a microscope that unveiled for me the secrets of life.

Lost to the world by renouncing the empty pleasure of Paris, I lived entirely within my own quarter of the city. Each morning I visited the departed in the Cemetery of Montparnasse, and afterwards walked down to the Luxembourg Gardens to say good morning to my flowers. Now and then some countryman of mine, on a visit to Paris, would call and invite me out to luncheon or to the theatre on the other side of the river. I always refused, as the right bank was forbidden territory. To me it represented the 'world' in the true sense of the word, the world of the living and of earthly vanity.

The fact was that a kind of religion had developed in me, though I was quite unable to formulate it. It was a spiritual state rather than an opinion founded upon theories, a hotch-potch of impressions that were far from being condensed into thoughts.

I had bought a Roman missal, and this I read and meditated over. The Old Testament comforted but also chastised me in a somewhat confused way, while the New Testament left me cold. This did not prevent a Buddhist work from making a far greater impression on me than all other sacred books, as it put the value of actual suffering

† This and "Tribulations" are from August Strindberg, *Inferno,* translated by Mary Sandback, London, 1962. Pp. 42-44, 164-68. Copyright 1962. Reprinted by permission of the publishers, Hutchinson Publishing Group Ltd.

far higher than that of mere abstention. Buddha had had the courage to give up his wife and children when he was in the prime of life and enjoying the happiness of married bliss, whereas Christ had avoided all contact with the legitimate pleasures of this world.

In other respects I did not brood upon the emotions that possessed me. I remained detached, let things take their course, and granted to myself the same freedom that I was bound to accord to others.

The great event in Paris that season was the call to arms raised by the critic Brunetière about the bankruptcy of science. I had been well acquainted with the natural sciences since my childhood and had tended towards Darwinism. But I had discovered how unsatisfying can be the scientific approach that recognizes the exquisite mechanism of the world but denies the existence of a mechanic. The weakness of the theory was revealed by the universal degeneration of science, which had marked out for itself a boundary line beyond which no one was allowed to go:

'We have solved all problems, the Universe has no secrets left.'

This presumptuous lie had annoyed me even in 1880, and for the past fifteen years I had been engaged upon revising the natural sciences. Thus, in 1884, I had cast doubts upon the accepted theory of the composition of the atmosphere, and upon the identification of the nitrogen found in air with that obtained by breaking down a compound of nitrogen. In 1891 I had gone to the Laboratory of Physical Science in Lund to compare the spectra of these two kinds of nitrogen, which I knew differed. Need I describe the sort of reception I got from the mechanistic men of science there? But with the year 1895 came the discovery of argon, which proved the rightness of the suppositions I had already advanced and infused new life into the investigations that had been interrupted by my rash marriage.

No, science had not gone bankrupt, only science that was out of date and distorted. Brunetière was right, though he was wrong.

Meanwhile, whereas all were agreed in recognizing the unity of matter and called themselves monists without really being so, I went further, drew the ultimate conclusions of this doctrine, and eliminated the boundaries between matter and what was called the spirit. In my book *Antibarbarus* I had discussed the psychology of sulphur and interpreted it in the light of its ontogeny—that is to say, the embryonic development of sulphur.

For further information I refer those interested to my book *Sylva Sylvarum*, published in 1896, in which, proudly aware of my clairvoyant faculty, I penetrated to the very heart of the secrets of creation, especially those of the animal and vegetable kingdoms. I would also refer them to my essay *In the Cemetery* (included in *Printed and Unprinted*) which shows how in solitude and in suffering I was brought back to a faltering apprehension of God and immortality.

Tribulations

Shut up in that little city of the Muses, without any hope of getting away, I fought out a terrible battle with the enemy, my own self.

Each morning, when I took my walk along the ramparts shaded by plane trees, the sight of the huge, red lunatic asylum reminded me of the danger I had escaped and of the future, should I suffer a relapse. By revealing to me the true nature of the terrors that had beset me during the past year, Swedenborg[1] had set me free from the electrical experts, the practitioners of the black arts, the wizards, the envious gold makers, and the fear of insanity. He had shown me the only way to salvation: to seek out the demons in their lair, within myself, and to destroy them by—repentance. Balzac, as the prophet's adjutant, had taught me in his *Séraphita* that 'remorse is the impotent emotion felt by the man who will sin again; repentance alone is effective, and brings everything to an end'.

To repent, then! But was not that to repudiate Providence, that had chosen me to be its scourge? Was it not to say to the Powers: 'You have misdirected my fate, you have allowed me to be born with a mission to punish, to overthrow idols, to raise the standard of revolt, and then you have withdrawn your protection and left me alone to recant and thus to earn ridicule. Do you now ask me to submit, to apologize, to make amends?'

Fantastic, but exactly the vicious circle that I foresaw in my twentieth year when I wrote my play *Master Olof*, which I now see as the tragedy of my own life. What is the good of having dragged out a laborious existence for thirty years only to learn by experience what I had already anticipated? In my youth I was a true believer and you made of me a free-thinker. Of the free-thinker you made an atheist, of the atheist a monk. Inspired by the humanitarians, I extolled socialism. Five years later you showed me the absurdity of socialism. You have cut the ground from under all my enthusiasms, and suppose that I now dedicate myself to religion, I know for a certainty that before ten years have passed you will prove to me that religion is false.

Are not the Gods jesting with us mortals, and is that why we too, sharing the jest, are able to laugh in the most tormented moments of our lives?

How can you require that we take seriously something that appears to be no more than a colossal jest?

Jesus Christ our Saviour, what is it that he saved? Look at our

1. Emanuel Swedenborg (1688–1772), a Swedish philosopher, scientist, theologian, and mystic [*Editor*].

Swedish pietists, the most Christian of all Christians, those pale, wicked, terror-stricken creatures, who cannot smile and who look like maniacs. They seem to carry a demon in their hearts and, mark you, most of their leaders end up in prison as malefactors. Why should their Lord have delivered them over to the enemy? Is religion a punishment, and is Christ the spirit of vengeance?

All the ancient Gods reappeared as demons at a later date, The dwellers in Olympus became evil spirits. Odin and Thor, the Devil himself, Prometheus—Lucifer, the Bringer of Light, degenerated into Satan. Is it possible—God forgive me—that even Christ has been transformed into a demon? He has brought death to reason, to the flesh, to beauty, to joy, to the purest feelings of affection of which mankind is capable. He has brought death to the virtues of fearlessness, valour, glory, love, and mercy.

The sun shines, daily life goes on in its accustomed way, the sound of men at their everyday tasks raises our spirits. It is at such moments that the courage to revolt rears up and we fling our challenge and our doubts at Heaven.

But at night, when silence and solitude fall about us, our arrogance is dissipated, we hear our heart-beats and feel a weight on our chests. Then go down on your knees in the bush of thorns outside your window, go; find a doctor or seek out some comrade who will sleep with you in the same room.

Enter your room alone at night-time and you will find that someone has got there before you. You will not see him, but you will feel his presence. Go to the lunatic asylum and consult the psychiatrist. He will talk to you of neurasthenia, paranoia, angina pectoris, and the like, but he will never cure you.

Where will you go, then, all you who suffer from sleeplessness, and you who walk the streets waiting for the sun to rise?

The Mills of the Universe, the Mills of God, these are two expressions that are often used.

Have you had in your ears the humming that resembles the noise of a water-mill? Have you noticed, in the stillness of the night, or even in broad daylight, how memories of your past life stir and are resurrected, one by one or two by two? All the mistakes you have made, all your crimes, all your follies, that make you blush to your very ear-tips, bring a cold sweat to your brow and send shivers down your spine. You relive the life you have lived, from your birth to the very day that is. You suffer again all the sufferings you have endured, you drink again all the cups of bitterness you have so often drained. You crucify your skeleton, as there is no longer any flesh to mortify. You send your spirit to the stake, as your heart is already burned to ashes.

Do you recognize the truth of all this?

There are the Mills of God, that grind slow but grind exceeding small—and black. You are ground to powder and you think it is all over. But no, it will begin again and you will be put through the mill once more.

Be happy. That is the Hell here on earth, recognized by Luther, who esteemed it a high honour that he should be ground to powder on this side of the empyrean.

Be happy and grateful.

What is to be done? Must you humble yourself?

But if you humble yourself before mankind you will arouse their arrogance, since they will then believe themselves to be better than you are, however great their villainy.

Must you then humble yourself before God? But it is an insult to the All-Highest to drag Him down to the level of a planter who rules over slaves.

Pray! What? Will you arrogate to yourself the right to bend the will of the Eternal and His decrees, by flattery and by servility?

Seek God and find the Devil. That is what has happened to me.

I have done penance, I have mended my ways, but no sooner do I begin the work of resoling my soul than I have to add yet another patch. If I put on new heels the uppers split. There is no end to it.

If I give up drinking and come home sober at nine o'clock of an evening to a glass of milk, my room is full to overflowing with all manner of demons, who pluck me from my bed and smother me under the bedclothes. If, on the other hand, I come home drunk, towards midnight, I fall asleep like a little angel and wake up in the morning as fresh as a young god, ready to work like a galley-slave.

If I shun women unwholesome dreams come upon me at night. If I train myself to think well of my friends, if I confide my secrets to them or give them money, I am betrayed, and if I lose my temper over a breach of faith it is always I who am punished.

I try to love mankind in the mass, I close my eyes to their faults, and, with limitless forbearance, forgive them their meanness and their back-biting, and then, one fine day, I find that I am an accomplice. If I withdraw from the company of people I consider bad I am immediately attacked by the demon of solitude. If I then seek for better friends I fall in with worse.

Furthermore, when I vanquish my evil passions, and reach at least some measure of tranquillity by my abstinence, I experience a feeling of self-satisfaction that makes me think I am superior to my fellow men, and this is the mortal sin of egotism, which brings down instant punishment.

How are we to explain the fact that each apprenticeship in virtue is followed by a new vice?

Swedenborg solves this riddle when he says that vices are the punishments man incurs for more serious sins. For instance, those who are greedy of power are doomed to the Hell of Sodomy. If we admit that the theory holds good we must endure our vices and profit by the remorse that accompanies them as things that will help us to settle our final account.

Consequently, to seek to be virtuous is like attempting to escape from our prison and our torments. This is what Luther was trying to say in article XXXIX of his reply to the Papal Bull of excommunication, where he proclaims that 'The Souls in Purgatory sin incessantly, since they are trying to gain peace and to avoid their torments.'

Similarly in article XXXIV: 'To struggle against the Turks is nothing more than rising in rebellion against God, who is chastising us for our sins throughout the medium of the Turks.'

Thus it is clear that 'all our good deeds are mortal sins', and that 'the world must be sinful in the eyes of God, and must understand that no one can become good except by the grace of God'.

Therefore, O my brethren, you must suffer without hope of a single lasting happiness in this life, since we are already in Hell. We must not reproach the Lord if we see innocent little children suffer. None of us can know why, but divine justice makes us suppose that it is because of sins committed before ever they arrived in this world. Let us rejoice in our torments which are so many debts repaid, and let us believe that it is out of pure compassion that we are kept in ignorance of the primordial reasons for our punishment.

Author's Note [to *A Dream Play*]†

In this dream play, as in his former dream play *To Damascus*, the Author has sought to reproduce the disconnected but apparently logical form of a dream. Anything can happen; everything is possible and probable. Time and space do not exist; on a slight groundwork of reality, imagination spins and weaves new patterns made up of memories, experiences, unfettered fancies, absurdities and improvisations.

The characters are split, double and multiply; they evaporate, crystallise, scatter and converge. But a single consciousness holds sway over them all—that of the dreamer. For him there are no secrets, no incongruities, no scruples and no law. He neither condemns nor acquits, but only relates, and since on the whole, there is more pain than pleasure in the dream, a tone of melancholy, and of compassion for all living things, runs through the swaying narrative.

† From August Strindberg, *Six Plays of Strindberg*, translated by Elizabeth Sprigge. Copyright 1955 by Elizabeth Sprigge. Reprinted by permission of Willis Kingsley Wing.

Sleep, the liberator, often appears as a torturer—and is thus reconciled with reality. For however agonising real life may be, at this moment, compared with the tormenting dream, it is a joy.

H. V. E. PALMBLAD

[A "Conscious Will" in History: Summary]†

The first suggestion of a departure from the anti-religious and atheistic attitude of the later eighties and early nineties on the part of Strindberg is probably to be found in what Lamm terms a note of weariness of dogmatic atheism in *Himmelrikets nycklar* in 1892. This attitude away from materialism and atheism emerges more clearly by August, 1894. By the end of the year, he has arrived at a definite belief in the existence of an "Invisible Hand" guiding his fate. This belief becomes strengthened by degrees, particularly under the influence of Swedenborg. Strindberg's belief in a personal God does not immediately carry with it a belief in Christianity. His acceptance of the latter dates from 1896. His religion from that time is a kind of "creedless Christianity."

The first expression in a critical work of a belief in Providence as an active factor in history, we find in "Världshistoriens mystik" (1903), although the idea was evidently in his mind before this time.

In this work, he expounds the following theory. He sees in history the working out of a definite plan conceived by a "Conscious Will." He sees this plan worked out through the agency of men, partly acting as free agents, partly under the restraint imposed by the Divine Will, often trying to accomplish ends of their own and ignorant of the purposes they are called to further. In this plan, Strindberg sees everything serving: error serving truth, and evil serving good. Each country has its mission to fulfill, and having fulfilled this mission, relinquishes its place in world history.

In the execution of this divine plan, in 1903 he sees an attitude of impartiality on the part of the Supreme Being, who is equally favorable toward all nations and all religions. As the final purpose of the "Conscious Will," he sees integration or unification, including the unification of religion. By 1906, the latter has come to mean the gradual merging of all religions into one Christian faith. With this new attitude toward Christianity, we note a changed idea of the "Conscious Will." The Supreme Being, who in the earlier conception was considered as impartial, has now become the God of the Christians, ready to protect his own and leading them to final victory.

† From H. V. E. Palmblad, *Strindberg's Conception of History*, New York, 1927. Pp. 88-90. Copyright 1927. Reprinted by permission of the publishers, Columbia University Press.

The relation between Strindberg's personal religious faith and his interpretation of history offers some interesting points. His conception of a "Conscious Will" guiding the events of history is merely the application to world history of the belief in the "Invisible Hand" guiding the events of his own life. His interpretation of God is the same in his personal religious convictions and in his studies on historical themes, that of the deist.[1] In the *Inferno*, he says that the Powers ("makterna") have revealed themselves to him as one or more persons governing the progress of the world and the fates of men consciously and hypostatically; in "Världshistoriens mystik," he sees the "Conscious Will" standing above everything, guiding the world from without, conducting the affairs on the plan of a big chess game. Just as he feels that there is a definite plan in his own life, so he sees a design in the events of history.

Finally, it may be noted that Strindberg's idea of the triumph of Christianity, the merging of all Christian faiths into one, and the absorption of other religions into this one faith, is paralleled in his own religious attitude. At times he dreamed of a return of the different Protestant churches to the Roman Catholic Church. He suggested this as early as 1890; then, however, as an academic theory which has no basis in his own religious conviction, since he was at this time an atheist. Later he sees it as something indicated by the actual progress of events. It is then associated in his own religious experience with a personal longing for a return to the Mother Church. Lastly the religion of the future becomes in his mind a kind of a creedless Christianity, a conception with which his own later religious belief is in accord.

MAURICE VALENCY

[A *Dream Play*: The Flower and the Castle]†

Like *Peer Gynt*, *Lucky Per's Journey*, and *To Damascus*,[1] A *Dream Play* traces the steps of a mythical journey. The plot—if it can be called a plot—is rudimentary, another and more abstract version of the narrative which underlies the action of *To Damascus*. A *Dream Play* develops the situation of a lady who becomes, presumably, the mistress of an officer, through whom she meets a lawyer, who marries her. She bears him a child. But in time she

1. I am using the word "deist" here in the sense given it by H. H. Lane in his *Evolution and Christian Faith*, p. 158-160, i.e., one who conceives God as governing the universe from the outside, emphasizing the transcendence of God to the exclusion of his immanence. Cf. also Hibben's *Problems of Philosophy*, pp. 67-68, and the article on "deism" in the *Encyclopedia Britannica*.

†From Maurice Valency, *The Flower and the Castle*, New York, 1963. Pp. 326-42. Copyright Maurice Valency, 1963. Reprinted by permission of the publishers, The Macmillan Company, Inc.
1. *Peer Gynt* (1866) is a verse play by Ibsen; *Lucky Per's Journey* (1882) and *To Damascus* (1898) are plays by Strindberg [*Editor*].

finds life with the lawyer unendurable, and she sets off with her first love on a long journey which she does not enjoy, but in the course of which she meets a poet, whom she finds congenial. The lawyer now attempts to assert his conjugal rights, whereupon the lady puts an end to her troubles by withdrawing from the world. Such, at least, are the bones of the action; and seldom has a plot had less relation to a play.

Though *A Dream Play* in many ways recalls *To Damascus*, the narrative patterns necessarily differ a good deal. *To Damascus*— the story of a man hunted by God—belongs to the tradition of the medieval chase-allegory, and very properly, has a medieval coloring. *A Dream Play* belongs to the *topos*[2] of the visitor from another sphere. Since, in this play, the Daughter of Indra is on a sight-seeing tour of the Christian world, she grows and develops, but she maintains her identity from beginning to end; she is, essentially, a constant in variable circumstances, and in this she somewhat resembles the Unknown in the earlier play. She is, however, unlike the Unknown, fundamentally an observer, and her perceptions are therefore much more objective than would be the case were she the primary subject of the action as he is. Nevertheless, in a general way, it is as if in *A Dream Play* the story of *To Damascus*, or something near it, were told from the viewpoint of the Lady.

The play, we are told in the foreword, is intended to produce on the stage the effect of a dream. Its shapes arise out of chaos half formed, with wisps of chaos, so to speak, still clinging to them. In its effects of abstraction and its bizarre groupings, it clearly announces the art of the twentieth century; yet its subject matter and its mood are unmistakably romantic. It is, moreover, as I have suggested, only seemingly amorphous. Its episodes are grouped quite systematically within the rigid frame that encloses them. It has a beginning, middle, and end; and its conclusion follows from the *données*[3] of its beginning in a way that is by no means characteristic of dreams. Beyond doubt it was a brilliantly revolutionary departure in its day, far ahead of the theatre of its time. It is only when we compare it with more completely developed examples of the genre it inaugurated—the brothel scene in *Ulysses*,[4] for example —that its connections with the romantic tradition of the nineteenth century become apparent.

It is customary to say that in this play Strindberg explored the workings of the subconscious during sleep,[5] but it must be obvious that the unconscious elements of *A Dream Play* do not come into consciousness here any more readily than they would in any

2. "Well known topic" or, in this case, well known story type [*Editor*].
3. "The things given" or premises [*Editor*].

4. The stream-of-consciousness novel (1922) by James Joyce [*Editor*].
5. *E.g.* Elizabeth Sprigge, *Six Plays by Strindberg* (New York, 1955), p. 188.

other play. A *Dream Play* is a play, not a dream. It is a montage of scenes in prose and verse composed in accordance with a conscious artistic aim, and for a wholly rational purpose. The play has therefore the enigmatic character of a work of art, and not at all the enigmatic character of a dream, and while much of its beauty, and its power, are derived from what is suggested by and to the unconscious, on the whole it is directed to the intellectual faculty and is meant to be understood.

Within the mythological frame which Strindberg imposed upon it, A *Dream Play* consists of a series of vignettes abstracted from the autobiographical sources which customarily provided him with his subject matter. It is, like *To Damascus*, essentially a personal statement, the complete comprehension of which would entail an impossibly intimate knowledge of the author's life and works. Consequently, although it has been the subject of the most careful study, much of the detail remains, and very likely will always remain, puzzling. Underlying the entire conception is the Brahmanic myth of self-sacrifice, to which Strindberg gave a vaguely Christian tone. As he understood the myth, the diversification of Brahma was the result of a sexual act, a seduction, and in the union of Brahma with Maya, the world mother, was figured the primal union of spirit and matter, corresponding to the creation of the world.

The Daughter's name, Agnes, was doubtless suggested by Agni the fire-god and heavenly messenger, often associated mythologically with Indra, the principal god of the Vedas, lord of the sky and the lightning, and dispenser of the fructifying rain. The Daughter's incarnation in A *Dream Play*, and her life on earth, is a species of sacrifice in the course of which she experiences all the evil she can bear in order to carry to her heavenly father a full report of the miseries of mankind. Through Agnes, Strindberg once more rationalizes the desire for suffering as a spiritual yearning for deliverance. The Daughter says, in words which come somewhat closer to Hartmann's *Philosophy of the Unconscious* than to the *Upanishads*:[6]

> But in order to be freed from the earthly element, the descendants of Brahma sought renunciation and suffering . . . And so you have pain as the deliverer . . . But this yearning for pain comes in conflict with the longing for joy and love . . . now you understand what love is: the highest joy in the greatest suffering, the most beautiful in the most bitter!

6. Eduard Hartmann (1842-1906) was a German philosopher whose key work concerns the relations between the will, the intellect, and the unconscious. The *Upanishads* is a collection of treatises on the nature of man and the universe; they form part of the Vedic writings and constitute the oldest speculative writing of the Hindus (10th century B.C.) [*Editor*].

Strindberg's position in A Dream Play is thus entirely consistent with his earlier views on the subject of pain and pleasure. Deliverance is a matter of freeing the spirit from its material involvements. This necessitates suffering. Pleasure binds us to the flesh; pain liberates us from it. It was through woman that the spirit was first entangled in matter, and it is through her that it is trapped in the flesh forever in the irresistible process of reproduction. But woman, who seduces the spirit through joy, also chastens it through suffering, and thus she teaches us the way of renunciation by which the spirit may be freed from the misery of being. Meanwhile the lot of mankind is pitiable, for man is continually torn between the craving for joy, which enslaves him, and the desire for suffering, which liberates him from the flesh. Such, according to the Daughter, is the answer to the riddle of life—as much of it, as least, as the Poet is privileged to hear.

There is nothing to indicate that Strindberg's acquaintance with the complexities of Eastern philosophy was other than superficial; but it was amply sufficient to support the poetic groundwork of A Dream Play. The Daughter's explanation of the riddle of the universe is based on the fundamental myth of atma-yajna, the act of self-sacrifice through which God brought the world into existence, and through which man eventually resumes his godhead. In the beginning, according to the myth, the Consciousness behind the universe, in the guise of Brahma, created the world by an act of self-forgetting, or self-dismemberment, through which the One became many. The diverse universe was the result. But this diversity of nature is only a seeming, maya. Accordingly, all attempts at definition and classification are merely an expression of the viewpoint of the beholder. In reality, there is only the flux of being; the forms exist only with relation to one another; and the play of contraries is simply the result of a poetic fiction, since order would be meaningless without disorder, and good would have no special character without evil.

The play of God does not go on eternally; only for countless kalpas of time: ultimately, the God comes to himself again, but only to forget himself once more in the endless game of improvisation. In the meantime, the individual consciousness, "that which knows" in each mind, is none other than God himself, the primal consciousness, and each individual life is a role in which the mind of God is absorbed in the course of the play in which is our reality. Thus, the one divine actor plays all the parts, and when the play of existence comes to an end, the individual consciousness awakens to its own divinity.[7]

7. These ideas were by no means new to Western thought in Strindberg's day. It was more than a half-century since Friedrich Schlegel first brought Brahmanism within reach of Western readers (Uber die Sprache und Weisheit der Indier, 1808). See: Rigveda, ed. Max Müller, 2nd ed., (London, 1890-92), X, 90 ff.; Brihadaranyaka Upanishad, tr. F. M. Müller, Sacred Books of the East, Vol. XV, I, 4-5; IV, 2-4; Chandogya Upanishad, VIII, 3.12. On the general subject see A. B. Keith, The Religion and Philosophy of the Veda and Upanishads (Cambridge, Mass., 1925).

The sacrificial act by which God gives birth to the world, and by which men in turn reintegrate themselves into God, involves the giving up of the individual life. This act is the same whether it be considered from the standpoint of creation or of cessation. For Strindberg this act had an erotic connotation. He symbolized it through the Growing Castle, where life begins and, in its flowering, ends. The Swedenborgian influence is seen in the manner in which the correspondence is indicated between the dream of man and the dream of God, the micro-macrocosmic relation. In Strindberg's play, the dreamer—with relation to his dream—is Brahma; and his single consciousness becomes multiple as he bodies forth through his fancy the dream-characters who live their independent lives while his mind is absorbed in them, and yet have no being aside from his.

The dreamer's personal experience, moreover, has universal character. In his dream, all begins and ends, and begins again through the Growing Castle which endlessly initiates the cycle of birth-and-death, *samsara*.[8] In the Mahayana scriptures, the castle is sometimes used as a symbol for the personality, the ego, in which the individual fortifies himself against the external world, isolating himself in the belief that there is a sacred difference between one individual and another, while the truth is that there are no individuals; and the external world is merely the externalization of mind, which casts its shadow, as the French symbolists would say, in order to see itself.

The characters of *A Dream Play* thus stand in a complex relationship to one another. They are at the same time different and the same, many and one. In *To Damascus*, which makes use of a similar relationship for symbolic purposes, these identities are rationalized in metaphysical terms, though even there we are aware of the psychological undercurrent as one by one the personalities of the Unknown are integrated into his single person until at the end only the Tempter remains unresolved. In *A Dream Play*, the identification is wholly psychological—all the characters, and all their experiences, and manifestations of the personality of the dreamer, from whose sole consciousness they derive their being, and whose fantasy is their life.

Aside from the Daughter of Indra, *A Dream Play* has four principal characters: the Officer, the Lawyer, the Quarantine Master, and the Poet. Whatever else they may be or represent, these characters, evidently, are four aspects of the author, the dreamer, and in their composite life is indicated his manifold nature. Moreover, since Strindberg cherished the idea that men lead several lives simultaneously, the four characters are thought of sometimes as four independent personages, sometimes as a single individual, depending on the circumstances. It is much the same in *To Damascus*. Here, the

---

8. The word *brahman* has the root *brih*, to grow.

Officer represents the romantic hero, the Lawyer is the bickering husband, the Quarantine Master, the merciless critic, while the Poet is the lover of beauty in his creative aspect, and is consequently more closely identified with the author, as dreamer, than the others, since *A Dream Play*, in a strict sense, is the Poet's dream.

To the Daughter of Indra, however, the dream gives a degree of autonomy that the other characters have not. She is the subject of all the dreamer's experience, the mirror which reflects his consciousness, and she is also, like the Lady in *To Damascus*, the woman he has endlessly wooed and lost. In that play, the Unknown has relations with the Lady in her various guises, chiefly, but not exclusively, as himself; but in *A Dream Play* the dreamer wins and loses her as Officer, Lawyer, and Poet in turn: he experiences her from every angle. Ultimately, of course, she too is an aspect of the dreamer; but, it is implied, an aspect of his truest and inmost self, which is conversant with God.

It is consistent with this idea that the Daughter is the only personage who developes organically in the course of the action; and this action is, on the whole, her biography. In the beginning she is relatively innocent, eager to experience life, energetic, and full of curiosity. At the end, she is weary and heavy with suffering, but yet as knowing and as fierce as Beatrice in the *Purgatorio*, whom she recalls:

DAUGHTER: . . . Look into my eyes.
POET: I cannot endure your gaze.
DAUGHTER: How then will you endure my words, if I speak in my own language?

In keeping with its dream-like character, the action of *A Dream Play* involves a wealth of detail, not all of which comes into focus, and not all of which admits of a ready interpretation. The Daughter of Indra is first seen outside the Growing Castle in which the Officer is found imprisoned. She appears in the company of the Glazer (*Glasmäster*), whom she calls father. There is no certain way to identify the Glazer, whose diamond is capable of opening all doors, including the doors of the castle. Possibly this character was suggested by Baudelaire's prose-poem *Le Mauvais Vitier*; possibly, Strindberg had in mind the great Leverrier, director of the Paris Observatoire; there are certainly other, and perhaps better, possibilities.[9]

With the Growing Castle, we are on safer ground. The figure appears to have been suggested by the vaulted roof of the cavalry barracks, with its crown-shaped cupola, which Strindberg could see above the treetops from the window of his study at Karlavägen

9. *Le verrier* would mean, of course, the glass-maker, not the glazier. Cf. Baudelaire, *Oeuvres*, p. 290, for *Le Mauvais Vitrier*. The Swedish glasscutter, a kind of Lorraine cross surmounted by the diamond cutting-point, resembles a skeleton key. The symbol is by no means abstruse.

40 in Stockholm.[1] In A *Dream Play* the castle grows quite appropriately out of the heaps of manure and straw that accumulate around stables, and, since it is a growing thing, it is topped by a blossom. The symbol of the flower, rooted in the soil and aspiring to the heavens, was a favorite figure with Strindberg: in *The Ghost Sonata,* there is the shallot which grows out of the lap of Buddha. The phallic character of this symbol need hardly be pointed out; doubtless Strindberg intended to suggest through it the reproductive process by which through pain the material world little by little becomes spirit.

In the interior of the castle, the restive Officer somewhat hesitantly permits the Daughter to draw him into the outer world, in order that he may see how, in spite of the pitiable condition of mankind, love conquers all. The allusion is clear in this scene to the role of Harriet Bosse in drawing Strindberg from his self-imposed seclusion, and the feelings of guilt and impotent fury which his seclusion involved.[2] Having liberated the Officer, the Daughter passes, without any transition, from the castle to the stage-door corridor of the opera. There is a giant monkshood growing behind the gate; for Strindberg, the monkshood, with its charming blue flower and its deadly root, was a symbol of worldly desire. The Officer appears, top-hatted and frock-coated, bearing a bouquet of roses: he has come to wait for his beloved Victoria. He has been waiting for her to come out, we learn, for seven years, and while he waits, he is overcome with a longing to see what lies beyond the mysterious clover-leaf door which opens off the theatre alley. The tempo of the action is suddenly accelerated. Day follows night, flash upon flash. The Officer comes and goes. His hair grows white. His clothes become shabby. His roses wilt. Victoria never comes out. The Officer preserves his good humor; he does not despair, but at last he insists on having the mysterious door opened, behind which, he is told, is the answer to the riddle of life. He sends for a locksmith. Instead, the Glazer comes with his diamond. He is about to open the door with this instrument when a policeman commands him to stop in the name of the law. The Officer resolves that the law which forbids us to know the riddle of life must be changed, and he dashes off, in the company of the Daughter of Indra, to find a lawyer.

The opera corridor now literally dissolves into the law office. The clover-leaf door, which remains on the stage as a visible reminder of the unsolved enigma of existence, thus becomes the door to the Lawyer's document file. For a time, the Officer gives place to the Lawyer as the focus of attention, and the Daughter becomes the principal witness of the Lawyer's pain. Like the Lady of *To Damascus II,* the Lawyer has grown hideous because of the evil absorbed

1. Paulson, *Letters to Harriet Bosse,* p. 41; Lamm, *August Strindberg,* p. 292.

2. Letter of 4 September 1901, Paulson, *op. cit.,* p. 61.

from his clients. The law office suddenly turns into a church; the clover-leaf door becomes the entrance to the vestry; and the Lawyer, who is passed over in the conferring of degrees which takes place in the church, is crowned not with laurel but with thorns. The Daughter sits at the organ, from which she elicits screams of human pain; then the organ turns into the resonant wall of Fingal's grotto, which is called the ear of the world. In this symbolic setting, the Daughter joins her destiny to that of the Lawyer, so that she may experience with him the supreme joy of life, which is love and marriage. The scene at once dissolves into the squalid apartment which they share, and in which the Daughter has so far savored the joys of marriage that when the Officer comes to her rescue, she gladly goes away with him.

The Officer means to take the Daughter to the beautiful seaside resort of Fairhaven. Instead, they land at Shamestrand. There they meet the Quarantine Master. In this worthy, whom the Officer greets as "old chatterbox" (Ordström: literally, word-stream), we are invited to recognize Strindberg in person. He is in blackface, because, as he says, he finds it best to show himself to the world a shade blacker than he is; and he tells us that it is in order to forget himself that he has taken up masquerade and play-acting. Now the Poet appears, his eyes on the heavens, and a bucket of mud in his hand, and gradually the suggestion takes form that it is essentially he who is the dreamer whose dream we are witnessing. There ensues an interlude in which a pair of lovers, one of whom is the Officer's beloved Victoria, are mercilessly fumigated by the Quarantine Master, in spite of the Poet's protest.

The symbolism once again grows transparent. The fumigation scene is evidently intended to represent comically the inner conflict of the dreamer in his trinary capacity as hero, critic, and poet. As the hero of the play, he recognizes his lost love, and he feels jealousy; as poet, he feels compassion; but in his capacity as national watchman, it is his duty to apply the severest measures to prevent the spread of the disease of love. While the lovers go sadly into the quarantine shed to be purified of passion, the Officer prepares to take up the hated profession of schoolmaster in order to support his mistress. Accompanied by the Daughter, he enters Fairhaven, the earthly paradise, a rich resort where a ball is constantly in progress. As it turns out, nobody is happy in Fairhaven; and the Officer suffers deep and undeserved humiliation as a student in the very school where he meant to teach.

The dream now becomes fragmentary. The cry of human anguish swells higher, and the Daughter, utterly weary, and faced with the obligation of returning to the Lawyer's home, yearns mightily for the peace of the upper world. To be rid of the Lawyer, and his domestic entanglements, however, she must retrace her steps until she is once again her own true self. She begins the backward journey in the company of the Poet. They find themselves first in a Mediterranean resort where two coal heavers demonstrate how society makes a hell of paradise. Then they are once again in the marine grotto, and the play begins to unwind. The Poet presents the Daughter with a petition for the lord of the universe. From the grotto they witness a shipwreck at sea: Christ himself appears on the waters, but his appearance merely serves to inspire the mariners with terror. While these visions appear and dissolve, the ship's mast turns into a tree, the cave turns into the opera-house corridor, and now the Daughter summons the chancellor and the faculties of the university to witness the opening of the door which conceals the secret of the universe.

Time rolls back. The Officer appears, young and fresh, with his bouquet of roses for Victoria. Before the assembled faculties, constantly at odds with each other, the Glazer solemnly springs the lock with his diamond. The door swings open: there is nothing behind it. The university faculties grow angry. They threaten to stone the Daughter. But by now the Daughter has recovered herself sufficiently so that she offers to reveal the secret to the Poet if he will come with her into the wilderness. The Lawyer opposes this, asserting his claims and the needs of his child. It is in vain. The corridor scene turns back into the Growing Castle. The Daughter reveals to the Poet the secret of the origin of pain, the nature of love, and the source of power; but she stops short of the ultimate answer, and the riddle remains unsolved as she shakes the dust of the world from her feet and prepares to enter the fire which will make her one with the air. The flame springs up spontaneously. While the characters of the play appear one by one and cast into the flames the poor things they have prized on earth, the Daughter speaks her farewell to mankind.

DOTTERN: ... O, nu jag känner hela varat's smärta,
            så är det då att vara människa . . .
            Man saknar även det man ej värderat
            man ångrar även det man icke brutit . . .
            Man vill gå bort, och man vill stanna . . .
            Sa rivas hjärtats hälfter var åt sitt hall . . .
            . . . Farväl!
(DAUGHTER   ... Oh, now I know the whole pain of existence.
            This, then, it is to be a human being . . .
            To regret even what one never valued,
            and feel remorse for what one never did . . .
            To wish to go, and to wish to stay,
            Thus the heart is cleft this way and that . . .
            . . . Farewell!)

She enters the castle. Silhouetted against the wall of human faces, the castle burns, and as the flames rise high, the chrysanthemum bud that tops it burst into flower.

The symbolism of *A Dream Play* thus ranges from the simplest and most amenable sort of signification to the most baffling. The train of thought that underlies it is at once straightforward and labyrinthine; yet the general impression is one of spontaneous improvisation. This is unquestionably the effect Strindberg aimed at, and the degree of success he attained is the more remarkable when we consider that the play was not developed from a unified conception, but is the result of the assimilation of several quite independent ideas, the full significance of which was avowedly not realized by the poet until after the play was substantially finished. The Growing Castle and the Corridor Drama were not, in the beginning, related at all; the unifying figure of the Daughter of Indra came quite late into the frame, and the Mediterranean episode was interpolated unfortunately, without much reference to the organic nature of the whole. In consequence, the progression is not uniformly smooth, nor is the play consistently meaningful. The first two scenes are original beyond anything that has ever been done in modern drama; the kaleidoscopic sequence that separates the first grotto scene from the second makes the effect of a series of exempla; the Mediterranean scene is in an obviously discordant style of allegory; the end is magnificently Wagnerian. The whole work, with its recurrent figures, transpositions and inversions, its thematic development, and the management of its modes and rhythms, makes less the effect of a dream than of a musical composition, a symphony, perhaps, or a tone-poem. A work of this sort might not be expected to convey very much to the mind by way of meaning. Its power of suggestion, however, is enormous, and this is to a considerable degree the result of the intricate scheme of correspondences by means of which the action and its symbols are laced together.

The Growing Castle, for example, evidently symbolizes the aspiration of the earthbound spirit, rooted in matter, and striving eternally to rise above it. The Officer who is liberated from the castle exemplifies a similar aspiration in the living individual, drawn out of himself by a vision of divine beauty into the hurly-burly of life. These two ideas are certainly not precisely correspondent, but they are related, and the result is a composite metaphor which has great cogency. Like the Castle of Alma in *The Faerie Queene*, the Growing Castle is the soul's prison; but the Growing Castle symbolizes also, and in quite another way, the aspiration of the flesh through which the germinal substance seeks its fulfillment. This is a visual figure, and the superposition of this image, with its wealth of erotic implication, involves the suggestion that the physical desire for procreation through beauty is identical with the longing of the spirit to expand and to exalt itself beyond its bodily confines.

It is precisely the point of A *Dream Play* that this identity of aims involves a tragic paradox. In man the inclination of the flesh is toward woman, but the aspiration of the spirit is toward God. The two desires, and their consequences, are quite distinct. The one tends to bind us ever more firmly to the earth, the other to deliver us, and the confusion of the two desires is, inevitably, a source of pain. Yet in the nature of things, this confusion is inescapable, for it is to woman that we turn, first of all, for a glimpse of paradise. Man seeks his happiness in woman; it is exactly for this reason that happiness eludes him, for woman, the representative of the material principle, cannot deliver the spirit through love. She can only imprison it. Her beauty, therefore, though it is God's beauty, is a snare; and though the spirit is irresistibly drawn to it, it must transcend this beauty or suffer disappointment. The elucidation of this time-honored mystery, the root of *The Divine Comedy*, seems to have been Strindberg's chief concern as a dramatist in the post-Inferno period.

The opera-corridor episode, half comic, half tragic in mood, is closely related to the episode of the Growing Castle. It illustrates, sardonically—as, indeed does all the rest of the play—in what way love conquers all. Doubtless, also, this episode reflected Strindberg's mood during rehearsals of *Easter*, when he played stagedoor Johnny for Harriet Bosse, as, in his youth, he had for Siri von Essen. Harriet Bosse notes that, in fact, Strindberg's curiosity had once been aroused by a disused door with a clover-leaf airhole cut into it, which led off the theatre alley where he was accustomed to wait for her. Since it was out of such details that Strindberg created the symbolism of these scenes, their interpretation is no simple matter, and the ever-widening ripples of significance tease the mind beyond certainty into precisely the mood which the symbolists considered proper to the poetic experience.

In the Officer's unwearied attendance upon the elusive Victoria we may certainly see the unhappy plight of one who had spent a lifetime, as it seemed, waiting in theatre corridors for a lady who never came; beyond that, the figure unquestionably symbolizes Strindberg's inhumanly protracted wait for a victory in the theatre, a period during which he had ample time to ponder the riddle of the closed door; beyond that still, is suggested the predicament of man waiting eternally for the One who never comes. But while this web of meaning gives the play something of the rich texture we admire in the intricately loomed allegories of a former age, A *Dream Play* differs from these allegories even more markedly than does *To Damascus*. *The Romance of the Rose*, for example, is also ostensibly, an erotic dream; but as a dream it has no verisimilitude; it is actually a play of abstractions arranged in a perfectly logical sequence, and would lose none of its quality if the dream framework were dropped. The logic of *A Dream Play*, which is also not a dream, comes somewhat closer to the logic of revery. The action involves effects of the sort actually experienced in dreams; it has something of the local color of dreams; and the result is something which is much less precise and more mysterious than allegory.

The flowering of the Growing Castle illustrates this point clearly. The symbol is obviously crucial to the total conception. It may be variously interpreted. From the moral standpoint, it suggests the liberation of the spirit, its release from matter, and its resumption into Godhead, its reawakening. But this moral superstructure evidently rests upon a deeper basis. In his celebrated production of *A Dream Play*, Olaf Molander piously changed the flower into a cross. The association of a Christian symbol with the assumption of the Daughter of Indra may be regarded as a somewhat arbitrary display of creative showmanship, but we must remember that Strindberg himself saw no inconvenience in presenting Indra's Daughter with a view of Christ walking on the waves. Moreover, the Growing Castle is not, like the Castle of Alma, a rigid figure which can admit of but a single interpretation. If one wishes to crown it with Christian significance, it will serve.

Nevertheless, in poetry, the preferable interpretation is that which gives greatest efficacy to the figure, and the efficacy of the figure ordinarily depends more on what is suggested than on what is rationally conveyed. On the intellectual level, there is no particular objection to the substitution of the cross for the flower, save that Strindberg did not write it so. Moreover, the cross is immediately comprehensible, while the chrysanthemum bud by itself tells us nothing. But for that faculty of the mind which is able to understand without understanding, and is therefore chiefly amenable to suggestion, the bud-capped edifice which grows until the moment of conflagration, and then bursts into flower, is not only comprehensible, but unmistakable.

Into this symbol is gathered, at the end, all the force of the play. The dream of life is essentially erotic. The Officer, the Lawyer, the Quarantine Master, the Poet himself, are all aspects of the lover. The Daughter of Indra, like all Strindberg's women, offers herself freely. She offers herself, in fact, to each in turn—to all save the Quarantine Master, who is an enemy of love—and in the end she offers herself to the burning tower. It is precisely at the moment when she unites with it that the castle bursts into flower. The suggestion is tolerably clear—it is the moment of orgasm that mortality merges with immortality, and pain with peace. The moment of flowering is extraordinarily ambiguous. It is release and captivity, pain and ecstasy, death and resurrection. The quest for the secret of life which lies concealed behind the clover-leaf door which connects the theatre with the law office, and also with the church, the grotto, and the home, ultimately leads us to the *linga*, Siva's symbol,[3] in the supreme moment which brings about the union of form and matter, Atman and Maya, the creative spirit and its creation, together with all the tragic implications of this union—for the individual, birth, suffering, old age, and death; for society, greed, cruelty, injustice, hatred, and violence. The process is clear. But the riddle remains unanswered. The clover-leaf door conceals nothing.

Nevertheless, the significance of the conceit is unmistakable. In the final moment of conflagration, all the elements of this creation, the physical, the spiritual, the concrete and the abstract, are fused in the bud which all this time has been maturing, and which is now offered up to the lord of heaven. In this respect, at least, the figure is superbly precise. The golden bud which crowns the castle in the beginning grows little by little as the fantasy of life develops. When the pain of life is more than the soul can bear, it flowers. For Strindberg, at least, this was the way of creation. Therefore the petition which the Poet addresses to God in the scene in Fingal's grotto seems pathetically insufficient to the Daughter:

DOTTERN: Är det så du ämnar nalkas
                stoftets son, den allerhögste . . . ?
DIKTAREN: Hur skall stoftets son väl finna
                ord nog ljusa, rena, lätta,
                att från jorden kunna stiga . . .
                Gudabarn, vill du vår klagan
                sätta över i det språk
                de Odödlige bäst fatta?
DOTTERN: Jag vill!
(DAUGHTER: Is it so that you intend to approach,
                son of dust, the All-highest?
POET: How shall the son of dust ever find
                a word so bright, so pure, so light,
                that it may rise up from the ground . . . ?
                Child of God, our complaint will you
                set over into the speech
                that the immortals best comprehend?
DAUGHTER: I will!)

Indeed, at the proper time, the Daughter translates the Poet's complaint into the language of the gods by taking it with her through the fire—thus, through her example, the Poet learns how the thing is done. It is in fact through the artist's experience of evil, the artist's pain, his passion, that poetry is made; but the complaint which ul-

---

3. Siva or Shiva is the third person in the Hindu trinity and represents both a destructive and a renovative principle. In many localities he is worshipped in the form of the *linga*, a phallic image [*Editor*].

timately reaches the All-Highest is nothing like the poor jingle lost in the confused roar of Fingal's cave. To reach God one must pass through the fire. What the Daughter of God takes with her into the burning castle is the dream of life in all its wretchedness. But what comes out of the purifying flame is something precious and beautiful; not pain, but the flower of pain; not evil, but the flower of evil; the golden flower, the poem.

A *Dream Play*, "child of my greatest pain," was Strindberg's most ambitious attempt to formulate the passion of the artist in modern conceptual terms. Others had written of this, but it is safe to say that nothing of this magnitude had ever been conceived for the stage. A *Dream Play* is perhaps not wholly successful; but there is nothing in the modern theatre to surpass it.

ROBERT BRUSTEIN

[August Strindberg: *A Dream Play*]†

* * * Of all the works that Strindberg wrote during this period, A *Dream Play* is probably the most typical and the most powerful. To judge from the parallel dreams of Jean and Julie,[1] Strindberg always believed in the significance of the dream life; but here he has converted this conviction into a stunning dramatic technique. Though the "dream play," as a genre, is probably not Strindberg's invention —Calderón, and possibly even Shakespeare in *The Tempest*, anticipated his notion that "life is a dream," while Maeterlinck certainly stimulated his interest in the vague, spiritual forces "behind" life— the form is certainly his own, in which time and space dissolve at the author's bidding and plot is almost totally subordinate to theme. The Dreamer, whose "single consciousness holds sway" over the split, doubled, and multiplied characters is, of course, Strindberg himself, who is also present as the Officer, the Lawyer, and the Poet, and, possibly, as Indra's Daughter. As he describes the Dreamer in his preface, "For him there are no secrets, no incongruities, no scruples and no law. He neither condemns nor acquits, but only relates, and since on the whole, there is more pain than pleasure in the dream, a tone of melancholy, and of compassion for all living things, runs through the swaying narrative."

Because of the absence of "secret," A *Dream Play* is even more self-exploratory than *The Father*; but although a direct revelation of Strindberg's unconscious mind, it is almost entirely free from any

---

† From Robert Brustein, *The Theatre of Revolt*, Boston, 1964. Pp. 126-33. Copyright © 1962, 1963, 1964 by Robert Brustein. Reprinted by permission of the publishers, Atlantic-Little, Brown & Co.

1. Jean and Julie are the leading characters in Strindberg's *Miss Julie*. Julie dreams she is on top of a pillar and cannot get down; Jean that he is climbing with great difficulty a large tree.

personal grievance. For Strindberg, the drama is no longer an act of revenge, but rather a medium for expressing "compassion for all living things." In *A Dream Play* the world is a pestilent congregation of vapors; the miseries of mankind far exceed its pleasures; but, for these very reasons, humans must be pitied and forgiven. The prevailing mood of woe in the work stems from the author's sense of the contradictions of life, some of which are suggested by the Poet in the Fingal's Cave section. After chancing upon the sunken wrecks of ships called *Justice, Friendship, Golden Peace*, and *Hope*, this Poet offers a petition to God in the form of anguished questions:

> Why are we born like animals?
> We who stem from God and man,
> whose souls are longing to be clothed
> in other than this blood and filth.
> Must God's image cut its teeth?

Indra's Daughter quickly silences this rebellious questioning—"No more. The work may not condemn the master! Life's riddle still remains unsolved"—but it is the unraveling of this painful enigma of existence which is the purpose of the play. Consequently, the work is structured on similar contrasts, conflicts, and contradictions: Body versus Spirit, Fairhaven versus Foulstrand, Winter versus Summer, North versus South, Beauty versus Ugliness, Fortune versus Misfortune, Love versus Hate. Even the sounds of the play communicate Strindberg's sense of the dissonance of life: a Bach toccata in four-four time is played concurrently with a waltz; a bell buoy booms in chords of fourths and fifths. For, in this work, life itself is no more than a disordered and chaotic struggle between opposites, and the movement of the play is towards explaining the cause of these divisions.

Like *Faust*, the play begins with a prologue in Heaven, a celestial colloquy over the lot of mortals. The god Indra explains to his Daughter that the earth is both fair and heavy because "revolt followed by crime" destroyed its almost perfect beauty. Listening to the wail of human voices rising from below, he determines to send the Daughter through the foul vapors to determine if human lamentation is justified. Indra's Daughter, descending, becomes the central character of the play. Indicating how far Strindberg has come from his old misogyny, she is—like Eleanora in *Easter*—a "female Christ," expressing the author's sympathy for the fate of humanity and his readiness to redeem man by sharing in man's sufferings. She is also Strindberg's Eternal Feminine; each man finds in her sweet, forgiving nature the realization of his own particular ideal. To the Officer, the first of Strindberg's dream surrogates, the Daughter is Agnes, "a child of heaven," and in her encounter with this embittered character, the Daughter is already beginning to see some motive for human complaint. He is imprisoned in a Castle which grows, throughout the action, out of manure and stable muck. Likened to the flowers (they "don't like dirt, so they shoot up fast as they can into the light—to blossom and to die"), the Castle is an image of life itself: the human spirit, trying to escape from the excremental body, aspires upwards toward the Heaven, but is always rooted in filth.[2]

Against this paradox of life, the Officer strongly protests, striking his sword on the table in his "quarrel with God." For despite his urge to aspire, he, too, is mired in filth. Like the Captain in *The Father*, he is another Hercules, doomed to an unpleasant labor: he must "groom horses, clean stables, and have the muck removed." Imprisoned in eternal adolescence, he is being punished for a childhood sin, for he once permitted his brother to be blamed for the theft of a book which he himself had torn to pieces and hidden in a cupboard. When the Daughter offers to set him free from the Castle (i.e., from his neurotic fears and guilts), he is, however, equally dubious: "Either way I'll suffer!" And when time and space dissolve back to the Officer's childhood, we see why adulthood is just as painful as adolescence. In this scene, the Officer's Father has given his Mother a silk shawl—still a symbol of maternal compassion for Strindberg. But she gives it away to a needy servant, and the Father feels insulted. In this life of shifting sands, what seems a generous act to one is an evil act to another; all of existence is suffering; and, as the Daughter observes now and throughout the play, "Humankind is to be pitied."

But the Daughter, still believing in worldly redemption, exclaims, "Love conquers all"; and the scene dissolves again for the first demonstration that she is wrong. The setting is a stage door, much like the place where Strindberg used to wait for Harriet to finish at the theatre, and the motif of the scene is—waiting. Waiting for Victoria, his heart's desire, with a bunch of flowers is the Officer, now freed from the Castle. But Victoria never comes. Time passes, with an accelerated whirring of lights; the Officer grows older and shabbier; the roses wither. The Daughter sits with the Doorkeeper, having taken from her the shawl (once the Mother's), now grown gray from its absorption of human misery. For nobody is contented except a Billsticker who, after fifty years of waiting, has attained *his* heart's desire: a net and a green fishbox. Yet, even he grows unhappy after a

---

2. In *The Ghost Sonata*, Strindberg uses the image of the Hyacinth in the same manner. The bulb is the earth; the stalk is the axis of the world; and the six-pointed flowers are the stars. Buddha is waiting for the Earth to become Heaven: i.e., for the Hyacinth to blossom, aspiring above its mired roots. Both the Castle and the Hyacinth, of course, are also phallic images—the sexual organ is pitched in the place of excrement.

time: the net was "not quite what I had in mind," the fishbox not quite as green as he had expected. Suffering the twin tragedies of getting and not getting what one wants, everybody in the world is afflicted with unhappiness. But behind a cloverleaf door (the Officer, poking at it, has an *intermittence du coeur*, recalling the guilty cupboard of his youth) lies the explanation of human misery and the secret of life. Yet, the Law forbids the opening of it.

The scene dissolves once again to the Lawyer's office, where the Daughter and the Officer hope to get the door opened. Everyone there has grown ugly from "unspeakable suffering." And the Lawyer's face, like the Mother's shawl, is marred by the absorption of human crime and evil. The second of Strindberg's dream surrogates, the Lawyer shares with the Daughter some of the qualities of Christ. Like Jesus, he has taken on himself all the sins of the world; and like Jesus, he is in conflict with the righteous, who condemn him for defending the poor and easing the burdens of the guilty. When he is denied his Law degree during an academic procession, the Daughter's shawl turns white, and she fits him with a crown of thorns. But since he too is a rebel, quarreling with God, she must explain to him the reasons for injustice: Life is a phantasm, an illusion, an upside-down copy of the original.[3] And the four Faculties (Theology, Philosophy, Medicine, and Law) are merely voices in the madhouse, each claiming wisdom for itself while scourging the sane and the virtuous.

Determined to put her theory of redemption through love to the test, the Daughter marries the Lawyer. But it is in this familiar Strindberg domestic scene that the irreconcilable conflicts of life are most agonizingly dramatized. While Kristin, the Maid, pastes all the air out of the apartment, the couple engage in sharp quarrels over their conflicting tastes in food, furnishings, and religious beliefs. Neither is right or wrong. It is simply a condition of life that one's sympathies are the other's antipathies, "one's pleasure is the other's pain."[4] The Daughter, stifling in the house, tied to her husband by their child, and revolted by the dirty surroundings, feels herself "dying in this air." And when the Officer—now at the top of the seesaw of fortune—enters seeking his Agnes, the Daughter and the Lawyer decide to part. The Lawyer dissolves their marriage, comparing it to a hairpin. Like a hairpin, a married couple remain one, no matter how they are bent—until they are broken in two.

3. This idea, like so many others, Strindberg probably found in Nietzsche, who writes in *Zarathustra:* "This world, the eternally imperfect, an eternal contradiction and imperfect image—an intoxicating joy to its imperfect creator. . . ."
4. This, like everything else in the play, is a perception which Strindberg achieved through personal suffering. As he writes in *Inferno:* "Earth, Earth is hell, the prison constructed by a superior intelligence in such a way that I cannot take a step without affecting the happiness of others, and others cannot be happy without giving me pain."

The Officer has decided to take the Daughter to Fairhaven, the land of youthful summer love, but through some miscalculation, they find themselves in Foulstrand, an ugly burnt-out hell, dominated by a Quarantine Station.[5] In this land, where life itself is a form of prolonged quarantine, young people are robbed of their color, hopes, and ideals, fortune turns to misfortune, youth becomes age. Strindberg's third dream surrogate enters, a visionary Poet who embodies the theme of opposition. Alternating between ecstasy and cynicism, he carries a pail of mud in which he bathes. The Quarantine Officer explains that "he lives so much in the higher spheres he gets homesick for the mud," leading the Officer to comment, "What a strange world of contradictions." Yet, even in Fairhaven, the heavenly paradise, contradictions mar the holiday atmosphere. The pleasure of the rich is attained only through the suffering of the poor; the fulfilled love of beautiful Alice leaves the passions of ugly Edith unrequited; the "most envied mortal in the place" is blind. Even in this place, in short, happiness is fleeting and ephemeral; and the only way to sustain pleasure is to die at the moment of achieving it, as a newlywed couple proceed to do, drowning themselves in the sea.

It is, to be sure, a grim vision that informs this work, combining the woeful sense of vanity in Ecclesiastes with the Sophoclean plaint that it is better never to have been born. Despite his conviction that life is universal suffering, however, Strindberg seems to have exonerated human beings from responsibility for it. It is not mankind but the system which is evil—not human character but the immutable conditions of existence. For, as we learn in the Schoolmaster scene, where the Officer, once again imprisoned in adolescence, is forced to learn his lessons over and over like a child, life takes the form of an eternal recurrence, a cycle of return which defeats all efforts at progress, change, or development.[6] "The worst thing of all," as the Lawyer tells the Daughter, is "repetitions, reiterations. Going back. Doing one's lessons again." Caught in his own repetition compulsion, locked in the pattern of his neurosis, Strindberg has found in his personal torment the universal agony of mankind, where one is forced to repeat mistakes, despite the consciousness of error. Thus, when the cloverleaf door is finally opened, the secret of life is discovered to be—nothing. The area behind the door is a vast emptiness.

5. The Quarantine Station is closely modeled on Swedenborg's Excremental Hell. Describing this Hell in *Inferno*, Strindberg recognizes it "as the country of Klam, the country of my zinc basin, drawn as if from life. The hollow valley, the pine knolls, the dark forests, the gorge with a creek, the village, the church, the poor house, the dunghills, the streams of muck, the pigsty, all are there."

6. Evert Sprinchorn, in his interesting article, "The Logic of *A Dream Play*," *Modern Drama*, December 1962, demonstrates how Strindberg invests the very structure of the play with this cyclical development—something he had already done with Part I of *The Road to Damascus*.

Condemned by the righteous for bringing man the truth,[7] the Daughter has had enough. She has suffered with all humanity—more extremely than others because of her sensitive nature—and now she knows that human complaint *is* justified. Shuffling off her earthly bonds, as her companions cast their sorrows into the purifying flames, the Daughter prepares to leave the world behind. But first she must provide the answer to the Poet's riddle, explaining the origin of the conflicts she has seen. Her interpretation, expressed in images of Buddhist and Hindu philosophy, is the perfect symbolization of Strindberg's dualism. In the dawn of time, she says, when Brahma, the "divine primal force," let himself be seduced by Maya, the "world Mother," the issue was the world—compounded ever since of elements both spiritual and fleshly, male and female, sacred and profane. Trying to escape from female matter, the descendants of Brahma sought "renunciation and suffering," but this, in turn, conflicted with their need for sexual love. Torn in two directions at once, pulled towards Heaven and dragged down to Earth, man became the victim of "conflict, discord, and uncertainty"—the "human heart is split in two"—and that is why the immortal soul is clothed in "blood and filth." Having given her answer, the Daughter blesses the Poet for his prophetic wisdom, and ascends to Indra, as the Castle blossoms into a giant chrysanthemum. It is the end of the dream, for the Dreamer has awakened; it is the orgiastic vision of the Poet, his mind dressed in its visionary Sunday clothes; but it is also the continual aspiration of the soul after the body has died.[8] In death only, Strindberg seems to be saying, is there redemption—for only in death are contradictions resolved, and the fleshly recoil finally stilled.

It was only through death, too, that Strindberg was able to resolve his own contradictions. When he succumbed to cancer in 1912, hugging a Bible to his breast and muttering, "Everything is atoned for," he had at last found his way to that peace which, half in love with death, he had been seeking all his waking life. The conflicts within him had almost torn him in two; but his art is witness to the fact that he had never surrendered to his own despair. Always ashamed of being human, Strindberg rejected the external world so completely that he often bordered on insanity. But except for his most disordered years, he was usually able to convert pathology into a penetrating, powerful, and profound drama. This transformation was perhaps his most impressive achievement, for his art was in a constant state of flux, always yielding to the pressures from his unconscious.

7. Another Nietzschean idea, that the righteous are those who crucified Christ: "And be on thy guard against the good and the just!" he affirms in *Zarathustra*. "They would fain crucify those who devise their own virtue—they hate the lonesome ones."

8. The image of the bursting Castle, as Professor Sprinchorn has suggested, is clearly sexual; and it is significant that Strindberg, like most Romantics, identifies sex with death.

When he learned to control his misogyny in later years, and soften his resistance to the female principle, he faced life with the quietism of a Buddhist saint, sacrificing his defiant masculinity to the need for waiting, patience, ordeals, and expiation. But though his mood had changed and his spirit was chastened, his quarrel with God was never far from the surface. His rebellious discontent, expressed through a drama of perpetual opposition, had simply found its way into a dissatisfaction with the essence of life itself. Strindberg left instructions before he died that his tomb be inscribed with the motto of *Crimes and Crimes:* Ave Crux Spes Unica.[9] But in view of his lifelong unrest and uncertainty, and his inability to commit himself to any particular creed, a more appropriate epitaph might have been the final lines from his last play, *The Great Highway:*

> Here Ishmael rests, the son of Hagar
> whose name was once called Israel,
> because he fought a fight with God,
> and did not cease to fight until laid low,
> defeated by His almighty goodness.
> O Eternal One! I'll not let go Thy hand,
> Thy hard hand, except Thou bless me.
> Bless me, Your creature, who suffers,
> Suffers Your sundering gift of life!
> Me first, who suffers most—
> Whose most painful torment was this—
> I could not be the one I longed to be!

9. "Hail, Cross, my sole salvation."

Eugene O'Neill
and
Desire Under the Elms

EUGENE O'NEILL

From the *New York Tribune*, February 13, 1921†

Diff'rent, as I see it, is merely a tale of the eternal, romantic idealist who is in all of us—the eternally defeated one. In our innermost hearts we all wish ourselves and others to be "Diff'rent." We are all more or less "Emmas"—the more or less depending on our talent for compromise. Either we try in desperation to clutch our dream at the last by deluding ourselves with some tawdry substitute; or, having waited the best part of our lives, we find the substitute time mocks us with too shabby to accept. In either case we are tragic figures, and also fit subjects for the highest comedy, were one sufficiently detached to write it.

I have been accused of unmitigated gloom. Is this a pessimistic view of life? I do not think so. There is a skin deep optimism and another higher optimism, not skin deep, which is usually confounded with pessimism. To me, the tragic alone has that significant beauty which is truth. It is the meaning of life—and the hope. The noblest is eternally the most tragic. The people who succeed and do not push on to a greater failure are the spiritual middle classers. Their stopping at success is the proof of their compromising insignificance. How pretty their dreams must have been! The man who pursues the mere attainable should be sentenced to get it—and keep it. Let him rest on his laurels and enthrone him in a Morris chair, in which laurels and hero may wither away together. Only through the unattainable does man achieve a hope worth living and dying for—and so attain himself. He with the spiritual guerdon of a hope in hopelessness, is nearest to the stars and the rainbow's foot.

† Reprinted by permission of the *New York Herald Tribune*.

This may seem to be soaring grandiloquently—and somewhat platitudinously—far above "a poor thing but mine own" like *Diff'rent*; but one must state one's religion first in order not to be misunderstood, even if one makes no rash boast of always having the strength to live up to it.

Diff'rent whatever its faults may be, has the virtue of sincerity. It is the truth, the inevitable truth, of the lives of the people in it as I see and know them. Whether it is psychoanalytically exact or not I will leave more dogmatic students of Freud and Jung than myself (or than Freud and Jung) to decide. It is life, nevertheless. I stick out for that—life that swallows all formulas. Some critics have said that Emma would not do this thing, would undoubtedly do that other. By Emma they must mean "a woman." But Emma is Emma. She is a whaling captain's daughter in a small New England seacoast town—surely no feminist. She is universal only in the sense that she reacts definitely to a definite sex-suppression, as every woman might. The form her reaction takes is absolutely governed by her environment and her own character. Let the captious be sure they know their Emmas as well as I do before they tell me how she would act.

There are objections to my end; but given Caleb and Emma the end to me is clearly inevitable. The youthful Emma refuses to accept the compromise of a human being for her dream Caleb. As the years go by she lives alone with her dream lover, the real Caleb fading into a friend. But suddenly she realizes youth is gone and the possibility of her dream lover forevermore. She snatches after him in a panic—and gets a Benny. She must re-create her god in this lump of mud. When it finally is brought home to her that mud is mud, she cries after the real Caleb, seeing him now for the first time. But he is gone. There is nothing for her to do but follow him. As for Caleb, he dies because it is not in him to compromise. He belongs to the old iron school of Nantucket-New Bedford whalemen whose slogan was "A dead whale or a stove boat." The whale in this case is transformed suddenly into a malignant Moby Dick who has sounded to depths forever out of reach. Caleb's boat is stove, his quest is ended. He goes with his ship.

There are objections to the play as pathological, but I protest that is putting the accent where none was intended, where only contributing circumstance was meant. And someone has said to me that all the people in the play were either degenerates or roughs —at which I was properly stunned, because I consider all of the characters, with the exception of Benny, to be perfectly regular human beings even as you and I. Dividing folks into moral castes has never been one of my favorite moral occupations.

And then there was someone, I have heard, who attributed to the author Caleb's remark that "folks be all crazy and rotten to the core." Upon which I grab the shoelace (but did they have them, though?) of the author of Hamlet, and going aloft to the dizzy height of his instep, inquire pipingly whether it was he or Macbeth who said, "It is a tale told by an idiot, full of sound and fury, signifying nothing."

Damn the optimists anyway! They make life so darned hopeless!

Letters to George Jean Nathan†

[*On* Welded]

Brook Farm / *Ridgefield, Connecticut* / *May 7, 1923*

Dear Nathan:

Nevertheless, I am convinced "Welded" is the best yet. I'm glad to get Mencken's[1] letter but I must confess the greater part of his comment seems irrelevant as criticism of my play. To point out its weakness as realism (in the usual sense of that word) is to confuse what is obviously part of my deliberate intention.

Damn that word, "realism"! When I first spoke to you of the play as a "last word in realism," I meant something "really real," in the sense of being spiritually true, not meticulously life-like—an interpretation of actuality by a distillation, an elimination of most realistic trappings, an intensification of human lives into clear symbols of truth.

Here's an example: Mencken says: "The man haranguing the street-walker is surely not a man who ever actually lived." Well, he surely is to me and, what is more to my point, he is also much more than that. He is Man dimly aware of recurring experience, groping for the truth behind the realistic appearances of himself, and of love and life. For the moment his agony gives him vision of the truth behind the real.

I can't agree that the speeches in this scene are "banal" or the ideas "rubber stamp." In fact, I'm positive it's the deepest and truest, as well as the best written scene I've ever done. Perhaps it isn't "plausible"—but the play is about love as a life-force, not as an intellectual conception, and the plausibilities of realism don't apply. Reason has no business in the theatre anyway, any more than it has in a church. They are both either below—or above it.

But I won't rave on. I'll grant this much for your criticisms—that parts of the dialogue are still, I find, "speechy" and artificial but that will all be gone over and fixed. It's the slopping-over of too much eagerness to say it all.

Thank Mencken for me for reading it. I'm sorry it didn't "knock

† The first two letters to Nathan are in the collection at the Cornell University Library, and are reprinted by permission of the Cornell University Library and Mrs. Carlotta Monterey O'Neill. The third letter was published in George Jean Nathan, *Intimate Notebooks* (New York: Alfred A. Knopf, Inc., 1932) and is reprinted by permission of Mrs. Carlotta Monterey O'Neill. Nathan was for many years the dean of New York drama critics (1882-1958).

1. An American journalist, editor, essayist, and critic.

him dead" to repay him for his trouble.

Well, just wait until you see it played! (if it's done right). I'm hoping that may make you recant.

My best to you both.

Sincerely,

Eugene O'Neill

[On Desire Under the Elms]

"Camprea" / South Shore, Paget W. / Bermuda / March 26, 1925
Dear Nathan:

* * * What I think everyone missed in "Desire" is the quality in it I set most store by—the attempt to give an epic tinge to New England's inhibited life-lust, to make its inexpressiveness poetically expressive, to release it. It's just that—the poetical (in the broadest and deepest sense) vision illuminating even the most sordid and mean blind alleys of life—which I'm convinced is, and is to be, *my* concern and justification as a dramatist. * * *

Sincerely,

Eugene O'Neill

[On the Playwright Today]

The playwright today must dig at the roots of the sickness of today as he feels it—the death of the Old God and the failure of science and materialism to give any satisfying new One for the surviving primitive religious instinct to find a meaning for life in, and to comfort its fears of death with. It seems to me that anyone trying to do big work nowadays must have this big subject behind all the little subjects of his plays or novels, or he is simply scribbling around on the surface of things and has no more real status than a parlor entertainer.

[A Conversational Remark]†

Most modern plays are concerned with the relation between man and man, but that does not interest me at all. I am interested only in the relation between man and God.

A Letter to Arthur Hobson Quinn‡

It's not in me to pose much as a "misunderstood one," but it does seem discouragingly (that is, if one lacked a sense of ironic humor!) evident to me that most of my critics don't want to see

---

† From the Introduction by Joseph Wood Krutch to *Nine Plays by Eugene O'Neill*, New York, 1924. Copyright 1924 and renewed 1952 by Eugene O'Neill. Reprinted by permission of Random House, Inc.
‡ From a letter to Arthur Hobson Quinn published in Quinn's *History of the American Drama*, Volume II (New York: F. S. Crofts & Company, 1945). Reprinted by permission of Mrs. Carlotta Monterey O'Neill. Quinn is a professor of English and historian of the American drama (b. 1875).

what I'm trying to do or how I'm trying to do it, although I flatter myself that end and means are characteristic, individual and positive enough not to be mistaken for anyone's else, or for those of any "modern" or "pre-modern" school. To be called a "sordid realist" one day, a "grim, pessimistic Naturalist" the next, a "lying Moral Romanticist" the next, etc. is quite perplexing—not to add the *Times* editorial that settled *Desire* once and for all by calling it a "Neo-Primitive," a Matisse of the drama, as it were! So I'm really longing to explain and try and convince some sympathetic ear that I've tried to make myself a melting pot for all these methods, seeing some virtues for my ends in each of them, and thereby, if there is enough real fire in me, boil down to my own technique. But where I feel myself most neglected is just where I set most store by myself —as a bit of a poet, who has labored with the spoken word to evolve original rhythms of beauty, where beauty apparently isn't— *Jones, Ape, God's Chillun, Desire,* etc.—and to see the transfiguring nobility of tragedy, in as near the Greek sense as one can grasp it, in seemingly the most ignoble, debased lives. And just here is where I am a most confirmed mystic, too, for I'm always, always trying to interpret Life in terms of lives, never just lives in terms of character. I'm always acutely conscious of the Force behind—Fate, God, our biological past creating our present, whatever one calls it—Mystery certainly—and of the one eternal tragedy of Man in his glorious, self-destructive struggle to make the Force express him instead of being, as an animal is, an infinitesimal incident in its expression. And my profound conviction is that this is the only subject worth writing about and that it is possible—or can be—to develop a tragic expression in terms of transfigured modern values and symbols in the theatre which may to some degree bring home to members of a modern audience their ennobling identity with the tragic figures on the stage. Of course, this is very much of a dream, but where the theatre is concerned, one must have a dream, and the Greek dream in tragedy is the noblest ever!

From an Interview with Oliver M. Sayler†

The theatre to me *is* life—the substance and interpretation of life. . . . [And] life is struggle, often, if not usually, unsuccessful struggle; for most of us have something within us which prevents us from accomplishing what we dream and desire. And then, as we progress, we are always seeing further than we can reach. I suppose that is one reason why I have come to feel so indifferent toward po-litical and social movements of all kinds. Time was when I was an active socialist, and, after that, a philosophical anarchist. But today I can't feel that anything like that really matters. It is rather amusing

† Published in *Century Magazine*, Jan-uary, 1922; later incorporated into Say- ler's book, *Our American Theatre*, New York, 1923.

to me to see how seriously some people take politics and social questions and how much they expect of them. Life as a whole is changed very little, if at all, as a result of their course. It seems to me that, as far as we can judge, man is much the same creature, with the same primal emotions and ambitions and motives, the same powers and the same weaknesses, as in the time when the Aryan race started toward Europe from the slopes of the Himalayas. He has become better acquainted with those powers and those weaknesses, and he is learning ever so slowly how to control them. The birth-cry of the higher men is almost audible, but they will not come by tinkering with externals or by legislative or social fiat. They will come at the command of the imagination and the will.

JOSEPH WOOD KRUTCH

Desire Under the Elms †

* * * O'Neill had, in *Desire Under the Elms* (1924), already discovered how the problem of writing tragedy significant for him could be approached in a different way: objectively not subjectively, and through the interpretation to be put upon a series of realistically imagined events rather than in terms of symbols invented directly for the purpose. The life of early New England had always appealed to him even as mere history or romance and to it he turned for a fable in which the conflict of violent passions leads to violent deeds.

Outwardly the play is a realistic, if heightened, study of the manners, morals, and psychological processes of a definite society—that of puritan New England in the middle of the last century. But it is impossible not to realize that the author is interested in New England as such no more, at least, than he is interested in an aspect of the eternal tragedy of man and his passions. He chose this particular time and particular place, partly because he knew something about them; partly because the stern repressions of puritan customs make the kind of explosion with which he proposed to deal particularly picturesque and particularly violent; but chiefly because it is necessary to give every dramatic story *some* local habitation and name. Questions concerning the historical accuracy of any detail are not strictly relevant. Realistic in manner though the presentation is, this puritan society is treated as already half fabulous, and the events, though feigned to occur in New England, also happen out of place and out of time.

The chief characters are Ephraim Cabot, a hard and self-righteous patriarch; Eben, a son by his second wife; and Abbie Putnam, a proud and ambitious young woman who has married Ephraim in

† From Joseph Wood Krutch, *The American Drama Since 1918*, New York, 1957. Pp. 94-100. Copyright 1957 by Joseph Wood Krutch. Reprinted by permission of the publisher, George Braziller, Inc.

his old age. There is a three-cornered struggle for power. The patriarch will yield nothing; Abbie schemes to secure for herself and her children the farm on which they all live; Eben is determined to escape the domination of the patriarch and also to retain the rights of an eldest son now threatened by Abbie. She realizes that an heir of her own would be the surest road to her purpose and undertakes to seduce Eben by whom she hopes to bear a son to be foisted upon the patriarch as his own. Eben resents her as the usurper of his own mother's place but he succumbs, not so much merely to lust, as to the feeling that he will revenge his mother and establish his own spiritual independence if he steals Ephraim's wife. Presently the son is born. Ephraim is now beside himself with triumph, quarrels with Eben whom he tells that Abbie has always despised him, and gloats over the fact her son will inherit the farm. Feeling now that Abbie has merely used him, Eben rejects her protestations that it is now he whom she loves, and Abbie, taking the only way to prove that she no longer cares chiefly for her claim on the farm, kills the child. Eben, horrified and furious, goes off to call the sheriff but when the sheriff comes he declares himself a partner in the crime and wins the grudging admiration even of Ephraim.

Eben, thinks his father, is at least hard—not soft like the other sons who have left the farm to seek gold in California. "God's hard, not easy! Mebbe they's easy gold in the West but it hain't God's gold. It hain't for me. I kin hear his voice warnin' me agen t'be hard and stay on my farm. I kin see his hand usin' Eben t' steal t' keep me from weakness. I kin feel I be in the palm o' His hand, His fingers guidin' me. (A *pause—then he mutters sadly*) It's a-goin' t'be lonesomer now than ever it was afore—an' I'm gittin' old, Lord—ripe on the bow—(*Then stiffening*) Waal—what d'ye want? God's lonesome, haint He? God's hard an' lonesome." As the sheriff is about to lead the two murderers away Abbie turns to say, "I love ye, Eben" and he replies, "I love ye, Abbie." Then the sheriff looks enviously about and remarks to a companion "It's a jim-dandy farm, no denyin'. Wished I owned it." And the curtain goes down.

The success of *Desire Under the Elms* was in part a success of scandal. Many saw it either to giggle at the scene in which Eben is seduced or to raise righteous hands in indignation that such obscenity should be permitted. Still others, fashionably intellectual, took it as an attack upon puritanism, a bold muckraking exposé of what really went on in the prim houses of our revered forebears. But what the prudish and the advanced, as well as the merely ribald, failed to perceive is the fact that the themes of *Desire Under the Elms* are the themes of the oldest and the most eternally interesting tragic legends here freshly embodied in a tale native to the American soil. The intense, almost religious possessiveness felt by Ephraim

and Eben and Abbie for the soil of New England is set off sharply
from the mere impersonal greed of the sheriff. But this is not all or
even the most important thing. The struggle of the son against the
father, the son's resentment of the intruding woman, canonical incest itself, are part of the story whose interest is deeper than any
local creed or any temporary society, whether of our own time or
of another. It is one of the great achievements of the play that it
makes us feel them not merely as violent events but as mysteriously
fundamental in the human story and hence raises the actors in
them somehow above the level of mere characters in a single play,
giving them something which suggests the kind of undefined meaning which we feel in an Oedipus or a Hamlet.

O'Neill's fondness for violent situation has always offended some.
Others who had accepted it in *The Hairy Ape* or *All God's Chillun
Got Wings* because it seemed there to enforce a moral relevant to
contemporary society, found it merely gratuitous in a play like *Desire
Under the Elms* whose plot seemed invented for no purpose beyond
that of providing blood and horror. "What's Hecuba to him or he
to Hecuba?" they asked. The tragedy of mere lust and blood belongs, they argued, to a more primitive age, and incest is not one
of the crimes by which contemporary society finds itself seriously
threatened. But sensible as such criticisms may at first sight appear,
it is worth remembering that they might have been made with almost equal pertinence against Aeschylus or Sophocles. The adven-
tures of Oedipus or Jason do not suggest the home life of a Greek
in the Periclean age. Their legends were already remote, archaic,
and monstrous. The horror of the plays was for the Greeks as it is
for us, nightmarish rather than immediately pertinent, and the singular hold which they continue to have upon the imagination is
somehow connected with the fact. Nor is it necessary to agree upon
any explanation of that fact in order to agree upon recognizing it.
Perhaps archaic desires and fears lead even in us a more vivid sub-
terranean life than we know. Perhaps tragedy seems grandest when
the soul is purged of just such terrors for the very reason that, being
so buried and so cut off from conscious life, they can be reached
in no other way and find in stories concerned with the ancient themes
the only channels through which they may be discharged. That
O'Neill should be led back to them as the result, not of academic
imitations of older literature, but of the independent exercise of his
imagination, is one more indication of the power of that imagination.
There is, to say the very least, no *a priori* objection to such themes.
He has a right to be judged according to his success in making something of them, and not prejudged merely because he has discovered
for himself situations akin to those which have occupied some of
the greatest tragic writers.

Not until he came some years later to *Mourning Becomes Electra*, probably the finest of his plays, did O'Neill find another story so well suited to development in a spirit fundamentally related to that of classical tragedy. It is not only that the personages of *Desire Under the Elms* are involved in a story which suggests their kinship with the enduring legends of the race. They are also personages who, in the sense so important to their creator, "belong" to something. They "belong" both to their soil and to the traditions of their culture; to both of these they feel an obligation which, when it comes into conflict with individual desires, is the source of conflicts which shake them to the bottom of their souls. And old Ephraim at least belongs also to God. That God may be, as he says, hard and lonesome. Rationally there may be something absurd in his thoroughgoing identification of himself and his will with the personality and the will of God. But that identification gives him stature. It gives him strength of passion in his struggle with the son whom he feels it necessary to subdue and with the young wife in whose arms he hopes to defy time. It also gives dignity and elevation and a kind of grandeur to the end where he is spiritually triumphant in defeat.

RICHARD DANA SKINNER

Desire Under the Elms: Dragons of Youth†

In much of Greek tragedy, as well as in northern mythology, such as the Niebelungen cycle, the theme of incest is predominant. In its poetic expression, this theme quite evidently has implications far broader than its literal meaning. In spite of such tawdry phrases as "Oedipus complex," drawn from a nebulous jargon of certain early schools of psychiatry, and implying an acutely personal problem of neurotic individuals, the incest problem as we find it in the great tragedies and the enduring myths seems to symbolize very clearly a critical stage in the break between childhood and manhood. It is a moment of fateful hesitancy just beyond adolescence when the soft irresponsibility of childhood and its egotistical little empire become an enthralling dream from which it is exceedingly hard to awake to harsh realities.

In this larger sense, the apparently innocuous legend of Peter Pan, the boy who did not want to grow up, takes its place among the legends of fateful regression. If, instead of desiring passionately to remain a child, Peter had been hounded by an inner will to grow up, we might have had a very different kind of story—a story of struggle against "monsters" that seemed to block his advance at

† From Richard Dana Skinner, *Eugene O'Neill, A Poet's Quest*, New York, 1935. Pp. 143-56. Copyright 1935. Reprinted by permission of the publisher, Longmans, Green.

every turn, against the temptation to return to the softly protecting mother principle that had previously stood between him and the clash of the outside world. In short, we should have had an "incest" story in its true psychological and poetic sense as distinct from its distorted personal sense. In mythology, the incest theme is generally used as the prelude to the development of a "hero," that is, of a man who has at last become strong enough to stand on his own feet and fight the obstacles of a real world. Later on, Christianity was to find in sacrifice and suffering and self-discipline the true prelude to the rebirth of the soul, free from the contamination of the incest symbol. The Christian saints were to find in the Cross and in the idea of death to the old self the all-sufficient road to a spiritual resurrection, and the Christian poets, for the most part, were to use the same high symbols of purgation. But Greek tragedy was for centuries, and still is to a large extent, the model for the "hero" theme in the theatre, and this fact is of the utmost importance if we are to appraise correctly several of Eugene O'Neill's most important plays in that second period following the writing of "All God's Chillun."

We must remember that in "All God's Chillun," the poet accepted himself at last as intellectually a man, but still enslaved to the emotional and creative instincts of a child. Clearly, then, the next great struggle of the soul—unlike the sentimental contentment in childhood of Peter Pan—would be to seek maturity and reality, and to battle it out with all the inner obstacles seeking to prolong the alluring state of childhood. In spite of Jim Harris' brave words, "I'll play right up to the gates of Heaven with you," the stern fact remained that the soul could not find its heaven, its true inner harmony, in "play." More was needed. The emotions as well as the intellect and the understanding must throw off completely the desire to turn back to protecting motherly arms and a world of make-believe. O'Neill chose to express the idea of this struggle in the terms and symbols of Greek incest tragedy, and the first play of this new struggle was called "Desire Under the Elms."

Nothing could explain more clearly the exact implications of this play than O'Neill's description of the elm trees brooding over the Cabot farmhouse in New England in which the entire action takes place. These two enormous elms "bend their trailing branches down over the roof. They appear to protect and at the same time subdue. There is a sinister maternity in their aspect, a crushing jealous absorption. They have developed from their intimate contact with the life of man in the house an appalling humanness. They brood oppressively over the house. They are like exhausted women resting their sagging breasts and hands and hair on its roof, and when it rains their tears trickle down monotonously and rot on the shingles."

If O'Neill had intended to write a sordid story of crime on an isolated New England farm, such a description as the above would have been totally unnecessary and irrelevant. But he was not writing an ordinary story of sordid crime. He was writing a play of extraordinary emotional intensity in which, consciously or unconsciously, he was using the incest formula of Greek tragedy to express that first terrific battle of the soul to escape from its own chains to childhood. In such a mood, every symbol associated with childhood becomes "sinister"—much as the encompassing sea appeared sinister to old Chris. For the time being, there is no distinction between tender and strength-giving motherhood, on the one hand, and on the other the "sinister maternity" from which the soul seeks escape. The very fact of the desire to escape completely distorts the perspective. The loving arms of a moment ago become in an instant the crushing absorbing arms of something sinister and appalling. The real change is entirely within the soul of the poet—a new attitude which becomes all the more intense because the desire to escape is thwarted by an almost equally intense desire to remain. The core of the tragedy in this first play of the second stage lies in this—that the desire of the soul to remain in its prison conquers, for the moment, the desire to escape. Unless the play is understood in this perspective, and in this profound relationship to the pagan symbols of similar soul struggles, it loses all meaning in the scheme of the poet's quest.

The main characters of "Desire Under the Elms" are old Ephraim Cabot, hard fisted and stony hearted owner of the old farm, who frequently confuses himself with an "old testament" God, Whom he believes to be both hard and lonesome; Simeon and Peter Cabot, Ephraim's sons by a first wife; Eben Cabot, his son by a second wife, now dead, from whom he inherited the farm; and Abbie Putnam, a proud and possessive younger woman whom Ephraim brings back to the farm as his third wife, to the consternation of his sons, who see their inheritance threatened. Although old Ephraim Cabot dominates the entire play, and is felt when not seen, it is Eben who is the dramatic hero, who becomes the symbol of youth seeking escape, only to find itself hopelessly entangled in old yearnings. The very first description of him gives the key to his character. "His face is well formed, good-looking, but its expression is resentful and defensive. His defiant, dark eyes remind one of a wild animal's in captivity. Each day is a cage in which he finds himself trapped but inwardly unsubdued. There is a fierce repressed vitality about him." In other words, he is O'Neill's equivalent of the young Siegfried in the dwarf's cave—or of Orestes driven on by the furies.

But O'Neill's equivalent of these mythological heroes is of a very different texture from the originals, wholly without the benefit of mythological proportions. Eben Cabot is the personification of youthful lust driven on by devotion to his dead mother's image and the suppressed rage he feels at her early death, which he believes was brought on by his father's cruelty. He believes the farm to be rightly his, because it was his mother's before him; his father, in his eyes, is an interloper and a robber, fit only to be hated and cheated at every turn. When Eben goes brutally to a notorious woman in the village, it is revenge as well as lust that drives him, because he has heard that his father once knew this woman too. He boasts of it to his brothers: "She may've been his'n—and yourn', too—but she's mine now! . . . The p'int is she was his'n—and now she b'longs t' me!" So deeply has Eben identified himself with his mother's wrongs that his every act is motivated in large part by the desire for revenge on his father. The older brothers resent old Ephraim, too, but for a simpler reason. He has driven them like slaves, made them hedge their lives around with the stone fences lifted from the rebellious soil, and given them nothing in exchange. In sudden rebellion, when they hear their father has married again, thus destroying their last chance of inheriting the farm, they leave for the California gold hills, making over their worthless shares in the farm to Eben in exchange for Ephraim's hidden hoard of gold which Eben discloses to them. In Eben's mind, the gold was the result of his mother's slavery and death—it belongs to his mother and to him!

With this setting of suppressed desires and distorted passions we are fully prepared for the consequences of Ephraim's third marriage to a young wife. At first, Eben resents her furiously as an intruder in his mother's place. Then he succumbs to his attraction toward her youth and coarse beauty and to the same frantic feeling he held toward the woman in the village—to make his own everything that his father has possessed. The play becomes a three-cornered battle, for imperious domination by the father, for the destruction of the father by the son, and for the possession of the farm and all else by Abbie. Abbie is described as "thirty-five, buxom, full of vitality. Her round face is pretty but marred by its rather gross sensuality. There is strength and obstinacy in her jaw, a hard determination in her eyes, and about her whole personality the same unsettled, untamed, desperate quality which is so apparent in Eben." Ephraim Cabot, in contrast, is described as "seventy-five, tall and gaunt, with great, wiry, concentrated power, but stoop-shouldered from toil. His face is as hard as if it were hewn out of a boulder, yet there is a weakness in it, a petty pride in his own narrow strength. His eyes are small, close together, and extremely near-sighted, blinking continually in the effort to focus on objects, their stare having a straining, ingrowing quality."

It is well worth noting at this point a strong characteristic of

O'Neill's method, particularly evident in his later plays, of dealing with evil. He does not romanticize it. He is blunt to the point of brutality in describing evil passions, whether those of lust or pride or possessiveness. But even though the motivations he gives his characters may explain their evil actions, they are not motivations that seek to excuse, palliate or romanticize the evil they bring. Abbie's face is "marred" by her gross sensuality. The criticism is always valid that the grosser forms of evil need not be depicted on the stage—that drama, after the Greek fashion, can deal with the consequences of evil rather than with the description of evil itself. But once an author makes the decision to depict evil at all in the body of his play, the whole question of the integrity of his work from that point on depends on a complete discarding of that oily, narcotic deception of pretending that good and evil are one and the same, to be distinguished only by custom or convention. With such a premise, the whole core of serious drama vanishes, and with it all sense of the spiritual integrity which is the hall mark of the true poet.

From her first appearance on the farm, Abbie takes deep and full possession of everything, including Eben, who becomes at once, in her eyes, a means to an end—further undisputed possession of all that Eben holds dear. To this end she tries to gain his sympathy by telling him of her own hard life, and to gain his affection by pointed reference to the youth they share. At first, Eben tries furiously to resist his growing feeling for her. "I'm fightin' him—I'm fightin' yew," he tells her defiantly, "fightin' fur Maw's rights t' her hum! An' I'm onto ye. Ye hain't foolin' me a mite. Ye're aimin' t' swaller up everythin' an' make it your'n. Waal, you'll find I'm a heap sight bigger hunk nor yew kin chew!"

In the meantime, old Ephraim begins to develop a curious tolerance of the "softness" he sees in Eben, and Abbie begins to be frightened. What if Ephraim, who feels he is getting old and "ripe on the bow," should decide to leave the farm to Eben instead of to her? But when she taunts him with the idea, Ephraim's own petty pride rises up. "If I could, in my dyin' hour," he says, "I'd set it afire an' watch it burn—this house an' every ear o' corn an' every tree down to the last blade o' hay! I'd sit an' know it was all a-dyin' with me an' no one else'd ever own what was mine, what I'd made out o' nothin' with my own sweat 'n' blood!" Then he adds: "'Ceptin' the cows. Them I'd turn free." And when Abbie asks harshly what he would do with her, he replies, none to reassuringly, "Ye'd be turned free, too." This scene leads to her discovery that what Ephraim most desires in the world is another son, that if Abbie can bring him this last blessing on his old age, he will give her anything she asks, even the farm.

This discovery only strengthens Abbie's determination to make Eben love her—to be more than ever the means to her great possessive end. She plays upon his love for his mother, covers her evil desires with a veneer of mother love, and finally, in the parlor of the house, the room in which Eben's mother was laid out before burial, she persuades him that in loving her he is only revenging his mother's death. Thus Eben, by the false road of an incestuous love, thinks he has discovered freedom from the softness and humiliation of his youthful resentment.

But Eben's false sense of freedom is short lived. Within a year, Abbie has a son by Eben—but Eben finds once more that his father stands above him. "I don't like this," he exclaims. "I don't like lettin' on what's mine is his'n. I been doin' that all my life. I'm gettin' t' the end of b'arin' it!" Abbie's efforts to comfort him, her assurances that "somethin's bound t' happen" are of no avail. The seed of dark evil has been sown, and Eben is beginning to watch the strange plant grow.

It is old Ephraim, boastful and derisive in what he believes to be his new fatherhood, who strikes the second blow at Eben. He gloats over the boy, and then tells him that Abbie always despised him, and wanted to have a son only to make sure that she and not Eben would have the farm. In a rage, Eben attacks his father and the two men struggle until Abbie rushes out to separate them. Then, when his father has gone, Eben vents his rage on Abbie—tells her what he has heard, and refuses to believe her wild protests that she really loves him now, and that all she once said was simply in resentment when he hated and ignored her. As for his son, "I wish he never was born!" cries Eben. "I wish he'd die this minit! I wish I'd never sot eyes on him! It's him—yew havin' him—a-purpose t' steal—that's changed everythin'!" When Abbie pleads that she might make it "'s if he'd never come up between us," Eben answers bitterly, "But ye hain't God, be ye?" As he leaves her, threatening never to see her again, Abbie, who does love Eben now with a tortured intensity, says strangely, "Mebbe I kin take back one thin' God does!" The tragedy sweeps on. To prove her love for Eben, Abbie kills her new-born son!

She comes to Eben to tell him what she has done. At first he thinks she has killed his father, and takes a sort of grim delight in the idea, but when he at last understands that it is his son who has been killed—the one thing really his in the world—a new rage sweeps over him. "I kin see why ye done it!" he yells, " 'cause ye wanted t' steal agen—steal the last thin' he'd left me—my part o' him—no, the hull o' him—ye saw he looked like me—ye knowed he was all mine—an' ye couldn't bar it—I know ye! Ye killed him fur bein' mine!" He rushes off to get the Sheriff.

Then comes Abbie's complete confession to old Ephraim—Eben's frantic return to Abbie, whom he still loves in spite of himself—his plea that they run away together before the Sheriff comes, and Abbie's calm statement: "I got t' take my punishment—t' pay fur my sin." But it is the sin of murder, and not her love for Eben that she means. "I don't repent that sin!" she says proudly, "as if defying God." When the sheriff comes, Eben gives himself up as a partner in the crime—his one and only act of true manliness. Even old Ephraim gives him one look of grudging admiration. "Purty good—fur yew!" he exclaims—and then goes off to follow the precepts of his peculiar god—"God's lonesome, hain't He? God's hard an' lonesome!"

In many respects, "Desire Under the Elms" is unlike all O'Neill's other plays in its complete absorption in the sins of lust, and in its description of those sins—proudly unrepented to the end. In this lies its sense of almost overwhelming defeat. Using the incest symbol of old mythology and tragedy to describe the first battle of youth against the ties of childhood, it describes a battle without an outcome. Eben is victorious in only one thing—a final acceptance of one responsibility of manhood. But he goes off to prison with Abbie, still loving her—the person who has symbolized his mother in his antagonism to his father. The feminine tie to childhood is still as much a part of the poet's struggle as in the closing scenes of "All God's Chillun." Only the masculine side begins to break free, no longer with the idea of 'playing right up to the gates of Heaven," but with the serious purpose of accepting full responsibility for the realities of life and the consequences of evil deed. Eben, at the close of the play, is no longer living in a world of make-believe.

But the feminine side of the poet's soul is still mightily in possession—and again, the child born of that longing for the childish past cannot live. It is killed—by the woman, the symbol of the sheltering maternity, now turned "sinister," to which the child can never return if he wishes to become wholly a man. The brooding elms retain their appalling quality. The desire bred under them is an unholy desire, from which Eben is not yet free. It is not difficult to know that the Ebens of future plays will be driven by the fates and furies within their souls, demanding the price of redemption.

But, of course, as we know, every character in such a play represents a part of the poet's soul—one of those countless voices of tumult which must some day be resolved into a harmony. Ephraim Cabot is also part of the complex struggle—the near-sighted one, of narrow vision and narrow pride, imperious, yet in many ways completely a man, identifying himself with a lonesome and hard God. We must reckon with that quality, too, in the poet's soul—the overharsh and unforgiving judge of his own weaknesses, all too likely to drive him from one compensating extreme to another, unless a true woman, like Maria de Cordova, in "The Fountain," can bring him "tenderness." Of the "dreamer," we would expect to hear less and less—for the manhood in Eben has grown up. But of the proud, imperious thinker, there is too much left. Then, too, there are the brothers to be heard from—the brothers who, like Andrew in "Beyond the Horizon," were able to break away in a search for wealth. The strange persistency of all of these qualities of soul is not the least amazing quality in a play so utterly different from all earlier plays in texture and treatment and immediate theme as "Desire Under the Elms."

This play will always be subject to the criticism of being too brutal and realistic a treatment of a universal theme which the classic dramatists have always approached with a grandiose and coldly symbolic attitude. It is a torrential outpouring of crude feeling, almost terrifying in its raw projection upon a realistic stage. But aside from this aspect—admittedly a very important one in a purely dramatic discussion of O'Neill's work—the meaning of the play as an integral part of the long struggle of a poet's soul toward inner harmony should be accepted at its own worth. It is the first great struggle to emerge into maturity. The significance of its failure can only be measured in the light of renewed conflicts to come and of their greater measure of achievement.

S. K. WINTHER

Desire Under the Elms, A Modern Tragedy†

Many critics of O'Neill have commented on *Desire Under the Elms* as marking a turning point in his development as a dramatist. Some have seen it as O'Neill's expression of extreme violence represented in brutal characters who exemplify "greed, lechery, incest, adultery, revenge, murder." O'Neill ". . . declared them good, and sanctified them."[1] This emphasis on all forms of violence and human degradation is the critical counterpart of popular public revulsion which reached its height in Los Angeles where the whole cast of the play was arrested, tried and convicted of giving a public performance of a play that was "mere smut, and filth . . . , morbid, lewd and obscene."[2] From this psychological approach the critic and the public indicate that in this play O'Neill had made a new departure into the lower depths of the psyche. They find it false, revolting, and

† From *Modern Drama* III (1960), pp. 326-32. Reprinted by permission of the editors of *Modern Drama*.
1. Edward A. Engel, *The Haunted Heroes of Eugene O'Neill* (Cambridge, Mass., 1953), p. 126.
2. *Nation*, CXXII (1926), p. 549.

since it sets its approval on bestiality, it deserves the moral condemnation it receives.

Another critical attack sees the play as centered on overblown pride that balks at no crime to achieve its own ends. In this view Ephraim "has dedicated his entire life to God, who is, of course, only an image of his own ego."[3] From this it follows that all the characters who come in contact with Ephraim are sacrificed to his lust for power. His God is in the rocks, hard, uncompromising and pitiless. This judgment of the play is based on the Aristotelian theory of *hamartia,* and so marks a turning point in O'Neill's conception of tragedy. According to this idea, there must be a "flaw" and the "flaw" must account for the hero's "fall."

Joseph Wood Krutch also emphasizes *Desire Under the Elms* as a turning point in O'Neill's development as a dramatist. He regards it as the first play "which clearly revealed the kind of artistic problem with which O'Neill's genius was destined to grapple."[4] His conception of the "problem" deals with the manner in which O'Neill succeeded in divorcing the action from the reality of the particular, and thereby concentrating on the interpretation of the abstract, or the idea. By this approach he lifts the play out of the muck of detail to which moralistic criticism is inevitably attached. He considered the play as "interested less in New England as such than in an aspect of the eternal tragedy of man and his passions." He holds that "the events really occur out of place and out of time."

This, however, is only a prelude to the real difference between *Desire Under the Elms* and the earlier plays. In this play, for the first time, O'Neill begins to see the problem of tragedy in modern drama as opposed to the classical and traditional interpretation. In this play he departs from the traditional interpretations of Aristotle, a departure that made it possible to develop his later and greater tragedies such as *Mourning Becomes Electra, The Iceman Cometh,* and *Long Day's Journey Into Night.*

O'Neill had, of course, read Aristotle's *Poetics,* but it does not follow that he studied the *Poetics,* analyzed twenty centuries of criticism, and then exemplified his own theory in a conscious dramatic structure. He began in a simpler manner, as no doubt Sophocles did, by seeking an answer to man's relation to the invisible forces that control his destiny. "I am interested only in the relation between man and God," states a point of view that O'Neill expressed many times in many different ways, but always emphasizing the essential and the only problem that is inseparable from any theory of tragedy.

In his notes to *Mourning Becomes Electra* O'Neill states the

3. Doris V. Falk, *Eugene O'Neill and the Tragic Tension* (New Brunswick, 1958), p. 95.

4. Joseph Wood Krutch, "Introduction," *Nine Plays by Eugene O'Neill* (New York, 1954), p. xvi.

problem, recognizing that a modern version of the Electra story needs a psychological equivalent which in turn requires a modern conception of tragedy. By the time he wrote this play he had formulated his theory, but it was in *Desire Under the Elms* that he first conceived of tragedy as based on a theory of life and art that rests upon an idea, "a way of life,"[5] as Abercrombie states it.

The difference between a modern theory of tragedy as exemplified in drama from Ibsen and Strindberg to O'Neill is that it discards all the superficial requirements of a tragedy as set forth by Aristotle. Of course one should not forget that Aristotle was applying an inductive method to the analysis of Greek practice, and not laying down laws as was assumed by the neo-classics. This is now news, but neither is it an accepted fact that modern tragedy has entirely escaped from the Aristotelian "laws" and the moral implications of *hamartia*.

Such substantial critics of O'Neill as Engel, Falk and Eric Bentley make their judgment within the moral limits of the traditional Aristotelian framework. Even when Bentley can not like O'Neill because he can't do a successful stage production, it is quite obvious that his real difficulty lies in his inability to grasp O'Neill's concept of tragedy. Miss Falk's study of "The Tragic Tension" is penetrating and profound even when it assumes that O'Neill accepted the moral view of *hamartia*, which he certainly did not. On this point he followed Ibsen and Strindberg, and in following them he violated the doctrine so hallowed by tradition that it is very nearly sacred.

No recent critic has developed the contrast between the classical and the modern on this issue better than Whitman in his study of Sophocles. He rejects Aristotle's interpretation of the tragic hero as in some way or other deserving his fall from good fortune to bad because of a flaw in his character, a frailty, or an error in judgment. This as the traditional approach was never better stated than by Butcher in his rejection of Ibsen's plays:

> Some quality of greatness in the situation as well as in the characters appears to be all but indispensable, if we are to be raised above the individual suffering and experience a calming instead of a disquieting feeling at the close. The tragic katharsis requires that suffering shall be exhibited in one of its comprehensive aspects; that the deeds and fortunes of the actors shall attach themselves to larger issues, and the spectator himself be lifted above the special case and brought face to face with universal law and the divine plan of the world.[6]

This is the very essence of the traditional approach to tragedy. Butcher has carried the moral interpretation of *hamartia* to its logical conclusion and perhaps the inescapable conclusion implied by Aris-

5. Lascelles Abercrombie, *Principles of Literary Criticism* (London, 1932), p. 99.

6. Samuel H. Butcher, *Aristotle's Theory of Poetry and Fine Art* (New York, 1951), p. 271.

totle. It provides a perfect escape from the grim truth that tragedy does not justify a moral order or "a divine plan of the world." This interpretation of the flaw makes the unbelievable assumption that the moral failure or error in judgment justifies the fearful doom that falls upon the tragic hero. It sings a lullaby of dawn after the midnight storm, it offers a pious, little Sunday school moral and actually implies that Sophocles, Shakespeare and O'Neill saw man's tragic conflict in the terms of piety divorced from reason. Whatever Aristotle may have meant by katharsis or for what matter by pity and fear it must have been something greater than this Victorian sense of pious acceptance of a divine order. And it is that something more that lays the foundation for modern tragedy in Strindberg and Ibsen, and this is more fully developed in a conscious conception of tragedy by O'Neill.

2

In *Desire Under the Elms* the tragic hero is a man apart from other men. He does not accept their manner of living, their morality is beneath his contempt, their ideals are to him the petty dreams of weaklings and cowards. He despises his weak and loutish sons, he scorns the morality so valuable to all those who work in the market place for profit, the church and the dogma it represents is not even worthy of mention, the legal system with its special morality he uses, but only to further his own end. As a man he stems from Ibsen's Brand and the supreme and powerful pride of Strindberg. He is as proud as any man who ever walked onto a stage demanding an answer from the unanswerable. Like Job he wants to know why, with this difference that he knows he must become like the rocks and the hills if he would know God, and then he would be like Him, perhaps even equal to Him.

3

As a drama every scene in *Desire Under the Elms* is developed with skill to enhance and clarify the nature and meaning of the tragic hero. All other characters are made small in contrast. The two older sons are ignorant and loutish. Eben is a complex of delicate and sentimental love for the memory of his dead mother. Mixed with this emotion is a passion for the farm which is nothing more than a superficial attitude learned from his father. He will steal in the name of his mother to acquire his brother's rights to the land. He will desecrate her love in the company of a whore; he will commit incest and console himself with the thought that the restless spirit of his mother finds peace at last in the approval of his action. Abbie has no fixed value by which she can live. Greed, ambition, power and carnal love are so mixed in her behavior that she never finds a principle by which she can reconcile her practice with a fixed standard of conduct.

Within this network of ignorance and doubtful values that form the outer framework of the plot the character of Ephraim stands hard as the rocks that represent God. He knows that God and the rocks are one, that if he would know God he must know the rocks of the field that are the voice and spirit of God. "God is hard. He ain't easy" is the all-enveloping idea of the play, and the plot is the arrangement of characters in action to emphasize this truth as the all-enveloping idea of man and his world.

This man is a giant in comparison with the human beings who surround him. There is never any suggestion in the play that anyone, either man or woman, understood him. In his presence they can conceal neither their fear nor their awe. He was larger, stronger, older, more daring than other men. He encompassed in his being an understanding of life that embraced all living things. He was a part of the stony hills, the blue sky, the changing seasons; age did not weaken him, and the laws and the morality that are necessary to the essential weakness of most human beings were nonexistent for him. The sense of guilt, sin, and the fear of the law before which other characters of the play cringe, never crossed the threshold of his mind or touched him with either sorrow or regret. He lived in the presence of God as manifested in the stones on his farm. He read the lessons of these stones as the true symbol of God's reality: cold, impersonal, strong, powerful, everlasting; a God untouched and unmoved by the petty, sensuous needs of men. Their pitiful cries for help, their intermittent faith, their identification with the soft and the sentimental was scorned by Ephraim as the God he understood so well also scorned them.

There are four scenes in Part I. Not until near the end of Scene Four does Ephraim appear, yet he dominates the actions and the thoughts of his three sons in the preceding scenes. The older sons are longing to escape from "makin' stone walls fur him to fence us in!" From that reference to "stones atop o' stones" and "Him," Ephraim dominates the action although he is not there in person. He had left the farm two months before. "Hitched up an' druv off into the West." They are puzzled by his queer behavior in leaving the place for the first time in thirty years. Simeon recognized a strange power, an unexplained force which he calls "Somethin'— driving him—t' drive us." He told his son why he was going, but to the younger man's dull mind it had no meaning. As Simeon recalls it his father was "lookin' kinder queer an' sick," and saying, "I been hearin' the hens cluckin' an' the roosters crowin' all the durn day. I been lisenin' t' the cows lowin' an' everthin' else kickin' up till I can't stand it no more. It's spring an' I am feelin' damned. . . . An' now I'm ridin' out t' learn God's message t' me in the spring, like the prophets done."

His sons scorn his avowed purpose, but he was speaking a deep conviction of his own. A little less than fifty years before, he had fled from the stones to seek an easy life in the rich lands of the Mississippi valley. Ephraim tells Abbie that as his crops in the rich soil began to flourish he heard the voice of God saying, "This hain't wuth nothin' to Me," and goes on to say, "God's hard, not easy! God's in the stones! Build my church on a rock—out of stones an' I'll be in them! That's what He meant t' Peter! . . . Stones."

In his seeking for identification with the God of Stone, he was set apart from other human beings. He neither shared in their lives nor felt bound by their laws. They in turn could not enter into his (Ibsen) Brand-like conception of man's relations to God. He married and his wife bore him two sons. "She was a good woman. She wuked hard. We was married twenty year. She never knowed me. She helped but she never knowed what she was helpin'. I was allus lonesome. She died." He took a second wife. "She never knowed me for nothin'. It was lonesomer'n hell with her. After a matter o' sixteen odd years, she died." His sons grew up hating him and coveting the farm not knowing what they coveted; not knowing as Ephraim knew that possession of the farm was equal to the knowledge of God. Then he went forth in the spring to listen to the voice of the Prophets and he found a third wife who for a fleeting instant seemed to grasp the meaning of the farm and then lost it to a calculated carnal desire, because, she like all the others, did not know that this stony stronghold of Ephraim and God could not be possessed by love, illegal or otherwise.

As Part II develops, the battle of love and greed between Abbie and Eben controls the action. It seems to have turned away from Ephraim. He is lost once more in the wilderness of his lonesome world. While Abbie is plotting to deceive him, he makes a last effort to enlist her sympathy and understanding. "Then this spring the call come—the voice o' God cryin' in my wilderness, in my lonesomeness—t' go out an' seek an' find! (Turning to her with strange passion) I sought ye an' I found ye! Yew air my Rose O' Sharon! Yer eyes air like. . . ." He gives up trying to make her understand.

In the blank ignorance of her expression Ephraim realizes that she, like his other wives, like his sons, does not understand his vision of God, his desire to become like God, hard as stone. In disgust he leaves her to join the cows in the barn. They are close to nature. They have accepted God as a stone. "They'll give me peace." But in leaving the scene he only emphasizes the fact that he dominates it. The next two scenes bring the lovers together. They believe that in deceiving Ephraim they have avenged Eben's mother. But the closing scene of Part II shows Ephraim contemplating the beauty of the sky and completely scornful of Eben's petty sense of triumph, which he senses without knowing exactly what its source is.

As the play moves to its conclusion in Part III all the action seems to center on the fearful clash between Eben and Abbie. Hate, fear, greed and love dominate their thoughts, feelings and action. It seems for a time as though they had finally taken over the play and the tragedy belonged to them. Then once more the shadow of the rock which is Ephraim looms over them like the ominous shadows of the elms that cover the house of Cabot. The lovers in their attempt to destroy Ephraim destroy themselves. Their end is ignominious defeat. Their actions are ignorant and cowardly. Their cringing acceptance of their fate deserves the towering contempt of Ephraim.

He in turn suffers a moment of weakness. It seems to him that at last the forces against him have won the battle. He has freed the cattle from the barn. "I'll set fire t' house an' barn an' watch 'em burn, an' I'll leave yer Maw t' haunt the ashes, an' I'll will the fields back t' God, so nothin' human kin ever touch 'em!"

He finds that Eben had stolen his money, so his easy plan to escape fails. His moment of weakness is over. He turns back to God. "I kin feel I be in the palm of His hand, His fingers guidin' me. It's a-goin' t' be lonesomer now than ever it war afore— . . . Waal —what d'ye want? God's lonesome, hain't He? God's hard an' lonesome!"

The Sheriff comes to take away the sin-sick, contrite lovers. Ephraim is to be left alone with the farm, the stones and God. He is seventy-five years old, he has had three wives and three sons. They have all, each in his own way, betrayed him. Through their weakness, their inability to understand that Nature has no special concern for their well-being, they deserted him.

4

In the character of Ephraim, O'Neill has developed a modern tragedy. The traditional conception of the tragic hero with his flaw, the idea of purification through suffering, the sense of a divine order based on the punishment of evil and reward for good—all his is irrelevant to the tragedy of this play. Ephraim has a sense of the ultimate realities, the forces that relate man to the physical world. He senses the need for a living force in the inanimate earth, and he knows that it is hard as stone and as impersonal as the wind. He listens to the voice of nature, he is exalted by her beauty, and he identifies himself with the quality of lonesomeness which must be the character of power divorced from purpose.

His God of stone embodies the spirit of the earth from which mankind has its being. It brings forth the life that flourishes for a moment on the stony hillside under the blue sky in the warmth of the sun. As it brings to life the spirit of man, it likewise invites him to his doom. There is no escape either from birth or death. All this is part of Ephraim's character. In his futile battle to know God's way and be like God he is doomed to defeat; in his determination never to submit or yield, he is heroic. In this struggle that has dominated his life he can never win. At the age of seventy-five, he walks out into the stony fields, into the beauty of dawn.

His great pride, one of the most hackneyed "flaws" in all criticism of tragedy, is no "frailty" in his character. It is pride that sustains him, it is by pride that he has endured his failures, it has strengthened him in his search for God. Not through humility but by pride does man attain his true humanity as a being that measures the extent of his universe and develops the courage to face his doom. Ephraim's exit is heroic. "Waal—what d'ye want? God's lonesome hain't He? God's hard an' lonesome."

Luigi Pirandello
and
Henry IV

LUIGI PIRANDELLO

From Umorismo†

The humorist is best defined by his special capacity for reflection,
a kind of reflection that typically generates a sense of contradiction,
perplexity, uncertainty, a certain wavering state of consciousness. It
is precisely this that distinguishes him from the comic writer, the
ironist, and the satirist. A sense of contradiction does not breed in
them; if it were to, it would lead the comic writer to seize on some
abnormality or other and would defeat the comic by making his
laughter bitter; it would defeat the ironic because the ironist's wholly
verbal contradiction between what he says and what he wishes to be
understood would no longer be merely verbal, but real and substantial; it would defeat the satiric because it would put an end to
the disdain and aversion for reality which are satire's reason for
being. Not that the humorist is pleased by reality! It is sufficient
for him that he be pleased by it only for a little while, so that,
reflecting on his own pleasure, he might destroy it.

By nature fine and sharp, this reflection insinuates itself everywhere and unmakes everything: every semblance of feeling, every
visionary fancy, every appearance of reality, every illusion. Guy de
Maupassant used to say that human thought "goes around like a fly
in a bottle." All phenomena are either illusory or inexplicable—
their reason for being escapes us. That objective value which we
commonly presume to attribute to our knowledge of the world and
of ourselves does not exist; it's a continuous illusory construction.

But let's consider the struggle between illusion and the humorist's
reflection, illusion which also insinuates itself everywhere, construct-

† From Luigi Pirandello, *Umorismo*
(The Mondadori Edition), Rome, 1960.
Pp. 145-57. Copyright 1960 by the Pir-
andello Estate. Reprinted by permission
of Toby Cole Actors and Authors
Agency. Translated by Anthony Caputi.

ing in its own way, and this reflection which one by one unmakes these constructions.

Let's begin with what illusion does for each one of us, with the construction, that is, which each of us by means of illusion makes of himself for himself. Do we see ourselves as we are, in our true, undiluted reality, and not as we wish to be? By means of a trick worked inside us, spontaneously, the product of hidden tendencies or of unconscious imitation, do we not in good faith believe ourselves different from what substantially we are? And yet we think, we work, and we live according to this fictional and even sincere interpretation of ourselves.

Now reflection can discover in this illusory construction as much for the comic writer and the satirist as for the humorist. But the comic writer will merely laugh at it, contenting himself with deflating the metaphor of ourselves that illusion spontaneously creates, while the satirist will be offended by it. Not the humorist: through the ridiculousness of the discovery he will see its serious and painful side. He will dismantle the construction, but not merely to laugh at it; and even though he laughs, he will sympathize instead of being offended.

Reflection has taught the comic writer and the satirist how much thread the spider of experience takes from social life in composing the web of mentality in this or that individual, and how this web supports, often envelops, what is called the moral sense. What is, fundamentally, the internal social structure of what is called convention? A system of elements derived from convenience, they reply, in which morality is almost always sacrificed. The humorist goes deeper and, without getting angry, laughs at discovering how with the greatest good faith, indeed ingenuously, we are induced by the impulsive working of fancy to believe that this responsibility and that moral sentiment are true, in themselves, when, in reality, they are only the responsibilities and sentiments of convention, that is, based on convenience. And he goes still further and discovers that even the need for a thing to appear worse than it actually is can become conventional, if being a member of some social group requires that one display ideals and feelings appropriate to the group yet contrary and inferior to the private feelings of the one who participates in it.

The communal lie provides a more practicable basis on which to reconcile jarring tendencies, conflicting feelings, and opposing opinions than one which openly and explicitly tolerates dissent and opposition; indeed, falsehood seems altogether more effective than truthfulness in that it can unite whereas veracity separates. Moreover, none of this prevents falsehood, even as it is tacitly unmasked and recognized, from enlisting this same veracity as a guarantee of its efficacy and in this way making hypocrisy seem like honesty. Reserve, discretion, the practice of letting others believe more than one says or does, silence itself when accompanied by a knowledge of the conditions which justify it—oh unforgettable Conte Zio of the Secret Council![1]—all these arts are met frequently in practical life; so too are the practice of not revealing what one is thinking, of letting others believe that one thinks less of oneself than one actually does, of pretending that one is thought to be different from what, at bottom, one is. . . .

The more one's own weakness is felt in the struggle for life the more important becomes the need for reciprocal deceit. The simulation of strength, of honesty, of sympathy, of prudence, in fact, of each of the major virtues relating to truthfulness, is a form of adaptation, a serviceable tool for use in the struggle. The humorist readily collects the various impersonations used in the life-struggle; he amuses himself by unmasking them. But he does not become angry: life is like that! While the sociologist describes social life as it appears in external observations, the humorist, armed with his instinctive shrewdness, shows how profoundly different the appearances are from the intimate private life of its members. Yet one lies in psychological matters just as one does in social ones, and the lie to ourselves, as we knowingly live only on the surface of our psychic being, is a result of the social lie. The spirit that ponders itself is a solitary spirit; but inward solitude is never so great that the influence of everyday life, with the dissimulations and transfiguring arts that characterize it, does not penetrate the consciousness of even the solitary spirit. There lives in our spirit the spirit of the race or of the collectivity of which we are a part; we respond, unconsciously, to the pressure of others, to their ways of judging, their ways of feeling and functioning.

Further, just as simulation and dissimulation dominate in the social world, the less evidently as they become more habitual, so we simulate and dissimulate with ourselves, now halving and now multiplying ourselves. We are driven by vanity to appear different from the person we give form to in society, and we take refuge from the analysis which, revealing this vanity, would prompt the bite of conscience and humiliate us before ourselves. But the humorist performs this analysis for us; it is his function to unmask all vanities and to represent society, as Thackeray did, a *Vanity Fair*.

Moreover, the humorist knows perfectly well that in the long run the pretence of logic frequently overcomes actual logical coherence in us. Even as we pretend, in theory, to be logical men, the logic of action is capable of belying the logic of thought, capable of

1. A character in Alessandro Manzoni's *The Betrothed;* a master in the arts of dissimulation.

demonstrating that a belief held with absolute sincerity is a sham. Habit, imitation, irresponsibility, and mental laziness compete to create misunderstanding. And even when logic rigorously informs our reasoning processes, with respect and love, let's assume, for certain fixed ideals, the reason is not always honest in its treatment of them. Is the true and exclusive source of our ideals and of our perseverance in cultivating them only to be found in pure, disinterested reason? Or is it more consistent with reality to suspect that sometimes they are evaluated, not by an objective and rational criterion, but by special emotional impulses and obscure tendencies?

The barriers and limits that we set on our consciousness are also illusory: they are the conditions for our relative individuality, but actually they have no existence. And this applies not only to us such as we are now and live in ourselves now, but also to us such as we were previously and lived then and felt and reasoned with thoughts and emotions long since forgotten, cancelled, spent in our present consciousness, but which with a jolt, a sudden turmoil of spirit, can still spring to life to reveal in us an unsuspected being within our present being. The limits of our private memory and consciousness are not rigidly fixed; beyond lie further memories and perceptions and reasonings. What we are aware of in ourselves is only a part, and perhaps a small part, of what we are. At certain unusual moments we come upon so many surprising things within ourselves—perceptions, reasonings, states of consciousness, things actually beyond the relative limits of our normal conscious existence. Certain ideals which we think we have put aside and believe no longer capable of exerting influence on our thoughts, emotions, and actions perhaps continue to survive, if not in a pure, intellectual form, on a stratum of their own, re-enforced by emotional tendencies and habit. Certain tendencies which we believe ourselves free of can be real motives for action, while new beliefs which we think we hold truly and deeply have no practical influence on us.

It is precisely the variety of tendencies that goes to make up the personality which ultimately forces the conclusion that the individual spirit is not one. How can we affirm that it is one, in fact, if passion and reason, instinct and will, indistinct tendencies, and ideals constitute numerous separate and mobile systems functioning so that the individual, now living by this one, now by that, now by some compromise between two or more psychic orientations, seems as if he contained several different and even opposed spirits, several conflicting personalities? There is no man, Pascal observed, who differs from another more than, in time, he differs from himself. The spirit in its natural state contradicts the historical concept of the human spirit. Its life is a moving equilibrium, a continuous rising and falling away of emotions, tendencies, ideas, an incessant fluctuation between conflicting ends, an oscillation between such opposing poles as hope and fear, true and false, beautiful and ugly, just and unjust. If in the obscure image of the future a bright design for action suddenly appears, or the flower of delight vaguely glimmers, it is not long before our memory of the past, that avenger in the name of experience, appears, usually dim and sad, or our riotous sense of the present intervenes and restrains our too lively imagination. This struggle between memories, hopes, forebodings, perceptions, and ideals can be seen as a struggle among spirits who oppose the domination of a firm and definitive personality.

Here is an important functionary who believes himself and who is in fact, poor soul, a man of honor. In him the moral spirit dominates. Yet one fine day instinct, like a primal beast crouched in the depths of each of us, lets fly with a kick at the moral spirit, and this man of honor steals. Oh, he himself, poor soul, is the first, shortly afterwards, to be stupefied by what has happened, to weep, to ask himself in despair: "How, how were you ever able to do such a thing?" But yes, my dear sir, you have stolen. And that one there? An upright man, indeed, an exceedingly good man: yes, my dear sir, he has killed. Moral idealism furnished his personality with a spirit which conflicted with his instinct and even to some extent with his emotions; it bodied forth an acquired spirit which fought the inherited one, which, in turn, left briefly to itself, seized suddenly on theft and crime.

Life is a continuous flux and we seek to arrest it, to fix it in stable and determined forms, inside and outside us, because we are already fixed forms, forms which move in the midst of immobile ones and which can therefore follow the flux of life until, as it gradually becomes rigid, the movement, which has already slowed down little by little, ceases. The forms in ourselves by which we seek to arrest and fix this continuous flux are the concepts and ideals which we would like to keep consistent, all the pretenses we create, the conditions, the state in which we endeavor to stabilize ourselves. But inside ourselves, in what we call the soul, which is the center of our lives, the flux continues, indistinct, sliding under the barriers we have set up, beyond the limits we have imposed, fashioning a consciousness and constructing a personality for us. At certain violent moments, assailed by the flux, all our make-believe forms crumble miserably; and even what does not slither under the barriers and beyond the limits, even what is clearly a part of us, what we have channelled into the affections and duties we have assumed and the habits we have marked out for ourselves, overflows in certain moments of fullness and throws everything into confusion.

There are reckless spirits who, almost continuously in a state of melting and blending, resist congealing or hardening into this or that form of personality. But even for the more placid ones who have settled into one form or other the melting and blending is always possible.

Even our own bodies, fixed perpetually in their immutable features, can sometimes represent a torture for the moving, melting spirit. Why must we be just like this, we sometimes ask ourselves at the mirror, with this face and this body? We raise a hand, unconsciously, and the gesture remains suspended. It seems strange that *we* have done it. *We are seeing ourselves live.* With this suspended gesture we can liken ourselves to a statue, to that statue of the ancient orator, for example, which one sees in a niche as one ascends the staircase of the Quirinale. With a scroll in one hand and the other extended in a sober gesture, how distressed and amazed he seems to have remained there, in stone, for all those centuries, suspended in that attitude, before all those people who have ascended, who ascend, and who will ascend that staircase!

In certain moments of interior silence, in which our spirit divests itself of its habitual pretences and our eyes become sharper and more penetrating, we see ourselves in life, and life itself, as if in a sterile nudity, and we are troubled; we feel ourselves assaulted by a strange impression, as if, in a flash, a different reality from that which we normally perceive were clarifying itself, a living reality beyond human sight, outside the forms of human reason. At such times the fabric of daily existence, almost suspended in the void of our interior silence, appears with blinding clarity to be without sense and purpose; and as all our habitual sham connections for sentiments and images are disjointed and broken up, the new reality seems horrible in its impassive and mysterious severity. The inward void gets larger, goes beyond the limits of our body, becomes a void around us, a strange emptiness, like a pause in time and in life, as if our interior silence were sinking into the abysses of mystery. With a supreme effort we try to re-acquire our normal consciousness of things, to re-establish the usual ties between them, to re-connect ideas, to feel ourselves alive again in the usual way, as before. But in this normal consciousness, in these re-connected ideas, in this habitual sense of life, we can no longer have faith because by now we know that they comprise a deception for the purpose of living, that beneath them is something else which man cannot confront except at the cost of dying or going mad. The whole experience has taken only an instant, but its impression endures in us for a long time, like a dizziness to which is contrasted the stability, however unreal in actuality, of things—ambitious, paltry appearances. The life that wanders about, small and habitual, among these appearances seems almost to be no longer real, to be a mechanical fantasmagoria. How can we give it importance? How can we respect it?

Today we are, tomorrow we are not. What sort of face have they given us with which to play the role of someone alive? An ugly nose? What misery to have to carry around an ugly nose all one's life . . . It's fortunate that in the long run we cease to notice it. Others notice it, it's true, when we have succeeded in believing that we have a beautiful nose; and then we can no longer understand why they laugh when they look at us. They are such fools! We console ourselves by noticing what ears that one has and what lips that other, yet they are not aware of them and they have the nerve to laugh at us. Masks, masks . . . A puff of wind and they pass and make way for others. That poor cripple there . . . Who is he? To run towards death on crutches . . . Here life crushes someone's foot; there it pulls out someone's eye . . . A wooden leg, a glass eye, and forward! Everyone tidies up his mask as best he can—that is, the exterior mask. But inside there is still that other, which often does not agree with the exterior one.

Nothing is true! The sea is true, yes, and the mountain, and the stone, and the blade of grass; but man? Eternally masked, without wishing to be or knowing it, by those very things that he in good faith believes himself to be: handsome, good, gracious, generous, unhappy. To think of all this is to laugh; yes, laugh. What does a dog do when he has overcome the first fever of living? He eats and sleeps; he lives as he can live, as he must live. He closes his eyes patiently and lets time pass; he's cold if it's cold, hot if it's hot; and if they kick him, he takes it because this too is a sign of his lot. But man? Even as an old man he always has fever: he is delirious and he is not aware of it; he cannot do less than assume a pose, even, somehow, to beguile himself with; and with his imagination he creates things, a great many things, which he needs to believe and needs to take seriously.

He is helped in this by a certain infernal little machine that nature gave him and adjusted to him inwardly as a conspicuous proof of its benevolence. In the interests of their health men ought to have let it rust, ought never to have started it, or touched it. But no. Certain individuals felt so proud and deemed themselves so happy to have it that they quickly dedicated themselves with relentless zeal to perfecting it. Aristotle wrote a book about it, a graceful little treatise that is still adopted in the schools because children learn how to play with toys so quickly and well. It's a kind of pump and filter which puts the brain in communication with the heart. The esteemed philosophers call it logic.

By means of logic the brain pumps feelings from the heart and extracts ideas. The feeling passes through the filter and leaves whatever it contains that is hot and cloudy; then it is refrigerated, purified, and i-de-a-lized. By this process a poor feeling, initially evoked by a particular circumstance, by some occurrence or other, often a sorrowful one, now pumped and filtered by this little machine used by the brain, becomes an abstract, general idea. And what follows? It follows that we not only must worry about this particular circumstance and that passing occurrence, but we also must poison our lives with the concentrated extract, the corrosive sublimate of logical deduction. Many unfortunates believe that in this way we shall cure the world of all its ills: they pump and filter, pump and filter, until their hearts are as dry as cork and their brains are like cabinets in a pharmacy, full of those little bottles with the black label bearing the skull and crossbones and the legend "Poison."

Man does not have an idea or an absolute conception of life, but a sense of it that is mutable and variable, depending on the times, circumstances, and chance. Now logic, abstracting ideas from feelings tends to fix what is mobile, mutable, and fluid, tends to give an absolute value to what is relative. It makes worse an evil that is already grave to begin with. For the root of our trouble is precisely that we have a sense of life. The tree lives but does not feel: for it the earth, sun, air, light, wind, and rain are not things beyond it. Man, on the other hand, is at birth endowed with the sad privilege of feeling himself alive, and this leads to that happy illusion by which he accepts his inward sense of life, mutable and variable as it is, as if it were a reality outside him.

The ancients told the story that Prometheus stole a spark from the sun to make a gift of it to men. Now the sense we have of life is precisely this Promethean spark of the fable. It causes us to see ourselves lost on the earth; it projects all around us a more or less full circle of light beyond which is dark shadow, the fearful shadow that would not exist if it were not for the lighted spark within us, a shadow, however, that we must unfortunately believe real as long as the spark lives in our breast. When it is extinguished at the last by the breath of death, what has apparently been a shadow will gather us up for good; after the smoky day of illusion perpetual night will receive us. Or, even then, perhaps, we shall continue to be at the mercy of Being, which will have broken only the futile forms of reason. All that shadow, that enormous mystery on which so many philosophers have speculated in vain and which now science, though it denies its interest in it, does not exclude, will it not be, perhaps, finally a deception like any other, a trick played by our minds, a fantasy that comes to nothing? What if ultimately all this mystery does not exist outside us, but only within us, and necessarily within us by virtue of the famous privilege of our sense of life? What if death were only the breath that extinguishes this sense in us, this sense so painful and terrifying because it is limited, defined by the circle of fictional shadow beyond the slight orbit of faint light which we project around us and within which our life remains as if imprisoned, as if excluded for a time from the universal, eternal life which it seems to us we must one day re-enter? What if actually we are already there and there we shall remain, though no longer with this sense of exile that aggrieves us? Is not this limit also illusory and relative to the scant light of our individuality? Perhaps we have always lived, always shall live with all of life; perhaps even now, in our present form, we participate in all the manifestations of the universe. We do not know it and we do not see it because unfortunately the Promethean spark enables us to see only that little which it illuminates.

Tomorrow a humorist could picture Prometheus on his rock in the Caucasus in the act of pondering sadly his lighted torch and perceiving in it, at last, the fatal cause of his infinite suffering. He has finally understood that Zeus is no other than a vain fantasm of his own creating, a pitiable deception, the shadow of his own body projected in gigantic dimensions in the sky precisely because he holds the torch burning in his hand. Zeus would disappear on one condition only, on condition that Prometheus extinguish his torch. But he does not know how, he does not wish it, he cannot; and the shadow remains, terrifying and tyrannical, for all men who do not succeed in understanding the fatal deception.

Thus the conflict proves itself irremovable and unresolvable, like shadow and substance. In this brief humorist vision we have seen it enlarge itself gradually, go beyond the limits of our individual being whence it takes root, and extend itself around us. Reflection, which sees in everything a construction that is either illusory, or pretended, or fictional, discovers it and by shrewd, subtle, minute analysis disassembles and unmakes it.

One of the greatest humorists, without knowing it, was Copernicus, who disassembled, not really the machine of the universe, but the proud image which we had made of it. * * * It was the discovery of the telescope, yet another infernal little machine which could make a pair with the one that nature made us a present of, which administered the coup de grace to us. But we invented this one so as not to be inferior. While the eye looks at one end, through the smaller lense, and sees enlarged what nature had providentially intended us to see small, what does our soul do? It leaps to look through the other end, through the larger lense. In this way the telescope becomes a terrible instrument which overwhelms the earth and man and all our glories and grandeur.

It is fortunate that humorist reflection does provoke a sense of contradiction: in this case it says, "But is man really as little as the reversed telescope causes us to see him? If he can understand and conceive of his infinite littleness, that means he understands and conceives of the infinite grandeur of the universe. How, then, can we say that man is a small creature?" Yet it is also true that if man believes himself great and a humorist comes to know it, he can go the way of Gulliver and be both a giant in Lilliput and a toy among the giants of Brobdingnag.

DOMENICO VITTORINI

[Being and Seeming: *Henry IV*]†

After the objective attitude towards reality shown in varying degree in the plays that give evidence of inspiration from Sicilian naturalism, Pirandello appears in a mood that he qualifies as humorous or grotesque. He distinguishes very sharply between humor and irony. To him irony is a rhetorical figure of speech that means the opposite of what it says with the purpose of hurting. It does not possess the deep and tragic implications of humor. Humor is a peculiarly philosophical attitude that obliterates the dividing line between laughter and grief, and it presents man as harboring in his heart a strange feeling of exaltation and of scorn, of pity and of derision for himself. Humor is understanding and compassionate, and, if the humorist laughs, there is a vein of grief in his laughter.

Pirandello's aesthetic ideas are discussed in a book that he published in 1908 under the title of *Umorismo* (*Humor*) which shows the vastness and depth of his intellectual background and also the seriousness with which he prepared himself for his art. It is fortunate that his reflective attitude has not marred the spontaneity of his inspiration. In this book the author studies the nature of humor in European literature, insisting especially on English, Spanish, and Italian humorists. He considers a typical expression of humor to be Giordano Bruno's attitude towards art and life inclosed in his saying, "Sad in mirth, mirthful in sadness." Pirandello also ponders admiringly over Machiavelli's profession of literary faith: "If at times I laugh or sing, I do it because this is the only way I have to provide an outlet for my painful tears."

Pirandello's ideas on the grotesque, which he believes to be the artistic expression of humor, have led many critics astray in that the latter have tried to interpret the whole of Pirandello's production through the æsthetic canons expressed in his book on humor. To apply these æsthetic beliefs to the whole of Pirandello's drama would be the same as to study Dante's *Divine Comedy* in the light of the

† From Domenico Vittorini, *The Drama of Luigi Pirandello*, Philadelphia, 1935. Pp. 89-94, 157-59. Copyright 1935. Reprinted by permission of the publishers, University of Pennsylvania Press.

æsthetic ideas of the *Convito*, or Tasso's *Jerusalem Delivered* in that of his discourse on the heroic poem. The critic and the poet do not necessarily harmonize in every writer, and often the poet sees distances and heights and depths that the vision of the critic can neither encompass nor fathom.

The ideas expressed in his *Humor*, however, dovetail with a section of his drama, the foreground of which is occupied by the ludicrous appearance of reality which hides or veils a ghastly anguish that torments the characters. Indeed, these ideas are the genesis of the drama of "being and seeming."

In this new field of artistic search and creation Pirandello's master is no longer, as in the days of his naturalism, Giovanni Verga. His place has been taken by the humorists of European literatures, and especially by Alessandro Manzoni[1] and a younger writer, Alfredo Cantoni, who had coined the phrase "Smiling in appearance, grieving in reality," and about whom Pirandello wrote a masterful critical essay.[2]

Humor detects contrasts and shadows, and reaches especially the fundamental clash in man—that of sentiment and of reason. It considers reason as an infernal mechanism that reduces life into concepts. When a situation is looked upon and lived as an abstract concept, we can move in it with the utmost ease because we can mold concepts to suit our taste and pleasure, since concepts do not possess the unwieldy and unbending solidity of actual facts. Concepts, however, being the result of intellect and reason, are the negation of life, which in its essence is fluid and spontaneous. We seek a refuge in them only when we have become so cerebral as to be deprived of spontaneity of feeling and of living.

For Pirandello good and simple people possess spontaneity of life (a characteristic also shared by plants and animals), but their life is necessarily limited, uneventful, and prosaic. Over-intellectual people enlarge the boundary and scope of their life, but they fall prey to intellectual complications and to artificiality. Their inner life is a place that fears light, since terrible shames are hidden there. Since they are compelled to go among men and they want to appear decent and even heroic, they hide themselves behind a fictitious personality that expresses itself with exalted gestures and idealistic words.

Pirandello calls this process *"costruirsi"* or "to build up oneself." In its simplest forms this process refers to the social mask we wear when we go among our fellow-men and lavish smiles that hide grimaces, honeyed words that are spoken in order to conceal real feelings. In its essential character, however, this process portrays a con-

1. See D. Vittorini, *The Modern Italian Novel,* Philadelphia, 1930.
2. "L'opera di Alfredo Cantoni." In *L'illustrissimo — Nuova Antologia.* Rome 1906.

scious self-deception which we force on ourselves, because without it we could not stand the weight of a painful situation in which we are caught. There are moments in life—the author had experienced them—when it is not possible to appear to others as we actually are; to show our poor souls stripped of the many veils that we throw around them.

Pirandello has shown in his plays that there are cases when loathing for life and for ourselves is so great that it transforms us into madmen. The typical Pirandellian character of this stage of his drama is a man distressed, with mobile eyes, tense, and unable to relieve that tension, for fear that his whole being, moral and physical, may disintegrate. When all alone, he grits his teeth and clenches his fists, while within him disgust rises like a polluted tide. Who could then show himself as he is, not only to others but to himself? It is then that reason begins to function, and it covers with idealistic hues a situation which is inwardly putrid. Reason lends to Pirandello's characters beautiful masks which they press against their faces while they walk among their fellow-men, composed and stately. However, there is the face and there is the mask which never become one, and Pirandello's characters know it. They feel from time to time that the face wants to appear or that circumstances in life threaten to remove the mask. They desperately cling to it, and press it with agonizing strength over their faces, feeling the hurt, the bruise, the burn, yet ready to endure that suffering because it is more bearable than the one inflicted on them by what they know about themselves.

This process, which has given life to immortal characters in Pirandello's drama, presupposes a ghastly moral shame and an acute and tormented sensitiveness. It is also predicated on the assumption that all men are, to a varying degree, theatrical, especially if highly intellectual. An intellectual man acquires in reflection what he loses in spontaneity. It is a law of life, and the mask that man dons is a logical means of self-defense. Since Pirandello's drama begins when the voice of instinct has been silenced and his characters are stranded on the bleak shore of disillusionment, all their life centers in their intellectual raving. Pirandello listens to them, smiles at them, sometimes cruelly, sometimes pitifully, and he shows them that in reality there is no use gesticulating like energumens, shouting and protesting. They are face to face with life, and they must accept it as it is.

Pirandello is compassionate with his characters, but he is also aware that their exaltation is artificial. He knows that as soon as we become exalted, since exaltation appears in people who are not endowed with simplicity, it becomes artificial and conscious of itself. Sentiment is then absent from us, and we must make up for it with the cold power of reason. Then we exaggerate, we shout, and we try to persuade others and ourselves to something of which we are not convinced. As long as we endure in the tension of exaltation, we are not conscious of the extreme lack of sincerity in us, but, if we should happen to look into a mirror and see ourselves in it, we immediately realize the unbearable ugliness of our deception. Seeing ourselves live suspended in the revolting image of our falseness destroys our exaltation, and we appear in all the pity of our betrayed humanity.

The result of this intuition is that the plays of the "grotesque," which largely make up the section of the drama of "being and seeming," move from ridicule to pathos. This prevents Pirandello's drama from being either low farce or an evanescent dream.

It is well to point out that the process of self-deception does not destroy the initial ego in Pirandello's characters. The natural and normal self becomes temporarily obliterated by hard and cruel necessity, and through the juxtaposition of these two selves, the original and the artificial, there arises the drama of "being and seeming," with the inevitable clash between them. More than from his brain the drama derives from the heart of Pirandello, and his work is a delicate and passionate analysis of a humanity that suffers and tries to appear at least calm; that inwardly bleeds through shame and outwardly puts on the veneer of decency. It is not at all necessary to think of the subconscious or of Freud, unless we wish to appear erudite to make an impression on the unsophisticated. Let us see how pitiful are the characters of the plays that we are going to study in this section: Ciampa, Ersilia Drei, Elma, Henry IV. Under the masks there suffers in them the human heart with an agonizing sorrow. It is unjust, therefore, to state that between "being and seeming" there is no difference, and that in Pirandello there is not a point at which the actual reality ends and the fantastic one begins, a statement very dear to Pirandello's critics. Pirandello's characters wilfully and consciously try to destroy the actual reality because it is unbearable for them, but they cannot free themselves of it.

It is evident that Pirandello's characters have at least temporarily the postures and mannerisms of supermen. It must not be forgotten, however, that their author does not take them seriously, and that the drama consists in dissecting their artificiality. In this fashion the drama is urged towards its climax, and after a moment of exaltation the characters reënter their ordinary life, either like Ciampa with a loud and jarring laughter, or tragically like Henry IV plunging into a lucid madness that is the only solution life has left for him.

From an aesthetic point of view the intuition of the grotesque transforms man into his own enemy, and the center of the play is transported into his very heart, affording to the author the opportunity of a searching and tormenting analysis.

The real genesis of these plays is in Pirandello's experience. With the secret of his painful and tragic domestic life hidden in his heart, he moved among men for years. Could he have revealed to them the truth of that condition? He learned then what it is to "build up oneself," and he discovered that most human beings had to seek in that process a screen for the cruel pranks that life had played on them. These plays reflect the most distressed period of Pirandello's inner life. This period begins with Ciampa's laughter in *Cap and Bells;* it develops through the cynical, but pain-giving utterances of Leone Gala in *Each in His Own Rôle;* it scoffs and jeers at everything human with Diego in *Each in His Own Way;* it softens before the calamities that befell Martino Lori and Ersilia Drei in *All for the Best* and *Naked;* it rises to a tragic height before the mental tortures of the emperor Henry IV; and finally it opens the haven of a peaceful and pure life before Elma in *As You Desire Me,* although the author does not allow her to find a shelter there for her harassed and tortured flesh and soul.

The immense surge of humanity that suffered in these plays cannot be the result of an abstract process. In the silence of long years of work Pirandello has created a galaxy of true and great characters, a crowd of poor, grieving creatures whose mouths are twisted in a grimace that tries to be a smile, whose eyes are staring and dull, and whose hearts are pierced by a long pin that they try to remove from their hearts to let it transfix their brains, for, though that may be more painful, at least it allows them to live.

* * *

Pirandello has projected in Henry IV the desperate passiveness to which he resigned himself when haunted by the inescapable but crushing event of his poor wife's madness. In the words of Henry IV, there echoes Pirandello's feeling of powerlessness in his despair. "I believe that phantasms are nothing but a little unbalanced condition of our mind: images that we fail to hold within the boundaries of the kingdom of sleep. They appear even in the daytime; and they terrify. I am greatly frightened when at night time I see them before me—disorderly images that, having dismounted from their horses, laugh. I am sometimes afraid, even of my blood that throbs in my veins like the thud of steps resounding in distant rooms in the silence of the night."

The drama is a subtle study of the interplay of the conscious and the subconscious, the rational and the irrational, as they may be observed in human actions. To what extent are our acts conscious? If we, without being seen, should look at the valets as they stand around the throne of Henry IV, we should believe, judging by their actions and words, that they were true and real. What difference is there between seeing them and seeing ordinary persons moving in the realm of actual life? As with grave mien they discuss matters of state with the emperor, we have no proof that they are acting. Conversely, we cannot ascertain when they are not acting when they speak and act in their capacity of men of today. We can be led in a most convincing manner to these paradoxical extremes by a process of logical and complete subjectiveness. Pirandello goes more deeply into the question of the reality of human personality. For twenty years, these valets have lived as men of the eleventh century. It is highly improbable that they have not merged to some extent with that superimposed rôle, even so far as to have their identity obliterated for hours at a time at least.

This play makes us realize more than any other how unjust is the accusation of abstract and cerebral so often applied to Pirandello. One feels constantly the author's reaction against those who lack spontaneity in life. He focuses his attention both on the worldly people of whom Henry IV, Donna Matilda, and Belcredi are the exponents and on the scientists, represented by the doctor. Pirandello finds himself at odds with both of them. The exaltation with which Henry IV lived before the tragedy speaks of a lack of real emotion and simplicity which led him to complicate life and to rationalize it. The doctor's stand is pure abstraction, and Pirandello ridicules him. The man of science is sure that the madman will react just as he expects and prescribes. It seems very peculiar to the author that the doctor, in his scientific dogmatism, has the courage to classify as demented one from whom he expects such a logical and certain reaction. Reasoning for Pirandello is a useless encumbrance that bespeaks man's inability to seize life in its essential points. The fantastic ravings of Henry IV before the accident were more cerebral and useless than his illusion centering around the belief that he was an historical character who lived eight hundred and eighty years before.

The power of the living reality is one of the strongest *motifs* in the play. What compelled Henry IV to leave the artificial groove into which he had gathered whatever débris of his life was left to him, was the call of the living life that reached him through the youth and charm of Frida. There was a violent clash between the desolate coldness of his solitude and the warm breath of the world that he had forsaken. That clash made it impossible for him to cling to his illusion and, therefore, it revealed the tragedy of his lucid madness. But it also made him feel that he was unfit to reënter the swift current of life that goes on and on, leaving behind all those who cannot keep pace with it. Tragedy stalks in, superinduced by this harrowing contrast. Critics are apt to put abstraction in Pirandello where it does not exist. If, upon seeing Donna Matilda as she is in the picture and as she is today, we should state that Pirandello conceives reality as existing on two planes, we might succeed in displaying brilliancy, but we should fail to feel what the author meant to be seen. The predominating element is the author's feeling of the swift passing of time with its transforming and ravaging power. The doctor thought and spoke of the two planes, but he is the butt of Pirandello's ridicule, and critics who follow him will share the same fate.

All the characters in the play are molded with that vividness and clear-cut contour that Pirandello lends to the creatures of his imagination. Henry IV, however, towers above them all. His madness is a case of lucid madness, a madness that is kinder than sanity; a madness to which one goes for shelter when life becomes crushing and unbearable. Were we to view Henry IV as an ordinary man, feigning madness, he would arouse indignation in us for his prolonged pretending. If we accept his conscious madness, we stand before him appalled by the greatness of the sorrowful and tragic existence of one who has willfully cut himself off from life because he knew that life held no promise for him. We see him as a tragic figure, enmeshed in the contradictions of life, immobilized in the merciless fate of his madness, but surrounded by the warm sympathy and pity of the author. He stands unforgettable before us as one for whom a conscious, planned madness is more tragic, harrowing, and devastating than one of which an ordinary individual is unaware. The madman as illuminated by the poet has eclipsed the one diagnosed by the physician.

JOSEPH WOOD KRUTCH

[Pirandello and the Dissolution of Ego]†

The objection may be raised that I have persistently defined my dramatists in terms of what they deny rather than of what they affirm. Ibsen denies the existence of absolutes. Strindberg denies the possibility of reconciling conflicting impulses. Shaw denies that man as he exists is capable of solving his problems. Now Chekhov denies, among other things, the significance of the drama.

Perhaps this objection would be valid if I were pretending to give a complete account. I say only "perhaps" because part of my thesis is that the playwrights whom we have been discussing actually deny more and affirm less than is commonly supposed. In any event my procedure is both inevitable and necessary in view of my special

† From Joseph Wood Krutch, *Modernism in Modern Drama: A Definition and an Estimate*, New York, 1953, 1962. Pp. 77-87. Copyright 1953. Reprinted by permission of the publishers, Russell and Russell, Inc.

purpose, and I shall apply it still more narrowly in the discussion of the last of my negative dramatists, the Italian Luigi Pirandello. Pirandello's plays have been variously interpreted, and a well-known contemporary critic has recently assigned him a very high place in the modern drama. Without questioning that judgment I shall treat him exclusively, from the point of view of my thesis, as the dramatist who made—or, as perhaps it would be safer to say of so ambiguous a dramatist, seems to me to have made—the most inclusive denial of all, namely, the denial that the persistent and more or less consistent character or personality which we attribute to each individual human being, and especially to ourselves, really exists at all.

This is perhaps the most elusive subject which I shall have to discuss, partly because the assumption that "I am I" and that "You are You" is one of the most fundamental which we make—because it seems self-evident to us, not only that the realities exist but also that they persist, so that the "I" of today and the "I" of yesterday are in some way continuous no matter what developments may occur. Upon this assumption all moral systems must rest, since obviously no one can be good or bad, guilty or innocent, unless he exists as some sort of continuous unity. Ultimately, not only all moral systems but all other attempts to deal systematically with the phenomena of human life depend upon it. Even the mechanists who deny free will and insist that an individual personality or character is merely the product of the conditioning influences which have come to bear upon it need nevertheless to assume that this externally determined character is some sort of persistent entity. For the mechanist too, the "I" must at least exist.

If Pirandello were a completely isolated phenomenon or even if similar attitudes had been exhibited only in the drama, he would be too aberrant a phenomenon to find a place in the present discussion. In his case, however, as in the case of all the other playwrights whom we have considered, the dramatist represents attitudes which appear in other writers and which he took, not necessarily from these other writers, but perhaps out of the air—as Ibsen said he got his ideas. So conspicuously is this true that what I am about to discuss, namely the phenomenon which has been called "the dissolution of the ego," has sometimes been described as one of the most significant processes in modern thought.

I do not mean to deny that a certain paradox in the common-sense concept of the "I" has not been recognized for a very long time. After all, Heraclitus maintained that nothing persisted except change, and an ancient Greek joke turns upon the case of the wrongdoer who protests that he should not be punished today for what "he" did yesterday, since no "he" has really persisted from one day into the next. Despite the occasional toying with such paradoxes,

Greek ethics no less than Christian ethics depend upon the assumption that separate and internally continuous personalities do exist.

We know that men are often inconsistent, but it would not mean anything to say that they are inconsistent if we did not assume that there is something consistent with which they are temporarily inconsistent. We say of a man's action that it was "unlike him" to do this or that. We solemnly adjure him to be "true to himself," or we flippantly advise him, "Be yourself!" The recognition of an inconsistency implies a prior and more significant recognition of a consistency. You cannot be true to yourself unless there is a self to whom you can be true.

I have just said that all classical and all Christian ethics assume this persistent, continuous reality of the ego and could not exist without it. I might add that without it history and storytelling also would be, in any ordinary form of either, likewise impossible, since a narrative moving through time implies something, namely man, recognizably continuous which moves with the narrative and through it. Yet in Pirandello we have the case of a playwright who does attempt to write some sort of drama while seeming to deny this generally indispensable assumption. After a very brief illustration of what I mean by this, I shall say a few words about the parallel between this odd enterprise and certain other literary phenomena of recent days. First let us take for discussion one play by Pirandello.

He is the author of several, more or less well known, and they exhibit a strong family resemblance to one another. However, in this country at least, the best known is *Six Characters in Search of an Author*, which had a successful Broadway run almost a generation ago in a fine production with Florence Eldridge as star.

In *Six Characters* the curtain goes up on the stage of a theater occupied by a director who is considering a new production. Six persons force their way in, declare that they are characters created by a playwight who abandoned them, and insist upon their right to act out the events they were created to stage. Against the manager's protests they take over the stage and do enact a sordid and complicated story about the relations of a man with the wife from whom he is separated and with her children by him and by a lover. Everyone in the play is tortured by jealousy, love, hatred, and, above all perhaps, by a sense of shame.

Without the peculiar setting of play within play and without all the metaphysical embellishments, what we should have is a rather lurid tragic melodrama. But we are obviously intended to be primarily interested, not in this story as a story, but in what the author uses it to say about the nature of reality. Psychological dramas are common. *Six Characters in Search of an Author* is not so much psychological as it is metaphysical.

The skepticism to which it would persuade us is almost all-inclusive. The thesis seems to be that the human being cannot distinguish between appearance and reality—even, perhaps, that no such distinction exists. Reality is merely that appearance in which I happen to believe, merely that form of insanity of which I happen to be the victim. Or to quote the title of another Pirandello play: "Right You Are If You Think You Are."

Thus at the very beginning the distinction between "real life" and make-believe is broken down when the six characters enter the world of "real life" and begin to operate on the same plane as that of the theatrical manager. Art, it seems, is no less real than nature. Perhaps it is even more real because the imagined character exists in eternity, the living man only temporarily in time, and also, perhaps, because a character in fiction may be given a consistent ego which a character in real life does not have.

Moreover, even within the framework of the play within a play, everything is almost equally dubious. The various characters see the various events, and especially they see one another, in various lights. The playwright remains neutral. One character is not right, or sane, or logical, and the others somehow wrong. There is no assumed version of things "as they really are" because no one, not even the playwright, could know what that version is even if it exists.

Inevitably the most dubious and elusive in the midst of all this dubiety are the characters, personalities, and motives of the dramatis personae. Every individual has many "I's." He is, of course, what he seems to himself, but he is also all the things which he seems to all the different people who know him. And there is no guarantee that his version of himself is any truer than any one of the others.

Merely as a passing fancy this sort of Pyrrhic skepticism[1] is no doubt as old as critical thought. From its paralyzing effect we are ordinarily saved by what Santayana calls "animal faith." We admit that life may be only a dream and that we may know nothing outside the fancies of our own brains, but the animal faith which bids us believe in the external world is much stronger than any metaphysical arguments. Everybody acts as though he believed that the external world exists; nearly everybody acts as though he believed that his version of it is a dependable one; and the majority act as though they could also make valid value judgments about it. Not merely in one play, but in a whole series of plays, Pirandello carries on an attack against our animal faith and seems determined to persuade us not merely that we cannot make value judgments, not merely that we cannot distinguish appearance from reality, but that the whole concept of reality as opposed to appearance is inadmissible.

1. Extreme skepticism, tracing from the Greek philosopher Pyrrho (365— 275 B.C.), who believed that all knowledge was uncertain.

Moreover and in the process, the "I" itself, the thing which perceives appearances and becomes the victim of illusions, disintegrates —if, at least, one means by the "I" any continuous, persisting, relatively stable thing. Every "I" is not merely all the things which at various times it seems to itself to be or all the things which at various times it seems to various people to be. It is also all the different things which at different times it has been. There are the "I's" of yesterday, today, and tomorrow, as well as what every observer has taken each of them to be. At one point in the play the husband, who has been caught in a ridiculous and even, in his judgment, a reprehensible act, protests against being judged by it; protests, that is, against the assumption that this action is typical of him or that, as we should say, he is "that kind of man." But from the standpoint of the play this is, of course, absurd. It assumes that he has a character as distinguished from the sum of all the inconsistent things which he does, that he is "being himself" at certain moments and not "being himself" at others. What, Pirandello seems to ask, can a "self" be except what it is being from moment to moment?

I have already remarked that the tendency which Pirandello carries to a logical or illogical extreme is not unique in him and that, as a matter of fact, this tendency to "dissolve the ego" has been sometimes regarded as one highly characteristic of our times. No doubt the direction taken by much psychological investigation has a good deal to do with the tendency. This investigation has tended to pay particular attention to "states of mind" rather than to what is loosely called "character." It has made us very much aware of inconsistencies and illogicalities in our feeling and conduct, of conflicts and opposing impulses. As a result we tend to think of others and sometimes of ourselves not in terms of a hard core of character occasionally obscured by "uncharacteristic" attitudes but as being simply, from moment to moment, the temporary resultant of the various forces being brought to bear at that moment upon our consciousness and our unconsciousness.

The Christian, and to an almost equal extent the classic, conception of the "persona" or of the "ego" seems to have been of a fully conscious unity, of a soul captain, born with us at birth and perhaps created by God. It is an ultimate, even *the* ultimate continuous reality persisting through time. This ego may develop itself or it may corrupt itself, but it can never cease to *be* itself. To its integrity and to its will we may appeal, and we may, more or less sternly, hold it to some extent accountable for what it does.

Inevitably the tendencies of modern psychology at least modify somewhat this classical conception of the "I." If we accept the theory of the unconscious and its role, if we assume that the "I" is a sort of iceberg at least three-fifths below the water line of awareness, then the "I" must become at least a double rather than a single thing. Whether or not the concepts of modern psychology, even assuming that they are entirely correct, really necessarily lead to the complete dissolution of the "I" is another question. I have no intention of opening it directly here; I have only the intention of suggesting that this tendency to dissolve it is characteristic and that, if I may return once more to the central metaphor, one of the most significant differences between the past which lies on one side of a chasm and the future which is presumed to lie on the other is simply that the past is dominated by egos, by actors who are assumed to be directed by a hard-core personality, while in the future there will be only states of consciousness—continuous only in the sense that they function for a time by means of a given brain, housed in a given skull.

Earlier I said that I wanted to say something about other manifestations in recent literature of the dissolving ego. I shall note only two things, first, that the whole "stream of consciousness" method tends to stress the fluid as opposed to the hard-core aspect of the individual personality even when there is no dogmatic assertion that the stream is either the only or the most significant aspect of the personality. Secondly, let me say that Marcel Proust's *Remembrance of Things Past* is both one of the most impressive works of modern literature and one in which the "dissolution of the ego" is most conspicuous. This dissolution was a theme of which the author himself was fully conscious and one to which he returned again and again. Swann, the Duchesse de Guermantes, and Monsieur de Charlus persist as names. But much of the book depends upon Proust's own sense that the personalities bearing these names are not at any moment what they were at any previous time and that the conception which he first formed when he heard about them is much more enduringly real than the manifestations in the flesh which from time to time he encounters. No doubt Pirandello was influenced, as Proust was, by Bergson's insistence that the ultimate reality is change in time. Whatever the reason, Proust's denial of the classical ego is only less fanatically stated, not much less thoroughgoing in fact, than Pirandello's.

It is a curious fact that the three most revolutionary new hypotheses of the nineteenth century—Darwinism, Marxism, and Freudism—should have had one thing and one thing only in common. All three are, or at least were popularly taken to be, hypotheses which tended to take man's fate out of his own hands, to assure him that he could not do the supremely important things for himself, and then to tell him also, by way of compensation, that he therefore could not be blamed for anything which happened to him.

According to Darwinism, the evolution from lower to higher is in the hands of an automatic process called natural selection. According to Marx, the development of social justice is in the hands of an automatic process called dialectical materialism. According to Freud —or at least according to Freud's popular interpreters—the character and the conduct of the individual depends, not upon his own free choice, but upon the experiences, traumatic or otherwise, to which he has been exposed and especially to those which he underwent in infancy. All three of these hypotheses lend themselves to what I should call philosophies of exculpation. Each is discouraging in the sense that it denies us the power radically to control our destiny, soothing in the sense that it assures us we are at least not to blame.

About each of these hypotheses I had said something before we came to the dissolution of the ego with which we are at present concerned. Unfortunately this last cannot be reduced to terms as simple as the others, and on the part of the general public there is not so acute a realization of it. The average literate man knows that he accepts or rejects what he thinks of as Darwinism, Marxism, or Freudism; but he is much less likely to be aware of the extent to which he has lost the classical sense of the "I" as an ultimate, persistent, unified thing whose continuous existence is the most self-evident of realities and without which the whole world of his mental and physical awareness would be a meaningless flux. Yet in so far as he has, even without knowing it, lost that sense he has undergone a very fateful change. Few things could cut him off more completely from any understanding of or participation in a past which did think of the universe as inhabited by "I's."

No doubt Darwinism, Marxism, and Freudism all contributed to the dissolution of the ego. The sense that we are directing our destiny is one of the things which convinces us that our "I" is real, and anything which casts doubt upon the power of self-direction weakens our belief in the reality of the ego. But I have chosen to discuss the dissolution of the ego as a separate topic, not merely because Pirandello and Proust afford us striking examples in contemporary literature of the artist's concern with the phenomenon, but also because it is something more than an obvious and predictable result of Darwin and Marx and Freud. It is one thing to say: "I am not a free agent. What I am and what I do is the result of natural selection, of the dialectic of the material universe, and of the psychic traumas of my infancy." Another step must be taken before one can add that the "I" is not only not self-determining but that it does not, in any easily understandable sense, exist at all except as a perpetually shifting configuration.

From any attempt even to suggest the major consequences for society, philosophy, religion, and morals of a general and complete renunciation of the classical concept of the ego, I retire appalled. I shall simply leave them to your imagination and conclude with a consideration comically less portentous. What would be the effect upon the drama if the theories and the procedure of both Chekhov and Pirandello were universally adopted by playwrights and carried to their logical conclusions?

Theorists have generally maintained that the soul of the drama is either action or character. Aristotle seems to maintain the supremacy of the first when he declares that "the fable" is the most important part of a tragedy. Many moderns, on the other hand, have insisted that the revelation of character through conflict is more important than story. Offhand I cannot think of any analyst who has maintained that you could have a play without either action on the one hand or the revelation of character on the other. Yet Chekhov gets rid of action and Pirandello gets rid of character. One is tempted to suggest somewhat light-mindedly that whatever else we may or may not be able to predict about the future which lies across the chasm one thing seems fairly certain: There will not be any plays in it.

Selected Bibliography

Books and articles quoted from earlier have not been included in this list.

Archer, William. *The Old Drama and the New*, New York, 1923.
Clark, Barrett H. *A Study of the Modern Drama*, New York, 1938.
Dickinson, Thomas H., ed. *The Theater in a Changing Europe*, New York, 1937.
Downer, Alan S. *Fifty Years of American Drama*, Chicago, 1951.
Fuerst, W. R., and Samuel J. Hume. *Twentieth-Century Stage Decoration*, two volumes, New York, 1929.
Gassner, John. *Form and Idea in Modern Theater*, New York, 1956.
Gorelik, Mordecai. *New Theaters for Old*, New York, 1940.
Jones, Robert Edmond and Kenneth Macgowan. *Continental Stagecraft*, New York, 1922.
Lamm, Martin. *Modern Drama*, trans. K. Elliott, Oxford, 1952.
Lumley, Frederick. *Trends in 20th Century Drama*, Fairlawn, N.J., 1956.
Moderwell, Hiram Kelly. *The Theater of Today*, New York, 1927.
Williams, Raymond. *Drama from Ibsen to Eliot*, London, 1952.

HENRIK IBSEN

Downs, Brian W. *Ibsen, the Intellectual Background*, Cambridge, 1946.
Downs, Brian W. *A Study of Six Plays by Ibsen*, Cambridge, 1950.
Jorgenson, Theodore. *Henrik Ibsen: Life and Drama*, Northfield, Minn., 1963.
Koht, Halvdan. *The Life of Ibsen*, New York, 1931.
Lavrin, Janko. *Ibsen, an Approach*, London, 1950.
McCarthy, Mary. "The Will and Testament of Ibsen," *Sights and Spectacles*, London, 1959.
McFarlane, James W. *Ibsen and the Temper of Norwegian Literature*, London, 1960.
Northam, John. *Ibsen's Dramatic Method*, London, 1953.
Raphael, Robert. "Illusion and the Self in *The Wild Duck*," *Scandinavian Studies*, XXXV (February 1963), pp. 37-42.
Tennant, P. F. D. *Ibsen's Dramatic Technique*, Cambridge, 1948.
Weigand, Hermann J. *The Modern Ibsen: A Reconsideration*, New York, 1925.
Zucker, Adolph E. *Ibsen, the Master Builder*, London, 1929.

ANTON CHEKHOV

Bruford, W. H. *Chekhov and His Russia*, New Haven, 1947.
Bruford, W. H. *Anton Chekhov*, London, 1957.
Gorki, Maxim. *Reminiscences of Tolstoy, Chekhov, and Andreyev*, New York, 1921.
Hingley, Ronald. *Chekhov*, London, 1950.
Koteliansky, S. S. *Anton Tchekhov: Literary and Theatrical Reminiscences*, New York, 1925.
Magarshack, David. *Chekhov the Dramatist*, London, 1952.
Magarshack, David. *Chekhov: A Life*, London, 1952.
Perry, Henry Ten Eyck. *Masters of Dramatic Comedy and their Social Themes*, Cambridge, Mass., 1939.
Simmons, Ernest J. *Chekhov, a Biography*, Boston, 1962.
World Theater, IX (1960), "Chekhov Centenary Issue."

GEORGE BERNARD SHAW

Bentley, Eric. *Bernard Shaw*, New York, 1947.
Chesterton, G. K. *George Bernard Shaw*, London, 1909.
Ervine, St. John. *Bernard Shaw, His Life, Works, and Friends*, New York, 1956.
Henderson, Archibald. *George Bernard Shaw: Man of the Century*, New York, 1956.

Joad, C. E. M. *Shaw*, London, 1949.
Kronenberger, Louis, ed. *George Bernard Shaw. A Critical Survey*, New York, 1953.
Nethercot, Arthur H. *Men and Supermen: The Shavian Portrait Gallery*, Cambridge, Mass., 1954.
Pearson, Hesketh. *G. B. S. A Full-Length Portrait*, New York, 1942.
Strauss, Ernest. *Bernard Shaw, Art and Socialism*, London, 1942.
Winsten, Stephen. ed. *G.B.S. 90*, New York, 1946.

AUGUST STRINDBERG

Campbell, George A. *Strindberg*, New York, 1933.
Dahlström, Carl E. W. L. *Strindberg's Dramatic Expressionism*, Ann Arbor, Mich., 1930.
Gustafson, Alrik. *A History of Swedish Literature*, Minneapolis, Minn., 1961.
Johnson, Walter. "Strindberg and the Danse Macabre," *Modern Drama* III (May 1960), pp. 8-15.
Lucas, F. L. *The Drama of Ibsen and Strindberg*, London, 1962.
McGill, V. J. *August Strindberg: The Bedevilled Viking*, London, 1930.
Milton, J. R. "The Esthetic Fault of Strindberg's Dream Plays," *Tulane Drama Review*, IV (March 1960), No. 3, pp. 108-116.
Modern Drama, V (December 1962), "Strindberg Issue."
Mortenson, Brita M. E., and Brian W. Downs. *Strindberg: An Introduction to His Life and Works*, Cambridge, 1949.
Sprigge, Elizabeth. *The Strange Life of August Strindberg*, New York, 1949.

EUGENE O'NEILL

Alexander, Doris. *The Tempering of Eugene O'Neill*, New York, 1962.
Carpenter, Frederic I. *Eugene O'Neill*, New York, 1964.
Clark, Barrett H. *Eugene O'Neill, The Man and His Plays*, New York, 1947.
Engel, Edwin. *The Haunted Heroes of Eugene O'Neill*, Cambridge, Mass., 1953.
Falk, Doris V. *Eugene O'Neill and the Tragic Tension*, New Brunswick, N. J., 1958.
Gelb, Barbara and Arthur. *O'Neill*, New York, 1962.
Granger, Bruce Ingham. "Illusion and Reality in Eugene O'Neill," *Modern Language Notes*, LXXIII (1958), pp. 179-186.
Krutch, Joseph Wood. "O'Neill's Tragic Sense," *American Scholar*, XVI (1947), pp. 283-290.
Leech, Clifford. *Eugene O'Neill*, New York, 1963.
Modern Drama, III (December 1960), "O'Neill Issue."
Winther, Sophus K. *Eugene O'Neill: A Critical Study*, New York, rev., 1961.

LUIGI PIRANDELLO

Bishop, Thomas. *Pirandello and the French Theater*, New York, 1960.
Fergusson, Francis. "The Theatricality of Shaw and Pirandello," *The Idea of a Theater*, Princeton, N.J., 1949, pp. 190-206.
Fioco, Achille. "The Heritage of Pirandello," *World Theater*, III (1953), No. 3, pp. 24-30.
MacClintock, Lander. *The Age of Pirandello*, Bloomington, Ind., 1951.
May, Frederick. "Drama of Reality," *Drama*, Nos. 32-35 (Winter 1954), pp. 21-26.
Palmer, John. *Studies in the Contemporary Theater*, Boston, 1927.
Starkie, Walter. *Luigi Pirandello: 1867-1936*, New York, 1937.
Vittorini, Domenico. *High Points in the History of Italian Literature*, New York, 1958.
Young, Stark. *Immortal Shadows*, New York, 1948, pp. 46-49, 76-80.